Cardinals Journal

Year by Year & Day by Day with
the St. Louis Cardinals Since 1882

Cardinals Journal

JOHN SNYDER

emmis
books

For further information, contact the publisher at:

Emmis Books
1700 Madison Road
Cincinnati, OH 45206

www.emmisbooks.com

Library of Congress Cataloging-in-Publication Data

Snyder, John, 1951-
  Cardinals journal : year by year & day by day with the St. Louis Cardinals since 1882 / by John Snyder.
    p. cm.

  ISBN-13: 978-1-57860-254-4
  ISBN-10: 1-57860-254-8
  1. St. Louis Cardinals (Baseball team)--History. I. Title.
  GV875.S74S69 2006
  796.357'640977866

                2005034649

Edited by Brad Crawford
Cover designed by Stephen Sullivan
Interior designed by Mary Barnes Clark
Production design by Carie Adams

Cover photo by Focus on Sport/Getty Images
Back cover photos by Transcendental Graphics/theruckerarchive.com

About the Author

John Snyder has a master's degree in history from the University of Cincinnati and a passion for baseball. He has authored fifteen books on baseball, soccer, hockey, tennis, football, basketball, and travel and lives in Cincinnati.

Acknowledgments

This book is part of a series that takes a look at Major League Baseball teams. The first was *Redleg Journal: Year by Year and Day by Day with the Cincinnati Reds Since 1866*, the winner of the 2001 Baseball Research Award issued by *The Sporting News* and SABR. That work was followed by *Cubs Journal: Year by Year and Day by Day with the Chicago Cubs Since 1876* and *Red Sox Journal: Year by Year and Day by Day with the Boston Red Sox Since 1901*. Each of these books is filled with little-known items that have never been published in book form.

Greg Rhodes was my co-author on *Redleg Journal*, in addition to publishing the book under his company's name, Road West Publishing. While Greg did not actively participate in the books about the Cubs, Cardinals and Red Sox, he deserves considerable credit for the success of those books because they benefited from many of the creative concepts he initiated in *Redleg Journal*.

The idea for turning *Redleg Journal* into a series of books goes to Richard Hunt, president and publisher of Emmis Books, and editorial director Jack Heffron. Mary Barnes Clark developed the series design. Thanks go also to Brad Crawford and Carie Adams for their editorial and design work on *Cardinals Journal*.

I would also like to than the staff at the Public Library of Cincinnati and Hamilton County. The vast majority of research for this book came from contemporary newspapers and magazines. The library staff was extremely helpful with patience and understanding while retrieving the materials for me, not only for this book but for all of my previous endeavors as well. Dick Miller deserves thanks for providing me with material from his personal collection of baseball books. Dick was a lifelong friend of my father, who passed away in 1999, and instilled in me a love of both history and baseball.

And finally, although they should be the first, thanks to my wife and sons, Derek and Kevin, whose encouragement and support helped me through another book.

Contents

❖ ❖ ❖

PART TWO: CARDINALS BY THE NUMBERS

Foreword

Growing up a Cardinals fan in the shadows of Busch Stadium made access to the team easy for me. I didn't need a ticket or anything official like a press pass. Occasionally when the team was in town, my friends and I would be listening to the game on the radio. At the start of the sixth inning, we would hop on our bikes and ride 10 blocks north to Busch Stadium. We would lock the bikes with a chain to the iron fencing that circled the large catwalk along the south end of the stadium, and when they opened the gates for fans to exit the game in the seventh inning, we were poised to enter and watch the final 12 outs. I remember thinking how cool it would be to have a job at the stadium as a vendor or a concessionaire. Being able to see Major League Baseball while you got paid would sure be nice.

Not only did I get to see great Cardinals history while getting paid, I went from unpaid late-inning bleacher bum to Busch Stadium's announcer. I was sort of a bleacher bum but with air-conditioning. I have been the Cardinals' stadium announcer for 21 full seasons and have been fortunate to introduce and to be around some of the greatest men ever to play the game. Even though I've seen almost every one of the Cardinals' home games in that 21-year period of time along with a bunch of those eighth and ninth innings and I've watched hundreds of road games, I loved reading this book, which highlights all the things I have forgotten I saw. This book on the Cardinals franchise is a refresher

course on one of the true storied teams in America. Their rich history is documented year by year in a succinct fashion that makes reading it easy and fun. The trivia buff will enjoy the advantage it will give you when trying to take money from beloved friends who think they know more than you'll ever know about the Cardinals. *Cardinals Journal* covers all the team's seasons, from the first year to the present. The recent passing from one stadium to the next has given many of us a renewed desire to read and remember the things that have occurred throughout Cardinals history and over the years at Busch Stadium, and this book puts you right there— minus, of course, the late-night bike ride.

—John Ulett

When Does Time Begin?

The present-day St. Louis Cardinals have been a part of the National League since 1892 but have their roots in the American Association, where the club played from 1882 through 1891. The official beginning of the franchise dates from November 2, 1881, with the creation of the American Association in a meeting held at the Gibson Hotel in Cincinnati. The six founding clubs represented St. Louis, Baltimore, Cincinnati, Louisville, Pittsburgh, and Philadelphia.

The foundations of the franchise that would become the Cardinals extend a few years earlier, however. The 1869 Cincinnati Red Stockings were baseball's first professional club. The Red Stockings toured the country and made two visits to St. Louis, playing local amateur teams. In September 1869, the Red Stockings defeated the Unions 70–9 and the Empires 31–9. The Empires were managed by Jeremiah Fruin, a young man from Brooklyn who was posted in St. Louis while serving in the Union Army's

Transcendental Graphics/theruckerarchive.com

Quartermaster Corps. At the time, Brooklyn was a hotbed of baseball, and Fruin learned the game in the city as a youngster. He is recognized as the "father of baseball in St. Louis" because he helped teach the sport to the citizens of the city.

Baseball's first organized league was the National Association, formed in 1871. Two St. Louis clubs joined the NA in 1875. The St. Louis Red Stockings played at Compton and Gratiot. The Brown Stockings used the site at Grand and Dodier, which acquired the name Sportsman's Park.

At the end of 1875, both the Red Stockings and the National Association folded. The Brown Stockings became part of the National League, established in February 1876. The first club had a 45–19 record and finished second to Chicago, now the Cubs. But after the 1877 season, St. Louis dropped out of the NL after finishing fourth, leaving the city without a major league ball club.

Al Spink, later the founder of *The Sporting News*, was among those who decided to try to do something about the problem. He formed the Sportsman's Park and Club Association. Its first task was to put the Grand Avenue park back into playing shape. Once the ballpark was in order, Spink and his compatriots assembled a team and began to book exhibition games against the best opposition available.

The primary investor in the Sportsman's Park and Club Association was German immigrant Chris Von der Ahe, an ambitious entrepreneur who owned a saloon and boarding house near the site. Von der Ahe knew next to nothing about baseball, but the fact that business at his saloon increased every time a baseball game took place at Grand and Dodier did not escape his notice. Von der Ahe steered the club into the American Association and adopted the nickname Brown Stockings, later shortened to Browns, and the brown-trimmed uniforms used by previous clubs at Grand and Dodier. The franchise's story begins here with that first American Association season of 1882.

What Is a Cardinal?

For purposes of simplicity and consistency, St. Louis's National League baseball team is called the "Cardinals" throughout this book. A fan of the club prior to 1900 would have been confused by the name "Cardinals," however, because it wasn't until that year that the nickname was coined. Prior to 1900, the Cardinals were known as the Browns or Perfectos. The franchise was called the Browns from the time it joined the American Association in 1882 until the end of the 1898 season.

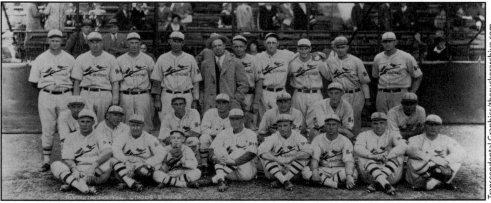

Frank and Stanley Robison, a pair of brothers from Cleveland, bought the club from controversial owner Chris Von der Ahe just prior to the 1899 season. Looking for a fresh start, the Robisons changed the predominate color on the club's uniforms from brown to vivid red. Local sportswriters in 1899 began referring to the club as the Perfectos.

According to legend, Willie McHale, a reporter for the *St. Louis Republic*, overheard a female fan remark, "What a lovely shade of cardinal" after gathering a look at the club's red uniforms just after the start of the 1900 season. McHale began using the nickname "Cardinals" to describe the ball club. Other newspapermen in St. Louis followed suit.

That the nickname originated in a newspaper was typical of the period. Many of the most famous nicknames in baseball, such as Cubs, Reds, Yankees, Phillies, Dodgers, Giants, Braves, Pirates, Indians, Tigers, and Orioles, were created not by the clubs themselves but by enterprising sportswriters. The editors and authors of many baseball histories have attempted retroactively to attach a single nickname to clubs from the 19th and early 20th centuries, when in fact many of these nicknames were seldom used. Clubs of the period often were called the name of the city instead of a nickname, for instance, the "Chicagos," the "New Yorks," the "Bostons," or the "Pittsburghs."

The Browns, the name the Cardinals originally used, gained new life in 1902 when the American League moved the Milwaukee franchise to St. Louis and called it the Browns. Befitting the name, players wore uniforms trimmed in brown. Orange was added about a decade later. The St. Louis Browns existed until 1953, when the team moved to Baltimore and was renamed the Orioles.

Transcendental Graphics/theruckerarchive.com

THE STATE OF THE CARDINALS

St. Louis was one of the six original members of the American Association, which existed as a major league from 1882 through 1891. The present-day Cardinals franchise (known as the Browns during the 1880s) dominated the fledgling league by capturing the pennant in 1885, 1886, 1887, and 1888 and finishing second place finishes in 1883, 1889, and 1891.

THE BEST TEAM

The .705 winning percentage posted by the 1885 club was the best of the decade, based on a record of 79–33. The 1887 Cardinals won the most games with a 95–40 record after an expansion of the playing schedule, and the .704 winning percentage was only a shade behind the 1885 team.

THE WORST TEAM

The first team in club history was in 1882 and won 37 while losing 43. It was the only team to compile a losing record during the 10 seasons that St. Louis was in the American Association.

THE BEST MOMENT

The popularity of baseball in the 19th century was evident on October 7, 1885, when an estimated 250,000 turned out in St. Louis for a parade honoring the 1885 pennant-winning Cardinals.

THE WORST MOMENT

The Cardinals refused to board a train for a series in Kansas City on May 2, 1889, after club owner Chris Von der Ahe fined second baseman Yank Robinson $25 for wearing a dirty uniform.

THE ALL-DECADE TEAM • YEARS W/CARDS

Doc Bushong, c	1885–87
Charlie Comiskey, 1b	1882–89, 1891
Yank Robinson, 2b	1885–89, 1891
Arlie Latham, 3b	1883–89
Bill Gleason, ss	1882–87
Tip O'Neill, lf	1884–89, 1891
Curt Welch, cf	1885–87
Hugh Nicol, rf	1883–86
Bob Caruthers, p	1884–87, 1892
Dave Foutz, p	1884–87
Silver King, p	1887–89
Jumbo McGinnis, p	1882–86

Among the players on the 1880s All-Decade Team, only Comiskey is in the Hall of Fame. His plaque at Cooperstown is based not on his playing ability, however, but on his management of four consecutive pennant winners in St. Louis beginning in 1885 and ownership of the Chicago White Sox from 1900 until his death in 1931. Bill James in 2001 ranked the top 125 players in baseball history at each position. Among the 1880s Cardinals, O'Neill ranks the highest at number 48. Latham (54th), Welch (83rd), Robinson (86th), and Caruthers (89th) were all in the top 100 in James's rankings and were considered the top stars of the era.

THE DECADE LEADERS

Batting Ave:	O'Neill	.348
On-Base Pct:	O'Neill	.407
Slugging Pct:	O'Neill	.498
Home Runs:	O'Neill	28
RBIs:	(not compiled every season)	
Runs:	Latham	829
Stolen Bases:	(not compiled every season)	
Wins:	Foutz	114
Strikeouts:	Foutz	619
ERA:	Caruthers	2.51
Saves:	Nine tied with 1	

THE HOME FIELD

The Cardinals played at Sportsman's Park at Grand and Dodier from 1882 through 1892 and again from 1920 through 1966.

THE GAME YOU WISH YOU HAD SEEN

Outfielder Curt Welch crossed the plate with the winning run in the tenth inning of Game Six of the 1886 World Series, played on October 23 against the National League champion Chicago White Stockings (today's Chicago Cubs) to clinch the World Championship for St. Louis.

THE WAY THE GAME WAS PLAYED

The first all-professional team was established in Cincinnati in 1869, and the game was still very much in the evolutionary and experimental stage during the 1880s. American Association teams averaged about 11 runs per game during this period, but about half of them were unearned, as rough fields made defensive play an adventure. Many players still played bare-handed when the St. Louis franchise began play in 1882, but gloves were nearly universal by 1890, although they were fingerless and meant only to protect the palm of the hand. Also in 1882, pitchers had to throw from a position below the waist in a sidearm or underhanded motion. By the mid-1880s, the overhand delivery was legalized, giving hurlers more speed and leverage on the breaking pitches. The pitching distance was 50 feet in 1882 and 55 feet in 1887. In 1882, seven balls were needed for a batter to draw a walk. The number of balls necessary for a walk was gradually reduced until the four ball–three strike count was established in 1889.

THE MANAGEMENT

Chris Von der Ahe, one of the most colorful and controversial owners in baseball history, ran the Cardinals from their inception until selling the club just prior to the 1899 season. The field manager in 1882 was Ned Cuthbert, who lasted only one season. Ted Sullivan was hired in 1883 but resigned in August after tangling once too often with Von der Ahe. Charlie Comiskey finished out the season. Jimmy Williams ran the club at the beginning of the 1884 campaign, but he too resigned before the season came to a close because of difficulties with Von der Ahe. Comiskey succeeded Williams and remained at the helm for the rest of the decade. With an uncommon drive and a win-at-all-costs approach, Comiskey led St. Louis to four consecutive pennants.

THE BEST PLAYER MOVE

The Cardinals' best all-around player during the 1880s was Bob Caruthers, who was not only one of the top pitchers of his era but also doubled as a hard-hitting outfielder in between pitching assignments. The team purchased Caruthers in 1884 from Grand Rapids of the Northwestern League for $250.

THE WORST PLAYER MOVE

After the Cardinals lost the 1887 World Series to the Detroit Wolverines, Chris Von der Ahe sold pitchers Bob Caruthers and Dave Foutz to Brooklyn. The move cost the club at least one pennant, and possibly more.

1882

Season in a Sentence

St. Louis finishes fifth in a six-team league but is second in attendance and turns a significant profit in the franchise's first year.

Finish • Won • Lost • Pct • GB

Fifth   37   43   .463   18.0

Manager

Ned Cuthbert

Stats

	Cards	• AA •	Rank
Batting Avg:	.231	.244	5
On-Base Pct:	.260	.271	5
Slugging Pct:	.302	.312	4
Home Runs:	11		2
ERA:	2.92	2.68	4
Fielding Avg:	.875	.886	5
Runs Scored:	399		5
Runs Allowed:	496		5

Starting Lineup

Sleeper Sullivan, c
Charlie Comiskey, 1b
Bill Smiley, 2b
Jack Gleason, 3b
Bill Gleason, ss
Ned Cuthbert, lf
Oscar Walker, cf
George Seward, rf
Harry McCaffery, rf
Eddie Fusselback, c

Pitchers

Jumbo McGinnis, sp
Jack Schappert, sp
Bert Dorr, sp

Attendance

135,000 (second in AA)

Club Leaders

Batting Avg:	Gleason	.288
On-Base Pct:	Gleason	.310
Slugging Pct:	Walker	.396
Home Runs:	Walker	7
Runs:	Gleason	63
Wins:	McGinnis	25
Strikeouts:	McGinnis	134
ERA:	McGinnis	2.60
Saves:	Fusselback	1

MAY 2   A month after Jesse James is shot by a member of his own gang, the Cardinals (then known as the Browns) play their first American Association regular-season game and defeat Louisville 9–7 before approximately 2,000 at Sportsman's Park. St. Louis led 8–2 after six innings before hanging on for the win. In celebration of the opening of the season, a band played on the field before the game. The first batting order looked like this:

Jack Gleason, 3b
Bill Gleason, ss
Oscar Walker, cf
Charlie Comiskey, 1b
Bill Smiley, 2b
Sleeper Sullivan, c
Ned Cuthbert, cf
Jumbo McGinnis, p
George Seward, ss

Jack and Bill Gleason were brothers who played side by side in the infield and also hit one-two in the batting order for most of the season.

Sportsman's Park was located on the west side of Grand at Dodier Street. Ballparks of the 1880s were made entirely of wood and were very primitive by today's standards. Sportsman's Park was no exception but was more luxurious than most of the others housing big-leagues teams during the period. Because of the wooden construction, fire was a constant concern. Sportsman's Park was seriously damaged by fire six times between 1882 and 1892. A diamond had been laid out at Grand and Dodier as early as 1866. The site was later used by the Browns of the National Association in 1875 and the National League in 1876 and 1877. In 1882, the permanent seating capacity was 6,000, although crowds were sometimes more than double that amount. The main grandstand, which had two decks and was located behind home plate, stretched approximately from first base to third base. Later, in 1886, the bleachers were extended around the outfield fences and down the left- and right-field foul lines, increasing capacity to 12,000. The outfield distances were approximately 350 feet down the left-field line, 460 feet to center, and 285 feet to right. The right-field wall was actually a two-story house where Augustus Solari had been living. The Cardinals leased the land from Solari. After Solari vacated the house, Cardinals owner Chris Von der Ahe transformed the residence into a beer garden with handball courts and lawn bowling. The area was regarded as part of the playing field until October 1888, and right fielders often raced through the beer garden to chase down long drives. Another feature of the ballpark was a Japanese fireworks cannon made of bamboo and wrapped with steel wire.

MAY 11   The Cardinals score seven runs in the second inning and defeat the Pittsburgh Alleghenies 7–2 in a game in Pittsburgh called after five innings by rain. The game was played at Exposition Park, which was located on the approximate site of present-day PNC Park. According to the newspapers reports, the Allegheny River was "steadily rising" during the game and right field should have been "guarded by a man in a skiff."

The Pittsburgh Alleghenies are the present-day Pittsburgh Pirates. The franchise moved from the American Association to the National League in 1887. The club began to be known as the Pirates in 1891.

MAY 23   The Cardinals wallop the Philadelphia Athletics 12–8 in Philadelphia.

The Cardinals' manager in 1882 was 37-year-old Ned Cuthbert, who doubled as the club's left fielder. A former pro player in St. Louis, Cuthbert had retired to tend bar at a local saloon before being brought back into baseball by Chris Von der Ahe. The 1882 club was in first place in a six-team league as late as June 8 and was eight games over .500, just a game behind first-place Cincinnati, in late June. But a dreadful seven-week stretch in which the Cardinals lost 14 of 18 games on a month-long road trip ended any hopes of contending. Cuthbert lasted only one season on the job.

MAY 30   Behind the shutout pitching of Jumbo McGinnis, the Cardinals defeat Baltimore 12–0 in Baltimore.

George W. McGinnis was known as "Jumbo" because of his big belly. Standing five foot ten and weighing 197 pounds, his build was attributed to his offseason occupation as a glass blower. McGinnis was only 18 years old in 1882 but had a 25–17 record on a club that was 37–43. He pitched for St. Louis until 1886 and posted an 88–61 record for the club. McGinnis was only 23 when he pitched his last big-league game, no doubt due to his workload. He pitched 388$\frac{1}{3}$ innings in 1882, 382$\frac{2}{3}$ in 1883, and 354$\frac{1}{3}$ in 1884. Despite his success, baseball historians have been unable to determine for certain whether McGinnis was left-handed or *right-handed, although all evidence points to the right side. Southpaws were so rare during the period that their appearance was duly noted.*

JUNE 1   The game between the Cardinals and the Alleghenies in Pittsburgh is postponed because the rising waters of the Allegheny River invade the playing field at Exposition Park. In order not to disappoint those who showed up to watch the game, the teams held an exhibition contest.

Befitting the Browns nickname St. Louis used during much of the 1880s and 1890s, the 1882 club was outfitted in white uniforms with brown caps, brown stockings, and uniforms with brown trim. The trim remained a feature of the jerseys until 1899, when the predominate color was switched to red.

JUNE 13   The Cardinals have their way with Baltimore, winning 12–5 at Sportsman's Park.

JUNE 20   On a miserably cold and wet day at Sportsman's Park, the Cardinals defeat the Athletics 11–9.

JUNE 29   The Cardinals win a game by forfeit when the Louisville club leaves the field in the fourth inning in protest over the decisions of umpire Paul McGee at Sportsman's Park.

McGee was the only umpire on the field. Except in rare circumstances, only one umpire was used in major league games until around 1910. Louisville also refused to play the last game of the series between the two clubs at Sportsman's Park, resulting in another forfeit. At a special American Association meeting, the St. Louis and Louisville clubs agreed to replay the two forfeits.

JULY 6   The Cardinals win a free-swinging 21–17 decision from Louisville at Sportsman's Park.

AUGUST 1   Jumbo McGinnis pitches the Cardinals to a 1–0 win over the Reds in Cincinnati.

SEPTEMBER 3   The Cardinals' 10–2 win over Baltimore in St. Louis is stopped at the end of the fourth inning so that first baseman Charlie Comiskey could be presented with "a handsome gold watch by some of his admirers."

The son of a Chicago alderman, Comiskey played for the Cardinals from 1882 through 1891 and managed the club from 1883 through 1891, with the exception of the 1890 season when he was a member of the Chicago club in the Players League. He was never a consistently strong hitter but was considered the best defensive first baseman of his day. He revolutionized the position. Before Comiskey, first basemen traditionally were practically bolted to the bag to serve as a target for the other three infielders. According to contemporary accounts, Comiskey showed remarkable mobility by ranging far and wide to cut off numerous base hits. He stationed himself 10 to 15 feet deeper than most first basemen as well. Comiskey was only 23 when he was appointed the manager in St. Louis, but his leadership qualities were evident at that early age. He would do anything it took to win. Comiskey was one of the greatest agitators the game has ever known, encouraging teammates and fans into baiting and belittling the opposition and umpires with a combative nature on the field and off. At the start of the 1880s, baseball was a rather genteel sport, and aggressive play was considered unseemly. Comiskey helped to change that with such tactics as running into the opposing second baseman to break up a double play and sliding hard into a fielder to dislodge the ball on a close play. As a consequence, his St. Louis clubs earned the enmity of just about everyone in the American Association outside of St. Louis. Comiskey's belligerence helped guide the club to four consecutive AA championships from 1885 through 1888. Comiskey left St. Louis to become manager of the Cincinnati Reds in 1892. Later, he was one of the founders of the American League by becoming owner of the Chicago White Sox in 1900, a position he held until his death in 1931. His early teams in Chicago were a huge success, winning the World Series in both 1906 and 1917. Unfortunately, he was also a tightwad, and his penny-pinching tactics helped inspire his White Sox players to throw the 1919 World Series.

Chris Von der Ahe

Chris Von der Ahe owned the St. Louis franchise from its inception in 1882 until 1899. Easily the most colorful baseball owner of the 19th century, he never fully understood the game yet built a dynasty during the club's 10 seasons in the American Association, winning four consecutive pennants beginning in 1885 and becoming a very wealthy man in the process. St. Louis was still one of the strongest teams in the American Association when the AA folded after the 1891 season. St. Louis moved to the National League, where it immediately began serving as a doormat, a situation that brought Von der Ahe financial ruin.

Von der Ahe wasn't just a winner in his early years in St. Louis—he won with flair. His personal style incorporated checked slacks, spats, gaudy waistcoats, and diamond stickpins. He often brought his pet greyhounds to the games. He spoke in a thick German accent and referred to himself as Der Boss President. Von der Ahe also spent extravagantly. Among his indulgences was a sequence of very expensive and very public mistresses. He traveled in private trains and stayed in the most lavish hotels.

On the negative side, Von der Ahe had an abysmal knowledge of the finer points of the game. But he didn't let his ignorance stop him from constantly interfering with the managers. With the exception of Charlie Comiskey, who managed the club for six seasons and parts of two others and won all four American Association pennants, Von der Ahe hired and fired managers at whim, sometimes employing as many as five

in a single year. He imposed fines for routine errors and demanded that his players live in rooming houses he owned and drink only at his establishments. When the club played below his standards, he turned vindictive. After St. Louis lost the 1887 World Series against the National League champion Detroit Wolverines, Von der Ahe refused to pay them for their work in the postseason. They lost the 1888 World Series as well playing the New York Giants, and again Von der Ahe declined to pay his players. Only Comiskey's intervention defused a player revolt.

Little is known about Von der Ahe's early life. He was born in Germany, came to the United States in 1867 at the age of 15, and, like many immigrants, settled in New York. In 1870, he moved to St. Louis, where he worked as a grocery clerk and eventually opened a tavern called the Golden Lion Saloon at Grand and St. Louis Avenues, in what then was a largely undeveloped area of the city. Von der Ahe bought real estate and increased his earnings as a landlord. His saloon was near Sportsman's Park, where large crowds attended games before heading to the Golden Lion. Von der Ahe became owner of the franchise we know today as the Cardinals in 1881. With a successful team, Von der Ahe turned a tidy profit. After games, flanked by two armed guards, he would ceremoniously cart the day's receipts in a wheelbarrow to a bank a block away.

Fellow owners viewed Von der Ahe as a buffoon. His club began unraveling in the early 1890s with the Cardinals' move to the National League, after Comiskey took his managerial skills and diplomatic talents to the Cincinnati Reds. In an attempt to compensate for his wretched club, Von der Ahe surrounded it with what he called the Coney Island of the West. His ballpark had carousels, carnival rides, band concerts, and boxing matches before and after each game. Von der Ahe brought in a Wild West show with real Indians and put a racetrack around his park.

The end came in 1898. Sportsman's Park burned down, Von der Ahe's wife sued him for divorce because of his infidelity, his mistress sued him for breach of promise, his son took him to court over a property matter, and he ended up in a Pittsburgh jail after former Pirates owner William Nimick had him kidnapped by private detectives and shanghaied to Pennsylvania over a seven-year-old debt of $2,500. The National League agreed to pay the debt if Von der Ahe got out of organized baseball. Destroyed financially, Von der Ahe couldn't even sell his team because a Missouri court had appointed a receiver to dispose of it. The team was eventually sold at auction. Von der Ahe died nearly penniless from cirrhosis of the liver in 1913. On top of his gravesite at Bellefontaine Cemetery is a life-sized statue of Von der Ahe. In keeping with his outsized and eccentric personality, he had arranged for the adornment in 1885 when he was flush with cash.

1883

Season in a Sentence

After overhauling almost the entire roster, the Cardinals finish only one game out of first place in an exciting pennant race with the Philadelphia Athletics.

Finish • Won • Lost • Pct • GB

Second   65   33   .663   1.0

Managers

Ted Sullivan (53–26) and Charlie Comiskey (12–7)

Stats

Stats	Cards	AA	Rank
Batting Avg:	.255	.252	3
On-Base Pct:	.280	.282	3
Slugging Pct:	.321	.331	6
Home Runs:	7		6
ERA:	2.23	3.30	1
Fielding Avg:	.909	.885	1
Runs Scored:	549		4
Runs Allowed:	409		2

Starting Lineup

Pat Deasley, c
Charlie Comiskey, 1b
George Strief, 2b
Arlie Latham, 3b
Bill Gleason, ss
Tom Dolan, lf-cf-c
Fred Lewis, cf
Hugh Nicol, rf
Tony Mullane, p-lf-cf

Pitchers

Tony Mullane, sp
Jumbo McGinnis, sp

Attendance

243,000 (second in AA)

Club Leaders

Batting Avg:	Comiskey	.294
On-Base Pct:	Nicol	.321
Slugging Pct:	Comiskey	.397
Home Runs:	Comiskey	2
	Gleason	2
Runs:	Comiskey	87
Wins:	Mullane	35
Strikeouts:	Mullane	191
ERA:	Mullane	2.19
Saves:	Mullane	1

MAY 1   The Cardinals lose the season opener 6–5 in 11 innings to the Reds in Cincinnati.
         St. Louis plated a run in the top of the eleventh, but Cincinnati rallied with a run in
         its half.

         *The American Association expanded from six to eight clubs in 1883 with new
         teams in New York City and Columbus, Ohio. The schedule called for 98 games,
         14 against each club.*

         *The Cardinals' manager at the start of the 1883 season was Ted Sullivan. Born in
         County Clare, Ireland, in 1851, Sullivan grew up in Milwaukee and came to St.
         Louis as a student at St. Louis University. The Cardinals had a record of 53–26
         in late August, when Sullivan was relieved of his duties after one too many
         clashes with meddling owner Chris Von der Ahe. Charlie Comiskey took over for
         the rest of the season.*

MAY 2   The Cardinals lose 12–1 to the Reds in Cincinnati. Jumbo McGinnis was the starting
         pitcher for St. Louis and tried to leave the game after allowing seven runs in the first
         inning, claiming injury to his arm. According to the rules of the day, a player couldn't
         be replaced unless he was completely disabled. The umpire believed that McGinnis
         was not hurt seriously and ordered him back to the mound.

         *McGinnis (45) and Tony Mullane (49) started 94 of the Cardinals' 98 games
         in 1883. McGinnis had a record of 28–16 while Mullane was 35–15. Born
         in County Cork, Ireland, Mullane had only one season in St. Louis, but his
         matinee-idol good looks and flamboyant handlebar mustache made quite an
         impression on female fans in the city and the six others metropolises he played
         in during his 13-year big-league career. Among his nicknames were "The Count"
         and "The Apollo of the Box." The* Cincinnati Enquirer *once observed that
         Mullane possessed an "arm like a freight car axle and calves that would have
         wooed the daughter of the Capulets away from Romeo." Although one of the
         best pitchers of his era, with 284 wins in the majors, Mullane was stubborn
         and temperamental and was often more trouble than he was worth. In his first
         five years in the major leagues, he played for five different clubs, infuriating
         owners by jumping his contract at a time in which baseball moguls were trying
         to establish the reserve clause. Mullane played for Louisville in 1882 but refused
         to sign a contract and joined the Cardinals in 1883 on a one-year contract.
         When that deal expired, Mullane joined St. Louis of the new Union Association
         during the 1883–84 offseason, then signed another contract with Toledo in the
         American Association. When the Toledo club folded after the 1884 season, the
         Cardinals bought his contract, but Mullane signed with Cincinnati. As a result,
         he was suspended for the 1885 season but was allowed to play for the Reds in
         1886. By that time, Mullane was unable to move from club to club of his own
         free will because the reserve clause held every player in the game to one club for
         life, a situation that would prevail until free agency was instituted in 1976.*

MAY 15   The Cardinals open their home season with a 7–4 win over Cincinnati before 4,000
         at Sportsman's Park.

         *The Cardinals made use of a new invention in 1883 patented just seven years
         earlier by Alexander Graham Bell. A telephone connection was made between
         Sportsman's Park and the club's downtown headquarters that enabled the club to
         report events on the field as fast as they occurred and also to post scores of other*

American Association games in progress on the scoreboard at the ballpark. The scores were relayed to St. Louis by telegraph.

MAY 20   The Cardinals defeat Columbus 5–1 at Sportsman's Park on a day that was so cold that players donned jackets during the last two or three innings of play.

The exact origin of the term "fan" to describe the enthusiastic follower of a sport or a performing art is open for debate, but many sources claim it was first used to describe baseball devotees in St. Louis in 1883. Up until then, baseball fans were most commonly called "cranks" or "fanatics." Some say that Cardinals manager Ted Sullivan first used the expression "fan" as a short term for fanatic. Others say that it came from owner Chris Von der Ahe, who had difficulty pronouncing the word "fanatic" with his thick German accent.

MAY 22   Charlie Comiskey scores a run without a hit during a 5–3 win over Columbus at Sportsman's Park. Comiskey swung and missed at a third strike, but the ball eluded catcher Rudy Kemmler and Comiskey made it all the way to second base. A moment later, Comiskey scored from second base on a wild pitch from pitcher Frank Mountain.

Comiskey was the club's top hitter in 1883 with an average of .294.

JULY 22   The Cardinals trounce Louisville 14–4 in Louisville.

AUGUST 3   After being held hitless by Tony Mullane for eight innings, the Reds erupt for four runs in the ninth inning to defeat the Cardinals 4–3 in Cincinnati. Later that evening, outfielder Tom Mansell, whose nickname was "Brick," suffered an injury that might have cost St. Louis the pennant. After a tour of Cincinnati's finest drinking establishments, Mansell stumbled back to his hotel and fell like a brick down an open elevator shaft and broke his leg. Mansell missed several weeks, and the Cardinals fell short of winning the pennant by only one game.

AUGUST 11   The Cardinals score two runs in the ninth inning to beat Columbus 7–5 in Columbus. In the seventh inning, umpire Robert McNichol was hit in the throat by a foul ball that, according to the newspaper dispatches, "paralyzed the muscles and took away his voice. He umpired the game out, however, making use of the deaf and dumb alphabet. He was applauded for his pluck."

During the evening following the game, Cardinal players Pat Deasley and Fred Lewis got drunk and assaulted manager Ted Sullivan. Deasley and Lewis were arrested and spent the night in jail before Sullivan dropped the charges.

AUGUST 31   The Cardinals score four runs in the ninth inning and defeat the New York Metropolitans 5–4 in New York.

SEPTEMBER 3   In a key game in the 1883 American Association pennant race, the Cardinals defeat the Athletics 7–5 before 12,000 on a Monday afternoon in Philadelphia. The win put St. Louis into first place by half a game.

The Athletics won the final three games of the four-game series, however, by scores of 11–1, 5–4, and 4–3, and the Cardinals left the City of Brotherly Love trailing by 2½ games.

SEPTEMBER 10   Hugh Nicol collects five hits, including a double, and scores five runs during a 15–4 pounding of Baltimore at Sportsman's Park.

Like many players of his era, Nicol immigrated to the United States from the British Isles as a youngster. Born in Campsie, Scotland, and raised in Rockford, Illinois, Nicol played for St. Louis from 1883 through 1886 as an outfielder. Despite standing only five foot four and weighing 145 pounds, Nicol played in 888 major league games. Many sources credit him with inventing the head-first slide.

SEPTEMBER 21   A crowd of 10,000 turns out amid swirling winds at Sportsman's Park for the pennant showdown between the Cardinals and the Philadelphia Athletics. Among those in attendance were Missouri Governor Thomas Crittenden and Congressman John O'Neill. Despite the enthusiastic throng, the Cardinals lost 13–11 in the first game of a three-game series. St. Louis committed 12 errors, 5 of them by third baseman Arlie Latham, who had so much difficulty fielding at the hot corner that Charlie Comiskey had him switch with catcher Pat Deasley in the eighth inning despite the fact that Latham hadn't caught a game all year. Latham allowed three passed balls in his one inning as a backstop, which helped Philadelphia score four runs to increase its lead to 13–8. Amazingly, the Athletics were even worse defensively, making 16 errors during the afternoon. The win gave Philadelphia a lead of 3½ games.

SEPTEMBER 22   The Cardinals win the second game of the pennant showdown series against the Athletics 9–8 at Sportsman's Park.

SEPTEMBER 23   Before 16,800 at Sportsman's Park, the Cardinals lose 9–2 to the Athletics in the final game of the series, all but eliminating any chance that the club had of winning the American Association pennant. The newspapers called the crowd "the largest that was ever assembled on such an occasion west of the Alleghenies."

The Cardinals ended the season one game behind Philadelphia. St. Louis was 5–9 against the Athletics in 1883.

SEPTEMBER 26   The Cardinals pick up 30 hits and wallop Pittsburgh 20–3 at Sportsman's Park. All nine starters had at least two hits. Fred Lewis collected five hits, including a triple, in six at-bats. Tom Mansell was also 5 for 6.

SEPTEMBER 28   Philadelphia clinches the American Association pennant with a 10-inning, 7–6 victory over Louisville at Louisville.

SEPTEMBER 30   The Cardinals close the season with a 6–3 win over Pittsburgh at Sportsman's Park.

The Cardinals took out their frustration over losing the 1883 pennant on peppery third baseman Arlie Latham, who was one of the most unique personalities in baseball history. The St. Louis players were angry because Latham had an extraordinary talent for badgering the opposition and the umpires with his derisive wit, but he often directed his sarcasm at teammates. His ability to use his mouth as a weapon with his merciless heckling earned Latham the nickname "The Freshest Man on Earth." At the end of the September 30 game, Cardinals players trapped Latham in the clubhouse, and the entire roster fought him one by one. As soon as Latham fended off one teammate, another took his place. A few knocked Latham out cold, but, once revived, he had to fight the next player in line. Latham had the last laugh, however, as his baseball career lasted over 70 years. He played in St. Louis from 1883 through 1889 and was the sparkplug on four American Association champions with his enthusiasm, fielding acumen, and base stealing abilities. After his playing days ended, Latham became the first individual appointed specifically as a coach when the Reds hired him in 1900, and he later coached the New York Giants under John McGraw. Latham lived in England for 17 years during the 1910s and 1920s, promoting the American pastime as England's Administrator of Baseball. While there, he mingled with royalty and became friends with the Prince of Wales, who later became King George VIII. After returning to the States, Latham worked for both the Giants and the Yankees as a press box custodian at the Polo Grounds and Yankee Stadium, a position he enjoyed until his death at the age of 92 in 1952.

1884

Season in a Sentence

Players involved in drunken scrapes with the law receive nearly as much attention as the on-field action as the Cardinals sink to fourth place.

Finish • Won • Lost • Pct • GB

Finish	Won	Lost	Pct	GB
Fourth	67	40	.626	8.0

Managers

Jimmy Williams (51–33) and Charlie Comiskey (16–7)

Stats

Stats	Cards	• AA •	Rank
Batting Avg:	.250	.240	5
On-Base Pct:	.288	.278	5
Slugging Pct:	.327	.326	6
Home Runs:	11		9
ERA:	2.67	3.24	3
Fielding Avg:	.900	.897	7
Runs Scored:	658		4
Runs Allowed:	539		6

Starting Lineup

Pat Deasley, c
Charlie Comiskey, 1b
Joe Quest, 2b
Arlie Latham, 3b
Bill Gleason, ss
Tip O'Neill, lf-p
Fred Lewis, cf
Hugh Nicol, rf
George Strief, lf
Tom Dolan, c

Pitchers

Jumbo McGinnis, sp
Dave Foutz, sp
Daisy Davis, sp
Tip O'Neill, sp

Attendance

212,000 (first in AA)

Club Leaders

Batting Avg:	Lewis	.323
On-Base Pct:	Lewis	.368
Slugging Pct:	Lewis	.427
Home Runs:	O'Neill	3
Runs:	Latham	115
Wins:	McGinnis	24
Strikeouts:	Davis	143
ERA:	Foutz	2.18
Saves:	None	

APRIL 20

The St. Louis Maroons of the new Union Association open their season with a 7–2 win over Chicago before about 10,000 fans at Union Grounds in St. Louis.

The St. Louis Maroons were part of a new eight-team major league started in 1884 to compete with the National League and American Association. The chief backer of the Union Association was Henry Lucas of St. Louis, whose family had large real estate holdings and owned several trolley car lines. He built Union Grounds for his club at the southeast corner of Cass and Jefferson. The park had a capacity of 10,000 and included upholstered folding opera chairs and leisure facilities. A cage of canaries serenaded patrons entering the park. With such amenities, the park was dubbed "The Palace Park of America." Lucas set about to build a strong team, but it might have been too good—destroying the pennant race and interest in baseball in many of the league's seven other cities. The Maroons won their first 20 games and finished the season with a record of 94–19. The UA also hoped to lure top players away from the NL and AA but generally failed as most major leaguers chose to remain in the two established leagues rather than risk their future on an untested organization. The NL and AA also won the battle at the box office. In St. Louis, the Cardinals outdrew the Maroons 212,000 to 116,000. Three of the original eight teams drew too few fans to succeed financially and either folded or moved to another city before the season ended, and the Union Association lasted only one year (see January 6, 1885). In order to better compete with the new league, the American Association expanded to 12 teams in 1884, adding clubs in Brooklyn, Indianapolis, Toledo, and Washington. The Washington club moved to Richmond, Virginia, in midseason.

MAY 1

The Cardinals win the season opener 4–3 over Indianapolis at Sportsman's Park. According to the wire service report, "Five thousand invitations had been sent to ladies and gentleman in the best classes of society, and all preparations made for a grand opening." A morning rain prevented a gala musical and militia program, but the United States Cavalry Depot Band was present and "played at intervals during the game, as did also the celebrated cornet player Levy. About five thousand persons witnessed the game, one thousand of them ladies."

The manager of the Cardinals at the start of 1884 was Jimmy Williams. Like Ted Sullivan the previous season, Williams directed a winning team but felt the wrath of owner Chris Von der Ahe and resigned in late August. Charlie Comiskey replaced Williams. The 1884 Cardinals won 10 of their first 11 games and went 51–33 under Williams and 16–7 under the direction of Comiskey.

MAY 4

Jumbo McGinnis pitches a one-hitter to defeat Toledo 4–0 at Sportsman's Park. Tony Mullane, who played for the Cardinals in 1883 but jumped his contract to sign with Toledo for the 1884 season, collected the lone hit off McGinnis. Every time that Mullane "picked up the ball or went to bat he was vigorously hissed" by the partisan St. Louis crowd.

MAY 6

African-American catcher Fleet Walker makes his first appearance in a regular-season game in St. Louis by playing for Toledo during a 5–3 Cardinal win at Sportsman's Park.

Fleet's brother Welday also played for Toledo in 1884. The two were the first African Americans to play in the big leagues. The 1884 campaign was their only one in the majors, however. Not until 1947 when Jackie Robinson played for the Brooklyn Dodgers would another African American appear in a major league game. The first black player on the Cardinals' roster was Tom Alston in 1954.

MAY 7   The Cardinals inflict a 16–0 thrashing on Toledo at Sportsman's Park.

MAY 13   Cardinals catcher Pat Deasley is arrested for drunkenness and for making "insulting comments to ladies" during a drunken spree in Indianapolis. He apparently propositioned them, and when his overtures were rejected, Deasley grabbed one of the women by her arm. Both women escaped to the safety of a store that sold ladies' hats. Deasley steadfastly pursued them, and the police quickly arrived to arrest him.

Deasley was fined $20 in court the following day, but six days later he was seriously injured in a fight with teammates Tom Dolan and Joe Quest. The Cardinals asked Deasley's wife to join the team on future road trips to keep him in line. He was released at the end of the season. Deasley and Dolan, both catchers, feuded all season. Dolan was furious that Deasley was drawing a higher salary and receiving more playing time. Later in the season, Dolan paid a teammate to beat up Deasley so that Dolan could be the first-string catcher. When that didn't work, Dolan jumped to the St. Louis Maroons in the Union Association.

MAY 16   The Cardinals rescue umpire John Valentine following a 14–4 win at Indianapolis. Angered over his calls, a mob followed Valentine for two blocks. He hopped into a carriage conveying some of the Cardinal players, who protected the ump until he reached his downtown hotel.

MAY 29   The Cardinals play the present-day Los Angeles Dodgers for the first time and lose 2–1 in Brooklyn.

The Dodgers moved to the National League in 1890 and from Brooklyn to Los Angeles in 1958.

JUNE 11   Jumbo McGinnis pitches a two-hitter to defeat Pittsburgh 3–0 in Pittsburgh. The only hits off McGinnis were singles by Ed Swartwood and Jack Neagle. The crowd was livid over a decision by umpire Jack Brennan, and at the close of the game, the demonstration became so violent that Brennan left the park guarded by a policeman.

McGinnis had a record of 24–16 in 1884.

JUNE 12   The Cardinals wallop Washington 13–2 in Washington.

JULY 1   Trailing 3–0, the Cardinals score seven runs in the second inning and win 11–5 over Baltimore at Sportsman's Park.

JULY 4   The Cardinals lose twice to the New York Metropolitans 17–0 and 11–8 at Sportsman's Park.

JULY 5   The wife of Arlie Latham unsuccessfully attempts to take her own life by swallowing the contents of a bottle of chloroform at the St. James Hotel in St. Louis. In the suicide note, she said she was distraught because Latham was physically abusive and had left her and their four-year-old son for another woman.

Hotel officials stated that Latham showed no concern over his wife's brush with death. A year later, the couple was divorced. Latham remarried in 1886, and that union also ended in divorce. He was married several more times during his life, which ended at the age of 92. No one knows his exact number of marriages.

JULY 12   The Cardinals outslug the Brooklyn Dodgers 15–12 at Sportsman's Park.

JULY 13   Jumbo McGinnis pitches a one-hitter for an 11–0 win over Brooklyn at Brooklyn. The only hit off McGinnis was a single by Fred Warner in the first inning.

JULY 15   Jumbo McGinnis pitches his second consecutive one-hitter and beats Brooklyn 6–0 at Sportsman's Park. Opposing pitcher Sam Kimber chalked up the hit, a single off McGinnis in the ninth inning. During his July 13 and July 15 appearances, McGinnis pitched 16 consecutive hitless innings.

JULY 20   The Cardinals blow a 6–1 lead by allowing Louisville to score five runs in the ninth inning and two in the tenth for an 8–6 loss at Sportsman's Park.

JULY 29   In his major league debut, Cardinal pitcher Dave Foutz strikes out 13 batters in a 13-inning, 6–5 win over the Reds in Cincinnati.

Foutz left his native Maryland in the late 1870s to seek a fortune as a gold miner in Leadville, Colorado. Pitching for the Leadville nine, he posted a 40–1 record and caught the attention of major league scouts. Standing six foot two and weighing 165 pounds, Foutz was nicknamed "Scissors" and "His Needles." In his first 20 days with St. Louis, he pitched in 10 games and won 8 of them before being put out of action for three weeks with malarial fever in late August and early September. Foutz recovered from the ailment to forge an excellent career. In four seasons with St. Louis, he had a record of 114–48. Among Cardinal pitchers with at least 100 decisions and 1,000 innings, Foutz ranks first in winning percentage (.704) and second in ERA (2.67). At the end of the 2005 season, he was also fourth in complete games (156 in 166 starts) and eighth in victories. A broken thumb suffered in August 1887 curtailed his pitching effectiveness, and at the end of the season, Foutz was dealt to the Brooklyn Dodgers. There, Foutz played nine seasons primarily as a hard-hitting first baseman and outfielder. In addition to his excellent pitching, he had a career .276 batting average and appeared in more big-league games at first base (596) and in the outfield (320) than as a pitcher (251). Six weeks after Foutz made his big-league debut, the Cardinals unveiled 20-year-old pitcher Bob Caruthers. Foutz and Caruthers were a potent 1–2 punch at the top of the rotation for the Cardinals' 1885, 1886, and 1887 pennant-winning teams. The son of a wealthy Memphis doctor, Caruthers stood only five foot seven and weighed just 138 pounds. Despite his small stature, he had a 108–48 record, a winning percentage of .692, in five seasons in St. Louis during a big-league career in which he was 218–89. Like Foutz, Caruthers was an excellent hitter who played more games as an outfielder (366) than as a pitcher (340). Caruthers had a career .282 batting average.

AUGUST 14   The Cardinals defeat Columbus 3–2 in 11 innings in Columbus with the help of an obtrusive fan. Batting in the eleventh inning with two outs, Columbus's Fred Mann hit a drive into the right-field bleachers. According to the rules of the day, a ball hit into the seats behind the outfielders was in play. A fan stopped the ball and laid it on a seat where St. Louis right fielder Hugh Nicol picked it up and fired the ball into the infield, holding Mann to a double. Had the fan let the ball go, Mann would have easily circled the bases for a home run.

AUGUST 15   The Cardinals wallop Columbus 16–6 at Columbus.

SEPTEMBER 13   The Cardinals collect 22 hits and roll to a 15–6 win over Brooklyn at Sportsman's Park.

SEPTEMBER 20   Outfielder Fred Lewis is released despite his team-leading .323 batting average.

The release was prompted by Lewis's habitual drunkenness, which often ended in brawls. The breaking point occurred when Lewis got drunk at the Marble Saloon in St. Louis, challenged every man in the room to a fight, and was asked to leave the premises. In a rage, Lewis threw a beer keg and a box full of soda water through the window of the establishment, leading to his arrest. Lewis had a career .296 batting average, but he played for six clubs in five years and was released by each of them because of his excessive alcohol consumption and combative demeanor. He was only 27 when he played in his last big-league game. Lewis apparently cleaned up his act at some point because he lived to the age of 86.

SEPTEMBER 21   The Cardinals trounce the Dodgers 15–4 at Sportsman's Park.

SEPTEMBER 23   Six weeks before Grover Cleveland wins the presidential election and succeeds Chester Arthur in the White House, the Cardinals wallop the Dodgers 18–5 at Sportsman's Park. The game was stopped after seven innings to allow the Brooklyn club to catch a train. Bill Gleason collected five hits, including a double, in five at-bats.

1885

Season in a Sentence

In a dominating performance, the Cardinals win the American Association pennant before playing in a controversial postseason series against the National League champions from Chicago.

Finish • Won • Lost • Pct • GB

First   79   33   .705 +16.0

Manager

Charlie Comiskey

Stats

	Cards	• AA •	Rank
Batting Avg:	.246	.246	5
On-Base Pct:	.297	.292	2
Slugging Pct:	.321	.328	5
Home Runs:	17		5 (tie)
ERA:	2.44	3.24	1
Fielding Avg:	.920	.909	1
Runs Scored:	677		2
Runs Allowed:	461		1

Starting Lineup

Doc Bushong, c
Charlie Comiskey, 1b
Sam Barkley, 2b
Arlie Latham, 3b
Bill Gleason, ss
Yank Robinson, lf
Curt Welch, cf
Hugh Nicol, rf
Tip O'Neill, lf

Pitchers

Bob Caruthers, sp
Dave Foutz, sp
Jumbo McGinnis, sp

Attendance

129,000 (second in AA)

Club Leaders

Batting Avg:	Welch	.271
On-Base Pct:	Welch	.318
Slugging Pct:	Barkley	.380
Home Runs:	Three tied w/ 3	
RBIs:	Welch	69
Runs:	Welch	84
	Latham	84
Wins:	Caruthers	40
Strikeouts:	Caruthers	190
ERA:	Caruthers	2.07
Saves:	None	

JANUARY 6   The St. Louis Maroons of the Union Association merge with the Cleveland club of the National League. With the collapse of the UA, the new team moved to the NL but stayed in St. Louis. Henry Lucas continued as the owner of the Maroons and kept his club at the Union Grounds at Cass and Jefferson, which was also known as the "Palace Park of America." The ballpark burned to the ground in July 1885, however, and Lucas moved his Maroons to a lot at the junction of Natural Bridge and Vandeventer. Lucas hadn't insured the ballpark for fire, and he suffered huge financial losses. Shortly thereafter, a hurricane-force storm struck St. Louis, demolishing his fleet of barges on the Mississippi River. The barges were also uninsured. The Maroons lasted only two years in the National League, finishing in last place in 1885 and sixth in an eight-team league in 1886. By contrast, the Cardinals won the American Association pennant both seasons. The Maroons were also hindered at the ticket window by the National League's strictures against playing on Sunday and on alcohol sold at the ballpark. St. Louis would lack an NL team until the Cardinals moved to the circuit in 1892 and the bans on Sunday ball and alcohol had been lifted. Lucas suffered further losses in subsequent business ventures. Once one of the richest men in St. Louis, he spent his last years working as a railroad ticket taker and as a city street inspector.

APRIL 11   In a preseason exhibition matchup of St. Louis's two Major League Baseball teams, the American Association Cardinals defeat the National League Maroons 7–0 in frigid temperatures at Sportsman's Park. Dave Foutz pitched a one-hitter.

The Cardinals and Maroons met twice more. On April 13, the Maroons won 6–4 at Union Grounds. On April 14, the Cardinals were victorious, winning 8–0 back at Sportsman's Park.

APRIL 18   The Cardinals open the season with a 7–0 loss to Pittsburgh at Sportsman's Park.

With the collapse of the Union Association, the American Association abandoned its one-year experiment with 12 teams. In 1885, eight teams competed for the pennant in St. Louis, Baltimore, Brooklyn, Cincinnati, Louisville, New York, Philadelphia, and Pittsburgh.

APRIL 24   The Cardinals score seven runs in the ninth inning and defeat Louisville 12–2 at Sportsman's Park.

MAY 5   The Cardinals score seven times in the eighth inning and win 12–4 at Louisville.

MAY 7   The Cardinals take first place with a 13–4 win over the Athletics at Sportsman's Park.

St. Louis remained in first place for the rest of the season, clinching the pennant on September 12.

MAY 17   The Cardinals explode for eight runs in the ninth inning and win 15–4 over the New York Metropolitans at Sportsman's Park.

MAY 21   The New York Metropolitans take a 7–0 lead in the first inning, but the Cardinals rally to win 11–9 in a contest at Sportsman's Park called after eight innings by darkness.

JUNE 1   The Cardinals extend their winning streak to 17 games with a 10–4 win over the Orioles in Baltimore.

JUNE 2   The Cardinals' 17-game winning streak comes to an end with a 7–1 loss to the Orioles in Baltimore.

The 17-game winning streak is the longest in club history. The longest since 1892, when the club joined the National League, has been 14 games, in 1935.

JUNE 17   Dodgers pitcher "Phenomenal" Smith makes his debut with the club and loses 18–5 to the Cardinals in Brooklyn. All 18 runs against Smith were unearned due to 14 Brooklyn errors, most of them intentionally committed by players who took an immediate dislike to the brash youngster. When he first joined the team, Smith, who gave himself the nickname, said he was so good that he didn't need his teammates to win.

Dodgers owner Charles Byrne fined his players $50 each and threatened them with expulsion for their disgraceful conduct, but he also released Smith in the interest of team harmony. The following day, the Dodgers played errorless ball and defeated the Cardinals 3–1.

JUNE 30   Dave Foutz pitches no-hit ball for 7²/₃ innings before losing 5–2 against Louisville in
           Louisville. With two outs in the eighth, Foutz surrendered four consecutive hits that
           netted Louisville three runs and the lead. Two more runs and three hits followed in
           the ninth.

           Bob Caruthers and Dave Foutz were the starting pitchers in 99 of the Cardinals'
           112 games in 1885 and completed all 99. Jumbo McGinnis started the other
           13 contests and completed 12 of them. Caruthers led the American Association
           in wins and winning percentage, compiling a 40–13 record. He also topped the
           circuit in ERA with a 2.07 mark while pitching 482¹/₃ innings. Foutz pitched
           407²/₃ innings and had a 33–14 record.

JULY 3   Jumbo McGinnis pitches a one-hitter to defeat Baltimore 2–1 at Sportsman's Park.
           The only hit off McGinnis was an infield single by Dennis Casey. McGinnis was late
           covering first base, and Casey just beat Charlie Comiskey to the bag.

JULY 4   The Cardinals score five runs in the top of the eleventh inning to defeat Baltimore 7–2
           in the first of two games at Sportsman's Park. St. Louis also won the second tilt, 2–1.

           The Cardinals batted first despite playing at home because of the rules of the day.
           Prior to 1900, there was a pregame coin flip, and the winner of the toss chose
           whether to bat or take the field first.

JULY 7   The Cardinals wallop the Baltimore Orioles 13–2 at Sportsman's Park.

JULY 16   The Cardinals extend their home winning streak to 27 games. St. Louis scored nine
           times in the second to take a 9–1 lead, allowed Philadelphia to tie the game, and then
           scored two in the ninth for a 13–11 victory.

JULY 18   The Cardinals' 27-game home winning streak ends with an 11–6 loss to Philadelphia
           at Sportsman's Park.

           The 27-game streak is still the record for most consecutive games won at home
           in a season. Next best is the New York Giants' 26-game streak in 1916.

AUGUST 9   Cardinal catcher Dan Sullivan sets a major league record for most passed balls in an
           inning with five in the third inning of a 6–3 loss to Pittsburgh at Sportsman's Park.

           Sullivan played only 17 games for St. Louis. In addition to his inability to
           adequately field his position, he batted only .117 for the Cardinals.

AUGUST 11 The Cardinals defeat Pittsburgh 3–1 in 14 innings at Sportsman's Park. Curt Welch's
           infield single drove in the winning run.

           Welch was the top St. Louis hitter in 1885 with a .271 average. He played for
           the Cardinals from 1885 through 1887 and, like many players of his generation,
           had an unhealthy fondness for alcohol that ended his career at 31 and led to
           his death at 34. Welch kept bottles of beer hidden behind the billboards on the
           outfield fences at Sportsman's Park to imbibe between innings.

SEPTEMBER 15 The Cardinals win a controversial 3–2 decision in 11 innings over the Athletics in
           Philadelphia. With nightfall fast approaching, players from both teams appealed

to umpire John Kelly to call the game, but he refused. In the eleventh, Athletics outfielder John Coleman dropped two fly balls that he had trouble tracking in the gloom, leading to the winning run.

SEPTEMBER 16   The Cardinals score nine runs in the third inning and win 15–6 in Philadelphia.

OCTOBER 7   The city of St. Louis stages a nighttime parade and a sumptuous banquet at Schnaider's Beer Garden to honor the 1885 American Association champion Cardinals. An estimated 250,000 people lined the streets. The procession through the principal thoroughfares of the city was led by mounted police, the United States Cavalry band, and the state militia. Local amateur clubs marched during the festivities, as did the Cincinnati Reds and New York Giants. A pretty young woman sat atop a Sportsman's Park float that contained pictures of Cardinal players. Chris Von der Ahe rode just behind the float in a carriage with his guests. The Atchison Flambeau Club provided a wagonload of ammunition and fireworks, and many in the crowd came equipped with pyrotechnics of their own, including live bombs, torches, Roman candles, and pinwheels. Shotguns blasts from upper-story windows punctuated the night air. Not surprisingly, the event was marred by a series of injuries. Vice President Thomas A. Hendricks was in St. Louis to attend the 25th annual Mississippi River Valley Agricultural and Mechanical Fair. Under the mistaken notion that the parade was being held in his honor to welcome him to town, Hendricks began to make a speech from the balcony of his room at the Southern Hotel thanking St. Louisans for their hospitality.

Once the regular season concluded, the Cardinals met the National League champion Chicago White Stockings in a "World Series" to determine the "World Championship" of baseball. It was the second time that the American Association and National League pennant winners had met in a postseason championship series. In 1884, the Providence Grays of the NL played the New York Metropolitans of the AA. The 1885 White Stockings were managed by Cap Anson, who was also the club's first baseman. The Chicago White Stockings franchise today is known as the Chicago Cubs. The Cubs nickname surfaced in 1902. Thus, the 1885 World Series between the two clubs was the beginning of the longstanding Cardinals-Cubs rivalry. The original schedule for the 1885 series called for one game in Chicago, three in St. Louis, and seven more contests split among Pittsburgh, Cincinnati, Baltimore, Philadelphia, and Brooklyn. The games in the last three cities were never played, however, as the Series turned into a complete fiasco.

OCTOBER 14   In Game One of the 1885 World Series, the Cardinals and the White Stockings play to a 5–5 tie, called after eight innings by darkness before a crowd of 2,000 in Chicago. St. Louis took a 5–0 lead in the fourth and was still on top 5–1 heading into the eighth when Chicago scored four runs on a walk, two singles, and Fred Pfeffer's three-run homer.

OCTOBER 15   The White Stockings win Game Two before 2,000 at Sportsman's Park by forfeit. Chicago led 5–4 in the sixth inning when Cardinals manager Charlie Comiskey pulled his team off the field, objecting to the decisions of umpire David Sullivan. The crowd swarmed all over the grounds, and Sullivan needed police protection to leave the ballpark. Once in the safety of his hotel room, Sullivan forfeited the game to Chicago. He didn't umpire any more games in the Series.

OCTOBER 16   The Cardinals take Game Three against the White Stockings, scoring five unearned runs with two outs in the top of the first and holding on for a 7–4 win before 3,000 at Sportsman's Park.

OCTOBER 17   The Cardinals win Game Four 3–2 before 3,000 at Sportsman's Park. St. Louis scored first with a run in the third inning, but Abner Dalrymple hit a two-run homer in the fifth to give Chicago a 2–1 lead. In the bottom of the eighth, however, the Cardinals scored twice and held on for the victory. The right fielder for Chicago was 17-year-old St. Louis amateur Bug Holliday. He was pressed into service after White Stockings outfielder George Gore was suspended for showing up to Game Two drunk and unable to play.

After the fourth game, the Series took a five-day break. During the interruption, the White Stockings played two exhibition games against the Reds in Cincinnati, and the Cardinals played their crosstown rival, the Maroons.

OCTOBER 22   The Cardinals–White Stockings series moves to Pittsburgh for Game Five. Only 500 fans watched Chicago win 9–2. The contest was called after seven innings by darkness.

OCTOBER 23   The White Stockings win Game Six 9–2 in Cincinnati. Jim McCormick stopped the Cardinals on two hits.

Poor crowds in Pittsburgh and Cincinnati compelled the Cardinals and White Stockings to cancel the games at the neutral sites in the Eastern cities of Baltimore, Philadelphia, and Brooklyn. It was also agreed to throw out Game Two, which was forfeited to Chicago. That left the series with each team winning two games and the other ending in a tie. The two clubs further consented to make the October 24 game in Cincinnati the last of the series, with the victor winning the championship and the winner-take-all prize money of $1,000.

OCTOBER 24   The Cardinals take the 1885 championship by defeating the White Stockings in a 13–4 runaway in Cincinnati. John Clarkson was scheduled to pitch for Chicago, but he missed the carriage taking the club to the ballpark because he overslept. Although Clarkson arrived in another conveyance in time to start the game, manager Cap Anson put in Jim McCormick as the pitcher. McCormick had pitched nine innings the day before and wasn't up to the task. He gave up 10 runs in the first four innings.

After St. Louis won the title, Chicago manager Cap Anson decided his club should retain its forfeit win after all, and a select committee agreed, leaving the Series in a draw with three wins for St. Louis, three for Chicago, and one tie. The winning prize money of $1,000 was split evenly between the two teams.

1886

Season in a Sentence

The Cardinals easily set the pace in the American Association pennant race and defeat the Chicago White Stockings in a postseason series for the World Championship.

Finish • Won • Lost • Pct • GB

First   93   46   .669 +12.0

Manager

Charlie Comiskey

Stats

Stats		Cards •	AA •	Rank
Batting Avg:	.273	.243	1
On-Base Pct:	.333	.305	1
Slugging Pct:	.380	.323	1
Home Runs:	20		3 (tie)
Stolen Bases:	336		1
ERA:	2.49	3.44	1
Fielding Avg:	.915	.906	2
Runs Scored:	944		1
Runs Allowed:	592		1

Starting Lineup

Doc Bushong, c
Charlie Comiskey, 1b
Yank Robinson, 2b
Arlie Latham, 3b
Bill Gleason, ss
Tip O'Neill, lf
Curt Welch, cf
Hugh Nicol, rf
Dave Foutz, p-rf
Bob Caruthers, p-rf

Pitchers

Dave Foutz, sp
Bob Caruthers, sp
Nat Hudson, sp
Jumbo McGinnis, sp

Attendance

205,000 (first in AA)

Club Leaders

Batting Avg:	O'Neill	.328
On-Base Pct:	O'Neill	.385
Slugging Pct:	O'Neill	.440
Home Runs:	Caruthers	4
RBIs:	O'Neill	107
Runs:	Latham	152
Wins:	Foutz	41
Strikeouts:	Foutz	283
ERA:	Foutz	2.11
Saves:	Foutz	1
	Hudson	1

March 13   From Paris, Bob Caruthers agrees to a salary of $3,200 with Chris Von der Ahe for the coming season via transatlantic telegraph. Caruthers was in France on a trip with teammate Doc Bushong. Caruthers's well-publicized holdout, which consisted of cables sent back and forth across the ocean, earned him the nickname "Parisian Bob."

Caruthers had a 30–14 record and a 2.32 ERA as a pitcher in 1886. In between starts, he played in 43 games as an outfielder and overall batted .334 while leading the club in home runs with four.

April 18   The Cardinals open the season with a separate-admission doubleheader against Pittsburgh with one contest played in the morning and the other in the afternoon. The twin bill was the result of a postponement of the scheduled season opener the previous day because of rain. St. Louis won the morning tilt 8–4 before 3,000 and the afternoon affair 10–3 in front of 12,000 fans.

April 24   Arlie Latham collects six hits, including a triple, in six at-bats during a 15–9 win over Louisville at Sportsman's Park. The Cardinals broke a 5–5 tie with four runs in the seventh inning.

Latham hit .301 and led the American Association in runs scored with 152 in 1886.

APRIL 25   The Cardinals win another slugfest from Louisville 15–10 at Sportsman's Park. Down 10–9, St. Louis scored a run in the eighth inning and five in the ninth.

APRIL 26   The Cardinals score two runs in the tenth inning and outlast the Reds 14–12 at Sportsman's Park.

APRIL 27   The Cardinals hammer the Reds 20–3 at Sportsman's Park, giving St. Louis 64 runs in a span of four games in four days. Tip O'Neill and Curt Welch both had five hits in six at-bats. Among O'Neill's hits were two triples and a double.

> *A native of Woodstock, Ontario, James "Tip" O'Neill played for the Cardinals from 1884 through 1889 and in 1891. He came to St. Louis as a pitcher but was soon converted to the outfield and became one of the top hitters of the late 1880s. O'Neill could not only hit for average, but for power as well. Among players in franchise history with at least 2,000 plate appearances at the end of the 2005 season, O'Neill ranked second to Rogers Hornsby in batting average (.343), seventh in on-base percentage (.406), and twelfth in slugging percentage (.498).*

MAY 8   The Cardinals rout Louisville 21–5 at Sportsman's Park, scoring in all eight at-bats. Pitcher Dave Foutz collected five hits.

> *Foutz was 41–16 in 1886 and led the league in wins, winning percentage (.719), and earned run average (2.11). He also played in 34 games as an outfielder in between pitching assignments and hit .280.*

MAY 14   Charlie Comiskey prevents a double play by running full-tilt into Reds second baseman Bid McPhee in the ninth inning, enabling the winning run to cross the plate for a 2–1 victory in Cincinnati. Reds fans were irate at the roughhouse tactic, but the umpire allowed the play to stand. The Cardinals gradually made "breaking up the double play" an accepted part of the game.

MAY 19   At the conclusion of a 7–3 win over the Dodgers in Brooklyn "a gang of roughs" attacks umpire Jim Clinton. The Brooklyn players, headed by Ed Swartwood, ran to Clinton's assistance and with their bats kept the mob at bay until police arrived.

MAY 23   Shortstop Bill Gleason commits six errors during a 10-inning, 13–12 loss to the Dodgers at the Long Island Athletic Club Grounds in the Ridgewood section of Queens. The Cardinals scored seven runs in the ninth inning only to lose in the extra frame.

> *The Dodgers played in Ridgewood on Sundays from 1886 through 1889 because games on the Christian Sabbath were illegal in Brooklyn at the time.*

MAY 29   The Cardinals pummel the Athletics 18–1 and 11–5 in a doubleheader in Philadelphia. St. Louis scored seven runs in both the first and fourth innings of the opener.

> *In order to slow down the speedy Cardinals, Philadelphia manager Lew Simmons piled sand on the right side of the infield. Charlie Comiskey reported that the sand was a foot deep. Comiskey refused to play unless the sand was removed, and umpire George Bradley agreed. A groundskeeper trotted in with a wheelbarrow and shovels. After one load was hauled away, Comiskey told the*

groundskeeper to get a bigger cart. Comiskey and Arlie Latham also grabbed a shovel and joined in the excavation. Without enough tools to go around, other players used their hands. The game began 15 minutes late.

JUNE 3   Cardinals teammates Arlie Latham and Doc Bushong get into a fistfight on the field during a 9–5 win over the Orioles in Baltimore.

Albert (Doc) Bushing earned his nickname by practicing dentistry during the offseason after earning his Doctor of Dental Surgery Degree from the University of Pennsylvania in 1882. A catcher, he pioneered the use of a padded glove and catching primarily with one hand.

JUNE 9   At an American Association meeting in Columbus, Chris Von Der Ahe pays the many fines Charlie Comiskey incurred as a result of his arguments with umpires. Comiskey had refused to pay the fines and was threatened with expulsion.

JUNE 16   Dave Foutz pitches the Cardinals to a 1–0 win over Pittsburgh at Sportsman's Park.

Transcendental Graphics/theruckerarchive.com

Charles Comiskey was a baseball player, manager, and owner for a half century. He was player-manager of the American Association's St. Louis Browns in 1883 and helped the team win four consecutive pennants from 1885 to 1888. Comiskey was one of the founders of the American League in 1901 and owned the Chicago White Sox for 31 years, winning five pennants. In 1910, he built famed Comiskey Park, home of the Chicago White Sox for 81 years.

| June 18 | The Cardinals score seven runs in the first inning and win 11–0 over the Reds at Sportsman's Park. Bob Caruthers pitched a two-hitter, allowing only singles to John Reilly and Kid Baldwin. |

June 26
The Cardinals eke out a 10-inning, 1–0 victory over the Reds in Cincinnati. Dave Foutz pitched the complete-game shutout and started the game-winning rally with a triple. He scored on a squeeze bunt by Yank Robinson.

> *Robinson was the Cardinals' starting second baseman from 1885 through 1889 but often filled in elsewhere on the field when others were injured and played at all nine positions before his big-league career ended in 1892. Shortly thereafter, Robinson became ill with pulmonary problems and died in 1894 a few weeks shy of his 35th birthday.*

June 30
The Cardinals and the Metropolitans set a major league record with just one putout by outfielders during a 7–3 St. Louis win in New York. Cardinal center fielder Curt Welch made the putout.

July 8
Jumbo McGinnis pitches the Cardinals to a 10–0 win over Baltimore at Sportsman's Park. The following day, McGinnis was sold to the Baltimore club.

July 11
A rowdy crowd in Cincinnati riots on a Sunday afternoon during the sixth inning of an 11–7 St. Louis win over the Reds. Umpire George Bradley was struck by a beer mug and retreated to the safety of the director's box under a shower of debris. Many of the seats in the grandstand were smashed, the press stand was demolished, and the game was delayed for 20 minutes.

July 13
After a 7–1 win over Philadelphia at Sportsman's Park, Chris Von der Ahe gives the two clubs and the press "an elegant banquet on the lawn of the park, at which several prominent citizens were present and made pleasant speeches, and a royal good time was had." Tables were "loaded down with good things," and "wine flowed like water."

July 17
The Cardinals wallop the Metropolitans 13–2 at the St. George Grounds on Staten Island.

> *The St. George Grounds overlooked New York Harbor. During the 1886 season, fans at the ballpark could not only see a major league game, but also look out over the water and watch the Statue of Liberty being assembled.*

July 24
Dodgers pitcher Adonis Terry no-hits the Cardinals 1–0 in Brooklyn.

July 27
After a 4–2 loss in Baltimore, Arlie Latham and Yank Robinson fight in a carriage waiting to take them back to the hotel. The fisticuffs occurred in full view of several thousand fans leaving the ballpark.

August 2
The Cardinals score eight runs in the fifth inning and defeat the Metropolitans 13–2 at Sportsman's Park.

August 11
The Cardinals trounce Baltimore 18–7 at Sportsman's Park. All 18 runs were scored off former teammate Jumbo McGinnis.

AUGUST 12	The Cardinals rout the Baltimore Orioles again, this time 13–1 in St. Louis.
AUGUST 13	The Cardinals win hands down against Baltimore for the third day in a row with a 14–2 triumph at Sportsman's Park.
AUGUST 15	The Cardinals win their 11th decision in a row and continue their incredible batting streak with a 19–0 pasting of the Dodgers at Sportsman's Park.
AUGUST 16	Bob Caruthers collects two homers, a triple, and a double but is the losing pitcher in an 11–9 loss to the Dodgers at Sportsman's Park that ends the Cardinals' 11-game winning streak. Caruthers allowed only two hits through the first seven innings and had an 8–1 lead, but he gave up 10 runs in the eighth. He was tagged out at the plate for the final out in the ninth inning when he tried to stretch a triple into his third home run of the game.

The other two pitchers in major league history with four extra-base hits in a game are Snake Wiltse of the 1901 Philadelphia Athletics (two triples and two doubles) and Babe Ruth of the Red Sox in 1918 (three doubles and a triple).

AUGUST 29	The Cardinals pummel Louisville 11–0 at Louisville.

The top St. Louis batters in 1886 were Tip O'Neill and Curt Welch. O'Neill hit .328, drove in 107 runs, and scored 106. Welch hit .281 and scored 114 runs.

SEPTEMBER 5	The day after Apache warrior Geronimo surrenders to the U.S. Army for the last time, Dave Foutz pulls off a strange play during an 8–2 loss at Louisville. Pete Browning was the Louisville base runner on first base, and Charlie Comiskey played deep behind the bag to encourage Browning to take a big lead. Foutz suddenly darted over from the pitcher's mound to tag Browning out in the only documented instance of a pitcher picking off a runner unassisted without a rundown.
SEPTEMBER 7	The Cardinals score two runs in the ninth inning to win 2–1 at Pittsburgh. Dave Foutz threw a two-hitter, allowing only a double and a single to former teammate Sam Barkley.
SEPTEMBER 28	The Cardinals clinch the pennant with a 16–3 victory in the second game of a doubleheader against Baltimore at Sportsman's Park. The Orioles delayed the celebration a few hours by winning the opener 6–3.

The Cardinals played the Chicago White Stockings (today's Chicago Cubs) in the 1886 World Series in a matchup of the 1885 Fall Classic, which ended in a less-than-classic manner (see October 24, 1885). Managed by Cap Anson, Chicago won the National League title with a record of 90–34. The two clubs were scheduled to meet in a best-of-seven series in 1886 with the winner taking all of the prize money, which amounted to about $14,000.

OCTOBER 18	The 1886 World Series begins in Chicago with the White Stockings defeating the Cardinals 6–0 behind the five-hit shutout pitching of John Clarkson.
OCTOBER 19	The Cardinals even the Series by trouncing the White Stockings 12–0 in Chicago in a game shortened to eight innings by darkness. Bob Caruthers pitched a one-hitter for St. Louis, allowing only a leadoff single to George Gore in the first

inning. Caruthers also hit a triple and a double. Tip O'Neill had three hits, two of them homers that landed among a number of carriages parked in the most distant regions of left field.

OCTOBER 20   The White Stockings regain the lead in the Series by winning 11–4 over the Cardinals in Chicago. Caruthers, pitching for the second day in a row, walked four of the first five batters he faced.

OCTOBER 21   The Cardinals rally from a 3–0 deficit, then break a 5–5 tie by scoring three times in the sixth inning to beat the White Stockings 8–5 before 6,000 at Sportsman's Park in Game Four. The contest was called after seven innings by darkness. The game fell shy of nine innings in part because of a delay in the fifth inning when a St. Louis rooter and a Chicago partisan duked it out in the left-field bleachers. The Chicago fan was thrown onto the field, and a Cardinal supporter leaped on top of him with a flurry of punches. Approximately 200 fans jumped onto the field to get a closer look at the fight.

OCTOBER 22   The Cardinals move within one win of the World Championship by defeating the White Stockings 10–3 before 10,000 at Sportsman's Park in Game Five.

OCTOBER 23   The Cardinals defeat the White Stockings 4–3 in 10 innings before 8,000 at Sportsman's Park in Game Six to win the 1886 World Series. The contest was interrupted by rain and a rowdy crowd that poured onto the field in the fifth inning with Chicago leading 2–0. The White Stockings added another tally in the sixth, but St. Louis tied the game with three in the eighth and won it in the tenth. The winning run scored when Chicago hurler John Clarkson threw the ball past catcher King Kelly and Curt Welch raced in from third base.

> Contemporary newspapers differ on exactly what took place when Welch scored the winning run. Some called it a passed ball and others a wild pitch. There is also a dispute over when Welch broke for the plate. Did he move forward after the ball sailed past the catcher, or did he break with the pitch in an attempt to steal? In later years, Charlie Comiskey and Arlie Latham claimed that Welch was trying to steal home and that he slid across the plate, although there is no concrete evidence that Welch went into a slide. Regardless, the play has gone into history as the "$15,000 slide," an amount slightly above the $13,920.10 in prize money the Cardinals took.

NOVEMBER 15   The Cardinals trade Hugh Nicol to the Reds for Jack Boyle. It was the first trade in major league history of players on the reserve list.

1887

Season in a Sentence

The Cardinals score an astonishing 1,131 runs and easily win the American Association pennant for the third year in a row.

Finish • Won • Lost • Pct • GB

First   95   40   .704 +14.0

Manager

Charlie Comiskey

Stats

	Cards	• AA •	Rank
Batting Avg:	.307	.273	1
On-Base Pct:	.371	.337	1
Slugging Pct:	.413	.387	1
Home Runs:	39		1
Stolen Bases:	581		1
ERA:	3.77	4.29	2
Fielding Avg:	.917	.906	1
Runs Scored:	1,131		1
Runs Allowed:	761		2

Starting Lineup

Jack Boyle, c
Charlie Comiskey, 1b
Yank Robinson, 2b
Arlie Latham, 3b
Bill Gleason, ss
Tip O'Neill, lf
Curt Welch, cf
Bob Caruthers, rf-p
Dave Foutz, rf-p
Doc Bushong, c

Pitchers

Silver King, sp
Bob Caruthers, sp
Dave Foutz, sp
Nat Hudson, sp

Attendance

244,000 (second in AA)

Club Leaders

Batting Avg:	O'Neill	.435
On-Base Pct:	O'Neill	.490
Slugging Pct:	O'Neill	.697
Home Runs:	O'Neill	14
RBIs:	O'Neill	123
Runs:	Latham	163
Stolen Bases:	Latham	129
Wins:	King	32
Strikeouts:	King	128
ERA:	Caruthers	3.30
Saves:	Caruthers	1
	Robinson	1

APRIL 16   In the season opener, the Cardinals lose 8–3 in Louisville.

The American Association voted on a new rule in 1887 that created the coach's box. It was passed with St. Louis in mind and was particularly directed at the antics of player-manager Charlie Comiskey, Arlie Latham, and Bill Gleason. At the time, teams didn't hire full-time coaches. Those serving as first and third base coaches during games were players who either weren't playing that day or were not batting during the inning. When serving as base coaches, Comiskey, Latham, and Gleason would chase the umpire around the field in order to be near enough to intimidate him on close calls. The Cardinal trio also ran onto the infield to urge teammates around the bases. With his quick and sarcastic wit, Latham could be particularly vicious in taunting umpires and opposing players who could be easily rattled. Latham would often edge near the grandstand to address the crowd. The "Arlie Show" was worth the price of admission as many fans came to the park solely to watch him torment the opposition and the umpires. If he had been born 100 years later, it's likely that Latham would have become famous as a stand-up comic or as a television commentator. The creation of the coach's box helped to corral the Cardinals' players, but it failed to curb their tongues, and umpires and the opposition still received an earful.

APRIL 22   The Cardinals play their first regular-season game at home in 1887 and defeat the Reds 5–2.

The Cardinals lost three of the first five games in 1887, then won 29 of their next 31.

APRIL 27   The Cardinals score eight runs in the eighth inning and roll over the Cleveland club 19–3 at Sportsman's Park.

Cleveland was a new club in the American Association in 1887, replacing one in Pittsburgh. The Pittsburgh team, today's Pirates, moved to the National League.

APRIL 28   The Cardinals build a 12–1 lead after 6½ innings, then hang on to defeat Cleveland 13–11 at Sportsman's Park.

APRIL 30   The Cardinals continue their assault on Cleveland pitching with a 28–11 win in a contest called after eight innings by darkness at Sportsman's Park. Tip O'Neill hit for the cycle with two homers, a triple, a double, and a single. All 28 runs scored in the first six innings, Cleveland hurler Mike Morrison allowed all 28.

MAY 1   The Cardinals complete a four-game sweep of Cleveland in which they score 74 runs with a 14–13 triumph at Sportsman's Park.

The Cardinals scored 1,131 runs in 138 games in 1887. The run explosion was in part due to a rule change that gave the batters four strikes. Five balls were necessary for a walk that season. Previous ball-strike counts in Major League Baseball were nine balls and three strikes from 1876 through 1879, eight balls and three strikes in 1880, seven balls and three strikes from 1881 through 1883, six balls and three strikes in 1884 and 1885, and five balls and three strikes in 1886. The count went back to five balls and three strikes in 1888. The present format of four balls for a walk and three strikes for an out was established in 1889.

MAY 7   Tip O'Neill hits for the cycle for the second time in a week, leading the Cardinals to a 12–7 win over Louisville at Sportsman's Park.

O'Neill had one of the best seasons in Cardinal history in 1887. He had a batting average of .435 that still ranks as the second best in the major league record books. Hugh Duffy is number one with a .440 mark for Boston in the National League in 1894. In 1887, O'Neill also led the American Association in on-base percentage (.490), slugging percentage (.691), hits (225), doubles (52), triples (19), home runs (14), runs scored (167), and RBIs (123). O'Neill is the only individual in big-league history to lead any league in doubles, triples, and homers in the same season. Other outstanding hitters on the 1887 Cardinals were Charlie Comiskey (.335 and 139 runs), Arlie Latham (.316 and 163 runs), and Yank Robinson (.305).

MAY 12   The Cardinals earn their 12th win in a row by scoring 12 runs in the fifth inning of a 22–14 victory over Baltimore at Sportsman's Park. Bob Caruthers let up after St. Louis built the big lead and surrendered 10 runs in the eighth.

MAY 16   The Cardinals stretch their winning streak to 15 games with a 7–2 decision over Philadelphia at Sportsman's Park.

MAY 17   The 15-game winning streak comes to an end with a 4–3 loss to Philadelphia at Sportsman's Park.

MAY 20   The Cardinals win a 15–9 slugging match against Brooklyn at Sportsman's Park.

MAY 28   The Cardinals score eight runs in the ninth inning and defeat New York 16–12 at Sportsman's Park.

JUNE 9   Curt Welch is fined $15 during the fifth inning of a 7–5 win over the Athletics in Philadelphia. Welch was docked for running in from center field to punch Philadelphia's Gus Weyhing to prevent him from reaching second base.

JUNE 16   Curt Welch is arrested during a game against the Orioles in Baltimore that results in an 8–8 tie. In the ninth inning, Welch tried to steal second base but ran outside the base line and slammed hard into second baseman Bill Greenwood, causing Greenwood to drop the ball and turn a complete somersault. As Baltimore players ran onto the field to check on Greenwood's condition, they found he had severely injured his back. A number of spectators ran onto the field and rushed toward Welch. Policemen sprang into action to head off the mob, and surrounded the St. Louis players. Welch was arrested for assault on Greenwood, and the Cardinal outfielder was marched to the clubhouse. Fearing a riot, umpire Jack McQuaid ended the contest and declared it a draw. Welch was taken to jail, where he was released on $200 bail. The following day, Welch stood trial and was fined $4.50.

JUNE 19   The Cardinals explode for 12 runs in the fourth inning and wallop the Reds 23–4 in Cincinnati.

JUNE 24   The Cardinals pummel the Cleveland Spiders 17–7 in Cleveland.

JUNE 28   In his first game in St. Louis since his June 16 arrest, Curt Welch is welcomed back with a standing ovation at the start of a 6–0 win over Louisville at Sportsman's Park. The first time Welch stepped to the plate, the cheering was so prolonged that umpire Jack McQuaid was compelled to call time. The second time he stepped to the plate, Welch was presented with a diamond stud valued at $300.

JULY 4   Playing right field in both games, Dave Foutz has a terrific day during a doubleheader against New York at Sportsman's Park. In the morning game, Foutz hit a homer and a double during a 15–2 victory. In the afternoon Foutz drove in nine runs with two homers and a double among his five hits.

            As a pitcher, Foutz had a record of 25–12. In addition to making 40 appearances on the mound, Foutz played 50 games in the outfield and 15 at first base. Overall, he batted .357 with 26 doubles, 13 triples, and 4 homers. Foutz's broke his thumb on August 14, however, fielding a line drive. The injury all but ended his days as an effective pitcher, although he continued to play in the majors until 1896, mainly as an outfielder and first baseman. Bob Caruthers matched Foutz as a duel threat. Caruthers had a 29–9 record, leading the AA in winning percentage (.763), and had a 3.30 ERA on the mound. He also played 54 games as an outfielder and 7 at first base. Like Foutz, Caruthers batted .357 in addition to collecting 23 doubles, 11 triples, and 8 homers.

JULY 10   Enforcing a law barring business on Sundays, St. Louis police stop the game against
               Baltimore at Sportsman's Park.

               *The law was enacted in 1839 by the Missouri legislature to prevent business or
               "labor" from being conducted on Sundays, but exempted places of amusements.
               The Cardinals had played on Sundays since 1882 as a "place of amusement,"
               but many in the community disagreed, claiming that baseball was a "business,"
               and they organized efforts to stop it. Police had warned Chris Von der Ahe of
               arrests if the July 10 game was played, but the Cardinals owner said that the
               contest would start as scheduled. Some 12,000 were present, and at the opening
               of the second inning, a police sergeant stepped forward and informed Von der
               Ahe that he was under arrest for violating the Sunday law. The crowd booed,
               and many broke onto the field, but umpire Bob Ferguson kept the contest going
               several minutes before he too was threatened with arrest. At this point, Ferguson
               called off the game. The fans were given "rain checks" to use for another contest
               later in the season. The following Friday, a judge ruled that the Cardinals
               could continue to play on Sundays in the future without interference from law
               enforcement officials.*

JULY 16   Charlie Comiskey stops a runaway team of horses during a 9–2 win over
               Philadelphia at Sportsman's Park.

               *Those who arrived at the ballpark in carriages were allowed to park the vehicles
               on the playing field along the outfield fence. At the close of the third inning, a
               runaway team broke onto the field and dashed at terrific speed, making several
               circuits around the park. After a hard run, Comiskey cleverly captured the team
               and saved the carriage from destruction.*

JULY 24   Trailing 3–0, the Cardinals score four runs in the fifth inning and defeat the Dodgers
               4–3 in Brooklyn. Yank Robinson scored the winning run when he cut third base, an
               incident noticed by nearly everyone in the ballpark except umpire Charles Mitchell.
               Brooklyn manager argued with the umpire to no avail, then plopped down next to
               Robinson on the St. Louis bench to lecture the Cardinal second sacker on proper
               sportsmanship.

JULY 29   The Cardinals score seven runs in the first inning and defeat the Orioles 12–9 at
               Baltimore. St. Louis won despite committing 14 errors, 6 of them by catcher Jack
               Boyle. Many of the errors were attributed to the conditions, as a pregame rain
               soaked the playing surface and made the ball slippery.

AUGUST 2   The Cardinals thrash the Athletics 14–6 in Philadelphia.

AUGUST 8   Tip O'Neill collects four hits, including a double, during an 8–4 win over Cleveland
               at Sportsman's Park.

AUGUST 9   Tip O'Neill runs his streak of consecutive hits to nine with a 5-for-5 day that includes
               a double and a triple during an 11–8 victory over Cleveland at Sportsman's Park.

AUGUST 15   The Cardinals score eight runs in the eighth inning of a 15–3 triumph in Cleveland.

AUGUST 19   The Cardinals trounce Philadelphia 22–8 at Sportsman's Park.

The winning pitcher was St. Louis amateur Joe Murphy, who was also the sports editor of the St. Louis Globe-Democrat. *Murphy pitched to give the overworked Cardinal pitching staff a rest.*

AUGUST 24   The Cardinals wallop Baltimore 23–6 at Sportsman's Park.

AUGUST 25   The Cardinals again whip Baltimore 14–6 at Sportsman's Park.

AUGUST 26   The Cardinals continue their hot hitting with a 14–6 victory over New York at Sportsman's Park.

SEPTEMBER 3   The Cardinals sweep a doubleheader from the New York Metropolitans 20–6 and 7–4 at St. George Grounds on Staten Island.

There were two unusual incidents during the twin bill because St. George Grounds in 1887 was one of the most unique venues ever to host a big-league game. Metropolitans owner Erastus Wiman moved his club from Manhattan to Staten Island in 1886, but attendance plummeted. In order to recoup some of his losses, Wiman built a theater in right field in 1887 and put on a play in the evenings called The Fall of Babylon *that featured live animals. The theater was in play, and outfielders could run across the stage and catch a fly ball. A ball that fell safely onto the stage was only a single. In the first game, Tip O'Neill hit a ball clear over the stage for a home run. In the second contest, St. Louis center fielder Curt Welch backed onto the steps leading to the stage while tracking a pop fly and fell sprawling, but he held on to ball.*

SEPTEMBER 4   The Cardinals earn their 12th win in a row with an 18–6 win over the Metropolitans amid chaos in a contest at Weehawken, New Jersey, called after six innings. St. Louis scored nine runs in the fourth inning.

The Metropolitans played at Weehawken because games on Sunday in New York were illegal. The grandstand at Weehawken held only 500, but between 12,000 and 13,000 showed up. The excess ringed the outfield, and there was little police presence to control the crowd. By prior agreement, any ball hit into the crowd was ruled a single. All 34 hits in the six-inning contest were singles. During the first inning, the mob inched forward, making further play impossible. The St. Louis players got into the carriages that brought them from their hotel in New York and drove around the grounds asking fans to move back. The ploy failed to work. One of the horses became detached from one of the carriages and rode through the crowd. After a 30-minute delay, the arrival of police forced the crowd far enough away from the infield to allow the game to continue, and it lasted five more innings before darkness ended play. The Cardinals brought only nine players from New York to save on transportation expenses. In the fourth inning, Tip O'Neill let the bat slip out of his hands, and it hit Curt Welch flush in the face. Welch was unable to continue, and the Cards finished the game with only eight players.

SEPTEMBER 11   The Cardinals' players refuse to play an exhibition game that Chris Von der Ahe scheduled against the New York Cuban Giants in West Farms, New York. The Cuban Giants were a club made of entirely of African Americans. A telegram sent the previous day to Von der Ahe and signed by eight St. Louis players read, "We, the undersigned members of the St. Louis Base-Ball Club do not agree to play against negroes to-morrow. We will cheerfully play against white people any time, and think by refusing to play we are only doing what is right, taking everything into consideration and the shape the team is in at present."

SEPTEMBER 15 Cardinal pitcher Silver King pitches a two-hitter to defeat the Orioles 4–2 in the second game of a doubleheader in Baltimore. The only hits off King were a double by Joe Sommer and a single by Matt Kilroy. St. Louis also won the opener, 3–0.

King had a record of 32–12 as a 19-year-old in 1887. He was born Charles Frederick Koenig in St. Louis, but sportswriters translated his name to King during his days as an amateur. The nickname "Silver" came from his white hair. King played three years with the Cardinals before defecting to the Players League in 1890. With St. Louis, he had a record of 111–49. At the end of the 2005 season, King still ranked ninth all time among Cardinal hurlers in wins, second in winning percentage (.694), and fifth in complete games (154 in 161 starts).

SEPTEMBER 17 The Cardinals clinch the American Association pennant with an 11-inning, 9–7 win over Cleveland at Sportsman's Park. The game was tied 3–3 at the end of the tenth inning. Umpire Jack McQuaid insisted on continuing play despite rapidly approaching darkness. With fielders having trouble seeing the ball, St. Louis scored six runs in the eleventh, and Cleveland scored four.

OCTOBER 4 The Cardinals outlast the Louisville Colonels 13–9 at Louisville.

OCTOBER 7 The Cardinals trounce Cleveland 12–2 at Sportsman's Park.

St. Louis played the National League champion Detroit Wolverines in the 1887 World Series. Managed by Bill Watkins, the Wolverines were 79–45 during the season. The owners of the two clubs agreed to a 15-game series played in 10 different cities over 17 days. All 15 games were to be played regardless of the outcome.

OCTOBER 10 The Cardinals defeat the Detroit Wolverines 6–1 in Game One of the 1886 World Series on a rainy and cold day before 4,208 at Sportsman's Park. Bob Caruthers pitched a five-hitter.

OCTOBER 11 Detroit wins Game Two 5–3 before 6,408 at Sportsman's Park.

OCTOBER 12 Despite being outhit 16–7, the Cardinals lose a 13-inning marathon by a 2–1 score in Game Three, played in Detroit. Bob Caruthers went all 13 innings. Opposing pitcher Charlie Getzein started the game-winning rally with a single, advanced to third on two infield outs, and scored on an error.

OCTOBER 13 Game Four of the World Series is played in Pittsburgh, and Detroit wins 8–0 behind a shutout by Lady Baldwin.

OCTOBER 14 The World Series moves to Brooklyn, and the Cardinals win 3–2.

After the win, the Cardinals trailed Detroit three games to two. The Wolverines won the next four.

OCTOBER 15 The Cardinals and Wolverines cross the East River for Game Six, and Detroit wins 9–0 at the Polo Grounds in New York. Charlie Getzein pitched the shutout.

OCTOBER 16   With an open date in the Series against Detroit, Chris Von der Ahe takes the Cardinals to Brooklyn for an exhibition game against the Dodgers. Brooklyn won 10–3.

OCTOBER 17   In Game Seven in Philadelphia, Detroit defeats the Cardinals 3–1.

OCTOBER 18   Bob Caruthers pitches for the second day in a row and loses 9–2 to Detroit in Boston.

OCTOBER 19   Back in Philadelphia for Game Nine, the Wolverines defeat the Cardinals 4–2.

OCTOBER 21   The Cardinals and the Wolverines play two games in two different cities. In the morning at Swampdoodle Grounds in Washington, St. Louis won 11–4. In the afternoon in Baltimore, Detroit was victorious, 13–2. The win gave Detroit the championship eight games to three. The final four games were played as scheduled.

OCTOBER 22   In Brooklyn in the twelfth game of the series, the Cardinals win 5–1. The game ended after 6½ innings because of cold and high winds. Fewer than a thousand fans attended the contest.

OCTOBER 24   Before the home fans in Detroit, the Wolverines defeat the Cardinals 6–3.

OCTOBER 25   Only 378 fans in Chicago show up for Game 14, a 4–3 Detroit win.

OCTOBER 26   Just 859 fans brave bitter cold in St. Louis to watch the Cardinals win the 15th and final game of the 1887 World Series against Detroit 9–2. The game was called after six innings because of the wintry weather.

Expressing his displeasure with his team's play in the World Series, Chris Von der Ahe refused to pay them for the postseason. Consequently, the Cardinals appeared in 16 games (including one exhibition) and earned nothing for their effort. On October 30, the Cardinals embarked on a long barnstorming tour that lasted until February. The club played the Chicago White Stockings in Charleston, South Carolina, Atlanta, Memphis, Nashville, New Orleans, and several Texas, New Mexico, and Arizona towns before reaching San Francisco for a series of contests, including one on Christmas Day.

NOVEMBER 21   The Cardinals trade Bill Gleason and Curt Welch to the Athletics for Fred Mann, Chippy McGarr, and Jocko Milligan plus $3,000.

Chris Von der Ahe was so angry and embarrassed by his team's showing in the 1887 World Series that he traded or sold many of the Cardinals' top stars. After dealing Gleason and Welch, Von der Ahe sold Bob Caruthers and Dave Foutz, who were not only his best two pitchers but who also doubled as outfielders, to the Brooklyn Dodgers. Few thought that the Cardinals could repeat in 1888 after the loss of many of their top stars, but they defied the experts by taking their fourth consecutive pennant. St. Louis finished two games behind Brooklyn in the 1889 race, however, with Caruthers and Foutz playing significant roles.

1888

Season in a Sentence

Despite selling their top two pitchers to Brooklyn, the Cardinals win their fourth consecutive American Association pennant.

Finish • Won • Lost • Pct • GB

First   92   43   .681   +6.5

Manager

Charlie Comiskey

Stats

Stats	Cards	• AA •	Rank
Batting Avg:	.250	.328	2
On-Base Pct:	.316	.297	1
Slugging Pct:	.324	.315	2
Home Runs:	36		1
Stolen Bases:	468		2
ERA:	2.09	3.06	1
Fielding Avg:	.924	.917	1
Runs Scored:	789		2
Runs Allowed:	501		1

Starting Lineup

Jack Boyle, c
Charlie Comiskey, 1b
Yank Robinson, 2b
Arlie Latham, 3b
Bill White, ss
Tip O'Neill, lf
Harry Lyons, cf
Tommy McCarthy, rf
Jocko Milligan, c
Ed Herr, ss

Pitchers

Silver King, sp
Nat Hudson, sp
Elton Chamberlain, sp
Jim Devlin, sp
Ed Knouff, sp

Attendance

166,000 (third in AA)

Club Leaders

Batting Avg:	O'Neill	.335
On-Base Pct:	O'Neill	.390
Slugging Pct:	O'Neill	.446
Home Runs:	Comiskey	6
RBIs:	O'Neill	98
Runs:	Latham	119
Stolen Bases:	Latham	109
Wins:	King	45
Strikeouts:	King	258
ERA:	King	1.64
Saves:	None	

APRIL 18   In the season opener, the Cardinals defeat the Louisville Colonels 8–0 at Sportsman's Park. Arlie Latham collected a homer and three singles. Silver King pitched a three-hit shutout. At the end of the first inning, the 1887 championship pennant was presented to the club by a St. Louis councilman and a local judge.

The Cardinals played in a partially rebuilt Sportsman's Park in 1888. The previous November, a suspicious blaze occurred at the ballpark. The fire destroyed the player's dressing room, handball court, gymnasium, and clubhouse. The conflagration also spread to Von der Ahe's nearby Golden Lion Saloon. Some of his critics suspected arson to collect insurance, but nothing was ever proved.

APRIL 19   The Cardinals defeat Louisville 13–7 at Sportsman's Park.

A new franchise was added to the American Association in Kansas City in 1888 after the New York Metropolitans went bankrupt.

APRIL 21   Trailing 7–2, the Cardinals score eight runs in the seventh inning and beat Louisville 11–7 at Sportsman's Park.

APRIL 22   The Cardinals defeat Louisville 11–6 during a quarrelsome afternoon at Sportsman's Park.

At the time, umpires had the power to levy fines. Umpire Jack McQuaid fined Louisville second baseman Reddy Mack for profanity and ordered him to the bench. Mack refused and was fined several more times. McQuaid called for the police to remove Mack, and three officers took hold of the Louisville player. Louisville outfielder Hub Collins grabbed a bat and ordered Mack's release. The police let go of him, but the game was delayed 20 minutes while Mack continued to jaw with McQuaid. Play resumed after Mack was allowed to remain in the game.

MAY 5	The Cardinals lambaste the Colonels 18–1 in Louisville.
MAY 24	The Cardinals stomp on the Spiders 17–5 in Cleveland.
JUNE 10	The Cardinals score six runs in the first inning and seven in the fourth and win 17–8 over the Reds in Cincinnati.
JUNE 14	The Cardinals wallop Louisville 13–7 at Sportsman's Park.
JUNE 27	The Cardinals take first place with a 7–5 win over Cleveland in St. Louis. Ed Herr hit a key home run that was only the third to clear the distant left-field fence at Sportsman's Park, a distance of about 350 feet, since the ballpark opened in 1882.
JULY 6	The Dodgers, led by former Cardinals Bob Caruthers and Dave Foutz, make their first appearance of the season in St. Louis and are feted with a parade from their downtown hotel to Sportsman's Park. The parade included about 20 carriages and a brass band. The ex-Cardinals were enthusiastically cheered. With Caruthers pitching and Foutz playing first base, Brooklyn won 6–2.
JULY 13	Tip O'Neill collects five hits, including a double, in six at-bats during a 16–9 win over Baltimore at Sportsman's Park.

O'Neill led the American Association in batting average (.335) and hits (177) in 1888.

JULY 15	The Cardinals struggle past Baltimore 12–9 at Sportsman's Park. St. Louis took a 9–7 lead with three runs in the sixth inning.
JULY 17	Tommy McCarthy collects five hits, including a double, in five at-bats during a 10–3 win over the Kansas City Cowboys at Sportsman's Park. McCarthy was also credited with six stolen bases.

A future Hall of Fame outfielder, McCarthy played for St. Louis from 1888 through 1891.

JULY 20	The Cardinals take first place with a one-sided 18–5 win over Kansas City at Sportsman's Park.

St. Louis remained in first place for the rest of the year.

JULY 29	The Cardinals defeat Cleveland 7–4 at Geauga Lake, Ohio. The Cleveland club played four Sunday games at Geauga Lake in 1888.
AUGUST 1	Following a 4–3 win in Cleveland, one unnamed Cardinal and two players from the

Cleveland team are hauled off to jail after being charged with "visiting a house of ill-repute." According to newspaper reports, "The arrested men declared that they stepped into the den where they were found by the police during a rainstorm, and intended moving on when the clouds rolled by."

AUGUST 12   Silver King pitches a two-hitter to defeat the Athletics 2–0 before a crowd of 10,000 at Sportsman's Park. The only Philadelphia hits were singles by Harry Stovey and opposing pitcher Ed Seward.

After the game, a 30-foot section of a walkway leading from the ballpark collapsed. The walkway was on the south side of Sportsman's Park and was about six feet wide and 15 feet above the ground. The posts supporting the walk gave way, and about 100 people crashed to the earth. Two were seriously injured.

AUGUST 20   Silver King pitches the Cardinals to a 1–0 win over the Dodgers at Sportsman's Park. The only Brooklyn hits were singles by George Pinkney. The lone run of the game scored when Arlie Latham led off the first inning with a single, stole second, and scored from second base on an infield out.

AUGUST 22   Silver King carries a no-hitter into the ninth inning before settling for a one-hitter and a 4–2 win over the Dodgers at Sportsman's Park. The lone hit occurred when Jack O'Brien popped a high fly that fell between shortstop Bill White and left fielder Tip O'Neill.

Silver King had a record of 45–21 in 1888. He led the American Association in wins, games pitched (66), games started (65), complete games (64), innings pitched (585⅔), opponent's on-base percentage (.224), shutouts (six), and ERA (1.64). The figures for wins, games started, complete games, innings pitched, and opponent's on-base percentage are Cardinal records. King's ERA in 1888 ranks second to Bob Gibson's mark of 1.12 in 1968.

AUGUST 25   Nat Hudson pitches the Cardinals to a 1–0 win over Cleveland in Cleveland.

Hudson was 25–10 for St. Louis in 1888. His winning percentage of .714 led the American Association. The 333 innings he pitched in 1888 placed too great a strain on his arm, however, and wrecked a promising career. Hudson was finished as a major league hurler after appearing in nine games in 1889.

SEPTEMBER 14   The Cardinals drub the Reds 14–2 at Sportsman's Park.

SEPTEMBER 28   Silver King carries a no-hitter into the eighth inning and defeats Brooklyn 7–0 on a two-hitter at Sportsman's Park. The only Dodger hits were singles by Dave Orr in the eighth and George Pinkney in the ninth.

SEPTEMBER 30   Over 15,000 people watch the Cardinals beat the Dodgers 13–4 at Sportsman's Park.

OCTOBER 3   The Cardinals clinch their fourth consecutive American Association pennant with a 14–5 win over Kansas City at Sportsman's Park.

The Cardinals played the National League champion New York Giants in the 1888 World Series. Managed by Jim Mutrie, the Giants were 84–47 in 1888. The clubs agreed to an 11-game series. Two contests were scheduled for Brooklyn and Philadelphia.

OCTOBER 16   In the opener of the 1888 World Series, the Cardinals lose 2–1 to the Giants at the Polo Grounds in New York in a brilliant pitchers' duel. Silver King pitched a two-hitter while New York pitcher Tim Keefe allowed just three hits.

OCTOBER 17   The Cardinals even the series with a 3–0 win over the Giants in New York. Elton Chamberlain pitched a six-hitter. Tommy McCarthy scored the first St. Louis run in the second inning when he hit a single, moved around to third on two passed balls by Giants catcher Buck Ewing, and came home on Ewing's failed attempt to throw out a runner stealing second. The Cardinals added two insurance runs in the ninth.

OCTOBER 18   The Giants win Game Three 4–2 over the Cardinals in New York.

OCTOBER 19   In Brooklyn, the Giants defeat the Cardinals 6–3 in Game Four.

OCTOBER 20   Back at the Polo Grounds, the Giants beat the Cardinals 6–4 in a contest called after eight innings by darkness.

OCTOBER 22   In Philadelphia, the Giants take a five-games-to-one lead in the World Series by pounding the Cardinals 12–5. The win put New York one victory from the championship. St. Louis had a 4–0 lead after three innings before the Giants exploded for 11 runs in the sixth, seventh, and eighth. The game was called at the end of the eighth by darkness.

OCTOBER 23   On the travel day, charges that umpires John Kelly and John Gaffney had wagered on the Giants are attributed to Cardinals owner Chris Von der Ahe and are reported by the Associated Press. Both umpires threatened to sit out the rest of the series. Von der Ahe claimed he was misquoted and affirmed the honesty of the umpires.

OCTOBER 24   The Cardinals stay alive by coming back from a 5–3 deficit to beat the Giants 7–5 before 4,624 at Sportsman's Park. St. Louis scored four runs in the eighth inning before darkness ended the game.

OCTOBER 25   The Giants wrap up the 1888 World Championship by defeating the Cardinals 11–3 before 4,865 at Sportsman's Park. New York broke open a close game by scoring six runs in the ninth.

              Although the Giants claimed the championship, the final three games of the 11-game series were played as scheduled.

OCTOBER 26   A crowd of only 711 watches the Cardinals rally to win 14–11 after scoring two runs in the ninth inning and three in the tenth.

OCTOBER 27   The Cardinals wallop the Giants 18–7 before only 412 at Sportsman's Park.

OCTOBER 28   In the final game of the Series, Silver King shuts out the Giants 6–0 at Sportsman's Park.

              After losing the Series, team owner Chris Von der Ahe called his team "chumps," and for the second straight season he paid his players nothing for participating in the World Series. The club played 27 postseason games in 1887 and 1888 and received no money in return.

1889

Season in a Sentence

The Cardinals lead the American Association for most of the season but fail to win their fifth straight pennant by losing a tight race with the Dodgers.

Finish • Won • Lost • Pct • GB

Second   90   45   .667   2.0

Manager

Charlie Comiskey

Stats

Stats	Cards	• AA •	Rank
Batting Avg:	.266	.262	3
On-Base Pct:	.339	.333	4
Slugging Pct:	.370	.354	3
Home Runs:	58		1
Stolen Bases:	336		4
ERA:	3.00	3.84	4
Fielding Avg:	.925	.916	3
Runs Scored:	957		2
Runs Allowed:	680		1

Starting Lineup

Jack Boyle, c
Charlie Comiskey, 1b
Yank Robinson, 2b
Arlie Latham, 3b
Shorty Fuller, ss
Tip O'Neill, lf
Charlie Duffee, cf
Tommy McCarthy, rf
Jocko Milligan, c

Pitchers

Silver King, sp
Elton Chamberlain, sp
Jack Stivetts, sp

Attendance

175,000 (third in AA)

Club Leaders

Batting Avg:	O'Neill	.335
On-Base Pct:	O'Neill	.419
Slugging Pct:	O'Neill	.478
Home Runs:	Duffee	16
RBIs:	O'Neill	110
Runs:	McCarthy	136
Stolen Bases:	Latham	69
Wins:	King	34
Strikeouts:	Chamberlain	202
ERA:	Stivetts	2.25
Saves:	Three tied w/	1

APRIL 17   Six weeks after the inauguration of President Benjamin Harrison, the Cardinals open the 1889 season with a 5–1 win over the Reds in Cincinnati. Silver King was the winning pitcher.

King had a 34–16 record and a 3.14 ERA for St. Louis in 1889. He never pitched for the Cardinals again after the season. He opted to play for Chicago in the Players League in 1890 (see December 16, 1889) and when the league folded, joined the Pittsburgh Pirates in 1891. After compiling a 111–49 record as a Cardinal, King finished his career in 1897 with 203 wins and 153 losses.

APRIL 21   The Cardinals score two runs in the ninth inning and slip past the Colonels 12–10 at Louisville.

APRIL 22   The Cardinals rout the Colonels 13–6 in Louisville.

APRIL 25   In the first home game of the season, the Cardinals defeat the Reds 10–5 before 10,000 at Sportsman's Park. Before the game, a brass band played and the crowd enjoyed a fireworks display.

MAY 2   Cardinals owner Chris Von der Ahe fines second baseman Yank Robinson for wearing a dirty uniform prior to a 5–1 win owner Louisville at Sportsman's Park. Robinson sent the clubhouse boy to his hotel for a fresh set, but the youngster was refused entrance back into the ballpark by the ticket taker, whom Robinson cursed. Von der Ahe fined Robinson $25 for his actions, and Robinson left the park. The Cardinals owner threatened him with suspension and blacklisting. In support of Robinson, the Cardinals refused to board a train for Kansas City for the next game until persuaded to do so by team secretary George Munson. Robinson, however, stayed behind in St. Louis under suspension.

MAY 3   The Cardinals fall behind 10–0 after two innings and lose 16–3 to the Cowboys in Kansas City.

MAY 4   The Cardinals commit 13 errors and lose 16–9 in Kansas City.

MAY 5   The Cardinals lose 18–12 in Kansas City. Jim Devlin was the starting pitcher for St. Louis but left after two scoreless innings with a leg injury. The Cardinals led 11–7 before Kansas City scored 11 runs off King in the ninth inning.

             The three consecutive losses to Kansas City, a club that was 55–82 in 1889, brought accusations that the Cardinals were losing on purpose in retaliation for Robinson's suspension. The players vehemently denied the charge.

MAY 6   The Cardinals salvage the fourth game of the series at Kansas City with an 11–9 victory.

MAY 7   The Cardinals level Columbus 21–0 at Sportsman's Park in the most lopsided shutout in club history. In his first game back from his suspension, and after Chris Von der Ahe rescinded the $25 fine imposed on May 2, Yank Robinson collected four hits.

             The 1889 season was the first in which the four ball–three strike count was used. Robinson drew 118 walks, then a record, while batting only .208.

MAY 10   The Cardinals wallop Columbus 16–5 at Sportsman's Park.

             Columbus replaced Cleveland in the American Association lineup in 1889. The Cleveland club moved to the National League.

MAY 11   Arlie Latham collects five hits, including a homer and a double, in six at-bats during a 20–4 thrashing of Baltimore at Sportsman's Park.

JUNE 2   Silver King pitches a one-hitter to defeat the Dodgers 2–1 in Ridgewood, New York. King also broke a 1–1 tie with a single in the seventh inning. The only Brooklyn hit was a single by Tommy Burns in the fourth.

             The game started late because the train carrying the Cardinals from Columbus had to take an alternative route through Pennsylvania because of the great Johnstown flood, which occurred on May 31 and claimed the lives of 2,200 people.

JUNE 8   The Cardinals nearly forfeit a game against the Orioles in Baltimore because of another train that was delayed by heavy rains in West Virginia. The Cardinals arrived at Baltimore's Union Station at 4:45 PM, more than an hour after the scheduled start. They commenced a quick warmup while Charlie Comiskey argued with John

Gaffney, who had declared a forfeit before the St. Louis club reached the ballpark. Orioles owner Billy Barnie insisted that the game be played, however, and the Cardinals won 5–1.

JUNE 16   The Cardinals defeat the Philadelphia Athletics 10–5 in Gloucester City, New Jersey. The game was played in Gloucester because Sunday games were illegal in Philadelphia.

JUNE 22   Louisville extends its major league record losing streak to 26 games by losing twice to the Cardinals 7–6 and 3–2 in 10 innings in a doubleheader at Louisville.

JUNE 23   Louisville's 26-game losing streak comes to an end with a 7–3 win over the Cardinals at Louisville.

JULY 11   Trailing 12–9, the Cardinals score two runs in the eighth inning and two in the ninth to win 13–12 against Philadelphia at Sportsman's Park.

JULY 13   The Cardinals score seven runs in the fifth inning and win with ridiculous ease, 25–5, against Baltimore at Sportsman's Park.

JULY 29   Matt Kilroy of the Orioles pitches a seven-inning no-hitter against the Cardinals in the second game of a doubleheader in Baltimore. The game ended after seven innings because of darkness with the score 0–0. Kilroy cost himself the game by failing to touch third base while attempting to score a run. St. Louis won the opener 4–3.

AUGUST 8   The Cardinals thump the Cowboys 12–2 in Kansas City.

AUGUST 11   The Cardinals take a 2½-game lead over the second-place Dodgers with a 14–4 win before 16,000 at Sportsman's Park.

> *Because of the importance of the game, the American Association assigned two umpires to the contest against the Dodgers. The overflow from the grandstand ringed the outfield, and a rule was adopted that any ball hit into the crowd would be a double. With one out in the seventh, St. Louis outfielder Charlie Duffee knocked the ball over the fence for a home run. The hit caused a scrap that lasted for half an hour. The Dodgers claimed that the drive should be a double because of the ground rule. The Cardinals asserted that it was a home run since it left the park. Umpire John Kerins ruled the play a home run. Fellow arbiter Bob Ferguson said it should be a double. While an argument ensued, many in the crowd surged onto the field, and it took the combined efforts of the police and Cardinal players to clear the diamond. Ferguson and the Dodgers finally got their way, and Duffee went to second base. Later, Duffee collided with Brooklyn catcher Bob Clark, who claimed he was injured and couldn't continue. At the time, substitutions could not be made without the consent of the opposition and the umpires. Charlie Comiskey refused to allow Clark to leave the game. Four doctors were called to examine Clark, creating another delay of approximately 30 minutes as hundreds of fans again stormed the field. Clark was compelled to stay in the game.*

AUGUST 12   Elton Chamberlain pitches a two-hitter to defeat the Dodgers 11–0 at Sportsman's Park. The only Brooklyn hits were singles by Joe Visner in the sixth and eighth innings.

Chamberlain was 32–15 with a 2.97 ERA in 1889. His nickname was "Icebox" because of his cool demeanor on the mound.

AUGUST 20   The Cardinals roll to a 14–2 victory over Philadelphia at Sportsman's Park.

AUGUST 25   The Cardinals score 12 runs in the third inning and win 16–9 over Baltimore at Sportsman's Park.

AUGUST 27   The Cardinals score eight times in the first inning and wallop Kansas City 19–1 at Sportsman's Park.

SEPTEMBER 1   The Cardinals are knocked out of first place with a 6–5 loss at Columbus. Dave Orr ended the game with a home run that not only cleared the left-field fence but also a row of houses behind the barrier as well. The St. Louis defeat put Brooklyn in first place.

SEPTEMBER 6   The Cardinals lose a controversial 3–2 decision to the Orioles in Baltimore.

In the top of the eighth with the Orioles leading 3–2, rain stopped play. After a 10-minute wait, the rain began to let up and umpire Fred Goldsmith ordered the teams back onto the field. Baltimore manager Billy Barnie protested, preferring to wait until the rain ceased completely. To emphasize the point, Baltimore first baseman Tommy Tucker took the field hoisting an umbrella. Cardinals second sacker Yank Robinson pulled the umbrella down, and Tucker responded by planting his foot in Robinson's posterior. A fight seemed imminent, but Goldsmith and four police officers separated Tucker and Robinson. Before the eighth inning was finished, a downpour ensued, and the game was called.

SEPTEMBER 7   In the first game of a pennant showdown against the Dodgers in Brooklyn, the Cardinals lose in a forfeit.

The Cardinals led 4–2 in the ninth inning. Charlie Comiskey tried convincing umpire Fred Goldsmith that it was too dark to continue, serving only to aggravate Goldsmith, who had listened to a steady stream of complaints from St. Louis players all day long. Chris Von der Ahe attempted to make his point by buying candles from a nearby grocery store and then lit and arranged them around the St. Louis bench like footlights, which did not improve Goldsmith's mood or that of the partisan Brooklyn fans. Some threw beer steins at the candles. They succeeded in knocking down a number of the candles, which ignited stray paper nearby and in turn created a small fire that briefly threatened to set the wooden grandstand ablaze. Fortunately, the flames were extinguished before any real damage was done. Determined to finish the game, the umpire forced the players to begin the ninth. Soon, Comiskey refused to play and ordered his men off the field. Goldsmith threatened to declare a forfeit. When he did so, the crowd of 15,143 cheered the decision. The Cardinals left the grounds under a shower of bottles and stones. Von der Ahe was fined $1,500 for the forfeit, but he decided not to send his players out the following day, which fell on a Sunday. Von der Ahe refused to field his club because the Dodgers played Sunday games in Ridgewood, in Queens, even though state laws prohibited Sunday amusements. The Queens County sheriff tacitly allowed the games to continue without interference, but since he was technically violating the law by doing so, he could not send any of his officers to the grounds. With no police *presence, and a large crowd inflamed by the pennant race and the tensions of the September 7 game, Von der Ahe feared for the safety of his players. The last two games of the four-game series were rained out. On September 23, a special American Association meeting awarded the 4–2 victory of September 7 to the Cardinals, but the forfeit of September 8 stood.*

SEPTEMBER 18   Tommy McCarthy steals second, third, and home in the seventh inning of a 7–2 win at Kansas City.

McCarthy hit .291 and scored 136 runs in 1889. Tip O'Neill was the top overall hitter for St. Louis during the year with a .335 average, 123 runs scored, and 110 RBIs. Charlie Comiskey batted .286 and had 105 runs scored and 102 RBIs.

OCTOBER 2   The Cardinals trounce Kansas City 15–5 at Sportsman's Park.

OCTOBER 15   An 8–3 loss to the Reds in Cincinnati eliminates the Cardinals from the pennant race. St. Louis finished the year two games behind Brooklyn.

NOVEMBER 14   A week after North Dakota, South Dakota, Montana, and Washington are granted statehood, the Cincinnati Reds and Brooklyn Dodgers are granted admission to the National League. The defection of the Reds and the Dodgers further weakened the American Association, which lost franchises in Pittsburgh following the 1886 season and Cleveland after the 1888 campaign to the NL. In place of the Cincinnati and Brooklyn clubs and the bankrupt franchise in Kansas City, teams were added to the American Association in 1890 in the much smaller cities of Syracuse, Rochester, and Toledo. Also, the Baltimore Orioles folded and were replaced by another team from Brooklyn. The new Brooklyn club in the AA couldn't compete with the more established Dodgers, however, and the club moved back to Baltimore in August 1890.

DECEMBER 16   The Players League is formally organized.

The new league grew out of dissatisfaction among players over their salaries and contracts. Many top stars left their National League and American Association teams to join the new league. The Players League located clubs in Boston, Brooklyn, Buffalo, Chicago, Cleveland, New York, Philadelphia, and Pittsburgh. The new organization, also known as the Brotherhood, devastated the Cardinals roster. Among those who left St. Louis for the Players League were front-liners like player-manager Charlie Comiskey, catcher Jack Boyle, second baseman Yank Robinson, third baseman Arlie Latham, outfielder Tip O'Neill, and pitcher Silver King. All of the aforementioned players joined the Chicago club, where Comiskey was the manager and first baseman, except for Robinson, who played for Pittsburgh.

THE STATE OF THE CARDINALS

After winning four consecutive American Association pennants from 1885 through 1888, the Cardinals were no longer the class of the league at the start of the decade, but they were still a strong team at the start of the 1890s, finishing third in 1890 and second in 1891. The American Association folded at the end of the 1891 season, and the Cards moved to the National League. The transition was far from smooth. St. Louis was 11th in a 12-team league in 1892, 10th in 1893, 9th in 1894, 11th in 1895, 11th in 1896, and last in both 1897 and 1898, which brought an end to mercurial owner Chris Von der Ahe's regime. Frank and Stanley Robison, a pair of brothers from Cleveland, bought the Cardinals in 1899. The two also owned the Cleveland Spiders of the NL and arranged a series of "trades" in which the best players on the Cleveland roster were sent to St. Louis, while the worst players from the Cardinals went to the Spiders. As a result, the 1899 Cardinals were 84–67, while the Spiders, at 20–134, became one of the worst teams in baseball history.

THE BEST TEAM

The 1891 Cardinals had a record of 85–51 and finished the season in second place, 8½ games behind Boston.

THE WORST TEAM

The 1897 club was the worst in club history, thudding into last place in a 12-team league with 29 wins and 102 losses, a winning percentage of .221.

The Cardinals that season were 23½ games behind the next-worst team in the National League. The 1898 club wasn't much better, posting a mark of 39–111.

THE BEST MOMENT

The best moment occurred in 1899 when Chris Von der Ahe was forced to sell the Cardinals, ending one of the most controversial ownership regimes in baseball history. Just prior to the start of the 1900 season, the National League reduced its membership from 12 to 8, eliminating franchises in Baltimore, Cleveland, Louisville, and Washington. Had the reduction occurred a year or two earlier when the Cardinals were in sorry shape under Von der Ahe's mismanagement, it's likely that St. Louis's franchise would have been one of those abolished.

THE WORST MOMENT

A fire swept through Sportsman's Park on April 16, 1898, with 6,000 people in the stands for a game against the Cubs. The players on both teams did heroic work rescuing many fans from the fire. Far from being appreciative, Chris Von der Ahe ordered his players to work all night clearing debris from the fire to help carpenters build 1,700 temporary seats for a game the following day.

THE ALL-DECADE TEAM • YEARS W/CARDS

Heinie Peitz, c	1892–95
Roger Connor, 1b	1894–97
Jack Crooks, 2b	1892–93, 1898
Lave Cross, 3b	1898–1900
Shorty Fuller, ss	1889–91
Jesse Burkett, lf	1899–1901
Tommy Dowd, cf	1893–98
Tommy McCarthy, rf	1888–91
Ted Breitenstein, p	1891–96, 1901
Jack Stivetts, p	1889–91
Cy Young, p	1899–1900
Willie Sudhoff, p	1897–1901

Young, McCarthy, Burkett, and Connor are all in the Hall of Fame, but their stays in St. Louis were brief. In fact, Ted Breitenstein and Tommy Dowd are the only members of the 1890s All-Decade Team to play for the Cardinals for five seasons or more as the club searched desperately for a winning combination.

THE DECADE LEADERS

Batting Avg:	Connor	.304
On-Base Pct:	Connor	.390
Slugging Pct:	Connor	.490
Home Runs:	Connor	27
RBIs:	Dowd	489
Runs:	Dowd	277
Stolen Bases:	Dowd	187
Wins:	Breitenstein	94
Strikeouts:	Breitenstein	625
ERA:	Stivetts	3.18
Saves:	Breitenstein	3

THE HOME FIELD

When the Cardinals joined the American Association in 1882, they played at Sportsman's Park on Grand Avenue between Dodier and Sullivan. With their move to the National League in 1892, Chris Von der Ahe wanted a larger ballpark. He moved the club to a new facility at the corner of Vandeventer and Natural Bridge in 1893. The Cardinals' new home was named New Sportsman's Park. By 1896, Von der Ahe had added other amusements, most notably a horse racing track and water chutes that fans could ride down for a quarter. The ballpark burned in 1898 and was rebuilt. When the Robison brothers bought the club in 1899, the name of the ballpark was changed from New Sportsman's Park to League Park.

THE GAME YOU WISH YOU HAD SEEN

Making his first major league start, Cardinal pitcher Ted Breitenstein pitched a no-hitter on October 4, 1891, against Louisville at Sportsman's Park.

THE WAY THE GAME WAS PLAYED

In 1893, the pitcher was moved from 55 feet to 60 feet, 6 inches from home plate. The added pitching distance put more offense in the game. League batting averages jumped from .245 in 1892 to .280 in 1893 and to .309 in 1894. The decade is known for its rough, even dirty, baseball, with many managers encouraging players to bend every rule and challenge every call. Brawling became commonplace.

THE MANAGEMENT

Chris Von der Ahe was the owner of the Cardinals when the franchise played its first game in a major league in 1882 and continued in that role until March 14, 1899, when the club was sold at auction to Frank and Stanley Robison. The sale was prompted by Von der Ahe's severe financial problems, which resulted in the club's filing for bankruptcy and going into receivership. Field managers changed often because of Von der Ahe's impatience. During the 1890 season alone, there were five managers: Tommy McCarthy, John Kerins, Chief Roseman, Count Campau, and Joe Gerhardt. Charlie Comiskey, who managed the club from 1883 through 1889 before moving to the Players League, returned in 1891. Tired of Von der Ahe's interference, Comiskey joined the Cincinnati Reds as player-manager in 1892. For the remainder of the Von der Ahe regime, the revolving door of Cardinals managers included Jack Glasscock (1892), Cub Stricker (1892), Jack Crooks (1892), George Gore (1892), Bob Caruthers (1892), Bill Watkins (1893), Doggie Miller (1894), Al Buckenberger (1895), Joe Quinn (1895), Lew Phelan (1895), Harry Diddlebock (1896), Arlie Latham (1896), Roger Connor (1896), Tommy Dowd (1896–97), High Nicol (1897), and Tim Hurst (1898). Von der Ahe even took over the club himself as manager for a few games in 1895, 1896, and 1897. The Robison brothers hired Patsy Tebeau as field manager. Tebeau ran the club in 1899 and part of the 1900 season.

THE BEST PLAYER MOVE

Although it was highly unethical, the Cardinals obtained the services of future Hall of Famers Cy Young, Jesse Burkett, and Bobby Wallace from Cleveland in 1899. The Robison brothers owned both the Cardinals and the Cleveland Spiders and transferred almost all of the Spiders' best players to St. Louis.

THE WORST PLAYER MOVE

The Cardinals inexplicably released Clark Griffith to Boston late in the 1891 campaign despite his 11–6 record. A 21-year-old rookie that season, Griffith landed in Chicago with the Cubs in 1893 and went on to win 237 career games.

1890s

1890

Season in a Sentence

With an almost entirely new roster due to Players League defections, the Cardinals finish in third place.

Finish • Won • Lost • Pct • GB

Third   77   58   .570   12.5

Managers

Tommy McCarthy (11–11), John Kerins (9–8), Chief Roseman (7–8), Count Campau (26–14), Tommy McCarthy (4–1), and Joe Gerhardt (20–16)

Stats

Stats	Cards	• AA •	Rank
Batting Avg:	.273	.253	2
On-Base Pct:	.350	.329	1
Slugging Pct:	.370	.332	1
Home Runs:	48		1
Stolen Bases:	307		5
ERA:	3.67	3.86	5
Fielding Avg:	.916	.923	7
Runs Scored:	870		1
Runs Allowed:	738		5

Starting Lineup

John Munyan, c
Ed Cartwright, 1b
Bill Huggins, 2b
Charlie Duffee, 3b-cf
Shorty Fuller, ss
Count Campau, lf
Chief Roseman, cf
Tommy McCarthy, rf
Tom Gettinger, lf
Pete Sweeney, 2b-3b

Pitchers

Jack Stivetts, sp
Todd Ramsey, sp
Billy Hart, sp
Bill Whitrock, sp
Joe Neale, sp

Attendance

105,000 (third in AA)

Club Leaders

Batting Avg:	McCarthy	.350
On-Base Pct:	McCarthy	.430
Slugging Pct:	McCarthy	.467
Home Runs:	Campau	9
RBIs:	Campau	75
Runs:	McCarthy	137
Stolen Bases:	McCarthy	83
Wins:	Stivetts	27
Strikeouts:	Stivetts	289
ERA:	Stivetts	3.52
Saves:	Whitrock	1

APRIL 18   In the season opener, the Cardinals rally from a 5–0 deficit to defeat the Colonels 11–8 at Louisville. A seven-run eighth inning put St. Louis ahead 11–5.

Charlie Comiskey managed the Cardinals from August 1884 through the end of the 1889 season before he moved to the Chicago club in the Players League for the 1890 season (see December 16, 1889). In 1890, Chris Von der Ahe changed managers five times during the season. Tommy McCarthy started the season as the St. Louis manager. The son of Irish immigrants from Boston, McCarthy cracked the Cardinals' starting lineup as an outfielder in 1888. The club was 11–11 when Von der Ahe relieved McCarthy of his duties, although he remained with the club as a player and batted .350, scored 137 runs, and stole a league-leading 83 bases. Von der Ahe next hired John Kerins as manager. Kerins was 9–8 as manager but hit only .127 as the club's starting first baseman and was released. Chief Roseman was next and managed the 1890 Cardinals for 15 games, winning 7. The impatient Von der Ahe replaced Roseman as manager but kept him around as the starting center fielder. Count Campau was brought from the Detroit club in the International League to follow Roseman and play left field. A descendent of one of the founding families of Detroit, Campau directed St. Louis to a 27–14 record, but he was demoted to player-only status on another Von der Ahe whim. Although he played only part of the season, Campau led the American Association in home runs in 1890 (9) and batted .322. Next, McCarthy was given another stint as manager and won four of five before

Von der Ahe turned to Joe Gerhardt, who finished out the season with a 20–16 record. Although he isn't officially credited with managing any games in 1890, newspaper reports indicate that Von der Ahe directed the Cardinals from the bench for a few games in September.

APRIL 19   Cardinal pitcher Jack Stivetts strikes out 13 batters, but St. Louis loses 5–3 in 10 innings at Louisville.

APRIL 20   The Cardinals lose at Louisville by forfeit.

A crowd of 10,000 overflowed the grandstand and stood in the outfield. According to a pregame agreement, any batter who hit a ball into the crowd was limited to two bases. In the third inning, Louisville's Chicken Wolf sent a drive into the crowd that scored Jack Ryan from first base. St. Louis manager Tommy McCarthy said that Ryan could advance just two bases and should be sent back to third, but umpire Terence Connell disagreed. McCarthy pulled his team off the field, and Connell declared a forfeit. To appease an angry crowd expecting to see a complete game, the two teams played an exhibition game that resulted in a 13–13 tie.

APRIL 22   In the first home game of the season, the Cardinals defeat Toledo 9–5 before 2,500 at Sportsman's Park.

APRIL 27   Jack Stivetts strikes out the first seven batters to face him and retires twelve in the game, leading the Cardinals to a 14–1 win over Columbus at Sportsman's Park.

JUNE 4   The Cardinals score seven runs in the third inning and win 9–2 at Louisville.

JUNE 10   Jack Stivetts strikes out 10 batters and hits two home runs, including a walk-off grand slam, to beat Toledo 9–8 at Sportsman's Park. In addition to the two homers, Stivetts collected two singles. The grand slam came with one out in the ninth off Fred Smith. The drive cleared the center-field fence.

Stivetts was 27–21 with a 3.52 ERA and struck out a team record 289 batters in 419$\frac{1}{3}$ innings in 1890. As a batter, he hit .288 with seven homers.

JUNE 25   Charlie Duffee hits a three-run homer into the left-field seats in the tenth inning to defeat Louisville 10–7 at Sportsman's Park.

JUNE 29   The Cardinals rout Rochester 13–7 at Sportsman's Park.

JULY 5   The Cardinals score seven runs in the eighth inning and wallop Brooklyn 18–7 at Sportsman's Park.

JULY 8   The Cardinals trounce Syracuse 13–5 at Sportsman's Park.

JULY 10   The Cardinals score seven runs in the first inning and two in the second to take a 9–0 lead but wind up losing 15–12 to Syracuse at Sportsman's Park.

JULY 12   Toad Ramsey strikes out 13 batters during a 12–4 win over Syracuse at Sportsman's Park.

Thomas (Toad) Ramsey had a 24–17 record with a 3.63 ERA and 257 strikeouts in 348²/₃ innings in 1890. Despite his winning record, Ramsey was released in September because of habitual drunkenness. He never pitched in the majors again.

JULY 28   The Cardinals thrash the Syracuse Stars 12–1 at Syracuse.

AUGUST 10   The Cardinals trounce Brooklyn 14–2 at Sportsman's Park.

AUGUST 12   The Cardinals pummel Brooklyn 21–4 at Sportsman's Park.

AUGUST 16   After falling behind 9–0 in the second inning against Philadelphia at Sportsman's Park, the Cardinals stage an incredible rally to win 12–11. St. Louis took the lead with four runs in the eighth inning.

Philadelphia outfielder Curt Welch, an ex-Cardinal serving as the Athletics' captain during the game, caused a brouhaha late in the game. With St. Louis trailing 9–7 in the seventh, Welch tried to replace pitcher Ed Seward with Sadie McMahon. Umpire Bob Emslie cited a new substitution rule that stipulated that two designated subs had to be listed on the lineup card before the game. McMahon was not one of them. Welch launched into a tirade and Emslie backed down, allowing McMahon into the game. This decision raised the ire of Cardinals manager Count Campau. Still seething as his club continued to blow a huge lead, Welch created two more long delays in both the eighth and ninth innings arguing Emslie's calls. Welch was ejected and replaced in center field by Seward, who re-entered the contest in another illegal substitution. The Cardinals were too exhausted to object to Seward's presence, and the tilt was completed without further incident.

AUGUST 25   The Cardinals pummel the Louisville Colonels 13–2 in a contest at Sportsman's Park called after seven innings by darkness.

AUGUST 27   The Cardinals outlast the Orioles 11–10 in Baltimore. St. Louis was ahead 8–1 after four innings, but Baltimore chipped away at the lead and took a 10–9 lead in the top of the ninth. The Cardinals won with two runs in the bottom of the inning.

AUGUST 31   The Cardinals score seven runs in the eighth inning and win 12–1 against the Athletics in Philadelphia.

SEPTEMBER 4   The Cardinals win 13–6 over the Stars in Syracuse.

SEPTEMBER 13   Jack Stivetts pitches the Cardinals to a 1–0 victory at Toledo.

SEPTEMBER 21   The Cardinals win two games during a contentious afternoon against the Rochester Hop Bitters at Sportsman's Park. The Cardinals won the first game 12–1. St. Louis led 10–3 in the second tilt when Rochester outfielder Sandy Griffin was ordered out of the game by umpire Jack Doescher for excessive arguing. When Griffin refused to leave, the umpire forfeited the contest to the Cardinals.

SEPTEMBER 23   Two Cardinals make the record books during a 21–2 pounding of the Athletics in a contest at Sportsman's Park called after seven innings by darkness. Making his major league debut, pitcher George Nicol pitched an abbreviated seven-inning no-hitter. First baseman Ed Cartwright drove in seven runs during an 11-run third inning. Cartwright hit a grand slam and a three-run homer, both off Ed Green.

Nicol pitched only three games with the Cardinals and had a 2–1 record. During his three-year big-league career, Nicol had a 5–7 record and a 6.68 ERA. Although he is credited with a seven-inning no-hitter, he didn't pitch a shutout in the majors. Nicknamed "Jumbo" for carrying 220 pounds on his five-foot ten-inch frame, Cartwright held the major league record for most RBIs during an inning for more than 100 years. His mark was broken on April 23, 1999, when the Cardinals' Fernando Tatis drove in eight runs in an inning with a pair of grand slams.

OCTOBER 22   After only one season, the Players League folds.

With the demise of the Players League, Charlie Comiskey returned to the Cardinals as player-manager along with regulars such as Jack Boyle, Yank Robinson, and Tip O'Neill. Arlie Latham and Silver King, two individuals suspected by Chris Von der Ahe to have thrown games during the 1889 season, did not return to St. Louis.

The Kidnapping of Chris Von der Ahe

Mark Baldwin, a pitcher in the majors from 1887 through 1893, and Cardinals owner Chris Von der Ahe battled each other in court for eight years during the 1890s. The trouble began in the fall of 1890 when the National League and American Association clubs were stealing players and claiming leftovers from the short-lived Players League. Baldwin signed with the Pittsburgh club of the National League and tried to persuade Silver King to join him. King had played for the Cardinals from 1887 through 1889 before jumping to the Players League in 1890. At the time, he was arguably the best pitcher in baseball. When Von der Ahe discovered that Baldwin had been trying to lure King away, the Cardinals owner had Baldwin arrested in a St. Louis poolroom on charges of conspiracy. Baldwin spent the next 24 hours in jail, but the case was thrown out of court. As Baldwin stepped out of the courtroom, Von der Ahe had Baldwin arrested again on new charges. In retaliation, Baldwin filed a $20,000 lawsuit in Pittsburgh against Von der Ahe for false arrest and malicious prosecution.

The case dragged on for years. It was still not resolved on May 5, 1894, when Von der Ahe went to Pittsburgh to watch his club play a game against the Pirates. As he emerged from his room at the Monongahela Hotel, a deputy sheriff arrested Von der Ahe. The warrant was issued at Baldwin's insistence. The case went to court in May 1895, and

a Pittsburgh jury awarded Baldwin $2,500. Baldwin still had not collected the money by January 1897. He sued Von der Ahe again and won a judgment for $10,000 in damages. The case eventually went to the Pennsylvania Supreme Court. The high court upheld Baldwin's case, but Von der Ahe still refused to pay.

In order to collect, Baldwin helped set up a plan to kidnap Von der Ahe in February 1898 in conjunction with private detectives, attorneys, and former Pirates owner W. A. Nimick. A private detective posed as a sportswriter to meet with Von der Ahe with the ruse that he wanted to talk about a business proposition that would be very much to his advantage. Instead, Von der Ahe was hustled into a carriage and handcuffed. The carriage sped across the Mississippi River to East St. Louis, Illinois, where he was forced onto a train bound for Pittsburgh, a 22-hour journey. On arrival in Pittsburgh, Von der Ahe was taken to an Allegheny County jail, where he spent several days before making bail. Despite the kidnapping, Baldwin still had trouble squeezing any money out of Von der Ahe, who was almost broke. In addition, the Pennsylvania court had no jurisdiction to seize any of the money Von der Ahe held in Missouri. Baldwin collected only a small portion of the judgment against Von der Ahe by claiming a percentage of the Cardinals' gate receipts whenever the club played in Pittsburgh and Philadelphia.

1891

Season in a Sentence

With most of the Players League defectors returning to St. Louis, the Cardinals stay in the thick of the American Association pennant race for most of the summer.

Finish · Won · Lost · Pct · GB

Second   85   51   .625   8.5

Manager

Charlie Comiskey

Stats

	Cards	AA	Rank
Batting Avg:	.266	.255	2
On-Base Pct:	.357	.338	2
Slugging Pct:	.355	.344	3
Home Runs:	58		1
Stolen Bases:	283		3
ERA:	3.27	3.72	2
Fielding Avg:	.920	.922	5
Runs Scored:	976		2
Runs Allowed:	753		2

Starting Lineup

Jack Boyle, c
Charlie Comiskey, 1b
Bill Eagan, 2b
Denny Lyons, 3b
Shorty Fuller, ss
Tip O'Neill, lf
Dummy Hoy, cf
Tommy McCarthy, rf
John Munyan, c

Pitchers

Jack Stivetts, sp
Willie McGill, sp
Clark Griffith, sp-rp
George Rettger, sp
Joe Neale, sp

Attendance

220,000 (first in AA)

Club Leaders

Batting Avg:	O'Neill	.321
On-Base Pct:	Lyons	.445
Slugging Pct:	Lyons	.455
Home Runs:	Lyons	11
RBIs:	O'Neill	95
	McCarthy	95
Runs:	Hoy	136
Stolen Bases:	Hoy	59
Wins:	Stivetts	33
Strikeouts:	Stivetts	259
ERA:	Stivetts	2.86
Saves:	Five tied w/	1

APRIL 8   The Cardinals open the 1891 season with a 7–7 tie, called after eight innings by darkness, against Cincinnati at Sportsman's Park. The umpire was ex-Cardinal Bill Gleason, whose calls were so impartial that the partisan St. Louis fans jeered him even though most of Gleason's decisions favored the local club. Cincinnati manager King Kelly was naturally incensed. When the ninth inning started, it was so dark that it was next to impossible to see the ball. Still, Gleason ordered that play continue into the tenth. The Cardinals quickly scored in the top of the inning, and Cincinnati began to stall in the bottom half hoping that the inning couldn't be completed and that the score would revert back to the 7–7 tie at the end of the ninth. When Gleason refused to halt the contest, Kelly took matters into his own hands and pulled his team off the field. The umpire declared a forfeit in favor of St. Louis. Chris Von der Ahe protested the forfeit, claiming that his club preferred to win on its own merits and not because of an incompetent umpire. Gleason was so abysmal that the American Association fired him after one game.

Cincinnati was one of three new franchises in the American Association in 1891. Others were in Boston and Washington, replacing those in Toledo, Syracuse, and Rochester. The Cincinnati club moved to Milwaukee in August.

APRIL 11   Clark Griffith wins his major league debut, defeating the Reds 13–5 at Sportsman's Park.

Griffith had an 11–6 record with St. Louis as a 21-year-old rookie in 1891 but was inexplicably released by the club in August. Griffith landed in Chicago with the Cubs in 1893 and went on to post a career record of 237–146. In 1901, he was the player-manager of the first Chicago White Sox club, which won the American League pennant that season. Later, Griffith was the owner of the Washington Senators from 1912 until his death in 1955.

APRIL 13   In a replay of the Opening Day tie, the Cardinals win 13–6 over Cincinnati at Sportsman's Park.

APRIL 15   Trailing 8–4, the Cardinals score eight runs in the sixth inning and defeat Columbus 13–8 at Sportsman's Park.

APRIL 27   The Cardinals outflank the Louisville Colonels 13–3 at Sportsman's Park.

APRIL 28   The Cardinals clobber the Colonels for the second day in a row, winning 13–6 at Sportsman's Park.

MAY 1   The Cardinals win 3–1 despite collecting only one hit off Cincinnati's Frank Dwyer in Cincinnati. Dummy Hoy got St. Louis's only hit, a pop-up that landed for a single just behind third base in the fourth inning. The hit by Hoy didn't figure in the scoring, however. The Cardinals scored two runs in the first and one in the sixth with the benefit of walks and errors.

William "Dummy" Hoy was deaf, stood only five foot six, and weighed just 160 pounds, but he played in the major leagues from 1888 through 1902. The 1891 season was his only one in St. Louis. An average hitter for most of his career, Hoy lasted more than a decade in the majors largely because of his speed and abilities in the outfield. Many histories call him a "deaf-mute," but that is not true. Hoy learned to speak a few phrases to help him in his profession, such as "You are rotten," which he directed at umpires who displeased him. Hoy could also make himself heard when calling for fly balls, although he couldn't hear the calls of his fellow fielders. Many historians also claim that Hoy was the reason that umpires adopted hand signals to go along with the vocal calls of "out," "safe," and "strike." This is also not true. Hand signals were not used by umpires until 1905, three years after Hoy's playing career ended. At the age of 99, he threw out the ceremonial first pitch in Cincinnati prior to the third game of the 1961 World Series.

MAY 5   The Cardinals win 11–1 in Cincinnati.

MAY 7   The Cardinals score nine runs in the second inning of a 14–2 victory in Washington.

MAY 8   The Cardinals drub the Washington Senators in Washington for the second day in a row, winning 20–4.

MAY 27   The Cardinals thrash Washington 10–0 at Sportsman's Park.

MAY 28   The Cardinals continue to hammer Washington pitching with a 14–5 triumph at Sportsman's Park.

MAY 30   The Cardinals whip the Philadelphia Athletics 17–2 and 15–3 in a Memorial Day doubleheader at Sportsman's Park. Jack Stivetts started both games for St. Louis, but he was taken out of each one after the club built a big lead.

Stivetts had a record of 33–22 in 1891, compiling a 2.86 ERA. In 440 innings, Stivetts walked a team record 232 batters and struck out 258.

JUNE 3   The Cardinals rout Baltimore 11–0 at Sportsman's Park.

Five Cardinals scored at least 100 runs in 1891. They were Dummy Hoy (134), Denny Lyons (124), Tommy McCarthy (124), Tip O'Neill (111), and Shorty Fuller (105).

JUNE 4   Jack Stivetts pitches a two-hitter to defeat Baltimore 12–1 at Sportsman's Park. The only Orioles hits were singles by Bill Johnson and opposing pitcher Bert Cunningham.

JUNE 6   The Cardinals take first place with a 10-inning, 11–10 win over the Boston Red Stockings at Sportsman's Park. St. Louis scored eight runs in the second inning to take a 10–3 lead but let Boston tie the score before winning in the tenth.

Boston won the last two games of the series to reclaim first place. The Cardinals and the Red Stockings battled for first place for several weeks until Boston pulled away in late August. Boston won the pennant by 8½ games, and St. Louis finished second.

JUNE 24   The Cardinals thrash Cincinnati 14–3 at Sportsman's Park.

JUNE 25   Long delays frustrate the crowd during a 9–1 win over Cincinnati at Sportsman's Park.

The trouble started in the first inning when Cincinnati shortstop Yank Robinson, an ex-Cardinal, tripped Tip O'Neill on the base paths. O'Neill was tagged out in a rundown, but umpire Jumbo Davis called him safe because of interference. Cincinnati manager King Kelly was livid and threw the ball over the outfield fence. Kelly argued with Davis for 10 minutes before play resumed. Unfortunately for Davis, Kelly was also the Cincinnati catcher, and Kelly continued to berate the umpire from his position behind the plate. Finally Davis couldn't take it anymore and tossed Kelly from the premises. He took his team with him, causing another delay of 45 minutes before the game proceeded. When the nine innings were finally completed, St. Louis had a 2–1 win.

JUNE 26   The Cardinals win with ease 15–4 over Cincinnati at Sportsman's Park.

JUNE 29   The Cardinals blow a 10–1 lead when Columbus scores six runs in the eighth inning and four in the ninth to win 11–10 at Sportsman's Park.

JULY 2   The Cardinals bury Louisville 15–7 at Sportsman's Park.

JULY 24   The Cardinals score seven runs in the fourth inning to break a 4–4 tie and go on to win a 20–12 slugfest in Cincinnati.

AUGUST 6   Jack Stivetts hits two home runs, but the Cardinals lose 7–5 to the Athletics at Sportsman's Park. On the mound, Stivetts allowed two homers among the 14 Philadelphia hits.

AUGUST 20   The Cardinals bury Columbus 15–8 at Sportsman's Park.

Charlie Comiskey seemed to lose control of the team in August. Both Jack Boyle and Denny Lyons disappeared for a few days on a drinking spree in Atlantic City. Bill Eagan became so drunk on a train trip that he tweaked owner Chris Von der Ahe on the nose. At the insistence of the Cardinals owner, the conductor evicted Eagan from the train in the dead of night miles from the nearest town. Willie McGill was another player who had issues with sobriety. McGill was only 17 years old in 1891 and started the season with the Cincinnati club, but it released him in May after he got into a drunken brawl at a saloon. Picked up by the Cardinals, he had an 18–9 record. Combined with his two wins in Cincinnati, McGill became the youngest 20-game winner in big-league history, but St. Louis released him in September. McGill's big-league career ended when he was 22.

SEPTEMBER 20   The Cardinals score nine runs in the seventh inning to take a 16–11 lead over Washington at Sportsman's Park. They proved to be the winning runs as the game was called by darkness at the end of the seventh.

SEPTEMBER 22   After allowing eight runs in the sixth inning to give Washington a 9–8 lead, the Cardinals score two runs in the seventh and two in the eighth to win 12–9 at Sportsman's Park. The tilt was called at the end of the eighth by darkness.

OCTOBER 2   The Cardinals slip past Louisville 13–8 at Sportsman's Park.

The Cardinals won 86 games in 1891. It would be 1921 before the franchise won that many times in a season again.

OCTOBER 4   Making his first major league start, Cardinal pitcher Ted Breitenstein pitches a no-hitter, defeating Louisville 8–0 in the first game of a doubleheader at Sportsman's Park. The only man to reach base off Breitenstein was Harry Taylor, who drew a walk. Breitenstein struck out

Workhorse pitcher Ted Breitenstein was one of the few Cardinals to play under owner Chris Von der Ahe for more than five seasons.

six batters. Prior to the no-hitter, Breitenstein made five relief appearances for the Cardinals totaling $19\frac{2}{3}$ innings in which he was 1–0 with an ERA of 3.20. Louisville won the second contest, called after eight innings by darkness, 4–2.

A native of St. Louis, Breitenstein was 22 when he made his big-league debut and pitched for the Cardinals from 1891 through 1896 and again in 1901. He had a lifetime record of 160–170.

OCTOBER 29   Cardinal stars Charlie Comiskey, Tip O'Neill, Jack Stivetts, Tommy McCarthy, and Denny Lyons announce their intention to sign with National League clubs in 1892.

The National League and American Association had each agreed since 1883 to honor the player contracts of the other, but the understanding came apart shortly after the end of the 1891 season when the NL began raiding the rosters of their AA rivals. Many American Association clubs were tottering on the brink of bankruptcy. As a result, all of the Cardinals were free to sign with NL clubs. Few wanted to cast their lot in St. Louis after years of abuse from capricious owner Chris Von der Ahe, who was becoming increasingly irrational and paranoid. Von der Ahe lost almost every key player he employed to National League teams. Tired of constant interference from Von der Ahe, Charlie Comiskey signed with the Cincinnati Reds as player-manager on November 4. Later, Tip O'Neill also signed with Cincinnati. Tommy McCarthy and Jack Stivetts signed with Boston, Jack Boyle, Denny Lyons, and Shorty Fuller went to New York, and Dummy Hoy got on with Washington. Von der Ahe made some signings of his own, inducing many National League regulars to come to St. Louis, such as Jack Glasscock and Kid Gleason, but the losses far outweighed the gains. The only two members of the 1891 Cardinals who played for the club the following season were pitchers Ted Breitenstein and John Easton, who had a combined 13 games of big-league experience prior to 1892. There were many players on the 1892 Cardinals that were familiar to 19th-century fans, but most were well past their prime. As a result, the Cardinals went from an 85–52 record in 1891 to 56–94 in 1892.

DECEMBER 17   After 10 years of existence, the American Association folds. Four of the eight clubs in the AA were absorbed into the National League. The Cardinals were one of the four. The other three were the Baltimore Orioles, Louisville Colonels, and the Washington Senators. The rest of the NL was composed of franchises in Boston, Brooklyn, Chicago, Cincinnati, Cleveland, New York, Philadelphia, and Pittsburgh, giving the circuit 12 clubs. With 12 teams and a 154-game schedule in 1892, the NL split the pennant race into two halves. The winners of the two halves were Boston and Cleveland, and the two met in a postseason series, which Boston won. With the exception of the strike-interrupted 1981 campaign, the 1892 season was the only time that a major league had two pennant races in a season.

As part of the agreement for allowing the four American Association teams into the National League, the NL allowed Sunday games to be played for the first time since the league was established, in 1876. Also, the ban on alcohol at the ballparks was lifted, as was the minimum ticket price of 50 cents. Fans could now enter National League ballparks for a quarter as they had in the American Association.

1892

Season in a Sentence

The Cardinals join the more prestigious National League after 10 seasons in the American Association, but the transition is far from smooth as the club finishes 11th in a 12-team league.

Finish • Won • Lost • Pct • GB

Eleventh   56   94   .373   46.0

Managers

Jack Glasscock (1–3), Cub Stricker (6–17), Jack Crooks (27–33), George Gore (6–9), and Bob Caruthers (16–32)

Stats

Stats	Cards	NL	Rank
Batting Avg:	.226	.245	12
On-Base Pct:	.312	.317	8
Slugging Pct:	.298	.327	11
Home Runs:	45		2
Stolen Bases:	205		12
ERA:	4.20	3.28	11
Fielding Avg:	.929	.928	7
Runs Scored:	703		10
Runs Allowed:	922		11

Starting Lineup

Dick Buckley, c
Perry Werden, 1b
Jack Crooks, 2b
George Pinkney, 3b
Jack Glasscock, ss
Cliff Carroll, lf
Steve Brodie, cf
Bob Caruthers, rf-p
Gene Moriarty, lf

Pitchers

Kid Gleason, sp
Ted Breitenstein, sp
Pink Hawley, sp
Charlie Getzein, sp
Bill Hawke, sp
Pud Galvin, sp
Bob Caruthers, sp

Attendance

192,442 (third in NL)

Club Leaders

Batting Avg:	Caruthers	.277
On-Base Pct:	Crooks	.400
Slugging Pct:	Caruthers	.357
Home Runs:	Werden	8
RBIs:	Werden	84
Runs:	Brodie	85
Stolen Bases:	Carroll	30
Wins:	Gleason	20
Strikeouts:	Gleason	133
ERA:	Hawley	3.19
Saves:	Caruthers	1

APRIL 12   In the season opener, the Chicago Cubs defeat the Cardinals 14–10 before 10,000 at Sportsman's Park. Chicago led 7–1 in the fifth inning and 14–5 in the seventh before allowing St. Louis back in the game. In his first game as a Cardinal, Cliff Carroll hit a home run.

The franchise's first day in the National League began with an extravagant morning parade that started at Sportsman's Park, moved down Grand to Washington, and proceeded to the Lindell Hotel and back through the principal streets to the park. A marching band led the procession, which included carriages toting world champion boxer John L. Sullivan, Chicago manager Cap Anson, celebrated actress Lillian Russell, Missouri Governor Dave Francis, and St. Louis Mayor Edward Noonan. The two teams entered Sportsman's Park with a brass band leading the way. With the move to a new league, the Cardinals were third in attendance despite being an 11th-place team.

APRIL 15   The Cardinals win their first National League game. In his first start since his no-hitter on October 4, 1891, Ted Breitenstein carried a no-hitter into the seventh inning before winning 9–3 over the Pirates at Sportsman's Park.

The win evened the Cardinals' record at 1–1, but the club lost its next eight games to drop to 1–9. Jack Glasscock started the year as manager. One of the best shortstops in baseball during the 1880s, Glasscock was 34 years old in 1892 and past his peak, but he was still an effective player. Unfortunately, he couldn't stomach Chris Von der Ahe's interference and lasted only four games as manager, although Glasscock remained in St. Louis as the starting shortstop. He was the first of five individuals who ran the Cardinals from the bench in 1892, each of them player-managers. Cub Stricker, a feisty infielder, followed Glasscock. Stricker had a 6–17 record as manager before Von der Ahe dismissed him. Two weeks prior to being fired, Stricker jumped into the Sportsman's Park seats following a 10–2 loss and punched a fan who had been heckling the team. Jack Crooks was the third of five St. Louis managers in 1892 and had a record of 27–33. George Gore, a star outfielder with Chicago during the 1880s, became the next man to guide the Cardinals. Gore was 35 and near the end of his career as player. He was 6–9 as a manager and batted .205 in 20 games. Bob Caruthers, another 1880s star in the last throes of his playing career, finished out the season and was 16–32 as manager.

APRIL 17 In the first Sunday game in National League history, the Cardinals lose 5–1 to the Reds at Sportsman's Park.

Sunday games were permitted at National League ballparks for the first time in 1892, local laws permitting. The only three clubs allowed to play on the Christian Sabbath by local authorities that season were in St. Louis, Cincinnati, and Louisville. Chicago was cleared to play on Sundays in 1893, but it would be well into the 20th century before teams in New York, Brooklyn, Boston, Philadelphia, and Pittsburgh were allowed to play on the first day of the week. The ballparks in the two Pennsylvania cities were vacant on Sundays until 1934.

APRIL 22 The Pirates score 12 runs in the first inning off Ted Breitenstein and Bob Caruthers and roll to a 14–2 win over the Cardinals at Pittsburgh. The contest was called after seven innings by darkness.

MAY 6 Ted Breitenstein carries a no-hitter into the ninth inning before defeating the Dodgers 14–2 at Sportsman's Park. The only Brooklyn hits were singles by Dan Brouthers and Bill Hart.

MAY 10 Perry Werden hits a grand slam off Kid Carsey in the fifth inning of an 8–4 win over the Phillies during the first game of a doubleheader at Sportsman's Park. Jack Crooks led off the first inning of the second game with a home run. St. Louis built a 9–0 lead before hanging on for a 9–8 victory.

A native of St. Louis, Werden played for the Cardinals in 1892 and 1893. In his second season, he set a club record for most triples in a season. Some sources credit him with 29 triples, others with 33. For unknown reasons, the Cardinals didn't ask Werden back in 1894, nor did any other big-league club. He didn't play in the majors again until 1897, his last season in the National League.

MAY 11 Jack Crooks leads off the first inning with a home run for the second game in a row, but the Cardinals lose 5–3 to Baltimore at Sportsman's Park.

JUNE 10 Orioles catcher Wilbert Robinson collects seven hits in seven at-bats and drives in eleven runs in pacing his club to a 25–4 thrashing of the Cardinals in the first game of a doubleheader in Baltimore. The Orioles also won the second tilt, 9–8.

JUNE 13	The Cardinals score 11 runs in the fifth inning and win 15–11 over the Senators in Washington.
JUNE 24	The Cardinals and the Cleveland Spiders play to a 16-inning, 3–3 tie at Sportsman's Park. Both Ted Breitenstein and Cy Young pitched complete games. St. Louis tied the game 2–2 in the ninth inning. Both teams scored in the fifteenth.
JULY 12	The Cardinals score two runs in the ninth inning to beat Baltimore 4–3 in the first game of a doubleheader at Sportsman's Park, then win the second tilt 12–1.
JULY 13	The Cardinals win easily, 20–3, over the Braves in Boston.
JULY 27	The Orioles tie a National League record with four triples in the seventh inning of a 12–0 win over the Cardinals in Baltimore. Pud Galvin surrendered each of the triples.

> *Like many of the 1892 Cardinals, Galvin was a star in the 1880s and well past his peak by the time he played for the Cardinals. He was 5–6 with the Cards to close out his career with a record of 361–308. Galvin's short stay in St. Louis was marked by tragedy when he learned that his nine-year-old son died after falling into a large salt vat in Allegheny City, Pennsylvania.*

AUGUST 2	The Cardinals score seven runs in the first inning for a 7–0 lead, but they lose 12–10 to the Spiders in Cleveland.
AUGUST 18	Cardinal left fielder Cliff Carroll is suspended after being involved in a bizarre play during a 13–4 win over Baltimore at Sportsman's Park. Carroll attempted to field a ground ball but misjudged it, and the ball miraculously became lodged in his shirt pocket. Carroll looked around on the ground for the missing ball for a few seconds before locating it. By the time he could extricate the ball, the Oriole runner reached third base. Chris Von der Ahe was so outraged that he fined Carroll $50 and suspended him without pay for the remainder of the season. Carroll appealed the fine and suspension at the end of the season but was denied.
AUGUST 24	The Cardinals wallop the Giants 16–4 at Sportsman's Park.
AUGUST 30	The Cardinals edge past Washington 12–9 at Sportsman's Park.
OCTOBER 1	The Cardinals build a 12–4 lead in the sixth inning, then hang on to defeat Cleveland 12–11 at Sportsman's Park in a contest called after eight innings by darkness.
OCTOBER 2	The Cardinals score eight runs in the first inning but lose 12–10 to the Reds in the first game of a doubleheader in Cincinnati. The Reds also won the second clash, 4–1, called after five innings by darkness.
OCTOBER 4	Because of dwindling attendance and competition from the fall horse racing season at St. Louis tracks, the Cardinals play a "home" game in Indianapolis and defeat the Reds 9–8.
OCTOBER 15	Three weeks before Grover Cleveland defeats Benjamin Harrison in the presidential election, the Cardinals finish the 1892 season by playing another "home" game out of town and lose 1–0 to the Cubs in Kansas City.

The 1892 season was the last that the Cardinals played at the corner of Grand and Dodier for nearly three decades. In 1893, the club moved to new digs at Vandeventer and Natural Bridge (see April 27, 1893) at a facility dubbed New Sportsman's Park. The Cardinals played at Vandeventer and Natural Bridge for 27 years at ballparks that underwent several renovations and name changes, including New Sportsman's Park (1893–98), League Park (1899–1911), Robison Field (1912–17), and Cardinal Field (1918–20). The Cards returned to Grand and Dodier in 1920 (see June 6, 1920). During the interval, old Sportsman's Park was used for other athletic events, such as bicycle races, until 1902, when the American League placed a franchise in St. Louis and began play at Grand and Dodier (see December 3, 1901).

1893

Season in a Sentence

The Cardinals lead the National League in earned run average, but a feeble offense brings about a 10th-place finish.

Finish • Won • Lost • Pct • GB

Tenth   57   75   .432   30.5

Manager

Bill Watkins

Stats

Stats	Cards	• NL •	Rank
Batting Avg:	.264	.280	10
On-Base Pct:	.343	.356	9
Slugging Pct:	.341	.379	11
Home Runs:	10		12
Stolen Bases:	250		4
ERA:	4.06	4.66	1
Fielding Avg:	.930	.931	6
Runs Scored:	745		11
Runs Allowed:	829		4

Starting Lineup

Heinie Peitz, c
Perry Werden, 1b
Joe Quinn, 2b
Jack Crooks, 3b
Jack Glasscock, ss
Charlie Frank, lf
Steve Brodie, cf
Tommy Dowd, rf-lf
Frank Shugart, ss-cf-lf
Bones Ely, ss
Joe Gunson, c

Pitchers

Kid Gleason, sp
Ted Breitenstein, sp
Dad Clarkson, sp
Pink Hawley, sp

Attendance

195,000 (fifth in NL)

Club Leaders

Batting Avg:	Brodie	.318
On-Base Pct:	Crooks	.408
Slugging Pct:	Werden	.442
Home Runs:	Brodie	2
RBIs:	Werden	94
Runs:	Dowd	114
Stolen Bases:	Dowd	59
Wins:	Gleason	21
Strikeouts:	Breitenstein	102
ERA:	Breitenstein	3.18
Saves:	Four tied w/	1

APRIL 27   The Cardinals open the 1893 season with a 4–2 win over Louisville before 12,000 at New Sportsman's Park. Pink Hawley took a no-hitter into the ninth inning before emerging with the win.

This was the first game at New Sportsman's Park. It was located on the southeast corner of Vandeventer and Natural Bridge across from Fairgrounds Park. To celebrate the opening of the new facility, Chris Von der Ahe and city officials staged a grand parade. According to the newspaper reports, "There were in line a sufficient number of carriages to cover more than three blocks." The vehicles contained state and city officials, prominent citizens, officers and directors of the Cardinals club, and players from the St. Louis and Louisville teams. One of the carriages was led by four of Adolph Busch's finest black Arabian horses with Busch himself handling the reins. The Italian-American cavalry and two brass bands furnished the music along the route. Many of the buildings in the city were decorated with flags and flowers, and bunting adorned New Sportsman's Park. The players on the two clubs entered the ballpark in carriages to the cheers of the crowd. After a series of speeches, the "Star Spangled Banner" was played, an anthem that at the time was performed only on special occasions. (The "Star Spangled Banner" didn't officially become the National Anthem until 1933 and wasn't played regularly at sporting events until the 1940s.) Two bands that had taken part in the parade played 53 pieces of music in an hour-long concert before the game. A ceremony was also held in which souvenirs and copies of the daily newspapers were buried in a time capsule under home plate. There were nearly 2,000 women present, "dressed in their latest and prettiest spring finery."

The diamond at New Sportsman's Park was originally laid out for the St. Louis Maroons' stay in the National League in 1885 and 1886. Chris Von der Ahe moved to Vandeventer and Natural Bridge because the lot was much larger than the one at Grand and Dodier. New Sportsman's Park had an enormous playing field. It was 470 feet down the left-field line, 520 to the deepest part of left-center, 500 to straightaway center field, 330 to right-center, and 290 down the right-field line. The backstop was 120 feet from home plate. The field was ringed by a bicycle track. There were 14,500 seats at the ballpark, which was constructed entirely of wood. Streetcar service brought fans right to the main gate after Von der Ahe gave the Lindell Railway Company 200 feet of land for a loop. There were private boxes, a clubhouse, a pavilion, a rooftop press box, and a ladies' powder room. A long bar located on the ground floor sold beer and sandwiches for a nickel. The new ballpark proved to be an attraction. In 1892 the Cardinals were third in the NL in attendance with an 11th-place club and fifth in attendance in 1893 despite finishing 10th. The bloom withered quickly, however, as fan patronage plummeted over the following five years.

MAY 1   The Cardinals drub the Louisville Colonels 11–1 at New Sportsman's Park.

The Cardinals hit only ten home runs in 1893 from nine different players. Steve Brodie led the club in homers with two.

MAY 10   The Cardinals wallop the Cubs 14–2 at New Sportsman's Park.

The manager in 1893 was Bill Watkins, who had led the Detroit Wolverines to a championship in the 1887 World Series against St. Louis. A native of Canada, Watkins's playing career ended in 1884 when, as a member of the Indianapolis club in the American Association, he was struck in the temple by a pitch from Gus Shallix of the Cincinnati Reds. While Watkins hovered between life and death for several weeks in the hospital, his hair turned from black to white. Watkins lasted only a year as the Cardinals' manager, but that was longer than most of the team's skippers during the 1890s.

MAY 12   The Cardinals score four runs in the ninth inning to beat Cleveland 8–7 at New Sportsman's Park. Trailing 7–4, St. Louis batted in the top of the inning (as determined by a pregame coin flip). Cy Young loaded the bases on walks and gave up a pair of two-run singles to Jack Glasscock and Perry Werden. In the bottom of the inning, Kid Gleason loaded the bases on walks but got out of the inning without any damage.

The win gave the Cardinals an 8–3 record and a spot in first place. By the end of May, the Cardinals dipped below the .500 mark, however, where they remained for the rest of the season.

MAY 15   The Cardinals win 10–6 over the Reds at New Sportsman's Park in a contest punctuated by a fight between St. Louis outfielder Steve Brodie and Cincinnati catcher Farmer Vaughn. In a collision at the plate, Brodie hit Vaughn with a clenched fist as he slid home. Vaughn responded by throwing a bat at Brodie, striking him on the shoulder.

Vaughn was arrested for assault by the St. Louis police force. Rather than fight the case in court, Vaughn pleaded guilty and was fined $15, plus $10 in court costs.

MAY 21   The Cardinals score three runs in the ninth inning to beat the Reds 9–8 in Cincinnati. Jack Glasscock drove in Tommy Dowd with the winning run.

JUNE 21   On the day that Lizzie Borden is convicted of the ax murder of her parents, Steve Brodie hits a grand slam off Bill Rhodes in the third inning of a 9–6 win over Louisville at New Sportsman's Park.

JUNE 28   The Cardinals break open a close game with eight runs in the seventh inning and win 14–5 over Baltimore at New Sportsman's Park. All eight runs scored with two outs.

JULY 21   The Cardinals and the Reds play to a 10–10 tie in a contest at New Sportsman's Park called after 10 innings by darkness.

JULY 22   Trailing 7–3, the Cardinals score four runs in the ninth inning and two in the eleventh to defeat the Reds 9–7 at New Sportsman's Park. The tallies in the ninth were driven home on two-run singles by Steve Brodie and Perry Werden. Frank Shugart keyed the eleventh-inning rally with an RBI triple.

Before the year was over, Brodie was dealt to Baltimore in a terrible transaction for the Cardinals. Brodie was the center fielder for the National League champion Oriole teams of 1894, 1895, and 1896. He played in 727 consecutive games with the Cardinals and Orioles, a 19th-century record. Brodie was born Walter Scott Brodie in Virginia. His father, a Scottish immigrant, was a tailor by trade and a Shakespearean actor by avocation and named his son after the most famous actor of his native land. Brodie earned the nickname Steve from a popular daredevil of that time as fans saw him as a player who gave his all. Brodie often carried on conversations with himself in the outfield, quoted

Shakespeare while at bat, and delighted fans by catching fly balls behind his back while facing away from home plate. After his playing days ended, Brodie coached at both Rutgers University and the US Naval Academy.

JULY 29   An umpiring controversy highlights a doubleheader against the Spiders in Cleveland. Tom Lynch umpired the first game, but his questionable decisions led to a 7–6 Cardinals loss. Chris Von der Ahe said he would rather have a Cleveland player umpire the second game than Lynch. As a result, a pair of brothers umpired the second game, Cleveland pitcher John Clarkson and St. Louis hurler Arthur "Dad" Clarkson. The Spiders won again 3–2. Von der Ahe was so angry over the second-game loss that he fined Clarkson $5 for making a decision unfavorable to the Cardinals.

AUGUST 1   The Cardinals lose a doubleheader 25–2 and 6–1 against the Pirates at Sportsman's Park.

                 Dad Clarkson was scheduled to start the first game but refused to take the mound after Chris Von der Ahe fined him for his umpiring decisions three days earlier (see July 29, 1893). With no one else available, outfielder Jimmy Bannon started the game as a pitcher and gave up 15 runs in four innings. Von der Ahe rewarded Bannon for pitching under trying circumstances by releasing him. At the time, Bannon was batting .336.

AUGUST 6   The Cardinals score five runs in the eighth inning to beat the Reds 12–8 in the first game of a doubleheader in Cincinnati. St. Louis lost the second contest, called after six innings by darkness, 3–2.

                 With a new ballpark, Chris Von der Ahe believed he could make money by scheduling other events. A bicycle race was staged in July, churning up cinder and dust from the track surrounding the field. Players complained about the conditions, and Von der Ahe promised his men a share of the gate receipts from an upcoming Civil War reenactment at New Sportsman's Park called "The Bombardment of Fort Sumter," held during a long road trip in August. Von der Ahe said the amount could reach $2,500. To collect, Cardinal players had to win 20 of their next 40 games. Instead, the club embarked on a long losing streak. The reenactment was a financial flop. All it accomplished was further destruction of the grounds. Numerous animals traipsed around the field, leaving deep divots, and spent fireworks casings littered the diamond.

AUGUST 29   The Cardinals suffer through several anxious hours on a ferry while traveling from Washington to New York when a gale nearly sweeps the vessel out to sea.

SEPTEMBER 12   Pink Hawley pitches a one-hitter but loses 3–1 to the Dodgers at New Sportsman's Park. The Cardinals lost the game on four walks, fielding miscues, and a single by Brooklyn's Tommy Corcoran.

                 Emerson "Pink" Hawley played for the Cardinals from 1892 through 1894 and had a 30–58 record on some awful clubs. He acquired his nickname at birth. He was an identical twin, and his parents differentiated between the infants by pinning a blue ribbon on the other twin's diaper and a pink one on the future big leaguer. The two played together on semipro teams in their native Wisconsin with "Blue" Hawley serving as catcher. Major league clubs were scouting "Blue" when he died of pneumonia at the age of 18.

SEPTEMBER 15   The Cardinals score seven runs in the fourth inning and beat the Washington Senators 13–6 at New Sportsman's Park.

SEPTEMBER 16   Down 6–0, the Cardinals score two runs in the third inning, three runs in the fourth, one in the sixth, and one in the ninth to win 7–6 against Washington at New Sportsman's Park.

SEPTEMBER 30   On the last day of the season, the Cardinals pummel the National League champion Boston Braves 17–6 and 16–4 at New Sportsman's Park. Before the games, *The Sporting News* honored Cardinal second baseman Joe Quinn as the most popular player in America. Quinn received a gold watch with a diamond setting from the St. Louis–based publication. Quinn responded by collecting eight hits in the doubleheader. In the second game, Duff Cooley picked up six hits, including a triple and a double, in six at-bats. Frank Shugart scored eight runs in the two contests, five of them in the second tilt.

> *Quinn was born on Christmas Day in 1864 in Sydney, Australia. His family settled in Dubuque, Iowa, as a young boy. Quinn was the first native of Australia to reach the majors. The second was Craig Shipley, who debuted with the Dodgers in 1986. Cooley stood out among the rough types involved in baseball during the 1890s and was nicknamed "Sir Richard" for his aristocratic manner. After his playing days ended, Cooley owned minor league clubs in Topeka and Salt Lake City.*

1894

Season in a Sentence

With a manager whose nickname was "Doggie," the Cardinals finish ninth in a 12-team National League horse race.

Finish • Won • Lost • Pct • GB

Ninth   56   76   .424   35.0

Manager

Doggie Miller

Stats

Stats	Cards	NL	Rank
Batting Avg:	.286	.309	11
On-Base Pct:	.354	.379	11
Slugging Pct:	.408	.435	11
Home Runs:	54		5
Stolen Bases:	190		12
ERA:	5.29	5.32	4
Fielding Avg:	.923	.927	9
Runs Scored:	771		11
Runs Allowed:	953		4

Starting Lineup

Doggie Miller, c-3b
Roger Connor, 1b
Joe Quinn, 2b
Heinie Peitz, 3b-c
Bones Ely, ss
Charlie Frank, lf
Frank Shugart, cf
Tommy Dowd, rf-lf
Duff Cooley, lf

Pitchers

Ted Breitenstein, sp
Pink Hawley, sp
Dad Clarkson, sp

Attendance

155,000 (eighth in NL)

Club Leaders

Batting Avg:	Miller	.339
On-Base Pct:	Miller	.414
Slugging Pct:	Connor	.582
Home Runs:	Ely	12
RBIs:	Ely	89
Runs:	Shugart	103
Stolen Bases:	Dowd	31
Wins:	Breitenstein	27
Strikeouts:	Breitenstein	140
ERA:	Breitenstein	4.79
Saves:	None	

APRIL 19   The Cardinals open the season with an 11–3 win over the Pirates before 8,000 at New Sportsman's Park. Ted Breitenstein was the winning pitcher. Heinie Peitz and Joe Quinn each collected four hits. Like the 1892 and 1893 openers, the game was preceded by a street parade from downtown to the ballpark with players of both teams in large carriages waving to the crowd assembled on the city's main thoroughfares. The Cardinals and Pirates entered New Sportsman's Park behind a brass band. The parade became an annual event on Opening Day in St. Louis into the early 1900s.

> *The Cardinals started with six wins in their first seven games under new manager George (Doggie) Miller. He was only five foot six and weighed 145 pounds, but he was known as "Foghorn" and "Calliope" because of his booming voice. Miller was in his 11th big-league season when he arrived in St. Louis and had already logged time as a regular in the outfield, at third base, and as a catcher as a member of the Pirates. After the fast start in 1894, the Cardinals quickly slid in the standings and finished the year in ninth place, costing Miller his job as manager. He batted .339 in 127 games that season, however, and returned to the Cards as a player in 1895, splitting time between third base and catcher.*

MAY 5   An altercation in the fifth inning highlights a 6–5 loss to the Pirates in Pittsburgh. Pirate shortstop Jack Glasscock, believing that Pink Hawley deliberately threw at him, hurled his bat at the pitcher and then confronted Hawley on the mound. The two began throwing punches before Pittsburgh outfielder Patsy Donovan intervened. While the Cardinals' Heinie Peitz was at bat in the next half-inning, opposing catcher Connie Mack twice threw dirt in his face.

MAY 10   Frank Shugart becomes the first Cardinal to hit three homers in a game and the club smack six home runs for the first time in history, but St. Louis loses 18–9 in Cincinnati. Tom Parrott gave up all six home runs, though Parrott helped himself with the bat by hitting a homer of his own along with a double and two singles. The Reds scored 11 runs in the fifth inning off Pink Hawley. Heinie Peitz hit two homers for the Cardinals, and Doggie Miller clubbed one. Shugart, Peitz, and Miller hit consecutive homers in the seventh inning. The back-to-back-to-back feat was also a Cardinal first.

> *The Cardinals hit only 10 homers all season in 1893. The club struck 54 home runs in 1894. The next Cardinal batter to hit three homers in a game was George Watkins in 1928. The Cards didn't hit six home runs in a game again until 1940, and the club didn't hit three home runs in a row again until 1944.*

JUNE 21   Owner Chris Von der Ahe suspends Duff Cooley. The club gave Cooley permission to visit his parents in Topeka, Kansas. When he was a day late in returning, Von der Ahe laid Cooley off for a month without pay.

JUNE 23   The Cardinals maul the Cleveland Spiders 14–3 at New Sportsman's Park.

JUNE 24   The Cardinals outlast the Spiders 14–10 at New Sportsman's Park.

JULY 4   Pink Hawley ties a major league record by hitting three batters in the seventh inning of a 10–5 loss to Washington in the first game of a doubleheader at New Sportsman's Park. Hawley's errant control was attributed to a wet ball as the grounds were soaked by a morning rain. The Cardinals won the second tilt 15–8, scoring seven runs in the third inning.

JULY 5   Brooklyn scores seven runs in the first inning to take a 7–0 lead, but the Cardinals rally to win 13–12 at New Sportsman's Park.

JULY 10   The Cardinals pummel the Phillies 17–8 at New Sportsman's Park.

JULY 11   A game at New Sportsman's Park is marked by heavy slugging for the second day in a row as the Cardinals prevail 13–12 over the Phillies. Philadelphia scored five times in the eighth inning to tie the contest 12–12 before the Cardinals scored a run in the ninth.

JULY 13   The Cardinals slip past the Orioles 11–10 at New Sportsman's Park.

The top pitcher on the 1894 Cardinals was Ted Breitenstein, who had a record of 27–25 and an ERA of 4.79. He led the NL in games (56), games started (50), complete games (46), and innings pitched (447^{1}/$_{3}$). The top hitter was Roger Connor, who batted .321 and had seven homers and 25 triples.

JULY 29   After winning the opener of a doubleheader 13–2 against Louisville at New Sportsman's Park, the Cardinals lose the nightcap 9–2.

AUGUST 1   The Cubs hammer the Cardinals 26–8 in Chicago.

AUGUST 20   The Cardinals lose 20–4 to the Dodgers in Brooklyn. Dad Clarkson gave up all 20 runs.

AUGUST 21   The Dodgers score 20 runs for the second day in a row, walloping the Cardinals 20–11 in Brooklyn. Ted Breitenstein allowed all 20 runs along with 25 hits.

Unable to draw people to New Sportsman's Park with a disintegrating ball club, Chris Von der Ahe staged a Wild West Show at the ballpark. The show featured 40 cowboys and 50 full-blooded Sioux Indians. Cardinals manager Doggie Miller even participated as payment for money he owed Von der Ahe. The debt was wiped out when Miller agreed to shoot blanks from a Winchester at stage coach–robbing Sioux. The show was not a financial success.

SEPTEMBER 5   The Cardinals lose by forfeit to the Senators in Washington. The game was tied 4–4 at the end of eight innings with sunset approaching. Washington batted in the top of the ninth and scored three times. The Cardinals began to stall, making no attempt to retire anyone hoping that darkness would end play before the inning could be completed. Umpire William Betts put a stop to the tomfoolery by declaring a forfeit.

SEPTEMBER 9   Roger Connor collects eight hits in a doubleheader against the Dodgers at New Sportsman's Park. Connor had five hits, including a triple, in five at-bats to help the Cardinals to a 7–5 win. Connor collected three hits, including a homer, in five second-game at-bats, but St. Louis lost 11–7 in a tilt called after eight innings by darkness.

After pitching 34 innings in the first eight days of September, Ted Breitenstein pitched a complete game in the opener. Still, when Dad Clarkson allowed 10 runs in the first two innings of the second game, Chris Von der Ahe called upon Breitenstein to pitch again in relief. Breitenstein refused, claiming exhaustion, and was fined $100 and suspended indefinitely.

SEPTEMBER 14   Dad Clarkson pitches the Cardinals to a 1–0 win over the Giants in St. Louis.

SEPTEMBER 21   The Phillies smack the Cardinals 21–1 at New Sportsman's Park. Dad Clarkson pitched the complete game.

> *Chris Von der Ahe was so disgusted by the turn of events that he named official scorer Harry Martin to take over as manager in the middle of the game. Doggie Miller, who was hung over from the previous evening's merriment, was happy to oblige, and left the ballpark. The next day, Martin and Miller were back at their old jobs.*

SEPTEMBER 25   The Cardinals score seven runs in the eighth inning to break a 7–7 tie and defeat the Phillies 14–7 at New Sportsman's Park.

SEPTEMBER 29   A Saturday afternoon "crowd" of 150 watches the Cardinals beat the Senators 6–4 at New Sportsman's Park.

SEPTEMBER 30   On the final day of the season, the Cardinals down the Senators 14–2 and 10–4 in a doubleheader at New Sportsman's Park. The second game was called after six innings by darkness.

1895

Season in a Sentence

The Cardinals split 12 games with the pennant-winning Baltimore Orioles but have difficulty beating anyone else and win fewer than 30 percent of their games.

Finish • Won • Lost • Pct • GB

Eleventh   39   92   .298 48.5

Managers

Al Buckenberger (16–34), Chris Von der Ahe (1–0), Joe Quinn (11–28), and Lew Phelan (11–30)

Stats

Stats	Cards	NL	Rank
Batting Avg:	.281	.286	11
On-Base Pct:	.338	.361	12
Slugging Pct:	.374	.400	11
Home Runs:	38		6
Stolen Bases:	205		8
ERA:	5.76	4.78	11
Fielding Avg:	.930	.930	8
Runs Scored:	747		11
Runs Allowed:	1,032		10

Starting Lineup

Heinie Peitz, c
Roger Connor, 1b
Joe Quinn, 2b
Doggie Miller, 3b-c
Bones Ely, ss
Duff Cooley, lf
Tom Brown, cf
Tommy Dowd, rf-cf
Biff Sheehan, rf
Denny Lyons, 3b

Pitchers

Ted Breitenstein, sp
Red Ehret, sp
Harry Staley, sp
Bill Kissinger, sp-rp
John McDougal, sp

Attendance

170,000 (ninth in NL)

Club Leaders

Batting Avg:	Cooley	.339
On-Base Pct:	Connor	.423
Slugging Pct:	Connor	.508
Home Runs:	Connor	8
RBIs:	Connor	77
Runs:	Cooley	106
Stolen Bases:	Dowd	30
Wins:	Breitenstein	19
Strikeouts:	Breitenstein	127
ERA:	Breitenstein	4.44
Saves:	Breitenstein	1

MARCH 12   On a street near New Sportsman's Park, Chris Von der Ahe assaults an African-American man named George Stevenson.

> *Defenseless and bewildered, Stevenson took a few punches to the face from Von der Ahe and then several shots at his feet from the Cardinals owner's pistol. The attack was unprovoked, and Von der Ahe was arrested for felonious assault. He protested the charge, claiming that African Americans had repeatedly robbed his saloons to carry away cases of alcohol. During the trial, Von der Ahe's son Eddie, who was treasurer of the saloons, testified that his father had routinely sent alcohol to his two mistresses and covered up the loss of inventory with bogus charges of robbery. Unfortunately for Stevenson, he lost the case when he failed to give security for court costs.*

APRIL 18   In the season opener, the Cardinals lose 10–7 to the Cubs before 8,000 at New Sportsman's Park.

> *Chris Von der Ahe continued to rotate managers, using three of them in 1895. Al Buckenberger started the year. He previously had managed Columbus in the American Association in 1889 and 1890 and the Pirates from 1892 through 1894. Unlike most of his predecessors in St. Louis, Buckenberger was not a player-manager, but he couldn't revive a moribund club and lasted just 50 games, losing 34 of them before being dismissed by Von der Ahe, who took over the club for a game and won. Unwilling to pay anyone just to manage, Von der Ahe turned to starting second baseman Joe Quinn to run the club from the bench. Quinn resigned after 39 games and a record of 11–28. Lew Phelan followed Quinn. So little is known about Phelan that the dates of his birth and death remain a mystery. He never appeared in a big-league game. The* Post-Dispatch *referred to Phelan as a "well-known sporting man." In those days a "sporting man" was a bookie. Phelan had been a partner in an Olive Street saloon the previous winter. "Just where he got his experience as a baseball manager is a mystery to the local fans," reported the St. Louis daily. Von der Ahe's mistress, Della Wells, was a relative of Phelan, which probably explains his hiring. Eventually Phelan was fired before the season was over. Although not credited as such in the official record books, contemporary newspapers reported that Von der Ahe ran the club from the bench during the last weeks of the season.*

APRIL 23   The Cardinals outlast the Cleveland Spiders 13–11 at New Sportsman's Park.

MAY 5   Heinie Peitz collects five hits, including two doubles and a triple, in five at-bats during a game against the Reds in Cincinnati. Despite the three extra-base hits and two singles, Peitz failed to score. Enough of his teammates crossed the plate, however, to enable the Cardinals to defeat the Reds 11–4.

MAY 11   Duff Cooley hits a grand slam off George Hodson in the third inning of a 12–0 win over the Phillies at New Sportsman's Park.

> *Cooley produced an odd set of statistics in 1895—9 doubles and 20 triples.*

MAY 24   Catcher Doggie Miller makes four throwing errors in the second inning of an 8–4 loss to Washington at New Sportsman's Park. Miller moved to third base in the third inning and committed yet another error.

MAY 26 — The Cardinals maul Washington 23–7 at New Sportsman's Park. St. Louis scored five runs in the first inning and seven in the eighth. Doggie Miller hit a grand slam.

JUNE 1 — The Cardinals score seven runs in the sixth inning and eight in the seventh and rout the Giants 23–2 in New York. Roger Connor collected six hits, including two doubles and a triple, in six at-bats. St. Louis picked up 30 hits as a team.

Connor hit .326 with eight homers in 1895.

JUNE 3 — Roger Connor becomes the all-time major league home run leader, passing Harry Stovey during a 5–2 loss to the Dodgers in Brooklyn.

The home run on June 3, 1895, was the 12th of Connor's career. He finished his stay in the majors in 1897 with 139 homers. Connor remained the career home run leader until Babe Ruth passed him in 1921. Connor also had a .318 lifetime batting average, 1,620 runs scored, 441 doubles, and 233 triples. The Hall of Fame began inducting players in 1936, with Ruth in the first class of five. Despite better numbers than many of his contemporaries, Connor didn't become a Hall of Famer until 1976. Although the honor came 45 years after his death in 1931, Connor has Hank Aaron to thank for his induction. After Aaron passed Ruth as the all-time home run king in 1974, reporters and historians began writing about Connor as the man who preceded Ruth at the top of the home run list. The publicity helped boost Connor into immortality in Cooperstown. He played in St. Louis from 1894 through 1897, the last four seasons of his big-league career. Connor came by his power naturally. He was six foot three and weighed 230 pounds during an era when players who were over six feet tall or weighed more than 200 pounds were a distinct minority.

JUNE 5 — The Cardinals win easily, 13–2, over the Phillies in Philadelphia.

JUNE 11 — The Cardinals score seven runs in the sixth inning but lose 15–10 to the Senators in Washington.

JUNE 23 — Roger Connor hits two home runs during a 9–3 win over the Reds at New Sportsman's Park. A policeman and an overflow crowd that ringed the outfield helped with one of the homers. In the first inning, Cincinnati center fielder Dummy Hoy settled under Connor's high fly but collided with the officer, who was assigned to crowd control. By the time Hoy retrieved the ball, Connor had circled the bases.

JULY 2 — The Cardinals score 11 runs in the first inning and move on to defeat the Cubs 15–5 in Chicago. Heinie Peitz tied a major league record by collecting two triples in the big inning. The Cardinals also tied a major league mark for most triples by one club in an inning with four. Roger Connor and Tom Brown collected the other two.

A catcher for most of his career, Peitz teamed with pitcher Ted Breitenstein to form the famous "Pretzel Battery." According the legend, they were named "The Pretzel Battery" when a fan found them at a bar at a local saloon munching on a bowl of pretzels. Peit z and Breitenstein were teammates in St. Louis from 1892 through 1895 and in Cincinnati from 1897 through 1900.

JULY 25 — The Cardinals collect 29 hits and slaughter the Dodgers 20–3 in Brooklyn. Joe Quinn had five hits, including a double, in six at-bats. Bones Ely was also 5 for 6 with three singles and two doubles.

JULY 31	The Colonels score 10 runs in the ninth inning off Ted Breitenstein and defeat the Cardinals 15–7 at Louisville.
AUGUST 7	The Pirates score 11 runs in the third inning off Red Ehret and Bill Kissinger and trounce the Cardinals 18–1 in Pittsburgh.
AUGUST 16	Tommy Dowd hits for the cycle during an 8–5 victory over Louisville at Sportsman's Park. All four hits came off Bert Inks.
AUGUST 17	The Cardinals score seven runs in the eighth inning and beat the Colonels 12–8 at Sportsman's Park.
SEPTEMBER 23	Only 100 fans endure a 15–6 loss to the Reds at Sportsman's Park.
SEPTEMBER 30	A horse racing track opens at New Sportsman's Park.

Chris Von der Ahe opened the track in another money-making scheme. Portions of the left- and right-field bleachers were altered and the grass sod torn up in a circle around the yard. One straightaway was beyond the outfield and the other behind home plate. The reconfigured grounds contained another bar so that patrons could enjoy an alcoholic beverage and place a bet. Sportswriters and fellow National League owners were outraged at the combination baseball park and horse racing track but were powerless to stop Von der Ahe from carrying out the plan since the races occurred after the baseball season ended. The new configuration was filled with festive flags and contained a flower garden and beer pavilion with red chairs and tables near right field. The grandstands, painted salmon-pink, were lined with geranium beds. Nearby were water fountains. Von der Ahe wasn't finished. Before the 1896 season started, he added other amusements and referred to his ballpark as the "Coney Island of the West." A water-chute ride was built behind the left-field wall that patrons in boats could slide down into an artificial lake for a quarter. A section of the fence was missing, and a batted ball could travel through the opening and roll more than 600 feet into the lake. In the winter, the 750-foot-by-250-foot lake accommodated ice skaters. The ride lasted only two seasons, however. Like most of Von der Ahe's financial ventures during the 1890s, it failed to recoup the cost of construction. The firm that built the contraption sued him for non-payment, and another company that invented the ride took Von der Ahe to court over patent infringement.

NOVEMBER 21	The Cardinals trade Heinie Peitz and Red Ehret to the Reds for Arlie Latham, Tom Parrott, Morgan Murphy, and Ed McFarland.

1896

Season in a Sentence

Chris Von der Ahe adds amusements to his ballpark, hailing it as "the Coney Island of the West," but fans are unamused by a 40–90 record.

Finish • Won • Lost • Pct • GB

Eleventh   40   90   .308   50.5

Managers

Harry Diddlebock (7–10), Arlie Latham (0–3), Chris Von der Ahe (2–0), Roger Connor (8–37), and Tommy Dowd (25–38)

Stats

Stats	Cards	• NL •	Rank
Batting Avg:	.257	.290	12
On-Base Pct:	.313	.354	12
Slugging Pct:	.346	.387	12
Home Runs:	37		4 (tie)
Stolen Bases:	185		11
ERA:	5.33	4.38	12
Fielding Avg:	.936	.938	7
Runs Scored:	593		12
Runs Allowed:	929		11

Starting Lineup

Ed McFarland, c
Roger Connor, 1b
Tommy Dowd, 2b-cf
Al Myers, 3b
Monte Cross, ss
Klondike Douglass, lf-rf
Tommy Parrott, cf
Tuck Turner, rf
Joe Sullivan, lf
Joe Quinn, 2b
Morgan Murphy, c
Duff Cooley, lf

Pitchers

Ted Breitenstein, sp
Bill Hart, sp
Red Donahie, sp
Bill Kissinger, sp

Attendance

184,000 (tenth in NL)

Club Leaders

Batting Avg:	Parrott	.291
On-Base Pct:	Connor	.356
Slugging Pct:	Connor	.433
Home Runs:	Connor	11
RBIs:	Connor	72
Runs:	Dowd	93
Stolen Bases:	Dowd	40
	Cross	40
Wins:	Breitenstein	18
Strikeouts:	Breitenstein	114
ERA:	Breitenstein	4.48
Saves:	Kissinger	1

APRIL 16 — Three months after Utah is admitted to the Union as the 45th state, the Cardinals defeat the Cleveland Spiders 5–2 before 15,000 at New Sportsman's Park. Ted Breitenstein was the winning pitcher, outdueling Cy Young. Duff Cooley contributed two singles and a triple.

MAY 3 — The Cubs and the Cardinals combine for nine triples, five of them by St. Louis, during a 16–7 win by the Cubs in Chicago. Neither team hit a double or a home run. The unusual situation was created by a large crowd that overflowed the grandstand and ringed the outfield. It was agreed before the game that any ball hit into the crowd would be a ground-rule triple.

MAY 8 — Two days after the Supreme Court case *Plessy vs. Ferguson* approves racial segregation under the "separate but equal" doctrine, the Cardinals fire Harry Diddlebock as manager.

Diddlebock was the first of five Cardinals managers in 1896. He was 41 years old with no prior playing or managing experience in the majors. Diddlebock had spent the previous 11 years as a sportswriter for the Philadelphia Inquirer *and the* Philadelphia Times. *The Cardinals won six of their first ten games in 1896, then lost six of seven. Diddlebock was late reporting to the ballpark on May 8 and arrived with his face smashed up and his eyes nearly swollen shut. He claimed he had been beaten up by six thugs. Chris Von der Ahe hired a private detective to investigate and learned that Diddlebock had spent the previous evening bar-hopping after winning a bundle on a long shot at a local racetrack. At his last stop, Diddlebock passed out while sitting on a bar stool and hit the floor face first. While Von der Ahe searched for a replacement, Arlie Latham was hired as manager. The players intensely disliked Latham, however, and he managed only three games. Von der Ahe led the club from the bench for two games before deciding on first baseman Roger Connor, who was 8–37 as manager. On July 8, outfielder–second baseman Tommy Dowd became manager number five in 1896 and somehow managed to finish out the season. The club won 13 of its first 20 games under Dowd but soon returned to its losing ways.*

JUNE 5
Nine days after a tornado kills 306 people in St. Louis and East St. Louis, the Cardinals lose their twelfth straight game, dropping a 7–3 decision to the Giants in New York.

JUNE 24
Tom Parrott's two-run homer in the ninth inning beats Louisville 4–3 in Louisville.

Parrott played in the majors with the Cubs (1893), Reds (1893–95), and Cardinals (1896) as a pitcher and an outfielder. He was an accomplished cornet player who performed during the offseason with the Portland (Oregon) Orchestra. Parrott loved to play the cornet into the wee hours of the morning to the annoyance of his fellow rooming-house tenants. A man with myriad eccentricities, Parrott slathered himself with iodine before each game because he believed it warded off sore muscles.

JULY 6
A timely thunderstorm saves the Cardinals from defeat at the hands of the Giants at New Sportsman's Park. The Giants broke a 6–6 tie with two runs in the ninth. After the Cards scored a run in the bottom half, rain stopped play. Since the inning wasn't completed, the score reverted to the end of the eighth and went into the books as a 6–6 tie.

Umpire Tim Keefe wasn't around for the finish. He left the ballpark in the fifth inning disgusted over the heckling he received from both clubs over his calls. Ed McFarland of the Cardinals and Jouett Meekin of the Giants served as umpires for the rest of the contest.

JULY 8
The Cardinals lose their 14th game in a row, dropping a 5–2 decision to the Giants at New Sportsman's Park.

Among the attractions amid the losing atmosphere at New Sportsman's Park in 1896 was the Silver Cornet Band, made up of two dozen attractive young girls. They wore long striped skirts, wide, white sailor hats, and leg-of-mutton sleeves. The group played all of the tunes then in vogue.

JULY 10
The Cardinals outlast the Boston Braves 12–11 at Sportsman's Park.

JULY 24
The Cardinals lose by forfeit to the Orioles at New Sportsman's Park. Baltimore scored five runs in the top of the thirteenth inning to break an 8–8 tie, and the Cardinals began stalling to prevent the inning from being completed before the sun set. The ploy failed to work, as umpire Bob Emslie forfeited the game to the Orioles.

JULY 25   The Cardinals score three runs in the ninth inning without a man being retired to defeat the Orioles 3–2 at New Sportsman's Park. Roger Connor drove in the tying run with a double and scored the winning tally on a single by Roger Connor.

JULY 28   Helped by 13 Louisville errors and 11 walks, the Cardinals win 20–5 over the Colonels at New Sportsman's Park.

The game was delayed a few minutes by the death of a sailor at the chutes water ride behind the left-field fence. The man died when a boat fell on him.

SEPTEMBER 2   The Cardinals suffer through a laborious Labor Day doubleheader, losing 18–3 and 12–8 to the Braves in Boston. The second game was called after eight innings by darkness.

SEPTEMBER 3   The Cardinals lose another doubleheader in Boston, 28–7 and 8–3. The second contest was called after six innings by darkness. The 28 runs the Cardinals allowed are the most in a single game in franchise history.

SEPTEMBER 4   The Braves continue to fatten their batting averages at the expense of St. Louis pitching with a 13–3 win in Boston. The Cardinals gave up 79 runs in five consecutive games over three days.

SEPTEMBER 8   Chris Von der Ahe marries former mistress Della Wells in Erie, Pennsylvania. Von der Ahe's first wife divorced him in January 1895 on grounds of infidelity and physical and mental abuse. Von der Ahe had also been at odds with his son Eddie over a nasty property dispute since the summer of 1894 that ended with each suing the other. Eddie sided with his mother in the divorce proceeding and ended his relationship with his father.

Temperamental and capricious, Cardinals owner Chris Von der Ahe alienated his players, managers, fellow owners, and, eventually, fans in his 17 years of ownership.

At the time he married Della, Von der Ahe was carrying on an affair with Anna Kaiser, who had been working as a servant in the Von der Ahe household. Kaiser claimed that the Cardinals owner had promised to marry her and sued for breach of promise. The case was settled out of court. The legal action didn't end the affair and put a strain on Chris and Della's marriage. A year later, Von der Ahe evicted Della's mother from an apartment he owned for non-payment of rent. The two divorced in January 1898. Von der Ahe, then 47 years old, married 24-year-old Kaiser in September 1898. The two divorced in 1902.

SEPTEMBER 20   Seven weeks before William McKinley defeats William Jennings Bryan in the presidential election, Ed McFarland hits a two-run, walk-off homer over the left-field fence in the ninth inning to beat the Cubs 3–2 at New Sportsman's Park.

1897

Season in a Sentence

The Cardinals continue their role as the laughingstock of the National League and win only 29 games all year.

Finish • Won • Lost • Pct • GB

Twelfth   29   102   .221   63.5

Managers

Tommy Dowd (6–22), Hugh Nicol (8–32), Bill Hallman (13–36), and Chris Von der Ahe (2–12)

Stats	Cards	• NL •	Rank
Batting Avg:	.275	.292	11
On-Base Pct:	.336	.354	11
Slugging Pct:	.356	.386	12
Home Runs:	31		6 (tie)
Stolen Bases:	172		10
ERA:	6.21	4.31	12
Fielding Avg:	.933	.939	9
Runs Scored:	588		12
Runs Allowed:	1,083		12

Starting Lineup

Klondike Douglass, c-lf
Mike Grady, 1b
Bill Hallman, 2b
Fred Hartman, 3b
Monte Cross, ss
Dan Lally, lf
Dick Harley, cf
Tuck Turner, rf
John Houseman, 2b-rf
Morgan Murphy, c
Tommy Dowd, cf

Pitchers

Red Donahue, sp
Bill Hart, sp
Kid Carsey, sp
Willie Sudhoff, sp

Attendance

136,400 (eleventh in NL)

Club Leaders

Batting Avg:	Douglass	.329
On-Base Pct:	Douglass	.403
Slugging Pct:	Douglass	.405
Home Runs:	Grady	7
RBIs:	Hartman	67
Runs:	Douglass	77
Stolen Bases:	Cross	38
Wins:	Donahue	10
Strikeouts:	Hart	67
ERA:	Donahue	6.13
Saves:	Donahue	1

APRIL 21   The Cardinals lose the season opener 4–1 to the Pirates before 5,000 at New Sportsman's Park.

The Cardinals finished the season with a record of 29–102 to place twelfth in the 12-team league. The next-worst team was Louisville, which ended the year at 52–78. Had the standings been turned upside down, St. Louis would have won by 23½ games. The club gave up 1,083 runs, an average of 8.2 per game, and scored 588. Like many previous seasons during the 1890s, managers were changed often. Tommy Dowd, who ended the season as manager in 1896, started the 1897 campaign in the same capacity but was traded to the Phillies after a 6–22 start. Hugh Nicol followed. Nicol played on the 1885 and 1886 American Association champions, but couldn't save a sinking ship. Under Nicol's leadership in 1897, the Cardinals were 8–32. Second baseman Bill Hallman, who worked as an actor and a vaudevillian during the offseason, succeeded Nicol as manager and posted a 13–36 record. Chris Von der Ahe managed himself during the final two weeks, in which the Cardinals lost 12 of 14.

MAY 15   The Orioles humiliate the Cardinals 20–3 at New Sportsman's Park.

MAY 31   The Braves hammer the Cardinals 25–5 in Boston.

JUNE 3   After the pitching staff allows 61 runs in the previous four games, Red Donahue tosses a shutout to beat the Dodgers 1–0 in Brooklyn. Klondike Douglass drove in the lone run of the game with a single in the third inning.

Donahue had a record of 17–62 in three seasons with the Cardinals (1895–97). He was 10–35 in 1897. Freed from the Cardinals by a trade to the Phillies in 1898, Donahue was 147–113 over the rest of his career and won 20 or more games in a season three times.

JUNE 24   Batting eighth in the lineup, Cardinal outfielder Dick Harley collects six hits, including a double, in six at-bats during a 12-inning, 7–6 win over the Pirates in Pittsburgh.

JULY 10   St. Louis fans throw eggs at umpire Jack Sheridan during a game against the Dodgers at New Sportsman's Park. With the score tied 2–2 in the fifth inning, Sheridan made a call that infuriated the hometown crowd. The game was halted, and Sheridan threatened the Cardinals with a forfeit unless he was granted police protection. Owner Chris Von der Ahe made the concession, and the Cardinals went on to win 4–3.

JULY 11   The Orioles wallop the Cardinals 22–4 at New Sportsman's Park.

JULY 30   Mike Grady hits a two-run, walk-off single in the ninth inning to defeat Louisville 7–6 at New Sportsman's Park.

JULY 31   The Cardinals and the Colonels split an unusual doubleheader at New Sportsman's Park. In the first game, won by Louisville 11–6, St. Louis pitchers Mike McDermott and John Grimes combined to hit six batters to tie a major league record by one club in one game. Louisville hurler Bill Magee plunked two batters. The combined eight hit batsmen in one game tied another big-league mark. In the second tilt, Louisville scored three times in the top of the eighth to take a 5–3 lead, but the Cardinals picked up four runs in their half to win 7–5 before darkness prevented the ninth inning from being played.

AUGUST 1   The Cardinals win the second game of a doubleheader against Louisville at New Sportsman's Park by forfeit.

Louisville won the first game 3–1 with Horace McFarland as umpire. McFarland was unable to umpire the second tilt because of injury, however, and Red Donahue of the Cardinals and Charlie Dexter of the Colonels served as arbiters. With Louisville winning 5–4 and St. Louis at bat in the last of the ninth, Tuck Turner fouled a pitch out of play. Donahue gave pitcher Bert Cunningham a new ball. At the time, players used one ball until it literally came apart at the seams or was hit into the crowd and not returned by the fans. (Fans were subject to arrest if they failed to return a foul ball.) New balls put into play always caused a controversy because they traveled farther, giving the team at bat an advantage. Cunningham promptly rolled the new ball into the dirt. Donahue objected and gave him another new ball. Cunningham gave five fresh balls the same treatment. Donahue then forfeited the contest to his own club. Three weeks later, the National League reversed the forfeit, depriving the Cardinals of a victory.

AUGUST 4   The Cardinals outlast the Cubs 13–12 in Chicago.

SEPTEMBER 3   The Orioles pummel the Cardinals 22–1 in Baltimore. Jack Doyle and Willie Keeler of the Orioles each collected six hits in six at-bats.

SEPTEMBER 18   Monte Cross of the Cardinals and Pink Hawley of the Pirates fight during a 13–10 St. Louis loss at Pittsburgh. Hawley struck out Cross to end the fifth inning. As they passed each other to change sides, Cross made an "ugly remark" to Hawley. The Pittsburgh pitcher responded by punching Cross in the jaw. Both players were ejected.

SEPTEMBER 26   Reds first baseman Jake Beckley hits three homers off Cardinal pitcher Willie Sudhoff during a 10–4 Cincinnati win in the first game of a doubleheader at New Sportsman's Park. All three balls cleared the left-field fence. Two of the three drives landed in the artificial lake created for the chutes water ride. The Cardinals also lost the second tilt, 8–6, to run the club's losing streak to 18 games.

During the 1897–98 offseason, owner Chris Von der Ahe removed the chutes water ride, the lake, and the racetrack from New Sportsman's Park. By Opening Day in 1898, baseball was the only attraction at the ballpark.

SEPTEMBER 27   The Cardinals end two long losing streaks with a 5–4 victory over Cincinnati at New Sportsman's Park. The win brought to a close an 18-game losing streak, the longest in club history. A 23-game losing streak to the Reds dating back to September 25, 1895, also came to an end. The Cardinals were 0–12 against Cincinnati in 1896 and 1–11 in 1897.

OCTOBER 3   On the final day of the season, the Cardinals trail the Cubs 8–0 in the first game of a doubleheader at New Sportsman's Park before scoring seven runs in the seventh inning. Four runs scored on a grand slam by Tuck Turner off Clark Griffith. After Chicago increased its lead to 9–7 in the top of the ninth, the Cards responded with three runs in their half to win 10–9. The Cubs won the second game, called after seven innings by darkness, 7–1.

1898

Season in a Sentence

While Teddy Roosevelt's Rough Riders storm San Juan Hill during the Spanish-American War, the Cardinals experience a rough ride to the National League cellar, losing a club record 111 games.

Finish • Won • Lost • Pct • GB

Twelfth   39   111   .260   63.5

Manager

Tim Hurst

Stats

Stats	Cards	• NL •	Rank
Batting Avg:	.247	.271	12
On-Base Pct:	.309	.354	12
Slugging Pct:	.305	.347	12
Home Runs:	13		11
Stolen Bases:	104		11
ERA:	4.53	3.60	12
Fielding Avg:	.939	.942	7
Runs Scored:	571		12
Runs Allowed:	929		12

Starting Lineup

Jack Clements, c
George Decker, 1b
Joe Quinn, 2b-ss
Lave Cross, 3b
Germany Smith, ss
Dick Harley, lf
Jake Stenzel, cf
Tommy Dowd, rf-cf
Jack Crooks, 2b
Joe Sudgen, c
Tommy Tucker, 1b

Pitchers

Jack Taylor, sp
Willie Sudhoff, sp
Jim Hughey, sp
Kid Carsey, sp

Attendance

151,700 (seventh in NL)

Club Leaders

Batting Avg:	Cross	.317
On-Base Pct:	Cross	.348
Slugging Pct:	Cross	.405
Home Runs:	Cross	3
	Clements	3
RBIs:	Cross	79
Runs:	Harley	74
Stolen Bases:	Stenzel	21
Wins:	Taylor	15
Strikeouts:	Taylor	89
ERA:	Taylor	3.93
Saves:	Taylor	1
	Sudhoff	1

APRIL 15   The Cardinals lose 2–1 to the Cubs in the season opener before 10,000 at New Sportsman's Park.

Chris Von der Ahe surprised Cardinal fans by hiring Tim Hurst as manager. Prior his appointment, Hurst had been a National League umpire from 1891 through 1897, in addition to serving as an official at numerous running, walking, and bicycle races and boxing and wrestling matches. A former coal miner in Pennsylvania, he had a reputation for being able to tame the rowdy players of the day. Hurst often settled disputed calls by striking disgruntled players with his fists or his mask. In 1897, an irate fan in Cincinnati tossed a beer stein at him. The umpire threw it back, hit another fan, and was arrested. The NL suspended him. It was hoped that Hurst's toughness would rub off on the Cardinals, but it failed to work as the club posted a 39–111 record in 1898. Despite his belligerent temperament, Hurst was considered to be one of the top umpires in the game, and the National League hired him back to officiate in 1900. He was serving as an ump in the American League in 1909 when he spit in the eye of Athletics second baseman Eddie Collins, inciting a riot. The incident ended Hurst's career in baseball, but he continued to work for many years as a boxing referee.

APRIL 16   A fire destroys almost all of New Sportsman's Park during a game against the Cubs. In addition to the ballpark, Chris Von der Ahe's saloon and dwelling were also reduced to ashes.

The ballpark was crowded with 6,000 people when the flames broke out. The Cubs had just gone into the field in the second inning when a column of smoke ascended from the lower corner of the northwest section of the grandstand. Small fires were an almost yearly occurrence at the wooden ballparks of the day. Trash piled up for weeks underneath the seats without anyone bothering to remove it. The invention of tarpaulins to cover the field during rainstorms was still in the future, and teams kept large mounds of sawdust at the ballparks to help dry out the fields. Add thousands of cigar-smoking fans discarding their stogies into the debris below, and you have a potentially lethal mix. These small fires were usually extinguished without endangering fans, and there was no sense of concern at first. But as the fire spread, a panic ensued. There was a rush for the front of the stands, and fans jumped onto the playing field, a distance of 12 feet, and stampeded toward the four stair cases at the rear of the ballpark. Within three minutes, the roof caught fire. When spectators surged toward the exit between the clubhouse and the saloon, they found the gate closed. The crowd formed a human battering ram to crash though the barrier. The players of both teams did heroic work and rescued many fans. No one was killed, but at least 100 were burned, and many had broken limbs. The flames also spread to an adjacent railway depot and the fairgrounds across the street. The only part of the ballpark left standing was the right-field bleachers. Von der Ahe lost all of his personal effects, including trophies and correspondence files. Insurance covered only part of the loss. He had also taken out thousands of dollars in loans for improvements to the ballpark, carried out during the previous offseason, only to see it all go up in smoke.

APRIL 17   A day after fire destroys much of the stands, an exhausted group of Cardinal players makes 11 errors and loses to the Cubs 14–1 on a Sunday afternoon at New Sportsman's Park. Ten of the Chicago runs scored in the fourth inning.

Despite the fact that most of the ballpark was destroyed the previous day, Chris Von der Ahe was not about to lose a lucrative Sunday date. With the help of electric lights, he assembled a group of carpenters to clear the debris and assemble 1,700 temporary seats overnight. He ordered his players to be part of the construction crew. A crowd of 7,500 attended the game, lured by excellent spring weather and a curiosity to see the ruins. Most of the fans were placed behind ropes strung across the outfield. Kid Carsey, who pitched two innings before the April 16 fire, then spent several evening hours unloading lumber for the rebuilding project. He started the April 17 contest and allowed only one run in the first three innings before Cubs batters used their lumber to unload for 10 runs off of his deliveries in the fourth. A homestand of about a dozen games was transferred to other cities while New Sportsman's Park was rebuilt. It was completed by July 4. This configuration lasted only three years, when it was destroyed by another fire (see May 4, 1901).

APRIL 24   The day before the United States declares war on Spain, starting the Spanish-American War, the Cardinals wallop the Pirates 13–1 at New Sportsman's Park.

The win was the only one the Cardinals recorded in the first nine games of the season. The players weren't paid from April 15 through May 19, further diminishing morale, because of Chris Von der Ahe's financial difficulties exacerbated by the fire of April 16. The issuance of paychecks was haphazard all season.

MAY 14   The Cardinals survive a four-base error by shortstop Russ Hall to win 5–4 over the Pirates in Pittsburgh. A grounder by Pittsburgh Patsy Donovan rolled through Hall's legs and into deep center field, allowing Donovan to circle the bases and scoring Frank Killen ahead of him.

MAY 18   Cubs pitcher Walter Thornton ties a major league record by hitting three batters in a row with pitches in the fourth inning of an 11–4 St. Louis win in Chicago. Those plunked by Thornton were Tommy Dowd, Tuck Turner, and Dick Harley.

MAY 21   Helped by 10 walks from Giants pitcher Cy Seymour and six errors by his teammates, the Cardinals win 14–5 at New Sportsman's Park.

MAY 22   Cardinal starting pitcher Bert Daniels lasts only three batters before being removed by manager Tim Hurst at the beginning of a 10–5 loss to the Giants at New Sportsman's Park. Daniels allowed a single and made two errors on routine grounders.

MAY 24   The Cardinals win a 12–10 slugging match against Boston at New Sportsman's Park.

MAY 30   The morning game of a Memorial Day doubleheader against the Senators in Washington is postponed when a railroad bridge washes out, which delays the Cardinals' train from St. Louis. In order to make the afternoon contest, the Baltimore and Ohio train traveled the 152 miles from Cumberland, Maryland, to Washington in three hours and five minutes, which at the time was a speed record. Oddly, manager Tim Hurst wasn't on the train. He disembarked at the station in East St. Louis to eat a frankfurter only to watch the train pull away without him. Hurst took another locomotive to Washington. After finally arriving in the nation's capital, the Cardinals lost to the Senators 5–3.

JUNE 27   The Cardinals make 17 errors in a doubleheader and lose 16–4 and 12–1 to Boston at New Sportsman's Park.

JULY 4   The day after Theodore Roosevelt and the Rough Riders storm San Juan Hill against Spanish forces in Cuba, the Cardinals score eight runs in the fourth inning of a 12–7 win over the Pirates in the second game of a doubleheader in Pittsburgh. The Pirates won the opener 9–1.

AUGUST 4   Trailing 7–3, the Cardinals stun the Dodgers with five runs in the ninth inning to win 8–7 at New Sportsman's Park. The game ended on an RBI single by Tommy Tucker. Brooklyn pitcher Brickyard Kennedy provided comic relief during the rally by throwing the ball over the grandstand after center fielder Mike Griffin made an error. Umpire Bob Emslie ejected Kennedy.

AUGUST 6   Umpire John Hunt is subjected to a hail of bottles and beer glasses during a game against the Giants at Sportsman's Park that ends in a 6–6 tie when called on account of darkness at the end of the tenth inning.

AUGUST 13   When the regular umpires are late in arriving, Cardinals manager Tim Hurst and Phillies catcher Morgan Murphy serve as arbiters during a game in Philadelphia. The Phillies won 5–4 in 11 innings (see August 28, 1898).

AUGUST 24   The Cardinals score seven runs in the second inning and defeat the Senators 14–5 at New Sportsman's Park.

AUGUST 28   Tim Hurst again umpires a game involving a team he manages during the second game of a doubleheader against the Orioles at New Sportsman's Park. Bob Emslie umpired the opener, won by the Orioles 13–2, but he was too ill to continue. An indication of Hurst's esteem as an umpire and his honesty, Baltimore manager Ned Hanlon suggested that Hurst umpire the nightcap. At the time, the Orioles were involved in a heated pennant race with Boston. Hurst obviously showed no favoritism in front of a partisan St. Louis crowd, as the Cardinals lost 6–2.

SEPTEMBER 21   Tommy Dowd collects five hits, including a double, in five at-bats, during a 7–3 win over the Dodgers in Brooklyn.

1899

Season in a Sentence

Under the new ownership of brothers Frank and Stanley Robison, St. Louis baseball takes a dramatic turn for the better.

Finish • Won • Lost • Pct • GB

Fifth   84   67   .556   18.5

Manager

Patsy Tebeau

Stats	Cards	NL	Rank
Batting Avg:	.285	.282	6
On-Base Pct:	.347	.343	4
Slugging Pct:	.378	.366	4
Home Runs:	47		1 (tie)
Stolen Bases:	210		8
ERA:	3.36	3.85	4
Fielding Avg:	.939	.942	8
Runs Scored:	619		8
Runs Allowed:	739		4

Starting Lineup

Lou Criger, c
Patsy Tebeau, 1b
Cupid Childs, 2b
Lave Cross, 3b
Bobby Wallace, ss-3b
Jesse Burkett, lf
Harry Blake, cf
Emmett Heidrick, rf
Jack O'Connor, c-1b
Ossie Schreckengost, 1b-c
Ed McKean, ss
Mike Donlin, cf

Pitchers

Cy Young, sp
Jack Powell, sp
Willie Sudhoff, sp
Nig Cuppy, sp
Cowboy Jones, sp

Attendance

373,909 (second in NL)

Club Leaders

Batting Avg:	Burkett	.396
On-Base Pct:	Burkett	.463
Slugging Pct:	Burkett	.500
Home Runs:	Wallace	12
RBIs:	Wallace	108
Runs:	Burkett	116
Stolen Bases:	Heidrick	55
Wins:	Young	26
Strikeouts:	Young	111
ERA:	Young	2.58
Saves:	Young	1

JANUARY 26   The Mississippi Valley Trust Company forecloses the deed of trust on the Sportsman's Park and Club, the legal name for the Cardinals franchise, for non-payment of loans. The bank then made plans to sell the club at auction to satisfy creditors (see March 14, 1899).

MARCH 14   At an auction held at the Old Courthouse in downtown St. Louis, the Cardinals are sold to G. A. Gruner for $33,000. Gruner represented all of the ball club's creditors except St. Louis attorney Edward C. Becker, who was the only other bidder. Becker stopped at $31,600.

Chris Von der Ahe's wealth, once estimated at $1 million, had vanished by 1899. He owed creditors thousands of dollars. Von der Ahe had been steadily losing money for decades on his business ventures, including the Cardinals, while spending lavishly. The fire of April 16, 1898, had sealed his fate. The cost of rebuilding the ballpark was $60,000, but insurance covered only about half of that. Von der Ahe was also bombarded by lawsuits from many of those injured in the blaze. Gruner quickly sold the Cardinals to Becker for $40,000 on March 17. Becker had been acting for Frank and Stanley Robison, owners of the Cleveland Spiders. At the time, there was no rule against an individual owning stock in more than one club in the league. The Spiders had been one of the best clubs in the National League during the 1890s. They never won a pennant, but were usually in the thick of the pennant chase. The Robison brothers, who had *amassed a fortune by operating streetcars in Cleveland and Fort Wayne, Indiana, failed to turn a profit in baseball, however, because the Spiders were always at or near the bottom of the National League in attendance. Every season from 1892 through 1898, the Cardinals outdrew the Spiders despite putting a vastly inferior product on the field. The Robisons decided on a novel strategy. They would transfer the best of Cleveland's player to St. Louis in an attempt to field a strong club in a better market. Among those they sent from the Spiders to the Cardinals were future Hall of Famers Cy Young, Jesse Burkett, and Bobby Wallace, each of them at or near the peaks of their careers. Altogether, the Cardinals received seven of Cleveland's eight starting position players, the top utility player, and the two best pitchers. The Cardinals, a club with a record of 39–111 in 1898, leaped to 84–67 in 1899 with the infusion of new talent. The Spiders, 81–68 in 1898, became the worst team in the history of baseball in 1899, winning only 20 times while losing a major league record 134. So few fans showed up for Spiders games that the club played 112 of its 154 games on the road. At the close of the 1899 season, the franchise was disbanded (see March 8, 1900).*

Von der Ahe lived out his final days in relative obscurity as a bartender at his saloon. His drinking became worse and worse. In 1908, Von der Ahe filed for bankruptcy, listing his assets at $200. A benefit game was staged between the National League Cardinals and the American League Browns to raise money for him. It raised $5,000 to help the former owner through his final years. He died in 1913.

APRIL 15   In the season opener, the Cardinals win 10–1 over the Spiders before 16,000 in St. Louis. The entire Cardinals starting lineup of Jesse Burkett, Cupid Childs, Ed McKean, Bobby Wallace, Emmett Heidrick, Patsy Tebeau, Jack O'Connor, Harry Blake, and Cy Young played for Cleveland in 1898.

Among the modifications the Robison brothers made in 1899 was to change the name of the ballpark at Vandeventer and Natural Bridge from Sportsman's Park to League Park. They also changed the club's uniforms colors from brown to red. Thus, the nickname Browns passed out of use temporarily (the new American League team in the city revived it in 1902). Most St. Louis sportswriters in 1899 used the nickname "Perfectos" to describe the club. A year later, the red-trimmed uniforms inspired the name "Cardinals" (see April 28, 1900).

APRIL 25   The Cardinals run their season record to 7–0 with an 11-inning, 3–2 win over the Cubs at League Park.

The 1899 Cardinals were in first place on May 19 with a record of 19–6 before dropping in the standings. The manager of the club was 34-year-old Patsy Tebeau, who had been manager of the Spiders since July 1891. A native of a gang-infested section of St. Louis known as Goose Hill, Tebeau was known as a tough, aggressive leader who would fight for every advantage and insisted on like-minded players on his clubs. Although none of his clubs won a pennant, they usually led the league in fights. Tebeau's outfits baited umpires, spiked opponents, beaned batters, and circumvented rules with regularity. The contemporary press often referred to his Spiders and Cardinals as "hooligans." Tebeau managed the Cardinals until August 1900 and never returned to baseball. While operating a saloon in St. Louis in 1918, Tebeau committed suicide, shooting himself with a revolver that he had tied to his right wrist.

APRIL 30   A crowd of 27,489 jams into West Side Grounds in Chicago for a game between the Cardinals and the Cubs. The crowd surrounding the field was so large it was ruled that any ball hit into the overflow would be a single. Many routine fly balls and drives that normally would have gone for extra bases fell into the crowd for singles. Each team had 12 singles in the game. Cubs pitcher Nixey Callahan did a better job of scattering the hits and won 4–0.

MAY 7   Harry Blake's three-run double in the ninth inning beats the Reds 4–3 in Cincinnati.

MAY 10   The Cardinals wallop the Spiders 12–2 in Cleveland.

MAY 12   Ed McKean's home run in the tenth inning defeats the Spiders 5–4 in Cleveland.

MAY 19   The Cardinals win a game over the Giants in New York by forfeit. At the end of the fifth inning, the Giants led 10–3. St. Louis scored six times in the top of the sixth, with the help of some questionable calls by umpire Oyster Burns. New York second baseman Kid Gleason was apoplectic and was ejected after berating Burns. Gleason refused to leave the field even being ordered to do so by Giants manager John Day. Burns had had enough of the shenanigans and declared a forfeit.

JUNE 8   Umpire Oyster Burns is at the center of another controversy during a Cardinals-Phillies game in Philadelphia. The Cardinals scored three times in the top of the sixth inning to take a 4–3 lead as it began to rain steadily. Phillies manager Bill Shettsline wanted Burns to call the game, but Burns refused, and the Cardinals skipper ridiculed Shettsline by calling him a "quitter." The Phillies responded with five tallies in their half to take an 8–4 advantage, and Burns called the contest because of the driving rain. Tebeau objected strenuously and followed Burns under the grandstand looking for a fight. Burns called for a policeman, who threatened to put Tebeau out into the street in full uniform in the midst of exiting Philadelphia fans. Tebeau promised to be "good" and was allowed to sit on the bench while Burns left the ballpark safely.

JUNE 16   Four days after Butch Cassidy and the Sundance Kid rob a train in Wyoming of $60,000, the Cardinals lose a heart-rending 13–12 decision to the Colonels in Louisville. The Cards led 12–6 before Louisville scored six runs in the ninth inning and one in the tenth for the win. Cy Young gave up all 13 Louisville runs.

             Although he failed to hold the big lead on this day, Young was one of the greatest pitchers of all time. The annual awards for best pitcher in each league are named after him. In 1899, the first of his two seasons with the Cardinals, Young was 26–16 with a 2.58 ERA. He is the all-time major league leader among pitchers in victories (511), games started (815), complete games (749), and innings pitched (7,355⅓).

JULY 9   The Cardinals play two teams in one day, winning both by 11–4 scores at League Park. In the opener, the Cardinals beat Louisville. In the nightcap, St. Louis downed Cleveland in a contest called after 7½ innings on account of darkness. Lave Cross struck a grand slam in the second tilt off Crazy Schmit.

JULY 16   With Sunday games in New York illegal, the Cardinals and the Giants travel across the Hudson River for a game in West New York, New Jersey. St. Louis won 10–2.

AUGUST 1   The Cardinals win a thrilling game 8–7 in 14 innings over the Boston Braves at League Park. The Cards scored one run in the ninth to tie the game 3–3. After the Braves scored in the top of the tenth, St. Louis rallied again for a tie. Boston plated three more runs in the top of the twelfth, and again the Cards knotted the contest with a furious rally. Jack Powell, who pitched all 14 innings for the Cardinals, led off the fourteenth with a walk-off, inside-the-park home run off future Hall of Famer Kid Nichols. The game was scheduled to be the first of a twin bill, but after the 14-inning encounter lasted four hours, it was too dark to start the second contest.

> *The homer was the first of Powell's career. He struck eight homers in 1,613 big-league at-bats over 16 years. During the 1899 season, he had a record of 23–19 and an ERA of 3.52.*

AUGUST 10   Patsy Tebeau is arrested following a 7–4 loss to the Orioles in Baltimore. Tebeau was charged with disorderly conduct and taken to the Central Police Station. During the game, Tebeau attempted to block the path of Baltimore's John McGraw from first base to second. When McGraw objected, Tebeau punched him viciously. Candy LaChance of the Orioles stepped between the combatants, and Tebeau and LaChance agreed to meet after the game. Tebeau backed down from fighting LaChance, however, and the Cardinals manager was called "yellow" by a bevy of Baltimore fans. Tebeau let loose with some "vile" language, leading to his arrest. He waived a hearing by paying a $25 fine.

AUGUST 23   Down 7–3, the Cardinals score two runs in the eighth inning and three in the ninth to win 8–7 over the Cubs in the first game of a doubleheader at League Park. Chicago won the second tilt 12–7, called after eight innings by darkness.

AUGUST 27   After winning the first game of a doubleheader 16–2 against the Senators at League Park, the Cardinals drop the second contest 15–9. Jesse Burkett collected seven hits, including two triples, in ten at-bats during the twin bill.

AUGUST 28   Jesse Burkett hits two inside-the-park homers during a 12–11 win over Washington at League Park.

> *Burkett played for the Cardinals from 1899 through 1901. A future Hall of Famer, he hit .348 in 424 games with the club. In 1899, he batted .396 with 116 runs and 221 hits. Standing only five foot eight and weighing 155 pounds, he played in the majors from 1890 through 1905 and compiled a .338 lifetime average while collecting 2,850 hits. Playing for 10 seasons under hard-nosed manager Patsy Tebeau in Cleveland and St. Louis, Burkett earned the nickname "The Crab" because of his disagreeable disposition. His bat control also led to a change in the rules. With two strikes, Burkett would foul off pitch after pitch until he received one to his liking. Beginning in 1902, a foul bunt with two strikes resulted in a strikeout. Third baseman Bobby Wallace was another future Hall of Famer on the 1899 Cardinals. He hit .295 with 12 homers and 108 RBIs. Like Burkett, he was with the Cardinals from 1899 through 1901, coming to the club from the Spiders and leaving the club when the American League Browns were formed (see December 3, 1901).*

SEPTEMBER 7   Arlie Latham tries his hand as an umpire and is assaulted by Cardinals players and fans during a 4–2 loss to the Reds at League Park.

The trouble started when Latham called Jesse Burkett out in the ninth inning on a fly ball that short-hopped into the glove of Cincinnati right fielder Algie McBride. Patsy Tebeau rushed toward Latham and gave the umpire a shove. Latham was soon surrounded by an angry mob of St. Louis players. Mike Donlin and Cy Young also pushed him. Spectators rushed onto the field to get their shots at Latham. With the help of police officers, he reached the clubhouse. About 500 fans followed Latham and the officers and threatened to tear down the clubhouse. It took nearly an hour to disperse the mob.

SEPTEMBER 9   St. Louis players again attack Arlie Latham during a game against the Reds at League Park. In the sixth inning, Latham called Jesse Burkett out on a stolen base attempt. Burkett shoved Latham around before the Cardinal outfielder was escorted from the field by two police officers. The game was called after eight innings by darkness with the Cardinals ahead 11–6.

During his long playing career, Latham was one of the greatest umpire baiters in the game. After the incidents of September 7 and 9, he decided that umpiring wasn't a profession he wished to pursue.

SEPTEMBER 14   The Cardinals win a doubleheader 11–1 and 7–4 over the Braves in Boston. The second contest was called after six innings by darkness.

SEPTEMBER 19   The Cardinals score seven runs in the sixth inning of a 13–2 win over the Giants in New York. The game was called after eight innings on account of darkness.

SEPTEMBER 24   An unusual doubleheader takes place at League Park in St. Louis. The Cardinals lose the opener 7–6 to Louisville. The Colonels played Cleveland in the second tilt with the Spiders as the "home" team. Louisville won again 5–1 before darkness stopped play in the seventh inning.

SEPTEMBER 26   The Cardinals score in each of their eight turns at bat and defeat the Spiders 15–3 at League Park.

OCTOBER 8   Trailing the Reds 7–5 in the first game of a doubleheader at League Park, the Cardinals score two runs in the ninth inning and one in the tenth to win 8–7. In the ninth, Emmett Heidrick tripled in one run, then scored on Jesse Burkett's single. Tim Flood's walk-off single drove in the winning run. The second contest ended in a 1–1 tie when it was called after six innings by darkness.

THE STATE OF THE CARDINALS

The first decade of the 20th century was the Cardinals' worst in history. The club had a record of 580–888. Its .395 winning percentage was the worst in the National League and the second worst in the majors, trailing only the Washington Senators. Three Cardinal teams finished in last place. National League pennant winners were the Dodgers (1900), Pirates (1901, 1902, 1903, and 1909), Giants (1904 and 1905), and Cubs (1906, 1907, and 1908).

THE BEST TEAM

The only Cardinal club with a winning record was the 1901 outfit, which finished in fourth place with a record of 76–64.

THE WORST TEAM

The 1903 club posted the worst winning percentage (.314) of the decade with a record of 43–94. The 1908 Cards lost the most games, finishing with a mark of 49–105.

THE BEST MOMENT

During a decade-high nine-game winning streak, Ed Karger pitched a seven-inning perfect game in the second game of a doubleheader on August 8, 1907. The game was limited to seven innings by prior agreement.

THE WORST MOMENT

Club owner Frank Robison made public a $10,000 bet he placed in 1902 that the Pittsburgh Pirates would not repeat as NL champions. The Pirates won the pennant by 27½ games.

THE ALL-DECADE TEAM • YEARS W/CARDS

Mike Grady, c	1897, 1904–06
Ed Konetchy, 1b	1907–13
John Farrell, 2b	1902–05
Bobby Byrne, 3b	1907–09
Bobby Wallace, ss	1899–1901, 1917–18
Jesse Burkett, lf	1899–1901
Homer Smoot, cf	1902–06
Patsy Donovan, rf	1900–03
Jack Taylor, p	1904–06
Mike O'Neill, p	1901–04
Ed Karger, p	1906–08
Jack Powell, p	1899–1901

Few of those who played for the Cardinals during the decade had a lasting impact on the franchise. The only individual on the 1900s All-Decade Team to play for the Cardinals for more than five seasons was Ed Konetchy, and four of his seven seasons with the club came between 1910 and 1920. Burkett and Wallace are in the Hall of Fame, but both signed with the cross-town Browns after the 1901 season.

THE DECADE LEADERS

Batting Avg:	Donovan	.314
On-Base Pct:	Donovan	.360
Slugging Pct:	Smoot	.385
Home Runs:	Burkett	17
RBIs:	Smoot	252
Runs:	Donovan	303
Stolen Bases:	Donovan	132
Wins:	Taylor	43
Strikeouts:	Beebe	434
ERA:	Karger	2.46
Saves:	Powell	3
	Melter	3

THE HOME FIELD

The Cardinals played at a ballpark constructed at the corner of Vandeventer and Natural Bridge Road from 1893 through 1920. Better known today as Robison Field, it didn't acquire that name until 1912. Throughout the decade, the facility was known as League Park. The grandstand there in 1900 was built in 1898 after a fire destroyed most of the previous structure. Another major fire swept through the wooden stands on May 4, 1901, in the tenth inning of a game against the Reds destroying all but the bleachers in center field. It was rebuilt and ready by the start of a homestand on June 3. The playing field at League Park was enormous. It was 470 feet down the left-field line, 520 to the deepest part of left-center, 500 to straightaway center, 330 to right-center, and 290 feet to right. The peculiar angle of the field, with a gargantuan left field and a short right field, was necessary because of the lot's restrictive rectangular shape. Lexington Avenue was just beyond the right-field fence, which was fronted by a few rows of bleacher seats. In addition, there was a vast expanse of foul territory. The distance from home plate to the backstop was 120 feet, which also meant that fans in the best seats were a good distance from the action on the field. Fences were brought in before the 1909 season, and that lopped 90 feet off the distance to left and 120 feet to the fence in left-center.

THE GAME YOU WISH YOU HAD SEEN

In a season in which the Cardinals hit only eight home runs, Homer Smoot hit a three-run, inside-the-park, walk-off homer to beat the Reds on July 22, 1903. It was his second three-run, inside-the-park, walk-off homer of 1903, both against the Reds.

THE WAY THE GAME WAS PLAYED

In this decade of pitching and defense, the NL set all-time lows in ERA and batting average. The hit and run, base stealing, and sacrifice plays dominated strategy. In part, this was the result of a 1901 rule change that for the first time counted fouls balls as strikes. The merits of the foul-strike rule were hotly debated for years afterward. Offense started a gradual decline that was not reversed until the introduction of the cork-center ball in 1910.

THE MANAGEMENT

The club was owned by brothers Frank Robison and M. Stanley Robison, who bought the club in 1899. At the start of the decade, Frank was the club president, but after a succession of losing clubs, he began to lose interest and in 1906 turned the presidency over to his brother. Frank died in September 1908. Stanley also managed the club from the dugout for 50 games in 1905. Other field managers were Patsy Tebeau (1899–1900), Louis Heilbroner (1900), Patsy Donovan (1901–03), Kid Nichols (1904–05), John McCloskey (1906–08), and Roger Bresnahan (1909–12).

THE BEST PLAYER MOVE

Most of the great players who played for the Cardinals during this stretch were either at the tail end of their careers, were traded, or left the club to sign with the newly formed American League. The best move was the purchase of Ed Konetchy from LaCrosse, in the Wisconsin State League, in 1907. Konetchy was the Cards' starting first baseman through 1913.

THE WORST PLAYER MOVE

In one of the worst trades in club history, the Cardinals sent future Hall of Fame pitcher Three Finger Brown to the Cubs in December 1903 along with Jack O'Neill for Jack Taylor and Larry McLean. The Cardinals also let an All-Star team get away to the American League in 1901 and 1902, including future Hall of Famers Cy Young, Jesse Burkett, Bobby Wallace, John McGraw, and Wilbert Robinson.

1900s

1900

Season in a Sentence

The Cardinals finish in a tie for fifth place despite the presence of five future Hall of Famers in the lineup.

Finish • Won • Lost • Pct • GB

Fifth (tie)   65   75   .464   19.0

Managers

Patsy Tebeau (42–50) and Louis Heilbroner (23–25)

Stats

Stats	Cards	NL	Rank
Batting Avg:	.291	.279	2
On-Base Pct:	.356	.339	3
Slugging Pct:	.375	.366	3
Home Runs:	36		2
Stolen Bases:	243		2
ERA:	3.75	3.69	4
Fielding Avg:	.943	.942	6
Runs Scored:	744		4
Runs Allowed:	748		5

Starting Lineup

Lou Criger, c
Dan McGann, 1b
Bill Keister, 2b
John McGraw, 3b
Bobby Wallace, ss
Jesse Burkett, lf
Emmett Heidrick, cf
Patsy Donovan, rf
Mike Donlin, of-1b
Wilbert Robinson, c
Pat Dillard, cf-3b

Pitchers

Cy Young, sp
Jack Powell, sp
Cowboy Jones, sp
Willie Sudhoff, sp
Jim Hughey, sp-rp

Attendance

255,000 (second in NL)

Club Leaders

Batting Avg:	Burkett	.363
On-Base Pct:	Burkett	.429
Slugging Pct:	Burkett	.474
Home Runs:	Donlin	10
RBIs:	Keister	72
Runs:	Burkett	88
Stolen Bases:	Donovan	45
Wins:	Young	19
Strikeouts:	Young	115
ERA:	Young	3.00
Saves:	None	

MARCH 8   The National League votes to reduce its membership from 12 teams to 8, dropping Baltimore, Cleveland, Louisville, and Washington. The NL roster of Boston, Brooklyn, Chicago, Cincinnati, New York, Philadelphia, Pittsburgh, and St. Louis remained unchanged from 1900 until the Boston Braves moved to Milwaukee in March 1953.

The Cardinals went shopping during the 1899–1900 offseason, acquiring several stars from the four defunct clubs. John McGraw and Wilbert Robinson, both future Hall of Famers, came from Baltimore, although neither signed until after the season started (see May 8, 1900). Dan McGann and Gus Weyhing were purchased from Washington. The Robison brothers already owned the Cleveland club and inherited its players, among them Otto Krueger, Jim Hughey, Joe Quinn, and Jack Harper. With the new additions and future Cooperstown enshrinees Cy Young, Jesse Burkett, and Bobby Wallace, it appeared as though the Cardinals would field one of the strongest teams in the National League. The club was a huge disappointment, however, finishing with a record of 65–75.

APRIL 19   The 1900 season opens with a 3–0 win over the Pirates before 15,000 at League Park. Cy Young pitched the shutout. All three Cardinal runs scored in the fourth inning off Rube Waddell. After a parade through the streets of St. Louis between downtown and the ballpark, manager Patsy Tebeau was presented with a diamond pin and ring in pregame ceremonies.

Young had a record of 19–19 with an ERA of 3.00 in 1900.

APRIL 22   The Cardinals win a thrilling 6–5 win over the Pirates before 20,000 at League Park, the largest ever in St. Louis at the time. The crowd overflowed from the stands and ringed the outfield. The Pirates scored three in the ninth to tie the contest 5–5. The Cardinals stopped the rally when Pittsburgh's Ginger Beaumont hit a drive to deep center with two on. Cardinal outfielder Emmett Heidrick waded into the crowd and caught the ball. The Cards won the game in the bottom of the inning on a walk-off single by Dan McGann.

McGann played two seasons with the Cardinals as the club's starting first baseman before jumping to the Baltimore Orioles after the 1901 season. He died in 1910 when he was shot in the heart with a revolver while staying at the Besler Hotel in Louisville. The coroner ruled the cause of death to be suicide, but his two surviving sisters believed he was murdered. Violence ran in the McGann family. Before Dan's death, a brother and sister committed suicide, and another brother died in an accidental shooting.

APRIL 28   The Cardinals defeat the Cubs 3–1 in 10 innings in Chicago. The game was a scoreless battle through nine between Cy Young and Ned Garvin. Jesse Burkett hit a two-run double in the tenth to put the Cards ahead 2–0 and scored on Patsy Donovan's single.

The 1900 season was the first in which the nickname Cardinals was used in conjunction with the St. Louis baseball club. It had nothing to do with the bird. The nickname was prompted by the change in the color of the trim and stockings on the club's uniforms from brown to vivid red. According to legend, Willie McHale, a reporter for the St. Louis Republic, *overheard a female fan remark, "What a lovely shade of cardinal" after getting a look at the new jerseys. Most newspapermen began calling the club the Cardinals, and it quickly gained acceptance from the fans. A few reporters held out, however, and continued to call the club the "Perfectos" for a few years before succumbing to the popular will of the people.*

MAY 8   John McGraw and Wilbert Robinson sign contracts with the Cardinals.

McGraw and Robinson were purchased from the defunct Baltimore Orioles on February 11, but the two refused to sign with the Cardinals. Both agreed only after the club struck the reserve clause from their contracts, making them free agents at the end of the season, an unheard-of concession. When McGraw and Robinson arrived in St. Louis, the Robison brothers arranged to have them met at the train station by a brass band. McGraw was one of the top third basemen in baseball at the time, and Robinson ranked among the elite catchers, but the Cardinals should have passed on both. McGraw hit .344 but was limited to 99 games because he missed two lengthy stretches. He was spiked during a play in June and was out with boils in August. To make room for McGraw, the Cards sold Lave Cross to the Dodgers. Cross was 34 but still had five solid seasons ahead of him. When McGraw and Robinson caught a train out of St. Louis at season's end, the two ceremoniously tossed their Cardinals uniforms out the window and into the Mississippi River while crossing the Eads Bridge. They both signed with the new Baltimore franchise in the American League in 1901 (see January 28, 1901).

MAY 9   The game between the Cardinals and Reds at League Park is postponed because of a streetcar strike in St. Louis that all but paralyzed transportation in the city. The previous day, the first day of the strike, the Cardinals drew only 200 fans for a 9–7 win over Cincinnati.

The Cardinals hoped for a quick resolution to the strike, but it wasn't settled until early July and cut into the club's attendance figures.

MAY 12   John McGraw plays in his first game with the Cardinals, and makes an error that contributes to three Dodger runs in the ninth and a 5–4 loss at League Park.

The arrival of McGraw and Wilbert Robinson brought a clamor for tickets, but the streetcar strike made it difficult to reach the ballpark. Between 6,000 and 7,000 attended the game. According to newspaper reports, "The crush of wagons around the park made a sight long to be remembered." There was gridlock for blocks in every direction. It was estimated that 1,500 wagons and 2,000 horses were crowded around the park and the confusion was "beyond description." Amid the traffic crush were a few of the first automobiles to ever traverse the streets of St. Louis. Before the game, McGraw and Robinson were presented with a gold cane, silk umbrella, and several floral horseshoes.

MAY 22   The Cardinals sell Jack O'Connor to the Pirates.

JUNE 2   Mike Donlin collects five hits, including a homer and a triple, in five at-bats, but the Cardinals waste a seven-run lead and lose 17–16 in 10 innings to the Braves in Boston. The Cards had a 9–2 advantage in the fourth inning, then fell behind 12–11 before regaining the lead 16–12 with five runs in the eighth. The Braves plated four runs in the ninth and one in the tenth to win, however.

JUNE 5   The Cardinals again blow a big lead and fall to the Braves in a slugfest in Boston. The Cards were ahead 9–3 in the third inning but lost 15–11.

JUNE 13   The Cardinals sell Joe Quinn to the Reds.

Mike Donlin posted a .333 batting average in 1,050 major-league games, but he ended up making more money in his touring vaudeville act.

JUNE 18   Pat Dillard sets a modern major league record for most putouts by a third baseman with nine in a 9–8 loss to the Reds at League Park.

Dillard played only 21 career games at third base.

JUNE 24   Cardinal outfielder Mike Donlin is stabbed during an altercation outside of a St. Louis saloon at 4 AM. Donlin and Gus Weyhing were carousing on Washington Avenue near Eleventh Street. Donlin began teasing a man about his large red beard when his companion took offense and tore at Donlin with a knife. Donlin was stabbed several times in the cheek and in the neck, just missing the jugular vein. He grabbed at the knife and his fingers were cut badly. The assailant took off and was never apprehended. At the hospital, Donlin hoped to avoid publicity by giving his occupation as "machinist," but he was recognized and the story hit the papers. Donlin missed nearly two months recuperating from his injuries.

> *Nicknamed "Turkey Mike" for his strutting walk, Donlin played for the Cardinals in 1899 and 1900. He was one of the most fascinating personalities in big-league history and might have been one of the greatest stars in the game if he had taken the sport more seriously. He had a .333 lifetime batting average in 1,050 games between 1899 and 1914. In March 1902, while playing for the Orioles, Donlin was sentenced to a six-month jail term for assaulting an actress and her escort. Later, while with the Giants, Donlin missed the entire 1907 season in a salary dispute, then came back in 1908 to hit .334, a season in which he married actress Mabel Hite. Donlin and Hite put together a successful stage act, and he sat out the 1909 and 1910 seasons touring the country on the vaudeville circuit, making much more money than he ever did in baseball. Donlin returned to the diamond in 1911 following his wife's untimely death. After his baseball days ended, Donlin made movies in Hollywood, playing supporting roles until his death in 1933.*

JUNE 25   Jack Powell pitches a two-hitter to defeat the Reds 2–0 at League Park. The only Cincinnati hits were a triple by Jake Beckley and a single by Jimmy Barrett.

JUNE 30   Because of an illness to umpire Ed Swartwood, Gus Weyhing of the Cardinals and Pop Foster of the Giants serve as umpires in a 6–1 St. Louis win at League Park. The contest was called after eight innings by darkness.

JULY 8   Jesse Burkett hits two inside-the-park homers during a 17–3 pounding of the Pirates at League Park.

> *Burkett hit .363 with 203 hits in 1900.*

JULY 12   The Cardinals score two runs in the ninth inning to beat the Braves 2–1 at League Park. Jack Powell pitched a two-hitter. The only two Boston hits were singles by Billy Sullivan.

JULY 25   In Boston, the Braves score 13 runs in the first inning off Jim Hughey and Gus Weyhing with the help of six Cardinal errors. The Braves won 19–5 in a contest mercifully called at the end of six innings by rain.

JULY 26   Gus Weyhing is released by the Cardinals.

> *Weyhing didn't receive the 10 days' pay he was entitled to following his release. He got a deputy sheriff to seize a share of the Cardinals' proceeds from the gate for a game a few days later at Brooklyn, but it amounted to less than the $100 he was claiming.*

AUGUST 14   Cards first baseman Dan McGann and Harry Wolverton of the Phillies fight during a 6–2 win at League Park. After grounding out, Wolverton spiked McGann as he crossed the bag. McGann turned around and threw the ball he had just caught, nailing Wolverton in the back of the head. Wolverton staggered for a few steps, then rushed at McGann. The two squared off and landed several blows, and it took a pair of policemen to separate them.

Three weeks later, Wolverton nearly died of a head injury. While on a Philadelphia streetcar, his straw hat blew off his head. Wolverton reached out to grab the hat, and his head smacked against a lamppost, fracturing his skull.

AUGUST 19   Patsy Tebeau resigns as manager of the Cardinals.

Tebeau was frustrated that his lineup of All-Stars failed to produce a winning record. The Cardinals were 42–50. When John McGraw refused the job as manager, the Robison brothers appointed four-foot nine-inch business manager Louis Heilbroner to run the team for the remainder of the season. The diminutive Heilbroner admitted that he didn't know much about baseball, and many of the players refused to take orders from him. Although Heilbroner held the title, McGraw actually ran the club during games. Discipline was a severe problem with the underperforming Cardinals all year in 1900. "There is no use trying to duck it," one unidentified player said. "Booze is the cause of our being where we are." At the end of the season, Heilbroner returned to the front office, and outfielder Patsy Donovan became player-manager. Previously, Donovan had managed the Pirates, in 1897 and again in 1899.

Donovan led the National League in stolen bases with 45 in 1900. He was born in County Cork, Ireland, in 1865 and immigrated with his family to Lawrence, Massachusetts, when he was three.

AUGUST 25   Emmett Heidrick steals four bases during a 2–0 win over the Cubs at League Park.

SEPTEMBER 12   The Braves beat the Cardinals 18–3 in Boston in a game called after six innings because of high winds. Jack Powell gave up all 18 runs.

SEPTEMBER 17   In five plate appearances, John McGraw draws four walks and is hit by a pitch, but the Cardinals lose 7–5 to the Dodgers in Brooklyn.

SEPTEMBER 19   With the Dodgers leading 2–0 in the third inning in Brooklyn, Cardinal catcher Wilbert Robinson objects to the call of umpire John Gaffney, who called a Dodger runner safe at home. Robinson jumped up and threw the ball at the ump, then punched him in the chest. Gaffney swung his mask at Robinson, grazing his nose, and threw the Cardinal catcher out of the game. John McGraw refused to put in another catcher, claiming one was injured and the other was suspended. Gaffney responded by forfeiting the game to the Dodgers. Brooklyn president Charles Ebbets issued refunds to any fans who requested one.

SEPTEMBER 24   Cy Young outduels Rube Waddell to beat the Pirates 1–0 at League Park. Dan McGann drove in the lone run of the game with a single.

SEPTEMBER 29   The Cardinals allow seven runs to the Cubs in the first inning but rally to win 10–7 in the first game of a doubleheader at League Park. The second game ended after seven innings due to darkness with the score 0–0.

October 5	Mike Donlin hits two inside-the-park homers during a 6–1 win over the Reds in Cincinnati. Otto Krueger and Donlin hit back-to-back homers in the second inning, and Donlin added another one in the sixth.
October 7	Umpire Bob Emslie causes a riot by calling a game against the Pirates at League Park after the seventh inning on account of darkness with the Cardinals trailing 3–2. Most observers believed there was enough daylight to complete at least two more innings. The crowd rushed onto the field and began hollering and jeering the umpire. Several threw rocks and sticks. Police came to Emslie's rescue and protected him from the howling mob, which followed at his heels until he reached the hotel.
October 14	Catcher Harry Stanton, a St. Louis native, completes one of the shortest careers in major league history during a 7–0 win over the Reds at League Park. In the final game of the season, Stanton played one inning in his big-league debut and never appeared in the majors again. He is so obscure that baseball researchers have been unable to determine his date of birth or death.

1901

Season in a Sentence

Despite the loss of Cy Young, John McGraw, and Wilbert Robinson to the American League, the Cardinals win 11 more games than in 1900 against competition also weakened by defections to the new league.

Finish • Won • Lost • Pct • GB

Fourth   76   64   .543   14.5

Manager

Patsy Donovan

Stats

Stats	Cards	NL	Rank
Batting Avg:	.284	.267	3
On-Base Pct:	.337	.321	2
Slugging Pct:	.381	.348	2
Home Runs:	39		1
Stolen Bases:	190		4
ERA:	3.68	3.32	6
Fielding Avg:	.949	.947	5
Runs Scored:	792		1
Runs Allowed:	689		5

Starting Lineup

Jack Ryan, c
Dan McGann, 1b
Dick Padden, 2b
Otto Krueger, 3b
Bobby Wallace, ss
Jesse Burkett, lf
Emmett Heidrick, cf
Patsy Donovan, rf
Art Nichols, c-cf
Pop Schriver, c-1b

Pitchers

Jack Harper, sp
Jack Powell, sp
Willie Sudhoff, sp
Ed Murphy, sp
Cowboy Jones, sp

Attendance

379,988 (first in NL)

Club Leaders

Batting Avg:	Burkett	.376
On-Base Pct:	Burkett	.440
Slugging Pct:	Burkett	.509
Home Runs:	Burkett	10
RBIs:	Wallace	91
Runs:	Burkett	142
Stolen Bases:	Heidrick	32
Wins:	Harper	23
Strikeouts:	Powell	133
ERA:	Sudhoff	3.52
Saves:	Powell	3

JANUARY 28   The American League formally organizes as a second major league with clubs in Baltimore, Boston, Chicago, Cleveland, Detroit, Milwaukee, Philadelphia, and Washington, DC. The AL also announced plans to raid National League rosters by offering more lucrative contracts.

The Cardinals were hit hard by defections to the American League before the 1901 season began. Cy Young signed with the Boston Red Sox, along with catcher Lou Criger. Young was 34 years old but posted a 33–10 record for the Red Sox in 1901 and 32–11 in 1902. He would win 225 more games after leaving the Cardinals before his big-league career ended in 1911. John McGraw, Wilbert Robinson, Bill Keister, and Mike Donlin went to Baltimore. In addition to Young, the Cardinals lost their best two catchers (Robinson and Criger) and their starting second baseman (Keister) and third baseman (McGraw). Although a reserve outfielder with the Cardinals, Donlin developed into one of the best hitters of the dead ball era. Fortunately, many other clubs in the National League were raided as well, and the Cardinals improved from a 65–75 record in 1900 to 76–64 in 1901. The Cards lost more players during the 1901–02 offseason, however, after the American League placed a club in St. Louis (see December 3, 1901).

APRIL 18   The season opener against the Cubs at League Park is postponed by rain.

APRIL 19   The Cardinals lose 8–7 to the Cubs on Opening Day at League Park. The Cards led 4–0 in the fourth inning before the Cubs mounted a comeback. Emmett Heidrick collected four hits, including two triples and a double, and Jesse Burkett had three singles. St. Louis pitcher Jack Powell took the loss but hit a home run. It was the only home run hit by a Cardinal on Opening Day between 1892 and 1912. The next Cardinal pitcher to homer on Opening Day was Joe Magrane in 1988.

Burkett led the NL in batting average (.376), on-base percentage (.440), hits (226), total bases (306), and runs (142) in 1901. Heidrick batted .339 in 1901.

APRIL 20   The Cardinals outlast the Cubs 11–9 at League Park.

APRIL 21   The Cardinals wallop the Cubs again, 12–5, at League Park.

APRIL 23   The Cardinals reach double digits in runs for the third game in a row, defeating the Pirates 10–4 at League Park.

APRIL 29   Trailing 14–4, the Cardinals turn a blowout into an interesting affair by scoring eight runs in the ninth inning, but they lose 14–12 to the Pirates in Pittsburgh.

MAY 4   In the bottom of the tenth inning with the score 4–4 against the Reds, fire breaks out at League Park. Most of the ballpark, built in 1898 in the wake of an earlier fire (see April 16, 1898), was destroyed.

The fire was caused by a cigar or cigarette dropped into a pile of refuse beneath the stands at the foot of one of the main stairways. There was little alarm at first among the 6,000 in attendance as smoke curled up through the seats, and fans leisurely left the structure. The game was interrupted more from the curiosity of the players and the umpire than any sense of imminent danger. But the flames, fanned by a stiff breeze, spread rapidly, leading to a general panic. Many leapt to the ground from the top of the grandstand, a distance of eight to ten feet, to escape the flames. When firemen reached the park, the grandstand, pavilion, and club's offices were a mass of flames. Most of the park couldn't be saved from the advance of the fire. The north fence and part of the east and west fences were also destroyed. Some of the fencing of the racetrack across Natural Bridge Road was also burned. In addition, a few streetcars sitting outside the ballpark awaiting passengers for their return home caught fire. Umpire Frank Dwyer lost his civilian clothes and a wad of cash that he left in the dressing room. He had to borrow money for car fare to return to his hotel room in his umpiring uniform. Only the bleachers in deep center field were saved. Fortunately, there were no reports of serious injuries.

MAY 5   The Reds defeat the Cardinals 7–5 before a crowd of 7,000 at Sportsman's Park.

League Park was destroyed by fire on a Saturday afternoon, and with a big crowd expected on Sunday, May 5, the Cards' management didn't want to postpone the game. It was played at Sportsman's Park, three blocks away from Robison Field. Sportsman's Park was used by the Cardinals from 1882 through 1892 and had since been converted into a facility for cycle races and other events. A diamond was hastily laid out inside the oval of the race track, but the opening was much too small for an adequate baseball field, and according to one newspaper report, the outfield "resembled a plowed field." Furthermore, much of the crowd of 7,000 was placed behind ropes in the outfield. This turned the contest into a complete farce. According to the ground rules, balls hit into the crowd were doubles. The crowd was located just a dozen feet behind the outfielders, and routine fly balls landed in the crowd as two-base hits. There were 22 base hits in the contest, 13 of them doubles and two of them homers hit over the crowd. Fortunately, the Cardinals began a six-city road trip the following day, which gave the club ample time to build a new facility after the ashes of League Park were cleared. The Cardinals moved into a rebuilt League Park on June 3. By order of the St. Louis building commissioner, the new wooden ballpark had to provide a water source for 11 reels of hose to help prevent another fire and be painted with two coats of a "fire-resisting mixture." There were three separate structures, consisting of a grandstand, pavilion, and bleachers. The three structures were placed with gaps of between 55 and 90 feet to help retard the spread of fire. This new League Park (renamed Robison Field in 1912) served the Cardinals until 1920, when the club moved to Sportsman's Park.

MAY 6   The Cardinals wallop the Reds 13–8 in Cincinnati.

MAY 8   Emmett Heidrick collects five hits in five at-bats during a 14–3 win over the Reds in Cincinnati.

MAY 22   Jesse Burkett leads off the first inning with a home run in the second game of a doubleheader against the Dodgers in Brooklyn, but the Cardinals lose 5–4. In an unusual play in the third inning, the Cards scored on a triple play. The play started with the bases loaded, and Cupid Childs scored from third base before Dick Padden, caught in a rundown, was tagged for the third out. The Dodgers won the first game by the same 5–4 score.

MAY 23   Jesse Burkett leads off the first inning with a homer for the second game in a row, and the Cardinals get seven runs in the ninth inning to defeat the Phillies 10–6 in Philadelphia.

MAY 28   Jack Powell pitches the Cardinals to a 1–0 win over Christy Mathewson and the Giants in New York.

Powell led the Cardinals in games started (37), games as a relief pitcher (eight), saves (three), strikeouts (133), and innings pitched (338$\frac{1}{3}$) in 1901. He had a record of 19–21 with an ERA of 3.54.

JUNE 17   The Cardinals trounce the Reds 12–1 in Cincinnati.

JUNE 22   The Cardinals overwhelm the Giants 13–3 in New York.

JUNE 25   A six-run rally in the ninth inning beats the Giants 12–8 in New York.

JULY 8   An eighth-inning decision by umpire Hank O'Day infuriates the crowd at League Park. When the contest ended with a 7–6 Dodgers win, hundreds of fans rushed at O'Day, who suffered a split lip before police, with revolvers drawn, could rescue him. The crowd milled around after the contest for an hour, and O'Day needed police protection again to move from his dressing room to a waiting police carriage. While the carriage was stalled in traffic on the way to O'Day's hotel, the umpire was recognized and pelted with stones. Once again, police drew their revolvers to quell the disturbance.

O'Day couldn't make it to the ballpark for the remaining two games of the series because of the injuries he suffered at the hands of St. Louis fans. One player from each team served as substitute umpires during the two contests.

JULY 15   Christy Mathewson of the Giants pitches a no-hitter to defeat the Cardinals 5–0 before a crowd of 5,000 at League Park. The final out was recorded when Dick Padden grounded to shortstop Piano Legs Hickman.

JULY 21   Jesse Burkett collects five hits, including a homer, in five at-bats during a 15–2 trouncing of the Reds at League Park.

JULY 25   In a game marked by great pitching and shoddy defense, the Cardinals defeat the Cubs 5–3 at League Park. The Cardinals made five errors, but Jack Harper pitched a two-hitter. The only Chicago hits were singles by Jock Menefee and Charlie Dexter.

Harper was 23–12 with an ERA of 3.62 as a rookie pitcher with the Cardinals in 1901.

JULY 26   Fisticuffs and beanballs enliven a 12–7 win over the Pirates at League Park. Pittsburgh catcher Jack O'Connor slugged Patsy Donovan in the third inning, and in retaliation, Cardinals hurler Jack Powell threw a pitch at O'Connor that struck him in the jaw.

AUGUST 5 The Cardinals break open a close game with 11 runs in the eighth inning and win 20–6 over the Pirates in Pittsburgh. The Cards collected 21 hits in the contest.

AUGUST 9	The Cardinals crush the Reds 13–6 in Cincinnati.
AUGUST 28	Down 6–0, the Cardinals score three runs in the fifth inning, one in the sixth, two in the seventh, and three in the ninth to win 9–7 over the Pirates in Pittsburgh.
AUGUST 31	Dick Padden collects five hits, including a triple, in five at-bats during a 15–4 slaughter of the Reds at League Park.
SEPTEMBER 2	The morning game of a Labor Day doubleheader against the Dodgers in Brooklyn is postponed because the Cardinals' train is delayed by a bridge washout in Cleveland while the club is traveling from St. Louis to New York. The afternoon tilt was played as scheduled, and the Cardinals lost 11–5. Dick Padden shoved umpire Billy Nash after a close play went against the Cardinals, but Padden was allowed to remain in the game.
SEPTEMBER 3	The Cardinals score four runs in the ninth inning to beat the Dodgers 8–7 in the second game of a doubleheader in Brooklyn. The Dodgers won the first game 8–3.
SEPTEMBER 15	Seven days after a hurricane in Galveston, Texas, claims 6,000 lives, the Cardinals clobber the Cubs 13–6 in Chicago.
SEPTEMBER 19	All National League games are postponed due to the funeral of President William McKinley. McKinley was shot by Leon Czolgosz during a reception in Buffalo on September 6 and died on September 14. Theodore Roosevelt became the president.
SEPTEMBER 23	Bobby Wallace collects five hits, including a triple and a double, during a 9–3 win over the Braves at League Park.
	Wallace hit .322 for the Cardinals in 1901.
SEPTEMBER 25	Rookie first baseman Bill Richardson hits a walk-off homer in the eleventh inning off future Hall of Famer Vic Willis to defeat the Braves 2–1 at League Park. Jack Harper pitched a complete game for his 23rd win of the season.
	The homer was Richardson's first in the majors. He hit only two home runs in a big-league career that lasted just 15 games.
SEPTEMBER 27	Rookie pitcher Mike O'Neill tosses a two-hitter to defeat the Phillies 9–0 at League Park. The only two Philadelphia hits were singles by Ed McFarland and Ed Delahanty.
SEPTEMBER 28	The Cardinals receive a 5–4 gift victory from the Phillies at League Park. The Cards trailed 4–3 in the ninth with two on and two out when pinch hitter Mike O'Neill lifted a fly ball to center. Phillies center fielder Roy Thomas fell down while chasing the ball, and both runners scored.
DECEMBER 3	The American League votes to transfer the Milwaukee Brewers to St. Louis.
	The new club in St. Louis was owned by Robert Lee Hedges, who took the Cardinals' former nickname, former playing field, and many of the club's top players by the start of the 1902 season. Hedges named his club the Browns and signed a lease to play at Sportsman's Park at Grand and Dozier, where the

Cardinals played from 1881 through 1892. There, Hedges built a completely new grandstand. He then went to work on recruiting the Cardinals' best players for his club. In this, Hedges was enormously successful. Jesse Burkett, Jack Harper, Emmett Heidrick, Dick Padden, Jack Powell, Willie Sudhoff, and Bobby Wallace all signed with the Browns. In addition, Dan McGann inked a deal with the Orioles. Thus, during the 1901–02 offseason, the Cardinals lost two starting outfielders, three of their starting infielders, and three pitchers who had combined for 59 of the club's 76 victories in 1901. Combined with the six players who moved to the AL between the 1900 and 1901 seasons, the Cardinals lost 14 players in two years. Among the regulars from the 1900 season, only Patsy Donovan was still with the Cards in 1902. It took the club years to recover from the blow. The Cards, who had a 76–64 record in 1901, slumped to 56–78 in 1902, and 43–94 in 1903. The Browns, with a roster full of ex-Cardinals, landed in second place in the American League in 1902. With the arrival of the Browns, St. Louis would have a team in both the National League and American League from 1902 through 1953. From 1920 through 1953, both teams played at Sportsman's Park.

1902

Season in a Sentence

With a roster decimated by the cross-town Browns, the Cardinals sink to sixth place.

Finish • Won • Lost • Pct • GB

Finish	Won	Lost	Pct	GB
Sixth	56	78	.418	44.5

Manager

Patsy Donovan

Stats

Stats	Cards	NL	Rank
Batting Avg:	.258	.259	3
On-Base Pct:	.306	.312	6
Slugging Pct:	.304	.319	5
Home Runs:	10		5
Stolen Bases:	158		3
ERA:	3.47	2.78	7
Fielding Avg:	.944	.949	7
Runs Scored:	517		6
Runs Allowed:	695		8

Starting Lineup

Jack Ryan, c
Roy Brashear, 1b
John Farrell, 2b
Fred Hartman, 3b
Otto Krueger, ss
George Barclay, lf
Homer Smoot, cf
Patsy Donovan, rf
Art Nichols, 1b
Jack O'Neill, c

Pitchers

Mike O'Neill, sp
Steve Yerkes, sp
Ed Murphy, sp
Bob Wicker, sp
Clarence Currie, sp
Alex Pearson, sp

Attendance

226,417 (fourth in NL)

Club Leaders

Batting Avg:	Donovan	.315
On-Base Pct:	Donovan	.363
Slugging Pct:	Smoot	.380
Home Runs:	Smoot	3
	Barclay	3
RBIs:	Barclay	53
Runs:	Barclay	79
Stolen Bases:	Donovan	34
Wins:	O'Neill	16
Strikeouts:	O'Neill	105
ERA:	O'Neill	2.90
Saves:	Murphy	1
	Dunham	1

APRIL 17   The Cardinals lose the season opener 1–0 to the Pirates before a crowd of 10,000 at League Park. Starting pitcher Stan Yerkes allowed only one run, unearned, in the sixth inning on an error by shortstop Otto Krueger. Deacon Phillippe pitched the shutout for Pittsburgh.

APRIL 19   The Cardinals set a modern National League record by making 11 errors in a 10–4 loss to the Pirates at League Park.

APRIL 23   The St. Louis Browns play their first regular-season game, and win 5–2 over the Cleveland Indians before 18,000 at Sportsman's Park.

On the same day, Cardinals owner Frank Robison offered to put up $10,000 that the Pirates would not repeat as National League champions. Pittsburgh players accepted the challenge with a matching pool. The Pirates won the pennant by a whopping 27½ games with a record of 103–36.

APRIL 25   The Cardinals win their first game of 1902 after opening the season with five straight losses with a 9–8 victory over the Reds in 10 innings in Cincinnati. Homer Smoot hit two inside-the-park homers in the game. His second one broke a 7–7 tie in the tenth before each club added another run.

All three Cardinal outfielders hit .300 or better in 1902. Smoot batted .311, Patsy Donovan .309, and George Barclay .300. Smoot and Barclay were rookies.

MAY 8   A two-run, walk-off single by Roy Brashear in the ninth inning beats the Phillies 2–1 at League Park.

MAY 12   Ed Murphy pitches a two-hitter to defeat the Giants at League Park. The only New York hits were a double by Jimmy Jones and a single by opposing pitcher Brickyard Kennedy.

JUNE 3   Trailing 8–5, the Cardinals score six runs in the ninth inning and defeat the Braves 11–9 in Boston. During the six-run rally, pitcher Mike O'Neill hit the first pinch-hit grand slam in major league history.

O'Neill was primarily a pitcher but was used often as a pinch hitter and occasionally as an outfielder between starts. During his five-year career, he had a 34–43 record, and hit .255 with nine homers in 380 at-bats. O'Neill was one of four brothers who played in the majors. The four O'Neill brothers were Jack (born in 1873), Mike (1877), Steve (1891), and Jim (1893). The two oldest brothers were born in Maam, Ireland, and the two youngest in the coal mining town of Minooka, Pennsylvania. Jack, who was a catcher, was Mike's teammate with the Cardinals in 1902 and 1903.

JULY 5   Mike O'Neill pitches the Cardinals to a 1–0 win over the Giants at League Park. The only Cardinal run scored in the sixth inning on a wild pitch by Christy Mathewson.

JULY 9   At League Park, the Cardinals and Braves play to a 5–5 tie, called after 10 innings by darkness.

JULY 10   The Cardinals play a tie game for the second day in a row. The contest with the Dodgers at League Park ended in a 2–2 tie after 12 innings before darkness prevented further play.

JULY 12   A three-run homer by Art Nichols in the fourth inning provides all of the runs in a 3–0 Cardinals win over the Braves at League Park. Stan Yerkes pitched the shutout.

The home run by Nichols was the only one that he hit in 1902 and was the last of three that he struck during a six-year big-league career.

JULY 19   The Cardinals beat the Reds 2–1 at League Park in a contest called in the top of the seventh inning by rain.

When it began to rain steadily, Patsy Donovan argued with umpire Tom Brown that the game should be stopped. A mob of rooters jumped out of the bleachers to join in the discussion. They were met by policemen, but by the time the field was cleared, the rain had turned into a deluge and the contest was called. The Reds protested to the National League office that the game should have been forfeited to them because of a lack of crowd control, but the protest was denied.

AUGUST 4   Clarence Currie pitches the Cardinals to a 1–0 win over the Braves in Boston in a contest called after seven innings by rain. Currie allowed only two hits, singles by Charlie Dexter and Ed Gremminger.

AUGUST 7   The Cardinals steal seven bases in an 11–1 win over the Dodgers in Brooklyn.

AUGUST 12   The Cardinals score three runs in the ninth inning and three in the tenth to beat the Phillies 12–9 in Philadelphia.

AUGUST 17   The Cardinals and the Dodgers play to an 18-inning, 7–7 tie at Robison Field. Most of the scoring was done in the first two innings. Brooklyn led 5–4 at the end of the second, the Cardinals scored two in the sixth, and the Dodgers tied the game with a run in the ninth. Both clubs tallied one in the thirteenth. Wild Bill Donovan pitched a complete game for Brooklyn. Clarence Currie pitched 16 innings of relief for St. Louis.

AUGUST 21   The Cardinals admit 12,000 school children free of charge to a doubleheader against the Braves at League Park. The Cards lost the first game 6–1 but won the second 7–4.

SEPTEMBER 14   The game between the Pirates and Cardinals at League Park is delayed for an hour because a railroad accident made the Pirates late. Pittsburgh won 9–6 in a contest called after eight innings by darkness.

OCTOBER 1   On a cold afternoon, only 250 fans attend a game between the Cardinals and Cubs at League Park. The tilt was called on account of darkness after seven innings with the score 4–4.

The Cardinals drew 226,417 fans to Robison Field in 1902. The Browns, in their first year in St. Louis, attracted 272,283 to Sportsman's Park.

1903

Season in a Sentence

No Cardinal pitcher wins as many as 10 games, and the club thuds into last place.

Finish • Won • Lost • Pct • GB

Eighth   43   94   .314   46.5

Manager

Patsy Donovan

Stats

Stats	Cards	NL	Rank
Batting Avg:	.251	.269	7
On-Base Pct:	.297	.331	8
Slugging Pct:	.313	.349	8
Home Runs:	8		8
Stolen Bases:	171		5
ERA:	3.67	3.26	7
Fielding Avg:	.940	.946	7
Runs Scored:	505		8
Runs Allowed:	795		8

Starting Lineup

Jack O'Neill, c
John Hackett, 1b
John Farrell, 2b
Jimmy Burke, 3b
Dave Brain, ss-3b
George Barclay, lf
Homer Smoot, cf
Patsy Donovan, rf
Jack Ryan, c
Jack Dunleavy, rf-p
Otto Williams, ss
Art Nichols, 1b

Pitchers

Chappie McFarland, sp
Three Finger Brown, sp
Clarence Currie, sp
Bob Rhoads, sp
Mike O'Neill, sp
Jack Dunleavy, sp
Ed Murphy, sp

Attendance

228,538 (fifth in NL)

Club Leaders

Batting Avg:	Donovan	.327
On-Base Pct:	Donovan	.370
Slugging Pct:	Smoot	.396
Home Runs:	Smoot	4
RBIs:	Brain	60
Runs:	Farrell	83
Stolen Bases:	Burke	28
Wins:	Brown	9
	McFarland	9
Strikeouts:	Brown	83
ERA:	Brown	2.60
Saves:	Currie	1
	Hackett	1

JANUARY 9   The National and American Leagues reach a peace accord at a meeting in Cincinnati. The two leagues agreed to refrain from raiding one another's rosters and set up a three-man governing body consisting of the presidents of the two leagues and Cincinnati Reds president Garry Herrmann.

APRIL 4   The Browns and the Cardinals play each other for the first time in a spring training exhibition game. The Browns won 13–4 at Sportsman's Park. The two St. Louis clubs met four times in the spring of 1903, each winning twice.

APRIL 16   In the season opener, the Cardinals defeat the Cubs 2–1 before 6,500 at League Park. Clarence Currie pitched the complete-game victory, and John Farrell collected three hits.

APRIL 19   In his major league debut, Three Finger Brown pitches a one-hit shutout for a 3–0 win over the Cubs in a contest at League Park called after five innings by rain.

Mordecai Peter Centennial "Three Finger" Brown was 9–13 with a 2.60 ERA as a rookie in 1903. Born in 1876, he received one of his two middle names because the year of his birth coincided with the 100th anniversary of the signing of the Declaration of Independence. Brown's nickname was the result of an accident he suffered at the age of seven while visiting his uncle's farm in Indiana. Brown stuck his right hand into a corn chopper, and half of the right index finger was shorn off. The thumb and middle finger were also badly injured. A few weeks later he fell while chasing a hog and further mangled the hand by breaking the third and fourth fingers. As it healed, each finger bent and twisted unnaturally. The disfigured hand gave Brown a unique spin on the ball. Unfortunately, the Cardinals sent Brown to the Cubs following the end of the 1903 season before he developed into an outstanding pitcher (see December 12, 1903).

National Baseball Hall of Fame Library/Major League Baseball/Getty Images

Mordecai "Three Finger" Brown debuted as a right-handed pitcher with the Cardinals in 1903 but stayed for only that season and spent most of his Hall of Fame career with the Chicago Cubs. His pitching hand, disfigured in a pair of childhood farm accidents, gave his pitches remarkable movement.

APRIL 26   Down 5–0, the Cardinals score three runs in the eighth inning and three in the ninth to beat the Reds 6–5 at League Park. The game ended on a thrilling three-run, inside-the-park homer by Homer Smoot, who just beat the throw to the plate by a whisker.

Smoot hit another three-run, walk-off, inside-the-park homer against the Reds on July 22. The Cardinals hit only eight homers all season, and Smoot accounted for four of them. No one else on the club hit more than one home run.

MAY 25   The Cardinals make 10 errors by eight different players in a 13–4 loss to the Giants in New York.

The Cardinals' starting first baseman in 1903 was John Hackett. His career ended the following offseason in a bizarre manner. While hunting, Hackett absentmindedly rubbed poison ivy in one of his eyes. The resulting infection permanently damaged his eyesight.

JUNE 2

Chappie McFarland pitches a two-hitter to defeat the Phillies 1–0 at League Park. The only Philadelphia hits were a double by Bill Hallman and a single by Harry Wolverton.

JUNE 15

Playing right field, Patsy Donovan pulls off an unassisted double play during a 4–3 loss to the Reds in Cincinnati. Cy Seymour of the Reds was running on the pitch that Joe Kelley lifted into right. Donovan caught it and raced to first base, beating Seymour to the bag.

JUNE 23

The Cardinals defeat the Braves 3–0 in 11 innings in Boston. Bob Rhoads pitched the complete-game shutout.

JUNE 25

The Cardinals defeat the Braves 5–3 and 1–0 in a doubleheader in Boston. Clarence Currie pitched a two-hitter in the opener. The only two Boston hits were a double and a single by Duff Cooley.

JULY 1

Homer Smoot hits into a "quadruple" play during a 5–2 loss to the Giants in New York. Smoot hit a fly ball to Roger Bresnahan in center field with the bases loaded. Bresnahan threw to catcher John Warner to retire Clarence Currie trying to score from third for the second out. Warner then fired the ball to shortstop George Davis to nail Patsy Donovan attempting to advance to second from first for the second out. Even though the inning was over, neither club seemed to realize it, and play continued. Davis saw John Farrell, who started the play on second, trying to score, and he instinctively threw home. Warner tagged Farrell for the "fourth out" of the inning.

JULY 22

Homer Smoot beats the Reds 8–7 at League Park with a three-run, inside-the-park homer in the ninth inning. With two outs and two strikes, Smoot hit a drive to right field. Cincinnati outfielder Cozy Dolan didn't see the ball in the darkness and stood still as a statue as the ball sailed past him. First baseman Jake Beckley had to retrieve the ball, but by the time he tracked it down, Smoot had scored. Reds pitcher Jack Harper angrily picked up the ball and heaved it into the stands as fans poured onto the field and carried Smoot around the diamond on their shoulders.

JULY 25

The day before H. Nelson Jackson completes history's first coast-to-coast trip by automobile, John Farrell collects five hits, including a triple and a double, in five at-bats during a 14–6 win over the Pirates in Pittsburgh.

SEPTEMBER 14

In his major league debut, Giants pitcher Red Ames throws a five-inning no-hitter against the Cardinals in the second game of a doubleheader in New York. The Giants won 5–0. The contest was called on account of darkness. The Giants also won the first game, 8–2.

SEPTEMBER 20

Rookie Cardinal pitcher Charlie Moran walks 10 batters in an 8–3 loss in the second game of a doubleheader against the Braves in Boston. The Braves also won the first game, 7–3.

OCTOBER 3   The Cardinals and Browns begin a seven-game postseason series to determine the champion of St. Louis. The Browns won the game 3–0 at Sportsman's Park.

OCTOBER 10   After losing the first four games of the series, the Cardinals score seven runs in the third inning and wallop the Browns 12–1 at Sportsman's Park.

> *The Browns won five of the seven games to claim the championship of St. Louis. The fall series between the Cardinals and Browns was played every year from 1903 through 1917, with the exception of 1908, 1909, and 1910.*

DECEMBER 12   Five days before the Wright brothers' first successful flight, the Cardinals trade Three Finger Brown and Jack O'Neill to the Cubs for Jack Taylor and Larry McLean.

> *This proved to be one of the worst trades in Cardinals history. At the time of the trade, Mordecai "Three Finger" Brown was 27 years old and had won only nine major league games. Once in Chicago, he became one of the best pitchers of his generation. After leaving St. Louis, Brown played in the majors for 13 more seasons and posted a record of 230–117 and an ERA of 2.56. He was elected to the Hall of Fame in 1949. Taylor was 29 and had records of 23–11 in 1902 and 21–14 in 1903 for the Cubs. He gave the Cardinals one good season. In 1904, Taylor was 20–19 with an ERA of 2.22 in 352 innings and completed each one of his 39 starts. Taylor went back to the Cubs in another trade in 1906.*

1904

Season in a Sentence

St. Louis hosts a World's Fair and the Olympics, but not a winning baseball club, although the Cardinals win 32 more games than the previous season.

Finish • Won • Lost • Pct • GB

Fifth   75   79   .487   31.5

Manager

Kid Nichols

Stats

Stats	Cards	• NL •	Rank
Batting Avg:	.253	.249	4
On-Base Pct:	.306	.306	4
Slugging Pct:	.327	.322	4
Home Runs:	24		2 (tie)
Stolen Bases:	199		4
ERA:	2.64	2.73	4
Fielding Avg:	.952	.950	5
Runs Scored:	602		4
Runs Allowed:	595		5

Starting Lineup

Mike Grady, c
Jake Beckley, 1b
John Farrell, 2b
Jimmy Burke, 3b
Dave Brain, ss-3b
George Barclay, lf
Homer Smoot, cf
Spike Shannon, rf
Danny Shay, ss
Jack Dunleavy, rf

Pitchers

Jack Taylor, sp
Kid Nichols, sp
Chappie McFarland, sp
Mike O'Neill, sp
Joe Corbett, sp

Attendance

228,538 (fifth in NL)

Club Leaders

Batting Avg:	Beckley	.325
On-Base Pct:	Beckley	.375
Slugging Pct:	Beckley	.403
Home Runs:	Brain	7
RBIs:	Brain	72
Runs:	Shannon	84
Stolen Bases:	Shannon	50
Wins:	Nichols	21
Strikeouts:	Nichols	134
ERA:	Nichols	2.02
Saves:	Taylor	1
	Nichols	1

JANUARY 9   The Cardinals hire 34-year-old Kid Nichols as manager, replacing Patsy Donovan.

Charles "Kid" Nichols compiled a record of 329–183 as a pitcher with the Boston Braves from 1890 through 1901. The Braves believed that Nichols's best years were behind him, however, and didn't offer him a contract for 1902. Nichols accepted an offer to manage and pitch for the minor league Kansas City club in the Western League, and led the team to first-and third-place finishes while posting a pitching record of 48–19. Under Nichols's leadership, the Cardinals improved from 43–94 in 1903 to 75–79 in 1904. On the mound, he was 21–13 with an ERA of 2.02. But Nichols was fired 14 games into the 1905 season and sold to the Phillies. Donovan later managed the Senators (1904), Dodgers (1906–08), and Red Sox (1910–11).

FEBRUARY 1   The Cardinals purchase Jake Beckley from the Reds.

A native of Hannibal, Missouri, and a future member of baseball's Hall of Fame, Beckley came to the Cardinals as a 36-year-old first baseman. Beckley gave the Cardinals one great season, batting .325 in 1904, before his career went into decline.

APRIL 15   In the season opener, the Cardinals lose 5–4 to the Pirates before 7,000 at League Park. The Cards scored only four times despite collecting 15 hits. John Farrell had three hits, including a double. In his big-league debut, catcher Bill Byers had three hits.

Byers played in only 19 big-league games, in which he batted .217 with 13 hits, all singles. Mike Grady soon took over as the regular catcher and hit .313.

APRIL 17   A crowd of 23,350, the largest ever to see the Cardinals play in St. Louis up to that time, squeezes into League Park to see the Cardinals beat the Pirates 6–5 with three runs in the eighth.

MAY 10   The Cardinals score five runs in the first inning off Christy Mathewson en route to a 14–1 thrashing of the Giants at League Park.

The city of St. Louis hosted both a World's Fair and the Olympic Games in 1904. The fair was held at Forest Park to mark the 100th anniversary of the Louisiana Purchase and drew 20 million visitors in seven months. For the mammoth event, fair officials planted 1,679,000 trees, shrubs, and vines and constructed 1,576 buildings and other structures. According to legend, both the ice cream cone and iced tea were invented at the fair. The Olympics in 1904 wasn't the international event it is today. Only 13 nations participated (compared with 202 in 2004). Most of the European nations declined the invitation. The United States won 80 of the 100 gold medals and 238 of the 284 total medals.

MAY 30   The Cardinals collect 20 hits and wallop the Pirates 13–0 in Pittsburgh.

JUNE 3   Jack Taylor pitches 12²/₃ innings, but loses 1–0 to the Braves in Boston on an unearned run caused by a wild throw from shortstop Danny Shay with two outs in the thirteenth.

Joe Corbett pitched 108²/₃ innings for the Cardinals in 1904 with an ERA of 4.39. He was the brother of heavyweight boxing champion "Gentleman Jim"

Corbett, who held the title from 1892 through 1897. Joe Corbett previously pitched in the majors with the Baltimore Orioles in 1897 and had a record of 24–8, but quit after manager Ned Hanlon reneged on a promise to buy him a $40 suit of clothes. Corbett refused to pitch for the Orioles or any other big-league club for seven years. The 1904 season was his last in the big leagues.

JUNE 17   During the fifth inning of a 6–3 loss to the Pirates in Pittsburgh, Chappie McFarland is hit in the head by a line drive and carried off the field in an unconscious condition. He was out of action for two weeks.

JULY 3   The Cardinals score seven runs in the ninth inning to cap a 19–2 drubbing of the Cubs in Chicago.

AUGUST 4   Kid Nichols pitches the Cardinals to a 1–0 win over the Braves in the second game of a doubleheader in Boston. In the ninth inning, Nichols loaded the bases with no outs, and worked his way out of the jam. The Braves won the first game 2–1.

AUGUST 11   The Cardinals win a 17-inning marathon by a 4–3 score over the Dodgers in Brooklyn. A two-run single by Dave Brain put the Cardinals ahead 4–2 in the top of the seventeenth before the Cards survived a Dodger rally in the bottom half. Both Kid Nichols of the Cardinals and Oscar Jones of the Dodgers pitched complete games. Nichols struck out 14 batters.

               Brain was born in Hereford, England. He hit .266 with seven homers for the Cardinals in 1904.

AUGUST 17   The Cardinals stun the Phillies with six runs in the ninth inning to win 9–7 in Philadelphia.

AUGUST 22   Dave Brain hits a grand slam off Ned Garvin during a 13–3 win over the Dodgers in Brooklyn.

SEPTEMBER 7   Kid Nichols pitches a two-hitter to beat the Cubs in the second game of a doubleheader at League Park. The only Chicago hits were a home run by Davy Jones and a single by Jimmy Slagle. The Cardinals also won the first game, 5–4.

SEPTEMBER 11   The Cardinals sell George Barclay to the Braves.

SEPTEMBER 24   Jack Taylor pitches two complete games in one day against the Phillies in Philadelphia. Taylor won the first game 3–2, but lost the second 2–0 in a contest called after 6½ innings on account of darkness.

SEPTEMBER 29   Kid Nichols earns his 21st win of the season with a 3–0 decision over the Dodgers in Brooklyn. The game took only 1 hour and 10 minutes to complete.

OCTOBER 1   Jack Taylor earns his 20th win of the season with a 5–1 win in 10 innings over the Giants in New York.

OCTOBER 4   The Cardinals win a forfeited game against the Giants in the second game of a doubleheader in New York. A crisis arose in the fourth inning when Umpire Jim Johnstone ruled that Danny Shay of the Cardinals had stolen second base before

Giant shortstop Bill Dahlen applied the tag. Dahlen and the entire Giants infield encircled Johnstone and argued against the call. Johnstone ejected Dahlen for using profane language, but his teammates continued to argue. The whole Giants team then refused to play. Johnstone gave the men a time limit, and when they still refused to take their places, he announced the game forfeited to the Cardinals. After learning of the decision, the spectators rushed onto the field and surrounded Johnstone. One knocked him down with a blow to the face. While Johnstone was down, the infuriated Giants partisans started to kick and punch him. The police got into the melee, and with their clubs rescued the umpire and escorted him to the dressing room. The first game was completed without untoward incident, the Cardinals winning 7–3.

OCTOBER 10   In the first game of the St. Louis city championship, the Cardinals defeat the Browns 3–1 on a two-run homer by Mike Grady in the tenth inning before 1,500 at Sportsman's Park.

> *The series was supposed to go seven games, but Game Seven was scheduled for October 16 and the contracts of the players on both teams expired on October 15. The Cardinals said they wouldn't play the seventh game unless the players on both clubs received 100 percent of the gate receipts. The owners of the Cardinals and Browns refused the ultimatum, and the series ended in a tie with each club winning six games.*

1905

Season in a Sentence

The Cardinals lose 96 games under three different managers, one of them owner Stanley Robison.

Finish • Won • Lost • Pct • GB

Sixth   58   96   .377   47.5

Managers

Kid Nichols (5–9), Jimmy Burke (34–56), and Stanley Robison (19–31)

Stats

Stats	Cards	• NL •	Rank
Batting Avg:	.248	.255	5
On-Base Pct:	.307	.315	6
Slugging Pct:	.321	.332	5
Home Runs:	20		5
Stolen Bases:	162		7
ERA:	3.59	2.99	7
Fielding Avg:	.957	.954	5
Runs Scored:	535		6
Runs Allowed:	734		7

Starting Lineup

Mike Grady, c
Jake Beckley, 1b
Harry Arndt, 2b
Jimmy Burke, 3b
George McBride, ss
Spike Shannon, lf
Homer Smoot, cf
Jack Dunleavy, rf
Danny Shay, ss-2b
Josh Clarke, rf-2b
Dave Brain, ss

Pitchers

Jack Taylor, sp
Jake Thielman, sp
Chappie McFarland, sp
Buster Brown, sp
Wish Egan, sp

Attendance

386,750 (fourth in NL)

Club Leaders

Batting Avg:	Smoot	.311
On-Base Pct:	Smoot	.359
Slugging Pct:	Smoot	.433
Home Runs:	Smoot	4
	Grady	4
RBIs:	Smoot	58
Runs:	Smoot	73
	Shannon	73
Stolen Bases:	Shannon	27
Wins:	Taylor	15
	Thielman	15
Strikeouts:	Taylor	102
ERA:	Brown	2.97
Saves:	Taylor	1
	McFarland	1

APRIL 14   The Cardinals lose 6–1 to the Cubs in the season opener at League Park. Temperatures in the low 50s kept the crowd to 2,500.

APRIL 23   Down 7–3 in the second inning, the Cardinals rally to beat the Reds 12–8 in Cincinnati.

MAY 1   Cardinal catcher John Warner and Otto Clymer of the Pirates fight during a 2–1 loss to the Pirates at League Park. Hostilities surfaced in the fifth inning when Clymer tried to score from third base on the back end of a double steal. Clymer was easily out, but he drove into Warner, and his impetus knocked the catcher on his back. Warner got up as Clymer turned toward the bench and fired the ball into the back of the retreating Pirate. Clymer headed back, and before he could react, received a blow from Warner on the neck. Umpire Hank O'Day stepped between them and ejected both players from the premises.

MAY 3   With the club holding a record of 5–9, Kid Nichols is replaced as manager by 30-year-old third baseman Jimmy Burke.

            Burke grew up in the tough, brawling Goose Hill district of north St. Louis, which was settled by Irish immigrants and produced numerous big-league ballplayers. He was known as a hustling firebrand who looked for any edge he could to win a game. Burke lasted only three months as the Cardinals' manager, however (see August 4, 1905). Nichols remained with the Cards as a pitcher until he was sold to the Phillies on July 16.

MAY 9   The Cardinals score four runs in the ninth inning and defeat the Giants 8–7 in New York.

MAY 16   The Cardinals score seven runs in the third inning and defeat the Phillies 11–8 in Philadelphia.

MAY 20   The Cardinals defeat the Braves 3–2 in Boston. Win Kellum earned the complete-game victory.

MAY 29   Dave Brain collects three triples in a 6–3 win over the Pirates in Pittsburgh.

JUNE 1   The Cardinals score six runs in the ninth inning to beat the Reds 9–3 in Cincinnati.

JUNE 3   Jack Taylor pitches the Cardinals to a 1–0 win over the Reds in Cincinnati. Danny Shay drove in the lone run of the game with a single in the seventh inning.

JUNE 13   Umpire Bill Klem needs police protection to leave the field after being surrounded by a mob following a 6–1 Cardinals loss to the Dodgers at League Park. The crowd was angry over an eighth-inning decision by Klem that led to the ejections of Jimmy Burke and Mike Grady.

JUNE 18   Trouble brews at League Park for the second time in less than a week as Giants manager John McGraw battles St. Louis fans following the conclusion of an 8–2 Cardinals win before a crowd of 9,000. The Cards overcame a 2–1 deficit with seven runs in the seventh inning on eight consecutive singles, a walk, and a hit batsman.

*While the New York players were entering an omnibus, a group assembled and
began jeering the New York skipper. He replied, and instantly the crowd set
upon him. Somebody struck McGraw on the shoulder with an umbrella, and this
was followed by a shower of stones. A number of police officers hurried up and
dispersed the crowd. The omnibus was accompanied from the grounds by several
officers.*

JUNE 19   The Cardinals score seven runs in the third inning to break a 2–2 tie in a 10–6
           victory over the Braves at League Park.

JUNE 24   The Cardinals lose a long, drawn-out 18-inning battle by a 2–1 score against the
           Cubs at League Park. Jack Taylor of the Cardinals and Ed Reulbach of the Cubs
           both pitched complete games. The winning run scored on a triple by Wildfire Schulte
           and a sacrifice fly by Billy Maloney.

JULY 4   The Cardinals trade Dave Brain to the Pirates for George McBride.

JULY 13   Chappie McFarland pitches a two-hitter to beat the Phillies in the first game of a
           doubleheader in Philadelphia. The only hits off McFarland were singles by Ernie
           Courtney and Sherry Magee. The Phillies won the first game 2–1.

JULY 15   Cardinal pitcher Wish Egan gives up back-to-back home run balls in Boston that
           travel several miles, but the Cardinals defeat the Braves 11–8.

           *Just beyond the short left field wall of South End Grounds in Boston, and
           only about 300 feet from home plate, were the tracks of the New York, New
           Haven & Hartford Railroad. Jim Delahanty smacked a ball that took a bounce
           and plopped into a gondola car of a moving freight train heading south.
           Someone finally retrieved the ball when the train reached the end of the line
           in Willimantic, Connecticut, 75 miles away. Harry Wolverton was the next
           batter and, incredibly, hit a home run into a northbound passenger train, which
           traveled another six miles to City Point in South Boston.*

JULY 30   The Cardinals sweep the Braves 1–0 and 6–5 in a doubleheader at League Park.
           Buster Brown pitched the first game shutout, defeating future Hall of Famer Vic
           Willis.

           *The top hitter for the Cardinals in 1905 was Homer Smoot, who batted .311.
           Mike Grady hit .286.*

AUGUST 4   Jimmy Burke is relieved of his duties as manager and is replaced by club owner
           Stanley Robison.

           *Burke had a record of 34–56 as skipper of the Cardinals. He remained as the
           Cards' third baseman for the remainder of the season. Burke later managed the
           Browns from 1918 through 1920. Under Robison, the Cardinals were 19–31.
           He hired John McCloskey at the end of the season to run the club.*

AUGUST 10 The Cardinals sell John Warner to the Tigers.

AUGUST 18 The Cardinals score three runs in the ninth inning to defeat the Phillies 11–9 in
           Philadelphia.

AUGUST 22   Jack Taylor is the star of a 1–0 win over the Braves in Boston. Not only did he pitch a shutout, but he also drove in the lone run of the game with a triple in the third inning off Vic Willis.

AUGUST 31   Jimmy Burke of the Cardinals and Honus Wagner of the Pirates are ejected for fighting during an 11-inning, 2–1 St. Louis loss in the first game of a doubleheader at Pittsburgh. According to the newspaper reports, "They rolled up in great shape, kicking, biting and gouging each other until the other players split them out." The Pirates also won the second game, 10–6.

SEPTEMBER 4   The Cardinals score seven runs in the seventh inning of a 9–2 win over the Reds in the first game of a doubleheader at League Park. The Cards completed the sweep with a 3–2 triumph in the second tilt.

SEPTEMBER 12   Harry Arndt makes a sensational steal of home with two outs in the ninth inning to beat the Pirates 2–1 in Pittsburgh. The Pirates won the second game 8–2.

SEPTEMBER 28   Buster Brown outduels Joe McGinnity to beat the Giants 1–0 at League Park.

OCTOBER 9   The St. Louis city championship series begins with a 4–1 win over the Browns before 2,800 at Sportsman's Park.

OCTOBER 14   At Sportsman's Park, Buster Brown pitches the Cardinals to a 1–0 win over the Browns in Game Five to take a three-games-to-two lead in the St. Louis city championship series. The winning run scored in the ninth inning on a triple by Spike Shannon and a single by Homer Smoot.

OCTOBER 15   The Browns sweep a doubleheader 7–6 and 3–0 over the Cardinals to take the city championship series four games to three. The Cards seemed to have the first game well in hand with a 6–2 lead, but the Browns scored five times in the eighth inning. The second tilt was called after six innings by darkness.

DECEMBER 30   The Cardinals hire John McCloskey as manager.

Before hiring McCloskey, Robison contacted several managerial candidates but had trouble convincing anyone to come to St. Louis to head a losing club with little hope of immediate improvement. McCloskey was 45 years old and had previously managed the Louisville Colonels in the National League in 1895 and 1896 to a record of 37–113. He led the Cardinals for three abysmal seasons in which the club won 153 and lost 302.

1906

Season in a Sentence

A 5–21 record in June is the lowlight of a season in which the Cardinals finish 63 games out of first place.

Finish • Won • Lost • Pct • GB

Seventh   52   98   .347   63.0

Manager

John McCloskey

Stats

Stats	Cards	• NL •	Rank
Batting Avg:	.235	.244	7
On-Base Pct:	.291	.310	7
Slugging Pct:	.296	.310	7
Home Runs:	10		8
Stolen Bases:	110		7
ERA:	3.04	2.62	6
Fielding Avg:	.957	.959	5
Runs Scored:	470		7
Runs Allowed:	607		6

Starting Lineup

Mike Grady, c
Jake Beckley, 1b
Pug Bennett, 2b
Art Hoelskoetter, 3b
George McBride, ss
Spike Shannon, lf
Homer Smoot, cf-rf
Al Burch, rf-cf
Harry Arndt, 3b
Shad Barry, rf-1b
Sam Mertes, lf
Jack Himes, cf
Forrest Crawford, ss

Pitchers

Buster Brown, sp
Fred Beebe, sp
Jack Taylor, sp
Ed Karger, sp
Carl Druhot, sp
Gus Thompson, sp
Wish Egan, sp

Attendance

283,770 (sixth in NL)

Club Leaders

Batting Avg:	Bennett	.262
On-Base Pct:	Bennett	.334
Slugging Pct:	Bennett	.318
Home Runs:	Grady	3
RBIs:	Beckley	44
Runs:	Bennett	66
Stolen Bases:	Bennett	20
Wins:	Beebe	9
Strikeouts:	Beebe	116
ERA:	Taylor	2.15
Saves:	Karger	1
	McFarland	1

APRIL 12   The Cardinals lose the season opener 2–1 to the Pirates in 13 hard-fought innings before 5,000 at League Park. Jack Taylor pitched the complete-game loss in a duel with Vic Willis.

APRIL 18   On the day of the great San Francisco earthquake and fire, Babe Adams makes his major league debut in an 11–1 loss to the Cubs in Chicago.

The Cardinals were not impressed by Adams, who gave up six unearned runs in four innings. He never pitched for the Cardinals again. It proved to be one of the worst personnel decisions in club history. The Pirates acquired Adams in 1907, and he went on to win 194 regular-season games for the club. In the 1909 World Series, Adams won three times.

MAY 10   Umpire Bill Carpenter calls police to have Cardinal catcher Mike Grady removed from the premises during an 8–5 loss to the Cubs at League Park. Grady was ejected for disputing Carpenter's calls, but refused to leave.

MAY 23   Jack Taylor pitches a two-hitter to defeat the Phillies 3–0 at League Park. The only hits off Taylor were singles by Roy Thomas and Mickey Doolan.

MAY 24   The Cardinals trounce the Phillies 11–1 at League Park.

| MAY 30 | The Cardinals defeat the Cubs 4–2 in 15 innings in the first game of a doubleheader in Chicago. In the 15th, Homer Smoot drove in a run with a triple and scored on an error. The Cardinals also won the second game 6–1. |

The doubleheader sweep of the Cubs, a club which posted a record of 116–36 in 1906, was the high point of the season. The Cardinals had a record of 20–21 at the conclusion of the twin bill, but lost 22 of their next 27 games.

| JUNE 3 | The Cardinals trade Chappie McFarland to the Pirates for Ed Karger. |

| JUNE 11 | Eleven Braves errors, five of them by ex-Cardinals third baseman Dave Brain, leads to an 8–1 Cardinals victory in Boston. |

| JULY 1 | The Cardinals send Jack Taylor to the Cubs for Fred Beebe, Pete Noonan, and cash. |

| JULY 4 | Fred Beebe pitches a three-hitter to beat the Reds 2–1 in 10 innings in the second game of a doubleheader at League Park. Cincinnati won the first game 12–0. |

During the two games, St. Louis fans shot toy pistols into the air and threw firecrackers at Reds left fielder Joe Kelley, who at times was obscured by a cloud of smoke. During the late 19th and early 20th centuries, it wasn't unusual for fans to attend July 4 doubleheaders with toy pistols, firecrackers, and fireworks to celebrate the nation's independence. In 1903, the American Medical Association began tracking the deaths and injuries suffered on July 4 and was appalled by the findings. From 1903 through 1909, 1,360 Americans died on the holiday from accidents, an average of 170 per year, mostly from fireworks and firearms, with a peak of 213 in 1909. Beginning in 1911, government agencies and newspapers campaigned to urge Americans to practice a "safe and sane" holiday. Toy pistols, fireworks, and cannons used in the celebrations were outlawed in many cities and towns. The crusade spread rapidly, and the deaths dropped to 41 in 1912.

| JULY 13 | The Cardinals trade Spike Shannon to the Giants for Sam Mertes and Doc Marshall. |

With numerous mid-season trades, the Cardinals didn't have anything resembling a stable lineup in 1906. Second baseman Pug Bennett was the only Cardinal to play in as many as 100 games.

| JULY 17 | Fred Beebe pitches a two-hitter to beat the Dodgers 2–1 at League Park. The only Brooklyn hits were singles by Harry Lumley and opposing pitcher Harry McInytre. |

| JULY 20 | Mal Eason of the Dodgers beats the Cardinals 2–0 with a no-hitter at League Park. Sam Mertes made the last out of the game on a grounder back to Eason. |

Mertes was nicknamed "Sandow" after a renowned strongman of the day.

| JULY 22 | Fred Beebe pitches a two-hitter and strikes out 12 batters to beat the Braves 4–1 at League Park. The only two hits off Beebe were singles by Del Howard. |

| JULY 25 | The Cardinals trade Homer Smoot to the Reds for Shad Barry and Carl Druhot. |

During World War I, Barry was in charge of all baseball programs for the American Expeditionary Forces.

AUGUST 29   Buster Brown pitches a two-hitter, but loses 1–0 to the Pirates at League Park.

SEPTEMBER 1   Umpires Jim Johnstone and Bob Emslie are unable to report to West Side Grounds in Chicago because of food poisoning. Pete Noonan of the Cardinals and Carl Lundgren of the Cubs served as substitute umpires, and the Cubs won 8–1.

SEPTEMBER 24   Pitching in only his second major league game, Cardinal hurler Stoney McGlynn pitches a seven-inning no-hitter in the second game of a doubleheader against the Dodgers in Brooklyn. The contest ended in a 1–1 tie when it was called on account of darkness. The Brooklyn run scored in the first inning on a walk, a stolen base, and an error. The Dodgers won the first tilt 6–5 in 11 innings.

OCTOBER 8   In the opening game of the St. Louis city championship, the Cardinals lose 4–3 to the Browns at Sportsman's Park.

In the seven games of the 1906 series, the Browns won four and the Cardinals took one. They tied twice.

1907

Season in a Sentence

The Cardinals lose 75 of their first 96 games and tumble into last place.

Finish • Won • Lost • Pct • GB

Eighth   52   101   .340   55.5

Manager

John McCloskey

Stats

Stats	Cards	• NL •	Rank
Batting Avg:	.232	.243	7
On-Base Pct:	.283	.308	8
Slugging Pct:	.288	.309	8
Home Runs:	19		3 (tie)
Stolen Bases:	125		6
ERA:	2.69	2.46	7
Fielding Avg:	.948	.960	8
Runs Scored:	419		8
Runs Allowed:	608		7

Starting Lineup

Doc Marshall, c
Ed Konetchy, 1b
Art Hoelskoetter, 2b
Bobby Byrne, 3b
Ed Holly, ss
Red Murray, lf
Jack Burnett, cf
Shad Barry, rf
Pug Bennett, 2b
Pete Noonan, c
John Kelly, rf-cf
Tom O'Hara, lf-rf
Al Burch, cf

Pitchers

Stoney McGlynn, sp
Ed Karger, sp
Fred Beebe, sp
Johnny Lush, sp
Art Fromme, sp-rp

Attendance

185,377 (eighth in NL)

Club Leaders

Batting Avg:	Murray	.262
On-Base Pct:	Byrne	.307
Slugging Pct:	Murray	.367
Home Runs:	Murray	7
RBIs:	Murray	46
Runs:	Byrne	55
	Holly	55
Stolen Bases:	Murray	23
Wins:	Karger	15
Strikeouts:	Beebe	141
ERA:	Karger	2.03
Saves:	Karger	1
	McGlynn	1

APRIL 11   In the season opener, the Cardinals lose 6–1 to the Cubs at Chicago.

The 1907 season was the first that the Cardinals opened on the road since entering the National League in 1892. From 1892 through 1906, St. Louis was granted the opener because it was, along with Cincinnati, the southernmost city in the league, and therefore, had a better chance of warmer weather. From 1907 though 1953, the Cardinals opened the season on the road in odd-numbered years and at home in even-numbered years, alternating with the Browns.

APRIL 13   The Cardinals-Cubs contest in Chicago is postponed by snow.

APRIL 18   The Cardinals' scheduled home opener against the Reds at League Park is postponed by foul weather.

APRIL 19   In the first game of the season at League Park, the Cardinals defeat the Reds 4–1. Cold and damp conditions kept the crowd to 1,500.

MAY 8   The Cardinals break a 12-game losing streak with a 6–4 win over the Phillies in Philadelphia. There were many anxious moments, however, when the Phillies scored all four of their runs in the ninth inning.

MAY 20   The Cardinals break the 17-game winning streak of the Giants with a 6–4 victory in New York. Entering the game, the Giants had a record of 24–3, while the Cardinals were 6–22.

JUNE 2   Fred Beebe pitches the Cardinals to a 1–0 win over the Reds in Cincinnati. Pete Noonan drove in the winning run with a single in the ninth inning.

JUNE 3   Stoney McGlynn pitches two complete nine-inning games against the Reds in Cincinnati. McGlynn won the first tilt 1–0, but lost the second 5–1. Pete Noonan drove in the lone run of the opener with a sacrifice fly in the seventh inning. It was the second game in a row that Noonan drove in the only run of a 1–0 decision.

Ulysses Simpson (Stoney) McGlynn posted a record of 14–25 in 1907. He led the National League in losses, games started (39), complete games (33), innings pitched (352⅓), hits (329), runs (129), earned runs (114), and walks (112). McGlynn lasted only one more season after 1907, and finished his career with a record of 17–33.

JUNE 10   The Cardinals trade Charlie Brown to the Phillies for Johnny Lush.

JUNE 13   Ed Karger pitches the Cardinals to a 1–0 victory over the Braves at League Park.

JULY 2   Three days after his major league debut, Cardinal first baseman Ed Konetchy is honored before a 4–3 loss to the Pirates in Pittsburgh.

Konetchy (pronounced CONE-uh-chee) was greeted by a delegation of Greek-Americans before the contest by a band, a large stand of flowers, and a gold watch. The group incorrectly believed that Konetchy was of Greek descent. He corrected them by saying he was Bohemian, but was allowed to keep the gifts.

JULY 8   Ed Karger pitches a shutout and hits a fifth-inning home run to defeat the Giants 2–0 in New York.

JULY 15   Fred Beebe pitches the Cardinals to a 1–0 win in the first game of a doubleheader in Boston. The Braves took the second tilt 4–2.

JULY 28   Stoney McGlynn pitches a 10-inning shutout to beat the Dodgers 1–0 at League Park. The second game was limited to seven innings by mutual agreement, with Brooklyn winning 4–2.

                 The Cardinals closed the month of July with a record of 21–75. The Cards pulled off a nine-game winning streak in early August and had a 31–26 record from August 1 through the end of the season, but it wasn't enough to extricate the club from last place.

AUGUST 4   Fred Beebe pitches a 10-inning shutout to beat the Phillies 1–0 at League Park. Pete Noonan drove in the winning run with a single.

                 It was the third time in 1907 that Noonan drove in the lone run of a 1–0 game. He drove in only 16 runs all season.

AUGUST 8   Ed Karger pitches a two-hitter to beat the Braves 3–0 at League Park. The only Boston hits were singles by Claude Ritchey and Bill Sweeney.

AUGUST 11   Ed Karger retires all 21 batters he faces in a seven-inning perfect game, defeating the Braves 4–0 in the second game of a doubleheader at League Park. The game was limited to seven innings by mutual agreement between the two clubs, in part because it was a brutally hot day in St. Louis. The Cardinals also won the first game, 5–4.

                 According to a National League rule in effect for only the 1906 and 1907 seasons, two clubs by prior mutual agreement could shorten the second game of a doubleheader to seven innings.

SEPTEMBER 1   Cubs pitcher Ed Reulbach shuts out the Cardinals through eight innings, then allows seven runs in the ninth for a 7–2 St. Louis victory in Chicago. During the big inning, the Cardinals collected eight consecutive hits.

SEPTEMBER 2   Art Fromme and Johnny Lush both pitch shutouts for the Cardinals against the Cubs in a doubleheader in Chicago. Fromme defeated the Cubs 6–0 and Lush spun a 9–0 victory. The second game was limited to seven innings by mutual consent.

SEPTEMBER 5   Trailing the Reds 5–0, the Cardinals score one run in the fifth inning, four in the seventh, and one in the eighth to win 6–5 at League Park.

SEPTEMBER 30   The Cardinals set a major league record (since tied) with three steals of home during a 5–1 win over the Braves at League Park. Ed Konetchy tied a big-league mark for an individual by accounting for two of the three steals. Joe Delahanty also stole home for the Cards.

                 In addition, the September 30 game was Joe Delahanty's major league debut. An outfielder, Joe was one of five Delahanty brothers to play in the majors. Hailing from Cleveland, they are the only family in history from which five siblings reached the big leagues. Joe was born in 1875 and played for the Cardinals from 1907 through 1909. The other Delahantys in the majors were Ed (born in 1867), Tom (1872), Jim (1879), and Frank (1883). Ed died tragically in 1903 while playing for the Senators in a mysterious fall while crossing a bridge over the Niagara River. He was swept over Niagara Falls. Ed was elected to the Hall of Fame in 1945.

OCTOBER 5   The Cardinals win a game by forfeit over the Cubs in the first game of a doubleheader at League Park. After umpire Cy Rigler called Cubs second baseman Johnny Evers out at third base in the fourth inning, he was surrounded by Cubs players emphatically questioning the decision. When the Cubs refused to give up the argument, Rigler forfeited the contest to the Cards. The second game went off without a hitch, as the Cardinals won 4–3.

OCTOBER 7   A month before Oklahoma becomes the 46th state in the Union, the Cardinals fire the first salvo in the St. Louis city championship by defeating the Browns 6–1 at Sportsman's Park.

OCTOBER 9   In Game Three of the series against the Browns, the Cardinals score two runs in the second inning and six in the ninth to win 8–5 at Sportsman's Park.

The Cardinals claimed the city championship by winning five of the seven games played against the Browns in the 1907 series. The two St. Louis clubs didn't play each other again in the postseason until 1911.

1908

Season in a Sentence

The Cardinals score the fewest runs in the NL, give up the most runs, make the most errors, and lose 105 games in an abysmal last-place finish.

Finish • Won • Lost • Pct • GB

Eighth   49   105   .318   50.0

Manager

John McCloskey

Stats

Stats	Cards	NL	Rank
Batting Avg:	.223	.239	7
On-Base Pct:	.271	.299	7
Slugging Pct:	.283	.306	7
Home Runs:	17		5 (tie)
Stolen Bases:	150		6
ERA:	2.64	2.35	7
Fielding Avg:	.946	.961	8
Runs Scored:	371		8
Runs Allowed:	626		8

Starting Lineup

Bill Ludwig, c
Ed Konetchy, 1b
Chappy Charles, 2b-ss
Bobby Byrne, 3b
Patsy O'Rourke, ss
Joe Delahanty, lf
Al Shaw, cf
Red Murray, rf-cf
Billy Gilbert, 2b
Shad Barry, rf
Art Hoelskoetter, c

Pitchers

Bugs Raymond, sp
Johnny Lush, sp
Fred Beebe, sp
Ed Karger, sp-rp
Art Fromme, sp
Irv Higginbotham, rp
Slim Sallee, rp-sp

Attendance

205,129 (eighth in NL)

Club Leaders

Batting Avg:	Murray	.282
On-Base Pct:	Murray	.332
Slugging Pct:	Murray	.400
Home Runs:	Murray	7
RBIs:	Murray	62
Runs:	Murray	64
Stolen Bases:	Murray	48
Wins:	Raymond	15
Strikeouts:	Raymond	145
ERA:	Raymond	2.03
Saves:	Raymond	2

APRIL 14 The scheduled season opener against the Pirates in St. Louis is rained out.

APRIL 15 The Cardinals open the season by losing 3–1 in 10 innings to the Pirates before 6,000 at League Park. Johnny Lush took the complete-game loss. The contest was a scoreless duel between Lush and Howie Camnitz until both clubs scored in the ninth.

APRIL 20 Bugs Raymond pitches a one-hitter, but loses 2–0 to the Cubs at League Park. Both runs scored in the sixth inning on two walks, an error, and a single by Harry Steinfeldt on a questionable scoring decision.

> *Pitching in his first full season in the majors at the age of 26, Arthur Lawrence (Bugs) Raymond had a 2.03 ERA in 1908, but posted a 15–25 record because of hard-luck losses like this one. The Cardinals were shut out 11 times when he pitched. An out-of-control drunk, his alcoholism led to numerous escapades, constant trouble, the end of a promising career in 1911, and probably to Raymond's death at the age of 30 a year later. Although his career was relatively short, Raymond earned a lasting reputation as one of the sport's more humorous characters. On one occasion, he showed a waiter how to throw a curve ball by throwing a beer glass through a plate-glass window. To deter Raymond's ardor for drink, managers tried fines and sending his paychecks directly to his wife so that he wouldn't have any money for drink. Raymond responded by trading baseballs for bottles of beer. With the Giants, John McGraw hired a detective to keep tabs on him. The surveillance ended when McGraw found Raymond and the detective in the midst of a drinking contest. In September 1912, Raymond was found dead in his room in Chicago with a cerebral hemorrhage. During the previous month, he was involved in two drunken brawls. In one he was hit repeatedly with a baseball bat in a barroom altercation, and in another was kicked in the head in a fight during an amateur baseball game.*

MAY 17 Ed Karger allows only one hit in a 1–0 victory over the Braves at League Park in a contest shortened to six innings by rain.

MAY 20 Bugs Raymond pitches the Cardinals to a 1–0 win over Joe McGinnity and the Giants at League Park.

> *National League teams averaged only 3.3 runs per game in 1908, the lowest in league history. The Cardinals finished last in the NL in runs with only 371 in 154 games, average of 2.4 per contest. As a team, the Cardinals hit .223 with an on-base percentage of .271 and a slugging percentage of just .283. The runs scored, batting average, on-base percentage, and slugging percentage are all-time club-record lows for a season.*

MAY 23 Slim Sallee pitches a shutout in his first major league start, defeating the Giants 3–0 in the second game of a doubleheader in New York. The Cards also won the first game, 6–2.

MAY 29 Bugs Raymond stings the Cubs by pitching a complete game and driving in the winning run with an eleventh-inning, walk-off single for a 4–3 victory at League Park.

JUNE 1 Irv Higginbotham pitches the Cardinals to a 1–0 win over the Reds in the second game of a doubleheader in Cincinnati. Bobby Byrne drove in the winning run with a single in the third inning. The Reds won the first game 3–2.

JUNE 10   Johnny Lush pitches a 10-inning complete game to beat the Phillies 1–0 in Philadelphia. Billy Gilbert drove in the winning run with a double.

JUNE 13   The Cardinals score three runs in the ninth to defeat the Dodgers 4–3 in Brooklyn.

JUNE 22   Bugs Raymond pitches the Cardinals to a 1–0 win over the Braves in Boston. Bill Ludwig drove in the winning run with a single in the fourth inning.

JULY 4   Bugs Raymond finishes an extra-inning complete game with a walk-off single for the second time in 1908, defeating the Reds 3–2 in 12 innings in the first game of a doubleheader at League Park. Cincinnati won the second game 6–2.

JULY 13   The Cardinals tie a National League record with three consecutive triples in the seventh inning of a 3–2 over the Dodgers in Brooklyn. The triples were hit by Ed Konetchy, Shad Barry, and Joe Delahanty.

AUGUST 6   Johnny Lush pitches a six-inning no-hitter to beat the Dodgers 2–0 in Brooklyn in a contest called by rain.

**ST. LOUIS BASE BALL CLUB OF 1908.
NATIONAL LEAGUE.**

1—Beebe   7—Wolters   13—Noonan
2—Konetchy   8—Holly   14—Hoelsketter
3—Murray   9—McGlynn   15—Gilbert
4—J. Delahanty   10—Higginbotham   16—Lush
5—Fromme   11—Karger   17—Byrne
6—Marshall   12—Barry

Transcendental Graphics/theruckerarchive.com

A 1908 composite reveals the faces of one of the most ignominious teams in Cardinal's history: Fred Beebe, Ed Konetchy, Red Murray, Joe Delahanty, Art Fromme, Doc Marshall, Harry Wolter, Ed Holly, Stoney McGlynn, Irv Higgenbotham, Ed Karger, Shad Barry, Pete Noonan, Art Hoelskoetter, Billy Gilbert, Johnny Lush, and Bobby Byrnes.

SEPTEMBER 1   Trailing 4–0, the Cardinals score one run in the eighth inning, three in the ninth, and one in the tenth to defeat the Cubs 5–4 in Chicago. The winning run scored on a triple by Red Murray and a single by Joe Delahanty.

SEPTEMBER 19   The Cardinals record 6–1 and 1–0 wins over the Dodgers in Brooklyn. Bugs Raymond pitched the shutout in the second game.

The Cardinals tied a National league record for most losses in a month by posting a 7–27 record in September 1908. Oddly, during the same month, the Dodgers were even worse, compiling a mark of 6–27.

SEPTEMBER 25   Part-owner Frank Robison dies of a stroke at the age of 54 at his palatial lakefront home near Cleveland. Control of the Cardinals passed to his brother Stanley.

DECEMBER 12   Five weeks after the election of William Howard Taft as president, the Cardinals trade Ed Karger and Art Fromme to the Reds for Admiral Schlei, then ship Schlei, Bugs Raymond, and Red Murray to the Giants for Roger Bresnahan. Bresnahan was immediately named manager, replaced John McCloskey.

> *Bresnahan was 29 years old and the best catcher in the game when he arrived in St. Louis. In 1908, he was John McGraw's top lieutenant with the Giants, and hit .283 while playing in 139 games. Bresnahan didn't come cheaply. The Cardinals gave up their best hitter (Murray) and pitcher (Raymond) to bring him to St. Louis. Bresnahan wasn't one to take losing gracefully, and battled umpires, players, and club owners while gradually building the Cardinals into a winner. Inheriting a 49–105 club, the Cards were 54–98 in 1909, 63–90 in 1910, and 75–74 in 1911. Bresnahan was rewarded with a five-year contract before the 1912 season, but was fired at the end of the season after the club sank into sixth place.*

1909

Season in a Sentence

After showing some initial promise under new manager Roger Bresnahan, the Cardinals lose 15 consecutive games in September, but finish the season with five more wins than the previous season.

Finish • Won • Lost • Pct • GB

Seventh   54   98   .355   56.0

Manager

Roger Bresnahan

Stats

Stats	Cards	NL	Rank
Batting Avg:	.243	.244	5
On-Base Pct:	.326	.310	3
Slugging Pct:	.303	.314	6
Home Runs:	15		6
Stolen Bases:	161		6
ERA:	3.41	2.59	8
Fielding Avg:	.950	.956	7
Runs Scored:	583		5
Runs Allowed:	731		8

Starting Lineup

Ed Phelps, c
Ed Konetchy, 1b
Chappy Charles, 2b
Bobby Byrne, 3b
Rudy Hulswitt, ss
Rube Ellis, lf
Jim Delahanty, cf-2b
Steve Evans, rf
Al Shaw, cf
Roger Bresnahan, c
Jap Barteau, 3b
Alan Stroke, ss

Pitchers

Fred Beebe, sp
Johnny Lush, sp
Slim Sallee, sp
Bob Harmon, sp
Les Backman, sp
John Raleigh, sp

Attendance

299,982 (seventh in NL)

Club Leaders

Batting Avg:	Konetchy	.286
On-Base Pct:	Konetchy	.366
Slugging Pct:	Konetchy	.396
Home Runs:	Konetchy	4
RBIs:	Konetchy	80
Runs:	Konetchy	88
Stolen Bases:	Konetchy	25
Wins:	Beebe	15
Strikeouts:	Beebe	105
ERA:	Sallee	2.42
Saves:	Meller	3

APRIL 14   In the first game of the season, the Cardinals lose 3–1 to the Cubs in Chicago.

On the same day, the Browns opened the 1909 season with a new grandstand at Sportsman's Park, but the club lost 4–2 to the Indians before 25,000. It was one of the first two double-decked, concrete-and-steel grandstands in baseball. The other was Shibe Park in Philadelphia, the home of the Athletics, which opened two days earlier. In 1909, only the stands behind home plate stretching from first to third base at Sportsman's Park were constructed of concrete and steel, however. The pavilions farther down the foul lines and the bleachers behind the outfield fences were made of wood, but were replaced by more formidable materials in later years. The concrete-and-steel portion was still in place when the ballpark was abandoned in favor of Busch Memorial Stadium in 1966.

APRIL 22   The Cardinals lose the home opener 7–3 to the Cubs at League Park.

The Cardinals' home at Natural Bridge and Vandeventer was also expanded in 1909, although with wood and not concrete and steel. A 60-foot addition to the grandstand was built on the third-base side and 50 feet added along the first-base line. A new bleacher section was also constructed in right field bringing the overall capacity to 20,000. The fences were also brought in, reducing the home run distance from 470 feet to 380 in left field, 520 to 400 in left-center, and 500 feet to 435 in straightaway center. Right field was also shortened from 290 to 280 by the new bleachers. Due to the reverse logic of the dead ball era, the shorter fences turned League Park from an above-average home run park to one that was below the NL average. During the period, a drive of 350 feet was noteworthy. Most home runs were inside-the-park, splitting the gaps between the outfielders and rolling to the distant fences. The new shorter fences erected in 1909 at League Park stopped many of these drives, and what had formerly been inside-the-park homers became triples or doubles.

MAY 12   Fred Beebe pitches a two-hitter to defeat the Dodgers 10–0 in Brooklyn. The only hits off Beebe were a double by Whitey Alperman and a single by John Hummel.

MAY 24   Returning to New York for the first time since leaving the Giants, Roger Bresnahan is given a silver loving cup by his admirers prior to a 6–4 Cardinals win over the Giants at the Polo Grounds. Christy Mathewson took the loss, breaking a personal 24-game winning streak over the Cardinals that dated back to May 10, 1904. That evening, a banquet was held in Bresnahan's honor in which he received a punch bowl among other gifts.

MAY 30   The Cardinals score 11 runs in the first inning and defeat the Reds 12–2 in Cincinnati.

JUNE 5   Before a game against the Giants at League Park, Roger Bresnahan is presented with a diamond ring and the rest of the team with silk umbrellas. Once the game started, the Cardinals were in a giving mood, committing six errors in an 8–7 loss.

JULY 3   The Cardinals tie a modern major league record for most errors in a doubleheader (17) and tie a National League mark for most errors in a game (11 in the second tilt), and lose 10–2 and 13–7 to the Reds at League Park.

Ed Konetchy, starting first baseman for the Cardinals from 1907 to 1913, often led the team in batting average, slugging, and RBIs. Konetchy was traded to the Pirates after a pitiful last-place finish for the Cards in 1913.

Transcendental Graphics//theruckerarchive.com

July 13   Fred Beebe pitches a two-hitter to defeat the Phillies 3–1 in Philadelphia. The only hits off Beebe were a double by Ossie Osborn and a single by Eddie Grant.

July 17   The Cardinals score seven runs in the ninth inning and defeat the Giants 7–1 in New York.

July 19   The Cardinals win 4–3 over the Giants in a 16-inning marathon in New York. Ed Konetchy led off the sixteenth with a single and scored on a two-out error. Ed Harmon of the Cardinals and ex-Cardinal Bugs Raymond of the Giants both pitched complete games. New York won the second game, called after 6½ innings by darkness, 3–0.

July 30   Chappy Charles accounts for all of the Cardinals runs with a three-run, walk-off triple to beat the Braves 3–2 at League Park.

August 6   The Cardinals collect only two hits, but defeat the Phillies 3–2 at League Park.

August 11   The Giants score 10 runs in the sixth inning and wallop the Cardinals 19–3 at League Park. In his major league debut, Cards pitcher Harry Sullivan gave up a home run to the first batter he faced. The homer was struck by opposing pitcher Doc Crandall. Late in the game, Giants manager John McGraw thrilled the St. Louis crowd by inserting ex-Cardinal Arlie Latham into the lineup at second base. Latham, who was a 49-year-old coach with the Giants, was hitless in one at-bat.

            Sullivan's career lasted only two games, in which he pitched one inning and had an ERA of 36.00.

August 14   A two-run, walk-off double by Joe Delahanty beats the Dodgers 4–3 at League Park.

August 15   At the age of 16 years and 301 days, Connie Blank becomes the youngest player in Cardinals history. He entered a 9–3 loss to the Dodgers at League Park as a substitute catcher for Jack Bliss. A native of St. Louis, Blank was hitless in two at-bats and never played another big-league game.

August 17   The Cardinals take an 8–0 lead in the fourth inning, but lose 11–8 to the Pirates in Pittsburgh. The contest was called after eight innings on account of darkness.

            This was the first time that the Cardinals played at Forbes Field, which was the home of the Pirates from June 30, 1909, through June 28, 1970.

August 18   Cardinal pitcher John Raleigh pitches a two-hitter, but loses 2–1 to the Pirates in the second game of a doubleheader at Forbes Field. Pittsburgh won the first game 6–3.

            Raleigh pitched two seasons in the majors, and had a record of 1–10.

August 19   The Cardinals trade Bobby Byrne to the Pirates for Jap Barbeau and Alan Storke.

            Storke attended Harvard Law School in the offseason. He played 48 games with the Cardinals as a shortstop. Storke died on March 18, 1910, of a lung disease at the age of 26.

AUGUST 20   The Cardinals defeat the Dodgers 3–1 in 11 innings in Brooklyn. All four runs were scored in the final inning. Fred Beebe and Nat Rucker battled through 10 scoreless innings, but neither received credit for a shutout.

AUGUST 23   The Cardinals set a modern major league record (since tied) for most times caught stealing in a game, but beat the Dodgers 9–1 in the second game of a doubleheader in Brooklyn. The Cards tried to steal six times on Dodgers catcher Bill Bergen, but were nabbed each time. Brooklyn won the first game 7–0.

AUGUST 25   Joe Delahanty hits a grand slam in the first inning off Lew Richie to help the Cardinals to a 5–0 lead, but the Braves rally to win 9–8 in Boston.

SEPTEMBER 20   Cardinals rookie pitcher Eddie Higgins takes a no-hitter into the seventh inning, but loses 2–0 to the Phillies at League Park.

SEPTEMBER 24   The Cardinals lose their 15th game in a row, with a 12–6 loss to the Dodgers at League Park.

               The 15-game losing streak is the longest in the modern era, and second all time to the 18 in a row lost by the 1897 Cardinals.

SEPTEMBER 25   The Cardinals break their 15-game losing streak with a 12–4 triumph over the Dodgers at League Park.

               The 15-game losing streak came on the back end of a 27-game stretch in which the club won only twice.

SEPTEMBER 26   Al Shaw hits a walk-off homer in the tenth inning to defeat the Dodgers 4–3 in the first game of a doubleheader at League Park. Brooklyn won the second tilt, called by darkness after six innings, 1–0.

OCTOBER 5   The Cardinals score three runs in the ninth inning to beat the Cubs 4–3 in the second game of a doubleheader at League Park. Chicago won the first game 6–1.

THE STATE OF THE CARDINALS

The Cardinals posted the worst overall record in the National League for the second consecutive decade. The Cards were 652–830 during the 1910s, a winning percentage of .440. Winning baseball games was a tough proposition in St. Louis during the 1910s. The only major league team worse than the Cardinals was the Browns, who were 597–892. The Cardinals were also the only NL team that did not finish a season in first place from 1909 through 1919. National League pennant winners during that period were the Pirates (1909), Cubs (1910), Giants (1911, 1912, 1913, and 1917), Braves (1914), Phillies (1915), Dodgers (1916), and Reds (1919).

THE BEST TEAM

The best club the Cardinals could muster was the 1914 outfit, which was 81–72 and finished the year in third place, 13 games out. It was one of three winning clubs during the decade. The others were in 1911 and 1917, but the Cardinals were never able to sustain the momentum and resumed their losing habits.

THE WORST TEAM

The worst club was in 1913, finishing with a 51–99 record in last place.

THE BEST MOMENT

The best moment took place in 1917 when Branch Rickey was hired to run the front office. Rickey turned one of the worst-run organizations in the majors into a dynasty.

THE WORST MOMENT

The Cardinals fired Roger Bresnahan following the 1912 season one year into a five-year contract. The cash-strapped Cards had to pay most of the remaining four years on the deal after Bresnahan filed a law suit against the club.

THE ALL-DECADE TEAM • YEARS W/CARDS

Frank Snyder, c	1912–19
Ed Konetchy, 1b	1907–13
Miller Huggins, 2b	1910–16
Mike Mowrey, 3b	1909–13
Rogers Hornsby, ss	1915–26, 1933
Rube Ellis, lf	1909–12
Rebel Oakes, cf	1910–13
Steve Evans, rf	1909–13
Bill Doak, p	1913–24, 1929
Slim Sallee, p	1908–16
Bob Harmon, p	1909–13
Red Ames, p	1915–19

Hornsby and Huggins are in the Hall of Fame, as is catcher Roger Bresnahan, who was the player-manager of the Cardinals from 1909 through 1912. Hornsby is considered by many to be the greatest second baseman in baseball history, but he didn't play there regularly until 1920. During the 1910s, he was primarily a shortstop with occasional forays at third base. Konetchy was among the top first basemen in baseball during the 1910s. Others who played significant roles with the club during the 1910s were first baseman–second baseman Dots Miller (1914–19), and catcher Mike Gonzalez (1915–18, 1924–25, 1931–32).

THE DECADE LEADERS

Batting Avg:	Hornsby	.310
On-Base Pct:	Huggins	.402
Slugging Pct:	Hornsby	.440
Home Runs:	Hornsby	27
RBIs:	Konetchy	316
Runs:	Huggins	507
Stolen Bases:	Huggins	174
Wins:	Sallee	93
Strikeouts:	Doak	629
ERA:	Doak	2.63
Saves:	Sallee	26

THE HOME FIELD

At the start of the decade, the Cardinals' home field was known as League Park, and was made entirely of wood. Following the deaths of team owners Frank Robison in 1908 and Stanley Robison in 1911, Frank's daughter, Helene Robison Britton, assumed control of the club. She renamed the ballpark Robison Field in 1912 in honor of her family. Britton sold the club in 1917, and the ballpark was renamed Cardinal Field that season by the new owners. By then it was an outdated, ramshackle facility that was arguably the worst ballpark in the majors. Beginning in 1909, clubs began building double-decked, concrete-and-steel ballparks. Among these were Sportsman's Park in St. Louis, used by the Browns three blocks away from the Cardinals' field. Others built between 1909 and 1914 were such gems as Fenway Park in Boston, Wrigley Field and Comiskey Park in Chicago, Tiger Stadium in Detroit, Ebbets Field in Brooklyn, the Polo Grounds in New York, Shibe Park in Philadelphia, and Forbes Field in Pittsburgh. By the end of the decade, the Cardinals' playing field was the last completely wooden ballpark in the big leagues.

THE GAME YOU WISH YOU HAD SEEN

The Cardinals pulled within one game of first place on August 27, 1914, with a 10-inning, 3–2 win over the Braves at Robison Field. It was the closest that the Cards would be to first place in August or September between 1891 and 1926.

THE WAY THE GAME WAS PLAYED

Pitching and defense continued to dominate baseball. Offense spiked in the early years of the decade after the NL adopted the cork-centered ball in 1910, but by the mid-teens, the league batting average was back around .250. Home runs were at a premium. There were more than twice as many triples as home runs and speedy outfielders were a necessity to cover playing fields that were much larger than those common today. NL pitchers completed 55 percent of their starts, but this was a significant drop from the 79 percent of the previous decade. During the 1910s, the strategic use of relief pitching, pinch hitters, and platooning became an important aspect of the game for the first time.

THE MANAGEMENT

When the decade began, Stanley Robison owned the Cardinals. Stanley jointly owned the club with his brother Frank, who died suddenly in 1908. Stanley too suffered an untimely death in March 1911 when he was 54 years old. The club passed to Helene Robison Britton, who was Frank's daughter and Stanley's niece. Britton became the first female owner of a professional sports team. She sold the club before the 1917 season to a syndicate headed by James Jones. To help run the front office, Jones hired Branch Rickey, who assumed the role of a modern-day general manager. Rickey remained with the Cardinals until 1942, and helped turn the club from perennial doormats into a club that would dominate the NL with nine pennants and six world championships from 1926 through 1946. Field managers during the 1910s were Roger Bresnahan (1909–12), Miller Huggins (1913–17), Jack Hendricks (1918), and Rickey (1919–25).

THE BEST PLAYER MOVE

The best player move was the purchase of Rogers Hornsby from a minor league club in Denison, Texas, in 1915. The best trade with a major league club brought Miller Huggins, Rebel Oakes, and Frank Corriden from the Reds in February 1910 for Fred Beebe and Alan Storke.

THE WORST PLAYER MOVE

The worst move was the demotion of Charlie Grimm to the minors in 1919, which allowed him to be snapped up by the Pirates. The worst trade took place on July 14, 1919, when the Cardinals dealt Lee Meadows to the Phillies.

1910s

1910

Season in a Sentence

The worst pitching staff in the league dooms the Cardinals to their ninth consecutive losing season, although with a modest improvement from eighth place to seventh.

Finish • Won • Lost • Pct • GB

Seventh   63   90   .412   40.5

Manager

Roger Bresnahan

Stats	Cards •	NL •	Rank
Batting Avg:	.248	.256	6
On-Base Pct:	.345	.328	2
Slugging Pct:	.319	.338	6
Home Runs:	15		8
Stolen Bases:	179		4
ERA:	3.78	3.02	8
Fielding Avg:	.959	.959	5
Runs Scored:	639		5
Runs Allowed:	718		8

Starting Lineup

Ed Phelps, c
Ed Konetchy, 1b
Miller Huggins, 2b
Mike Mowrey, 3b
Arnold Hauser, ss
Rube Ellis, lf
Rebel Oakes, cf
Steve Evans, rf
Roger Bresnahan, c

Pitchers

Johnny Lush, sp-rp
Bob Harmon, sp
Vic Willis, sp-rp
Frank Corridon, sp-rp
Slim Sallee, sp
Les Backman, rp-sp

Attendance

335,668 (fifth in NL)

Club Leaders

Batting Avg:	Konetchy	.302
On-Base Pct:	Huggins	.399
Slugging Pct:	Konetchy	.425
Home Runs:	Ellis	4
RBIs:	Konetchy	78
Runs:	Huggins	101
Stolen Bases:	Huggins	34
Wins:	Lush	14
Strikeouts:	Harmon	87
ERA:	Lush	3.20
Saves:	Willis	3
	Corridon	3

FEBRUARY 3   The Cardinals trade Fred Beebe and Alan Storke to the Reds for Miller Huggins, Rebel Oakes, and Frank Corridon.

This was an enormously successful trade for the Cardinals. A future Hall of Famer who was only five-foot-six and weighed 140 pounds, Huggins was the Cards' starting second baseman and leadoff hitter for six seasons, and their manager from 1913 through 1917. Oakes started in center field for the club for four years.

APRIL 14   The Cardinals lose the season opener 5–1 to the Pirates at League Park.

APRIL 20   The Cardinals' eighth-inning rally against the Cubs at League Park is halted by umpire Hank O'Day to allow both teams to catch a train. By prior agreement, the game was to end at precisely 5 PM. When the appointed hour arrived, the Cardinals were trailing 4–3 and had the bases loaded and one out.

MAY 4   President William Howard Taft visits both St. Louis ballparks. Taft started the day by watching two innings of the Cardinals 12–3 win over the Reds at League Park. The portly president, who weighed over 300 pounds, was provided with a comfortable armchair to watch the game. In order to avoid showing favoritism, Taft walked the three blocks to Sportsman's Park to watch part of the Browns-Indians game, which ended in a 3–3 tie when it was called by darkness after 14 innings. By leaving early, Taft missed one of the strangest games in Cardinals history. The Cards scored their 12 runs on only four hits as three Cincinnati pitchers combined to walk 16 hitters. St. Louis plated seven runs in the third inning without a base hit.

MAY 13   The Cardinals score eight runs in the second inning off Christy Mathewson and move on to defeat the Giants 13–4 at League Park.

MAY 19   The Cardinals win their eighth game in a row by defeating the Phillies 9–1 at League Park. The victory gave the Cards a 14–13 record on the season.

MAY 21   The Cardinals score two runs in the ninth inning and one in the tenth to defeat the Dodgers 4–3 at League Park. The winning run scored on a double by Rebel Oakes and a single by Steve Evans.

MAY 23   The Cardinals score five runs in the eighth inning to defeat the Braves 5–0 at League Park.

JUNE 1   The Cardinals score six runs in the ninth inning to beat the Phillies 10–5 in Philadelphia. Miller Huggins had six plate appearances without an official at-bat. He walked four times and had a sacrifice fly and a sacrifice hit.

            In his first season with the Cardinals, Huggins was first in the National League in walks with 116 and second in runs with 101. He batted .265. Other offensive leaders for the Cards in 1910 were Ed Konetchy and Mike Mowrey. Konetchy hit .302 and Mowrey batted .282. Konetchy also had a 20-game hitting streak.

JUNE 30   After the Cubs score five runs in the top of the first inning, the Cardinals bounce back with nine runs in their half. The nine runs scored on only three hits. The Cards won the contest at League Park 13–9.

JULY 14   The Dodgers score three runs in the ninth inning to defeat the Cardinals 3–1 during a contentious afternoon at League Park. During the game, umpire Bill Klem ejected Brooklyn manager Bill Dahlen and two of his players. After the contest, a spectator criticized Roger Bresnahan and his team for blowing the game. Bresnahan and third baseman Mike Mowrey started after the fan, Mowrey armed with a couple of baseball bats, but they were prevented from doing any harm by a police officer.

JULY 27   Trailing 5–0, the Cardinals score eight runs in the sixth inning off Three Finger Brown and beat the Cubs 8–6 at League Park. All eight runs scored with two outs.

JULY 31   King Cole of the Cubs pitches an abbreviated no-hitter in the second game of a doubleheader against the Cardinals at League Park. The game was called with one out in the bottom of the seventh inning with the Cubs leading 4–0 to allow both teams to catch a train. Chicago also won the first game, 9–3.

AUGUST 3   Disgusted after using three ineffective pitchers, Roger Bresnahan discards his mask and chest protector to take the mound himself in the fifth inning of a 5–3 loss to the Dodgers in Brooklyn. Bresnahan allowed an unearned run and six hits in $3^2/_3$ innings. It was his first pitching appearance since 1901. He never pitched again in the majors.

AUGUST 12	The Cardinals break a 14-game losing streak by defeating the Phillies 11–2 in Philadelphia.
AUGUST 30	The Cardinals clobber the Dodgers 14–3 at League Park.
SEPTEMBER 10	The Cardinals trounce the Reds 14–7 in Cincinnati.
SEPTEMBER 23	The Cardinals collect only two hits, but defeat the Dodgers 6–2 in a game in Brooklyn called after seven innings by darkness. Dodgers pitcher Sandy Burk walked 11 batters.
OCTOBER 10	In the final game of the season, the Cardinals rout the Cubs 15–7 in Chicago.

1911

Season in a Sentence

Under the first female owner in professional sports, the Cardinals are in pennant contention in July and finish with their first winning season since 1901.

Finish • Won • Lost • Pct • GB

Fifth   75   74   .503   22.0

Manager

Roger Bresnahan

Stats

Stats	Cards	NL	Rank
Batting Avg:	.252	.260	7
On-Base Pct:	.337	.335	6
Slugging Pct:	.340	.356	7
Home Runs:	26		7
Stolen Bases:	175		5
ERA:	3.68	3.39	7
Fielding Avg:	.960	.958	5
Runs Scored:	671		6
Runs Allowed:	745		7

Starting Lineup

Jack Bliss, c
Ed Konetchy, 1b
Miller Huggins, 2b
Mike Mowrey, 3b
Arnold Hauser, ss
Rube Ellis, lf
Rebel Oakes, cf
Steve Evans, rf
Roger Bresnahan, c
Wally Smith, 3b-ss

Pitchers

Bob Harmon, sp
Bill Steele, sp
Slim Sallee, sp
Roy Golden, sp
Rube Geyer, rp

Attendance

447,768 (third in NL)

Club Leaders

Batting Avg:	Evans	.294
On-Base Pct:	Huggins	.385
Slugging Pct:	Konetchy	.433
Home Runs:	Konetchy	6
RBIs:	Konetchy	88
Runs:	Huggins	106
Stolen Bases:	Huggins	37
Wins:	Harmon	23
Strikeouts:	Harmon	144
ERA:	Sallee	2.76
Saves:	Harmon	4

MARCH 24	Cardinals owner Stanley Robison dies suddenly at the age of 54 of heart failure.

Robison owned nearly all of the stock in the Cardinals. He bought the club in 1899 with his older brother Frank. Stanley assumed control of the Cards in September 1908 when Frank also died suddenly when he was only 54. Stanley never married. His three heirs, a sister, sister-in-law (Frank's widow), and niece (Frank's daughter), were all women. The niece was Helene Robison Britton. Fellow National League owners did not want a woman running the

Cardinals. After all, this was 1911, and women did not even have the right to vote, a privilege that wasn't granted until the passage of the 19th Amendment in 1920. Britton was also only 32 years old with no prior experience running a business. At the funeral, the NL owners, some of whom were pallbearers, gently tried to persuade the grieving family to put the club up for sale. The family ignored the pleas, and four days after Stanley's death, it was announced that Britton would assume control of the Cardinals. She would become the first woman to own a professional team in any sport. A militant, early advocate of woman's rights, Britton took an active role in running the club. Known as "Lady Bee," she had been raised around baseball

Helene Robison Britton, the first female owner of a baseball team, inherited the Cardinals from her uncle in 1911. She owned the team for six years before selling it in 1917.

with a father and uncle owning two big-league clubs in Cleveland and St. Louis, and attended and participated in every league meeting, much to the discomfort of a group of her fellow owners. A native of Cleveland, she and her husband, Schuyler, a printing executive, moved to St. Louis and resided in a mansion in the 4200 block of Lindell Boulevard. Mrs. Britton lacked the financial resources to compete with other teams in the league, however, and the Cardinals desperately needed either a new ballpark or a massive rebuilding of League Park, which she renamed Robison Field in honor of her family in 1912. By 1917, Britton had grown weary of running a baseball club, and sold the Cardinals.

APRIL 7   The Cardinals' Board of Directors elects Edward A. Steininger as club president.

Helene Britton didn't assume active control of the club immediately. Steininger, who was the administrator of Stanley Robison's estate, was appointed president to run the day-to-day operations of the front office. He was a building contractor whose firm built the Moolah Temple and the Shriners Hospital for Crippled Children in St. Louis. Steininger and Britton disagreed over the direction of the Cardinals almost immediately, and the battle for control became ugly. Britton took Steininger to court claiming that he overstepped his authority as the administrator of the estate, and a judge agreed in May 1912. As a result of the decision, Steininger was forced to relinquish his office as club president. James Jones, Britton's legal adviser, succeeded Steininger briefly as president. Jones would later own the Cardinals from 1917 through 1920. Britton's husband, Schuyler, became club president in February 1913, but the couple divorced in November 1916, and Helene took over full control of the club. Like most pioneering women, Britton had to undergo a great deal of chauvinism,

Transcendental Graphics/theruckerarchive.com

particularly in a male-dominated profession like baseball, and struggled to gain the respect of her fellow owners, her managers, players, and the sportswriters who covered the club.

APRIL 12

The Cardinals open the 1911 season in Chicago, and play to a 3–3 tie against the Cubs in a contest called after 11 innings on account of darkness. The Cards held a 3–0 lead in the first inning, but couldn't score again. Slim Sallee pitched a complete game for St. Louis.

APRIL 17

After a 10-inning game against the Reds in Cincinnati is called by darkness with the score 1–1, Reds outfielder Bob Bescher punches Roger Bresnahan in the mouth, loosening several teeth. The two were separated before Bresnahan could retaliate or Bescher could inflict further damage.

Three of the Cardinals' first six games in 1911 ended in ties. In the third game of the season, played on April 15 in Chicago, the Cubs and Cards played to a 3–3 tie, in a contest called after 10 innings by darkness. Overall, the Cardinals played nine ties in 1911, a National League record.

APRIL 20

In the home opener, the Cardinals lose 9–5 to the Cubs at League Park.

The Cardinals started the season with a 3–11 record, and it looked like another losing season was in the offing. But the club won 47 of it's next 72 games. On July 24, the Cards had a record of 50–36 and were just 3½ games from the top of the National League. It was the first time that St. Louis was involved in a National League pennant race that late in the year since joining the circuit in 1892. The Cardinals were 25–38 over the rest of the season, however, although the final regular-season record of 75–74 was the first winning season for the club since 1901. Roger Bresnahan's crew posted a winning record in spite of being outscored 745–671. The success of the club helped boost attendance over the 400,000 mark for the first time. The Cardinals drew 447,768, a figure that wouldn't be reached again until 1922.

MAY 13

The Giants score 13 runs in the first inning off Slim Sallee, Bob Harmon, and Grover Lowdermilk and cruise to a 19–5 win over the Cardinals in New York.

Sallee drew his nickname from his six-foot-three, 180-pound frame. In nine seasons with the Cardinals from 1908 through 1916, he had a record of 106–107, but his losing record was the result of pitching for some awful teams in St. Louis. He also had problems with alcohol abuse along with little regard for training and practice. Sallee was suspended several times during his nine years with the Cardinals for insubordination and drinking binges in which he would disappear for days. Sallee's ERAs were well below the NL average for the period. His earned run average of 2.67 with the Cards ranks first among all pitchers in franchise history among those with at least 1,000 innings. In addition to serving as a mainstay in the Cardinals rotation, he was also called upon to come into games out of the bullpen in crucial situations. He led the NL in saves three times, twice with the Cardinals. Sallee finished his career with a record of 173–143, and might have merited Hall of Fame consideration if he had pitched for one of the top teams of the 1910s, instead of one of the worst. Sallee demonstrated what he could do with a good team behind him by posting a record of 18–7 with the Giants in 1917 and 21–7 with the Reds in 1919, both NL pennant-winners.

*Grover Cleveland Lowdermilk, who was born two months after Grover
Cleveland won the 1884 presidential election, was another pitcher nicknamed
"Slim" because he was six-foot-four, weighed 190 pounds, and appeared to be
all arms and legs. He pitched for the Cardinals in 1909 and 1911. His younger
brother Lou also pitched for the Cards in 1911 and 1912.*

MAY 23   The Cardinals score eight runs in the fourth inning and beat the Phillies 12–4 in
          Philadelphia.

MAY 31   Down 8–0, the Cardinals stage an astonishing rally with two runs in the sixth inning,
          ten in the seventh, and three in the eighth to beat the Reds 15–8 in the second game
          of a doubleheader at League Park. The Cards also won the first game, 4–2.

JUNE 1   The Cardinals put together another incredible rally by scoring six runs in the ninth
          inning to defeat the Reds 6–5 in the first game of a doubleheader at League Park.
          The six runs were scored on a triple by Steve Evans, five singles, and two walks. The
          winning run scored on a single by Rube Ellis. Cincinnati won the second game 6–4.

          *Because of the need to make up two April postponements and a tie game,
          plus a scheduled Memorial Day twin bill, the Cardinals and the Reds played
          doubleheaders four days in a row from May 29 through June 1.*

JUNE 10   The Cardinals score three runs in the ninth inning to defeat the Phillies 9–8 at
          League Park.

JUNE 11   Fans in the left-field stands at League Park throw bottles at umpire Bill Brennan
          during the eighth inning of a 6–5 win over the Phillies. The crowd was angry because
          Brennan called Cardinal catcher Jack Bliss out at third base. The contest was stopped
          until police cleared the field of glass.

JUNE 17   The Cardinals collect only two hits off Christy Mathewson, but win 2–1 over the
          Giants at League Park.

JUNE 23   Umpire Bill Klem punches Roger Bresnahan after an 8–7 loss to the Reds in
          Cincinnati. Bresnahan made a remark about Klem's decision-making as the teams
          left the field. Klem responded with a right hook to Bresnahan's jaw. The Cardinal
          manager made no attempt to retaliate.

JUNE 30   For the second time in 1911, a bombardment of bottles is directed at an umpire
          during a game at League Park. Jim Johnstone was the object of the barrage after he
          called Honus Wagner of the Pirates safe at third base. Two fans were arrested. The
          Cardinals beat Pittsburgh 5–3.

JULY 6   The Cardinals outslug the Phillies 13–9 in Philadelphia. Rube Ellis collected a homer,
          two triples, and a single.

JULY 11   The Cardinals survive a deadly train wreck at 3:35 AM on the New York, New
          Haven & Hartford Railroad. Running from Washington to Boston, the train
          crashed into a viaduct and plunged down an 18-foot embankment 1½ miles west of
          Bridgeport, Connecticut, killing 14 people and leaving 47 others injured. The cause
          of the accident was attributed to the engineer, who tried to negotiate a switch at a

high speed. After realizing that none of their teammates was injured seriously, the Cardinal players labored in the midst of the wreckage until the last body had been pulled out 15 hours later. Ironically, the Pullman sleeping car of the St. Louis team was repositioned from near the front of the nine-car train to a spot near the rear shortly before the wreck because Bresnahan complained that his players couldn't sleep as a result of the engine noise after the club boarded the train in Philadelphia. The day coach, which took the place of the Pullman car in which the Cardinals were riding, was so badly crushed and splintered that it was unrecognizable. Most of those who died in the accident were sitting in the day coach. Many of the Redbird players later credited Bresnahan's complaint with saving their lives. The railroad paid the players $25 apiece for their efforts and lost possessions.

JULY 12   After arriving safely in Boston, the Cardinals win 13–6 in the first game of a doubleheader against the Braves. The second game ended in a 6–6 tie, called after 10 innings by darkness.

JULY 19   The Cardinals score seven runs in the fifth inning of an 8–5 win in the second game of a doubleheader against the Dodgers in Brooklyn. The Cards also won the first game, 4–2.

SEPTEMBER 9   Cardinals rookie pitcher Gene Woodburn pitches a one-hitter to defeat the Pirates 7–2 in the second game of a doubleheader at League Park. Woodburn carried a no-hitter into the ninth inning before allowing a single to Vin Campbell. Pittsburgh won the first game 4–1.

This was a rare moment of success for Gene Woodburn. He lasted only two years in the majors and had a record of 2–9 and an ERA of 5.50.

SEPTEMBER 19   A sensational four-run rally in the ninth inning beats the Braves 13–12 at League Park in the first game of a scheduled doubleheader. The Cards trailed 8–2 before scoring three runs in the sixth inning and four in the seventh to take a 9–8 lead. The Braves wiped out the advantage by plating four in the eighth to pull ahead 12–9. St. Louis collected 21 hits in the contest. The second game was canceled to allow the Braves to catch a train for Pittsburgh.

SEPTEMBER 23   President William Howard Taft watches the Cardinals beat the Phillies 3–2 in St. Louis. The League Park grandstand was decorated for the occasion. Taft stayed to the finish and saw the Cards score a run in the ninth for the victory.

The Cardinals' top hitters in 1911 were Ed Konetchy and Miller Huggins. Konetchy hit .289 and led the NL in doubles with 38. Huggins batted .261, drew 98 walks, and scored 106 runs.

OCTOBER 8   Bob Harmon wins his 23rd game of the season by hurling a two-hitter to defeat the Reds 5–0 in Cincinnati. The only hits off Harmon were singles by Tommy Clarke in the second inning and Armando Marsans in the ninth.

Harmon had a record of 23–16 and an ERA of 3.13 in 1911. He led the NL in games started with 41 and also appeared as a reliever in 10 other contests. Harmon was on the mound at the end of 35 games—28 as a starter and 7 in relief—and pitched 348 innings. He was only 23 and looked like a promising star, but the extreme workload hindered his progress. Harmon never had another *winning season, and finished his career with a record of 107–133. Bill Steele was another young pitcher who pitched far too many innings in 1911. A 26-year-old, Steele was 18–19 while appearing in 287^1/$_3$ innings. He lasted only three more years in the majors with a record of 15–20 and a 4.45 ERA.*

OCTOBER 11   The Cardinals and Browns play to a 0–0 tie at Sportsman's Park in the first game of the St. Louis city championship series. The pitchers were Lou Lowdermilk of the Cardinals and Earl Hamilton of the Browns. The game was called at the end of nine innings by darkness.

This was the first time that the Cardinals and Browns met in the postseason since 1907. The two clubs played seven games in 1911, with the Browns winning five and the Cardinals one after a first-game tie.

1912

Season in a Sentence

After a winning season in 1911, optimism is rampant heading into 1912, but the club loses 16 of the first 21 games and Roger Bresnahan is fired only one year into a five-year contract.

Finish • Won • Lost • Pct • GB

Sixth   63   90   .412   41.0

Manager

Roger Bresnahan

Stats

Stats	Cards	NL	Rank
Batting Avg:	.268	.272	5
On-Base Pct:	.340	.340	4
Slugging Pct:	.352	.369	7
Home Runs:	27		7
Stolen Bases:	193		3
ERA:	3.85	3.40	7
Fielding Avg:	.957	.960	6
Runs Scored:	659		6
Runs Allowed:	830		7

Starting Lineup

Ivy Wingo, c
Ed Konetchy, 1b
Miller Huggins, 2b
Mike Mowrey, 3b
Arnold Hauser, ss
Lee Magee, lf
Rebel Oakes, cf
Steve Evans, rf
Rube Ellis, lf
Wally Smith, 3b-ss

Pitchers

Bob Harmon, sp
Slim Sallee, sp-rp
Bill Steele, sp
Joe Willis, sp-rp
Rube Geyer, rp-sp

Attendance

241,759 (seventh in NL)

Club Leaders

Batting Avg:	Konetchy	.314
On-Base Pct:	Huggins	.422
Slugging Pct:	Konetchy	.415
Home Runs:	Konetchy	8
RBIs:	Konetchy	82
Runs:	Huggins	82
Stolen Bases:	Huggins	35
Wins:	Harmon	18
Strikeouts:	Sallee	108
ERA:	Sallee	2.60
Saves:	Sallee	6

APRIL 11   Two months after New Mexico is granted statehood and six weeks after Arizona becomes the 48th state in the Union, the Cardinals defeat the Pirates 7–0 in the season opener before a crowd of 15,000 in St. Louis. Bob Harmon pitched a four-hit shutout and Steve Evans hit a home run. It was the only homer by a Cardinal player on Opening Day between 1901 and 1922.

The Cardinals' ballpark had a new name in 1912. Known as League Park from 1899 through 1911, the field at Natural Bridge and Vandeventer was christened Robison Field by Helene Britton. She changed the name of the facility to honor her father, Frank Robison, and her uncle Stanley.

APRIL 16   Two days after the sinking of the *Titanic*, the Cardinals trounce the Cubs 20–5 in a game called after 7½ innings by darkness at Robison Field. The Cards scored 10 runs in the fourth inning and tied a major league record for most players scoring two or more runs in a game with nine. Steve Evans clubbed a grand slam.

The Cardinals opened the season with three straight wins, but quickly went into a slide. By May 9, the Cards were in last place with a record of 5–16.

APRIL 21   The Cardinals play their first game at Redland Field in Cincinnati, which opened nine days earlier. The Cards lost 7–1 to the Reds.

Renamed Crosley Field in 1934, the ballpark served as the home of the Reds until 1970.

MAY 15   The Cardinals score seven runs in the second inning and defeat the Dodgers 10–1 at Robison Field.

MAY 23   The Cardinals score four runs in the seventh inning, the last two on a homer by Ivy Wingo, to defeat the Reds 11–10 at Robison Field.

JUNE 4   Trailing 11–1, the Cardinals make things interesting with eight runs in the seventh inning, but lose 14–9 to the Giants in New York.

JUNE 5   Following an 8–5 win over the Phillies in Philadelphia, Cardinal infielder Arnold Hauser is informed that his mother committed suicide in Chicago.

A year later, Hauser and his wife suffered the death of an infant son, and he sat out most of the year due to a knee injury that required surgery. A despondent Hauser missed the entire 1914 season when he was confined to a mental hospital.

JUNE 25   Cardinals pitchers are knocked all over the lot in a 10–4 and 19–3 doubleheader loss to the Pirates at Robison Field. Pittsburgh scored 10 runs in the seventh inning of the second game.

JULY 6   Miller Huggins scores five runs in a 12–7 win over the Cubs at Robison Field.

Huggins batted .304 for the Cardinals in 1912.

JULY 9   The Cardinals score two runs in the ninth inning and one in the eleventh to defeat the Braves 8–7 in the second game of a doubleheader at Robison Field. The winning run scored on a double by Roger Bresnahan and a pinch-single by Jack Bliss. The Cards also won the first game, 3–0.

JULY 24   The Cardinals score three runs in the ninth inning to beat the Phillies 5–4 at Robison Field.

AUGUST 1   Roger Bresnahan causes a balk that leads to a 4–3 loss to the Phillies in Philadelphia. With the bases loaded with Phillies and the Cardinals leading 3–2 in the fifth inning,

Bresnahan gave a yell and ran toward home plate. Pitching to Sherry Magee, Slim Sallee had already started his motion but stopped when he heard his manager. Umpire Al Orth called a balk, which scored the tying run. The Phils added another run before the inning was over, and it held up for the win.

AUGUST 5   Ed Konetchy hits two inside-the-park homers during an 8–4 win over the Dodgers in Brooklyn.

Konetchy batted .314 with eight homers in 1912.

AUGUST 12   The Cardinals are accused by Cubs owner Charles Murphy of failing to use their best efforts against the Giants to help the New York club win the pennant because of Roger Bresnahan's friendship with Giants skipper John McGraw.

Later, Phillies owner Horace Fogel, who was seen as a front for Murphy, echoed the accusation against Bresnahan, and in a letter to Murphy, accused NL umpires of fixing the pennant race of favor of the Giants. The Cubs owner turned the letter over to the Chicago Post for publication. At a league meeting on November 27, Fogel was drummed out of baseball. Bresnahan was acquitted of all charges. There is no evidence that the Cardinals played any worse against the Giants than they did against the Cubs. During his four seasons as manager in St. Louis, the Cardinals were 27–61 playing the Cubs and 29–58 facing the Giants. No charges were made against Murphy, who in a strange twist, signed Bresnahan to a contract to play for the Cubs for the 1913 season after the Cards fired him (see October 22, 1912).

AUGUST 25   The Cardinals score nine runs in the fourth and wallop the Dodgers 11–4 at Robison Field.

AUGUST 31   With the score 1–1 in the third inning against the Cubs in Chicago, umpire Bill Brennan orders the Cardinals players to stop ridiculing his decisions. When they failed to comply, Brennan ejected all of the players who were not participating in the game. The 10 extra players were forced to march to the clubhouse, located in center field, in front of a jeering crowd. Despite the handicap, the Cards won the game 5–1.

OCTOBER 9   In the opener of the St. Louis city championship series against the Browns, the Cardinals win 7–6 at Sportsman's Park.

The Cardinals won the series four games to three with one contest ending in a tie.

OCTOBER 22   Two weeks before Woodrow Wilson's election as president, the Cardinals fire Roger Bresnahan as manager and replace him with Miller Huggins.

Bresnahan took over the Cardinals after a 49–105 season in 1908 and turned the club into a winner by 1911 when the Cards were 75–74. He was rewarded by Helene Britton with a five-year contract calling for $10,000 a year plus 10 percent of the profits. Things turned sour almost immediately after the 1912 season began, however, when the Cardinals lost 16 of their first 21 games. Britton offered Bresnahan a few suggestions on how to improve the club, and in a vulgar and profanity-filled response, the Cards skipper said that no woman was going to tell him what to do. The two argued all season. Bresnahan also wanted to purchase the Cardinals, and Britton refused to listen to any offer to sell. *In August, Bresnahan tried to trade Huggins, who was Britton's favorite player, to the Reds. She blocked the deal. Cardinals president James Jones said that the players had been complaining that Bresnahan had been "riding them" too hard and accused him of having an "insane desire" to trade Huggins. Bresnahan had the support of the majority of the fans, however, and many of the players, minority stockholders, and reporters who covered the club. His firing was not a popular move in St. Louis. In January 1913, the Cubs signed Bresnahan as a catcher. He managed the Chicago club in 1915. Meanwhile, Bresnahan took the Cardinals to court when the club refused to pay the final four years of his five-year deal. He received $20,000 in a settlement.*

Huggins was a native of Cincinnati and received a degree from the University of Cincinnati Law School before entering professional baseball. He had been a player in the majors since 1904 and with the Cardinals since 1910. He was 33 when hired as the club's manager. Standing only five-foot-six and weighing only 140 pounds, Huggins became a star player with his defense at second base and a pesky lead off hitter by drawing walks. He led the NL in bases on balls four times and was in the top five nine seasons from 1904 through 1915. Huggins also ranked among the top five in on-base percentage five years and in runs four times. He lasted five seasons as manager of the Cardinals, but had only a 346–415 record with the financially strapped club.

1913

Season in a Sentence

Though Miller Huggins would eventually reach the Hall of Fame because of his abilities as a manager, those qualities aren't evident in his first season as the Cardinals skid into last place.

Finish • Won • Lost • Pct • GB

Eighth   51   99   .340   49.0

Manager

Miller Huggins

Stats

Stats	Cards	NL	Rank
Batting Avg:	.247	.262	8
On-Base Pct:	.316	.325	8
Slugging Pct:	.316	.354	8
Home Runs:	15		8
Stolen Bases:	171		8
ERA:	4.23	3.20	8
Fielding Avg:	.965	.962	2
Runs Scored:	528		8
Runs Allowed:	755		8

Starting Lineup

Ivy Wingo, c
Ed Konetchy, 1b
Miller Huggins, 2b
Mike Mowrey, 3b
Charley O'Leary, ss
Lee Magee, lf
Rebel Oakes, cf
Steve Evans, rf
Possum Whitted, cf-rf-ss-3b
Ted Cather, rf
Larry McLean, c
Jimmy Sheckard, lf-rf

Pitchers

Slim Sallee, sp-rp
Dan Griner, sp
Bob Harmon, sp-rp
Pol Perritt, sp-rp
Bill Doak, sp
Rube Geyer, rp

Attendance

203,531 (eighth in NL)

Club Leaders

Batting Avg:	Oakes	.293
On-Base Pct:	Huggins	.432
Slugging Pct:	Konetchy	.427
Home Runs:	Konetchy	8
RBIs:	Konetchy	68
Runs:	Konetchy	75
Stolen Bases:	Konetchy	27
Wins:	Sallee	19
Strikeouts:	Sallee	106
ERA:	Sallee	2.71
Saves:	Sallee	5

JANUARY 24   The Cardinals sign Larry McLean to a contract.

A catcher and a native of Fredericton, New Brunswick, McLean previously played 37 games for the Cardinals in 1904. He was well-traveled during his career, which lasted from 1901 through 1915, because of his notorious problems with alcohol. Larry was six-foot-five and weighed 225 pounds in an era when a ballplayer over six feet was in a distinct minority. He was a likable man of gentle disposition when sober, but turned violent during his drinking binges. The Reds gave up trying to reform him, and granted McLean his release. Miller Huggins played with McLean in Cincinnati, and recommended that the Cardinals sign him. McLean's second tour of duty in St. Louis was brief. He reported to spring training with a broken arm suffered in a brawl in a poolroom. The Cardinals dealt him to the Giants in August 1913. His career ended in 1915 in the wake of a drunken encounter with John McGraw in which McLean challenged the Giants' manager to a fight in a St. Louis hotel lobby. Prohibition failed to subdue McLean's ardor for alcohol. He died in 1921 at the age of 39 when shot to death by a bartender in a Boston speak-easy.

MARCH 29   The Cardinals lose most of their equipment in a flood in Indianapolis. The uniforms, bats, gloves, and shoes were destroyed. The gear was located at Washington Park in Indianapolis, where the Cards were scheduled to play exhibition games for a week. None of the games was played because of rain and the subsequent floods that put the ballpark under 10 feet of water. Moreover, the Cards were marooned in Indianapolis and were unable to even engage in a practice session because all of the highways and railroads out of the city were inundated in massive flooding, which caused the deaths of 467 people and left 200,000 homeless in Indiana and Ohio.

APRIL 8   The Cardinals purchase Jimmy Sheckard from the Cubs.

APRIL 10   The season opener against the Cubs in Chicago is postponed by rain. The April 11 contest was also called off.

APRIL 12   The Cardinals finally open the 1913 season and defeat the Cubs 5–3 in Chicago. Dan Griner pitched the complete-game victory.

APRIL 17   In the home opener, the Cardinals lose 7–1 to the Cubs at Robison Field. Roger Bresnahan, who was the manager of the Cardinals from 1909 through 1912, was the starting catcher in the game for the Cubs. Before the contest, St. Louis mayor Henry Kiel presented Bresnahan with a diamond watchfob.

Helene Britton instituted a few changes at Robison Field in 1913. She arranged for flowers to be passed out to women as they entered the park, scorecards were complimentary to all fans, and a male singer crooned through a megaphone between innings. Britton promised that the Cardinals would have a new ballpark by the start of the 1914 season, but she never obtained the financing necessary to build the facility.

APRIL 20   Lee Magee hits a grand slam in the third inning off Marty O'Toole that gives the Cardinals a 4–0 lead, but the Pirates rally to win 5–4 at Robison Field.

Born Leopold Hoernschemeyer, Lee Magee played for the Cardinals from 1911 through 1914. His turbulent career ended with a lifetime ban from baseball when a jury found him guilty of having bet against his own team while playing for the Reds in 1918.

APRIL 22   Rookie Cardinal pitcher Pol Perritt throws a two-hitter, but loses 1–0 to the Pirates at Robison Field. Perritt's error in the seventh inning in between singles by Chief Wilson and Alex McCarthy scored the lone run of the game.

APRIL 23   A day after losing despite allowing only two hits, the Cardinals collect just two safeties and hit into a triple play, but defeat the Pirates 3–1 at Robison Field.

APRIL 26   After the Reds score two runs in the top of the tenth inning, the Cardinals roar back with three in their half to win 6–5 at Robison Field. A two-run single by Jimmy Sheckard ended the game.

> *In their first year under Miller Huggins, the Cardinals won 11 of their first 19 games, but were 51–99 and in last place by season's end, a worse record than any of the four years under Roger Bresnahan. There were rumors flying all season that Huggins's dismissal was imminent.*

MAY 4   Miller Huggins uses outfielder Ted Cather and first baseman Ed Konetchy as pitchers in a 13-inning, 10–8 win over the Cubs in Chicago. After Cather pitched one-third of an inning and gave up two runs, Konetchy went 4²/₃ innings, allowed no runs and only one hit while striking out three, and was the winning pitcher. The Cardinals trailed 6–2 before scoring six runs in the ninth inning, but allowed two runs in the bottom of the inning to knot the contest at 8–8 when Konetchy was called in with one out. A triple by Possum Whitted drove in both thirteenth-inning runs.

> *Huggins turned to Cather and Konetchy because he took only three pitchers to Chicago. The Cardinals played in Pittsburgh on Saturday, May 3, in Chicago on May 4 and, after an off day on May 5, began an East Coast road trip in Philadelphia on May 6. The usual scheduling was set up because Sunday baseball was illegal in Pennsylvania, and the Cards traveled to Chicago rather than sit idle on a day of the week that usually drew the largest crowds. Huggins didn't believe he needed more than three pitchers in the May 4 contest in Chicago, so he sent the rest of the staff on to Philadelphia to save on train fare. Cather had been a pitcher in the minors, and Konetchy pitched in an indoor baseball league in St. Louis during the off-season.*

MAY 15   The Cardinals play at Ebbets Field in Brooklyn for the first time, and lose 8–6.

> *Ebbets Field was the home of the Dodgers from 1913 through 1957.*

MAY 16   Shortstop Al Cabrera becomes the first Latin player in Cardinals history by playing shortstop in a 6–5 loss to the Dodgers in Brooklyn.

> *Cabrera was hitless in two at-bats in what proved to be the only game of his major league career. He was born in the Canary Islands of Spain and grew up in Cuba.*

MAY 20   Bob Harmon pitches a two-hitter to defeat the Giants 8–0 at the Polo Grounds. The only two New York hits were singles by Red Murray in the second inning and George Burns with two outs in the ninth.

JUNE 10 — The Cardinals win a thrilling 11-inning, 8–7 game against the Braves at Robison Field. Down 5–0 in the sixth, the Cards pecked away at the Boston lead and sent the contest into extra innings with the score 6–6. After the Braves scored in the top of the eleventh, St. Louis came back with two runs to win the game. Ed Konetchy contributed a home run, a triple, and two singles.

The Cardinals had only 15 homers all season in 1913. Konetchy hit eight of them.

JUNE 24 — Dan Griner allows 11 hits and walks a batter, but beats the Cubs 1–0 at Robison Field. Miller Huggins drove in the lone run of the game with a single. Oddly, it was the second game of a doubleheader following a first game that was rained out. The Cardinals and Cubs played two innings of the opener, but it was called by rain. After the sun came out, the two clubs decided to play the second game.

Huggins had a batting average of .285, a league-leading on-base percentage of .432, and a slugging percentage of .317 in 1913. He drew 92 walks with only 12 extra-base hits, all doubles.

JUNE 25 — The Cardinals score a run in the ninth to send the game into extra innings, but the Pirates explode for eight runs in the tenth inning and beat the Cards 9–1 at Robison Field.

JULY 4 — The Cardinals defeat the Pirates 12–8 in the afternoon game of a split admission doubleheader in Pittsburgh. A sandstorm interrupted play for 20 minutes in the seventh inning. In the ninth, Bobby Byrne of the Pirates was struck in the jaw by a pitch from Cardinals hurler Rube Geyer. Once Byrne came to his senses, he made a rush at Geyer with intent to inflict bodily harm, but was restrained. The morning game of the twin bill was called after 11 innings with the score 3–3. The tilt was stopped in order to allow sufficient time to clear the grandstand for those who bought tickets for the afternoon encounter.

JULY 6 — After losing the first game of a doubleheader 6–0 against the Cubs in Chicago, the Cardinals win the second contest by forfeit.

By prior agreement, the second game was to end at 5 PM to allow both teams to catch a train. Five innings had to be played to make it an official game. After the Cardinals took a 3–0 lead in the third, the club began to make outs deliberately in order to keep the game moving so that five innings would be played on time. The Cubs, on the other hand, stalled as much as possible. The last straw for umpire Mal Eason was a play in which Cards catcher Ivy Wingo bunted to Cubs pitcher Ed Reulbach, who threw the ball wildly to first base. Second baseman Johnny Evers, who was also the Cubs manager, retrieved it but made no attempt to retire Wingo, who slowly trotted around the bases. Eason declared the game a forfeit. Evers punched Eason but somehow escaped a suspension from the National League office.

JULY 17 — A 3–2 loss to the Giants in the second game of a doubleheader in New York is marred by a fight in the dugout between Cardinal teammates Lee Magee and Ted Cather. The two became engaged in an argument over the way Cather played Larry Doyle's fly ball in left field, which dropped for a single. Cather didn't care for the remarks, and tore into Magee. Police broke up the fight and umpire Bill Brennan ejected them both. The Cards won the first game 4–2.

JULY 22

Slim Sallee steals home and pitches a complete game to beat the Dodgers 3–1 in Brooklyn.

Sallee was 18–15 with an ERA of 2.70 in 1913.

AUGUST 2

A triple play by the Cardinals highlights a 4–2 win over the Braves at Robison Field. In the seventh inning with Bill Sweeney on second base and Hap Myers on first, Wilson Collins hit a liner to Cards second baseman Possum Whitted on a hit-and-run play. Whitted stepped on second to force Sweeney and could have easily tagged Myers for an unassisted triple play. Whitted elected to throw to Ed Konetchy at first, however.

AUGUST 6

The Cardinals trade Larry McLean to the Giants for Doc Crandall.

AUGUST 16

Slim Sallee beats the Dodgers 1–0 in the first game of a doubleheader in Brooklyn. Lee Magee drove in the winning run with a sacrifice fly in the first inning. The Dodgers' bats erupted in the second tilt, a 14–5 victory over the Cards.

AUGUST 18

Twelve days after trading for Doc Crandall, the Cardinals sell him back to the Giants.

Crandall played in only two games with the Cardinals, both as a pinch hitter. He was unhappy over being dealt to the cellar-dwelling Cardinals and his disposition didn't improve when the club tried to cut his salary. Crandall threatened to sit out the rest of the season if he wasn't sent back to New York, and the club complied with the request.

SEPTEMBER 10

Slim Sallee outduels Christy Mathewson for a 10-inning, 1–0 win over the Giants in the first game of a doubleheader at Robison Field. Ivy Wingo started the game-winning rally with a triple, but was knocked unconscious when the relay throw from shortstop Art Fletcher struck him in the back of the head. Miller Huggins pinch ran for Wingo and scored on a single by Finners Quinlan. New York won the second game 2–0.

Quinlan played only 13 games with the Cardinals. The game-winning hit off Mathewson came just four days after his major league debut and was his only run batted in with the Cards.

OCTOBER 4

Third baseman Mike Mowrey loses his false teeth in an 11–2 win over the Reds at Robison Field. In the eighth inning, a grounder hit by Heinie Groh took a bad hop and struck Mowrey in the mouth, knocking loose a set of three false teeth. After the teeth hit the ground, they were struck by the ball, which glanced into foul territory. The ball drove the teeth into the ground, and players from both teams sifted through the infield dirt looking for Mowrey's choppers. After they were found, Mowrey had to leave the game for repairs.

OCTOBER 9

The Cardinals defeat the Browns 1–0 at Sportsman's Park in the first game of the St. Louis city championship series. Slim Sallee outdueled Carl Weilman for the victory.

The 1913 city championship series was a battle between two clubs that had finished in last place in their respective leagues. The Cardinals went up two games to none by winning the October 10 contest 4–1. Two games were played at Sportsman's Park on October 11, with the Browns winning the first game 8–5 and the second ending in a 2–2 tie, called after six innings by darkness. The Browns won both ends of another twin bill on October 12 by scores of 7–6 and 6–2, with the second concluding after six innings on account of darkness. A third doubleheader was scheduled for October 13 with the Browns leading the best-of-seven series three games to two.

OCTOBER 13   The St. Louis city championship series ends in controversy. In the first game of a doubleheader, first baseman Del Pratt of the Browns fielded a ball that took a wicked hop and hit him in the eye. Pratt failed to throw the ball to the pitcher covering the bag because he thought the ball was foul. Umpire George Hildebrand disagreed and called it fair and ruled that the runner was safe. Pratt rushed toward Hildebrand to argue. During the course of the discussion, Pratt was jeered by the Cardinals bench. A former football player at the University of Alabama, Pratt sprinted toward the Cardinals dugout and fought with Zinn Beck. After the two were separated, Pratt resumed his argument with Hildebrand and was banished. Meanwhile, the crowd surged onto the field, and the contest was delayed while police cleared the diamond. The remainder of the game went on in peace, with the Cardinals winning 5–2. When the Cardinals took the field for the second game, they objected to Pratt's presence in the lineup. Umpires Hildebrand and Bill Brennan agreed that Pratt was ineligible to play in the second game according to the rules then in force. Browns manager Branch Rickey argued that Pratt should remain, and the umpires walked off the field in disgust. They eventually returned once Rickey agreed to keep Pratt out of the game, but there was only enough time to play five innings before the sun set, and the contest ended with the score 1–1. Due to the ill feeling surrounding the event, the management of both clubs agreed to end the series with each team having three victories.

DECEMBER 12   The Cardinals trade Ed Konetchy, Mike Mowrey, and Bob Harmon to the Pirates for Dots Miller, Art Butler, Cozy Dolan, Chief Wilson, and Hank Robinson.

After a dismal last-place finish, the Cardinals pulled off a blockbuster deal by swapping their regular first baseman, third baseman, and a starting pitcher for the Pirates' starting first baseman, right fielder, two top reserves, and a promising young pitcher. Miller, Butler, Dolan, and Wilson were all in the Cardinals' starting lineup in 1914, while Robinson was in the pitching rotation. The quintet contributed to a surprising season in which the Cards rose from last place to third, but none had a long-term impact on the club's success.

The biggest news in the sports pages during the 1913–14 offseason was not the Cardinals-Pirates trade, but the creation of the Federal League, which intended to become a third major league and to raid the National and American League rosters with the inducement of more lucrative contracts. The Federal League established franchises in St. Louis, Baltimore, Brooklyn, Buffalo, Chicago, Indianapolis, Kansas City, and Pittsburgh for the 1914 season. The St. Louis franchise, nicknamed the Terriers and headed by Philip Ball, an artificial-ice plant manufacturer, and brewer Otto Stifel. President of the club was Edward Steininger, who was president of the Cardinals in 1912 and 1913. The Terriers played their home games at the northeast corner of Grand and Laclede on what had been an old circus grounds and a private park owned by the Handlin family and called Handlin's Park. The Terriers constructed a ballpark seating 12,000, although with a small playing field that was 325 feet down the left-field line, 375 to center, and 300 to right. Today, the property is part of St. Louis University. The Cardinals lost all three starting outfielders in the Federal League players raids. Steve Evans went to Brooklyn and Rebel Oakes to Pittsburgh between the 1913 and 1914 seasons, and Lee Magee signed a deal with Brooklyn a year later. Between the big trade with Pittsburgh and the Federal League losses, only three of the eight regulars with the 1913 Cardinals returned in 1914, and only one was left by 1915. The lone 1913 regular remaining in 1915 was 36-year-old player-manager Miller Huggins, who had benched himself by the start of the 1916 campaign. In addition, the four members of the 1913 starting pitching rotation were gone by the end of 1916 as the Cardinals were completely made over under Huggins's aggressive leadership. Huggins had a difficult time turning the club into a winner, however, because Helene Britton didn't have the cash to compete with most of the other major league clubs for top talent. Her finances took another hit when salaries escalated due to inducements offered by the Federal League and the fact that the Cardinals, with the introduction of the Terriers and the presence of the Browns, were one of three major league teams in St. Louis.

1914

Season in a Sentence

In a stunning turnaround after a last-place finish in 1913, the Cardinals are only one game out of first place in the last week of August with the best pitching staff in the NL, before fading in September.

Finish • Won • Lost • Pct • GB

Third   81   72   .529   13.0

Manager

Miller Huggins

Stats

Stats	Cards	• NL •	Rank
Batting Avg:	.248	.251	5
On-Base Pct:	.314	.317	6
Slugging Pct:	.333	.334	6
Home Runs:	33		4
Stolen Bases:	204		3
ERA:	2.38	2.78	1
Fielding Avg:	.964	.956	1
Runs Scored:	558		6
Runs Allowed:	540		1 (tie)

Starting Lineup

Frank Snyder, c
Dots Miller, 1b-ss
Miller Huggins, 2b
Zinn Beck, 3b
Art Butler, ss
Cozy Dolan, lf
Lee Magee, cf
Chief Wilson, rf
Walton Cruise, lf-cf
Ivy Wingo, c

Pitchers

Slim Sallee, sp-rp
Bill Doak, sp
Pol Perritt, sp
Hub Perdue, sp
Hank Robinson, sp-rp
Dan Griner, rp-sp

Attendance

256,099 (third in NL)

Club Leaders

Batting Avg:	Miller	.290
On-Base Pct:	Huggins	.396
Slugging Pct:	Miller	.393
	Wilson	.393
Home Runs:	Wilson	9
RBIs:	Miller	88
Runs:	Huggins	85
Stolen Bases:	Huggins	32
Wins:	Doak	19
Strikeouts:	Doak	118
ERA:	Doak	1.72
Saves:	Sallee	6

Transcendental Graphics/theruckerarchive.com

Miller Huggins, played for and managed the Cardinals from 1913 to 1917. His aggressive leadership helped the team, but the competition for players with three teams in St. Louis drained the Cardinals' finances. He went on to manage the famed Yankee teams of the 1920s and was inducted into the Hall of Fame in 1964.

APRIL 14   In the season opener, the Cardinals defeat the Pirates 2–1 before 7,500 at Robison Field. The winning run scored in the ninth inning on a single by Chief Wilson, who was making his debut with the Cardinals. Wilson came to St. Louis in a trade with Pittsburgh the previous December. Dan Griner pitched the complete-game shutout.

The Cardinals were 4–10 in April and had a 22–26 record on June 8, but a 10-week hot streak in June, July, and August put the club into the thick of the pennant race.

APRIL 16   The St. Louis Terriers open the Federal League season with a 7–3 win over Indianapolis before an overflow crowd of 18,000 at Handlin's Park.

The Terriers finished in last place in the eight-team Federal League with a record of 62–89. At the start of the season, they were managed by future Hall of Famer and ex-Cardinal Three Finger Brown, who also pitched for the club. Brown was fired in August and replaced by Fielder Jones.

MAY 1   Hank Robinson pitches a two-hitter to defeat the Cubs 2–0 in Chicago. The only hits off Robinson were singles by Wildfire Schulte and opposing pitcher George Pierce. The Cards scored in the first inning on a triple play. Dots Miller was the runner on third, Lee Magee on second, and Walton Cruise on first when Frank Snyder flied to Cubs center fielder Jimmy Johnston. Miller scored from third. Cruise was out trying for second when tagged by shortstop Heinie Zimmerman after a relay by third baseman Tommy Leach. Magee was retired trying to score as Zimmerman threw to catcher Roger Bresnahan.

MAY 11   Lee Magee of the Cardinals and Bill Sweeney of the Cubs battle in the eleventh inning of a 13-inning, 5–5 tie called by darkness at Robison Field. Magee tried to steal second base and was greeted by a hard tag from Sweeney in the small of the back. Magee got up and struck Sweeney, but received the worst of the altercation when the Chicago second baseman dropped him with several punches to the head.

MAY 16   Bill Doak pitches the Cardinals to a 1–0 win over the Phillies at Robison Field. The lone run of the contest scored on a sacrifice fly by Chief Wilson off Grover Alexander in the second inning.

Doak entered the season as a 23-year-old with a lifetime record of 2–8, but erupted in 1914 with a league-leading ERA of 1.72 and a mark of 19–6 with seven shutouts. Throwing a spitball, he played for the Cardinals for 13 seasons over a 17-year career. With St. Louis, he was 144–138. Doak ranks fifth all time among Cardinals since 1900 in wins, and is fourth in games started (319), third in complete games (144), second in shutouts (32), fourth in innings pitched (2,387), sixth in ERA (2.93), and seventh in strikeouts (938). Doak's greatest contribution to baseball was the invention of a baseball glove. Before Doak came along, fielders' mitts were little more than small leather pillows. The gloves helped protect the hand but did not aid the fielder in making a catch, particularly before being broken in. Players often spent several seasons pounding out a satisfactory pocket. Some even cut out the palm of the glove to form a pocket. In 1919, Doak sketched a glove with a pocket already formed. He inserted a lace of leather strips between the thumb and forefinger, which were previously connected with a single slab of leather. He took his sketches to the Rawlings Sporting Goods Company, and within a few years, the Doak glove was the most *popular mitt on the market. It still protected the hand, but for the first time, helped the fielder snag the ball. Fielding improved dramatically in the 1920s after the introduction of the mitt based on Doak's prototype. He continued to receive royalties from Rawlings, which earned him as much as $25,000 year, until he passed away in 1954. After his playing days ended, Doak made more money in real estate in Bradenton, Florida, and operated a candy store in town called Bill Doak's Sweet Shop.*

MAY 28   Dan Griner and Ted Cather are fined $100 each by Miller Huggins for fighting in the clubhouse.

JUNE 11 Miller Huggins mixes it up with shortstop Ollie O'Mara of the Dodgers during a 2–1 Cardinals win at Brooklyn. Huggins tried to knock the ball out of O'Mara's hands during a tag play at second base. Umpire Bill Byron stepped between them. Neither player was ejected.

Huggins drew 105 walks in 1914 to lead the NL.

JUNE 12 The Cardinals win a 16-inning marathon 8–7 against the Dodgers in Brooklyn. In the sixteenth, Possum Whitted doubled, took third on a fly out and scored on a passed ball. The Cards trailed 6–2 after two innings and were still down 7–4 before tying the game with three tallies in the ninth.

A few days later, the Cardinals traded Whitted and Ted Cather to the Braves for pitcher Hub Perdue, who was nicknamed the "Gallatin Squash." It wasn't a good move. Whitted was a regular outfielder with the Braves and Phillies until 1921, while Perdue pitched only two more seasons with a record of 14–20.

JUNE 30 Two days after the assassination of Archduke Ferdinand, an event that precipitates the start of World War I in August, Slim Sallee bests ex-Cardinal Bob Harmon for a 1–0 win over the Pirates at Robison Field. The lone run of the game scored in the seventh inning on a single by Chief Wilson.

JULY 14 Joe Riggert's two-run, walk-off double in the ninth inning beats the Braves 3–2 at Robison Field. Miller Huggins scored the winning run, which was a better result than the three previous times he reached base during the contest. Huggins tied a major league record when he was caught stealing three times.

JULY 19 The Cardinals score three runs in the ninth inning to defeat the Phillies 5–4 at Robison Field. Zinn Beck hit a two-run triple to tie the game, then scored on a single by Frank Snyder.

JULY 20 A great play by Chief Wilson in right field saves the Cardinals' 7–6 win over the Dodgers at Robison Field. The Dodgers scored four runs in the ninth inning to pull within a run. With one out, Wilson made a sensational catch, then threw to third to double the runner trying to advance.

Wilson holds the all-time record for most triples in a season by collecting 36 with the Pirates in 1912. It was the only season in a nine-year career in which Wilson had more than 14 three-baggers.

JULY 30   Dan Griner pitches a one-hitter but loses 2–1 to the Braves in Boston because his
               teammates make four errors. The only hit off Griner was a single by Les Mann in the
               second inning.

               *The Cardinals led the NL in earned run average in 1914 with a mark of 2.38. It
               was a deep staff, as none of the nine pitchers who won 20 or more games in the
               National League in 1914 played for the Cardinals, nor did any of the 10 hurlers
               who pitched at least 290 innings. The 1914 season began a strange three-year
               progression for the Cardinals. In 1914, the club was sixth in runs scored and led
               the league in fewest runs allowed per game, outscoring opponents 558–540. In
               1915, the Cards jumped to first in runs scored with 590, but dropped to sixth
               in ERA and in runs given to the opposition (601). In 1916, the club plated only
               476 runs to finish last in the NL, and also surrendered the most runs with 629.*

AUGUST 7   The Cardinals sell Bill Steele to the Dodgers.

               *The Cardinals were involved in one of the strangest pennant races in big-league
               history in 1914. At the start of July, it looked like a two-team race between
               the Giants and the Cubs. The Braves had a record of 26–40 and were in last
               place, 15 games out of first. But suddenly the Braves were virtually unbeatable,
               winning 68 of their last 87 games. As the Braves surged forward, the Giants fell
               back, and the Cubs dropped out of contention, the Cardinals found themselves
               in a late-summer pennant race for the first time since joining the National League
               in 1892. At the conclusion of play on August 25, the Giants had a record of
               59–48, the Braves 60–49, and the Cards 62–53.*

AUGUST 26   With a chance for the Cardinals to take first place, 27,000 turn out at Robison Field
               to see the local club play a doubleheader against the Giants. Played on a Wednesday
               afternoon, it was the largest weekday crowd in St. Louis history up to that time. The
               crowd overflowed the grandstand, and about 10,000 fans ringed the field. In the first
               game, Bill Doak outdueled Rube Marquard for a 1–0 win. Miller Higgins scored
               from second base on a wild pitch for the lone run of the game. The Giants won the
               second tilt 4–0 behind the two-hit pitching of Christy Mathewson. At the end of
               the day, the Giants were in first place with the Braves one-half game behind and the
               Cardinals still one back.

AUGUST 27   The Cardinals leap into second place one game back of the Giants with a 10-inning,
               3–2 win over the Braves at Robison Field. Cozy Dolan hit a walk-off double off the
               left-field wall for the winning run. The game was played in steady rain from start to
               finish. The first two St. Louis runs scored on homers by Walton Cruise in the second
               inning and Lee Magee in the eighth.

AUGUST 29   The Cardinals and Braves play a doubleheader at Robison Field to make up a
               postponement of a contest scheduled for the previous day, and the Braves win both
               games, 4–0 and 6–4.

               *The two defeats started a seven-game Cardinal losing streak. Unable to keep pace
               with the streaking Braves, the Cards ended the season in third place, 13 games
               behind.*

SEPTEMBER 5   The Cardinals thrash the Reds 12–2 in Cincinnati.

SEPTEMBER 10   The Cardinals collect only one hit, but defeat the Reds 3–2 in Cincinnati. The Reds led 2–0 heading into the seventh with Rube Benton pitching a no-hitter, but Benton walked the first three batters in the inning before yielding to Phil Douglas. Douglas allowed a single to Ivy Wingo and walked two more to give the Cards three runs.

SEPTEMBER 18   Bill Doak pitches 12 innings, allowing only three hits, but the game against the Braves in Boston ends in a 1–1 tie when called on account of darkness.

SEPTEMBER 23   Prior to a doubleheader against the Giants in New York, Cardinal infielder Dots Miller is honored by the Elks Club of Kearny, New Jersey, his hometown. Miller received a diamond-studded watchfob containing an elk's tooth. The Cardinals won both games, 2–1 and 9–0.

Miller hit .290 in 1914, his first season with the Cardinals. He played in the majors from 1909 through 1921 and was a regular at both first base and second base. Miller managed the San Francisco Seals to the 1922 Pacific Coast League pennant, but contracted tuberculosis and died in September 1923, four days before his 37th birthday.

SEPTEMBER 30   Dots Miller hits an inside-the-park homer off Wilbur Cooper in the sixth inning to beat the Pirates 1–0 in Pittsburgh. Bill Doak pitched the shutout.

OCTOBER 6   The Browns defeat the Cardinals 2–1 at Sportsman's Park in the first game of the St. Louis city championship.

The Browns won the series with four victories to one for the Cardinals. Another contest ended in a tie.

1915

Season in a Sentence

The Cardinals lead the NL in runs, but the pitching staff fails and the club careens into sixth place.

Finish • Won • Lost • Pct • GB

Sixth   72   81   .471   18.5

Manager

Miller Huggins

Stats

	Cards	• NL •	Rank
Batting Avg:	.254	.248	1
On-Base Pct:	.320	.309	2
Slugging Pct:	.333	.331	4
Home Runs:	20		5
Stolen Bases:	162		3
ERA:	2.89	2.74	6
Fielding Avg:	.964	.964	5
Runs Scored:	590		1
Runs Allowed:	601		6

Starting Lineup

Frank Snyder, c
Dots Miller, 1b-2b
Miller Huggins, 2b
Bruno Betzel, 3b
Art Butler, ss
Bob Bescher, lf
Chief Wilson, cf
Tom Long, rf
Cozy Dolan, cf-lf-rf
Ham Hyatt, 1b
Zinn Beck, 3b

Pitchers

Bill Doak, sp
Slim Sallee, sp
Lee Meadows, sp-rp
Red Ames, sp
Dan Griner, rp-sp
Hank Robinson, rp-sp
Hub Perdue, rp-sp

Attendance

252,666 (fifth in NL)

Club Leaders

Batting Avg:	Snyder	.298
On-Base Pct:	Snyder	.353
Slugging Pct:	Long	.446
Home Runs:	Bescher	4
RBIs:	Miller	72
Runs:	Miller	73
Stolen Bases:	Miller	27
	Bescher	27
Wins:	Doak	16
Strikeouts:	Doak	124
ERA:	Doak	2.64
Saves:	Sallee	3
	Griner	3

FEBRUARY 18   The Cardinals trade Pol Perritt to the Giants for Bob Bescher.

The Cardinals ended up on the short end of this transaction. Bescher was a former star outfielder who was 31 years old and near the end of the line. Perritt was a 22-year-old pitcher who would post records of 18–11, 17–7, and 18–13 for the Giants from 1916 through 1918.

FEBRUARY 28   The Cardinals purchase Ham Hyatt from the Pirates.

APRIL 8   The Cardinals trade Ivy Wingo to the Reds for Mike Gonzalez.

This was a trade of two young catchers who would have a major impact on their new clubs. Wingo played for the Reds for 13 seasons. A native of Cuba, Gonzalez was a player (1915–19, 1924–25, and 1931–32), coach (1934–46), and interim manager (1938 and 1940) for the Cardinals.

APRIL 14   The Cardinals lose the season opener 7–2 in Chicago.

APRIL 19   Cardinals pitcher Lee Meadows makes his major league debut in a 4–1 loss to the Reds in Cincinnati, and becomes the first player to wear glasses regularly on the field since Will White in 1886.

The nearsighted Meadows pitched 15 seasons in the majors, five of them with the Cardinals. He ended his career with the record of 188–180 in seasons that varied from a 12–23 record with the Cardinals in 1916 to a 20–9 mark for the Pirates in 1926.

APRIL 22   In the home opener at Robison Field, the Cardinals lose 9–5 to the Cubs.

APRIL 24   Slim Sallee pitches a two-hitter to defeat the Cubs 3–0 at Robison Field. The only Chicago hits were a double by Art Phelan and a single by Wildfire Schulte.

APRIL 25   With the score tied 1–1, the Cardinals erupt for seven runs in the eighth inning and beat the Pirates 8–1 at Robison Field.

MAY 27   Eighteen days after the sinking of the *Lusitania* by a German submarine, Dan Griner faces the minimum 27 batters and pitches a two-hitter to defeat the Phillies 2–0 at Philadelphia. The only two hits off Griner were singles by Bobby Byrne and Bud Weiser. Both were erased on double plays.

MAY 25   Trailing 4–2, the Cardinals score seven runs in the seventh inning and trounce the Giants 11–5 in New York.

MAY 31   Umpire Bill Byron is mobbed after the second game of a doubleheader against the Reds at Robison Field, which ended in a 4–4 tie after nine innings due to darkness. During a Cardinals rally in the ninth, Miller Huggins, coaching third base, patted Bob Bescher on the back offering encouragement. It was illegal for a coach to touch a runner, however. Byron strictly enforced the rule and called Bescher out, inciting the Cardinal faithful after the next batter hit a single that would have scored Bescher with the winning run. After the game, thousands rushed onto the field, pelting Byron with debris, including a couple of bricks. The umpire fought off his attackers and reached the dressing room without serious injury. The Reds won the first game 2–1.

> *Byron was known as "The Singing Umpire" because he would sing some of his calls. He was an NL umpire from 1913 through 1919, and would be involved in two more altercations with Cardinals fans (see August 15, 1915, and July 30, 1917).*

JUNE 5   Cardinal shortstop Art Butler breaks up Grover Alexander's no-hit bid by hitting a single with two outs in the ninth. It was the lone St. Louis hit in a 3–0 loss to the Phillies at Robison Field.

> *Alexander won 373 games and threw 90 shutouts during his major league career, but never pitched a no-hitter.*

JUNE 9   Trailing 9–4, the Cardinals explode for seven runs in the seventh inning and outlast the Giants 11–10 at Robison Field.

JUNE 10   Bob Bescher hits a grand slam off Ferdie Schupp in the third inning of a 13–2 thrashing of the Giants at Robison Field.

JUNE 20   The Cardinals defeat the Braves 8–2 at Robison Field. The victory gave the Cardinals a 32–26 record and second place, 1½ games behind the first place Cubs. It was the high point of the season. By the end of July, the Cards had tumbled into seventh.

JUNE 24   The Cardinals score four runs in the top of the ninth inning to take a 13–10 lead over the Cubs in Chicago, but allow four tallies in the bottom half to lose 14–13.

JULY 2   Lee Meadows pitches a one-hitter to defeat the Reds 2–0 in Cincinnati. The only hit off Meadows was a double by Heinie Groh in the fifth inning.

JULY 22   After losing the first game of a doubleheader 1–0 to the Dodgers in Brooklyn, Cardinal bats come alive in the second tilt to defeat the Dodgers 11–1.

JULY 24   The Cardinals purchase Red Ames from the Giants.

AUGUST 4   A seven-run rally in the eighth inning comes much too late as the Cardinals lose 11–9 to the Giants in the first game of a doubleheader at Robison Field. New York completed the sweep with a 7–0 win in the nightcap.

AUGUST 7   Miller Huggins dupes Dodgers rookie pitcher Ed Appleton into an error in the seventh inning of a 6–4 win at Robison Field. As Appleton stepped to the mound with Cardinal runner Dots Miller at third base, Huggins, coaching at third, called for the ball. Appleton obliged, Huggins stepped aside, and Miller scored.

               A change in the rules prevented such trickery in the future.

AUGUST 14   The Cardinals clobber the Cubs 12–2 at Robison Field.

AUGUST 15   The Cardinals lose 3–1 and 8–1 to the Cubs during a contentious doubleheader at Robison Field. Cubs manager Roger Bresnahan had to be stopped by umpire Mal Eason and a police officer from climbing into the stands to attack a heckling fan. Cardinals fans, upset over the calls by Eason's fellow ump Bill Byron, littered the field with bottles and vegetables, which halted the first game for five minutes. The fans took exception to Byron's ruling that Dots Miller was out at second. It was the second time in 1915 that Byron was the target of Cardinal fans (see May 31, 1915). A week before the second incident, Cardinal owner Helene Britton stopped Byron on the field immediately after a game to complain about the umpire's decisions in full view of the throng in the grandstand.

AUGUST 18   The Cardinals play in the first game ever played at Braves Field in Boston, losing 3–1 to the Braves. The ballpark held 43,500, which then the largest in baseball. The Braves played at Braves Field through the end of the 1952 season. A year later, the club relocated to Milwaukee.

AUGUST 24   The Cardinals trounce the Giants 12–1 in New York.

AUGUST 27   Dots Miller hits an inside-the-park homer off Sherry Smith in the eighth inning of an 11–7 win over the Dodgers in Brooklyn.

AUGUST 30   A freak walk-off homer by ex-Cardinal Possum Whitted in the tenth inning gives the Phillies a 4–3 win over the Cards in Philadelphia. Whitted's drive struck the top of the left-field fence, caromed off the shoulder of St. Louis outfielder Bob Bescher, and went over the wall for a homer.

SEPTEMBER 6   The Cardinals sweep the Cubs 3–2 in 12 innings and 10–0 in 7½ in a doubleheader at Robison Field. The second game was called by darkness. The Cards won the first game with the help of a batter hitting out of turn. The batting order called for Frank Snyder to bat seventh and Bruno Betzel eighth, but in the second inning, Betzel hit ahead of Snyder. Betzel tripled and scored on Snyder's single, but no one on the Cubs observed the error and the run counted. Had it been noticed that Betzel batted out of turn, he would have been declared out after hitting his triple and the side would have been retired without a run.

Snyder hit .298 for the Cardinals in 1915. Tom Long, a 25-year-old rookie outfielder, batted .294. His 25 triples not only led the NL in 1915, but also set a modern record for rookies. He slumped after his rookie campaign, however, and played only two more seasons.

SEPTEMBER 10   Rogers Hornsby makes his major league debut in a 7–1 loss to the Reds at Robison Field. Hornsby subbed for shortstop Art Butler in the sixth inning and was hitless in two at-bats.

Hornsby was 20 years old and was purchased by the Cardinals from the Denison, Texas, entry in the Texas-Oklahoma League. At the time, teams did not have farm systems and acquired much of their talent by buying them directly from minor league clubs. The Cardinals were perpetually short of cash during this period, and spent little time trying to purchase athletes from the top minor leagues such as the American Association, International League, and Pacific Coast League because the club couldn't afford the prices. Instead, the Cards trolled through the low minors looking for hidden gems like Hornsby.

SEPTEMBER 14   Rogers Hornsby collects his first major league hit, a single off Rube Marquard, during a 6–2 win over the Dodgers at Robison Field.

The hit was the first of 2,930 hits that Hornsby collected during his Hall of Fame career. His lifetime batting average of .358 is the second best all time to Ty Cobb's .366, and is the best of any right-handed batter. Hornsby had 301 career homers, 541 doubles, 169 triples, 1,579 runs, 1,584 RBIs, a .434 on-base percentage, and a .577 slugging percentage. He played for the Cardinals from 1915 through 1926 and again in 1933, and ranks first all time among Cardinal players in batting average (.359), second in on-base percentage (.427), third in slugging percentage (.568), second in triples (143), third in hits (2,110), third in runs (1,069), fourth in home runs (193), fourth in RBIs (1,072), fourth in doubles (367), and eighth in games played (1,580). Hornsby achieved those lofty figures by becoming one of the most driven and dedicated players in history. He was fanatical about staying in shape. He never smoked or drank, and even refused to read books or magazines or go to the movies for fear of damaging his eyes. Hornsby's only vice was playing the horses. He was cold, nasty, rude, and mean, however. With an utter disregard for tact, Hornsby insulted teammates, owners, his own players when he managed, and even commissioner Kenesaw Landis. His difficult personality led to frequent changes of address. While he still ranked among the greatest players in the game, Hornsby played for four teams in four seasons, moving from the Cardinals (1926) to the Giants (1927), Braves (1928), and Cubs (1929).

SEPTEMBER 17   Bill Doak pitches the Cardinals to a 1–0 win over the Braves in the first game of a doubleheader at Robison Field. Miller Huggins drove in the lone run of the game with a single in the sixth inning. The second tilt was called on account of darkness at the end of the ninth inning with the score 2–2.

SEPTEMBER 18   The Cardinals are walloped 20–1 and 6–3 by the Braves in a doubleheader at Robison Field. In the first-game disaster, Bob Bescher nearly came to blows with Boston pitcher Dick Rudolph, who buzzed a pitch near Bescher's head. Both were ejected.

SEPTEMBER 19   Red Ames pitches a 10-inning one-hitter to defeat the Phillies 1–0 in the second game of a doubleheader at Robison Field. The only Philadelphia hit was a bloop single to center field by Possum Whitted in the eighth inning. The winning run scored on a single by Miller Huggins, a wild pitch by George Chalmers and a single by Bob Bescher. Philadelphia won the first game 6–2.

OCTOBER 5   In the first game of the St. Louis city championship series, the Browns defeat the Cardinals 3–2 at Sportsman's Park.

The Browns won the series four games to two.

DECEMBER 22   In Cincinnati, the American and National Leagues sign a peace treaty with the Federal League. The NL and AL owners paid $600,000 to the eight owners of the Federal League franchises, and the FL ceased to exist after two seasons.

The end of the Federal League had long-term consequences for St. Louis baseball. As part of the peace treaty, St. Louis Terriers owner Phil Ball was promised the right to purchase either the Cardinals or the Browns. He preferred to buy the Cardinals, but Helene Britton refused to sell despite being pressured by her fellow NL owners to do so. Instead, Ball bought the Browns. One of Ball's first acts was the fire Branch Rickey as field manager and replace him with Fielder Jones, who had been Ball's skipper with the Terriers. Rickey remained with the Browns as business manager but didn't get along with Ball. In March 1917, Rickey was hired by the Cardinals and turned the club into a winner.

1916

Season in a Sentence

Despite the contributions of Rogers Hornsby, a Cardinals club that scored the most runs in the NL in 1915 scores the fewest in 1916, resulting in a tie for last place.

Finish • Won • Lost • Pct • GB

Seventh   63   90   .392   33.5
(tie)

Manager

Miller Huggins

Stats	Cards	• NL •	Rank
Batting Avg:	.243	.247	5
On-Base Pct:	.295	.303	8
Slugging Pct:	.318	.328	6
Home Runs:	25		5
Stolen Bases:	182		3
ERA:	3.14	2.61	8
Fielding Avg:	.957	.963	8
Runs Scored:	476		8
Runs Allowed:	629		8

Starting Lineup

Frank Snyder, c-1b
Dots Miller, 1b
Bruno Betzel, 2b
Roger Hornsby, 3b-ss
Roy Corhan, ss
Bob Bescher, lf
Jack Smith, cf
Tom Long, rf
Chief Wilson, rf-cf
Mike Gonzalez, c
Zinn Beck, 3b

Pitchers

Lee Meadows, sp-rp
Red Ames, sp-rp
Bill Doak, sp
Bob Steele, sp
Milt Watson, sp
Steamboat Williams, rp
Hi Jasper, rp-sp

Attendance

224,308 (eighth in NL)

Club Leaders

Batting Avg:	Hornsby	.313
On-Base Pct:	Hornsby	.369
Slugging Pct:	Hornsby	.444
Home Runs:	Three tied	6
RBIs:	Hornsby	65
Runs:	Bescher	78
Stolen Bases:	Bescher	39
Wins:	Meadows	12
	Doak	12
Strikeouts:	Meadows	120
ERA:	Meadows	2.58
Saves:	Ames	8

APRIL 12   The Cardinals seize the opener by defeating the Pirates 2–1 before 13,000 at Robison Field. The winning run scored on a squeeze bunt by Rogers Hornsby that brought Bruno Betzel home from third base. Bill Doak pitched the shutout.

During the 1915 season, Hornsby hit .246 in 18 games. The Cardinals went into the 1916 season intending to send him to the minors for more seasoning. Hornsby worked hard on his father's farm during the offseason and gained 30 pounds of muscle. He also changed his stance from a crouch to an upright position to gain more power. After an impressive spring training, Hornsby won the starting shortstop job, but hit seventh in the batting order during the opening week of the regular season. With the change in physique and approach at the plate, Hornsby was soon elevated to the cleanup spot and hit .313 in 1916. In a season in which he turned 21 shortly after Opening Day, Hornsby ranked fourth in the NL in batting average, fourth in slugging percentage (.444), and second in triples (15).

APRIL 16   Lee Meadows (eight innings) and Slim Sallee (two innings) combine to defeat the Cubs 1–0 in 10 innings at Robison Field. Frank Snyder's walk-off double drove in the winning run.

APRIL 27   The Cardinals play for the first time at present-day Wrigley Field in Chicago and lose 9–5 to the Cubs.

Known as Weeghman Park in its early days, Wrigley Field opened in 1914 for the Federal League Chicago Whales. The Cubs moved into the facility in 1916 after the Federal League folded.

MAY 2   Bill Doak pitches a two-hitter to defeat the Cubs 3–0 in Chicago. The only hits off Doak were singles by Wildfire Schulte and Steve Yerkes.

MAY 7   The Cardinals collect only two hits off Reds pitcher Fred Toney, but win 1–0 at Robison Field. The run scored in the fourth inning on a double by Dots Miller and a single by Tom Long. Red Ames pitched the shutout.

MAY 14   Rogers Hornsby hits his first career homer in a 3–2 loss to the Dodgers at Robison Field. The pitcher was Jeff Pfeffer. Hornsby's first homer could hardly be described as majestic. It was a spinning blooper that landed just inside the left-field line, bounced toward the grandstand, and skipped off the railing and into the stands.

MAY 23   Rogers Hornsby scores both runs in a 2–0 win over the Braves at Robison Field. Hornsby scored after hitting a single in the second inning an clubbed an inside-the-park homer in the fifth.

JUNE 10   The Cardinals defeat the Dodgers 3–2 in 14 innings at Brooklyn. A two-run double by Chief Wilson put the Cards ahead 3–1 before the Dodgers scored once in the bottom of the inning.

JUNE 23   Tom Long collects five hits, including two doubles, in five at-bats during an 8–7 win over the Pirates in Pittsburgh.

JUNE 28   Rogers Hornsby collects five hits, including a homer and two triples, during a 9–6 win over the Reds in Cincinnati. The Cardinals scored four runs in the ninth inning for the win.

JULY 23   The Cardinals sell Slim Sallee to the Giants for $10,000.

After nine seasons of playing for Cardinals clubs that lost far more often than they won, Sallee had had enough and announced his retirement in June. The Cards capitulated to his demands to move to a winning club, and sold Sallee to the Giants. He pitched in the World Series for the Giants in 1917 and the Reds in 1919.

AUGUST 2   Peeved at remarks by Boston fans during a 5–3 win over the Braves, Miller Huggins throws a handful of dirt into the stands.

AUGUST 13   The Cardinals split an odd doubleheader against the Pirates at Robison Field. In the first game, the Cardinals collected 23 hits, but left 17 men on base and eked out a 9–8 win in 11 innings. Bob Bescher drove in the winning run with a walk-off double. The second game ended after five innings by darkness with the Pirates winning 9–5. Despite losing the game and batting only five times, the Cards tied a National League record by stealing 11 bases. Jack Smith, Roy Corhan, Rogers Hornsby, Dots Miller, and Frank Snyder each swiped two bases, and Chief Wilson stole one. The Pirate catcher was ex-Cardinal Bill Fischer.

AUGUST 21   Milt Watson bests ex-Cardinal Slim Sallee in a 1–0 duel over the Giants at Robison Field. The lone of the game scored in the first inning on a triple by Rogers Hornsby.

SEPTEMBER 9   Red Ames pitches the Cardinals to a 1–0 win over the Reds in the second game of a doubleheader at Robison Field. Bob Bescher drove in the winning run with a walk-off single in the ninth. Cincinnati won the first game 6–3 in 10 innings.

SEPTEMBER 14   Bob Bescher hits a grand slam off Erskine Mayer in the fifth inning of a 5–3 win over the Phillies in Philadelphia.

OCTOBER 1   The Cardinals close the regular season with a 6–3 loss to the Cubs in Chicago.

The Cardinals lost their last 14 games in 1916 and 28 of their last 33.

OCTOBER 4   In the first game of the St. Louis city championship series, the Cardinals lose 5–3 to the Browns at Robison Field.

The Browns won the series four games to one.

1917

Season in a Sentence

New ownership brings the arrival of Branch Rickey but causes the departure of Miller Huggins.

Finish • Won • Lost • Pct • GB

Third	82	70	.539	15.0

Manager

Miller Huggins

Stats	Cards	• NL •	Rank
Batting Avg:	.250	.249	3
On-Base Pct:	.303	.305	5
Slugging Pct:	.333	.328	4
Home Runs:	26		3 (tie)
Stolen Bases:	159		2
ERA:	3.03	2.70	8
Fielding Avg:	.946	.961	8
Runs Scored:	531		6
Runs Allowed:	567		6

Starting Lineup

Frank Snyder, c
Gene Paulette, 1b
Dots Miller, 2b-1b
Doug Baird, 3b
Rogers Hornsby, ss
Walton Cruise, lf-cf
Jack Smith, cf-rf
Tom Long, rf
Bruno Betzel, 2b
Mike Gonzalez, c
Fred Smith, 3b

Pitchers

Bill Doak, sp
Lee Meadows, sp
Marv Goodwin, sp
Red Ames, rp-sp
Milt Watson, rp-sp
Oscar Horstmann, rp-sp
Gene Packard, rp-sp

Attendance

288,491 (fourth in NL)

Club Leaders

Batting Avg:	Hornsby	.327
On-Base Pct:	Hornsby	.385
Slugging Pct:	Hornsby	.484
Home Runs:	Hornsby	8
RBIs:	Hornsby	66
Runs:	Hornsby	86
Stolen Bases:	Smith	25
Wins:	Doak	16
Strikeouts:	Doak	111
ERA:	Ames	2.71
Saves:	Ames	3

MARCH 5   Helene Britton sells the Cardinals to a group of St. Louis investors headed by James
               C. Jones.

               *Mrs. Britton let it be known that she intended to sell the club after the divorce
               from her husband, Schuyler, the previous November. Many had been advising
               her that she lacked the cash and the knowledge of the sport to turn the Cardinals
               into winners, and she began to realize that quite possibly they were correct.
               Losing teams and the competition from the Federal League had also strained her
               cash reserves. In addition, there was the probability that the United States would
               soon be involved militarily in World War I, which added to her uncertainty over
               the future. Miller Higgins wanted to buy the club, and went to Cincinnati to
               talk to wealthy yeast manufacturers Julius and Max Fleischmann for financial
               backing. The Fleischmann brothers agreed, but by the time Huggins was ready
               to take the proposal to Britton, she had already sold the club to Jones, who was
               Helene's legal advisor and served briefly as club president in 1912. Jones was
               worried that out-of-town interests would buy the Cardinals and pull the club
               out of the city. His idea was to make the Cardinals community-owned. He paid
               $375,000 for the club by lining up 1,200 investors who bought stock in $25
               shares with $10,000 as the maximum amount. As an added incentive to purchase
               the stock, Jones came up with a clever idea. Anyone who bought a share of stock
               had the right to give a season pass to a deserving underprivileged youngster
               between the ages of 10 and 16. Large organizations serving St. Louis youth
               were contacted to help identify those in need. Called the Knothole Gang, the
               program was credited with helping to curb juvenile delinquency. The free tickets
               also helped turn many St. Louis youngsters away from the Browns and made
               them lifelong Redbird fans. Helene Britton married Charles Bigsby, an electrical
               appliance distributor, and moved to Philadelphia. She died in 1950.*

MARCH 20   The Cardinals hire 35-year-old Branch Rickey to run the club with the title of
               president.

               *James Jones bought the Cardinals as a civic duty and knew he had no expertise
               in running a successful baseball operation. He asked seven civic leaders and
               local sportswriters whom he should hire to bring a winning team to St. Louis.
               The unanimous choice was Branch Rickey, who was then the business manager
               of the St. Louis Browns. Rickey wanted more control over running a baseball
               operation than he had with the Browns, and jumped at the chance to take over
               the Cardinals. He was under contract with the American League club, however,
               and Browns owner Phil Ball went to court to force Rickey to live up to the deal.
               After two weeks of legal wrangling, a compromise was reached between the two
               clubs, freeing Rickey to join the Cards. Branch Wesley Rickey was born in 1881,
               the son of a poor farmer in Lucasville, Ohio. Raised by strict Methodist parents
               who scrimped and saved for his education, Rickey attended Ohio Wesleyan
               University, and graduated 1½ years ahead of schedule. He starred on semi-pro
               football and baseball teams, and coached Ohio Wesleyan's baseball team. Rickey
               caught the attention of major league scouts, and played 118 games as a catcher
               with the Browns and the Yankees from 1905 through 1907. After his playing
               days ended, Rickey attended the University of Michigan Law School and earned
               a degree by squeezing a three-year course of study into two years while coaching
               the baseball team. He came to St. Louis as manager of the Browns, a job he held
               from 1913 through 1915, when he moved into the club's front office. Building*

National Baseball Hall of Fame Library/Major League Baseball/Getty Images

Branch Rickey managed the Cardinals from 1919 to 1925 while also serving in the team's front office. In the latter arena where he worked until 1942, he created the first extensive farm system, pioneered the use of baseball statistics, and developed and promoted the first batting helmet.

baseball's first extensive farm system, Rickey would run the Cardinals' front office for 25 years and transformed one of the worst operations in baseball into a dynasty that would win nine NL pennants and six World Championships from 1926 through 1946.

APRIL 11   Five days after the United States declares war on Germany and enters World War I, the Reds defeat the Cardinals 3–1 on Opening Day in Cincinnati.

War fever ran at the opener. The Cincinnati Enquirer *reported that "at least 10,000 flags were carried by patrons." Other than overt displays of patriotism, the war had little effect on baseball in 1917. The changes were dramatic in 1918, however, as many players were drafted and the season ended a month early.*

APRIL 14   Milt Watson carries a no-hitter into the seventh inning and figures in both runs in a 2–1 victory over the Reds in Cincinnati. Watson drove in a run with a single in the sixth inning to put the Cardinals up 1–0. The Reds scored in the seventh after collecting their first hit with two outs. Watson then doubled and scored in the eighth. Tom Long tied a major league record when he was caught stealing three times.

APRIL 19   In the first game of the season in St. Louis, the Cardinals defeat the Reds 4–1.

With the change in ownership, the name of the ballpark was changed from Robison Field to Cardinal Field. The capacity of the ballpark shrunk by 1,500, however, because the city building commissioner decided that the top portion of the left-field bleachers was unsafe and ordered it to be removed. The new owners also used cheerleaders in 1917 as young men stood in front of the stands with megaphones to stir the crowd. Although cheerleaders are a staple of many sports, most notably football and basketball, the idea never caught on in baseball.

APRIL 20   The Cardinals win a strange 7–6 decision over the Reds at Cardinal Field. The Cards scored six runs in the first inning on only one hit, a single, thanks to four walks, a hit batsman, two errors, and several mental blunders by Cincinnati fielders. The Cards carried a 7–1 lead into the ninth, but the Reds made it close by scoring five times in the final inning.

MAY 2   Red Ames pitches a two-hitter to defeat the Pirates 4–0 at Forbes Field. The only Pittsburgh hits were from Carson Bigbee and Jesse Altenburg.

MAY 6   The Cardinals defeat the Reds 4–0 in Cincinnati and slip into first place with a record of 12–7.

The stay in first lasted only one day. The Cardinals were out of contention by July, as the Giants ran away with the NL pennant, but the Cards won 82 games, the highest win total by any St. Louis team since 1899.

MAY 15   Red Ames wins his own game by driving in the winning run with a single in the tenth inning for a 5–4 decision over the Giants in New York.

MAY 26   Bill Doak pitches a two-hitter to defeat the Braves 6–1 in Boston. The hits off Doak were a double by Red Smith and a single by Joe Wilhoit.

MAY 29   Rogers Hornsby's brother William is shot and killed during an argument with a bartender in a Fort Worth, Texas, saloon.

JUNE 6   Rogers Hornsby hits a grand slam off Art Nehf in the third inning to put his club up 5–0, but the Cardinals barely eke out an 8–7 win over the Braves at Cardinal Field. Boston scored six runs in the eighth to tie the game 7–7. Hornsby started the game-winning rally in the bottom half with a double.

Hornsby hit .327 and led the NL in total bases (253), slugging percentage (.484), and triples (17) in 1917.

JUNE 7   Two Cardinal left fielders are injured in consecutive innings during a 9–4 win over the Braves at Cardinal Field. Walton Cruise hurt his leg rounding second base in the third inning. Bob Bescher replaced Cruise, and sprained his ankle in the fourth chasing a fly ball. Bruno Betzel subbed for Bescher and managed to make it through the remainder of the game unscathed.

Cruise played in 153 of the Cardinals' 154 games in 1917 and hit .295. Center fielder Jack Smith also had an excellent season, batting .297.

JUNE 11   Mike Gonzalez steals home in the fifteenth inning to defeat the Phillies 5–4 at Cardinal Field. Gonzalez doubled and took third on an infield out before crossing the plate with the winning run. Bill Doak pitched the complete game. He allowed four runs in the first inning, then pitched 14 consecutive scoreless innings. Over the final seven innings, Doak allowed only one runner to reach base.

JUNE 14   A triple steal in the fifth inning with Dots Miller swiping home highlights a 5–4 win over the Dodgers at Cardinals Field.

               On the same day, the Cardinals traded Bob Steele to the Pirates for Doug Baird.

JUNE 15   In his first game with the Cardinals, Doug Baird triples in the twelfth inning and scores on a squeeze bunt by Mike Gonzalez for a 3–2 victory over the Dodgers at Cardinal Field.

JUNE 24   The Reds pound out 25 hits in a 15–4 win over the Cardinals in the second game of a doubleheader at Cardinal Field. The Cards won the first game 4–2.

               The Cardinals made the most of their opportunities in 1917. They ranked sixth in runs scored (531) and sixth in runs allowed (567), but finished the year in third place with a record of 82–70.

JUNE 26   The Cardinals win a 15-inning marathon by a 5–4 score over the Cubs in the first game of a doubleheader at Cardinal Field. The Cards should have won the contest in regulation, but Walton Cruise was called out for failing to touch second base on a home run. Chicago won the second tilt, called after seven inning by darkness, 8–6.

JUNE 27   Rogers Hornsby, Walton Cruise, and Dots Miller hit consecutive triples in the seventh inning of a 6–3 win over the Cubs in the second game of a doubleheader at Cardinal Field. Chicago won the first game 4–2.

JULY 26   Bill Doak pitches a two-hitter to defeat the Braves 2–0 at Cardinal Field. The only Boston hits were singles by Ed Konetchy and Joe Kelly.

JULY 30   Umpire Bill Byron is once again the target of a fusillade of bottles in St. Louis during a 3–2 loss to the Phillies. In the seventh inning, fans in the left field bleachers disagreed when Tom Long was called out on strikes. The contest was stopped while the field was cleared of glass.

AUGUST 6   Milt Watson pitches the Cardinals to a 1–0 win over the Dodgers at Cardinal Field. The lone run of the game scored on a walk-off double by Jack Smith.

AUGUST 20   A double steal in the ninth with Walton Cruise swiping home beats the Braves 7–6 in Boston.

AUGUST 21   Marv Goodwin pitches a one–hit, 1–0 victory against the Braves in a contest shortened to six innings by rain.

Goodwin was the first major leaguer to die as a result plane crash while piloting a plane that went down on October 18, 1925, in Houston. Goodwin was a flying instructor during World War I.

AUGUST 31   The Cardinals beat the Pirates 1–0 in the second game of a doubleheader at Forbes Field which was stopped by rain at the end of the fifth inning. Red Ames pitched the shutout. Pittsburgh won the first game 3–0.

SEPTEMBER 1   The Cardinals defeat the Pirates twice by 1–0 scores in a doubleheader at Pittsburgh. Bill Doak and Milt Watson were the shutout pitchers. Watson's gem was a one-hitter. The only Pirate hit was a single by Jake Pitler in the third inning.

SEPTEMBER 18   Bill Doak pitches two complete-game victories in one day against the Dodgers at Cardinal Field. In the first contest, Doak defeated Brooklyn 2–0. The only Dodger hits were Casey Stengel and George Cutshaw. In the second tilt, Doak won 12–4.

SEPTEMBER 22   The Cardinals and the Braves battle to a 0–0 tie called after 14 innings before darkness ended play. Both Lee Meadows and Art Nehf pitched complete-game shutouts without receiving credit for a victory.

OCTOBER 3   In the first game of the St. Louis city championship series, the Cardinals defeat the Browns 3–2 at Cardinal Field.

The Cardinals captured the 1917 city championship by winning four games to two over the Browns, with one ending in a tie. With the exception of the 1944 World Series, this was the last postseason series between the Cardinals and Browns. The Cardinals and Browns continued to meet in spring training exhibition games in St. Louis until 1953.

OCTOBER 25   Miller Huggins resigns as manager of the Cardinals.

Huggins seethed all season over losing his opportunity to purchase the Cardinals (see March 5, 1917). Huggins moved from St. Louis to New York, where he took a job as manager of the Yankees. At the time, the Yankees had yet to win a single American League pennant. Under the guidance of Huggins, and the acquisition of such players as Babe Ruth, the Yankees established one of the most enduring winning traditions in professional sports. With Huggins as manager, the Yanks won six AL titles and three World Championships in an eight-year span from 1921 through 1928, before his untimely death on September 22, 1929. He died of erysipelas, a skin disease, at the age of 50.

DECEMBER 31   The Cardinals hire 42-year-old Jack Hendricks as manager.

Hendricks earned a law degree from Northwestern University in 1897 and practiced law off and on for 15 years, but couldn't get baseball out of his system. After a brief major league career as an outfielder, Hendricks had managed in the minors for 13 years when hired by the Cardinals. He was signed to a two-year contract, but lasted only one year as the St. Louis skipper. Hendricks feuded all year with Rogers Hornsby as the Cards skidded into last place with a record of 51–78.

1918

Season in a Sentence

Because of World War I, the season ends on Labor Day, which is none too soon for the last-place Cardinals.

Finish • Won • Lost • Pct • GB

Eighth   51   78   .395   33.0

Manager

Jack Hendricks

Stats

Stats	Cards	NL	Rank
Batting Avg:	.244	.254	6
On-Base Pct:	.301	.311	7
Slugging Pct:	.325	.328	4
Home Runs:	27		1
Stolen Bases:	119		5
ERA:	2.96	2.76	6
Fielding Avg:	.962	.965	7
Runs Scored:	454		5
Runs Allowed:	527		8

Starting Lineup

Mike Gonzalez, c
Gene Paulette, 1b
Tom Fisher, 2b
Doug Baird, 3b
Rogers Hornsby, ss
Austin McHenry, lf
Cliff Heathcote, cf
Walton Cruise, rf-lf
Bruno Betzel, 3b-rf
Jack Smith, cf
Charlie Grimm, 1b
George Anderson, rf

Pitchers

Gene Packard, sp
Bill Doak, sp
Red Ames, sp
Lee Meadows, sp
Jakie May, sp
Bill Sherdel, rp-sp

Attendance

110,599 (sixth in NL)

Club Leaders

Batting Avg:	Hornsby	.317
On-Base Pct:	Hornsby	.349
Slugging Pct:	Hornsby	.416
Home Runs:	Cruise	6
RBIs:	Hornsby	60
Runs:	Hornsby	51
Stolen Bases:	Baird	25
Wins:	Packard	12
Strikeouts:	Doak	74
ERA:	Ames	2.31
Saves:	Packard	2

APRIL 16   In the season opener, the Cardinals defeat the Cubs 4–2 at Cardinal Field. Lee Meadows pitched the complete-game victory. The losing pitcher was Grover Alexander, who had won 30 or more games in each of the previous three seasons. Red Smyth collected three hits off Alexander, including a double.

Before the game, fans were treated to a concert from the Great Lakes Naval Training Station Band. Colonel George K. Hunter, commanding officer at Jefferson Barracks, an army post located in St. Louis County south of the city, threw out the first ball. World War I had a huge impact on baseball in 1918. Dots Miller, who had been a starting infielder for the Cardinals since 1914, missed the entire season while serving in the military. Other Cards who were in the service on Opening Day were pitchers Marv Goodwin, Lou North, and Bruce Hill. Before the season ended, the Cards lost four more regulars to the military in Walton Cruise, Doug Baird, Jack Smith, and Frank Snyder. Oscar Horstmann and Tony Brottem also went into the service. The Cardinals were so strapped for players that 44-year-old coach Bobby Wallace appeared in 32 games even though he batted .153 with one extra-base hit in 98 at-bats.

APRIL 23   The Cardinals overcome a 5–0 Pirate lead with two runs in the second inning, three in the third, and one in the sixth to win 6–5 at Cardinal Field.

The 1918 season was the first in which the nickname "Cardinals" appeared on the club's uniform. Prior to 1918, the club was identified on the jersey's by the name of the city or by an interlocking "S," "T," and "L."

APRIL 24   Prior to the home opener in Chicago, Cardinals manager Jack Hendricks, a native of the Windy City, is presented with a chest of silver. The Cubs won the game 2–0.

MAY 2   Red Ames pitches a two-hitter, but loses 1–0 to the Pirates at Forbes Field. With one out in the first inning, Fritz Mollwitz singled and Max Carey doubled for the only Pittsburgh run. Ames retired the last 22 batters to face him.

MAY 8   The Cardinals carry a 6–0 lead over the Reds into the ninth inning at Cardinals Field, but lose 9–6 when Cincinnati stages an astonishing nine-run rally in the final inning off Jakie May and Lee Meadows.

MAY 13   The Cardinals score two runs in the ninth inning and one in the tenth to beat the Braves 3–2 at Cardinal Field. Doug Baird's walk-off single drove in the winning run.

It was "Bat and Ball Day" in St. Louis. A portion of the gate proceeds went to purchase baseball equipment for soldiers in France. Before the game, there was a military ceremony in which a company from Jefferson Barracks participated.

MAY 25   The Cardinals score three runs in the ninth inning to defeat the Dodgers 7–6 at Cardinal Field. A two-run triple by Walton Cruise tied the score. Marty Kavanaugh, in his first game with the Cardinals following his purchase from the Indians, drove in Cruise with a single to account for the winning run.

JUNE 3   The Cardinals win a weird 12-inning, 15–12 decision over the Dodgers at Ebbets Field. In the first inning, the Cards scored two runs before the Dodgers plated six in their half. St. Louis countered with seven runs in the second to take a 9–6 lead after only an inning and a half had been played. Brooklyn took an 11–9 advantage with five in the fourth. The Cards retook the lead 12–11 in the eighth, but the Dodgers sent the contest into extra innings with a tally in the ninth. Three Cardinal runs in the twelfth settled the issue. The Cards were helped by an application of the rules by umpire Cy Rigler. In the sixth inning with Doug Baird as a base runner on second, Walton Cruise knocked a low liner to center, which Dodger outfielder Dave Hickman held momentarily then dropped. Baird reached third and, believing the ball was caught, started back for second. After going about 20 feet, Baird realized that Hickman had failed to hold onto Cruise's drive. Instead of touching third again, Baird cut across the diamond and scored. Rigler counted the run despite the protests of the Dodgers. According to Rigler, Baird had already legally touched third base, and didn't need to do so again. At the time, there was nothing in the rule book specifically addressing the situation.

JUNE 4   The Cardinals explode for seven runs in the thirteenth inning to defeat the Dodgers 8–1 in Brooklyn. Cy Rigler was once again a source of controversy. With the score tied 1–1 and the bases loaded, Marty Kavanaugh drove a ball down the third-base line. Rigler ruled it fair, but the Dodgers made no attempt to field the ball, claiming it was foul. During the course of the argument, Kavanaugh rounded the bases for a grand slam home run. Dozens of fans rushed onto to the field to get at Rigler. Players prevented them from reaching the umpire, with the exception of one individual who punched Rigler in the neck.

Kavanaugh played only 12 games as a member of the Cardinals. The fluke grand slam accounted for four of his eight RBIs with the club.

JUNE 13   The Cardinals and Phillies play to a 19-inning, 8–8 tie before the contest is called by darkness at Baker Bowl in Philadelphia. The Phillies led 8–1 after fourth inning, but the Cards battled back with three runs in the fifth inning, three in the sixth, and one in the seventh. The final 12 innings of the game were scoreless. Cardinal rookie outfielder Cliff Heathcote hit for the cycle in nine at-bats. The big day came only nine days after Heathcote's major league debut.

JUNE 19   Five Cardinals and the wife of one of the players narrowly escape death or serious injury in an accident north of Buffalo, New York. The Cards were traveling from Boston to St. Louis, a trip that required a four-hour layover in Buffalo for a change in trains. Bill Doak, Jakie May, Walton Cruise, Cliff Heathcote, Doug Baird, and Baird's wife decided to take advantage of the delay by taking a quick jaunt to Niagara Falls. The group rented a car, but 15 miles out of Buffalo a tire blew out, causing the auto to turn over. The top was down and the six were thrown clear, escaping with only scrapes and bruises. Mrs. Baird was drenched in gasoline, which fortunately did not ignite.

JUNE 20   The Cardinals sell Hank Robinson to the Yankees.

JUNE 21   The Cardinals score eight runs in the first inning and defeat the Reds 12–6 at Cardinal Field. Mike Gonzalez collected five hits, including a homer and two doubles, in five at-bats.

JULY 2   Lee Meadows starts both ends of a doubleheader against the Cubs at Cardinal Field, and loses both games. In the first tilt, Meadows was knocked out in the first inning of a 7–1 defeat. In the second, Meadows lasted only until the fourth as the Cards went down 6–2.

JULY 3   Second baseman Bobby Fisher pulls off a hidden-ball trick with one out in the ninth inning to help defeat the Cubs 2–1 at Cardinal Field. Fisher covered first base for the first out of the inning, then went to the mound to confer with pitcher Red Ames. Fisher faked putting the ball into Ames's glove, then ambled back to his position. When base runner Dode Paskert stepped off the bag, Fisher snuck in behind Paskert and tagged him out.

JULY 4   The Cardinals lose a pair of 1–0 decisions to the Cubs at Cardinal Field. Bill Doak and Red Ames were the hard-luck losing pitchers.

JULY 16   After the Braves score four runs in the top of the ninth inning to take a 6–4 lead, the Cardinals stage a sensational rally with three runs in their half to win 7–6. All three scored after the first two batters of the inning were retired. After a single and a walk, Austin McHenry tripled and scored on Johnny Beall's pinch-hit single.

JULY 20   The Cardinals lose 6–4 to the Giants at Cardinal Field, but fans raise more than $10,000 for charity. Gate receipts went toward a fund being collected by the St. Louis Tuberculosis Society to care for soldiers and sailors who contracted the disease during World War I. The contest with the Giants was preceded by teams from Jefferson Barracks and the Great Lakes Naval Training Station competing for the service title of the Midwest. The army nine won 6–5.

JULY 27

The Cardinals move from one extreme to the other, losing the first game of a doubleheader against the Dodgers in Brooklyn 2–0, then erupting for 26 hits in the second tilt to win 22–7. The big inning was the seventh, when the Cards scored seven runs.

AUGUST 1

The National Commission, baseball's governing body, announces that the 1918 season will end on September 2 in order to comply with an order issued by the federal government requiring all men of draft age to either enter the military service or find a war-related job.

AUGUST 3

The Cardinals sweep a doubleheader from the Phillies 16–12 and 7–1 in Philadelphia. The Cards had a 10–0 lead in the opener, but nearly frittered it away.

AUGUST 18

Rogers Hornsby hits a grand slam off Gary Fortune in the third inning to break a 1–1 tie and lead the Cardinals to a 5–1 victory over the Phillies in the first game of a doubleheader at Cardinal Field. The slam followed three walks. The Cards also won the first contest 3–0.

Hornsby hit .281 for the Cardinals in 1918.

AUGUST 26

Rogers Hornsby is ejected from the first game of a doubleheader, a 2–0 loss to the Giants at Cardinal Field. He was tossed by the home plate umpire for arguing a called third strike. According to the rules of the day, Hornsby was ineligible to play in the second game because he was banished from the opener.

Manager Jack Hendricks believed that Hornsby had been ejected on purpose so that he wouldn't have to play in the nightcap. Hornsby was fined $50 and insisted once the season ended that he wouldn't play for the Cards in 1919 if Hendricks was still the manager.

SEPTEMBER 2

Gene Paulette pitches to two batters in a 6–3 loss to the Reds in Cincinnati in the first game of a doubleheader on the final day of the season. The Reds also won the second game, 1–0.

By pitching, Paulette played all nine positions in 1918. He appeared in 97 games at first base, twelve at shortstop, seven at second base, three in right field, two at third base, and one each as a right fielder, a center fielder, a catcher, and a pitcher. The second game on September 2 was also historic. The starting pitchers were Oscar Tuero of the Cardinals and Dolf Luque of the Reds. It was the first time that two Latins faced each other as starters. Earlier in the year, Tuero and catcher Mike Gonzalez formed the first all-Latin battery in the majors. Tuero, Luque, and Gonzalez were all from Cuba.

NOVEMBER 11

An armistice is signed with Germany ending World War I.

When the 1918 season came to a close, it appeared that there would be no baseball in 1919 because the end of the war was nowhere in sight. But a series of victories by the Allies, led by the United States, Great Britain, and France, sped the conflict to a conclusion by November 1918. Owners hastily made plans for the 1919 season, but due to the late start in preparing for the campaign and the anticipation of a poor year at the gate, baseball executives shortened the season to 140 games. It was a decision that officials came to regret, as attendance reached record levels in 1919.

1919

Season in a Sentence

Branch Rickey takes over as manager, but the club falls out of contention early and finishes last in the major leagues in attendance.

Finish • Won • Lost • Pct • GB

Seventh   54   83   .394   40.5

Manager

Branch Rickey

Stats

	Cards	NL	Rank
Batting Avg:	.256	.258	5
On-Base Pct:	.305	.311	6
Slugging Pct:	.326	.337	6
Home Runs:	18		7
Stolen Bases:	148		4
ERA:	3.23	2.91	7
Fielding Avg:	.963	.967	7
Runs Scored:	463		7
Runs Allowed:	552		6

Starting Lineup

Verne Clemons, c
Dots Miller, 1b
Milt Stock, 2b-3b
Rogers Hornsby, 3b-ss
Doc Lavan, ss
Austin McHenry, lf
Cliff Heathcote, cf
Jack Smith, rf-cf
Burt Shotton, lf
Joe Schultz, rf
Frank Snyder, c
Gene Paulette, 1b

Pitchers

Bill Doak, sp
Marv Goodwin, sp-rp
Jakie May, sp-rp
Lee Meadows, sp-rp
Ferdie Schupp, sp
Oscar Tuero, rp-sp
Bill Sherdel, rp-sp
Red Ames, rp
Elmer Jacobs, rp

Attendance

167,059 (eighth in NL)

Club Leaders

Batting Avg:	Hornsby	.318
On-Base Pct:	Hornsby	.384
Slugging Pct:	Hornsby	.430
Home Runs:	Hornsby	8
RBIs:	Hornsby	71
Runs:	Hornsby	68
Stolen Bases:	Smith	30
Wins:	Doak	13
Strikeouts:	Doak	69
ERA:	Goodwin	2.51
Saves:	Tuero	4

JANUARY 21   The Cardinals trade Doug Baird, Gene Packard, and Stuffy Stewart to the Phillies for Milt Stock, Pickles Dillhoefer, and Dixie Davis.

This proved to be an excellent trade for the Cardinals. Stock was a five-year starter at third base for the club. In 1919, he hit .316 for the Cards.

JANUARY 25   Jack Hendricks is relieved of his duties as manager and replaced by Branch Rickey.

Hendricks was fired after serving only one year of a two-year contract. The Cardinals bought him off rather than bring him back for another year. Hendricks later managed the Reds from 1924 through 1929. Rickey continued to run the front office operation as the Cardinals' president in addition to his duties as manager. He remained as manager until 1925.

FEBRUARY 1   The Cardinals purchase Burt Shotton from the Senators.

Earlier in his career, Shotton played for Branch Rickey with the Browns. Shotton played for the Cardinals from 1919 through 1923 and was a coach from 1923 through 1925. He was also Rickey's "Sunday manager." Rickey made a promise to his mother that he would never enter a ballpark on a Sunday, a pledge he kept to his dying day.

APRIL 16   An auto driven by Lee Meadows with four teammates aboard is involved in a collision with a streetcar on a rain-slickened St. Louis street. The car overturned, tossing Meadows through the windshield. Fortunately, he was only bruised and not seriously hurt. Nor were fellow pitchers Bill Doak, Bill Sherdel, and Oscar Horstmann. Red Ames, a fifth pitcher riding in the car, had to miss a month because of his injuries.

The Cardinals held their spring training drills in St. Louis because the club didn't have the cash to head south. Branch Rickey had the team work out at Washington University. Stockholder A. M. Diaz, who had made money selling shoemakers' tools and supplies, agreed to house the players and buy equipment for spring training. The coaches guarded the baseballs so the team wouldn't have to foot the bill for new ones. The uniforms from the year before that were salvageable were sent to seamstresses for patching, and borrowed others from semipro and high school teams. Rickey found a sporting goods store that would make the rest of the jerseys and extend him credit. With the exception of World War II, when travel was restricted, the 1919 Cardinals and Philadelphia Athletics were the last two clubs to conduct spring training in their home city.

APRIL 23   The Cardinals open the season with a 6–2 loss to the Reds in Cincinnati. The Cards led 2–0 before allowing a run in the seventh inning and five in the eighth.

APRIL 29   After opening the season with five straight losses, the Cardinals finally win with a 1–0 victory over the Cubs in Chicago. Jakie May pitched the shutout and Frank Snyder drove in the lone run of the game with a single in the second inning.

MAY 1   In the home opener, the Cardinals lose 6–2 to the Reds before a paltry crowd of 2,100 at Cardinal Field.

MAY 11   Hod Eller of the Reds hurls a no-hitter against the Cardinals in Cincinnati. Burt Shotton closed out the 6–0 St. Louis loss by grounding out to second base.

MAY 19   The Cardinals sell Mike Gonzalez to the Giants.

MAY 20   The Cardinals head into the bottom of the ninth inning in Philadelphia leading 7–2, but blow the advantage when Marv Goodwin and Bill Sherdel allow six runs for an 8–7 Phillies victory.

MAY 28   Oscar Tuero pitches a 13-inning complete game and drives in two runs in the top of the thirteenth with a single to beat the Dodgers 7–5 in Brooklyn.

JUNE 5   Bill Doak pitches the Cardinals to a 1–0 win over the Reds at Cardinal Field. The game ended when pinch-hitter Joe Schultz drew a bases-loaded walk in the ninth inning from Hod Eller.

JUNE 6   A two-run, walk-off single by Cliff Heathcote beats the Phillies 6–5 at Cardinal Field.

JUNE 29   The Cardinals collect 22 hits and wallop the Reds 14–9 in Cincinnati.

JULY 9   The Cardinals outlast the Giants 12–8 in New York.

Gene Paulette was tossed by umpire Pete Harrison before taking his position. After first baseman Dots Miller was injured, Branch Rickey called on Paulette as a substitute. Before a pitch was thrown, Paulette made a remark that caused Harrison to eject him from the premises.

JULY 14   The Cardinals trade Lee Meadows and Gene Paulette to the Phillies for Elmer Jacobs, Frank Woodward, and Doug Baird.

> *This was a bad move. After the trade, Meadows won 136 games and lost 113 for the Phillies and Pirates. He pitched for Pittsburgh in both the 1925 and 1927 World Series.*

JULY 16   The Cardinals trade Frank Snyder to the Giants for Ferdie Schupp.

> *For the second time in three days, the Cardinals made a terrible trade. Schupp gave St. Louis one good season before suffering from arm miseries. Snyder was the starting catcher on Giants clubs that played in the World Series four consecutive seasons from 1921 through 1924.*

JULY 17   In his first game since his trade to the Phillies, Lee Meadows beats his former mates 1–0 in 12 innings at Philadelphia. Elmer Jacobs, acquired in the same deal, pitched the complete-game loss.

AUGUST 26   The Cardinals sell Doug Baird to the Dodgers.

> *To recap, the Cardinals traded Baird to the Phillies on January 21, 1919, reacquired him from the Phils in another trade on July 14, then sold him to Brooklyn on August 26.*

AUGUST 28   Cardinal pitcher Ferdie Schupp leads off the ninth inning with a walk-off, inside-the-park homer that beats the Dodgers 4–3 at Cardinal Field.

SEPTEMBER 5   The Cardinals sell Red Ames to the Phillies.

SEPTEMBER 27   Rogers Hornsby hits a grand slam off Wilbur Cooper in the first inning of a 5–3 win over the Pirates at Cardinals Field.

> *Hornsby closed out the 1919 season with a .318 batting average, eight homers, and 71 RBIs.*

THE STATE OF THE CARDINALS

From 1892, the year that the Cardinals entered the National League, through 1920, the club had only five winning seasons, none of them consecutively. Things began to change for the better in 1921 when the Cards finished in third place, only seven games out of first, with record of 87–66. The Cardinals took a giant leap forward in 1926 by capturing their first National League pennant, which was followed by a World Series victory over the Yankees. After a close second in 1927, another NL crown followed in 1928. Overall, the Cardinals had a record of 822–712, a winning percentage of .536. It was the fourth-best record in the majors, trailing only the Yankees, Giants, and Pirates. Besides the two won by the Cards, NL pennants during the 1920s were taken by the Dodgers (1920), Giants (1921, 1922, 1923, and 1924), Pirates (1925 and 1927), and Cubs (1929).

THE BEST TEAM

The 1926 club took the only World Championship of the decade, but the 1928 outfit had the best record with a mark of 95–59.

THE WORST TEAM

The progress the Cardinals made early in the decade began to look like a mirage when the 1924 club finished a disappointing 65–89 and landed in sixth place.

THE BEST MOMENT

Grover Alexander came out of the bullpen in Game Seven of the 1926 World Series to snuff out a Yankee rally and claim the first World Series title for the city of St. Louis.

THE WORST MOMENT

Promising young outfielder Austin McHenry died of a brain tumor on November 27, 1922, at the age of 27. It was the second death of an active player during the year. In February, catcher Pickles Dillhoefer died of typhoid fever.

THE ALL-DECADE TEAM • YEARS W/CARDS

Verne Clemons, c	1919–24
Jim Bottomley, 1b	1922–32
Rogers Hornsby, 2b	1915–26, 1933
Milt Stock, 3b	1919–23
Doc Lavan, ss	1919–24
Chick Hafey, lf	1924–31
Taylor Douthit, cf	1923–31
Jack Smith, rf	1915–26
Jesse Haines, p	1920–37
Bill Sherdel, p	1918–30, 1932
Grover Alexander, p	1926–29
Flint Rhem, p	1924–28, 1930–32, 1934, 1936

Other top players with the Cardinals during the 1920s were second baseman Frankie Frisch (1927–37), outfielder Jack Smith (1915–26), left fielder Ray Blades (1922–32), left fielder Austin McHenry (1918–22), third baseman Les Bell (1923–27), first baseman Jack Fournier (1920–22), catcher Bob O'Farrell (1925–28, 1933, 1935), and pitcher Bill Doak (1913–24, 1929). Hornsby, Frisch, Bottomley, Haines, and Hafey are all in the Hall of Fame. The strength of the team was at second base, where Hornsby and Frisch patrolled. The club was unable to secure an adequate shortstop to team with them, however.

THE DECADE LEADERS

Batting Avg:	Hornsby	.386
On-Base Pct:	Hornsby	.456
Slugging Pct:	Hornsby	.638
Home Runs:	Hornsby	164
RBIs:	Bottomley	885
Runs:	Hornsby	807
Stolen Bases:	Smith	119
Wins:	Haines	153
Strikeouts:	Haines	742
ERA:	Doak	3.38
Saves:	Sherdel	24

THE HOME FIELD

The Cardinals moved out of ramshackle Cardinal Field, the last wooden ballpark in the majors, and into Sportsman's Park during the middle of the 1920 season. The Cardinals shared Sportsman's Park with the Browns, who owned the facility. Renamed Busch Stadium in 1953, it remained the home of the Cardinals until 1966. The capacity of the ballpark was increased from 18,000 to 32,000 between the 1925 and 1926 seasons.

THE GAME YOU WISH YOU HAD SEEN

Most of the Cardinals' best moments during the 1920s, including the 1926 and 1928 pennant clinchings and the dramatic Game Seven win in the 1926 World Series, took place out of town. The best game in St. Louis occured on July 17, 1924, when Jesse Haines pitched the first Cardinal no-hitter in 33 years, and the first ever since the club joined the National League in 1892, in front of a large crowd assembled for the annual benefit for the Tuberculosis Society.

THE WAY THE GAME WAS PLAYED

Rule changes in 1920, and the emergence of Babe Ruth as a star changed baseball from a low-scoring defensive affair to a high-scoring offensive carnival. This was the first decade that baseball embraced the home run. Teams went from averaging 3.5 runs a game in 1917 to 5.0 runs a game in 1922 to 5.7 per game in 1930. Team batting averages in the NL ballooned from .249 in 1917 to .292 in 1922 and .303 in 1930. Not surprisingly, team ERAs jumped nearly two runs. The 1928 season was the first in National League history in which there were more home runs than stolen bases. There wouldn't be another season in which the number of steals exceeded the numbers of homers in the NL until 1975. Pitchers completed less than half of their starts in the NL in 1922, the first time that happened as relief pitching continued to gain importance.

THE MANAGEMENT

The Cardinals began to win during the 1920s because of the team of owner Sam Breadon, who took over the presidency of the club in 1920, and Branch Rickey, who assumed the duties of a modern-day general manager. Rickey also directed the Cardinals from the dugout from 1919 to 1925, when Rogers Hornsby became player-manager. Hornsby led the Card to the 1926 World Championship. Other Cardinal managers were Bob O'Farrell (1927), Bill McKechnie (1928), Billy Southworth (1929), and Bill McKechnie again (1929). Despite a run of success in the late 1920s, St. Louis was somewhat of a graveyard for managers. Hornsby was traded to the Giants in December 1926 two months after guiding the club to its first World Championship. O'Farrell was canned following a 1927 season in which the Cards finished second, only 1½ games out of first. McKechnie was let go after the Cards won the pennant in 1928. He was replaced by Southworth, who was fired in July 1929. McKechnie was brought back to succeed Southworth, only to be released at the end of the 1929 season. Gabby Street, who served as interim manager for one game in 1929, was hired for the 1930 campaign.

THE BEST PLAYER MOVE

The best player move was the signing of Chick Hafey out of Berkeley High School in Berkeley, California, in March 1923. He was one of the many players mined by the Cardinals in the newly developed farm system. The best deal with another club was the purchase of Grover Alexander from the Cubs in June 1926.

THE WORST PLAYER MOVE

The worst trade sent Jack Fournier to the Dodgers in February 1923 for Hy Myers and Ray Schmandt.

1920

Season in a Sentence

The Cardinals make progress, staying in the pennant race until June in a season in which the club moves out of rickety Cardinal Field and into Sportsman's Park.

Finish • Won • Lost • Pct • GB

Fifth (tie)   75   79   .487   18.0

Manager

Branch Rickey

Stats

Stats	Cards	NL	Rank
Batting Avg:	.289	.270	1
On-Base Pct:	.337	.322	1
Slugging Pct:	.385	.357	1
Home Runs:	32		4
Stolen Bases:	128		4
ERA:	3.43	3.13	6
Fielding Avg:	.961	.968	8
Runs Scored:	675		2
Runs Allowed:	682		7

Starting Lineup

Verne Clemons, c
Jack Fournier, 1b
Rogers Hornsby, 2b
Milt Stock, 3b
Doc Lavan, ss
Austin McHenry, lf
Cliff Heathcote, cf-rf
Joe Schultz, rf
Jack Smith, cf
Hal Janvrin, ss-1b-lf
Pickles Dillhoefer, c
Burt Shotton, lf

Pitchers

Bill Doak, sp
Jesse Haines, sp
Ferdie Schupp, sp
Bill Sherdel, rp
Marv Goodwin, rp-sp
Lou North, rp
Elmer Jacobs, rp-sp

Attendance

326,836 (seventh in NL)

Club Leaders

Batting Avg:	Hornsby	.370
On-Base Pct:	Hornsby	.431
Slugging Pct:	Hornsby	.559
Home Runs:	McHenry	10
RBIs:	Hornsby	94
Runs:	Hornsby	96
Stolen Bases:	Fournier	26
Wins:	Doak	20
Strikeouts:	Haines	120
ERA:	Doak	2.53
Saves:	Sherdel	6

JANUARY 13   Three days before the Prohibition amendment to the Constitution goes into effect, Sam Breadon is elected president of the Cardinals. Branch Rickey, who had been club president, was named vice president and remained as manager.

The plan of James Jones to turn the Cardinals into a community-owned organization (see March 5, 1917) was unworkable. The club was on the verge of bankruptcy when the group headed by Jones bought the Cards, and the situation didn't improve under his leadership. Breadon proved to be the financial angel that the Cardinals needed. He served as club president until 1947, during which the Cards won nine NL pennants and six World Series. The son of Irish immigrants, Breadon left his native New York City in 1903 at the age of 24 at the urging of a friend to move to St. Louis with plans to open a garage and an automobile agency. He started as a mechanic in the fast-growing, fledgling industry, but was fired after only a few months on the job. To make ends meet, Breadon sold popcorn at the 1904 World's Fair and caught the attention of Marion Lambert, a member of a prominent St. Louis family that owned a pharmaceutical company that marketed Listerine. Impressed by Breadon's plans for the future, Lambert offered him a partnership in the Western Automobile Company. The auto company distributed Pierce-Arrows and Fords and made

Breadon, a man with only a grade-school education, a millionaire. Breadon was merely one of the 1,200 individuals who bought shares in the Cardinals in 1917 under the scheme of James Jones to make the club a community-owned affair. Breadon had little interest in baseball, but was persuaded to invest in Jones's organization at the insistence of a friend named Fuzzy Anderson. Initially, Breadon owned only four shares, which he purchased for $200, but became consumed by the sport and soon began buying the stock of others in large chunks. As time passed, the ownership group found itself frequently strapped for cash. At Jones's instance, Breadon took an active role in the group's business dealings. Breadon kept purchasing more stock until he became the majority owner in 1922.

FEBRUARY 9   Baseball's rules committee adopts new regulations that usher in the era of the lively ball. The changes were spurred in part by the owners' recognition of the positive impact of Babe Ruth upon the game. Ruth clubbed a then-record 29 home runs for the Red Sox in 1919 and helped the American League set an all-time attendance records. The committee adopted a more lively ball, agreed to keep a fresh ball in play at all times, and banned pitchers from using any foreign substances to deface the ball. These included paraffin, resin, powder, emery boards, files, and saliva. There were 17 pitchers, however, who were allowed to continue to use the spitball for the remainder of their career, however, because they had come to rely heavily on the pitch. One of the 17 was Cardinal pitcher Bill Doak.

APRIL 14   On Opening Day, the Cardinals lose 5–4 in 10 innings to the Pirates at Cardinal Field. Burt Shotton collected three hits.

MAY 18   Jesse Haines pitches a one-hitter, but loses 1–0 to the Phillies at Cardinal Field. The lone run of the game scored in the fifth inning on a triple by Casey Stengel and a throwing error by catcher Pickles Dillhoefer.

Jesse Haines was purchased by the Cardinals from Kansas City of the American Association in November 1919 for $10,000 when he was 26 years old. He went on to pitch more years (18) in a Cardinal uniform than anyone in history. Haines pitched his last game at the age of 44. He ranks second among Cardinal pitchers in career wins (210), first in games (554), third in games started (388), second in complete games (209), fifth in shutouts (24), second in innings pitched (3,203²/₃), and fifth in strikeouts (979). Haines was elected to the Hall of Fame in 1970.

MAY 21   Eppa Rixey of the Phillies throws a bat into the Cardinal Field stands during a 3–1 Cardinal win. Rixey threw the bat after being hit by a pitch from Marv Goodwin. The bat hit the top of the dugout before reaching the seats. Rixey said the incident was accidental.

MAY 22   The Cardinals score two runs in the ninth inning and one in the tenth to beat the Giants 3–2 at Sportman's Park. In the top of the tenth, the Cardinals pulled off a triple play. With George Burns as the New York runner on third and Ross Youngs on first, Art Fletcher drove a ball to right, where Joe Schultz made a spectacular catch. Schultz threw to home plate to retire George Burns. Youngs, who was off and running because he didn't believe that Schultz had a chance of making the out, had to scamper back to first and was thrown by catcher Verne Clemons to Jack Fournier.

MAY 26   A boneheaded mistake by Reds left fielder Pat Duncan leads to a 10–8 win by the
           Cardinals at Cardinal Field. With the score tied 8–8 in the bottom of the eighth
           inning and a St. Louis runner on third base, Rogers Hornsby dropped a hit in front
           of Duncan. Believing it was the ninth inning and that the winning run had crossed
           the plate, Duncan trotted off the field while Hornsby raced around the bases for an
           inside-the-park homer.

MAY 27   The Cardinals outslug the Reds 16–9 at Cardinals Field.

MAY 29   A rally in the eighth inning of an 8–5 loss to the Cubs in Chicago comes up short in
           part due to a base-running blunder by Cardinal shortstop Doc Lavan. Lavan tried to
           steal third base, only to discover a teammate already occupying the bag.

           *Lavan's mental lapse wasn't due to a lack of education. A practicing medical
           doctor with a degree from the University of Michigan, Lavan was an officer
           in the US Navy Medical Corps during both World War I and World War II,
           retiring with the rank of Commander in the Naval Reserves. He was also a
           health officer in New York City, St. Louis, Kansas City, Toledo, Kalamazoo, and
           Grand Rapids, and served as director of research for the National Foundation
           for Infantile Paralysis.*

JUNE 1   The Cardinals win 5–4 in a 15-inning marathon in Pittsburgh. The winning run
           scored after Austin McHenry doubled, then crossed the plate after two errors.

JUNE 6   The Cardinals defeat the Cubs 5–2 at Cardinal Field.

           *No one knew it at the time, but this was the last game at Cardinal Field,
           baseball's last ballpark constructed entirely of wood. One of the first problems
           facing new club owner Sam Breadon was a dilapidated ballpark that was in
           danger of being condemned by St. Louis officials. Cardinal Field needed massive
           renovation to bring it up to major league standards, and it would have been
           more cost effective to simply tear down the facility and start over. This was long
           before local or state governments built new stadiums for sports teams. Breadon
           would have to bear the cost of a renovation or a new ballpark. Instead, Breadon
           wanted to rent Sportsman's Park from the Browns. National and American
           League schedules were drawn so that the Cardinals and Browns never played
           at home at the same time, and the Cardinals could use the facility while the
           Browns were on the road. Breadon approached Browns owner Phil Ball while
           the Cardinals were on a five-city road trip beginning on June 7. The Cardinals
           owner reasoned that it was a good deal for both clubs. The Cardinals wouldn't
           have to spend the money to build a new ballpark. Ball had blueprints drawn
           up to expand the capacity of Sportsman's Park from 18,000 to 32,000, but
           didn't have the money to carry out the plan. The rent he would receive from the
           Cardinals would finance the expansion. Ball was resistant to the idea, however.
           Part of it was personal. Ball was still angry at Branch Rickey for leaving the
           Browns to run the Cardinals three years earlier. Ball was persuaded to allow the
           Cardinals to rent his ballpark when Breadon walked away from the negotiations
           by threatening to build a ballpark of his own. Breadon may have been bluffing,
           but Ball couldn't take a chance. If Breadon build a larger, more modern, and
           more accessible ballpark than Sportsman's Park, it would hinder the Browns'
           ability to attract fans. Ball gave in on June 24 and leased the ballpark to the
           Cardinals for 10 years at $20,000 annually. The Cards played their first game*

at Sportsman's Park on July 1. After tearing down Cardinal Field, Breadon sold most of the property for $200,000 to the St. Louis board of education, which built Beaumont High School. A corner of the lot was sold for $75,000 for a streetcar loop. With the money realized from the real estate sale, Breadon invested in baseball's first farm system, which helped transform the Cardinals into perennial winners.

JUNE 10   Umpire Cy Rigler needs police protection following a 9–3 Cardinals win over the Dodgers at Ebbets Field. Brooklyn fans were angry over a safe call of St. Louis first baseman Jack Fournier in the seventh inning. As soon as the game ended, several hundred fans leaped onto the field and made a rush at Rigler.

JUNE 17   Austin McHenry homers off future Hall of Famer Eppa Rixey in the fifth inning to defeat the Phillies 1–0 in Philadelphia. Jesse Haines pitched the shutout.

The victory was the seventh in a row for the Cardinals. The club was 30–23 and in third place, one game back of the first-place Reds. The Cards lost their next five games, however, and were never again a serious factor in the race.

JULY 1   The Cardinals play at Sportsman's Park for the first time, and lose 6–2 when the Pirates score four runs in the tenth inning. The crowd numbered about 20,000, overflowing the grandstand. Some 2,000 were located behind a temporary fence in the outfield.

JULY 7   During an 8–5 loss to the Cubs at Sportsman's Park, Chicago outfielder Dode Paskert tries to climb into the grandstand after engaging in an argument with two hecklers. Paskert stayed in the game, and the two offending spectators were escorted from the premises by police officers.

JULY 12   Cliff Heathcote scores from second base on a Fred Toney wild pitch in the tenth inning to beat the Giants 4–3 at Sportsman's Park.

JULY 17   Doc Lavan is ejected from the sixth inning of a 1–0 loss to the Phillies at Sportsman's Park after throwing a bat at Philadelphia pitcher George Smith. Lavan was nearly hit by a pitch in the fourth inning, then was plunked by Smith in the sixth.

JULY 19   Bill Sherdel pitches 12 innings and scores the winning run in a 3–2 win over the Phillies at Sportsman's Park. Sherdel started the twelfth with a double and scored on Jack Fournier's single.

AUGUST 9   The Cardinals outlast the Phillies 12–10 at Baker Bowl. The Cards overtook Philadelphia leads four times in the seesaw affair to either tie the score or take the lead themselves. The Cardinals were behind 5–0 in the first inning, 6–5 in the fourth, 7–6 in the fifth, and 9–8 in the seventh. Lou North, the fifth Cardinal pitcher, drove in both runs in the twelfth inning with a single.

AUGUST 10   Bill Doak pitches a one-hitter to beat the Phillies 5–1 in Philadelphia. Doak's own fielding lapse cost him a no-hitter. In the seventh inning, Cy Williams hit a ball that eluded first baseman Jack Fournier, moving to his right, but was fielded by second baseman Rogers Hornsby. Hornsby had plenty of time to throw out Williams, but Doak was late covering the bag and the batter was safe with a single.

Doak pitched three one-hitters during his career, and in each case the lone hit was an infield single in which Doak failed to cover first base in time (see May 11, 1922, and July 13, 1922).

AUGUST 11   The Cardinals collect 25 hits and wallop the Phillies 18–9 in Philadelphia. Jack Fournier had five hits, including two doubles, in seven at-bats. Jesse Haines picked up four hits, including a homer.

In his first season with the Cardinals, Fournier batted .306.

AUGUST 14   Bill Doak pitches the Cardinals to a 1–0 win over the Pirates in the first game of a doubleheader at Forbes Field. The lone run of the game scored in the third inning on a double by Milt Stock and a single by Rogers Hornsby. The second tilt ended in a 1–1 tie after eight innings, called to allowed both teams to catch a train.

Stock collected 204 hits and batted .319 in 1920 while playing in all 155 games.

AUGUST 20   The 6–4 win over the Braves at Sportsman's Park is stopped for five minutes at 4 PM with the players standing in silence as a tribute to the memory of Indians shortstop Ray Chapman, who died three days earlier from the effects of being hit in a head by a pitched ball thrown by Carl Mays of the Yankees.

SEPTEMBER 10   Two weeks after women are granted the right to vote with the passage of the 19th Amendment, the Cardinals score three runs in the eleventh inning to take an 8–5 lead, but the Dodgers rally with four in their half off Bill Sherdel to win 9–8 in Brooklyn. The Dodgers scored twice in the ninth to send the contest into extra innings.

SEPTEMBER 17   The Cardinals launch 12 straight hits in the fourth and fifth innings to set a major league record for most consecutive hits during a 9–4 win over the Braves in Boston. With one out in the fourth, the Cards got 10 hits in succession and scored eight runs. The last two men in the inning were thrown out trying on the base paths trying to take an extra base. Milt Stock was out attempting to make second on a single, and Austin McHenry was retired trying to stretch a double into a triple. Doc Lavan opened the fifth with a double, and Cliff Heathcote followed with a single before Verne Clemons popped out to shortstop Rabbit Maranville to end the streak. McHenry, Lavan, and Heathcote each collected two of the 12 consecutive hits. The others were picked up by Clemons, Bill Doak, Mike Knode, Jack Fournier, Milt Stock, and Rogers Hornsby. Boston pitcher Mule Watson gave up the first five hits, George McQuillan the next five, and Leo Townsend the final two. The winning pitcher was Bill Doak, who earned his 20th victory of the year.

Doak was 20–12 with a 2.53 earned run average in 1920.

SEPTEMBER 18   Ferdie Schupp starts both ends of a doubleheader against the Braves in Boston. In the opener, Schupp lasted only three innings and received a no-decision in a 7–6 win in 13 innings. In the second tilt, Schupp went 3²/₃ and was the losing pitcher in a 5–3 decision.

SEPTEMBER 27   The Cardinals collect 25 hits and score in every inning from the second through the ninth in a 16–1 hammering of the Cubs in Chicago. Cliff Heathcote had five hits, including a double, in five at-bats.

The Cardinals hit 96 triples in 1920, a club record.

OCTOBER 1   The Cubs defeat the Cardinals 3–2 in 17 innings in Chicago. Jesse Haines and Grover Alexander, two hurlers destined for the Hall of Fame, pitched complete games. Haines held the Cubs hitless for 10 consecutive innings from the seventh through the sixteenth while walking only two batters, before losing the game in the seventeenth.

DECEMBER 29   The Cardinals turn down a $200,000 offer from the Giants for Rogers Hornsby.

Playing second base on a regular basis for the first time in his career, Hornsby led the NL in batting average (.370), on-base percentage (.431), slugging percentage (.559), hits (218), doubles (44), total bases (329), and RBIs (94), in addition to collecting 20 triples during the 1920 season. The Giants had been after Hornsby for more than a year, and the $200,000 offer was $75,000 more than the Yankees paid the Red Sox for Babe Ruth in January 1920. The Giants' lucrative proposition spurred great debate among the Cardinals' seven-man board of directors, some of whom believed that the Cards should take the money and run. The club held onto Hornsby, however, hoping to build a pennant-contending team around one of the best players in the game.

1921

Season in a Sentence

Propelled by winning streaks of ten games in June and eight in August, the Cardinals win 87 times, the highest single-season total by the club since 1889.

Finish • Won • Lost • Pct • GB

Third   87   66   .569   7.0

Manager

Branch Rickey

Stats

Stats	Cards	• NL •	Rank
Batting Avg:	.308	.289	1
On-Base Pct:	.358	.338	2
Slugging Pct:	.437	.397	1
Home Runs:	83		2
Stolen Bases:	94		5 (tie)
ERA:	3.62	3.78	4
Fielding Avg:	.965	.967	6
Runs Scored:	809		2
Runs Allowed:	681		4 (tie)

Starting Lineup

Verne Clemons, c
Jack Fournier, 1b
Rogers Hornsby, 2b
Milt Stock, 3b
Doc Lavan, ss
Austin McHenry, lf
Les Mann, cf
Jack Smith, rf
Joe Schultz, rf
Heinie Mueller, cf
Pickles Dillhoefer, c
Cliff Heatcote, cf

Pitchers

Jesse Haines, sp
Bill Doak, sp
Bill Pertica, sp
Roy Walker, sp-rp
Jeff Pfeffer, sp
Lou North, rp
Bill Sherdel, rp

Attendance

384,773 (fifth in NL)

Club Leaders

Batting Avg:	Hornsby	.397
On-Base Pct:	Hornsby	.458
Slugging Pct:	Hornsby	.639
Home Runs:	Hornsby	21
RBIs:	Hornsby	126
Runs:	Hornsby	131
Stolen Bases:	Fournier	20
Wins:	Haines	18
Strikeouts:	Haines	84
ERA:	Doak	2.59
Saves:	North	7

MARCH 24	Three weeks after the inauguration of Warren Harding as US president, Gene Paulette is banned from baseball for life for his association with gamblers while playing for the club. Paulette played for the Cardinals from 1916 through 1919. It was alleged that during that period, he accepted money from St. Louis gamblers Elmer Farrar and Carl Zork in 1919 in order to throw games to the opposition. Paulette claimed his innocence, but admitted accepting money from Farrar after Farrar and Zork approached him about throwing selected games on which gamblers had placed large bets. Paulette said the money he received was a loan, but admitted that it was never repaid. Zork was implicated in the 1919 World Series scandal in which the White Sox agreed to throw games in collusion with gamblers.
APRIL 13	The Cardinals usher in the 1921 season with a 5–2 loss to the Cubs in Chicago.
APRIL 16	The final game of the series against the Cubs in Chicago is postponed by snow.
APRIL 21	The scheduled home opener against the Cubs is rained out. The April 22 contest was also postponed.
APRIL 23	The Cardinals finally get the home opener under way and lose 5–1 to the Cubs at Sportsman's Park. Mayor Henry Kiel threw out the ceremonial first pitch. He was accompanied by Sao-Ke Alfred Sze, the Chinese Minister to the United States.

APRIL 29 — Rogers Hornsby is presented with an eight-cylinder limousine before a 7–3 loss to the Reds at Sportsman's Park. Hornsby received the gift from the Missouri State Life Insurance Company, for which he worked during the previous offseason.

> *The loss dropped the Cardinals' record to 1–9 at the start of a streaky season for the club. On May 13, the Cards were 5–15, then hit period of success. A 10-game winning streak raised the Cardinals record to 27–22 on June 13. After dropping to 42–47 on July 26, St. Louis won 45 of its last 64 games to finish at 87–66.*

MAY 1 — Jesse Haines pitches the Cardinals to a 1–0 win over the Reds at Sportsman's Park. The lone run of the game scored on a triple by Jack Fournier and a sacrifice fly by Doc Lavan off Rube Marquard.

> *Haines had a record of 18–12 and an ERA of 3.50 in 1921.*

MAY 21 — The Cardinals trounce the Phillies 13–3 at Philadelphia.

MAY 28 — The Cardinals score three runs in the ninth inning to beat the Cubs 8–7 in the first game of a doubleheader in Chicago. The Cards also won the second tilt, 9–2.

JUNE 4 — The Cardinals outlast the Phillies 11–9 at Sportsman's Park.

JUNE 6 — The Cardinals wallop the Phillies 11–0 at Sportsman's Park.

JUNE 7 — The Cardinals score seven runs in the first inning and clobber the Dodgers 14–5 at Sportsman's Park.

JUNE 12 — After the Giants score two runs in the top of the ninth to take a 3–2 lead, the Cardinals come back with a pair in their half on Milt Stock's two-run, walk-off double to win 4–3 at Sportsman's Park. It was the club's ninth victory in a row.

JUNE 13 — The Cardinals record their tenth win in a row with a 10–1 decision over the Giants at Sportsman's Park.

JUNE 18 — The Cardinals trade Ferdie Schupp and Hal Janvrin to the Dodgers for Jeff Pfeffer.

JUNE 19 — Austin McHenry hits a three-run walk-off double in the ninth inning to beat the Braves 5–4 at Sportsman's Park.

> *McHenry looked like a rising star when he finished the 1921 season third in the NL in batting average (.350), fourth in homers (17), and third in RBIs (102). The following season, McHenry suffered from severe headaches and blurred vision. At first, it was diagnosed as a sinus infection, but further tests revealed a brain tumor. An operation was unsuccessful, and McHenry died at the age of 27 on November 27, 1922.*

JUNE 21 — The Cardinals hammer the Cubs 17–5 in the first game of a doubleheader at Sportsman's Park before losing the nightcap 6–3. Rogers Hornsby hit a home run in the opener.

> *Hornsby started the season as a left fielder, but the experiment lasted only six*

games and he returned to second base. Hornsby had another terrific season in 1921, leading the NL in batting average (.397), on-base percentage (.458), slugging percentage (.639), runs (131), hits (235), doubles (44), triples (18), RBIs (126), and total bases (378), and finished second in home runs (21). From July 3 through July 20, Hornsby set a National League record (since tied) for most games consecutive games scoring a run with 17. He scored 21 runs during the streak.

JUNE 25   Trailing 3–0, the Cardinals score seven runs in the sixth inning and defeat the Pirates 7–4 in the first game of a doubleheader at Sportsman's Park. Pittsburgh won the second game 5–2.

JULY 7   The Cardinals break open a close game with five runs in the seventh inning and seven in the eighth to beat the Phillies 15–2 in Philadelphia. The Cards collected 20 hits in the contest.

JULY 9   With the consent of the Phillies, the Cardinals use a courtesy runner during a 7–1 win in Philadelphia. In the first inning, Jack Fournier was hit by a Bill Hubbell pitch and collapsed on the way to first base. Specs Toporcer went in to run for Fournier, who was allowed to return to his defensive position in the bottom of the inning after a brief recovery period. Two weeks later, the Cardinals returned the favor (see July 26, 1921).

             Fournier hit .343 with 16 homers, 86 RBIs, and 103 runs scored in 1921.

JULY 11   Rain stops a game-tying Cardinal rally against the Phillies in Philadelphia. The Cards tied the score 9–9 in the top of the ninth, but a downpour prevented a continuation of the game. The score reverted back to the end of the eighth inning, and the Phillies were declared 9–8 winners.

JULY 26   The good sportsmanship of Branch Rickey backfires in an 8–7 loss to the Phillies at Sportsman's Park.

             Phillies catcher John Peters was put out the game in the second inning for arguing with the umpires. Philadelphia manager Wild Bill Donovan had only Frank Bruggy available to catch, but Bruggy could barely stand because of an injured leg. Rickey allowed the Phils to use pinch runners for Bruggy twice in the game with Bruggy allowed to remain in the lineup. The Cardinals led 7–3 at the end of the sixth inning, but the Phillies rallied to win with five runs over the last three innings.

JULY 29   Jeff Pfeffer pitches the Cardinals to a 1–0 win over the Dodgers at Sportsman's Park. Austin McHenry accounted for the lone run of the game with a homer in the fifth inning off Clarence Mitchell. The contest was played in an hour and 15 minutes.

AUGUST 4   Rookie pitcher Bill Pertica pitches the Cardinals to a raucous 1–0 win over the Giants at Sportsman's Park. Catchers Pickles Dillhoefer of the Cards and Frank Snyder of the Giants were put out of the game following a fistfight. In the eighth inning, New York hurler Art Nehf hit Joe Schultz in the head with a pitch. While Schultz was being revived, a remark by Dillhoefer angered Snyder, and several blows were exchanged before the umpires separated them. When Snyder left the New York bench shortly afterward, he was greeted by a shower of bottles from the stands, and police were called upon to restore order and see the opposing players safely off the field.

Dillhoefer played to give regular catcher Verne Clemons a day off. Clemons hit .320 for the Cards in 1921.

AUGUST 6   The Cardinals clobber the Braves 12–2 at Sportsman's Park.

AUGUST 7   The Cardinals rout the Braves for the second day in a row, winning 11–0 at Sportsman's Park.

AUGUST 20   Joe Schultz hits a grand slam homer off Rosy Ryan in the fifth inning of a 10–1 win over the Giants in New York.

AUGUST 27   The Cardinals sweep the Braves 7–3 and 2–1 in Boston to run their winning streak to eight games.

AUGUST 31   The Cardinals collect 23 hits and crush the Phillies 12–5 in Philadelphia. Jack Smith had five hits in five at-bats.

SEPTEMBER 2   The Cardinals defeat the Pirates 1–0 in Pittsburgh. The lone run of the contest scored in the eighth inning on a double by Jack Fournier and a single by Milt Stock. Bill Doak started the game but pitched to only one batter. He was taken out because it started raining and the Cards didn't want to risk his nagging back injury on a wet mound. Jesse Haines went the rest of the way for the combined shutout.

Doak was 15–6 with a league-leading 2.59 earned run average in 1921.

SEPTEMBER 6   The Cardinals sweep the Cubs 1–0 and 3–2 at Sportsman's Park. Bill Bailey pitched the first-game shutout. He also started the second tilt, but lasted only one inning.

The shutout by Bailey was his first in the majors since 1915 when he was in the Federal League. It was also his first shutout in either the National or American Leagues since 1909. Bailey never pitched another one in the big leagues.

SEPTEMBER 17   Jack Smith collects five hits, including two doubles, in five at-bats during a 9–5 win over the Phillies at Sportsman's Park.

SEPTEMBER 30   Rogers Hornsby is honored before a 12–4 win over the Pirates at Sportsman's Park. He was presented with two diamond rings, one from the Masonic Lodge, and another from a fund made up of subscriptions. A diamond stickpin was given to him by the Chamber of Commerce. Two thousand dollars' worth of liberty bonds were also provided to him to be used for the purchase of a home in St. Louis, in addition to a baseball autographed by President Warren Harding.

Hornsby clouted a homer and two doubles in five at-bats to raise his batting average to .402. There were two games left in the season, and Hornsby could have sat on the bench to keep his average above .400, but he hadn't missed a game all year and decided to play. In those final two contests, he was hitless in eight at-bats to finish the year with an average of .397.

1922

Season in a Sentence

In a season of highs and lows, the Cardinals hold first place as late as the second week of August, but two players die of illnesses.

Finish • Won • Lost • Pct • GB

Third (tie) 85   69   .552   8.0

Manager

Branch Rickey

Stats

Stats	Cards	• NL	• Rank
Batting Avg:	.301	.292	3
On-Base Pct:	.357	.348	4
Slugging Pct:	.444	.404	1
Home Runs:	107		2
Stolen Bases:	73		6
ERA:	4.44	4.10	7
Fielding Avg:	.961	.967	8
Runs Scored:	863		2
Runs Allowed:	819		6

Starting Lineup

Eddie Ainsmith, c
Jack Fournier, 1b
Rogers Hornsby, 2b
Milt Stock, 3b
Specs Toporcer, ss
Joe Schultz, lf-rf
Jack Smith, cf-rf
Max Flack, rf
Doc Lavan, ss
Austin McHenry, lf
Verne Clemons, c
Heinie Mueller, cf

Pitchers

Jeff Pfeffer, sp
Bill Sherdel, sp-rp
Jesse Haines, sp
Bill Doak, sp
Lou North, rp
Clyde Barfoot, rp
Bill Pertica, rp-sp

Attendance

536,998 (third in NL)

Club Leaders

Batting Avg:	Hornsby	.401
On-Base Pct:	Hornsby	.459
Slugging Pct:	Hornsby	.722
Home Runs:	Hornsby	42
RBIs:	Hornsby	152
Runs:	Hornsby	141
Stolen Bases:	Smith	18
Wins:	Pfeffer	19
Strikeouts:	North	84
ERA:	Pfeffer	3.58
Saves:	North	4

FEBRUARY 23   Cardinals catcher Pickles Dillhoefer dies of typhoid-pneumonia at St. John's Hospital in St. Louis at the age of 27. Dillhoefer was taken ill on January 19, only five days after marrying Massie Slocum, a schoolteacher from Mobile, Alabama. His funeral was held in the same Mobile church where he was married six weeks earlier.

APRIL 12   The season opens with a 10–1 trimming of the Pirates before 18,000 at Sportsman's Park. Rogers Hornsby hit a homer and Bill Sherdel pitched a complete game. Del Gainer, playing first base in place of injured Jack Fournier, drove in five runs. It was Gainer's first game with the Cardinals and his first in the majors in three years.

The 1922 season was the first appearance on the club's uniforms of the unique graphic symbol featuring two redbirds perched on a sloping bat that passed through the letter "C" in the word Cardinals. It appeared on both the home and road jerseys. The design motif has been included on Cardinals' uniforms to this day with the exception of a one-year absence in 1956.

APRIL 30   The Cardinals rout the Cubs 10–0 in Chicago.

MAY 4   The Cardinals defeat the Reds 8–7 at Sportsman's Park after one of the wildest ninth innings in club history. The Cards led 3–1 heading into the ninth, but the Reds scored six times to take a 7–3 lead. St. Louis bounced back with five in their half to win 8–7. The first two runs in the incredible rally scored on a bases-loaded single by Joe Schultz. Eddie Ainsmith singled to load the bases again, and Jack Fournier and Specs Torpocer drew walks to tie the game 7–7. A long drive to right field by Rogers Hornsby drove in the game winner.

Ainsmith hit .293 for the Cards in 1922.

MAY 8

Sam Breadon buys the stock of James Jones, which gives Breadon controlling interest in the Cardinals. The purchase gave Breadon 67 percent of the club. In 1923, he bought the holdings of his friend Fuzzy Anderson, who had convinced Breadon to make his initial $200 investment in 1917. Anderson later became a minority stockholder with the Giants.

MAY 11

Bill Doak pitches a one-hitter to beat the Giants 2–0 at Sportsman's Park. The lone hit was an infield single by Dave Bancroft leading off the first inning in which Doak was late reaching first base for the putout.

MAY 15

The Cardinals collect 23 hits and swamp the Phillies 19–7 in Philadelphia. The Cards scored in every inning except the fifth.

MAY 19

The Cardinals score seven runs in the third inning and defeat the Dodgers 10–6 at Sportsman's Park.

MAY 25

Before a 7–3 loss to the Pirates at Sportsman's Park, a charity auction is held to raise money for playground equipment for St. Louis youngsters. Among the items auctioned was a ball autographed by President Warren Harding.

MAY 30

The Cardinals trade Cliff Heathcote to the Cubs for Max Flack.

The trade was pulled off between games of a separate-admission doubleheader between the Cardinals and Cubs in Chicago. Flack and Heathcote both appeared in the morning game, won 4–1 by the Cubs, traded uniforms, and played for their new teams in the afternoon, a 3–1 Chicago victory. Heathcote was 0 for 3 as a Card and 2 for 4 as a Cub. Flack went 0 for 4 in the first game and 1 for 4 in the second. Flack and Heathcote had remarkable similar careers. Flack played in 1,411 games and Heathcote in 1,415. Flack hit .278 and Heathcote .275. Flack stole 200 bases to Heathcote's 190. Flack had 212 doubles and Heathcote collected 206. Heathcote outhomered Flack 42 to 35. The only other player besides Flack and Heathcote to play for two teams in one day was Joel Youngblood with the Mets and Expos on August 4, 1982.

JUNE 3

Down 5–0, the Cardinals score six runs in the sixth inning to spur a 9–6 win over the Pirates in Pittsburgh.

JUNE 12

The Cardinals record 10 consecutive hits in a seven-run, sixth inning against the Phillies in Philadelphia. The Cards trailed 6–3 heading into the inning, and won 14–7. Jack Fournier collected the first and tenth hit. The others were by Milt Stock, Eddie Ainsmith, Doc Lavan, Specs Toporcer, Max Flack, Jack Smith, Rogers Hornsby, and Austin McHenry. Lavan had five hits in the game, including a double, in five at-bats.

Batting as a pinch hitter for Roy Walker, Toporcer's hit in the sixth came on a ball he hit over the right-field wall, but he was credited with only a single because he passed Doc Lavan between first and second base. Toporcer may have been confused at the rare sight of one of his drives clearing the wall. He hit only nine homers in 1,566 at-bats during a nine-year career.

June 15   Down 3–0, the Cardinals score once in the eighth inning, twice in the ninth on a Milt Stock homer, and once in the tenth to win 4–3 over the Dodgers in Brooklyn.

June 25   The Cardinals hammer the Cubs 11–1 at Sportsman's Park.

July 6   The Cardinals score eight runs in the fifth inning of a 14–2 pounding of the Dodgers at Sportsman's Park.

July 7   A two-run, walk-off homer by Rogers Hornsby in the ninth inning beats the Dodgers 6–5 at Sportsman's Park. The Cards trailed 5–0 before scoring three times in the sixth inning and once in the eighth to set the stage for the game-winning rally.

July 9   The Cardinals score three runs in the ninth inning to defeat the Dodgers 6–5 at Sportsman's Park. Specs Toporcer drove in the tying run with a pinch-double and scored on a single by Max Flack.

> *A grammar school classmate of James Cagney in New York City, George "Specs" Torpocer played as an infielder for the Cardinals from 1921 through 1928. He was the first non-pitcher to wear glasses in the major leagues. In 1944, Toporcer wrote a book called* Baseball, from Backyards to the Big Leagues, *which was among the leading training manuals of instruction for coaches and youngsters for several decades. Despite five operations, he lost his eyesight while managing Buffalo in the International League in 1951. He died in 1989 at the age of 89 following a fall down a flight of stairs.*

July 11   Jesse Haines pitches a two-hitter to defeat the Phillies 3–0 at Sportsman's Park. The only Philadelphia hits were an infield single by Art Fletcher and a double by Goldie Rapp.

July 13   Bill Doak pitches a one-hitter to defeat the Phillies 1–0 at Sportsman's Park. The only Philadelphia hit was an infield tapper by Curt Walker which was fielded by first baseman Jack Fournier. Doak had ample time to cover first base, but failed to do so in time. The lone run of the game scored in the fifth inning on a double by Fournier and a single by rookie catcher Harry McCurdy.

> *This was the second time in 1922 and the third time in his career that Doak lost a no-hitter because he failed to reach first base in time to prevent a hit on an infield grounder (see August 10, 1920, and May 11, 1922). Doak was nicknamed "Lumbago Bill" because of a chronic bad back, which may explain his inability to properly field his position. Ironically, Doak became a wealthy man by inventing a baseball glove (see May 16, 1914).*

July 14   Trailing 4–2, the Cardinals score seven runs in the seventh inning and win 9–5 over the Phillies at Sportsman's Park.

July 16   Bill Sherdel pitches the Cardinals to a 1–0 win over the Giants at Sportsman's Park. The lone run of the contest was driven in on a single by Jack Fournier. Sherdel caught a break in the second inning. With one out and the bases loaded in the second inning, Jesse Barnes of the Giants attempted to duck an inside pitch on a 3–0 count, but the ball hit his bat and deflected to third baseman Milt Stock, who made an unassisted double play to end the inning. The win put the Cardinals only one-half game behind the first-place Giants.

Sherdel had a 17–13 record and a 3.88 ERA in 1922. The most effective Cardinal pitcher was Jeff Pfeffer, who was 19–12 with a 3.58 earned run average.

JULY 19   Rogers Hornsby hits a three-run, walk-off homer to defeat the Braves 7–6 at Sportsman's Park. The homer was his 25th of the season, breaking the modern (since 1900) National League record of 24, previously held by Gavvy Cravath of the Phillies since 1915. Many in the Sportsman's Park crowd carried Hornsby off the field.

Photo File/Hulton Archive/Getty Images

Rogers Hornsby, a Cardinal player from 1915 to 1926 and again in 1933, holds the major league record for total bases in a single season (450), and is the only player in history to hit at least 40 homers and bat .400 or better in a single season. Hornsby was inducted into the Hall of Fame in 1942.

JULY 21   Jack Fournier hits a grand slam in a six-run, eighth inning off Mule Watson in a 6–1 win over the Braves at Sportsman's Park.

JULY 22   The Cardinals take first place with a thrilling 9–8 win over the Braves at Sportsman's Park. Down 8–3, the Cards scored six runs in the eighth inning. The victory gave St. Louis a 1½-game lead over the Giants in the NL pennant race.

AUGUST 5   Rogers Hornsby breaks the all-time National League record for homers in a season with his 28th of 1922 in a 2–1 loss to the Phillies in Philadelphia. The previous record of 27 was held by Ned Williamson of Chicago in 1884.

Hornsby finished the season with 42 homers. He was the second individual to hit at least 40 homers in a season. The other was Babe Ruth, who passed Williamson for the major league record when he connected for 29 with the Red Sox in 1919. Ruth followed that season by shattering his own mark with 54 homers with the Yankees in 1920, and 59 in 1921. Hornsby held the National League standard for homers in a season until 1929 when Chuck Klein struck 43 for the Phillies in 1929. Until the arrival of Mark McGwire in 1997, the only two Cardinals with 40 or more homers in a season were Hornsby in 1922 and Johnny Mize, who had 43 in 1940.

AUGUST 12 A 6–5 loss to the Cubs at Sportsman's Park drops the Cardinals out of first place.

The pennant aspirations of the Cardinals were all but over in less than three weeks. By the end of August, the Cards were eight games behind the Giants. Before the club's nosedive in the National League race, there was talk of an all–St. Louis World Series. The Browns were in the American League lead as late as September 7 and finished the season only one game behind the Yankees with a record of 93–61. The 93 wins were the most of any Browns team in their 52-year history.

AUGUST 18 The Cardinals defeat the Phillies 3–2 in 14 innings at Sportsman's Park. After the Phils scored once in the top of the fourteenth, the Cards countered with two in their half. Jack Smith tripled in the first run, then scored on a single by Specs Toporcer.

On the same day, Giants pitcher Phil Douglas was banned from baseball for life by Commissioner Kenesaw Landis for writing a letter to Cardinals outfielder Les Mann. Angered over being suspended by New York manager John McGraw for his drunken behavior, Douglas wrote Mann, his former roommate when the two played for the Cubs, offering to leave the Giants in exchange for an "inducement" to help the Cards win the NL pennant. Mann turned the letter over the Branch Rickey, who relayed it to Landis.

AUGUST 20 After trailing 6–1 in the sixth inning, the Cardinals rally to defeat the Phillies 9–6 at Sportsman's Park.

AUGUST 24 Les Mann hits a grand slam off Garland Braxton in the sixth inning to put the Cardinals ahead 6–3, but the Braves rally to win 12–11 at Sportsman's Park.

After his playing days, Mann formed the National Amateur Baseball Association. In 1936, he persuaded the World Olympic Committee to add baseball as an exhibition event. Two American teams played before a crowd in Berlin of over 100,000, but baseball did not become an Olympic sport until 1984.

SEPTEMBER 9 The Cardinals outlast the Reds 12–10 in Cincinnati. The Cards scored five runs in the ninth inning to take a 12–6 lead, then survived a four-run rally by the Reds to preserve the win.

SEPTEMBER 13 The Cardinals pound the Phillies 13–4 and 11–1 in a doubleheader in Philadelphia. Rogers Hornsby collected seven hits, including two doubles, in ten at-bats during the two games.

SEPTEMBER 15 Rogers Hornsby hits a grand slam in the fourth inning off Jimmy Ring to put the Cardinals ahead 7–0, but the Phillies rally to win 10–9 in Philadelphia. The winning runs were scored on back-to-back homers in the ninth inning by Butch Henline and Cliff Lee off Bill Sherdel. It was Henline's third home run of the game. Hornsby also had another homer and a single in the game to run his hitting streak to 30 games.

SEPTEMBER 19 Rogers Hornsby runs his hitting streak to 33 games during an 8–4 win over the Braves in Boston.

SEPTEMBER 20 After losing the first game of a doubleheader 6–1 to the Dodgers in Brooklyn, the Cardinals score eight runs in the ninth inning of the second tilt to win 13–7. Rogers Hornsby had his 33-game hitting streak snapped in the opener, but homered twice in the second contest.

Hornsby's 33-game hitting streak in 1922 is the longest in Cardinals history. The second longest is 30 games by Stan Musial in 1950 and Albert Pujols in 2003.

SEPTEMBER 23 Rogers Hornsby hits his 40th homer of the season during a 7–5 loss to the Giants in New York.

SEPTEMBER 24 Rogers Hornsby hits his 41st and 42nd homers of 1922 during a 10–6 triumph over the Giants in New York. He hit his homers off a pair of brothers. The first was an inside-the-park homer off Virgil Barnes. The second went into the stands facing Jesse Barnes.

SEPTEMBER 26 Incensed at being taken out in the fifth inning of a 6–3 loss to the Giants in New York, Jesse Haines throws the ball over the grandstand roof.

SEPTEMBER 30 Doc Gainer homers in what proves to be his last major league at-bat during a 5–3 win over the Cubs in the second game of a doubleheader in Chicago, called by darkness after five innings. The Cardinals also won the first game 9–8. Rogers Hornsby collected four hits in seven at-bats to raise his batting average to .39968, which rounded to the nearest thousandth of a point, gave him an average of .400. There was one game left on the schedule.

Gainer played 10 years in the majors and hit 14 homers.

OCTOBER 1 Rogers Hornsby collects three hits in five at-bats in the final game of the season, a 7–1 win over the Cubs in Chicago, to end the year with an average of .401.

Hornsby not only led the NL in batting average, but in on-base percentage (.459), slugging percentage (.722), runs (141), hits (250), doubles (46), homers (42), total bases (450), and RBIs (152). The runs, hits, and total bases figures are Cardinals single-season records. The 450 total bases by Hornsby are a National

League record and the second highest in major league history behind the 457 by Babe Ruth in 1921. Hornsby is also the only player in major league history to hit at least 40 homers with a batting average of .400 or better in a single season. He nearly did it again in 1925 with 39 homers and a .403 average.

NOVEMBER 27   Austin McHenry dies at his home in Blue Creek, Ohio, at the age of 27 from a brain tumor.

1923

Season in a Sentence

After contending for the pennant in 1921 and 1922, the Cardinals take a step backward.

Finish • Won • Lost • Pct • GB

Fifth   79   74   .516   16.0

Manager

Branch Rickey

Stats

Stats	Cards	NL	Rank
Batting Avg:	.286	.286	4
On-Base Pct:	.343	.343	5
Slugging Pct:	.398	.395	5
Home Runs:	63		4
Stolen Bases:	89		5
ERA:	3.87	3.99	4
Fielding Avg:	.963	.966	7
Runs Scored:	746		6
Runs Allowed:	732		5

Starting Lineup

Eddie Ainsmith, c
Jim Bottomley, 1b
Rogers Hornsby, 2b
Milt Stoock, 3b
Howard Freigau, ss
Jack Smith, lf
Hy Myers, cf
Max Flack, rf
Ray Blades, lf
Specs Toporcer, 2b-ss
Heinie Mueller, cf
Verbe Clemons, c

Pitchers

Jesse Haines, sp
Bill Sherdel, sp-rp
Fred Toney, sp
Bill Doak, sp
Jeff Pfeffer, sp-rp
Johnny Stuart, rp
Lou North, rp
Clyde Barfoot, rp

Attendance

338,551 (sixth in NL)

Club Leaders

Batting Avg:	Hornsby	.384
On-Base Pct:	Hornsby	.459
Slugging Pct:	Hornsby	.627
Home Runs:	Hornsby	17
RBIs:	Stock	96
Runs:	Hornsby	89
Stolen Bases:	Smith	32
Wins:	Haines	20
Strikeouts:	Sherdel	78
ERA:	Haines	3.11
Saves:	Stuart	3

FEBRUARY 17   The Cardinals trade Jack Fournier to the Dodgers for Hy Myers and Ray Schmandt.

The Cardinals deemed Fournier expendable because Jim Bottomley was ready to take over as the starter at first base. Fournier didn't want to leave St. Louis, and declared that he would quit baseball rather than report to the Dodgers. He changed his mind shortly after the 1923 season started, and gave Brooklyn three excellent seasons. From 1923 through 1925, he hit .345 with 71 homers and 348 RBIs. The Cardinals received next to nothing in return. Myers batted .276 with three homers in 141 games for the Cards while Schmandt never played a game for the club.

MARCH 6   The Cardinals announce that they will use uniform numbers in 1923. At the time, no club in the majors placed numbers on uniforms, although the numerals on jerseys had been in use by leading college football teams for many years. Previously, baseball clubs had numbers for each player on the scorecards and posted the corresponding number on the scoreboard as each player came to bat to help the fans identify the players, and in some cases, the full batting order was placed on the scoreboards. The numbers on the 1923 Cardinals' uniforms were about six inches high on the left sleeve, but were so small that it was almost impossible to read them from the stands. The experiment was dropped before the season was over, in part because concessionaires complained about the drop in scorecard sales. The first club to use permanent numbers on the backs of uniforms was the Yankees in 1929. By 1932, all clubs in the majors affixed numbers to their uniforms.

APRIL 17   The Cardinals lose 3–2 to the Reds in 11 innings in the season opener in Cincinnati. A single by George Burns off Hi Bell drove in the winning run.

           Branch Rickey had 10 Prohibition agents from the Cincinnati area as his guests at the opener.

APRIL 21   Jim Bottomley hits a grand slam off Virgil Cheeves in the first inning to help the Cardinals to a 5–0 lead, but the Cubs rally to win 10–8 in Chicago.

           In his first full season in the majors, Bottomley hit .371 with eight homers in 1923. He played 11 seasons with the Cardinals (1922–32) and batted .325 during that period in 1,392 games with 921 runs, 1,727 hits, 344 doubles, 119 triples, 161 homers, and 1,105 RBIs. Nicknamed "Sunny Jim" because of his pleasant, easygoing nature, Bottomley had a habit of wearing his cap tilted over his left eye. He played in four World Series with the Cards and was elected to the Hall of Fame in 1971.

APRIL 25   In the home opener, the Cardinals lose 3–1 to the Reds before 7,500 at Sportsman's Park. Jeff Pfeffer took a 1–0 lead into the ninth inning before allowing three runs.

MAY 2   The Cardinals pound the Pirates 13–1 at Sportsman's Park.

MAY 6   The Cardinals score seven runs in the second inning to take an 11–2 lead and roll to a 16–4 victory over the Cubs at Sportsman's Park.

MAY 8   Rogers Hornsby tears muscles in his knee rounding second base in the fifth inning of an 11–3 win over the Phillies in Philadelphia.

           After playing in every game in both 1921 and 1922, Hornsby was limited to 107 games in 1923 because of the knee injury and other incidents. He tried playing two weeks later but eventually spent two weeks in a cast. When he returned June 14, he homered in a 3–2 victory over the Braves, but quickly left the lineup again. Hornsby also missed time because of the illness of his mother and personal problems, including a divorce. He was suspended by Branch Rickey for five games and fined $500 when Hornsby left the club feigning to be ill despite a doctor's diagnosis to the contrary. Rickey and Hornsby actually duked it out in the clubhouse one day. Despite all of the problems, Hornsby led the NL in batting average (.384), on-base percentage (.459), and slugging percentage (.627) and hit 17 homers. The Cardinals brass decided they no longer required his *services, however, and shopped Hornsby all winter. The Giants, Cubs, Braves, and Dodgers all made lucrative offers, but Rickey and Sam Breadon pulled him off the market (see February 21, 1924).*

MAY 11   At Baker Bowl in Philadelphia, the Cardinals and Phillies combine for 10 home runs and 79 total bases in a game won by the Phillies 20–14. Three of the ten homers belonged to Philadelphia's Cy Williams. The other home run hitters for the Phils were Johnny Mokan, who had two, and Frank Parkinson. For the Cardinals, Les Mann hit two and Eddie Dyer and losing pitcher Bill Sherdel one each. St. Louis had 22 hits in the game.

The 79 total bases were a major league record for two teams in a game until the Reds and Rockies combined for 81 in a contest at Coors Field in 1999. There were 23 different Cardinals and Phillie players who collected hits in the contest, which is still a big-league record. Eddie Dyer, who was normally a pitcher, started the game in left field and batted second in an eight-game experiment to try to turn him into an outfielder. Les Mann pinch hit for Dyer and remained in the game, so the Cards got three homers out of their left fielders and the number two slot in the batting order. The homer by Dyer was the second of two that he hit in 157 career at-bats. The first came three days earlier at Baker Bowl in his first major league start. Later, Dyer tossed a shutout in his first starting assignment as a pitcher (see September 9, 1923).

MAY 15   Jim Bottomley ties a Cardinal and modern major league record with three triples during a 10–5 win over the Braves in Boston.

MAY 16   The Cardinals suffer an agonizing 14-inning, 7–6 loss to the Braves in Boston. Down 6–1, the Cards scored two runs in the eighth inning and three in the ninth to send the game into extra innings but lost on a walk-off homer by Billy Southworth. The Cards also executed a triple play in the eleventh inning. Shortstop Howard Freigau caught a liner off the bat of Tony Boeckel, then threw to Jim Bottomley at first base to double Southworth. Bottomley relayed to Milt Stock before Walton Cruise could return to third.

MAY 18   Specs Toporcer hits a fluke homer in the sixth inning of a 3–1 win over the Dodgers at Ebbets Field. The drive went down the right-field line, hit the fence, and caromed into an alleyway at the end of the right-field stands.

MAY 23   Right fielder Les Mann completes an unassisted double play in the fourth inning of a 4–1 loss to the Giants in New York. Mann caught Frank Snyder's drive in the sixth inning and ran to first base before Jimmy O'Connell could return to the bag.

MAY 28   After the Reds score two runs in the top of the tenth inning, the Cardinals rally for three in their half to win 5–4. Jim Bottomley drove in the game-winner with a single. A thunderstorm rolled toward Sportsman's Park during the rally. Rain let loose in a torrent as fans filed out of the ballpark.

JUNE 6   The Cardinals beat the Phillies 7–6 at Sportsman's Park in 12 innings. The winning run scored on a triple by Jim Bottomley and a sacrifice fly by Hy Myers. Both teams scored twice in the tenth inning.

JUNE 7 Jeff Pfeffer pitches a 10-inning shutout to defeat the Phillies 1–0 at Sportsman's Park. A walk-off triple by Ray Blades accounted for the lone run of the game.

JUNE 20 Rotary International, holding its national convention in St. Louis, presents gifts to Giants manager John McGraw and New York players Art Nehf and Dave Bancroft, each of them Rotarians, before a game at Sportsman's Park. The Cardinals led 6–2 before the Giants scored five runs in the ninth inning to win 7–6.

JUNE 23 The Cardinals score seven runs in the fourth inning of a 9–5 win over the Cubs in Chicago.

> *The contest was enlivened by an argument on the field between pitcher Fred Toney and shortstop Specs Toporcer. Toney wanted Toporcer to move closer to third base when Cliff Heathcote came to bat. Toporcer refused to budge, and Heathcote drove the ball through the spot where Toney had suggested Toporcer position himself. Toney blew up and dressed Toporcer down on the field in full view of the fans. Specs took off his glasses and raised his fists before Toney returned to the mound. In the bottom of the inning, Toporcer was cheered when he stepped to the plate and Toney was booed. Toney refused to take his place in the batter's box and stormed off the field. The pitcher said he was quitting baseball, but Branch Rickey, who was critical of Toporcer for refusing to move, convinced Toney to return to the club two days later.*

JUNE 28 In his first game since his two-day "retirement" following his argument with Specs Toporcer, Fred Toney outduels Grover Alexander to beat the Cubs 1–0 in Chicago.

JULY 5 The Cardinals win a 16–12 slugfest against the Phillies in Philadelphia. The Cards led 10–1 in the fifth inning before allowing Philadelphia to narrow the gap to 12–11 in the eighth. The Cardinals put the game on ice with four runs in the ninth.

JULY 10 Cardinals rookie pitcher Johnny Stuart pitches two complete game wins over the Braves in Boston, winning 11–1 and 6–3. Only three days earlier, Stuart pitched four innings of relief.

> *Stuart was only 22 years old when he pitched the two complete games in one day. He lasted only four seasons in the majors with a record of 20–18.*

JULY 11 The Braves strand 18 runners in losing 10–4 to the Cardinals in Boston. Cardinals pitchers Lou North, Bill Doak, and Jesse Haines combined to allow 13 hits and seven walks in addition to three errors by their teammates.

JULY 12 The Cardinals score seven runs in the fifth inning of a 9–6 win over the Braves in Boston.

JULY 13 Rogers Hornsby collects five hits, including a triple and a double, in five at-bats during a 10–6 victory over the Braves in Boston.

JULY 16 The Cardinals score seven runs in the second inning and defeat the Phillies 13–7 in Philadelphia. The Cards collected 22 hits in the contest.

JULY 19 The Cardinals defeat the Giants 3–0 in New York on three solo homers. Heinie Mueller homered in the second and sixth innings, and Jim Bottomley also homered in the sixth.

AUGUST 1	The Cardinals win a thrilling doubleheader against the Dodgers at Sportsman's Park. The Cards won the first game 11–10 with two runs in the ninth inning and the second 7–6 in 14 innings.
AUGUST 3	There are no games in Major League Baseball due to the death of President Warren Harding the previous day. All of the games on August 10, the day of Harding's funeral, were also postponed. Calvin Collidge succeeded Harding as president.
AUGUST 9	The Cardinals win 13–12 in 15 innings against the Giants at Sportsman's Park. Lou North, the sixth Cardinal pitcher, hurled four hitless innings of relief and drove in the winning run with a single. The Cardinals led 10–6 before the Giants scored one in the eighth inning and three in the ninth to send the game into extra innings. The Giants took a 12–10 lead in the eleventh, but the Cards tied the game on a two-run homer by Rogers Hornsby.
AUGUST 17	The Cardinals defeat the Dodgers 8–5 in 12 innings at Ebbets Field. Heinie Mueller put the Cards up 5–4 with an inside-the-park homer when Brooklyn center fielder Bernie Neis misjudged the long fly ball. After the Dodgers tied the score in their half of the inning, Eddie Ainsmith cleared the bases with a three-run double in the twelfth.
AUGUST 23	The Cardinals score seven runs in the second inning of a 7–4 win over the Giants in the second game of a doubleheader at the Polo Grounds. New York won the first game 8–7.
SEPTEMBER 3	Rogers Hornsby homers off Vic Keen in the eighth inning to lift the Cardinals to a 1–0 win over the Cubs in the first game of a doubleheader in Chicago. Johnny Stuart pitched the shutout. The Cubs won the second game 3–2 in 10 innings.
SEPTEMBER 8	The Cardinals defeat the Reds 5–4 in 13 innings and 13–4 during a doubleheader at Sportsman's Park.
SEPTEMBER 9	In his first major league start as a pitcher, Eddie Dyer hurls a shutout to defeat the Cubs 3–0 at Sportsman's Park. *Used mostly as a reliever during his six-year career, all with the Cardinals, Dyer was 15–15 with two shutouts. He later managed the Cardinals to a World Championship in 1946.*
SEPTEMBER 15	At Sportsman's Park, the Cardinals score six runs in a doubleheader against the Phillies, and all six runs are in one inning. In the first game, the Cards lost 2–0. In the second, St. Louis parlayed a six-run second into a 6–0 victory.
SEPTEMBER 30	Jesse Haines records his 20th win of the season with an 8–5 win over the Reds in Cincinnati. *Haines finished the season with a 20–13 record and a 3.11 ERA.*

1924

Season in a Sentence

In a season of individual accomplishment, Rogers Hornsby bats .424, Jim Bottomley drives in 12 runs in a game, and Jesse Haines pitches the first Cardinal no-hitter in 33 years, but the club tumbles into sixth place.

Finish • Won • Lost • Pct • GB

Sixth   65   89   .422   28.5

Manager

Branch Rickey

Stats	Cards •	NL •	Rank
Batting Avg:	.290	.283	2
On-Base Pct:	.341	.337	3
Slugging Pct:	.411	.392	2
Home Runs:	67		4
Stolen Bases:	86		4
ERA:	4.15	3.87	6
Fielding Avg:	.969	.970	5
Runs Scored:	740		2
Runs Allowed:	750		6

Starting Lineup

Mike Gonzalez, c
Jim Bottomley, 1b
Rogers Hornsby, 2b
Howard Freigau, 3b
Jimmy Cooney, ss
Ray Blades, lf
Wattie Holm, cf
Jack Smith, rf
Heinie Mueller, of
Max Flack, of
Specs Toporcer, 3b-ss
Taylor Douthit, of

Pitchers

Allen Sothoron, sp
Jesse Haines, sp
Johnny Stuart, sp
Eddie Dyer, sp
Leo Dickerman, sp
Jeff Pfeffer, sp
Bill Sherdel, rp
Hi Bell, rp-sp

Attendance

272,885 (seventh in NL)

Club Leaders

Batting Avg:	Hornsby	.424
On-Base Pct:	Hornsby	.507
Slugging Pct:	Hornsby	.696
Home Runs:	Hornsby	25
RBIs:	Bottomley	111
Runs:	Hornsby	121
Stolen Bases:	Smith	24
Wins:	Haines	10
Strikeouts:	Haines	69
ERA:	Sothoron	3.57
Saves:	Doak	3

FEBRUARY 21   Branch Rickey and Rogers Hornsby bury the hatchet after feuding for much of the 1923 season, and after Rickey spent much of the 1923–24 offseason trying to trade his star second baseman. In a meeting with St. Louis reporters, Hornsby said, "There is no longer and misunderstanding between us. I want to have the best year in baseball I ever had and I want the Cardinals to have the best year it ever had."

Hornsby responded with one of the greatest seasons of any player in big-league history. He set a modern major league record for the highest batting average in a single season by hitting .424. He led the NL in on-base percentage (.507), slugging percentage (.696), runs (121), hits (227), doubles (43), total bases (373), and walks (89). Hornsby's 25 homers were second in the league and he drove in 94 runs. It was not a good year for the ballclub, however. The progress the Cardinals made by competing for the pennant in 1921 and 1922 looked like a mirage when the team fell into sixth place with a record of 65–89.

MARCH 12   The Browns evict the Cardinals from Sportsman's Park.

In January, the Cardinals failed to make their quarterly rent payment. The Cards claimed that it was an oversight, and immediately paid the money upon realizing the error, but Browns owner Phil Ball carried out the eviction proceedings. The real reason for the eviction wasn't non-payment of rent, but stalled negotiations over who would pay for the expansion of Sportsman's Park. Ball had plans to increase the capacity of the facility from 18,000 to 32,000, but wanted the Cards to pay part of the cost. Sam Breadon and Branch Rickey refused to spend any money on the improvements. The Cardinals went to court to prevent the eviction, and received a temporary restraining order on March 31 and a permanent one on July 12 which allowed them to remain at the corner of Grand and Dodier. The judge administering the case admonished the Cardinals, however, for the refusal to pay a share of the cost of expanding the ballpark in light of the fact that it would likely increase the club's profitably (see July 15, 1924).

APRIL 15   In an exciting season opener, the Cardinals score three runs in the ninth inning to beat the Cubs 6–5 before 15,000 st Sportsman's Park. Commissioner Kenesaw Landis threw out the ceremonial first pitch with St. Louis mayor Henry Kiel serving as the "catcher."

APRIL 21   Trailing 9–5, the Cardinals score six runs in the seventh inning to beat the Pirates 11–9 at Sportsman's Park.

APRIL 27   The Cardinals trade Milt Stock to the Dodgers for Mike Gonzalez.

MAY 11   Ray Blades leads off the first inning with a home run on the first pitch from Dinty Gearin and the Cards move on to beat the Giants 3–2 at Sportsman's Park.

            Blades hit .311 with 11 homers in 1924.

MAY 16   Max Flack hits a walk-off homer in the eleventh inning to beat the Dodgers 6–5 at Sportsman's Park.

MAY 18   Max Flack strikes again with a two-run, walk-off double in the ninth inning to defeat the Braves 5–4 at Sportsman's Park.

MAY 25   Eddie Dyer stars with his bat and his arm in a 10-inning, 5–4 win over the Phillies at Sportsman's Park. In addition to pitching a complete game, Dyer tied the score 4–4 with a triple in the sixth inning, then drove in the winner with a two-out, walk-off single.

JUNE 4   Howard Freigau steals four bases and collects four hits, including a double, during a 12–5 win over the Phillies in Philadelphia.

JUNE 6   Heinie Mueller and Phillies shortstop Heinie Sand of the Phillies fight during a 7–6 Philadelphia win at Baker Bowl. After a close play at second base, Sand accused Mueller of throwing dirt in his eyes. It took the combined efforts of both teams to separate the combatants.

            On the same day, the Cardinals sold Joe Schultz to the Phillies.

JUNE 13   The Cardinals trade Bill Doak to the Dodgers for Leo Dickerman.

JUNE 17	The Cardinals sell Lou North to the Braves.
JULY 4	The Cardinals win the opener of a holiday doubleheader 11–0 over the Cubs at Sportsman's Park before falling 6–5 in the second tilt.
JULY 7	The Cardinals score in every inning except the third and wallop the Cubs 15–3 at Sportsman's Park.
JULY 11	The Cardinals sell Jeff Pfeffer to the Pirates.
JULY 14	The Cardinals trounce the Dodgers 12–0 at Sportsman's Park.
JULY 15	Sam Breadon purchases 6.7 acres of land at the corner Spring and Choteau near Grand Avenue just south of St. Louis University. Breadon said that a new ballpark for the Cardinals would be built at the site within five years. The plans went by the boards after the capacity of Sportsman's Park increased by 14,000 with an expansion between the 1925 and 1926 seasons. Breadon added to the tract over the years, however, with the idea of building a ballpark. He still owned the property when he sold the Cardinals in 1947.
JULY 17	Jesse Haines pitches a no-hitter to defeat the Braves 5–0 at Sportsman's Park. It was the first no-hitter by a Cardinal pitcher since Ted Breitenstein threw one in 1891 and the first since the club joined the National League a year later. A crowd of 13,000 turned on Tuberculosis Day. Haines walked three and fanned five. In the ninth inning, he retired Gus Felix on a fly ball to Jack Smith in right field, a pop-up by Bill Cunningham to Jimmy Cooney at shortstop, and Casey Stengel on a grounder to Rogers Hornsby at second.

> *Tuberculosis Day was an annual event at Sportsman's Park that was staged to benefit the efforts of the St. Louis Tuberculosis Society to eradicate the disease. The benefit took place each year from 1915 through 1942.*

JULY 19	Cardinals rookie pitcher Hi Bell pitches two complete-game victories in one day, defeating the Braves 6–1 and 2–1 allowing only six hits in 18 innings of pitching. In the opener, Bell held the Braves hitless until Don Padgett doubled in the eighth. Cotton Tierney followed with a single to drive in the lone Boston run. Bell finished the contest with a two-hitter and followed with a four-hitter in the nightcap.

> *The two wins accounted for two-thirds of Bell's victories in 1924. He finished the season with a record of 3–8 and was 32–34 during an eight-year career, five of which were spent in St. Louis.*

JULY 25	The Cardinals rout the Giants 13–5 in New York.
JULY 30	Bill Sherdel is called out of the bullpen in the second inning with none out and runners on first and second to pitch to pinch hitter Johnny Mokan of the Phillies, and records a triple play on the first pitch. Mokan bunted the ball into the air. First baseman Jim Bottomley caught the pop-up and threw to shortstop Jimmy Cooney, who doubled the runner at second and threw to Rogers Hornsby, who covered first. The Cardinals trailed 4–1 when recording the triple play and went on to win 9–8. Sherdel pitched eight innings and earned the victory.

AUGUST 8   Jim Bottomley hits a fluke homer in the ninth inning, but it's too late to prevent a 4–3 loss to the Dodgers in Brooklyn. The drive by Bottomley glanced off the glove of right fielder Bernie Neis and into the stands.

AUGUST 9   Jim Bottomley drives in all five Cardinals runs with a three-run homer and a two-run single to defeat the Dodgers 5–1 in Brooklyn.

Bottomley hit .316 with 14 homers and 111 RBIs in 1924.

AUGUST 20   The Cardinals take a doubleheader from the Phillies at Sportsman's Park by scores of 3–1 and 13–10. Wattie Holm collected seven hits in ten at-bats and Rogers Hornsby was 6 for 7, including two doubles.

AUGUST 21   Rogers Hornsby collects seven hits, including two homers, in seven at-bats during a doubleheader in New York, but the Cardinals lose twice, 6–4 and 12–1, to the Giants at Sportman's Park. In consecutive doubleheaders, Hornsby picked up 13 hits in 14 at-bats.

AUGUST 22   Rogers Hornsby runs his streak of hits in consecutive at-bats to nine with a homer in his first at-bat of a 6–4 loss to the Giants at Sportsman's Park. The hit also gave Hornsby 14 hits in a span of 15 at-bats over five games.

AUGUST 24   The Cardinals swamp the Dodgers 7–6 and 17–0 in a doubleheader at Sportsman's Park. In the opener, Rogers Hornsby hit a walk-off homer in the ninth. The second tilt, the Cards collected 25 hits. Verne Clemons was 5 for 5 on a double and four singles.

AUGUST 26   Rogers Hornsby collects three doubles and a homer, but the Cardinals lose 7–4 to the Dodgers at Sportsman's Park.

From August 20 through 29, Hornsby had an incredible streak of 34 hits in 51 at-bats. Among the 34 hits were seven homers, two triples, and seven doubles, a total of 66 total bases. The streak ended when Hornsby wrenched his back in the fourth inning of a 12–5 win over the Cubs in Chicago that put him out of the lineup for nine days.

AUGUST 28   Chick Hafey makes his major league debut by going hitless in four at-bats during a 6–2 loss to the Cubs in the first game of a doubleheader in Chicago. Hafey went 1 for 3 in the second tilt, an 8–3 Cardinals loss.

A future Hall of Famer, Hafey played for the Cardinals until 1931 and in the majors until 1937. Known for his screaming line drives and rifle arm, he hit 164 homers and batted .317 in 1,283 games. Hafey's numbers would have been much greater if antihistamines and other present-day allergy remedies had been available during his playing career. A chronic sinus condition caused diminished eyesight. He had three sets of glasses because his sight would vary from day to day. John McGraw said, "If Chick Hafey had two good eyes, he'd be the best ballplayer anybody ever saw."

SEPTEMBER 7   After losing the opener 3–1, the Cardinals rebound to smack the Cubs 15–4 in the second tilt.

Ed Clough, who played in 11 games for the Cardinals from 1924 through 1926, had one of the most unusual careers in history. His three-year stay in the majors ended before he turned 20. He made his big league debut on August 25, 1924, when he was only 17 years old. In addition, Clough appeared in four games as a pitcher and six in the outfield, with the remainder as a pinch hitter. He wasn't successful as a pitcher or a batter. Clough had two hits, both singles, in 19 at-bats for an average of .105. As a pitcher, he was on the mound for 12 innings and posted an ERA of 10.50.

SEPTEMBER 9   Less than two weeks after his major league debut, Chick Hafey accounts for all seven runs in a 7–4 win over the Pirates in the first game of a doubleheader at Sportsman's Park. In the four-run first, Hafey hit a three-run triple and scored on a single. He hit a two-run homer in the third and drove in his sixth run with a sacrifice fly in the seventh.

SEPTEMBER 16   Jim Bottomley collects six hits in six at-bats and sets a major league record for most RBIs in a game with 12 during a 17–3 thrashing of the Dodgers in Brooklyn.

Bottomley drove in 12 runs off five Dodgers pitchers. In the first inning, Bottomley connected for a two-run single off Rube Ehrhardt. In the second, Bottomley had a run-scoring double against Bonnie Hollingsworth. Art Decatur gave Bottomley a grand slam homer in the fourth and a two-run homer in the sixth. The Cardinal first baseman had a two-run single against Tex Wilson in the seventh for his 10th and 11th RBIs. The record-breaking 12th RBI came on a single facing Jim Roberts in the ninth. The only other player in major league history who has collected 12 RBIs in a game was Mark Whitten of the Cardinals on September 7, 1993.

1925

Season in a Sentence

A 13–25 start causes a switch in managers from Branch Rickey to Rogers Hornsby.

Finish • Won • Lost • Pct • GB

Fourth   77   76   .503   16.0

Manager

Branch Rickey (13–25) and Rogers Hornsby (64–51)

Stats	Cards	NL	Rank
Batting Avg:	.299	.292	2
On-Base Pct:	.356	.348	2
Slugging Pct:	.445	.414	2
Home Runs:	109		2
Stolen Bases:	70		6
ERA:	4.36	4.27	4
Fielding Avg:	.966	.966	4
Runs Scored:	828		2
Runs Allowed:	764		4

Starting Lineup

Bob O'Farrell, c
Jim Bottomley, 1b
Rogers Hornsby, 2b
Les Bell, 3b
Specs Toporcer, ss
Ray Blades, lf
Heinie Mueller, cf
Chick Hafey, rf-lf
Ralph Shinners, cf
Jack Smith, cf-rf
Max Flack, rf
Jimmy Cooney, ss
Tommy Thevenow, ss

Pitchers

Bill Sherdel, sp-rp
Jesse Haines, sp
Allen Sothoron, sp
Art Reinhart, sp
Flint Rhem, sp
Leo Dickerman, sp-rp
Duster Mails, sp-rp
Eddie Dyer, rp

Attendance

404,959 (sixth in NL)

Club Leaders

Batting Avg:	Hornsby	.403
On-Base Pct:	Hornsby	.489
Slugging Pct:	Hornsby	.756
Home Runs:	Hornsby	39
RBIs:	Hornsby	143
Runs:	Hornsby	133
Stolen Bases:	Smith	20
Wins:	Sherdel	15
Strikeouts:	Sothoron	67
ERA:	Sherdel	3.11
Saves:	Dyer	3

APRIL 14   The Cardinals open the season with a 4–0 loss to the Reds in Cincinnati. Pete Donohue pitched the shutout.

APRIL 18   The Cardinals thrash the Cubs 20–5 in Chicago. Les Bell tied a club record for most extra base hits in a game with four on two homers and two doubles. Bell also singled for a 5-for-6 day. Rogers Hornsby tied a modern club mark with five runs scored following two doubles, a single and two walks in five plate appearances before being taken out of the game in the eighth inning. Jim Bottomley, Ray Blades, and Taylor Douthit also homered for the Cardinals.

Hornsby won his sixth consecutive National League batting title in 1925 by hitting .403. He led the NL in on-base percentage and slugging percentage for the sixth straight year. In 1925, his on-base percentage was .489 and his slugging percentage was .756, a club record for a season. In addition, Hornsby led the league in home runs (39), total bases (381), and RBIs (143), scored 133 runs, and collected 41 doubles. From 1921 through 1925, Hornsby hit .402. He is the only player in major league history to post a batting average of .400 or better over five consecutive seasons. Bottomley was the runner-up in the batting race with a .367 average and led the league in hits (227) and doubles (44). He hit 21 homers and drove in 128 runs. Blades hit .342 with 12 homers.

APRIL 22   In the home opener, the Cardinals thrill the Sportsman's Park crowd by scoring 11 runs in the first inning of a 12–3 walloping of the Reds before a crowd of 12,000. The 11 runs were scored on 12 hits. Eleven of them were singles and one a double. Victor Miller, who was sworn in as mayor the previous day, threw out the ceremonial first pitch.

The Cardinals lost their first three games, then won five in a row before a seven-game losing streak sent the club to a 5–10 record. By May 30, the Cards were 13–25 bringing about a change in leadership (see May 30, 1925).

APRIL 25   Reds president Garry Herrmann and seven Reds fans known as the Royal Rooters arrange for 25 barrels of beer to be delivered to the Hotel Statler in St. Louis and are arrested by Prohibition agents for illegal possession of alcohol. Herrmann and his cronies paid a substantial fine for the indiscretion.

MAY 7   The Cardinals overcome an unassisted triple play by Pirate shortstop Glenn Wright to defeat the Pirates 10–5 at Forbes Field. The Cards collected 20 hits in the game. The triple play occurred in the ninth inning. With Jimmy Cooney on second and Rogers Hornsby on first, Jim Bottomley hit a liner to Wright, who stepped on second to force Cooney, then tagged Hornsby, who was only a few feet from the bag.

There have been only 11 unassisted triple plays in major league history during the regular season and another in the World Series. Cooney is the only individual to be involved in one both as a fielder and a base runner. Cooney pulled off an unassisted triple play while playing shortstop for the Cubs in 1927.

MAY 23   The Cardinals trade Mike Gonzalez and Howard Freigau to the Cubs for Bob O'Farrell.

O'Farrell played in the majors from 1915 through 1935. He was the starting catcher on the 1926 World Champion Cardinals and was named the league's MVP for his all-around leadership and play. He hit .293 that season and caught 146 of the club's 156 games. O'Farrell was named manager of the club in December 1926 after the trade of Rogers Hornsby to the Giants. He guided the Cards to a strong second place finish, but was fired after the end of the season.

MAY 29   With the score tied 5–5 and the bases loaded with Pirates in the bottom of the ninth in Pittsburgh, Cardinals pitcher Leo Dickerman hits Kiki Cuyler with a pitch for a 6–5 loss.

MAY 30   Cardinals hurlers Pea Ridge Day and Eddie Dyer allow a modern major league record eight triples during a 15–5 loss to the Pirates in the first game of a doubleheader at Forbes Field. Pittsburgh also won the opener 4–1.

Following the doubleheader loss, Sam Breadon relieved Branch Rickey of his duties as manager and replaced him with Rogers Hornsby. Rickey retained his position as vice president, however, and continued to run the front office operation. "We decided Rickey was trying to do too much," Breadon said. "He was trying to manage the team and look after the vast organization of a major league club." Dwindling attendance along with the club's 13–25 record was also a heavy influence on the decision. Rickey wanted to remain as manager, and peevishly told Breadon that he wanted to sell his stock in the club if he couldn't remain as manager. Hornsby was only 29 years old, but it was an era in which star players managed clubs. At the same time, Ty Cobb managed the Tigers, George Sisler the Browns, Tris Speaker the Indians, Eddie Collins the White Sox, and Dave Bancroft the Braves. Hornsby was reluctant to take the Cardinals job, but relented when Breadon agreed to help him purchase stock that Rickey was putting up for sale. The stock transfer gave Hornsby a 12.5 percent interest in the club. Hornsby scrapped Rickey's platoon system and many of his strategy sessions. The club won 15 of their first 19 games under Hornsby and were 64–51 under his simplified direction over the remainder of the 1925 season.

JUNE 2   Jim Bottomley hits two homers, one a grand slam in the fifth inning off Neal Brady, to lead the Cardinals to an 8–2 win over the Reds at Sportsman's Park.

Bottomley hit three grand slams in 1925 to set a club record. It was since been tied by Keith Hernandez in 1977 and Fernando Tatis in 1999.

JUNE 10   The Cardinals score eight runs in the fifth inning and defeat the Dodgers 11–2 at Sportsman's Park.

JUNE 16   Rogers Hornsby throws a right jab at Phillies manager Art Fletcher during a 6–4 win on a hot afternoon in Philadelphia. In the fifth inning, Phillie catcher Jimmie Wilson wanted umpire Cy Pfirman to stop the game to allow pitcher Jimmy Ring to go to the clubhouse to change his undershirt, which was soaked with sweat. Pfirman informed Wilson that the pitcher would have the wait until the inning was completed for the wardrobe change. When Wilson refused to give up the debate, Pfirman threw him out of the game. Fletcher took up the argument with the umpire, and tired of the stalling tactics, Hornsby joined in the discussion. Quickly, Hornsby and Fletcher became involved in a heated discussion which escalated into a fight with Hornsby striking the first blow. In the course of all of the commotion, Ring went to the clubhouse and changed into a dry shirt. Hornsby was fined $100 by the National League.

JUNE 22   The Pirates score 10 runs in the eighth inning and overwhelm the Cardinals 24–6 at Sportsman's Park. It is the most runs ever given up by a Cardinal club since joining the National League in 1892. Only two pitchers absorbed the pounding. Flint Rhem started and gave up eight runs in $^2/_3$ of an inning. Johnny Stuart went the rest of the way, surrendering 16 runs in $8^1/_3$.

JUNE 28   Jim Bottomley hits a grand slam off Wilbur Cooper in the fifth inning of an 8–3 win over the Cubs in the second game of a doubleheader at Sportsman's Park. The Cards also won the first game 3–1.

JULY 21   Trailing 5–3, the Cardinals score four runs in the ninth inning to take a two-run lead, then survive a Phillies rally to win 7–6 at Philadelphia. Jim Bottomley's two-run homer broke the 5–5 tie.

JULY 28   Four days after John Scopes is convicted and fined $100 for teaching evolution following the "Monkey Trial" in Tennessee, Rogers Hornsby hits a grand slam in the eighth inning off Burleigh Grimes, but the Cardinals lose 12–9 to the Dodgers in Brooklyn.

AUGUST 5   Center fielder Jack Smith pulls off an unassisted double play in the second inning a 14–5 win over the Braves in Boston. Smith caught Doc Gautreau's drive then ran to first base to double Joe Genewich.

AUGUST 22   Trailing 3–2, the Cardinals score nine runs in the seventh inning and defeat the Phillies 11–2 in the first game of a doubleheader at Baker Bowl. Philadelphia won the aftermath of the twin bill 5–0.

AUGUST 24   The Cardinals sweep the Phillies 14–5 and 6–4 in Philadelphia. Jim Bottomley was 5 for 5 in the first game and 2 for 5 in the second. Three of his seven hits were doubles.

SEPTEMBER 10   Jim Bottomley hits a grand slam off Vic Aldridge in the ninth inning, but the Cardinals lose 9–5 to the Pirates at Sportsman's Park.

SEPTEMBER 15   The Cardinals clobber the Dodgers 15–3 at Sportsman's Park.

SEPTEMBER 27   After the Braves score two runs in the top of the tenth inning, the Cardinals rally for three in their half to win 6–5 in the first game of a doubleheader at Sportsman's Park. The Braves took the second tilt, called after seven innings by darkness, 7–6.

DECEMBER 11   The Cardinals trade Jimmy Cooney to the Cubs for Vic Keen.

                  During the 1925–26 offseason, the seating capacity Sportsman's Park was expanded from 18,000 to 32,000 by Browns owner Phil Ball. In 1925, the ballpark consisted of a double-decked, concrete-and-steel grandstand, built in 1909, which ran from just behind third base around to a point just past first base, two wooden pavilions down the left and right field lines, and wooden bleachers behind the outfield fences. In the expansion, all of the wooden seats were removed. The concrete-and-steel grandstand was extended to the ends of the foul lines and built of the same architecture as the original 1909 stands. A covered pavilion was built behind the right field wall, and open bleachers in center and left fields. Compared to other ballparks of the era, Sportsman's Park was rather nondescript, lacking in the architectural flair and quirks that characterize many of the others. The right field foul pole was only 310 feet, to dead center 422 feet, and down the left field line 351 feet. The new seats were rarely used during Browns games, however, as meager crowds turned out for teams that were usually at or near the bottom of the American League standings. Sportsman's Park was often filled for Cardinals games, however. The Cards played in 10 World Series at the ballpark.

1926

Season in a Sentence

The Cardinals take their first National League pennant and defeat the Yankees for seven games in the World Series.

Finish • Won • Lost • Pct • GB

First   89   65   .578   +2.0

World Series—The Cardinals won, four games to three, over the New York Yankees

Manager

Rogers Hornsby

Stats

Stats	Cards	• NL •	Rank
Batting Avg:	.286	.280	2
On-Base Pct:	.348	.338	2
Slugging Pct:	.415	.386	1
Home Runs:	90		1
Stolen Bases:	83		4
ERA:	3.67	3.82	4
Fielding Avg:	.969	.968	4
Runs Scored:	817		1
Runs Allowed:	678		4

Starting Lineup

Bob O'Farrell, c
Jim Bottomley, 1b
Rogers Hornsby, 2b
Les Bell, 3b
Tommy Thevenow, ss
Ray Blades, lf
Taylor Douthit, cf
Billy Southworth, rf
Chick Hafey, of
Heinie Mueller, of
Wattie Holm, of

Pitchers

Flint Rhem, sp
Bill Sherdel, sp
Jesse Haines, sp
Vic Keen, sp
Grover Alexander, sp-rp
Art Reinhart, rp-sp
Hi Bell, rp

Attendance

668,428 (sixth in NL)

Club Leaders

Batting Avg:	Hornsby	.317
On-Base Pct:	Blades	.409
Slugging Pct:	Bell	.518
Home Runs:	Bottomley	19
RBIs:	Bottomley	120
Runs:	Bottomley	98
Stolen Bases:	Douthit	23
Wins:	Rhem	20
Strikeouts:	Rhem	72
ERA:	Rhem	3.21
Saves:	Alexander	2
	Bell	2

APRIL 10	The first game is played at expanded Sportsman's Park as 22,632 turn out on a bitterly cold day to watch the Browns defeat the Cardinals 4–2 in an exhibition contest.
APRIL 13	The Cardinals open the season with a 7–5 win over the Pirates at Sportsman's Park. A three-run homer by Jim Bottomley in the sixth inning put the Cardinals up 6–0.
	Bottomley hit .299 with 19 homers and led the NL in total bases (305), doubles (40), and RBIs (120) in 1926.
APRIL 19	The Cardinals sell Jack Smith to the Braves.
APRIL 22	A two-run homer by Chick Hafey in the tenth inning beats the Pirates 5–3 in Pittsburgh.
MAY 16	The Cardinals rout the Braves 13–2 at Sportsman's Park.

MAY 21
The Cardinals score seven runs in the seventh inning and defeat the Phillies 12–4 at Sportsman's Park.

MAY 24
Trailing 6–0, the Cardinals score two runs in the sixth inning, two in the seventh, and seven in the eighth to beat the Reds 11–6 at Sportsman's Park.

MAY 26
The Cardinals overcome a large deficit against the Reds again at Sportsman's Park. Down 5–1, the Cardinals scored seven times in the eighth inning for an 8–5 victory. The Cards also pulled off a triple play in the second inning. With Red Lucas on second base, Chuck Dressen on first and Curt Walker batting, Rogers Hornsby leaped high into the air for a one-handed catch, then threw to shortstop Tommy Thevenow for the second out. Thevenow relayed the ball to first baseman Jim Bottomley to complete the triple killing.

> *When the 1926 season began, Cardinals fans hadn't seen a pennant-winning club since 1888 when the club was in the American Association. From 1892, the year the Cards moved into the National League, until 1925, St. Louis had never finished a season higher than third place in the standings or closer than seven games from first place. The Cardinals were the only team in the eight-team National League in 1926 that had failed to appear in a modern World Series since the event was inaugurated in 1903. (By 1926, the Browns were the only American League club that had failed to play in the Fall Classic, a distinction the club would hold until 1944.) The 1926 edition of the Cardinals looked like another losing club in April and May. The team had a record of 12–17 in seventh place on May 13 and was still under .500 at 21–23, in fifth position in the NL, on May 29 before catching fire in June and surging into pennant contention.*

JUNE 2
The Cardinals wallop the Cubs 14–6 in Chicago.

JUNE 14
The Cardinals trade Heinie Mueller to the Giants for Billy Southworth.

> *Southworth was in his 14th year in the majors and 33 years old when acquired by the Cardinals. He was brought to St. Louis for outfield depth, became the starter in right field, and had the best season of his career. In 99 games with the Cardinals in 1926, he batted .317 with 11 homers. Southworth also provided the club with one clutch hit after another and veteran leadership in the clubhouse.*

JUNE 22
The Cardinals purchase Grover Alexander from the Cubs.

> *Alexander was 39 years old, but had a 318–171 lifetime record when acquired by the Cardinals. He was 3–3 in 1926 when purchased from the Cubs. Chicago wanted to get rid of Alexander because he constantly feuded and defied the authority of new manager Joe McCarthy. Alexander showed up drunk six of his last ten days with the club and twice failed to show up for a game. During one contest, he collapsed on the bench in a drunken stupor. The Cards picked up Alexander at the urging of coach Bill Killefer, who was a teammate of the pitcher with the Phillies and Cubs and was his manager in Chicago from 1921 through 1925. Killefer had long been a steadying influence on Alexander, who helped the Cardinals win two pennants and one World Championship. He was 9–7 over the remainder of the 1926 season, won Game Six of the World Series and earned a dramatic save in the seventh game clincher. In 1927, Alexander was 21–10 and posted a 16–9 mark in 1928 before age caught up with him.*

Hulton Archive/Getty Images

(L–R) Taylor Douthit (center field), Les Bell (third base), Jim Bottomley (first base), Chick Hafey (outfield), and Bob O'Farrell (catcher). Douthit, Bell, Bottomley, and O'Farrell were the core of the World Series–winning 1926 team.

JUNE 23   Rogers Hornsby hits a homer off Don Songer in the seventh inning of a 6–2 win over the Pirates at Sportsman's Park. Earlier in the contest, Hornsby collected his 2,000th career hit with a single off Songer.

JUNE 27   A crowd of 37,196, the largest ever to see a baseball game in St. Louis up to that time, turns up at Sportsman's Park for a doubleheader against the Cubs. Grover Alexander, making his first appearance with the Cardinals, was the attraction. In the first game of the twin bill, Alexander defeated the Cubs 3–2 in 10 innings gaining a measure of revenge against the club which sold him to the Cards five days earlier. Chicago won the second game 5–0, which was interrupted in the ninth inning when thousands of bottles descended onto the field after St. Louis fans objected to a call by umpire Charlie Moran.

             On July 6, the Cardinals were 40–36 in third place, six games behind the first-place Reds.

JULY 10   The Cardinals score in every inning but the fifth and romp to an 18–6 triumph over the Braves at Sportsman's Park.

JULY 13	The Cardinals overcome three homers by Jack Fournier of the Dodgers to win 12–10 at Sportsman's Park. The Cards scored seven runs in the fifth inning to take an 11–3 lead before hanging on for the victory.
JULY 17	The Cardinals plate seven runs in the fifth inning of a 13–5 win over the Phillies at Sportsman's Park.
JULY 18	The Cardinals score three runs in the ninth inning, the last two on a walk-off homer by Billy Southworth, to defeat the Phillies 9–7 at Sportsman's Park.
JULY 25	Billy Southworth's walk-off homer in the eleventh inning ends an exciting 6–5 win over the Giants at Sportsman's Park. The Cards tied the score 4–4 in the ninth and 5–5 in the tenth to stay alive in the contest. Ray Blades and Jesse Haines were both ejected from the premises. Blades argued with umpire Jim Sweeney after being called out at second base and grabbed Sweeney by the coat. A shower of bottles was thrown by the fans, and Haines made a gesture to the crowd urging them to throw more.
JULY 30	Les Bell extends his hitting streak to 21 games with a homer during a 5–3 win over the Giants in New York.

Bell hit .325 with 17 homers and 100 RBIs for the Cards in 1926.

AUGUST 5	The Cardinals win a 10-inning battle over the Dodgers 11–9 at Ebbets Field. The Cards scored a run in the ninth to tie the game 7–7 and send it into extra innings, then added four in the tenth before surviving a Brooklyn rally in the bottom of the inning. Rogers Hornsby became involved in an altercation with a fan seated behind the St. Louis dugout in the eighth and was prevented from climbing into the stands after his tormentor by umpire Frank Wilson.
AUGUST 11	A two-run double by Bob O'Farrell in the eighth inning beats the Braves 2–0 in Boston. Jesse Haines pitched the shutout.
AUGUST 22	The Cardinals win their eighth game in a row with a 4–2 decision over the Giants at Sportsman's Park. The win put the Cards within one percentage point of the first-place Pirates.
AUGUST 23	The Cardinals are rained out against the Braves at Sportsman's Park, but take first place when the Pirates lose 10–2 to the Dodgers in Pittsburgh.

The Cardinals, Pirates, and Reds were in and out of first place over the next week in a dizzying three-team race. The Cards dropped out of first place on August 24, regained the top spot a day later, then dropped out of first again on August 26.

AUGUST 31	The Cardinals send 24,000 delirious fans home from a doubleheader at Sportsman's Park with a 6–1 and 2–1 sweep of the Pirates that enables St. Louis to take first place.
SEPTEMBER 1	The Cardinals sweep the Pirates in a doubleheader at Sportsman's Park for the second day in a row with 3–1 and 5–2 victories.

The two wins closed the Cardinals home schedule in 1926. The club finished the year with a seven-city road trip through Chicago, Pittsburgh, Boston, Philadelphia, Brooklyn, New York, and Cincinnati.

SEPTEMBER 2   Playing in Chicago for the first time since being sold by the Cubs to the Cardinals, Grover Alexander pitches a two-hitter to win 2–0 in the first game of a doubleheader. The Chicago only hits were singles by Hack Wilson and Clyde Beck. Alexander also scored the first run of the game following a double in the third inning. The Cards completed the sweep with a 9–1 victory. It was the fourth consecutive day that the Cards played a doubleheader, a period that included a train trip from St. Louis to Chicago. The Cardinals were 7–1 in those four twin bills and the pitching staff allowed only 12 runs.

The Cardinals had no National League games scheduled for September 8 and 9, but Sam Breadon insisted on playing exhibition games in Buffalo and Syracuse to showcase his club and earn some extra money. Rogers Hornsby wanted his pennant-contending club to rest, but Breadon insisted that the exhibitions be played. Hornsby countered by refusing to play any of his regulars. Without the star players on the field, crowds at the exhibitions were meager, cutting into Breadon's profit margin. The incident would influence Breadon's decision to trade Hornsby at the end of the season (see December 20, 1926).

SEPTEMBER 10   The Cardinals begin a four-game series in Boston against the last-place Braves and lose 11–2.

The Cardinals went into Boston with a three-game lead, lost three of four, and left in a tie for first place with the Reds. While the Cards were idle on September 14, the Reds won to take a one-half game lead.

SEPTEMBER 16   The Cardinals move into a first place tie with the Reds with a 23–3 and 10–2 pasting of the Phillies in Philadelphia. In the opener, the Cardinals scored 12 runs in the third, a club record for most runs in an inning. St. Louis collected 23 hits in the contest and Taylor Douthit scored five runs.

SEPTEMBER 17   The Cardinals take sole possession of first place with a 10–1 bombing of the Phillies in Philadelphia. The Cards won three straight over the Phillies in a little more than 24 hours by a combined score of 43–6.

SEPTEMBER 18   The Cardinals hold on to first place by splitting a doubleheader against the Phillies at Baker Bowl. The Cards won the opener 7–3 before the Phils sprang to life in the second tilt with a 3–2 victory.

Flint Rhem was the winning pitcher in the first game, earning his 20th triumph of the season. In a career year, he was 20–7, including an 11-game winning streak, with a 3.21 ERA in 1926. Rhem entered the 1926 campaign with a 10–15 lifetime record. He never again won more than 12 games in a season.

SEPTEMBER 22   Coming into the game with a three-game losing streak, the Cardinals club the Dodgers 15–7 in Brooklyn. Les Bell starred with three triples and a double. The win gave the Cardinals a 1½-game lead.

SEPTEMBER 24   The Cardinals clinch their first National League pennant with a 6–4 win over the Giants in New York. Bill Terry hit a three-run homer off Flint Rhem in the first inning, but the Cards rebounded with five runs in the second.

Some 50 loudspeakers were set up in the downtown business area carrying the radio broadcast of the Cardinals-Giants game. Thousands were gathered on the streets listening to the play-by-play from New York. Once the last out was made, the pent-up feelings of Cardinals fans, who hadn't celebrated a pennant since 1888, erupted in spontaneous jubilation. According to the report in The Sporting News, *"Great cheers went up from these many assemblages, and immediately a demonstration was on. Factory whistles shrieked, automobilists tooted their horns, trucks went about with cutouts open and the drivers backfiring their engines, impromptu bands and parades were organized and howling thousands surged through the streets, tying up traffic in general. From office buildings, great wads of paper, ticker tape and confetti were released, falling like the snow of a Dakota blizzard on the pavement below."*

SEPTEMBER 29   Rogers Hornsby's mother Mary dies in Austin, Texas, following a long illness. It was Mary Hornsby's dying wish that her son stay with the Cardinals until after the World Series was over. Her funeral and burial was delayed until October 13.

The Cardinals played the New York Yankees in the World Series. Managed by ex-Cardinal Miller Huggins, the Yankees were 91–63 in 1926 and won the AL pennant by three games.

OCTOBER 2   The Yankees win Game One of the 1926 World Series 2–1 in New York. Taylor Douthit opened the first inning with a double and scored on a single by Jim Bottomley, but over the final eight innings, the Cards collected only one hit off Herb Pennock. The Yanks scored their runs in the first and sixth off Bill Sherdel.

A humorous situation took place in the third inning when Babe Ruth advanced from first base to second on a grounder and split his pants in the process. The game was halted while Yankee Stadium groundskeeper Phil Schenck cut a few yards out of the tarpaulin that was used to cover the infield in wet weather, and trainer Doc Woods showed the piece onto Ruth's pants with a needle and thread.

OCTOBER 3   The Cardinals even the series with a 6–2 victory over the Yankees in New York. Grover Alexander allowed two runs in the second to fall behind 2–0, but shutout the Yankees the rest of the way, retiring the last 21 batters to face him. He fanned 10 batters in the game. The Cards tied the score 2–2 in the third on a single by Jim Bottomley. A three-run homer by Billy Southworth in the seventh broke the deadlock. Tommy Thevenow, who hit only two regular-season homers in 4,164 regular-season at-bats during his career, hit an inside-the-park home run in the ninth Thevenow hit a drive into the farthest corner of right field. Babe Ruth gave chase, hesitated just before arriving to avoid a collision with the concrete wall, then hit the wall anyway. By the time Ruth found the ball, Thevenow rounded the bases.

OCTOBER 5   In the first World Series game played in St. Louis in the modern era, the Cardinals beat the Yankees 4–0 before 37,708 at Sportsman's Park. Jesse Haines pitched the six-hit shutout and hit a two-run homer in the fourth inning.

Haines is one of only two pitchers with a shutout and a homer in the same World Series game. The other was Bucky Walters of the Reds in 1940.

OCTOBER 6   Babe Ruth hits three homers and the Yankees even the World Series with a 10–5 win before 38,825 at Sportsman's Park. Ruth homered in the first inning off Flint Rhem, in the third off Rhem and in the sixth facing Hi Bell. The third-inning blast cleared the right field roof and crashed through the window of an auto dealer across the street. Ruth's third homer traveled some 500 feet before settling into the center field bleachers. In the fourth, Chick Hafey and Taylor Douthit collided in the outfield. Douthit was sidelined for the rest of the series.

OCTOBER 7   The Yankees take a three games to two lead over the Cardinals with a ten-inning 3–2 win before 39,552 at Sportsman's Park. Herb Pennock and Bill Sherdel both pitched complete games. The Yankees tied the game 2–2 with a run in the ninth. A sacrifice fly by Tony Lazzeri in the tenth drove in the winning run. To claim a World Championship, the Cardinals had to win two games at Yankee Stadium.

OCTOBER 9   The Cardinals force a seventh game by defeating the Yankees 10–2 in New York. Grover Alexander went the distance. At 39, he is the oldest pitcher in World Series history with a complete game. The Cards put the game away with three runs in the first inning. Les Bell was the hitting star with a homer, two singles, and four RBIs. Rogers Hornsby drove in three runs and Billy Southworth scored three times.

OCTOBER 10   The Cardinals claim their first modern World Championship with a 3–2 win over the Yankees in Game Seven at Yankee Stadium. Jesse Haines and Waite Hoyt took the mound in the decisive match, which was played in a steady drizzle. Babe Ruth homered off Haines in the third for a 1–0 lead. But shoddy Yankee fielding in the fourth helped give the Cardinals a 3–1 lead. Tommy Thevenow broke the 1–1 tie with a two-run single. After getting a run back in the sixth, the Yanks loaded the bases with two outs in the seventh against Haines, who had worn a blister on his index finger. Rogers Hornsby held a long conference on the mound with catcher Bob O'Farrell and the rest of the infield and decided to bring Grover Alexander into the game. Alexander had not only pitched a complete game the day before, but according to legend, celebrated far into the evening believing that he wouldn't pitch again. According to many teammates, Alexander reported to Game Seven severely hung over and was sleeping in the bullpen when summoned by Hornsby. The 39-year-old veteran pitcher worked carefully to Tony Lazzeri, going to a 1–1 count, before serving a pitch that Lazzeri drilled foul. Alexander proceeded to strike out Lazzeri on the next pitch. In the eighth, Alexander set the Yankees down in order. With a 3–2 lead and the world title on the line, Alexander retired Earle Combs and Mark Koenig to start the ninth, then walked Babe Ruth. With Bob Meusel at the plate, Ruth impulsively decided to try and steal second. Catcher Bob O'Farrell gunned the ball to Hornsby, who slapped the tag on the Babe in plenty of time to end the game and make the Cards the champs.

There was another celebration on the streets of St. Louis following the World Series win. Property damage was extensive and two teenagers were killed when struck by automobiles. Approximately 80 individuals were treated at local hospitals for injuries.

DECEMBER 20   In a trade of superstar second basemen of the top of their game, the Cardinals deal Rogers Hornsby to the Giants for Frankie Frisch. The Giants also sent pitcher Jimmy Ring to the Cardinals in the transaction.

Hornsby was never shy about expressing his opinion and didn't hesitate to crudely and tactlessly criticize Sam Breadon when he disagreed with the policies *of the Cardinals owner. Hornsby also wanted a three-year contract, while Breadon was offering only a one-year deal, although at $50,000 which would make him the highest-paid player in baseball behind Babe Ruth. Breadon also wanted Hornsby to stop betting on horse racing, but Hornsby refused. (A year later, Hornsby was sued by a Newport, Kentucky, bookmaker, who claimed Hornsby owed him $92,000 in gambling debts. The case was settled out of court.) An off-year by Hornsby at the bat was another influence. After batting .403 in 1925, Hornsby fell to .317 in 1926 and Breadon was convinced that he was slowing down. John McGraw and the Giants had been trying to convince the Cards to send Hornsby to New York for nearly a decade, and the trade was completed by sending Frisch to St. Louis. It was a gutsy move by Breadon to trade the best player in club history and a man who had just taken the Cardinals to a World Championship. Cardinals fans were up in arms over the exile of Hornsby. Mayor Victor Miller and the St. Louis Chamber of Commerce contacted baseball commissioner Kenesaw Landis and National League president John Heydler to see of the trade could be cancelled. Mark Steinberg, a member of the Cardinals board of directors, called the trade "an insult" to St. Louis fans. At a downtown intersection, an irate fan jumped on the running board of Breadon's Piece-Arrow and shouted insults until police chased him away. The Cardinals owner received so many abusive calls to his home that he disconnected his phone. Breadon's home and auto agency were festooned with black crepe by angry fans. The trade was also criticized heavily in the media. One sportswriter vowed he would never cover another Cardinals game, and kept the pledge for 10 years. Breadon justified the move by stating that "flattering friends" gave Hornsby "too big of an opinion of himself" and added that the Cardinals were "a good team with Hornsby and they will be a great team without him." With that last statement, Breadon was correct. The Cardinals continued to be a great team without Hornsby. In the years that Frisch was the starting second baseman, the Cards won pennants in 1928, 1930, 1931 and 1934. He also was the manager of the 1934 club. Hornsby still had three great years ahead of him, however. From 1927 though 1929, he hit .376 with 86 homers, but he did it for three different teams as his prickly personality led to trades from the Giants to the Braves in 1928 and to the Cubs in 1929. Hornsby later managed the Braves (1928), Cubs (1930–32), Browns (1933–37 and 1952), and Reds (1952–53). He never managed another club in a World Series, although he played in one with the Cubs in 1929. Although Hornsby had better years than Frisch in 1927, 1928, and 1929, Frisch was still a productive player well into the 1930s at a time when Hornsby was benched because of injuries. Ultimately, the Cardinals got the better of the deal.*

DECEMBER 27   The Cardinals hire Bob O'Farrell as manager to replace Rogers Hornsby.

O'Farrell was 30 years old and he won the National League Most Valuable Player Award in 1926. He was in the unenviable position of replacing Hornsby after a World Championship year and after Hornsby went to the Giants in an unpopular trade. O'Farrell's 1927 Cardinals were 92–61 and finished a close second to the Pirates, but at the end of the 1927 season, he was replaced by Bill McKechnie.

1927

Season in a Sentence

The 1927 Cardinals win three more games than the 1926 World Championship club, but finish second and replace Bob O'Farrell as manager after only one year on the job.

Finish • Won • Lost • Pct • GB

Second   92   61   .601   1.5

Manager

Bob O'Farrell

Stats

Stats	Cards	NL	Rank
Batting Avg:	.278	.282	6
On-Base Pct:	.343	.339	4
Slugging Pct:	.408	.386	3
Home Runs:	84		2
Stolen Bases:	110		1
ERA:	3.57	3.91	3
Fielding Avg:	.966	.968	6
Runs Scored:	754		3
Runs Allowed:	665		5

Starting Lineup

Frank Snyder, c
Jim Bottomley, 1b
Frankie Frisch, 2b
Les Bell, 3b
Heinie Schulte, ss
Chick Hafey, lf
Taylor Douthit, cf
Billy Southworth, rf
Wattie Holm, lf-cf
Specs Toporcer, 3b-ss
Tommy Thevenow, ss
Ray Blades, lf-rf
Bob O'Farrell, c
Johnny Schulte, c

Pitchers

Jesse Haines, sp
Grover Alexander, sp
Bill Sherdel, sp-rp
Flint Rhem, sp
Bob McGraw, sp
Art Reinhart, rp-sp

Attendance

749,340 (fourth in NL)

Club Leaders

Batting Avg:	Frisch	.337
On-Base Pct:	Frisch	.387
	Bottomley	.387
Slugging Pct:	Bottomley	.590
Home Runs:	Bottomley	19
RBIs:	Bottomley	124
Runs:	Frisch	112
Stolen Bases:	Frisch	48
Wins:	Haines	24
Strikeouts:	Haines	89
ERA:	Alexander	2.52
Saves:	Sherdel	6

APRIL 8   Rogers Hornsby sells his stock in the Cardinals.

The trade involving Hornsby and Frankie Frisch, completed on December 20, 1926, hit a snag because Hornsby owned 12.5 percent of the stock in the Cardinals. According to major league rules, an individual could not own stock in one team while playing for another. Hornsby knew he had Sam Breadon over a barrel and took advantage of the situation by asking an exorbitant price for his shares. Breadon paid Hornsby $86,000 for the stock, the Giants paid $12,000, and each of the other major league clubs contributed $2,000. Hornsby received $110,000 for stock he bought for less than half that price in May 1925.

APRIL 12   The defending World Champion Cardinals open the 1927 season by losing 10–1 to the Cubs in Chicago. Grover Alexander was the starting pitcher and allowed six runs in four innings.

Alexander recovered from the Opening Day debacle to post a record of 21–10 for the Cards in 1927 with a 2.52 ERA.

APRIL 13   Jesse Haines pitches a two-hitter to beat the Cubs 5–0 at Wrigley Field. The only Chicago hits were singles by Jimmy Cooney and Cliff Heathcote.

Haines was 24–10 with a 2.72 earned run average in 300⅔ innings in 1927.

APRIL 15   Bill Sherdel holds the Cubs to two hits, but one is a homer by Hack Wilson in the second inning resulting in a 1–0 loss in Chicago.

The Cardinals' uniforms in 1927 featured the depiction of a single Cardinal perched on a bat on the left breast of the shirt with the words "WORLD CHAMPIONS" over and under the bird.

National Baseball Hall of Fame Library/Major League Baseball/Getty Images

Frankie Frisch, acquired by the Cardinals in exchange for Rogers Hornsby, was not a fan favorite in his Cardinal debut. Frisch won over the fans by putting up solid offensive and defensive numbers. He played for the Cards for 11 years and was inducted into the Hall of Fame in 1947.

APRIL 20   In the home opener, the Cardinals defeat the Cubs 4–2 before 12,000 at Sportsman's Park. The 1926 National League pennant was unfurled from the flagpole before the game.

When the season started, Cardinal fans were still seething over the Hornsby-for-Frisch trade, and much of the crowd at Sportsman's Park chanted, "We

want Hornsby, we want Hornsby," whenever Frisch stepped to the plate. Frisch himself wasn't happy leaving the Giants and moving to the Midwest because he was a native New Yorker. Saddled with the almost impossible task of replacing the town's baseball idol, Frisch won over the fans with an excellent season in 1927. He hit .337 with 112 runs, 208 hits, 10 homers, and a league-leading 48 stolen bases. On defense, Frisch had 641 assists and 1,037 total chances, which are still major league records. The highly competitive switch-hitting second baseman played for the Cardinals until 1937 and managed the club from 1933 through 1938. In his years in St. Louis, Frisch played in 1,311 games, scored 831 runs, and collected 1,577 hits, 286 doubles, 61 triples, and 195 stolen bases. With a remarkable ability to make contact, he struck out only 272 times in 9,112 career at-bats with both the Giants and Cardinals. Frisch played in eight World Series, the most of any National Leaguer in history. He played in four Fall Classics with the Giants and four with the Cards. Frisch was elected to the Hall of Fame in 1947.

APRIL 23   Flint Rhem pitches a two-hitter to beat the Cubs 7–0 at Sportsman's Park. The only Chicago hits were singles by Howard Freigau and opposing pitcher Percy Jones. It was the third two-hitter by a Cardinal pitcher against the Cubs in less than two weeks.

APRIL 25   Taylor Douthit hits a homer in the sixth inning off Ray Kremer to defeat the Pirates 1–0 at Sportsman's Park. Jesse Haines pitched the shutout.

That fans were quickly mollified over the Hornsby trade is reflected in the attendance figures at Sportsman's Park. Although the club drew a record 668,428 in 1926, the standard was broken again in 1927 when 749,340 paid their way into Sportsman's Park. After that experience, Sam Breadon never again hesitated to trade a star player. Others dealt by Breadon in later years included Burleigh Grimes (1931), Chick Hafey (1932), Jim Bottomley (1932), Dizzy Dean (1938), Joe Medwick (1940), Johnny Mize (1941), and Walker Cooper (1946).

MAY 8   Flint Rhem pitches a two-hitter to beat the Dodgers 5–1 at Ebbets Field. The only Brooklyn hits were a single by Jigger Statz and a double by Harvey Hendrick, both in the sixth inning.

MAY 12   Les Bell strikes out five times in an 11-inning, 3–2 loss to the Giants in New York.

MAY 13   The Cardinals score seven runs in the first inning and two in the second to spark an 11–1 win over the Giants in New York.

MAY 14   Tragedy strikes at Baker Bowl in Philadelphia bringing an end to a game between the Phillies and the Cardinals. During the seventh inning with the Phillies leading 12–4, a full section of the right-field stands collapsed. Fans in other sections of the park were in a panic, and Cardinals players came out of their dugout and ranged along the edge of the playing field, imploring the crowd to stay calm. Some 50 fans were injured and one died of a heart attack.

MAY 16   While Baker Bowl is closed for repairs, the Cardinals and Phillies play at Shibe Park, home of the Philadelphia Athletics. The Cardinals won 2–1.

MAY 25	Four days after Charles Lindbergh lands in Paris after his historic solo flight across the Atlantic in *The Spirit of St. Louis*, Les Bell hits a grand slam in the fifth inning off Tony Kaufmann during an 8–5 win in the first game of a doubleheader at Wrigley Field. Chicago won the second tilt by the same 8–4 score.
MAY 31	Taylor Douthit hits a homer in the eighth inning off Jakie May to beat the Reds 1–0 at Sportsman's Park. Bob McGraw pitched the shutout. It was his only shutout in a nine-year big-league career.
JUNE 7	US Vice President Charles Dawes watches the Cardinals lose 12–5 to the Braves at Sportsman's Park.
JUNE 9	Cardinals catcher Johnny Schulte receives a concussion before a 6–1 win over the Braves at Sportsman's Park which struck in the head by a bat which slipped from the hands of Wattie Holm during batting practice.
JUNE 12	Les Bell hits a two-run, walk-off homer in ninth that defeats the Phillies 5–4 at Sportsman's Park.
JUNE 15	Jesse Haines pitches a two-hitter to defeat the Giants 5–0 at Sportsman's Park. The only New York hits were singles by Edd Roush and Travis Jackson.

> *The contest was also the first appearance by Rogers Hornsby in St. Louis since his trade to the Giants. Before the game, Mayor Victor Miller presented Hornsby with a watch engraved "from the fans of St. Louis."*

JUNE 16	Rogers Hornsby collects four hits, including a homer, in four at-bats to lead the Giants to a 10–5 win over the Cardinals at Sportsman's Park.
JUNE 18	With Charles Lindbergh in attendance, the World Championship banner is raised before a crowd of 27,000 at Sportsman's Park prior to a 6–4 victory over the Giants.

> *It was Lindbergh's first appearance in St. Louis since becoming the first individual to fly solo across the Atlantic on May 20 and 21 in a plane that was financed in the city and named The Spirit of St. Louis. That Lindbergh was on hand to help the Cardinals raise the world championship banner was a happy coincidence because the Cardinals announced the date of the flag-raising in late April before the historic flight took place. The following day, a ticker-tape parade was held in St. Louis honoring Lindbergh, attended by an estimated 100,000.*

JUNE 21	The Cardinals win an exciting 13-inning, 6–5 victory over the Cubs at Sportsman's Park. In the twelfth inning, Earl Webb of the Cubs homered to put his club up 4–3, but Johnny Schulte hit a home run for the Cards in the bottom half to tie the contest. In the thirteenth, Mike Gonzalez homered to once again put Chicago in the lead. St. Louis came roaring back with two in their half on a triple by Taylor Douthit, a single by Jim Bottomley and a hit from Les Bell. The Cardinals completed the sweep in the second tilt with a 12–3 victory behind three triples from Bottomley.

> *The Cards received a setback when starting shortstop Tommy Thevenow broke his ankle sliding into second base, an injury that put him out for the season.*

JULY 7   The Cardinals trounce the Braves 12–1 in Boston.

                Heading into the game, the Cards had a record of 39–31 and were in third place,
                5½ games out of first.

JULY 15   Jim Bottomley hits for the cycle, leading the Cardinals to a 9–7 win over the Phillies
                in Philadelphia. Bottomley collected a total of five hits, including two singles.

                Bottomley hit .303 with 19 homers, 124 RBIs, and 15 triples in 1927.

JULY 17   The Cardinals score three runs in the ninth inning off Dazzy Vance to defeat the
                Dodgers 5–3 in Brooklyn. Johnny Schulte hit a two-run triple and scored on a pinch-
                hit single by Danny Clark.

JULY 27   The Cardinals win a hectic 11-inning, 9–8 win over the Phillies at Sportsman's Park.
                Frankie Frisch hit a homer in the ninth to tie the game 7–7. After Philadelphia scored
                in the tenth, Les Bell deadlocked the game again with a homer. The Cards won the
                contest on a two-out single by Ray Blades.

                On the same day, Flint Rhem left the club after being fined $2,500 for drinking
                during a road trip. Rhem had a 20–7 record in 1926, but was constantly in
                trouble with club management for his drunken behavior. His contract for 1927
                called for a bonus of $2,500 if he didn't take a drink during the season. Rhem
                forfeited the bonus when he got drunk at the Elks's Club in Boston, which had
                just been converted into a hotel. Though it was Prohibition, a nightclub had been
                set up on the third floor, and in violation of club rules, Rhem, Grover Alexander,
                and others partied late into the night and by morning were in a drunken stupor.
                Citing that others were involved in the indiscretion, Rhem asked, "Why should
                I be penalized for enjoying myself on a trip?" He also came up with the lame
                excuse that he drank the booze only to keep it away from Alexander, who was
                a noted alcoholic. "They were passing drinks at Alex so fast, I had to drink 'em
                up. I wanted to keep him sober; he's more important to the club than I am."
                Rhem returned to the club four days later when Sam Breadon gave him $500 of
                his $2,500 abstinence bonus because he made it into July before taking a drink.
                Rhem was 105–97 in 12 seasons in the majors, 10 of them with the Cardinals,
                in a career plagued by inconsistency. He came from a wealthy family in South
                Carolina. His hometown of Rhems was named for his grandfather, who founded
                the village and established its economy by owning virtually every business in
                the area. Rhem studied engineering at Clemson, where his pitching earned the
                attention of Cardinal scouts. The club suspended Rhem many times during his
                career because of his excessive drinking habits, and even sent him to the minors
                for the entire 1929 season, but he continued to struggle with alcoholism until his
                big-league career closed in 1936.

AUGUST 11   With the Cardinals trailing 1–0. Jim Bottomley hits a two-run homer to lift the club
                to a 2–1 win over the Pirates at Sportsman's Park.

AUGUST 12   Jim Bottomley hits a walk-off homer in the eleventh inning defeating the Pirates 2–1
                at Sportsman's Park. Jesse Haines pitched a complete game allowing four hits.

                On August 14, the Cardinals had a record of 61–47 record and were in third
                place, seven games out of first.

AUGUST 16	Bob O'Farrell collects five hits in six at-bats during a 5–3 win in 11 innings over the Braves in Boston.
AUGUST 22	Chick Hafey's homer off Dutch Ulrich in the second inning beats the Phillies 1–0 at Philadelphia. Jesse Haines pitched the shutout.
AUGUST 23	The Cardinals score eight runs in the fifth inning and maul the Phillies 13–3 in Philadelphia.
SEPTEMBER 2	The Cardinals purchase Rabbit Maranville from Rochester in the International League. Maranville was one of best shortstops in baseball through most of the 1910s and early 1920s, but heavy drinking brought about a trip back to the minors. He quit drinking early in the 1927 season while at Rochester, and earned a call back to the majors. Maranville was the Cardinals' regular shortstop on the 1928 National League championship club.

> *On the day that Maranville was purchased by the Cardinals, the club was involved in a four-team race. The Pirates were in first, the Cubs in second (½ game behind), the Cards third (1 game back), and the Giants fourth (1½ games out).*

SEPTEMBER 6	The Cardinals hammer the Cubs 12–1 at Sportsman's Park.
SEPTEMBER 9	With the Cardinals trailing 6–5 in the tenth inning, Les Bell hits a two-out, three-run, walk-off homer to beat the Giants 8–6 at Sportsman's Park.
SEPTEMBER 12	Jim Bottomley's two-run homer in the fifth inning off Jumbo Jim Elliott gives the Cardinals a 2–0 win over the Dodgers at Sportman's Park. Art Reinhart pitched the shutout.
SEPTEMBER 14	A three-run, walk-off homer by Chick Hafey beats the Giants 6–3 in the first game of a doubleheader at Sportsman's Park. New York won the second game 9–3.
SEPTEMBER 17	The Cardinals crush the Phillies 11–0 at Sportsman's Park. Despite the victory, the Cardinals lost a half a game in the pennant race when the Pirates swept a doubleheader. At the end of the day, the Cards appeared to be out of pennant contention, trailing by six games with 14 contests left on the schedule.
SEPTEMBER 18	The Cardinals sweep the Phillies 7–3 and 8–3 in a doubleheader at Sportsman's Park. Grover Alexander picked up his 20th win in the opener.
SEPTEMBER 22	The Cardinals keep their slim hopes for a pennant alive with two runs in the ninth inning to defeat the Braves 6–5 at Sportsman's Park. The win put the Cardinals three games behind the Pirates with nine left to play.

> *Fred Frankhouse, a 23-year-old rookie, made his major league debut on September 11 and was a tremendous addition during the 1927 pennant drive. He won his first five major league games, each with complete-game starts.*

SEPTEMBER 25	The Cardinals sweep the Braves 4–1 and 6–5 at Sportsman's Park. The wins put the Cardinals two games behind the Pirates with five games remaining.

SEPTEMBER 29   The Cardinals are eliminated from the pennant race with a 3–2 loss to the Reds in
                Cincinnati.

                *On the same day, a tornado ripped through St. Louis resulting in the deaths of
                87 people. Some 500 more were injured in a path of devastation that covered
                six square miles in a diagonal path through the city and into Illinois towns just
                across the Mississippi River. At Sportsman's Park, the twister flipped the pavilion
                roof onto Grand Avenue, bent the flagpole in center field, and scattered debris
                all over the ballpark. The Cards played their final home game as scheduled on
                October 1, but had the club reached the World Series, the extensive damage
                to Sportsman's Park would probably have prompted the moving of the event
                outside of St. Louis since it would be been difficult to make the repairs necessary
                to handle capacity crowds. Many major traffic arteries near the ballpark were
                also closed.*

NOVEMBER 7   Despite finishing a close second in 1927 with three more victories than the 1927
                club, Bob O'Farrell is deposed as manager of the Cardinals and replaced by
                41-year-old Bill McKechnie.

                *Although relieved of his duties as manager, O'Farrell was given a $5,000 raise
                not to manage the club. He remained with the Cardinals as a player, but was
                traded to the Giants in May 1928. O'Farrell later managed the Reds in 1934.
                McKechnie managed the Pirates to a World Championship in 1925, but was
                fired after the 1926 season. He served as a coach with the Cardinals under
                O'Farrell in 1927.*

DECEMBER 13   The Cardinals trade Jimmy Ring and Johnny Schulte to the Phillies for Jimmy
                Cooney, Johnny Mokan, and Bubber Jonnard. Five days later, the Cardinals sold
                Cooney to the Braves.

1928

Season in a Sentence

The Cardinals rebound to win the National League pennant, but change managers again after being swept by the Yankees in the World Series.

Finish • Won • Lost • Pct • GB

First   95   59   .617   +2.0

World Series—The Cardinals lost, four games to none, to the New York Yankees

Manager

Bill McKechnie

Stats	Cards	• NL •	Rank
Batting Avg:	.281	.281	3
On-Base Pct:	.353	.344	2
Slugging Pct:	.425	.397	2
Home Runs:	113		2
Stolen Bases:	82		3
ERA:	3.38	3.99	2
Fielding Avg:	.974	.971	2
Runs Scored:	807		2 (tie)
Runs Allowed:	636		2

Starting Lineup

Jimmie Wilson, c
Jim Bottomley, 1b
Frankie Frisch, 2b
Wattie Holm, 3b
Rabbit Maranville, ss
Chick Hafey, lf
Taylor Douthit, cf
George Harper, rf
Andy High, 3b
Wally Roettger, rf-lf
Tommy Thevenow, ss

Pitchers

Bill Sherdel, sp-rp
Jesse Haines, sp
Grover Alexander, sp
Flint Rhem, sp
Clarence Mitchell, sp
Syl Johnson, rp
Fred Frankhouse, rp-sp

Attendance

761,574 (third in NL)

Club Leaders

Batting Avg:	Hafey	.337
On-Base Pct:	Hafey	.416
Slugging Pct:	Bottomley	.628
Home Runs:	Bottomley	31
RBIs:	Bottomley	136
Runs:	Bottomley	123
Stolen Bases:	Frisch	29
Wins:	Sherdel	21
Strikeouts:	Haines	77
ERA:	Sherdel	2.86
Saves:	Haid	5

MARCH 25   The Cardinals send Les Bell to the Braves in exchange for Andy High and $25,000.

APRIL 11   The Cardinals get off to a flying start in 1928 by winning the opener 14–7 against the Pirates before 20,745 at Sportsman's Park. Jim Bottomley hit a homer and double and drove in three runs. Frankie Frisch also had three RBIs on a homer and two singles.

> *Bottomley had the best season of his career in 1928 with a .325 batting average, 31 homers, a league-leading 136 RBIs, 123 runs, 42 doubles, and 20 triples. He also topped the NL in total bases with 362. Frisch hit .300 with 10 homers and 29 stolen bases.*

APRIL 19   The Cardinals outlast the Pirates 13–10 in Pittsburgh. The Cards were down 4–1 before a five-run fifth inning put them in the lead.

APRIL 25   Rabbit Maranville plays shortstop for the Cardinals after being ejected from a 17-inning, 5–4 loss to the Reds in Cincinnati. Maranville was ejected in the twelfth inning for heckling the decisions of umpire Charlie Moran from the dugout. In the fourteenth, however, the Cardinals replaced Tommy Thevenow, who was lifted for a pinch-hitter, with Maranville at shortstop. Cincinnati manager Jack Hendricks objected to Maranville's presence in the game, but Moran allowed Maranville to remain.

The Cardinals were off to a rough start in 1928 with a 10–11 record on May 6.

MAY 8   The Cardinals score nine runs in the eighth inning and defeat the Phillies 15–4 at Sportsman's Park.

MAY 10   The Cardinals trade starting catcher and ex-manager Bob O'Farrell to the Giants for George Harper.

MAY 11   The Cardinals trade Spud Davis and Homer Peel to the Phillies for Jimmie Wilson. The trade took place while the Cardinals were in the process of beating the Phillies 3–2 at Sportsman's Park. Wilson was the Phils starting catcher in the contest and was taken out of the game in the second inning was the swap was completed.

Wilson filled the void at catcher left when O'Farrell was dealt to the Giants a day earlier. Wilson was the Cardinals starting catcher until 1933 and played for the club in three World Series. Davis had several excellent seasons as a catcher with the Phils. On November 15, 1933, Wilson was traded to the Phillies in order for him to become manager of the team. In exchange, Davis came back to St. Louis.

MAY 14   Chick Hafey hits a two-run, walk-off single in the ninth inning which beats the Braves 4–3 at Sportsman's Park.

The Cardinals drew 761,574 fans in 1928, a club record that would stand until 1946.

MAY 21   The Cardinals win an unusual 8–7 game over the Cubs at Sportsman's Park. The Cards left no one on base in the game. Of the ten batters who reached base, eight scored, one was erased on a double play, and another was picked off base. Four home runs helped the cause. Jim Bottomley hit two, and George Harper and Wally Roettger one each.

JUNE 1   Art Reinhart pitches the Cardinals to a 1–0 win over the Phillies in Philadelphia.

JUNE 2   The Cardinals win a 13–12 slugfest over the Phillies in Philadelphia. The Cards led 7–2 in the fifth inning, fell behind 9–7, then regained the lead with six runs in the eighth. A pinch-hit grand slam by Wattie Holm put St. Louis in the lead. It was one of three pinch-hit homers in the game, a major league record. The other two were by Johnny Schulte and Cy Williams of the Phillies.

JUNE 6   Down 5–1, the Cardinals score six runs in the seventh inning and beat the Giants 11–6 in New York.

JUNE 10   The Cardinals score seven runs in the eighth inning and beat the Dodgers 15–7 in Brooklyn.

National Baseball Hall of Fame Library/Major League Baseball/Getty Images

Grover Alexander was a remarkable pitcher who in his 20-year career
won 373 games and appeared in three World Series, two with the Cards.
Alexander, who suffered from epilepsy, struggled even more with alcoholism
after he left the game than he had before and died in 1950 with little money.

JUNE 13   The Cardinals hit five home runs and defeat the Braves 11–8 in Boston. Chick Hafey
struck two of the homers, and Jim Bottomley, Frankie Frisch, and Taylor Douthit one
each.

JUNE 14   A two-run homer by Chick Hafey in the ninth inning beats the Braves 3–2 in Boston.

Hafey hit .337 with 27 homers and 111 RBIs in 1928.

JUNE 15   A three-run homer by Jim Bottomley in the fourteenth inning defeats the Dodgers
5–2 in Brooklyn.

*The win put the Cardinals into first place. With the exception of a five-day
stretch in August, the Cards remained on top of the National League for the rest
of the year, although the pennant wasn't assured until the final weekend of the
season.*

JUNE 16   The Cardinals win a thrilling 11-inning, 6–5 win over the Dodgers in Brooklyn. With
               the Dodgers leading 4–2 with two out in the ninth and a runner on base, George
               Harper pinch-hit for Rabbit Maranville, but after the Dodgers switched from
               right-hander Ray Moss to lefty Jesse Petty, Ray Blades was sent to the plate for
               Harper. Blades responded with a homer to tie the score 4–4. Both teams scored in the
               tenth before the Cardinals won the contest in the eleventh.

JUNE 25   With the score 1–1 in the eleventh inning against the Reds in Cincinnati, Ray Blades
               hits a bases loaded triple then scores on an error. The Reds scored in the bottom of
               the inning to make the final 5–2.

               *Three starting pitchers had excellent seasons for the Cardinals in 1928. Bill
               Sherdel was 21–10 with an ERA of 2.86. Jesse Haines had a 20–8 record and an
               earned run average of 3.19. Grover Alexander, at the age of 41, was 16–9 with a
               3.36 ERA.*

JULY 12   The Cardinals wallop the Giants 11–1 at Sportsman's Park in a contest called in the
               sixth inning by rain.

               The win gave the Cardinals a 52–30 record and a 5½-game lead over the Giants.

JULY 28   Chick Hafey ties a major league record for most extra base hits in a doubleheader
               with six against the Phillies in Philadelphia. In the opener, Hafey hit a homer in the
               12th inning to left the Cardinals to a 7–6 victory. Earlier in the game, he doubled
               twice. In the second tilt, he was 5 for 5 with a homer, two doubles, and two singles in
               a 12–3 win.

JULY 31   The Cardinals collect 20 hits and administer an 18–5 trouncing of the Phillies in
               Philadelphia. Taylor Douthit had five of the hits, including a double, in five at-bats.
               The Cards were helped by a mental error by the Phillies. With the score 2–2 in
               the fifth, Phillie shortstop Heinie Sand threw the ball toward the pitcher's mound
               believing that the third out had been recorded. His teammates followed him off the
               field. There were only two out, however, and Jimmie Wilson scored from first base
               before the Phillies realized the inning hadn't ended.

AUGUST 8   The Cardinals defeat the Giants 6–4 in 15 innings at the Polo Grounds. The Cards
               led 4–0 in the third inning before allowing New York to tie the contest. Neither team
               scored from the sixth through the fourteenth.

AUGUST 19   The Giants knock the Cardinals out of first place by completing a three-game sweep
               of the Cardinals at Sportsman's Park with a 3–2 win.

AUGUST 24   Ernie Orsatti's homer in the first inning off Ray Benge is enough to defeat the Phillies
               1–0 at Sportsman's Park. Jesse Haines pitched the shutout.

               *The win put the Cardinals back in first place, where they remained for the rest of
               the year.*

SEPTEMBER 6   The two-run, pinch-hit, walk-off homer by George Harper in the tenth inning defeats
               the Pirates 4–3 at Sportsman's Park.

SEPTEMBER 14   The Cardinals clobber the Phillies 13–6 in Philadelphia.

SEPTEMBER 15   The Cardinals leave 29 men on base in a doubleheader, but manage to sweep the Phillies 3–2 and 8–6 in Philadelphia. The Cards left 11 on base in the first game and tied a National League record by stranding 18 in the nightcap.

SEPTEMBER 20   George Harper becomes the first Cardinal batter to collect three homers in a game during an 8–5 victory in the first game of a doubleheader against the Giants at the Polo Grounds. Harper hit a solo homer off Rube Benton in the second inning, a three-run shot off Benton in the sixth, and another solo home run against Jack Scott in the eighth. Harper batted in the ninth with the bases loaded, but was called out on strikes. Harper was so incensed over the call by umpire Cy Rigler, that he had to be dragged into the dugout by teammate Rabbit Maranville. New York won the second game 7–4. The day ended as it started, with the Cardinals holding a two-game edge over the Giants in the NL pennant race.

SEPTEMBER 22   The Cardinals lead over the Giants drops to one game after an 8–5 loss in New York. Both teams had eight games left to play.

SEPTEMBER 25   The Cardinals maintain their one-game lead with 4–3 victory in a tense 15-inning battle against the Dodgers in Brooklyn. Bill Sherdel pitched a complete game and had a hand in the game-winning rally. Sherdel sacrificed Rabbit Maranville to second, where Maranville scored on a Taylor Douthit double.

SEPTEMBER 27   Jesse Haines earns his 20th victory of the season with an 8–3 decision over the Braves in Boston. The win kept the Cardinals margin over the Giants at one game. Both clubs had three games left on the schedule.

SEPTEMBER 28   The Cardinals clinch a tie for the pennant with seven runs in the fifteenth inning to defeat the Braves 10–3 in Boston.

SEPTEMBER 29   The Cardinals clinch the pennant on the second-to-last day of the season with a 3–1 victory over the Braves in Boston. It was Bill Sherdel's 21st victory of the season.

                 The Cardinals played the Yankees in the World Series. The Yankees were managed by Miller Huggins and won their sixth AL pennant in eight years with a record of 101–53. The Yanks were also defending World Champs, having swept the Pirates in the 1927 World Series. The Yankees were also looking for revenge after losing the 1926 Fall Classic to the Cardinals.

OCTOBER 4   The Yankees defeat the Cardinals 4–1 in the first game of the 1928 World Series by a 4–1 score in New York. Waite Hoyt held the Cards to three hits. Bill Sherdel was the losing pitcher. Jim Bottomley accounted for the lone Cardinal run with a homer in the seventh inning when the Cards trailed 3–0.

OCTOBER 5   The Yankees win again in Game Two with a 9–3 victory over the Cardinals at Yankee Stadium. Grover Alexander started for the Cards but was unable to summon his heroic efforts of 1926. He gave up eight runs in 2$\frac{1}{3}$ innings. After tying the score 3–3 with three runs in the second, the Cards failed to dent the plate again off George Pipgras.

OCTOBER 7   The Yankees take a three-games-to-none lead in the Series with a 7–3 win before 39,602 at Sportsman's Park. Lou Gehrig rocketed a pair of homers off Jesse Haines. One was inside-the-park in the fourth inning on a ball misplayed by centerfielder Taylor Douthit. The score was 3–3 in the sixth when Jimmie Wilson made two errors on one play. Wilson dropped a throw from Jim Bottomley when Babe Ruth tried to score, then threw the ball into center field trying to nab Bob Meusel trying to advance from first to second.

OCTOBER 8   Rain postpones Game Four.

OCTOBER 9   The Yankees complete a sweep of the Cardinals with another 7–3 victory before 37,331 at Sportsman's Park. Babe Ruth hit three homers, two off Bill Sherdel in the fourth and seventh innings and one facing Grover Alexander in the eighth. Ruth's home run off Sherdel in the seventh inning was controversial. Sherdel thought he caught the Babe looking at a third strike on an 0–2 pitch, but umpire Cy Pfirman ruled it was a quick pitch because Ruth wasn't in the batter's box. After looking at two pitches to even the count, Ruth smacked Sherdel's offering over the right-field pavilion. Lou Gehrig and Cedric Durst also hit home runs for the Yankees. Cardinal catcher Earl Smith, who played on the 1927 Pirate club that was swept by the Yankees in the Fall Classic, collected three hits.

In the four games, Ruth and Gehrig combined for 16 hits in 27 at-bats with 7 homers and 13 RBIs.

NOVEMBER 21   Two weeks after Herbert Hoover defeats Al Smith in the presidential election, Billy Southworth replaces Bill McKechnie as manager of the Cardinals.

Southworth and McKechnie actually traded jobs. Southworth had been manager of the Cardinals' top farm club at Rochester in the International League. McKechnie took Southworth's job in Rochester. McKechnie was demoted despite winning the National League pennant in his first season as manager of the Cardinals. It was the second time that he was relieved of his duties shortly after winning a pennant. In 1925, he led the Pirates to their first NL pennant in 16 years, won the World Series, but was fired at the end of the 1926 season. Sam Breadon was angry over being swept by the Yankees in the World Series and believed that McKechnie had been too soft on his players and instructed Southworth to get tough on the club. Southworth, then 35, played outfield for the Cardinals 1926 World Championship club, and the get-tough policy drew resistance from players who had been Southworth's teammates only two years earlier. Eight months later, Southworth and McKechnie traded jobs again (see July 23, 1929).

DECEMBER 8   The Cardinals sell Rabbit Maranville to the Braves.

DECEMBER 11   The Cardinals trade Tommy Thevenow to the Phillies for Heinie Sand and $10,000.

Thevenow holds the all-time record for most consecutive regular-season at-bats without hitting a home run. Thevenow failed to homer in the regular season from September 24, 1926 through the end of his career in 1938 while playing with the Cardinals, Phillies, Pirates, Reds, and Braves, a span of 3,347 at-bats. He hit a total of two regular-season homers, both inside-the-park and both in 1926, in 4,164 at-bats. Thevenow also hit an inside-the-park homer during the 1926 World Series.

1929

Season in a Sentence

Following an 11-game losing streak in July, Billy Southworth and Bill McKechnie trade jobs again.

Finish • Won • Lost • Pct • GB

Fourth   78   74   .513   20.0

Manager

Billy Southworth (43–45), Gabby Street (0–1), and Bill McKechnie (34–29)

Stats	Cards	• NL •	Rank
Batting Avg:	.293	.354	5
On-Base Pct:	.354	.357	6
Slugging Pct:	.438	.426	3
Home Runs:	100		4
Stolen Bases:	72		6
ERA:	4.66	4.71	5
Fielding Avg:	.971	.971	4
Runs Scored:	831		5
Runs Allowed:	806		5

Starting Lineup

Jimmie Wilson, c
Jim Bottomley, 1b
Frankie Frisch, 2b
Andy High, 3b
Charlie Gelbert, ss
Chick Hafey, lf
Taylor Douthit, cf
Ernie Orsatti, rf
Wally Roettger, rf
Wattie Holm, rf

Pitchers

Jesse Haines, sp
Bill Sherdel, sp-rp
Pete Alexander, sp
Clarence Mitchell, sp
Wild Bill Hallahan, sp-rp
Syl Johnson, rp-sp
Hal Haid, rp-sp
Fred Frankhouse, rp-sp

Attendance

399,887 (fifth in NL)

Club Leaders

Batting Avg:	Hafey	.338
On-Base Pct:	Douthit	.416
Slugging Pct:	Hafey	.632
Home Runs:	Hafey	29
	Bottomley	29
RBIs:	Bottomley	137
Runs:	Douthit	128
Stolen Bases:	Frisch	24
Wins:	Haines	13
Strikeouts:	Johnson	80
ERA:	Mitchell	4.27
Saves:	Haid	4

APRIL 16   The Cardinals defeat the Reds 5–2 on Opening Day in Cincinnati. Grover Alexander pitched a complete game in a contest that took only 1 hour and 17 minutes to complete. Three Cardinal runs in the first inning settled the issue. Chick Hafey hit a home run.

The Cardinals were 19–3 against the Reds in 1929.

APRIL 24   The scheduled home opener against the Reds is postponed. The April 25 contest was also called off.

APRIL 26   The Cardinals finally get their home opener under way and defeat the Reds 9–2 before 11,000 at Sportsman's Park. The 1928 National League pennant was raised before the contest.

A new press box was built in 1929 at Sportsman's Park under the roof of the second deck. It wasn't popular with sports writers because to reach it required a perilous climb. One writer said that the best way to reach the press box would have been by "airplane or dirigible." It was replaced in 1947.

MAY 8   The Cardinals score eight runs in the first inning and cavort to a 10–2 win over the Braves in Boston.

MAY 12	The Cardinals hammer the Dodgers 13–7 in Brooklyn.

MAY 21   The Cardinals score seven runs in the fourth inning and defeat the Reds 12–1 in Cincinnati.

MAY 25   The Cardinals take first place with a 7–6 win in 12 innings against the Cubs at Sportsman's Park. Syl Johnson starred with two innings of shutout relief, then drove in the winning run with a walk-off single. During his two-inning stint, Johnson fanned future Hall of Famers Kiki Cuyler, Rogers Hornsby, and Hack Wilson in order.

MAY 26   Taylor Douthit collects seven hits in ten at-bats during a doubleheader against the Pirates at Sportsman's Park. Douthit hit a grand slam in the fifth inning of the first game, in addition to two doubles and four singles. The Cardinals lost both contests, however, by scores of 12–8 and 7–5.

MAY 29   Cardinal pitcher Hal Haid carries a no-hitter into the eighth inning before settling for a four-hit, 4–1 win over the Reds in the first game of a doubleheader at Sportsman's Park. The Cards completed the sweep with a 6–2 win in the second fray.

JUNE 15   Down 4–2, the Cardinals score two runs in the ninth and one in the tenth to defeat the Braves 5–4 at Sportsman's Park. Chick Hafey hit a two-run homer in the ninth to tie the score. A bases-loaded, walk-off single by Ernie Orsatti drove in the winning run.

          The victory gave the Cardinals a 34–19 record and a hold on first place. The club went into a quick tailspin, however, losing 22 of their next 27 games, including an 11-game losing streak.

JUNE 17   The Cardinals score eight runs in the sixth inning of a 13–3 win over the Cubs in Chicago.

JUNE 22   The Cardinals score seven runs in the eighth inning to take a 10–1 lead, then hang on to beat the Reds 11–8 in Cincinnati.

JULY 1   The Cardinals and Cubs play to an 11–11 tie, called after six innings to allow the Cards to catch a train to Pittsburgh.

          During the first week of July, while the Browns were playing at home, a 21.5-foot high-wire screen was placed on top of the 11.5-foot concrete wall in front of the right field pavilion. The screen was erected to cut down on the number of home runs in that direction. The screen remained until the Cardinals vacated the ballpark in 1966, with the exception of the 1955 season when it was removed to try and help the Cardinals left-handed power hitters.

JULY 6   After losing the first game of a doubleheader 10–6 to the Phillies in Philadelphia, the Cardinals 11th loss in a row, the Cards explode for 28 hits and a 28–6 victory. The 28 runs is a modern National League record. The only two clubs with more runs in a game since 1900 are the Red Sox in a 29–4 win over the Browns in 1950 and a 29–6 triumph by the White Sox over the Athletics in 1955. The Cardinals scored ten runs in the first inning, one in the second, two in the fourth, and ten in the fifth to take a 23–4 lead. The Cards closed the scoring with five tallies in the eighth. The Phillies pitchers were Jim Willoughby and Elmer Miller, neither of whom retired a batter,

Luther Roy (4$^{1}/_{3}$ innings), and June Green (4$^{2}/_{3}$ innings). Jim Bottomley hit a grand slam and drove in six runs. Chick Hafey collected five hits, including a grand slam and two doubles, in seven at-bats. Taylor Douthit had five singles in six at-bats. The 50 runs during the afternoon tied a modern National League record for most runs by two clubs in a doubleheader. The Cardinals and Phillies also set modern major league records for most hits in a double with 73 (43 by the Cardinals), and a National League mark for most total bases in a twin bill with 108 (59 by the Cards).

JULY 9

Two Cardinals batters extend hitting streaks during a 7–4 win over the Phillies in Philadelphia. Chick Hafey tied a National League record with hits in 10 consecutive at-bats in a streak that started in the 28–6 win on July 6. Bottomley hit a home run, giving him homers in five consecutive games from July 5 through 9. He hit seven homers in the five games.

Bottomley is one of three Cardinals to homer in five consecutive games. The other two are Ripper Collins in 1935 and Jim Edmonds in 2004. In 1929, Bottomley hit .314 with 29 homers and 137 RBIs. He was one of six regulars to bat .314 or better. Chick Hafey had a .338 average with 47 doubles, 29 homers, and 125 RBIs. Taylor Douthit hit .336, scored 128 runs, and collected 206 hits. Frankie Frisch batted .334, Ernie Orsatti .332, and Jimmie Wilson .325. By the standards of 1929, however, the Cardinals' offense wasn't anything special. The club batting average of .293 was one point below the NL average. There were 6,609 runs scored in the league that season, an average of 826 per club. The Cardinals scored 831.

JULY 12

The Cardinals suffer a crushing 8–7 loss to the Dodgers at Ebbets Field. The Cards scored five runs in the top of the ninth off Dazzy Vance to take a 7–2 lead, but Brooklyn tallied six times in their half off Syl Johnson, Hal Haid, and Fred Frankhouse for the stunning comeback win.

Greasy Neale was a Cardinals coach at the start of the season, but was let go in July because he spent more time talking about football than baseball. Neale was a collegiate football coach during the 1920s, and led tiny Washington and Jefferson to a 0–0 tie against heavily favored California in the 1922 Rose Bowl. Later, Neale won NFL championships in 1948 and 1949 as coach of the Philadelphia Eagles. He was inducted into the Pro Football Hall of Fame in 1969.

JULY 13

The Cardinals again blow a lead in Brooklyn when the Dodgers score nine runs in the eighth inning to win 13–8.

A pitching meltdown contributed to the Cardinals decline. In 1928, Bill Sherdel, Jesse Haines, and Grover Alexander combined for a record of 57–24. In 1929, the trio was 32–33.

JULY 17

Taylor Douthit collects a homer, triple, and double in a 6–1 win over the Giants in New York.

In five consecutive games from July 15 through 20, Douthit had 14 hits in 19 at-bats.

JULY 23

With the club floundering with a record of 43–45, the Cardinals change managers once again, sending Billy Southworth back to the minors to manage the farm club in Rochester, while bringing Bill McKechnie back from Rochester to run the Cards. Coach Gabby Street was the interim manager for one game until McKechnie could arrive.

> *It was the second time in eight months that Southworth and McKechnie traded jobs (see November 21, 1928). "I myself took the World Series of 1928 too much to heart," Sam Breadon said, "and now realize I made a mistake. I still think we have the best ball club in the National League and believe that under McKechnie we will again get into the race for the pennant." McKechnie failed in that pursuit, however, and was fired by Breadon at the end of the season (see October 31, 1929). Southworth returned to manage the Cardinals in 1940, and won National League pennants in 1942, 1943, and 1944 and the World Series in 1942 and 1944.*

JULY 24   Wally Roettger hits a grand slam off Les Sweetland in the sixth inning of a 6–4 win over the Phillies at Sportsman's Park.

> *The drop in the standings had a severe effect on attendance. After drawing 761,574 in 1928, the Cardinals attracted only 399,887 in 1929.*

JULY 30   The Cardinals score two runs in the ninth inning and one in the eleventh to defeat the Dodgers 10–9 at Sportsman's Park.

JULY 31   Wild Bill Hallahan lives up to his nickname by issuing 10 walks to the Dodgers in an 8–2 loss to the Dodgers in the second game of a doubleheader at Sportsman's Park. The Cardinals won the first game 5–2.

> *A left-hander, Hallahan was 109–94 during a 12-year big-league career. He was 102–94 in nine seasons with the Cardinals. Hallahan led the National League in victories once in his career (with 19 in 1931), three times in walks (1930, 1931 and 1933), and twice in strikeouts (1930 and 1931). He pitched in four World Series for St. Louis and was the starting pitcher for the National League in the very first All-Star Game, played in 1933.*

AUGUST 2   The Cardinals pummel the Dodgers 14–7 at Sportsman's Park.

AUGUST 10 Grover Alexander wins the 373rd game of his major league career as a reliever in an 11-inning, 11–9 victory over the Phillies in the second game of a doubleheader in Philadelphia. The Cards trailed 8–0 after five innings before mounting a comeback with three runs in the sixth, four in the seventh, one in the eighth, one in the ninth, and two in the eleventh. Chick Hafey drove in five runs. The Phillies won the first game 7–1.

> *The victory tied the National League record for most victories by a pitcher. Christy Mathewson also won 373 games. Alexander and Mathewson are third all-time behind Cy Young (511) and Walter Johnson (417). Alexander never won another game after August 10, 1929. Nine days later he was indefinitely suspended for showing up drunk for a game. The Cards lifted the suspension two days later, but sent Alexander home with pay for the rest of the season. In December, he was traded to the Phillies. He pitched nine games for Philadelphia in 1930, but failed to earn a victory. The remainder of Alexander's life was a sad one. He was broke by the time he left the majors, and pitched for the*

barnstorming House of David team, which featured players who wore long beards to emulate the look of Orthodox Jews. Later, he appeared in a sideshow at Hulbert's Museum on Times Square in New York. Living on small pensions from both the government and the Cardinals, Alexander slipped deeper into alcoholism. He drifted from job to job and disappeared for months at a time. Hospitalized for cancer, Alexander had an ear removed, and went completely deaf. He died penniless in 1950 in a rented room in his hometown of St. Paul, Nebraska.

SEPTEMBER 4 The Cardinals break an 8–8 tie with six runs in the eighth inning and defeat the Cubs 14–8 in the first game of a doubleheader at Sportsman's Park. Chicago won the second fray, called after eight innings by darkness.

SEPTEMBER 22 The Cardinals and Dodgers combine to set a record for the fewest walks in a doubleheader with one. The lone walk was issued by Jim Lindsay of the Cards. The Dodgers won the first tilt at Sportsman's Park 7–2, while the Cards nabbed the second one 4–0. The twin bill took only 3 hours and 12 minutes to complete.

SEPTEMBER 29 Chick Hafey collects three doubles and a homer during a 10–2 win over the Pirates in the second game of a doubleheader at Sportsman's Park. Pittsburgh won the first game 5–1.

OCTOBER 31 Two days the historic stock market crash, which starts the country on the road to the Great Depression, the Cardinals release Bill McKechnie as manager and hire Gabby Street.

It was the sixth managerial change by the Cardinals in a span of 54 months. To recap, Rogers Hornsby replaced Branch Rickey in May 1925. Hornsby won the World Championship in 1926, but was traded to the Giants following the season, and was replaced by Bob O'Farrell. O'Farrell lasted only a year despite 92 wins and a second-place finish in 1927. O'Farrell was succeeded by Bill McKechnie, who won the 1928 National League pennant but lost his job after the Yankees swept the Cardinals in the World Series. Billy Southworth started the 1929 season, but McKechnie was brought back when the Cards stumbled into July with a losing record. Then McKechnie was canned again after the season was over. Charles "Gabby" Street was 48 years old when hired to manage the Cardinals. He earned his nickname because he was never at a loss for words. Street played in the majors as a catcher from 1904 through 1912, and saw combat in both the Spanish-American War (at the age of 15) and World War I. He was a manager in the Cardinals minor league system for six years before becoming a coach with the Cardinals in 1929. Street won National League pennants in 1930 and 1931, his first two years as a big-league manager, and won the World Series in 1931. But like his predecessors, he had little job security with Sam Breadon running the Cardinals. Street was fired during the 1933 season. McKechnie wasn't out of work for long. He managed the Braves from 1930 through 1937 and the Reds from 1938 through 1946. McKechnie's Reds won the National League pennant in 1939 and 1940 and the World Series in 1940.

DECEMBER 11 The Cardinals trade Grover Alexander and Harry McCurdy to the Phillies for Homer Peel and Bob McGraw.

Alexander was at the end of the line. He was 0–3 with a 9.14 ERA for the Phillies in 1930.

THE STATE OF THE CARDINALS

The Cardinals continued their success of the late 1920s by winning the National League pennant in 1930, 1931, and 1934 and the World Series in 1931 and 1934. Included were some of the most colorful players in baseball history, such as Dizzy Dean, Pepper Martin, Leo Durocher, Joe Medwick, and Frankie Frisch, a core group of athletes known as "The Gas House Gang." Overall, the Cardinals had a record of 869–665, a winning percentage of .566 that was the fourth best in the majors during the decade behind the Yankees, Cubs, and Giants. National League pennants won outside the city of St. Louis were captured by the Cubs (1932, 1935, and 1938), Giants (1933, 1936, and 1937), and Reds (1939).

THE BEST TEAM

The 1931 Cardinals were 101–53, won the National League pennant by 13 games, then took the World Series in seven games from the Athletics. The 101 wins were the most of any NL club between 1913 and 1942.

THE WORST TEAM

The 1932 club was one of two during the 1930s to post a losing record, with a mark of 72–82, good only for a tie for sixth, 18 games out of first.

THE BEST MOMENT

Pepper Martin's heroics in the 1931 World Series made him a national hero. He had 12 hits in 24 at-bats and stole five bases.

THE WORST MOMENT

The worst moment came when 23-year-old catcher Bill DeLancey was diagnosed with tuberculosis in 1935, ending his career. Before contracting the disease, many were predicting that DeLancey would become one of the greatest catchers of all time.

THE ALL-DECADE TEAM • YEARS W/CARDS

Jimmie Wilson, c	1928–33
Johnny Mize, 1b	1936–41
Frankie Frisch, 2b	1927–37
Pepper Martin, 3b	1928, 1930–40, 1944
Charley Gelbert, ss	1929–32, 1935–36
Joe Medwick, lf	1932–40, 1947–48
Terry Moore, cf	1935–42, 1946–48
George Watkins, rf	1930–33
Dizzy Dean, p	1930, 1932–37
Wild Bill Hallahan, p	1925–26, 1929–36
Jesse Haines, p	1920–37
Lon Warneke, p	1937–42

Dean, Mize, Frisch, Medwick, and Haines are all in the Hall of Fame. Other Cardinals who played prominent roles during the 1930s were first baseman Ripper Collins (1931–36), third baseman-second baseman Jimmy Brown (1937–43), outfielder Ernie Orsatti (1927–35), shortstop Leo Durocher (1933–37), outfielder-catcher Don Padgett (1937–41), and catcher Spud Davis (1928, 1934–36).

THE DECADE LEADERS

Batting Avg:	Mize	.346
On-Base Pct:	Mize	.426
Slugging Pct:	Mize	.605
Home Runs:	Medwick	145
RBIs:	Medwick	771
Runs:	Medwick	873
Stolen Bases:	Martin	136
Wins:	Dean	147
Strikeouts:	Dean	1,144
ERA:	Dean	2.96
Saves:	Dean	30

THE HOME FIELD

There were few monumental changes at Sportsman's Park during the 1930s, a decade in which the success of the tenant Cardinals far exceeded that of the Browns, who owned the ballpark.

THE GAME YOU WISH YOU HAD SEEN

The Cardinals completed an upset of the Philadelphia Athletics in Game Seven of the 1931 World Series with a 4–2 win on October 10.

THE WAY THE GAME WAS PLAYED

The offensive explosion that changed baseball during the 1920s peaked in 1930, when the National League batting average was .303 and teams averaged 5.7 runs per game. As the top offensive club in the top offensive year in modern times, the 1930 Cardinals set a modern National League record by scoring 1,004 runs. They also set club records for hits (1,732) and total bases (2,595). The NL moguls deadened the ball for 1931, and batting averages dipped to 4.5 runs per game in 1931 and 4.0 runs a game in 1933. From 1934 through 1939, batting averages were generally around .270. There were only 354 stolen bases in the National League in 1938, less than half the total of 1924.

THE MANAGEMENT

President and majority owner Sam Breadon and vice president Branch Rickey, whose duties closely followed those of a modern-day general manager, ran the Cardinals throughout the 1930s. It was their second full decade running the club. Breadon assumed the presidency in 1920, and bought controlling interest in 1922. Rickey ran the front office from 1917 through 1942. The Breadon-Rickey tandem was noted for the frequency with which it changed managers, even following pennant-winning seasons. During the 1930s, managers included Gabby Street (1930–33), Frankie Frisch (1933–38), Mike Gonzalez (1938), and Ray Blades (1939–40). The Cardinals won nine National League pennants under Breadon from 1926 through 1946, but those nine pennants came under six different managers. The six were Rogers Hornsby (1926), Bill McKechnie (1928), Street (1930 and 1931), Frisch (1934), Billy Southworth (1942, 1943, and 1944), and Eddie Dyer (1946). World Championships were won by Hornsby (1926), Street (1931), Frisch (1934), Southworth (1942 and 1944), and Dyer (1946).

THE BEST PLAYER MOVE

The best player move was the signing of Stan Musial out of high school in Donora, Pennsylvania, in 1938. Musial arrived in the majors in 1941. He was at the top of a list of Cardinals system products who joined the Cards during the 1930s, a group that included Dizzy Dean, Joe Medwick, Johnny Mize, and Harry Brecheen. The best trade brought Lon Warneke from the Cubs for Ripper Collins and Roy Parmelee in October 1936.

THE WORST PLAYER MOVE

The worst player move was the sale of Johnny Mize to the Reds in December 1934. Fortunately, the Reds returned Mize to the Cardinals because of a severely torn groin muscle. The worst permanent move sent Paul Derringer to the Reds in a six-player trade in May 1933.

1930

Season in a Sentence

The Cardinals win 39 of their 49 games to come from 12 games out of first place to win a thrilling National League pennant race.

Finish • Won • Lost • Pct • GB

First   92   62   .597   +2.0

World Series—The Cardinals lost four games to two to the Philadelphia Athletics

Manager

Gabby Street

Stats

Stats	Cards	• NL •	Rank
Batting Avg:	.314	.303	3
On-Base Pct:	.372	.360	2
Slugging Pct:	.471	.448	3
Home Runs:	104		5
Stolen Bases:	72		2
ERA:	4.36	4.97	2
Fielding Avg:	.970	.970	6
Runs Scored:	1,004		1
Runs Allowed:	784		2

Starting Lineup

Jimmie Wilson, c
Jim Bottomley, 1b
Frankie Frisch, 2b
Sparky Adams, 3b
Charlie Gelbert, ss
Chick Hafey, lf
Taylor Douthit, cf
George Watkins, rf
Showboat Fisher, rf-lf
Gus Mancuso, c
Andy High, 3b

Pitchers

Wild Bill Hallahan, sp
Jesse Haines, sp
Syl Johnson, sp
Burleigh Grimes, sp
Flint Rhem, sp-rp
Hi Bell, rp
Jim Lindsay, rp
Al Grabowski, rp

Attendance

508,591 (fourth in NL)

Club Leaders

Batting Avg:	Frisch	.346
On-Base Pct:	Frisch	.407
	Hafey	.407
Slugging Pct:	Hafey	.652
Home Runs:	Hafey	26
RBIs:	Frisch	114
Runs:	Frisch	121
Stolen Bases:	Frisch	15
Wins:	Hallahan	15
Strikeouts:	Hallahan	177
ERA:	Haines	4.30
Saves:	Bell	8

APRIL 10   The Cardinals trade Wally Roettger to the Giants for Showboat Fisher and Doc Farrell.

APRIL 15   The Cardinals lose the season opener 9–8 against the Cubs before 14,000 at Sportsman's Park. Chicago scored four runs in the eighth to pull ahead 9–4, then survived three Cardinal runs in the home half of the inning and one in the ninth. In his first game as a Cardinal, right fielder Showboat Fisher collected four hits.

> *Fisher also had four hits in the second game of the season, giving him eight hits in his first nine at-bats with the Cardinals. After 12 games, Fisher had 23 hits in 44 at-bats, a batting average of .523. Prior to 1930, Fisher's only big-league experience was 28 games with the Senators in 1923 and 1924 in which he hit .234. During the 1930 season, Fisher batted .374 with eight homers in 254 at-bats. After 1930, he played in only 18 more games with an average of just .182. Thanks to his one great season, Fisher left the majors with a lifetime average of .335. He died in 1994 at the age of 94.*

APRIL 16   The Cardinals launch a 20-hit attack to defeat the Cubs 13–3 at Sportsman's Park.

APRIL 18   Wild Bill Hallahan two-hits the Cubs for an 11–1 victory at Sportsman's Park. He walked nine batters and fanned 11. The only Chicago hits were singles by Danny Taylor and Chuck Tolson.

MAY 2   The Dodgers score five runs in the top of the tenth inning against the Cardinals at Sportsman's Park to take an 11–6 lead, but need every one of them when the Cards rally for four in their half to make the final 11–10.

            On May 4, the Cardinals were 6–12, 5½ games out of first.

MAY 7   The Cardinals score nine runs in the fifth inning to take a 13–7 lead and move on to defeat the Phillies 16–11 at Sportsman's Park. Chick Hafey drove in five runs in the big inning. George Watkins scored five runs in the game.

            Watkins was a 30-year-old rookie outfielder in 1930 and hit .373 with 17 homers in 119 games. His batting average that season is the best of any rookie in major league history with a minimum of 300 at-bats. He was a regular for seven seasons with the Cardinals, Giants, Phillies, and Dodgers, but never matched the numbers he achieved in his rookie season. Watkins reached the .300 mark in only one other season, when he hit .312 for St. Louis in 1932. He finished his career with a batting average of .288.

MAY 14   The Cardinals score four runs in the ninth inning for a thrilling 9–8 win over the Cubs at Sportsman's Park. Taylor Douthit drove in the last two runs with a single. It was the Cardinals' 21st hit of the game and Douthit's fifth. The victory was the ninth in a row for St. Louis to run the club's record on the season to 15–12.

MAY 15   The Cardinals trade Clarence Mitchell to the Giants for Ralph Judd.

MAY 20   Charlie Gelbert hits a grand slam off Al Shealy in the eighth inning of a 10–3 win over the Cubs at Sportsman's Park.

MAY 26   The Cardinals win their eighth straight game, and their 17th in the last 18, with a 10–3 decision over the Pirates in Pittsburgh.

            With the victory, the Cardinals had a record of 23–13 and were in first place. The Cards lost 12 of their next 13 contests, however, and were 30–32 on June 27.

JUNE 3   The Cardinals break a seven-game losing streak by defeating the Phillies 11–10 in Philadelphia.

JUNE 16   The Cardinals trade Fred Frankhouse and Bill Sherdel to the Braves for Burleigh Grimes.

            Grimes was a 36-year-old future Hall of Famer with a record of 227–174 when acquired by the Cardinals. He gave the club two excellent seasons with a 13–6 record in 1930 and 17–9 in 1931, and made two World Series starts both seasons. Grimes was one of the heroes of the 1931 Fall Classic with a two-hitter in the third game and a victory in Game Seven.

JULY 1   The Cardinals erupt for 11 runs in the third inning and defeat the Dodgers 15–7 at Sportsman's Park.

JULY 4   The Cardinals celebrate the holiday with 15–4 and 6–2 wins over the Reds at Sportsman's Park. The Cards scored eight runs in the fourth inning of the first game.

JULY 6   The Cardinals collect only two hits off Glenn Spencer, but defeat the Pirates 2–1 in the first game of a doubleheader at Sportsman's Park. The second hit was a walk-off homer by Taylor Douthit in the ninth inning. The Cards completed the sweep with a 12–4 victory in the second tilt.

JULY 17   The Cardinals collect 20 hits, but leave 17 men on base and lose 12–9 to the Giants in New York.

JULY 20   The Cardinals score seven runs in the second inning and pound the Dodgers 15–6 at Sportsman's Park.

JULY 21   After losing the first game of a doubleheader against the Dodgers 9–8 at Ebbets Field, the Cardinals bounce back with seven runs in the second inning of the second fray to win 17–10. In the opener, the two clubs tied a major league record for most home runs by pinch hitters with three. Jim Bottomley and George Puccinelli hit pinch-homers for the Cardinals and Harvey Hendrick for the Dodgers. In addition, Hal Lee hit a pinch-homer for Brooklyn in the nightcap. It was also the first major league hits for both Puccinelli and Lee.

             An outfielder, Puccinelli had nine hits, including three homers, in 16 at-bats, a batting average of .563 in 1930. He had an odd four-year big-league career in which he only played in even-numbered years. Puccinelli played for the Cardinals in 1930, 1932, and 1934 and the Phillies in 1936. He appeared in a total of 187 games, had 602 at-bats, and hit .283 with 19 homers, 102 RBIs, and 109 runs scored, but fielding deficiencies prevented him from becoming a regular.

JULY 27   The Cardinals sweep the Braves 2–0 and 6–1 in a doubleheader in Boston. Solo homers by Showboat Fisher in the fourth inning and Chick Hafey in the sixth won the first game. Syl Johnson pitched the shutout.

             Hafey batted .336 with 28 homers and 107 RBIs in 1930.

AUGUST 2   Down 6–0 to the Reds in Cincinnati, the Cardinals score three runs in the fifth inning, one in the seventh, and two in the ninth to send the game into extra innings. The Cards scored three runs in the top of the eleventh, then survived a two-run rally in the Cincinnati half of the inning to win 9–8.

             The Cardinals were on the road from July 10 through August 4. Fortunately, the club missed the brunt of one of the worst heat waves in St. Louis history. A total of 133 died in the city when temperatures reached 100 degrees 18 days in a row.

AUGUST 8   The Cardinals lose 11–5 to the Dodgers at Sportsman's Park.

             The defeat was the low point of the season. The Cards had a record of 53–52 and were in fourth place 12 games back of the first-place Dodgers.

AUGUST 10   The Cardinals sweep the Dodgers 8–2 and 4–0 at Sportsman's Park. Wild Bill Hallahan struck out 12 batters in the second-game shutout.

The Cardinals were 92–62 in 1930 without a single pitcher winning more than 15 games. Wild Bill Hallahan was the club's leading winner with a 15–9 record and a 4.67 ERA. He led the NL in both strikeouts (177) and walks (128).

AUGUST 11   The Cardinals score three runs in the ninth inning to defeat the Dodgers 7–6 at Sportsman's Park. A single by Frankie Frisch drove in the winning run.

Frisch hit .346 with 10 homers, 114 RBIs, and 121 runs scored in 1930.

AUGUST 14   Jimmie Wilson's two-run, walk-off, pinch-single in the ninth inning beats the Braves 4–3 in the first game of a doubleheader at Sportsman's Park. Boston won the second game 3–2.

AUGUST 17   After losing the opener of a doubleheader 12–4 to the Giants at Sportsman's Park, the Cardinals rebound with eight runs in the sixth inning of the second skirmish to win 14–4.

AUGUST 21   Chick Hafey hits for the cycle in a 16–6 win over the Phillies at Sportsman's Park. Hafey started his cycle with a two-run home run off Claude Willoughby in the first inning.

AUGUST 22   Down 5–0 after three innings, the Cardinals rally to win 10–8 over the Phillies at Sportsman's Park. The Cards still trailed when Gus Mancuso hit a three-run double in the eighth inning.

The Cardinals tried to send Mancuso to the minors before the season started, but commissioner Kenesaw Landis ruled that Mancuso was out of options and ordered the Cards to keep him or put him on waivers. The Cards hung on to Mancuso, and he hit .366 in 76 games as a backup catcher to Jimmie Wilson.

AUGUST 28   The Cardinals outlast the Cubs 8–7 in a 20-inning marathon at Wrigley Field. The Cards led 5–0 with Burleigh Grimes on the mound, but the Cubs rallied with three runs in the seventh inning and two in the eighth. St. Louis scored twice in the fifteenth, but Chicago matched that figure. In the twentieth, Taylor Douthit singled, advanced to second on an infield out, and scored on a single by Andy High. Syl Johnson was the winning pitcher, hurling the final 12 innings in relief.

AUGUST 29   The Cardinals pennant express takes a detour with a 9–8 loss in 13 innings to the Cubs at Wrigley Field. The Cards led 5–0, but the Cubs scored five runs in the ninth off Jesse Haines and Hi Bell to send the contest into extra innings. The Cards added three runs in the eleventh, but Chicago tied it again with three in the bottom half, then won out in the thirteenth.

AUGUST 30   The Cubs clobber the Cardinals 16–4 in Chicago.

The loss put the Cardinals 7½ games behind the first-place Cubs with a record of 70–58. The Cards would win 21 of their next 24 games to clinch the pennant.

AUGUST 31   Wild Bill Hallahan strikes out 12 batters in an 8–3 win over the Cubs in Chicago.

SEPTEMBER 4   The Cardinals lambaste the Reds 13–2 at Sportsman's Park. Eight runs in the sixth inning broke a 1–1 tie.

SEPTEMBER 11   The Cardinals edge the Giants 5–4 in New York to pull within one-half game of the first-place Cubs in a tension-filled, four-team NL pennant race. The Dodgers were also one-half game back. The Giants were in fourth, three games out of first.

SEPTEMBER 13   The Cardinals take first place with an 8–2 win over the Braves in Boston to pull two percentage points ahead of the Dodgers and one-half game in front of the Cubs.

SEPTEMBER 14   The Cardinals topple back out of first place by splitting a doubleheader against the Braves in Boston while the Dodgers won 8–3 over the Reds in Brooklyn. The Cards won the first game 9–2, but lost the second 7–4, called after eight innings by a Massachusetts law which stipulated that Sunday games must end at 6 PM.

SEPTEMBER 16   The Cardinals take first place again with a dramatic, ten-inning, 1–0 victory over the Dodgers at Ebbets Field. Wild Bill Hallahan and Dazzy Vance both pitched complete games. Pitching with a sore finger on his right (non-pitching) hand he injured when it was caught in the door of a cab, Hallahan retired the first 20 batters to face him before Babe Herman reached on an error when Hallahan fumbled a grounder. The first Brooklyn hit was a single by Harvey Hendrick with one out in the eighth. In the tenth, Andy High hit a pinch-double. Hallahan sacrificed High to third with two strikes on him, and Taylor Douthit singled for the 1–0 lead. In the bottom of the inning, the Dodgers loaded the bases, but a double play ended the contest. The twin killing started when shortstop Sparky Adams barehanded a sizzling grounder by Al Lopez.

The victory put the Cards one percentage point ahead of the Dodgers and 1½ games up on the Cubs.

SEPTEMBER 17   The Cardinals take a one-game lead in the pennant race with a 5–3 decision over the Dodgers in Brooklyn behind emergency starter Syl Johnson. Andy High broke a 3–3 tie with a two-run pinch-double in the ninth.

Flint Rhem was scheduled to start, but showed up at the ballpark after disappearing for 48 hours bleary-eyed, hung over, and in no condition to pitch. He covered his tracks with an outlandish tale. Rhem claimed he was standing in front of the Cardinals' hotel in Manhattan when two men called him over to a limousine. Flint said he walked over, and the pair pushed him into the vehicle and pointed a gun. The men drove him to New Jersey, and forced him to drink raw whiskey. According to Rhem, the kidnappers were gamblers and threatened him with bodily harm if he pitched and won his start against the Dodgers. Cardinal management was skeptical, but called police. Rhem couldn't find the place in New Jersey where he was taken, however, and law enforcement officials dropped the pursuit of the "abductors."

SEPTEMBER 18   The Cardinals complete a three-game sweep of the Dodgers in Brooklyn with a 4–3 decision. The win gave St. Louis a two-game lead in the NL race.

SEPTEMBER 22   The Cardinals get another step closer to the National League pennant with a 15–7 win over the Phillies in Philadelphia. The victory put the Cards 2½ games ahead of the second-place Cubs. The Cardinals had five games left to play, and the Cubs four.

SEPTEMBER 23   The Cardinals collect 26 hits and outslug the Phillies 19–16 at Baker Bowl. The Cards led 11–0 in the fourth inning before surviving a Philadelphia comeback.

SEPTEMBER 26   The Cardinals score seven runs in the second inning and clinch the National League pennant with a 10–5 win over the Pirates at Sportsman's Park. It was the Cardinals' 38th win in their last 47 games.

> *It was the Cardinals' third NL pennant in five years, a feat accomplished under three different managers. Gabby Street followed Rogers Hornsby (1926) and Bill McKechnie (1928).*

SEPTEMBER 28   On the last day of the season, 20-year-old Dizzy Dean makes his major league debut and beats the Pirates 3–1 on a three-hitter at Sportsman's Park. Dean pitched shutout ball after allowing a run in the first inning on two walks and a single.

> *After the sterling debut, Cardinals manager Gabby Street compared Dean to Walter Johnson. Street was Johnson's catcher from 1908 through 1911 when the two played for the Senators. Dean was signed by the Cardinals during the spring of 1930, and won 17 games for St. Joseph in the Western League and Houston in the Texas League. Despite the great record, Gabby Street and Branch Rickey became so annoyed with Dean's insufferable braggadocio and immature behavior that they decided another year in the minors might give him a needed dose of humility. Dean would return in 1932 and quickly establish himself as one of the best pitchers in baseball.*

> *The Cardinals met the Philadelphia Athletics in the 1930 World Series. Managed by Connie Mack, the A's had a 102–52 record during the season and were defending World Champions. The Athletics defeated the Cubs in five games in the 1929 World Series.*

OCTOBER 1   In the opening game of the World Series, the Athletics defeat the Cardinals 5–2 at Shibe Park in Philadelphia. The Cards took a 2–1 lead in the third, but the A's scored single runs in the fourth, sixth, seventh, and eighth innings off Burleigh Grimes, who allowed only five hits in five separate innings, but each was for extra bases, including homers to Mickey Cochrane and Al Simmons. Lefty Grove pitched the complete-game victory for Philadelphia.

> *Among those in attendance was President Herbert Hoover.*

OCTOBER 2   The Athletics win Game Two by a 6–1 score over the Cardinals in Philadelphia. Starter Flint Rhem gave up all six runs in 3⅓ innings. The lone St. Louis run scored on a homer in the second inning by George Watkins.

OCTOBER 4   Wild Bill Hallahan gives the Cardinals some hope in Game Three with a seven-hit, 5–0 win over the Athletics before 36,944 at Sportsman's Park. Taylor Douthit broke a scoreless tie with a solo homer in the fourth inning after A's starter Rube Walberg retired the first nine batters he faced. Jim Bottomley helped preserve the shutout with a spectacular catch of Jimmie Foxx's foul pop in the sixth inning. Bottomley leaped over the heads of box-seat patrons to snare the ball.

> *Otherwise, Douthit had a miserable series with two hits in 24 at-bats. Jim Bottomley was 1 for 22 with nine strikeouts.*

OCTOBER 5   The Cardinals even the series with a 3–1 win over the Athletics in Game Four in front of 39,946 at Sportsman's Park. Haines allowed only four hits, none of them after the third inning, to defeat Lefty Grove and drove in a run with a single in the third inning to tie the score 1–1.

OCTOBER 6   The Athletics move within one game of a World Championship with a 2–0 victory over the Cardinals before 38,844 at Sportsman's Park. Both runs scored in the ninth on a one-out homer by Jimmie Foxx off Burleigh Grimes. George Earnshaw (seven innings) and Lefty Grove (two innings) combined on the three-hit shutout.

OCTOBER 8   The Athletics claim the World Championship for the second year in a row with a 7–1 victory over the Cardinals in Game Six in Philadelphia. St. Louis starter Wild Bill Hallahan lasted only two innings. Pitching on one day of rest, George Earnshaw threw the complete game for the A's, allowing only five hits. Despite the splurge of offense during the 1930 regular season, the two clubs in the World Series combined for 33 runs and a .198 batting average in six games.

Transcendental Graphics/theruckerarchive.com

The pennant-winning 1930 St. Louis Cardinals (L-R). (back row) Jim Lindsey, Hi Bell, Syl Johnson, Jesse Haines, Burleigh Grimes, Jim Bottomley, Chick Hafey, Showboat Fisher, Jimmie Wilson, George Puccinelli; (middle row) Al Grabowski, Wild Bill Hallahan, Gus Mancuso, Ernie Orsatti, Frankie Frisch, Charlie Gelbert, Ray Blades; (front row) George Watkins, Buzzy Wares (coach), unnamed "mascot," Gabby Street (manager), Audy High, Sparky Adams, Taylor Douthit, Earl Smith.

1931

Season in a Sentence

The Cardinals cruise to their second NL pennant in a row before Pepper Martin almost single-handedly knocks off the Athletics in the World Series.

Finish • Won • Lost • Pct • GB

First   101   53   .656 +13.0

World Series—The Cardinals defeated the Philadelphia Athletics four games to three

Manager

Gabby Street

Stats	Cards	• NL •	Rank
Batting Avg:	.286	.277	3
On-Base Pct:	.342	.334	2
Slugging Pct:	.411	.387	3
Home Runs:	60		5
Stolen Bases:	114		1
ERA:	3.45	3.86	2
Fielding Avg:	.974	.971	1
Runs Scored:	815		2
Runs Allowed:	614		2

Starting Lineup

Jimmie Wilson, c
Jim Bottomley, 1b
Frankie Frisch, 2b
Sparky Adams, 3b
Charlie Gelbert, ss
Chick Hafey, lf
Pepper Martin, cf
George Watkins, rf
Ripper Collins, 1b
Gus Mancuso, c
Ernie Orsatti, lf
Wally Roettger, rf

Pitchers

Wild Bill Hallahan, sp
Paul Derringer, sp-rp
Burleigh Grimes, sp
Flint Rhem, sp
Syl Johnson, sp
Jesse Haines, sp

Attendance

608,535 (fourth in NL)

Club Leaders

Batting Avg:	Hafey	.349
On-Base Pct:	Hafey	.404
Slugging Pct:	Hafey	.569
Home Runs:	Hafey	16
RBIs:	Hafey	95
Runs:	Adams	97
Stolen Bases:	Frisch	28
Wins:	Hallahan	19
Strikeouts:	Hallahan	159
ERA:	Johnson	3.00
Saves:	Lindsey	7

APRIL 14   Six weeks after Congress adopts "The Star-Spangled Banner" as the national anthem, the Cardinals open the season with a 7–3 win over the Reds in Cincinnati. Jimmie Wilson collected three hits, including a double. Flint Rhem pitched the complete-game shutout.

The Cardinals opened the season with a 4–0 record. The club was out of first only three days all season—on April 27 and May 27 and 28.

APRIL 19   During a 4–1 loss to the Cubs before an overflow crowd at Sportsman's Park, an odd call by umpire Charley Evans triggers a Cardinals protest. Chicago left fielder Riggs Stephenson momentarily held a drive by Jim Bottomley, then dropped it into the crowd. Evans called Bottomley out, claiming that the crowd verbally interfered with Stephenson. The Cards filed an official protest with National League president John Heydler, but the protest was denied.

APRIL 22   In the home opener, the Cardinals defeat the Reds 3–2 before 7,500 at Sportsman's Park. Prior to the game, the 1930 National League pennant was raised. Missouri Governor Henry Caulfield threw out the first ball.

The first public address system at Sportsman's Park was installed in 1931. The innovation first appeared at the Polo Grounds in New York in 1929.

MAY 3   A squeeze bunt by Charlie Gelbert in the eleventh inning scores the winning run for a 5–4 victory over the Cubs at Sportsman's Park. It was the first Cardinal run since the first inning, when the club scored four times.

Gelbert had the best season of his career in 1931 with a .289 batting average.

MAY 9   The Cardinals win their eighth game in a row with a 4–2 decision over the Pirates in Pittsburgh. The victory gave the Cards a 14–3 record on the season.

MAY 24   The Cardinals' 19-game winning streak over the Reds dating to the previous season is broken with a 3–2 loss in the first game of a doubleheader in Cincinnati. The Cards won the second tilt 13–6.

MAY 26   The Cardinals beat the Pirates 11–9 at Sportsman's Park. After seven innings, the Cards led 5–1. Pittsburgh scored five times in the top of the eighth to take a 6–5 lead before the Cards countered with six in their half. The Pirates had three runs in the ninth.

MAY 29   The Cardinals outslug the Reds 14–9 at Sportsman's Park.

The win put the Cards into first place, a spot they held for the remainder of the season. The club had an 8½-game lead at the end of July and was never challenged over the final two months of the season, winning the pennant by 13½ games.

MAY 30   After trailing 4–0 in both ends of a doubleheader against the Reds at Sportsman's Park, the Cardinals rally to win 12–4 and 5–4. Seven runs in the sixth inning of the first game broke a 4–4 tie.

MAY 31   The Cardinals win the opener of a doubleheader against the Reds at Sportsman's Park 7–5, the 25th consecutive win over Cincinnati in St. Louis dating back to April 1929. The Reds broke the jinx with a 7–2 victory in the second game.

After the defeat, the Cardinals won the next 11 games against the Reds at Sportsman's Park. The Cards also had a 12-game winning streak over the Reds in St. Louis in 1934 and 1935. From April 1929 through August 1936, the Cardinals had an incredible 72–8 record against the Reds in Sportsman's Park.

JUNE 10   The Cardinals submerge the Braves 13–4 at Sportsman's Park.

JUNE 14   The Cardinals sweep the Phillies 7–3 and 13–4 at Sportsman's Park. The Cards scored nine runs in the first inning of the second game and held a 13–2 lead at the end of three innings.

JUNE 15   The Cardinals trade Taylor Douthit to the Reds for Wally Roettger.

JUNE 16   George Watkins and Frankie Frisch hit back-to-back homers in the ninth inning off Ray Benge with one out to lift the Cardinals to a 2–1 victory over the Phillies at Sportsman's Park. Watkins pinch hit for Burleigh Grimes and hit a 3–2 pitch into the right-field pavilion. Frisch hit the next pitch onto the pavilion roof to win the game.

Frisch hit .311 in 1931, led the NL in stolen bases with 28, and won the Most Valuable Player Award.

JUNE 21   Pepper Martin's homer in the sixth inning off Socks Seibold beats the Braves 1–0 in the second game of a doubleheader in Boston. Burleigh Grimes pitched the shutout. The Braves won the first game 6–2.

At the age of 37, Grimes had a record of 17–9 with a 3.65 ERA in 1931.

JUNE 24   George Watkins hits three homers and drives in all of the Cardinals' runs in a 4–2 win over the Phillies in the second game of a doubleheader at Baker Bowl. Watkins had a two-run homer off Phil Collins in the fourth inning, a solo shot off Collins in the sixth, and another solo homer against Hal Elliott in the ninth. The Cardinals also won the first game by the same 4–2 score with three runs in the ninth.

JUNE 25   George Watkins steals home for the lone run of a 1–0 win over the Dodgers at Ebbets Field. Dazzy Vance retired the first 20 Cardinals to face him before Watkins bunted safely with two outs in the seventh. Jim Bottomley singled Watkins to third. While Vance threw to first to hold Bottomley on base, Watkins swiped home. Paul Derringer pitched the shutout.

Derringer was a 24-year-old rookie in 1931. He had to overcome a thumb injury and blood poisoning and didn't pitch regularly until late May. Despite the late start, Derringer won his first six decisions and finished the season with a record of 18–8 with a 3.35 earned run average.

JUNE 30   The Cardinals outlast the Giants 11–10 in New York.

JULY 12   During a doubleheader at Sportsman's Park, the Cardinals and Cubs combine for a record 32 doubles, 23 of them in the second game. The twin bill attracted a record crowd of 45,715 at the St. Louis ballpark, about 13,000 more than the stands could hold. The remainder encircled the outfield. The Cubs couldn't take infield practice because the mob stole the balls. The start of the first game was delayed as fans wandered around the field overwhelming the ushers and law enforcement officers. When police were successful in pushing the crowd back in one area, it would surge forward in another sector. The game started with spectators in fair territory only about 70 feet beyond first base, about 100 feet behind third and not more than 150 feet behind second. Balls hit into the overflow during the two games were ground rule doubles, which contributed mightily to the record number of two-baggers, many of which were mere pop flies. The throng turned the game into a farce. Outfielders played practically on the heels of the infielders. The Cubs won the first game 8–5, with nine doubles in the contest, five by the Chicago batters.

Between the two games, the crowd occupied the entire field and it had to be cleared again. This time it edged a few feet closer to the infield, further squeezing the playing area. The Cardinals bounced back in the second contest, winning 17–13. St. Louis scored seven runs in the second inning to take a 10–6 lead, and after the Cubs tied it 10–10 with four in the fifth, the Cards broke the deadlock with three in their half. There were 23 doubles, the most ever in a single game by two teams. The 13 doubles by the Cards is the most by a club in a single game since 1900. The Cards also set an all-time major league record for most doubles in a doubleheader with 17. The 17 doubles were by Ripper Collins (4), Gus Mancuso (3), Chick Hafey (2), Frankie Frisch (2), Ernie Orsatti (2), George Watkins (2), Andy High (1), and Jake Flowers (1).

JULY 13   The Cardinals score seven runs in the fourth inning and defeat the Cubs 12–5 at Sportsman's Park.

JULY 24   The Cardinals sweep the Phillies 10–0 and 7–2 at Sportsman's Park.

JULY 28   Jesse Haines pitches the Cardinals to a 1–0 win over the Braves at Sportsman's Park. Jake Flowers drove in the lone run of the game with a sacrifice fly in the eighth inning.

AUGUST 5   Jim Bottomley collects six hits, including a double, in six at-bats during a 16–2 win over the Pirates in the second game of a doubleheader in Pittsburgh. The Cardinals scored eight runs in the fifth inning. Bottomley was 2 for 4 in the first game, a 12-inning, 5–4 loss.

             It was Bottomley's second career six-hit game. The first was on September 16, 1924. The only other players in major league history with a more than one six-hit game in their careers are Cal McVey (both in 1876), Jimmie Foxx (1930 and 1932), and Kirby Puckett (1987 and 1991).

AUGUST 8   The Cardinals score seven runs in the fifth inning of a 14–7 victory over the Cubs at Sportsman's Park.

AUGUST 9   On "Paul Derringer Day" at Sportsman's Park, Derringer loses a 1–0 duel to Guy Bush of the Cubs. Bush pitched a one-hitter. The only Cardinal hit was an infield single by George Watkins, who just beat the throw from shortstop Woody English.

             Before the game, Derringer was given a radio and a set of golf clubs.

AUGUST 12   Jesse Haines gives up 11 hits and walks one, but pitches a complete-game shutout to defeat the Dodgers 5–0 in the first game of a doubleheader in Brooklyn. The Cards also won the first game, 8–5.

AUGUST 23   The Cardinals defeat the Braves 16–1 and 1–0 in a doubleheader in Boston. In the first game, Chick Hafey drove in eight runs on two homers, one of them a grand slam, two doubles, and a single in six at-bats. The second tilt was an 11-inning duel between Paul Derringer and Ed Brandt, both of whom pitched complete games. Jim Bottomley drove in the lone run of the game with a homer.

AUGUST 30   Wild Bill Hallahan strikes out 13 batters in a 4–1 win over the Pirates in the second game of a doubleheader at Sportsman's Park. The Cardinals also won the first game, 5–0, behind Paul Derringer.

             Hallahan was 19–9 in 1931, leading the league in victories in a season in which there no were 20-game winners in the NL. Hallahan also led the league in strikeouts (159) and walks (112) for the second straight year. His ERA was 3.29.

SEPTEMBER 6   The Cardinals sweep the Reds with a pair of shutouts in Cincinnati. Flint Rhem won the first game 3–0, and Syl Johnson the second 7–0. The Cards were the victims of an unusual triple play in the second contest. With the bases loaded in the sixth inning, Jimmie Wilson flied to Reds left fielder Nick Cullop. Jim Bottomley, the runner on third, tagged and headed for home but was thrown out for the second out of the inning. Catcher Lena Styles then threw the ball to shortstop Leo Durocher, who held onto it. When Chick Hafey, the runner on second, took his lead, Durocher tossed the ball to second baseman Tony Cuccinello, who applied the tag to complete a 7–2–6–4 triple play.

SEPTEMBER 7   The Cardinals sweep the Cubs 1–0 and 8–3 in a doubleheader in Chicago. Paul Derringer pitched the first-game shutout. It was the third consecutive shutout by Cardinals pitchers and the third in three starts by Derringer, who had a streak of 33 consecutive shutout innings over five starts in late August and early September.

SEPTEMBER 14   The Cardinals defeat the Phillies 13–5 and 10–3 in a doubleheader at Sportsman's Park. Chick Hafey collected six hits, including two homers and two doubles, in seven at-bats.

SEPTEMBER 16   The Cardinals clinch their fourth National League pennant in six years during a 6–3 win over the Phillies at Sportsman's Park. The clinching actually took place before the final out when the second-place Giants lost 7–3 to the Reds in Cincinnati. When word reached St. Louis that the Giants lost, Gabby Street pulled all eight starting position players out of the game and inserted substitutes.

SEPTEMBER 18   Chick Hafey scores from first base on a Pepper Martin single in the ninth inning to beat the Giants 4–3 at Sportsman's Park. Hafey barely beat the throw to the plate at the end of his 270-foot dash.

SEPTEMBER 20   Gabby Street catches the first three innings of a 6–1 loss to the Dodgers at Sportsman's Park. It took place 10 days before Street's 49th birthday and was his first major league game since 1912.

               A track and field event took place before the game involving players from both clubs. The event was marred by a sprained ankle suffered by starting third baseman Sparky Adams, who missed the rest of the regular season and was limited to four at-bats in the World Series because of the injury.

SEPTEMBER 21   The Cardinals overtake the Dodgers 11–10 in 10 innings at Sportsman's Park. Ripper Collins drove in the winning run with a walk-off double.

SEPTEMBER 24   With the country mired in the Great Depression, the Cardinals and Browns play a charity exhibition to raise money for the unemployed in St. Louis. Fans attending the contest contributed $30,250. The Browns won 7–4.

SEPTEMBER 27   The Cardinals close the season with their 100th and 101st wins of 1931 with 6–3 and 5–3 win over the Reds in a doubleheader in Cincinnati. After going hitless in four at-bats in the first game, Chick Hafey was 2 for 4 in the nightcap to wrap up the batting title by a razor-thin margin in one of the closest races in history. Hafey's average of .3489 just nosed out Bill Terry of the Giants, who finished at .3486 after picking up a hit in four at-bats on the final day. Jim Bottomley was a close third with an average of .3482 after collecting four hits in eight at-bats in the season-ending doubleheader.

The Cardinals were the first NL club since the 1913 Giants to win at least 100 games in a season. It didn't happen again until the Reds won 100 in 1940. The Cards' World Series opponents in 1931 was the Philadelphia Athletics. The A's were gunning for their third consecutive world title after defeating the Cubs in five games in 1929 and the Cardinals in six games in 1930. Managed by 68-year-old Connie Mack, the Athletics were 107–45. The A's winning percentage of .704 was the highest of any big-league club between 1927 and 1954.

OCTOBER 1   The Cardinals open the 1931 World Series with a 6–2 loss to the Athletics before 38,529 at Sportsman's Park. The Cards scored two runs in the first, but Lefty Grove shut them down the rest of the way. The A's took the lead with four runs in the third against Paul Derringer. Rookie center fielder Pepper Martin collected three hits, including a double, in four at-bats for the Cards. He also stole a base.

Seven individuals were on the World Series eligibility rosters of the Cardinals in each of the club's four appearances in the Fall Classic in 1926, 1928, 1930, and 1931. They were Ray Blades, Jim Bottomley, Jesse Haines, Wild Bill Hallahan, Chick Hafey, Syl Johnson, and Flint Rhem.

In Game Two of the 1931 World Series, it was Pepper Martin's slide home that sealed the 2–0 win over the Athletics. During the Series, Martin collected a team-high 12 hits, 5 RBIs, and 5 steals to go with a .500 batting average. The cap he wore in this series is on display at the Hall of Fame.

OCTOBER 2 — Spurred by the efforts of Pepper Martin and Wild Bill Hallahan, the Cardinals even the Series by defeating the Athletics 2–0 before 35,947 at Sportsman's Park. Martin stretched a routine single into a double with a head-first slide in the second inning, stole third just ahead of Mickey Cochrane's throw, and came home on Jimmie Wilson's fly to center. In the seventh, Martin reached first on a single, stole second, went to third on an infield out, and dived across the plate in a cloud of dust on a squeeze bunt by Charlie Gelbert. The game nearly got away on a boneheaded play by the usually reliable Jimmie Wilson. With two on base in the ninth and two outs, pinch hitter Johnny Moore swung at the ball and missed. Believing the game was over, Wilson threw the ball to third baseman Jake Flowers. Umpire Dick Nallin ruled that Wilson trapped the third strike, however, and Moore reached first safely to load the bases. Fortunately, Jim Bottomley made a sensational catch leaning into the box seats to get the final out on a pop foul by Max Bishop. Hallahan struck out eight, walked seven, and allowed just three hits.

> *There were no games on Saturday, October 3 or Sunday, October 4. Saturday was a travel day, and Pennsylvania law banned baseball on Sundays.*

OCTOBER 5 — Pepper Martin again leads his teammates to victory with a 5–2 decision over the Athletics in Philadelphia before a crowd that included President Herbert Hoover. Martin had a single and a double in four at-bats and scored twice. Jimmie Wilson collected three hits for the Cards. Burleigh Grimes pitched no-hit ball until Bing Miller singled with none out in the eighth. The only Athletics runs came with two outs in the ninth inning when Mickey Cochrane walked and Al Simmons homered. Grimes also had two hits and drove in two runs.

OCTOBER 6 — The Athletics even the Series with a 3–0 win in Philadelphia in Game Four. George Earnshaw pitched a two-hitter. Pepper Martin had both St. Louis hits with a single in the fifth inning and a double in the eighth.

OCTOBER 7 — The Cardinals move within one game of the World Championship with a 5–1 win over the Athletics in Philadelphia in Game Five. Pepper Martin had three hits, one of them a home run, in four at-bats. He drove in four of the five Cardinal runs. Wild Bill Hallahan pitched the complete game.

> *Martin batted sixth during the first four games of the Series, but because of his hit hitting, he was elevated to the cleanup spot in Game Five. After five games, Martin had 12 hits in 18 at-bats. Among his hits were four doubles and a home run. He also stole four bases, scored five runs, and drove in five. Although he would add his fifth stolen base of the Series, Martin would go hitless in six at-bats in the final two games. But his teammates picked up the slack and the Cardinals managed to win the Series.*

OCTOBER 9 — The Athletics even the World Series by winning game six 8–1 before 39,401 disappointed fans at Sportsman's Park. Lefty Grove held the Cardinals to five hits.

> *During fielding practice before Game Six, a man with a rifle rushed toward Pepper Martin. It turned out to be a gun manufacturer, who presented the rifle to Martin, an avid hunter, as a gift.*

OCTOBER 10 — The Cardinals take the World Championship with a 4–2 win over the Athletics in Game Seven at Sportsman's Park. George Watkins was the hitting star. He contributed to a two-run first inning with a single and hit a two-run homer in the third over the right-field pavilion. Burleigh Grimes took a 4–0 lead into the ninth before running into trouble. With two outs and a runner on first, Grimes allowed a walk and two singles to score two runs. Wild Bill Hallahan came in from the bullpen and retired Max Bishop on a fly ball to Pepper Martin in center field. The pivotal game drew only 20,805. Tickets for the games in St. Louis were sold in three-game strips with the seventh game omitted. Game Seven tickets didn't go one sale until after the sixth game ended, resulting in a diminished crowd.

When the 1931 World Series began, Martin was an unheralded 27-year-old rookie who hit .300 with seven homers in 123 games during the regular season. By the end of the Series, Martin was a national hero for his play in the defeat of the Athletics. He was a stocky five-foot-eight and hailed from rural Oklahoma. Making up for a limited store of talent, Martin won over fans with his desperate, reckless all-out hustle that earned him the nickname "The Wild Horse of the Osage." His craggy face and dirty uniform seemed to define the Depression era.

DECEMBER 2   The Cardinals send Andy High to the Reds for Nick Cullop and cash.

DECEMBER 9   The Cardinals trade Burleigh Grimes to the Cubs for Hack Wilson and Bud Teachout.

Grimes was a 1931 World Series hero, but was 38 years old and near the end of the line. He pitched only three more seasons in the majors with a record of 13–22. Wilson, who like Grimes was destined for the Hall of Fame, hit 56 homers and drove in 191 runs for the Cubs in 1930. The 56 homers stood as the NL record until it was surpassed by Mark McGwire and Sammy Sosa in 1998. The 191 RBIs is still the major league record. But in 1931, Wilson slumped badly and hit only 13 homers with 61 RBIs. He never played for the Cardinals, however. The Cards wanted to cut his salary by $25,000 and Wilson objected. He was sent to the Dodgers on January 23, 1932, in exchange for Bob Parham and $45,000. Wilson had one good year for the Dodgers before his career ended in 1934.

1932

Season in a Sentence

The glow of the World Championship wears off quickly as an aging roster loses 82 games, the most of any Cardinal team between 1924 and 1954.

Finish • Won • Lost • Pct • GB

Sixth (tie) 72   82   .468   18.0

Manager

Gabby Street

Stats

Stats	Cards	NL	Rank
Batting Avg:	.269	.276	6
On-Base Pct:	.324	.328	6
Slugging Pct:	.385	.396	6
Home Runs:	76		4
Stolen Bases:	92		1
ERA:	3.97	3.88	6
Fielding Avg:	.971	.971	3
Runs Scored:	684		6
Runs Allowed:	717		6

Starting Lineup

Gus Mancuso, c
Ripper Collins, 1b-rf
Frankie Frisch, 2b-3b
Jake Flowers, 3b
Charlie Gelbert, ss
Ernie Orsatti, lf-cf
Pepper Martin, cf
George Watkins, rf
Jim Bottomley, 1b
Jimmy Reese, 2b
Jimmie Wilson, c
Ray Blades, rf

Pitchers

Dizzy Dean, sp-rp
Paul Derringer, sp
Tex Carleton, sp
Wild Bill Hallahan, sp
Syl Johnson, sp-rp
Jesse Haines, sp-rp
Jim Lindsey, rp

Attendance

279,219 (seventh in NL)

Club Leaders

Batting Avg:	Watkins	.312
On-Base Pct:	Watkins	.384
Slugging Pct:	Collins	.474
Home Runs:	Collins	21
RBIs:	Collins	91
Runs:	Collins	82
Stolen Bases:	Watkins	18
	Frisch	18
Wins:	Dean	18
Strikeouts:	Dean	191
ERA:	Hallahan	3.11
Saves:	Lindsey	3

JANUARY 26   The Cardinals purchase Hod Ford from the Reds.

APRIL 11   Six weeks after the kidnapping of the Lindbergh baby, the Cardinals send Chick Hafey to the Reds for Harvey Hendrick, Benny Frey, and cash.

> *After the 1930 season, Hafey wanted an increase in salary from $9,000 to $15,000. He held out until Opening Day and finally signed for $12,500. Branch Rickey inserted a clause that stated Hafey would not be paid until he was "ready to play." He then kept Hafey on the bench and deducted $2,100 from his pay. After winning the batting title in 1931, Hafey demanded the $15,000 plus the restoration of the $2,100. When the demands were rejected, Hafey held out again. Rickey responded by trading Hafey to the Reds on the eve of Opening Day for two players and $45,000. The Cardinals had no use for either Frey or Hendrick and sold Frey back to the Reds in May and Hendrick to the Cincinnati club in June. Hafey gave the Reds three good years, but was benched frequently with sinus trouble and other assorted injuries. By the end of the 1932 season, the Cardinals had Joe Medwick ready to take over Hafey's spot in left field.*

APRIL 12   The two-time defending National League champion and defending World Champion Cardinals play before an Opening Day crowd of only 5,937 at Sportsman's Park, but defeat the Pirates 10–2. Flint Rhem pitched the complete-game victory. Ripper

Collins hit a home run and Ray Blades contributed three hits. The 1931 National League pennant was raised before the game.

The low attendance figure was due to cold weather, the sluggish economy of the Great Depression, and unpopular offseason trades. After an attendance figure of 608,535 in 1931, the Cardinals drew only 279,219 fans in 1932 and 256,171 in 1933.

APRIL 13   An incredible five-run rally in the ninth inning beats the Pirates 9–8 at Sportsman's Park. A two-out, two-run double by Frankie Frisch drove in the tying and winning runs.

The Cardinals won their first two games of 1932, then lost six in a row setting the stage for the club's first losing season since 1924.

APRIL 15   Ripper Collins hits a homer and three doubles, but the Cardinals lose 9–7 to the Pirates at Sportsman's Park.

James "Ripper" Collins quit school to work in the Altoona, Pennsylvania, coal mines at the age of 13. He might have spent his whole life there were it not for a miners' strike five years later that gave him a shot at professional baseball. He was 27 when he reached the Cardinals in 1931, and beat out Jim Bottomley for the starting first base job a year later. Despite standing five-foot-nine and weighing 165 pounds, Collins could hit for power. In back-to-back seasons in 1934 and 1935, he batted .323 with 58 homers and 250 RBIs. During a 30-year association with baseball, he also worked as a minor league manager, sporting goods representative, and broadcaster.

MAY 1   Wild Bill Hallahan walks ten batters, but allows only three hits and defeats the Cubs 7–1 in Chicago.

MAY 9   The Cardinals score three runs in the ninth inning to defeat the Dodgers 7–6 at Sportsman's Park. Sparky Adams tied the game with a two-run triple and scored on a single by Ripper Collins.

MAY 11   Wild Bill Hallahan throws three wild pitches in the twelfth inning contributing to three Dodger runs in a 6–3 loss at Sportsman's Park.

MAY 15   The Cardinals raise the 1931 World Championship banner, then lose 8–3 to the Braves. Commissioner Kenesaw Landis attended the festivities and presented diamond rings to the Cardinal players who were a part of the championship club.

MAY 18   The Cardinals purchase Bill Sherdel from the Braves.

JUNE 1   Frankie Frisch and Eddie Delker lose home runs in a 1–0 win over the Cubs in Chicago. Both homered in the top of the eighth, but rain began to fall and the game was called. Since the inning wasn't completed, the home runs were wiped off the books and the final score reverted back to the end of the seventh. Dizzy Dean pitched the shutout.

The home run would have been Delker's first in the majors. He was sold to the Phillies three days later. In 187 big-league at-bats, Delker hit only one official homer, which was struck on June 14, 1932.

JUNE 4   The Cardinals sell Flint Rhem and Eddie Delker to the Phillies.

JUNE 8   The Cardinals swat the Braves 15–8 in Boston. The Cards trailed 5–4 before scoring seven times in the fifth inning.

JUNE 15   Rookie pitcher Dizzy Dean jumps to the club in Philadelphia in a salary dispute. Dean had been threatening to quit for weeks, claiming mistreatment from Cardinal management, which repeatedly denied Dean's demands for a pay boost. Dean claimed his contract should be voided because he was underage when he signed it and petitioned Kenesaw Landis to declare him a free agent. After an investigation by Landis revealed that Dean was 21 when he signed the document, the commissioner denied the request. Dean returned to the Cardinals two days later.

Jay Hanna (Dizzy) Dean exploded onto the big-league scene in 1932. Only 22, he was 18–15 with an ERA of 3.30. He led the NL in innings pitched (286), strikeouts (191), and shutouts (four). The son of a poor Arkansas sharecropper, Dean was an immediate fan favorite with his winning personality. His pitching alone would have been enough to immortalize him, but his bold and zany antics on and off the field made him one of the most recognizable figures in America. A relentless braggart who had a burning need to be the center of attention and overreacted to the slightest personal affront, he usually backed up his boasts. As he put it, "It ain't bragging if you can do it." Dean was difficult to handle, and was constantly at loggerheads with club management. His eccentricities were tolerated because of his performance on the mound and his tremendous drawing power whenever he pitched. In seven seasons as a Cardinal, he was 150–83 with a 3.02 ERA, 26 shutouts, and 1,163 strikeouts in 1,967⅓ innings. During his three peak seasons (1934–36), Dean won 72 games and lost 32.

JUNE 16   Jesse Haines pitches a shutout and hits a third-inning homer to defeat the Phillies 2–0 in Philadelphia.

JUNE 19   Tex Carleton earns his first major league victory with a two-hitter to defeat the Giants 7–0 at the Polo Grounds. The only New York hits were singles by Joe Moore and Shanty Hogan.

JUNE 22   The National League directs all clubs to sew numbers onto the backs of their uniforms to help fans identify the players.

Within a few days, the Cardinals complied with the new rule. The numbers were issued to Skeeter Webb (1), Pepper Martin (2), Frankie Frisch (3), Jim Bottomley (4), Ernie Orsatti (5), George Watkins (6), Ray Blades (7), Ripper Collins (8), Jimmy Reese (9), Jake Flowers (10), Charlie Gelbert (11), Jimmie Wilson (12), Gus Mancuso (14), Mike Gonzalez (15), Jesse Haines (16), Dizzy Dean (17), Tex Carleton (18), Jim Lindsey (19), Paul Derringer (20), Allyn Stout (21), Wild Bill Hallahan (22), Syl Johnson (23), Wattie Holm (24), manager Gabby Street (25), and coach Buzzy Wares (26).

JUNE 26   Jimmie Reese hits a two-run, pinch-hit, walk-off double in the ninth inning that beats the Cubs 4–3 in the first game of a doubleheader at Sportsman's Park. The Cubs reversed the score and won the second contest 4–3.

Reese was a roommate of Babe Ruth while the two played for the Yankees in

1930 and 1931. Reese was a popular coach with the Angels from 1973 until his death at the age of 89 in 1994. The Angels honored Reese by retiring his number 50.

JUNE 28   The Cardinals purchase Rube Bressler from the Phillies.

JULY 12   Down 6–0, the Cardinals rally with one run in the fourth inning, two in the sixth, two in the eighth, and two in the ninth to beat the Phillies 7–6 in Philadelphia. The final two runs scored on a two-out homer by George Watkins.

                 Watkins hit .312 with nine homers in 1932.

JULY 20   The Cardinals collect 22 hits and wallop the Dodgers 16–5 at Sportsman's Park. Jake Flowers had five hits, including a homer, in six at-bats. Ernie Orsatti was 4 for 5 with two doubles during an eight-run seventh inning.

                 Orsatti played for the Cardinals from 1927 through 1935, mostly as a reserve outfielder. Before entering professional baseball, he worked as a stunt double for silent screen star Buster Keaton. Orsatti also drew paychecks from Hollywood studios as a cameraman and assistant director. After his playing career ended, he was an agent and managed some of the top names in show business including Sonja Henie, Veronica Lake, Ann Miller, Jack Haley, and the comedy team of Stan Laurel and Oliver Hardy.

JULY 24   The Cardinals sweep the Reds 7–3 and 1–0 in a doubleheader in Cincinnati. The second tilt lasted 13 innings. A single by Jimmie Reese drove in the winning run. Dizzy Dean (nine innings), Syl Johnson (three innings), and Jim Lindsey (one inning) combined on the shutout.

JULY 26   The Dodgers score 11 runs in the seventh inning and defeat the Cardinals 12–6 in the first game of a doubleheader in Brooklyn. The Dodgers also won the second contest, 8–4.

AUGUST 8   After the Phillies score six runs in the seventh inning to take a 6–1 lead, the Cardinals rally with three runs in the eighth and three in the ninth to win 7–6 in the first game of a doubleheader in Philadelphia. The Cardinals completed the sweep with an 11-inning, 6–4 victory in the nightcap. Both extra-inning runs scored on a homer by Ripper Collins.

AUGUST 9   The Cardinals collect 25 hits and hammer the Phillies 18–13 at Baker Bowl. Jim Bottomley hit two homers and drove in six runs. Philadelphia took an 8–2 lead with an eight-run second inning, but the Cards forged ahead with five runs in the third inning and six in the fifth.

AUGUST 10   The Cardinals erupt for six runs in the eleventh inning and defeat the Phillies 11–5 in Philadelphia.

AUGUST 20   Tex Carleton allows 7 runs and 12 hits, but pitches a 10-inning complete game and drives in the winning run with a walk-off single to defeat the Dodgers 8–7 at Sportsman's Park.

AUGUST 24   Dizzy Dean drives in four runs on a homer and a single and pitches a complete game to defeat the Giants 6–2 at Sportsman's Park.

AUGUST 26   Pitching on one day of rest, Dizzy Dean pitches a complete game to defeat the Giants 4–2 at Sportsman's Park.

AUGUST 28   Making his third start in five days, Dizzy Dean pitches eight innings to defeat the Dodgers 6–3 in the second game of a doubleheader at Sportsman's Park. The Cardinals won the first game 4–1.

SEPTEMBER 15   Ray Starr pitches a shutout in his major league debut to defeat the Dodgers 3–0 at Ebbets Field. The only Brooklyn hits were singles by Joe Stripp and Johnny Frederick.

Starr pitched only three games for the Cardinals before being dealt to the Giants between the 1932 and 1933 seasons. His September 15 debut was his only victory in a St. Louis uniform. Starr didn't win another big-league game until 1941 when he was 35 years old and had battled his way back to the big leagues spending eight years in the minors.

SEPTEMBER 22   An intimate gathering of only 450 watches the Cardinals defeat the Reds 8–5 at Sportsman's Park.

SEPTEMBER 23   Dizzy Dean participates in a calf-roping contest at a rodeo in St. Louis. Unable to lasso the calf from his horse, Dean dismounted, ran down the animal, and then tied it up to the delight of the crowd.

OCTOBER 10   The Cardinals trade Gus Mancuso and Ray Starr to the Giants for Bill Walker, Ethan Allen, Bob O'Farrell, and Jim Mooney.

Walker gave the Cardinals a couple of good seasons at the back end of the starting pitching rotation, but he wasn't worth the loss of Mancuso, who was the Giants' starting catcher for five seasons and appeared in two All-Star games.

OCTOBER 25   The Cardinals sign Rogers Hornsby to a contract.

Hornsby was been let go as player-manager of the Cubs the previous August. He played in 46 games with the Cards in 1933 as a spare infielder and pinch hitter and hit .325 in 83 at-bats. In July 1933, the Cards released Hornsby so he could take a job as manager of the Browns.

NOVEMBER 16   Charlie Gelbert shoots himself in the leg in a hunting accident.

Gelbert was out hunting rabbits near McConnellsburg, Pennsylvania, when he tripped over a vine. In the process, his 12-gauge shotgun discharged and opened a nasty wound about his left ankle. At the time of the accident, Gelbert had just completed his fourth season as the Cardinals' shortstop, and at the age of 26, it looked as though the club was set at the position for several more years. Gelbert was unable to play during the 1933 and 1934 seasons while recovering. Nerves were severed, the instep blown away, gangrene set in, and three operations were performed to repair the damage caused by the shotgun blast. By the time he was healthy enough to return in 1935, Gelbert's speed was gone and he lasted only two more seasons as a utility infielder. After his playing career ended, Gelbert was a coach at Lafayette College for 21 years.

DECEMBER 17   Six weeks after Franklin Roosevelt defeats Herbert Hoover in the presidential election, the Cardinals trade Jim Bottomley to the Reds for Estel Crabtree and Ownie Carroll.

Bottomley was near the end of his career. He was traded because the Cardinals had a better alternative at first base in Ripper Collins.

1933

Season in a Sentence

A slump in July forces another switch in managers, as Frankie Frisch replaces Gabby Street.

Finish • Won • Lost • Pct • GB

Fifth   82   71   .536   9.5

Managers

Gabby Street (46–45) and Frankie Frisch (36–26)

Stats	Cards	NL	Rank
Batting Avg:	.276	.266	2
On-Base Pct:	.329	.317	2
Slugging Pct:	.378	.362	3
Home Runs:	57		5
Stolen Bases:	99		1
ERA:	3.37	3.33	5
Fielding Avg:	.973	.973	2
Runs Scored:	687		1
Runs Allowed:	609		4

Starting Lineup

Jimmie Wilson, c
Ripper Collins, 1b
Frankie Frisch, 2b
Pepper Martin, 3b
Leo Durocher, ss
Joe Medwick, lf
Ernie Orsatti, cf
George Watkins, rf
Ethan Allen, cf-rf
Pat Crawford, 1b-2b
Bob O'Farrell, c

Pitchers

Dizzy Dean, sp
Tex Carleton, sp
Wild Bill Hallahan, sp
Bill Walker, sp-rp
Jesse Haines, rp-sp
Syl Johnson, rp
Dazzy Vance, rp-sp
Jim Mooney, rp-sp

Attendance

256,171 (sixth in NL)

Club Leaders

Batting Avg:	Martin	.316
On-Base Pct:	Martin	.387
Slugging Pct:	Medwick	.497
Home Runs:	Medwick	18
RBIs:	Medwick	98
Runs:	Martin	122
Stolen Bases:	Frisch	26
Wins:	Dean	20
Strikeouts:	Dean	199
ERA:	Dean	3.04
Saves:	Dean	4

FEBRUARY 8   The Cardinals trade Jake Flowers and Ownie Carroll to the Dodgers for Dazzy Vance and Gordon Slade.

Vance had 187 victories to his credit when acquired by the Cardinals, but was 42 years old on Opening Day in 1933. He pitched two seasons for the Cards and had a 7–3 record. Slade was acquired to replace Charlie Gelbert at shortstop following Gelbert's hunting accident the previous November. Slade hit only .113 in 39 games for St. Louis, however. Fortunately, the Cards gave up little of value in the transaction.

APRIL 12   Five weeks after Franklin Roosevelt proclaims, "The only thing we have to fear is fear itself," at the depths of the Great Depression, the Cardinals lose the season opener 3–0 to the Cubs in Chicago. Lon Warneke pitched the shutout.

APRIL 20   In the home opener, the Cardinals down the Cubs 3–1 at Sportsman's Park.

With the end of Prohibition, beer was sold at Sportsman's Park for the first time since 1919.

APRIL 27   The Cardinals score three runs in the ninth inning to defeat the Reds 3–2 at Sportsman's Park. Ethan Allen drove in the winning run with a sacrifice fly.

Allen had an interesting life after his 13-year major league career ended in 1940. During World War II, he served in Italy in the Special Services sports program. Later, Allen was the motion picture director in the National League publicity department, authored several books, invented two scientific baseball games, and coached at Yale for two decades. One of his table-top games, called All-Star Baseball, was extremely popular in the days before the advent of video games. In 1947 and 1948, Allen's Yale teams made it to the NCAA championship game with future President George Bush playing first base.

MAY 2   The Cardinals slaughter the Dodgers 13–4 in Brooklyn.

MAY 5   Pepper Martin hits for the cycle in a 5–3 win over the Phillies in Philadelphia. All four hits were struck off Frank Pearce.

Following his terrific performance in the 1931 World Series, Martin slumped in 1932 with a .238 average in 85 games. He rebounded in 1933 by hitting .316 in addition to leading the NL in runs (122) and stolen bases (26).

MAY 7   The Cardinals trade Paul Derringer, Sparky Adams, and Allyn Stout to the Reds for Leo Durocher, Butch Henline, and Jack Ogden.

The Cards were in desperate need of a shortstop, and Durocher filled the void. A talkative and nasty brawler who would do anything to win a game, Durocher fit right in with the hell-raising "Gas House Gang" Cardinals of the 1930s. He was a poor hitter, but was one of the top defensive shortstops of his era, and was the club's starter at the position for five seasons. Durocher didn't come cheaply, however. Derringer recorded 194 victories after leaving the Cardinals, won 20 or more games in four seasons, was named to six All-Star teams, and pitched in two World Series for the Reds and another with the Cubs.

MAY 19   Down 7–2, the Cardinals cut loose with five runs in the eighth inning and one in the tenth to win 8–7 over the Giants at Sportsman's Park. Pat Crawford drove in the winning run with a bases-loaded single.

MAY 21   Wild Bill Hallahan pitched a two-hitter to defeat the Giants 2–1 in the first game of a doubleheader at Sportsman's Park. Johnny Vergez had both New York hits, a pair of singles. The Cards completed the sweep with an 8–4 victory in the second tilt.

MAY 22   A two-out, three-run, walk-off homer by Pepper Martin in the tenth inning beats the Braves 3–0 at Sportsman's Park. Bill Walker pitched the complete-game shutout.

MAY 26   Dizzy Dean pitches a 14-inning complete game and scores the winning run in the 5–4 victory over the Phillies at Sportsman's Park. Dean scored on a walk-off single by Ernie Orsatti.

JUNE 6   Numerous sideshows highlight a 6–2 win over the Reds in Cincinnati. The chaotic day began with Dizzy Dean fighting Paul Derringer in front of the grandstand during batting practice. Dazzy Vance stepped between them and broke up the Dizzy-Derringer duel. During the game George Watkins and Reds acting manager Jewel Ens were ejected for arguing too strenuously with the umpiring crew. In the ninth inning, Reds outfielder Harry Rice was knocked silly from a collision with the outfield wall while chasing a drive off the bat of Joe Medwick, who circled the bases for an inside-the-park homer. Finally, Cardinal infielder Burgess Whitehead innocently leaned out of the dugout and was conked on the shoulder by a bottle thrown by a woman from the second deck.

JUNE 9   The Cardinals move into first place with a 12–2 win over the Cubs at Sportsman's Park.

              The win was the high point of the season, with the Cards holding a 30–18 record. By the end of the season, the club was in fifth place with an 82–71 record.

JUNE 11   The Cardinals suffer a stunning setback in the first game of a doubleheader against the Pirates at Sportsman's Park. The Cards led 7–1 heading into the ninth before Pittsburgh scored 10 runs off Wild Bill Halahan, Tex Carleton, and Dizzy Dean to win 11–7. The Pirates also won the second fray, 3–0.

JUNE 17   The Cardinals score eight runs in the eighth inning and wallop the Reds 17–2 in Cincinnati. George Watkins collected five hits, including a triple, in six at-bats.

JUNE 18   The Cardinals coast to a 13–1 win over the Reds in the first game of a doubleheader in Cincinnati before losing 6–5 in the nightcap.

JUNE 20   The Cardinals score eight runs in the eighth inning of a 15–4 win over the Dodgers in Brooklyn.

JUNE 29   Ethan Allen hits an inside-the-park homer in the second inning against the Giants in New York, only to be called out because he batted out of turn. The lineup had Joe Medwick batting fifth and Allen sixth, but Allen hit ahead of Medwick, who according to the scoring rules was charged with the at-bat. Allen then hit in his regular spot in the order, and grounded out. Despite the gaffe, the Cardinals won 7–3.

JUNE 30   Joe Medwick hits a homer with two outs in the ninth off Hal Schumacher to beat the Giants 1–0 in New York. Dizzy Dean pitched the shutout.

              Medwick hit .306 with 40 doubles and 18 homers in 1933.

JULY 2   The Cardinals play 27 innings only to suffer a pair of crushing 1–0 losses against the Giants at the Polo Grounds. The Cards collected only 10 hits in the doubleheader.

The first game lasted 18 innings. In a remarkable pitching performance, future Hall of Famer Carl Hubbell hurled a complete-game shutout for New York, allowing only six hits and no walks. St. Louis wasted the pitching excellence of Tex Carleton who tossed the first 16 innings for the Cards before being lifted for a pinch hitter. Jesse Haines pitched the seventeenth and eighteenth innings. The game ended on a single by Hughie Critz. In the second contest, Dizzy Dean lost a 1–0 duel to Roy Parmelee. A homer by Johnny Vergez in the fourth inning produced the lone run of the game.

Carleton had a record of 17–11 with a 3.38 ERA in 1933.

JULY 3   Dizzy Dean misses an exhibition game in Elmira, New York.

Dean was among the Cardinals instructed to board the train to Elmira. A few players who were excused from the exhibition game took a train to Pittsburgh, where the Cards were scheduled to play on July 4. Dean got on the train bound for Pittsburgh. He claimed it was an innocent mistake, but the club fined him $100. Frankie Frisch promised to rescind the fine if Dean won his next start, which he accomplished with a shutout (see July 8, 1933).

JULY 5   Pepper Martin collects five hits, including a double, in five at-bats, but the Cardinals lose 7–6 to the Pirates in Pittsburgh.

JULY 6   Four Cardinals are in the National League starting lineup in the first All-Star Game, played at Comiskey Park and won by the American League 4–2. Pepper Martin started at third base, Frankie Frisch at second, Jimmie Wilson as the catcher, and Wild Bill Hallahan on the mound. Martin was the leadoff batter, and thus became the first batter in All-Star history. He grounded out. In the sixth, Frisch hit the first National League All-Star homer off General Crowder. Hallahan took the loss, surrendering three runs in two innings, including the first All-Star homer to Babe Ruth.

Frisch hit .303 with four homers during the regular season in 1933.

JULY 8   Dizzy Dean pitches the Cardinals to a 1–0 win over the Dodgers at Sportsman's Park. Ernie Orsatti drove in the lone run of the game with a single in the eighth inning. Earlier, Joe Medwick saved the game in the seventh inning. With a Brooklyn runner on third and two outs, Medwick made a diving catch in left field and slid 20 feet on the slippery turf.

JULY 21   Dizzy Dean walks into a St. Louis drugstore while a robbery is in progress. A pistol was shoved into Dean's ribs and he was told to join the other herded customers and keep still. Three days later, the two bandits sent Dean a half-dozen neckties as a gift, with a note stating that they had nothing against him personally.

JULY 23   The Cardinals smoke the Braves 12–0 in the first game of a doubleheader at Sportsman's Park. Boston won the second contest, called after six innings by rain, 2–1.

JULY 24   Frankie Frisch replaces Gabby Street as Cardinals manager.

Street won two NL pennants in his first two years as manager, but the Cardinals had a regular-season record of 117–128 under Street since winning the 1931

World Series. At the time Street was fired, the Cards had lost 28 of their last 43 games. Frisch remained in his role as the Cardinals' starting second baseman. He was the Cardinals' manager until September 1938, a period in which the "Gas House Gang" reigned in St. Louis and the Cardinals won a World Championship in 1934. Street later managed the Browns in 1938 and was a popular radio and television broadcaster in St. Louis broadcasting both the Cardinals' and Browns' games from 1940 through 1946, and the Cardinals' alone from 1947 through 1950 when he teamed with Harry Caray.

JULY 26   The Cardinals release Rogers Hornsby to allow him to take a job as player-manager of the Browns. Hornsby remained as Browns manager until 1937.

JULY 29   A three-run walk-off homer by Pepper Martin in the tenth inning beats the Cubs 9–6 at Sportsman's Park.

JULY 30   Dizzy Dean strikes out 17 Cubs during a 6–2 win in the first game of a doubleheader at Sportsman's Park. Dean was the first pitcher to strike out as many as 17 batters in a nine-inning game since the four-ball-three-strike count was established in 1889. The Cardinals also won the second fray, 6–5.

The next day, Dean hurled two innings of an exhibition game in Columbus, Ohio. His brother Paul pitched for Columbus. The Cardinals won 4–3.

AUGUST 1   A fight enlivens a 9–3 loss to the Pirates at Forbes Field. The scrap came after Leo Durocher was hit by a pitch in the seventh inning. George Watkins made the last out of the inning and exchanged words with Pittsburgh hurler Steve Swetonic. The two squared off and began trading punches before the umpires separated them and ejected both from the premises.

AUGUST 2   Hostilities flare again during the Cardinals' 12-inning, 4–3 win over the Pirates at Forbes Field. In the seventh, Cardinal pitcher Bill Walker covered first and Pittsburgh shortstop Arky Vaughan crashed into him. Walker swung at Vaughan sparking a 12-minute melee.

AUGUST 6   The Cardinals waste brilliant pitching and lose 2–1 in 11 innings and 1–0 in 13 innings to the Reds in Cincinnati. Tex Carleton pitched a complete game in the opener and Jesse Haines in the second.

AUGUST 16   Ripper Collins hits a homer in the twelfth inning to defeat the Phillies 7–6 in the first game of a doubleheader at Baker Bowl. Philadelphia won the second tilt 2–0.

Collins hit .310 with 10 homers in 1933.

AUGUST 28   The Cardinals score seven runs in the ninth inning to defeat the Giants 12–8 in New York. Bob O'Farrell put the Cardinals into the lead with a two-run homer. It was his second home run of the game.

The homers were O'Farrell's first since the 1931 season and the only two that he hit during the 1933 campaign in 163 at-bats.

AUGUST 31   The Cardinals sweep the Dodgers 10–3 and 10–4 in a doubleheader in Brooklyn.

SEPTEMBER 8   The Cardinals extend their record at home under new manager Frankie Frisch to 14–0 with a 6–5 win over the Phillies.

SEPTEMBER 13   Dizzy Dean wins his 20th game of 1933 with a 4–1 decision over the Dodgers at Sportsman's Park.

Dean was a 20–18 record with a 3.04 ERA in 1933. He led the NL in games pitched with 48, making 34 starts and 14 relief appearances. Dean also topped the league in complete games (26) and strikeouts (199 in 293 innings).

SEPTEMBER 16   The Cardinals outlast the Dodgers 14–13 in 10 innings in the first game of a scheduled doubleheader at Sportsman's Park. The Cards trailed 6–2 in the third inning before moving ahead 12–9, only to allow the Dodgers to score three in the ninth and one in the tenth. The Cardinals won the contest with two in their half of the tenth. A walk-off double by Pepper Martin drove across the winning run. The second contest started, but by the fourth inning it was so dark the players could barely follow the ball. Umpire Ted McGrew insisted on continuing play, however. One fan leaped out of the stands to attack McGrew but was stopped by the players. Another group of fans built a bonfire in the bleachers. Sam Breadon sent word to McGrew that he would sue the umpires if any of his players were injured. McGrew finally called a halt to play in the top of the fifth before it became an official game.

SEPTEMBER 17   Dizzy Dean is presented with a new Buick on Dizzy Dean Day at Sportsman's Park, then loses 4–3 to the Giants. Dean also received a crate of chicks and five tiny pigs.

NOVEMBER 15   The Cardinals trade Jimmie Wilson to the Phillies for Spud Davis and Eddie Delker.

Wilson was named manager of the Phillies, a position he held until 1938. Davis gave the Cardinals three excellent seasons as the club's starting catcher. On the 1934 pennant winners, he batted .300 with nine homers.

1934

Season in a Sentence

Led by 30 wins from Dizzy Dean and 19 more from his brother Paul, the free-spirited Cardinals, known as the Gas House Gang, win an exciting pennant race, then take the World Series against the Tigers.

Finish • Won • Lost • Pct • GB

First   95   58   .621   +2.0

World Series—The Cardinals defeated the Detroit Tigers four games to three

Manager

Frankie Frisch

Stats

Stats	Cards	NL	Rank
Batting Avg:	.288	.279	1
On-Base Pct:	.337	.333	4
Slugging Pct:	.425	.394	1
Home Runs:	104		2
Stolen Bases:	69		1
ERA:	3.69	4.06	2
Fielding Avg:	.972	.972	3
Runs Scored:	799		1
Runs Allowed:	656		3

Starting Lineup

Spud Davis, c
Ripper Collins, 1b
Frankie Frisch, 2b
Pepper Martin, 3b
Leo Durocher, ss
Joe Medwick, lf
Ernie Orsatti, cf
Jack Rothrock, rf
Burgess Whitehead, 2b-ss-3b
Bill DeLancey, c
Chick Fullis, cf

Pitchers

Dizzy Dean, sp-rp
Paul Dean, sp-rp
Tex Carleton, sp
Bill Walker, sp
Wild Bill Hallahan, sp
Jesse Haines, rp
Jim Mooney, rp

Attendance

325,056 (fifth in NL)

Club Leaders

Batting Avg:	Collins	.333
On-Base Pct:	Collins	.393
Slugging Pct:	Collins	.615
Home Runs:	Collins	35
RBIs:	Collins	128
Runs:	Collins	116
Stolen Bases:	Martin	23
Wins:	D. Dean	30
Strikeouts:	D. Dean	195
ERA:	D. Dean	2.66
Saves:	D. Dean	7

JANUARY 11   The Cardinals trade Syl Johnson and Bob O'Farrell to the Reds for Glenn Spencer.

O'Farrell was immediately named manager of the Reds. He was the second Cardinal catcher in two months to be traded to another club to become a manager. The first was Jimmie Wilson, who was dealt to the Phillies in November 1933. O'Farrell, who had previously managed the Cardinals in 1927, was fired by the Reds in July 1934.

FEBRUARY 3   The Cardinals and the Browns bar radio broadcasts of their games. Since 1926, the weekday home games of the two clubs had been broadcast. The Cards and Browns stopped the radio transmissions because they believed they were harmful to attendance. The broadcasts were restored in 1935.

One announcer tried to get around the 1934 ban by bootlegging the games from a stepladder atop the YMCA across the street in deepest center field, but Sam Breadon put a stop to the practice.

FEBRUARY 11   The Cardinals sell Flint Rhem to the Phillies.

Transcendental Graphics/theruckerarchive.com

1934 Gas House Gang starters (L–R): Dizzy Dean, Leo Durocher, Ernie Orsatti, Bill DeLancey, Ripper Collins, Joe Medwick, Frankie Frisch, Jack Rothrock, Pepper Martin.

APRIL 17   Dizzy Dean pitches the Cardinals to a 7–1 win over the Pirates in the season opener before 7,500 at Sportsman's Park. Joe Medwick contributed a homer and two singles.

> *Dean had one of the greatest seasons by a pitcher in Cardinals history in 1934. He had a 30–7 record and a 2.66 ERA in 311²/₃ innings over 50 games, 34 of them starts. In addition to his 30 wins, Dean recorded seven saves in his 16 relief appearances. He led the majors in strikeouts with 195, completed 24 games, and won the Most Valuable Player Award. The only pitcher since 1934 with 30 or more wins in a season is Denny McLain, who was 31–6 with the Tigers in 1968. Dizzy was one of two Deans on the 1934 Cardinals. His younger brother Paul, a rookie, won his first seven decisions and finished with a record of 19–11 and a 3.43 ERA in a season in which he didn't turn 21 until August. Cardinal pitchers outside the Dean family gene pool were 46–40 in 1934. Although the press nicknamed Paul Dean "Daffy" as a gimmick to echo his brother's nickname, Paul was actually shy, quiet, and serious, unlike the boisterous, talkative Dizzy.*

MAY 1   Ripper Collins hits two clutch homers during an 11-inning, 3–2 win over the Reds at Sportsman's Park. His first homer tied the score 1–1 in the ninth. After the Reds scored in the top of the eleventh, Collins tied the contest again with his second home run. The Cardinals won the game on a double by Bill DeLancey and a single by Burgess Whitehead.

DeLancey hit .316 with 13 homers in 253 at-bats as a 22-year-old rookie catcher in 1934. He tragically contracted tuberculosis in 1935, however. Except for a 15-game comeback in 1940, DeLancey never played again. He died in 1946 on his 35th birthday.

MAY 3   Joe Medwick hits a grand slam off Phil Collins in the fourth inning of an 8–7 win over the Phillies at Sportsman's Park.

The Cardinals were 2–7 on April 28, but got on the right course by winning 12 of their next 13 games.

MAY 10   An alert steal by Pepper Martin highlights a 5–4 win over the Giants at Sportsman's Park. While New York pitcher Hal Schumacher and shortstop Blondy Ryan held a confab on the mound in the fifth inning, Martin stole second base and later scored on a single.

There were ten player-managers in baseball in 1934. They were Frankie Frisch, Bill Terry (Giants), Charlie Grimm (Cubs), Pie Traynor (Pirates), Jimmie Wilson (Phillies), Bob O'Farrell (Reds), Mickey Cochrane (Tigers), Rogers Hornsby (Browns), Joe Cronin (Senators) and Jimmy Dykes (White Sox).

MAY 15   Jack Rothrock collects five hits, including a homer and a double, in five at-bats, but the Cardinals lose 6–5 to the Dodgers at Sportsman's Park.

Before the game, Joe Medwick and Tex Carleton fought during batting practice. Carleton objected to Medwick taking a turn while the pitchers were hitting.

MAY 18   The Cardinals purchase Phil Collins from the Phillies.

MAY 22   Joe Medwick's bases-loaded triple in the ninth inning beats the Giants 7–4 in New York.

Medwick hit .319 in 1934 and led the league with 18 triples. He also had 40 doubles, 18 homers, 110 runs scored, and 106 RBIs.

MAY 27   Dizzy Dean's homer against a stiff wind in the tenth inning breaks a 2–2 tie against the Phillies in Philadelphia. The Cards added two more runs for a 5–2 victory.

MAY 28   The Cardinals trounce the Phillies 10–0 in Philadelphia.

MAY 30   Joe Medwick collects five hits, including two triples and a double, in five at-bats during a 9–2 victory over the Reds in the second game of a doubleheader in Cincinnati. The Cards also won the first tilt, 9–6.

Although the 1934 World Championship Cardinals, featuring the rowdy, passionate crew that included Dizzy Dean, Joe Medwick, Pepper Martin, Frankie Frisch, and Leo Durocher, has gone into history as the "Gas House Gang," the name wasn't firmly established until late in the 1935 season. The origins of the name are somewhat murky. The most probable explanation derived from a doubleheader the Cards played in Boston in June 1935. It rained during the second game, leaving their uniforms were caked with dirt. The team had to grab a late train to New York for a game against the Giants and there was no time to dry-clean the jerseys. They were still mud-stained when they took the field at the Polo Grounds. A reporter in the press box commented that the Cardinals looked as though they were from the Gas House District, an area on the Lower East Side of Manhattan that housed a number of large gas tanks. It was a rough neighborhood and the subject of many novels and newspaper stories. The neighborhood included a vicious band of thugs known as the Gas House Gang. Influential New York writers and cartoonists began calling the Cardinals the Gas House Gang because of the club's unkempt appearance and its willingness to do anything possible to win, including fisticuffs, and the nickname stuck.

JUNE 1   Dizzy Dean goes on "strike" for a day. He was scheduled to start against the Pirates on June 1 in Pittsburgh, but claimed he had a "sore arm." The Cards lost 4–3 with Wild Bill Hallahan as the starter. Dizzy said he would not work again until Paul received a raise above his $3,000 salary to $5,000. Dizzy returned a day later.

JUNE 2   The Dean brothers pitch the Cardinals to a sweep of the Pirates in Pittsburgh. Dizzy won the opener 13–4 in a complete-game start, and Paul the second 6–3 in a one-inning relief stint.

JUNE 3   Frankie Frisch collects his 2,000th career hit, but the Cardinals lose 4–2 to the Pirates in Pittsburgh.

JUNE 6   Frankie Frisch is banished from a loss against the Cubs at Sportsman's Park after he grabs umpire Cy Rigler's arm in protesting that Joe Medwick was not out at the plate. Rigler responded by striking Frisch with his mask and the other Cardinals attempted to punch the umpire before order was restored. Frisch was not around to see the Cubs scored six runs in the thirteenth inning to win 12–6.

JUNE 13   Leo Durocher makes four errors at shortstop in a 9–0 loss to the Braves at Sportsman's Park.

JUNE 14   Leo Durocher hits an inside-the-park grand slam in the fifth inning off Leo Mangum to break a 6–6 tie and sparks the Cardinals to a 12–9 win over the Braves at Sportsman's Park. Durocher also singled twice and had a total of six RBIs.

JUNE 22   Frankie Frisch collects five hits, including two doubles, in five at-bats to lead the Cardinals to a 7–2 win over the Dodgers at Sportsman's Park.

JUNE 23   The Cardinals sell Flint Rhem to the Red Sox.

JUNE 24   With the temperature in St. Louis at 102 degrees, Dizzy Dean makes light of the situation during a 9–7 loss to the Giants at Sportsman's Park. Dean collected paper wrappers, sticks, old scorecards, and other rubbish and built a bonfire in front of the Cardinal dugout and huddled in front of the fire with several of his teammates, all of them covered in blankets. Dean concluded the act by performing an Indian war dance.

The temperature in St. Louis was 100 or above 30 days during the stifling summer of 1934.

JUNE 25   The Cardinals sell Dazzy Vance to the Reds.

JUNE 26   The Cardinals' hitting rampage results in a 13–7 win over the Dodgers at
             Sportsman's Park.

             Before the game a scene from the movie Death on the Diamond *was filmed.
             The scene started with two Cardinals on base and Ernie Orsatti at bat. Orsatti
             slammed a long drive into left-center where it was kicked around by the fielder,
             who then threw wildly past third. Sprinting toward the plate, Orsatti suddenly
             collapsed in a heap. The Brooklyn catcher rushed out, retrieved the ball, and
             tagged Orsatti, and umpire Bill Klem signaled him out with a grand, sweeping
             gesture. The Cardinals rushed out of the dugout and surrounded their fallen
             teammate.* Death on the Diamond, *starring Robert Young, was released in
             September. In the story, Cardinals players were being murdered one by one.
             Young played a rookie pitcher who solved the mystery.*

JUNE 27   On a day in which the temperature in St. Louis reaches 102 degrees, Bill DeLancey
             hits a walk-off homer in the ninth to beat the Giants 8–7 at Sportsman's Park.

JULY 1   The Cardinals win an 18-inning, 8–6 decision over the Reds at Crosley Field. The
             game developed into a heated battle between Dizzy Dean and Cincinnati's Tony
             Freitas, each of whom hurled 17 innings. The score was 5–5 after nine innings, and
             the tie wasn't broken until the seventeenth inning, when Joe Medwick broke an 0-for-
             19 slump with a solo home run that struck the top of the left-field wall and bounced
             onto the roof of a laundry building across the street. The Reds tied it again 6–6 in the
             bottom of the inning. In the eighteenth, the Cards scored twice off Paul Derringer to
             take an 8–6 lead on RBI singles by Jack Rothrock and Frankie Frisch, but the Reds
             rallied in their half, loading the bases off Jim Lindsey, who relieved Dean. Medwick
             ended the game with a leaping one-handed catch in front of the scoreboard off Jim
             Bottomley's drive. If Medwick had missed the ball, all three runs would have scored.
             The second game resulted in a 2–2 tie, called after five innings by darkness.

JULY 6   The Reds edge the Cardinals 16–15 in a slugfest at Sportsman's Park. The game
             ended when Leo Durocher was thrown out at the plate on a close play. Ripper
             Collins scored five runs after reaching base on a homer, a triple, a single, and two
             walks.

JULY 8   The Dean brothers challenge the Reds bench during an 8–4 loss in the second game
             of a doubleheader at Sportsman's Park. Paul Dean left the mound and headed for
             the Cincinnati dugout after Ray Kolp, whose nickname was "Jockey" for his ability
             to insult opponents, made a stinging remark. Paul was restrained by Ripper Collins.
             Dizzy took up his brother's cause and motioned for Kolp to come out and fight, but
             Dizzy was held back by coach Mike Gonzalez.

JULY 10   Frankie Frisch and Joe Medwick both hit home runs in the All-Star Game, but
             the National League loses 9–7 at the Polo Grounds in New York. Frisch homered
             off Lefty Gomez leading off the first inning, and Medwick hit a three-run shot off
             Gomez in the third.

             *Cardinal batters accounted for three of the first four All-Star Game home runs,
             and Frisch had two of the first three. In the first Midsummer Classic, played in
             1933, Frisch and Babe Ruth both hit home runs.*

JULY 20   In Boston, Tex Carleton retires the first 20 batters to face him before Wally Berger of the Braves homers. Carleton settled for a five-hit, 5–1 complete-game win.

JULY 22   On the day that John Dillinger is shot by FBI agents outside of a movie theater in Chicago, Dazzy Vance records his 2,000th career strikeout during a 6–4 win over the Braves in the second game of a doubleheader in Boston. Wally Berger was the victim of the milestone in the eighth inning. The Cardinals also won the first game, 5–4.

JULY 23   Ripper Collins collects five hits, including a homer, in five at-bats during a 6–5 win over the Giants in New York. Dizzy Dean recorded his 10th win in a row and 18th on the season.

> *Collins was sensational in 1934 with a .333 batting average and league-leading totals in home runs (35) and slugging percentage (.615). He also had 116 runs scored, 40 doubles, 12 triples, and 126 RBIs.*

AUGUST 7   Dizzy Dean records his 20th win with a 2–0 decision over the Reds in the first game of a doubleheader at Crosley Field. Cincinnati won the second contest 9–2.

AUGUST 8   The Cardinals score six runs in the twelfth inning to defeat the Reds 10–4 in Cincinnati. Just a day after pitching a complete game, Dizzy Dean earned his 21st victory with three innings of relief.

AUGUST 9   The Cardinals sign Elmer Dean, the older brother of Dizzy and Paul, to work as a ballpark vendor. Elmer lasted just three days and returned to his former job—selling peanuts at the home games of the Houston Buffs, a Cardinals minor league team.

AUGUST 10   The Cardinals score nine runs in the third inning and hammer the Cubs 17–3 at Sportsman's Park.

AUGUST 13   Dizzy Dean and Paul Dean leave the Cardinals.

> *After the Dean brothers were the losing pitchers in both ends of a doubleheader against the Cubs at Sportsman's Park on August 12, they refused to go to Detroit for an exhibition game. Dizzy was fined $100 and Paul $50 by Frankie Frisch. When Frisch refused to rescind the fines, Dizzy declared, "Then me and Paul are through with the Cardinals." The Deans refused to take the field for the August 14 game against the Phillies in St. Louis. Frisch asked for their uniforms and Dizzy ripped his to shreds. Then he destroyed another one for the benefit of photographers. (The club billed him $36 for the cost of two new uniforms.) Dizzy was suspended for ten days, but Frisch reduced it to seven. Dizzy requested a hearing with Commissioner Landis, held on August 20. Landis upheld the suspension. Paul was suspended for three days and returned to the club on August 17.*

AUGUST 17   Paul Dean, pitching for the first time since his suspension, pitches seven innings of relief and is the winning pitcher in a 12–2 decision over the Phillies at Sportsman's Park.

AUGUST 18   The Cardinals collect 20 hits and swamp the Braves 15–0 at Sportsman's Park.

AUGUST 28   The Cardinals collect only four hits, but all four are by consecutive batters in the sixth inning that produce two runs for a 2–0 win over the Dodgers at Sportsman's Park. The hits were singles by Leo Durocher, Paul Dean, and Burgess Whitehead and a double by Jack Rothrock, all off Ray Benge. Dean pitched the complete-game shutout.

Whitehead was a Phi Beta Kappa at the University of North Carolina.

SEPTEMBER 4   While the Cardinals are idle, the Giants win a doubleheader 3–2 and 6–5 against the Phillies. The wins put the Giants seven games ahead of the Cardinals and Cubs, who were tied for second with records of 75–53. The Giants had 24 games left to play, and the Cardinals and Cubs had 26.

The Cardinals won 20 of the remaining 25 games. One postponed game was not rescheduled.

SEPTEMBER 9   Joe Medwick extends his hitting streak to 28 games in the first game of a doubleheader at Philadelphia, a 6–1 Cardinal win. The Cardinals also won the second contest 7–3, but Medwick was unable to play because of injury. Medwick's streak ended when he returned to action on September 11.

SEPTEMBER 13   Heading into action trailing the Giants by 5½ games, the Cardinals beat the New York club 2–0 in 12 innings at the Polo Grounds. Paul Dean pitched the complete-game shutout. The twelfth-inning runs scored on a sacrifice fly by Joe Medwick and a single by Leo Durocher. The Cards survived a score in the bottom of the twelfth when Dean issued a walk and George Watkins hit a long foul drive that missed being a home run by three feet.

SEPTEMBER 16   Before 62,573 in New York, the Cardinals sweep the Giants 5–3 and 3–1. The second game went 11 innings. Pepper Martin's homer in the eleventh broke a 1–1 tie. Dizzy Dean was the winning pitcher in the opener, and Paul Dean in the nightcap.

The wins cut the Giants' pennant race margin to 3½ games. The Cards had 12 games left and the Giants 14.

SEPTEMBER 20   The Cardinals sweep the Braves 4–1 and 1–0 in Boston behind the pitching of Tex Carleton in the first game and Bill Walker in the second.

SEPTEMBER 21   After Dizzy Dean pitches a three-hit shutout for a 13–0 victory in the first game of a doubleheader against the Dodgers in Brooklyn, Paul Dean follows with a no-hitter in the second tilt for a 3–0 win. Dizzy had a no-hitter until Buzz Boyle beat out a slow roller for a single with one out in the eighth inning. Paul struck out six. The only base runner off Paul was Len Koenicke on a walk in the first inning. After that, the younger Dean brother retired 25 batters in a row. In the ninth he fanned Jim Bucher, Johnny McCarthy on a pop-up to Frankie Frisch at second, and Buzz Boyle on a grounder to Leo Durocher at short.

SEPTEMBER 25   Dizzy Dean pitches the Cardinals to a 3–2 win over the Pirates at Sportsman's Park while the Giants lose 4–0 to the Phillies. The win put the Cardinals one game back of the Giants. The Cards had six games left, and the Giants four.

FPG/Hulton Archive/Getty Images

The more serious and shy brother, rookie Paul "Daffy" Dean (left) joined his brother Dizzy on the 1934 Cardinals pitching staff. Dizzy predicted that they would combine to win 45 games. Instead, they won 49.

SEPTEMBER 27   The Cardinals beat the Reds 8–5 at Sportsman's Park to pull within one-half game of the Giants.

SEPTEMBER 28   With the Giants idle, the Cardinals defeat the Reds 4–0 at Sportsman's Park to tie for first place. On two days' rest, Dizzy Dean pitched the shutout for his 29th win. The Cards and Giants each had two games left.

SEPTEMBER 29   Paul Dean pitches the Cardinals into first place with a 6–1 win over the Reds at Sportsman's Park. The Giants lost 5–1 to the Dodgers in New York. The Cards had a one-game lead with one game left to play.

SEPTEMBER 30   The Cardinals clinch the pennant with a 9–0 victory over the Reds before 35,274 at Sportsman's Park. Dizzy Dean hurled the shutout on only one day of rest. It was his 30th win of the season. The Giants lost 8–5 to the Dodgers in New York.

The Cardinals' opponent in the World Series was the Detroit Tigers. Mickey Cochrane was the manager and starting catcher. The Tigers reached the Series for the first time since 1909 with a record of 101–53.

OCTOBER 3   The Cardinals open the 1934 World Series with an 8–3 win over the Tigers in Detroit. Dizzy Dean pitched the complete game, allowing eight hits. The Cards scored twice in the second inning to take a 2–0 lead and never trailed in the contest. Joe Medwick was the batting star with a homer and three singles in five at-bats. The Tigers contributed to their demise by making five errors.

The Cardinals were almost completely rebuilt between winning the pennants of 1931 and 1934. The only players on the World Series roster on both clubs were Ripper Collins, Frankie Frisch, Jesse Haines, Wild Bill Hallahan, Pepper Martin, and Ernie Orsatti. Haines and Hallahan were the only players on the World Series rosters of the Cardinals in 1926, 1928, 1930, 1931, and 1934.

OCTOBER 4   The Tigers even the Series with a 12-inning, 2–1 victory over the Cardinals in Detroit. The Cards led 2–1 heading into the bottom of the ninth, but Wild Bill Hallahan allowed a run to tie the contest. The Tigers won it in the twelfth on two walks and a walk-off single by Goose Goslin against Bill Walker. Schoolboy Rowe went all 12 innings for Detroit.

OCTOBER 5   The Cardinals regain the lead in the Series with a 4–1 win over the Tigers in Game Three before 34,073 at Sportsman's Park. Paul Dean stranded 13 runners in pitching a complete game.

Policemen worked in two-hour shifts guarding Dizzy Dean while he slept in his room at the Forest Park Hotel in St. Louis because Sam Breadon feared a possible kidnapping.

OCTOBER 6   The Tigers even the Series again by belting the Cardinals 10–4 in Game Four before 37,492 at Sportsman's Park. The Cards made five errors. The game was tied 4–4 after six innings before the Tigers scored a run in the seventh and five in the eighth off Bill Walker. Dizzy Dean pinch-ran in the fourth inning, failed to slide while running to second, and caught shortstop Billy Rogell's throw right on the head. Dean was carried off the field on a stretcher and taken to the hospital. X-rays of his noggin found nothing amiss.

OCTOBER 7   A day after being conked in the head, Dizzy Dean takes the mound and loses 3–1 to the Tigers before 38,536 at Sportsman's Park. Tommy Bridges pitched a complete game for Detroit. The lone St. Louis run scored on a homer by Bill DeLancey in the seventh inning. The loss put the Cardinals behind three games to two in the Series. To take the World Championship, the Cards needed to win twice in Detroit.

OCTOBER 8   The Cardinals stay alive in the World Series by taking Game Six 4–3 in Detroit. The score was 3–3 in the seventh when Leo Durocher hit a one-out double and scored on Paul Dean's single. The younger Dean brother went on to pitch a complete game.

OCTOBER 9   The Cardinals take their third World Championship by defeating the Tigers 11–0 in Game Seven in Detroit. Frankie Frisch sent Dizzy Dean to the mound in the winner-take-all contest on just one day of rest. Dean responded with a six-hit shutout and hit a double and a single. The drama was over quickly as the Cards jumped all over Tiger starter Eldon Auker for seven runs in the third inning. St. Louis added two more runs in the sixth to make the score 9–0. During the inning, Joe Medwick slid hard into third baseman Marv Owen on a triple. Medwick knocked Owen over, and as he fell, Owen stepped on Medwick's shin. As both lay on the ground, Medwick kicked Owen in the chest. As they scrambled to their feet, the two squared off but were separated before any blows could be struck. When Medwick took his defensive position in left field in the bottom of the sixth, he was pelted with bottles and garbage by angry Detroit fans. The Tigers sold the bleachers on an unreserved general admission basis, and many fans arrived early in the morning to get the choice seats, bringing their lunches in picnic baskets and brown paper bags. With plenty of leftover food in their possession, in addition to apple cores, banana peels, chicken bones, and other assorted remnants of their midday meal, the fans seemed to have an inexhaustible supply of ammunition to throw at Medwick. He went to the field three times and retreated to the dugout on each occasion under a barrage of refuse. Efforts to quell the crowd proved futile, and faced with the possibility of a riot with the Cardinals holding an almost insurmountable nine-run lead, Commissioner Kenesaw Landis removed Medwick from the game "for his own safety." The delay lasted 17 minutes, and Chick Fullis took Medwick's place in left. Dean had to wait out the delay, and when play resumed, he retired Mickey Cochrane, Charlie Gehringer, and Goose Goslin, all future Hall of Famers, on three pitches.

Before the Series began, Dizzy Dean boasted, "Me and Paul'll win four games." He was proved correct as Dizzy and Paul Dean accounted for all four Cardinals victories in the World Series, each winning twice. "I'm glad the Deans aren't triplets," said Tiger pitcher Schoolboy Rowe. Counting the postseason, the duo won 53 games in 1934. From September 25 through October 9, Dizzy made six starts in a span of 15 days, and completed each of them with three shutouts.

OCTOBER 20   St. Louis businessman Samuel Long is judged to be legally competent because he predicted that the Cardinals would play in the World Series. Long was the 81-year-old president of a warehouse company who sought in probate court to have a guardianship imposed by his children removed so that he could run his own business. During the court proceedings, Long testified that with two weeks remaining in the 1934 season, he predicted the Cards would play in the Fall Classic even though they were four games out of first place. Long cited baseball prophecy as proof of his mental alertness. The judge agreed, and Long was free to make his own decisions.

OCTOBER 26   The Cardinals trade Ken O'Dea to the Cubs for Pat Malone.

NOVEMBER 3   The Cardinals sell Ivan Goodman and Lew Riggs to the Reds for $60,000.

The Cardinals gave up two good ballplayers. Goodman and Riggs became starters with the Reds for several years, with Goodman in right field and Riggs at third base. Riggs appeared in the 1936 All-Star Game. Goodman played for Cincinnati in both the 1939 and 1940 World Series and appeared in two All-Star games.

NOVEMBER 21   The Cardinals send Tex Carleton to the Cubs for Bud Tinning, Dick Ward, and cash.

DECEMBER 12   The National League votes to allow its club to install lights for night baseball beginning with the 1935 season.

Three clubs—the Reds, Cubs, and Cardinals—expressed interest in staging night games. The Reds went ahead with plans, and played the first of seven 1935 night games on May 24 against the Phillies. Cubs owner P. K. Wrigley was intrigued with the notion, but decided against night play. By 1948, the Cubs were the only club in the majors playing day games only. The first night game at Wrigley Field didn't occur until 1988. An enthusiastic proponent of night baseball, Sam Breadon would have installed lights at Sportsman's Park in 1935 if he owned the ballpark. The Browns held title to the facility, however, and refused to allow the lights to be added. The Cards didn't play regular-season night games at home until 1940. The Cards did, however, play night exhibition games at Sportsman's Park as early as 1932. The barnstorming House of David team traveled with a portable lighting system, and the Cardinals played several games against the club at night.

DECEMBER 13   The Cardinals sell Johnny Mize to the Reds for $55,000.

The Reds acquired Mize on a conditional basis from the Cardinals. He played well enough for the Reds during spring training to win the starting first base job, but doctors determined that a groin injury would require surgery and put him out of action for months. Leery of investing in "damaged goods," the Reds returned his contract to St. Louis. The Cardinals were extremely fortunate that the Reds passed on Mize. He had the operation and began playing in mid-season in 1935 with the Cardinals farm club in Rochester. A future Hall of Famer and one of the greatest sluggers ever to wear a Cardinals uniform, Mize played for the club from 1936 through 1941, and had a batting average of .336, an on-base percentage of .419, and a slugging percentage of .600. He clubbed 158 homers. Mize remained in the majors until 1953 and hit 359 home runs despite missing three full seasons during World War II.

1935

Season in a Sentence

After trailing by 9½ games in the pennant race in July, the Gas House Gang Cardinals take a three-game lead in September only to finish second to the Cubs.

Finish • Won • Lost • Pct • GB

Second   96   58   .623   4.0

Manager

Frankie Frisch

Stats

	Cards	NL	Rank
Batting Avg:	.284	.277	4
On-Base Pct:	.335	.331	4
Slugging Pct:	.405	.391	3
Home Runs:	86		4
Stolen Bases:	71		2
ERA:	3.52	4.02	3
Fielding Avg:	.972	.968	1
Runs Scored:	829		2
Runs Allowed:	625		2

Starting Lineup

Bill DeLancey, c
Ripper Collins, 1b
Frankie Frisch, 2b
Pepper Martin, 3b
Leo Durocher, ss
Joe Medwick, lf
Terry Moore, cf
Jack Rothrock, rf
Burgess Whitehead, 2b
Spud Davis, c
Ernie Orsatti, rf-cf
Charlie Gelbert, 3b-ss

Pitchers

Dizzy Dean, sp-rp
Paul Dean, sp-rp
Bill Walker, sp-rp
Wild Bill Hallahan, sp-rp
Ed Heusser, rp-sp
Jesse Haines, rp-sp
Phil Collins, rp-sp

Attendance

506,084 (third in NL)

Club Leaders

Batting Avg:	Medwick	.353
On-Base Pct:	Medwick	.386
Slugging Pct:	Medwick	.576
Home Runs:	Medwick	23
	Collins	23
RBIs:	Medwick	126
Runs:	Medwick	132
Stolen Bases:	Martin	20
Wins:	D. Dean	28
Strikeouts:	D. Dean	190
ERA:	D. Dean	3.04
Saves:	D. Dean	5
	P. Dean	5

MARCH 26   The Cardinals sell Pat Malone to the Yankees for $15,000.

MARCH 28   Sam Breadon states that he might transfer the Cardinals to Detroit, but that there was no immediate prospect of the shift. Breadon was concerned because of low attendance figures for Cardinals games at Sportsman's Park. In 1934, with one of the most colorful clubs in big-league history and that won a pennant on the final day of the season, the Cards drew only 325,056 at home, the fifth-best figure in the National League and the tenth-best in the majors. The average home attendance for clubs in the big leagues in 1934 was 435,232. The Cardinals' attendance in 1935 improved to 506,084.

APRIL 16   The Cardinals lose 4–3 to the Cubs in the season opener at Wrigley Field on a day in which the high temperature in Chicago was 34 degrees. Dizzy Dean left the game in the first inning when he was hit in the left ankle on a drive by Freddie Lindstrom. Dean was carried from the field, but was able to make another start five days later.

APRIL 18   Paul Dean pitches the Cardinals to a 1–0 win over the Cubs in Chicago. Joe Medwick accounted for the lone run of the game with a homer in the sixth inning off Larry French.

Paul Dean followed a rookie season in which he won 19 games with a 19–12 record and a 3.37 ERA in 1935. It was his last effective season, however, as arm miseries curtailed his abilities when he was only 23 years old. After winning five games early in the 1936 season, Dean won only seven more big-league games.

APRIL 23   In the home opener, the Cardinals win 9–5 over the Cubs before 10,000 at Sportsman's Park.

APRIL 28   The Central Trades and Labor Union of St. Louis votes to boycott the Cardinals because of remarks and actions by Leo Durocher.

The previous February, Durocher caused the arrest of a female picket of the Garment Workers' Union for disturbing the peace. The woman was fined $240 in city court when Durocher prosecuted the case. Durocher's wife, Grace, was employed as a buyer and designer at the place being picketed. Leo accused the woman of trying to molest his wife as she entered the factory and trying to strike him as he sat in his automobile. The Cardinals' shortstop also publicly criticized the pickets. The citation of the Central Trades body asked union members to stay away from Sportsman's Park. The union also set up pickets at the ballpark.

MAY 5   Dizzy Dean faces Babe Ruth for the first time during the regular season when the Cardinals play the Braves in Boston. Before Ruth's second at-bat, Dean waved his outfielders back to the fences, then proceeded to strike out the Babe on four pitches. Dean not only beat the Braves 7–0, but also hit a home run.

Dean had a record of 28–12 with an ERA of 3.04. His workload was brutal. Dean led the league in starts with 36 and complete games with 29, in addition to making 14 relief appearances. He recorded five saves in addition to the 28 wins. He also topped the NL in innings pitched (325$\frac{1}{3}$) and strikeouts (190).

MAY 11   The Cardinals wallop the Phillies 15–6 in the first game of a doubleheader in Philadelphia before losing the nightcap 5–2.

MAY 13   Leo Durocher's two-out homer in the tenth inning beats the Giants 3–2 in New York.

The Cardinals started slowly in 1935 with a 12–12 record after 24 games.

MAY 21   Dizzy Dean is ejected from a 7–6 loss to the Phillies at Sportsman's Park. In the fourth inning with Paul Dean pitching for the Cards, Philadelphia coach Hans Lobert made a remark that inspired Paul to challenge Lobert, who was 53 years old, to a fight. Dizzy jumped off the bench to defend his younger brother. In the fifth inning, Phillies catcher Al Todd was hit by a pitch thrown by Paul. Todd headed for the mound, but was blocked by Dizzy, who again leaped from the dugout to protect his sibling. Several punches were thrown, and Dizzy was escorted off the field by police officers to the cheers of the home crowd, which was upset over his actions.

JUNE 1   Paul Dean pitches a 12-inning complete game and scores the winning run in a 4–3 win over Cubs in the first game of a doubleheader in Chicago. The Cards also won the second game, 8–4.

JUNE 2   The Cardinals stage a sensational five-run rally in the ninth inning to beat the Cubs 6–5 in Chicago. The rally was climaxed by a grand slam by Ripper Collins off Larry French.

JUNE 3   Pepper Martin extends his hitting streak to 23 games during a 6–2 loss to the Cubs in Chicago.

JUNE 4   During a 9–4 loss to the Pirates in Pittsburgh, Dizzy Dean turns petulant when his Cardinal teammates make two errors in the third inning leading to four unearned runs. Dean began lobbing the ball and the Pirates scored four more times leading to a dispute in the dugout with Joe Medwick. Dizzy and Paul Dean advanced on Medwick, who grabbed a bat to defend himself before their teammates got between them. Frisch threatened to fine Dean $5,000 and suspend him indefinitely if he ever had reason to believe that Dean was not bearing down at any time in the future. Dean responded by demanding a trade.

JUNE 8   Ripper Collins hits a walk-off homer in the eleventh inning to defeat the Cubs 6–5 in the second game of a doubleheader at Sportsman's Park. Chicago won the first game 4–3. Charlie Gelbert made his first start since 1932. He missed the entire 1933 and 1934 seasons following a hunting accident (see November 16, 1932).

Collins hit .313 with 23 homers, 122 RBIs, and 109 runs scored in 1935. He hit homers in five consecutive games from June 20 through 23.

JUNE 9   At Sportsman's Park, Dizzy Dean is the target of fans, who threw lemons and booed lustily as he took the mound against the Cubs. Fans were still seething over Dean action's in his previous start (see June 4, 1935). Dean went on to beat Chicago 13–2. The Cards scored in every inning.

The June 4 incident in Pittsburgh marked a turning point in the relationship between Dean and baseball fans nationwide. During his first three seasons in the majors, he was one of the most popular athletic heroes in America and made several hundred thousand dollars in the depths of the Great Depression in personal appearances and endorsements. But by 1935, his self-absorbed, hot-tempered, emotional outbursts were no longer viewed as the work of a fun-loving eccentric. Because of the adverse publicity, businesses stopped contacting him to help to endorse their products. Sales of those already on the market came to a virtual halt. Dean would eventually realize that his actions were counterproductive. With a more mature attitude, he restored his reputation, but it took several years.

JUNE 10   The Cardinals suffer rough treatment during an exhibition game against a semipro team called the Automotive Twins at Bridgeport, Connecticut. In center field, Terry Moore was accosted and thrown to the crowd by a group of ruffians who stole his cap and tried to take his shoes before Moore fought them off. Many gloves, caps, and baseballs were stolen. Reserve infielder Charlie Wilson was dragged from a taxicab outside the park and was badly bruised. Others who were assaulted included Ernie Orsatti, Spud Davis, and Ray Harrell.

JUNE 23   The Cardinals hammer the Dodgers 16–2 in the first game of a doubleheader at Ebbets Field. Brooklyn won the second contest 10–6.

JUNE 28   Joe Medwick hits for the cycle, but the Cardinals lose 8–6 to the Reds in Cincinnati. The homer was struck in the ninth inning and hit the foul pole just above the fence.

Medwick hit .353 with 132 runs, 224 hits, 46 doubles, 13 triples, 23 homers, and 126 RBIs in 1935.

JULY 4   Ernie Orsatti collects five hits, including a triple, in six at-bats to lead the Cardinals to a 12-inning, 5–3 win over the Cubs in the first game of a doubleheader in Chicago. The Cards completed the sweep with a 6–4 victory in the second fray.

JULY 8   With Frankie Frisch as manager of the National League squad, Bill Walker starts for the NL in the All-Star Game, but allows three runs in two innings. The American League won 4–1 at Municipal Stadium in Cleveland.

JULY 13   Wild Bill Hallahan pitches a two-hitter to defeat the Phillies 4–0 at Sportsman's Park. The only Philadelphia hits were singles by Johnny Moore and Dolph Camilli. It was the Cardinals' eighth win in a row.

JULY 14   The 1934 World Championship pennant is raised in ceremonies before a doubleheader against the Phillies at Sportsman's Park. Commissioner Kenesaw Landis and NL president Ford Frick handed out diamond rings to players on the 1934 club. The Cardinals swept the twin bill 5–1 and 10–1 to extend their winning streak to 10 games.

JULY 15   The St. Louis winning streak reaches 11 with a 13–6 victory over the Braves at Sportsman's Park.

JULY 17   A walk-off homer by Terry Moore in the ninth inning beats the Braves 2–1 at Sportsman's Park. It was the Cardinals' 13th win a row.

JULY 18   The Cardinals crush the Braves 13–3 for their 14th consecutive win.

              The winning streak cut the Giants' margin over the Cards to three games in the NL pennant race. The 14-game winning streak is the modern club record. No other Cardinal team since 1900 has won more than 12 in succession.

JULY 21   The Cardinals sweep the Dodgers 13–7 and 7–5 at Sportsman's Park.

JULY 22   Paul Dean strikes out 12 batters to beat the Giants 6–1 in the first game of a doubleheader at Sportsman's Park. The win was the 18th in a span of 19 games for the Cards and put them into first place. The Giants regained the top spot with an 8–2 win in the nightcap.

JULY 31   In the first regular-season night game ever played by the Cardinals, an uncontrollable sellout crowd witnesses a 10-inning, 4–3 Reds victory over the Cards in Cincinnati.

              The capacity of Crosley Field at the time was 26,000, but an estimated 35,000 to 40,000 squeezed into the park. Fans stood 12 deep all around the diamond and against the outfield wall. The contest was delayed for 25 minutes in the third inning when many of the unruly fans scampered across the outfield. Order was restored by the arrival of the riot squad of the Cincinnati police and the threat of a forfeit to the Cardinals. Players couldn't see the action from the dugout and had difficulty making their way to the playing field through the crush of fans. The two managers had to call out to fans to find out what was happening on the field. In the eighth, when play was stopped to tend to an injured player, Kitty Burke, a young woman in the crowd near home plate, grabbed the bat from the hands of Reds outfielder Babe Herman and pranced up to the batter's box. Paul Dean tossed an underhanded pitch that Miss Burke grounded to first base. She later toured the burlesque circuit as the only woman to "bat" in the major leagues. Somehow, in the midst of the pandemonium, a baseball game was played. The Reds won it on a walk-off single by Billy Sullivan.

AUGUST 6   Dizzy Dean hits a three-run, walk-off homer in the tenth inning to defeat the Reds 6–3 at Sportsman's Park.

AUGUST 16   Dizzy Dean pitches the Cardinals to a 1–0 win over the Giants in New York. Joe Medwick's sacrifice fly in the ninth inning drove in Pepper Martin with the winning run.

Martin hit .299 and scored 121 runs in 1935.

AUGUST 18   Leo Durocher hits a grand slam off Huck Betts in the Cardinals' five-run tenth inning that defeats the Braves 9–4 in the second game of a doubleheader in Boston. The Braves won the first game 2–1.

AUGUST 21   The Cardinals trounce the Braves 13–3 in Boston. Pepper Martin hit the first pitch of the game for a homer off Bob Smith.

AUGUST 23   The Cardinals score seven runs in the sixth inning of an 11–5 win over the Dodgers in Brooklyn. The Cards also won the first game, 6–1.

AUGUST 24   The Cardinals score four runs in the ninth inning to defeat the Dodgers 10–7 in Brooklyn.

AUGUST 25   The Cardinals extend their winning streak to eight games and take first place by sweeping a doubleheader 10–3 and 6–1 over the Dodgers in Brooklyn.

AUGUST 28   The Cardinals sweep a doubleheader from the Phillies 5–1 and 13–5 in Philadelphia. In the opener, Terry Moore had three doubles and a homer. In the second tilt, a nine-run St. Louis second inning broke a 2–2 tie.

> *The best defensive outfielder of his era, and one of the best of all time, Moore was with the Cardinals from 1935 through 1948. He played in four All-Star games in each season from 1939 through 1942, and might have appeared in a few more, if he hadn't spent the 1943, 1944, and 1945 seasons in the service. In addition to his play on the field, Moore was a respected leader in the clubhouse.*

SEPTEMBER 2 The Cardinals win 4–3 in 16 innings in the first game of a doubleheader against the Pirates at Sportsman's Park. Two Cardinal runs in the ninth sent the game into extra innings. The winning run scored on a double by Joe Medwick and a single by Ripper Collins. The second game lasted only five innings because of darkness. The Cards also won that contest, 4–1.

SEPTEMBER 5 Terry Moore collects six hits, including a double, in six at-bats during a 15–3 win over the Braves at Sportsman's Park. The win put the Cardinals three games up on the Giants and Cubs, who were tied for second.

SEPTEMBER 8 The Cardinals win the opener of a doubleheader 11–0 against the Phillies at Sportsman's Park, before falling 4–2 in the second game.

SEPTEMBER 11   The Cardinals score seven runs in the third inning of a 10–2 win over the Phillies at Sportsman's Park.

SEPTEMBER 14   The Cardinals are knocked out of first place with an 11-inning, 5–4 loss to the Giants at Sportsman's Park. The Cubs, in the midst of a 21-game winning streak, took over the top spot in the National League.

SEPTEMBER 15   An overflow crowd of 41,284, the largest ever for a single game at Sportsman's Park, watches the Cardinals lose 7–3 to the Giants. The defeat dropped the Cards two games behind the Cubs. In the eighth, a bottle fell at the feet of Giants right fielder Mel Ott. He charged toward the crowd ringing the outfield to find the individual who threw the bottle, and other members of the New York team rushed to the scene. Fans gathered around the players, but police quickly restored order.

SEPTEMBER 16   Paul Dean pitches the Cardinals to a 1–0 win over the Dodgers at Sportsman's Park. Frankie Frisch drove in the lone run of the game with a single in the first inning.

SEPTEMBER 22   The Cardinals sweep the Reds 14–4 and 2–1 in a doubleheader at Sportsman's Park. The second game was Dizzy Dean's 28th win.

SEPTEMBER 27   The pennant hopes of the Gas House Gang are gassed when the Cubs clinch the pennant with 6–2 and 5–3 wins over the Cardinals at Sportsman's Park.

SEPTEMBER 28   Joe Medwick's two-run, walk-off homer in the eleventh inning beats the Cubs 7–5 at Sportsman's Park. The Cardinal victory ended Chicago's 21-game winning streak.

DECEMBER 9   The Cardinals send Burgess Whitehead to the Giants for Roy Parmelee, Phil Weintraub, and cash.

1936

Season in a Sentence

The Cardinals spend 85 days in first place, but one of the worst pitching staffs in the league results in a second-place finish.

Finish • Won • Lost • Pct • GB

Second (tie) 87 67 .565 5.0

Manager

Frankie Frisch

Stats

Stats	Cards	NL	Rank
Batting Avg:	.281	.278	3
On-Base Pct:	.336	.335	5
Slugging Pct:	.410	.386	1
Home Runs:	88		3
Stolen Bases:	69		1
ERA:	4.47	4.02	7
Fielding Avg:	.974	.969	2
Runs Scored:	795		2
Runs Allowed:	794		7

Starting Lineup

Spud Davis, c
Johnny Mize, 1b
Stu Martin, 2b
Charlie Gelbert, 3b-ss
Leo Durocher, ss
Joe Medwick, lf
Terry Moore, cf
Pepper Martin, rf
Frankie Frisch, 2b
Ripper Collins, 1b
Bruce Ogrodowski, c
Art Garibaldi, 3b-2b

Pitchers

Dizzy Dean, sp-rp
Roy Parmelee, sp
Jim Winford, sp-rp
Paul Dean, sp
Bill Walker, sp-rp
Ed Heusser, rp
Jesse Haines, rp-sp

Attendance

448,078 (fourth in NL)

Club Leaders

Batting Avg:	Medwick	.351
On-Base Pct:	Mize	.402
Slugging Pct:	Mize	.577
	Medwick	.577
Home Runs:	Mize	19
RBIs:	Medwick	138
Runs:	Martin	121
Stolen Bases:	Martin	23
Wins:	D. Dean	24
Strikeouts:	D. Dean	195
ERA:	D. Dean	3.17
Saves:	D. Dean	11

MARCH 5   The Cardinals begin a four-game series in Havana, Cuba, playing a team of Cuban all-stars.

APRIL 14   The Cardinals lose the season opener 12–7 to the Cubs before 14,000 at Sportsman's Park. Dizzy Dean went six innings and allowed seven runs and 14 hits. Leo Durocher collected four hits, including three doubles, in four at-bats. Terry Moore picked up three hits. Appearing in the game as a pinch hitter in the seventh inning, Eddie Morgan stroked a home run in his first major league at-bat.

Morgan played in only six games with the Cardinals and just 37 in his career. The home run struck in his first plate appearance proved to be the only one of his big-league career. Morgan hit .212 in 66 at-bats in the majors.

APRIL 16   Johnny Mize makes his major league debut during a 5–3 loss to the Cubs at Sportsman's Park. He was hitless in one at-bat as a pinch hitter.

Mize started the season on the bench behind Ripper Collins. Mize soon worked his way into the starting lineup and finished his rookie campaign with a .329 batting average and 19 home runs.

APRIL 20   The Cardinals score five runs in the ninth inning to stun the Reds 8–7 at Sportsman's Park. Frankie Frisch closed the gap to 7–6 with a bases-loaded double. After an error put another Cardinal on base, Joe Medwick hit a two-run, walk-off double.

Due to an agreement between the Cardinals and Browns, only the home games of both clubs were broadcast on radio. Sunday and holiday contests were blacked out. The games were broadcast simultaneously on two stations. France Laux was the main announcer on KMOX and Ray Schmidt on KWK. Both men covered both St. Louis clubs.

APRIL 22   Cardinal rookie right fielder Lou Scoffic loses a fly ball in the sun, which leads to a 7–6 loss to the Reds at Sportsman's Park. In the sixth inning, Cincinnati's Calvin Chapman hit an easy fly ball toward Scoffic that landed 30 feet away from him. Chapman circled the bases for what proved to be the only home run of his big-league career. Scoffic's stay in the majors lasted only four games, although he left with a .429 batting average in seven at-bats.

APRIL 29   The Cardinals win a 17-inning marathon 2–1 over the Giants at Sportsman's Park. Both Roy Parmelee, whom the Cardinals acquired from New York the previous offseason, and Carl Hubbell pitched all 17 innings. Parmelee allowed only six hits. The game was scoreless until the twelfth when both clubs plated a run. The winning run scored on a double by Spud Davis, a walk, and two Giants errors.

APRIL 30   Johnny Mize hits his first major league homer during a 3–2 win over the Giants at Sportsman's Park. The pitching victim was Harry Gumbert.

MAY 1   The Cardinals clobber the Dodgers 12–0 at Sportsman's Park.

MAY 8   The Cardinals score in every inning but the second and defeat the Cubs 11–9 in Chicago.

MAY 12   Leo Durocher and Dodgers manager Casey Stengel tangle after a 5–2 Cardinal loss against the Dodgers at Ebbets Field.

Stengel and Durocher bickered at each other across the diamond all afternoon and settled their differences under the grandstand immediately after the game. Durocher claimed Stengel hit him with a bat, but Casey said that Leo merely thought it was a bat that hit him. Stengel said that it was just a good old-fashioned right hook.

MAY 14   The Cardinals score seven runs in the seventh inning and defeat the Dodgers 12–4 in Brooklyn.

MAY 17   Joe Medwick collects a homer, two triples, and a single during a 10–3 win over the Phillies in Philadelphia.

During the club's stay in Philadelphia, Pepper Martin, Dizzy Dean, and Heinie Schuble pulled a prank at the Bellevue-Stratford Hotel. Garbed in overalls, donning long-peaked caps, and carrying ladders and hammers, the three posed as carpenters. They first visited the banquet room, where about 200 people were attending a Rotary luncheon, and went about the business of inspecting the place for repairs by moving tables and unseating many of Philadelphia's leading citizens. After those attending the banquet learned the identity of the "carpenters," the three ballplayers were invited to join those at the head table. Later, Martin, Dean, and Schuble visited several other parts of the hotel, going through the same antics, finally invading a meeting of the United Boys' Club of America, where they got into a mock disagreement over work to be done and Dean bashed Martin to the floor with a resounding crack of his open hand. Cardinal management took a dim view of the shenanigans, however, which squashed a repeat performance.

MAY 29   The Cardinals come from behind to defeat the Pirates 9–7 at Sportsman's Park. Down 5–0, the Cards scored six runs in the fifth, trailed again 7–6 heading into the eighth, then scored three times for the victory.

MAY 31   Dizzy Dean gives up nine hits, eight of them for extra bases, but beats the Reds 8–7 in 12 innings at Sportsman's Park. The Cardinals scored twice in the ninth to send the game into extra innings. Stu Martin drove in the winning run with a single.

On the same day, the Cardinals sold Wild Bill Hallahan to the Reds.

JUNE 3   The Cardinals defeat the Dodgers 7–3 at Sportsman's Park.

The win gave the Cards a record of 30–14 and a four-game lead in the NL pennant race.

JUNE 9   A grand slam by Johnny Mize off Johnny Lanning in the first inning sparks the Cardinals to a 7–5 win over the Braves at Sportsman's Park.

Mize played the outfield for the first time in his career during the game. The experiment lasted only eight games, and Mize returned to first base.

JUNE 12   Ripper Collins hits a walk-off homer in the eleventh inning that beats the Phillies 3–2 at Sportsman's Park.

JUNE 14   The Cardinals win a 12–10 slugfest against the Phillies at Sportsman's Park. The Cards scored three times in the eighth inning to break a 9–9 tie.

JUNE 17   A pregame wrestling match leads to a 9–6 loss in the first game of a doubleheader against the Braves in Boston. The Cardinals won the second tilt 10–3.

Before the opener, Pepper Martin and Paul Dean engaged in a friendly wresting match in the clubhouse. Dean slammed Martin against a wall, causing an injury to Martin's leg. Martin played two innings in the opener, then had to withdraw for the day with a bad limp. With the club already short-handed because of injuries to other infielders, Spud Davis replaced Martin at third base in both ends of the doubleheader, the only two games that Davis played at third during his 16-year big-league career. Dean, who had used up much of his energy wrestling with Martin, was knocked out in the second inning. At the end of the afternoon, Frankie Frisch issued an edict banning wrestling.

JUNE 23   Dizzy Dean creates a commotion at the Democratic National Convention in Philadelphia, where Franklin Roosevelt is nominated for a second term.

With the Cardinals in town to play the Phillies, Dean stopped at the Convention Hall to call on the Missouri delegation. After he was recognized, hundreds in the hall rushed to meet him or to catch a glimpse of the star pitcher, and those making speeches at the rostrum were completely ignored.

JUNE 25   In a strange reversal of fortune at Baker Bowl, the Cardinals lose the opener to the Phillies 13–4, then win by the same 13–4 score in the second tilt with the aid of nine runs in the second inning.

JULY 5   The Cardinals sweep the Reds 8–6 and 17–7 in a doubleheader in Cincinnati. Terry Moore collected seven hits, including four doubles, during the twin bill.

JULY 7   Dizzy Dean is the starting pitcher in the All-Star game, and pitches three hitless and scoreless innings to lead the National League to a 4–3 victory at Braves Field in Boston. Joe Medwick drove in a run in the fifth inning with a single.

A Cardinal pitcher was a starter in four of the first five All-Star games. Wild Bill Hallahan was the starter in 1933, Bill Walker in 1935, and Dean in 1936 and 1937.

JULY 10   With the temperature in St. Louis reaching 104 degrees, the Cardinals play 13 innings and defeat the Giants 5–4 at Sportsman's Park. Frankie Frisch inserted himself into the game as a pinch hitter and drove in the winning run with a double.

JULY 11   Dizzy Dean is knocked unconscious during a 9–3 win over the Giants at Sportsman's Park. A line drive off the bat of Burgess Whitehead struck Dean on the right side of the head in the sixth inning.

The high temperature in St. Louis that day was 102 degrees. A freak dust storm interrupted play in the eighth inning when a revolving funnel of dust swirled over the infield, forcing the Giants infielders to fall back on the outfield grass.

JULY 12   The stifling heat continues as the Cardinals play a doubleheader at Sportsman's Park on a day in which the high temperature in St. Louis is 104 degrees. The Cards lost twice, 6–3 and 11–4, to the Dodgers.

JULY 14   On a day in which the official high temperature in St. Louis is 108 degrees, Pepper Martin drives in six runs on a two-run homer in the fourth inning and a walk-off grand slam off George Jeffcoat in the ninth to lead the Cardinals to an 11–7 victory over the Dodgers at Sportsman's Park.

Martin led the National League in stolen bases in 1936 with 23 in addition to hitting .306. He collected 11 homers and scored 121 runs.

JULY 19   Joe Medwick collects seven hits, including a double, in seven at-bats during a doubleheader against the Braves at Sportsman's Park. The Cardinals won both games, 8–1 and 7–2.

JULY 21   By collecting two doubles and a single in his first three plate appearances, Joe Medwick ties a National League record with hits in 10 consecutive at-bats during a 10-inning, 2–1 loss to the Giants in New York. The three hits followed a 7-for-7 performance in the July 19 doubleheader.

On the same day, the Cardinals purchased George Earnshaw from the Athletics.

JULY 23   Joe Medwick extends his consecutive game hitting streak to 23 during a 4–2 loss to the Giants in New York.

JULY 29   After a humiliating 22–7 loss in the first game of a doubleheader against the Dodgers in Brooklyn, the Cardinals bounce back to win the second tilt 5–4.

JULY 31   Dizzy Dean pitches a complete game and hits a two-run single in the tenth inning to beat the Dodgers 8–6 in Brooklyn.

> *Dean had a record of 24–13 and a 3.17 ERA in 1936. He continued to perform double duty as the club's number one starter and reliever, leading the NL in games pitched with 51. Dean started 34 games, completing 28 of them. He appeared in 17 contests as a relief pitcher, and was on the mound at the end of the game in each one of them. He had a 2–3 record and 11 saves out of the bullpen. He led the league in both complete games and saves. Dean's 315 innings pitched also topped the NL, and he was second in strikeouts with 195. Dean was the first Cardinal to reach double digits in saves in a season. It didn't happen again until Ted Wilks collected 13 in 1948.*

AUGUST 2   The Cardinals sweep the Phillies 13–4 and 11–8 in Philadelphia.

AUGUST 6   Johnny Mize hits a homer in the eleventh inning that beats the Cubs 3–2 in Chicago.

> *On the same day, the Cardinals traded Bill Walker to the Reds for Si Johnson.*

AUGUST 7   Pepper Martin pitches the seventh and eighth innings of a 14–5 loss to the Cubs in Chicago. Martin didn't allow a run. It was the second, and last, pitching performance of his career. In a game in 1934, Martin pitched two innings and surrendered a run.

AUGUST 10   A fight between Dizzy Dean and Cubs pitcher Tex Carleton highlights a 7–3 win over the Cubs at Sportsman's Park.

> *In the top of the first with Billy Herman at bat, Dean raced from the mound toward the Cubs dugout in response to taunts from Carleton, who played for the Cards from 1932 through 1934. Carleton leaped off the bench and met Dean near the first-base line. Dean got Carleton into a headlock and punched him in the face. The two scuffled until members of both teams, aided by the umpires, separated them. Paul Dean started after Carleton and had to be pulled away. The umpires wanted to eject Dizzy, but Cubs manager Charlie Grimm pleaded with them to let the ace hurler stay in the game in a gesture of sportsmanship that may have cost him the game.*

AUGUST 25   The Cardinals are knocked out of first place with 20–3 and 5–4 losses to the Braves at Sportsman's Park. Boston scored 11 runs in the first inning of the opener off Si Johnson and Ed Heusser. The two Cardinal pitchers allowed a major league record seven doubles in the inning.

> *The Cardinals spent 85 days in first place in 1936, but none of them was after the devastating doubleheader loss on August 25. The Cards finished the season five games behind the Giants.*

AUGUST 27   Roy Parmelee loses a 1–0 duel with Danny MacFayden of the Braves in 10 innings at Sportsman's Park. Parmelee held the Braves hitless until Al Lopez singled in the eighth inning.

SEPTEMBER 1   The game between the Cardinals and Dodgers at Sportsman's Park is halted by rain after 3½ innings, but the inclement weather fails to prevent pregame festivities celebrating the 60th anniversary of the National League. First there was a three-inning game between St. Louis firemen and St. Louis policemen that ended in a 2–2 tie. The firemen and policemen dressed in 1876 replica uniforms and played the game in accordance with 1876 rules and equipment, or lack of equipment. Players of the 1876 period did not wear fielding gloves, and neither did those participating in the vintage contest in 1936. Another three-inning exhibition was played in which the 1936 Cardinals played those from the 1926 World Championship club. The 1936 team won 1–0.

SEPTEMBER 9   The Cardinals defeat the Braves 3–1 in 15 innings in Boston. In the fifteenth, Leo Durocher singled in a run with his fifth hit of the game, and scored on a double by Johnny Mize.

SEPTEMBER 11   Playing in only his fifth big-league game, Don Gutteridge collects two homers, a triple, and a single along with five RBIs during a 12–8 win in the first game of a doubleheader against the Dodgers at Ebbets Field. Brooklyn won the second tilt 5–4.

SEPTEMBER 12   Dizzy Dean is the winning and losing pitcher in a doubleheader against the Dodgers in Brooklyn. As a reliever in the opener, Dean pitched two-thirds of an inning and allowed two runs for a 9–8 loss. He started the second tilt, and pitched a complete game for a 10–3 victory.

SEPTEMBER 13   The Cardinals and Giants play before an overflow crowd of 64,417 at the Polo Grounds. Heading into the game trailing the Giants by 3½ games, the Cards remained even by losing the first game 8–4 before winning the second 4–3. Dizzy Dean, pitching in his third game in two days, saved the nightcap with two innings of scoreless relief. Playing in only his third major league game, pitcher Cotton Pippen ran his Cardinals out of a rally in the third inning of the opener. Pippen was the base runner on second and Terry Moore was on first when Art Garibaldi slashed a hit over the head of right fielder Mel Ott. Pippen held at second waiting to see if the ball would be caught. Late leaving the bag, Pippen was caught in a rundown between third and home and was tagged out. Moore was then caught between second and third and retired. Garibaldi scrambled back to first base just in time to avoid being the victim of a triple play on what should have been a double.

                 Pippen played in only six games as a Cardinal. He didn't collect another hit in the majors until 1939, and finished his big-league career with a record of 5–16, a 6.38 ERA, and a .111 batting average.

SEPTEMBER 14   The Giants all but end the Cardinals' flickering hopes for a pennant with a 7–5 win in New York. The defeat left the Cards 4½ games behind with 12 contests remaining on the schedule. The afternoon was enlivened by a fistfight on the Cardinals bench in the sixth inning between Joe Medwick and Ed Heusser. The incident occurred after Heusser chided Medwick for a poor throw from the outfield.

SEPTEMBER 19   A pinch-hit grand slam by Ripper Collins off Curt Davis in the seventh inning carries the Cardinals to a 9–6 win over the Cubs in Chicago.

SEPTEMBER 25   The Cardinals sweep the Reds 5–4 in 12 innings and 2–0 in six innings in a doubleheader in Cincinnati. The second tilt was shortened by darkness. Joe Medwick hit his 64th double in the first game. Dizzy Dean recorded his 24th victory of the season in the nightcap.

Medwick set a National League record with 64 doubles in 1936. The only major leaguer with more two-base hits in a season is Earl Webb, who had 67 for the Red Sox in 1931. Medwick also led the NL in 1936 in hits (223), RBIs (138), and total bases (367). In addition, he hit .351, scored 115 runs, hit 18 homers, and collected 13 triples.

SEPTEMBER 27   On the final day of the season, the Cardinals lose 6–3 to the Cubs at Sportsman's Park. The defeat dropped the Cards into a tie for second place with Chicago.

Walter Alston made his major league debut during the game. Johnny Mize was banished by the umpires in the seventh inning, and Alston entered the contest at first base to replace Mize. Facing Lon Warneke, Alston struck out in what proved to be his only big-league plate appearance. He later managed the Dodgers from 1954 through 1976, winning seven NL pennants and four World Championships. He was elected to the Hall of Fame in 1983.

OCTOBER 8   The Cardinals trade Ripper Collins and Roy Parmelee to the Cubs for Lon Warneke.

Warneke gave the Cardinals five effective seasons, posting a record of 77–45 from 1937 through 1941.

DECEMBER 2   A month after Franklin Roosevelt wins a second term as president in an election against Alf Landon, the Cardinals sell Spud Davis and Charlie Gelbert to the Reds.

1937

Season in a Sentence

Joe Medwick wins the Triple Crown by leading the NL in batting average, home runs, and RBIs, but an injury to Dizzy Dean in the All-Star Game hampers a thin pitching staff.

Finish • Won • Lost • Pct • GB

Fourth   81   73   .526   15.0

Manager

Frankie Frisch

Stats

Stats	Cards	• NL •	Rank
Batting Avg:	.282	.272	3
On-Base Pct:	.331	.332	5
Slugging Pct:	.406	.382	2
Home Runs:	94		3
Stolen Bases:	78		1
ERA:	3.98	3.91	6
Fielding Avg:	.973	.971	4
Runs Scored:	789		2
Runs Allowed:	733		6

Starting Lineup

Bruce Ogrodowski, c
Johnny Mize, 1b
Jimmy Brown, 2b
Don Gutteridge, 3b
Leo Durocher, ss
Joe Medwick, lf
Terry Moore, cf
Don Padgett, rf
Pepper Martin, rf-cf
Frenchy Bordagaray, 3b-rf
Mickey Owen, c
Stu Martin, 2b

Pitchers

Lon Warneke, sp
Bob Weiland, sp
Dizzy Dean, sp
Si Johnson, sp-rp
Mike Ryba, rp
Roy Harrell, rp-sp

Attendance

430,811 (fifth in NL)

Club Leaders

Batting Avg:	Medwick	.374
On-Base Pct:	Mize	.427
Slugging Pct:	Medwick	.641
Home Runs:	Medwick	31
RBIs:	Medwick	154
Runs:	Medwick	111
Stolen Bases:	Moore	13
Wins:	Warneke	18
Strikeouts:	Dean	120
ERA:	Dean	2.69
Saves:	Five tied w/	1

MARCH 13   The Cardinals and Giants play the first of two exhibition games in Havana.

During the two-day stay in Cuba, Johnny Mize met 19-year-old St. Louis socialite Jene Adams. The two were married the following August.

APRIL 2   Dizzy Dean and Joe Medwick fight with reporters in the lobby of the Tampa Terrace Hotel in Tampa, Florida.

Dean got into an argument with New York Daily News *columnist Jack Miley over an article written by Miley that claimed that Dean's wife, Pat, "wore the pants of the family." Dean and Miley began exchanging roundhouse swings. Irving Kupcinet of the* Chicago Daily News, *who had played in the NFL with the Philadelphia Eagles as recently as 1935, tried to intervene and was punched by Medwick. Kupcinet sprawled backward into a potted palm tree that started a chain reaction, knocking down floor lamps, plants, and four other palms. Miley was struck in the forehead by the spiked shoe of an unidentified Cardinal player and sported a cut on his scalp. Kupcinet suffered a black eye. Dean and Medwick apologized and promised never to strike a sportswriter again.*

APRIL 20   The Cardinals defeat the Reds 2–0 in 10 innings on Opening Day at Crosley Field. Dizzy Dean pitched a complete-game shutout despite allowing 13 hits, two walks, and committing a fielding error. Cincinnati stranded 14 runners. The Cardinal runs scored on doubles by Joe Medwick and Johnny Mize, a single by Leo Durocher, and a sacrifice fly by Bruce Ogrodowski.

Transcendental Graphics/theruckerarchive.com

Joe Medwick played for the Cardinals from 1932 to 1940 and again in 1947 and 1948. Medwick was a powerhouse at the plate accumulating 1,383 RBIs in his 17-year career. He won the Triple Crown in 1937, the last NL player to do so.

In his first five starts in 1937, Dean won each one of them with complete games, hurling 46 innings and allowing only three runs, two of them earned.

APRIL 22   The Cardinals outlast the Reds 14–11 at Crosley Field. The Cards led 7–1 when Cincinnati scored nine runs in the fourth inning. The Cards broke an 11–11 tie with three runs in the eighth.

APRIL 23   In the home opener, the Cardinals win 5–4 over the Cubs with two runs in the eighth inning and two in the ninth before 18,000 at Sportsman's Park. A two-out, bases-loaded single by Johnny Mize drove in the tying and winning runs.

Mize hit .364 with 25 homers, 113 RBIs, 103 runs, 204 hits, and 40 doubles in 1937.

MAY 5   The Cardinals bury the Braves 13–1 in Boston. Joe Medwick hit a grand slam in the first inning off Jim Turner. It was the first of five Cardinal homers. The others were by Don Gutteridge, Frenchy Bordagaray, Pepper Martin, and Bruce Ogrodowski.

Medwick had one of the greatest seasons in Cardinals history in 1937. He won the Triple Crown by leading the NL in batting average (.374), home runs (31), and RBIs (154). No National Leaguer since Medwick has won the Triple Crown. Medwick also topped the league in 1937 in runs (111), hits (237), doubles (56), total bases (406), and slugging percentage (.641). The figures earned him the Most Valuable Player Award.

MAY 8   Two days after the German dirigible *Hindenberg* erupts in flames in Lakehurst, New Jersey, killing 36 people, the Cardinals collect 20 hits and wallop the Giants 12–5 in New York.

MAY 12   Behind a 20-hit attack, the Cardinals clout the Phillies 15–3 in Philadelphia. Joe Medwick tied a Cardinals record for most extra-base hits in a game with two homers and two doubles.

During the 1937 season, Pepper Martin put the Gas House Gang to music by forming the Mudcat Band. Martin was the master of ceremonies and played the harmonica. Lon Warneke played the guitar and sang. Bill McGee was the fiddle player. Bob Weiland blew into a jug and Frenchy Bordagaray played a contraption that included a washboard, whistle, auto horn, and electric light. Max Lanier later joined as a singer. The Mudcat Band adorned themselves in cowboy attire, dress boots, and sombreros and specialized in country and western tunes. The club appeared in venues all over the country, including national radio shows.

MAY 19   The Cardinals brawl with the Giants during a 4–1 loss at Sportsman's Park.

With the Cardinals holding a 1–0 lead in the sixth inning, umpire George Barr called a balk on Dean. National League president Ford Frick had put in a new interpretation that season, instructing pitchers to come to a full stop after their wind-up stretch when a runner was on base before delivering a pitch to the plate. The argument between Dean and Barr over the balk and the interpretation of the full-stop ruling lasted five minutes. Dean returned to mound and completely lost his composure, allowing three runs before the third out was recorded. In *the ninth, the still fuming Dean threw at every Giant who stepped to the plate. Jimmy Ripple bunted down the line, and he and Dizzy collided on the play at first base. Ripple slugged Dean, who came up swinging. Both benches emptied and a free-for-all ensued. Giant catcher Gus Mancuso tried to get at Dean when Mickey Owen of the Cardinals plunked him on the chin. It took a contingent of park police to break the two clubs apart. Don Gutteridge was among those who tried to act as peacemaker, and came out of the fray with two shiners. Although the entire Giants team wanted to tear him limb from limb, Dean escaped without a scratch. Dean was not ejected, but was fined $50 by Frick for "tending to precipitate a riot." (See May 23, 1937.)*

MAY 23   Dizzy Dean makes a mockery of the balk rule during a 6–2 win over the Phillies at Sportsman's Park.

Taking heed of Ford Frick's ruling to come to a full stop between his wind-up and delivery, Dean came to a stop for three minutes before pitching to Jimmy Wilson with a runner on first in the second inning. On the next pitch, Dean stopped and stood still as a statue for four minutes before the umpires called a balk for holding up the game unnecessarily. Dean responded by sitting on the mound for another four minutes and was called for yet another balk for stalling. A few days later at a father-son luncheon in Belleview, Illinois, Dean called Frick and umpire George Barr "the two biggest crooks in baseball." Frick suspended Dean for three days for the remarks, but after a stormy meeting with Dean in New York, reduced the suspension to two days with no loss of pay. Frick wanted Dean to sign a document retracting his remarks calling the NL president a "crook," but Dean refused.

JUNE 4   The Cardinals trounce the Dodgers 14–4 in Brooklyn.

JUNE 6   The Cardinals sweep a doubleheader against the Phillies in Philadelphia, the second by forfeit. The opener was a conventional 7–2 St. Louis victory. Pennsylvania law in 1937 stated that baseball games played on Sunday must end at 6 PM. Baseball rules stipulated that a game must last five innings before it is official. In the top of the fourth, the Cards led 8–2. The Phillies stalled as long as possible so that the clock would strike six before the fifth inning could be completed. Umpires Ziggy Sears, Lee Ballanfant, and Bill Klem had enough of the stalling tactics and forfeited the contest to the Cardinals.

JUNE 13   Dizzy Dean pitches the Cardinals to a 1–0 win over the Braves in the second game of a doubleheader in Boston. The Cards also won the first game, 6–2.

JUNE 15   The Cardinals rout the Phillies 13–4 at Sportsman's Park.

JUNE 19   After the first two batters in the ninth inning are retired, the Cardinals rally for three runs to defeat the Braves 7–5 at Sportsman's Park. After Jimmy Brown and Don Padgett singled, Joe Medwick struck a walk-off homer. It was his second home run of the game.

JUNE 24   The Cardinals rip the Dodgers 13–3 at Sportsman's Park.

The Cards were one-half game out of first place on June 29 when they began a three-game series against the Cubs at Sportsman's Park. Chicago won all three contests, which sent the Cards reeling out of the race.

JULY 4   The Cardinals sweep the Reds 1–0 and 5–2 in a doubleheader in Cincinnati. Dizzy Dean pitched the shutout in the opener, with Leo Durocher driving in the lone run with a single in the second inning. The second contest was shortened to six innings by a torrential downpour.

JULY 7   Dizzy Dean breaks his big toe when struck by a line drive off the bat of Earl Averill of the Indians in the All-Star Game, played at Griffith Stadium in Washington and won by the American League 8–3. Dean was the starting pitcher and slated to go three innings. He had one out to go when Averill lined the drive off his toe (see July 21, 1937). Joe Medwick collected four hits, including two doubles, in five at-bats. Johnny Mize drove in a run with a sacrifice fly.

JULY 16   The Cardinals stun the Phillies 10–3 and 18–10 in a doubleheader in Philadelphia. The second game went into extra innings and was climaxed by an eight-run explosion by the Cardinals in the tenth inning. Johnny Mize had six hits, including four doubles, in the twin bill.

JULY 21   Three days after the disappearance of Amelia Earhart, Dizzy Dean makes his first appearance after breaking his toe in the All-Star Game. Dean lost 2–1 in the second game of a doubleheader against the Braves in Boston. The Cards also lost the opener, 5–1, on a walk-off grand slam by Ray Mueller in the eleventh inning.

The toe injury had serious consequences for Dean. Pitching just two weeks after the toe was broken, Dean came back much too soon. He was unable to properly push off the mound, which dramatically reduced the velocity of his pitches, and the stress ruined his arm. Dean made seven starts in 1937 after the All-Star break before being shut down for the season during the last week of August. Only 27 when the injury occurred, Dean had already accumulated 133 wins in the majors. After breaking his toe in the 1937 All-Star Game, Dean had only 17 more wins. Although there is no question that the toe injury was the turning point in Dean's career, there is some question as to which came first. Was it the toe injury or the arm injury? Dean had been complaining of a sore arm before breaking his toe, and there is little doubt that a brutal workload was an overriding factor. Dizzy's first professional season was in 1930 when he was 20 years old, and he pitched 311 innings in 47 games. In 1931, he went 304 innings in 41 games while still in the minors. Reaching the majors in 1932, Dean averaged 306 innings and 49 games per year over his first five seasons. He also pitched often in exhibition games during the season as the Cardinals spent many off days playing in minor league towns to earn some extra money. At the 1937 All-Star break, Dean had pitched 147²/₃ innings, a pace that would have given him 339 innings by season's end. Given the number of innings and games that he pitched at such a young age, it's amazing that Dean's arm didn't break down before 1937 and it's likely that an arm injury would have occurred even if Earl Averill's All-Star Game drive had missed his toe.

JULY 24   The Cardinals crush the Dodgers 20–2 in Brooklyn. Leading 2–0 at the end of the third, the Cards scored in each of the last six innings.

JULY 27   A walk-off homer by Joe Medwick with two outs in the ninth inning beats the Giants 9–8 at Sportsman's Park. The Cards appeared to have the game won when they scored eight runs in the fourth to take an 8–1 lead, but allowed the Giants back in the contest.

AUGUST 3 Rookie catcher Mickey Owen pulls off an unassisted double play during a 5–2 win over the Braves at Sportsman's Park. With Roy Johnson attempting to score from third on a squeeze play, Rabbit Warstler popped the bunt into the air. Owen caught the ball and tagged Johnson.

AUGUST 4 The Cardinals erupt for five runs in the ninth inning to defeat the Braves 7–6 at Sportsman's Park. Frankie Frisch put himself into the game as a pinch hitter and drove in the tying and winning runs with a walk-off single. Joe Medwick tied a major league record with four doubles during the afternoon.

Frisch accumulated only seven hits in 1937, the last season for Frisch as a player. He finished his 19-year career with 2,880 hits, and was elected to the Hall of Fame in 1947.

AUGUST 17-18 The Cardinals and the Reds become the first two major league teams to finish a game after midnight in an 8–6 St. Louis win in Cincinnati.

AUGUST 22 The Cardinals sweep the Pirates 12–0 and 9–7 in a doubleheader in Pittsburgh. Bob Weiland pitched the shutout and hit a three-run homer.

One of the tallest pitchers of his era at six-foot-four, Weiland entered the 1937 campaign as a 30-year-old with a big-league record of 21–57 and a 4.79 earned run average with four American League clubs. He spent the entire 1936 season in the minors. Despite the less-than-stellar credentials, Weiland helped the Cards with a 15–14 record in 1937 and 16–11 in 1938.

AUGUST 29 Cardinals rookie Ray Harrell pitches a one-hitter to defeat the Braves 3–0 in the second game of a doubleheader at Braves Field. The only Boston hit was a single by Ray Mueller with none out in the sixth inning. The Braves won the first game 5–2.

The effort was not typical of Harrell's career. He lasted six seasons in the majors and had a record of 9–20 with an ERA of 5.70. The August 29, 1937, one-hitter was Harrell's only career shutout.

SEPTEMBER 5 Lon Warneke pitches the Cardinals to a 1–0 win over the Reds in the second game of a doubleheader at Crosley Field. Cincinnati won the first game 3–2.

In his first season with the Cards, Warneke had an earned run average of 4.53, but posted a record of 18–11.

SEPTEMBER 14 The Cardinals sweep the Phillies in a pair of odd-sized games at Sportsman's Park. The Cards won the first contest 9–8 in 14 innings. The Phillies scored two runs in the top of the thirteenth inning to take an 8–8 lead, but the Cardinals tied it in their half. Joe Medwick won the game with a walk-off double. The second tilt went only five innings because of darkness with St. Louis winning 1–0.

SEPTEMBER 17 Johnny Mize hits a two-run homer in the eighth inning to beat the Braves 2–0 at Sportsman's Park. Si Johnson pitched the shutout.

Mike Ryba, who played for the Cardinals from 1935 through 1938, is one of the few individuals to appear in games as both a pitcher and a catcher. With the Cards, he was a pitcher in 57 games and a catcher in seven.

SEPTEMBER 21   Trailing 5–1, the Cards score seven runs in the seventh inning and defeat the Dodgers 8–5 in the first game of a doubleheader at Sportsman's Park. The Cards completed the sweep with a 6–2 victory in the second tilt.

SEPTEMBER 23   Don Padgett hits a homer and two triples in an 8–4 victory against the Dodgers at Sportsman's Park.

SEPTEMBER 26   The Cardinals score four runs in the ninth inning to beat the Cubs 6–5 in the first game of a doubleheader at Sportsman's Park. A bases-loaded double by Joe Medwick drove in the last three runs. Chicago won the second game, called after eight innings by darkness, 8–6.

OCTOBER 4   The Cardinals trade Leo Durocher to the Dodgers for Johnny Cooney, Joe Stripp, Roy Henshaw, and Jim Bucher.

Durocher began a long and controversial career as a big-league manager less than two years later. He led the Dodgers (1939–46, 1948), Giants (1948–55), Cubs (1966–72), and Astros (1972–73). During his years in Brooklyn, the Cardinals and Dodgers were bitter rivals with pennant races between the two clubs undecided until the final weekend in 1941, 1942, and 1946.

1938

Season in a Sentence

The Cardinals score more runs than any other club in the National League, but a weak pitching staff dooms the Cardinals to a losing record and costs Frankie Frisch his job as manager.

Finish • Won • Lost • Pct • GB

Sixth   71   80   .470   17.5

Managers

Frankie Frisch (63–72) and Mike Gonzalez (8–8)

Stats

Stats	Cards	NL	Rank
Batting Avg:	.279	.267	1
On-Base Pct:	.331	.329	5
Slugging Pct:	.407	.376	1
Home Runs:	91		3
Stolen Bases:	55		2
ERA:	3.84		6
Fielding Avg:	.967	.972	7
Runs Scored:	725		1
Runs Allowed:	721		7

Starting Lineup

Mickey Owen, c
Johnny Mize, 1b
Stu Martin, 2b
Don Gutteridge, 3b
Lynn Myers, ss
Joe Medwick, lf
Terry Moore, cf
Enos Slaughter, rf
Don Padgett, rf
Jimmy Brown, 2b-ss-3b
Pepper Martin, cf-rf
Joe Stripp, 3b
Frenchy Bordagaray, cf-rf

Pitchers

Bob Weiland, sp
Lon Warneke, sp
Curt Davis, sp-rp
Bill McGee, sp-rp
Roy Henshaw, sp-rp
Max Macon, rp-sp
Clyde Shoun, rp-sp

Attendance

291,418 (seventh in NL)

Club Leaders

Batting Avg:	Mize	.337
On-Base Pct:	Mize	.422
Slugging Pct:	Mize	.614
Home Runs:	Mize	27
RBIs:	Medwick	122
Runs:	Medwick	100
Stolen Bases:	Gutteridge	14
Wins:	Weiland	16
Strikeouts:	Weiland	117
ERA:	McGee	3.21
Saves:	McGee	5

FEBRUARY 2   The Cardinals purchase Guy Bush from the Braves.

FEBRUARY 23   The Cardinals sign Sammy Baugh to a contract.

Baugh was the number one overall pick in the 1937 National Football League draft. After establishing himself as one of the best quarterbacks in football while playing for the Washington Redskins during his rookie season, Baugh decided to give baseball a try. He had been a star in both football and baseball at Texas Christian University. Baugh played in 53 games for the Cardinals' minor league clubs in Columbus and Rochester in 1938, but hit only .200. He returned to football, and had a career that lasted until 1951. Baugh was in the first class of 16 inductees in the Pro Football Hall of Fame in 1963.

MARCH 23   Commissioner Kenesaw Landis frees 91 players in the Cardinals' minor league system.

Landis had always disliked farm systems, believing that minor league clubs should be locally owned and operated and free from any association with major league teams. Landis also had an intense loathing for Branch Rickey, whom the commissioner believed was a religious hypocrite. Landis allowed the 91 farm hands to become free agents over alleged irregularities in the Cardinals' farm system. The situation didn't cripple the Cardinals, as the club went on to post the best record of any club in the majors during the 1940s. Pete Reiser and Skeeter Webb were the only two of the 91 players released by Landis to reach the majors. Reiser developed into a star, however, and was one of the best players on a 1941 Dodgers club that beat out the Cardinals for the NL pennant by just 2½ games.

APRIL 16   The Cardinals send Dizzy Dean to the Cubs for Curt Davis, Clyde Shoun, Tuck Stainback, and $185,000.

Three days before the opening game of the season, the Cardinals made a huge news splash by trading Dean. The deal was a complete surprise and was announced with no advance warning. Dean injured his arm shortly after the 1937 All-Star Game (see July 21, 1937), and the Cards gambled that he would never recover. The gambit paid off. Dizzy was 28 years old when he was traded to the Cubs, but his arm never came around. He won only 16 more big-league games after being dealt to Chicago. Davis gave the Cards a 12–8 record in 1938 and was 22–16 in 1939 before a trade to the Dodgers in 1940. Shoun provided St. Louis with two solid seasons out of the bullpen.

APRIL 19   The Cardinals open the season with a 4–3 loss to the Pirates before 19,856 at Sportsman's Park. The Cards led until the ninth inning when Arky Vaughan hit a two-run homer off Bob Weiland. In his major league debut, Enos Slaughter was 3 for 5 with a double and two singles. Joe Medwick missed the game because of lumbago, ending a streak of 485 games played dating back to 1934.

The Cardinals trained in St. Petersburg, Florida, for the first time in 1938. St. Petersburg hosted the Cardinals until 1997, with the exception of three seasons during World War II when travel restrictions forced the Cardinals to train in Cairo, Illinois.

APRIL 22   The Cardinals score four runs in the ninth inning and defeat the Cubs 6–5 in
               Chicago. Enos Slaughter hit a bases-loaded triple and scored on an error.

               *Slaughter played for the Cardinals from 1938 through 1942 and again from
               1946 through 1953, with the intervening three years spent in the service during
               World War II. Slaughter was known for his endless hustle on the diamond. The
               nickname "Charlie Hustle" was applied to Pete Rose in 1963, but Slaughter was
               the original. Rose patterned his hell-bent-for-leather style, including running
               to first base on a walk, after Slaughter while watching the Cardinal star play
               the Reds at Crosley Field in Rose's hometown of Cincinnati. Slaughter ranks
               fourth all time in games played as a Cardinal with 1,820 and batted .300 with
               169 homers. He also ranks second in RBIs (1,148), third in walks (839), third
               in triples (135), fourth in runs (1,071), fourth in hits (2,064), fourth in total
               bases (3,138), fifth in doubles (366), and fifth in at-bats (6,775). Slaughter trails
               Stan Musial in each of those categories, however, and played under Musial's
               shadow for much of his career. This in part accounts for the fact that Slaughter
               wasn't elected to the Hall of Fame until 1985. He should have had a plaque at
               Cooperstown much sooner than that. In 1996, the Cardinals retired Slaughter's
               uniform number 9.*

APRIL 24   Dizzy Dean faces his former Cardinals teammates for the first time and pitches a 5–0
               complete-game victory for the Cubs in Chicago.

APRIL 26   Cardinal pitcher Curt Davis hits a grand slam off Al Hollingsworth that helps the
               Cardinals to a 7–0 lead, but Davis and his relievers fail to hold the lead and the Reds
               rally to win 8–7 in 10 innings in Cincinnati.

               *Cardinals and Browns home games were aired on KMOX, KWK, and WIL
               in 1938, with the exception of those played on Sundays and holidays. Road
               games were not carried. The Cardinals also set up a radio network consisting
               of out-of-town stations for the first time in 1938. Games were aired on stations
               in Columbia and Jefferson City in Missouri; Lincoln, Nebraska; Terre Haute,
               Indiana; Cedar Rapids, Des Moines, and Shenandoah in Iowa; Yankton, South
               Dakota; and Jonesboro, Arkansas. The far-flung radio network would help
               transform the Cardinals into a regional franchise and boost attendance by
               inducing fans to travel hundreds of miles to see the Cardinals play in person.*

MAY 14   The Cardinals win a thrilling 7–6 come-from-behind victory in 10 innings against the
               Reds at Sportsman's Park. Trailing 5–1 heading into the ninth, the Cardinals scored
               four runs to forge a tie. After Cincinnati plated a run in the top of the tenth, the
               Cards came back with two in their half of the inning on a walk-off homer by Enos
               Slaughter for the win.

               *In the end, the dramatic victory didn't count. The Reds filed a protest over a
               disputed hit by Reds outfielder Dusty Cooke. At Sportsman's Park, the roof
               of the right-field pavilion projected over the playing field. In the sixth inning,
               Cooke hit a ball that struck the facing of the roof and bounced back onto the
               outfield grass. Cooke reached third base for a triple, but the Reds argued the
               call should have been a home run, because if Cooke had hit the ball a few inches
               lower it would have missed the roof and settled into the grandstand. On June 3,
               NL president Ford Frick upheld the protest and ruled that the game be replayed
               in its entirety as part of a doubleheader on August 20. That day, the Cardinals*

lost the first game 4–2, but won the second 5–4. As a result of the incident, white markings were applied along the roof from the edge of the pavilion screen to center field, including two poles that supported the screen separating the pavilion seats from the center field bleachers. A new ground rule provided that any ball hitting any of the white marks and bouncing back onto the field was a home run.

MAY 15   The Cardinals edge the Reds 12–11 in 10 innings at Sportsman's Park. The Cards led 11–4 in the fourth inning before allowing the Reds back in the game. The winning run scored on a triple by Mickey Owen and a single by Pepper Martin.

A massive scoreboard was built in 1938 behind the left-field bleachers at Sportsman's Park.

MAY 17   Bill McGee pitches a one-hitter to defeat the Dodgers 2–1 at Ebbets Field. The only Brooklyn hit was a single by Goody Rosen in the sixth inning. Rosen scored on a three-base error by Joe Medwick.

Medwick led the NL in RBIs (122) and doubles (47) in 1938. He also batted .322 with 100 runs, 190 hits, and 21 homers.

MAY 29   Bob Weiland pitches a two-hitter to defeat the Reds 3–0 at Crosley Field. The only Cincinnati hits were singles by Dusty Cooke in the first inning and Frank McCormick in the seventh.

JUNE 3   Mickey Owen hits a two-out, bases-loaded, walk-off single that beats the Phillies 8–7 at Sportsman's Park. Don Padgett hit a grand slam in the seventh inning off Pete Sivess that broke a 2–2 tie, but the Cards allowed the Phils to tie the contest and send it into extra innings.

JUNE 5   The Cardinals score three runs in the ninth inning to defeat the Braves 6–5 in the first game of a doubleheader at Sportsman's Park. Pepper Martin hit a two-run double to tie the score, then crossed the plate on an error by Boston first baseman Elbie Fletcher.

On the same day, the Cardinals signed 17-year-old left-handed pitcher Stan Musial from Donora High School in Donora, Pennsylvania, to a contract. Musial was instructed to report to the Cardinals' farm club in Williamson, West Virginia, in the Mountain State League.

JUNE 16   The Cardinals play at Baker Bowl in Philadelphia for the last time, and lose 3–2 to the Phillies.

The Phillies moved into Shibe Park in July. The Phillies shared Shibe Park, built in 1909, with the Athletics until the Philadelphia American League entry moved to Kansas City in 1955. The Phillies were the lone occupants of the ballpark until Veterans Stadium opened in 1971. Shibe Park was renamed Connie Mack Stadium in 1953.

JUNE 28   The Cardinals score seven runs in the third inning to beat the Cubs 9–3 in Chicago.

JULY 6   Joe Medwick drives in the first run of the All-Star Game with a sacrifice fly sparking the National League to a 4–1 win at Crosley Field in Cincinnati.

July 13   Johnny Mize hits three consecutive homers, but the Cardinals lose 10–5 to the Braves at Sportsman's Park. Mize drove in all five St. Louis runs on a two-run homer in the fourth inning, a solo blast in the fifth, and another two-run home run in the eighth. All three came at the expense of Jim Turner.

Mize hit .337 in 1938, and had 27 homers, 102 RBIs, 179 hits, and league-leading totals in triples (16) and slugging percentage (.614) in 1938.

July 20   Johnny Mize connects for three homers in a game for the second time in a span of eight days, leading the Cardinals to a 7–1 victory over the Giants in the second game of a doubleheader at Sportsman's Park. Mize homered off Slick Castleman in the first and third innings and against Bill Lohrman in the eighth. The Cardinals also won the first game, 7–2.

Mize had six games in his career in which he hit three homers to set a major league, later tied by Sammy Sosa. In addition to his two three–home run games in 1938, Mize hit three for the Cardinals twice in 1940, for the Giants in 1947, and with the Yankees in 1950. Oddly, his club won only one of the six games in which Mize struck three homers. Four resulted in losses and another in a tie.

July 27   The Cardinals parlay a seven-run sixth inning into a 7–0 win over the Giants in New York.

August 1   The Cardinals sell Joe Stripp to the Braves.

August 2   The Cardinals and Dodgers experiment with dandelion yellow baseballs during a 6–2 Brooklyn win in the first game of a doubleheader at Ebbets Field. The switch to a conventional white ball in the second tilt failed to aid the Cards, as the Dodgers won again 9–3.

The motivating force behind the yellow ball was scientist Frederick Rahr, who made an agreement with the Spalding Baseball Company to manufacture the balls. Rahr believed that its high visibility would lessen the dangers of players being hit by pitched balls. Larry MacPhail, Brooklyn's general manager took it from there and persuaded National League president Ford Frick and the Cardinal management team of Sam Breadon and Branch Rickey to sanction the test. Player reaction was mixed, but most agreed that the ball was easier to follow. One drawback surfaced when the yellow dye came off on the hands of the pitchers. The entire side of the uniform of Dodgers hurler Fred Fitzsimmons was stained where he had wiped off the dye. The yellows balls were used in two more games involving the Dodgers and Cardinals in 1939 (see July 23, 1939, and July 30, 1939), and another that season between the Dodgers and Cubs.

August 23   Terry Moore hits a grand slam off Vito Tamulis in the fourth inning of a 9–7 win over the Dodgers at Sportsman's Park.

August 24   Curt Davis pitches a one-hitter to defeat the Dodgers 5–0 at Sportsman's Park. The only Brooklyn hit was by Ernie Koy, who beat out a drag bunt by inches in the second inning.

August 26   Don Gutteridge's second triple of the game drives in the game-winner to beat the Braves 7–6 at Sportsman's Park. Gutteridge also hit a double in the contest.

Frenchy Bordagaray had a tremendous season as a pinch hitter in 1938 with 20 hits in 43 at-bats, an average of .465.

SEPTEMBER 1   Terry Moore collects five hits in five at-bats during a 6–5 win over the Phillies in Philadelphia.

SEPTEMBER 2   The Cardinals edge the Pirates 11–10 in Pittsburgh. The Cards led 11–3 after six innings before hanging on for the win.

The 1938 club was the first Cardinal club to finish a season with a losing record since 1932. It didn't happen again until 1954.

SEPTEMBER 11   The Cardinals fire Frankie Frisch as manager. Coach Mike Gonzalez finished out the season as interim manager.

Frisch had managed the Cardinals since July 1933 and played for the club from 1927 through 1937. He was a member of four NL champions in St. Louis and won the World Championship in 1934 as a manager. Frisch kept the club in contention in 1935, 1936, and the first half of the 1937 season, but the Gas House Gang was aging and the club was in a rebuilding mode by 1938. After spending the 1939 season as a radio broadcaster in Boston, Frisch later managed the Pirates (1940–46) and Cubs (1949–51), but never came close to another pennant.

SEPTEMBER 14   The Cardinals sweep the Phillies 12–9 and 3–2 in Philadelphia.

SEPTEMBER 21   Joe Medwick drives in all four St. Louis runs in a 4–0 win over the Braves in the first game of a doubleheader in Boston. Medwick hit a solo homer in the first inning and a three-run homer in the eighth. Paul Dean pitched the shutout. The second game lasted 3½ innings before it was called off because of high winds.

Within a few hours, the high winds in Boston reached hurricane force. It was part of a vicious storm that struck Long Island and New England and resulted in the deaths of 600 people. The storm also resulted in the first trip by airplane for the Cardinals as a team. The club's next stop on the schedule was Chicago and train travel was interrupted because of rail damage out of Boston. The Cards flew to Newark, New Jersey, then boarded a train to the Windy City.

NOVEMBER 6   The Cardinals hire 42-year-old Ray Blades as manager.

Blades was a hustling former outfielder who played on four Cardinals World Series clubs from 1926 through 1931. He managed the Cardinals' top farm clubs in Columbus and Rochester from 1933 through 1938. Blades looked like a genius in 1939 when the Cardinals won 92 games and finished second, but he was fired after a 14–26 start in 1940.

1939

Season in a Sentence

Under new manager Ray Blades, the Cardinals contend for the pennant until late September.

Finish • Won • Lost • Pct • GB

Second   92   61   .601   4.5

Manager

Ray Blades

Stats

Stats	Cards	NL	Rank
Batting Avg:	.294	.272	1
On-Base Pct:	.354	.335	1
Slugging Pct:	.432	.386	1
Home Runs:	98		2 (tie)
Stolen Bases:	44		4 (tie)
ERA:	3.59		2
Fielding Avg:	.971	.972	6
Runs Scored:	779		1
Runs Allowed:	633		2

Starting Lineup

Mickey Owen, c
Johnny Mize, 1b
Stu Martin, 2b
Don Gutteridge, 3b
Jimmy Brown, ss-2b
Joe Medwick, lf
Terry Moore, cf
Enos Slaughter, rf
Pepper Martin, cf-3b
Don Padgett, c

Pitchers

Curt Davis, sp-rp
Mort Cooper, sp-rp
Lon Warneke, sp-rp
Bob Weiland, sp
Tom Sunkel, sp-rp
Clyde Shoun, rp
Bob Bowman, rp
Bill McGee, rp-sp

Attendance

400,245 (fifth in NL)

Club Leaders

Batting Avg:	Mize	.349
On-Base Pct:	Mize	.444
Slugging Pct:	Mize	.625
Home Runs:	Mize	28
RBIs:	Medwick	117
Runs:	Mize	104
Stolen Bases:	Four tied w/	6
Wins:	Davis	22
Strikeouts:	Cooper	130
ERA:	Cooper	3.25
Saves:	Shoun	9
	Bowman	9

APRIL 18   The Cardinals win 3–2 over the Pirates at Forbes Field in the season opener. The Cards scored all three of their runs in the seventh inning to wipe out a two-run Pittsburgh lead. Joe Medwick tied the score with a two-run single and Johnny Mize hit a sacrifice fly to break the deadlock.

Mize and Medwick again headed the St. Louis batting attack and were joined in 1939 by Enos Slaughter. Slaughter, Medwick, and Mize finished 1-2-3 in the league in doubles. Mize led the NL in batting average (.349), slugging percentage (.628), home runs (28), and total bases (353) in addition to scoring 104 runs and collecting 197 hits, 44 doubles, 14 triples, and 108 RBIs. Medwick hit .332 with 201 hits, 48 doubles, 117 RBIs, and 14 homers. Enos Slaughter batted .320, clubbed 12 home runs and led the NL in doubles with 52. Despite playing right field, he topped National League outfielders in putouts in addition to assists and double plays. Slaughter had to overcome illness and personal tragedy to reach those figures. When he arrived for spring training, he was suffering from rabbit fever. On New Year's morning, Enos and his father had gone rabbit hunting near their home in North Carolina. As they waded through the underbrush, they were scratched by sharp thorns, and then shot and handled infected rabbits. That afternoon Slaughter's father became ill and was bedridden. Eleven days later he died of the disease, called tularemia. Enos also contracted the ailment and hovered for weeks between life and death. Rabbit fever strikes its victims with a high temperature that comes and goes. Weakness, deep depression, and abscesses develop. Still suffering from the ailment, Slaughter reported to spring training against the wishes of his doctor and family. He shivered under the hot Florida sun and the abscesses caused great pain with almost every move, but he kept the illness secret from Cardinal management for fear of losing his job. Slaughter beat off the remnants of tularemia to have a terrific season.

Transcendental Graphics/theruckerarchive.com

Johnny Mize finished second in MVP voting to Cincinnati's Bucky Walters in 1939. "We always did know who to pitch to him," Dodger legend Roy Campanella once said, "but some days when you're squatting behind the plate, Mr. Mize's bat swells up."

APRIL 21   In the home opener, the Cardinals lose 4–2 to the Cubs before 10,373 at Sportsman's Park.

APRIL 22   Lon Warneke beats the Cubs 9–0 at Sportsman's Park. Warneke drove in the first three runs of the contest with a three-run double in the second inning.

APRIL 26   Curt Davis pitches the Cardinals to a 1–0 win over the Reds in Cincinnati and drives in the lone run of the game with a two-out single in the fourth inning.

The two shortstops in the game were brothers, with Lynn Myers playing for the Cardinals and Billy Myers for the Reds.

APRIL 29   Lon Warneke pitches a one-hitter to defeat the Cubs 2–0 at Wrigley Field. The only Chicago hit was a single by Stan Hack to start the seventh inning on a weak roller between Warneke and Johnny Mize that neither was able to field in time.

MAY 8   Pepper Martin steals home in the sixth inning for the only run in a 1–0 victory over the Dodgers in Brooklyn. Martin singled and moved to second and third on infield outs before swiping home. Bob Weiland pitched the shutout.

MAY 9   The Cardinals slaughter the Dodgers 13–1 in Brooklyn.

MAY 16   Down 5–0, the Cardinals score one run in the fourth inning, two in the fifth, three in the sixth, and one in the seventh to beat the Giants 7–6 at Sportsman's Park. A pinch-single by Lynn Myers broke a 1–1 tie.

MAY 25   The Cardinals win their seventh game in a row with a 7–1 decision over the Braves at Sportsman's Park.

The win gave the Cardinals a 20–9 record and a hold on first place. The Cards were knocked out of the top spot the following day by the Reds, however. By July 15, St. Louis had a record of 37–37 and had fallen to fifth place, 9½ games out of first. The Cardinals rose to second place by the end of July, but were 12 games behind the Reds. A surge of 19 wins in 21 games during the first three weeks of August cut Cincinnati's lead to 3½ games. From July 16 through September 24, the Cardinals had a record of 52–20 and remained within striking distance of first place until the last week of the season.

JUNE 1   Bill McGee pitches the Cardinals to a 1–0 win over the Giants at the Polo Grounds. In the ninth inning, Johnny Mize doubled on a close play at second. Two Giants were ejected arguing the call. Lynn Myers ran for Mize, and scored when New York pitcher Manny Salvo threw wildly to first after fielding a bunt by Don Gutteridge.

JUNE 11   The Cardinals save a split with a four-run rally in the ninth inning to win the second game of a doubleheader against the Phillies in Philadelphia 4–1. The Cards started the ninth-inning rally with two outs and no one on base. Don Padgett broke the 1–1 tie with a bases-loaded triple. The Phils won the opener 5–4 in 11 innings.

JUNE 21   The Cardinals score eight runs in the fourth inning and rout the Phillies 14–2 at Sportsman's Park.

The Cardinals defeated the Phillies in St. Louis 17 games in a row from August 30, 1938, through June 1, 1940.

JUNE 28   Dizzy Dean takes the mound at Sportsman's Park for the first time since the April 1938 trade, but is knocked out in the first inning as the Cardinals defeat the Cubs 8–4.

JULY 3

Johnny Mize collects two homers, a triple, and a double during a 5–3 win over the Cubs in Chicago.

JULY 23

The Cardinals sweep the Dodgers 12–0 and 8–2 in Brooklyn. The first game was the second experiment in the use of yellow baseballs (see August 2, 1938). The Cards collected 20 hits in the opener. Cardinal pitcher Bob Bowman retired the first 20 batters to face him before Ernie Koy singled with two outs in the seventh inning. Bowman settled for a three-hitter.

JULY 26

Cardinals hurler Tom Sunkel pitches a two-hitter for a 10–0 win over the Giants at Sportsman's Park. The bid for a no-hitter was spoiled when Tom Hafey singled with one out in the eighth inning. Billy Jurges added another single in the ninth. It was Sunkel's first major league complete game, and proved to be his only shutout in a Cardinal uniform.

> Sunkel had a career record of 9–15, but it was remarkable that he reached the majors at all considering that he was blind in one eye due to an inoperable cataract. The condition dated back to when he was four years old and was shot in the left eye with a stick fired from a toy gun. Despite the handicap, Sunkel compiled a .212 batting average in 66 big-league at-bats.

JULY 27

Don Padgett hits a pinch-hit grand slam off Manny Salvo during a 9–4 win over the Giants at Sportsman's Park.

JULY 30

The experiment with yellow baseballs continues during a doubleheader between the Cardinals and Dodgers at Sportsman's Park. The Cards won both games by 5–2 scores.

AUGUST 1

Joe Medwick throws a tantrum after being removed for defensive purposes in the ninth inning of a 4–3 win over the Braves at Sportsman's Park.

> Ray Blades made the switch to Lynn King with two outs in the inning, one man on base, and a 2–1 count on Boston hitter Tony Cuccinello. As King made his way to Medwick's position, Medwick heaved his glove high into the air. Then he trudged belligerently after the glove, kicked it a couple of times, picked it up, and stomped off the field. Medwick did not use the customary dugout exit to the clubhouse, but headed for a vehicle gate near third base. Just as he swung the latch, Clyde Shoun put over a third strike on Cuccinello and the game was over.

AUGUST 4

After spotting the Phillies a 7–0 lead in the fifth inning, the Cardinals rally to win 9–5 in 13 innings at Sportsman's Park. Joe Medwick hit an RBI-double in the ninth to tie the score 8–8, then drove in the winner with a walk-off double in the thirteenth.

AUGUST 6

The Cardinals sweep the Phillies 11–0 and 8–3 at Sportsman's Park. Joe Medwick collected six hits, including a homer, a triple, and a double, in nine at-bats during the twin bill.

AUGUST 9

The Cardinals run their winning streak to 10 games with a 5–3 decision over the Pirates at Sportsman's Park.

AUGUST 13

An overflow crowd of 40,087 at Sportsman's Park watches the Cardinals sweep the first-place Reds in a pair of 4–3 decisions that cut Cincinnati's lead to 6½ games.

Uncounted thousands entered for free after club management closed the bleacher gate and the mob tore the gate off its hinges. The start of the first game was delayed 10 minutes in an attempt to get the overflow behind the ropes in the outfield. The second tilt was delayed another 10 minutes after Don Padgett homered in the seventh inning and dozens of fans ran onto the field in celebration.

AUGUST 14   The Cardinals purchase Lyn Lary from the Dodgers.

AUGUST 15   On Terry Moore Day at Sportsman's Park, Moore collects three hits and scores the winning run in a 10-inning, 7–6 win over the Cubs.

The day began with a parade from the southern end of the city to the Cardinals' ballpark. A prize of $10 was offered for the most brilliantly decorated car. Before the game, Moore was showered with gifts, which included a 20-gauge shotgun, a hunting dog, a fishing outfit, a $50 check, a tent, a gold pin, wearing apparel, and coupons for free shaves at a St. Louis barber shop.

AUGUST 16   Terry Moore drives in all four Cardinal runs on a pair of inside-the-park homers during a 4–3 win over the Pirates in the first game of a doubleheader at Forbes Field. Both of the homers came on drives that were badly misplayed by Pittsburgh left fielder Johnny Rizzo. The first homer, struck in the fifth inning, tied the score 2–2. The second came in the ninth with the Cardinals trailing 3–2. The Cards completed the sweep with a 3–0 triumph in the second tilt.

AUGUST 20   Johnny Mize drives in six runs on two homers and a double in a 7–5 win over the Reds in the second game of a doubleheader against the Reds at Crosley Field. The Cards also won the first game, 3–1, to cut Cincinnati's lead to 3½ games.

AUGUST 22   Johnny Mize and Jimmy Brown come together in a frightening collision during an 8–5 loss to the Dodgers in Brooklyn.

The collision took place in the seventh inning at second base when both infielders ran to the bag to take a throw. The 160-pound Brown was struck in the head and went out like a light while the 230-pound Mize suffered a bruised shoulder and jaw. Brown was rushed to a nearby hospital with a severe concussion. The accident was witnessed by his mother, who was visiting from North Carolina and was watching her son play a big-league game for the first time. Brown missed 10 games.

AUGUST 26   Johnny Mize draws a National League record six walks in a doubleheader as the Cardinals sweep the Phillies 5–0 and 11–4 in Philadelphia.

SEPTEMBER 2   A day after Germany invades Poland, triggering a declaration of war from England and France and the start of World War II, Johnny Mize misses an 11–2 loss to the Pirates at Sportsman's Park when a bat slips out of the hands of Pepper Martin during batting practice and strikes Mize on the shoulder. The shoulder was already sore from his collision with Jimmy Brown 11 days earlier.

SEPTEMBER 3   The Cardinals sweep the Pirates 14–6 and 3–0 at Sportsman's Park. The Cards piled up 20 hits in the opener.

SEPTEMBER 9   The Cardinals rout the Pirates 12–2 in Pittsburgh.

SEPTEMBER 10   The Cardinals sweep the Pirates 9–3 and 11–4 in a doubleheader in Pittsburgh. Curt
                   Davis picked up his 20th victory of the season in the opener. The Cards scored eight
                   runs in the fifth inning of the second tilt.

                   *Davis was 22–16 with seven saves and a 3.53 ERA while making 31 starts and
                   18 relief appearances for the Cardinals in 1939.*

SEPTEMBER 15   The Cardinals outlast the Braves 1–0 in 14 innings at Sportsman's Park. The winning
                   run scored on a double by Enos Slaughter and a single by Joe Medwick. The shutout
                   was achieved by the combined efforts of Bob Bowman (11 innings), Bill McGee ($^{1}/_{3}$
                   of an inning), Clyde Shoun ($^{2}/_{3}$ of an inning), and Lon Warneke (1 inning).

SEPTEMBER 18   After absorbing a 7–2 loss to the Giants in the first game of a doubleheader at
                   Sportsman's Park, the Cardinals rebound to win 15–5. The Cards collected 22 hits in
                   the second contest. Johnny Mize had five of the hits, including a homer and a triple,
                   in five at-bats.

SEPTEMBER 21   The Cardinals score two runs in the ninth inning to defeat the Dodgers 6–5 at
                   Sportsman's Park. The rally started after two were out on singles by Jimmy Brown,
                   Don Gutteridge, and Enos Slaughter and a double by Joe Medwick. The win put the
                   Cardinals 2½ games behind the Reds with 11 contests left on the schedule.

SEPTEMBER 27   Bill McGee keeps the Cardinals' slim hopes for a National League pennant alive
                   by defeating the Reds 4–0 in Cincinnati. The Cards were 2½ games out with four
                   contest left.

SEPTEMBER 28   The Cardinals are eliminated from the National League pennant with a 5–3 loss to
                   the Reds in Cincinnati.

OCTOBER 1   During a 2–1 loss to the Cubs in Chicago on the last day of the season, Don Padgett
                   loses a chance at finishing the season with a batting average of .400.

                   *Padgett entered the game with a .399 average in 253 at-bats. Pinch hitting in the
                   eighth inning, Padgett lined a clean single up the middle, but upon reaching first
                   base learned that the first-base umpire had called time a split second before the
                   pitch because a ball rolled loose in the bullpen. Padgett returned to the plate and
                   drew a walk in what proved to be his last plate appearance to finish the season
                   with an average of .39914. Had the hit stood, his season batting average would
                   have been .402. Padgett had an unusual career, because he was converted from
                   an outfielder to a catcher in 1938, his second season in the majors at a time when
                   he was 26 years old after a string of injuries hit the Cardinal catchers. Padgett
                   played 251 games as a catcher and 246 in the outfield during his big-league
                   career.*

DECEMBER 27   The Cardinals send Ken Raffensberger to the Cubs for Steve Mesner and Gene
                   Lillard.

THE STATE OF THE CARDINALS

The 1940s was the best decade in Cardinals history. The club posted a record of 960–580, a winning percentage of .623 that topped the majors. The Yankees were second best during the 1940s, with a record of 955–582 (.621), although the Yankees claimed four World Championships to the Cardinals' three. The Cards won the National League pennant in 1942, 1943, 1944, and 1946 and claimed the World Series title in 1942, 1944, and 1946. St. Louis finished either first or second every season from 1941 through 1949. Other NL clubs that won pennants were the Reds (1940), Dodgers (1941, 1947, and 1949), and Cubs (1945). The Dodgers, managed for much of the decade by ex-Cardinal Leo Durocher, were a bitter rival. There were four pennant races (1941, 1942, 1946, and 1949) between the two clubs that were not decided until the final week. The feud erupted into a major on-field brawl almost every year during the 1940s.

THE BEST TEAM

The 1942 Cardinals had the best record of the decade at 106–48, topping the Dodgers by two games in a heated pennant race. The 1943 and 1944 clubs were both 105–49, although neither was at full strength because many regulars were serving in the military. The 1943 Cards won the NL pennant by 18 games.

THE WORST TEAM

Every Cardinal club during the 1940s posted a winning record. The worst club was in 1940, but it was still strong enough to compile an 84–69 mark.

THE BEST MOMENT

The best moment happened on October 1, 1944, when the Browns clinched the American League pennant, setting up the only all–St. Louis World Series in history. The Cardinals defeated the Browns in six games.

THE WORST MOMENT

The worst moment occurred in the final week of the 1949 season when the Cardinals blew a 1½-game lead by losing four in a row to the lowly Pirates and Cubs.

THE ALL-DECADE TEAM • YEARS W/CARDS

Walker Cooper, c	1940–45, 1956–57
Ray Sanders, 1b	1942–45
Red Schoendienst, 2b	1945–56, 1961–63
Whitey Kurowski, 3b	1941–49
Marty Marion, ss	1940–50
Stan Musial, lf	1941–44, 1946–63
Terry Moore, cf	1935–42, 1946–48
Enos Slaughter, rf	1938–42, 1946–53
Harry Brecheen, p	1940, 1943–52
Mort Cooper, p	1938–45
Howie Pollet, p	1941–43, 1946–51
Al Brazle, p	1943, 1946–54

Other outstanding players for the Cardinals during the 1940s were pitchers Max Lanier (1938–46, 1949–51), George Munger (1943–44, 1946–52), Murry Dickson (1939–40, 1942–43, 1948–48, 1956–57), and Ted Wilks (1944–51), outfielder–first baseman Johnny Hopp (1939–45), infielder Jimmy Brown (1937–43), and first baseman Johnny Mize (1936–41). Musial, Slaughter, Schoendienst, and Mize are in the Hall of Fame, while Marion and Walker Cooper are among those who have drawn consideration from voters in the past.

THE DECADE LEADERS

Batting Avg:	Musial	.346
On-Base Pct:	Musial	.426
Slugging Pct:	Musial	.578
Home Runs:	Musial	146
RBIs:	Musial	706
Runs:	Musial	815
Stolen Bases:	Hopp	69
Wins:	Brecheen	103
Strikeouts:	Brecheen	743
ERA:	Lanier	2.66
Saves:	Wilks	28

THE HOME FIELD

Night baseball was played at Sportsman's Park for the first time in 1940. Other than the addition of light towers, the ballpark changed little during the decade. Four World Series and two All-Star games were played at the facility during the forties.

THE GAME YOU WISH YOU HAD SEEN

One of the most thrilling Game Sevens in World Series history took place at Sportsman's Park on October 15, 1946. Enos Slaughter made his "mad dash" around the bases in the eighth inning to score the winning run for a 4–3 victory over the Red Sox.

THE WAY THE GAME WAS PLAYED

The most significant change in the game was integration with the arrival of Jackie Robinson in 1947. The Cardinals did not integrate until 1954, however. League statistics and averages in 1949 looked very similar to those of 1940, although offense dipped during the war years and there was a surge in home runs at the end of the decade. Home runs in the NL jumped from 562 in 1946 to 1,100 in 1950.

THE MANAGEMENT

When the decade started, the hugely successful team of president and majority owner Sam Breadon and vice president Branch Rickey had been running the Cardinals for 20 years. The two gradually developed a mutual resentment over the years, however, and Rickey left St. Louis in October 1942 to take over as president of the Dodgers. Breadon sold the Cards in November 1947 to a group headed by Fred Saigh, who owned 51 percent of the stock. Although Saigh was majority owner, he held the title of vice president with Robert Hannegan as president. Hannegan died of a heart attack in October 1949 at the age of 46, and Saigh succeeded him as president. Field managers were Ray Blades (1939–40), Mike Gonzalez (1940), Billy Southworth (1940–45), and Eddie Dyer (1946–50).

THE BEST PLAYER MOVE

The best player move was the signing of Red Schoendienst to a contract during a tryout camp in St. Louis in 1942. Schoendienst reached the majors in 1945. There were no outstanding trades.

THE WORST PLAYER MOVE

The worst player move was the trade of Johnny Mize to the Giants in December 1941.

1940

Season in a Sentence

Consensus picks by sportswriters to win the National League pennant, the Cardinals dispel that illusion by losing 29 of their first 44 games, leading to two managerial changes.

Finish • Won • Lost • Pct • GB

Third   84   69   .549   16.0

Managers

Ray Blades (14–24), Mike Gonzalez (1–5), and Billy Southworth (69–40)

Stats

Stats	Cards	NL	Rank
Batting Avg:	.275	.264	2
On-Base Pct:	.336	.326	2
Slugging Pct:	.411	.376	1
Home Runs:	119		1
Stolen Bases:	97		1
ERA:	3.83	3.85	5
Fielding Avg:	.971	.972	3
Runs Scored:	747		2
Runs Allowed:	699		5

Starting Lineup

Mickey Owen, c
Johnny Mize, 1b
Joe Orengo, 2b-ss
Stu Martin, 3b-2b
Marty Marion, ss
Ernie Koy, lf
Terry Moore, cf
Enos Slaughter, rf
Jimmy Brown, 2b-3b-ss
Don Padgett, c
Pepper Martin, rf-lf

Pitchers

Lon Warneke, sp
Bill McGee, sp
Mort Cooper, sp
Bob Bowman, sp-rp
Clyde Shoun, rp
Max Lanier, rp-sp
Carl Boyle, rp-sp

Attendance

324,078 (sixth in NL)

Club Leaders

Batting Avg:	Mize	.314
On-Base Pct:	Mize	.404
Slugging Pct:	Mize	.536
Home Runs:	Mize	43
RBIs:	Mize	137
Runs:	Mize	111
Stolen Bases:	Moore	18
Wins:	Warneke	16
	McGee	16
Strikeouts:	Cooper	95
ERA:	Warneke	3.14
Saves:	Shoun	5

JANUARY 31   The Cardinals and Browns jointly announce plans to install lights for night games at Sportsman's Park. The two clubs agreed to split the $150,000 cost of installing the lighting plant (see May 24, 1940, and June 4, 1940).

APRIL 16   In the season opener, the Cardinals lose 6–4 to the Pirates before 16,599 at Sportsman's Park. The Cards trailed 6–0 when they scored all four of their runs during a sixth-inning rally. Marty Marion made his big-league debut and went 1 for 4 with a double.

> *Marion was a fixture at shortstop for the Cardinals from 1940 through 1950. He wasn't a great hitter, hitting just .263 and slugging .345 during his career, but most contemporaries hail Marion as the best defensive shortstop of his generation, if not all time. He played in four World Series for the Cards and was named to seven All-Star teams. During his career, Marion played in 1,502 games and collected 1,402 hits and 261 doubles.*

APRIL 22   The Reds defeat the Cardinals 6–1 in a game in Cincinnati that was nearly postponed by rising flood waters.

Crosley Field was located near Mill Creek, which flooded frequently. The water in the dugout was three feet deep when the April 22 game began, and the players had to sit on benches in foul territory. The flood crept up inch by inch during the contest and by the ninth inning had begun to spill onto the field and into the first few rows of box seats. Both the April 23 and 24 games between the Reds and Cardinals were called off because the diamond was underwater.

APRIL 25   The Cardinals rap 22 hits and defeat the Pirates 10–9 in Pittsburgh.

For the 1940 season, the Cardinals dropped the white cap with red stripes the club had worn since 1920 and that defined the Gas House Gang teams. The new cap was navy blue with the intertwined S-T-L monogram in red on the front, and a red bill. An extra stripe was also added down the shoulder on the jersey. With a few minor alterations, the Cardinals would use this style uniform through 1955.

MAY 7   The Cardinals set club records with seven homers and 49 total bases during an 18–2 annihilation of the Dodgers in Brooklyn. Johnny Mize and Eddie Lake each hit two homers, and Don Padgett, Stu Martin, and Joe Medwick added one each. The 49 total bases came on seven homers, two triples, four doubles, and seven singles.

The homers by Lake were the first two of his major league career, his only two in 1940, and the only two he struck in 79 games as a Cardinal. Lake didn't hit another big-league homer until 1943, when he was playing for the Red Sox.

MAY 9   In his major league debut, Ernie White pitches 7²/₃ innings of hitless relief and collects three hits in three at-bats to lead the Cardinals to an 8–4 defeat of the Phillies at Sportsman's Park.

White pitched in only eight games in 1940 but emerged in 1941 with a 17–7 record and a 2.40 ERA at the age of 24. He looked like a coming star, but he ran into arm problems and missed two years in the service during World War II. He finished his career with a 30–21 record, and none of his wins came after 1943. One of White's high school classmates in Pacolet, South Carolina, was General William Westmoreland.

MAY 13   Johnny Mize hits three homers during a 14-inning, 8–8 tie against the Reds in Cincinnati in a contest called by darkness. Mize homered in the second and third innings against Johnny Vander Meer and in the thirteenth off Milt Shoffner. The third homer gave the Cards an 8–7 lead, but the Reds came back to tie the game in the bottom of the inning.

When game time arrived, there were no umpires on hand. The contest was played to make up one of the games lost to the flood in April on what was originally an open date in the schedule, and the league neglected to assign umpires. Fortunately, National League umpire Larry Goetz was at his home in the Cincinnati neighborhood of Walnut Hills, and was called to officiate. The start of the game was delayed for 29 minutes until Goetz arrived. Reds coach Jimmie Wilson umpired at first base, and Cardinals pitcher Lon Warneke was stationed at third. Wilson and Warneke each received $50 from the league office for performing the extra duty. Warneke became an umpire after his playing days were over, serving the National League in that capacity from 1949 through

1955. Crosley Field had lights, but the game was called by darkness because of an anachronistic major league rule stipulating that the lights couldn't be turned on to finish day games. The rule wasn't changed until 1950.

MAY 18   The Cardinals strike five homers during a 6–2 win over the Dodgers in Brooklyn. Johnny Mize and Terry Moore each hit two homers, and Joe Medwick added the other.

With another outstanding season, Mize topped the NL in home runs (43), RBIs (137), total bases (368), and slugging percentage (.636). He scored 111 runs and collected 182 hits, 31 doubles, and 13 triples and batted .314.

MAY 24   In the first major league night game played in St. Louis, the Browns lose 3–2 to the Indians before 24,627 at Sportsman's Park. Bob Feller pitched a complete game for Cleveland and hit his first major league home run (see June 4, 1940).

JUNE 4   Seven days after Holland's and Belgium's surrender to Germany and on the same day that 350,000 British troops are evacuated at Dunkirk, the Cardinals play their first regular-season night game at home and lose 10–1 to the Dodgers before 23,500 at Sportsman's Park. Joe Medwick collected five hits, including three doubles in five at-bats, but received little help from his teammates. The opening night game was spoiled by a barrage of bottles thrown onto the field by disgruntled fans.

The Browns and the Cardinals were the eighth and ninth major league clubs to play home games at night. Rules in force in 1940 limited both National and American League teams to seven night games a season.

JUNE 7   The Cardinals fire Ray Blades as manager and replace him with coach Mike Gonzalez on an interim basis. A week later Billy Southworth took over as manager of the club.

The Cards were expected to contend in 1940 after Blades brought the team from a sixth-place finish in 1938 to second in 1939. But the Cards were off to a disappointing start, and Blades was fired with St. Louis holding a 14–24 record. A drop in attendance was another reason. Breadon was livid because the Cardinals' first night game at home three days earlier failed to sell out. Blades kept detailed notes on the strengths and weaknesses of every player in the National League, something few of his contemporaries did. He made more pitching changes and used more pinch hitters and pinch runners than anyone else of his time. It worked in 1939. The Cardinals were second in the NL in ERA while using pitchers in relief 210 times, 47 more than any other club in the league. The Cards also finished last in complete games. But when the club began losing in 1940, Blades drew considerable heat for his frequent lineup changes. With the exception of one game as interim manager with the Dodgers in 1948, Blades never managed another club, although he was a big-league coach as late as 1956. Southworth previously managed the Cardinals for the first part of the 1929 season but was released from his duties in July when the defending NL champions had a record of 43–45. The Cardinals kept Southworth in the organization as a minor league manager. While managing in the minors in 1932, his wife and twin babies died in childbirth. Already a heavy drinker, Southworth's alcohol consumption increased after the tragedy. A few years later he gave up the booze and remarried a woman 19 years his junior in 1935. After winning several league championships in the minors, Southworth earned a trip back to the big leagues. It proved to be a wise choice. Unlike his first term as a big-league manager, Southworth was laid-back, patient, and understanding. Under his guidance, the Cards were 1,001–659 from 1940 through 1945, a winning percentage of .603. The Cardinals won the NL pennant in 1942, 1943, and 1944 and the World Series in 1942 and 1944.

JUNE 8   Another shower of bottles, the second such occurrence in less than a week, and a doubleheader loss to the Giants by scores of 4–2 and 5–2 mar Bill DeLancey Day at Sportsman's Park. After umpire Tom Dunn ruled that Terry Moore had short-hopped a drive off the bat of Babe Young, fans in the bleachers and grandstand threw hundreds of glass bottles onto the field. Fans in the lower stands were in danger because many of the missiles thrown from the upper deck fell short of their mark and smashed in the seats and aisles.

DeLancey was presented with a car in pregame ceremonies. He appeared to be on the way to becoming a star before he contracted tuberculosis in 1935, when he was only 23. DeLancey missed four straight seasons from 1936 through 1939 while recovering in Phoenix, Arizona. He returned in 1940 but appeared in only 15 games. DeLancey died in 1946 on his 35th birthday.

JUNE 12   The Cardinals shock their fans by sending superstar outfielder Joe Medwick to the Dodgers along with Curt Davis for Ernie Koy, Carl Doyle, Sam Nahem, Bert Haas, and cash.

The amount of cash wasn't disclosed, but it was in excess of $100,000. The Cardinals had grown weary of Medwick's salary demands and believed that he was on the decline. While Medwick was past his peak, he was still among the top outfielders in the game. It proved to be a horrible deal that cost the Cardinals a championship. Medwick gave the Dodgers three stellar seasons and helped his new club beat out the Cards for the 1941 National League pennant. The Cardinals could also have used Davis during the 1941 season when he was 13–7 for the Dodgers. None of the four players acquired in the deal aided the Cards in any significant manner.

JUNE 15   The Cardinals wallop the Phillies 14–1 in Philadelphia.

JUNE 18   Just six days after being traded from the Cardinals to the Dodgers, Joe Medwick is beaned by St. Louis pitcher Bob Bowman in the first inning of an 11-inning, 7–5 victory over Brooklyn at Ebbets Field.

Bowman denied throwing at Medwick intentionally, but few believed him. Bowman had exchanged words with Medwick and Dodgers manager Leo Durocher that morning at Manhattan's Hotel New Yorker. According to Durocher, Bowman shouted, "I'll take care of both of you guys! Wait and see!" On Medwick's first at-bat, he was hit in a temple with a fastball, which gave him a severe concussion. The next day, Durocher sought out Bowman at the hotel, and the two nearly came to blows. National League president Ford Frick spent several days accumulating testimony from nearly everyone on both clubs but absolved Bowman of any blame in the incident. Medwick was playing again in four days.

JUNE 19   The Cardinals make seven errors during an 8–3 loss to the Dodgers in Brooklyn. Shortstop Marty Marion committed four of the errors, three of them in one inning. It was the first defeat the Cardinals suffered since Billy Southworth took over as manager, breaking a six-game winning streak.

With tensions high following the beaning of Joe Medwick the previous day, Mickey Owen and Leo Durocher engaged in a fistfight. Owen took exception to a remark by Durocher as the Cardinal catcher walked off the field in the third inning. Owen charged Durocher. Players from both teams joined in the melee, which was broken up by the umpires. Owen was fined $50 by Ford Frick for "conduct tending to incite disorder." Less than six months later, Owen was traded to the Dodgers, where he played under Durocher.

JUNE 22   On the day that France surrenders to Germany, the Cardinals score seven runs in the sixth inning and defeat the Braves 9–2 in Boston.

JUNE 26   The Cardinals lose 10–9 in 10 innings at the Polo Grounds. There were 13 runs scored in the seventh inning by the two clubs. The Cards scored seven runs in the top of the inning to take a 9–3 lead, but the Giants roared back with six tallies in their half to tie the contest.

JUNE 28   Pepper Martin hits a grand slam off Dick Lanahan in the ninth inning of an 8–2 win over the Pirates in Pittsburgh.

JUNE 30   Mort Cooper pitches the Cardinals to a 1–0 win over the Pirates in the first game of a doubleheader at Forbes Field. Pittsburgh won the second tilt 2–0.

JULY 9   The All-Star Game is played at Sportsman's Park for the first time, and the National League wins 4–0 before a crowd of 32,373. Five NL pitchers combined on a three-hitter. Max West of the Braves hit a three-run homer off Red Ruffing in the first inning. West left the game in the second when he was injured crashing into the right field wall.

Future Hall of Famers on the playing rosters of the two clubs included Luke Appling, Lou Boudreau, Joe DiMaggio, Bill Dickey, Leo Durocher, Bob Feller, Jimmie Foxx, Hank Greenberg, Billy Herman, Carl Hubbell, Ernie Lombardi, Joe Medwick, Johnny Mize, Mel Ott, Red Ruffing, Arky Vaughan, and Ted Williams.

JULY 13   Johnny Mize hits for the cycle in a 7–6 win over the Giants in the first game of a doubleheader against the Giants at Sportsman's Park. Mize completed the cycle with a triple in the ninth inning and scored the winning run on an error when New York catcher Harry Danning couldn't handle the throw to the plate. The Cards also won the second game, 4–3, with a run in the ninth.

JULY 15   The Cardinals pound out 20 hits and hammer the Braves 12–2 at Sportsman's Park.

JULY 21   Enos Slaughter drives in all five runs with two homers and a single during a 5–2 win over the Dodgers in the second game of a doubleheader at Sportsman's Park. Brooklyn won the first game 3–1.

Slaughter hit .306 with 17 homers in 1940.

JULY 30   The Cardinals clobber the Braves 13–5 in Boston.

JULY 31   The Cardinals win both ends of a doubleheader, 3–1 in 11 innings in the first tilt and 17–8 in the second, in Boston.

AUGUST 7   Trailing 8–0, the Cardinals score seven runs in the seventh inning and tie the game 8–8 in the eighth, but wind up losing 10–9 to the Pirates in Pittsburgh.

AUGUST 11   Mort Cooper pitches a two-hitter to down the Reds 3–2 in the first game of a doubleheader at Crosley Field. The only Cincinnati hits were singles by Billy Werber and Ernie Lombardi in the fourth inning. The Cardinals completed the sweep with a 3–1 win in the second contest.

AUGUST 24   The Cardinals run their winning streak to nine games with a 1–0 decision over the Phillies at Sportsman's Park. Lon Warneke pitched the shutout. Terry Moore drove in the lone run of the game with a single in the fifth inning.

                 Warneke had a record of 16–10 with a 3.14 ERA in 1940.

AUGUST 29   The Cardinals score five runs in the first inning to provide all of the scoring in a 5–0 victory over the Giants at Sportsman's Park. Bill McGee pitched a two-hit shutout. The only New York hits were singles by Johnny Rucker and Tony Cuccinello.

SEPTEMBER 8   Johnny Mize hits three consecutive homers and drives in six runs, but the Cardinals lose a 16–14 slugfest to the Pirates in the first game of a doubleheader at Sportsman's Park. Pittsburgh also won the nightcap, 5–4.

SEPTEMBER 15   Enos Slaughter hits a grand slam in the seventh inning off Ike Pearson during a 7–0 win over the Phillies in the first game of a doubleheader in Philadelphia. The Cards also won the second fray, 3–1.

SEPTEMBER 18   Two days after the passage of the Selective Service Act, America's first peacetime draft, Johnny Mize drives in six runs on four singles as the Cardinals crush the Dodgers 14–7 in Brooklyn.

SEPTEMBER 27   Lon Warneke pitches a two-hitter to defeat the Cubs 11–1 at Sportsman's Park. The only Chicago hits were a single by Bill Nicholson and a double by Rip Russell in the fourth inning. Johnny Mize hit his 43rd home run of the season during the contest to break the club record of 42 set by Rogers Hornsby in 1922.

                 Mize held the club record for home runs in a season until Mark McGwire clubbed 70 in 1998. No Cardinal batter reached the 40–home run mark from 1941 through 1997.

SEPTEMBER 29   With his brother Walker as the catcher, Mort Cooper pitches a shutout to defeat the Cubs 6–0 at Sportsman's Park on the final day of the season.

                 Mort and Walker Cooper starred together on the Cardinals from 1940 through 1944. The two formed one of the best sibling batteries in baseball history. Mort compiled a composite record of 65–22 for the Cardinals from 1942 through 1944, all on pennant-winning teams. Walker, who was 22 months younger than Mort, was on every All-Star roster from 1942 through 1950 with the exception of 1945, when he was in the Navy. Mort was the NL MVP in 1942. Walker was the runner-up to Stan Musial in the balloting in 1943. Like many Cardinals during the years that Sam Breadon ran the club, the Cooper brothers were dissatisfied with the size of their paychecks, and both were dealt after disagreements over money. Mort was traded to the Braves in 1945 after leaving the club in a salary dispute. Walker was dealt to the Giants a year later. During his years with the Cardinals, Mort posted a record of 105–50. His winning percentage of .677 is the best of any Cardinal pitcher since 1900 with at least 100 decisions. Mort's earned run average of 2.77 in St. Louis is the best of any pitcher with at least 1,000 innings with the club since 1920. He completed 105 of his 186 starts, pitched 1,480¹/₃ innings and posted 28 shutouts, third best in Cardinals history behind only Bob Gibson (56) and Bill Doak (32).

NOVEMBER 25   Three weeks after Franklin Roosevelt wins a third term as president by defeating Wendell Willkie, the Cardinals sell Joe Orengo to the Giants.

Orengo hit .287 in 129 games as a 25-year-old rookie second baseman for the Cardinals in 1940 but batted only .209 over the remaining four seasons of his sojourn in the big leagues.

DECEMBER 2   The Cardinals sell Stu Martin to the Pirates.

DECEMBER 4   The Cardinals send Mickey Owen to the Dodgers for Gus Mancuso, John Pinrat, and $65,000.

Owen was named to the National League All-Star team each season from 1941 through 1944, but the Cardinals had a better option at catcher in Walker Cooper.

DECEMBER 5   The Cardinals sell Bob Bowman to the Giants.

1941

Season in a Sentence

Despite injuries to nearly every hitter in the starting lineup, the Cardinals win 97 games and hang in the pennant race until the final week of the season.

Finish • Won • Lost • Pct • GB

Second   97   56   .634   2.5

Manager

Billy Southworth

Stats

Stats	Cards	• NL •	Rank
Batting Avg:	.272	.258	2
On-Base Pct:	.340	.326	2
Slugging Pct:	.377	.361	2
Home Runs:	70		4
Stolen Bases:	47		5
ERA:	3.19	3.63	3
Fielding Avg:	.973	.972	4
Runs Scored:	734		2
Runs Allowed:	589		3

Starting Lineup

Gus Mancuso, c
Johnny Mize, 1b
Creepy Crespi, 2b
Jimmy Brown, 3b
Marty Marion, ss
Johnny Hopp, lf
Terry Moore, cf
Enos Slaughter, rf
Don Padgett, lf
Walker Cooper, c
Coaker Triplett, lf
Estel Crabtree, rf-lf-cf

Pitchers

Lon Warneke, sp
Ernie White, sp
Mort Cooper, sp
Harry Gumbert, sp-rp
Max Lanier, sp-rp
Howie Krist, rp
Sam Nahem, rp

Attendance

633,645 (fourth in NL)

Club Leaders

Batting Avg:	Mize	.317
On-Base Pct:	Mize	.406
Slugging Pct:	Mize	.535
Home Runs:	Mize	16
RBIs:	Mize	100
Runs:	Moore	86
Stolen Bases:	Hopp	15
Wins:	Warneke	17
	White	17
Strikeouts:	Cooper	118
ERA:	White	2.40
Saves:	Hutchinson	5

APRIL 15   In the season opener, the Cardinals defeat the Reds 7–3 in Cincinnati. Lon Warneke earned the complete-game victory. Johnny Mize collected three hits, including a homer and a double, and three RBIs. Terry Moore had three hits, including a double, and scored three runs. Enos Slaughter and Ernie Koy also homered for the Cardinals.

The Cardinals started the season with three straight wins against the defending World Champion Reds.

APRIL 18   In the home opener, the Cardinals lose 6–4 to the Cubs before 11,989 at Sportsman's Park.

Sam Breadon tossed a party at the Fairgrounds Hotel for mayors of towns and cities within a 150-mile radius of St. Louis. The party was an annual event. All of the mayors were guests of the Cardinals at the opener.

APRIL 26   Max Lanier pitches a two-hitter to defeat the Cubs 6–2 at Wrigley Field. The only Chicago hits were singles by Dom Dallesandro and Bill Nicholson. The two Cubs runs scored in the third inning on four walks and a balk.

Born a right-hander, Lanier converted to a southpaw after breaking his right arm twice as a child. That didn't prevent him from a major league career that started in 1938 and ended in 1953. Max's son Hal was later a major league player and manager. As a Cardinal, Lanier was 101–69. He would have won many more if he hadn't missed the 1945 season due to World War II or had remained with the club in 1946 instead of defecting to the Mexican League (see May 23, 1946). Lanier was barred from organized baseball until 1949 because of the move. In addition to his 101 wins in St. Louis, Lanier posted a 2.84 ERA with 754 strikeouts and pitched 20 shutouts and 1,454²/₃ innings.

MAY 3   Making his first major league start, Hank Gornicki of the Cardinals pitches a one-hitter to defeat Phillies 6–0 at Philadelphia. The only Philadelphia hit was a single by Stan Benjamin with two outs in the sixth inning.

A native of Niagara Falls, New York, Gornicki was 30 years old when he made his big-league debut. Despite the one-hitter, he never made another start for the Cardinals, in part because he gave up four runs in 2²/₃ innings in three relief appearances. The Cardinals also had a staff full of great young pitchers: Howie Pollet (age 20), Ernie White (24), Max Lanier (25), and Howie Krist (25). Gornicki was sent back to the minors, then sold to the Cubs later in the 1941 season. He finished his career in 1946 with a record of 15–19.

MAY 5   The Cardinals win their 10th game in a row with a 5–1 decision over the Braves at Boston. The victory gave the Cardinals a 15–3 record on the 1941 season.

The Cards recorded the 10-game winning streak with eight different starting pitchers. The eight were Lon Warneke, Max Lanier, Mort Cooper, Bill McGee, Sam Nahem, Howie Krist, Hank Gornicki, and Ernie White.

MAY 14   The Cardinals sell Ernie Koy to the Reds and swap Bill McGee to the Giants for Paul Dean, Harry Gumbert, and cash.

MAY 26   The Cardinals blow a nine-run lead before defeating the Cubs 12–11 in 11 innings at Sportsman's Park. The Cardinals went up 9–0 with two runs in the second inning and seven in the third, but the Cubs scored six in the fourth, one in the fifth, and three in the seventh to go up 10–9. Don Padgett's double in the ninth tied the game 10–10. Bill Nicholson homered in the top of the eleventh before the Cards came back with two in their half to win. Jimmy Brown homered to lead off the inning, and with one out Padgett hit a walk-off homer. Padgett didn't enter the game until the fifth inning, replacing Coaker Triplett.

Brown had the best season of his career in 1941, batting .306.

MAY 28   A three-run uprising in the ninth inning beats the Cubs 6–5 at Sportsman's Park. Coaker Triplett tripled in the first run and then scored on Steve Mesner's single. A walk-off single by Don Padgett scored the winning run. It was the Cardinals' ninth win in a row.

MAY 29   The Cardinals defeat the Reds 10–9 at Sportsman's Park for their 10th win in a row, including the last five by one run. Cincinnati rallied for three runs in the ninth inning, but shortstop Marty Marion leaped high in the air to catch Ernie Lombardi's liner and threw to second base, doubling off Ernie Koy to end the game.

The win gave the Cardinals a 30–9 record and a three-game lead in the NL pennant race.

JUNE 10   Lon Warneke pitches a one-hitter to defeat the Phillies 3–0 at Shibe Park. Emmett Mueller, the leadoff batter in the first inning, lined a single to right field, and Warneke shut Philadelphia down the rest of the way.

Warneke had a 17–9 record and 3.15 ERA in 1941.

JUNE 13   Max Lanier pitches the Cardinals to a 1–0 win over the Dodgers in Brooklyn. Don Padgett drove in the lone run of the game with a single in the third inning.

Sam Nahem, who pitched for the Cardinals in 1941 and 1942, held a law degree from Brooklyn's St. John's College. He was nicknamed "Subway Sam" because he commuted from his home in Manhattan to Brooklyn while attending school.

JUNE 15   After losing the first game of a doubleheader at Sportsman's Park to the Dodgers 8–1, the Cardinals come back and win the nightcap 3–0 behind Ernie White's two-hitter. The only Brooklyn hits were doubles by Pee Wee Reese and opposing pitcher Hugh Casey. Two wins by the Dodgers would have knocked the Cardinals out of first place.

JUNE 21   On the day Germany invades the Soviet Union, Ernie White pitches a two-hitter for the second start in a row, defeating the Giants 6–0 at Sportsman's Park. The only New York hits were singles by Billy Jurges in the second inning and Mel Ott in the fourth.

White had a streak of 27 consecutive scoreless innings in June.

JUNE 24   The Cardinals smother the Braves 13–1 at Sportsman's Park.

During the 1940 All-Star break, an executive at General Mills gave Sam Breadon some Vitamin B-1 tablets. Breadon found that he had more pep and endurance and that his golf game improved. The Cardinals owner began giving them to his players in 1941, and the use of the vitamins was cited as one of the reasons that the Cardinals dominated the National League during the first half of the 1940s.

JUNE 28   The Cardinals break open a close game by scoring eight runs in the seventh inning of a 14–4 win over the Reds at Sportsman's Park.

JUNE 29   Lon Warneke loses a 6–2 decision to the Reds on Lon Warneke Day at Sportsman's Park.

In pregame ceremonies, Warneke was given a car, a shotgun, two hunting dogs, a heifer, and a silver tea set.

JULY 7   After being released by the Cubs, Dizzy Dean signs with St. Louis radio station KWK as a broadcaster for Cardinals and Browns games. He did the color with Johnny O'Hara on the play-by-play. When the Cardinals and Browns broadcasts were split in 1947 and each club had its own set of announcers, Dean did the Browns games exclusively. Dean's broadcasting career included the infancy of television and lasted into the 1960s. With his malaprops, humorous stories, and fracturing of English grammar, Dean was enormously popular behind the mic and announced the National Game of the Week on CBS television during the 1950s.

There were no members of the 1934 World Champion "Gas House Gang" Cardinals remaining with the club by 1941.

JULY 10   The Cardinals defeat the Giants 13–9 in a weird game at the Polo Grounds. The Cards led 8–0 when New York scored eight times in the seventh to deadlock the contest. St. Louis came right back with five tallies in the eighth.

Howie Krist had a 10–0 record in 1941, his first full season in the majors. He was 4–0 in eight games as a starter, and 6–0 with two saves as a reliever. Krist ended his career in 1946 with a record of 37–11. He had a 20–6 record as a starter and was 17–5 out of the bullpen. Krist's 10 wins without a loss are the third most in major league history. Tom Zachary was 12–0 with the Yankees in 1929, and Dennis Lamp had an 11–0 mark as a Blue Jay in 1985.

JULY 15   The Cardinals win a 16-inning battle with the Phillies 3–2 in Philadelphia. A sacrifice fly by Jimmy Brown with the bases loaded drove in the winning run.

Outfielder Estel Crabtree hit .341 for the Cardinals in 167 at-bats over 77 games in 1941, despite turning 38 in August. Crabtree had previously played for the Cards in 1933 and then spent eight years in the minors before earning a trip back to the big leagues. Crabtree hailed from the tiny town of Crabtree, Ohio.

JULY 22   Ernie White pitches 5^2/$_3$ innings as a starter and is the winning pitcher in a 7–6 decision over the Giants at Sportsman's Park.

JULY 23   The Cardinals defeat the Giants 5–4 in 12 innings at Sportsman's Park. Ernie White was the winning pitcher for the second day in a row by pitching an inning of relief.

JULY 24   In sweltering 102-degree heat, the Cardinals score a run in the ninth inning and one in the tenth to down the Giants 3–2 at Sportsman's Park. Pitching two-thirds of an inning of relief, Ernie White was the winning pitcher for the third game in a row, all against the Giants.

More than 9,000 women were admitted free upon the presentation of a piece of aluminum as part of a nationwide National Defense drive. A total of 35,235 pieces were collected. The prize for the most unusual piece was given to a woman who contributed a set of false teeth with aluminum plates.

JULY 26   Ernie White pitches a complete game to earn his fourth win in five days by defeating the Braves 9–2 at Sportsman's Park. Each of the four wins was achieved on days in which the temperature in St. Louis was 97 degrees or higher.

JULY 29   The Cardinals and Dodgers battle 12 innings at Sportsman's Park in 103-degree heat for nothing as the contest ends in a 7–7 tie when called by darkness.

JULY 30   Ernie White picks up his fifth win in nine days defeating the Dodgers 6–4 in a complete game at Sportsman's Park on a day in which the high temperature in St. Louis is 101 degrees.

The victory gave the Cardinals a 62–33 record and a three-game lead over the Dodgers.

AUGUST 2   Johnny Mize hits a grand slam off Boom Boom Beck in the second inning to give the Cardinals a 7–0 lead in an 11–7 victory over the Phillies at Sportsman's Park.

Mize hit .317 with 16 homers, 100 RBIs, and a league-leading 39 doubles in 1941, but his power numbers were down from 1940, when he clubbed 43 home runs. Hampered by a broken finger and a bad shoulder, Mize's play was limited to 126 games. The Cardinals were concerned that Mize, only 28, was on his way down. When Mize balked at a pay cut following the 1941 season, the Cards traded him (see December 11, 1941).

AUGUST 4   Creepy Crespi is hit in the face by a line drive off the bat of Lon Warneke, who was knocking fungoes to the outfielders during fielding practice at Wrigley Field. Ernie White won his sixth game in 14 days, defeating the Cubs 4–2 with a complete game on a 94-degree day in Chicago.

A native of St. Louis, Frank "Creepy" Crespi was the Cardinals' starting second baseman in 1941 and a top reserve in 1942 before entering the service. Unfortunately, an army camp accident ended a promising career. In 1943, he broke his leg playing baseball, then broke it again in another place when he crashed into a wall in a wheelchair race.

AUGUST 10   Enos Slaughter breaks his collarbone during a doubleheader against the Pirates at Sportsman's Park. The Cardinals won twice by scores of 3–2 and 4–2. In the second inning of the second game, both Slaughter and Terry Moore were pursuing a long fly ball near the right–center field wall. The two collided, and Slaughter hit the wall. Slaughter bounced off the barrier and fell on his left shoulder.

Slaughter didn't start another game for the rest of the year. He returned on September 13 but was limited to pinch-hitting duties. The loss of Slaughter was a tremendous blow to the Cardinals' pennant drive. He hit .311 in 113 games in 1941.

AUGUST 20   Terry Moore is felled when the Braves' Art Johnson hits him behind the left ear during a doubleheader in Boston. The Cardinals swept the Braves, 2–0 and 3–2.

Moore was out of action until September 14. Until 1941, there was no head protection for batters at the plate. Two months before Moore's injury, the Cardinals received a shipment of one-ounce plastic shields to be inserted into players' regulation caps to help prevent head injuries. The new device was a subject of great debate among big-league players. Pirates manager and former Cardinal Frankie Frisch refused to allow his players to use the shields, calling any one who wanted to wear one at the plate a "sissy." Cardinal players were among those who declined to wear them in games. After watching Moore being rushed to a hospital in an ambulance, many on the club began wearing the shields. Big-league clubs didn't use batting helmets until the 1950s.

AUGUST 22   Coaker Triplett hits an inside-the-park homer with a man on base in the tenth inning to defeat the Phillies 4–2 at Shibe Park. The Cardinals lost Johnny Hopp to injury when Philadelphia shortstop Bobby Bragan stepped on his hand in a play at second base in the fourth inning. Hopp was the third starting outfielder injured inside of two weeks, following Enos Slaughter and Terry Moore.

Hopp hit .303 in 1941, his first season as a regular.

AUGUST 30   Lon Warneke pitches a no-hitter to defeat the Reds 2–0 at Crosley Field. Warneke previously pitched four one-hitters, two of them with the Cubs and two as a Cardinal. Warneke struck out two batters and walked one. Two others reached on errors. Only three balls were hit out of the infield. In the ninth inning, Lloyd Waner popped out to Marty Marion at shortstop, Ernie Koy went down on a grounder to Marion, and Billy Werber flied out to Johnny Mize.

SEPTEMBER 4   The Cardinals are knocked out of first place with a doubleheader defeat to the Cubs in Chicago 3–0 and 4–3 in 11 innings.

The Cardinals had an 83–43 record heading into the twin bill and had spent 81 days in first place. The Dodgers held the top spot in the NL for the rest of the year as the Cardinals went 14–13.

SEPTEMBER 10   The Cardinals sweep the Phillies 3–2 and 1–0 at Sportsman's Park. Harry Gumbert pitched the second-game shutout. Marty Marion drove in the lone run of the game with a single in the fourth inning.

SEPTEMBER 12   At Sportsman's Park, the Cardinals defeat the Dodgers 4–3 to remain one game behind the Brooklyn in the NL pennant race.

Among the key individuals on the 1941 Dodgers were ex-Cardinals Curt Davis, Mickey Owen, Joe Medwick, and Pete Reiser. Ex-Cardinal Leo Durocher managed the Dodgers.

SEPTEMBER 13   The Cardinals drop two games back in the NL race after suffering a crucial 1–0 loss to the Dodgers at Sportsman's Park. Mort Cooper held the Dodgers hitless until the eighth inning, when Dixie Walker and Billy Herman hit back-to-back doubles to produce the lone run of the game. Brooklyn hurler Whitlow Wyatt held the Cards without a hit until the fifth and tossed the complete-game shutout.

SEPTEMBER 14   The Cardinals sweep the Giants 1–0 and 6–5 at Sportsman's Park. Lon Warneke pitched the shutout in the opener. The lone run of the game scored on a single by Gus Mancuso. The Cards won the nightcap after trailing 5–3 with two runs in the eighth inning and one in the ninth.

SEPTEMBER 17   The Cardinals sweep the Braves 6–1 and 3–2 to stay one game back of the Dodgers. They won the second game on Estel Crabtree's walk-off homer. At the age of 20, Stan Musial made his major league debut in the nightcap. Playing right field and batting third, Musial went 2 for 4. He popped out on Jim Tobin's knuckleball in his first at-bat. Musial's first hit was a two-run double against Tobin in the third inning.

Musial was given number 6 for his big-league debut. He was the third player to wear number 6 in 1941. The other two were Harry Walker and Pep Young. Musial wore number 6 for the remainder of his career, which ended in 1963. At that time, the Cardinals retired number 6.

SEPTEMBER 20   The Cardinals suffer a crushing 7–3 loss to the Cubs at Sportsman's Park to drop two games behind the Dodgers. The Cards entered the ninth leading 3–1, but Chicago scored six runs.

SEPTEMBER 23   Stan Musial hits his first major league homer during a 9–0 win over the Pirates in the second game of a doubleheader in Pittsburgh near his hometown of Donora,

Pennsylvania. The pitcher was Rip Sewell. The Pirates won the first game 4–0.

Musial made a spectacular rise through the Cardinals' farm system after he was signed out of high school as a pitcher in 1938. With Daytona Beach in the Florida State League in 1940, he played in 113 games, splitting his time between pitching and the outfield, compiling a record of 18–4 and a .313 batting average. An arm injury ended his days as a pitcher. He became a full-time outfielder during spring training in 1941. Musial gave the Cardinals an inkling of what the future held by hitting .426 in 47 at-bats in his late-season trial. Howie Pollet was another September rookie star. After posting a 20–3 record and a 1.16 ERA at Houston in the Texas League, Pollet was 5–2 with a 1.93 ERA for the Cards.

SEPTEMBER 25   A 3–1 loss to the Pirates in Pittsburgh eliminates the Cardinals from the pennant race.

DECEMBER 7   The Japanese attack Pearl Harbor. A day later, the United States declared war on Japan and on December 11 declared war on Germany.

The attack on Pearl Harbor prevented a possible move of the St. Louis Browns to Los Angeles. With a contending team, the Cardinals boosted their attendance from 324,078 in 1940 to 633,345 in 1941. The Browns, meanwhile, dropped from 239,591 in 1940 to 176,240 during the 1941 campaign despite winning 70 games for the first time since 1929. Even the 1940 figure was well above those during the 1930s. The Browns attracted only 88,113 for the entire 1933 season, 80,922 in 1935, and 93,267 in 1936. St. Louis had long been considered large enough for only one successful big-league club, but neither the Cardinals nor the Browns would leave town. Despairing of ever turning a decent profit in St. Louis, Browns owner Don Barnes finally set his sights on Los Angeles. At the time, no major league franchise had left a city since 1903, and there was no big-league club west of St. Louis. Barnes made an agreement with Cardinals owner Sam Breadon in which Breadon would pay Barnes $350,000 for the exclusive rights to the St. Louis market. Barnes used part of the loot to negotiate the purchase of the Los Angeles Angels, a minor league franchise in the Pacific Coast League owned by Cubs owner P. K. Wrigley. The Los Angeles Browns would play at Wrigley Field in Los Angeles, a facility built in 1925 and a smaller version (22,000 seats) of Wrigley Field in Chicago.

The distance from Los Angeles to other American League cities, the nearest being Chicago, posed a problem. Teams in 1941 traveled exclusively by train, and a train from Chicago to Los Angeles took two days, which would disrupt the playing schedule. Barnes made arrangements with Trans World Airlines to fly two ballplayers on each of the 21 daily flights from Chicago to L.A. to avoid the possible loss of an entire ball club to a crash. The plan was impractical, however, and illuminated the prevailing notion of the period that airplanes were dangerous. Schedules were drawn to accommodate train travel so that the other seven AL clubs would travel to the West Coast only twice a season, playing one five-game series and another of six contests. The proposal was supposed to come to a vote of American League owners at a meeting on December 8, 1941, but Pearl Harbor changed all that.

By the time the war ended, Barnes had grown weary of baseball and sold much of his stock in the Browns to Richard Muckerman. Also, an American

League pennant in 1944, a season in which the Browns outdrew the Cardinals, gave Browns owners the delusion that they could compete with their National League intracity rivals. Muckerman, Bill DeWitt, and Bill Veeck, who followed Barnes as owners of the Browns in the postwar period, decided to remain in St. Louis and continue to fight what became an increasingly futile battle with the Cardinals over fan patronage. The Browns would remain in St. Louis until September 1953, when the club moved to Baltimore and was renamed the Orioles. Los Angeles would not gain a major league team until the Dodgers moved from Brooklyn in October 1957.

DECEMBER 10   The Cardinals sell Don Padgett to the Dodgers for $30,000.

DECEMBER 11   The Cardinals send Johnny Mize to the Giants for Ken O'Dea, Bill Lohrman, Johnny McCarthy, and $50,000.

Like many Cardinal stars before him, Mize was dealt during a salary dispute. Trading him was a huge mistake. Mize led the NL in RBIs and slugging percentage in 1942. After missing three years due to World War II and much of 1946 with a broken hand, Mize clubbed 51 homers for the Giants in 1947 and 40 more in 1948. He closed his career by playing on five consecutive World Championship clubs with the Yankees from 1949 through 1953.

1942

Season in a Sentence

Trailing the Dodgers by 10 games in early August, the Cardinals win 43 of their last 51 games to take the NL pennant, then upset the Yankees in the World Series.

Finish • Won • Lost • Pct • GB

First   106   48   .688   +2.0

World Series—The Cardinals defeated the New York Yankees four games to one

Manager

Billy Southworth

Stats	Cards	• NL •	Rank
Batting Avg:	.268	.249	1
On-Base Pct:	.338	.318	1
Slugging Pct:	.379	.343	1
Home Runs:	60		6
Stolen Bases:	71		2
ERA:	2.55	3.31	1
Fielding Avg:	.972	.973	5
Runs Scored:	755		1
Runs Allowed:	482		1

Starting Lineup

Walker Cooper, c
Johnny Hopp, 1b
Jimmy Brown, 2b-3b
Whitey Kurowski, 3b
Marty Marion, ss
Stan Musial, lf
Terry Moore, cf
Enos Slaughter, rf
Creepy Crespi, 2b
Ray Sanders, 1b
Ken O'Dea, c
Harry Walker, cf
Coaker Triplett, lf

Pitchers

Mort Cooper, sp
Johnny Beazley, sp-rp
Max Lanier, sp-rp
Harry Gumbert, sp-rp
Ernie White, sp
Lon Warneke, sp
Murry Dickson, rp
Howie Krist, rp
Howie Pollet, rp-sp

Attendance

552,552 (fourth in NL)

Club Leaders

Batting Avg:	Slaughter	.318
On-Base Pct:	Slaughter	.412
Slugging Pct:	Slaughter	.494
Home Runs:	Slaughter	13
RBIs:	Slaughter	98
Runs:	Slaughter	100
Stolen Bases:	Hopp	14
Wins:	Cooper	22
Strikeouts:	Cooper	152
ERA:	Cooper	1.72
Saves:	Gumbert	5

JANUARY 15   President Franklin Roosevelt gives baseball commissioner Kenesaw Landis the go-ahead to play ball for the duration of World War II. In his statement, Roosevelt said that he believed the continuation of the sport would be beneficial to the country's morale.

There were 71 players who appeared in the majors in 1941 who were in the service at the start of the 1942 season, an average of 4.4 players per team. The only 1941 Cardinals in the military in 1942 were Johnny Grodzicki and Walter Sessi, who combined to play 10 games in the big leagues. The enlistments and the selective service draft didn't have a major impact on baseball until 1943.

APRIL 14   In the season opener, the Cardinals lose 5–4 to the Cubs before 12,821 at Sportsman's Park. Ken O'Dea homered for the Cards. The game was played five days after the fall of Bataan, one of the many shocking military defeats the United States suffered at the hands of Japan early in 1942.

For the duration of World War II, balls hit into the stands at Sportsman's Park were returned by the fans and donated to the recreation departments of the Armed Forces.

MAY 1   Two weeks after Major General James Doolittle's air raid on Tokyo, Ken O'Dea hits a walk-off homer in the tenth inning to beat the Braves 8–7 at Sportsman's Park. Stan Musial hit a two-run homer in the ninth inning that tied the score 7–7.

MAY 3   The Cardinals sweep the Dodgers 14–10 and 4–2 at Sportsman's Park. The second game was called by darkness after six innings. Ken O'Dea drove in seven runs in the opener. He hit a grand slam in the first inning off Whitlow Wyatt and a bases-loaded double in the seventh. The Cards led the first tilt 10–2 after three innings before allowing Brooklyn to tie the game 10–10. A four-run Cardinal seventh broke the deadlock.

MAY 5   The Cardinals sell Gus Mancuso and Bill Lohrman to the Giants.

MAY 6   The Cardinals sell Clyde Shoun to the Reds.

MAY 18   The Cardinals rout the Giants 16–4 in New York.

               Heading into the game, the Cardinals had a 15–15 record and were tied for fourth place 7½ games behind the Dodgers.

MAY 20   The Cooper brothers star in a 2–0 win over the Dodgers at Ebbets Field. Mort pitched a two-hitter, and Walker smacked a homer off Whitlow Wyatt in the fifth inning for the first Cardinal base hit. The only Brooklyn hits were singles by Joe Medwick in the second inning and Billy Herman in the ninth.

               Mort had a record of 22–7 in 1942 and won the Most Valuable Player Award by leading the National League in wins, ERA (1.77), shutouts (10), lowest opponent batting average (.204), and lowest opponent on-base percentage (.258). He was second in strikeouts (152) and innings pitched (278²/₃). Walker hit .281 with seven homers.

JUNE 3   The gate proceeds from the 11,477 attending the Cardinals-Braves game at Sportsman's Park go to the Army-Navy Relief Fund. The Cardinals lost 4–3.

               The gate proceeds from many games played from 1942 through 1945 were designated for various war charities.

JUNE 16   Ten days after America's victory over Japan in the Battle of Midway, Enos Slaughter hits a homer in the tenth inning to defeat the Giants in New York. It was his second homer of the game.

               Slaughter hit .318 in 1942 to finish second in the batting race to Ernie Lombardi of the Braves, who batted .330. Under today's rules, Slaughter would have been the batting champion. In 1942, a player needed to play in 100 games to qualify for the batting title. Today, a player would require 477 plate appearances in a 154-game schedule. In 1942, Lombardi appeared in 105 games but had only 347 plate appearances. Slaughter did lead the NL in hits (188), triples (17), and total bases (292), in addition to scoring 100 runs, driving in 98, and hitting 13 home runs.

JUNE 17   Mort Cooper holds the Giants hitless until the seventh inning but settles for a five-hit, 3–0 win at New York.

JUNE 18   A fistfight erupts during a 5–2 loss to the Dodgers in Brooklyn. In the sixth inning Joe Medwick tried to advance from first to second on a passed ball. Walker Cooper recovered in time to make the play at second, and Medwick went in with his spikes high at shortstop Marty Marion. As soon as Medwick was called out, Marion pounced on him, and as they were getting up, Creepy Crespi rushed up and knocked Medwick down. Both clubs emptied out of the dugouts. It was nearly 10 minutes before peace was restored. Medwick and Crespi were ejected. Dixie Walker of the Dodgers had to come out because he had twisted an ankle during the rumpus.

JUNE 21   Mort Cooper shuts out the Dodgers 11–0 in the first game of a doubleheader at Ebbets Field. Brooklyn won the second fray 5–2.

JUNE 25   Mort Cooper pitches a two-hitter to defeat the Braves 4–0 in Boston. It was Cooper's third consecutive shutout. Cooper retired the first 16 batters he faced. The only Braves hits were singles by Chet Ross in the sixth inning and Ernie Lombardi in the seventh.

JUNE 30   Mort Cooper's streak of 33 consecutive innings comes to an end with a first-inning homer by Elbie Fletcher of the Pirates, but Cooper pitches the complete game to win 4–2 at Sportsman's Park.

JULY 6   Mort Cooper is the starting pitcher in the All-Star Game. He allowed three runs in three innings, and the American League won 3–1 at the Polo Grounds in New York.

JULY 8   The Cardinals sell Lon Warneke to the Cubs for $75,000.

> *After a 17-win season in 1941 that included a no-hitter, Warneke's effectiveness dropped dramatically in 1942. He had a career record of 10–13 after his contract was sold to the Cubs.*

JULY 10   The Cardinals score two runs in the ninth inning and one in the tenth to defeat the Giants 3–2 at Sportsman's Park. The ninth-inning rally started with two outs, none on, and two strikes on Whitey Kurowski. After Kurowski singled, Walker Cooper hit a pinch-double and Coaker Triplett singled. The tenth-inning tally came on two singles and an error.

> *Kurowski overcame many obstacles to become one of the finest third basemen of the 1940s. A childhood accident in which he was cut severely by a piece of glass caused osteomyelitis, which required that doctors cut four inches of infected bone out of his arm between the wrist and elbow and made his right arm shorter than his left. His brother died in 1937 in a mine cave-in. During spring training in 1942, Kurowski's father passed away from a heart attack. He went home for the funeral and came back to win the starting third base job. A top performer on both offense and defense, Kurowski was named to four All-Star games before injuries shortened his career. He played in only 87 games after his 30th birthday.*

JULY 12   Harry Gumbert pitches a two-hitter to beat the Braves 5–1 in the first game of a doubleheader at Sportsman's Park. The only Boston hits were a double by Tony

Cuccinello and a single by Nanny Fernandez. The Cards completed the sweep with a 9–3 victory in the second tilt.

The number of Cardinals night games, which had been limited to 7 in both 1940 and 1941 by league rule, increased to 14 for 1942 and 1943.

JULY 14   Stan Musial's two-run walk-off homer in the eleventh inning beats the Braves 7–5 at Sportsman's Park. The Cardinals trailed 5–0 before scoring three runs in the sixth inning and two in the eighth.

Musial was only 21 in 1942, his first major league season. He hit .315 with 10 homers. Beginning in 1943, Musial made the All-Star team every year of his career until he retired in 1963. He leads the Cardinals in almost every offensive record category. Among all major league hitters, Musial ranks sixth in games played (3,036), ninth in at-bats (10,972), eighth in runs (1,949), fourth in hits (3,630), third in doubles (725), second in total bases (6,134), second in extra-base hits (1,377), and fourth in RBIs (1,951). Through the 2005 season, the only other players with at least 1,900 runs and 1,900 RBIs were Hank Aaron, Ty Cobb, Willie Mays, and Babe Ruth. In addition, Musial hit 475 homers and compiled a .331 lifetime batting average. He hit better than .300 17 times, 16 of them consecutively. Musial also led the NL seven times in batting average, six in on-base percentage, six in slugging percentage, six in hits, eight in doubles, five in triples, six in total bases, five in runs, and two in RBIs.

JULY 15   The Cardinals score seven runs in the sixth inning to beat the Phillies 9–4 in the second game of a doubleheader in Philadelphia. The Cardinals also won the first game, 7–3.

JULY 19   A walk-off, inside-the-park homer by Enos Slaughter in the tenth inning gives the Cardinals a 7–6 victory and caps a sweep of the Dodgers before 34,443 at Sportsman's Park. Brooklyn right fielder Pete Reiser attempted to make a one-handed catch on Slaughter's drive, but the ball popped free. The Cards won the first contest 8–5. In the third inning, Stan Musial had to be restrained from charging Les Webber after the Brooklyn hurler threw two pitches at Musial's head.

Terry Moore missed four games in July when he tore the nail off one of his fingers trying to untangle two automobile bumpers that had become locked together.

JULY 28   The Cardinals score seven seventh-inning runs in a 9–1 win during the second game of a doubleheader at Ebbets Field. Brooklyn won the first game 7–6.

AUGUST 5   The Cardinals drop 10 games behind the Dodgers in the National League pennant race.

The Cardinals overcame the 10-game deficit by posting a 43–8 record over the final 51 games of the season.

AUGUST 8   The Cardinals and Pirates battle to a 5–5, 16-inning tie in Pittsburgh that was called by darkness. The Cardinals trailed 5–0 in the third inning before rallying to tie. Neither team scored in the last eight innings. Howie Krist, Harry Gumbert, and Murry Dickson combined for $13\frac{2}{3}$ innings of scoreless relief in which they allowed only four hits.

AUGUST 14   Mort Cooper pitches a two-hitter to defeat the Reds 4–0 at Sportsman's Park. The
                 only Cincinnati hits were singles by Frank McCormick and Bert Haas.

                 *Cooper, who normally wore number 13, had been trying to win his 14th game
                 for more than a month. To change his luck, Cooper donned Gus Mancuso's
                 number 14 for the game against the Reds. Following the win, Cooper changed
                 his uniform after every victory for the rest of the season.*

AUGUST 19   Wearing the uniform of his brother Walker, number 15, Mort Cooper earns his 15th
                 victory of the season by defeating the Cubs 5–1 at Sportsman's Park.

AUGUST 22   The Cardinals record their eighth win in a row by defeating the Pirates 7–6 at
                 Sportsman's Park.

AUGUST 25   The Cardinals cut the Dodgers' lead to 5½ games by defeating Brooklyn 2–1 in 14
                 innings in St. Louis. Mort Cooper, wearing Ken O'Dea's number 16, pitched all
                 14 innings to earn his 16th victory of the season. The game was scoreless until the
                 thirteenth. The Dodgers scored in the top of the inning, but the Cardinals came back
                 with a run in their half on a single driven in by Mort's brother Walker. Terry Moore's
                 bases-loaded single brought across the winning run in the fourteenth. In addition
                 to enjoying a thrilling victory over their archrival in a tight pennant race, fans at
                 Sportsman's Park were treated to a lunar eclipse during the game.

AUGUST 26   The Cardinals beat the Dodgers 2–1 in 10 innings at Sportsman's Park. The winning
                 run scored when Coaker Triplett hit a slow roller with Jimmy Brown on third.
                 Brooklyn pitcher Max Macon fell trying to field the ball. He recovered in time to
                 throw to catcher Mickey Owen, but Owen dropped the ball when Brown crashed
                 into him.

AUGUST 29   Wearing Erv Dusak's number 17, Mort Cooper earns his 17th win of the season with
                 a 5–2 decision over the Phillies at Sportsman's Park.

SEPTEMBER 1   Mort Cooper dons Sam Narron's uniform, number 18, and earns his 18th win of the
                 season with a 4–3 decision over the Braves at Sportsman's Park.

SEPTEMBER 6   Mort Cooper earns his 19th victory of the season with a 10–2 decision over the Reds
                 in Cincinnati. He of course wore Harry Gumbert's uniform, number 19.

SEPTEMBER 7   Leading 5–0, the Cardinals allow the Pirates to score 11 runs in the sixth inning
                 and lose 11–6 in the first game of a doubleheader at Forbes Field. The 11 runs were
                 surrendered by Max Lanier, Murry Dickson, and Howie Pollet. The Cards won the
                 second game, called after eight innings by darkness, 6–4.

SEPTEMBER 11   Wearing Coaker Triplett's number 20, Mort Cooper earns his 20th victory and
                 eighth shutout by defeating the Dodgers 3–0 in Brooklyn. The win cut the Dodgers'
                 lead to one game. The contest was a scoreless duel between Cooper and Whitlow
                 Wyatt through seven innings. Cooper also collected two hits and scored once. He
                 led off the sixth inning and eighth inning with singles and came around to cross the
                 plate in the eighth.

SEPTEMBER 12   The Cardinals tie the Dodgers for first place with a 2–1 win at Brooklyn. Both

Cardinal runs scored on a homer by Whitey Kurowski in the second inning. Max Lanier pitched the complete game.

Cardinal pitcher Johnny Beazley was assaulted by an unidentified assailant that night when the club arrived at the train station in Philadelphia. The man approached Beazley and offered to carry his bags. When Beazley refused, the man cursed him, pulled out a knife, and slashed the pitcher on the thumb. Fortunately, the laceration was minor.

SEPTEMBER 13   The Cardinals split a doubleheader with the Phillies in Philadelphia but move into first place when the Dodgers lose twice to the Reds in Brooklyn. The Cards lost the first game 2–1 in heartbreaking fashion when the Phillies scored twice in the ninth inning on a series of fielding misplays. The Cards recovered to take the nightcap 3–2.

SEPTEMBER 14   The Cardinals score four runs in the ninth inning to defeat the Phillies 6–3 in Philadelphia.

SEPTEMBER 15   The Cardinals take a two-game lead in the National League race by defeating the Phillies 3–2 in 14 innings in Philadelphia. Murry Dickson, who relieved Mort Cooper with none out in the ninth, pitched six shutout innings and scored the winning run. Dickson doubled in the fourteenth and scored on Jimmy Brown's single.

SEPTEMBER 17   Trailing 3–1, the Cardinals score five runs in the ninth inning then hold off a Braves uprising in the bottom half to win 6–4 in Boston. The win gave the Cards a three-game lead with eight contests left on the schedule.

SEPTEMBER 20   Mort Cooper wears Johnny Beazley's uniform, number 21, and records his 21st win of the season with a 1–0 victory over the Cubs in the first game of a doubleheader at Wrigley Field. The lone run scored in the fourth inning. With Johnny Hopp on third base, first base runner Whitey Kurowski broke for second. When Cubs catcher Chico Hernandez threw to head off Kurowski, Hopp came home. Chicago won the second game 3–0.

SEPTEMBER 21   The Cardinals defeat the Pirates 2–1 at Sportsman's Park on a walk-off single by Jimmy Brown in the ninth inning.

SEPTEMBER 22   Stan Musial hits a grand slam off Rip Sewell in the fifth inning of a 9–3 win over the Pirates at Sportsman's Park.

SEPTEMBER 23   Rookie Johnny Beazley earns his 20th win of the season with a 4–2 decision over the Reds at Sportsman's Park to virtually sew up the NL pennant. The victory gave the Cardinals a 2½-game lead with three games left to play. The Dodgers still had four to go.

Beazley was a tremendous find. Only 24, he had a 21–6 record and a 2.13 ERA in 1942, then beat the Yankees twice in the World Series. Beazley spent the 1943, 1944, and 1945 seasons in the Army Air Corps, rising to the rank of captain. He spent much of his time in the South Pacific and pitched on service teams in between combat assignments. Beazley developed arm trouble in the military, however, because he was out of shape and didn't warm up properly before an exhibition staged for the benefit of the Army Relief Fund. Beazley tried to beg off the assignment because of the injury risk due to his lack of physical conditioning, but his commanding officer ordered him to pitch. Beazley came back to the majors in 1946 but lasted only one season with a 7–5 record and a 4.46 ERA.

SEPTEMBER 24   Wearing the uniform of Murry Dickson, bearing the number 22, Mort Cooper defeats the Reds 6–0 at Sportsman's Park with a two-hitter for his 22nd win of the season. The only Cincinnati hits were singles by Gee Walker and Ray Lamanno.

To continue the uniform number superstition he had started weeks earlier, Cooper had to squeeze himself into Dickson's uniform. Cooper stood six foot two and weighed 210 pounds. Dickson was five foot ten and 157 pounds.

SEPTEMBER 27   On the last day of the season, the Cardinals clinch their first National League pennant since 1934 with a 9–2 win over the Cubs in the first game of a doubleheader at Sportsman's Park. The Cards also won the second game, 4–1.

The Cardinals were 106–48 in 1942, barely beating out a strong Dodgers club that was 104–50. The 106 wins are the most in Cardinals history and the most of any National League club between the 1909 Pirates and the 1975 Reds. The Cards met the Yankees in the World Series. The Yanks were managed by Joe McCarthy and were 103–51 in 1942, taking the American League pennant by nine games. The Yankees were favored, having won the World Series five of the previous six seasons: 1936, 1937, 1938, 1939, and 1941.

SEPTEMBER 30   In the first game of the World Series, the Cardinals lose 7–4 to the Yankees before 34,769 at Sportsman's Park. The jittery Cardinals made four errors and didn't get their first hit off Red Ruffing until Terry Moore singled with two outs in the eighth inning. The Cards salvaged a little pride by scoring four runs in the ninth in a resilient, furious, and almost miraculous comeback. Stan Musial grounded out to end the contest with the bases loaded.

OCTOBER 1   The Cardinals edge the Yankees 4–3 before 34,355 at Sportsman's Park to even the Series. Walker Cooper started the scoring with a two-run single in the first inning. The Cards scored another run in the seventh to take a 3–0 lead, but the Yankees tied the contest with three tallies in the eighth off Johnny Beazley. St. Louis came back in its half, however, with an Enos Slaughter double and a Stan Musial single that scored a run. A Yankee ninth-inning rally died when Slaughter, playing right field, gunned down Tuck Stainback at third base with a bullet throw.

OCTOBER 3   The Cardinals take a two-games-to-one lead in the Series with a 2–0 win over the Yankees in New York. Ernie White pitched a six-hit shutout. Spectacular outfield defense helped preserve the victory. With the Cardinals leading 1–0 with one on and two outs in the Yankee half of the sixth, Joe DiMaggio lined a shot into the left–center field gap, but center fielder Terry Moore galloped after it and hauled it in with a diving catch. In the seventh, Joe Gordon drove the ball deep to left, but Stan Musial grabbed it just as it was heading into the seats. Then Charlie Keller blasted the ball to deep right, and Enos Slaughter made a leaping catch at the fence to rob the Yankees of another homer.

OCTOBER 4   The Cardinals move within one game of a World Championship by taking Game Four 9–6 at Yankee Stadium. The Cards scored six runs in the fourth inning to take a 6–1 lead but allowed the Yankees to tie the contest with five tallies in the sixth.

Two runs in the seventh and one in the ninth gave St. Louis the victory. Max Lanier pitched three innings of shutout relief and singled in the insurance run in the ninth.

OCTOBER 5   The Cardinals win Game Five 4–2, and the World Series, over the Yankees in New York. A homer by Enos Slaughter in the fourth inning tied the score 1–1. Walker Cooper's sacrifice fly in the sixth deadlocked the contest at 2–2. The Cardinals won the tilt in the ninth when Whitey Kurowski hit a two-run home run just inside the left-field foul pole with one out facing Red Ruffing. Pitcher Johnny Beazley earned the complete-game win.

Counting the World Series, the Cardinals were 47–9 in their last 56 games in 1942.

OCTOBER 29   Branch Rickey resigns as Cardinals vice president and takes a position as president and general manager of the Brooklyn Dodgers.

Rickey and majority owner Sam Breadon began their working relationship in 1920 and had built the Cardinals into a model franchise, but the two gradually developed a mutual resentment, in large part because they had vastly different political and moral outlooks. In addition, Breadon believed that Rickey received more credit for the Cardinals' success than he deserved and itched to prove that he could build a winning club without Rickey. Rickey felt that Breadon

Hulton Archive/Getty Images

Whitey Kurowski hits a game-winning home run in Game Five of the 1942 World Series against the Yankees. Kurowski played third base for St. Louis from 1941 to 1949 and was a huge part of the Cardinals' winning three World Series in that time.

meddled too much in the club's affairs, and Breadon responded by making key decisions without consulting him. By 1942, a working relationship was no longer possible even after the club had won the World Series. Rickey had an opportunity to replace Larry MacPhail as the Dodgers' president and general manager. (MacPhail, who had been an officer in the Army during World War I, left the club to help with the war effort as an assistant to the Secretary of State in Washington and a lieutenant colonel.) MacPhail had worked under Rickey in the Cardinal organization running the club's farm team in Columbus during the early 1930s, and he arranged for Rickey to purchase a 25 percent interest in the Dodgers.

In Brooklyn, Rickey had much more freedom to operate the club by his own standards than he had in St. Louis. He expanded the Dodgers' farm system and built a club that won six NL pennants from 1947 to 1956. Most important, Rickey integrated the major leagues in 1947 with the signing of Jackie Robinson. With Rickey's move from St. Louis to Brooklyn, the Dodgers' gain was the Cardinals' loss. The Cards won pennants in 1943, 1944, and 1946 and were in the race until the final weekend in 1949, but it was accomplished largely with players signed and developed under the Rickey regime. Once those players aged, replacements from the once fruitful farm system were no longer available, and the Cardinals went through a long period of mediocrity that lasted into the early 1960s. Stan Musial concluded each of his first four full seasons in the majors with World Series appearances, but he spent the last 17 seasons of his career without playing in the Fall Classic.

1943

Season in a Sentence

The Cardinals take control of the pennant race by July and win 105 regular-season games, but they're unable to repeat their 1942 World Series victory over the Yankees.

Finish • Won • Lost • Pct • GB

First   105   49   .682 +18.0

World Series—The Cardinals lost to the New York Yankees four games to one

Manager

Billy Southworth

Stats

Stats	Cards •	NL •	Rank
Batting Avg:	.279	.258	1
On-Base Pct:	.333	.324	4
Slugging Pct:	.391	.347	1
Home Runs:	70		2
Stolen Bases:	40		6
ERA:	2.57	3.38	1
Fielding Avg:	.976	.974	2
Runs Scored:	679		2
Runs Allowed:	475		1

Starting Lineup

Walker Cooper, c
Ray Sanders, 1b
Lou Klein, 2b
Whitey Kurowski, 3b
Marty Marion, ss
Danny Litwhiler, lf
Harry Walker, cf
Stan Musial, rf
Dens Garms, rf-lf
Johnny Hopp, lf-1b
Ken O'Dea, c

Pitchers

Mort Cooper, sp
Max Lanier, sp
Howie Krist, sp-rp
Harry Gumbert, sp
Howie Pollet, sp
Al Brazle, sp
Harry Brecheen, rp
Murry Dickson, rp
George Munger, rp

Attendance

517,135 (second in NL)

Club Leaders

Batting Avg:	Musial	.357
On-Base Pct:	Musial	.425
Slugging Pct:	Musial	.562
Home Runs:	Musial	13
	Kurowski	13
RBIs:	Kurowski	81
	Cooper	81
Runs:	Musial	108
Stolen Bases:	Klein	9
	Musial	9
Wins:	Cooper	21
Strikeouts:	Cooper	141
ERA:	Lanier	1.90
Saves:	Brecheen	4

FEBRUARY 23   A month after Franklin Roosevelt and Winston Churchill begin meetings in Casablanca, Morocco, to formulate strategy for the war in Europe, the Cardinals advertise for players in *The Sporting News*.

> *With the military draft and enlistments taking players out of the organization, both at the major and minor league levels, the Cardinals took an unusual step in securing replacements for the clubs in the farm system. They took out ads in several issues of* The Sporting News. *"If you are now a free agent and have previous professional experience, we may be able to place you to your advantage on one of our clubs," the ad read. "We have positions open on our AA, B and D classification clubs." The ad asked players to submit their previous professional experience, playing position, martial status, date of birth, height, weight, and Selective Service classification. Players on the 1942 Cardinals who were in the service before the start of the 1943 season were Enos Slaughter, Terry Moore, Johnny Beazley, Creepy Crespi, Erv Dusak, Jeff Cross, and Whitey Moore. Howie Pollet, Jimmy Brown, and Murry Dickson were called to the service during the season. With their deep farm system, the Cardinals were better*

equipped to replace departed players than most of their National League rivals. As a result, the Cardinals won the pennant in 1943 by 18 games.

MARCH 21   The Cardinals open spring training in Cairo, Illinois.

During World War II, teams had to train north of the Ohio River and east of the Mississippi to save on travel expenses. The Cards trained at Cairo, a town at the confluence of the Ohio and Mississippi, prior to the 1943, 1944, and 1945 seasons before returning to St. Petersburg, Florida, in 1946. When the Midwest spring weather prevented outdoor practice, the Cardinals trained at a high school gymnasium in Cairo.

APRIL 21   Johnny Vander Meer of the Reds outduels Mort Cooper for a 1–0 Cincinnati victory in 11 innings on Opening Day at Crosley Field. The only St. Louis hits were singles by Whitey Kurowski in the first inning and Frank Demaree in the third. Cooper allowed only six hits. The winning run scored on Max Marshall's single.

Kurowski hit .287 with 13 homers in 1943.

APRIL 22   In the second game of the season, the Reds beat the Cardinals 1–0 in extra innings in Cincinnati again, this time in 10 innings. Ernie White pitched the complete game.

APRIL 24   After failing to score in 26 consecutive innings, the Cardinals finally plate runners in the sixth and eighth innings of a 2–1 win over the Reds in Cincinnati. Stan Musial scored both runs, one on an error and another on a passed ball.

Musial was the National League MVP in 1943. He led the league in batting average (.357), on-base percentage (.425), slugging percentage (.562), total bases (347), hits (220), doubles (48), and triples (20). He scored 108 runs, drove in 81, and hit 13 homers.

APRIL 25   Howie Pollet shuts out the Reds 1–0 in Cincinnati. The lone run scored in the fifth inning on a triple by Walker Cooper and a squeeze bunt by Buster Adams. It was the first RBI for the Cards in 1943, and it came in the 35th inning of the season.

The opening four-game series between the Cardinals and Reds produced only six runs, the result of an inferior batch of baseballs manufactured with different specifications due to wartime shortages. A more resilient ball was soon rushed into use.

APRIL 27   In the home opener, the Cardinals defeat the Cubs 7–0 before 6,934 at Sportsman's Park. Mort Cooper pitched the shutout. In the first five games of the 1943 season, Cardinal pitchers allowed only three runs in 48 innings.

Cooper was 21–8 with a 2.30 ERA in 1943, completing 24 of his 32 starts, six of them shutouts. Max Lanier also had a terrific season with a 15–7 record and a 1.90 ERA.

APRIL 29   The Cardinals score two runs in the ninth inning and one in the twelfth to defeat the Cubs 4–3 at Sportsman's Park. Ray Sanders hit a single to drive in the winning run.

Sanders grew up playing softball on the south side of St. Louis. He didn't take up baseball until he was 20, playing for a team in the St. Louis Muny League. A scout offered Sanders an invitation to a Cardinals tryout camp, where he was signed. Sanders reached the majors in 1942 at the age of 25 and was the Cardinals' starting first baseman during the war years. He was exempt from military service because of an irregular heartbeat.

MAY 16   Four days after Germany surrenders in North Africa, a squeeze bunt by Whitey Kurowski scores Johnny Hopp from third base in the eleventh inning to defeat the Phillies 4–3 in the first game of a doubleheader at Shibe Park. Philadelphia won the second game 2–1.

MAY 31   Mort Cooper pitches a one-hitter to defeat the Dodgers 7–0 in the first game of a doubleheader at Sportsman's Park. The only Brooklyn hit was a Billy Herman single in the fifth inning. Rookie second baseman Lou Klein's 21-game hitting streak came to an end in the contest. The Dodgers won the second tilt 1–0.

Klein played every inning of every game in 1943 and hit .287. After missing almost two years to World War II, he returned in 1946 but lost his second base job to Red Schoendienst. Disgusted with the turn of events, Klein jumped to the Mexican League and was barred from organized baseball until 1949. Klein played 154 games in his first season in the majors but only 149 after World War II. His career ended in 1951.

JUNE 1   Harry Walker's two-run walk-off homer in the twelfth inning beats the Dodgers 11–9 at Sportsman's Park. The drive hit the roof of the right-field pavilion over his brother Dixie, who was playing right field for the Dodgers.

On the same day, the Cardinals traded Buster Adams, Coaker Triplett, and Dain Clay to the Phillies for Danny Litwhiler and Earl Naylor.

JUNE 4   Mort Cooper pitches a one-hitter in his second consecutive start, defeating the Phillies 5–0 at Sportsman's Park. The no-hit bid ended in the eighth inning when Jimmy Wasdell lashed a single into left field.

JUNE 5   The Cardinals wrest first place from the Dodgers with a 1–0 win over the Phillies at Sportsman's Park. Howie Krist pitched the shutout. Stan Musial drove in the lone run of the game with a single in the sixth inning, extending his hitting streak to 22 games.

The Cardinals started the season with a 13–10 record before going 92–39 the rest of the way.

JUNE 12   Howie Pollet pitches the Cardinals to a 1–0 win over the Pirates at Sportsman's Park.

JUNE 15   Harry Gumbert pitches a two-hitter to defeat the Reds 3–1 at Sportsman's Park. The only Cincinnati hits were singles by Steve Mesner in the second inning and Gee Walker with two outs in the ninth.

JUNE 16   Harry Walker extends his hitting streak to 22 games during a 3–1 win over the Reds at Sportsman's Park.

JUNE 18   The Cardinals are awarded their 1942 World Championship rings, then lose 3–1 to the Cubs at Sportsman's Park.

JUNE 27

Danny Litwhiler's two homers beat the Cubs 3–2 in the first game of a doubleheader in Chicago. With the Cardinals down 2–0, Litwhiler hit a solo homer in the seventh inning. The Cards still trailed 2–1 when Litwhiler hit a two-run shot over the wall to win the game. St. Louis also won the second tilt, 4–3. Howie Krist was the winning pitcher in both contests in a pair of relief appearances.

> *After his playing career ended, Litwhiler became an innovative coach at Florida State and Michigan State. He is credited as the first to use a radar gun to clock pitchers.*

JULY 4

The Cardinals defeat the Dodgers 2–0 in 10 innings in the first game of a doubleheader in Brooklyn. Howie Pollet not only pitched a three-hit shutout, but also started a ninth-inning rally with a single. The Cards completed the sweep with a 7–2 win in the nightcap.

JULY 10

Howie Pollet pitches his third consecutive shutout, defeating the Braves 4–0 in Boston.

> *Pollet posted an 8–4 record and a 1.75 ERA. He entered the service with the Army Air Corps before the end of July and didn't return to baseball until 1946, when he won 21 games for the Cardinals. He won 20 more for the club in 1949. In his career with the Cardinals, Pollet was 97–65 with an ERA of 3.06. He pitched 20 shutouts and 96 complete games in 177 starts in addition to striking out 635 batters in 1,401²/₃ innings.*

JULY 13

For the second straight year, Mort Cooper is the starting pitcher in the All-Star Game, and for the second straight year, he is also the losing pitcher. Cooper allowed four runs in 2¹/₃ innings during a 5–3 National League loss at Shibe Park in Philadelphia. In his first All-Star at-bat, Stan Musial hit a sacrifice fly in the first inning and later added a double.

JULY 21

The Cardinals sweep the Giants 3–1 and 14–6 in a doubleheader at Sportsman's Park. The Cards were held to three hits in the opener but collected 19 in the second game. The Cardinals broke open the nightcap with nine runs in the fifth inning.

JULY 23

Howie Krist pitches the Cardinals to a 1–0 win over the Giants at Sportsman's Park. George Fallon drove in the lone run of the game with a sacrifice fly in the second inning.

JULY 26

After allowing three runs and five hits in the first two innings, Mort Cooper retires 21 batters in a row from the third through the ninth to beat the Braves 6–3 at Sportsman's Park. It was the Cardinals' ninth win in a row.

JULY 27

The Cardinals' winning streak reaches 11 games with a sweep of the Phillies in a doubleheader at Sportsman's Park. The Cards triumphed 6–2 and 5–2.

JULY 28

The start of the Cardinals-Phillies game at Sportsman's Park is delayed 40 minutes because Philadelphia players threaten to go on strike to protest manager Bucky Harris's firing. The Phils were finally persuaded to take the field, and they beat the Cardinals 6–4, ending the Redbirds' 11-game winning streak.

JULY 29   The Cardinals score nine runs in the fourth inning and beat the Phillies 13–5 at Sportsman's Park.

AUGUST 1   The Cardinals win two from the Dodgers, 7–1 and 5–4, at Sportsman's Park. The opener was marred by a fight between opposing catchers Walker Cooper and Mickey Owen. The mix-up began when Cooper, thrown out on a close play at first, nearly spiked first baseman Augie Galan. Owen charged into Cooper, and the two began exchanging punches. Both were ejected.

AUGUST 14   After pasting the Giants 11–1 in the opener of a doubleheader in New York, the Cards lose 8–0 in the nightcap.

AUGUST 17   Harry Walker extends his hitting streak to 29 games in a 7–3 win over the Dodgers in Brooklyn.

               "Harry the Hat" Walker came from a baseball family. His father, uncle, and brother were all major leaguers. Walker's nickname derived from his habit of constantly tugging on his cap. In an 11-year playing career, 9 of them with the Cardinals, Walker hit .296, although he hit only 10 homers in 2,651 at-bats.

AUGUST 22   In the first game of a doubleheader in Boston, Walker Cooper hits a grand slam off the Braves' Jim Tobin in the ninth inning of a 6–1 win. The Cards also won the second tilt, 5–1.

               Cooper finished second to Stan Musial in the MVP balloting in 1943 by hitting .318 with nine home runs.

AUGUST 23   The Cardinals pound the Braves 14–5 in Boston.

AUGUST 24   Mort Cooper allows 11 hits and walks 1 but beats the Braves 1–0 in 10 innings in Boston. Stan Musial's triple drove in the lone run of the game.

AUGUST 31   A two-run, inside-the-park homer by Harry Walker in the ninth inning beats the Pirates 4–2 in Pittsburgh.

SEPTEMBER 5   Two days after the Allied invasion of the Italian mainland, Whitey Kurowski's homer in the fourth inning off Clyde Shoun accounts for the only run of a 1–0 win over the Reds in the first game of a doubleheader at Sportsman's Park. Mort Cooper pitched the shutout. Cincinnati won the second tilt 4–0.

SEPTEMBER 17   Mort Cooper wins his 20th game of the season with a 10-inning, 2–1 decision over the Cubs at Sportsman's Park.

SEPTEMBER 18   The Cardinals sweep the Cubs 2–1 and 5–0 at Sportsman's Park to clinch the 1943 pennant.

OCTOBER 1   Howie Krist pitches the Cardinals to a 1–0 win over the Giants at Sportsman's Park. Lou Klein drove in the lone run of the game with a single.

               The Cardinals met the Yankees, managed by Joe McCarthy, in the World Series for the second year in a row. The Yankees were 98–56 and won the AL pennant race by 13½ games. To save on travel expenses with the war raging in Europe,

Asia, and the South Pacific, there was only one travel day in 1943. The first three games were played in New York, and the remainder were in St. Louis.

OCTOBER 5

The Yankees open the World Series by defeating the Cardinals 4–2 in New York. A 2–2 tie was broken in the sixth inning when the Yankees scored twice by stringing together three singles before Max Lanier threw a wild pitch.

A scary moment took place in the eighth inning when a B-17 zoomed low over Yankee Stadium, startling the crowd of 68,676. It swung back two minutes later and returned again five minutes after the second pass. This third pass was frightening, as the huge four-engine bomber was no more than 200 feet off the ground and hedge-hopped over the roof, narrowly missing the flagpoles. The roar of the plane drowned out the nationwide radio broadcast and stopped play as the players stood and watched the aircraft. New York Mayor Fiorello LaGuardia demanded that the Army Air Force discipline the pilot. The AAF admitted that it had no idea who piloted the plane. If the military ever learned his identity, it was never revealed to the public.

OCTOBER 6

The Cardinals even the series by taking Game Two with a 4–3 decision over the Yankees in New York behind a complete game by Mort Cooper. Marty Marion started the scoring with a 320-foot home run down the left-field line to lead off the third inning. The Cards added three more in the fourth, two of them on a homer by Ray Sanders. St. Louis led 4–1 heading into the ninth when the Yankees scored twice. On the final out, Joe Gordon fouled out to Walker Cooper.

In the morning, Mort and Walker Cooper received word that their father had passed away in Independence, Missouri. After mulling it over, the Cooper brothers decided their dad would have wanted them to play in the game. The two put aside their grief long enough to beat the Yankees, with Walker calling the signals for Mort's complete game. At the plate, Walker was 1 for 3 with a sacrifice. Following the final out, Mort and Walker boarded a train to attend their father's funeral.

OCTOBER 7

The Yankees regain the lead in the Series by beating the Cardinals 6–2 in New York. The Cards made four errors in the game. St. Louis led 2–1 entering the eighth when the Yankees exploded for five runs off Al Brazle, the first three on Billy Johnson's bases-loaded triple.

The 1943 World Series was the first broadcast on radio to US troops overseas. It was also the first in which Major League Baseball produced an official World Series film. The film was also shipped overseas to members of the armed forces. Major League Baseball has produced an official film record of the World Series every year since 1943.

OCTOBER 10

The Yankees move within one game of a World Championship with a 2–1 win over the Cardinals before 36,196 at Sportsman's Park. The Yankees broke a 1–1 tie in the eighth when opposing pitcher Marius Russo doubled off Harry Brecheen, moved to third on a bunt, and scored on a sacrifice fly by Frankie Crosetti.

OCTOBER 11

The Yankees claim the World Championship with a 2–0 Game Five victory over the Cardinals before 33,782 at Sportsman's Park. Mort Cooper struck out the first five batters he faced. The only runs of the game scored in the sixth on a two-run homer by Bill Dickey. Spud Chandler pitched the complete-game shutout despite allowing 10 hits and walking two. The Cards left 11 runners on base. Murry Dickson, on a 10-day pass from the army, pitched two-thirds of an inning of relief. It was the Yankees' sixth World Championship in eight seasons from 1936 through 1943.

1944

Season in a Sentence

Making a shambles of the pennant race, the Cardinals top the National League for the third year in a row, then polish off the Browns in the only all–St. Louis World Series in history.

Finish • Won • Lost • Pct • GB

First   105   49   .682 +14.5

World Series—The Cardinals defeated the St. Louis Browns four games to two

Manager

Billy Southworth

Stats

	Cards	NL	Rank
Batting Avg:	.275	.261	1
On-Base Pct:	.344	.326	1
Slugging Pct:	.402	.363	1
Home Runs:	100		1
Stolen Bases:	37		6 (tie)
ERA:	2.67	3.51	1
Fielding Avg:	.982	.972	1
Runs Scored:	772		1
Runs Allowed:	490		1

Starting Lineup

Walker Cooper, c
Ray Sanders, 1b
Emil Verban, 2b
Whitey Kurowski, 3b
Marty Marion, ss
Danny Litwhiler, lf
Terry Moore, cf
Stan Musial, rf
Ken O'Dea, c
Augie Bergamo, of

Pitchers

Mort Cooper, sp
Max Lanier, sp
Ted Wilks, sp-rp
Harry Brecheen, sp
George Munger, sp-rp
Freddy Schmidt, rp
Al Jurisch, rp
Blix Donnelly, rp

Attendance

461,968 (fifth in NL)

Club Leaders

Batting Avg:	Musial	.347
On-Base Pct:	Musial	.440
Slugging Pct:	Musial	.549
Home Runs:	Kurowski	20
RBIs:	Sanders	102
Runs:	Musial	112
Stolen Bases:	Hopp	15
Wins:	Cooper	22
Strikeouts:	Lanier	141
ERA:	Cooper	2.46
Saves:	Schmidt	5

APRIL 18   In the season opener, the Cardinals win 2–0 over the Pirates before a crowd of only 4,030 on a rainy day at Sportsman's Park. Max Lanier pitched the shutout. Preacher Roe, a Cardinal castoff, pitched for Pittsburgh and allowed only two hits in a complete-game loss.

The Cardinals sold Roe to the Pirates during the 1943–44 offseason in a horrible miscalculation by the St. Louis front office. Roe pitched one game for the Cardinals in 1938 and got shellacked. He led the American Association in strikeouts in 1943 while pitching for the Cards' farm club in Columbus, but at 29, he was no longer a prospect. Roe went on to post a major league career record of 127–84 and pitched in three World Series for the Dodgers. In 1949, Roe was 15–6 for Brooklyn in a season in which the Cardinals finished one game behind the Dodgers in the NL pennant race.

APRIL 26   Al Jurisch pitches a complete game but loses a 1–0 heartbreaker to the Reds in Cincinnati when Frank McCormick hits a walk-off homer in the thirteenth inning at Crosley Field. Bucky Walters pitched the complete-game shutout for Cincinnati.

Players who finished the 1943 season with the Cardinals but were in the military by Opening Day in 1944 included Howie Pollet, Howie Krist, Al Brazle, Ernie White, Lou Klein, Harry Walker, Johnny Wyrostek, and Earl Naylor. George Munger was inducted into the service in midseason. Walker served in General Patton's Third Army and earned a Bronze Star (for capturing two dozen German soldiers) and a Purple Heart.

MAY 4   Segregation at Sportsman's Park comes to an end as African Africans are permitted to sit in all sections of the ballpark. Previously, only white patrons were allowed in the grandstand. African Americans were confined to the bleachers and the pavilion.

MAY 7   The Cardinals sweep the Reds 5–1 and 1–0 in a doubleheader at Sportsman's Park. Al Jurisch pitched the shutout in the second game. Danny Litwhiler provided the lone run of the game with a homer in the sixth inning off Tommy de la Cruz.

MAY 14   The Cardinals sweep the Phillies 6–3 and 1–0 in a doubleheader at Sportsman's Park. Ray Sanders's homer off the roof of the right-field pavilion against Al Gerheauser accounted for the only run in the second game. George Munger pitched the shutout.

Munger had a record of 11–3 and an ERA of 1.34 in 1944, his second season in the majors. He was selected to the All-Star team but was already in the service by the time the game was played. Munger returned in 1946 and played with the Cards until 1952.

MAY 15   The Cardinals score nine runs in the first inning and cruise to an 11–6 win over the Phillies at Sportsman's Park.

Despite the loss of four key pitchers, a starting second baseman, and a center fielder to military service, the Cardinals cruised to the NL pennant in 1944. After compiling a 92–39 record over the last 131 games in 1943, the Cardinals were 91–30 on September 1 in 1944 and led the league by 20 games. From May 1943 through September 1944, the Cardinals had a record of 183–69, a winning percentage of .726 that would translate to 118–44 for a 162-game regular season. The all-time record for wins in a season is 116, set by the 1906 Cubs and tied by the 2001 Mariners. The Cardinals had a shot at 116 wins heading into September in 1944 but lost 15 of 20 in a stretch during the first three weeks of the month.

MAY 18   The Cardinals collect only two hits but defeat the Braves 2–0 at Sportsman's Park. Both runs scored in the seventh inning on a walk, a fielder's choice, and a two-run single by Whitey Kurowski, the first hit off Boston starter Al Javery.

The Cardinals won 106 games in 1942, 105 in 1943, and another 105 in 1944. The Cards are the only club in major league history to record at least 105 victories three seasons in a row.

MAY 30   After losing the first game of a doubleheader 1–0 to the Braves in Boston, the Cardinals erupt for a 13–1 victory in the second contest.

JUNE 6   All major league games are postponed in observance of D-Day. President Franklin Roosevelt urged Americans to spend the day in prayer at home or in church.

JUNE 10   After scoring just one run in their last 25 innings, the Cardinals explode for an 18–0 win over the Reds at Crosley Field. The margin of victory set a club record for the most runs scored in a shutout victory. The carnage might have been worse, but the Cardinals tied a National League record for most runners left on base in a nine-inning game with 18. Reds pitchers gave up 21 hits and 14 walks. The last five runs were scored in the ninth inning off Cincinnati pitcher Joe Nuxhall, who was making his major league debut at the age of 15, thereby becoming the youngest player in modern major league history.

JUNE 11   The Cardinals sweep the Reds 3–1 and 4–1 in a doubleheader in Cincinnati. The Cardinals broke a 1–1 tie in the second game with three consecutive homers by Walker Cooper, Whitey Kurowski, and Danny Litwhiler off Clyde Shoun. The homers by Cooper and Kurowski were on successive pitches. It was the first time since 1894 that three Cardinals in a row connected for home runs.

Cooper hit .317 with 13 homers in 1944. Kurowski hit .270 with 20 home runs.

JUNE 14   The Cardinals sell Harry Gumbert to the Reds.

JUNE 18   The Cardinals pound the Pirates 12–2 in the first game of a doubleheader at Sportsman's Park, but they lose the second tilt 3–1.

JUNE 24   The Cardinals collect 22 hits and clobber the Pirates 16–0 in Pittsburgh.

JULY 1   The Cardinals pull off their first triple play in five years in the third inning of an 8–3 win over the Dodgers at Sportsman's Park. With runners on first and second, Marty Marion ran into short left field with his back to the plate and made a spectacular running catch of Frenchy Bordagaray's drive. Marion then whirled to second baseman Emil Verban, who threw to Ray Sanders at first base.

Marion won the Most Valuable Player Award in 1944 on the strength of his defense. His offensive statistics were rather ordinary, batting .267 with six homers, 63 RBIs, and 50 runs. Stan Musial led the NL in hits (197), doubles (51), on-base percentage (.440), and slugging percentage (.549) in addition to batting .347 with 112 runs, 14 triples, 12 homers, and 94 RBIs.

Hulton Archive/Getty Images

Marty Marion played shortstop for the Cardinals from 1940 to 1950 playing for and managing the St. Louis Browns. His defensive skills helped the Cards get to the World Series four times in the 1940s.

JULY 2   The Cardinals defeat the Dodgers 2–1 in 14 innings in the first game of a doubleheader at Sportsman's Park. There were no runs scored over the first 13 innings of the contest with Max Lanier dueling Rube Melton. Brooklyn tallied in the top of the fourteenth, but the Cards came back with two in their half for the victory. Johnny Hopp drove in the winner with a single. St. Louis completed the sweep with a 4–2 victory in the nightcap.

Lanier was 17–12 with a 2.65 ERA in 1944.

JULY 9   The Cardinals record a pair of shutouts against the Braves in a doubleheader at Sportsman's Park. Mort Cooper won the opener 1–0. His brother Walker drove in the lone run with a single in the sixth inning. Harry Brecheen won the second contest 9–0.

Nicknamed "The Cat" for his grace on the field, Brecheen was 28 before he finally established himself on a major league roster, and even that took the wartime departures of several top Cardinal pitchers. Brecheen was ineligible for the service because of a spinal malformation and a childhood ankle injury. Standing only five foot ten and weighing 160 pounds, Brecheen pitched well enough during the war years to secure a spot in the starting rotation when the veterans returned in 1946, and he held it into the 1950s. As a Cardinal, Brecheen was 128–79 with a 2.91 ERA. He pitched 1,790⅓ innings, completed 122 of his 224 starts with 25 shutouts, and recorded 857 strikeouts. Brecheen was also a World Series hero, earning three victories over the Red Sox in 1946. He was the pitching coach for the Orioles in 1966 on a staff that allowed only two runs in a four-game World Series sweep of the Dodgers.

JULY 11   Whitey Kurowski hits a two-run double in the seventh inning during the National League's 7–1 win in the All-Star Game at Forbes Field in Pittsburgh.

JULY 15   The Cardinals score seven runs in the first inning and thrash the Reds 12–1 at Sportsman's Park.

JULY 27   Mort Cooper pitches a two-hitter to beat the Phillies 5–0 in the second game of a doubleheader at Shibe Park. The only Philadelphia hits were singles by Buster Adams and Johnny Peacock. The Cards took an 8–0 lead in the second game and hung on to win 8–7.

JULY 29   The Cardinals extend their winning streak to nine games by defeating the Dodgers 14–2 and 12–7 in a doubleheader in Brooklyn. Danny Litwhiler hit a grand slam in the opener.

AUGUST 1   The Cardinals rout the Dodgers 14–3 in Brooklyn.

AUGUST 3   The Cardinals squash the Pirates 15–2 in Pittsburgh.

AUGUST 6   After 14 innings in Cincinnati, the Cardinals edge the Reds 5–4. Max Lanier scored the winning run on a double by Johnny Hopp. Ted Wilks was injured when struck in the head by a line drive from Steve Mesner. The ball bounced about 40 feet in the air before Whitey Kurowski caught it at third base. Fortunately, Wilks was pitching again within a few days.

                 Prior to 1944, Hopp had been a first baseman and corner outfielder, but he became a center fielder with Terry Moore and Harry Walker in the service. Hopp responded with the best season of his career, batting .336 and scoring 106 runs. First baseman Ray Sanders hit .295 with 12 homers and 102 RBIs in 1944.

AUGUST 10   A two-run homer by Whitey Kurowski off Al Gerheauser in the second inning is all the offense the Cards need to defeat the Phillies 2–0 at Sportsman's Park. Mort Cooper pitched the shutout.

                 The city of St. Louis was buzzing all summer about the possibility of a World Series between the Cardinals and Browns. For the first time since 1925, the Browns outdrew the Cardinals. Previously, the Browns had drawn more fans than the Cardinals in 1902 and 1903, 1905–1908, 1918 and 1919, and 1922–1925. The Cardinals' World Championship in 1926 gave the club a firm advantage in attendance over the Browns, one they held every year until the Browns left town in 1953, except for 1944. Attendance at Browns games jumped from 214,392 in 1943 to 508,644 in 1944 amidst the club's thrilling American League pennant race, which wasn't decided until the final day (see October 1,

1944). The Cardinals took all of the suspense out of the National League race by midseason, and attendance fell from 517,135 in 1943 to 461,968. By the end of the decade, the Cardinals had reestablished themselves as St. Louis's dominant club. In 1949, the Cardinals outdrew the Browns 1,430,767 to 270,936, a margin of more than 5-to-1.

AUGUST 20   The Cardinals build a 15–0 lead by the end of the fifth inning and roll to a 15–5 win over the Braves in the first game of a doubleheader at Sportsman's Park. It was the Cardinals' ninth win in a row. The Braves snapped the streak by winning the second contest 5–3.

AUGUST 22   Max Lanier pitches a one-hitter to defeat the Braves 2–1 in the second game of a doubleheader at Sportsman's Park. Butch Nieman's scratch single off the glove of third baseman Whitey Kurowski in the third inning was the lone Boston hit. The Cards also won the first game, 7–4.

AUGUST 23   The Cardinals drub the Cubs 11–1 at Sportsman's Park.

AUGUST 28   The Cardinals score three runs in the ninth inning and beat the Reds 3–2 at Sportsman's Park. The game ended on a two-run pinch-homer by Ken O'Dea that struck the top of the right-field pavilion.

AUGUST 29   Ted Wilks wins his 11th game in a row with a 3–0 decision over the Reds at Sportsman's Park. Wilks carried a no-hitter into the eighth inning before Frank McCormick singled, the first of three Cincinnati hits.

> *As a 28-year-old rookie in 1944, Wilks had a 17–4 record and a 2.65 ERA. Elbow problems curtailed his effectiveness after his fine rookie season, but Wilks was a valuable commodity out of the Cardinal bullpen in the postwar period. At the end of 1947, Wilks had an astonishing career record of 33–11 and retired in 1951 with a mark of 59–30.*

SEPTEMBER 5   Mort Cooper and Cincinnati's Bucky Walters both win their 20th games of the season during a doubleheader at Crosley Field. In addition, each won 4–0 and allowed six hits. Cooper won the first game and Walters the second.

> *Cooper was 22–7 in 1944 with an ERA of 2.46. He led the NL in shutouts with seven.*

SEPTEMBER 21   The Cardinals clinch the pennant with 5–4 and 6–5 wins over the Braves in a doubleheader in Boston. In the second game, the Cards scored twice in the ninth inning and once in the tenth for the victory.

SEPTEMBER 24   The Cardinals take two games from the Phillies 4–3 and 1–0 in a doubleheader at Shibe Park. The first game lasted 16 innings with Mort Cooper pitching a complete game. Cooper allowed no runs over the final 13 innings. Ken Raffensberger also pitched all 16 innings for Philadelphia. Whitey Kurowski capped the victory with a game-winning homer. Ted Wilks pitched the shutout in the second tilt with the Cards winning again in the last at-bat when Ken O'Dea singled in the ninth.

OCTOBER 1   On the final day of the regular season, the Browns clinch the American League pennant by defeating the Yankees 5–2 at Sportsman's Park.

Managed by Luke Sewell, the Browns were 89–65 in 1944. The pennant was the only one that the Browns captured during their 52 seasons in St. Louis and set up a World Series date with the Cardinals, the only all–St. Louis Fall Classic ever played. With both teams using Sportsman's Park as their home field, it was the third and most recent World Series played entirely in one ballpark. The first two were in 1921 and 1922 when the Giants and Yankees met at the Polo Grounds. The 1944 Fall Classic was the only one in which the tenant (the Cardinals) defeated the landlord (the Browns). The Cardinals-Browns matchup was also the first World Series played entirely west of the Mississippi. It didn't happen again until 1965 when the Dodgers met the Twins. In the 1944 Series, the Cardinals were the home team in the first two games, the Browns in the next three, and the Cardinals in Game Six. In compliance with an order from the Office of Defense Transportation to keep trains, planes, and buses open for military personnel, tickets were sold only to individuals living in the St. Louis metropolitan area.

OCTOBER 4

The Browns open the 1944 World Series with a 2–1 win over the Cardinals before 33,242 at Sportsman's Park. The Browns emerged with the victory despite collecting only two hits off Mort Cooper (seven innings) and Blix Donnelly (two innings). In the fourth inning, Gene Moore singled with two outs, and George McQuinn followed with a homer. The Cards scored their lone run in a futile ninth-inning rally. Denny Galehouse pitched a complete game for the Browns, surrendering seven hits.

On the same day, Tony La Russa was born in Tampa, Florida.

OCTOBER 5

The Cardinals even the Series with an 11-inning, 3–2 victory before 35,076 at Sportsman's Park. The winning run scored on a single by Ray Sanders, a walk to Marty Marion and a single by pinch hitter Ken O'Dea. Blix Donnelly pitched four innings of shutout relief, striking out seven.

A backup catcher for most of his 12-year career, O'Dea played in five World Series: with the Cubs in 1935 and 1938 and the Cardinals in 1942, 1943, and 1944. In Series play, he had six hits, including a homer, in 13 at-bats for a .462 average.

OCTOBER 6

The Browns retake the lead with a 6–2 win in Game Three in front of 34,737 at Sportsman's Park. Jack Kramer pitched a complete game for the Browns and struck out 10.

With a wartime housing shortage in effect, Billy Southworth and Browns manager Luke Sewell shared an apartment in the Lindell Towers during the 1944 season. The arrangement worked because the Cardinals and Browns were never in town at the same time. That was, until the World Series. During the week of the Fall Classic, Southworth moved into the apartment of another tenant, who was out of town.

OCTOBER 7

The Cardinals even the Series again with a 5–1 triumph in Game Four before 35,455 at Sportsman's Park. Harry Brecheen went all the way for the Cards and stranded 10 runners. Stan Musial collected a single, a double, and a two-run homer in four at-bats.

OCTOBER 8

The Cardinals move within one game of a World Championship with a 2–0 win over the Browns before 36,588 at Sportsman's Park. Mort Cooper pitched the complete-game shutout, allowing 7 hits while striking out 12 batters. The Cardinal runs scored on solo homers by Ray Sanders in the sixth inning and Danny Litwhiler in the eighth, both off Denny Galehouse, who fanned 10 Cardinals. It is the only game in World Series history in which two pitchers struck out at least 10 batters.

Newspapers of the day remarked about how quiet the crowds were during the 1944 World Series. Fans seemed to have trouble knowing whom to root for. In St. Louis, with the two clubs sharing one ballpark, fans weren't divided by neighborhood as in Chicago, where South Siders root for the White Sox and North Siders follow the Cubs.

OCTOBER 9   The Cardinals wrap up the World Championship with a 3–1 Game Six win over the Browns before 31,630 at Sportsman's Park. Max Lanier started and went 5⅓ innings, allowing a run and three hits. Ted Wilks went the final 3⅔ innings, retiring all 11 batters he faced and striking out four. Emil Verban was 3 for 3 and drove in a run during the Cardinals' three-run fourth inning.

Verban hit .412 in the Series. He was infuriated when Browns management, as the park's owners, assigned his wife a seat behind a post for their home games at Sportsman's Park.

1945

Season in a Sentence

The loss of Stan Musial and Walker Cooper to the service is too much to overcome, and the Cardinals finish second to the Cubs.

Finish • Won • Lost • Pct • GB

Second   95   59   .617   3.0

Manager

Billy Southworth

Stats

Stats	Cards	• NL	• Rank
Batting Avg:	.273	.265	2
On-Base Pct:	.338	.333	4
Slugging Pct:	.371	.364	6
Home Runs:	64		4
Stolen Bases:	55		6
ERA:	3.24	3.80	2
Fielding Avg:	.977	.971	2
Runs Scored:	756		2
Runs Allowed:	507		2

Starting Lineup

Ken O'Dea, c
Ray Sanders, 1b
Emil Verban, 2b
Whitey Kurowski, 3b
Marty Marion, ss
Red Schoendienst, lf
Buster Adams, cf
Johnny Hopp, rf
Augie Bergamo, rf
Del Rice, c
Debs Garms, 3b

Pitchers

Red Barrett, sp
Ken Burkhart, sp-rp
Harry Brecheen, sp
Blix Donnelly, sp
Ted Wilks, sp
Bud Byerly, rp
George Dockins, rp-sp
Jack Creel, rp-sp

Attendance

594,630 (fifth in NL)

Club Leaders

Batting Avg:	Kurowski	.323
On-Base Pct:	Kurowski	.383
Slugging Pct:	Kurowski	.511
Home Runs:	Kurowski	21
RBIs:	Kurowski	102
Runs:	Adams	98
Stolen Bases:	Schoendienst	26
Wins:	Barrett	21
Strikeouts:	Donnelly	76
ERA:	Brecheen	2.52
Saves:	Four tied with 2	

JANUARY 22   Stan Musial is drafted and chooses to enter military service with the Navy.

Members of the 1944 Cardinals who were in the service by the start of the 1945 season were Musial, George Munger, Danny Litwhiler, and Freddy Schmidt. Walker Cooper entered the service four games into the season. Soon after, Max Lanier and George Fallon answered the call. The losses in 1945, plus those of the three previous three years, were too much for even the Cardinals to overcome. The Cards were without not just Musial and Cooper in 1945, but also Enos Slaughter, Howie Pollet, Murry Dickson, Johnny Beazley, Al Brazle, George Munger, Terry Moore, Erv Dusak, Lou Klein, Harry Walker, and Ernie White. The Cards had a better team in the service in 1945 than the one they were able to put on the field. The Cardinals started the season with a 10–12 record before edging toward the top of the National League. The club stayed on the Cubs' heels until the last week of the season but couldn't close the gap and finished three games behind Chicago. The Cubs had fewer significant losses due to military commitments than any other NL team during World War II. If both the Cardinals and Cubs had been at full strength in 1945, the Cardinals easily would have finished first. Had the Cards won the 1945 pennant, they would have been NL champions five years in a row, combined with victories in 1942, 1943, 1944, and 1946.

FEBRUARY 15   Billy Southworth Jr., the son of the Cardinals manager, dies in a plane crash.

Billy Jr. was toiling in the minor leagues when he became the first professional baseball player to join the service in the 1940s, almost a year before the attack on Pearl Harbor. He flew B-17s and made more than 25 bombing runs in Europe. On February 15, 1945, Billy Jr. took off from Mitchel Field on Long Island as a pilot on a routine training flight to Florida. Soon afterward, the plane developed engine trouble, and he tried to land at LaGuardia Field. Instead, the plane plunged into Flushing Bay. It was several weeks before the body was recovered.

MARCH 26   The Cardinals are driven out of their wartime spring training base in Cairo, Illinois, by a flood of the Ohio and Mississippi rivers. The Cards spent the rest of the training period working out at Sportsman's Park.

APRIL 17   Five days after the death of Franklin Roosevelt and the succession of former Missouri Senator Harry Truman to the presidency, the Cardinals open the season with a 3–2 loss to the Cubs in Chicago. Red Schoendienst made his major league debut in the game. Playing left field and batting third, Schoendienst had one hit, a triple off Paul Derringer, in four at-bats.

Albert "Red" Schoendienst was moved from second base, his natural position, to the outfield in 1945 because so many of the regular outfielders had gone to war. Schoendienst also wore number 6 in his major league debut, a uniform that was available with Stan Musial in the military. Schoendienst switched to number 2 when Musial returned in 1946, and he also moved back to second base. After years of service to the Cardinals as a player, coach, and manager, Schoendienst's number 2 was retired in 1996. He was named to 10 All-Star teams, 9 of them as a Cardinal, and was elected to the Hall of Fame in 1989. On the Cardinals' career lists, he ranks fourth in at-bats (6,841), fifth in games (1,795), fifth in hits (1,980), fifth in runs (1,025), sixth in doubles (352), and seventh in total bases (2,657).

His career had a humble beginning. As a 19 year old in 1942, Schoendienst hitchhiked 40 miles from his hometown in Germantown, Illinois, to St. Louis for an open tryout with the Cardinals. Though 500 hopefuls attended, scout Joe Mathes chose Schoendienst and drove him home to get his father's signature. Overall, Schoendienst was in a Cardinal uniform for 39 seasons. He played with the Cardinals from 1945 through 1955 and was a player-coach from 1961 through 1963. After coaching exclusively in 1964, he was a manager from 1965 through 1976 and a coach from 1979 through 1989. Schoendienst was also the Cards' interim manager in 1980 and 1990.

APRIL 21   The Cardinals open the home schedule with a 3–2 win over the Cubs before 6,030 at Sportsman's Park. The winning run scored on a bases-loaded, walk-off single by Johnny Hopp.

On the day of the home opener, the war in Europe was drawing to a close, but the conflict with Japan had no end in sight. The country was well into its fourth year of war, and everyone at Sportsman's Park could claim a loved one, friend, or neighbor who had been or was currently fighting somewhere in the world. While the 1945 openers were taking place, US forces were involved in a deadly struggle to capture Okinawa.

APRIL 28   Rookie left fielder Jim Mallory drops a fly ball with the bases loaded and two outs in the ninth inning that scores the lone run in a 1–0 loss to the Reds in Cincinnati. Blix Donnelly took the tough complete-game loss.

Two stations with two sets of announcers carried the Cardinals and Browns home games in 1945. As a matter of policy that had been in effect for more than a decade, single games on Sundays and the first games of Sunday and holiday doubleheaders were blacked out, as were all of both teams' road games. France Laux and Johnny O'Hara were on WTMV. Harry Caray and Gabby Street were behind the mic on WIL. It was Caray's first season as a major league play-by-play announcer in a career that lasted until his death in 1998. Caray handled the Browns and Cardinals games in 1945 and 1946 and the Cardinals alone from 1947 until 1969. Caray was an immediate hit. In 1946, he was named the number one announcer in the National League by The Sporting News. *Caray replaced Dizzy Dean, who left the broadcasting booth for a year as a "goodwill ambassador" for Falstaff Beer. Dean toured Army bases and hospitals, showing baseball films and telling yarns about the Gas House Gang. He also pitched a few exhibitions games against Negro Leagues star Satchel Paige. Dean returned in 1946 and replaced France Laux.*

MAY 8   The day after Germany's surrender closes the European front in World War II, the Cardinals trade John Antonelli and Glenn Crawford to the Phillies for Buster Adams.

MAY 23   The Cardinals rout the Dodgers 11–1 at Sportsman's Park.

On the same day, the Cardinals sent Mort Cooper to the Braves for Red Barrett and $60,000. Cooper was traded after a nasty salary squabble with Sam Breadon. Cooper was 65–22 for the Cards from 1942 through 1944 and started the 1945 season 2–0, but the Cards traded him at the right time. He won only seven more games in 1945 and just 23 more over the rest of his career, which ended in 1949. Barrett was a huge surprise. When he arrived in the Cooper *trade, he was 30 years old and had a lifetime record of 26–37. With the Cards over the remainder of the 1945 season, he was 21–9 with a 2.74 ERA. Counting his 2–3 mark with the Braves, Barrett was 23–12 overall in 1945 and led the league in victories, complete games (24), and innings pitched (284²/₃). It proved to be the only run of success that Barrett would enjoy in the majors. Post-1945, his cumulative won-lost record was 22–23.*

MAY 30   A two-run homer by Ray Sanders in the twelfth inning beats the Braves 4–2 in the first game of a doubleheader at Sportsman's Park. Boston won the second game 9–2.

JUNE 1   A three-run rally in the ninth inning beats the Giants 4–3 at Sportsman's Park. The rally was interrupted for nearly an hour when strong winds and rain struck St. Louis. Time was called with two outs and the Cardinals trailing 3–2. When play resumed, Ray Sanders singled in the tying run, and Whitey Kurowski hit a walk-off triple.

               Kurowski hit 21 homers, drove in 102 runs, and batted .323 in 1945.

JUNE 8   In a 4–3 win over the Pirates at Sportsman's Park, Buster Adams collects five hits in six at-bats and drives in the tying run in the ninth inning and the winning run in the thirteenth.

JUNE 16   The Pirates score five runs in the first inning, but the Cardinals rally to win 13–10 in Pittsburgh.

JUNE 19   Red Barrett pitches a complete game and allows only four hits in 13 innings, but he loses 1–0 to the Reds at Crosley Field. Barrett retired 26 batters in a row from the first inning through the ninth. Joe Bowman pitched the complete game for the Reds.

JUNE 27   Blix Donnelly pitches a one-hitter for a 6–0 win over the Phillies in the second game of a doubleheader at Shibe Park. The only Philadelphia hit was a single by Vance Dinges. The Phillies won the first game 8–3.

JULY 4   The Cardinals score seven runs in the fifth inning of a 19–2 romp over the Giants in the second game of a doubleheader in New York. Outfielder Augie Bergamo drove in eight of the runs on two homers and three singles in six at-bats. One of the homers was a grand slam. In the opener, Bergamo was 3 for 5, including an RBI triple, as the Cards won 8–4.

JULY 6   The Cardinals score seven runs in the second inning of a 15–3 win over the Dodgers in Brooklyn.

JULY 10   The Cardinals and Browns meet at Sportsman's Park in a game for the benefit of war charities. It was one of eight exhibition games played in place of the All-Star Game, which was canceled due to travel restrictions. The Browns won 3–0 and limited the Cards to two hits. Nine different pitchers appeared in the game for the Browns, with each going one inning.

JULY 13   The Cardinals sweep the Giants 14–3 and 3–1 in a doubleheader at Sportsman's Park.

JULY 19   The Cardinals surge and score seven runs in the eighth inning to defeat the Phillies 9–4 in the second game of a doubleheader at Sportsman's Park. Philadelphia won the opener 3–2.

JULY 27   Buster Adams hits a two-run homer in the seventh inning off Preacher Roe that defeats the Pirates 2–0 at Sportsman's Park. Blix Donnelly pitched the shutout.

               Elvin (Buster) Adams's nickname stemmed from his resemblance to the Buster Brown shoe company logo.

AUGUST 1   The Cardinals score eight runs in the second inning and wallop the Reds 15–3 at Sportsman's Park. Johnny Hopp hit a grand slam over the right-field pavilion off Cincinnati's 47-year-old Hod Lisenbee.

AUGUST 13   Seven days after an atom bomb is dropped on Hiroshima, Japan, the Cardinals outlast the Dodgers 11–10 in 15 innings at Ebbets Field. A double by Ken O'Dea drove in the winning run. The Cardinals led 10–6 before Brooklyn scored three times in the eighth and once in the ninth.

AUGUST 16   Ken Burkhardt pitches a two-hitter to defeat the Phillies 4–0 at Shibe Park. The only Philadelphia hits were singles by Vince DiMaggio and Andy Seminick.

               Burkhardt was a 29-year-old rookie who posted an 18–8 record and a 2.90 ERA for the Cardinals in 1945. He was only 9–12 over the remainder of his career, however, which ended in 1949. After his playing days ended, Burkhardt went into umpiring. He was a National League arbiter from 1957 through 1973.

AUGUST 24   Harry Brecheen pitches the Cardinals to a 1–0 win over the Cubs in Chicago. Ray Sanders drove in the lone run of the game with a double in the sixth inning.

AUGUST 25   Red Schoendienst's bases-loaded triple in the second inning scores the only Cardinal runs in a 3–1 victory over the Cubs in Chicago.

AUGUST 31   Harry Brecheen pitches a two-hitter to defeat the Cubs 4–1 at Sportsman's Park. The only Chicago hits were Ed Sauer's homer and single.

SEPTEMBER 2   Red Barrett faces the minimum 27 batters during a one-hit, 4–0 win over the Cubs in the second game of a doubleheader at Sportsman's Park. The only Chicago base runner was Lennie Merullo, who singled in the second inning and then was thrown out in a stealing attempt. The Cardinals also won the opener, 4–1 in 10 innings. The two wins cut the Cubs' margin in the pennant race to two games.

SEPTEMBER 18   Red Barrett picks up his 20th win in 1945 as a Cardinal, and his 22nd overall, with a 3–2 decision over the Cubs at Sportsman's Park. The victory placed the Cards two games back of Chicago with 10 contests left on the schedule.

               The Cardinals had a 16–6 record against the first-place Cubs in 1945.

SEPTEMBER 26   The Cardinals stay alive in the pennant race with an 11–6 win over the Cubs in Chicago. The victory put the Cards 1½ games out.

SEPTEMBER 27   The Cardinals lose 5–2 to the Pirates in Pittsburgh while the Cubs sweep the Reds 3–1 and 7–4 in Cincinnati. With three games left in the season, the Cards were three games back and all but eliminated from the pennant race.

SEPTEMBER 29   The Cardinals sweep the Reds 5–3 and 6–2 but are eliminated from the pennant race when the Cubs win twice at Pittsburgh.

SEPTEMBER 30   On the last day of the season, Del Rice hits a homer in the twelfth inning to defeat the Reds 3–2 in Cincinnati. It was Rice's first career homer.

NOVEMBER 6   Billy Southworth resigns as manager of the Cardinals to take a position as manager of the Braves.

With Southworth's contract with the Cardinals set to expire at the end of the 1945 season, the Braves offered him a three-year deal and a substantial raise. It was a salary that Sam Breadon was unwilling to pay, and Southworth left with the blessings of the Cardinals owner. In Southworth's first season in Boston, the Braves finished fourth, their highest finish since 1934. In 1947, the Braves were third, their highest finish since 1916. In 1948, he led the Braves to their first pennant since 1914. Things soon went downhill, however, and Southworth resigned in 1951.

NOVEMBER 7   The Cardinals hire 46-year-old Eddie Dyer as manager to replace Billy Southworth.

Dyer was a pitcher with the Cardinals from 1922 through 1927, posting an unspectacular 15–15 record. As a manger in the Cardinals' vast minor league system, Dyer won nine pennants in 15 years from 1928 through 1942. After a two-year stint as the Cardinals' farm director, Dyer went into the oil and insurance business in Houston before being named Cardinals manager. Unlike most first-year skippers, Dyer was expected to win. The St. Louis roster was crammed with returning servicemen, most of whom were established major league stars before the war. He spent five seasons as manager in St. Louis.

1946

Season in a Sentence

In Eddie Dyer's first season as manager, the Cardinals win a playoff over the Dodgers for their ninth NL pennant since 1926, then win the World Series in seven games over the Red Sox.

Finish • Won • Lost • Pct • GB

First   98   58   .626 +2.0

World Series—The Cardinals defeated the Boston Red Sox four games to three

Manager

Eddie Dyer

Stats

Stats	Cards •	NL •	Rank
Batting Avg:	.265	.256	1
On-Base Pct:	.334	.329	3
Slugging Pct:	.381	.355	1
Home Runs:	81		2
Stolen Bases:	58		4
ERA:	3.01	3.41	1
Fielding Avg:	.980	.974	1
Runs Scored:	712		1
Runs Allowed:	545		1

Starting Lineup

Joe Garagiola, c
Stan Musial, 1b
Red Schoendienst, 2b
Whitey Kurowski, 3b
Marty Marion, ss
Erv Dusak, lf
Harry Walker, cf
Enos Slaughter, rf
Terry Moore, cf
Dick Sisler, 1b-lf
Buster Adams, cf-rf

Pitchers

Howie Pollet, sp
Harry Brecheen, sp
Johnny Beazley, sp
Ken Burkhardt, sp-rp
Murry Dickson, rp-sp
Ted Wilks, rp
Al Brazle, rp-sp

Attendance

1,061,087 (fourth in NL)

Club Leaders

Batting Avg:	Musial	.365
On-Base Pct:	Musial	.434
Slugging Pct:	Musial	.587
Home Runs:	Slaughter	18
RBIs:	Slaughter	130
Runs:	Musial	124
Stolen Bases:	Schoendienst	12
	Walker	12
Wins:	Pollet	21
Strikeouts:	Brecheen	117
ERA:	Pollet	2.10
Saves:	Pollet	5

JANUARY 5   The Cardinals sell Walker Cooper to the Giants for $175,000. On the same day, the Cards sold Jimmy Brown to the Pirates.

Cooper was one of the top catchers in the major leagues when he left for military service in April 1945. While he was away, the Cardinals traded his brother Mort to the Braves, and the club hired Eddie Dyer as manager. Walker had played for Dyer in Houston in the Texas League in 1939, and the two didn't get along. He demanded that the Cardinals send him to another club, and Sam Breadon complied, sending the All-Star catcher to the Giants for $175,000, which at the time was one of the largest figures ever paid for a player. The Cardinals made a huge mistake in letting Cooper leave town. In 1947, Cooper hit .305 with 35 homers and 122 RBIs. He was named to five consecutive All-Star teams beginning in 1946 and was a regular with the Giants, Reds, and Braves until 1952. Cooper played in the majors until 1957, when he was 42 years old, and spent his final two big-league seasons in a return engagement as a Cardinal.

FEBRUARY 5   The Cardinals sell Johnny Hopp to the Braves and Johnny Wyrostek and Al Jurisch
                to the Phillies.

                *The Cardinals had outfielders Stan Musial, Enos Slaughter, Terry Moore, and
                Harry Walker coming back from the war, and they viewed Hopp and Wyrostek
                as surplus. Hopp hit .333 in 129 games for the Braves in 1946 and was a
                productive semi-regular for several clubs until 1950. Wyrostek was a run-of-the-
                mill starter in the outfield for the Reds and Phillies from 1946 through 1953.*

FEBRUARY 20   The Cardinals lose their entire stock of 1946 uniforms when a fire sweeps the R. J.
                Liebe Athletic Lettering Company in St. Louis.

FEBRUARY 22   The Cardinals open spring training camp in St. Petersburg, Florida, the first held in
                peacetime in five years.

                *The 1946 major league training camps were unique as returning war veterans
                competed with wartime fill-ins for spots on the roster. The Cardinals' spring
                training roster included 22 players who had spent all or most of the 1945 season
                in the military. Many of them, such as Stan Musial, Enos Slaughter, Howie
                Pollet, Murry Dickson, Harry Walker, Erv Dusak, Terry Moore, Johnny Beazley,
                and Al Brazle, reclaimed their regular positions. Wartime players such as Augie
                Bergamo were released. The Cardinals also had a tremendous group of young
                players in Musial (age 25), Red Schoendienst (23), Pollet (25), Dusak (25), Dick
                Sisler (25), Joe Garagiola (20), and Del Rice (23). After years of assembling the
                best farm system of baseball, the Cardinals looked to be unbeatable and seemed
                to have enough talent to field two pennant-winning teams.*

                *As a result, Sam Breadon sold what he considered to be excess, including many
                of his regulars and promising youngsters, to other clubs. The process began
                before spring training with the sales of Walker Cooper, Johnny Hopp, and
                Johnny Wyrostek and would continue into the season. The sales weakened the
                Cardinals, however, while strengthening their rivals. The Cardinals nosed out
                the Dodgers for the NL pennant in 1946, then defeated the Red Sox in the
                World Series. It was the Cardinals' ninth National League title and sixth World
                Championship in 21 years. The dynasty was near an end, though. The 1946
                pennant would be the last for St. Louis until 1964, and Breadon's postwar fire
                sale was a primary reason for that. Given the close second-place finishes of
                1947, 1948, and 1949, Breadon cost the club at least one and possibly as many
                as three more pennants by selling many of his top players and by losing three
                players to the Mexican League (see May 23, 1946), in part due to his notoriously
                low salary structure.*

APRIL 15   The Cardinals sell Ray Sanders and Max Surkont to the Braves.

                *In a preseason poll of sportswriters, 115 of the 119 queried picked the Cardinals
                to win the 1946 NL pennant.*

APRIL 16   The Cardinals lose the season opener 6–4 to the Pirates before 14,003 at Sportsman's
                Park.

                After the Opening Day loss, the Cardinals won seven in a row.

MAY 2   The Cardinals trade Emil Verban to the Phillies for Clyde Kluttz.

MAY 9   Cardinal pitcher Johnny Grodzicki is placed on the disabled list due to a war wound. Grodzicki was wounded in the right thigh by a shell fragment while serving as a paratrooper in Germany. He missed four full seasons while in the military. Grodzicki returned to baseball late in the 1946 season but appeared in only 19 more big-league games.

MAY 14   The Cardinals sell Ernie White to the Braves.

MAY 15   Howie Pollet pitches the Cardinals to a 1–0 win over the Dodgers at Ebbets Field. The lone run of the game scored on a triple by Dick Sisler and a double by Whitey Kurowski. The contest was enlivened by a fight between Enos Slaughter and Brooklyn hurler Les Webber. In the fifth inning, Slaughter rolled a grounder down the first-base line that Webber fielded, and the pair collided at the bag. Both came up jawing and swinging before players and umpires broke up the duel.

MAY 16   Utility infielder Jeff Cross steals home as a pinch runner in the tenth inning to give the Cardinals a 9–8 win over the Braves in Boston.

               Cross had a four-year career in which he played in 119 games and hit .162 with a .190 slugging percentage in 142 at-bats.

MAY 23   Max Lanier, Lou Klein, and Freddie Martin accept offers to play in the Mexican League.

               The Mexican League was controlled by five Pasquel brothers who belonged to one of Mexico's richest and most politically powerful families. Jorge Pasquel was the one determined to upgrade Mexican baseball and create a third major league by attracting big leaguers with offers of much higher salaries than they were being paid in the States. In all, the brothers persuaded 18 players to take their offer, mostly notably Mickey Owen of the Dodgers and Sal Maglie of the Giants. Lanier was the biggest loss for the Cardinals. He had a record of 6–0 when he left for Mexico and appeared to be on the verge of developing into a staff ace. All of those who jumped to Mexico were suspended by commissioner Happy Chandler for five years.

               In June, Sam Breadon traveled south of the border to talk to Jorge, who had also made overtures to Stan Musial, Marty Marion, Enos Slaughter, Whitey Kurowski, and Terry Moore. The Cardinals' players were prime targets of the Pasquel brothers because of the talent on the roster and Breadon's stinginess. Musial had been offered $75,000 and a five-year contract calling for $125,000 at a time when he was making $13,500. Breadon received a promise from Pasquel that he wouldn't pursue any more Cardinal players. Chandler wanted to fine Breadon $5,000 for "talking to the enemy," but National League president Ford Frick persuaded him not to do it and Chandler backed down. The Mexican League was a financial and artistic failure, and most of the players who went there soon regretted the decision. Much of the promised money never materialized, and living and playing conditions were often primitive when compared with major league standards. Chandler lifted the suspensions in 1949, and Lanier, Klein, and Martin returned to the Cardinals.

MAY 24
The Cardinals take a rare journey by plane. The flight was from New York to Cincinnati due to a nationwide rail strike.

> *Thunderstorms forced the plane down in Dayton, Ohio, 50 miles north of Cincinnati. The Cardinals then piled into cabs for the drive to Crosley Field. In Stan Musial, Enos Slaughter, and Buster Adams's cab, the hood latch broke, requiring the cabbie to lie across the hood to keep it down while Musial drove to the park with his head out of the window so he could see the road.*

MAY 28
The Cardinals score eight runs in the fifth inning and defeat the Cubs 12–2 in Chicago. Dick Sisler highlighted the inning with a grand slam.

> *Sisler was the son of Hall of Fame first baseman George Sisler, who played for the Browns from 1915 through 1927.*

MAY 30
The Cardinals edge the Pirates 12–11 in the second game of a doubleheader at Forbes Field. Most of the scoring was done in the final two innings. St. Louis scored twice in the eighth to move ahead 7–2, but Pittsburgh responded with seven tallies in the bottom half to lead 9–7. The Cardinals countered with five runs in the ninth before squelching a two-run Pittsburgh rally for the victory. The Pirates won the first game 9–3.

JUNE 8
Red Barrett retires the first 22 batters to face him and pitches a one-hitter to beat the Phillies 7–0 at Shibe Park. The only Philadelphia base runner was Del Ennis, who hit a line-drive single to left field on a 1–2 count with one out in the eighth inning.

> *The Cardinals purchased red satin uniforms in 1946 for night games on the road instead of the traditional gray outfits. When the uniforms arrived, however, the club considered them to be too gaudy. The suits were donated to the North Side Teen Town team of the St. Louis Muny League. Several clubs tried the satin material during the 1940s. Baseball officials believed the reflective material would add to the enjoyment of the sport under the lights, but the outfits were almost impossible to keep clean and were uncomfortable to wear on hot and humid summer evenings.*

JUNE 9
The Cardinals sell Danny Litwhiler to the Phillies.

JUNE 17
The Cardinals sweep the Braves 9–6 and 1–0 in Boston. Howie Pollet pitched the second-game shutout. Erv Dusak drove in the lone run of the game with a single in the sixth inning.

> *Pollet was 21–10 in 1946 with a 2.10 ERA. He led the league in wins, ERA, and innings pitched (266) and completed 22 of his 32 starts, four of them shutouts. Pollet also led the Cards in saves with five.*

JUNE 20
The Cardinals break a 1–1 tie with eight runs in the eighth inning and defeat the Braves 9–1 in Boston.

JULY 2
A 7–5 loss to the Reds at Sportsman's Park leaves the Cardinals at 37–30, 7½ games behind the first-place Dodgers.

> *The Cardinals rallied from the deficit by winning 61 of their last 89 games.*

JULY 3   The Cardinals score 10 runs in the fourth inning and thrash the Reds 16–0 at Sportsman's Park. Enos Slaughter led the attack with six RBIs on two doubles and a single.

JULY 5   Harry Brecheen not only pitches the Cardinals to a 1–0 win over the Cubs at Sportsman's Park but also drives in the lone run of the game with a sacrifice fly in the eighth inning.

              Brecheen had hard luck all season. He hurled five shutouts and posted a 2.49 ERA but had only a 15–15 record to show for it.

JULY 12   Howie Pollet earns a win and a save in a doubleheader against the Dodgers at Sportsman's Park. In the opener, Pollet checked the Giants on five hits for a 2–1 victory. In the nightcap, the Cards had a 5–4 lead with no outs in the ninth inning and New York runners on first and third. Pollet entered the game and worked out of the jam without any runs scoring.

              There were 27 players on the National League roster at the 1946 All-Star Game. Six were Cardinals (Whitey Kurowski, Marty Marion, Stan Musial, Howie Pollet, Red Schoendienst, and Enos Slaughter), and six were ex-Cardinals (Mort Cooper, Walker Cooper, Johnny Hopp, Johnny Mize, Pete Reiser, and Emil Verban).

JULY 14   Stan Musial's walk-off homer in the twelfth inning beats the Dodgers 2–1 in the second game of a doubleheader at Sportsman's Park. The Cardinals also won the opener, 5–3. The sweep put the Cardinals 2½ games behind the Dodgers.

JULY 16   Erv Dusak's pinch-hit, three-run, walk-off homer defeats the Dodgers 5–4 at Sportsman's Park. The dramatic victory completed a four-game sweep of the Dodgers that put the Cardinals one-half game out of first place.

JULY 18   The Cardinals take first place with a 5–4 win over the Phillies at Sportsman's Park while the Dodgers lose to the Reds in Cincinnati.

              The Cardinals and Dodgers battled for the top spot in the NL until the final day of the season. The lead changed hands several times.

AUGUST 3   Johnny Beazley holds the Phillies to one hit in a 3–1 victory in Philadelphia shortened to five innings by rain.

AUGUST 4   Murry Dickson stifles the Phillies with two hits in a 7–0 win in the first game of a doubleheader at Shibe Park. Dickson also had three hits, including two doubles. The only Philadelphia hits were singles by Frank McCormick and Skeeter Newsome. The Phillies won the second tilt 3–2 in 12 innings.

AUGUST 11   Stan Musial collects eight hits in 10 at-bats as the Cardinals sweep the Reds 15–4 and 7–3 in Cincinnati. In the first game, Musial was 4 for 5, including a triple. In the finale, he was 4 for 5 again with a double and three singles. Enos Slaughter also starred with seven RBIs on five hits in the opener, including a homer and a double, in six at-bats.

AUGUST 12   Stan Musial is 4 for 4 with three singles and a double during a 5–0 win over the Cubs in Chicago. In three consecutive games over two days in two different cities,

Musial had 12 hits in 14 at-bats.

Moving to first base for the first time in his career, Musial was the National League's Most Valuable Player in 1946. It was his second MVP award, following the one he earned in 1943. Musial led the NL in batting average (.365), slugging percentage (.587), runs (124), hits (228), doubles (50), and triples (20) in addition to hitting 16 homers and driving in 103 runs. Enos Slaughter led the NL in RBIs in 1946 with 130, clubbed 18 homers, and batted .300. Whitey Kurowski hit .301 with 14 home runs for the Cards.

AUGUST 17   Les Wilson, a 37-year-old scout for the Cardinals, kills himself in a Dallas hotel, where his body is found naked and bloody. Two physicians, after performing an autopsy, reported he killed himself with alcoholic gluttony in an all-night wrestling match against "whiskey-inspired phantoms."

AUGUST 25   Heading into the day tied for first place, the Cardinals and Dodgers split a doubleheader at Sportsman's Park. Brooklyn won the first game 3–2, and the Cardinals captured the second 14–8 in a contest called after eight innings on account of darkness. The Cards nearly blew a 10–0 lead in the nightcap.

AUGUST 26   The Cardinals push the Dodgers out of first place with a 2–1 win at Sportsman's Park.

The Cardinals drew more than one million fans for the first time in 1946 with a total of 1,061,807. It shattered the old record of 761,574 set in 1928. Despite the record, the Cardinals were fourth in attendance in the National League in 1946 and seventh in the majors. By contrast, the team drew 1,518,545 on the road. Attendance at major league games zoomed that season with the end of World War II. The 16 big-league clubs drew 18,534,444 that season, a huge increase over the former mark of 10,951,502 set in 1945.

AUGUST 28   The Cardinals sweep the Giants 13–8 and 3–2 in a doubleheader at Sportsman's Park. Walter Sessi won the second game on a pinch-hit, walk-off homer.

This was Sessi's only major league home run, one of his two career RBIs, and one of his two hits. In 27 at-bats over 20 games, Sessi had a lifetime batting average of .074.

SEPTEMBER 5   On Joe Garagiola Day at Sportsman's Park, the Cardinals trounce the Cubs 10–1.

A 20-year-old rookie catcher in 1946, Garagiola was given an auto by a delegation of 1,500 from the Hill, the Italian St. Louis neighborhood where he grew up. Garagiola lived at 5446 Elizabeth Street across the street from boyhood chum Yogi Berra. (The Cardinals also scouted Berra but considered him to be too small to make it as a big leaguer.) Garagiola played for the Cardinals for six seasons of his nine-year career. After his playing days were over, he teamed with Harry Caray and Jack Buck to announce Cardinals games. Garagiola's insider knowledge of the game, humor, and exuberance made him an immediate hit. He worked with Caray and Buck for eight years, then moved onto a larger stage by signing a deal with NBC. From 1975 through 1983, he teamed with Tony Kubek on the network's Saturday-afternoon Game of the Week. *In addition to his baseball duties, Garagiola cohosted* The Today Show *and hosted syndicated talk shows and game shows. He was also a successful writer. Garagiola's book* Baseball Is a Funny Game *was a bestseller.*

SEPTEMBER 8   The Cardinals win two games from the Pirates, 5–4 in 11 innings and 12–2, at Sportsman's Park. The doubleheader sweep put the Cards two games ahead of the Dodgers with 18 contests left on the schedule.

SEPTEMBER 17   Howie Pollet wins his 20th game of the season with a 10–2 win over the Giants in New York. The Cards were two games ahead of the Dodgers with 10 left on the schedule.

SEPTEMBER 19   Stan Musial collects five hits, including a game-winning single in the ninth inning, for a 5–4 win over the Braves in Boston. Musial's five base knocks included two doubles.

SEPTEMBER 21   Murry Dickson protects the Cardinals' one-game lead over the Dodgers with a 2–1 victory over the Cubs in Chicago. Dickson pitched a complete game and scored the winning run in the ninth inning after starting the rally with a single.

SEPTEMBER 23   Harry Brecheen pitches the Cardinals to a 1–0 win over the Cubs in Chicago and drives in the lone run of the game with a single in the third inning. It was the second time in 1946 that Brecheen won a 1–0 game with his own RBI (see July 5, 1946).

SEPTEMBER 24   Erv Dusak's walk-off homer in the tenth inning beats the Reds 2–1 at Sportsman's Park. Stan Musial tied the game with a run-scoring single with two outs in the ninth. The victory kept the Cards one game up on the Dodgers with four contests left on the schedule.

SEPTEMBER 27   The Cardinals drop into a first-place tie with the Dodgers by virtue of a 7–2 loss to the Cubs in Chicago. Both the Cards and the Dodgers had two games remaining.

SEPTEMBER 28   Harry Brecheen pitches the Cardinals to a 4–1 win over the Cubs in Chicago. The Dodgers beat the Braves 7–4. The Cards and Dodgers were tied for first heading into the final day.

SEPTEMBER 29   On the final day, both the Cardinals and Dodgers lose to force a playoff for the league title. The Cards lost 8–3 to the Cubs in Chicago. The Dodgers dropped a 4–0 decision to the Braves with ex-Cardinal Mort Cooper hurling the shutout.

               The playoff between the Dodgers and Cardinals to determine the National League champion was the first in major league history. A best-of-three series was set up. NL president Ford Frick decided the sites by a flip of the coin. Sam Breadon called the toss incorrectly. The Dodgers chose to open in St. Louis, thereby giving Brooklyn the home-field advantage for the second and, if necessary, third games.

OCTOBER 1   The Cardinals win the first game of the playoff 4–2 over the Dodgers before 26,012 at Sportsman's Park. Howie Pollet, struggling with a pulled muscle in his side, pitched the complete game. The Cards broke a 1–1 tie with two runs in the third. Joe Garagiola collected three hits and drove in two runs.

OCTOBER 3   The Cardinals win the National League pennant with an 8–4 win over the Dodgers at Ebbets Field. Brooklyn scored a run in the first to take a 1–0 lead, but the Cardinals countered with eight unanswered tallies until the Dodgers crossed the plate three times in the ninth. Murry Dickson was the winning pitcher and hit a triple. Harry Brecheen earned the save by striking out the last two Brooklyn batters.

The Cardinals moved on to the World Series against the Red Sox. Managed by Joe Cronin, the Sox were 104–50 in 1946 and claimed the flag by 12 games. It was Boston's first pennant since 1918.

OCTOBER 6 The Red Sox open the 1946 World Series with a 10-inning, 3–2 win over the Cardinals before 36,218 at Sportsman's Park. Howie Pollet had a 2–1 lead before allowing a run in the ninth on three singles, the first of which took a bad hop and skipped past Marty Marion. Rudy York's homer in the tenth was the game-winner.

OCTOBER 7 The Cardinals even the Series with a 3–0 win over the Red Sox in Game Two before 35,815 at Sportsman's Park. Harry Brecheen pitched a four-hit shutout and drove in the first run of the game with a third-inning single.

OCTOBER 9 The Red Sox take a two-games-to-one lead by defeating the Cardinals 4–0 in Boston. Rudy York put the game away with a three-run homer in the first inning off Murry Dickson. Boo Ferriss pitched a six-hit shutout for the Red Sox.

OCTOBER 10 The Cardinals knot the Series at two games apiece with a 12–3 trouncing of the Red Sox in Boston. The Cardinals collected 20 hits in the game. Three different players had four hits each. Enos Slaughter went 4 for 6 and doubled and homered. Whitey Kurowski was 4 for 5, including two doubles. Joe Garagiola was also 4 for 5 and had a double and three RBIs. Marty Marion picked up three hits and three RBIs. George Munger went the distance for the win.

OCTOBER 11 The Red Sox move within one game of a World Championship with a 6–3 victory over the Cardinals at Fenway Park in Game Five.

OCTOBER 13 The Cardinals stay alive and force a seventh game by winning 4–1 over the Red Sox before 35,788 at Sportsman's Park. Harry Brecheen pitched the complete game for his second win of the series. In his two starts, Brecheen went 18 innings and allowed only one run and 11 hits.

OCTOBER 15 The Cardinals take the world title with a thrilling 4–3 win over the Red Sox before 36,143 at Sportsman's Park in Game Seven. Murray Dickson and Boo Ferriss were the starting pitchers. Dickson took a 3–1 lead for the Cardinals into the eighth, but the Red Sox scored two runs. Dickson put two runners on base on a single and a double and was replaced by Harry Brecheen, who surrendered a two-run double to Dom DiMaggio before recording the final out. DiMaggio twisted his ankle on the hit and was replaced in center field by Leon Culberson. In the bottom of the eighth, Enos Slaughter led off with a single facing Bob Klinger. After Whitey Kurowski and Del Rice were retired, Harry Walker drilled a pitch to left-center. Culberson fielded the ball and threw to shortstop Johnny Pesky. Slaughter got a terrific jump from first base, rounded third, and headed home. Pesky turned toward the plate expecting to find Slaughter standing on third base. Stunned to see Slaughter steaming toward the plate, Pesky hesitated for a split second and put little on the throw. Slaughter was safe, which gave St. Louis a 4–3 lead. Walker was credited with a double. Brecheen was now the pitcher of record and had a chance to nail down his third win of the Series to tie the all-time record. Brecheen started the ninth inning by issuing a walk to Rudy York and a single to Bobby Doerr, but he then retired three in a row to give the Cardinals the World Championship.

Whether Pesky could have thrown out Slaughter on the play, which has gone into history as "Slaughter's Mad Dash," is a subject baseball fans have debated endlessly. Game film shows that Slaughter had just rounded third when Pesky caught the ball in short left field. Pesky was about 120 feet from home plate, and Slaughter was about 70 to 80 feet from home and running at top speed. Pesky turned, and his body language showed his surprise that Slaughter was heading home. Pesky hesitated for only a fraction of a second, but even that little time gave the speedy Slaughter an extra 15 feet. More important, Pesky appeared to drop his glove slightly, which took him out of position to make a strong throw. Even so, it's likely that it would have taken an almost perfect throw from Pesky and a clean catch and quick tag from catcher Roy Partee to nail Slaughter.

DECEMBER 9   The Cardinals sell Red Barrett to the Braves.

Photo File/Hulton Archive/Getty Images

The final slide in Enos Slaughter's famous "Mad Dash" to win the 1946 World Series. Marty Marion is the batter on deck; the Red Sox' Roy Partee is taking the throw. Slaughter played 13 years as a Cardinal right fielder, hitting .300 or better eight times. He was inducted into the Hall of Fame in 1985.

1947

Season in a Sentence

The defending World Champion Cardinals are unable to overcome a horrid start and end the season second to the Dodgers.

Finish • Won • Lost • Pct • GB

Second   89   65   .578   5.0

Manager

Eddie Dyer

Stats

Stats	Cards	• NL •	Rank
Batting Avg:	.270	.265	4
On-Base Pct:	.347	.338	2
Slugging Pct:	.401	.390	3
Home Runs:	115		3
Stolen Bases:	28		7
ERA:	3.53	4.06	1
Fielding Avg:	.979	.976	1
Runs Scored:	780		2
Runs Allowed:	634		1

Starting Lineup

Del Rice, c
Stan Musial, 1b
Red Schoendienst, 2b
Whitey Kurowski, 3b
Marty Marion, ss
Enos Slaughter, lf
Terry Moore, cf
Ron Northey, rf
Erv Dusak, of
Joe Garagiola, c
Joe Medwick, of

Pitchers

George Munger, sp
Harry Brecheen, sp
Murry Dickson, sp-rp
Jim Hearn, sp-rp
Howie Pollet, sp-rp
Al Brazle, rp-sp
Ken Burkhardt, rp

Attendance

1,247,913 (sixth in NL)

Club Leaders

Batting Avg:	Musial	.312
On-Base Pct:	Kurowski	.404
Slugging Pct:	Kurowski	.544
Home Runs:	Kurowski	27
RBIs:	Kurowski	104
Runs:	Musial	113
Stolen Bases:	Schoendienst	6
Wins:	Munger	16
	Brecheen	16
Strikeouts:	Munger	123
ERA:	Dickson	3.07
Saves:	Wilks	5

April 12   The Cardinals appear on television for the first time. The telecast was carried over KSD-TV, which had just gone on the air as the first television station in St. Louis. The occasion was an exhibition game between the Cardinals and the Browns at Sportsman's Park that the Browns won 2–0.

April 15   The Cardinals open the season with a 3–1 loss to the Reds in Cincinnati. The Cards collected only three hits off Ewell Blackwell.

April 18   In the home inaugural, the Cardinals defeat the Cubs 4–1 before 11,863 at Sportsman's Park.

The Cardinals started the season with a 2–11 record and were 20–28 and in last place on June 12. The club pulled within three games of the Dodgers by August 11 but couldn't close the gap.

May 3   The Cardinals trade Harry Walker and Freddy Schmidt to the Phillies for Ron Northey.

Walker hit .237 for the Cardinals in 1946 and started slowly in 1947, batting .200 over the first 10 games. He suddenly found his stroke in Philadelphia and ended the season with a .363 average and the NL batting title. Walker and

Broadcast Legends

All of the Cardinals' and Browns' home games were on television in 1947. The announcers for the Cardinals' contests were Harry Caray and Gabby Street. The Browns had Dizzy Dean and Johnny O'Hara at the mic. There was also a change in the radio broadcasts. Prior to 1947, in a mutual agreement between the Cards and Browns, only the two teams' home games were broadcast for fear that airing road games while the other club was playing at home would harm attendance. Two broadcast tandems covered both teams. Caray and Street were on WTMV and WEW, and Dean and O'Hara were on WIL. Beginning in 1947, St. Louis radio stations broadcast the Cardinals' and Browns' road games for the first time, and each team had its own set of announcers. The Cardinals were the team that broke the agreement to black out road games. Cards owner Sam Breadon created controversy not only by broadcasting his team's away games while the Browns were at home, but also by choosing Caray and Street as his broadcast team over Dean and O'Hara. Caray had only two years under his belt as a play-by-play announcer, and many found his bombastic style difficult to take.

St. Louis baseball fans were already divided into pro-Caray and anti-Caray camps. Dean, on the other hand, was a St. Louis institution as the ace pitcher of the Gas House Gang during the 1930s and had announced Cardinals games since 1941. Caray and Street were also on WEW in St. Louis and WTMV in East St. Louis, Illinois, stations with less powerful signals than WIL, where Dean and O'Hara were working. Ultimately Breadon was vindicated in choosing Caray and Street. Caray became a fixture in the Midwest on the Cardinals Radio Network, which stretched hundreds of miles across eight states.

Caray, Street, Dean, and O'Hara didn't travel with the Cardinals and Browns, however. They remained in St. Louis and re-created the road games using updates from the Western Union ticker. Caray devised a system that made the reports seem more direct. He and Street placed a photograph of the out-of-town park in front of them that showed the park's size and dimensions along with the locations of the grandstands and bleachers. As each play came in on the ticker, in code, the Western Union operator interpreted the message and passed it on to Caray, who then reconstructed the scene as if he were actually present. Sound effects and crowd noises were added. Cardinals play-by-play announcers began traveling with the club and broadcasting games from road contests live on a regular basis during the 1950s.

Northey were traded for each other again on December 14, 1949, in another deal between the Cardinals and the Phillies.

MAY 6   The Cardinals play a regular-season game against an African-American opponent for the first time since 1884 and lose 7–6 to Jackie Robinson and the Dodgers in Brooklyn.

Two days later, the AP issued a story that the Cardinals threatened to strike over the presence of Robinson on the Dodgers' roster. According to the report, the strike was averted by the intervention of NL president Ford Frick and Cards owner Sam Breadon. Frick publicly threatened any player who refused to take the field with Robinson with an indefinite suspension. The Cardinals' "strike" remains a matter of controversy. Breadon and Cards manager Eddie Dyer denied the report. A number of Cardinal players insist to this day that there was never a strike threat. According to those on the club in 1947, there was grumbling about integration of the sport among Cardinals players, but no more than on any other club, including Robinson's Dodgers.

MAY 21   Jackie Robinson makes his first appearance at Sportsman's Park. Robinson was
              hitless in four at-bats, but the Dodgers defeated the Cardinals 4–3 in 10 innings.

              *An expansive new press box was added to Sportsman's Park in 1947, accessible
              by elevator. The old facility, built in 1929, was reached only by a narrow, rickety
              flight of stairs.*

MAY 25   Joe Medwick returns to the Cardinals after an absence of seven years. He was signed
              by the club after his release by the Yankees. In his first game back, Medwick drove in
              a run with a pinch-hit double, but the Cardinals lost 2–1 to the Pirates in the second
              game of a doubleheader at Sportsman's Park. The Cards won the opener 10–5.

              *During the season, Sam Breadon placed a sign at the northeast corner of Spring
              and Chouteau on property he had owned since 1924. The sign read, "New
              stadium for the Cardinals to be erected in this 14 acres." The 14 acres were
              bounded by Chouteau, Spring, Gratiot, and Grand Boulevard. The stadium
              was never erected, however. In the 1940s, government tax money wasn't used
              to build stadiums. Clubs had to bear 100 percent of the construction costs, and
              postwar inflation pushed the stadium project beyond what Breadon was willing
              to pay. He was also past his 70th birthday, and his health was failing. Breadon
              sold the Cardinals the following November.*

JUNE 2   Howie Pollet pitches a complete game and drives in the winning run with a single in
              the tenth inning to defeat the Dodgers 5–4 in Brooklyn.

JUNE 9   Red Schoendienst is hitless in 12 at-bats during a doubleheader against the Phillies at
              Shibe Park. Schoendienst was 0 for 5 in the first game, won by the Cardinals 4–2. He
              was 0 for 7 in the nightcap, with Philadelphia emerging with the victory 2–1 in 15
              innings.

JUNE 14   The Cardinals sweep the Dodgers 5–3 and 12–2 at Sportsman's Park.

JUNE 16   The Cardinals score three runs in the ninth inning to defeat the Phillies 7–6 at
              Sportsman's Park. The three runs scored on three walks and Stan Musial's triple.

              *Musial, weakened by acute appendicitis early in the season, was batting .140 as
              late as May 19. By season's end, he had a .312 average, 19 homers, 95 RBIs, and
              113 runs scored.*

JUNE 21   The Cardinals win their ninth game in a row with an 11–5 decision over the Giants
              at Sportsman's Park.

JUNE 26   A fan is mysteriously shot during a 6–3 loss to the Dodgers at Sportsman's Park.
              Kenneth Morris was shot in the right knee while sitting in row six of the grandstand
              along the left-field line. Discovering the wound in his knee after another spectator
              called attention to the blood on his trousers, Morris went to the first aid station for
              emergency treatment, but, unaware that he had been shot, he remained at the game.
              The next morning, when the knee became stiff and painful, he was sent to a hospital,
              where X-rays discovered a bullet lodged in the leg. Spectators reported the sound of
              what was later learned to be a gunshot, but at the time thought it was a firecracker.

JUNE 27 | The Cardinals hoist the 1946 World Championship pennant and players receive their World Series rings prior to a 6–5 11-inning win at Sportsman's Park. Cincinnati scored a controversial run on a close play at the plate in the top of the eleventh. Fans displayed their displeasure by throwing bottles onto the field, interrupting play until the debris was cleared. The Cardinals came back with two in their half on a walk, a double, and a two-run, walk-off single by Whitey Kurowski.

JUNE 28 | Whitey Kurowski provides walk-off heroics for the second game in a row. With the Cardinals trailing 7–5 heading into the bottom of the ninth, Terry Moore singled and Stan Musial tripled to narrow the gap to one. Kent Peterson was relieved by Harry Gumbert, and Kurowski hit Gumbert's first pitch for a game-winning homer.

Kurowski had the best year of his career in 1947. He batted .310, hit 27 homers, and drove in 104 runs.

JUNE 29 | After losing the opener of a doubleheader 9–7 when a six-run, eighth-inning rally falls short, the Cardinals shellac the Reds 17–2 in the finale. The Cards led 16–1 at the end of the fourth inning. Enos Slaughter drove in 10 runs during the twin bill at Sportsman's Park, seven of them in the second tilt. He had five hits on three doubles and two singles in 11 at-bats.

JULY 6 | The Cardinals shut out the Reds twice during a doubleheader in Cincinnati. Jim Hearn won the first game 3–0, and Murry Dickson won the second 2–0.

JULY 12 | Murry Dickson throws a one-hitter to defeat the Giants 4–0 in the first game of a doubleheader at the Polo Grounds. The only New York hit was a single by Ernie Lombardi in the second inning. All four St. Louis runs crossed the plate in the ninth inning. The Cards completed the sweep with an 11–3 victory in the second tilt.

JULY 17 | The infields of both clubs are busy during a 5–2 Cardinals win over the Braves at Braves Field. The Cards tied a National League record for most putouts by an infield in a game with 25, and the two clubs combined to tie a major league mark for putouts by infielders with 46.

The Cardinals outscored the opposition 780–634 in 1947 to lead the NL in run differential, and they scored more runs and allowed fewer than the pennant-winning Dodgers. Brooklyn scored 774 runs and surrendered 668.

JULY 20 | The Dodgers score three runs in the ninth inning to defeat the Cardinals 3–2 at Ebbets Field.

The game was later wiped off the books because of the Cardinals' protest. In the ninth inning with two outs and two Cardinals on base, umpire Beans Reardon signaled that Ron Northey's long hit had gone into the stands for a home run, and the Cards' outfielder slowed down to a jog on his trip around the bases. Northey arrived at the plate to find catcher Bruce Edwards waiting to tag him with ball in hand. The umpires conferred and ruled that the ball had struck the top of the wall and that Northey was out. After the game was over, the Cardinals filed a protest with NL president Ford Frick. After deliberation, Frick ruled that the game should go into the books as a 3–3 tie and that Northey should be credited with a homer. The contest was replayed on August 18, with the Dodgers winning 12–3. The proceeds of the replayed game totaled $46,000 and went toward the erection of a memorial to World War II veterans in Brooklyn.

JULY 23   Unleashing a four-run rally in the ninth inning, the Cardinals come from behind to
               pull out a 6–5 win over the Giants at Sportsman's Park. A two-run single by Red
               Schoendienst drove in the tying and winning runs.

               *Night games in St. Louis started at 8:30 during the 1940s. During the summer
               months, the time was pushed back to 8:45 because players complained they had
               trouble following the ball at dusk. The Cards scheduled 41 night games in 1947,
               the most of any club in the majors.*

JULY 30   The Cardinals overcome a 10-run deficit only to lose 11–10 to the Dodgers in 10
               innings at Sportsman's Park. Brooklyn led 10–0 when the Cardinals scored four runs
               in the sixth inning. The Cards still trailed 10–4 entering the ninth but scored six
               times to send the contest into extra innings. It was all for naught when the Dodgers
               scored in the tenth inning for the win. The game ended when Stan Musial was
               thrown out trying to steal second base.

AUGUST 2   A two-out, walk-off homer onto the pavilion roof by Ron Northey beats the Phillies
               4–3 at Sportsman's Park.

AUGUST 3   With the official high temperature in St. Louis reaching 103 degrees, the Cardinals
               defeat the Phillies 10–5 at Sportsman's Park.

AUGUST 5   Del Rice hits a grand slam off Claude Passeau in the fourth inning of an 8–2 win
               over the Cubs in Chicago.

AUGUST 8   The Cardinals win their eighth game in a row with a 6–0 decision over the Pirates at
               Sportsman's Park.

               *The Cardinals drew 1,247,913 fans in 1947, breaking the old mark of 1,061,807
               set the previous year. Despite the record, and a second-place finish, the Cardinals
               ranked sixth in attendance among eight National League teams and were tenth
               in attendance in the majors.*

AUGUST 16   The Pirates hit seven home runs to beat the Cardinals 12–7 in Pittsburgh. Ralph
               Kiner hit three of the home runs, and Hank Greenberg and Billy Cox each struck a
               pair.

AUGUST 20   Whitey Kurowski hits a homer in the twelfth inning to beat the Dodgers 3–2 in
               Brooklyn. The Cardinals were held without a hit through seven innings by Ralph
               Branca, and one hit through eight, before scoring twice in the ninth to send the
               contest into extra innings.

               *The game featured a controversial incident in which Enos Slaughter spiked
               Jackie Robinson, who was playing first base for the Dodgers, in the eleventh
               inning. Brooklyn players believed that Slaughter had spiked Robinson
               deliberately, and the accusations reached newspapers across the country the
               following day. As a result, Slaughter has been branded as a racist by many
               historians. Slaughter and his teammates asserted that the spiking was accidental.*

AUGUST 21   The Cardinals defeat the Phillies 13–3 in the second game of a doubleheader at Shibe
               Park. Stan Musial hit two homers, one of them a grand slam off Charley Schanz.
               Philadelphia won the opener 9–3.

AUGUST 31	The Cardinals outslug the Reds 15–8 in Cincinnati.
SEPTEMBER 1	After the Pirates score in the top of the tenth, the Cardinals come back with two in their half on two walks and a triple by rookie catcher Del Wilber to win 6–5 in the first game of a doubleheader at Sportsman's Park. The Cards completed the sweep with an 8–2 win in the second contest. Stan Musial collected four hits, including a double, in four at-bats.

The triple was the first of Wilber's career. He didn't hit another one until 1951, when he was playing for the Phillies.

SEPTEMBER 3	Led by Stan Musial's five hits and a pinch-hit grand slam by Ron Northey off Russ Meers in the ninth inning, the Cardinals win 11–1 over the Cubs in Chicago. Musial's five hits included a triple. Combined with his 4-for-4 game in the second contest of a September 1 twin bill, Musial recorded nine hits in ten at-bats.

Northey stood five foot ten and weighed 195 pounds, earning him the nickname "The Round Man." He set a major league record for most pinch-hit grand slams in a career with three, later tied by Rich Reese and Willie McCovey. Northey hit two of the three slams as a Cardinal. The second one was on May 30, 1948.

SEPTEMBER 6	Harry Brecheen pitches a 13-inning complete game and starts the game-winning rally with a bunt single for a 4–3 win over the Reds at Sportsman's Park. Brecheen made it around the bases on a subsequent single and two walks, the last one issued to Stan Musial.

Brecheen had a 16–11 record and a 3.30 ERA in 1947.

SEPTEMBER 7	The Cardinals rout the Reds 12–2 at Sportsman's Park in the first game of a doubleheader. Cincinnati won the nightcap 4–2.
SEPTEMBER 12	Ted Wilks wins his 12th game in a row with an 8–7 win over the Dodgers at Sportsman's Park. The Cards led 6–3 before Brooklyn scored four times in the ninth inning. St. Louis came back with two in their half. Enos Slaughter drove in the tying and winning runs with a bases-loaded double.

Wilks went undefeated for nearly three years, from September 3, 1945, through April 29, 1948. He was 8–0 in 1946 and 4–0 in 1947. During the 12-game streak, Wilks made four starts and 73 relief appearances. He was 12–0 over two seasons in spite of a 3.96 ERA.

SEPTEMBER 13	The Cardinals lose a crucial 8–7 decision to the Dodgers at Sportsman's Park. The defeat left them 5½ games behind with 16 contests left on the schedule and was the start of a six-game losing streak that eliminated the club from the pennant race.
SEPTEMBER 19	The Cardinals defeat the Cubs 5–2 on Terry Moore Night at Sportsman's Park.

In pregame ceremonies, Moore was given a Buick Roadmaster, a brass desk lamp, a wallet, a season's worth of theater passes, and a dozen neckties.

SEPTEMBER 25	Blasting out 22 hits, the Cardinals beat the Pirates 15–3 in the first game of a doubleheader in Pittsburgh. The Cards completed the sweep with a 3–1 victory in the second tilt.

SEPTEMBER 27   In his first major league starting assignment, 24-year-old Cardinal pitcher Ken Johnson pitches a one-hitter to defeat the Cubs 3–1 at Wrigley Field. The only Chicago hit was a single by Eddie Waitkus with two outs in the eighth inning.

Johnson pitched in one previous big-league game, a scoreless inning of relief, on September 18. Despite his impressive start, he proved to be a disappointment. Johnson didn't pitch another complete game until 1950 when he was playing for the Phillies. He finished his career in 1952 with a record of 12–14.

SEPTEMBER 28   On the last day of the season, the Cubs' Hank Borowy acts as a courtesy runner for Bill Nicholson during a 3–0 Chicago win over the Cardinals at Wrigley Field. In the third inning, Nicholson tore up his shoe sliding into third base. While Nicholson was replacing his footwear, Borowy ran for him, and Nicholson was allowed to remain in the game with the approval of Cards manager Eddie Dyer and the umpires.

NOVEMBER 25   Sam Breadon sells the Cardinals to a group headed by Fred Saigh and Robert Hannegan.

Breadon made his initial investment in the Cardinals in 1917 and became majority owner in 1920. Under his stewardship, the Cards developed from a weak, debt-ridden club into an organization rich in playing talent and pennant glory, winning nine National League pennants and six World Championships. By 1947, he was 71 years old and suffering from cancer. Breadon had seen the heirs of Colonel Jacob Ruppert forced into selling the New York Yankees to meet inheritance tax requirements, and he had no desire to inflict that responsibility on his wife, daughter, and stepdaughters. Breadon also wanted to choose his own successors. He shopped the Cardinals quietly and found willing buyers in Robert Hannegan, the US Postmaster General in Harry Truman's administration, and local attorney and real estate investor Fred Saigh. By putting up Saigh's downtown real estate holdings as collateral, Hannegan and Saigh managed to pay $4 million for the Cardinals with only $60,800 in cash. The rest was borrowed in a labyrinth of financial deals and what Saigh referred to as "tax gimmicks." The sale price was the highest in baseball history up to that point. Breadon didn't have long to enjoy his retirement, however. He died in May 1949.

Although Saigh held 51 percent of the stock, Hannegan became president and chairman of the board. Hannegan grew up in northwest St. Louis, the son of a police captain, and was a devoted Cardinals fan. At the age of 14, he sold peanuts at Robison Field. After starring in football at St. Louis University, Hannegan entered Democratic Party politics. Though married to the daughter of a prominent St. Louis Republican, Hannegan became chairman of the Democratic National Committee and was instrumental in securing the vice presidential nomination for fellow Missourian Harry Truman at the 1944 convention. At the time he bought stock in the Cardinals, Hannegan was on the board of directors for the Browns. Although only in his 40s, he suffered from ill health due to hypertension. Hannegan sold his shares in the club to Fred Saigh for $1 million in January 1949. He died the following October at the age of 46. The purchase of Hannegan's shares gave Saigh approximately 90 percent of Cardinals stock. The five-foot-five son of a Syrian immigrant who had built a chain of groceries and small department stores in northern Illinois, Saigh became *an accomplished tax and corporate attorney and accumulated a large fortune in real estate and stocks in the two years prior to purchasing the Cards. Known as a financial wizard, he owned two entire blocks of valuable property in the heart of downtown St. Louis. According to St. Louis sportswriter J. Roy Stockton, Saigh could "teach the mint about dollars." He was 42 years old when he bought the club. It's probable that no one ever acquired a major league club with as meager a knowledge of the game as Saigh had when he gained control of the Cardinals. Like many owners, he soon believed he was an expert on the game, and his impact would be felt for some time. In 1950, for instance, Saigh was instrumental in driving baseball commissioner Happy Chandler out of office. Saigh owned the Cardinals until February 1953, when a conviction for income tax evasion forced him to sell the club (see January 28, 1953).*

1948

Season in a Sentence

Stan Musial has the greatest season of his legendary career, but the Cardinals finish second again.

Finish • Won • Lost • Pct • GB

Finish	Won	Lost	Pct	GB
Second	85	69	.552	6.5

Manager

Eddie Dyer

Stats

Stats	Cards	NL	Rank
Batting Avg:	.263	.261	2
On-Base Pct:	.340	.333	2
Slugging Pct:	.389	.383	3
Home Runs:	105		3
Stolen Bases:	24		8
ERA:	3.91	3.95	3
Fielding Avg:	.980	.974	1
Runs Scored:	742		3
Runs Allowed:	646		2

Starting Lineup

Del Rice, c
Nippy Jones, 1b
Red Schoendienst, 2b
Don Lang, 3b
Marty Marion, ss
Enos Slaughter, lf
Terry Moore, cf
Stan Musial, rf-cf-lf
Erv Dusak, cf
Ron Northey, rf
Ralph LaPointe, 2b-ss
Whitey Kurowski, 3b

Pitchers

Harry Brecheen, sp
Murry Dickson, sp-rp
Howie Pollet, sp
George Munger, sp-rp
Al Brazle, sp-rp
Ted Wilks, rp
Jim Hearn, rp-sp

Attendance

1,111,240 (sixth in NL)

Club Leaders

Batting Avg:	Musial	.376
On-Base Pct:	Musial	.450
Slugging Pct:	Musial	.702
Home Runs:	Musial	39
RBIs:	Musial	131
Runs:	Musial	135
Stolen Bases:	Musial	7
Wins:	Brecheen	20
Strikeouts:	Brecheen	149
ERA:	Brecheen	2.24
Saves:	Wilks	13

Francis Miller/Time & Life Pictures/Getty Images

For a generation of fans, Stan Musial was the Cardinals. At the end of his 22-year career, Musial held 17 major league records and had won three MVPs. In 1999 the Society for American Baseball Research (SABR) placed him at no. 5 on its list of the 100 greatest baseball players.

MARCH 30   Murry Dickson pitches a nine-inning spring training no-hitter, defeating the Yankees 7–0 in St. Petersburg, Florida.

The Cardinals and Yankees both trained at St. Petersburg from 1938 through 1961, with the exception of the 1943, 1944, 1945, and 1951 seasons.

APRIL 7   The Cardinals send Dick Sisler to the Phillies for Ralph LaPointe and $50,000.

Sisler had an appointment with destiny. In 1950, he hit a home run in the final game of the season to win the pennant for the Phillies.

APRIL 20   Murry Dickson shuts out the Reds 4–0 on 10 hits before 14,071 at Sportsman's Park on Opening Day. St. Louis Mayor Aloys Kaufmann threw out the first pitch to Missouri governor Phil Donnelly.

APRIL 23   Harry Brecheen pitches the Cardinals to a 1–0 win over the Cubs in Chicago's home opener. In the ninth inning, Ralph LaPointe doubled to drive in Erv Dusak from first base for the lone run of the contest after twice failing to lay down a bunt. It was only the second Cardinal hit off Johnny Schmitz.

APRIL 30   Six days after the start of the Berlin airlift, Stan Musial collects five hits, including a homer and two doubles, during a 13–7 win over the Reds in Cincinnati. Joe Garagiola hit a grand slam off Harry Gumbert during a seven-run seventh inning.

MAY 1   Harry Brecheen pitches his second consecutive shutout, defeating the Cubs 4–0 at Sportsman's Park.

MAY 8   An infield single during a 5–0 win over the Phillies at Sportsman's Park deprives Harry Brecheen of a perfect game. Brecheen retired the first 20 batters to face him. With two outs in the seventh inning, Johnny Blatnik beat out a hopper down the third-base line. Whitey Kurowski fielded the ball near the bag and made a perfect throw to Nippy Jones at first, but the batter beat the ball by less than a step. Brecheen then retired the last seven batters for the win.

The May 8 victory was Brecheen's third consecutive shutout and came during a stretch in which he hurled 32 straight scoreless innings. He had the best season of his career in 1948, with a 20–7 record, and led the league in ERA (2.24), shutouts (seven), and strikeouts (149). Brecheen completed 21 of his 30 starts.

MAY 16   Ralph LaPointe sprinted all the way home from first base with two outs in the tenth inning on Terry Moore's pop fly to beat the Pirates 6–5 at Sportsman's Park. The ball fell between left fielder Ralph Kiner and center fielder Johnny Hopp while each waited for the other to catch it for the third out.

MAY 19   Stan Musial scores five runs and collects five hits in five at-bats to lead the Cardinals to a 14–7 win over the Dodgers in Brooklyn. Musial had a triple, a double, and three singles.

MAY 20   Stan Musial collects four hits, including two doubles and a homer, in six at-bats during a 13–4 pasting of the Dodgers in Brooklyn. The outburst gave Musial nine hits, five of them for extra bases, in consecutive games.

Musial won his third Most Valuable Player Award in 1948 with the best season of his career. He led the NL in batting average (.376), on-base percentage (.450), slugging percentage (.702), runs (135), hits (230), doubles (46), triples (18), total bases (429), and RBIs (131). If he had hit one more home run, Musial would have won the Triple Crown. As it stood, he hit 39 homers, one less than Ralph Kiner and Johnny Mize, who shared the league home run title. Musial's 429 total bases in 1948 are the sixth highest in major league history and the highest overall of any batter since 1932.

MAY 23   The Cardinals sweep the Phillies 18–3 and 4–1 during a doubleheader in Philadelphia. Nippy Jones drove in six runs in the opener on a home run and a double.

MAY 30   Ron Northey hits a pinch-hit grand slam in the sixth inning off Elmer Singleton, but the Cardinals lose 7–6 to the Pirates in the second game of a doubleheader at Forbes Field. Pittsburgh also won the opener, 9–3.

JUNE 5   Red Schoendienst collects three doubles and a single during a 9–6 win over the Dodgers at Sportsman's Park. Enos Slaughter hit a grand slam off Harry Taylor in the third inning.

JUNE 6   Red Schoendienst leads the attack as the Cardinals sweep the Phillies 11–1 and 2–0 during an eventful doubleheader at Sportsman's Park. Schoendienst collected three doubles and a homer in the opener.

Combined with his three doubles the day before, Schoendienst tied a major league record for most extra-base hits in consecutive games (seven) and another big-league mark for most doubles in consecutive games (six). He tied a Cardinals record for most extra-base hits in a game (four). Schoendienst continued his hot hitting in the second game with two doubles. This tied a major league for most extra-base hits in a doubleheader (six) and a National League record for most doubles in a doubleheader (five). Over three consecutive games, Schoendienst had eight doubles and a homer. The Cardinals also set a club record for most homers in an inning with four in the sixth inning of the opener. In a span of six batters, Erv Dusak, Schoendienst, Enos Slaughter, and Nippy Jones all went deep off Phillies pitcher Charlie Bicknell. It is the only time in Cardinals history that the club hit four homers in an inning.

At the end of the day, the Cardinals had a 24–17 record and were in first place. The Cards were knocked out of the top spot the following day but remained in the thick of the pennant race until the first week of September.

June 21   Al Brazle bests Warren Spahn and the Braves 1–0 at Sportsman's Park. Del Rice drove in the lone run of the game with a single in the seventh inning.

Although never a star pitcher, left-hander Brazle baffled big-league batters with a unique sidearm, herky-jerky delivery. He spent his entire career with the Cardinals, from 1943 through 1954. He never won more than 14 games in a season but had a lifetime record of 97–64 and an ERA of 3.31. Brazle also recorded 60 saves in the majors and led the NL in saves with 16 in 1952 and 18 in 1953, which at the time were club records. He completed 47 of his 117 career starts and is the only Cardinal with at least 40 complete games and 40 saves. A native of Loyal, Oklahoma, Brazle was 29 when he made his major league debut, and he pitched until he was 40.

June 22   Stan Musial collects five hits in five at-bats during a 5–2 win over the Braves in Boston.

July 10   A light failure at Sportsman's Park causes a 15-minute interruption during a 4–3 win over the Reds. In the second inning, a foul from Cincinnati's Grady Hatton hit a light standard on the grandstand roof. The impact blew a primary fuse, and the 60 bulbs on the tower went out until an electrician could make emergency repairs.

July 11   Ken Raffensberger of the Reds pitches a one-hitter against the Cardinals for the second time in six weeks, winning 1–0. Raffensberger beat the Cards 7–0 with a one-hitter on May 31. Both games were at Sportsman's Park.

July 13   The All-Star Game is played at Sportsman's Park, with the American League winning 5–2. The Browns were the hosts, and the AL was the home team. Stan Musial drove in both NL runs with a homer in the first inning off Walt Masterson. Musial added a single in the third.

Future Hall of Famers on the rosters of the two clubs included Richie Ashburn, Yogi Berra, Lou Boudreau, Joe DiMaggio, Bobby Doerr, Bob Feller, George Kell, Ralph Kiner, Bob Lemon, Johnny Mize, Stan Musial, Hal Newhouser, Pee Wee Reese, Red Schoendienst, Enos Slaughter, and Ted Williams.

JULY 17   Stan Musial hits a grand slam in the second inning, but the Cardinals lose 11–10 to the Phillies at Sportsman's Park.

JULY 18   Terry Moore hits a three-run, walk-off homer in the eleventh inning to beat the Dodgers 6–3 in the first game of a doubleheader at Sportsman's Park. The Dodgers took a 3–2 lead in the top of the tenth, but the Cards tied the contest on a double by Ron Northey and a triple by Red Schoendienst, both acting as pinch hitters, to set the stage for Moore's heroics. Brooklyn won the second game 13–4.

JULY 22   Trailing 5–0, the Cardinals erupt for six runs in the seventh inning against the Giants in the first game of a doubleheader at Sportsman's Park. New York came back with a run in the eighth, but the Cards won 7–6 with a tally in the eleventh. Nippy Jones's single drove in the winner. The Giants won the finale 6–3.

AUGUST 2   The Cardinals collects 20 hits and roll to a 21–5 thrashing of the Giants in New York. The Cards scored eight runs in the fifth inning to take a 17–2 lead.

AUGUST 14   Del Rice hits a grand slam off Fritz Ostermueller in the fourth inning of a 6–3 win over the Pirates in Pittsburgh. Nippy Jones was given an intentional walk to get to Rice, who was hitting .204 at the time.

               Rice had only a .237 career batting average but remained in the majors for 17 seasons, 12 of them with the Cardinals, because of his defensive abilities. He had modest power (79 lifetime homers) and no speed (two stolen bases in 1,309 games).

AUGUST 21   Ron Northey hits a grand slam off Kirby Higbe in the fourth inning of a 9–2 win over the Pirates at Sportsman's Park. The slam followed an intentional walk to Enos Slaughter.

               The victory put the Cardinals one game behind the first-place Braves. The Cards could draw no closer, however. The Braves, managed by ex-Cardinals skipper Billy Southworth, went on to win the pennant.

AUGUST 26   A two-run, walk-off homer by Stan Musial beats the Giants 7–5 in the second game of a doubleheader at Sportsman's Park. The Cards also won the first game, 7–2.

AUGUST 28   The Cardinals earn two come-from-behind victories from the Giants in a doubleheader at Sportsman's Park. In the opener, the Cards trailed 4–0 before rallying to send the game into extra innings. Stan Musial won the contest 5–4 with a walk-off homer in the twelfth. In the second tilt, the Cards scored four runs in the ninth inning to defeat the Giants 7–6. The deciding tally scored when Ralph LaPointe missed a squeeze bunt and New York catcher Walker Cooper dropped the ball. While Cooper was fumbling to pick it up, Nippy Jones slid across the plate with the winning run.

               During the offseason, LaPointe was an assistant football coach at the University of Vermont. He was the varsity baseball coach at the school when he died at age 45, in 1967.

AUGUST 31   Prior to a 5–0 win over the Phillies on Enos Slaughter Night at Sportsman's Park, the Cardinal outfielder is presented with two autos, a deep-freeze unit, a deer rifle, an outboard motor, fishing tackle, and a motion picture camera.

Slaughter hit .321 with 11 homers in 1948.

SEPTEMBER 6   The Cardinals lose 2–1 and 4–1 to Pittsburgh in an unusual doubleheader at Forbes Field. The two clubs tied a major league record for most double plays in a doubleheader with 13 (eight by the Pirates and five by the Cardinals), and tied a National League record for the fewest strikeouts in a twin bill with two (both by Cards pitcher Murry Dickson in the opener).

The two defeats were the start of a four-game losing streak that dropped the Cards out of the pennant race. The club finished second 6½ games behind the Braves.

SEPTEMBER 22   Stan Musial collects five hits, including a homer and a double, in five at-bats during an 8–2 win over the Braves in Boston. Enos Slaughter gets struck in the face by Nippy Jones's line drive while running between first and second base. Slaughter suffered a broken nose that put him out of action for the rest of the year.

Musial had four five-hit games in 1948. The only other players in the modern era with four five-hit games in a season are Ty Cobb (1922), Tony Gwynn (1993), and Ichiro Suzuki (2004).

SEPTEMBER 30   Harry Brecheen records his 20th win of the season with a 4–1 decision over the Pirates in the second game of a doubleheader at Sportsman's Park. The Cards also won the first game, 6–1.

OCTOBER 3   On the final day of the season, Erv Dusak pitches the ninth inning of a 4–3 loss to the Cubs at Sportsman's Park. Dusak faced four batters, walking one and retiring the other three.

Dusak played every position but first base and catcher in 1948, but he batted only .209. In 1949, at the age of 28, he went back to the minors to become a pitcher. Dusak made it back to the big leagues in 1950 as a pitcher, but he posted an 0–3 record and a 5.33 ERA over two seasons with the Cardinals and the Pirates.

NOVEMBER 8   Six days after Harry Truman upsets Thomas Dewey in the presidential election, the Cardinals trade Ken Burkhardt to the Reds for Babe Young.

1949

Season in a Sentence

After battling the Dodgers for first place all season, the Cardinals take a 1½-game lead into the final week, only to lose four straight to the lowly Pirates and Cubs.

Finish • Won • Lost • Pct • GB

Second   96   58   .623   1.0

Manager

Eddie Dyer

Stats

Stats	Cards	NL	Rank
Batting Avg:	.277	.262	1
On-Base Pct:	.348	.334	2
Slugging Pct:	.404	.389	2
Home Runs:	102		6
Stolen Bases:	17		8
ERA:	3.44	4.04	1
Fielding Avg:	.976	.975	4
Runs Scored:	766		2
Runs Allowed:	616		1

Starting Lineup

Del Rice, c
Nippy Jones, 1b
Red Schoendienst, 2b
Eddie Kazak, 3b
Marty Marion, ss
Enos Slaughter, lf
Chuck Diering, cf
Stan Musial, rf-cf
Ron Northey, rf
Tommy Glaviano, 3b
Rocky Nelson, 1b
Joe Garagiola, c

Pitchers

Howie Pollet, sp
Harry Brecheen, sp
George Munger, sp
Al Brazle, sp-rp
Max Lanier, sp
Ted Wilks, rp
Gerry Staley, rp-sp

Attendance

1,430,676 (third in NL)

Club Leaders

Batting Avg:	Musial	.338
On-Base Pct:	Musial	.438
Slugging Pct:	Musial	.624
Home Runs:	Musial	36
RBIs:	Musial	123
Runs:	Musial	128
Stolen Bases:	Schoendienst	8
Wins:	Pollet	20
Strikeouts:	Pollet	108
ERA:	Pollet	2.77
Saves:	Wilks	9

JANUARY 27   Fred Saigh purchases Robert Hannegan's team stock. The deal gave Saigh 1,665 of the 1,676 shares of stock in the club. The other 11 shares were held by three individuals who purchased stock in 1917 and held on to them for sentimental reasons.

JANUARY 29   The Cardinals sell Murry Dickson to the Pirates for $125,000.

The Pirates were owned at the time by Frank McKinney, who succeeded Bob Hannegan as chairman of the Democratic National Committee. It's likely that the sale was made to help finance Saigh's purchase of Hannegan's stock. It's also likely that the transaction cost the Cardinals the pennant in 1949. Dickson was 12–14 that season, but he posted a 3.29 ERA and beat St. Louis five times. In 1951, he won 20 games for a Pittsburgh club that finished the year in last place. Dickson was still in the majors in 1959, when he was 43 years old, and played for the Cardinals again in 1956 and 1957.

FEBRUARY 3   Brothers Bill and Charles DeWitt gain control of the Browns by acquiring 57 percent of the stock from Richard Muckerman for $1 million.

One of the DeWitt brothers' first acts was to try to raise the Cardinals' rent, which was $35,000. When Fred Saigh pointed out that the two clubs had a *written agreement until 1952 specifying that there would be no rent increase, the DeWitts tried to evict the Cardinals from Sportsman's Park, leading to a long legal battle.*

APRIL 19   The Cardinals lose 3–1 to the Reds on Opening Day in Cincinnati. Enos Slaughter homered for the lone Cardinal run.

Slaughter hit .336 with 191 hits, 13 homers, and a league-leading 13 triples in 1949.

APRIL 22   In the home opener, the Cardinals defeat the Cubs 9–2 before 10,121 at Sportsman's Park. Stan Musial hit a home run.

Musial topped the NL in hits (207), doubles (41), triples (13 in a tie with teammate Enos Slaughter), total bases (382), and on-base percentage (.438). He ranked second in batting average (.338), slugging percentage (.624), home runs (36), and runs (128) and finished third in RBIs (123).

APRIL 30   Rookie first baseman Rocky Nelson hits a bizarre home run for the Cardinals in the ninth inning to beat the Cubs 4–3 at Wrigley Field. With the Cubs leading 3–2 and a Cardinal runner on base, Chicago center fielder Andy Pafko, thinking he had made the final out of the game with a diving somersault catch off his shoe tops, held the ball while Nelson circled the bases for an "inside-the-glove" homer.

Pafko ran toward the Cubs' dugout with the ball, believing that the game was over. Second base umpire Al Barlick, in a delayed call, ruled that Pafko had trapped it. Pafko, ignoring his teammates' frantic pleas to throw the ball, headed for the umpire to protest the decision while Nelson circled the bases as the ball was inside Pafko's glove. Pafko finally made a belated throw home when Nelson was only steps from the plate, and the Cardinal batter was safe with what would be the game-winning run. The Cubs' arguing delayed the game for 10 minutes, and the crowd of 30,775 showed its disapproval by showering the field with debris.

MAY 9   Eddie Kazak hits a grand slam in the eighth inning of a 14–5 win over the Dodgers in Brooklyn. It was Kazak's first major league homer.

A 28-year-old rookie third baseman in 1949, Kazak played well enough during the first half of the season to make the All-Star team as a starter. A native of the coal mining region of Pennsylvania, where he worked in the mines alongside his father, it was remarkable that Kazak reached the majors at all. Born Edward Tzaczuk, he was wounded severely twice in the European theater during World War II. He was first bayoneted in the right arm in hand-to-hand fighting. Then, his right elbow was crushed by shrapnel and falling mortar in a small town near Brest, France. He spent 18 months in the hospital and underwent a delicate operation in which plastic was used to repair the elbow and restore movement to three paralyzed fingers. Surgeons advised Kazak to forget about baseball, but he battled back to play in the majors. Shortly after the All-Star Game, however, he suffered an on-field injury that all but ended his career. A chipped bone in his ankle shelved Kazak for two months, and afterward he was little more than a reserve and a pinch hitter until his career ended in 1952.

MAY 13   A collision between Joe Garagiola and Rip Sewell highlights a 3–2 loss to the Pirates at Forbes Field. Bad feelings already existed between the two clubs after Cardinal pitcher Ken Johnson had beaned Pittsburgh's Stan Rojek on April 27. In the fifth inning, Garagiola, who was charged with calling for the duster that decked Rojek, grounded to first base after being dropped to the ground by a close pitch. Sewell gave Garagiola a hip check in the base line and sent him sprawling. Players from both teams swarmed to the scene, but umpires kept the combatants apart.

          The Pirates had a 71–83 record in 1949 but geared up to play the Cardinals in what became a bitter rivalry. The Pirates had a 12–10 record against the Cards during the year (see September 5, 1949).

MAY 15   The Cardinals score two runs in the ninth inning to beat the Pirates 4–3 in Pittsburgh. Chuck Diering doubled in the tying run, then scored on a single by Red Schoendienst.

          The Cardinals had a record of 12–17 on May 23 but won 25 of their next 32 games to move into pennant contention. By June 24, the Cards were in first place and spent the rest of the season battling the Dodgers for the top spot in the league.

MAY 26   The Cardinals score seven runs in the first inning and defeat the Pirates 13–6 at Sportsman's Park.

MAY 28   Cardinals owner Fred Saigh announces plans for a new stadium. Plans called for a 47,000-seat stadium built for $4 million. Plans drawn up by architect Syl G. Schmidt had a horseshoe-shaped grandstand in three tiers and uncovered bleachers in the outfield. There would be no posts to obstruct the spectators' view, which at the time was a revolutionary concept. The design was somewhat similar to that of Memorial Stadium in Baltimore, which served as the home of the Orioles from 1954 through 1991, but with a cleaner, more modern approach, much like present-day Dodger Stadium, which opened in 1962. Saigh refused to disclose the location of the proposed ballpark but said it would be built on 18 acres he owned and that he hoped to acquire eight to nine more acres. At the time, only two ballparks in the majors had been built since 1915. They were Yankee Stadium, constructed in 1923, and Municipal Stadium in Cleveland, which opened in 1932. Saigh's proposed stadium never got past the planning stages.

JUNE 1   The Cardinals score four runs in the ninth inning to down the Dodgers 6–3 in Brooklyn.

JUNE 2   The Cardinals score three runs in the ninth inning to tie the score 4–4, then add three more in the fourteenth to win 7–4 in Brooklyn. In the fourteenth, Stan Musial tripled in two runs and then scored on a double by Chuck Diering.

JUNE 5   Commissioner Happy Chandler extends amnesty to the 18 players who jumped to the outlaw Mexican League in 1946 (see May 23, 1946). Among the 18 were Max Lanier, Lou Klein, and Freddie Martin of the Cardinals. The players, who received five-year suspensions when they bolted for Mexico, were notified that they must apply for reinstatement in writing and that the approval would be automatic. Chandler's action came after owners were threatened with antitrust lawsuits. Lanier, Klein, and Martin rejoined the Cards within a month.

June 15   Nippy Jones drives in six runs on a homer, a double, and a single during a 9–5 win over the Dodgers at Sportsman's Park.

June 22   Down 8–1, the Cardinals rally with three runs in the fourth inning, two in the sixth, and five in the seventh to beat the Giants 11–8 at Sportsman's Park.

July 7   The Cardinals suffer a tough 2–0 loss at the hands of the Pirates at Forbes Field. With two Pittsburgh runners on base in the sixth inning, Pirate rookie Dino Restelli stepped out of the batter's box to complain about the calls of home plate umpire Larry Goetz. With two strikes on Restelli, Goetz motioned for Cardinal pitcher Gerry Staley to throw the ball plateward. Believing that Goetz wanted to see the ball, Staley lobbed the ball to the plate. Joe Garagiola snapped the ball back to Staley, who realized that he had just missed a chance for an uncontested third strike. Staley quickly fired another pitch, but Restelli jumped into the box and lifted a double to score the only two runs of the game.

July 12   Cardinals batters collect six hits in eight at-bats in the All-Star Game, although the National League still loses 11–7 at Ebbets Field in Brooklyn. Stan Musial hit a homer in the first inning off Mel Parnell and added two singles for a 3-for-4 day. Eddie Kazak, in the lone All-Star appearance of his career, had two singles in two at-bats. Red Schoendienst contributed a pinch-single.

July 15   Howie Pollet pitches the Cardinals to a 1–0 win over Robin Roberts in Philadelphia. Pollet also drove in the lone run of the game with a single in the seventh inning.

               Pollet had a 20–9 record and a 2.77 ERA in 1949. He led the NL in shutouts with five.

July 23   Twice just one strike from defeat, the Cardinals score two runs in the ninth inning to defeat the Dodgers 5–4 at Ebbets Field. With two outs and Stan Musial on third, Lou Klein walked on a 3–2 pitch. Marty Marion, hitless in his previous 22 at-bats, singled on a 1–2 pitch to score Musial. Joe Garagiola followed with a single to score Klein with the winning run.

July 24   Stan Musial hits for the cycle during a 14–1 win over the Dodgers in Brooklyn. Musial tripled in the first inning off Don Newcombe, singled in the third against Paul Minner, and homered in the fifth and doubled in the seventh against Carl Erskine. In the ninth, Erskine walked Musial.

               During the 1948 and 1949 seasons, Musial played 22 games at Ebbets Field and had a .531 batting average on 43 hits, of which 11 were doubles, five were triples, and eight were homers. The nickname "Stan the Man" came from Brooklyn fans because of Musial's uncommon success against the Dodgers.

August 5   Gerry Staley pitches the Cardinals to a 1–0 win over the Giants at Sportsman's Park. Marty Marion drove in the lone run of the game with a single in the sixth inning.

August 6   A first-inning home run by Nippy Jones is wiped out because of a balk during a 3–1 loss to the Giants at Sportsman's Park. Jones drove the ball over the wall off New York pitcher Adrian Zabala, but a split second before the pitch, the third base umpire called a balk. According to the rules of the day, the home run didn't count because of the prior balk call. Later, the rules were changed to give the offensive club the option of taking the balk or the hit.

AUGUST 7   US Vice President Alben Barkley attends a 9–2 win over the Giants at Sportsman's Park. At the time, Barkley was dating St. Louis widow Jane Hadley. The 71-year-old Barkley had married the 38-year-old Hadley the following November.

AUGUST 8   Enos Slaughter hits a grand slam off Ken Burkhart in the fourth inning of a 9–3 win over the Reds at Sportsman's Park.

AUGUST 17   Relief pitcher Freddie Martin wins his own game by singling in a run in the thirteenth inning to beat the Reds 4–3 in Cincinnati. Martin also pitched five shutout innings.

AUGUST 29   The Cardinals score seven runs in the seventh inning of an 8–3 win over the Braves in Boston. The big inning was highlighted by a grand slam from Ron Northey against Bill Voiselle.

SEPTEMBER 3   The Cardinals and Reds play to a 9–9, 15-inning tie at Sportsman's Park, called by curfew because National League rules stipulated that no inning could start after 12:50 AM. The two teams combined to leave 40 men on base during the contest, 22 of them by the Cards.

The 15-inning night game was followed by two daytime doubleheaders. The Cardinals played 52 innings in fewer than 48 hours.

SEPTEMBER 4   The Cardinals sweep the Reds 6–4 and 11–2 at Sportsman's Park. Tommy Glaviano hit a grand slam during an eight-run third inning in the second game.

It was Radio Appreciation Day at the ballpark. Women representing each of the 60 stations in eight states carrying the Cardinals' games paraded around the infield. The Cardinals' 1949 contests were heard in Missouri, Illinois, Kentucky, Tennessee, Iowa, Kansas, Arkansas, and Oklahoma. Stations were added in Indiana and Mississippi in 1950 and Texas in 1958 to give the Cards an 11-state radio network.

SEPTEMBER 5   George Munger is both the winning and losing pitcher in a doubleheader against the Pirates at Sportsman's Park. He earned a complete-game 9–1 win in the opener. In the second tilt, Munger appeared in relief in the eighth inning but allowed a tenth-inning run to lose 5–4.

In the second inning of the second game, Enos Slaughter spiked Pittsburgh second baseman Danny Murtaugh in the chest trying to break up a double play. The blow was hard enough to draw blood. Murtaugh shouted at Slaughter while the Cardinal outfielder headed for the dugout. Slaughter whirled and motioned toward Murtaugh to fight. Murtaugh dropped his glove and started toward him but was stopped by teammates. The Cardinals and Pirates had feuded all season, and the Slaughter-Murtaugh incident fanned the flames. Pittsburgh was hopping mad and helped prevent the Cardinals from winning the pennant three weeks later (see September 27 and 29, 1949).

SEPTEMBER 7   The Cardinals score two runs in the ninth inning to defeat the Cubs 3–2 at
               Sportsman's Park. With one out and the Cards down 2–1, Nippy Jones hit a
               grounder to third. Just as Chicago third baseman Bob Ramazzotti was about to field
               it, the ball hit the bag and bounded away for a single with Rocky Nelson scoring on
               the play. Marty Marion drove in the winning run.

               *Before the game, Stan Musial was presented with $6,000 in bonds and a station
               wagon, among other gifts. Two weeks earlier, he received a Cadillac from fans
               living in his hometown of Donora, Pennsylvania, prior to a game in Pittsburgh.*

SEPTEMBER 13   George Munger pitches a one-hitter to defeat the Giants 1–0 at Sportsman's Park.
               The only Giants hit was a single by Sid Gordon in the second inning. After hitting
               a double, Stan Musial scored the lone run in the first inning on a single by Eddie
               Kazak.

               *The Cardinals drew 1,430,676 fans in 1949 to break the old record of 1,247,913
               set in 1947. Despite being in first place for 64 days and in a pennant race that
               lasted until the final day of the season, the Cards finished third in the NL in
               attendance and seventh in the majors in 1949. They didn't draw as many as 1.25
               million in a season again until 1966, the year the new Busch Memorial Stadium
               opened.*

SEPTEMBER 16   A 7–5 win over the Braves at Sportsman's Park gives the Cardinals a 2½-game lead
               over the Dodgers with 14 contests left on the schedule. It was the Cardinals' 17th
               win in their last 20 games to improve the club's record to 90–50.

               *Blowing a chance to put the pennant on ice, the Cardinals lost eight of their last
               14 games, six of their last nine, and four of their final five.*

SEPTEMBER 18   The Cardinals annihilate the Phillies 15–3 at Sportsman's Park. Ron Northey hit a
               grand slam off Robin Roberts in the third inning.

SEPTEMBER 20   Max Lanier pitches the Cardinals to a 1–0 win over the Dodgers at Sportsman's
               Park in the first game of a crucial three-game series. The victory gave the Cards a
               2½-game lead with 10 contests left to play. The lone run scored in the ninth inning.
               Enos Slaughter opened the inning with a double. After Ron Northey was walked
               intentionally, Bill Howerton sacrificed, but the bunt went for a bases-filling single
               when third baseman Eddie Miksis let the ball roll in the hope that it would trickle
               foul. At this point, play was interrupted for several minutes as Jackie Robinson
               resumed an argument with umpire Bill Stewart over a ball-and-strike decision on
               Robinson's last trip to the plate. Robinson was ejected, and Miksis replaced him
               at second base. Joe Garagiola subsequently singled off Miksis' glove to score the
               winning run.

               *The Cardinals lost the final two games of the series 5–0 and 19–6 to cut their
               margin over the Dodgers to half a game.*

SEPTEMBER 25   Two days after President Harry Truman announces that the Soviet Union had tested
               an atom bomb, the Cardinals defeat the Cubs 6–1 at Sportsman's Park.

               *The victory gave the Cardinals a 1½-game lead with a two-game advantage in
               the loss column. St. Louis had five games left, all on the road, but the games*

were against the sixth-place Pirates and last-place Cubs. The Dodgers had four games remaining.

SEPTEMBER 27   The Cardinals lose 6–4 to the Pirates in Pittsburgh, cutting their advantage over the Dodgers to one game. George Munger walked in two batters and allowed a grand slam to reserve outfielder Tom Saffell, who hit only six career home runs.

SEPTEMBER 29   After a rainout pushes the game back a day, the Cardinals lose 7–2 to the Pirates in Pittsburgh. Ex-Cardinal Murry Dickson was the winning pitcher. On the same day, the Dodgers swept a doubleheader against the Braves in Boston to take first place by half a game over St. Louis.

SEPTEMBER 30   The reeling Cardinals lose 6–5 to the Cubs in Chicago to fall one game behind Brooklyn with two contests remaining.

OCTOBER 1   The Cardinals lose their fourth straight game, their longest skid of the season, dropping a 3–1 decision to the Cubs in Chicago. The Cards left 12 runners on base. Fortunately, the Dodgers also lost, 6–4 to the Phillies in Philadelphia. This left the two contenders separated by a single game entering the final day of the season.

OCTOBER 2   In Chicago, the Cardinals finally snap the four-game losing streak to wallop the Cubs 13–5. When the contest ended, the Dodgers-Phillies tilt was still in progress. The Dodgers could clinch the pennant with a win. A loss would force a best-of-three playoff with the Cardinals for the NL pennant. Brooklyn took an early 5–0 lead, but the Phillies knotted the score 7–7 in the sixth. The two clubs went into extra innings, with the Dodgers pushing across two runs in the tenth on Carl Furillo's homer to win 9–7. The game ended on a spectacular catch by Jackie Robinson. The Dodgers went on to lose the World Series in five games to the Yankees.

The Cardinals finished either first or second nine consecutive times from 1941 through 1949, winning the NL pennant in 1942, 1943, 1944, and 1946. The glory years were coming to an end, however, as the roster was aging. During the 1930s and 1940s, the Cards traded or sold their top players just after they passed their peak and had ready replacements available from the minor leagues. The vast farm system had begun to deteriorate after Branch Rickey left for Brooklyn at the end of the 1942 season, however, and by the end of the 1940s, there were few top-quality prospects in the organization. As a result, the Cardinals began a long, slow decline to mediocrity during the 1950s.

DECEMBER 14   The Cardinals trade Ron Northey and Lou Klein to the Phillies for Harry Walker.

THE STATE OF THE CARDINALS

After posting the best record in the majors during the 1940s, the Cardinals ran with the middle of the pack in the National League during the 1950s, compiling 776 wins and 763 losses for a winning percentage of .504. The Cards had the fourth-best record in the NL, trailing the Dodgers, Braves, and Giants. National League pennant winners were the Phillies (1950), Giants (1951 and 1954), Dodgers (1952, 1953, 1955, 1956, and 1959), and Braves (1957 and 1958).

THE BEST TEAM

The 1957 edition was the only Cardinal club to hold first place after August 1 during the 1950s, but it ended the year in second place at 87–67, eight games behind the Braves.

THE WORST TEAM

The 1955 Cardinals were 68–86 and landed in seventh place. It was not only the worst record of any club during the 1950s but also the worst winning percentage compiled by a Cardinal outfit between 1924 and 1978.

THE BEST MOMENT

The best moment took place on May 13, 1958, when Stan Musial collected his 3,000th career hit with a pinch-double against the Cubs in Chicago.

THE WORST MOMENT

The Cardinals lost a game by forfeit to the Phillies on July 18, 1954, because of manager Eddie Stanky's stalling tactics.

THE ALL-DECADE TEAM • YEARS W/CARDS

Del Rice, c	1945–55, 1960
Stan Musial, 1b	1941–44, 1946–63
Red Schoendienst, 2b	1945–56, 1961–63
Ken Boyer, 3b	1955–65
Solly Hemus, ss	1949–56, 1959
Rip Repulski, lf	1953–56
Wally Moon, cf	1954–58
Enos Slaughter, rf	1938–42, 1946–53
Larry Jackson, p	1955–62
Vinegar Bend Mizell, p	1952–53, 1955–60
Gerry Staley, p	1947–54
Harvey Haddix, p	1954–58

Musial, Schoendienst, and Slaughter were also on the Cardinals All-Decade team of the 1940s. All three are also in baseball's Hall of Fame. Other prominent Cardinals of the 1950s were first baseman–outfielder Joe Cunningham (1954, 1956–61) and second baseman Don Blasingame (1955–59).

THE DECADE LEADERS

Batting Avg:	Musial	.330
On-Base Pct:	Musial	.421
Slugging Pct:	Musial	.568
Home Runs:	Musial	266
RBIs:	Musial	972
Runs:	Musial	948
Stolen Bases:	Blasingame	65
Wins:	Staley	72
Strikeouts:	Mizell	789
ERA:	Haddix	3.65
Saves:	Brazle	55

THE HOME FIELD

At the start of the decade, Sportsman's Park was in sorry shape. The moribund Browns built the ballpark in 1909. By 1950, the club treasury was all but depleted. Browns ownership had barely enough money for perfunctory repairs and upkeep, much less improvements. Things changed in February 1953 when August Busch purchased the Cardinals. One of his first acts was to buy Sportsman's Park from the Browns for $800,000 and change the name of the ballpark to Busch Stadium. Busch poured $1.5 million into upgrading almost every aspect of the facility. At the end of the 1953 season, the Browns moved to Baltimore, where they were renamed the Orioles. For the first time since 1901, the Cardinals were the only team in St. Louis.

THE GAME YOU WISH YOU HAD SEEN

The best day to be at Sportsman's Park/Busch Stadium during the 1950s was on May 2, 1954, when Stan Musial clubbed a record five home runs in a doubleheader against the Giants.

THE WAY THE GAME WAS PLAYED

The number of home runs continued to rise during the 1950s with NL teams averaging 140 homers per year, compared with 80 per year in the 1930s. The number of complete games continued to decline, from an average of 62 per club in 1950 to 47 in 1959. Relievers were making more appearances, and the relief specialist emerged. The increased use of relievers to close out victories led to a new statistic called the "save," although it wasn't officially recognized by Major League Baseball until 1969. Games were taking longer to play. The average length of a game rose from 2 hours, 23 minutes to 2 hours, 38 minutes. In addition, the Cardinals employed black players for the first time beginning with the addition of Tom Alston to the roster in 1954. Lastly, the first franchise relocation in more than 50 years took place during the 1950s. In the NL, the Braves moved from Boston to Milwaukee in 1953, and the Dodgers and Giants moved from New York to California after the 1957 season.

THE MANAGEMENT

Fred Saigh, who bought the club in 1947, was the owner at the start of the 1950s. He was forced to sell the club, however, after receiving a prison sentence because of income tax invasion. Saigh sold the Cardinals to August Busch in February 1953. General managers under Busch during the fifties were Dick Meyer (1954–55), Frank Lane (1955–57), and Bing Devine (1957–64). Field managers were Eddie Dyer (1946–50), Marty Marion (1951), Eddie Stanky (1952–55), Harry Walker (1955), Fred Hutchinson (1956–58), Stan Hack (1958), and Solly Hemus (1959–61).

THE BEST PLAYER MOVE

The best player move was the signing of Bob Gibson out of Creighton University in 1957. The Cardinals acquired center fielder Curt Flood from the Reds in December 1957 for three nondescript pitchers in the best trade of the decade.

THE WORST PLAYER MOVE

The Cardinals traded Harvey Haddix and Stu Miller to the Phillies in May 1956 for two washed-up pitchers.

1950

Season in a Sentence

In first place on July 24, the Cardinals fade to fifth by season's end, the club's worst finish since 1938.

Finish • Won • Lost • Pct • GB

Fifth   78   75   .510   12.5

Manager

Eddie Dyer

Stats	Cards	NL	Rank
Batting Ave.:	.259	.261	6
On-Base Pct.:	.339	.336	4
Slugging Pct.:	.386	.401	7
Home Runs:	102		7
Stolen Bases:	23		8
ERA:	3.97	4.14	3
Fielding Pct.:	.978	.975	2
Runs Scored:	693		5
Runs Allowed:	670		3

Starting Lineup

Del Rice, c
Rocky Nelson, 1b
Red Schoendienst, 2b
Tommy Glaviano, 3b
Marty Marion, ss
Stan Musial, lf-1b
Chuck Diering, cf
Enos Slaughter, rf
Bill Howerton, cf-lf
Eddie Kazak, 3b
Eddie Miller, ss
Harry Walker, c

Pitchers

Howie Pollet, sp
Gerry Staley, sp-rp
Max Lanier, sp
Harry Brecheen, sp
George Munger, sp-rp
Al Brazle, rp
Cloyd Boyer, rp-sp

Attendance

1,093,411 (fifth in NL)

Club Leaders

Batting Avg:	Musial	.346
On-Base Pct:	Musial	.437
Slugging Pct:	Musial	.596
Home Runs:	Musial	28
RBIs:	Musial	109
Runs:	Musial	105
Stolen Bases:	Glaviano	6
Wins:	Pollet	14
Strikeouts:	Pollet	117
ERA:	Lanier	3.13
Saves:	Brazle	6

April 18

In the first-ever season major league opening game played at night, the Cardinals defeat the Pirates 4–2 before 20,871 at Sportsman's Park. It was the largest crowd ever for an opener in St. Louis at the time. Red Schoendienst hit a homer in the first inning, and Stan Musial added another in the third. Joe Garagiola's single in the sixth inning broke a 2–2 tie. Gerry Staley pitched a complete game.

Night baseball had been played in the majors since only 1935, and in St. Louis since only 1940, and it was still somewhat of a novelty. The Cardinals scheduled 54 of their 77 home games at night in 1950, the most of any club in the majors. The Cards played 70 percent of their home games at night that season, while the other 15 clubs combined played 31 percent under the lights.

April 24

Max Lanier beats the Reds 1–0 in Cincinnati with his arm and his bat. Lanier not only pitched a complete game, he also drove in the lone run of the game with a single with two outs in the ninth.

April 30

Del Rice hits a walk-off homer in the thirteenth inning to defeat the Cubs 1–0 at Sportsman's Park. It was only the fourth hit off Chicago pitcher Johnny Schmitz, who pitched a complete game and had retired 20 Cardinals in a row before Rice's homer. Harry Brecheen also went all the way, allowing just five hits in the 13-inning shutout.

MAY 1	The Cardinals score three runs in the ninth inning to defeat the Dodgers 3–2 at Sportsman's Park. The Cards trailed 2–0 with two outs when Red Schoendienst singled in the first run. Bill Howerton drove in the tying run with a pinch-single. The winning tally crossed the plate on a wild pitch by Willie Ramsdell.
MAY 3	After the Dodgers score a run in the top of the thirteenth, the Cardinals come back with two in their half to win 6–5 at Sportsman's Park in the second thrilling rally during a final at-bat in three days. A single by Joe Garagiola in the ninth inning tied the game 4–4. With the bases loaded in the thirteenth, Garagiola singled in two runs with a walk-off single. Tommy Glaviano collected five hits, including a double, in six at-bats.

On the same day, the Cardinals purchased Eddie Miller from the Phillies.

MAY 9	The Cardinals collect 21 hits and rout the Braves 15–0 at Sportsman's Park.
MAY 13	Four errors by third baseman Tommy Glaviano, three of them in the ninth inning on balls struck by three consecutive batters, lead to a 9–8 loss to the Dodgers at Ebbets Field. The Cardinals led 8–0 before Brooklyn scored four runs in the eighth inning. With a light rain falling on a cold night, the Dodgers renewed their assault in the ninth, scoring one run and filling the sacks with one out to set the stage for the Glaviano debacle. First he threw wide to second trying for a force play on Roy Campanella's grounder, allowing a run to score and making the tally 8–6. Glaviano then pegged wide to the plate on Eddie Miksis' bounder to allow another run to cross the plate and narrow the gap to a run while leaving the bases full. When Glaviano let Pee Wee Reese's hopper go through his legs, the tying and winning runs scored. That night, Enos Slaughter and coach Terry Moore tried to keep the despondent Glaviano company by taking him to a movie at a Manhattan theater. The movie was *D.O.A.*, the story of a man attempting to find out who had given him a deadly, slow-acting poison.

> *Nicknamed "Harpo" for his curly blond hair reminiscent of Harpo Marx, Glaviano hit .285, had a .421 on-base percentage, and hit 11 homers in 1950, his first season as a regular. He had above-average range at third base, but a scatter-gun arm made him a liability on defense. After 1950, Glaviano played three more seasons and hit only .215. During spring training in 1951, the Cards tried Glaviano in center field. The first time he played the position in an exhibition contest, he crashed into the wall and fell to the ground unconscious in the second inning.*

MAY 21	A first-inning triple play highlights a 6–5 win over the Phillies in the first game of a doubleheader at Shibe Park. With Richie Ashburn on second and Granny Hamner on first for Philadelphia, Eddie Waitkus struck out. Catcher Joe Garagiola promptly whipped the ball to third baseman Tommy Glaviano, and Ashburn, who got a poor start on a stolen-base attempt, was trapped between second and third and tagged out by shortstop Marty Marion. Hamner, meantime, waited midway between first and second and was caught scrambling back to first base on Marion's snap throw to Stan Musial. The Phils won the second tilt 4–2.
MAY 28	Joe Garagiola hits a grand slam off Ewell Blackwell in the first inning of a 7–2 win over the Reds in the second game of a doubleheader in Cincinnati. The Cards also won the first game, 6–2.

Through May 29, Stan Musial had 53 hits in 120 at-bats for an average of .442. Musial finished the year leading the NL in batting average (.346) and slugging percentage (.596) and was second in on-base percentage (.437), hits (192), doubles (41), and total bases (331). Musial also hit 28 homers, drove in 109 runs, and scored 105.

MAY 30   The Cardinals use two explosive eighth innings to defeat the Pirates 17–13 and 8–5 in a doubleheader at Forbes Field. In the first game, the Cards scored seven times in the eighth to take a 17–7 lead, then withstood a rally by Pittsburgh to emerge with the win. In the nightcap, the Redbirds were down 4–0 before scoring six runs in the eighth.

JUNE 1   Down 2–0, the Cardinals' Marty Marion hits a grand slam off Preacher Roe for a 5–2 win over the Dodgers at Sportsman's Park.

It was a costly victory. Joe Garagiola grounded to the right side and tripped over Jackie Robinson's feet when Robinson covered first on the play. He suffered a separated shoulder and was out until September.

JUNE 4   Cardinals owner Fred Saigh creates controversy by scheduling the first Sunday-night game in major league history.

The Sunday-night game dispute originated with the postponement of a night game between the Dodgers and Cardinals in St. Louis on June 3. The next day, Saigh announced that Dodgers president Branch Rickey agreed to replay the contest on Sunday night, July 16, as part of a day-night doubleheader. The rescheduled contest was a sellout within days. On June 9, Commissioner Happy Chandler informed Saigh that he must find another day to play the game. Three days later, National League president Ford Frick backed Chandler, stating that league rules prohibited Sunday-night games, and the rained-out contest was rescheduled for Monday afternoon, July 17. The dispute between Saigh and Chandler would have long-lasting consequences. Chandler's contract as commissioner expired in April 1952. Saigh began a one-man campaign to oust Chandler and lined up enough fellow owners to prevent an extension of Chandler's contract when it came up for a vote in December 1950. Chandler resigned in July 1951, and Frick succeeded him as commissioner. The first Sunday-night game in the major leagues would not be played until 1963.

JUNE 8   The Cardinals score eight runs in the first inning and overwhelm the Braves 18–6 at Sportsman's Park. Boston opened the scoring with four tallies in the top of the first.

JUNE 14   The Cardinals extend their lead in the National League race to 3½ games with a 4–2 win over the Phillies in Philadelphia.

The Cards had a 32–17 record but lost seven of their next eight to drop out of first. Eddie Dyer's club regained first place during the first week of July and was in and out of the top spot in the NL throughout the month in a tight-four team race with the Phillies, Dodgers, and Braves. The Cardinals' last day in first was July 24, when the team was 51–37. The Cards soon began another slide and were out of the race by mid-August. With an old club, St. Louis lost 38 of its last 65 games. Seven players on the 1950 Cardinals had at least 300 plate appearances, and none was younger than 27. Six pitchers were on the mound for at least 125 innings during the season, and none was younger than 29.

JUNE 21   The Cardinals defeat the Giants 14–6 in New York.

JUNE 24   Johnny Lindell homers in the tenth inning to defeat the Braves 7–6 in Boston.

A day later, North Korean forces attacked South Korea. The US immediately became involved militarily. The Korean War would last until 1953, and the military draft claimed such stars as Ted Williams and Willie Mays. The Cardinals were not adversely affected, however. The only player on their major league roster drafted was pitcher Tom Poholsky, a 21-year-old rookie in 1951 who missed the 1952 and 1953 seasons. Vinegar Bend Mizell, a rookie hurler in 1952, was in the Army during the 1954 and 1955 campaigns after the Korean War ended and the draft remained in place as the Cold War intensified.

JULY 6   The Cardinals erupt for 10 runs in the first inning and trounce the Reds 13–1 at Sportsman's Park. Bill Howerton collected two doubles in the inning.

Howerton was a 28-year-old rookie outfielder in 1950 and batted .281 in 110 games. His nickname was "Hopalong" because he favored a leg injured in a horse-riding accident as a child. Howerton developed osteomyelitis, and doctors discovered that he had no ankle bone in his left leg. Despite the ailment, he played four years in the majors.

JULY 8   Jack Phillips of the Pirates hits a pinch-hit, walk-off grand slam in the ninth inning to defeat the Cardinals 7–6 at Forbes Field. Stan Musial, playing left field, made a gallant effort to snare Phillips's drive with a leap in front of the eight-foot-high wire fence, and for a moment it appeared that he might have made the catch. After several moments of confusion during which Musial laid on the ground after bouncing off the fence, Pittsburgh base runners remained glued to the bags. Finally, Pirate pitchers in the bullpen retrieved the ball and showed it to the umpires, who signaled the home run.

JULY 10   The Cardinals sell Jim Hearn to the Giants.

Hearn was 29 years old and had regressed each season after a 12–7 record as a rookie with the Cardinals in 1947. The club gave up on him because it believed he couldn't pitch under pressure. With the encouragement of Giants manager Leo Durocher, Hearn had an immediate turnaround in New York. Over the remainder of the 1950 season, he was 11–3 with a 1.94 ERA and posted records of 17–9 in 1951 and 14–7 in 1952.

JULY 11   Red Schoendienst hits a game-winning homer in the fourteenth inning of the All-Star Game to lift the National League to a 4–3 win at Comiskey Park in Chicago. The drive landed in the upper deck of the left-field stands. Enos Slaughter contributed a triple and a single in four at-bats.

Schoendienst hit only seven regular-season homers in 1950. Slaughter batted .290 with 10 homers and 101 RBIs, but he slumped badly during the Cardinals' nose dive down the stretch. After August 6, Slaughter hit a measly .181.

JULY 19   The Cardinals sweep the Giants 18–3 and 10–4 in a doubleheader at Sportsman's Park. The Cards led the opener 15–1 at the end of the fourth inning.

July 27   The Cardinals collect five home runs and hammer the Dodgers 13–3 in Brooklyn. Enos Slaughter and Chuck Diering each hit two homers, and Del Rice added the other. Despite the batting explosion by the Cards, Stan Musial was held without a hit, which snapped his batting streak at 30 games, the second longest in club history.

               The club record is 33 games by Rogers Hornsby in 1922. Albert Pujols matched Musial's 30-game streak in 2003.

August 6   Red Schoendienst collects five hits, including a double, in five at-bats as the Cardinals defeat the Phillies 7–1 in the first game of a doubleheader at Shibe Park. A two-run single by Eddie Kazak in the fourth inning accounted for all of the runs in a 2–0 victory in the second tilt. Max Lanier pitched the shutout.

August 19   Al Brazle helps his own cause by beating out an infield single in the ninth inning, then scoring on a walk-off triple by Red Schoendienst to defeat the Reds 3–2 at Sportsman's Park.

August 27   The Cardinals wallop the Dodgers 13–3 at Sportsman's Park.

               On the same day, Victor Papai, the older brother of Cardinal pitcher Al Papai, was shot in a Divernon, Illinois, tavern. Papai was wounded in the right shoulder, though not seriously. The shooting occurred during an argument over the international relationship between the United States and Hungary. The Papais were of Hungarian descent.

August 28   The Cardinals are held to four hits, but three of them are homers by Del Rice, Tommy Glaviano, and Stan Musial for a 3–1 win over the Dodgers at Sportsman's Park.

September 3   An unorthodox strategy by Eddie Dyer results in a 10-inning, 12–11 loss to the Pirates at Forbes Field. The Cardinals scored twice in the top of the tenth to tie the score, but Harry Brecheen gave up homers to Pete Castiglione and Bobby Dillinger in the bottom half to tie the score 11–11. With two outs and no one on base, Dyer ordered an intentional walk to Pittsburgh slugger Ralph Kiner, who had hit two homers earlier in the game. The tactic failed when Gus Bell drove in Kiner with a game-winning double.

September 6   Held to one hit through eight innings by Paul Minner of the Cubs, the Cardinals score three runs in the ninth inning and one in the tenth to defeat Chicago 5–4 in the first game of a doubleheader at Sportsman's Park. Bill Howerton, who homered in the fifth, drove in the tying run in the ninth. The Cards won on a walk-off homer by Stan Musial. St. Louis also took the nightcap, 7–3, with a five-run rally in the eighth.

September 7   The Cardinals purchase Peanuts Lowrey from the Reds.

September 10   The Cardinals stun the Pirates with four runs in the ninth inning and one in the tenth for a 6–5 win in the first game of a doubleheader at Sportsman's Park. Stan Musial's three-run homer capped the rally that tied the game. Peanuts Lowrey, in his first game with the Cards, drove in the winning run with a single, his third hit of the game. Pittsburgh won the second fray 6–2.

September 14   The Cardinals tie a National League record by leaving 18 men on base during a 3–2 loss to the Phillies in Philadelphia.

SEPTEMBER 15   Cardinal starting pitcher Cloyd Boyer injures his right elbow on the last pitch of his pregame warm-up. The Cardinals had to switch to George Munger, who pitched all nine innings of a 6–2 victory over the Dodgers in Brooklyn. In an unusual scoring decision, Boyer was listed as the starter since he appeared in the starting lineup after the lineup cards were given to the umpires. Munger was given a relief appearance in the official league statistics but was also credited with a complete game.

SEPTEMBER 20   After recovering from a sore elbow that forced him to miss his September 15 start, Cloyd Boyer pitches the Cardinals to a 1–0 win over the Braves in Boston. The lone run of the game scored on a single by Marty Marion in the eighth inning.

Boyer was part of a baseball family. There were 14 children, seven of them boys. All seven boys signed professional contracts, and three reached the majors. Cloyd (born in 1927 in Alba, Missouri) played for the Cardinals from 1949 through 1952 and with the Athletics in 1955. Ken (born in 1931 in Liberty, Missouri) reached the big leagues in 1955 as a third baseman with the Cards. He played 11 of his 15 seasons in the majors in St. Louis. Clete (born in 1937 in Cassville, Missouri) was in the majors as an 18-year-old third baseman with the Athletics in 1955. He also played for the Yankees and Braves in a career that lasted until 1971.

SEPTEMBER 27   Harry Brecheen pitches the Cardinals to a 1–0 win over the Reds at Sportsman's Park. Peanuts Lowrey drove in the lone run of the game with a single in the ninth inning.

SEPTEMBER 28   Howie Pollet shuts out the Reds 7–0 at Sportsman's Park.

SEPTEMBER 29   Replacing starting pitcher Cloyd Boyer, who pitched to only one batter before re-injuring his elbow, Al Brazle hurls nine innings of relief to beat the Cubs 5–1 at Sportsman's Park.

SEPTEMBER 30   The Cardinals throw two shutouts at the Cubs during a doubleheader at Sportsman's Park. Gerry Staley won the first game 2–0, and George Munger took the second 4–0.

In five consecutive games between the Reds and the Cubs from September 27 though 30, Cardinal pitchers allowed only one run.

OCTOBER 16   Sensing that Fred Saigh intends to fire him, Eddie Dyer resigns as manager of the Cardinals.

The Cardinals won a World Championship in Dyer's first season in 1946 and never had a losing year in the five years he ran the club. But age and a lack of depth had taken their toll on the team, and the 78–75 record and fifth-place finish in 1950 season was the worst by the franchise since 1938. With few prospects in the farm system ready to produce and the probability that others would be drafted because of the Korean War, there was little reason to believe that the Cardinals would contend again in the near future. Dyer never held another job in baseball. He became a partner in an insurance business in Houston and had extensive holdings in oil and other commercial enterprises. He died in 1964.

NOVEMBER 29   Fred Saigh ends six weeks of speculation over the identity of the new Cardinal manager by hiring Marty Marion to replace Eddie Dyer.

Marion was hired two days before his 33rd birthday. Suffering from back and knee problems, the 1950 season was the last of his 11 years as a player for the Cardinals. The Cardinals improved to 81–73 in 1951 under Marion, but Saigh fired him shortly after the season.

1951

Season in a Sentence

The Cardinals improve by three victories and two places in the standings, but it's not enough for Marty Marion to keep his job.

Finish • Won • Lost • Pct • GB

Third   81   73   .526   15.5

Manager

Marty Marion

Stats

Stats	Cards	NL	Rank
Batting Ave:	.264	.260	2
On-Base Pct:	.339	.331	3
Slugging Pct:	.382	.390	5
Home Runs:	95		7
Stolen Bases:	30		7
ERA:	3.95	3.96	6
Fielding Pct:	.980	.975	1
Runs Scored:	683		5
Runs Allowed:	671		3

Starting Lineup

Del Rice, c
Nippy Jones, 1b
Red Schoendienst, 2b
Bill Johnson, 3b
Solly Hemus, ss
Stan Musial, lf-1b
Peanuts Lowrey, cf
Enos Slaughter, rf
Wally Westlake, cf-rf
Hal Rice, lf
Stan Rojek, ss

Pitchers

Gerry Staley, sp
Tom Poholsky, sp-rp
Max Lanier, sp
Harry Brecheen, sp-rp
Cliff Chambers, sp
Joe Presko, sp
Al Brazle, rp
George Munger, rp-sp

Attendance

1,013,429 (third in NL)

Club Leaders

Batting Ave.:	Musial	.355
On-Base Pct:	Musial	.449
Slugging Pct:	Musial	.614
Home Runs:	Musial	32
RBIs:	Musial	108
Runs:	Musial	124
Stolen Bases:	Hemus	7
	Slaughter	7
Wins:	Staley	19
Strikeouts:	Poholsky	70
ERA:	Lanier	3.26
Saves:	Brazle	7

APRIL 17   Six days after President Harry Truman removes General Douglas MacArthur from his command in Korea, the Cardinals lose the season opener 5–4 in Pittsburgh. The temperature was in the low 40s, and snow fell during part of the game. Ex-Cardinal Murry Dickson pitched a complete game and hit his first major league homer, off 21-year-old Tom Poholsky, who making his second big-league start.

A surprise Opening Day starter, Poholsky was 7–13 with a 4.43 ERA in 1951. A civil engineering graduate of Washington University in St. Louis, he ended his career in 1957 with a record of 31–52.

APRIL 20   In the home opener, the Cardinals defeat the Cubs 5–1 before 15,592 at Sportsman's Park. Joe Garagiola hit a home run.

The Cardinals switched from their traditional red socks with blue and white stripes to all-blue stockings in 1951. The club went back to the red socks with the stripes during the first week of May, however, because the players complained that the blue ones made their legs appear too skinny.

APRIL 25   Tom Poholsky pitches a two-hitter for a 4–0 win over the Pirates at Sportsman's Park for his first major league win. He retired the last 19 batters to face him. The only Pittsburgh hits were singles by Catfish Metkovich and opposing pitcher Cliff Chambers.

The Cardinals were 11–5 on May 7 and were in first place. During a trip to New York from May 8 through 10, however, a flu bug swept through the club and put 13 players out of action for anywhere from a day to a week. At the nadir of the epidemic, the Cards lost 17–3 to the Giants. The Redbirds never recovered and were out of the race by the first of June.

MAY 11   The Cardinals defeat the Reds 8–6 in 10 innings in the second game of a doubleheader at Crosley Field. In the seventh inning, Bill Howerton hit a pinch-homer to make the score 4–3 in favor of Cincinnati. In the eighth, Marty Marion sent Eddie Kazak in to bat for Beryl Richmond. When the Reds countered by switching from left-handed pitcher Harry Perkowski to right-handed Frank Smith, Marion sent Musial to the plate. Musial had been on the bench because of the flu and wasn't able to hit the ball out of the infield during batting practice, but he responded with a three-run homer to put the Cards up 6–4. After the Reds tied the score 6–6 in the ninth, St. Louis scored two in the tenth with a single and four walks. The Reds won the first game 7–2.

Ex-Cardinal catcher Gus Mancuso replaced Gabby Street in the broadcast booth. Mancuso covered the Cardinals on radio and TV until 1953. Street passed away from cancer in February 1951 at the age of 68.

MAY 14   The Cardinals send Don Bollweg and $15,000 to the Yankees for Billy Johnson.

Johnson became the starting third baseman for the Cardinals, and at the age of 32 hit a career-high 14 homers.

MAY 24   Joe Presko carries a no-hitter into the seventh inning before beating the Reds 11–3 on a five-hitter at Sportsman's Park.

MAY 30   Stan Musial hits his fifth home run in four games to give the Cardinals a 4–3 victory over the Pirates in the first game of a doubleheader at Sportsman's Park. The Cards completed the sweep with a 7–3 win in the second tilt.

In 1951 Musial led the NL in batting average (.355), runs (124), total bases (355), and triples (12) and ranked second in on-base percentage (.449), slugging percentage (.614), and hits (205). He hit 32 homers and drove in 108 runs.

JUNE 14   The Cardinals lose 2–1 on a two-out, two-run homer by Gil Hodges in the ninth inning off Joe Presko at Ebbets Field. The Cards scored just once despite collecting 15 hits. In the fourth inning with men on first and third, Joe Garagiola grounded hotly to Hodges at first. Hodges's throw home nailed one runner, and Garagiola froze in the batter's box for a double play. In the fifth, the club put five runners on base and failed to score because Brooklyn catcher Roy Campanella picked two men off second base.

Presko, a 22-year-old rookie, had a 6–2 record heading into the game. Over the remainder of his career, which ended in 1958, he was 21–35.

JUNE 15   The Cardinals trade Howie Pollet, Ted Wilks, Joe Garagiola, Bill Howerton, and Dick Cole to the Pirates for Wally Westlake and Cliff Chambers.

Chambers was traded to the Cardinals only six weeks after pitching a no-hitter for the Pirates. At the time of the deal, Westlake was leading the NL in home runs and RBIs and played in the 1951 All-Star Game. Neither Chambers nor Westlake had much success with the Cards, however, although Chambers looked like a bargain at the beginning. He was 11–6 over the remainder of the 1951 season and had a 4–2 record in late May 1952 when he broke his wrist. Chambers won only three more games after the injury. Westlake hit only .246 with six homers in 341 at-bats with the Cards before being dealt to the Reds in 1952. Fortunately, none of the five players sent to Pittsburgh had much of an impact on a Pirates club that had a record of 42–112 in 1952. Garagiola spent much of his time during his broadcasting career spinning humorous tales about playing for that awful team.

JUNE 16   Playing in his first game with the Cardinals, Wally Westlake hits a three-run homer in the eighth inning to lead his new club to a 6–5 win over the Phillies at Sportsman's Park.

JUNE 24   On a day the 1926 World Champion Cardinals were honored in pregame ceremonies, the 1951 Cards trail 5–0, then score one run in the sixth inning, one in the eight, three in the ninth, and one in the fourteenth to defeat the Braves 6–5 at Sportsman's Park. Stan Musial's double capped the three-run rally in the ninth. In the fourteenth, Musial doubled again, moved to third on a fly ball, and scored on an infield single by Nippy Jones on a close play at first.

JUNE 27   The Cardinals wallop the Cubs 14–2 at Sportsman's Park.

Jay Van Noy, a 22-year-old rookie outfielder with the Cardinals in 1951, had a brief, unspectacular career in the majors. In seven plate appearances, he walked in his big-league debut, then struck out six consecutive times. A football star at Utah State University, Van Noy led the NCAA in interceptions in 1948 with eight.

JULY 2   Bill Veeck assumes ownership of the Browns from Bill and Charles DeWitt.

Veeck was highly successful as the owner of the Cleveland Indians from 1946 through 1949. The club won its first AL pennant in 28 years in 1948 and drew 2.6 million fans, a major league attendance record that stood until 1962. Veeck hoped to breathe life into a floundering, comatose Browns franchise by employing the same crowd-pleasing, unconventional gimmicks he had used in Cleveland. The Browns drew only 247,131 fans in 1950 amid rumors that the club was moving to Baltimore, Milwaukee, Houston, or Los Angeles. There were 18 minor league clubs that had higher attendance than the Browns that season. Upon buying the club, Veeck told reporters he had no plans to pull the Browns out of St. Louis. Veeck's intention was to promote the Browns and run the Cardinals out of town, leaving St. Louis all to himself (see August 19, 1951).

JULY 8   Red Schoendienst hits homers from both sides of the plate during a 9–8 win over the Pirates in the second game of a doubleheader at Forbes Field. Schoendienst homered off right-hander Ted Wilks in the sixth inning and lefty Paul LaPalme in the seventh. Pittsburgh won the first game 6–2.

JULY 10   Stan Musial hits a home run and a single and draws a walk in five plate appearances during an 8–3 National League win in the All-Star Game at Briggs Stadium in Detroit. Musial homered off Ed Lopat of the Yankees in the third inning.

JULY 12   Billy Johnson's two-run homer off Larry Jansen in the fifth inning accounts for the only runs in a 2–0 win over the Giants at Sportsman's park. Gerry Staley pitched the shutout.

               Staley was 19–13 with a 3.81 ERA in 1951.

AUGUST 7   The Cardinals score seven runs in the first inning and submerge the Pirates 16–7 at Sportsman's Park. Peanuts Lowrey collected five hits in five at-bats.

               During the 1951–52 offseason, Lowrey appeared in the movie The Winning Team, *which was the biography of pitching great Grover Alexander, with Ronald Reagan playing Alexander. Lowrey's scene in* The Winning Team *called for him to hit Reagan in the head with a baseball. As a youngster, Lowrey appeared in the* Our Gang *comedy series. As an adult, he was also in the baseball movies* Pride of the Yankees (1942) *and* The Stratton Story (1949).

AUGUST 10   Gerry Staley pitches four innings of shutout relief and contributes a bases-loaded, walk-off single in the tenth inning to beat the Reds 4–3 at Sportsman's Park. Cincinnati intentionally walked Hal Rice with two outs to get to Staley.

               In 525 career at-bats, Staley had a batting average of .126 and a slugging percentage of .139.

AUGUST 11   Max Lanier faces the minimum 27 batters and pitches a two-hitter to beat the Reds 2–0 at Sportsman's Park. Ted Kluszewski collected both Cincinnati hits with singles in third and sixth innings. He was erased both times on double plays.

AUGUST 19   In a promotional stunt, Browns owner Bill Veeck trots out a midget to pinch hit in the first inning of a doubleheader against the Tigers at Sportsman's Park. Eddie Gaedel, standing three foot seven and weighing 65 pounds, drew a walk on four pitches. Two days later, American League president Will Harridge barred Gaedel from playing in any future games (see August 24, 1951).

AUGUST 24   In another legendary Bill Veeck PR stunt, it's "Grandstand Managers Night" at Sportsman's Park as the Browns defeat the Athletics 5–3. The Browns coaches held up placards for 1,115 fans who voted on the options given them, such as setting the lineup, changing pitchers, or positioning the infield by responding to signs that read "yes" and "no."

               Cardinals owner Fred Saigh countered Veeck's moves by printing the following line in the club's scorecards: "The Cardinals, a dignified St. Louis institution."

AUGUST 26   The Cardinals stagger to a 12–10 win over the Braves in the first game of a doubleheader in Boston. The Cards broke a 1–1 tie with seven runs in the fourth inning and led 11–2 in the seventh before the Braves mounted a comeback. Boston won the second tilt 9–1.

SEPTEMBER 12   The game between the Giants and the Cardinals at Sportsman's Park is rained out.

The Giants were in a neck-and-neck race with the Dodgers for the NL pennant and had no more games scheduled in St. Louis. To solve the solution, a unique doubleheader was played the following day.

SEPTEMBER 13   The Cardinals play both the Giants and the Braves at Sportsman's Park. In the afternoon, the Cards beat the Giants 6–4. At night, the Braves defeated the Redbirds 2–0.

The Cardinals were the first club since 1899 to play two teams in one day. It didn't happen again until 2000, when the Indians met both the Twins and White Sox in Cleveland.

SEPTEMBER 15   Solly Hemus draws five walks during a 10–1 win over the Braves at Sportsman's Park.

Hemus was 28 years old in 1951, his first full season in the majors. He was a second baseman throughout his minor league career but in 1951 became the club's starting shortstop, replacing Marty Marion. Although limited defensively, Hemus was a valuable component in the Cardinals starting lineup from 1951 through 1953, during which he batted .276 with a .420 slugging percentage and .389 on-base percentage.

SEPTEMBER 16   Gerry Staley yields 14 hits and walks three but beats the Phillies 9–2 at Sportsman's Park. The Phils left 13 men on base.

SEPTEMBER 19   Presented with a Cadillac before the game by friends from Arkansas and southeast Missouri, Dodgers pitcher Preacher Roe beats the Cardinals 2–0 at Sportsman's Park.

SEPTEMBER 21   Jackie Collum pitches a two-hit shutout in his major league debut, defeating the Cubs 6–0 at Sportsman's Park. The only Chicago hits were singles by Bob Ramazzotti in the second inning and Eddie Miksis in the sixth.

Collum didn't have another win, complete game, or shutout until 1953 when he was a member of the Reds. He lasted in the majors until 1962, however, spending most of his time in relief. Collum's "out" pitch was a screwball that was aided by an accident he suffered as a youngster on his family's farm near Grinnell, Iowa. While loading hay into the loft of the barn, his hand was caught in a pulley, and Collum lost an inch off the finger of his left hand and a half-inch of his index finger.

OCTOBER 26   The Cardinals fire Marty Marion as manager.

The Cardinals improved from fifth place and a 78–75 record in 1950 to third and 81–73 in 1951 in Marion's first season as manager, but owner Fred Saigh didn't believe that Marion had the fire necessary to be a big-league manager. Marion later managed the Browns from June 1952 through the end of the 1953 season and the White Sox from 1954 through 1956.

DECEMBER 11   The Cardinals trade Chuck Diering and Max Lanier to the Giants for Eddie Stanky.

Stanky was immediately named manager of the Cardinals, replacing Marty Marion. Stanky's scrappy and fiery personality was the opposite of the laid-back Marion. Branch Rickey once said that Stanky "can't hit, he can't run, he can't field, he can't throw. He can't do a thing except beat you." That was the kind of man that Fred Saigh wanted to manage a Cardinals team that appeared to lack direction. Stanky was 35 when Saigh hired him and had been a starting second baseman in the majors since 1943. He had only a .268 lifetime batting average, but because of an innate ability to draw walks, Stanky's on-base percentage was .410. He went to the World Series with the Dodgers in 1947, the Braves in 1948, and the Giants in 1951. The 1951 Giants trailed the Dodgers by 13½ games in August and won the pennant in storybook fashion. The Cards improved to 88–66 in 1952 under Stanky, but they dropped to 83–71 in 1953 and 72–82 in 1954. He was fired 36 games into the 1955 season.

1952

Season in a Sentence

Under new manager Eddie Stanky, the Cardinals overcome a shaky start to win 88 games, seven more than the previous season.

Finish • Won • Lost • Pct • GB

Third   88   66   .571   8.5

Manager

Eddie Stanky

Stats

Stats	Cards	NL	Rank
Batting Ave:	.267	.253	1
On-Base Pct:	.340	.323	2
Slugging Pct:	.391	.374	3
Home Runs:	97		6
Stolen Bases:	33		3
ERA:	3.66	3.73	5
Fielding Pct:	.977	.976	3
Runs Scored:	677		3
Runs Allowed:	630		3

Starting Lineup

Del Rice, c
Dick Sisler, 1b
Red Schoendienst, 2b
Billy Johnson, 3b
Solly Hemus, ss
Peanuts Lowrey, lf-cf
Stan Musial, cf
Enos Slaughter, rf
Hal Rice, lf
Tommy Glaviano, 3b

Pitchers

Gerry Staley, sp
Vinegar Bend Mizell, sp
Joe Presko, sp-rp
Harry Brecheen, sp-rp
Cloyd Boyer, sp-rp
Al Brazle, rp
Eddie Yuhas, rp

Attendance

913,113 (fourth in NL)

Club Leaders

Batting Ave:	Musial	.336
On-Base Pct:	Musial	.432
Slugging Pct:	Musial	.538
Home Runs:	Musial	21
RBIs:	Slaughter	101
Runs:	Musial	105
	Hemus	105
Stolen Bases:	Schoendienst	9
Wins:	Staley	17
Strikeouts:	Mizell	146
ERA:	Staley	3.27
Saves:	Brazle	16

MARCH 24   Bobby Slaybaugh, a 20-year-old pitching prospect, suffers the loss of his right eye as the result of being stuck in the face by a line drive during spring training in St. Petersburg, Florida. Slaybaugh was pitching during batting practice when a drive by Jim Dickey hit him, shattering his left cheekbone and forcing the eyeball partly out of the socket. Efforts to save the eye proved unsuccessful, and it was removed April 3. Slaybaugh pitched again in the minors three months later but never reached the big leagues.

APRIL 11   *The Pride of St. Louis,* the film saga of Dizzy Dean, has its premiere at the Missouri Theater in St. Louis. Dan Dailey, who played Dean in the movie, was present along with Dean himself. The following day, a six-mile-long parade took place from downtown to Sportsman's Park.

APRIL 15   The Cardinals open the season with a 3–2 win over the Pirates before 15,850 at Sportsman's Park. Red Schoendienst homered in the first inning.

> *Flamboyant Browns owner Bill Veeck and straight-laced Fred Saigh were constantly at odds. During the 1951–52 offseason, Veeck installed photo murals of Browns players behind the concession stands at Sportsman's Park. When the Cardinals played at home, Saigh covered them with red cloth.*

APRIL 22   Umpire Scotty Robb shoves Eddie Stanky during a 2–1 loss to the Reds in Cincinnati. Solly Hemus was ejected by Robb, officiating at home plate, in the third inning for throwing his bat after being called out on a third strike. Stanky rushed to Hemus's defense and brushed Robb's coat in the ensuing argument. Robb then threw his mask aside, gave Stanky a vigorous shove, and appeared ready to square off. NL president Warren Giles fined Stanky $50 and Robb a "much greater" sum. In a huff, Robb quit the National League staff.

APRIL 29   A picket line established by union bartenders protesting the employment of non-organized concession-stand employees almost results in the cancellation of the Cardinals-Dodgers game at Sportsman's Park. Because of the picket line, electricians in charge of the lighting system at the ballpark refused to take their posts. After negotiation, the union agreed to lift the picket line, but the game began 65 minutes late. The Dodgers won the contest 4–1.

APRIL 30   The Cardinals trounce the Dodgers 14–2 at Sportsman's Park. Red Schoendienst hit a grand slam in the fifth inning off Bud Podbielan.

> *Schoendienst batted .303 with seven homers in 1952. During spring training, the Cards experimented with turning him into a shortstop and putting Stanky at second base. Stanky had lost a step, however, and was no longer up to playing regularly. Prospect Earl Weaver, a 21-year-old native of St. Louis, was given an extended look at second base during spring training. Weaver returned to the minors before Opening Day, Schoendienst went back to second, and Solly Hemus retained his job at short. Hemus responded with a .268 average and 15 homers and tied Stan Musial for the league lead in runs with 105. Weaver never played in the majors but reached the Hall of Fame because of his success as manager of the Orioles during the 1960, 1970s, and 1980s.*

MAY 3   The Cardinals trade George Munger to the Pirates for Bill Werle.

MAY 13   The Cardinals trade Eddie Kazak and Wally Westlake to the Reds for Dick Sisler and Virgil Stallcup.

MAY 18   Third baseman Tommy Glaviano's leaping catch beats the Phillies 4–3 at Shibe Park and gives Al Brazle a one-pitch save. The Cards led 4–0 heading into the ninth before the Phils scored three times. Brazle entered the game with two outs and a runner on second when Glaviano caught Bill Nicholson's line drive.

MAY 28

Eddie Stanky creates controversy by fining Harry Brecheen $50 during a 7–2 loss to the Cubs in Chicago.

Stanky fined Brecheen for failing to make a pitchout after the manager signaled. Several innings later, Stan Musial limped off the field, and when the press sought to learn the nature of the injury, Stanky replied with an unprintable tirade. Two days later, he had a meeting with his players to clear the air, lifted the levy against Brecheen, and eliminated all automatic fines. The Cardinals were 17–21 on May 28, then won 28 of their next 40 games.

JUNE 1

Enos Slaughter's two-out, walk-off homer in the ninth inning beats the Giants 8–7 in the first game of a doubleheader at Sportsman's Park. The Cardinals trailed 6–2 in the fifth inning before the comeback. The Cards completed the sweep with an 8–2 victory in the nightcap, called after 7½ innings by darkness because of a National League rule stipulating that lights couldn't be turned on to complete games played on a Sunday.

Slaughter hit .300 with 11 homers and 101 RBIs in 1952.

JUNE 10

Joe Presko pitches a 10-inning complete game to defeat the Dodgers 1–0 at Sportsman's Park. Red Schoendienst's walk-off triple provided the lone run of the contest.

JUNE 12

The Cardinals outslug the Dodgers 15–10 at Sportsman's Park. The Cards took a 10–7 lead with five runs in the fourth inning.

JUNE 15

Trailing 11–0, the Cardinals make an amazing comeback to win 14–12 in the first game of a doubleheader at the Polo Grounds. The Giants took the lead with five runs in the second inning and six in the third. Believing the game was in the bag, New York manager Leo Durocher removed two of his regulars to rest for the second game of the day. Eddie Stanky contemplated doing the same thing, but St. Louis struck back with seven in the fifth, three in the seventh, and two in the eighth to take a 12–11 lead. Cards shortstop Solly Hemus tied the game with a homer. Enos Slaughter broke the tie with a single. The Redbirds added two insurance tallies in the ninth before the Giants added one more. The rally set a National League record (since tied) for the largest deficit overcome to win a game. St. Louis failed to score for the rest of the day. New York won the second game 2–0 in a contest called after seven innings by darkness.

JUNE 20

After the Braves score 10 runs in the sixth inning to take an 11–0 lead, the Cardinals come back for seven runs in the seventh but lose 12–7 in Boston. Solly Hemus hit a grand slam off the Braves' Jim Wilson.

JUNE 28

Stan Musial extends his hitting streak to 24 games during a 4–3 win over the Pirates in Pittsburgh.

JULY 2

A three-run double by 37-year-old Enos Slaughter in the eighth inning beats the Reds 3–0 at Sportsman's Park. Harry Brecheen, 36, tossed the complete-game shutout.

JULY 4

The Cardinals sweep the Cubs 13–7 and 4–1 at Sportsman's Park. Hal Rice hits a grand slam off Johnny Klippstein in the third inning of the first game.

Rice was a tank lieutenant during World War II and received a Purple Heart.

JULY 6

A walk-off homer by Stan Musial in the ninth inning beats the Pirates 6–5 in the first game of a doubleheader at Sportsman's Park. The Cardinals completed the sweep with a 6–4 triumph in the second tilt to extend their winning streak to nine games.

JULY 8

Enos Slaughter contributes a double to the National League's 3–2 victory in the All-Star Game, played at Shibe Park in Philadelphia. The game was called after five innings by rain.

JULY 10

The Cardinals win their 10th game in a row with a 10–3 decision over the Phillies in Philadelphia.

JULY 16

Down 7–2, the Cardinals explode for five runs in the ninth only to lose 8–7 to the Giants at Sportsman's Park.

> *The top pitcher for the Cardinals in 1952 was Gerry Staley, who had a record of 17–14 and an ERA of 3.27.*

JULY 18

Billy Johnson hits a grand slam off Max Surkont in the fifth inning of a 7–2 win over the Braves at Sportsman's Park.

AUGUST 6

The Cardinals score five runs in the tenth inning to beat the Pirates 7–2 in the first game of a doubleheader in Pittsburgh. The Cards completed the sweep with a 3–2 victory in the second game.

AUGUST 9

Red Schoendienst collects five hits in five at-bats, but the Cardinals lose 12–3 to the Reds in Cincinnati.

AUGUST 10

The Cardinals score three runs in the ninth inning to beat the Reds 3–2 in the first game of a doubleheader at Crosley Field. Dick Sisler drove in the tying and winning runs with a single. Cincinnati won the second game 4–2.

AUGUST 12

In his major league debut, Stu Miller pitches the Cardinals to a 1–0 win over the Cubs at Wrigley Field. Miller allowed six hits and closed out the game by striking out Bill Serena with runners on first and third. Hal Rice drove in the lone run of the game with a single in the first inning.

AUGUST 17

Stu Miller comes within one out of pitching his second shutout in his second big-league start, beating the Reds 2–1 at Sportsman's Park. The lone run of the game scored in the ninth inning on two errors by shortstop Solly Hemus.

> *Play had to be suspended for several minutes in the sixth inning when fans tossed bottles and paper into left field over a decision by umpire Bill Stewart, who ruled that catcher Andy Seminick had tagged out the Cardinals' Vern Benson. After another bottle shower during a Browns-Yankees game in May 1953, park regulations prohibited bottles at games, and fans bought beverages served in paper cups.*

AUGUST 22

Stu Miller turns in his third brilliant start in his third big-league game, defeating the Giants 3–1 at Sportsman's Park. The lone run scored in the eighth inning. Miller allowed no earned runs in his first 25 big-league innings, and just two runs, one earned, in his first 33 innings.

AUGUST 23   The Cardinals record their eighth win in a row with a 3–1 decision over the Giants at Sportsman's Park.

The Cardinals had a record of 72–49 and were 7½ games behind the first-place Dodgers. The Cards lost four in a row to the Dodgers at Sportsman's Park from August 24 through 26, however, ending any dreams of a pennant.

AUGUST 27   Umpire Lon Warneke clears the Cardinal bench of all but Eddie Stanky and two coaches in the fifth inning of a 7–2 loss to the Phillies at Sportsman's Park. The Redbirds refused to stop heckling the umpires after Cards catcher Del Rice was chased in the third inning for objecting to a decision. The umps permitted Stanky to bring players back one by one as needed.

AUGUST 30   The Cardinals tie a National League record for most consecutive doubles with four during the third inning of a 12–2 win over the Pirates in Pittsburgh. The doubles were from Peanuts Lowrey, Red Schoendienst, Stan Musial, and Enos Slaughter.

SEPTEMBER 1   In the first game of a doubleheader against the Reds, Hal Rice hits a first-inning grand slam off Bubba Church in a 6–0 win at Crosley Field. Cincinnati won the second tilt 3–2.

SEPTEMBER 4   Stu Miller pitches the Cardinals to a 1–0 victory over the Cubs at Sportsman's Park. In a near repeat of his debut on August 12, Miller fanned Randy Jackson with runners on first and third to end the game. Enos Slaughter drove in the lone run of the game with a single in the first inning.

In his first season, Miller was 6–3 with a 2.05 ERA in 88 innings. In 1953 and 1954, he was 9–11 with an earned run average of 5.61, however, and the Cards gave up on him. Miller spent much of the 1954 season and all of 1955 in the minors and was traded to the Phillies early in the 1956 season.

SEPTEMBER 6   A three-run, walk-off homer by Enos Slaughter in the tenth inning beats the Pirates 7–4 at Sportsman's Park.

SEPTEMBER 7   Enos Slaughter stars with a walk-off hit for the second game in a row as the Cardinals defeat the Pirates 4–3 at Sportsman's Park. Down 3–0 in the eighth inning, Slaughter hit a bases-loaded triple to tie the score. He came to bat with the sacks filled again in the ninth and delivered a single.

SEPTEMBER 9   The Cardinals score five runs in the ninth inning to defeat the Phillies 7–4 in Philadelphia. Solly Hemus drove in the go-ahead run with a double. Stan Musial collected his 2,000th career hit with a single off Curt Simmons in the fourth inning.

SEPTEMBER 14 The Cardinals score 11 runs in the fifth inning to break a 3–3 tie and move on to defeat the Giants 14–4 in New York. Stan Musial walloped a homer and a double in the inning. Dave Koslo was the losing pitcher. Entering the contest, he had beaten the Cards 13 straight times dating back to 1950.

SEPTEMBER 16 The Cardinals play the Braves in Boston for the last time and sweep a doubleheader 8–6 and 5–1.

The Braves moved to Milwaukee before the start of the 1953 season.

SEPTEMBER 25   Eddie Yuhas wins his 10th game in a row with a 4–3 decision over the Reds at Sportsman's Park.

> *Yuhas was one of the surprises of the 1952 season. A 27-year-old rookie reliever, he had a 12–2 record and a 2.72 ERA. Yuhas hurt his arm during spring training in 1953, however, and pitched only two more big-league games, neither resulting in a decision.*

SEPTEMBER 28   On the final day of the season, Stan Musial makes the only pitching appearance of his big-league career in a 3–0 Cardinals loss to the Cubs at Sportsman's Park.

> *Musial went into the game with a .336 to .326 lead over Frank Baumholtz in the NL batting race. With one out in the first inning, Musial came in from his center field position to pitch to Baumholtz, while pitcher Harvey Haddix went to the outfield. A right-handed hitter, Baumholtz switched to the left side and hit a weak grounder to shortstop Solly Hemus, who fumbled the ball for an error. Musial returned to the outfield and won the batting championship by going 1 for 3 while Baumholtz was 1 for 4. Musial finished the year at .336 while Baumholtz ended with a .325 average. Musial also led the NL in slugging percentage (.538), runs (105), hits (194), doubles (42), and total bases (311). He hit 21 homers and drove in 91 runs.*

SEPTEMBER 30   Five weeks before Dwight Eisenhower defeats Adlai Stevenson in the presidential election, the Cardinals sell Tommy Glaviano to the Phillies.

1953

Season in a Sentence

As the Cardinals embark on a major youth movement with four rookies making the starting lineup and pitching rotation, August Busch buys the club, and the Browns leave town.

Finish • Won • Lost • Pct • GB

Third (tie) 83   71   .539   22.0

Manager

Eddie Stanky

Stats

Stats	Cards	NL	Rank
Batting Avg:	.273	.266	2
On-Base Pct:	.347	.335	2
Slugging Pct:	.424	.411	2
Home Runs:	140		5
Stolen Bases:	18		8
ERA:	4.23	4.29	4
Fielding Avg:	.977	.975	3
Runs Scored:	768		2 (tie)
Runs Allowed:	713		4

Starting Lineup

Del Rice, c
Steve Bilko, 1b
Red Schoendienst, 2b
Ray Jablonski, 3b
Solly Hemus, ss
Stan Musial, lf
Rip Repulski, cf
Enos Slaughter, rf
Peanuts Lowrey, rf

Pitchers

Harvey Haddix, sp
Gerry Staley, sp
Vinegar Bend Mizell, sp
Joe Presko, sp
Al Brazle, rp
Hal White, rp
Stu Miller, rp-sp
Cliff Chambers, rp

Attendance

880,242 (third in NL)

Club Leaders

Batting Avg:	Schoendienst	.342
On-Base Pct:	Musial	.437
Slugging Pct:	Musial	.609
Home Runs:	Musial	30
RBIs:	Musial	113
Runs:	Musial	127
Stolen Bases:	Slaughter	4
Wins:	Haddix	20
Strikeouts:	Mizell	137
ERA:	Haddix	3.06
Saves:	Brazle	18

JANUARY 28   Fred Saigh is convicted in federal court for income tax evasion. The judge sentenced him to 15 months in prison and imposed a $15,000 fine. The government charged that Saigh owed $558,901 in back taxes and penalties.

Saigh professed his innocence and declared that the sentence was too harsh, but under pressure from National League president Ford Frick, he decided to sell the Cardinals. Saigh's conviction also set off a chain of events that resulted in the Braves' moving from Boston to Milwaukee seven weeks later.

FEBRUARY 20   The Anheuser-Busch Brewery purchases the Cardinals for $3.75 million. August A. Busch became president of the club.

Saigh received lucrative bids from two groups in Houston that intended to move the Cardinals to Texas. Saigh himself had considered a move to Houston a year earlier, where he owned the minor league club in the Texas League. Saigh also entertained a deal from interests in Milwaukee, headed by Fred Miller, the president of Miller Brewing Company. The city had just completed County Stadium, opened in 1952, with the idea of luring a big-league club. Saigh said that he wanted to keep the Cardinals in St. Louis, however. Saigh said he *could have made another $700,000 to $750,000 by selling the club to a group that intended to move the Cards out of town. He did make money investing in Anheuser-Busch, though. Saigh realized that the brewery's ownership of the Cardinals would benefit the company, and just before selling the club, he purchased 28,000 shares of stock in Anheuser-Busch. The day after the sale, the stock rose $2 a share. For years, Saigh owned more stock in the brewery than any individual outside of the Busch family did. The stock made him millions as Anheuser-Busch leaped from third in the market, behind Schlitz and Miller, to number one. But Saigh remained bitter because he felt that Busch took advantage of him during negotiations for the sale of the Cardinals. He had bought the club in 1947 as a mere financial investment, but he soon discovered that baseball lifted him out of relative obscurity and placed him in the national spotlight. As the owner of the Cardinals, Fred Saigh was no longer a nobody. It pained him deeply to sell the club. He remained a diehard Cardinal fan but refused to see the team in person in St. Louis until the Busch family sold in 1996. At the time, Saigh was 91 years old. He died in 1999 when he was 94.*

August Busch was 53 years old when his brewery purchased the Cardinals. He had become president of the company in 1946. His great-grandfather Adolphus Busch founded A-B with Eberhard Anheuser in 1865. Until the sale, August Busch was known better in St. Louis social circles for hobbies such as horsemanship and hunting and for his lavish parties. He was a casual baseball fan, but he had the idea that buying the Cardinals would be good for the brewery's relationship with the city and to boost sales. Over time, Busch became a major power broker in baseball circles.

MARCH 3   Lou Perini, owner of the Boston Braves, blocks Bill Veeck's move of the Browns to Milwaukee. Perini was also owner the Milwaukee Brewers, which at the time was a minor league club in the American Association and a Braves farm club.

Perini and his Braves were having attendance problems, and he wanted to keep the Milwaukee territory as an escape hatch for his ball club if the situation in Boston continued to deteriorate. The Braves drew only 281,278 fans in 1952. Attendance at Browns games rose from 293,790 in 1951 to 518,796 in 1952, but Veeck believed that he was doomed in St. Louis as soon as August Busch bought the Cardinals. Veeck didn't have the cash reserves to compete with the millions that Busch had at his disposal. The Browns owner set his sights on Milwaukee, where he had owned the Brewers from 1941 through 1944. When Perini prevented Veeck from moving to the city, he began negotiations to move the Browns to Baltimore, a city that, like Milwaukee, had a new ballpark in Memorial Stadium. The maneuver by Perini in stopping Veeck from moving to Wisconsin placed the Braves and Brewers owner in a precarious predicament, however. He was now seen as the man who prevented Milwaukee from obtaining a major league franchise. Fans organized a boycott of his Brewers club in the American Association at brand new County Stadium. Perini, who had plans to transfer his Braves from Boston to Milwaukee perhaps as early as 1954, began to consider moving before the start of the 1953 campaign, barely a month away (see March 18, 1953).

MARCH 16   The American League prevents Bill Veeck from moving the Browns to Baltimore. AL owners said that it was too close to the start of the season to move the club (see

September 29, 1953). After the rejection, Veeck was faced with the almost impossible position of trying to draw resentful fans to Sportsman's Park with a losing club that he had tried to move out of town. In 1953, the Browns attendance was only 297,238. By the end of the season, Veeck was nearly bankrupt, and his franchise faced receivership.

MARCH 18   The National League approves the move of the Braves to Milwaukee. It was the first franchise shift in Major League Baseball since 1903. The Braves became an immediate financial success in Milwaukee, drawing 1,826,397 fans in 1953 and 2,131,388 in 1954.

APRIL 9   August Busch purchases Sportsman's Park from the Browns. The price was $800,000. Busch then leased it back to the Browns at $175,000 per season.

Busch immediately announced that he was changing the name of the ballpark to Budweiser Stadium. The name Sportsman's Park had been associated with baseball in St. Louis since 1875. The new name drew fire from temperance groups and other organizations, as well as other NL owners, objecting to naming the facility after an alcoholic beverage. A day later, Busch changed the name of his new ballpark to Busch Stadium. (A year later, the company introduced a new product called Busch Bavarian Beer.) The name wasn't the only thing that needed to be changed at the corner of Grand and Dodier. Busch Stadium, built in 1909, was in deplorable condition after years of neglect by the cash-strapped Browns, who couldn't afford normal upkeep. Even the tarp was virtually useless. It was so thin it that it left puddles all over the infield. Mounds of dirt and debris littered public areas under the lower grandstand. Over the next two years, Busch upgraded every aspect of the ballpark with an investment of $1.5 million. He put in new seats, restrooms, concession stands, drinking fountains, and longer and better dugouts, in addition to revamping the public address system, ticket offices, gate entrances, turnstiles, ramps, and aisles. The lighting system was upgraded, as was the field itself following the installation of new drainage and sprinkling systems. The playing field had long been regarded as the worst surface in the majors because it was used by two clubs and was subject to the searing St. Louis heat. The ballpark was painted red, green, jade, and metallic blue, selected by a color specialist for "eye appeal and sparkle under the lights to provide for a cheerful atmosphere for fans." The scoreboard in left field was also renovated. Busch couldn't call his ballpark Budweiser Stadium, but he could install a huge Budweiser sign on the scoreboard in left field. The ad contained 1,100 lamps with a large lighted "A" and an eagle that symbolized Anheuser-Busch. The scoreboard employed new design concepts using neon and animation. A large Redbird swinging a bat and hitting a ball would indicate whether the official scorer had ruled a hit or an error on a play.

APRIL 12   A fight breaks out during an exhibition game between the Browns and the Cardinals at Busch Stadium, won by the American Leaguers 8–5. In the second inning, Billy Hunter of the Browns charged hard into Del Rice, who kicked at Hunter. An exchange of words followed between Browns manager Marty Marion and Rice, but Eddie Stanky pulled Rice away.

APRIL 14   The Cardinals play the first ever Braves game in Milwaukee and lose 3–2 in 10 innings at County Stadium. It was the first major league game in Milwaukee since

1901. Bill Bruton ended the game with a home run off Gerry Staley. Enos Slaughter had his glove on the ball, but he was unable to hold onto it.

APRIL 18   In the home opener, the Cardinals defeat the Cubs 3–0 before 14,926 at Busch Stadium. Enos Slaughter hit a two-run homer. Harvey Haddix pitched the complete-game shutout.

APRIL 29   The Cardinals defeat the Phillies 1–0 in 11 innings in Philadelphia. Joe Presko (9$^1/_3$ innings) and Al Brazle (1$^2/_3$ innings) combined on the shutout. Billy Johnson drove in the winning run with a double.

The Cards stole only 18 bases as a team in 1953. Enos Slaughter, at age 37, was the club leader with four.

MAY 4   Vinegar Bend Mizell pitches a two-hitter to defeat the Pirates 9–0 at Forbes Field. A drizzle fell throughout the game. The only Pittsburgh hits were singles by Carlos Bernier and Frank Thomas.

Wilmer "Vinegar Bend" Mizell earned his nickname because he hailed from the small Alabama town of Vinegar Bend, although he was born in Leakesville, just across the border in Mississippi. With his appealing Southern drawl, many hailed him as the next Dizzy Dean. Mizell never came close to emulating Dean's Hall of Fame career, but he was an effective middle-of-the-rotation starter and compiled a record of 69–70 as a Cardinal from 1952 through 1960, and 90–88 during his career. After his playing days ended in 1962, Mizell went into politics. He was elected to the US Congress in 1968 as a Republican from North Carolina and served until losing a reelection bid in 1974. Later, Mizell served as Assistant Secretary of Commerce in the Ford administration, as Assistant Secretary of Agriculture under Ronald Reagan, and as executive director of the President's Council on Physical Fitness under the elder George Bush.

MAY 9   Harvey Haddix pitches a two-hitter to defeat the Reds 4–2 at Crosley Field. The only two Cincinnati hits were singles by Gus Bell and Roy McMillan.

MAY 10   Grant Dunlap's first major league hit is a pinch-hit home run, although the Cardinals lose 4–2 and 5–2 in Cincinnati. The homer came in the second game of the doubleheader and was struck during Dunlap's third big-league at-bat.

Dunlap was a World War II veteran who served in the South Pacific and China with the Marines. He never hit another homer. Dunlap had only 17 at-bats in the big leagues but left with a .353 batting average. He later coached baseball from 1954 through 1984 at Occidental College, where he was a professor in physical education and published a baseball novel called Kill the Umpire.

MAY 12   A pitcher's duel erupts into a slugfest when the Phillies break a 1–1 tie by scoring five runs in the ninth inning, then withstand a four-run Cardinal rally in the bottom half to win 6–5 at Busch Stadium.

MAY 20   Red Schoendienst and Solly Hemus star in an 11–6 win over the Pirates at Busch Stadium. Hemus tied a club record with five runs scored after reaching base on a triple, a double, and three walks. Schoendienst drove in six runs with a homer, two doubles, and a single.

Schoendienst had the best season of his career in 1953, batting .342 with 15 homers, 79 RBIs, and 107 runs.

MAY 21   The Cardinals come from behind twice to defeat the Reds 11–9 at Busch Stadium. Down 6–0, the Cards scored six runs in the sixth inning. After Cincinnati plated three in the seventh, St. Louis rallied with four in their half for the lead.

MAY 26   Stan Musial drives in six runs on a pair of homers and a single leading the Cardinals to a 14–3 win over the Cubs in Chicago.

Musial was off to an uncharacteristically slow start in 1953. He was batting just .251 on June 15 but just as quickly went off on a 24-for-43 tear from June 17 through 24 and hit .430 over the final 30 games of the season. He led the NL in on-base percentage (.437) and doubles (53) and batted .337 with 127 runs, 200 hits, 30 homers, and 113 RBIs.

MAY 28   Steve Bilko strikes out five times in a 10-inning, 10–10 tie against the Reds under the lights in Cincinnati. The game was called to allow the Cardinals to catch a train to St. Louis for a day game the next day.

MAY 29   The Cardinals score 10 runs in the fourth inning and coast to an 11–7 win over the Braves at Busch Stadium. Steve Bilko collected two doubles in the inning.

A first baseman, Bilko stood six foot one and weighed between 230 and 260 pounds, depending on the stage of his latest diet. He played in 600 games as a Cardinal from 1949 through 1954 and hit .249 with 76 homers in 1,738 at-bats. Bilko was hampered by the fluctuations in his weight, a tendency to strike out, and injuries. In 1952 he broke his arm when he tripped between first base and the dugout. Bilko was dealt to the Cubs in 1954 and went down to the minors a year later. With the minor league Los Angeles Angels in the Pacific Coast League, Bilko became a cult hero. From 1955 through 1957, he hit .330 with 148 home runs. The popular television character Sgt. Bilko played by Phil Silvers on The Phil Silvers Show *was named after Steve Bilko because he was series creator Nat Hiken's favorite player.*

JUNE 14   Harvey Haddix beats Sal Maglie and the Giants 1–0 in the first game of a doubleheader in New York. A double by Peanuts Lowrey and a single by Ray Jablonski in the fifth inning produced the lone run of the game. The Cards completed the sweep with a 9–4 victory in the second tilt.

Jablonski debuted as the Cardinals' regular third baseman in 1953, hitting 21 homers with 112 RBIs as a rookie. He developed an exuberant following with a large section of Busch Stadium frequently yelling, "Go-go, Jabbo." Jablonski was part of a group with Steve Bilko and Rip Repulski known as the "Polish Falcons." He followed his rookie campaign with 12 homers and 104 RBIs in 1954, but an iron glove and Ken Boyer's progression led to his being traded to the Reds before the start of the 1955 season.

JUNE 23   The Cardinals score seven runs in the first inning and seven more in the fourth to defeat the Giants 15–8 at Busch Stadium. Del Rice stroked a grand slam off Al Corwin in the fourth inning.

Peanuts Lowrey had two terrific seasons as a pinch hitter for the Cardinals. In 1952 he was 13 for 27, and in 1953 he went 21 for 59. His combined pinch-hit average over those two years was .407.

JUNE 27 The Cardinals sweep the Phillies 4–3 and 7–4 at Busch Stadium.

The wins gave the Cardinals a 40–26 record and placed the club in third place, one game back of first. The Cards were only 43–45 over the remainder of the season, however, and ended the season 22 games behind the Dodgers.

JULY 4 Stan Musial passes Rogers Hornsby as the all-time Cardinal hit leader with the 2,111th of his career during a 7–3 win over the Cubs in the first game of a doubleheader at Wrigley Field. Chicago won the second game 5–4.

JULY 8 Vinegar Bend Mizell pitches a two-hitter, and Ray Jablonski collects five hits, including a double, in five at-bats during a 7–3 win over the Reds at Crosley Field. The only Cincinnati hits were a single by Bob Borkowski in the fourth inning and a homer by Jim Greengrass in the ninth.

JULY 14 Enos Slaughter and Stan Musial each collect two hits during a 5–1 National League win in the All-Star Game, played at Crosley Field in Cincinnati. Slaughter also drove in a run and stole a base.

JULY 18 Enos Slaughter collects his 2,000th career hit during a 14–6 loss to the Dodgers in Brooklyn.

JULY 24 Granny Hamner collects two homers for the Phillies, one a walk-off blast in the ninth, to beat the Cardinals 2–1 in Philadelphia.

An embarrassing batting mix-up contributed to the defeat. After Eddie Stanky turned in a lineup card showing Solly Hemus batting first and Stanky himself second, Stanky opened the game as the leadoff batter and fanned. Hemus then went to the plate and singled. On appeal by Phillies manager Steve O'Neill, Hemus's hit was nullified because he had hit out of turn.

AUGUST 2 Six days after the armistice ending the Korean War, Steve Bilko hits a grand slam off Jim Hughes in the seventh inning of a 10–1 win over the Dodgers at Busch Stadium.

AUGUST 6 Harvey Haddix carries a no-hitter into the ninth inning before beating the Phillies 2–0 at Busch Stadium. Richie Ashburn broke up the no-hit bid with a single with no outs. Two batters later, Del Ennis also singled.

AUGUST 16 At the age of 18 years and 223 days, Dick Schofield becomes the youngest player in Cardinals history to hit a home run. It was struck off Frank Smith during a 6–2 win over the Reds in the second game of a doubleheader at Crosley Field. Cincinnati won the first game 3–2.

According to a major league rule passed in 1953, any amateur player who signed a contract worth more than $4,000 with a major league club had to remain on the active roster for two years and could not be farmed out to the minors without waivers. These players became known as "bonus babies." Schofield was the Cardinals' first "bonus baby," signing a deal worth $40,000 out of *high school. He played for the Cards until 1957 and remained in the majors until 1971, though mainly as a utility infielder. In 19 seasons, he played in 1,321 games and hit .227. Other Cardinal "bonus babies" were Lindy and Von McDaniel (see June 13, 1957). The rule was rescinded at the end of the 1957 season.*

AUGUST 19   On Red Schoendienst Night at Busch Stadium, Schoendienst collects a triple, double, and single, but the Cardinals lose 5–3 to the Cubs. Schoendienst was presented with a Lincoln convertible, a shotgun, a gun rack, a vacuum cleaner, an eight-piece set of china, a deep freeze, a TV set, and a basket of peaches.

AUGUST 21   The Cardinals overcome another batting mix-up to beat the Reds 4–0 at Busch Stadium. Steve Bilko led off the St. Louis half of the second and grounded out. Realizing that Bilko had batted in Ray Jablonski's turn, Eddie Stanky notified umpire Bill Stewart. When the arbiter ruled Jablonski out for missing his turn, Bilko batted again and hit a home run.

A 10-time All-Star at second base, Red Schoendienst gave the Cardinals 14 seasons of heady play before managing the team from 1965 to 1976 and again, temporarily, in 1980 and 1990.

Kidwiler Collection/Diamond Images/Getty Images

AUGUST 26   Dusty Rhodes of the Giants hits three homers off three different Cardinal pitchers in a 13–4 New York win at the Polo Grounds.

AUGUST 30   The Dodgers score 12 runs in the seventh inning and wallop the Cardinals 20–4 in Brooklyn. The Dodgers teed off on pitchers Eddie Erautt, Cliff Chambers, and Willard Schmidt. Oddly, all three outs in the 12-run seventh came on strikeouts.

The Cardinals were 0–11 at Ebbets Field in 1953.

SEPTEMBER 1   The Cardinals smash five homers, but all come with no one on base, and the Cardinals lose 12–5 in Brooklyn. Steve Bilko struck two homers, and Stan Musial, Harry Elliott, and Rip Repulski hit one each. The Dodgers hit no home runs in their victory.

Elliot's homer was the first of two he hit during his big-league career. He hit the other in 1955.

SEPTEMBER 7   The Cardinals sweep the Reds 4–3 and 1–0 at Busch Stadium. Harvey Haddix pitched the shutout. Stan Musial drove in the lone run of the game with a double in the third inning.

SEPTEMBER 10   In a weird game, the Cardinals are forced to return to the field from the clubhouse to close out a 7–6 win over the Giants at Busch Stadium. With two outs in the top of the ninth, New York runners on first and second, and the score 7–5, Dusty Rhodes grounded to shortstop Solly Hemus, who threw to Red Schoendienst at second for an apparent force-out. Umpire Lee Ballanfant signaled out but didn't notice that Schoendienst had dropped the ball. As the Cardinals raced for the clubhouse, the Giants intercepted the umpires, who conferred on the play. They reversed the decision and called the runner safe, which loaded the bases. The Cardinals were called back to the field. After Al Brazle gave up a walk that scored a run, he got the final out on a ground ball.

SEPTEMBER 13   The Cardinals trounce the Phillies 17–3 at Busch Stadium.

SEPTEMBER 20   Ernie Banks hits his first career homer during an 11–6 Cardinals win over the Cubs at Busch Stadium. Banks hit the homer off Gerry Staley.

Staley had an 18–9 record and a 3.99 ERA in 1953.

SEPTEMBER 23   Enos Slaughter's ex-wife sues him.

Mary Slaughter sued for $227,000 in damages in a Peoria (IL) County Circuit Court alleging that a razor blade advertisement referring to her courtship with Slaughter made her look "foolish, stupid and ridiculous." According to the suit, the ad implied that her ex-husband "courted and married her as a result of his use of the razor blades." In addition, said Mrs. Slaughter, the ad depicted her as a flaming redhead, although she asserted that her hair had never been red.

SEPTEMBER 25   Rookie pitcher Harvey Haddix wins his 20th game of the season with an 11–2 victory over the Cubs in Chicago.

Only five foot nine and 170 pounds, Haddix was 28 years old at the end of his rookie season. He was 20–9 in 1953 with six shutouts, a 3.06 ERA, and 163 strikeouts in 253 innings. Haddix earned the nickname "The Kitten" because of his resemblance to fellow Cardinal southpaw Harry "The Cat" Brecheen in size and felinelike quickness in fielding his position. Haddix finished second to Jim Gilliam in Rookie of the Year balloting. The only two rookies to have won 20 or more games in a season since 1953 are Bob Grim of the Yankees in 1954 and Tom Browning of the Reds in 1985.

SEPTEMBER 27   On the final day of the season, Red Schoendienst falls short in his bid to capture the batting title during a 3–2 loss to the Cubs in Chicago. Schoendienst was 2 for 5 and finished the year with a .342 average compared with .344 for Carl Furillo of the Dodgers.

On the same day, the Browns played their last game in St. Louis, losing 2–1 to the White Sox in 11 innings before 3,174 fans at Busch Stadium. Bill Veeck was hung in effigy from the right-field stands. As a final denouement, the club ran out of baseballs in the ninth inning. The rest of the contest was played with scuffed balls that had been discarded earlier. By the end of the game, "knocking the cover off the ball" nearly became a literal phrase instead of a figurative one as the balls were coming loose at the seams.

SEPTEMBER 29   The American League votes to allow the Browns to move to Baltimore. AL owners, who disliked Veeck because of his over-the-top promotional ideas, such as sending a midget to bat in a game (see August 19, 1951), and other grievances, forced Veeck to sell the Browns to a group of Baltimore investors. Following the move, the Browns were renamed the Orioles. The transfer ended 52 seasons of American League baseball in St. Louis. Veeck purchased the Chicago White Sox in 1959.

DECEMBER 2   The Cardinals send Jack Crimian and $100,000 to the Reds for Alex Grammas.

Solly Hemus had a great year in 1953 with a .279 batting average, 110 runs scored, 14 homers, and 61 RBIs, but the Cardinals purchased the untried Grammas to replace Hemus at shortstop. It was a terrible decision, as Grammas never panned out.

1954

Season in a Sentence

The youth movement continues but takes a wrong turn as the Cardinals suffer their first losing season since 1938.

Finish • Won • Lost • Pct • GB

Sixth   72   82   .468 25.0

Manager

Eddie Stanky

Stats

Stats	Cards	NL	Rank
Batting Avg:	.281	.265	1
On-Base Pct:	.354	.339	1
Slugging Pct:	.421	.407	3
Home Runs:	119		6
Stolen Bases:	63		1
ERA:	4.50	4.07	5
Fielding Avg:	.976	.976	4
Runs Scored:	799		1
Runs Allowed:	790		7

Starting Lineup

Bill Sarni, c
Joe Cunningham, 1b
Red Schoendienst, 2b
Ray Jablonski, 3b
Alex Grammas, ss
Rip Repulski, lf
Wally Moon, cf
Stan Musial, rf
Tom Alston, 1b
Solly Hemus, ss

Pitchers

Harvey Haddix, sp
Brooks Lawrence, sp-rp
Vic Raschi, sp
Tom Poholsky, sp-rp
Gordon Jones, sp
Al Brazle, rp
Gerry Staley, rp-sp

Attendance

1,039,698 (third in NL)

Club Leaders

Batting Avg:	Musial	.330
On-Base Pct:	Musial	.428
Slugging Pct:	Musial	.607
Home Runs:	Musial	35
RBIs:	Musial	126
Runs:	Musial	120
Stolen Bases:	Moon	18
Wins:	Haddix	18
Strikeouts:	Haddix	184
ERA:	Haddix	3.57
Saves:	Brazle	8

FEBRUARY 23   The Cardinals purchase Vic Raschi from the Yankees for $85,000.

Raschi was 35 years old and had a lifetime record of 120–50 when the Cardinals picked him up, and he was coming off a 13–6 season in which he led the American League in ERA. He played in six World Series with the Yankees. But Father Time had caught up with Raschi by the time he reached St. Louis. As a Cardinal he was 8–10 with a 4.88 ERA.

APRIL 11   The Cardinals trade Enos Slaughter to the Yankees for Bill Virdon, Mel Wright, and Emil Tellinger.

After playing with the club since 1938, Slaughter was crushed when the Cardinals traded him. A tough-as-nails competitor, Slaughter sat in front of his locker and wept openly when informed of the deal. He was never again an everyday player, but he appeared in three World Series with the Yankees. Wally Moon replaced Slaughter in the outfield and won the 1954 Rookie of the Year Award. Virdon reached the majors with the Cardinals in 1955 and won that season's Rookie of the Year Award. He was traded to the Pirates in May 1956 and had a 12-year big-league career.

APRIL 13   The Cubs clobber the Cardinals 13–4 in the season opener, played before 17,027 at

Busch Stadium. Facing Paul Minner, Wally Moon hit a home run in his first major league at-bat. The ball cleared the right-field pavilion. Stan Musial also homered.

The game was also notable because of the major league debut of 23-year-old first baseman Tom Alston, the Cardinals' first black player. The Cardinals purchased him from San Diego of the Pacific Coast League for $100,000. Alston was viewed as a can't-miss prospect but hit only .244 with four homers in 271 at-bats over four seasons in the majors. The Cardinals were the 10th of the then 16 major leagues clubs to integrate. The club continued to add black players throughout the remainder of the 1950s, and by 1959 there were seven African Americans on the roster, including Bob Gibson, Bill White, and Curt Flood. The only club with more black or Latin players in 1959 was the Giants, who had nine.

APRIL 17   The Cubs wallop the Cardinals 23–13 at Wrigley Field. Chicago did most of its scoring in the first five innings. It led 9–6 at the end of the third, then added three more in the fourth. After the Cards scored four runs in the fifth to make it 12–10 but still down two, the Cubs exploded for 10 runs in their half to lead 22–10. The Cubs got help from 12 walks and five Cardinal errors. One of the St. Louis runs scored on catcher Sal Yvars's steal of home. It was the only stolen base of his eight-year, 210-game career.

The Cardinals allowed 62 runs in the first six games of the 1954 season.

APRIL 20   Making his major league debut, starting pitcher Memo Luna fails to get out of the first inning of a 13–6 loss to the Reds at Busch Stadium.

The Cardinals purchased Luna for $100,000 from San Diego. It was a complete waste of money. He never pitched another game.

APRIL 23   Wally Moon collects five hits, including a triple, in five at-bats, but the Cardinals lose 7–5 in 11 innings to the Braves in Milwaukee. Facing Vic Raschi, Hank Aaron hit his first major league home run.

The Cardinals added Jack Buck and Milo Hamilton to the radio and TV broadcasting team in 1954, joining Harry Caray. On television, the Cardinals moved from KSD-TV to WTVI. KSD had been telecasting games since 1947, but through 1953 it was the only station in St. Louis and had trouble clearing air time to show Cardinals games. In 1954, WTVI aired all 77 road games. Hamilton lasted only a year with the club, but Buck became a St. Louis institution. He announced Cardinals games until 2001. His son Joe became part of the club's broadcasting staff in 1991.

APRIL 29   Harvey Haddix strikes out 13 batters but gives up a two-out, two-strike, two-run single to Dick Cole in the ninth inning to lose 4–3 to the Pirates at Busch Stadium. On the previous pitch, Cole barely fouled it off.

APRIL 30   The Cardinals sell Steve Bilko to the Cubs.

Stan Musial was on the May 1, 1954, cover of the Saturday Evening Post *in a painting by John Falter shown signing autographs for five youngsters. St. Louis youths Bill Fassett and Michael Lane served as models for the composition. Fassett actually appeared twice, once as a redhead and once with black hair. The two wound up receiving 40 Musial autographs. "Wow!" exclaimed one in awe, "will we clean up selling these at school!" The other two who modeled for the cover art were Belvedere, California, neighbors of Falter's.*

MAY 2   Stan Musial sets a major league record by striking five homers during a doubleheader against the Giants at Busch Stadium. In the first game, Musial hit three homers and drove in six runs in a 10–6 victory. Stan the Man hit a solo homer in the third inning and a two-run bomb in the fifth off Johnny Antonelli, as well as a three-run shot in the eighth against Jim Hearn to break a 6–6 tie. Wally Moon and Tom Alston also homered for the Cards. In the second tilt, Musial homered off Hoyt Wilhelm in the fifth and seventh innings, but the Cards lost 9–7. He also hit a 410-foot fly ball that Willie Mays caught in right-center.

            Musial is the only Cardinal in history with five homers in consecutive games. The only other individual in major league history with five homers in a doubleheader is Nate Colbert of the Padres on August 1, 1972. Colbert was also at Busch Stadium on the day that Musial hit his five home runs, but he was an eight-year-old St. Louis youngster at the time.

MAY 12   The Cardinals pile up 21 hits and defeat the Pirates 13–5 at Pittsburgh. Wally Moon scored five runs and drove in four. He had a homer and four singles in six at-bats.

            Stan Musial left the game in the eighth inning. His mother, watching from the stands, was rushed to the hospital for an emergency operation for a strangulated hernia.

MAY 20   Three days after the Supreme Court rules in the *Brown vs. Board of Education of Topeka* decision that segregation of public schools is illegal, the Cardinals score six runs in the first inning and seven in the seventh to overwhelm the Pirates 17–4 in Pittsburgh.

MAY 21   Although Stan Musial hits a grand slam in the seventh inning off Frank Smith, the Cardinals are forced to score two runs in the tenth inning to beat the Reds 8–7 at Busch Stadium. Rip Repulski drove in the game-winner with a single.

            The Cardinals had a 20–14 record and were in first place with a 1½-game lead. The club was out of the top spot two days later and began a slide that resulted in the first losing season in 16 years.

MAY 22   Reds manager Birdie Tebbetts tries a four-man outfield against Stan Musial at Busch Stadium. Cincinnati was ahead 4–2 in the ninth with two outs and Red Schoendienst on first base. With Musial coming to bat, Tebbetts removed shortstop Roy McMillan from the game and replaced him with Nino Escalera, whom he stationed in the outfield between Gus Bell and Wally Post. The shift wasn't needed because Art Fowler struck out Musial to end the game.

            Musial led the NL in runs (120) and doubles (41) in 1954. He also hit .330 with 195 hits, 35 homers, and 126 RBIs.

MAY 24   Wally Moon steals four bases in a 9–4 win over the Cubs at Busch Stadium. In the sixth inning, Moon singled, swiped second and third, and scored on a wild pitch.

The Cardinals stole only 18 bases in 1953, worst in the NL, but improved to 63 in 1954, best in the league. A 24-year-old rookie, Moon had the unenviable task of replacing Enos Slaughter, who had been a favorite of St. Louis fans for 15 years. Moon won over Cardinal followers by contributing 18 steals along with 12 homers, 106 runs, and a .304 average. Moon started in the Cardinals' outfield for five years.

JUNE 3   Hank Thompson of the Giants hits three homers during a 13–8 win over the Cardinals at Busch Stadium.

JUNE 9   Harvey Haddix pitches the Cardinals to a 3–0 win over the Dodgers at Busch Stadium.

JUNE 13   Harvey Haddix pitches his second consecutive shutout to defeat the Pirates 5–0 in the first game of a doubleheader at Busch Stadium. The Cardinals also won the second contest, 5–3.

JUNE 18   Harvey Haddix pitches his third straight shutout, defeating the Giants 5–0 in New York.

Haddix hurled 37 consecutive scoreless innings over five starts. Following up his 20–9 rookie season in 1953, he had a won-loss mark of 12–3 on June 23 in 1954. He slumped afterward, however, and finished the '54 campaign with 18 wins and 13 losses. Haddix had a 12–16 record in 1955 and was dealt to the Phillies in May 1956.

JUNE 24   Brooks Lawrence becomes the first African-American pitcher in Cardinal history and pitches the club to a 5–1 win over the Pirates with a complete game in Pittsburgh. On the same day, Rip Repulski set a major league record by collecting at least two hits in 10 consecutive games. During the spree, which began June 14, Repulski had 22 hits in 44 at-bats, including five homers, three triples, and three doubles.

Lawrence was 29 years old when he made his big-league debut. Even though he didn't pitch for the Cards until the last week of June, he was a rookie sensation, finishing the season with a record of 15–6. Plagued by ulcers, Lawrence slipped to 3–8 with a 6.36 ERA in 1955, however, and was traded to the Reds in January 1956.

JUNE 30   In his major league debut, Joe Cunningham hits a three-run homer in the fifth inning and a two-run single in the ninth during an 11–3 win over the Reds in Cincinnati.

JULY 1   In his second big-league game, Joe Cunningham clouts two homers and drives in four runs during a 9–2 win over the Braves in Milwaukee. Both homers came off Warren Spahn.

After two big-league games, Joe Cunningham had three homers and drove in nine runs. He is the only player in modern times to hit three homers in his first two games in the majors. Cunningham played for the Cardinals until 1961 and in the majors until 1966, but he was never really a home run hitter. As a Cardinal, Cunningham hit 52 homers in 2,183 at-bats but batted .304. Among retired Cardinals with at least 2,000 plate appearances with the club, Cunningham's .413 on-base percentage ranks fifth behind Mark McGwire,

Rogers Hornsby, Stan Musial, and Johnny Mize. After his playing days ended, Cunningham worked in the Cardinals front office in the speakers bureau and promotions department.

JULY 4   Royce Lint pitches a shutout in his first major league start, defeating the Cubs 7–0 in the second game of a doubleheader at Wrigley Field. Chicago won the first game 4–2.

Lint was 33 years old when he made his big-league debut. He had only four starts among his 30 appearances in the majors. The July 4 game was his only complete game and the last of his two victories.

JULY 9   Red Schoendienst extends his hitting streak to 28 games, but the Cardinals lose 6–4 in 11 innings to the Cardinals at Busch Stadium.

Schoendienst hit .315 with 195 hits, 38 doubles, and 5 homers in 1954.

JULY 10   A two-run, pinch-hit, walk-off homer by Joe Frazier in the ninth inning beats the Cubs 2–1 at Busch Stadium.

Frazier collected 20 hits in 62 pinch-hit at-bats in 1954.

JULY 13   Stan Musial collects two singles in five at-bats in the All-Star Game, but the National League loses 11–9 at Municipal Stadium in Cleveland.

JULY 17   Trailing 9–0, the Cardinals come back to force extra innings with five runs in the sixth inning, three in the seventh, and one in the eighth only to lose 10–9 to the Giants in 11 innings at Busch Stadium.

JULY 18   On a day in which the high temperature in St. Louis reaches a searing 112 degrees, the Cardinals play a contentious doubleheader against the Phillies at Busch Stadium. Rain caused a delay of more than an hour in the first game, which went 10 innings before the Phillies won 11–10. As a result, the second contest didn't start until 6:48. In the fifth inning, with the Phillies leading 8–1 and darkness setting in, Eddie Stanky, mistakenly believing that the lights could not be turned on to complete a Sunday contest, ordered the Cardinals to begin stalling. That was true prior to 1954, but the rule was changed just before the start of the season. Stanky changed pitchers twice during the inning, and his hurlers spent as much time as possible between deliveries, which were nowhere near the plate. When Stanky called for a third reliever, umpire Babe Pinelli gave the game to the Phillies. The decision drew a rousing, derisive cheer from St. Louis fans. NL president Warren Giles suspended Stanky for five days and fined him $100.

Just prior to Pinelli's decision to end the game, Cards catcher Sal Yvars and Phillies first baseman Earl Torgeson fought. They began exchanging words after Torgeson was nearly hit by a pitch, which touched off a melee in which players from both sides swarmed the field and began swinging and punching indiscriminately. Phillies manager Terry Moore, a longtime Cardinal star whom Stanky had fired as a coach two years earlier, grabbed Yvars. Stanky, in turn, sent Moore to the ground with an old-fashioned football tackle. Both Stanky and Moore sported facial injuries after the skirmish. The extreme heat created another unusual situation. In the first game, catcher Stan Lopata of the Phillies and Bill Sarni of the Cards discarded their chest protectors believing the risk of being hit in the shoulder, ribs, or abdomen outweighed being bogged down by extra equipment on the torrid day.

JULY 21   The Cardinals use eight pitchers and edge the Pirates 13–12 at Busch Stadium. The Cards trailed 7–6 in the sixth inning, 10–9 in the seventh, and 12–11 in the eighth but came back to take the lead on each occasion.

Bill Sarni hit .300 with nine homers as a 27-year-old rookie catcher in 1954.

JULY 24   Wally Moon hits a grand slam off Erv Palica in the seventh inning, but the Cardinals lose 7–6 to the Dodgers at Busch Stadium.

AUGUST 5   Stan Musial drives in seven runs on two homers and a sacrifice fly to pace the Cardinals to a 13–4 rout of the Dodgers at Busch Stadium. Tommy Lasorda, who was making his major league debut, gave up the sacrifice fly.

AUGUST 15   Trailing 8–2, the Cardinals score seven runs in the fourth inning and move on to beat the Reds 14–12 in Cincinnati.

AUGUST 25   The Cardinals trounce the Pirates 13–0 in Pittsburgh.

AUGUST 29   Stan Musial collects the 500th double of his career along with two homers during an 11-inning, 5–4 win over the Giants in the first game of a doubleheader at Busch Stadium. Alex Grammas drove in the winning run with a bases-loaded, walk-off single. New York won the second game 7–4.

SEPTEMBER 8   The Cardinals score three runs in the ninth inning and defeat the Dodgers 6–5 at Ebbets Field. Joe Cunningham hit a two-run double to tie the game, then scored on a single by Rip Repulski.

SEPTEMBER 20   The Cardinals score five runs in the tenth inning to defeat the Cubs 7–2 in Chicago.

SEPTEMBER 26   In the final game of the season, Wally Moon hits a two-run homer in the eleventh inning to defeat the Braves 2–0 in Milwaukee. Harvey Haddix (nine innings) and Brooks Lawrence (two innings) combined on the shutout. Moon also homered in his first at-bat of the season, which was his first in the major leagues.

Brooks was actually Lawrence's middle name. His first name was Ulysses. Lawrence was a high school football teammate of comedian Jonathan Winters in Springfield, Ohio.

DECEMBER 8   The Cardinals trade Ray Jablonski and Gerry Staley for Frank Smith.

The Cardinals relief pitching was abominable in 1954, and Smith had 20 saves for the Reds that season. He was a bust with the Cards, however. Staley converted to relief pitching a few years later and was a highly successful closer for several seasons with the White Sox, including the 1959 AL champions.

1955

Season in a Sentence

The Cardinals lose more games than in any season since 1924 and fire two managers.

Finish • Won • Lost • Pct • GB

Seventh   68   86   .442   30.5

Managers

Eddie Stanky (17–19) and Harry Walker (51–67)

Stats

Stats	Cards •	NL •	Rank
Batting Avg:	.261	.259	3
On-Base Pct:	.324	.331	6
Slugging Pct:	.400	.407	5
Home Runs:	143		5
Stolen Bases:	64		2
ERA:	4.56	4.04	8
Fielding Avg:	.975	.976	6
Runs Scored:	654		6
Runs Allowed:	757		7

Starting Lineup

Bill Sarni, c
Stan Musial, 1b-rf
Red Schoendienst, 2b
Ken Boyer, 3b
Alex Grammas, ss
Rip Repulski, lf
Bill Virdon, cf
Wally Moon, rf-cf-lf
Solly Hemus, 3b
Nels Burbrink, c

Pitchers

Harvey Haddix, sp
Luis Arroyo, sp-rp
Larry Jackson, sp-rp
Tom Poholsky, sp
Willard Schmidt, sp
Paul LaPalme, rp
Brooks Lawrence, rp

Attendance

849,130 (fifth in NL)

Club Leaders

Batting Avg:	Musial	.319
On-Base Pct:	Musial	.408
Slugging Pct:	Musial	.566
Home Runs:	Musial	33
RBIs:	Musial	108
Runs:	Musial	97
Stolen Bases:	Boyer	22
Wins:	Haddix	12
Strikeouts:	Haddix	150
ERA:	Poholsky	3.81
Saves:	Schultz	4

April 12   The Cubs hammer the Cardinals 14–4 in the opener in Chicago. Starting pitcher Brooks Lawrence allowed five runs in the first inning. Ken Boyer made his major league debut as the starter at third base and homered in the eighth inning. Boyer was assigned uniform number 14, which had previously been Gerry Staley's.

The Cardinals moved to KMOX radio in 1955. It was also the first year that Joe Garagiola was in the radio and TV booth, joining Harry Caray and Jack Buck in a trio of broadcasting legends.

April 14   Bill Virdon hits a walk-off homer in the eleventh inning to beat the Braves 8–7 in the home opener before 11,402. The Cardinals trailed 7–2 before scoring one run in the seventh inning, three in the eighth, and one in the ninth to force extra innings. Pitcher Frank Smith's base-running error in the tenth delayed the victory celebration, however. Smith inexplicably stopped between first and second on Wally Moon's apparent game-winning hit, which scored Bob Stephenson, and Smith was forced at second for the third out, nullifying the run.

The 21-foot-high screen in front of the right-field pavilion that was erected in 1929 was removed during the 1955 season to take advantage of the Cardinals' left-handed power hitters. The move boosted the number of homers as the Cardinals hit 57 at home in 1954 and 84 in 1955, but the screen was put back up at 25 feet in 1956. That season, the Cards clubbed 58 home runs at Busch Stadium.

National Baseball Hall of Fame

Hall of Fame broadcaster Jack Buck came to the Cardinals' booth in 1954 as the color commentator opposite Harry Caray. Though known for his eminent partnership with Caray, and later Mike Shannon, he also broadcast football games on radio and TV, including the famous 1967 Super Bowl between Dallas and Green Bay

APRIL 16   The Cardinals overcome six Cubs homers to defeat the Reds 12–11 in 14 innings at Busch Stadium. In the second inning, Randy Jackson, Ernie Banks, and Dee Fondy hit back-to-back-to-back homers off Tom Poholsky. In the eleventh, Banks and Fondy homered to put Chicago ahead 11–9. Wally Moon hit a two-run shot in the bottom of the inning to tie the game. In the fourteenth, Cubs left fielder Hank Sauer and shortstop Banks let a fly ball by pinch hitter Bill Sarni drop between them for a double. Moon hit a single on the next pitch to win the game.

APRIL 17   The Cardinals score 10 runs in the first inning of a 14–1 win over the Cubs in the second game of a doubleheader at Busch Stadium. The 10 runs scored on four singles, three doubles, a triple, two walks, and two errors. Larry Jackson held Chicago hitless until the seventh inning before allowing three singles. The Cubs won the opener 6–5. Harry Elliott, playing right field in place of Bill Virdon, who was sidelined with a fever, collected seven hits in eight at-bats during the afternoon.

APRIL 20

In his major league debut, Luis Arroyo pitches 7²/₃ innings of shutout ball in a 3–0 win over the Reds in Cincinnati. Herb Moford earned the save with 1¹/₃ innings of relief.

> *Arroyo won his first six major league decisions and had a record of 11–4 on July 17, but he didn't win another game and finished his rookie season at 11–8 with a 4.19 ERA. The Cardinals traded him to the Pirates in May 1956. Arroyo went back to the minors for several years, then made a spectacular comeback as the closer for the 1961 World Champion Yankees.*

MAY 10

Bill Virdon hits a two-run walk-off homer in the tenth inning to defeat the Phillies 5–3 at Busch Stadium. It was Virdon's second homer of the game.

MAY 16

Five days after the Milwaukee Hawks of the National Basketball Association move to St. Louis, Bill Sarni hit perhaps the shortest double in major league history during a 6–0 win over the Pirates at Busch Stadium. Sarni hit a fly ball almost straight up. Pittsburgh catcher Jack Shepard and first baseman Dale Long became confused over who would take the pop-up, and it landed five feet in front of the plate just before the hustling Sarni reached second base.

MAY 17

Before a 3–0 win against the Dodgers at Busch Stadium, Del Rice and Brooklyn catcher Rube Walker stage a race. The foot race was a result of good-natured bantering about the identity of the "slowest man in baseball," and whether the dubious distinction belonged to Rice or Walker. In a 50-yard dash across the outfield, Rice, coming from behind, won by about a foot. NL president Ford Frick was not amused because members of both clubs, including Eddie Stanky, made wagers on the event, although the total amount was only about $50.

MAY 28

Eddie Stanky is fired as manager of the Cardinals and is succeeded by Harry Walker.

> *With Stanky's testy disposition, sarcastic sense of humor, and ties as a player to the hated Dodgers, Cardinal fans never warmed to him. Declining win totals from 88 in 1952 to 83 in 1953 and 72 in 1954 didn't help. When he was fired, the Cards were 17–19. Stanky later returned to the Cardinals as director of player personnel from 1958 through 1964. He managed the White Sox from 1966 through 1968. When hired, Harry Walker was 38 years old and was the manager of the Cards' minor league affiliate in Rochester. (Harry's brother Dixie replaced him as manager at Rochester.) Walker had been an outfielder for the club for eight seasons during the 1940s and 1950s. His stint as manager of the Cardinals was short. The team was 51–67 over the remainder of the season, and Fred Hutchinson replaced Walker in 1956.*

JUNE 3

Facing Johnny Podres, Stan Musial hits the 300th homer of his career during a 12–5 loss to the Dodgers at Busch Stadium.

> *On the same day, the Cardinals traded Del Rice to the Braves for Pete Whisenant.*

JUNE 5

Ken Boyer hits two important homers during a 9–4 win over the Dodgers in the first game of a doubleheader at Ebbets Field. Boyer homered in the ninth inning to tie the score and went deep again during a five-run tenth. Brooklyn won the second game 10–6.

Boyer was a rookie third baseman in 1955, the first of 11 seasons with the club. The Cardinals signed him in 1949 as a pitcher, following his brother Cloyd in the organization (see September 20, 1950). But wildness on the mound and strong hitting led the team to convert him to a third baseman. During his career, Ken was named to seven All-Star teams, won five Gold Gloves, and was the NL MVP in 1964. As a Cardinal, Boyer ranks seventh in games played (1,667), second in home runs (255), seventh in runs (988), seventh in hits (1,855), fifth in RBIs (1,011), and fifth in total bases (3,011).

JUNE 13   Paul LaPalme stars with his arm and bat during a 13-inning, 6–5 victory over the Giants in the second game of a doubleheader at the Polo Grounds. LaPalme pitched seven scoreless innings, allowing only two hits, and drove in the winning run with a double. New York won the first game 8–3.

JUNE 18   After the Dodgers score three runs in the tenth inning to take a 4–1 lead, the Cardinals storm back with four in their half to win 5–4 at Busch Stadium. The rally was pulled off with a double, walk, error, and three singles, the last by Red Schoendienst with one out.

JUNE 29   Stan Musial collects his 2,500th career hit with a sixth-inning single off the Reds' Rudy Minarcin at Busch Stadium. The Cardinals won the game 9–5.

Musial hit .319 with 33 homers and 108 RBIs in 1955.

JULY 5   Harry Walker and Reds manager Birdie Tebbetts fight each other at home plate during a 5–4 Cardinals loss in Cincinnati. Tebbetts complained to umpire Jocko Conlan about the Cardinals' stalling tactics with the score tied 4–4 in the bottom of the ninth. When Walker joined in the discussion, Tebbetts stepped around Conlan and swung at the Cardinals skipper. The two managers wrestled each other to the ground, while both benches emptied and fights erupted all over the field. After the field was cleared of combatants, Johnny Temple drove in the winning run with a single. Tebbetts and Walker were ejected and fined $100 by the league office.

JULY 9   Stan Musial hits a grand slam off Warren Hacker in the sixth inning to account for the only St. Louis runs in a 4–2 victory over the Cubs at Busch Stadium.

JULY 12   Stan Musial hits a twelfth-inning, walk-off homer to lift the National League to a 6–5 win in the All-Star Game, played at County Stadium in Milwaukee. Musial struck the first pitch of the inning from the Red Sox' Frank Sullivan.

JULY 23   Del Ennis hits three homers for the Phillies during a 7–2 Cardinals defeat in Philadelphia.

JULY 27   Wally Moon hits a grand slam off Roy Face in the eighth inning of a 6–1 win over the Pirates at Busch Stadium.

AUGUST 9   Hoping to inspire his team, Harry Walker starts his first major league game since 1951. Batting leadoff, Walker doubled in five at-bats. He also started a double play from left field, but the Cardinals lost 9–6 at Sportsman's Park.

Walker used seven pitchers in the defeat and launched a 90-minute tirade at his players in the clubhouse after the game.

AUGUST 10	Stan Musial collects his 1,000th career extra-base hit with a first-inning double off Lew Burdette during a 7–2 win over the Braves in Milwaukee.

AUGUST 11   Willard Schmidt pitches a one-hitter to defeat the Braves 4–0 in the second game of a doubleheader at County Stadium. The only Milwaukee hit was a single by Johnny Logan in the seventh inning. The Cards also won the first game, 7–1.

The shutout was the only one of Schmidt's seven-year big-league career.

AUGUST 12   The Cardinals score three runs in the ninth inning to beat the Reds 8–7 at Busch Stadium. Ken Boyer hit a two-out, two-run double to tie the contest, then scored on Wally Moon's single.

AUGUST 14   Harry Walker's unorthodox strategy proves to be unsuccessful, but the Cardinals defeat the Reds 5–4 in 10 innings at Busch Stadium. With the Cardinals leading 4–2 in the Reds' half of the eighth and a runner on base, Walker took Tom Poholsky off the mound and brought in Luis Arroyo to face Ted Kluszewski for a lefty-lefty matchup. Poholsky went to left field so that he could remain in the game. The maneuver backfired when Kluszewski homered to tie the score.

AUGUST 25   A grand slam by Wally Moon off Robin Roberts in the fourth inning gives the Cardinals a 9–3 lead, but the Phillies rally to win 11–9 in the first game of a doubleheader at Connie Mack Stadium. Philadelphia won the second game 8–3.

AUGUST 30   Stan Musial extends his games-played streak with a bit of contrivance. It appeared as though his streak would end at 593 when he was hit on the right hand in a game against the Dodgers the previous day. But in the August 30 game, Musial played only defensively in the bottom of the first inning in a 3–1 loss to the Pirates in Pittsburgh. Listed in the batting order in the sixth slot in instead of third as usual, Musial was lifted by pinch hitter Pete Whisenant in the top of the second. On August 31, Musial was in the official starting lineup but never appeared in the game. Whisenant batted for him in the first inning as the Cardinals lost against 4–3 to the Pirates at Forbes Field. Musial's streak ended in 1957 at 895 games.

SEPTEMBER 4   Willard Schmidt retires the first 20 batters to face him, but the Cubs rally to win 4–3 in Chicago with one run in the seventh inning and three in the eighth.

SEPTEMBER 19   Rip Repulski hits a walk-off homer in the twelfth inning to beat the Cubs 6–5 at Busch Stadium.

SEPTEMBER 20   Solly Hemus's two-run homer in the first inning accounts for all of the runs in a 2–0 victory over the Cubs at Busch Stadium. Ben Flowers (six innings) and Harvey Haddix (three innings) combined on the shutout. Don Blasingame's single in his first big-league at-bat preceded Hemus's homer.

SEPTEMBER 25   In the last game of the season, Wally Moon hits a two-out, three-run, walk-off homer to beat the Braves 6–5 at Busch Stadium. It was Moon's second homer of the game. It was also the second straight year that he won a game with a homer in his last at-bat of the season (see September 26, 1954).

OCTOBER 6   The Cardinals hire 59-year-old Frank Lane as general manager.

Lane had worked in the front offices of the Reds and Yankees before becoming general manager of the White Sox at the end of the 1948 season, when the team lost 101 games. With a series of brilliant trades, Lane transformed the Sox from league doormats to pennant contenders. But Lane had a volatile personality and didn't back down from anyone, causing difficulties with his superiors throughout his career. Lane and White Sox owner Charles Comiskey II bickered constantly, leading to Lane's dismissal even though he had a contract through the 1960 season. Lane went to the Cardinals two weeks after leaving the Sox. With a flurry of deals that included trading fan favorites such as Red Schoendienst, Lane helped the Cardinals leap from seventh place in 1955 to second in 1957. He didn't get along with August Busch any better than he had with Charles Comiskey, however, and resigned at the end of the '57 season.

OCTOBER 12   The Cardinals hire 37-year-old Fred Hutchinson as manager to replace Harry Walker.

Hutchinson was a pitcher in the American League for 10 seasons and managed the Tigers from 1952 through 1954. In 1955, Hutchinson managed Seattle, his hometown, to the Pacific Coast League championship. He was tough, aggressive, and relentless with an explosive temper. Known to throw clubhouse furniture and smash light bulbs after tough defeats, Hutch always seemed to be angry about something, but his titanic rages were directed at inanimate objects. He had the utmost respect for and loyalty of his players because he rarely chewed them out or subjected them to public criticism. Under Hutchinson, the Cardinals went from 68 wins in 1955 to 76 in 1956 and 87 in 1957, but a bad year in 1958 led to his dismissal. Walker was a Cardinals coach from 1959 through 1962 and managed the Pirates (1965–67) and Astros (1968–72).

DECEMBER 4   The Cardinals purchase Ellis Kinder from the Red Sox.

1956

Season in a Sentence

The Cardinals show improvement under new manager Fred Hutchinson but finish with a losing record for the third year in a row.

Finish • Won • Lost • Pct • GB

Fourth   76   78   .494 17.0

Manager

Fred Hutchinson

Stats	Cards	• NL •	Rank
Batting Avg:	.268	.256	1
On-Base Pct:	.335	.324	3
Slugging Pct:	.399	.401	4
Home Runs:	124		6
Stolen Bases:	41		6
ERA:	3.97	3.77	7
Fielding Avg:	.976	.977	4
Runs Scored:	678		4
Runs Allowed:	698		6

Starting Lineup

Hal Smith, c
Stan Musial, 1b-rf
Don Blasingame, 2b-ss
Ken Boyer, 3b
Al Dark, ss
Rip Repulski, lf
Bobby Del Greco, cf
Wally Moon, rf-1b
Whitey Lockman, lf-cf
Ray Katt, c
Red Schoendienst, 2b
Hank Sauer, lf

Pitchers

Vinegar Bend Mizell, sp
Murry Dickson, sp
Herm Wehmeier, sp-rp
Tom Poholsky, sp
Willard Schmidt, sp-rp
Lindy McDaniel, rp

Attendance

1,029,773 (fourth in NL)

Club Leaders

Batting Avg:	Musial	.310
On-Base Pct:	Moon	.390
Slugging Pct:	Musial	.522
Home Runs:	Musial	27
RBIs:	Musial	109
Runs:	Blasingame	94
Stolen Bases:	Moon	12
Wins:	Mizell	14
Strikeouts:	Mizell	153
ERA:	Dickson	3.07
Saves:	Collum	7

JANUARY 31   The Cardinals trade Brooks Lawrence and Sonny Senerchia to the Reds for Jackie Collum.

The Cards gave up on Lawrence after an awful year in 1955, but he rebounded with a 19–10 record for the Reds in 1956 and was 16–13 in 1957. Collum was of little help to the Cardinals, and Senerchia never played in a big-league game.

MARCH 30   The Cardinals trade Pete Whisenant to the Cubs for Hank Sauer.

APRIL 17   On Opening Day in Cincinnati, Stan Musial's two-out, two-run homer in the ninth inning breaks a 2–2 tie and gives the Cardinals a 4–2 win over the Reds in 44-degree weather. Vinegar Bend Mizell, who missed the 1954 and 1955 seasons while serving in the Army, pitched $8^2/_3$ innings for the victory.

The Cardinals' uniforms received a major redesign in 1956. The boldest stroke was the removal of the longstanding birds-on-the-bat insignia from the front of the jersey. A cartoon figure of a redbird in a batting stance appeared on the left sleeve. The change was not popular with fans, however. The birds-on-the-bat motif returned in 1957 and has been a feature of the uniforms ever since.

APRIL 20   In the home opener, the Cardinals lose 5–4 to the Braves before 23,984. Ken Boyer hit a home run.

In just his second season in the big leagues, Boyer batted .306 with 26 homers and 98 RBIs in 1956.

APRIL 22   The Cardinals score eight runs in the sixth inning of a 10–4 triumph over the Braves in the first game of a doubleheader at Busch Stadium. Stan Musial hit a single off Lew Burdette and a grand slam against Phil Paine during the inning. Milwaukee won the second game 13–5.

Musial led the NL in RBIs with 109 in 1956 along with a .310 batting average and 27 homers.

APRIL 25   Harvey Haddix pitches a two-hitter to defeat the Cubs 6–0 at Busch Stadium. The only Chicago hits were singles by Ernie Banks in the second inning and Gene Baker in the sixth.

MAY 2   Stan Musial hits a grand slam in the fifth inning off Jack McMahan, but the Cardinals need two runs in the tenth inning to beat the Pirates 10–9 at Busch Stadium. A squeeze bunt by Alex Grammas drove in the winning run.

MAY 3   Stan Musial plays in his 2,000th career game, a 7–3 loss to the Dodgers at Busch Stadium.

MAY 5   Ken Boyer hits a grand slam off Roger Craig in the first inning to account for all the runs in a 4–1 win over the Dodgers at Busch Stadium.

MAY 6   The Cardinals trade Luis Arroyo to the Pirates for Max Surkont.

MAY 11   The Cardinals trade Harvey Haddix, Stu Miller, and Ben Flowers to the Phillies for Murry Dickson and Herm Wehmeier. On the same day, the Cardinals purchased Grady Hatton from the Red Sox.

At the time of the trade, Wehmeier had a lifetime 0–14 record against the Cardinals. Dickson previously had played for the Cardinals for seven seasons during the 1940s. In the short term, the deal worked out all right as Dickson and Wehmeier helped the Cardinals over the next two seasons. In the long run, it was a disaster because Haddix and Miller were effective pitchers well into the 1960s. A failure as a starter, Miller was converted to relief by the end of the 1950s and had a string of great seasons out of the bullpen with the Giants and Orioles. He led the league twice in saves, once in ERA, and once in games pitched.

MAY 13   The Cardinals rally from a 5–0 deficit to defeat the Cubs 14–7 in the second game of a doubleheader in Chicago, called by darkness after seven innings. The Cards also won the first game, 3–2.

MAY 14   The Cardinals trade Solly Hemus to the Phillies for Bobby Morgan.

MAY 16   The Cardinals lose 5–3 to the Brooklyn Dodgers at Roosevelt Stadium in Jersey City, New Jersey. The Dodgers played seven games at Jersey City in both 1956 and 1957 to express their dissatisfaction with the conditions at Ebbets Field.

On the same day, the Cardinals traded Alex Grammas and Joe Frazier to the Reds for Chuck Harmon.

MAY 17   The Cardinals trade Bill Virdon to the Pirates for Bobby Del Greco and Dick Littlefield.

The Cards would soon regret this deal as Virdon immediately became the Pirates' starting center fielder and remained there until 1965.

MAY 21   Umpire Stan Landes clears the Cardinal bench after being heckled in the second inning of a game against the Giants in New York. Reserves were eligible as needed, but the Cards used the minimum nine players to win 4–1.

MAY 27   The Cardinals sweep the Cubs 11–9 and 12–2 at Busch Stadium. In the first game, Jim Davis of the Cubs struck out four batters in an inning. The feat was possible because Davis's knuckler eluded catcher Hobie Landrith on a third strike to Lindy McDaniel, and McDaniel reached first base. Davis also struck out Hal Smith, Jackie Brandt, and Don Blasingame. The Cards led 8–1 in the third inning but allowed the Cubs to tie the contest 8–8 before securing the victory. Stan Musial drove in seven runs during the two games with three in the first and four in the second.

MAY 31   Vinegar Bend Mizell carries a shutout into the ninth inning before giving up consecutive homers to Ted Kluszewski, Frank Robinson, and Ray Jablonski, but he survives to defeat the Reds 9–3 at Busch Stadium.

JUNE 4   The Cardinals sign Jim Konstanty following his release from the Yankees.

JUNE 6   The Cardinals edge the Giants 3–2 in 11 innings at Busch Stadium. With two outs in the ninth, Stan Musial doubled. Jackie Brandt pinch ran for him and scored on Ken Boyer's single. Brandt remained in the game and clubbed a walk-off double in the eleventh.

JUNE 8   Murry Dickson holds the Pirates without a run for 10 innings but gives up two tallies in the eleventh to lose 2–0 at Busch Stadium. Bob Friend went the distance for Pittsburgh.

The Cardinals had a record of 29–21 on June 10 and were only percentage points out of first place. The club went into a slide, however and sank out of the race by mid-July. By the end of the season, the Cards were 76–78. It was the first time that they had three losing seasons in a row since 1918 through 1920. Since 1956, the Cardinals have never again had three seasons in a row below .500. The only consecutive losing seasons have been 1958–1959 and 1994–1995.

JUNE 14   The Cardinals' roster shake-up continues with the trade of Red Schoendienst, Jackie Brandt, Bill Sarni, Dick Littlefield, and Gordon Jones to the Giants for Al Dark, Whitey Lockman, Ray Katt, and Don Liddle.

The trade stunned Cardinals fans as the popular Schoendienst, who had been a starter since 1945, was dealt to the Giants. He went to the Braves in June 1957 and helped Milwaukee win the NL pennant in both 1957 and 1958. With Schoendienst near the end of his career and Don Blasingame ready to take over at second base, Brandt was the bigger loss, however. He was a regular outfielder in the majors until 1964. Sarni was the Giants' starting catcher for the remainder of 1956, but his career ended when he suffered a heart attack during spring training in 1957. Dark capably filled the shortstop position for the Cardinals for a season and a half. Before arriving in St. Louis, Dark was a college football star as a halfback at LSU, turned down an offer to play with the Philadelphia Eagles, and appeared in the World Series with the Braves in 1948 and the Giants in 1951 and 1954. Dark was also one of nine members of the 1956 Cardinals who later managed in the majors. The others were Ken Boyer, Joe Frazier, Alex Grammas, Grady Hatton, Solly Hemus, Whitey Lockman, Red Schoendienst, and Bill Virdon. Boyer, Hemus, and Schoendienst were later Cardinals managers.

JUNE 21   The Cardinals lead the Dodgers 8–5 in the ninth inning at Ebbets Field with two outs in the ninth but lose 9–8 when six straight batters reach base. After two singles, Roy Campanella hit a three-run homer off Murry Dickson to tie the score. A walk and two singles scored the game-winner.

JUNE 24   Ken Boyer hits two homers and a triple during an 8–4 win over the Phillies in the first game of a doubleheader at Connie Mack Stadium. Philadelphia won the second tilt 3–2.

JULY 1   Ted Kluszewski hits three homers in a 10-inning, 19–15 Cincinnati win over the Cardinals in the first game of a doubleheader at Busch Stadium. The Cards trailed 7–1 before rallying to tie the game with six runs in the fifth inning, aided by Wally Moon's grand slam off Brooks Lawrence. The Cards took a 9–7 lead in the sixth, fell behind 13–10, and then sent the game into extra innings with three tallies in the ninth. In the tenth, the Reds scored six runs to the Redbirds' two. Cincinnati won the second game 7–1.

            Moon hit .298 with 16 homers in 1956.

JULY 10   Stan Musial and Ken Boyer shine in the All-Star Game, which the National League wins 7–3 at Griffith Stadium in Washington. Boyer made three great defensive plays. Two were on diving stops of ground balls, the other a leaping stab of a line drive. He also collected three singles in five at-bats and drove in a run. Musial homered off Tom Brewer of the Red Sox in the seventh inning.

            In the first four games after the All-Star break, three of which were against his former Giants teammates, Al Dark collected 12 hits, including three doubles and a triple, in 16 at-bats and drove in 11 runs.

JULY 11   The Cardinals sell Ellis Kinder to the White Sox.

JULY 21   The Cardinals explode for 20 hits and defeat the Dodgers 13–6 at Busch Stadium.

JULY 26   The Cardinals outslug the Phillies 14–9 at Philadelphia.

AUGUST 1   The Cardinals sell Grady Hatton to the Orioles.

            Only nine players on the Cardinals' Opening Day roster were still with the club at the end of season.

AUGUST 7   Wally Moon collects five hits, including a double and a homer, in five at-bats to lead the Cardinals to an 8–4 win over the Reds in Cincinnati.

AUGUST 8   Herm Wehmeier pitches a 10-inning complete game and drives in the winning run
               with a single to beat the Braves 3–2 in the second game of a doubleheader at County
               Stadium. Milwaukee won the first contest 10–1.

AUGUST 19   Two days before his 40th birthday, Murry Dickson pitches a two-hitter to defeat the
               Cubs 6–0 in the first game of a doubleheader at Busch Stadium. Dickson retired the
               first 17 batters to face him before Monte Irvin singled. Hobie Landrith accounted for
               the second Chicago hit with a single in the eighth. The Cubs won the second game 3–1.

AUGUST 25   After spotting the Pirates a 5–0 lead in the first two innings, the Cardinals bounce
               back to chalk up an 8–5 victory at Busch Stadium with one run in the third inning,
               one in the fifth, two in the sixth, and four in the seventh. Wally Moon broke the 5–5
               tie with a two-run double.

SEPTEMBER 7   Ken Boyer and Vinegar Bend Mizell star in a 1–0 win over the Reds at Busch
               Stadium. Boyer accounted for the only run of the game with a homer in the seventh
               inning off Joe Nuxhall. The only two hits off Mizell were singles by Wally Post in the
               second inning and Frank Robinson in the ninth.

SEPTEMBER 9   After the Reds score in the top of the thirteenth inning, the Cardinals battle back
               with two in their half to win 6–5 at Busch Stadium. Walker Cooper hit a pinch-hit
               triple, and after two intentional walks, Ray Katt stroked a two-run single.

SEPTEMBER 16   A homer in the tenth inning by Rip Repulski beats the Pirates 3–2 in the first game of
               a doubleheader at Forbes Field. Pittsburgh won the second tilt 9–3.

SEPTEMBER 18   A two-out, two-run homer by Ken Boyer in the ninth inning defeats the Dodgers 6–5
               in Brooklyn.

SEPTEMBER 19   The Dodgers overwhelm the Cardinals 17–2 in Brooklyn.

               From 1953 through 1956, the Cardinals had a record of 8–35 at Ebbets Field.

SEPTEMBER 25   The Cardinals pull off an unusual triple play during a 5–1 win over the Cubs at
               Wrigley Field. The bases were loaded in the Chicago fifth, with Dave Hillman
               on first, Hobie Landrith on second, and Gene Baker on third when Solly Drake
               drilled a line drive to Musial at first base. Musial appeared to have trapped the ball
               but actually caught it at ankle height. In the ensuing confusion, Musial threw to
               shortstop Dick Schofield to double Landrith at second, but Schofield's return throw
               to second baseman Don Blasingame, covering first, was too late to catch Hillman off
               the bag. Blasingame flipped the ball to pitcher Lindy McDaniel, who heard manager
               Fred Hutchinson's shouts from the dugout and fired across the diamond to triple
               Baker, who had tried to run home on the play and was tagged out by third baseman
               Ken Boyer in a rundown.

SEPTEMBER 29   On the second-to-last day of the season, the Cardinals hand the Braves a crushing
               2–1 defeat in 12 innings at Busch Stadium. A win would have put the Braves into a
               tie for first place with the Dodgers. Bill Bruton hit a home run with one out in the
               first inning, but Herm Wehmeier shut Milwaukee out the rest of the way. Center
               fielder Bobby Del Greco saved the game with two sensational catches in the ninth
               inning. In the twelfth, Stan Musial and Rip Repulski doubled for the win. The Braves
               finished the season one game behind the Dodgers.

NOVEMBER 19   Two weeks after Dwight Eisenhower wins a second term as president by defeating Adlai Stevenson, the Cardinals trade Rip Repulski and Bobby Morgan to the Phillies for Del Ennis.

Ennis was an outfield starter for 11 seasons in Philadelphia, including six in which he drove in more than 100 runs, before moving to St. Louis. Ennis gave the Cardinals one good season, driving in 105 runs with 24 home runs in 1957.

NOVEMBER 27   Cardinals outfielder Charlie Peete dies in a plane crash in Venezuela along with his wife and three children. The plane on which they were traveling struck a fog-shrouded mountain peak near Caracas. Peete was en route to Caracas to play winter ball. He played 23 games for the Cards in 1956 as a rookie after winning the American Association batting title at Omaha. The Cardinals had planned to make him the starting center fielder in 1957.

DECEMBER 11   The Cardinals trade Tom Poholsky, Jackie Collum, Ray Katt, and Wally Lammers to the Cubs for Sam Jones, Hobie Landrith, Jim Davis, and Eddie Miksis.

The Cards gave up little of value to acquire Sam Jones, who gave the club two excellent seasons as a starting pitcher.

1957

Season in a Sentence

The Cardinals are surprise pennant contenders, holding first place as late as the first week of August before finishing second to the Braves.

Finish • Won • Lost • Pct • GB

Second   87   67   .565   8.0

Manager

Fred Hutchinson

Stats

Stats	Cards	NL	Rank
Batting Avg:	.274	.260	1
On-Base Pct:	.336	.325	2
Slugging Pct:	.405	.400	3
Home Runs:	132		6
Stolen Bases:	58		3
ERA:	3.78	3.88	3
Fielding Avg:	.979	.977	4
Runs Scored:	737		3
Runs Allowed:	666		4

Starting Lineup

Hal Smith, c
Stan Musial, 1b
Don Blasingame, 2b
Eddie Kasko, 3b
Al Dark, ss
Wally Moon, lf-rf
Ken Boyer, cf
Del Ennis, rf-lf
Joe Cunningham, 1b-rf
Hobie Landrith, c
Bobby Gene Smith, cf

Pitchers

Larry Jackson, sp-rp
Lindy McDaniel, sp
Sam Jones, sp
Herm Wehmeier, sp-rp
Vinegar Bend Mizell, sp-rp
Von McDaniel, sp
Hoyt Wilhelm, rp
Lloyd Merritt, rp
Willard Schmidt, rp

Attendance

1,183,575 (second in NL)

Club Leaders

Batting Avg:	Musial	.351
On-Base Pct:	Musial	.422
Slugging Pct:	Musial	.612
Home Runs:	Musial	29
RBIs:	Ennis	105
Runs:	Blasingame	108
Stolen Bases:	Blasingame	21
Wins:	Jackson	15
	McDaniel	15
Strikeouts:	Jones	154
ERA:	Jackson	3.47
Saves:	Wilhelm	11

FEBRUARY 26   The Cardinals trade Whitey Lockman to the Giants for Hoyt Wilhelm.

APRIL 16   Stan Musial collects four hits, including two doubles, in four at-bats to lead the Cardinals to a 13–4 win over the Reds in the season opener in Cincinnati. Bobby Gene Smith hit a homer and a single in his major league debut. Wally Moon also homered, and Al Dark rapped three hits. Herm Wehmeier pitched a complete game.

                   Dark hit .290 for the Cardinals in 1957.

APRIL 18   In the home opener, the Cardinals lose 10–2 to the Cubs before 17,255 at Busch Stadium.

APRIL 20   The Cardinals trade Bobby Del Greco and Ed Mayer to the Cubs for Jim King.

APRIL 30   Stan Musial homers in the thirteenth inning to beat the Pirates 6–5 at Forbes. The Cardinals seemed to have the game in hand with a 5–0 lead before Pittsburgh scored five runs in the ninth.

                   Wally Moon hit a titanic shot over the right field roof at Forbes Field, which was built in 1909. Only two drives had previously been hit over the roof in a regularly scheduled game, one of them by Babe Ruth. Moon batted .295 with 24 homers in 1957.

MAY 2   The Cardinals win a 16-inning marathon 3–2 over the Dodgers in Brooklyn. Don Blasingame drove in the winning run with a single. Herm Wehmeier pitched 12 innings and struck out 12 batters. Larry Jackson went the final four frames.

                   Blasingame hit .271 and scored 108 for the Cards in 1957. During the season, Blasingame began dating Sara Cooper, the daughter of teammate Walker Cooper. Sara was a finalist in the Miss America contest as Miss Missouri. Don and Sara married in 1960.

MAY 8   Hal Smith drives in six runs with a homer and two singles to lead the Cardinals to a 13–4 win over the Giants in New York.

MAY 15   The Cardinals outlast the Giants 6–5 in 14 innings at Busch Stadium. Hal Smith drove in the game-winning run with a single.

                   The Cardinals had a record of only 13–17 on May 23 but won 49 of their next 73 games and were in first place as late as August 5.

MAY 26   Stan Musial hits two homers, including a grand slam off Hal Jeffcoat in the eighth inning, but the Cardinals lose 7–6 to the Reds in Cincinnati.

                   At the age of 36, Musial led the league in batting average (.351) and on-base percentage (.422) in 1957. He also hit 29 homers and drove in 102 runs.

MAY 31   Wally Moon extends his hitting streak to 24 games during a 4–3 win over the Braves in Milwaukee.

JUNE 7   Del Ennis hits a two-run homer in the eleventh inning to defeat the Giants 5–3 in New York.

The McDaniel Brothers

A pair of brothers on the Cardinal pitching staff was the talk of the baseball world during the summer of 1957. Lindy McDaniel, only 21, was 15–9 that season with a 3.49 ERA. His brother Von, just 18, had a 7–5 mark and a 3.22 ERA. The McDaniels drew comparisons to the Dean bothers, who set baseball on its ear during the Cardinals' 1934 World Championship season. Dizzy and Paul Dean even came to St. Louis to meet the McDaniel siblings, posed for photographs, and predicted a bright future.

Lindy and Von McDaniel played for the Cardinals as teenagers because of a unique rule. In order to curb the large bonuses being paid to unproven players out of high school and college, owners passed a rule in 1953 that any player paid a bonus greater than $4,000 must remain on the active roster for two years.

The Cardinals signed Lindy in 1955 at the age of 19 after his freshman season at Abilene Christian College. He saw a bonus of $50,000. He pitched in only four games in 1955 but showed promise in 1956 with a 7–6 record and a 3.40 ERA in 39 games (116⅓) innings. By 1957, he was in the Cardinals' starting rotation.

Von joined Lindy in June 1957 when the Cardinals signed him for $50,000 less than two months after he celebrated his 18th birthday and just after he graduated from high school in Hollis, Oklahoma. Von was considered such a hot prospect that he received larger offers from other clubs, but his father insisted that he sign with the Cardinals because he didn't want the brothers separated and didn't want Von to receive more money than Lindy.

Von debuted on June 13. Pitching the last four innings of a blowout loss against the Phillies, he didn't allow a run. Four days later against the Dodgers, he pitched four more shutout innings of relief. This prompted the Cardinals to give the younger McDaniel a starting assignment. On June 21, Von pitched a two-hit complete game and beat the Dodgers 2–0 in St. Louis. A one-hitter against the Pirates followed on July 28.

Von McDaniel looked to be headed for the Hall of Fame, but he pitched only two games and two major league innings after 1957 in which he posted a 13.50 ERA. He suffered a severely torn muscle in his pitching shoulder during spring training in 1958, and his big-league career was over at 19. He moved to third base and played in the minors as late as 1964, but he never hit well enough to make it back to the majors.

Lindy also struggled in 1958 but became a relief pitcher in 1959. He played for the Cardinals until 1962 and in the majors until 1975. Although Lindy never pitched in the postseason, he capped his 21-year career by appearing in 987 big-league games, which at the time was second all time in games pitched behind only Hoyt Wilhelm.

During the magical summer of 1957, St. Louis newspapers reported on the exploits of 13-year-old Kerry Don McDaniel back in amateur games in Hollis. In 1962, Kerry Don became the third McDaniel brother to sign with the Cardinals for $50,000. By that time, the rule requiring players who signed for such an amount to remain in the majors for two years was no longer in effect. Kerry Don was allowed to start his professional career in the minors, but he never pitched a major league game.

JUNE 12   The Cardinals win their eighth game in a row with a 4–0 decision over the Phillies in Philadelphia.

JUNE 13   Von McDaniel, an 18-year-old rookie pitcher only weeks out of high school, makes his major league debut with four innings of relief during a 5–1 loss to the Phillies in Philadelphia. McDaniel allowed no runs and one hit.

Three days later, Von pitched four innings of relief during a 7–6 win over the Dodgers in Brooklyn, and again surrendered no runs and only one hit in four *innings. A native of Hollis, Oklahoma, he was signed by the Cardinals on May 27 for $50,000. His brother Lindy, who was three years older, was also signed by the Cards for $50,000 in 1955 and, like Von, went straight to the majors because of the bonus rule then in effect (see August 16, 1953).*

JUNE 20   The Cardinals take over control of first place with a 7–4 win over the Pirates at Busch Stadium. Stan Musial extended his hitting streak to 21 games.

JUNE 21   In his first major league start, Von McDaniel pitches a two-hit shutout to defeat the Dodgers 2–0 at Busch Stadium. The only Brooklyn hits were singles by Jim Gilliam and Duke Snider, both in the sixth inning.

           In his first 17 innings in the majors, McDaniel allowed no runs and only four hits while striking out 13.

JUNE 23   In the fourth inning, Wally Moon hits a three-run triple, then steals home, to lead the Cardinals to a 4–3 win over the Dodgers at Busch Stadium.

JUNE 27   Teenage sensation Von McDaniel stretches his streak of scoreless innings at the start of his career to 19 before allowing four runs to the Phillies at Busch Stadium. Nonetheless, McDaniel was the winning pitcher in a 6–4 decision.

JULY 2   Von McDaniel continues his spectacular mound work by retiring the first 18 Milwaukee batters to face him before Bill Bruton singles leading off the seventh. McDaniel gave up two runs and five hits in 7⅓ innings but was the winning pitcher in a 4–2 victory at Busch Stadium.

           McDaniel proved to a phenomenal drawing card. The July 2 contest drew 29,211 one night after the same two clubs played before 16,849.

JULY 6   The Cardinals slug their way to a 13–3 win over the Reds at Busch Stadium.

           The Cards headed into the All-Star break with a 46–31 record and a 2½-game lead.

JULY 9   The All-Star Game is played at Busch Stadium, with the American League winning 6–5 before 30,693. Both teams scored three runs in the ninth inning, but Minnie Minoso's running catch of a Gil Hodges drive with the bases loaded shut down the NL's last-ditch rally. Stan Musial contributed a double.

           Future Hall of Famers on the rosters of the two clubs included Hank Aaron, Ernie Banks, Yogi Berra, Jim Bunning, Nellie Fox, Al Kaline, George Kell, Mickey Mantle, Eddie Mathews, Willie Mays, Stan Musial, Frank Robinson, Red Schoendienst, Warren Spahn, and Ted Williams.

JULY 17   Sam Jones pitches a two-hitter to beat the Giants 5–1 at the Polo Grounds. The only two New York hits were a single by Whitey Lockman with two outs in the sixth inning and a homer by Willie Mays with two outs in the ninth.

           Jones was nicknamed "Toothpick Sam" because of the toothpick he always chewed on the mound.

JULY 18   The Cardinals lose an unbelievable 10–9 decision to the Dodgers in 11 innings at Ebbets Field. The Cardinals scored seven runs in the top of the ninth inning to take a 9–4 lead only to have Brooklyn plate five runs in its half, the last four on a Gil Hodges grand slam off Vinegar Bend Mizell, to tie the contest. The eleventh-inning run not only resulted in a loss but also knocked the Cards out of first place.

JULY 28   Von McDaniel pitches a one-hitter to defeat the Pirates 4–0 in the first game of a thrilling doubleheader at Busch Stadium. The only Pittsburgh hit was a single by Gene Baker in the second inning. McDaniel retired the last 22 batters to face him. In the second tilt, the Cardinals trailed 8–5 before scoring three runs in the ninth inning and one in the eleventh to win 9–8. Joe Cunningham's walk-off home run settled the issue.

            At 18 years and 91 days, McDaniel is the youngest pitcher in modern major league history to pitch a one-hitter or a no-hitter.

JULY 29   Vinegar Bend Mizell pitches a two-hitter to defeat the Pirates 4–0 at Busch Stadium. The only Pittsburgh hits were a single by Dick Groat and a double by Frank Thomas, both in the fourth inning.

JULY 30   Joe Cunningham hits a dramatic pinch-hit, walk-off grand slam to down the Giants 7–3 at Busch Stadium.

AUGUST 1   The Cardinals move back into first place with an 8–0 win over the Giants at Busch Stadium. Stan Musial contributed two homers and two singles.

AUGUST 2   Willard Schmidt wins his tenth game in a row with a 10-inning, 5–4 decision over the Phillies at Busch Stadium with four innings of relief.

            Schmidt finished the 1957 season with a 10–3 record and a 4.78 ERA.

AUGUST 3   The Cardinals win their eighth game in a row with a 3–1 decision over the Phillies at Busch Stadium.

AUGUST 6   An 8–2 loss to the Cubs at Busch Stadium knocks the Cardinals out of first place.

            The defeat started a nine-game losing streak, six of them to the lowly Cubs. By August 17, the Cardinals were 8½ games behind the first-place Braves.

AUGUST 18   Trailing 6–1 in the first game of a doubleheader in Milwaukee, the Cardinals score one run in the seventh inning, two in the eighth, two in the ninth, and two in the tenth to beat the Braves 8–6. The two tenth-inning runs scored on a Stan Musial home run. The Cards completed the sweep with a 6–0 triumph in the nightcap.

AUGUST 21   The Cardinals play the Giants for the last time in New York and lose 13–6 at the Polo Grounds.

            The game was played two days after the Giants announced they were moving to San Francisco at the end of the 1957 season. The Cardinals played at the Polo Grounds again in 1962 and 1963 when the Mets called it home.

AUGUST 23   Stan Musial's playing streak ends at 895 games when he fails to appear in a 3–2 loss to the Phillies in Philadelphia because of a torn muscle and chipped bone in his shoulder blade. He had sustained the injury whiffing at a high, outside pitch the previous day against the Phillies. Musial missed 15 games with the injury.

The 895-game streak, which dated to 1951, is a Cardinal record and the eighth-longest in big-league history.

AUGUST 25   The Cardinals play the Dodgers in Brooklyn for the last time and lose 6–5 at Ebbets Field.

The Dodgers officially announced the move to Los Angeles on October 8.

AUGUST 31   The Cardinals purchase Irv Noren from the Athletics.

SEPTEMBER 3   The Cardinals break loose with a 14–4 win over the Reds in Cincinnati.

SEPTEMBER 10   Ken Boyer hits a walk-off single with the bases loaded in the fourteenth inning to beat the Phillies 4–3 at Busch Stadium. The Cards stranded 11 base runners from the tenth through the thirteenth innings.

Without a dependable center fielder and with rookie Eddie Kasko available to play third base, the Cardinals moved Ken Boyer to center during the 1957 season. Boyer led all outfielders in fielding percentage but returned to third base in 1958 and remained there for the rest of his career.

SEPTEMBER 11   The Cardinals trounce the Phillies 14–6 at Busch Stadium.

SEPTEMBER 15   The Cardinals make the pennant race interesting with a 9–6 and 11–3 sweep of the Pirates in Pittsburgh. The victories placed the Cards 2½ games behind the Braves, but St. Louis lost 7 of its last 10 games.

SEPTEMBER 17   A seven-run seventh inning featuring an Irv Noren pinch-hit triple with the bases loaded leads to a 12–5 win over the Dodgers at Busch Stadium.

SEPTEMBER 20   A two-run homer by Joe Cunningham in the tenth inning beats the Reds 7–5 in Cincinnati. Cunningham entered the game as a pinch hitter in the eighth.

SEPTEMBER 21   Three days before President Eisenhower sends federal troops to Little Rock, Arkansas, to integrate Central High School, Roy McMillan of the Reds hits a tenth-inning, two-run homer off his landlord, Herm Wehmeier, to beat the Cardinals 9–8 at Crosley Field. McMillan rented Wehmeier's Cincinnati home during the baseball season. To make matters more embarrassing for Wehmeier, it was the only homer McMillan hit all season.

On the same day, the Cardinals sold Hoyt Wilhelm to the Indians. Wilhelm was 34 years old and had a 4.25 ERA in 40 relief appearances in 1957, but the Cardinals made a huge mistake by letting him go. Despite his age, Wilhelm used his dancing knuckleball to become one of the top relievers of the 1960s and pitched his last game in 1972 at the age of 49.

NOVEMBER 12   Frank Lane resigns as general manager of the Cardinals and immediately takes a position as general manager of the Indians. Bing Devine replaced Lane in the Cardinals organization.

Lane had upset August Busch during the 1956 season with several trades of fan favorites that failed to significantly improve the club. Lane had also tried to deal Stan Musial and Ken Boyer before Busch put a stop to it. The Cardinals owner believed that Lane was making trades just to make trades. Busch and Lane had incompatible visions of the future. Lane believed in the quick fix with rapid-fire trades. Busch wanted a more patient approach by building through the farm system and was upset over Lane deals that included young players such as Luis Arroyo, Bill Virdon, and Jackie Brandt in exchange for veterans past their prime. At a February 1957 dinner of the Knights of Cauliflower Ear, a St. Louis sportsmen's group, Busch said, "I expect the Cardinals to come close to winning a pennant in 1957, and 1958 is going to have to be a sure thing or Frank Lane will be out on his ass. I mean it." Publicly, Lane dismissed the remark as a joke. Privately, he knew Busch was serious. Lane spent the season looking for other options, and when he had an opportunity to take a job with the Indians, Lane submitted his resignation. Bing Devine replaced Lane as the Cardinals general manager. Devine had been in the Cardinals organization for 18 years, working his way up the ladder. He started as a publicity man in the front office and later ran minor league teams throughout the Cardinals farm system. At the time of his promotion to general manager, Devine was Lane's executive assistant.

DECEMBER 5   The Cardinals trade Willard Schmidt, Marty Kutyna, and Ted Wieand to the Reds for Curt Flood and Joe Taylor.

This proved to be one of the greatest trades in Cardinals history. In exchange for three pitchers of little or no value, the Cardinals acquired Flood, who played center field for the club for 12 seasons and in three World Series. With 1,738 games as a Cardinal, Flood ranks sixth on the club's all-time list behind Hall of Famers Stan Musial, Lou Brock, Ozzie Smith, Enos Slaughter, and Red Schoendienst. Flood had 845 runs, 1,853 hits, 271 doubles, and 633 RBIs. Beginning in 1963, he won seven straight Gold Gloves.

1958

Season in a Sentence

Optimism is high heading into the season after a second-place finish in 1957, but the Cards lose 14 of their first 17 games and finish last in the league in runs scored.

Finish • Won • Lost • Pct • GB

Fifth (tie) 72   82   .468 20.0

Managers

Fred Hutchinson (69–75) and Stan Hack (3–7)

Stats

Stats	Cards	NL	Rank
Batting Avg:	.261	.262	6
On-Base Pct:	.331	.331	5
Slugging Pct:	.380	.405	8
Home Runs:	111		8
Stolen Bases:	44		5
ERA:	4.12	3.95	5
Fielding Avg:	.974	.977	8
Runs Scored:	619		8
Runs Allowed:	704		5

Starting Lineup

Hal Smith, c
Stan Musial, 1b
Don Blasingame, 2b
Ken Boyer, 3b
Eddie Kasko, ss
Wally Moon, lf-rf
Curt Flood, cf
Gene Green, rf-c
Joe Cunningham, 1b-rf-lf
Del Ennis, lf
Gene Freese, ss-2b
Irv Noren, lf
Hobie Landrith, c

Pitchers

Sam Jones, sp
Vinegar Bend Mizell, sp
Lindy McDaniel, sp-rp
Larry Jackson, rp-sp
Jim Brosnan, rp-sp
Phil Paine, rp
Billy Muffett, rp
Bob Mabe, rp-sp

Attendance

1,063,730 (fifth in NL)

Club Leaders

Batting Avg:	Musial	.337
On-Base Pct:	Musial	.423
Slugging Pct:	Musial	.528
Home Runs:	Boyer	23
RBIs:	Boyer	90
Runs:	Boyer	101
Stolen Bases:	Blasingame	20
Wins:	Jones	14
Strikeouts:	Jones	225
ERA:	Jones	2.88
Saves:	Jackson	8

JANUARY 29   Stan Musial signs a contract making him the second player in baseball history to earn $100,000 in a season. The first was Ted Williams.

APRIL 2   The Cardinals trade Jim King to the Giants for Ray Katt.

APRIL 15   Three days after the St. Louis Hawks win the NBA championship in a six-game series over the Boston Celtics, the Cubs defeat the Cardinals 4–0 before 26,246 in the season opener at Busch Stadium. The Cards stranded 14 runners as four Cubs pitchers combined on the shutout.

The Cardinals started the season 0–4 and were 3–14 on May 8. By June 26, the Cards had a 34–29 record with a run of 31 victories in 46 games and were 1½ games out of first place. But after another slide, the club was in last place by August 2. A subsequent surge put the Cardinals into a tie for fifth by season's end.

APRIL 22   The Cardinals play the Giants in San Francisco for the first time and win 7–5 at Seals Stadium.

Before Candlestick Park opened in 1960, the Giants played at Seals Stadium, a former minor league facility seating 23,000.

APRIL 25   The Cardinals play the Dodgers in Los Angeles for the first time and lose 5–3 at Memorial Stadium.

From 1958 through 1961, the Dodgers played at Memorial Coliseum. Built for football and track, the 105,000-seat Coliseum had little to recommend it for baseball. The left-field foul line was only 251 feet long, topped by a 40-foot-high screen.

MAY 11   Coming from behind in the ninth inning of each game, the Cardinals sweep a doubleheader 8–7 and 6–5 against the Cubs in Chicago at Busch Stadium. Stan Musial collected four hits in the twin bill to raise his career total to 2,998. In the opener, Cardinal pitchers issued 14 walks, and the club trailed 7–6 into the last of the ninth before scoring twice to win. Irv Noren's walk-off single decided the contest. In the second fray, Chicago was in front 5–3 in the ninth. With two outs and the bases loaded, Hobie Landrith singled in two runs, and the winning tally crossed the plate when Bobby Thomson fumbled the hit in center field. The Cardinals tied a major league record for most pinch hitters used in a doubleheader with 10.

MAY 12   Stan Musial doubles in the first inning for his 2,999th career hit but was stopped in three subsequent at-bats in his quest for number 3,000. The Cardinals won the game against the Cubs in Chicago 6–4.

Al Fenn/Time & Life Pictures/Getty Images

May 13, 1958: Stan Musial notches his 3,000th career hit, a double, against the Cubs at Wrigley Field.

MAY 13	Stan Musial collects his 3,000th career hit during a 5–3 win over the Cubs at Wrigley Field. Musial was left out of the starting lineup so that he could accomplish the historic feat in front of the hometown fans in St. Louis. However, with the Cubs leading 3–1 and a runner on second in the sixth inning, Fred Hutchinson called on Musial as a pinch hitter. Musial responded with a run-scoring double off Moe Drabowsky. The umpires halted the game to award the ball to Musial, who was lifted for a pinch runner.

On the same day, the Cardinals sold Herm Wehmeier to the Tigers.

MAY 14   Stan Musial, honored in pregame ceremonies for his 3,000th hit, dramatically smashes a home run in the first inning and later adds a single as the Cardinals win 3–2 over the Giants at Busch Stadium.

Musial entered the 1958 season needing 43 hits to reach number 3,000 and got there in a hurry with 46 hits in his first 92 at-bats. He finished the season with a .337 average and 17 homers.

MAY 17   The Cardinals score seven runs in the fourth inning of a 10–1 win over the Dodgers at Busch Stadium.

MAY 18   Ken Boyer hits a grand slam off Fred Kipp in the first inning of a 6–5 win during the first game of a doubleheader at Busch Stadium. Los Angeles won the second game 4–0.

Boyer hit .307 with 23 homers, 90 RBIs, and 101 runs scored in 1958.

MAY 20   The Cardinals trade Al Dark to the Cubs for Jim Brosnan.

MAY 25   In his Cardinal debut, pitcher Jim Brosnan is literally hit three times during a 4–2 win over the Reds in his hometown of Cincinnati. In the third inning, a Jerry Lynch line drive struck his glove and bare hand, though he knocked down the ball and threw Lynch out at first. In the top of the sixth, as a base runner on second, Brosnan got picked off the base as Reds second baseman Johnny Temple fell on top of him. In the bottom half of the sixth, Gus Bell's hot liner drilled Brosnan in the groin. He finished out of the inning, but the last injury prevented him from continuing.

MAY 30   Playing as a catcher for the first time in the major leagues, Gene Green has his ups and downs during a 10-inning, 7–6 win over the Giants in the first game of a doubleheader at Busch Stadium. Green made two throwing errors trying to nab Willie Mays on stolen-base attempts. Shifted to right field late in the game, Green started the tenth-inning rally with a single. The Cardinals completed the sweep with an 8–1 victory in the nightcap.

MAY 31   The Cardinals wipe out a seven-run deficit to defeat the Giants 10–9 in 12 innings at Busch Stadium. Down 8–1, the Cards scored three runs in the fifth, two in the sixth, and three in the seventh to take a 9–8 lead. After letting San Francisco tie the contest in the eighth, the Cards won on Ken Boyer's walk-off homer.

JUNE 6   Sam Jones strikes out 12 batters in a 3–1 win over the Phillies at Busch Stadium.

JUNE 11   Ken Boyer smashes a walk-off homer in the twelfth inning to beat the Reds 3–2 at Busch Stadium.

JUNE 14	The Cardinals trade Joe McClain to the Yankees for Sal Maglie.
JUNE 15	The Cardinals send Dick Schofield and cash to the Pirates for Gene Freese and Johnny O'Brien.
JUNE 16	Down 3–1 heading into the ninth inning, the Cardinals emerge with an 11-inning, 6–5 victory over the Reds in Cincinnati. Joe Cunningham's two-run pinch-single in the ninth inning sent the game into extra innings. Cunningham remained in the game and singled in the eleventh to start a three-run rally. The Cards held off a two-run Cincinnati outburst in the bottom half to win the game.
JUNE 17	Joe Cunningham's bases-loaded triple highlights a six-run Cardinal rally in the ninth inning and helps defeat the Reds 10–4 in Cincinnati.
JUNE 21	Vinegar Bend Mizell holds the Braves hitless until Felix Mantilla homers with one out in the seventh before settling for a four-hit, 3–1 win at Milwaukee.
JUNE 24	Curt Flood's two-run homer in the ninth inning beats the Pirates 2–1 in Pittsburgh.
JUNE 28	Gene Green hits a grand slam off Curt Simmons in the first inning of an 8–1 win over the Phillies in Philadelphia.
JUNE 29	Left fielder Del Ennis ties a major league record with two assists in an inning on throws to second and third base in the eighth, but the Cards lose 5–4 in 13 innings in the first game of a doubleheader in Philadelphia. St. Louis won the second tilt, which took a month to complete. The game was suspended with the Cardinals leading 4–2 in the eighth because of a Pennsylvania law stipulating that contests must end by 7 PM. It was finished on July 29 with the Cardinals the victors, 4–3.
JULY 3	The Cardinals are the first team east of the Rockies to televise a game to local fans from the West Coast with a 4–2 win over the Giants at San Francisco.
JULY 5	The Cardinals' Larry Jackson walks in the winning run to hand the Giants a 5–4 win in San Francisco. Willie Kirkland took a 3–2 pitch with two outs and the bases loaded in the ninth inning.
JULY 6	In a situation eerily similar to the game the previous day, Larry Jackson is the goat again when he hits the Giants' Jim Davenport with a pitch with the bases loaded and two outs in the ninth. The hit batsman was the deciding tally in the Cards' 4–3 defeat in San Francisco.
JULY 9	The Cardinals purchase Chuck Stobbs from the Senators.
JULY 16	Del Ennis collects his 2,000th career hit during a 6–5 loss to the Braves at Busch Stadium. The milestone hit was a double off Warren Spahn. Ken Boyer hit a grand slam off Spahn during the third inning.
JULY 19	Ken Boyer leads off the tenth inning with a homer off Alex Kellner to beat the Reds 1–0 in Cincinnati, ending the Cardinals' seven-game losing streak. Larry Jackson pitched the complete-game shutout.

Jackson played eight seasons for the Cardinals (1955–62) and had a record of 101–86. The only other Cardinal hurlers with at least 100 wins since 1950 are Bob Gibson and Matt Morris. Jackson pitched in 330 games (209 of them starts) for the Cardinals in addition to his 1,672¹/₃ innings, 899 strikeouts, and 15 shutouts.

JULY 20   Sam Jones strikes out 12 batters to defeat the Reds 2–1 in Cincinnati.

JULY 21   Curt Flood hits a homer in the fourteenth inning to down the Braves 5–4 in Milwaukee.

AUGUST 4   Larry Jackson fans 12 during a 3–2 win over the Dodgers at Busch Stadium.

AUGUST 5   The Cardinals score seven runs in the fourth inning in a 13–3 trouncing of the Dodgers at Busch Stadium. The Cards collected 21 hits in the contest.

AUGUST 6   Trailing 5–0 in the second inning, the Cardinals rally to defeat the Giants 8–7 at Busch Stadium.

AUGUST 7   The Cardinals roll over the Giants 12–1 at Busch Stadium.

AUGUST 8   Del Ennis hits a grand slam off Dick Drott in the fifth inning of a 6–3 win over the Cubs in Chicago.

AUGUST 9   Curt Flood's homer in the tenth inning downs the Cubs 3–2 in Chicago.

AUGUST 18   Curt Flood and Gene Freese lead off the first inning with back-to-back homers off Sandy Koufax en route to a 12–7 Cardinal win over the Dodgers in the first game of a doubleheader at Memorial Coliseum. Los Angeles won the second game 9–3.

AUGUST 19   Former stars of the Cardinals and Browns are introduced to the crowd prior to a game against the Phillies at Busch Stadium. Among those honored were Hall of Famers Dizzy Dean, Rogers Hornsby, Frankie Frisch, Jesse Haines, and George Sisler. Future Hall of Famer Stan Musial smashed a homer and two singles in the 5–4 victory.

AUGUST 22   Sam Jones strikes out 14 batters and carries a no-hitter into the eighth inning in a 9–1 win over the Phillies at Busch Stadium. The first of three Philadelphia hits was a homer by Rip Repulski.

Jones became the first Cardinal pitcher to strike out at least 200 batters in a season by fanning 225 in 250 innings in 1958.

AUGUST 24   The Cardinals score five runs in the eighth inning to defeat the Pirates 12–8 in the second game of a doubleheader at Busch Stadium. Pittsburgh won the opener 6–4.

AUGUST 30   Sam Jones strikes out 13 batters but loses 3–1 in 10 innings to the Cubs at Busch Stadium.

SEPTEMBER 1   Vinegar Bend Mizell allows nine walks, four hits, and five stolen bases and strikes out only one batter, but he still beats the Reds 1–0 in the first game of a doubleheader at Busch Stadium. The game's only run scored on a Wally Moon single in the second inning. Cincinnati won the nightcap 9–3.

SEPTEMBER 9   Eddie Kasko hits a grand slam off Bill Henry in the fourth inning of an 8–7 win over the Cubs at Busch Stadium.

SEPTEMBER 17   With the club holding a disappointing 69–75 record, the Cardinals fire Fred Hutchinson as manager. Coach Stan Hack was named interim manager for the final 10 games of the season.

Hutchinson became manager of the Reds in July 1959 and led the club to a pennant in 1961. He was still the skipper in Cincinnati when he was diagnosed with cancer in January 1964. Hutch died the following November at the age of 45.

SEPTEMBER 23   Sam Jones is four outs from a no-hitter when Jim Gilliam of the Dodgers singles with two gone in the eighth. Jones surrendered two more hits before yielding to Jim Brosnan with no outs in the ninth but was the winning pitcher in a 5–1 decision in Los Angeles.

SEPTEMBER 29   The Cardinals trade Gene Freese to the Phillies for Solly Hemus.

The Cards made the deal to bring Hemus back to St. Louis as manager of the club. He played in St. Louis from 1949 through 1956 and was 35 years old when hired as manager. Hemus brought the same fire and intensity he had as a player to his role as manager. It earned him the nickname Mighty Mouse and worked in 1960 when the Cardinals finished a strong third with an 86–68 record. But overall he was 190–192 and was fired in July 1961.

OCTOBER 3   The Cardinals trade Del Ennis, Eddie Kasko, and Bob Mabe to the Reds for George Crowe, Alex Kellner, and Alex Grammas.

OCTOBER 8   The Cardinals trade Hobie Landrith, Billy Muffett, and Benny Valenzuela to the Giants for Ernie Broglio and Marv Grissom.

The Cards gave up little of value to obtain Broglio, who posted a 70–55 record and 18 shutouts over six seasons in St. Louis. He was 21–9 in 1960 and 18–8 in 1963. Despite some excellent pitching while with the Cardinals, Broglio will always be linked with a June 15, 1964, trade in which the Cards sent him to Chicago as part of a package deal that brought the Cubs' Lou Brock to St. Louis.

OCTOBER 9   The Cardinals leave St. Louis for a trip to Japan.

On the way, the Cards played games in Hawaii, Guam, the Philippines, Okinawa, and South Korea before arriving in Japan on October 17. The club returned to St. Louis on November 16.

DECEMBER 4   The Cardinals trade Wally Moon and Phil Paine to the Dodgers for Gino Cimoli.

Moon gave the Cardinals four solid seasons but was traded after hitting only .238 in 1958. He rebounded to give the Dodgers three more good years, batting .309 with 49 homers from 1959 through 1961, while the Cards sent Cimoli to the Pirates after one subpar season.

1959

Season in a Sentence

The Cardinals lose 16 of their first 21 games under new manager Solly Hemus and finish the year with a losing season for the second year in a row.

Finish • Won • Lost • Pct • GB

Seventh   71   83   .461   16.0

Manager

Solly Hemus

Stats	Cards	• NL •	Rank
Batting Avg:	.269	.260	2
On-Base Pct:	.333	.328	3
Slugging Pct:	.400	.400	4
Home Runs:	118		6
Stolen Bases:	65		3 (tie)
ERA:	4.34	3.95	8
Fielding Avg:	.975	.977	5
Runs Scored:	641		7
Runs Allowed:	725		6 (tie)

Starting Lineup

Hal Smith, c
Stan Musial, 1b
Don Blasingame, 2b
Ken Boyer, 3b
Alex Grammas, ss
Bill White, lf-1b
Gino Cimoli, cf-lf-rf
Joe Cunningham, rf
Curt Flood, cf
Gene Oliver, lf

Pitchers

Larry Jackson, sp
Vinegar Bend Mizell, sp
Ernie Broglio, sp
Lindy McDaniel, sp
Marshall Bridges, rp
Gary Blaylock, rp-sp

Attendance

929,953 (fifth in NL)

Club Leaders

Batting Avg:	Cunningham	.345
On-Base Pct:	Cunningham	.453
Slugging Pct:	Boyer	.508
Home Runs:	Boyer	28
RBIs:	Boyer	94
Runs:	Blasingame	90
Stolen Bases:	Blasingame	15
	White	15
Wins:	Jackson	14
	McDaniel	14
Strikeouts:	Jackson	145
ERA:	Jackson	3.30
Saves:	McDaniel	15

MARCH 25   Two months after Alaska becomes the 49th state, the Cardinals trade Sam Jones and Don Choate to the Giants for Bill White and Ray Jablonski.

> *The spring training deal was a short-term flop but paid huge dividends in the long run. In 1959, Jones had a record of 21–15 and a league-leading 2.83 ERA for the Giants, followed by an 18–14 mark in 1960. But Jones went into a quick decline after 1960 while White established himself as one of the best first basemen in baseball. He was named to five All-Star teams as a Cardinal and hit 140 homers and drove in 631 runs for the club. In addition to his batting credentials, White won seven Gold Gloves. After his playing career ended, he was a radio announcer for the Yankees for 17 seasons beginning in 1971. White was the first African American to broadcast games for a major league club. In 1989, he became president of the National League and broke new ground as the first African American to be named to that post in either league.*

APRIL 10   The Cardinals open the season with a 6–5 loss to the Giants before 20,998 at Busch Stadium. Jackie Brandt broke the 5–5 tie with a double in the ninth inning off Jim Brosnan. Don Blasingame and Alex Grammas each hit two singles and a double.

APRIL 15   Bob Gibson makes his major league debut during a 5–0 loss to the Dodgers in Los Angeles. He entered the game as a reliever in the seventh inning with the score 3–0 and gave up a homer to Jim Baxes, the first batter he faced. Gibson allowed two runs in two innings.

The Cardinals sent Gibson back to the minors a few days later, but he returned to St. Louis in July. Gibson wore number 58 in 1959. At the start of the 1960 season, he got number 31, but Gibson went back to the minors again. By the time his name appeared on the Cardinals' roster before the 1960 campaign ended, Curt Simmons had Gibson's number 31. The Cards gave Gibson number 45, which he wore for the remainder of his career. Number 45 was retired in 1975, the last year of Gibson's playing career. The last Cardinal prior to Gibson to wear number 45 in a regular-season game was Dean Stone in 1959.

APRIL 17   Solly Hemus sets a National League record (since tied) by using 25 players in a nine-inning game, but the Cardinals lose 7–5 to the Dodgers in Los Angeles.

APRIL 18   Stan Musial's single off Johnny Antonelli in the seventh inning is the lone Cardinals hit in an 8–1 loss to the Giants in San Francisco.

APRIL 21   Stan Musial breaks up his second no-hitter in four days when his double in the seventh inning off Glenn Hobbie is the only Cardinal hit in a 1–0 loss to the Cubs in Chicago.

MAY 5   The Phillies stun the Cardinals with five runs in the ninth inning to win 8–7 in Philadelphia.

The defeat gave the Cards a 5–16 record, setting the stage for a difficult year under new manager Solly Hemus. Part of the problem was a poorly constructed roster. The club had no outfielders who were above average both offensively and defensively, and four players—Stan Musial, Bill White, Joe Cunningham, and George Crowe—whose best position was first base. White and Cunningham played much of the season out of position in the outfield.

MAY 7   Stan Musial collects his 400th career homer with a walk-off blast off Don Elston in the ninth inning to beat the Cubs 4–3 at Busch Stadium.

At the age of 38, Musial spent much of the season on the bench as Solly Hemus wanted to give younger players such as Curt Flood, Bill White, and Gene Oliver a chance to get into the lineup. Musial had only 341 at-bats in 1959 and hit .255 with 14 home runs.

MAY 19   The Cardinals trade Irv Noren to the Cubs for Charlie King.

JUNE 8   The Cardinals trade Jim Brosnan to the Reds for Hal Jeffcoat.

The deal worked out horribly for the Cardinals. Jeffcoat never won another game while Brosnan won 29 games and saved 43 over the next four seasons. Club officials in both St. Louis and Cincinnati were unaware that Brosnan was writing an autobiographical diary of the 1959 campaign, titled The Long Season, *that became a best-seller in 1960. He followed with a similar book about the 1961 season called* The Pennant Race. *The books were the first of the diary genre that presented an inside look at Major League Baseball from a player's perspective.*

MAY 9   The Cardinals score seven runs in the eighth inning, highlighted by Ken Boyer's grand slam off Don Elston, and they defeat the Cubs at Busch Stadium. Hal Smith hit two homers on a difficult day. That morning he took his four-year daughter to the hospital to treat her kidney infection. When he learned she was out of danger, Smith rushed to the ballpark and arrived just before game time.

Boyer batted .309 with 28 homers and 94 RBIs in 1959.

MAY 10   Lindy McDaniel and Cubs pitcher Elmer Singleton figure in the decision in both ends of a doubleheader at Busch Stadium, each earning a win and a loss. The Cubs won the opener 10–9 in 11 innings. The Cards won the second tilt 8–7 with two runs in the ninth. Gino Cimoli doubled in the tying run and scored on a single by Curt Flood.

MAY 12   Gary Blaylock hits his first career homer and earns his first victory as a pitcher in a 7–4 decision over the Reds at Busch Stadium.

MAY 20   The Cardinals wallop the Pirates 11–1 at Busch Stadium.

 Two Balls in Play

One of the daffiest situations ever recorded in Cardinals history took place on June 30, 1959, when two balls were in play at the same time during a game against the Cubs at Wrigley Field. With the Cards batting in the fourth inning, the count was 3–1 on Stan Musial with Bob Anderson pitching. Anderson's next pitch sailed past Cubs catcher Sammy Taylor, entitling Musial to first base on the walk. Taylor claimed the ball hit Musial's bat and therefore was foul and failed to pursue the ball as it rolled back to the screen. Taylor began arguing with home plate umpire Vic Delmore, and Chicago manager Bob Scheffing joined Taylor in the discussion. Musial took first base and headed for second.

Third baseman Al Dark realized the ball was in play and ran full speed toward the backstop to get the ball. With Dark charging in, the batboy tossed the ball to field announcer Pat Pieper, who acted as though it were a hot potato and dropped it. Dark reached down, grabbed the ball, and threw it to shortstop Ernie Banks in an attempt to retire Musial on the base paths.

Meanwhile, Delmore gave Taylor a new ball as the two continued to argue. Anderson, who was also engaged in the debate with the umpire, saw Musial race for second. Anderson grabbed the ball out of Taylor's hand and threw it to second at almost the precise moment that Dark's throw was headed in the same direction.

Banks fielded Dark's throw on one hop. Anderson's throw sailed into center field. While all this was happening, Musial slid safely into second. Musial saw Anderson's throw head into the outfield and started for third. But he hadn't taken more than two or three steps past second when Banks tagged him. Bobby Thomson retrieved the second ball and lobbed it toward the Cubs dugout.

The umpires huddled for 10 minutes and ruled that Musial should return to first base. Scheffing protested, and the umps conferred again, this time calling Musial out. Cardinal manager Solly Hemus objected immediately, claiming interference by the batboy nullified the play. Hemus intended to file a formal protest with the National League office, but he never sent it because the Cardinals won 4–1.

MAY 22   The Cardinals outlast the Cubs 3–1 in 14 innings in Chicago. Jim Brosnan pitched six shutout innings, allowing only one hit, and started the game-winning rally with a bunt single.

JUNE 17   The Cardinals honor the Gas House Gang on the field before a 10–4 win over the Phillies at Busch Stadium. Fifteen players attended the reunion, held 25 years after the 1934 World Championship, including Dizzy and Paul Dean, Jesse Haines, Frankie Frisch, Pepper Martin, and Joe Medwick.

JUNE 21   Four straight doubles by Alex Grammas, Marshall Bridges, Don Blasingame, and Gino Cimoli highlight the third inning, but the Cardinals lose 10–8 in the second game of a doubleheader against the Pirates at Busch Stadium. The Cards won the first game 5–1.

JUNE 27   Ernie Broglio pitches a two-hitter to defeat the Reds 5–0 at Crosley Field. The only Cincinnati hits were singles by Whitey Lockman in the first inning and Ed Bailey in the fifth.

JUNE 28   After scoring seven runs in the first inning, the Cardinals battle to a 9–7 win over the Reds in the first game of a doubleheader at Crosley Field. The Cards nearly blew another big lead before winning the second tilt 11–8. St. Louis was ahead 9–0 when Cincinnati scored eight times in the seventh inning.

JULY 2   Solly Hemus is ejected from a 4–0 loss to the Dodgers at Busch Stadium for "repeated bodily contact" with umpire Shag Crawford following an argument over ball and strike calls. While Hemus jawed with Crawford, a fan leaped into the act by jumping onto the field and engaged in a boxing-wrestling match with umpire Bill Jackowski.

        Hemus was fined $250 and suspended for five days by NL president Warren Giles. He was ejected from eight games in 1959.

JULY 5   Bill White hits a grand slam off Jack Sanford in the fifth inning to drive in all four Cardinal runs in a 4–2 triumph over the Giants in the first game of a doubleheader at Busch Stadium. San Francisco won the nightcap by the same 4–2 score.

JULY 30   Making his first major league start, Bob Gibson pitches the Cardinals to a 1–0 win over the Reds in Cincinnati. After doubling, Ken Boyer scored the lone run of the game on a single by Joe Cunningham in the second inning. It was the first of Gibson's 56 career shutouts.

        Cunningham hit .345 with a league-leading .453 on-base percentage in 1959.

AUGUST 6   The Pirates score 10 runs in the ninth inning off Jack Urban and Hal Jeffcoat to cap an 18–2 walloping of the Cardinals at Busch Stadium.

AUGUST 7   A two-run, walk-off homer by Stan Musial in the ninth inning beats the Phillies 3–1 at Busch Stadium.

AUGUST 13   George Crowe hits a pinch-hit grand slam off Roger Craig during a five-run ninth inning, but the Cardinals come up short and lose 7–6 to the Dodgers at Busch Stadium.

Crowe hit 14 career pinch-hit home runs. Like many African Americans of his generation, he was in his 30s before he had an opportunity to play in the majors. An all-around athlete, Crowe played professional basketball for several teams during the 1940s. His brother Ray coached Crispus Attucks High School in Indianapolis to two state basketball championships on a team that included Oscar Robertson. In the 1986 film Hoosiers, *Ray portrayed the coach of the big-city school in the championship game.*

AUGUST 20   The Cardinals sell Ray Jablonski to the Athletics.

AUGUST 22   On the day after Hawaii becomes the 50th state in the Union, the Reds' Frank Robinson hits three homers off Cardinal pitchers in an 11–4 Cincinnati win at Crosley Field.

AUGUST 28   Joe Cunningham's two-out, two-run, walk-off double in the ninth inning beats the Reds 3–2 at Busch Stadium.

SEPTEMBER 1   Larry Jackson pitches a two-hitter to defeat the Dodgers 5–0 at Memorial Coliseum. The only Los Angeles hits were a single by Maury Wills and a double by Duke Snider in the seventh.

SEPTEMBER 6   Larry Jackson pitches the Cardinals to a 1–0 victory over the Giants in San Francisco. The lone run scored on a squeeze bunt by Alex Grammas in the eighth inning.

SEPTEMBER 10   Only 17 years old, Tim McCarver makes his major league debut with a fly-out as a pinch hitter in the ninth inning of a 7–4 loss to the Braves in Milwaukee.

SEPTEMBER 11   Tim McCarver makes his first major league start. The starting pitcher was 20-year-old Bob Miller, who attended Beaumont High School in St. Louis, site of the old Robison Field, where the Cardinals played from 1893 through 1920. The Cards lost 2–1 to the Cubs in Chicago.

Although a month shy of his 18th birthday, McCarver played eight games for the Cardinals in 1959 and even batted in the leadoff spot on occasion. He was signed the previous June out of Christian Brothers High School in Memphis for $75,000. It would be 1963 before McCarver secured a starting job with the Cardinals, but he was named to two All-Star teams and appeared in three World Series before a trade to the Phillies following the 1969 season.

SEPTEMBER 12   Ken Boyer runs his hitting streak to 29 games during a 6–4 win over the Cubs in Chicago.

SEPTEMBER 22   Hal Smith hits a grand slam off Sandy Koufax in the first inning of an 11–10 win over the Dodgers at Busch Stadium.

SEPTEMBER 26   Sam Jones pitches a seven-inning no-hitter to defeat the Cardinals 4–0 at Busch Stadium. The game was stopped at the conclusion of the seventh by rain.

SEPTEMBER 27   The Cardinals close out the season by sweeping the Giants 2–1 and 14–8 at Busch Stadium.

DECEMBER 2   The Cardinals trade Gene Green to the Orioles for Bob Nieman.

DECEMBER 15   The Cardinals trade Don Blasingame to the Giants for Leon Wagner and Daryl Spencer.

DECEMBER 21   The Cardinals trade Gino Cimoli and Tom Cheney to the Pirates for Ron Kline.

THE STATE OF THE CARDINALS

The Cardinals won three National League pennants and two World Championships during the 1960s. After a mediocre start to the decade, the Cards finished a strong second in 1963 before winning it all in 1964 with a dramatic turnaround during the final two weeks of the season to overtake the Phillies, followed by a seven-game World Series victory over the Yankees. After rebuilding seasons, the Cards won another World Series in 1967 and a second consecutive NL pennant in 1968. Overall, the club was 884–718 during the 1960s, a winning percentage of .552. The only big-league clubs with more wins were the Orioles (911–698), Giants (902–704), and Yankees (887–720). Other NL championships went to the Pirates (1960), Reds (1961), Giants (1962), Dodgers (1963, 1965, and 1966), and Mets (1969).

THE BEST TEAM

The 1967 Cardinals were 101–60 and won the World Championship. The .627 winning percentage was the best posted by a St. Louis club between 1946 and 2004.

THE WORST TEAM

After winning the 1964 World Championship, the 1965 club sank to seventh place with a record of 80–81.

THE BEST MOMENT

Trailing by 7½ games with two weeks left in the 1964 season, the Cardinals rallied to win the NL pennant on the final day.

THE WORST MOMENT

After taking a three-games-to-one lead in the 1968 World Series and a 3–0 lead in Game Five, the Cardinals wind up losing to the Tigers in seven games.

THE ALL-DECADE TEAM • YEARS W/CARDS

Tim McCarver, c	1959–61, 1963–69, 1973–74
Bill White, 1b	1959–65, 1969
Julian Javier, 2b	1960–71
Ken Boyer, 3b	1955–65
Dick Groat, ss	1963–65
Lou Brock, lf	1964–79
Curt Flood, cf	1958–69
Mike Shannon, rf	1962–70
Bob Gibson, p	1959–75
Curt Simmons, p	1960–66
Steve Carlton, p	1965–71
Ernie Broglio, p	1959–64

Other outstanding Cardinals of the 1960s included first baseman Orlando Cepeda (1966–68), shortstop Dal Maxvill (1962–72), outfielder Stan Musial (1941–44, 1946–63), and pitchers Lindy McDaniel (1955–62), Ray Washburn (1961–69), Nelson Briles (1965–70), Ray Sadecki (1960–66, 1975), and Larry Jackson (1955–62). Hall of Famers include Musial, Brock, Gibson, Carlton, and Cepeda. Underrated Boyer, McCarver, and Groat each deserve Hall of Fame consideration.

THE DECADE LEADERS

Batting Avg:	Flood	.297
On-Base Pct:	Boyer	.365
Slugging Pct:	Boyer	.481
Home Runs:	Boyer	141
RBIs:	Boyer	595
Runs:	Flood	771
Stolen Bases:	Brock	337
Wins:	Gibson	164
Strikeouts:	Gibson	2,071
ERA:	Gibson	2.74
Saves:	Hoerner	60

THE HOME FIELD

Professional baseball was played at the corner of Grand and Dodier beginning in 1875. The last version of Sportsman's Park, built in 1909 and expanded in 1925, served as the home of the Browns from 1909 through 1953 and the Cardinals from 1920 to 1966. The ballpark was renamed Busch Stadium in 1953 and hosted its final game on May 8, 1966. Four days later, Busch Memorial Stadium opened downtown. One of many multipurpose stadiums built during the 1960s and early 1970s, it was part of a major renewal project in what had been a shoddy and underdeveloped area.

THE GAME YOU WISH YOU HAD SEEN

There were many great games in St. Louis during the 1960s. There was the pennant-winning victory on the final day in 1964, the opening of the new Busch Stadium in 1966, and Bob Gibson's 17 strikeouts in the first game of the 1968 World Series. But nothing tops watching the home club taking the seventh game of a World Series. On October 15, 1964, the Cardinals did just that with a 7–5 win over the

THE WAY THE GAME WAS PLAYED

Baseball was played in several new cities and ballparks in the 1960s. Candlestick Park, Dodger Stadium, Shea Stadium, the Astrodome, Atlanta–Fulton County Stadium, and Busch Memorial Stadium were among the facilities to open. Expansion and franchise shifts brought National League baseball back to New York and major league ball to Houston, Atlanta, San Diego, and Montreal for the first time. Expansion to 12 teams in 1969 brought divisional play and a playoff between division champions to determine who would go on to the World Series. The Astrodome opened in 1965 and brought two more innovations: indoor baseball and artificial turf. In the wake of a strike zone expansion in 1963, offense declined in the 1960s until the owners lowered the mound for the 1969 season. The league ERA dipped to 2.99 in 1968, the first time since 1919 it had been below 3.00.

THE MANAGEMENT

August Busch, who bought the club in 1953, continued to run the operation throughout the successful 1960s. General managers were Bing Devine (1958–64), Bob Howsam (1964–67), Stan Musial (1967), and Devine again (1967–78). Field managers were Solly Hemus (1959–61), Johnny Keane (1961–64), and Red Schoendienst (1965–76).

THE BEST PLAYER MOVE

In the best trade in club history, the Cardinals acquired Lou Brock on June 15, 1964, along with Jack Spring and Paul Toth in a trade with the Cubs for Ernie Broglio, Bobby Shantz, and Doug Clemens.

THE WORST PLAYER MOVE

The Cardinals let Mike Cuellar go to the Astros on June 15, 1965, along with Ron Taylor for Hal Woodeshick and Chuck Taylor.

1960s

1960

Season in a Sentence

A summer surge puts the Cardinals just three games out of first place in mid-August on the way to a surprising third-place finish.

Finish • Won • Lost • Pct • GB

Third   86   68   .558   9.0

Manager

Solly Hemus

Stats

Stats	Cards	NL	Rank
Batting Avg:	.254	.255	5
On-Base Pct:	.323	.322	4
Slugging Pct:	.393	.388	3
Home Runs:	138		3
Stolen Bases:	48		6
ERA:	3.64	3.76	4
Fielding Avg:	.976	.977	6
Runs Scored:	639		6
Runs Allowed:	616		3

Starting Lineup

Hal Smith, c
Bill White, 1b
Julian Javier, 2b
Ken Boyer, 3b
Daryl Spencer, ss
Stan Musial, lf
Curt Flood, cf
Joe Cunningham, rf
Walt Moryn, rf-lf
Alex Grammas, ss-2b
Bob Nieman, lf
Carl Sawatski, c

Pitchers

Ernie Broglio, sp-rp
Larry Jackson, sp
Ray Sadecki, sp
Curt Simmons, sp
Ron Kline, sp-rp
Lindy McDaniel, rp
Bob Gibson, rp-sp

Attendance

1,096,632 (fourth in NL)

Club Leaders

Batting Avg:	Boyer	.304
On-Base Pct:	Spencer	.385
Slugging Pct:	Boyer	.562
Home Runs:	Boyer	32
RBIs:	Boyer	97
Runs:	Boyer	95
Stolen Bases:	Javier	19
Wins:	Broglio	21
Strikeouts:	Broglio	189
ERA:	Broglio	2.74
Saves:	McDaniel	26

MARCH 13   The National Football League votes to allow the transfer of the Chicago Cardinals to St. Louis.

The football Cardinals entered into an agreement to rent Busch Stadium from the baseball Cardinals. The NFL Cardinals played at Busch Stadium, despite its limited capacity of 32,500, until the new Busch Memorial Stadium opened in 1966. The football Cardinals remained in St. Louis until 1988, when owner Bill Bidwell relocated the franchise to Phoenix.

APRIL 12   The Cardinals play the first-ever game at Candlestick Park in San Francisco, home of the Giants from 1960 through 1999, and lose 3–1. The only St. Louis run scored on a home run by Leon Wagner, who was making his debut with the Cardinals. Vice President Richard Nixon was on hand for the opening ceremonies of the new ballpark and posed with Stan Musial in the dugout before the game.

Wagner also homered in his second game with the Cardinals, and it was the club's lone run in a 6–1 loss to the Giants on April 13. He batted .225 with five homers in 87 games during his only season with the Cardinals, however.

APRIL 13   At owner August Busch's urging, stockholders of Anheuser-Busch, Inc., approve the brewer's $5 million investment in a proposed downtown stadium (see December 17, 1960). The motion was carried by a 7–1 margin. The dissenting block was led by former Cardinals owner Fred Saigh, who owned about 28,000 shares in the company. Saigh still harbored hopes of building a stadium of his own on land he purchased in 1949 (see May 28, 1949).

APRIL 19   After opening the season with five straight losses, the Cardinals win their first home game of 1960 with a 5–2 decision over the Cubs before 25,888 at Busch Stadium.

APRIL 23   The Cardinals hit two home runs with one ball in the fourth inning of a 9–5 win over the Dodgers at Busch Stadium. Ken Boyer hit a homer into the right-field pavilion that a spectator deflected back into play. The ball was returned to Los Angeles hurler Danny McDevitt, and two batters later, Daryl Spencer launched the same ball against the scoreboard and into the bleachers, where a fan pocketed the ball.

Boyer hit .304 with 32 homers and 97 RBIs in 1960.

APRIL 29   The Cardinals explode for 10 runs in the eighth inning and defeat the Cubs 16–6 at Busch Stadium. The 10 runs scored on five singles, two doubles, a walk, a hit batsman, and a home run, hit by Bill White.

The Cardinals were 51–26 at home in 1950. As a result of losing their first 12 road games, the Cards were 35–42 in away contests.

MAY 5   Following a game against the Phillies, the Cardinals have a rough trip from St. Louis to Cincinnati. First, the bus waiting at Busch Stadium to ferry the team to the St. Louis airport wouldn't start without a push from the Phillies' bus. Then, when the Cardinals' chartered plane landed in Cincinnati, one of its engines caught fire.

MAY 15   The Cardinals are victims of a no-hitter by Don Cardwell in a 4–0 loss to the Cubs in the first game of a doubleheader at Wrigley Field. It was Cardwell's first game as a Cub following a trade with the Phillies two days earlier. It was also the first nine-inning no-hitter against the Cards since 1919. The final out was recorded when Joe Cunningham hit a hump-backed liner on a 3–2 pitch to left field. It looked like a certain hit, but Walt Moryn made a miraculous catch off his shoe tops. The Cards won the first game 6–1, breaking an eight-game losing streak that dropped the club's record to 9–15.

For the third straight season, the Cardinals were plagued by a slow start. The 1958 and 1959 clubs finished with losing records. The 1960 team overcame the early setbacks to pull within sight of first place by August.

MAY 20   The Cardinals sign Curt Simmons following his release by the Phillies.

When signed by the Cardinals, Simmons was 31 years old and had 115 major league wins, but he looked to be finished. He hadn't won a big-league game since September 1958. Once in St. Louis, Simmons turned his career around and was in the Cardinals' starting rotation from 1960 through 1965. He was 15–9 in 1963 and 18–9 in 1964.

MAY 21   The Cardinals score three runs in the ninth inning to defeat the Reds 6–5 at Busch Stadium. A walk-off single by Ken Boyer broke the 5–5 tie.

MAY 22   A walk-off homer by Daryl Spencer in the ninth inning beats the Reds 5–4 in the first game of a doubleheader at Busch Stadium. Cincinnati won the second game 5–3.

MAY 25   A two-run, pinch-hit, walk-off homer by George Crowe beats the Braves 5–3 at Busch Stadium.

MAY 28   The Cardinals trade Vinegar Bend Mizell and Dick Gray to the Pirates for Julian Javier and Ed Bauta.

This was the rare trade that benefited both clubs. Mizell had a 13–5 record over the remainder of the 1960 season, helping the Pirates reach the World Series. Pittsburgh had a better option than Javier at second base in Bill Mazeroski. While Javier wasn't Mazeroski's equal, he was good enough to start at second for the Cardinals immediately upon his arrival in St. Louis and held the job until 1970. He played on two All-Star teams and in three World Series. Javier's 1,547 games at second base for the Cards are the most in club history. Julian's son Stan, named for Stan Musial, was a major league outfielder for nine different teams from 1984 through 2001.

MAY 30   Bill White drives in six runs on two homers and two singles during a 15–3 trouncing of the Dodgers in Los Angeles.

JUNE 11   The Cardinals score three runs in the ninth inning to defeat the Pirates 7–6 at Busch Stadium. The final two runs scored on a walk-off double by Bob Nieman.

JUNE 12   Don Hoak of the Pirates hits a three-run homer that strikes the neon eagle on the Budweiser sign atop the scoreboard. The pitch was the first of Cardinal hurler Cal Browning's major league career. He entered the game as a reliever during a six-run first inning that led to a 15–3 loss in the first game of a doubleheader at Busch Stadium. The Cardinals salvaged a split with a 5–2 victory in the nightcap.

Browning never pitched another big-league game. He faced eight batters and allowed five hits, a walk, and three runs in two-thirds of an inning for a career ERA of 40.50.

JUNE 15   The Cardinals trade Jim McKnight to the Cubs for Walt Moryn.

JUNE 25   Curt Simmons pitches the Cardinals to a 1–0 win over his former Phillies teammates in Philadelphia. Simmons went 8²/₃ innings with a final-out save by Lindy McDaniel. Ken Boyer accounted for the lone run of the game with a home run in the ninth inning off Jim Owens.

McDaniel had an outstanding season out of the bullpen for the Cardinals in 1960. He pitched 116¹/₃ innings in 65 games and had a 12–4 record with 26 saves and a 2.09 ERA. McDaniel's 26 saves shattered the previous club record of 18 set by Al Brazle in 1953. Lindy held the record until Bruce Sutter recorded 36 saves in 1982.

JUNE 26   Hal Smith smacks a three-run homer in the ninth inning to defeat the Phillies 4–3 in the second game of a doubleheader at Philadelphia. Ernie Broglio pitched three innings of relief for the win. In the opener, Broglio was the losing pitcher, also as a reliever, when he surrendered a walk-off homer to Tony Gonzalez in the twelfth inning for a 3–2 defeat.

JULY 1   Ernie Broglio is the winning pitcher in relief in both ends of a doubleheader against the Braves at Busch Stadium. In the first game, the Cardinals led 7–0 after six innings, but the Braves rallied to tie the contest. The Cards won it 8–7 in the tenth on a walk-off single by John Glenn, who subbed for Stan Musial in left field in the ninth inning for his defense. The Redbirds had a 5–0 advantage at the close of the seventh inning of the second tilt, but they allowed Milwaukee to tie with five runs in the top of the eighth before winning 7–5 with two tallies in the bottom half.

Broglio started the 1960 season in the bullpen and worked his way into the starting rotation. He had a 21–9 record and a 2.75 ERA. Broglio was 14–7 in 24 starting assignments and 7–2 in 28 relief appearances.

JULY 12   Cardinal pitcher Bob Duliba suffers five rib fractures, a concussion, lacerations of the head, and contusions of the kidney and right knee in a two-car collision in which three people were killed 11 miles west of Columbia, Missouri. Duliba and his wife were en route to Kansas City to attend the wedding of Cardinal teammate Ray Sadecki. The nine-month-old daughter of a neighbor of Sadecki's, who was riding in Duliba's car, died in the accident. Two passengers in another vehicle, one of them also a nine-month old baby, were killed. Duliba recovered from his injuries and pitched in the majors until 1967.

JULY 13   At Yankee Stadium, Stan Musial hits a pinch-homer off Gerry Staley in the seventh inning of a 6–0 National League win in the second of two All-Star games played in 1960. Ken Boyer added a two-run homer in the ninth facing Gary Bell. (There were two All-Star games played each season from 1959 through 1962.)

Musial holds All-Star Game career records for most games played (24), most total bases (40), extra-base hits (8), and home runs (6). His home runs were in 1948, 1949, 1951, 1955, 1956, and 1960. Other Cardinals with All-Star Game home runs are Frankie Frisch (1933 and 1934), Joe Medwick (1934), Red Schoendienst (1950), Ken Boyer (1960 and 1964), and Reggie Smith (1974).

JULY 15   Ernie Broglio strikes out 15 batters and pitches a one-hitter to defeat the Cubs 6–0 at Busch Stadium. The lone Chicago hit was a single by Ed Bouchee in the second inning.

JULY 23   Walt Moryn clubs a two-run homer in the tenth inning to defeat the Reds 7–5 in Cincinnati.

JULY 29   Ernie Broglio fans 12 during a 3–0 victory over the Phillies at Busch Stadium.

JULY 31   Bill White hits a grand slam off Gene Conley in the fifth inning of a 9–2 win over the Phillies in the first game of a doubleheader at Busch Stadium. White hit a two-run homer in the second contest, a 5–3 Cards win.

AUGUST 3   The Cardinals outslug the Braves 13–8 at Busch Stadium. The Cards broke a 7–7 tie with five runs in the sixth inning.

AUGUST 6   After falling behind 5–0 to the Reds at Busch Stadium, the Cardinals rally with three runs in the fourth inning, one in the fifth, and two in the seventh to win 6–5 at Busch Stadium.

AUGUST 7   Shaking off an 18–4 walloping by the Reds in the first game of a doubleheader at Busch Stadium, the Cardinals come back to take the nightcap 4–2. Members of the 1930 National League Champion Cardinals were introduced between games.

AUGUST 11   Stan Musial's two-run homer in the twelfth inning puts the Cardinals up 3–1 against the Pirates at Pittsburgh. Ernie Broglio entered the twelfth inning having retired the last 20 batters to face him. He gave up a run but emerged with a 3–2, complete-game victory.

AUGUST 12   The Cardinals are just three games out of first place following a 9–2 triumph over the Pirates in Pittsburgh.

The Cardinals entered the five-game series at Forbes Field five games behind the first-place Pirates. The Cards won the first two games but dropped the final three, the start of a six-game losing streak.

AUGUST 14   Bill White hits for the cycle, but the Cardinals lose 9–4 to the Pirates in the first game of a doubleheader at Forbes Field. White hit his homer, triple, double, and single in five at-bats off Vern Law. Pittsburgh also won the second contest, 3–2 in 11 innings.

AUGUST 19   Larry Jackson pitches the Cardinals to a 1–0 win over the Dodgers at Busch Stadium. Bob Gibson, in the game as a pinch runner for Hal Smith, scored the winning run on a throwing error by third baseman Jim Gilliam.

Jackson led the NL in games started (38) and innings pitched (282) in 1960 while compiling an 18–13 record and a 3.48 ERA.

AUGUST 27   Stan Musial hits a walk-off homer in the ninth inning to beat the Pirates 5–4 at Busch Stadium.

The Cardinals swept a three-game series from the Pirates from August 26 through 28 to pull within 3½ games of first place, but they never seriously threatened the Pirates afterward. The Cards finished the year in third, nine games behind Pittsburgh, which claimed its first NL pennant in 33 years.

SEPTEMBER 7   The Cardinals sell Del Rice to the Orioles.

SEPTEMBER 18   Ernie Broglio earns his 20th win of the season with a 4–3 win over the Giants at Busch Stadium.

SEPTEMBER 19   Stan Musial's homer off Stan Williams in the sixth inning is enough to defeat the Dodgers 1–0 at Busch Stadium. Bob Miller (8⅓ innings) and Lindy McDaniel (⅔ of an inning) combined on the shutout.

SEPTEMBER 20   A two-run, walk-off homer by Charlie James in the ninth inning defeats the Dodgers 3–2 at Busch Stadium.

OCTOBER 2   The football Cardinals play their first game at Busch Stadium and lose 35–14 to the New York Giants before 26,089.

DECEMBER 17   The St. Louis City Planning Commission approves plans for a redevelopment project that will include a new 50,000-seat stadium for the baseball and football Cardinals.

1961

Season in a Sentence

A slow start leads to a change in managers in July from Solly Hemus to Johnny Keane.

Finish • Won • Lost • Pct • GB

Fifth   80   74   .519   13.0

Managers

Solly Hemus (33–41) and Johnny Keane (47–33)

Stats

Stats	Cards	•	NL	•	Rank
Batting Avg:	.271		.262		2
On-Base Pct:	.336		.330		2
Slugging Pct:	.393		.405		7
Home Runs:	103				7 (tie)
Stolen Bases:	46				6
ERA:	3.74		4.03		1
Fielding Avg:	.972		.976		7
Runs Scored:	703				5
Runs Allowed:	668				4

Starting Lineup

Carl Sawatski, c
Bill White, 1b
Julian Javier, 2b
Ken Boyer, 3b
Bob Lillis, ss
Stan Musial, lf
Curt Flood, cf
Charlie James, rf-lf
Joe Cunningham, rf
Don Taussig, lf-rf-cf
Alex Grammas, ss
Jimmie Schaffer, c
Carl Warwick, cf-lf

Pitchers

Ray Sadecki, sp
Larry Jackson, sp
Bob Gibson, sp
Curt Simmons, sp
Ernie Broglio, sp
Lindy McDaniel, rp

Attendance

855,305 (sixth in NL)

Club Leaders

Batting Avg:	Boyer	.329
On-Base Pct:	Boyer	.397
Slugging Pct:	Boyer	.533
Home Runs:	Boyer	24
RBIs:	Boyer	95
Runs:	Boyer	109
Stolen Bases:	Javier	11
Wins:	Sadecki	14
	Jackson	14
Strikeouts:	Gibson	166
ERA:	Simmons	3.13
Saves:	McDaniel	9

JANUARY 26   The Cardinals send Leon Wagner, Cal Browning, Ellis Burton, and cash to the Angels for Al Cicotte.

The Cards made a huge mistake in letting Wagner out of the organization. From 1961 through 1965 with the Angels and Indians, Wagner hit 150 homers, an average of 30 per season. St. Louis didn't have a single outfielder who hit as many as 30 homers in any season between 1954 (Stan Musial with 35) and 1996 (Ron Gant with 30).

FEBRUARY 2   A spokesman for the Vinoy Park Hotel in St. Petersburg, Florida, which served as the Cardinals' spring training headquarters, informed the Cardinals that African-American players would have to find quarters elsewhere. C. H. Alberding of Tulsa, Oklahoma, the president of the concern that operated the hotel, said that if the Cardinals insisted on housing all of their personnel in the same hotel, the club should "look for other hotels." The statement came after the Cardinals requested that the entire club be housed in one hotel. Bing Devine, the Cards' general manager, said segregation created problems, but added, "We don't make the rules and regulations for the various localities." Since the Cardinals had integrated their roster in 1954, African-American players lived and ate at private homes and rooming houses during spring training. It was a problem for all throughout baseball's spring training as clubs trained in towns and cities in Florida and Arizona where segregation had been entrenched by both law and custom for decades, including St. Petersburg. At the time, the walls of segregation were just beginning to crack in the South, however, led by civil rights groups such as the Southern Christian Leadership Conference and the Freedom Riders, which were in the news on an almost daily basis. Under prodding from African-American Cardinal players such as Bill White, Curt Flood, and Bob Gibson, the situation changed in 1962 when August Busch leased two adjoining hotels near the Skyway Bridge that allowed the club's black and white players to stay together. The Yankees left St. Petersburg after the 1961 season and moved to Ft. Lauderdale beginning in 1962, in part due to the racial restrictions in the Tampa Bay Area. The Yankees had trained in St. Petersburg since 1925. The Mets subsequently used St. Petersburg as a training site from 1962 through 1987. The Cardinals remained in St. Pete until 1997.

MARCH 15   Red Schoendienst signs a contract with the Cardinals after his release from the Braves.

            It was a homecoming for Schoendienst, who played for the Cards from 1945 through 1955. He returned in 1961 as a pinch hitter and spare infielder and was named player-coach in July. During the 1961 and 1962 seasons, Schoendienst hit .300 in 263 at-bats.

MARCH 27   On a Duke Snider line drive up the middle, Larry Jackson breaks his jaw when he's hit by a broken bat during a spring training game against the Dodgers in Vero Beach, Florida. The ball hit Jackson on the hip, and as he reached for the ball, the heavy end of the bat flew through the air and struck him in the face. He suffered two fractures of the lower jaw that put him out of action for a month. The Cards lost the game 11–2. Weakened by a liquid diet, Jackson started the season with a 3–8 record but finished at 14–11.

APRIL 10   The Cardinals sell Ron Kline to the Angels.

APRIL 11   In the season opener, the Cardinals defeat the Braves 2–1 in 10 innings in Milwaukee. Daryl Spencer won the contest with a homer off Warren Spahn. The St. Louis pitchers were Ernie Broglio (seven innings) and Lindy McDaniel (three innings).

APRIL 14   In the home opener before 19,077 at Busch Stadium, the Reds score five runs in the ninth inning to defeat the Cardinals 7–3. Cincinnati's Wally Post hit a tape-measure homer that struck the beak of the eagle on the Budweiser sign atop the scoreboard some 90 feet above the playing field 410 feet from home plate. Reds pitcher Jay Hook, who held an engineering degree from Northwestern University, estimated the ball would have traveled 569 feet if it hadn't hit the sign. Most observers considered it to be the longest home run ever hit at the former Busch Stadium. Stan Musial homered for the Cardinals.

APRIL 17   The day after the United States launches its unsuccessful Bay of Pigs invasion in Cuba, Daryl Spencer hits a grand slam off Larry Sherry in the ninth inning of a 9–5 win over the Dodgers in Los Angeles.

APRIL 21   Stan Musial and Red Schoendienst, along with coaches Harry Walker, Johnny Keane, and Howie Pollet, visit Alcatraz during a trip to San Francisco. At the time, Alcatraz was an active prison and not open to the public. The Cardinal contingent talked to many of the infamous inmates at the facility.

APRIL 23   The Cardinals score five runs in the ninth inning to defeat the Giants 7–4 in the second game of a doubleheader at Candlestick Park. Mickey McDermott hit a three-run pinch-double during the rally, then took the mound in the bottom half and retired the Giants in order for the save. San Francisco won the first game 2–1.

APRIL 28   A two-run, walk-off, pinch-hit home run by Red Schoendienst beats the Phillies 10–9 at Busch Stadium. Schoendienst was the 24th Cardinal to play in the game.

The homer was the only one Schoendienst hit in 1961.

MAY 10   Five days after Alan Shepard becomes the first American in space, three Cardinal pinch hitters strike out in the ninth inning of a 3–2 loss to the Reds at Busch Stadium. The three were Charlie James, Don Taussig, and Alex Grammas.

On the same day, the Cardinals sent Bob Nieman to the Indians for Joe Morgan and cash. Unfortunately, the Joe Morgan acquired in the deal was not the future Hall of Fame second baseman, but a utility infielder with an 88-game career.

MAY 26   Ken Boyer hits two homers and two singles during a 12–2 trouncing of the Pirates at Busch Stadium.

Boyer hit .329 with 24 homers, 95 RBIs, and 109 runs in 1961.

MAY 27   Julian Javier collects five hits in five at-bats during a 7–5 win over the Pirates at Busch Stadium.

MAY 30   The Cardinals trade Daryl Spencer to the Dodgers for Bob Lillis and Carl Warwick.

JUNE 5   Bill White hits a grand slam off Don Elston in the seventh inning of a 10–8 win over the Cubs at Busch Stadium.

JUNE 7   Stan Musial raps two homers and two singles during an 8–6 victory over the Cubs at Busch Stadium.

JUNE 15   The Cardinals sell Walt Moryn to the Pirates.

JUNE 20   Hal Smith is diagnosed with a "coronary artery condition."

The ailment ended Smith's career. He was only 30 and had played with the Cardinals since his rookie season in 1956. Smith served as a coach with the Cardinals in 1962 and later with the Pirates, Reds, and Brewers. He was one of two Hal Smiths to catch in the big leagues during the 1950s and 1960s, which created considerable confusion. The other Hal Smith was in the majors from 1955 through 1964 with the Orioles, Athletics, Pirates, Houston Colt .45s, and Reds. The two Hal Smiths were born only five months apart in 1930 and 1931.

JUNE 23   Stan Musial drives in seven runs on two homers during a 10–5 win over the Giants at Busch Stadium. Musial hit a three-run homer off Billy O'Dell in the third inning and a grand slam against Bobby Bolin in the fifth.

In his autobiography, Musial cited this game as proof that athletes can have some of their greatest games when they aren't feeling well because it raises their concentration level. Musial played despite suffering from a pulled leg muscle, a bad cold, and an abscessed tooth.

JUNE 25   Ray Sadecki pitches a two-hitter to defeat the Giants 3–1 in the second game of a doubleheader at Busch Stadium. The only San Francisco hits were a single by Felipe Alou in the second inning and a homer by Willie Mays in the ninth. The Giants won the first game 6–4.

Sadecki was only 19 years old when he became a major leaguer in 1960. It took him awhile to get his feet on the ground. Battling the pressures of pitching in the majors at such a young age (see June 5, 1962), Sadecki was 39–37 with a 4.12 ERA after his first four seasons before winning 20 games in 1964. He was 6–15 with a 5.21 earned run average in 1965, however, and in May 1966 was traded to the Giants for Orlando Cepeda. Sadecki pitched eight games for the Cardinals in 1975 near the end of an 18-year career in which he posted a 135–131 record.

JUNE 30   Jimmie Schaffer hits a grand slam off Jim Brewer in the first inning of an 11–4 win over the Cubs in Chicago.

JULY 4   Harry Caray brings a brief halt to a 10–7 win over the Phillies in the first game of a doubleheader at Busch Stadium. Caray reached for a foul ball and in the process knocked loose papers that fluttered through the air and landed behind first base. Umpires stopped play to retrieve the documents.

JULY 5   Bill White hits three homers and drives in four runs to help the Cardinals to a 9–1 win over the Dodgers in Los Angeles. White homered off Johnny Podres in the third inning, Roger Craig in the fourth, and Jim Golden in the eighth. With a shot at a record-tying fourth homer in the ninth inning, White smacked a double.

JULY 6   The Cardinals fire Solly Hemus as manager and hire 49-year-old Johnny Keane.

After 86 wins and a third-place finish in 1960, the Cardinals brass expected better results than the 33–41 mark the club posted on the morning of July 6. A native of St. Louis, Keane provided a steadier hand than the impulsive Hemus, and the Cards were 47–33 over the remainder of the 1961 season. A shortstop, Keane's playing career ended in the minors when he was beaned and spent six days in a coma and another six weeks in the hospital with a skull fracture seven inches long. Keane started managing in the Cardinals' minor league system in 1938. He was considered a top candidate for the Cardinals' managing job time and time again during the 1950s but was passed over for the likes of Marty Marion, Eddie Stanky, Fred Hutchinson, and Hemus. Keane finally reached the big leagues after nearly three decades in the minors as a coach under Hemus in 1959. But Hemus came to rely on Keane's advice less and less often as the years passed. The Cardinals front office valued Keane's baseball expertise, however, and hired him to succeed Hemus. Hemus never managed another big-league club, although he was a coach for four seasons with the Mets and the Indians.

JULY 8   Spotting the Giants a 5–0 lead after three innings, the Cardinals rally for a 9–7 victory over the Giants in San Francisco. A two-run eighth inning broke a 7–7 tie.

One of Johnny Keane's first acts was to give Bob Gibson a regular spot in the starting rotation. Gibson had played for Keane in the minors. When the 1961 season started, Gibson was 25 years old and had a 6–11 record and a 4.53 ERA. Control was his worst problem. Gibson walked 87 batters in 163 innings. Solly Hemus had lost confidence in Gibson and believed he would never develop into an effective major league pitcher. There was no question about his athletic ability or intensity. Gibson went to Creighton University on a basketball scholarship and played for the Harlem Globetrotters. The 1961 season was the turning point in his career. Gibson had a 13–12 record and a 3.24 ERA. His unusual self-discipline, intensity, and willingness to fight every batter on every pitch set him part. By the time his career ended, Gibson led the Cardinals in almost every pitching category, including wins (251), games started (482), complete games (255), shutouts (56), innings (3,684¹/₃), and strikeouts (3,117). If that weren't enough, he hit 24 career home runs and won nine Gold Gloves.

JULY 11   Bill White singles in a run in the fourth inning to help the National League to a 10-inning, 5–4 win in the first of two 1961 All-Star Games, played at Candlestick Park in San Francisco.

JULY 14   Carl Sawatski hits a walk-off homer in the ninth inning to defeat the Braves 2–1 at Busch Stadium.

JULY 15   An eight-run explosion in the eighth inning breaks a 4–4 tie for a 12–4 victory over the Braves at Busch Stadium.

JULY 17   Bill White collects eight hits in 10 at-bats during a doubleheader sweep of the Cubs at Busch Stadium. In the opener, White had four singles in five at-bats. Down 6–0, the Cardinals scored four runs in the seventh inning and six in the eighth for a 10–6 win. In the nightcap, White was 4 for 5 again with a double and three singles. The Redbirds won 8–5.

JULY 18   Bill White continues his torrid hitting with six hits in eight at-bats during 8–3 and 7–5 triumphs over the Cubs at Busch Stadium. White was 3 for 4 in each game. He had a homer and two singles in the first contest and two triples and a single in the second skirmish.

With 14 hits in 18 at-bats on July 17 and 18, White tied a major league record set by Ty Cobb for most hits in consecutive doubleheaders. Cobb's feat came on July 17 and 19, 1912, almost 49 years to the day before White's. White started the streak on the day that Cobb died at the age of 74 in Atlanta. There was a moment of silence prior to the July 18 doubleheader in St. Louis in Cobb's honor.

JULY 19   Bill White is the hero again with a walk-off single in the tenth inning to defeat the Giants 3–2 at Busch Stadium.

JULY 21   The Cardinals sell Mickey McDermott to the Athletics.

JULY 25   Ken Boyer hits a grand slam off Jack Curtis in the first inning of a 6–5 win over the Cubs in Chicago.

JULY 31   Bill White collects a double, a single, and an RBI in four at-bats in the second of two All-Star games played in 1961. The contest at Fenway Park in Boston ended in a 1–1 tie when it was called after nine innings by rain.

AUGUST 3	The Pirates drub the Cardinals 19–0 at Busch Stadium. Al Cicotte, Bob Miller, and Lindy McDaniel combined to allow 24 Pittsburgh hits.
AUGUST 6	Carl Sawatski comes off the bench to star in a 3–2 win over the Phillies in the second game of a doubleheader at Busch Stadium. Sawatski hit a two-run pinch-homer in the seventh that tied the scored 2–2. Staying in the game as a catcher, he drove in the winning run with a single in the ninth inning. The Cards also won the opener, 3–1.
AUGUST 8	Ken Boyer's second homer of the game is a walk-off wallop in the ninth inning that beats the Reds 6–5 at Busch Stadium.
AUGUST 9	On his 28th birthday, Julian Javier accounts for all four runs of a 4–0 win over the Pirates with a grand slam in the eighth inning off Joe Gibbon.
AUGUST 10	The Cardinals extend their winning streak to eight games with a 3–2 decision over the Pirates in Pittsburgh.
AUGUST 28	Two weeks after the construction of the Berlin Wall commences, the Cardinals extend their winning streak to eight games with a 5–4 decision over the Phillies in the first game of a doubleheader at Connie Mack Stadium. It was the Cards' second eight-game winning streak in August 1961. The streak ended when Philadelphia won the second tilt 4–3.
AUGUST 30	Bill White sets a club record by extending his RBI streak to 10 games by driving in two during a 4–3 loss to the Phillies in Philadelphia.
SEPTEMBER 2	Curt Flood collects five hits, including a double, in five at-bats, but the Cardinals lose 5–4 to the Pirates at Busch Stadium.
SEPTEMBER 4	Bill White's grand slam in the sixth inning off Al McBean is the feature of a 9–4 win over the Pirates at Busch Stadium.
SEPTEMBER 14	The Cardinals sweep a doubleheader against the Cubs at Busch Stadium, both in the final at-bats. In the opener, a passed ball with the bases loaded in the ninth scored Bob Lillis from third base for an 8–7 St. Louis victory. In the second game, Ken Boyer doubled in a run in the ninth to tie the game 5–5, then struck a walk-off homer in the eleventh for the win. The home run capped a great day for Boyer in which he collected 7 hits in 11 at-bats. In the opener, he had a triple and a single. In the nightcap, Boyer hit for the cycle. He also hit a second single in the game.
SEPTEMBER 30	The Cardinals score seven runs in the sixth inning of a 12–2 win over the Phillies in Philadelphia.
OCTOBER 10	The Cardinals lose six players in the first expansion draft. The new franchise in Houston selected Bob Lillis, Ed Oliveras, and Don Taussig. The New York Mets chose Jim Hickman, Bob Miller, Craig Anderson, and Chris Cannizzaro.
NOVEMBER 27	The Cardinals trade Joe Cunningham to the White Sox for Minnie Minoso.
	The Cardinals acquired Minoso two days before his 39th birthday, but he was still a productive outfielder. He played in only 39 games for the Cardinals,

however, and hit only .196 during an injury-marred 1962 season. Minoso fractured his skull and wrist when he struck the unpadded concrete left-field wall at Busch Stadium while chasing a Duke Snider drive. He was about to return to the lineup when he was hit by a pitch during batting practice on July 21 that made his vision blurry. On August 19, he broke his arm when he was struck by an offering from the Mets' Craig Anderson, and the injury put him out for the season.

1962

Season in a Sentence

The Cardinals open the season with seven straight wins and end it with four consecutive victories over pennant contenders, but they finish the year only six games above .500.

Finish • Won • Lost • Pct • GB

Sixth   84   78   .519   17.5

Manager

Johnny Keane

Stats

Stats	Cards	• NL •	Rank
Batting Avg:	.271	.261	2
On-Base Pct:	.337	.329	3
Slugging Pct:	.394	.393	6
Home Runs:	137		7
Stolen Bases:	86		2
ERA:	3.55	3.94	2
Fielding Avg:	.979	.975	2
Runs Scored:	774		4
Runs Allowed:	664		2

Starting Lineup

Gene Oliver, c
Bill White, 1b
Julian Javier, 2b
Ken Boyer, 3b
Julio Gotay, ss
Stan Musial, lf
Curt Flood, cf
Charlie James, rf
Carl Sawatski, c
Dal Maxvill, ss

Pitchers

Larry Jackson, sp
Bob Gibson, sp
Ernie Broglio, sp
Ray Washburn, sp
Curt Simmons, sp
Ray Sadecki, sp
Lindy McDaniel, rp

Attendance

953,985 (fifth in NL)

Club Leaders

Batting Avg:	Musial	.330
On-Base Pct:	Musial	.416
Slugging Pct:	Musial	.508
Home Runs:	Boyer	24
RBIs:	White	102
Runs:	Flood	99
Stolen Bases:	Javier	26
Wins:	Jackson	16
Strikeouts:	Gibson	208
ERA:	Gibson	2.85
Saves:	McDaniel	14

MARCH 6   Two weeks after John Glenn becomes the first American to orbit the earth, St. Louis voters approve a bond issue project for downtown redevelopment that paves the way for a new stadium to replace outdated Sportsman's Park. The stadium itself was privately financed. The bond issue covered the costs of the purchase of the land, the relocation of streets and the connection of utilities to the facility. The new Busch Stadium opened in May 1966. (See May 12, 1966.)

APRIL 10   The season opener against the expansion New York Mets at Busch Stadium is rained out.

APRIL 11   The Cardinals open the season with an 11–4 win over the Mets before 16,147 at

Busch Stadium. It was the first game in New York Mets history. Stan Musial collected three hits, including a double, in three at-bats. Julian Javier had four hits, and Bill White drove in three runs. Larry Jackson pitched a complete game.

At the age of 41, Musial played in 135 games, batted .330, and hit 19 home runs for his best season since 1958. Ken Boyer hit .291 with 24 homers and 98 RBIs. Bill White had a .324 average with 20 homers, 103 RBIs, and 199 hits.

APRIL 13   The Cardinals score three runs in the fifteenth inning to beat the Cubs 8–5 in Chicago. Don Landrum broke the 5–5 tie with a single. He entered the game as a pinch runner for Stan Musial in the ninth inning.

Before leaving the game, Musial set a new National League record by scoring the 1,869th run of his career, passing Mel Ott. He finished his career with 1,949 runs, and at the end of the 2005 season ranked fifth in the National League and eighth all time behind Rickey Henderson (2,295), Ty Cobb (2,246), Hank Aaron (2,174), Babe Ruth (2,174), Pete Rose (2,165), Bobby Bonds (2,070), and Willie Mays (2,062).

APRIL 16   After a weird first inning in which both teams score six runs, the Cardinals move on to defeat the Phillies 12–6 in 36-degree weather in Philadelphia. Bob Gibson allowed all six first-inning runs. Ernie Broglio followed with 8$^{1}/_{3}$ innings of shutout relief.

The Cardinals added numbers to the fronts of their uniforms for the first time in 1962.

APRIL 18   The Cardinals play the Mets in New York for the first time and win 15–5 at the Polo Grounds.

The Mets used the Polo Grounds as their home field for two seasons before moving into Shea Stadium in 1964.

APRIL 21   The Cardinals run their record to 7–0, the best start in club history, with an 8–0 win over the Cubs at Busch Stadium.

The seven consecutive wins, achieved largely over the Cubs and Mets, two clubs that combined to lose 223 games in 1962, proved to be an illusion. The Cardinals finished the season only six games above .500.

APRIL 24   The Cardinals play a regular-season game in Houston for the first time and lose 4–3 to the Colts at Colt Stadium.

During the first three years of their existence, the Houston franchise was officially known as the Colt .45s, and informally as the Colts. The nickname was changed to the Astros in 1965. Houston played for three years at Colt Stadium, a temporary facility built in what would become the parking lot for the Astrodome, baseball's first indoor stadium, which opened in 1965.

APRIL 25   The Cardinals and Colts battle to a 17-inning, 5–5 tie in Houston. The game was halted by a National League rule stating that no inning could start after 12:50 AM. Ed Bauta pitched eight shutout innings of relief for the Cards.

APRIL 26   Bob Gibson pitches a two-hitter for a 3–2 win over the Colts at Houston. The only hits off Gibson came in the eighth inning, when Roman Mejias homered and Al Heist hit a single.

Gibson overcame childhood adversity to become one of the greatest pitchers of his generation. He was born during the Depression in Omaha and spent his early years in a four-room shack without electricity. His father died three months before he was born, and he was one of seven children. His mother worked in a commercial laundry. While still a toddler, Gibson was bitten on the ear by a rat. He was small and sickly as a child, suffering from rickets, asthma, and a heart murmur, and he nearly died from pneumonia.

APRIL 27   The Cardinals score eight runs in the seventh inning and trample the Reds 14–3 at Busch Stadium.

APRIL 29   The Cardinals overwhelm the Reds 16–3 in the first game of a doubleheader at Busch Stadium. Cincinnati took the second contest 4–3.

MAY 1   Houston plays the Cardinals in St. Louis for the first time. The Cardinals scored five runs in the first inning and won 6–4 at Busch Stadium.

MAY 6   Stan Musial's homer off Moe Drabowsky with two men on base in the ninth inning accounts for all of the runs in a 3–0 win over the Reds in the second game of a doubleheader at Crosley Field. Bob Gibson pitched the shutout. Cincinnati won the opening tilt 5–4.

MAY 7   The Cardinals trade Carl Warwick and John Anderson to Houston for Bobby Shantz.

Standing only five foot six and weighing 142 pounds, Shantz was 36 years old and in the 14th season of a 16-year big-league career when he was acquired by the Cardinals. Before a trade to the Cubs in June 1964, Shantz pitched 99 games in relief for the Cards and posted an ERA of 2.51. In addition to his pitching, Shantz won the last of eight consecutive Gold Gloves in 1964. Warwick came back to the Cardinals in another trade in 1964.

MAY 12   The Cardinals outlast the Dodgers 6–5 in 15 innings at Busch Stadium. Julian Javier drove in the winning run with a single.

MAY 17   Bob Gibson pitches the Cardinals to a 1–0 win over the Giants in San Francisco. Charlie James drove in the winning run with a single in the ninth inning off Billy O'Dell.

James was a football star as a running back at the University of Missouri. He was drafted by the New York Giants in the 24th round of the NFL draft in 1959.

MAY 18   The Cardinals play at Dodger Stadium for the first time and defeat the Dodgers 8–3.

MAY 19   Stan Musial collects the 3,431st hit of his career to break the existing National League record set by Honus Wagner. The milestone was a single off Ron Perranoski in the ninth inning of an 8–1 win over the Dodgers in Los Angeles.

Musial finished his career with 3,630 hits and ranks second in the National League and fourth all time behind Pete Rose (4,256), Ty Cobb (4,189), and Hank Aaron (3,771).

MAY 22   Rookie catcher Roberto Herrera helps Ernie Broglio move his family and winds up on the disabled list. Broglio slammed his car door before Herrera could get the little finger of his right hand away in time. The result was a compound fracture. Herrera was sent to the minors before he appeared in a big-league game.

JUNE 5   Trailing 9–1, the Cardinals rebound with three runs in the sixth inning, five in the seventh, and one in the eleventh to beat the Reds 10–9 at Busch Stadium. Stan Musial's walk-off homer accounted for the winning run. The victory broke an eight-game losing streak.

Ray Sadecki entered the game in the sixth inning. He allowed a home run to Reds pitcher Bob Purkey on the first pitch he threw and left the contest allowing five runs without retiring a batter. Sadecki wasn't much better at fielding his position, making two errors. Manager Johnny Keane called it "the poorest exhibition I've ever seen on a major league diamond." The next night, Sadecki failed to report to the ballpark and demanded a trade. He was fined $250 and suspended for one day.

JUNE 9   In his first game since his suspension, Ray Sadecki allows three runs in the first inning but pitches a complete game to defeat the Giants 8–4 at Busch Stadium.

JUNE 10   The Cardinals sweep the Giants 6–5 and 13–3 at Busch Stadium.

JUNE 13   Bob Gibson strikes out 12 batters in a 6–1 win over the Phillies at Busch Stadium.

JUNE 19   In a duel of future Hall of Famers, Bob Gibson loses 1–0 to Sandy Koufax and the Dodgers in Los Angeles on a walk-off homer by Tommy Davis with one out in the ninth inning.

JUNE 22   Stan Musial becomes the all-time total-bases leader, raising his total to 5,864. He surpassed Ty Cobb's record during a 7–3 win in the first game of a doubleheader against the Phillies at Connie Mack Stadium. Philadelphia won the second game 11–3.

Musial closed his career with 6,134 total bases. At the end of the 2005 season, he ranked second in total bases to Hank Aaron's 6,856.

JUNE 26   The Cardinals score nine runs in the eighth inning and wallop the Cubs 15–3 in Chicago.

JUNE 27   The Cardinals win both ends of a doubleheader over the Cubs in Chicago with a shutout. The Cards won 4–0 behind Larry Jackson and 8–0 with Ray Sadecki on the mound.

JULY 1   A two-inning Old-Timers Game between the 1942 Cardinals and the 1942 Yankees precedes a game against the Pirates at Busch Stadium. Stan Musial, a member of both the 1942 and 1962 Cards, played in the both the Old-Timers Game and the regularly scheduled contest. The 1942 Cards won 6–0. The 1962 Cards lost 7–2.

JULY 4   Ken Boyer drives in both runs in a 2–0 victory over the Braves at Busch Stadium. Boyer had a home run in the second inning and an RBI single in the sixth.

> *In July, the Cardinals ordered all of the players to wear batting helmets. The last two holdouts were Boyer and Stan Musial. The National League passed a rule in 1958 requiring that all players wear batting helmets at the plate, but those who were in the majors prior to the season were exempt from the edict.*

JULY 7   Stan Musial homers off Craig Anderson in the eighth inning to beat the Mets 3–2 in the second game of a doubleheader at the Polo Grounds. New York won the first game 5–4.

JULY 8   Stan Musial hits three homers in his first three at-bats during a 15–1 pounding of the Mets at the Polo Grounds. Combined with the homer he struck in his last plate appearance the previous day, Musial tied a major league record with home runs in four consecutive at-bats. He homered off Jay Hook in the first and fourth innings and Willard Hunter in the seventh. In his bid for a fifth consecutive home run, Musial struck out in the ninth. Bill White, Fred Whitfield, and Bob Gibson also homered for the Cardinals.

> *Entering the 2005 season, four consecutive home runs by a player had been accomplished 24 times in the major leagues. At 41, Musial is the oldest person to accomplish the feat and the only Cardinal.*

JULY 15   Five days after the launching of Telstar, the world's first communications satellite, comedian Jerry Lewis takes batting practice with the Cardinals prior to a doubleheader against the Pirates at Forbes Field. Lewis was in Pittsburgh for an engagement. In the first game, Fred Whitfield hit a pinch-homer in the tenth inning for a 3–2 win. The Pirates won the second tilt 8–7.

JULY 18   Bob Gibson strikes out 12 batters in a 2–1 win over the Cubs at Busch Stadium.

JULY 25   Stan Musial becomes the National League's all-time RBI leader with 1,862 by driving in both Cardinal runs in a 5–2 loss to the Dodgers at Busch Stadium. Mel Ott was the previous record holder.

> *Musial closed his career with 1,951 RBIs. At the end of the 2005 season, he ranked second in the National League and fourth all time in RBIs behind Hank Aaron (2,297), Babe Ruth (2,213), and Lou Gehrig (1,995).*

AUGUST 4   Ray Washburn carries a no-hitter into the seventh inning before winning 2–0 with a four-hitter against Houston at Busch Stadium.

> *Washburn looked like a tremendous pitching talent when he reached the majors in 1961 as a 23-year-old. He never developed into the power pitcher the Cardinals envisioned, however. In nine years with the club, Washburn had a record of 72–64. His best season was in 1968, when he was 14–8 with a 2.26 ERA and a no-hitter.*

AUGUST 12   Six days after the death of Marilyn Monroe, Fred Whitfield hits a grand slam off Bill Smith that puts the Cardinals ahead 7–6, but the Phillies rally to win 9–7 in the second game of a doubleheader at Connie Mack Stadium. Philadelphia also won the opener, 7–3.

AUGUST 18   The Cardinals swamp the Mets 7–4 and 10–0 in a doubleheader in New York.

SEPTEMBER 1   The Cardinals explode for eight runs in the fourth inning and trounce the Mets 10–5 at Busch Stadium.

SEPTEMBER 9   The Cardinals score five runs in the ninth inning, four of them on a pinch-hit grand slam by Carl Sawatski off Jim Brosnan, to defeat the Reds 5–3 in Cincinnati.

SEPTEMBER 21   Charlie James hits a grand slam in the first inning off Sandy Koufax to spark an 11–2 win over the Dodgers at Busch Stadium. The Cards scored seven runs in the sixth inning.

SEPTEMBER 24   The Cardinals wallop the Dodgers 12–2 at Busch Stadium.

After the game, the Cardinals had a scare when their chartered airliner made an emergency landing at Schilling Air Force base in Salina, Kansas. The Cards were en route from St. Louis to San Francisco when one of the four engines of the American Airlines craft began sputtering. The pilot feathered the propeller and made an uneventful landing. Because Schilling was a Strategic Air Command base, the plane was met by an armed guard. The pilot stayed at the plane until an officer arrived to escort the players from "sensitive areas." Once the base officials ascertained that the "invaders" were ball players, the Cards became honored guests. They spent five hours in the Officers Club lounge while another plane was flown to Dallas so that the club could resume the trip west.

SEPTEMBER 27   Stan Musial collects five hits in five at-bats during a 7–4 win over the Giants in San Francisco.

The loss put the Giants two games back of the Dodgers with three games left in the season. The Dodgers played the Cardinals in each of those three contests in Los Angeles.

SEPTEMBER 28   Charlie James hits a single in the tenth inning to drive in the winning run in a 3–2 win over the Dodgers in Los Angeles.

SEPTEMBER 29   Ernie Broglio pitches a two-hitter to defeat the Dodgers 2–0 in Los Angeles. The only hits off Broglio were singles by Duke Snider in the first inning and Wally Moon in the second. Don Drysdale was the hard-luck losing pitcher. Both runs scored when Frank Howard dropped a fly ball.

SEPTEMBER 30   In the final game of the season, the Cardinals defeat the Dodgers 1–0 in Los Angeles. Curt Simmons pitched the shutout. Gene Oliver drove in the lone run of the game with a homer off Johnny Podres in the eighth inning. The three-game sweep at the hands of the Cardinals dropped the Dodgers into a first-place tie with the Giants, which forced a playoff to determine the NL champion. The Giants won the best-of-three series.

OCTOBER 17   The Cardinals trade Larry Jackson, Lindy McDaniel, and Jimmie Schaffer to the Cubs for Don Cardwell, George Altman, and Moe Thacker.

The Cardinals made a bad trade. Jackson had six years ahead of him as a good to excellent starting pitcher. He won 24 games for the Cubs in 1964. McDaniel was in the majors until 1975 as a relief pitcher and pitched in 651 more games after leaving St. Louis. An outfielder who hit 22 homers and batted .318 for the Cubs in 1962, Altman suffered a huge dropoff in production after the trade and lasted only a year in St. Louis. Fortunately, Cardwell was used 33 days later as bait in a trade that worked to the Cardinals benefit.

OCTOBER 29   The Cardinals hire 81-year-old Branch Rickey as a consultant.

August Busch had owned the Cardinals since 1953 and was becoming frustrated. The closest that any of his clubs had come to a pennant was in 1957, when the Cards ended up in second place, eight games out of first. In 1962, the team finished sixth, 17½ games out. At the suggestion of Los Angeles restaurateur Bob Cobb, who operated the minor league Los Angeles Angels in the Pacific Coast League during the 1950s, Busch hired Rickey to oversee the Cardinals organization. Rickey had previously run the Cardinals front office from 1917 through 1942, shepherding the club through the most successful period in the history of St. Louis baseball. After leaving the Cards, Rickey headed the Brooklyn Dodgers until 1950, where he integrated the sport and built a consistent pennant-winning club that author Roger Kahn dubbed the "Boys of Summer." From 1950 through 1955, Rickey was the general manager of the Pittsburgh Pirates franchise with much less success, but he laid the foundation for a club that won a World Championship in 1960. In 1958, Rickey became the president of the Continental League, which had designs on becoming a third major league with franchises in New York, Houston, Minneapolis-St. Paul, Buffalo, Atlanta, Toronto, Denver, and Dallas-Fort Worth. The league never came to fruition, but it forced the National and American Leagues to expand from eight teams to ten.

Upon returning to St. Louis, Rickey caused an immediate stir by suggesting that Stan Musial retire. Rickey also said that the Cardinals would finish in fifth place in 1963 and that 1965 seemed to be a "rational objective for a pennant." During his two years as a consultant, Rickey had a testy relationship with general manager Bing Devine. Rickey was used to running the show and believed he had the authority to make the final decisions on major matters. Devine had been a low-level office functionary during the late 1930s and early 1940s when Rickey was the vice president of the Cardinals, and Rickey still regarded him as a minion and constantly usurped his authority. The situation was unworkable. Rickey greased the skids for Devine's departure (see August 17, 1964) and was let go as a consultant shortly after the end of the 1964 season.

NOVEMBER 19   A month after America's nerves are frazzled by the Cuban missile crisis, the Cardinals trade Don Cardwell and Julio Gotay to the Pirates for Dick Groat and Diomedes Olivo.

The Cardinals had below-average production at shortstop for nearly a decade before acquiring Groat, who was 32 and won the NL MVP Award in 1960 as a Pirate. For short-term value, it was one of the best trades in Cardinals history. In his first two seasons with the Cardinals, Groat made the NL All-Star team and rounded out an infield that included Bill White, Julian Javier, and Ken Boyer. In 1963, Groat was the runner-up in National League MVP balloting after hitting .318 with 201 hits and a league-leading 43 doubles. In the World Championship season of 1964, Groat batted .292. As a collegian at Duke University, he not only starred at baseball, but was also an All-American basketball player. Although only five foot eleven, he scored 831 points for Duke's 1951–52 basketball team, which then was the all-time NCAA record. Groat played part of the 1952–53 season with the Fort Wayne Pistons in the NBA and averaged 11.9 points per game in 26 games.

DECEMBER 15   The Cardinals trade Fred Whitfield to the Indians for Ron Taylor and Jack Kubisyn.

Taylor is the only individual to serve as a player for one World Series and as a trainer for another. Taylor pitched for the Cardinals in the 1964 Fall Classic, and after earning a medical degree was the trainer for the Blue Jays in the Series in 1992 and 1993.

1963

Season in a Sentence

Given little chance of competing for a pennant in Stan Musial's last season, the Cardinals are within one game of first place with two weeks remaining after a stretch of 19 wins in 20 games.

Finish • Won • Lost • Pct • GB

Second   93   69   .574   6.0

Manager

Johnny Keane

Stats

Stats	Cards	NL	Rank
Batting Avg:	.271	.245	1
On-Base Pct:	.328	.308	1
Slugging Pct:	.403	.364	2
Home Runs:	128		3
Stolen Bases:	77		3
ERA:	3.32	3.29	7
Fielding Avg:	.976	.975	4
Runs Scored:	747		1
Runs Allowed:	628		7

Starting Lineup

Tim McCarver, c
Bill White, 1b
Julian Javier, 2b
Ken Boyer, 3b
Dick Groat, ss
Charlie James, lf
Curt Flood, cf
George Altman, rf
Stan Musial, lf

Pitchers

Bob Gibson, sp
Ernie Broglio, sp
Curt Simmons, sp
Ray Sadecki, sp
Lew Burdette, sp-rp
Bobby Shantz, rp
Lindy McDaniel, rp

Attendance

1,170,546 (fourth in NL)

Club Leaders

Batting Avg:	Groat	.319
On-Base Pct:	Groat	.377
Slugging Pct:	White	.491
Home Runs:	White	27
RBIs:	Boyer	111
Runs:	Flood	112
Stolen Bases:	Javier	18
Wins:	Broglio	18
	Gibson	18
Strikeouts:	Gibson	204
ERA:	Simmons	2.48
Saves:	McDaniel	11
	Shantz	11

MARCH 12   The model for the new Busch Stadium is unveiled. Edward Durell Stone, whose work included the United States Pavilion at the Brussels World's Fair in 1958 and the US Embassy in New Delhi, India, agreed to serve as collaborating architect with the St. Louis firms of Schwartz & Van Hoefen and Sverdrup & Parcel.

APRIL 2   The Cardinals sell Minnie Minoso to the Senators.

APRIL 9   In the season opener, the Cardinals win 7–0 over the Mets at the Polo Grounds. Ernie Broglio pitched a two-hitter. Larry Burright collected both New York hits: a single to lead off the first inning and a double in the ninth. In his first game as a Cardinal, George Altman starred with four hits in five at-bats. Dick Groat, also making his debut with the club, had three base hits. Bill White homered.

            Joe Garagiola, who handled radio and TV duties for the Cardinals from 1955 through 1962, left the club to take a job with NBC. Jerry Gross replaced Garagiola and joined Harry Caray and Jack Buck in the broadcast booth.

APRIL 10   The Cardinals open with two consecutive shutouts, as Ray Washburn defeats the Mets 4–0 in New York.

APRIL 12   The scheduled home opener against the Phillies is postponed by rain.

APRIL 13   Behind the pitching of Curt Simmons, the Cardinals defeat the Phillies 7–0 in the home opener before 22,050. Dick Groat, Carl Sawatski, and Julian Javier each homered.

            Cardinal pitchers started the 1963 season with three shutouts and 32 consecutive scoreless innings. The club had also ended the 1962 campaign with back-to-back shutouts for a streak of five shutouts in succession and 53 straight scoreless innings over two seasons.

APRIL 23   The Cardinals blast the Colts 15–0 in Houston. Ernie Broglio pitched a two-hitter, allowing a single to Al Spangler in the third inning and a double to Bob Lillis in the eighth.

            The Cardinals added names to the backs of their uniforms for the first time in 1963.

APRIL 26   Down 7–1, the Cardinals score two in the sixth inning, two more in the eighth, and three in the ninth to defeat the Dodgers 8–7 in Los Angeles. The key blow was a two-run double by Bill White in the ninth.

            White batted .304, scored 106 runs, collected 200 hits, smacked 27 homers, and drove in 109 runs in 1963.

APRIL 27   Ray Washburn retires the first 20 batters to face him before settling for a three-hitter and a 3–0 win over the Dodgers in Los Angeles. The perfect game was broken up by a walk to Ron Fairly with two outs in the seventh. The first Dodger hit was a single by Bill Skowron later in the inning.

MAY 8   A Stan Musial home run during an 11–5 loss to the Dodgers at Busch Stadium gives him 1,357 career extra-base hits, surpassing Babe Ruth's major league record.

Musial finished his career with 1,377 extra-base hits. At the end of the 2005 season, Musial ranked second behind Hank Aaron, who had 1,477.

MAY 9   The Cardinals score seven runs in the fifth inning of a 10–7 win over the Dodgers at Busch Stadium. Bill White led the batting display with a grand slam off Dick Scott.

The Cardinals installed padding to the outfield walls at Busch Stadium in 1963. Prior to the padding, collisions with the notoriously unforgiving concrete wall caused serious injuries to players such as Ray Blades (1927), Earle Combs (1934), Pete Reiser (1941), Enos Slaughter (1942), and Minnie Minoso (1962).

MAY 10   George Altman homers off Bob Friend with two outs in the ninth inning to defeat the Pirates 1–0 in Pittsburgh. Curt Simmons pitched the shutout.

MAY 15   Bob Hendley of the Braves is no-hitting the Cardinals until Curt Flood singles with one out in the ninth inning. Two more hits and three runs followed before Hendley closed out a 9–3 win over the Cards in Milwaukee.

MAY 23   Ernie Broglio pitches the Cardinals to a 1–0 win over the Cubs in Chicago. Gene Oliver accounted for the lone run of the game with a homer off Dick Ellsworth in the fifth inning.

MAY 26   Ken Boyer collects five hits, including two doubles, in five at-bats during a 7–4 win over the Mets in the first game of a doubleheader at Busch Stadium. New York won the second tilt 3–2 in 11 innings.

Boyer hit .285 with 24 homers and 111 RBIs in 1964.

MAY 29   Bill White hits a walk-off homer in the tenth inning to beat Houston 3–2 at Busch Stadium.

MAY 31   A fluke pop-up by Stan Musial in the ninth inning beats the Giants 6–5 at Busch Stadium. With the score 5–5, the Cardinals loaded the bases on a walk to Curt Flood and two late throws on attempted force plays at second base. Musial hit a high pop fly to the right of second base and was automatically out because of the infield fly rule. San Francisco second baseman Cap Peterson, who had been playing in, backpedaled as Willie Mays charged in from his center field spot and Felipe Alou raced in from right. The ball fell among the befuddled trio, and Flood crossed the plate with the winning run. In disgust, Mays kicked his glove about 30 feet.

During his career, Musial played 1,016 games at first base, 943 in left field, 750 in right field, and 325 in center.

JUNE 2   Willie Mays hits three homers against the Cardinals in a 6–4 Giants win at Busch Stadium.

JUNE 8   Ernie Broglio pitches a two-hitter to defeat the Mets 4–0 at the Polo Grounds. The only New York hits were singles by Chico Fernandez in the seventh inning and Rod Kanehl in the ninth.

JUNE 9   Tim McCarver's inside-the-park grand slam off Larry Bearnarth helps the Cardinals to a 10–4 win over the Mets in the second game of a doubleheader in New York.

Mets center fielder Rod Kanehl was set to make the catch but slipped and fell. The ball skidded past him into deep center field at the Polo Grounds, allowing McCarver to circle the bases. New York won the first game 8–7.

JUNE 15 Three days after the University of Alabama is integrated by federal troops over the objections of Governor George Wallace, the Cardinals trade Gene Oliver and Bob Sadowski to the Braves for Lew Burdette.

Burdette came to the Cardinals with a lifetime record of 179–120 but was 36 years old. The Cards hoped to squeeze another productive year or two out of him, but Burdette was a disappointment in St. Louis with a 4–8 record over parts of two seasons.

JUNE 17 The Cardinals take over first place with an 8–1 win over the Mets at Busch Stadium.

JUNE 19 Bill White hits a grand slam off Don Rowe in the fourth inning of a 9–4 win over the Mets at Busch Stadium.

JUNE 24 The Cardinals trade Leo Burke to the Cubs for Barney Schultz.

When acquired by the Cardinals, Schultz was a 36-year-old knuckleballing relief specialist with a 15–15 lifetime record and a 3.95 ERA. The Cards thought so little of him that Schultz spent the most of the 1964 season in the minors. Recalled on August 1, he helped the team win the pennant by posting a 1.64 ERA and 14 saves in 49$\frac{1}{3}$ innings over 30 games. Barney soon lost his touch, however, and 1965 was his last season in the majors. He was later the Cardinals pitching coach from 1971 through 1975.

JUNE 28 Bob Gibson strikes out 13 batters during a 9–2 win over the Colts in Houston.

JULY 2 The Cardinals are knocked out first place with a 1–0 loss to the Dodgers in Los Angeles. The defeat started an eight-game losing streak.

JULY 9 All four Cardinal infielders start in the All-Star Game, won by the National League 5–3 at Municipal Stadium in Cleveland. Bill White, Ken Boyer, and Dick Groat were voted to the starting lineup (then decided by a poll of players, managers, and coaches), while Julian Javier replaced an injured Bill Mazeroski. Groat drove in the first run of the game with a single in the second inning. Stan Musial played in his last All-Star Game and lined out as a pinch hitter in the fifth inning.

The four Cardinal infielders were remarkably durable in 1963. White played in all 162 games, Javier in 161, Boyer in 159, and Groat in 158.

JULY 16 Bobby Shantz strikes out 8 of the 11 batters he faces in relief during a 10–inning, 5–4 win over the Reds in Cincinnati. A squeeze bunt by Tim McCarver scored Bill White with the winning run.

McCarver batted .289 in 1963.

JULY 17 Bob Gibson strikes out 12 batters during a 3–1 win over the Reds in Cincinnati.

Gibson struck out 204 batters in 254$\frac{2}{3}$ innings while posting an 18–9 record and a 3.39 ERA in 1963.

AUGUST 3   Ernie Broglio pitches his fourth two-hitter of 1963, defeating the Phillies 7–0 at Busch Stadium. The only Philadelphia hits were singles by Ruben Amaro in the third inning and Clay Dalrymple in the ninth.

Broglio was 18–9 with a 2.99 ERA.

AUGUST 8   The Cardinals play at the Polo Grounds for the last time and lose 3–2 to the Mets.

The Mets moved into Shea Stadium in 1964.

AUGUST 12   Stan Musial announces his retirement, effective at the end of the season.

The announcement was made at the annual team picnic, held at Grant's Farm, the estate of August Busch. On September 25, Musial was named the team's vice president with duties that included signing free agents, coaching batters, scouting other clubs, and serving as a goodwill ambassador.

AUGUST 16   The Cardinals wallop the Giants 13–0 at Busch Stadium.

AUGUST 17   The Cardinals score two runs in the ninth inning and one in the tenth to beat the Giants 8–7 at Busch Stadium. Bill White tied the score 7–7 with a two-run homer. Stan Musial drove in the winning run with a pinch-single.

AUGUST 19   The Cardinals score three runs in the ninth inning to defeat the Giants 8–7 at Busch Stadium. Ken Boyer drove in two runs with a home run to tie the game 7–7. With a great burst of speed, Julian Javier scored from first base on Tim McCarver's pop-fly single to score the winning run.

AUGUST 21   The Cardinals lose a 16-inning marathon 2–1 to the Dodgers in Los Angeles. The loss put the Cards 7½ games behind the Dodgers in the NL pennant race.

AUGUST 29   The day after Martin Luther King Jr. delivers his "I Have a Dream" speech in Washington, the Cardinals defeat the Phillies 11–6 at Philadelphia.

The win started a streak in which the Cardinals won 19 times in a span of 20 games and had St. Louis fans dreaming of a pennant as the Dodgers' first-place margin over the Cards was cut to just one game by September 15.

AUGUST 31   Ken Boyer smacks a two-run homer in the eleventh inning that beats the Phillies 7–5 in Philadelphia.

Stan Musial played in his 3,000th career game that evening. He finished his career with 3,026 games and is currently tied with Eddie Murray for sixth place. The only players ahead of Musial are Pete Rose (3,562), Carl Yastrzemski (3,308), Hank Aaron (3,298), Rickey Henderson (3,061), and Ty Cobb (3,035).

SEPTEMBER 1   Curt Simmons triples in the second inning, then steals home to set the stage for a 7–3 win over the Phillies in Philadelphia.

Simmons was 15–9 with a 2.48 ERA in 1963.

SEPTEMBER 5   Curt Flood collects five hits, including a triple, in five at-bats during a 9–0 win over the Mets at Busch Stadium. Curt Simmons pitched the shutout.

Flood batted .302 with 122 runs and 200 hits in 1963.

SEPTEMBER 8   The Cardinals record their ninth win in a row with a 5–1 decision over the Pirates in the first game of a doubleheader at Forbes Field. The winning streak ended when Pittsburgh won the nightcap 5–0.

SEPTEMBER 9   Curt Simmons pitches his second consecutive shutout, blanking the Cubs 6–0 at Busch Stadium.

SEPTEMBER 10   Stan Musial hits a home run in his first at-bat as a grandfather, sparking the Cardinals to an 8–0 win over the Cubs at Busch Stadium.

Sharon Musial, the wife of Stan's son Dick, gave birth to a son about 4:30 AM at Fort Riley, Kansas. About 16 hours later, on the first pitch of his first at-bat as a grandfather, Musial hit a home run off Glenn Hobbie that landed on the pavilion roof. Bob Gibson pitched the shutout and smacked a three-run homer.

SEPTEMBER 13   Curt Simmons pitches his third consecutive shutout, defeating the Braves 7–0 at Busch Stadium.

SEPTEMBER 15   The Cardinals sweep the Braves 3–2 and 5–0 at Busch Stadium to run their winning streak to 10 games. It was the Cards' 19th win in a span of 20 games and put the club just one game behind the first-place Dodgers with a three-game series scheduled against the Los Angeles club at Busch Stadium on September 16, 17, and 18.

SEPTEMBER 16   In the first game of the pennant showdown series against the Dodgers at Busch Stadium, Johnny Podres handcuffs the Cardinals 3–1. Stan Musial homered in the seventh inning to tie the contest 1–1, but Los Angeles scored twice in the ninth for the win.

The home run was the 475th and last of Musial's big-league career.

SEPTEMBER 17   The Dodgers defeat the Cardinals 4–0 behind a shutout by Sandy Koufax.

SEPTEMBER 18   The Dodgers complete a three-game sweep of the Cardinals with a 6–5 victory in 13 innings at Busch Stadium. The Cards led 5–1 before Bob Gibson allowed three runs in the eighth. Dick Nen, who was making the second plate appearance of his major league debut, homered in the ninth to tie the game 5–5. Nen entered the contest the previous inning as a pinch hitter. The Dodgers won the skirmish with a tally in the thirteenth.

The loss put the Cardinals four games out of first. The Cards never seriously threatened the Dodgers again and finished the year in second place, six games behind. On the positive side, the 93–69 record by St. Louis was the club's best since 1949.

SEPTEMBER 29   Stan Musial plays the last of his 3,026 major league games, a 3–2 win in 14 innings over the Reds before 27,576 at Busch Stadium. Dal Maxvill drove in the winning run with a walk-off double.

During batting practice, many Reds players asked Musial to pose with them for photographs and asked for his autograph. Among them was rookie second baseman Pete Rose, who was five months old when Musial made his big-league debut and would later break Musial's National League career record for hits in 1981. Rose shook Musial's hand and wished him well. During pregame ceremonies, Musial was presented with a framed six-foot-by-four-foot painting of the statue that would later adorn the new Busch Stadium. He was also given a diamond ring with the number 6. Testimonial speeches were given by August Busch, baseball commissioner Ford Frick, NL president Warren Giles, AL president Joe Cronin, St. Louis Mayor Raymond Tucker, and Missouri Governor John Dalton. Two Cub Scouts presented Musial with a neckerchief, which remained around his neck for the duration of the program. Afterward, he was driven around the front of the stands in a convertible accompanied by his family and waved to the fans. In Musial's first plate appearance, Cincinnati pitcher Jim Maloney caught him looking at strike three. In the fourth inning, Musial smashed a single just past Rose for the Cardinals' initial hit. Two innings later, Musial slashed another single to right to score the game's first run. Gary Kolb went in as a pinch runner, and Musial received a tumultuous standing ovation as he trotted off the field for the last time as a player.

NOVEMBER 4   The Cardinals trade George Altman and Bill Wakefield to the Mets for Roger Craig.

Pitching for two of the worst teams in major league history, Craig was 10–24 with the Mets in 1962 and 5–24 in 1963. He was 7–9 as a Cardinal in 1964 before being dealt to the Reds.

1964

Season in a Sentence

In a season full of unexpected twists and turns, the Cardinals overcome a 6½-game deficit in the final two weeks to win the pennant, and they down the Yankees in seven games in the World Series.

Finish • Won • Lost • Pct • GB

First   93   69   .574 +1.0

World Series—The Cardinals defeated the New York Yankees four games to three

Manager

Johnny Keane

Stats

Stats	Cards •	NL •	Rank
Batting Avg:	.272	.254	2
On-Base Pct:	.326	.313	2
Slugging Pct:	.392	.374	2
Home Runs:	109		7
Stolen Bases:	73		3
ERA:	3.43	3.54	6
Fielding Avg:	.973	.975	9
Runs Scored:	715		2
Runs Allowed:	652		7

Starting Lineup

Tim McCarver, c
Bill White, 1b
Julian Javier, 2b
Ken Boyer, 3b
Dick Groat, ss
Lou Brock, lf
Curt Flood, cf
Mike Shannon, rf
Charlie James, lf

Pitchers

Bob Gibson, sp
Curt Simmons, sp
Ray Sadecki, sp
Barney Schultz, rp
Ron Taylor, sp
Roger Craig, rp-sp

Attendance

1,143,294 (fifth in NL)

Club Leaders

Batting Avg:	Brock	.348
On-Base Pct:	Brock	.387
Slugging Pct:	Brock	.527
Home Runs:	Boyer	24
RBIs:	Boyer	119
Runs:	Boyer	100
Stolen Bases:	Brock	33
Wins:	Sadecki	20
Strikeouts:	Gibson	245
ERA:	Gibson	3.01
Saves:	Schultz	14

FEBRUARY 14   Three months after the assassination of John Kennedy, Stan Musial is named as director of the President's Council on Physical Fitness by new President Lyndon Johnson.

APRIL 9   The Cardinals trade Gary Kolb and Jimmie Coker to the Braves for Bob Uecker.

Uecker hit only .215 with three homers in 251 at-bats in two seasons with the Cardinals as a reserve catcher, but he kept the clubhouse loose with his unique brand of humor. After his career ended, Uecker had a long broadcasting and acting career. He was one of many 1964 Cardinals to turn to announcing games after their playing careers ended, joining Tim McCarver, Bill White, and Mike Shannon.

APRIL 14   In the midst of Beatlemania, with the Fab Four holding the top five spots on the Billboard chart of the top-selling singles, the Cardinals open the season with a

4–0 loss to the Dodgers in Los Angeles. Sandy Koufax pitched the complete-game shutout.

APRIL 22   In the first game of the season at Busch Stadium, the Cardinals win 7–6 over the Dodgers before 31,410. It was the first time that the Cardinals drew more than 30,000 for a home opener.

The Cardinals switched from blue caps to red ones for home games in 1964. Blue continued to be worn on the road, but the club changed to red caps with both their home whites and road grays in 1965.

MAY 4   A bean-ball battle erupts during a 9–2 win over the Phillies at Busch Stadium. In the second inning, Dennis Bennett hit Julian Javier after giving up a homer to Curt Flood. An inning later, Bennett was the target of two high hard ones from Bob Gibson. In the fourth, Jack Baldschun relieved Bennett and plunked Gibson on the left thigh. Gibson flipped his bat toward the mound. Baldschun caught the bat with his gloved hand, and Gibson was ejected.

The ejection probably cost Gibson a 20-win season. He didn't receive credit for a victory in the May 4 game because he pitched only four innings. Gibson finished the 1964 season with a 19–12 record, a 3.01 ERA, and 245 strikeouts in 287¹/₃ innings. Three Cardinal pitchers combined to win 57 games during the season. Ray Sadecki was 20–11 with an ERA of 3.68. Curt Simmons was 18–9 and had an ERA of 3.43.

MAY 8   The Cardinals play at Shea Stadium for the first time and lose 5–4 to the Mets.

MAY 15   Jeoff Long's first major league homer is a tape-measure job that hits the top of the animated Redbird sign to the left of the scoreboard at Busch Stadium during a 10–6 win over the Braves. Long was playing first base for Bill White, who was missing his first game since 1961, ending a streak of 284 consecutive games. Julian Javier hit a grand slam in the first inning off Denny Lemaster.

The homer proved to be the only one of Long's career in 83 at-bats. Long was one of three 1963 Cardinals to be born after Stan Musial made his major league debut. The other two were Tim McCarver and Jerry Buchek.

MAY 19   Ernie Broglio throws three wild pitches in the seventh inning of a 7–4 loss to the Cubs at Busch Stadium.

Before the contest, NL president Warren Giles presented general manager Bing Devine with a plaque signifying Devine's election as the National League Executive of the Year for 1963 in a poll conducted by The Sporting News. *Devine was honored for his work in bringing the Cardinals from a sixth-place finish in 1962 to second in 1963. The accolade didn't save Devine's job, however. He was fired by the Cardinals three months later (see August 17, 1964) but won the award again in 1964 after the club captured the pennant.*

MAY 20   Bob Gibson strikes out 12 batters during a 1–0 win over the Cubs at Busch Stadium. He retired the last 17 batters to face him. Bill White drove in the lone run of the game with a single in the eighth inning.

MAY 24	Groundbreaking ceremonies take place at the site of the new Busch Stadium in downtown St. Louis, which opened on May 12, 1966.
JUNE 2	The Cardinals trade Lew Burdette to the Cubs for Glen Hobbie.
JUNE 9	Ray Sadecki outduels Juan Marichal to defeat the Giants 1–0 in San Francisco. Charlie James drove in the lone run of the contest with a single in the ninth inning.
JUNE 10	Glenn Hobbie pitches a two-hitter to defeat the Giants 2–1 in the second game of a doubleheader at Candlestick Park. Both San Francisco hits were singles in the first inning by Harvey Kuenn and Willie Mays. The Giants won the opener 3–0.
JUNE 13	The Cardinals send Jim Saul and cash to the Reds for Bob Skinner.
JUNE 15	In the most beneficial trade in club history, the Cardinals swap Ernie Broglio, Bobby Shantz, and Doug Clemens to the Cubs for Lou Brock, Jack Spring, and Paul Toth. That evening, Brock made his debut with the Cards and struck out on three pitches as a pinch hitter during a 9–3 loss to the Astros in Houston.

The Cardinals came into the season with high hopes after finishing second in 1963. Those hopes were dashed early in 1964. Following a June 15 loss to the Astros, the Cards had a 28–31 record and were in eighth place. The offense was anemic, scoring only 29 runs in the previous 14 games, 11 of them losses. The two corner outfield positions were particular weaknesses in the batting order. The Cardinals did have strength in starting pitching, however. Broglio, a pitcher with an 18–8 record in 1963, was a spot starter in 1964. Dealing a pitcher for a starting outfielder made perfect sense, and Broglio was dealt along with Shantz and Clemens for Brock and two marginal pitchers. The trade wasn't well-received in St. Louis, however, as most fans believed the Cardinals front office had been bamboozled. Most fans in Chicago were ecstatic, a feeling summed up by Bob Smith of the Chicago Daily News: *"Thank you, thank you, you lovely St. Louis Cardinals," Smith wrote. "Nice doing business with you. Please call again anytime."*

Broglio was a proven commodity. He was 28 years old and had a lifetime record of 70–55. He was 3–5 at the start of the 1964 season but attributed his problem to a sore arm and believed that the ailment was temporary. Shantz was 38 but had pitched well for the Cards since his acquisition from Houston in 1962. Brock, on the other hand, was viewed as a player who could do little but steal a base. He was three days shy of his 25th birthday, had a .257 batting average with just 20 homers in 1,207 at-bats, and was a liability on defense. Within weeks, however, it was apparent to both fans and the Cardinals management alike that the club had hit the bull's-eye with the trade. Over the remainder of the 1964 season, Brock played in 103 games and batted .348 with 12 homers and 33 stolen bases. He went on to a Hall of Fame career and played in three World Series for the Cards. In three seasons as a Cub, Broglio had a 7–19 record and a 5.40 ERA.

JUNE 16	Lou Brock makes his first start with the Cardinals. Batting second and playing right field, Brock went 2 for 4 and had a triple and a stolen base during a 7–1 win over the Colts in Houston. Ken Boyer hit for the cycle, collecting a single, double, triple, and homer in that order off Bob Bruce and Don Larsen.

Brock was given uniform number 20, which was last worn by Gary Kolb during the 1963 regular season and spring training in 1964. On the Cardinals' all-time career lists, Brock ranks first in stolen bases (888), second in games (2,289), second in at-bats (9,125), second in runs (1,427), second in hits (2,713), second in total bases (3,776), second in doubles (434), fourth in triples (121), fifth in walks (681), and ninth in RBIs (814). He batted .297 as a Cardinal and hit 129 home runs.

June 27   Julian Javier ties a National League record for most putouts by a second baseman in a game with 11 during a 7–4 win over the Phillies at Busch Stadium.

July 7   Five days after President Lyndon Johnson signs a Civil Rights act banning discrimination in voting, jobs, and public accommodations, Cardinal batters drive in the first three National League runs during a 7–4 win over the American League in the All-Star Game, played at Shea Stadium in New York. In the fourth inning, Ken Boyer hit a two-run homer off John Wyatt. In the fifth, Dick Groat doubled in a run. The NL won the contest with four runs in the ninth, the last three on a walk-off homer by Johnny Callison.

Groat was involved in controversy midway through the 1964 season. Manager Johnny Keane had given him the go-ahead to use the hit-and-run whenever the All-Star shortstop deemed necessary, but the ploy backfired twice in a game against the Dodgers. As a result, Keane revoked the privilege, and Groat fumed for weeks. During a contest against the Braves, Groat complained about Keane to Milwaukee third baseman Eddie Mathews, who happened to be dating Elizabeth Busch, the daughter of the Cardinals owner. Elizabeth told her father about Groat's complaints. August Busch was angry that he had to hear about the problem from his daughter and not Keane or general manager Bing Devine. The incident led to Devine's forced resignation (see August 17, 1964) as well as Keane's departure (see October 16, 1964).

July 9   Mets outfielder Frank Thomas, sidelined with a glandular infection, comes off the bench and delivers a two-run homer in the ninth inning off Curt Simmons to beat the Cardinals 4–3 in New York.

At the conclusion of the contest, the Cardinals had a record of 39–41 and were 11 games back of the Phillies. On July 24, the Cards were still under .500 with a mark of 47–48 in a position 10 games off the pace. From that point to the end of the season, St. Louis had a record of 46–21 to take the pennant.

July 13   Lou Brock collects 7 hits, including a homer, triple, and double, in 11 at-bats during a doubleheader against the Pirates at Forbes Field. Brock was 3 for 5 in the opener, a 12-inning, 5–4 Cardinal victory. In the second tilt, the Cards picked up 20 hits and won 12–5.

July 14   Trailing 7–2, the Cardinals stun the Dodgers with two runs in the eighth inning and four in the ninth to win 8–7 at Busch Stadium. Bob Skinner drove in the tying and winning runs with a pinch-single.

July 18   With the help of four errors, the Cardinals score 11 runs in the eighth inning and wallop the Mets 15–7 at Busch Stadium. During the inning, Ken Boyer, Bill White, and Tim McCarver hit consecutive home runs. Boyer's homer was a grand slam off Bill Wakefield.

McCarver batted .288 and hit nine home runs in 1964.

JULY 19 The Cardinals score four runs in the ninth inning to defeat the Mets 7–6 in the second game of a doubleheader at Busch Stadium. Dick Groat drove in the winning run with a walk-off single. New York won the opener 3–2.

JULY 25 Ken Boyer hits a grand slam off Dennis Bennett in the fifth inning of a 10–9 win over the Phillies at Connie Mack Stadium. The Cardinals led 10–2 heading into the ninth and had to weather a furious seven-run Philadelphia rally.

Boyer won the National League Most Valuable Player Award in 1964 by leading the league in RBIs with 119 and by batting .295 with 24 homers and 100 runs scored.

JULY 28 The Cardinals score five runs in the tenth inning to defeat the Cubs 12–7 in Chicago.

JULY 29 The Cardinals explode for seven runs in the eighth inning and defeat the Cubs 9–1 in Chicago.

AUGUST 9 Prior to a 2–1 win over the Giants at Busch Stadium, members of the 1944 Cardinals and Browns, participants in the only all–St. Louis World Series in history, are introduced to the crowd. In an old-timers game, the Cardinals won 5–2.

AUGUST 12 Bill White extends his hitting streak to 20 games during a 6–4 win over the Giants at Busch Stadium.

White batted .303 with 21 homers and 102 RBIs in 1964.

AUGUST 16 Curt Flood collects eight consecutive hits, two of them triples, during a doubleheader against the Dodgers in Los Angeles. Flood had four hits in each game and eight of the 16 hits that the Cardinals accumulated during the twin bill. The Cards lost the first game 3–0, but won the second fray 4–0.

AUGUST 17 August Busch ousts Bing Devine as general manager by demanding his resignation. Business manager Art Routzong, a protégé of Devine's, was also dismissed along with Eddie Stanky, the director of player development. Bob Howsam replaced Devine.

Dissatisfied with the team's performance, Busch ordered a shake-up of the front office. Busch was disgruntled over many of Devine's trades and believed the farm system had declined. At the time of Devine's dismissal, the Cardinals were in fifth place, nine games out of first. The removal of Devine, who had been an employee of the Cardinals for 25 years and general manager since 1957, was orchestrated by Branch Rickey, who was hired as a special consultant by Busch in 1962. Devine was popular with the players, who were angry about his discharge. Many cited Devine's departure as a catalyst for the incredible comeback that resulted in a pennant in 1964. Howsam had worked for Rickey in the Pirates farm system during the 1950s when Howsam was president of the Denver club in the Western Association, and then the American Association, from 1949 through 1961. When the Continental League was formed in 1958 with designs on becoming a third major league with Rickey as president, Howsam was set to own the Denver franchise. Howsam was also the original owner of the Denver Broncos in 1960, although he sold the club a year later. At the time of his hiring by the Cardinals, Howsam was 46 years old and had been out of baseball for three years while working as an assistant vice president at Westamerica Securities, Inc. The Cardinals went on to win the 1964 National League pennant largely because of previous Devine trades that brought the Cardinals the likes of Lou Brock, Curt Flood, Bill White, Dick Groat, Julian Javier, Curt Simmons, and Barney Schultz. Although Busch was upset about what he perceived as a lack of progress in the farm system, the Devine regime signed and developed Steve Carlton, Tim McCarver, Nelson Briles, Ray Sadecki, Mike Shannon, Dal Maxvill, and Bobby Tolan. Under Howsam, the Cardinals dropped to seventh place in 1965 and sixth in 1966. But his deals helped the Cards win pennants in both 1967 and 1968. By that time, however, Howsam was running the Cincinnati Reds (see January 23, 1967). After leaving the Cardinals, Devine worked for the Mets, serving first as assistant to president George Weiss, then as president following Weiss's retirement. Devine returned to the Cardinals as general manager in December 1967.

AUGUST 21   The Cardinals score three runs in the ninth inning to defeat the Giants 6–5 at Candlestick Park. With the Cards trailing 5–3 with two outs and Lou Brock on first base, San Francisco manager Al Dark intentionally walked Bill White to put the tying run on base to pitch to light-hitting Dal Maxvill. The unorthodox strategy was upset when Maxvill delivered a run-scoring single. Mike Shannon followed with another single. Giants second baseman Hal Lanier, handling the relay from the outfield, threw wildly to the plate trying to retire White. While the Giants were retrieving the errant toss, Maxvill crossed the plate with the winning run.

Maxvill played 14 seasons in the majors (1962–75), 11 of them with the Cardinals (1962–72) because of his defensive abilities at shortstop. In 3,443 at-bats, he had a lifetime .217 average, a .259 slugging percentage, and a .293 on-base percentage. He has the lowest batting average of anyone in major league history with at least 3,200 at-bats. Maxvill hit only six career home runs and stole just seven bases. Maxvill served as the Cardinals' general manager from 1985 through 1994.

AUGUST 23   The Cardinals lose 3–2 in 10 innings to the Giants in San Francisco.

The defeat gave the Cards a 65–58 record and dropped the club into fourth place, 11 games behind the first-place Phillies.

AUGUST 25   After the Pirates take a 6–4 lead in the twelfth inning, the Cardinals rally for two runs in their half and then win 7–6 in the thirteenth at Busch Stadium. Lou Brock ended the game with a home run.

SEPTEMBER 4   Ken Boyer hits a three-run, walk-off homer in the ninth inning to beat the Cubs 8–5 at Busch Stadium.

SEPTEMBER 6   The Cardinals score two runs in the ninth inning and one in the eleventh to defeat the Cubs 6–5 at Busch Stadium. Lou Brock drove in the winning run with a single.

SEPTEMBER 7   The Cardinals win both ends of a doubleheader by 3–2 scores against the Reds at Busch Stadium by scoring runs in the ninth inning. Tim McCarver's walk-off single drove in the winning run in the opener. Curt Flood ended the second tilt with another single.

Flood hit .311 with 211 hits in 1964.

SEPTEMBER 9   The Cardinals score five runs in the tenth inning to defeat the Phillies 10–5 in Philadelphia. Lou Brock collected five hits, including a homer, in six at-bats.

SEPTEMBER 11   Bob Gibson pitches a two-hitter to defeat the Cubs 5–0 at Wrigley Field. The only Chicago hits were singles by Jimmy Stewart in the first inning and Ellis Burton in the seventh.

SEPTEMBER 13   The Cardinals score in all nine innings to beat the Cubs 15–2 in Chicago. The Cards scored two runs in the first inning, one in the second, two in the third, two in the fourth, two in the fifth, one in the sixth, three in the seventh, one in the eighth, and one in the ninth. The only other major league clubs since 1900 to score in all nine innings are the New York Giants on June 1, 1923, and the Colorado Rockies on May 5, 1999.

SEPTEMBER 15   Bob Gibson strikes out 12 batters during a 3–1 win over the Braves in the second game of a doubleheader in Milwaukee. The Cards also won the opener, 11–6.

SEPTEMBER 19   The Cardinals' slim hopes of winning a pennant take a jolt when the club blows a 5–0 lead and loses 7–5 in the first game of a doubleheader in Cincinnati. The game ended on a three-run homer by Frank Robinson off Bob Gibson. The Cards rebounded to win the second game 2–0.

SEPTEMBER 20   Any thoughts of playing in the World Series appear to go out the window when the Cardinals blow a 6–0, fourth-inning lead and lose 9–6 to the Reds in Cincinnati.

At the end of the day, the Phillies had a record of 90–60 and seemed to have the pennant well in hand. The Cardinals and Reds were tied for second, 6½ games out, with records of 83–66.

SEPTEMBER 24   Behind the pitching of Bob Gibson and Ray Sadecki, the Cardinals sweep the Pirates 4–2 and 4–0 in Pittsburgh.

On the same day, the Phillies played the Braves at Connie Mack Stadium and lost 5–3. It was Philadelphia's fourth loss in a row. The Phils were swept by the Reds in Philadelphia in a three-game series played on September 21, 22, and 23. At the conclusion of play on September 24, the Phillies were three games ahead of the Reds and 3½ in front of the Cards. St. Louis had nine games left to play.

SEPTEMBER 27   The Cardinals complete a sweep of the Pirates in a five-game series in Pittsburgh with a 5–0 win. Roger Craig (seven innings) and Barney Schultz (two innings) combined on the shutout.

On the same day, the Reds completed a five-game sweep of the Mets in New York and the Phillies lost their seventh game in a row to drop out of first place. At the end of the day, the Reds were in first place, one game ahead of the Phillies and 1½ games in front of the Cardinals. The Phillies and Reds each had five games left to play, and the Cardinals had six. The September 27 victory capped a six-city road trip in which the Cardinals were 12–6. That night, an enthusiastic crowd of 8,000 greeted the club at Lambert Field in St. Louis. Coming up next was a three-game series against the Phillies at Busch Stadium on September 28, 29, and 30.

SEPTEMBER 28   The Cardinals move into second place with a 5–1 win over the Phillies at Busch Stadium behind the pitching of Bob Gibson. The Cards were one game behind the Reds.

SEPTEMBER 29   Ray Sadecki records his 20th win of the season, defeating the Phillies 4–2 at Busch Stadium. The victory put the Cardinals into a tie for first place with the Reds, who lost 2–0 to the Pirates in Cincinnati. The Phillies were 1½ games out.

SEPTEMBER 30   The Cardinals take sole possession of first place by completing a sweep of the Phillies with an 8–5 victory at Busch Stadium. It was the Cardinals' eighth win in a row and Philadelphia's tenth loss in a row. On the same day, the Reds lost 1–0 in 16 innings to the Pirates in Cincinnati. The lone run of the game at Crosley Field scored on a squeeze bunt by Jerry May.

OCTOBER 1   With the Cardinals and Phillies idle, the Reds defeat the Pirates 5–4 in Cincinnati.

Heading into the final three days of the season, the Cardinals were one-half game ahead of the Reds and 2½ in front of the Phils. The Cards had three games left against the Mets on October 2, 3, and 4 at Busch Stadium. The Mets didn't seem to pose much of a threat, heading into the series with a record of 51–108. The Reds and Phillies were set to play each other in Cincinnati on October 2 and 4.

OCTOBER 2   The Cardinals lose 1–0 to the Mets at Busch Stadium as Al Jackson outduels Bob Gibson. Fortunately, the Reds lost to the Phillies 5–4, which kept the Cards in first place by one-half game over the Reds. The Phillies were 1½ games behind. The Giants were in fourth place, two games out. With two days remaining, there was a remote possibility that four teams could end the regular season in a four-way tie for first place.

OCTOBER 3   The Mets overwhelm the Cardinals 15–5 at Busch Stadium to drop the Cards into a tie for first with the Reds. Houston eliminated the Giants from the race with a 10–7 win in San Francisco. Heading into play on October 4, the last day of the regular season, the Cardinals and Reds had identical 92–69 records. The Phillies were 91–70. A three-way tie for first place was still possible with a Phillies win and a Cardinals loss.

OCTOBER 4   The Cardinals complete their incredible stretch drive by clinching the pennant with an 11–5 win over the Mets at Busch Stadium. The Cards took a 5–3 lead with three runs in the fifth. Bob Gibson was the winning pitcher with four innings of relief just two days after pitching a complete game. Barney Schultz earned the save, his fifth in the Cards' last 12 games, a period in which he pitched 11 scoreless innings. The Reds were eliminated with a 10–0 loss to the Phillies in Cincinnati. The Cards concluded the season with a one-game lead over both Cincinnati and Philadelphia. St. Louis won the pennant despite spending only six days in first place all season.

It was the Cardinals' first pennant since 1946 and the first for August Busch, who had purchased the club in 1953. In the World Series, the Cards met the Yankees. Under first-year manager Yogi Berra, a native of St. Louis who replaced Ralph Houk at the end of the 1963 season, the Yanks won in 1964 with a record of 99–63. It was the fifth American League pennant in succession for New York. As a result, the Yankees were heavy favorites. Another significant development was the family connection between the two clubs. Ken Boyer's brother Clete played third base for the Yankees.

Tim McCarver (left) and Ken Boyer congratulate Mike Shannon on his home run in the sixth inning of Game One of the 1964 World Series.

OCTOBER 7   The Cardinals open the 1964 World Series with a 9–5 win over the Yankees before 30,805 at Busch Stadium. Trailing 4–2, the Cards took the lead for good with four runs in the sixth inning. Mike Shannon tied the score 4–4 with a one-out, two-run homer. The other two runs scored on a double by Tim McCarver, a pinch-single by

Carl Warwick, and a triple by Curt Flood. Ray Sadecki allowed four runs and eight hits in six innings but received credit for the victory. Whitey Ford took the loss. He entered the Series with an all-time record 10 wins in World Series play. Suffering from a sore arm, Ford didn't play for the remainder of the Series.

Cardinals reserve catcher Bob Uecker didn't play in the 1964 World Series as Tim McCarver caught every inning of every game. Uecker did find a new use for a tuba, however. During batting practice before Game One, he borrowed a tuba from a member of the band scheduled to play the National Anthem and tried to direct fly balls into its large opening. Uecker was billed $200 for the dents he put in the tuba.

OCTOBER 8   The Yankees even the Series by defeating the Cardinals 8–3 before 30,805 at Busch Stadium. Bob Gibson surrendered four runs in eight innings. The Yankees put the game away with four runs in the ninth off Barney Schultz and Gordie Richardson.

Julian Javier didn't start a game in the 1964 Series because of an injured hip. Dal Maxvill replaced him at second base.

OCTOBER 10   The Yankees take the lead in the Series by winning Game Three in New York 2–1 thanks to a run in the ninth. Curt Simmons allowed only one run and four hits in eight innings but was lifted for a pinch hitter in the top of the ninth. Barney Schultz relieved in the bottom half, and on his first pitch gave up a home run to Mickey Mantle that landed in the upper deck in right field. Jim Bouton pitched a complete game for the Yankees.

Simmons had been a member of the 1950 Phillies' starting rotation, which won the National League pennant, but he was unable to pitch in the World Series because he was drafted by the Army in August of that year. He had to wait until 1964 for an opportunity to appear in the postseason.

OCTOBER 11   The Cardinals even the Series at two games apiece with a 4–3 win over the Yankees in New York. The Yankees seemed to be on the way to another win with three runs in the first inning off Ray Sadecki. From there, the Cardinals' relievers took over. Roger Craig went 4²/₃ innings, allowing no runs and two hits. Ron Taylor pitched four hitless innings. Ken Boyer accounted for all four Cardinals runs with a one-out grand slam in the sixth against Al Downing. The bases were loaded on two singles and an error by second baseman Bobby Richardson, who threw wildly to second on what looked like a sure double play with one out.

OCTOBER 12   The Cardinals pull within one game of a World Championship with a 10-inning, 5–2 win over the Yankees in New York. The Cards took a 2–0 lead into the ninth with Bob Gibson working on a complete-game shutout. He recorded his 13th strikeout of the game for the first out of the ninth inning. But the Yankees tied the game on Tom Tresh's two-out, two-run homer. In the top of the tenth, Bill White walked, Ken Boyer beat out a bunt, and Tim McCarver hit a three-run homer on a 3–2 pitch from Pete Mikkelsen with one out. Gibson closed the victory in the bottom half.

OCTOBER 14   The Yankees force a seventh game by defeating the Cardinals 8–3 before 30,805 at Busch Stadium. The Yanks broke a 1–1 tie in the sixth inning on back-to-back homers by Roger Maris and Mickey Mantle, both of which reached the right-field pavilion roof. Joe Pepitone sealed the win with a grand slam off Gordie Richardson in the eighth inning.

OCTOBER 15   The Cardinals claim the World Championship with a 7–5 win over the Yankees before 30,346 at Busch Stadium. The starting pitchers were Bob Gibson and Mel Stottlemyre, each pitching on two days' rest. The Cards took a 3–0 lead with three runs in the fourth inning. One of the runs scored on a double steal: Tim McCarver swiped home, and Mike Shannon pilfered second. Three more runs followed in the fifth, the first on a solo homer by Lou Brock. With Bob Gibson on the mound, a 6–0 lead appeared to be secure, but the Yankees went down fighting. Mickey Mantle hit a three-run homer in the sixth. Ken Boyer homered in the seventh to give the Cardinals a 7–3 lead, and he gave his brother Clete, the Yankees' third baseman, a playful pat on the back just before rounding third on his home run trot. Clete returned the gesture when he kept the Yankees in the game with his home run in the ninth. Phil Linz followed with a two-out homer to make the score 7–5. Gibson closed out the game, however, by inducing Bobby Richardson, who had 13 hits in the Series, to pop out to second baseman Julian Javier.

The Boyers are the only pair of brothers to each hit a home run in the same World Series. McCarver is the only catcher to steal home in the Fall Classic and the only player to do it in Game Seven. He hit .478 in the 1964 Series with 11 hits in 23 at-bats. Gibson allowed 9 runs and 23 hits in 27 innings and struck out 31 batters. Carl Warwick collected three hits and a walk in five pinch-hit appearances.

OCTOBER 16   Just one day after winning the World Series, Johnny Keane stuns the Cardinals by submitting his resignation. He had worked in the organization since 1938. The Cardinals called a press conference to announce that Keane was being offered a new contract. Keane showed up 15 minutes late, however, and handed Busch a letter explaining the reasons for his resignation. Busch then had to tell the assembled media that Keane would not be returning in 1965.

Keane had a strong working relationship with general manager Bing Devine, business manager Art Routzong, and director of player development Eddie Stanky. When August Busch discharged those three (see August 17, 1964), Keane knew that he would be the next to go. Busch wanted to hire Leo Durocher as manager to replace Keane. A member of the Gas House Gang during the 1930s, Durocher had previously managed the Dodgers (1939–46, 1948) and Giants (1948–55). In 1964, Durocher was a coach with the Dodgers and told the club he wouldn't be returning in 1965, believing that his hiring by the Cardinals was a done deal. Then came the Cardinals' unbelievable turnaround during the final two weeks of the season—erasing a 6½-game deficit in just two weeks to win the pennant, and subsequently the World Series over the Yankees. Busch had no choice but to bring Keane back in 1965. Busch formally offered Keane a contract during the last week of September, but Keane said that he wanted to wait until after the season was over to make up his mind. Keane had already decided to quit, however. He could no longer work for Busch after the Cards owner had spent several weeks shopping for a different manager. Durocher spent the 1965 season working the Saturday Game of the Week for NBC and became manager of the Cubs in October 1965.

OCTOBER 19   Johnny Keane takes a job as the manager of the Yankees.

Yogi Berra won the 1964 pennant for the Yankees in his first season as manager, but the front office wasn't happy with his performance and fired him on October

16, the same day that Keane resigned his position with the Cards. In a strange twist, Keane turned around and accepted a job with the Yankees, the team he had just defeated in the World Series. From 1947 through 1964, the Yankees had won 15 pennants and 10 World Championships in 18 years. As soon as Keane took over, however, the club seemed to grow old overnight. The Yanks finished in sixth place in 1965 with a record of 77–85, the club's first losing season since 1925. After a 4–16 start in 1966, Keane was fired. On January 6, 1967, he died of a heart attack at the age of 55.

OCTOBER 20   The Cardinals hire Red Schoendienst as manager on the same day Branch Rickey is dropped as a consultant.

Schoendienst had been a coach under Johnny Keane since 1961. He played for the Cards from 1945 through 1955 and again from 1961 through 1963. Schoendienst's hiring was a popular move with the fans, who were angry over the ouster of Bing Devine and the resignation of Johnny Keane, two men who had just led the Cardinals to a World Championship. Schoendienst had never managed a team in the majors or in the minors. He had a rocky start as a skipper, as the Cards were 80–81 in 1965 and 83–79 in 1966. But the club won the NL pennant in 1967 and the world title in 1968. Schoendienst remained as the Cardinal manager through the end of the 1976 season, the longest stint of anyone in club history.

DECEMBER 7   Five weeks after Lyndon Johnson defeats Barry Goldwater in the presidential election, the Cardinals trade Johnny Lewis and Gordie Richardson to the Mets for Tracy Stallard and Elio Chacon.

DECEMBER 14   The Cardinals trade Roger Craig and Charlie James to the Reds for Bob Purkey.

DECEMBER 15   The Cardinals purchase Tito Francona from the Indians.

1965

Season in a Sentence

The glow of a World Championship wears out quickly as the Cardinals stumble out of the gate and close the season with a losing record.

Finish • Won • Lost • Pct • GB

Seventh 80   81   .497 16.5

Manager

Red Schoendienst

Stats

Stats	Cards	NL	Rank
Batting Avg:	.254	.249	4
On-Base Pct:	.316	.313	3
Slugging Pct:	.371	.374	6
Home Runs:	109		7
Stolen Bases:	100		2
ERA:	3.77	3.54	6
Fielding Avg:	.979	.977	2
Runs Scored:	707		3
Runs Allowed:	674		6

Starting Lineup

Tim McCarver, c
Bill White, 1b
Julian Javier, 2b
Ken Boyer, 3b
Dick Groat, ss
Lou Brock, lf
Curt Flood, cf
Mike Shannon, rf
Phil Gagliano, 2b-rf
Tito Francona, rf
Jerry Buchek, 2b-ss

Pitchers

Bob Gibson, sp
Tracy Stallard, sp-rp
Curt Simmons, sp
Ray Sadecki, sp
Bob Purkey, sp-rp
Ray Washburn, sp-rp
Hal Woodeshick, rp
Don Dennis, rp

Attendance

1,241,201 (fifth in NL)

Club Leaders

Batting Avg:	Flood	.310
On-Base Pct:	Flood	.361
Slugging Pct:	White	.481
Home Runs:	White	24
RBIs:	Flood	83
Runs:	Brock	107
Stolen Bases:	Brock	63
Wins:	Gibson	20
Strikeouts:	Gibson	270
ERA:	Gibson	3.07
Saves:	Brock	63

April 12 Five weeks after the first US combat troops arrive in Vietnam, the Cardinals tie the Cubs 10–10 in the season opener at Wrigley Field, called after 11 innings by rain. The Cards led 9–6 heading into the bottom of the ninth, but Chicago scored three times. The Redbirds went ahead again 10–9 in the eleventh but allowed the Cubs to tie once more. Curt Flood collected four hits, including two doubles. Lou Brock and Bill White each had three hits. Steve Carlton made his major league debut and faced one batter in the tenth, issuing a walk.

> *Carlton was only 20 years old at the time. He didn't reach the majors to stay, however, until 1967, when he became a part of the Cardinals' starting rotation on a club that won two consecutive pennants. Carlton was 77–62 with a 3.10 ERA in St. Louis before a trade to Philadelphia for Rick Wise in February 1972. It was one of the worst swaps in team history.*

April 16 In the home opener, the Cardinals lose 10–4 to the Reds before 24,364 at Busch Stadium.

April 17 The Cardinals are given their 1964 World Championship rings by commissioner Ford Frick prior to an 8–0 win over the Reds at Busch Stadium. It was the Cards' first win of 1965 after starting the season with a tie and three defeats.

APRIL 18   On Easter Sunday, the World Championship pennant is raised over Busch Stadium before an 8–2 loss to the Reds. Six fans selected at random helped raise the pennant.

MAY 2   Bill White hits a walk-off homer in the ninth inning to defeat the Pirates 5–4 in the second game of a doubleheader at Busch Stadium. The Cardinals also won the opener, 9–5. In an oddity, four Bobs served as starting pitchers in the twin bill. Bob Gibson and Bob Purkey went for the Cardinals, with Bob Friend and Bob Veale taking the hill for Pittsburgh.

            White hit .289 with 24 homers in 1965.

MAY 7   Bob Gibson pitches a one-hitter to defeat the Phillies 2–0 at Connie Mack Stadium. The only Philadelphia hit was a single in the fifth inning by Johnny Callison.

            Gibson started the 1965 season by winning his first eight decisions. He finished with a 20–12 record, 20 complete games, a 3.07 ERA, and 270 strikeouts in 299 innings.

MAY 14   The Cardinals score two runs in the ninth inning to beat the Pirates 8–7 in Pittsburgh. Dick Groat tripled in the first run and scored on a single by Bill White.

MAY 20   The Cardinals polish off the Phillies 12–2 at Busch Stadium.

MAY 23   Down 7–0, the Cardinals pull off an incredible rally with two runs in the eighth inning, five in the ninth, and one in the twelfth to win 8–7 over the Mets at Busch Stadium. With two outs in the ninth, the bases loaded, and the Mets leading 7–4, Dal Maxvill hit a sinking liner that skipped past right fielder Ron Swoboda to tie the score. Bill White's walk-off double drove in the winning run.

            The Cardinals were 22–15 on May 24, and a pennant repeat looked like a possibility, but the club lost 25 of its next 35 games.

MAY 27   The Cardinals play indoors for the first time and lose 6–1 to the Astros at the Astrodome in Houston.

JUNE 8   In the first amateur draft, the Cardinals select right-handed pitcher Joe DiFabio from Delta State College.

            DiFabio never made past Triple-A. The initial draft was one of the worst in Cardinal history. The only future major leaguers the Cardinals drafted and signed in 1965 were Harry Parker in the 4th round and Jerry Robertson in the 27th.

JUNE 13   The Cardinals score seven runs in the fourth inning and defeat the Braves 12–2 in the second game of a doubleheader at Busch Stadium. Milwaukee won the first contest 4–2.

JUNE 15   The Cardinals trade Mike Cuellar and Ron Taylor to the Astros for Hal Woodeshick and Chuck Taylor.

            At the time of the trade, Cuellar was 28 years old and had a 5–5 record and a 5.09 ERA as a major leaguer. Following a rough spring training in 1965, the Cardinals sent him to the minors. After four seasons in Houston, Cuellar was traded to the Orioles, where he became one of the top pitchers in baseball. From 1969 through 1974, Cuellar had a 125–63 record for Baltimore.

JUNE 18   Bill White homers in the tenth inning to defeat the Braves 5–4 in Milwaukee.

JUNE 27   Bob Gibson strikes out 12 batters during an 8–0 win over the Cubs in the first game of a doubleheader at Busch Stadium. Chicago won the first game 6–3.

JULY 2   Bob Gibson fans 13 hitters during a 6–2 victory over the Mets in New York.

JULY 3   Phil Gagliano's two-run homer off Jack Fisher in the sixth inning accounts for the only runs in a 2–0 victory over the Mets in New York. Tracy Stallard (seven innings) and Hal Woodeshick (two innings) combined on the shutout.

Gagliano and Tim McCarver not only played together with the Cardinals but also were teammates on an American Legion team in Memphis, Tennessee, that Gagliano's uncle coached.

JULY 7   Bob Gibson pitches a 13-inning complete game and strikes out 12 batters, but he loses 4–2 to the Giants at Busch Stadium.

JULY 13   Bob Gibson earns a save in the All-Star Game by pitching the eighth and ninth innings without allowing a run in a 6–5 National League victory at Metropolitan Stadium in Bloomington, Minnesota. Gibson closed out the contest by fanning Harmon Killebrew and Joe Pepitone.

JULY 31   Lou Brock's two-run, walk-off, bases-loaded single in the ninth inning beats the Dodgers 4–3 at Busch Stadium.

Brock hit .288 with 16 homers, 107 runs, and 63 stolen bases in 1965. He was the first Cardinal to swipe at least 60 bases since Tommy McCarthy had 83 steals in 1890.

AUGUST 12   On the second day of the Watts riots in Los Angeles, which resulted in the deaths of 34 people, the Cardinals play the Braves in Milwaukee for the last time and win 5–4 in 13 innings.

The Braves moved to Atlanta in 1966.

AUGUST 15   The Cardinals break loose for eight runs in the eighth inning and beat the Reds 12–7 at Busch Stadium.

AUGUST 16   Tim McCarver hits a grand slam off Billy O'Dell in the eighth inning to tie the game 8–8, but the Braves score two times in the ninth to win 10–8 at Busch Stadium.

McCarver hit .276 with 11 homers in 1965.

AUGUST 27   The Cardinals defeat the Reds 6–5 in 14 innings in Cincinnati. Ken Boyer drove in the winning run with a double.

AUGUST 31   Bob Gibson not only pitches a two-hitter but also smacks a home run during a 3–0 win over the Cubs at Wrigley Field. The only Chicago hits were singles by Don Landrum and Joey Amalfitano, both in the sixth inning.

SEPTEMBER 3   Jim Hickman of the Mets hits three homers in consecutive at-bats off Ray Sadecki
during a 6–3 Cardinals loss at Busch Stadium.

SEPTEMBER 4   Bob Gibson pitches his second consecutive two-hitter, matching his performance
of August 31, to defeat the Mets 3–0 in the first game of a doubleheader at Busch
Stadium. The only New York hits were singles by Johnny Lewis in the first inning
and Joe Christopher in the sixth. The Cards completed the sweep with a 3–1 victory
in the second tilt.

SEPTEMBER 8   Ray Sadecki strikes out 13 batters in seven innings but loses 2–1 to the Pirates at
Busch Stadium.

SEPTEMBER 15   Curt Flood collects five hits in six at-bats and drives in five runs to lead the Cardinals
to a 7–3 win over the Pirates in Pittsburgh. Flood had four singles and a double.

    Flood hit .310 with 11 homers in 1965.

SEPTEMBER 22   In his first major league start, Larry Jaster pitches a complete game to defeat the
Astros 4–1 at Busch Stadium.

    *Only 21 when he reached the majors, Jaster won all three of his first major
    league starts, each of them complete games in which he allowed only five
    runs. Jaster is best known for shutting out the Dodgers five times in 1966 (see
    September 28, 1966).*

SEPTEMBER 29   Bob Gibson hits a grand slam off Gaylord Perry in the eighth inning to give the
Cardinals an 8–0 lead over the Giants at Candlestick Park. San Francisco scored six
runs in the ninth, five off Gibson, but the Cardinals emerged with an 8–6 victory.

SEPTEMBER 30   The Cardinals score six runs in the first inning and swamp the Astros 19–8 in
Houston.

OCTOBER 3   On the last day of the season, Bob Gibson records his 20th victory of the season
with a 5–2 decision over the Astros in Houston.

OCTOBER 20   The Cardinals trade Ken Boyer to the Mets for Charley Smith and Al Jackson.

    *Following the disappointing 1965 season, Bob Howsam began his dismantling
    of the 1964 World Championship infield by dealing Boyer to the Mets. Boyer
    had been with the Cardinals for 11 seasons and was the NL's MVP in 1964, but
    he declined sharply in 1965 and was 34 years old at the time of the trade. The
    decline continued after leaving St. Louis. Boyer was a regular for only one more
    season. Smith gave the Cards one mediocre season before a trade to the Yankees
    in exchange for Roger Maris. Jackson was 13–15 with the Cards in 1966 but had
    an ERA of 2.51 and was a spot starter on the 1967 World Championship club.*

OCTOBER 27   The day before the keystone is installed in the Gateway Arch, the Cardinals trade
Bill White, Dick Groat, and Bob Uecker to the Phillies for Alex Johnson, Art
Mahaffey, and Pat Corrales.

    *Two more aging All-Star infielders were dealt just seven days after Boyer was
    traded to the Mets. White and Groat were both near the end of the line and*

spent only one more season each as big-league regulars, but none of the three players acquired in the swap aided the Cardinals in any significant way.

DECEMBER 9   Branch Rickey dies at the age of 83. Rickey had remained unconscious in a Columbia, Missouri, hospital since November 13, when he had collapsed from a heart attack. He had checked out of a St. Louis hospital that day against the advice of doctors and family so that he could attend the Missouri-Oklahoma football game and make his acceptance speech at the Missouri Sports Hall of Fame banquet that night. Rickey collapsed during the speech.

1966

Season in a Sentence

The Cardinals open a new stadium and have the second-best ERA in the NL, but they rank last in the league in runs scored and barely finish above the .500 mark.

Finish • Won • Lost • Pct • GB

Sixth   83   79   .512   12.0

Manager

Red Schoendienst

Stats

Stats	Cards	NL	Rank
Batting Avg:	.251	.305	8
On-Base Pct:	.300	.316	10
Slugging Pct:	.368		7
Home Runs:	108		8 (tie)
Stolen Bases:	144		1
ERA:	3.11	3.61	2
Fielding Avg:	.977	.977	5
Runs Scored:	571		10
Runs Allowed:	577		2

Starting Lineup

Tim McCarver, c
Orlando Cepeda, 1b
Julian Javier, 2b
Charley Smith, 3b
Dal Maxvill, ss
Lou Brock, lf
Curt Flood, cf
Mike Shannon, rf
Jerry Buchek, 2b-ss
Phil Gagliano, 3b
Tito Francona, 1b

Pitchers

Bob Gibson, sp
Al Jackson, sp
Ray Washburn, sp
Larry Jaster, sp
Joe Hoerner, rp
Hal Woodeshick, rp
Nelson Briles, sp-rp

Attendance

1,712,980 (fourth in NL)

Club Leaders

Batting Avg:	Cepeda	.303
On-Base Pct:	Cepeda	.362
Slugging Pct:	Cepeda	.469
Home Runs:	Cepeda	17
RBIs:	Flood	78
Runs:	Brock	94
Stolen Bases:	Brock	74
Wins:	Gibson	21
Strikeouts:	Gibson	225
ERA:	Gibson	2.44
Saves:	Hoerner	14

JANUARY 27   In anticipation of the closing of Busch Stadium in May, the Cardinals donate the land it occupies to the Herbert Hoover Boys Club (today known as the Herbert Hoover Boys and Girls Club). The site, at Grand and Dodier, where baseball was played for 100 years, was converted to a complex serving 2,500 youngsters, including a recreation center and swimming pool. August Busch said that he considered turning the park over to real estate interests for a shopping development but decided granting the land to the youth of St. Louis "would be more beneficial to the entire community."

MARCH 5   The Major League Players Association hires Marvin Miller as the new executive director of the organization. Miller formally took office on July 1. Under Miller's leadership, the association would take actions that led to a revolution in player-owner relations, including free agency beginning in 1967.

MARCH 26   A model of the new scoreboard to be installed at Busch Memorial Stadium, set to open on May 12, is unveiled to the public.

The scoreboard was in two units, each measuring 145 feet long and 21 feet high. The left-field unit carried the stats of the game in progress along with advertisements and public-service announcements. The right-field section displayed the scores of out-of-town contests and the message board. On the right-field side, a neon Cardinal streaked across each time a member of the home team hit a home run. The "flight" was accompanied by the actual studio recording of a redbird's chirp. At the same time, on the left-field portion, an eagle flapping its wings was superimposed over Anheuser-Busch's trademark "A." Able to show only four different colors and lacking animation, the scoreboard seems quaint by today's standards, but it was cutting edge at a time when there were few electronic scoreboards of its size in the country. The original scoreboard was replaced in 1983.

APRIL 7   The Cardinals sell Bob Purkey to the Pirates.

In the last 12 home games at old Busch Stadium, 12 St. Louis baseball greats were honored, one for each game. The 12 were Stan Musial, Jesse Haines, Joe Medwick, Frankie Frisch, Chick Hafey, Dizzy Dean, Terry Moore, Johnny Mize, Enos Slaughter, Marty Marion, Red Schoendienst, and George Sisler.

APRIL 13   In the season opener, the Cardinals lose 3–2 in 12 innings to the Phillies before only 8,219 at Sportsman's Park. John Herrnstein drove in the winning run with a single off Dennis Aust.

APRIL 15   The Cardinals tie a major league record by winning their 18th consecutive game at Forbes Field in Pittsburgh, a streak dating back to May 7, 1964, by defeating the Pirates 9–2.

APRIL 16   The Cardinals' 18-game winning streak in Pittsburgh ends with a 3–2 loss to the Pirates.

The only other major league clubs to win 18 games in a row on the road were the Red Sox, against the Yankees from 1911 through 1913, and the Dodgers, against the Phillies in 1945 and 1946.

APRIL 21   Curt Flood's two-out, two-run homer in the ninth inning beats the Mets 5–4 in New York.

APRIL 25   Rookie pitcher Larry Jaster shuts out the Dodgers 2–0 in Los Angeles.

APRIL 27   The Cardinals play on AstroTurf for the first time and lose 3–1 to the Astros at the Astrodome.

The Astrodome opened in 1965 with a conventional grass field, but fielders lost

fly balls in the glare of the glass panels in the roof. The glass had to be painted,
which killed the grass. The artificial surface, manufactured by Monsanto and
named AstroTurf, was the solution.

MAY 4   Ray Sadecki is the only Cardinal base runner in an 8–0 loss to the Mets at Busch
         Stadium. Sadecki robbed opposing pitcher Jack Hamilton of a perfect game when he
         beat out a bunt in the third inning.

MAY 6   Bob Gibson strikes out 13 batters but loses 4–2 to the Giants at Busch Stadium.

MAY 7   The Giants score 13 runs in the third inning off Art Mahaffey, Dennis Aust, and
         Tracy Stallard and roll to a 15–2 victory over the Cardinals at Busch Stadium.

MAY 8   In the last game at Busch Stadium, the Cardinals lose 10–5 to the Giants before
         17,503. Willie Mays accounted for the last run in the ballpark with a homer in the
         ninth inning. On the final play of the game, Alex Johnson bounced into a double
         play. In postgame ceremonies, August Busch presented the deed to the property to
         Richard Amberg, publisher of the *St. Louis Globe-Democrat* and president of the
         Herbert Hoover Boys Club. Stadium superintendent Bill Stocksick, who "planted"
         the original home plate in 1909, was given the honor of digging it up. He then
         carried the plate to a waiting helicopter, where it was taken to the new Busch
         Memorial Stadium.

         On the same day, the Cardinals traded Ray Sadecki to the Giants for Orlando
         Cepeda. For short-term value, it was one of the best trades in Cardinal history.
         At the time it was announced, it was not popular with fans in St. Louis, however.
         Sadecki had a 20–11 record in 1964, and although he was 6–15 with a 5.21
         ERA in 1965, he was only 25 and still seemed to have a bright future. Cepeda
         was 28, appeared to be damaged goods, and had an unjustified reputation as a
         malingerer. From 1958 through 1964, he hit .309 and averaged 32 homers and
         107 RBIs per season with the Giants. But in 1965, he was limited to 34 at-bats
         because of a knee injury, and at the start of the 1966 season, he found himself
         playing behind Willie McCovey. The Cardinals were in desperate need of a
         first baseman after trading Bill White the previous offseason and subsequently
         failing to find an adequate replacement. Cepeda more than filled the bill. Over
         the remainder of the 1966 season, he hit .303 with 17 homers in 123 games. In
         1967, Cepeda was the National League MVP when he batted .325, clubbed 25
         homers, and led the league in RBIs with 111.

MAY 10   In his Cardinal debut, Orlando Cepeda homers during an 8–0 win over the Cubs in
         Chicago.

MAY 12   The Cardinals open Busch Memorial Stadium before 46,048 and win 4–3 in 12
         innings over the Atlanta Braves on a 50-degree night. The first batter was Felipe
         Alou facing Ray Washburn. Later, Alou hit two home runs to give the Braves a 3–2
         lead. Mike Shannon hit the first Cardinal homer in the ballpark. The Cardinals tied
         the score in the ninth on a single by Jerry Buchek. Lou Brock won the contest with
         a walk-off single. Don Dennis was the winning pitcher, and Phil Niekro was the loser.

         Among those present were baseball commissioner William Eckert and NL
         president Warren Giles. A helicopter landed to deliver the American flag to open

the game's festivities. The stadium wasn't quite complete, however. In the city that gave baseball "The Gas House Gang," gas to the concession stands' grills hadn't been hooked up, so there were no hot dogs. Workers were still laying tile and hammering nails through the paneling in the elegant Stadium Club, which featured a large bar and numerous tables for dining. Attendants had to ice the bottles of beer by hand because the refrigeration equipment wasn't working. The message board and the mechanical rolling tarp weren't operating properly. The outfield was soggy, and the infield still had patches of dirt. Those problems were quickly corrected, however, and Cardinals fans arrived in record numbers. Prior to 1966, the Cardinals' record for season attendance was 1,430,676 in 1949. The club drew 1,241,201 in 1965. The 1966 Cardinals attracted 1,712,980 into the old and new Busch Stadiums.

A New Stadium for St. Louis

August Busch was a man who was used to getting his way. He wanted a new stadium for the Cardinals in downtown St. Louis that could comfortably hold 50,000 fans and demanded that the stockholders of Anheuser-Busch, Inc., approve a $5 million investment for the construction of the facility. The motion passed by a 7–1 margin on April 13, 1960. The other $21 million necessary to make the stadium a reality was raised by the Civic Center Development Corporation, headed by James P. Hickok, president of the First National Bank of St. Louis; Sidney Maestra, chairman of the board of the Mercantile Trust Co.; and Preston Eslep, president of the Transit Casualty Co. The Civic Center Development Corporation would become owners of the new ballpark, which opened on May 12, 1966, with the unwieldy name Civic Center Busch Memorial Stadium. (By 1983, it was known simply as Busch Stadium.) It was only the second privately financed stadium built for Major League Baseball since 1923. The other one was Dodger Stadium in Los Angeles, opened in 1962. (The only one built privately since the 1966 opening of Busch has been SBC Park in San Francisco, finished in 2000.)

August Busch wanted to replace the original Busch Stadium, opened in 1909 as Sportsman's Park, which was expensive to maintain because of its age, besides holding only 30,500 fans. Many of those seats were undesirable because of obstructing posts and girders. When it was built, there were few automobiles on the road, and nearly everyone traveled by streetcar. Located in a residential neighborhood, the initial Busch Stadium was difficult to reach by car and had limited parking.

The new Busch Stadium was part of the urban renewal of downtown St. Louis. The overall plan encompassed 31 blocks over 82 acres just south of the downtown shopping district. The area had deteriorated significantly and was the site of warehouses, fourth-rate hotels, greasy spoons, bars and burlesque houses. It was a period in which municipalities tried to fight the decay of the inner-city with a bulldozer, and all 31 blocks were slated for demolition and replaced by new structures. According to the plan, an eight-block, 30-acre section was scheduled to be razed to make way for the stadium, bounded by 7th Street, Walnut Street, Broadway and Spruce Street. A group of parking garages around the stadium could hold 7,400 cars. Other features of the development included an 800-unit motel, several office buildings and commercial facilities, restaurants, and shops.

The new stadium, also used by the football Cardinals, was a major impetus for rebuilding all of downtown since it would bring activity to the area. Part of a national trend, it was one of many multipurpose stadiums planned or built in or near downtowns of major cities during the 1960s and 1970s. Similar stadiums were constructed in Washington (opened in 1962), Atlanta (1966), Pittsburgh (1970), Cincinnati (1970), and Philadelphia (1971).

Edward Durell Stone, whose work included the United States Pavilion at the Brussels World's Fair in 1958 and the US Embassy in New Delhi, agreed to serve as collaborating architect with the St. Louis firms of Schwartz & Van Hoefen and Sverdrup & Parcel. The architectural signature of the new stadium was 96 arches along the roofline that echoed the Gateway Arch, which was completed on October 28, 1965. A circular design was used to accommodate both baseball and football more easily. The box seats were movable so they could follow the foul lines for baseball games and the sidelines for football.

Eventually, the multipurpose circular stadiums of the 1962–71 era were abandoned, and separate facilities were built for baseball and football. At the start of the 2006 baseball season, the only one still standing was RFK Stadium in Washington, which will be used by the Nationals until a new baseball-only ballpark is completed sometime around 2008.

MAY 22   After the first two batters in the ninth inning are retired, the Cardinals rally for two runs in the inning to defeat the Reds 4–3 at Busch Memorial Stadium.

When it first opened, Busch Memorial Stadium was 330 feet down each foul line, 386 feet to the power alleys, and 414 feet to center field with a 10½-foot-high fence.

MAY 25   The Cardinals score seven runs in the seventh inning and defeat the Cubs 9–1 at Busch Memorial Stadium. Curt Flood hit a grand slam off Bill Faul.

MAY 26   The Cardinals score three runs in the ninth inning to beat the Cubs 3–2 at Busch Memorial Stadium. Tim McCarver drove in the winning run with a single.

McCarver hit .274 with 12 homers in 1966 and led the National League in triples with 13. McCarver is the only catcher in history to lead the league in triples.

MAY 29   Nelson Briles carries a no-hitter into the seventh inning but gives up two runs and three hits to fall behind the Reds 2–1 at Busch Stadium. The Cardinals rallied to win, however, 3–2 in 10 innings.

JUNE 3   The Cardinals play the Braves in Atlanta for the first time and win 3–2.

JUNE 7   Bob Gibson strikes out 12 batters in seven innings, including a record-tying four in the fourth inning, but the Pirates score eight runs in the eighth inning, four of them off Gibson, to defeat the Cardinals 9–1 in Pittsburgh.

On the same day, the Cardinals selected outfielder Leron Lee from Grant High School in Sacramento, California, in the first round of the amateur draft. A top high school football player, Lee refused numerous scholarships in order to sign with the Cardinals. He had an eight-year big-league career (1969–76), three of them with the Cards, mainly as a reserve outfielder. He hit .250 with 31 homers in 614 big-league games. Others future major leaguers drafted and signed by the club in 1966 were Clay Kirby in the third round and Jerry DaVanon in the first round of the secondary phase, which consisted of previously drafted players who had failed to sign with their original clubs. Both Kirby and DaVanon were selected by the Padres in the expansion draft following the end of the 1968 season.

June 10   Orlando Cepeda survives a scare when he gets hit by a line drive from the Phillies' Johnny Callison before a 5–4 win in Philadelphia. Cepeda missed 15 days because of the mishap.

June 15   Bob Gibson pitches the Cardinals to a 1–0 win over the Pirates at Busch Memorial Stadium.

> *Gibson had a 21–12 record, a 2.44 ERA with 20 complete games, and 225 strikeouts in 280⅓ innings in 1966. It capped a progression in which he won 18 games in 1963, 19 in 1964, and 20 in 1965.*

June 19   Ray Washburn pitches a two-hitter to beat the Phillies 1–0 in the first game of a doubleheader at Busch Memorial Stadium. The only Philadelphia hits were singles by Clay Dalrymple in the fifth inning and Tony Taylor in the eighth. Tito Francona's homer off Jim Bunning in the sixth inning provided the lone run of the game. The Cardinals completed the sweep with a 5–1 victory in the second tilt.

June 22   The Cardinals sell Curt Simmons to the Cubs.

July 1   Mike Shannon's two-run homer in the seventh inning off Sandy Koufax provides all the runs needed to notch a 2–0 win over the Dodgers in Los Angeles. Al Jackson pitched the shutout.

July 3   Larry Jaster shuts out the Dodgers for the second time in 1966, winning 2–0 in Los Angeles.

July 5   Al Jackson pitches a two-hitter to defeat the Giants 3–1 at Candlestick Park. The only San Francisco hits were singles by Ozzie Virgil in the second inning and Willie Mays in the fourth.

July 12   The All-Star Game is played at Busch Memorial Stadium before a crowd of 49,936, and the National League wins 2–1 in 10 innings on a day in which the official high temperature in St. Louis hits 105 degrees. Hundreds of fans in the field-level boxes left their seats, at least temporarily, because of the broiling sun. The searing heat resulted in more than 130 people requiring first-aid care at the stadium. Asked to comment about the new stadium, Casey Stengel said that it "certainly holds the heat well." The winning run scored in the tenth inning when Tim McCarver singled, moved to second on a sacrifice, and scored on a single by Maury Wills.

> *The Cardinals had hosted an All-Star Game as recently as 1957, but the city of St. Louis was granted the Midsummer Classic in 1966 because of the new stadium and to help the city celebrate its bicentennial. It proved to be the only All-Star Game played at Busch Memorial Stadium. Future Hall of Famers on the rosters of the two All-Star clubs in 1966 included Hank Aaron, Jim Bunning, Roberto Clemente, Bob Gibson, Catfish Hunter, Al Kaline, Harmon Killebrew, Sandy Koufax, Juan Marichal, Willie Mays, Willie McCovey, Joe Morgan, Gaylord Perry, Brooks Robinson, Frank Robinson, Willie Stargell, and Carl Yastrzemski.*

July 19   The Cardinals take a thrilling 10–9 decision over the Braves at Busch Memorial Stadium. Down 7–0, the Cards scored seven times in the sixth inning. After Atlanta plated two runs in the top of the seventh, the Redbirds countered with two in their half. The winning run crossed the plate in the ninth inning on a double by Orlando

Cepeda and a single by Charley Smith.

The outburst was a rare sight in 1966. The Cards scored only 571 runs all season, the lowest figure of any Cardinal club since 1919. No team since 1966 has scored fewer than 571 runs in a non-strike season.

JULY 22   Mike Shannon collects five hits, including a double and a homer, in five at-bats during a 9–4 win over the Cubs in Chicago.

JULY 24   Lou Brock's three-run homer in the tenth inning beats the Cubs 7–4 in the second game of a doubleheader at Wrigley Field. In the eighth inning, Brock scored from first base on a single by Jerry Buchek to help send the game into extra innings. Chicago won the first game 10–7.

Brock led the National League in stolen bases in 1966 with 74.

JULY 29   Larry Jaster shuts out the Dodgers for the third time in 1966, winning 4–0 at Busch Memorial Stadium.

AUGUST 5   Steve Carlton records the first win of his career with a 7–1, complete-game victory over the Mets in New York.

Carlton finished his career with 329 wins.

AUGUST 14   The Cardinals score three runs in the ninth inning to defeat the Mets 4–3 in the second game of a doubleheader at Busch Memorial Stadium. The rally started with two outs and one on base. Mike Shannon drove in two runs with a bases-loaded single, and Charley Smith ended the contest with another single. The Mets won the first game 5–4.

AUGUST 19   Larry Jaster shuts out the Dodgers for the fourth time in 1966, winning 4–0 in Los Angeles.

AUGUST 21   A crowd of more than 23,000 at Busch Memorial Stadium ignores a steady, pouring rain to see the only St. Louis appearance by the Beatles. It was the second major league ballpark in which the Beatles had performed that day. The group played at Crosley Field in Cincinnati at noon, then flew to St. Louis for an evening concert.

Later artists to perform at the stadium included Billy Joel, Elton John, Fleetwood Mac, the Rolling Stones, and the Who.

SEPTEMBER 11   The football Cardinals play their first regular-season game at Busch Memorial Stadium and win 16–13 over the Philadelphia Eagles before a crowd of 39,065.

The NFL Cardinals played at Busch through the 1987 season, when the club moved to Phoenix.

SEPTEMBER 16   Bob Gibson records his 20th victory of 1966 with a 3–1 decision over the Cubs in the first game of a doubleheader in Chicago. The Cardinals also won the second game, 4–0.

SEPTEMBER 28   Larry Jaster shuts out the Dodgers for the fifth time in 1966 to tie a major league record for most shutouts against one club in a season with a 2–0 victory at Busch

Memorial Stadium. Ed Spezio drove in both runs with a single in the fourth inning.

The only other pitchers since 1900 to record five shutouts in one season over one club are Tom Hughes of the Washington Senators against Cleveland in 1905 and Grover Alexander of the Phillies versus the Reds in 1916. But Jaster stands alone in the record books in one respect. His shutouts were in consecutive appearances. The others were not. There were many oddities to Jaster's accomplishment, which is one of the strangest records on the books. The five shutouts against the Dodgers were his only five in 1966, were the first five of his career, and came in his first five career starts against Los Angeles. Jaster finished his career with a total of only seven shutouts. His 11–5 record in 1966 gave him a career mark of 14–5. After 1966, he was only 19–28. Despite being shut out five times by Jaster, the Dodgers won the National League pennant in 1966. The fifth shutout on September 28 came when the Dodgers were desperately clinging to first place in a close pennant race against the Giants and Pirates. In the five shutouts, Jaster allowed only 24 hits in 45 innings, each of them singles. Against the other eight clubs in the NL that season, Jaster pitched 106 2/3 innings and had an ERA of 4.64. His ineffectiveness led to a trip to the minors. Jaster spent six weeks in May and June of the 1966 season with Tulsa in the Pacific Coast League. While in the minors, Jaster missed a June series against the Dodgers in St. Louis, posted a 2–4 record with a 4.98 ERA, and failed to pitch a shutout.

OCTOBER 2   On the last day of the season, 23-year-old rookie pitcher Jim Cosman makes his major league debut and pitches a two-hitter to defeat the Cubs 2–0 at Busch Memorial Stadium. The only Chicago hits were singles by Ron Santo in the second inning and Glenn Beckert in the ninth.

Cosman never pitched another complete game during his major league career, much less a shutout. He pitched only 12 games in the majors, six of them starts, and had a 2–0 record and a 3.05 ERA. Control was a major problem. Cosman walked 27 batters in 41 1/3 innings.

DECEMBER 8   The Cardinals trade Charley Smith to the Yankees for Roger Maris.

Maris became a living legend in 1961 when he hit 61 homers for the Yankees to break Babe Ruth's single-season record of 60 set in 1927. Maris also won the second of two consecutive MVP awards in 1961. He went into a slow decline after 1961, however, largely due to injuries. The Yankees traded Maris to the Cardinals after he hit only .233 with 13 homers and 43 RBIs in 1966. The Yankees had questioned his courage and dedication for complaining constantly about a sore hand. It was only after the trade that he found out he'd played most of the season with a broken bone in his hand, which the Yankee doctors had been unable to diagnose. Maris lasted two seasons in St. Louis before retiring at the age of 34. Injuries had diminished his skill. He hit only .258 with 12 homers in 720 at-bats as a Cardinal, but he played in five World Series with the Yankees and knew what it took to win. With his quiet leadership and professionalism, he was a useful member of two pennant-winning teams in St. Louis. A grateful August Busch set Maris up with a beer distributorship after he retired.

DECEMBER 14   The Cardinals trade Walt Williams and Don Dennis to the White Sox for Johnny Romano and Lee White.

1967

Season in a Sentence

The Cardinals take control of the National League pennant race in August and defeat the Red Sox in the World Series.

Finish • Won • Lost • Pct • GB

First   101   60   .627   +10.5

World Series—The Cardinals defeated the Boston Red Sox four games to three

Manager

Red Schoendienst

Stats

Stats	Cards	NL	Rank
Batting Avg:	.263	.249	2
On-Base Pct:	.322	.312	2
Slugging Pct:	.379	.363	2
Home Runs:	115		4
Stolen Bases:	102		1
ERA:	3.05	3.38	3
Fielding Avg:	.978	.978	7
Runs Scored:	695		2
Runs Allowed:	557		2

Starting Lineup

Tim McCarver, c
Orlando Cepeda, 1b
Julian Javier, 2b
Mike Shannon, 3b
Dal Maxvill, ss
Lou Brock, lf
Curt Flood, cf
Roger Maris, rf
Bobby Tolan, cf-rf
Phil Gagliano, 2b-3b
Alex Johnson, rf

Pitchers

Dick Hughes, sp
Steve Carlton, sp
Bob Gibson, sp
Ray Washburn, sp
Larry Jaster, sp-rp
Joe Hoerner, rp
Ron Willis, rp
Nelson Briles, rp-sp
Al Jackson, rp

Attendance

2,090,145 (first in NL)

Club Leaders

Batting Avg:	Flood	.335
On-Base Pct:	Cepeda	.399
Slugging Pct:	Cepeda	.524
Home Runs:	Cepeda	25
RBIs:	Cepeda	111
Runs:	Brock	113
Stolen Bases:	Brock	52
Wins:	Hughes	16
Strikeouts:	Carlton	168
ERA:	Hughes	2.67
Saves:	Hoerner	15

JANUARY 22   Seven days after the first Super Bowl, between the Green Bay Packers and the Kansas City Chiefs, Bob Howsam resigns as general manager of the Cardinals to take a similar position with the Cincinnati Reds. A day later, Stan Musial was named as general manager to replace Howsam.

Howsam, who took over as general manager of the Cardinals in August 1964, was unpopular with August Busch, the players, and the fans because of some controversial trades. Many of those deals proved to be successful, however, and helped the Cardinals win the National League pennant in both 1967 and 1968. Howsam moved on to build a Cincinnati club that won four NL pennants and two World Championships from 1970 through 1976. Musial lasted less than a year as general manager (see December 5, 1967).

APRIL 1   The Cardinals send Art Mahaffey, Jerry Buchek, and Tony Martinez to the Mets for Ed Bressoud, Danny Napoleon, and cash.

APRIL 10   The Cardinals sell Tito Francona to the Phillies.

Orlando Cepeda slides into home. Cepeda, a Puerto Rican native, led the league with 111 RBIs for the 1967 World Champion Cardinals and was a unanimous choice for MVP in the National League, the first since Carl Hubbell in 1936. Cepeda was inducted into the Hall of Fame in 1999.

APRIL 11   The Cardinals defeat the Giants 6–0 before a crowd of 38,117 on Opening Day at Busch Memorial Stadium. Bob Gibson started the contest by fanning the first five batters he faced and finished with 13 strikeouts and a complete-game shutout. Lou Brock and Phil Gagliano each hit homers. Dal Maxvill collected three hits.

Sculptor Carl Christian Mose spent much of the year working on a statue of Stan Musial, which was to be installed on a pedestal in front of Busch Memorial Stadium (see August 4, 1968). The statue was 10 feet high and weighed 2,000 pounds. Musial visited Mose at his studio in Alexandria, Virginia, in February 1967 and was distressed because Mose's design showed him in "too straight a batting stance." The alignment of Musial's body in the statue was subsequently corrected to mimic his trademark crouched batting stance.

APRIL 14   After shutting out the Dodgers five times in 1966, Larry Jaster faces Los Angeles for the first time in 1967. Jaster didn't allow a run for the first six innings and emerged with an 8–4 win at Busch Memorial Stadium.

APRIL 15   Lou Brock collects two homers and two singles during a 13–4 pasting of the Dodgers at Busch Memorial Stadium.

APRIL 16   Lou Brock hits two homers and two singles for the second consecutive game, leading the Cardinals to an 11–8 victory over the Astros at Busch Memorial Stadium.

Brock led the league in runs (113) and stolen bases (52) in 1967 in addition to batting .299 with 206 hits, 32 doubles, 12 triples, and 21 homers.

APRIL 19   The Cardinals run their season record to 6–0 with a 7–5 victory over the Giants in San Francisco.

APRIL 25   Al Jackson carries a no-hitter into the eighth inning before Bob Aspromonte singles. Jackson had to settle for a one-hitter and a 4–0 win over the Astros in Houston.

MAY 2   Bob Gibson pitches a two-hitter and strikes out 12 batters to defeat the Reds 5–0 at Busch Memorial Stadium. The only Cincinnati hits were a double by Vada Pinson in the fourth inning and a single by Leo Cardenas in the fifth.

MAY 3   Ray Washburn pitches a two-hitter to defeat the Reds 2–0 at Busch Memorial Stadium. Mike Shannon drove in both St. Louis runs with a bases-loaded single in the fourth inning. The only Cincinnati hits were singles by Pete Rose in the fourth inning and Chico Ruiz in the fifth.

In his tenth professional season and fifth major league season, Shannon had to learn a new position in 1967. Roger Maris took over Shannon's old spot in right field, and he moved to third base. Shannon was the starter at third until he developed kidney problems in 1970 (see March 18, 1970).

MAY 17   A walk-off pinch-homer by Tim McCarver in the ninth inning defeats the Phillies 3–2 at Busch Memorial Stadium.

McCarver hit .295 with 14 homers in 1967.

MAY 19   A home run by Lou Brock off Jack Fisher on the first pitch of the game starts the Cardinals off toward a 6–3 win over the Mets in New York.

MAY 20   Down 9–4, the Cardinals score four runs in the seventh inning, one in the eighth, and two in the ninth to defeat the Mets 11–9 in New York.

MAY 25   Rookie Cardinal pitcher Dick Hughes throws a two-hitter to defeat the Braves 5–0 at Atlanta. The only hits off Hughes were singles by Woody Woodward in the third inning and Marty Martinez in the eighth.

MAY 30   Dick Hughes strikes out 13 batters but loses a heartbreaking 2–1 decision to the Reds at Crosley Field. Hughes retired the first 21 batters he faced before the Reds scored twice in the eighth on a Tony Perez triple, Vada Pinson double, and a Leo Cardenas single. In the Cardinal ninth, Orlando Cepeda and Tim McCarver opened with singles, and Cincinnati manager Dave Bristol replaced Jim Maloney with Don Nottebart. On Nottebart's first pitch, Phil Gagliano hit a grounder to shortstop Cardenas, who flipped to Tommy Helms at second to start what appeared to be a double play. Helms threw to Deron Johnson at first to record the second out. But Cepeda, running hard all the way from second base, headed home in an attempt to score the tying run. Johnson alertly fired the ball to catcher Johnny Edwards, who tagged out Cepeda for a 6–4–3–2 game-ending triple play.

Entering the 1967 season, Hughes was 29 years old and had appeared in only six big-league games. From 1958 through 1966, he played in 10 different cities in the minors. With thick glasses, the result of 20–300 vision in one eye and 20–350 in the other, Hughes didn't look like an athlete. But he was a revelation in 1967, posting a 16–6 record and a 2.67 ERA. He developed arm trouble after his stellar rookie season, however. In 1968, his last season in the majors, Hughes won only two games. Literally coming out of nowhere to post a 16-win rookie season, he returned just as quickly.

JUNE 1
The Cardinals score two runs in the ninth inning and one in the tenth to beat the Braves 5–4 at Busch Memorial Stadium. Bobby Tolan hit a walk-off triple to drive in the winning run. He entered the game in the top of the tenth in place of Curt Flood in a double-switch.

Tolan was the nephew of Eddie Tolan, who won two gold medals in track and field in the 1932 Olympics.

JUNE 6
Lou Brock runs his hitting streak to 20 games, but the Cardinals lose 3–2 to the Astros at Busch Memorial Stadium.

On the same day, the Cardinals selected catcher Ted Simmons from Southfield High School in Southfield, Michigan, in the first round of the amateur draft. The only three future major leaguers the Cardinals drafted and signed in 1967 were Simmons, Jerry Reuss (second round), and Bob Chlupsa (fifth round of the secondary phase), but the draft has to be rated as an unqualified success as Simmons and Reuss became stars with long careers. Simmons played in the majors for 21 seasons, and Reuss for 22.

JUNE 7
The Astros trounce the Cardinals 17–1 at Busch Memorial Stadium.

JUNE 10
A three-run, walk-off homer by Roger Maris in the eleventh inning beats the Dodgers 5–2 at Busch Memorial Stadium.

JUNE 15
Tim McCarver hits a grand slam off Billy O'Dell in the first inning of a 7–4 win over the Pirates in Pittsburgh.

JUNE 18
The Cardinals move into first place with a 4–1 win over the Giants in San Francisco.

The Cards stayed in first for the remainder of the season, although the club was tied for first with the Cubs following games on July 2, July 22, and July 24.

JUNE 19
An 11-inning, 5–4 win over the Astros in Houston ends with an unassisted double play by Curt Flood. With the Astros' Jim Landis on second base, Bob Lillis hit a looping fly into center field and Landis set sail for the plate. Flood made a shoestring catch and continued running to second base to double up the runner.

JUNE 29
The Giants score 11 runs in the first inning and rout the Cardinals 12–4 at Busch Memorial Stadium. Bob Gibson allowed nine runs, all of them earned, in just two-thirds of an inning.

JULY 3
The Cardinals score seven runs in the first inning and defeat the Reds 7–3 in a contest punctuated by a vicious brawl. Bob Gibson struck out 12, including 9 of the first 13 batters he faced.

Early in the game, two Cardinal batters were hit by pitches because the Reds were seething over Lou Brock's stolen base attempt when his club had a seven-run lead. In the fifth inning, Gibson dumped Tony Perez into the dirt with a pitch. After Perez flied out, he had words with Gibson on the way back to the dugout. Both benches emptied, but peace seemed to be restored until the Reds bullpen, led by Bob Lee, came flying into the action and fights broke out all over the field. It took 12 minutes and a contingent of 19 St. Louis policemen, some of them swinging billy clubs, to quell the melee. About two dozen players on the two teams had to be treated for cuts and bruises.

JULY 8   A three-run inside-the-park homer by Julian Javier in the twelfth inning sparks the Cardinals to a win over the Phillies at Connie Mack Stadium. Philadelphia center fielder Johnny Briggs misjudged Javier's drive, which broke a 3–3 tie. The Cards withstood a rally in the bottom of the twelfth to win 6–4.

                Javier hit .281 with 14 homers in 1967.

JULY 11   Tim McCarver collects two hits in the All-Star Game, won 2–1 in 15 innings by the National League at Anaheim Stadium.

JULY 15   Bob Gibson breaks his right leg when Roberto Clemente's line drive hits him in the fourth inning of a 6–4 loss to the Pirates at Busch Stadium. The drive cracked Gibson's fibula, the small bone in the lower part of the leg. Somehow, he stayed in the game and faced three more batters before sinking to the ground. He retired one and walked two.

                Gibson had a 10–6 record at the time of the injury. He returned on September 7, and finished the season at 13–7. Nelson Briles, who had been toiling in the bullpen in long relief, filled the void in Gibson's absence. Briles won his last nine decisions to finish the season with a 14–5 record. Before his nine-game winning streak, Briles had a career record of 12–23.

JULY 16   The Cardinals acquire Jack Lamabe from the Mets for a player to be named later. Al Jackson was sent to the Mets on October 13 to complete the deal.

JULY 24   The day after riots erupt in Detroit, resulting in the deaths of 40 people, the Cardinals lose 3–1 to the Cubs at Busch Memorial Stadium.

                As a result of the defeat, the Cards fell into a first-place tie with Leo Durocher's Cubs, who had posted a record of 59–103 the previous season. The Cards won 40 of their next 56 games, however, to put the pennant on ice.

JULY 25   The Cardinals take sole possession of first place with a dramatic 4–3 win over the Cubs at Busch Stadium. The Cardinals led 4–2 in the ninth inning with two outs. Ernie Banks and Ted Savage were on base for the Cubs when Al Spangler singled; Banks scored, but Curt Flood threw out Savage at the plate.

                Flood hit .335 in 1967.

AUGUST 14   The Cardinals score three runs in the ninth inning to beat the Cubs 6–5 at Busch Memorial Stadium.

AUGUST 19   The Cardinals win their eighth game in a row, defeating the Astros 7–4 at Busch Memorial Stadium.

AUGUST 30   Tim McCarver drives in both runs in a 2–0 win over the Mets at Busch Memorial Stadium. He homered in the second inning and hit a sacrifice fly in the sixth.

SEPTEMBER 1   Lou Brock homers on the first pitch from Astros pitcher Bruce Van Hoff to spark the Cardinals to a 5–0 win at Busch Memorial Stadium.

SEPTEMBER 3   The Cardinals rout the Astros 13–1 at Busch Memorial Stadium.

               From August 24 through September 3, the Cardinals allowed only 17 runs in a stretch of 13 games.

SEPTEMBER 15   Steve Carlton pitches a two-hitter to beat the Reds 4–0 at Crosley Field. The only Cincinnati hits were singles by Tommy Helms in the first inning and Johnny Bench in the second.

               Carlton had a streak of 28 scoreless innings in September.

SEPTEMBER 19   The Cardinals clinch the National League pennant with a 5–1 win over the Phillies in Philadelphia. The Cards had a 13-game lead with 11 contests left on the schedule.

SEPTEMBER 20   Steve Carlton strikes out 16 batters but loses 3–1 to the Phillies in Philadelphia.

SEPTEMBER 26   Lou Brock collects two homers and two singles, but the Cardinals lose 8–7 to the Cubs in Chicago.

               The Cardinals drew more than two million fans for the first time in club history in 1967, finishing with 2,090,145. The Cards also led the majors in attendance. Previously, St. Louis had never led the National League in attendance, much less the majors.

SEPTEMBER 30   The Cardinals record their 100th win of the season with a 3–1 decision over the Braves in Atlanta.

               The Cardinals met the Boston Red Sox in the 1967 World Series. In a season forever known in New England as "The Impossible Dream," the Sox leaped from ninth place in 1966 to first in 1967, ending the year with a 92–70 record. Four teams had a shot at the AL pennant heading into the final week, and Boston won it on the final day. The manager behind the miracle was Dick Williams.

OCTOBER 4   The Cardinals open the 1967 World Series with a 2–1 win over the Red Sox at Fenway Park in Boston. Bob Gibson pitched a complete game and struck out 10 batters. Both Cardinal runs scored on infield ground-outs by Roger Maris, one in the third inning and the other in the seventh. The Red Sox run came on a home run by opposing pitcher Jose Santiago in the third. Lou Brock had four singles in four at-bats and stole two bases.

OCTOBER 5   Jim Lonborg pitches a one-hitter against the Cardinals to lead the Red Sox to a 5–0 victory in Game Two, played in Boston. Lonborg allowed only two base runners the entire game. He retired the first 19 batters to face him before Curt Flood walked with one out in the seventh. The lone hit was Julian Javier's double with two gone in the eighth.

OCTOBER 7 The Cardinals regain the lead in the Series with a 5–2 victory over the Red Sox in Game Three, played before 54,575 at Busch Memorial Stadium. Mike Shannon struck the key blow with a two-run homer in the second that gave the Cards a 3–0 lead. Nelson Briles pitched the complete-game victory.

OCTOBER 8 The Cardinals move one game from a World Championship with a 6–0 win over the Red Sox in Game Four, played before 54,575 at Busch Memorial Stadium. Bob Gibson pitched the five-hit, complete-game shutout. The Cards scored four runs in the first inning and two in the third.

OCTOBER 9 The Cardinals' World Championship is delayed when the Red Sox win Game Five 3–1 before 54,575 at Busch Memorial Stadium. Jim Lonborg was brilliant again, pitching a three-hitter. The lone St. Louis run was a homer by Roger Maris in the ninth inning.

OCTOBER 11 The Red Sox force a seventh game by defeating the Red Sox 8–4 at Fenway Park. Dick Hughes became the only pitcher in World Series history to give up three homers in an inning when he yielded round-trippers to Carl Yastrzemski, Reggie Smith, and Rico Petrocelli in the fourth inning to give Boston a 4–2 lead. The Cards tied the game 4–4 in the top of the seventh on a two-run homer by Lou Brock that traveled some 450 feet into the right-center-field bleachers, but the Sox put the game away with four tallies in their half. The Cards used eight pitchers in the contest.

On the same day, the St. Louis Blues made their National Hockey League regular-season debut by playing the Minnesota North Stars to a 2–2 tie in St. Louis.

OCTOBER 12 In Game Seven, the Cardinals take the World Championship by defeating the Red Sox 7–2 at Boston. Bob Gibson allowed only three hits and struck out 10 in a complete game. He also hit one of two St. Louis homers off Jim Lonborg, who struggled pitching on two days' rest. Julian Javier struck the other Redbird home run with two runners on base in the sixth.

Gibson tied a World Series record by winning three times. In 27 innings, he allowed only three runs and 14 hits while walking five and striking out 26. He is also the only pitcher in history to win Game Seven of a World Series twice in his career. The first was in 1964. Lou Brock set a World Series record with seven stolen bases in seven attempts. He also had 12 hits, including two doubles, a triple, and a homer, and batted .414.

DECEMBER 5 Bing Devine replaces Stan Musial as general manager.

After winning a World Championship in his first year as general manager, Musial resigned because of the pressure of his outside business interests. He lost his longtime friend and business associate Julius (Biggie) Garagnani, who died on June 19. They were partners in "Stan and Biggie's Restaurant," a popular spot in St. Louis. The two also shared ownership in various real estate holdings. Musial remained with the club as senior vice president and consultant. It was a homecoming for the 50-year-old Devine. He had put in 25 years with the Cardinal organization before resigning under pressure in August 1964. From that point until his return to the Cardinals, he worked in the front office of the Mets and helped put together the club that won the 1969 World Championship. Devine's second tour with the Cardinals lasted until 1978.

1968

Season in a Sentence

Behind an incredible season by Bob Gibson, the Cardinals cruise to their second consecutive pennant and are on the brink of another World Series title before losing Games Five, Six, and Seven to the Tigers.

Finish • Won • Lost • Pct • GB

First   97   65   .599   +9.0

World Series—The Cardinals lost to the Detroit Tigers four games to three

Manager

Red Schoendienst

Stats

Stats	Cards	• NL •	Rank
Batting Avg:	.249	.243	4
On-Base Pct:	.298	.300	6
Slugging Pct:	.346	.341	3
Home Runs:	73		8
Stolen Bases:	110		2
ERA:	2.49	2.99	1
Fielding Avg:	.978	.978	7
Runs Scored:	583		5
Runs Allowed:	472		1

Starting Lineup

Tim McCarver, c
Orlando Cepeda, 1b
Julian Javier, 2b
Mike Shannon, 3b
Dal Maxvill, ss
Lou Brock, lf
Curt Flood, cf
Roger Maris, rf
Bobby Tolan, of
Johnny Edwards, c

Pitchers

Bob Gibson, sp
Nelson Briles, sp
Ray Washburn, sp
Steve Carlton, sp
Larry Jaster, sp-rp
Joe Hoerner, rp
Ron Willis, rp

Attendance

2,011,167 (first in NL)

Club Leaders

Batting Avg:	Flood	.301
On-Base Pct:	Flood	.339
Slugging Pct:	Brock	.418
Home Runs:	Cepeda	16
RBIs:	Shannon	79
Runs:	Brock	92
Stolen Bases:	Brock	62
Wins:	Gibson	22
Strikeouts:	Gibson	268
ERA:	Gibson	1.12
Saves:	Hoerner	17

JANUARY 11   The Cardinals trade Alex Johnson to the Reds for Dick Simpson.

There was no question that Johnson had All-Star talent, but after two seasons, the Cardinals had tired of his lackadaisical attitude and sent him to the Reds. Johnson moved on to bat .312 and .315 in two years in Cincinnati and won the AL batting title with a .329 average for the Angels in 1970. In 1971 alone, however, Johnson was suspended four times and fined on 29 occasions by California. During a 13-year career, he played for eight teams. Johnson might have been more trouble than he was worth and didn't fit on a pennant-winning Cardinals team full of self-motivated athletes, but the club received nothing in exchange in the trade. Simpson played only 26 games for St. Louis.

FEBRUARY 8   The Cardinals trade Pat Corrales and Jimmy Williams to the Reds for Johnny Edwards.

APRIL 9 — Martin Luther King Jr.'s funeral postpones the Cardinals' scheduled opener against the Braves in St. Louis. King was murdered on April 4.

After the assassination, Curt Flood painted a portrait of the civil rights leader that hung in the living room of King's widow, Coretta.

APRIL 10 — In the season opener, the Cardinals win 2–1 against the Braves before 34,740 at Busch Memorial Stadium. The Cards scored a run in the eighth inning to tie the contest 1–1. In the ninth, Dal Maxvill doubled, and Dave Ricketts hit a walk-off pinch-single. The pitchers were Bob Gibson (seven innings) and Ray Washburn (two innings).

Dave Ricketts had a brother who pitched for the Cardinals in 1959. Dave Ricketts also played in the NBA from 1955 through 1958 with the St. Louis Hawks, Rochester Royals, and Cincinnati Royals.

APRIL 13 — Curt Flood collects five hits in five at-bats during an 8–5 victory over the Cubs in Chicago.

The 1968 Cardinals were the first team in major league history with a payroll of more than $1 million.

APRIL 17 — Lou Brock collects five hits, including a homer and a double, in six at-bats, but the Cardinals lose 4–3 in 12 innings to the Reds in Cincinnati.

Brock led the NL in doubles (46), triples (14), and stolen bases (62) in 1968. He also scored 92 runs and batted .279.

APRIL 23 — Down 2–0, the Cardinals score two runs in the ninth inning and two in the tenth to win 4–2 against the Reds at Busch Memorial Stadium. Lou Brock ended the game with a walk-off homer.

APRIL 27 — Nelson Briles wins his 13th consecutive regular-season decision over two seasons, defeating the Pirates 7–5 at Busch Memorial Stadium. Briles won his last nine decisions in 1967 and his first four in 1968. He also won a game without taking any losses in the 1967 World Series.

Briles was 19–11 with a 2.80 ERA in 1968.

MAY 6 — Three days after the St. Louis Hawks move to Atlanta, Bob Gibson pitches 11 innings and allows only three hits for a 2–1 win over the Mets at Busch Memorial Stadium. The winning run scored in the bottom of the eleventh on Lou Brock's triple and an Orlando Cepeda single off Tom Seaver, who also pitched a complete game.

Gibson had one of the most incredible seasons by a pitcher in big-league history in 1968. He had a 22–9 record and a 1.12 ERA and won both the Most Valuable Player and Cy Young awards. Gibson's earned run average is the best by any pitcher in the majors with a minimum of 150 innings pitched since 1914. He completed 28 of his 34 starts. In the other six contests, he was lifted for a pinch hitter, and he averaged 8.96 innings per start. Gibson pitched 13 shutouts, the second highest in major league history. The record is 15 by Grover Alexander with the Phillies in 1916. Gibson also struck out 268 batters in 304²/₃ innings.

MAY 13   Nelson Briles pitches the Cardinals to a 1–0 win over the Pirates in Pittsburgh. The lone run of the contest scored in the first inning on a double by Curt Flood and a single by Roger Maris off Jim Bunning.

MAY 15   Julian Javier homers off Steve Blass in the fourth inning for the lone run of a 1–0 victory over the Pirates at Busch Memorial Stadium. Steve Carlton pitched the shutout.

          Before the game, Javier went to a St. Louis hospital, where he visited a six-year-old youngster whose legs had been crushed in an automobile accident. The boy, who wasn't expected to walk again, asked Javier to hit a home run for him. It was the first of only four homers that he hit all season.

MAY 20   In his first game of the season, Larry Jaster pitches a two-hitter to defeat the Dodgers 2–1 in Los Angeles. The only hits off Jaster were singles by Paul Popovich in the fifth inning and Wes Parker in the ninth.

MAY 29   The Cardinals' record drops to 22–21 after a 2–1 loss to San Francisco at Busch Memorial Stadium. The Cards were three games back of the first-place Giants.

          From May 30 through August 1, the Cardinals had a record of 49–15 to build a 15-game lead.

MAY 31   Larry Jaster retires the first 23 batters to face him before settling for a two-hitter and a 2–0 win over the Mets in New York. Greg Goossen broke up the perfect-game bid with a single with two outs in the eighth. Don Bosch added another single with two outs in the ninth.

JUNE 1   Mike Shannon hits a homer in the tenth inning to defeat the Mets 6–5 in New York. Joe Hoerner ended a four-inning relief stint by striking out the last six batters to face him. The win put the Cardinals into a tie for first place.

          Hoerner, who pitched for the Cardinals from 1966 through 1969, had 17 saves and a 1.47 ERA in 1968. Pitching for Davenport, Iowa, in 1958 at the age of 21, Hoerner suffered what at first was diagnosed a heart attack. He was given last rites and was unconscious for 3½ hours. Later, doctors learned that Hoerner had a weak muscle on his right side that, when strained, impaired his circulation severely. As a result, Hoerner began pitching with a sidearm motion to put less strain on the muscle. He was 29 when he finally reached the majors. Perhaps because of his medical condition, Hoerner kept his teammates loose with his carefree attitude. The most famous story involving Hoerner took place in Atlanta in 1967 when the team was sitting for a long time on the bus outside the ballpark. After it became obvious that no driver was coming to take the club back to the hotel, Hoerner grabbed the wheel himself and took the bus on a wild and harrowing ride through the downtown streets. He also liked to try to hit the roof of the Astrodome with fungoes during pregame drills. He accomplished the feat several times before Astros team officials put a stop to the practice.

JUNE 2   The Cardinals take sole possession of first place by sweeping the Mets 6–3 and 3–2 in New York.

          The Cards remained in first for the rest of the season. Their lead expanded to 10 games by July 8.

JUNE 6

The Cardinals win their ninth game in a row, as Bob Gibson shuts out the Astros 4–0 in Houston.

> *On the same day, the Cardinals selected outfielder James Hairston from Roth High School in Dayton, Ohio, in the first round of the amateur draft. Hairston was one of the worst first-round selections in club history as he failed to advance beyond Class A. The best player the Cardinals chose in 1968 was 26th-rounder Bob Forsch, who played for the club for 14 seasons. Other future major leaguers the team drafted and signed in 1968 were Tom Heintzelman (7th round), Tom Plodinec (33rd round), and Skip Jutze (4th round of the secondary phase in January).*

JUNE 8

The Reds-Cardinals game at Crosley Field is delayed for 45 minutes by a near walkout of Cincinnati players. Several objected to playing on a day of national mourning declared by President Lyndon Johnson in memory of slain presidential candidate Robert F. Kennedy, who was shot on June 5 and died a day later. The Cards won the game 7–2.

JUNE 9

The Cardinals split a strange doubleheader with the Reds at Crosley Field. In the opener, the Cards trailed 8–0 before exploding for 10 runs in the fifth inning to win 10–8. All 10 runs scored with two outs, coming on six singles, two walks, a double, and Lou Brock's three-run homer. In the nightcap, the Redbirds were ahead 6–0 in the fourth but wound up losing 7–6 in 12 innings.

JUNE 11

Bob Gibson pitches his second consecutive shutout, defeating the Braves 6–0 in Atlanta.

JUNE 13

Dick Schofield homers in the thirteenth inning to beat the Braves 3–1 in Atlanta. It was Schofield's only home run in 1968. In the third, Steve Carlton collected his first major league homer.

JUNE 15

Bob Gibson strikes out 13 and pitches his third straight shutout, beating the Reds 2–0 at Busch Memorial Stadium.

JUNE 18

Bobby Tolan homers off Bill Hands for the lone run in a 1–0 victory over the Cubs at Busch Memorial Stadium. Nelson Briles pitched the shutout.

JUNE 19

Steve Carlton pitches a one-hitter to down the Cubs 4–0 at Busch Memorial Stadium. The only Chicago hit was a single by Glenn Beckert in the fourth inning.

JUNE 20

Bob Gibson pitches his fourth consecutive shutout, beating the Cubs 1–0 at Busch Memorial Stadium. The lone St. Louis run scored on a triple by Lou Brock and a single by Curt Flood in the third inning off Ferguson Jenkins.

> *It was the third consecutive team shutout by Cardinal pitchers. The Cards put together a streak of 34 consecutive scoreless innings from June 16 through June 21.*

JUNE 21

Bobby Tolan provides the heroics during a 13-inning, 4–3 victory over the Braves at Busch Memorial Stadium. In the twelfth, Tolan saved the game by grabbing Marty Martinez's line drive into right field and making a perfect throw home to catch the runner. In the thirteenth, Tolan singled and scored on a double by Mike Shannon.

Transcendental Graphics/theruckerarchive.com

Bob Gibson pitched for the Cardinals from 1959 to 1975. In 17 seasons with the team, he won 20 or more games five times. In 1968 he put together one of the greatest seasons in major league history for a pitcher. Gibson was inducted into the Hall of Fame in 1981.

Shannon had the best season of his career in 1968, with 15 homers and a .266 batting average.

JUNE 26   Bob Gibson pitches his fifth consecutive shutout, one shy of the major league record, with a 3–0 win over the Pirates in the first game of a doubleheader at Busch Memorial Stadium. Pittsburgh won the second tilt 3–1.

During his five straight shutouts, Gibson allowed 21 hits, walked 5, and struck out 35 in 45 innings. The five shutouts were recorded on June 6, 11, 15, 20, and 26. Including the final two innings of a June 2 start, Gibson pitched 47 consecutive scoreless innings.

JULY 1   Gibson loses a chance for a sixth consecutive shutout but defeats the Dodgers 5–1 in Los Angeles. The only Dodger run scored on a first-inning wild pitch. With two outs, Gibson allowed singles to Len Gabrielson and Tom Haller to put runners on first and third, then delivered a pitch that hit the dirt and eluded catcher Johnny Edwards, allowing Gabrielson to score.

After surrendering the run, Gibson pitched 23 consecutive scoreless innings over three starts. Were it not for the first-inning run he allowed in the July 1 contest, Gibson would have pitched seven consecutive shutouts and 71 consecutive scoreless innings. The major league record for consecutive shutouts is six, set by Don Drysdale of the Dodgers from May 14 through June 4, 1968. The mark for consecutive scoreless innings is 59 by Orel Hershiser of the Dodgers from August 30 through September 28, 1988.

JULY 6   Bob Gibson records his sixth shutout in seven starts by defeating the Giants 3–0 in San Francisco.

JULY 9   Red Schoendienst manages the National League to a 1–0 win in the All-Star Game, played at the Astrodome in Houston.

JULY 10   The National League votes to divide into two divisions in 1969 because of the addition of expansion teams in Montreal and San Diego. The Cardinals were placed in the Eastern Division with Chicago, Montreal, New York, Philadelphia, and Pittsburgh.

The Cardinals were inserted into the Eastern Division in defiance of geographic logic because of the shortsightedness of Mets chairman of the board M. Donald Grant. In 1968, the three biggest road draws were the Cardinals, Dodgers, and Giants, and Grant insisted that the Mets be placed in a division with at least one of the three. Being the easternmost of those three teams, St. Louis thus moved into the Eastern Division, but the Cardinals would agree only if long-standing rival Chicago were included. That put Atlanta and Cincinnati, two cities east of St. Louis and Chicago, into the west. Shortly after division play began, the Cardinals declined from their perch as pennant-winners to mediocrity, while the Reds became one of the top attractions in baseball.

JULY 21   Bob Gibson strikes out 13 batters during a 2–0 win over the Mets in the first game of a doubleheader at Busch Memorial Stadium. There were no outfield putouts in the game. New York won the second game 2–1.

Gibson made 11 starts in June and July and completed all 11. He pitched shutouts in 8 of the 11 and allowed only one run in each of the other three. All 11 starts were Cardinal victories. In 99 innings, Gibson allowed only three runs, for an ERA of 0.27, and surrendered 56 hits and 13 walks while striking out 83.

JULY 22   The Cardinals score three runs in the ninth inning to defeat the Phillies 5–4 at Busch Memorial Stadium. Tim McCarver drove in the winning run with a sacrifice fly.

AUGUST 4   The statue of Stan Musial outside of Busch Memorial Stadium is unveiled prior to a 14-inning, 6–5 loss to the Cubs.

The bronze statue, sculpted by Carl Christian Mose, a former St. Louis native, is 10 feet, 5 inches high and rests on a marble pedestal 8½ feet high and was located on the sidewalk at the front of the stadium on the northeast side with Musial crouched in his trademark batting stance. The statue was engraved, "Here stands baseball's perfect warrior; here stands baseball's perfect knight." Commissioner Ford Frick uttered the words on the day that Musial retired, September 29, 1963. Among the guests at the event were 19 members of the 1941 Cardinals, Musial's first year with the club. Although flattered by the honor, Musial was never happy about the statue. He preferred a design that showed a bat resting on his hip while signing an autograph for a young boy. The design was rejected, however, largely due to the cost.

AUGUST 5   With Curt Flood at bat, the sprinkler system at Busch Memorial Stadium accidentally activates, bringing a brief halt to a 3–2 win over the Reds.

On the same day, Roger Maris announced his retirement effective at the end of the season. He made the announcement a month before his 34th birthday. Maris was suffering from an assortment of nagging injuries and desired to spend more time with his family and on his business. August Busch set Maris up with a beer distributorship in Gainesville, Florida (see August 3, 2001).

AUGUST 8   The Cardinals defeat the Reds 1–0 in 11 innings at Busch Memorial Stadium. Ray Washburn and Tony Cloninger each allowed only two hits over the first nine innings. Washburn was relieved in the eleventh by Joe Hoerner, who received credit for the win when Roger Maris drove in the lone run of the game with a walk-off double.

AUGUST 15   Mike Shannon hits a grand slam off Bill Stoneman in the second inning of an 8–0 win over the Cubs in Chicago.

The Cardinals were harassed during the four games at Wrigley Field from August 12 through August 15 by a group that called itself the "Bleacher Bums." On August 13, one bleacher fan threw a beer in Roger Maris's face as he was trying to catch a fly ball. The three outfielders were targets of debris almost constantly during the series. In the ninth inning of the August 15 contest, Lou Brock and Curt Flood spread a banner across the outfield grass that read, "We're No. 1."

AUGUST 19   Bob Gibson wins his club record 15th game in a row with a two-hit, 2–0 win over the Phillies at Connie Mack Stadium. The only Philadelphia hits were singles by opposing pitcher John Boozer in the fifth inning and Johnny Callison in the eighth. Ron Davis drove in both runs with a single in the second inning.

During the 15-game winning streak, which took place over 16 starts, including a no-decision, Gibson pitched 146 innings and allowed 11 runs, for an ERA of

0.68, along with 89 hits and 24 walks while striking out 124. Ten of his fifteen victories were shutouts. During the winning streak, he shut out eight of the Cardinals' nine National League rivals, missing only the Dodgers.

AUGUST 24   Two days before the start of the Democratic National Convention in Chicago, marred by violent confrontations between antiwar demonstrators and police, Bob Gibson strikes out 15 batters, but his 15-game winning streak comes to an end when he allows six runs over the final three innings of a 6–4 loss to the Pirates at Busch Memorial Stadium.

SEPTEMBER 2   Bob Gibson records his 20th win of 1968 by pitching a 10-inning complete game to defeat the Reds 1–0 in Cincinnati. It was Gibson's 12th shutout of the season. Julian Javier provided the lone run of the game with a homer off Ted Abernathy.

SEPTEMBER 15   The Cardinals clinch the National League pennant with a 7–4 win over the Astros in Houston. The win gave the Cards a 12½-game lead with 11 contests left on the schedule. Curt Flood collected five hits in five at-bats. Roger Maris hit the last of his 275 career home runs.

SEPTEMBER 17   Gaylord Perry no-hits the Cardinals to give the Giants a 1–0 win in a night game in San Francisco. Curt Flood struck out for the final out of the game. Bob Gibson was the losing pitcher.

SEPTEMBER 18   Following Gaylord Perry's no-hitter, Ray Washburn pitches a no-hitter to give the Cardinals a 2–0 victory over the Giants at Candlestick Park. Washburn's no-hitter ended a little more than 17 hours after Perry's. In the ninth, Ron Hunt hit a sharp ground-out to Phil Gagliano at second for the first out. Willie Mays followed with a hot grounder to Mike Shannon at third for out number two. Willie McCovey hit a fly ball to Curt Flood in center for the final out. Washburn walked five and struck out eight.

It was the first time that no-hitters had been pitched in consecutive games involving the same two teams. It has happened once since. On April 30, 1969, Jim Maloney of the Reds threw a no-hitter against the Astros at Crosley Field, and the following night, Don Wilson of Houston no-hit Cincinnati.

SEPTEMBER 21   Ted Simmons makes his major league debut. Simmons had a single in two at-bats during a 3–0 loss to the Dodgers in Los Angeles.

Simmons played 1,440 games as a catcher for the Cardinals, more than anyone else in club history. Overall, he played in 1,564 games in St. Louis from 1968 through 1980 and collected 736 runs, 1,704 hits, 332 doubles, 172 homers, and 929 RBIs while posting a .459 slugging percentage and a .298 batting average before being traded to the Brewers. One of the most underrated catchers of all time and one of the most underappreciated players of the 1970s, Simmons was ranked as the 10th-best catcher in baseball history by Bill James in 2001 behind eight Hall of Famers and Mike Piazza, who is certain to be enshrined at Cooperstown. Yet when Simmons's name appeared before Hall of Fame voters for the first time in 1994, he received only 17 votes out of 455 cast, short of the minimum 5 percent needed to stay on the ballot. Among players who played more games at catcher than at any other position, Simmons ranks first in hits (2,472), second in RBIs (1,389), and fifth in runs scored (1,074). He had the misfortune, however, of playing on mediocre Cardinal teams during the heydays of such catchers as Johnny Bench, Carlton Fisk, and Thurman Munson and was unfairly maligned for his defense.

SEPTEMBER 27   Bob Gibson makes his last start of the regular season and pitches his 13th shutout, defeating the Astros 1–0 at Busch Memorial Stadium. Curt Flood drove in the lone run of the game with a single in the fifth inning.

SEPTEMBER 29   In the final game of the season, the Cardinals smash the Astros 11–1 at Busch Memorial Stadium. The Cards scored nine runs in the second inning, three of them on a long bases-loaded single by Orlando Cepeda that scored Lou Brock from first base.

The Cardinals met the Detroit Tigers in the World Series. It was the first time since 1945 that Detroit had hosted a Fall Classic. Managed by Mayo Smith, the Tigers were 103–59 in 1968 and won the AL pennant by 12 games.

OCTOBER 2   Behind Bob Gibson's World Series record 17 strikeouts, the Cardinals win the first game of the 1968 World Series 4–0 over the Tigers before 54,692 at Busch Memorial Stadium. The Cards scored three runs in the fourth inning and added an insurance run on a homer by Lou Brock in the seventh.

The contest was a much-anticipated matchup of Bob Gibson and Denny McLain, two pitchers who won the Most Valuable Player Award in 1968. McLain had a record of 31–6 to become baseball's first 30-game winner since Dizzy Dean in 1934. Gibson was almost untouchable, allowing only five hits. He struck out two batters in the first inning, three in the second, two in the third, one in the fourth, one in the fifth, two in the sixth, two in the seventh, one in the eighth, and three in the ninth. Gibson headed into the ninth with 14 strikeouts, one shy of the World Series record set by Sandy Koufax of the Dodgers in 1963. After allowing a single to Mickey Stanley, Gibson fanned Al Kaline, Norm Cash, and Willie Horton in succession.

OCTOBER 3   The Tigers even the Series by defeating the Cardinals 8–1 in Game Two, played before 54,692 at Busch Memorial Stadium. Mickey Lolich pitched a complete game and hit the only home run of his professional career.

OCTOBER 5   At Tiger Stadium in Detroit, the Cardinals pound out a 7–3 victory in Game Three. Tim McCarver hit a three-run homer in the fifth inning, Orlando Cepeda added a three-run blast in the seventh, and Lou Brock stole three bases. Joe Hoerner pitched 3²/₃ innings of shutout relief.

OCTOBER 6   The Cardinals move within one victory of their second consecutive World Championship with a 10–1 trouncing of the Tigers in Detroit in Game Four. Bob Gibson went all the way, allowing five hits while striking out ten. He also hit a home run. Denny McLain lasted only 2²/₃ innings for Detroit. Lou Brock collected a homer, triple, and double in five at-bats while driving in four runs and scoring two. He also stole a base. Brock is the only player with a homer, triple, and double in a single World Series game. Tim McCarver collected three hits, one of them a homer.

The win was Gibson's seventh consecutive World Series victory, a record. He won his last two starts in 1964, all three in 1967, and the first two in 1968. Each of the seven wins was a complete game, and one of them lasted 10 innings. In those seven victories, Gibson allowed 11 runs, 9 of them earned, and 39 hits in

64 innings while striking out 75. In addition, Gibson is one of only two pitchers with two homers in the World Series. Gibson's first was in the seventh game in 1967. He is also the only pitcher with a homer and at least 10 strikeouts in the same Series game. Gibson did it twice.

OCTOBER 7   The Tigers delay the Cardinals' hopes for a World Championship by winning Game Five 5–3 in Detroit. When the Cardinals scored three times off Mickey Lolich in the top of the first inning, a win seemed to be assured. But Lolich settled down and pitched eight scoreless innings. The Tigers scored twice in the fourth to narrow the gap to 3–2. The Cards blew an opportunity in the fifth when Lou Brock was tagged out at the plate standing up while trying to score from second on a single by Julian Javier. If Brock had slid, he probably would have scored. The Tigers won the contest with three runs in the seventh. Al Kaline, playing in the only World Series of his career, drove in the tying and go-ahead runs with a single.

Jose Feliciano, a blind 23-year-old Puerto Rican soul singer, created a firestorm when he sang the National Anthem on national television before Game Five. Feliciano's interpretation was done to a slower beat in a blend of soul and folk styles with an acoustic guitar, and it differed greatly from the normal rendition. At a time when the country was bitterly divided over the Vietnam War, newspapers and radio and television stations were flooded with protests by irate viewers, many of whom considered the performance to be unpatriotic. Today, Felicano's rendition would barely raise an eyebrow, as individual expressions of "The Star-Spangled Banner" have become commonplace and the lyrics have been sung in a wide variety of musical styles since his groundbreaking appearance.

OCTOBER 9   The Tigers force a seventh game by walloping the Cardinals 13–1 before 54,692 at Busch Memorial Stadium. The Tigers blew the game wide open with 10 runs in the third inning off Ray Washburn, Larry Jaster, and Ron Willis. Jim Northrup hit a grand slam. Detroit manager Mayo Smith gambled by pitching Denny McLain on two days' rest, and McLain responded with a complete game. Fewer than 10,000 fans were in the stands at the finish as the rout and a 45-minute rain delay in the eighth sent most of the original crowd scurrying for home.

Dal Maxvill set a record for the most at-bats in a single World Series without collecting a hit when he went 0 for 22 in 1968. In three World Series with the Cardinals in 1964, 1967, and 1968, Maxvill had 7 hits in 61 at-bats for a .115 average.

OCTOBER 10   Rebounding from a three-games-to-one deficit, the Tigers take the World Championship by defeating the Cardinals 4–1 in Game Seven before 54,692 at Busch Memorial Stadium. The game was scoreless after six innings in a duel between Bob Gibson and Mickey Lolich, each seeking his third win of the Series. Gibson retired 20 of the first 21 batters he faced. Disaster struck for the Cards in the seventh. With two outs, Norm Cash and Willie Horton singled, and Jim Northrup lined a shot to center. Curt Flood misjudged the drive by breaking in, then slipped on the wet grass as the ball sailed over his head for a triple. Bill Freehan promptly drove in Northrup, and the Cards were down 3–0. The only St. Louis run scored on Mike Shannon's homer with two outs in the ninth.

Lou Brock tied two World Series records by collecting 13 hits and stealing seven bases. He hit .464. The hit record tied the mark set by Bobby Richardson of the Yankees in 1964. Marty Barrett also collected 13 hits for the Red Sox in 1986. Strangely, all three played for the losing side. Brock's seven steals tied his own record, set in 1967. Brock's 14 career steals in the Fall Classic are a record he shares with Eddie Collins. He also had 12 hits in 1967. His 25 hits in consecutive Series are also a record. In the three World Series of his career, Brock had 34 hits in 87 at-bats for a .391 average, the best of any player with at least 75 plate appearances.

OCTOBER 11   The Cardinals trade Wayne Granger and Bobby Tolan to the Reds for Vada Pinson. On the same day, the Cardinals traded Johnny Edwards and Tommy Smith to the Astros for Dave Giusti and Dave Adlesh.

The Cardinals believed that they had a dynasty in the making after winning the 1967 and 1968 pennants by a wide margin. With their sights set on a third consecutive pennant in 1969, the club needed a right fielder to replace the retired Roger Maris. Tolan was the best in-house option, but he hit only .230 with five homers in 92 games in 1968. Unwilling to gamble with unproven youngsters and wanting a veteran presence in right field, the Cardinals traded Tolan, along with Granger, to the Reds for Pinson, whom the club believed was 31 years old. (He was actually 33.) It proved to be a horrible deal for the Cardinals. At the time of the trade, Pinson had a .297 lifetime batting average with 1,897 hits, but he was in the decline phase of his career and hit only 10 homers with a .255 average in one season in St. Louis. Tolan, who was only 22 when traded by the Cards, blossomed in Cincinnati. He was the Reds' starting center fielder in two World Series. Granger pitched in 90 games in 1969 and as the Reds' closer saved 35 games on the 1970 pennant-winning team. In the end, the Cardinals front office miscalculated how much life the 1967 and 1968 pennant-winning players had left in their careers and as a result a 1968 club that won 97 times was 87–75 in 1969 and 76–86 in 1970. The youngest starting position player on the 1969 Cardinals was Tim McCarver, who was 27 on Opening Day. The others were Joe Torre (28), Lou Brock (29), Mike Shannon (29), Dal Maxvill (30), Curt Flood (31), Julian Javier (32), and Pinson (33).

OCTOBER 14   In the expansion draft, the Cardinals lose Dave Giusti, Clay Kirby, and Jerry DaVanon to the Padres and Larry Jaster, Jerry Robertson, and Coco Laboy to the Expos.

NOVEMBER 3   Harry Caray is hit by a car in rain-swept downtown St. Louis across the street from the Chase Park Plaza Hotel. He suffered a broken nose, shoulder separation, and multiple fractures of both legs below the knees.

DECEMBER 2   A month after Richard Nixon defeats Hubert Humphrey and George Wallace in the presidential election, the Cardinals trade Dick Schofield to the Red Sox for Gary Waslewski.

DECEMBER 3   The Cardinals trade Ed Spezio, Danny Breeden, Ron Davis, and Phil Knuckles to the Padres for Dave Giusti.

To recap, the Cardinals acquired Giusti in a trade with the Astros on October 11, lost him to the Padres in the expansion draft three days later, then reacquired him for four players. He pitched only 22 games for the Cards and had a 3–7 record.

1969

Season in a Sentence

The Cardinals allow fewer runs than any other team in the league but finish last in the league in home runs and fail to win a third straight pennant.

Finish • Won • Lost • Pct • GB

Fourth   87   75   .537   13.0

Manager

Red Schoendienst

Stats

Stats	Cards	NL	Rank
Batting Avg:	.253	.250	5
On-Base Pct:	.316	.319	7
Slugging Pct:	.359	.369	8
Home Runs:	90		12
Stolen Bases:	87		2
ERA:	2.94	3.59	1
Fielding Avg:	.978	.977	6
Runs Scored:	595		10
Runs Allowed:	540		1

Starting Lineup

Tim McCarver, c
Joe Torre, 1b
Julian Javier, 2b
Mike Shannon, 3b
Dal Maxvill, ss
Lou Brock, lf
Curt Flood, cf
Vada Pinson, rf

Pitchers

Bob Gibson, sp
Steve Carlton, sp
Nelson Briles, sp
Mike Torrez, sp-rp
Ray Washburn, sp-rp
Dave Giusti, sp-rp
Joe Hoerner, rp
Chuck Taylor, rp-sp

Attendance

1,682,783 (third in NL)

Club Leaders

Batting Avg:	Brock	.298
On-Base Pct:	Torre	.361
Slugging Pct:	Torre	.447
Home Runs:	Torre	18
RBIs:	Torre	101
Runs:	Brock	97
Stolen Bases:	Brock	53
Wins:	Gibson	20
Strikeouts:	Gibson	269
ERA:	Carlton	2.17
Saves:	Hoerner	15

January 21   Stan Musial is elected to the Hall of Fame in his first time on the ballot.

March 17   Two months after the Jets upset the Colts in the Super Bowl, the Cardinals trade Orlando Cepeda to the Braves for Joe Torre.

> *Most Cardinals fans were outraged when the St. Patrick's Day trade was announced because of Cepeda's popularity and his contributions both on and off the field to two pennant-winners. It turned out to be a great trade, however. In six seasons in St. Louis, all as a regular taking turns as a catcher, first baseman, and third baseman, Torre batted .308, hit 96 homers, and was the National League Most Valuable Player in 1971. By the end of Torre's run with the Cardinals, Cepeda had retired because of gimpy knees.*

April 3   The Cardinals trade Jerry Buchek and Jim Hutto to the Phillies for Bill White.

April 8   The Cardinals lose the season opener 6–2 in 14 innings to the Pirates before 38,163 at Busch Memorial Stadium. Bob Gibson pitched nine innings and left the game with the score 2–2. Joe Hoerner pitched four innings of hitless relief before Mel Nelson gave up four runs in the fourteenth.

APRIL 12   In his first appearance with the Cardinals, Dave Giusti pitches a 1–0 complete-game shutout to defeat the Mets 1–0 in New York. Giusti also scored the lone run of the game. In the third inning, he doubled and crossed the plate on Curt Flood's two-bagger.

APRIL 14   The Cardinals participate in the first major league regular-season game played outside the United States, losing 8–7 to the Expos at Jarry Park in Montreal. The Expos took a 6–0 lead after three innings before the Cards scored seven runs in the fourth. Montreal came back, however, with a run in their half of the fourth and another in the seventh to win. Lou Brock, facing ex-teammate Larry Jaster, was the first batter in the historic game.

APRIL 21   The Expos play in St. Louis for the first time and lose 5–4 to the Cardinals at Busch Memorial Stadium.

APRIL 26   With two outs in the ninth inning and the score tied 4–4, the Cardinals suddenly explode for six runs and defeat the Phillies 10–4 in Philadelphia. Tim McCarver hit a grand slam off Gary Wagner.

MAY 6   Rookie Jim Hicks ties a major league record for outfielders by recording two assists in one inning during a 3–0 win over the Giants at Busch Memorial Stadium. Playing right field, Hicks threw out Bobby Bonds, who was caught in a rundown between first and second, and Hal Lanier at the plate.

            Hicks played only 15 games as a Cardinal. The two assists in one inning were his only two as an outfielder during a major league career in which he played 93 games for three clubs over five seasons.

MAY 9   The Padres play in St. Louis for the first time and lose 7–6 to the Cardinals at Busch Memorial Stadium.

MAY 12   In the seventh inning against the Dodgers at Busch Memorial Stadium, Bob Gibson strikes out Len Gabrielson, Paul Popovich, and John Miller on the minimum nine pitches. At the plate, Gibson collected three singles and a walk in four plate appearances, leading the Cards to a 6–2 victory.

            Gibson led the National League in complete games in 1969 with 28 in 35 starts. He had a 20–13 record, a 2.18 ERA, and 269 strikeouts in 314 innings.

MAY 14   The Cardinals collect only two hits off Bill Singer but still defeat the Dodgers 2–1 at Busch Memorial Stadium.

MAY 16   The Cardinals play in San Diego for the first time and lose 2–1 to the Padres.

MAY 22   The Cardinals score six runs in the eleventh inning and defeat the Giants 8–3 in San Francisco.

MAY 23   Steve Carlton pitches the Cardinals to a 1–0 win over the Dodgers in Los Angeles. Lou Brock opened the game with a single, stole second, and scored on a Curt Flood single for the lone run of the contest.

            Carlton was 17–11 with an ERA of 2.17 in 1969.

MAY 30

Reds pitcher Clay Carroll hits a tenth-inning homer on a 3–2 pitch off Bob Gibson to give Cincinnati a 4–3 win at Busch Memorial Stadium. The drive struck the top of the left field wall and bounced over. It was the only home run of Carroll's career.

On the same day, the Cardinals traded Jim Hicks to the Angels for Vic Davalillo.

JUNE 1

In his first at-bat with the Cardinals, Vic Davalillo hits a three-run homer to help the Cardinals to an 11–3 triumph over the Reds at Busch Stadium.

JUNE 3

The Cardinals trade Gary Waslewski to the Expos for Mudcat Grant.

JUNE 5

In the first round of the amateur draft, the Cardinals select left-handed pitcher Charles Minott from Royal Oak High School in Covina, California.

For the second year in a row, the Cards made a horrible selection in the first round as Minott failed to advance beyond Class A ball. St. Louis had much better luck by picking Al Hrabosky out of Fullerton (CA) Junior College in the first round of the draft the previous January. Ed Crosby was chosen in the second round of the January draft and Ray Bare in the third. Future major leaguers drafted and signed by the Cards in June were Mick Kelleher (3rd round), Bill Stein (4th round), and Ken Reitz (31st round). Despite his low draft position, Reitz was the Cards' starting third baseman for eight seasons. The club also chose Bucky Dent (9th round) and Bill Madlock (11th round) but failed to sign either of them. Both were drafted out of high school and opted to go to college instead. Dent signed with the White Sox and Madlock with the Cubs in 1970.

JUNE 17

Curt Flood's two-run pinch-double in the seventh inning furnishes all the runs needed in a 2–0 win over the Expos at Busch Memorial Stadium. He started the game on the bench because of a slump.

JUNE 27

Steve Carlton strikes out 12 batters during a 3–1 win over the Cubs in Chicago. Ken Holtzman retired the first 20 batters to face him before allowing three runs and six hits.

JUNE 30

Vic Davalillo pitches during the ninth inning of a 10–2 loss to the Mets at Busch Memorial Stadium. Davalillo faced two batters and allowed a hit and a walk.

JULY 2

Vic Davalillo hits a pinch-hit grand slam in the eighth inning off Ron Taylor to tie the score 4–4, but the Cardinals lose 6–4 in 14 innings to the Mets at Busch Memorial Stadium.

JULY 4

Bob Gibson is relieved while an inning is in progress for the first time since 1967 when he allows two runs in the tenth inning to lose 3–1 to the Cubs at Busch Memorial Stadium. Over a stretch of 56 starts from 1967 through 1969, Gibson pitched 45 complete games and was lifted for a pinch hitter in the other 11.

The loss dropped the team, the two-time defending National League champions, to 37–44 on the 1969 season. The Cards had a 30–9 record from July 5 through August 17, but that wasn't enough to seriously challenge the division leaders.

JULY 13

Bob Gibson records his 2,000th career strikeout but loses 3–0 to the Pirates at Busch Memorial Stadium. The victim of the milestone strikeout was Roberto Clemente, in the sixth inning. Clemente exacted revenge by hitting a three-run homer in the eighth for the only three runs of the game.

JULY 16   Steve Carlton strikes out 12 batters during a 5–0 win over Phillies 5–0 Busch Memorial Stadium.

JULY 23   Three days after Neil Armstrong becomes the first man to walk on the moon, Red Schoendienst manages the National League to a 9–3 win in the All-Star Game, played at RFK Stadium in Washington. Steve Carlton was the starting pitcher and allowed two runs in three innings.

JULY 25   Bob Gibson pitches 13 innings and scores the winning run in a 2–1 victory over the Giants at Busch Memorial Stadium. In the thirteenth, Gibson singled, took second on a wild pitch, went to third on an intentional walk, and crossed the plate on a single by Curt Flood.

JULY 29   Trailing 4–3, the Cardinals score seven runs in the seventh inning and defeat the Padres 10–4 at Busch Memorial Stadium.

JULY 30   Bob Gibson strikes out 13 batters during a 5–2 win over the Padres at Busch Memorial Stadium.

AUGUST 1   Vada Pinson extends his hitting streak to 22 games during a 7–2 triumph over the Dodgers at Busch Memorial Stadium.

AUGUST 8   The Cardinals sell Ron Willis to the Astros.

            Willis led both the 1967 and 1968 pennant-winners in games pitched. He was only 34 when he died in an automobile accident in 1977.

AUGUST 20   Two days after the end of the Woodstock Music Festival in Bethel, New York, Chuck Taylor pitches a two-hitter to defeat the Reds 2–1 at Busch Memorial Stadium. The only Cincinnati hits were a single by Pete Rose in the first inning and a homer by Tony Perez in the seventh.

AUGUST 24   A total of 25 of the 37 living Hall of Famers are honored in pregame ceremonies prior to a 14-inning, 4–1 loss to the Braves at Busch Memorial Stadium. Hank Aaron, a future Hall of Famer, broke up the game with a three-run homer.

            The Hall of Famers in attendance were Luke Appling, Max Carey, Stan Coveleski, Dizzy Dean, Bill Dickey, Joe DiMaggio, Bob Feller, Frankie Frisch, Charlie Gehringer, Burleigh Grimes, Lefty Grove, Waite Hoyt, Carl Hubbell, Ted Lyons, Heinie Manush, Joe Medwick, Stan Musial, Sam Rice, Edd Roush, Red Ruffing, Ray Schalk, Casey Stengel, Pie Traynor, Lloyd Waner, and Zack Wheat.

AUGUST 26   Nelson Briles pitches the Cardinals to a 1–0 win over the Astros in the first game of a doubleheader at Busch Memorial Stadium. Julian Javier accounted for the lone run of the game with a homer in the third inning off Larry Dierker. Houston won the second game 4–2.

Javier hit .282 with 10 homers in 1969. In his first season with the Cardinals, Joe Torre batted .289 with 18 homers and 101 RBIs. Lou Brock hit batted .298, scored 97 runs, clubbed 12 homers, and led the NL with 53 stolen bases. It was the fourth consecutive year that Brock led the NL in steals. From 1966 through 1974, he topped the league in stolen bases eight times. The only year Brock missed during that span was in 1970, when ex-Cardinal Bobby Tolan stole 57 bases for the Reds while Brock swiped 51.

AUGUST 28   A walk-off homer by Steve Huntz in the tenth inning beats the Astros 2–1 at Busch Memorial Stadium. Huntz entered the game at shortstop in place of Dal Maxvill, who was lifted for a pinch hitter.

The homer was the first of Huntz's career. He hit just three home runs in 1969. The other two were in one game on September 26. Huntz was the only player for the Cardinals in 1969 to hit more than one homer in a game.

SEPTEMBER 5   Nelson Briles pitches the Cardinals to a 1–0 win over the Expos at Busch Memorial Stadium.

SEPTEMBER 15   Steve Carlton sets a major league record by striking out 19 batters, but the Cardinals lose 4–3 to the Mets at Busch Memorial Stadium. All four New York runs scored on a pair of two-run homers by Ron Swoboda in the fourth and eighth innings.

B. Bennett/Getty Images News/Getty Images

Steve Carlton's dazzling 19-strikeout performance against the Mets on September 15, 1969, was a highlight of his seven-year stint with the Cardinals. Following an ill-advised trade to the Phillies in February 1972, Carlton seemed to muster his best stuff when facing the Redbirds.

Heading into the contest, the modern major league mark for strikeouts in a nine-inning game was 18 by Bob Feller, Sandy Koufax (twice), and Don Wilson. The all-time record was 19 by Charlie Sweeney of Providence in 1884, when it took six balls to draw a walk. Carlton broke the modern record by striking out two batters in the eighth inning and three in the ninth. During the ninth, he also broke the Cardinals' team record of 17, set by Dizzy Dean in 1933 and Bob Gibson in the 1968 World Series. Carlton struck out the side four times, walked two, allowed nine hits, and threw 152 pitches.

Carlton later admitted that he was going for a strikeout while facing every batter in the late innings and that the strategy cost him the game. His major league record was tied by Tom Seaver in 1970 and Nolan Ryan in 1974 before Roger Clemens struck out 20 batters in 1986. Clemens also struck out 20 in 1996, and Kerry Wood matched it in 1998. Randy Johnson fanned 20 in the first nine innings of an 11-inning game in 2001. Carlton's strikeouts on September 15, 1969, are still the Cardinal record.

SEPTEMBER 18   The Cardinals score two runs in the ninth inning to defeat the Pirates 8–7 at Busch Memorial Stadium. The final run scored on a walk-off single by Ted Simmons. Vada Pinson collected his 2,000th career hit during the contest. The milestone came on a homer in the seventh inning off Joe Gibbon.

SEPTEMBER 26   The Cardinals wallop the Expos 12–1 in Montreal.

The Cardinals scored only 595 runs in 1969. The only teams with fewer runs were first-year expansion teams Montreal and San Diego. The Cardinals' 90 homers were the worst in the NL.

SEPTEMBER 27   Jerry Reuss makes his major league debut and allows no runs and two hits and delivers a run-scoring single as the Cardinals win a 2–1 decision over the Expos in Montreal. *Reuss made his debut three months after his 20th birthday. He helped lead Ritenour High School in suburban St. Louis to consecutive Missouri state titles in 1966 and 1967. In three seasons as a Cardinal, Reuss was 21–22 with a 4.43 ERA before he was dealt to the Astros in a terrible trade in the spring of 1972.*

OCTOBER 2   On the final day of the season, Bob Gibson records his 20th win of 1969, but he has to go 12 innings to beat the Phillies 3–2 at Busch Memorial Stadium. A bases-loaded walk to Curt Flood scored the winning run.

OCTOBER 7   The Cardinals trade Curt Flood, Tim McCarver, Joe Hoerner, and Byron Browns to the Phillies for Dick Allen, Cookie Rojas, and Jerry Johnson.

This became one of the most pivotal trades in major league history because of Flood's refusal to go to Philadelphia and his subsequent lawsuit against Major League Baseball to be declared a free agent. At the time, there was no free agency as the reserve clause, which was created in 1879, kept every player in professional baseball bound to one club for life. Flood was 32, had been with the Cardinals for 12 years, and had no desire to move to the Phillies, then a losing club with a reputation as a difficult place for African Americans to play. He first asked baseball commissioner Bowie Kuhn to be declared a free agent and was denied. Flood filed suit on January 16, 1970, stating that baseball had violated the nation's antitrust laws. Even though he was making $90,000, one of the top salaries in baseball at the start of the 1970s, Flood likened "being owned" to *"being a slave 100 years ago." Former Supreme Court Justice Arthur Goldberg argued Flood's case. Flood asked for changes in baseball's reserve clause and $1.4 million in damages. Goldberg agreed to work for expenses, which were paid by the Major League Baseball Players Association. Flood's request for free agency were denied by the US District Court in New York and the Court of Appeals before the US Supreme Court agreed to hear Flood's arguments. The ruling in the highest court in the land, which was rendered in June 1972, favored organized baseball in a 5–3 decision. Meanwhile, Flood sat out the 1970 season but signed with the Washington Senators in 1971 for $110,000. He played only 13 games for Washington and retired. The suit likely cost Flood several years of his career and hundreds of thousands of dollars. Although Flood lost the battle, the players won the war. Flood's suit paved the way for free agency, which started in 1976, and multi-million-dollar salaries (see April 8, 1970).*

OCTOBER 9

The Cardinals fire Harry Caray.

Caray had been the Cardinals' radio and television broadcaster since 1945, and he was enormously popular throughout the Midwest on the Cardinals vast radio network. He was fired amid rumors that he was having an affair with the wife of August Busch's son. Caray spent a year announcing games for the Oakland Athletics before moving to Chicago. Caray did the White Sox' games from 1971 through 1981 and the Cubs' from 1982 until his death in February 1998. It was with the Cubs that Caray achieved national fame as the club's contests were telecast on superstation WGN-TV over cable systems across the country. With Caray gone, Jack Buck became the Cardinals' lead announcer. Buck had teamed with Caray since 1954. Buck's broadcasting partner in 1970 and 1971 was Jim Woods.

OCTOBER 21

The Cardinals trade Dave Giusti and Dave Ricketts to the Pirates for Carl Taylor and Frank Vanzin.

This proved to be a horrible deal for the Cardinals. Giusti was 30 years old and had struggled throughout his career as a starter. The Pirates turned him into a reliever, and Giusti was Pittsburgh's closer for six years, five of which resulted in NL East pennants. He led the NL in saves in 1971, a season in which the Pirates won the World Series, and was an All-Star in 1973.

NOVEMBER 5

The Cardinals trade Ray Washburn to the Reds for George Culver.

NOVEMBER 21

The Cardinals trade Vada Pinson to the Indians for Jose Cardenal.

DECEMBER 5

The Cardinals sell Mudcat Grant to the Athletics.

Grant gave Oakland one terrific season, with a 6–2 record, 24 saves, and a 1.82 ERA in 1970.

DECEMBER 16

The Cardinals begin installing AstroTurf at Busch Memorial Stadium.

The stadium opened in 1966 with a grass field, but the grass had trouble taking root because of poor drainage, a clay-based soil, the brutal summer heat, and the facility's dual use for both baseball and football. From 1970 through 1977, there was a dirt infield at Busch Memorial Stadium similar to those on grass fields. From 1977 through 1995, the entire field was covered with artificial turf except for sliding pits around the bases.

THE STATE OF THE CARDINALS

The 1970s were an era of great individual accomplishments by the likes of Lou Brock, Bob Gibson, and Joe Torre, but the team was unable to finish a season in first place. Overall, the Cardinals were 800–813, a winning percentage of .496. It was the fifth-best record among the 12 teams in the National League. The only franchises to post winning records during the 1970s were the Reds, Dodgers, Pirates, and Phillies. NL pennants went to the Reds (1970, 1972, 1975, and 1976), Pirates (1971 and 1979), Mets (1973), and Dodgers (1974, 1977, and 1978). NL East titles went to the Pirates (1970, 1971, 1972, 1974, 1975, and 1979), Mets (1973), and Phillies (1976, 1977, and 1978).

THE BEST TEAM

The best club is terms of victories was the 1971 crew, which was 90–72 and finished in second place, seven games behind the Pirates. The 1973 and 1974 clubs finished only 1½ games out of first in a weak NL East. The 1973 club was 81–81, and the 1974 outfit had an 86–76 record.

THE WORST TEAM

The 1978 club had a record of 69–93, the worst winning percentage by a Cardinal club between 1924 and the present.

THE BEST MOMENT

Bob Gibson pitched the only no-hitter of his career on August 14, 1971, against the Pirates in Pittsburgh.

THE WORST MOMENT

Vern Rapp was fired 15 games into the 1978 season after calling Ted Simmons a "loser."

THE ALL-DECADE TEAM • YEARS W/CARDS

Ted Simmons, c	1968–80
Keith Hernandez, 1b	1974–83
Ted Sizemore, 2b	1971–75
Joe Torre, 3b	1969–74
Garry Templeton, ss	1976–81
Lou Brock, lf	1964–79
Bake McBride, cf	1973–77
Reggie Smith, rf	1974–76
Bob Gibson, p	1959–75
Bob Forsch, p	1974–88
Al Hrabosky, p	1970–77
John Denny, p	1974–79

Other prominent players on the Cardinals during the decade were third baseman Ken Reitz (1972–75, 1977–80) and second baseman–shortstop Mike Tyson (1972–79). Gibson and Brock were also on the 1960s All-Decade Team and are in the Hall of Fame. Simmons, Hernandez, Torre, and Smith are deserving of enshrinement at Cooperstown, but have thus far been overlooked by the voters.

THE DECADE LEADERS

Batting Avg:	Torre	.312
On-Base Pct:	Torre	.386
Slugging Pct:	Torre	.460
Home Runs:	Simmons	151
RBIs:	Simmons	828
Runs:	Simmons	652
Stolen Bases:	Brock	551
Wins:	Gibson	84
Strikeouts:	Gibson	998
ERA:	Gibson	3.20
Saves:	Hrabosky	59

THE HOME FIELD

Busch Memorial Stadium was covered with AstroTurf between the 1969 and 1970 seasons. The dirt infield was also covered in 1977. From 1977 until 1996, the only dirt on the field was around the sliding pits. Crews then ripped up the turf and reinstituted the grass. In 1973, an eight-foot-high inner fence reduced the power alleys from 386 feet to 376 and center field from 414 feet to 404. The Cardinals' home run production failed to increase significantly, however, and the inner fence was removed after four seasons.

THE GAME YOU WISH YOU HAD SEEN

Bob Forsch no-hit the Phillies on April 16, 1978. It was the first National League no-hitter in St. Louis in 54 years.

THE WAY THE GAME WAS PLAYED

In the 1970s speed and defense ruled, in part because of new stadiums with more distant fences and artificial turf. Opening in the NL during the decade were Riverfront Stadium in Cincinnati, Three Rivers Stadium in Pittsburgh, Veterans Stadium in Philadelphia, and Olympic Stadium in Montreal. The average number of stolen bases per team rose from 87 in 1970 to 124 in 1979, while home runs declined from 140 to 119.

THE MANAGEMENT

August Busch was in his third decade as owner. The Cardinals' general manager at the start of the 1970s was Bing Devine. Devine was fired at the end of the 1978 season and replaced by John Claiborne, who held the general manager position for only 22 months. Field managers were Red Schoendienst (1965–76), Vern Rapp (1977–78), Jack Krol (1978), and Ken Boyer (1978–80).

THE BEST PLAYER MOVE

The best move was the drafting of Keith Hernandez in the 42nd round of the amateur draft in 1971. The best trade brought George Hendrick from the Padres in exchange for Eric Rasmussen in May 1978.

THE WORST PLAYER MOVE

One of the worst trades in club history took place in February 1972 when the Cardinals sent Steve Carlton to the Phillies for Rick Wise. The Cardinals did a dreadful job of trading during the 1970s; the bad deals seemed to far outnumber the good ones. Among those dealt were, in chronological order, Willie Montanez, Cookie Rojas, Richie Allen, Cecil Cooper, Fred Norman, Mike Torrez, Jose Cardenal, Steve Carlton, Jerry Reuss, Larry Hisle, Jim Bibby, Jose Cruz, Larry Herndon, Ron Reed, Reggie Smith, Bill Caudill, Mike Caldwell, Bake McBride, Aurelio Lopez, Jim Dwyer, Jerry Mumphrey, and John Denny.

1970

Season in a Sentence

A July stretch of 20 losses in 24 games along with a pitching collapse leads to a losing season.

Finish • Won • Lost • Pct • GB

Fourth   76   86   .469   13.0

Manager

Red Schoendienst

Stats

	Cards	NL	Rank
Batting Avg:	.263	.258	5
On-Base Pct:	.333	.332	7
Slugging Pct:	.379	.392	9
Home Runs:	113		10
Stolen Bases:	117		3
ERA:	4.06	4.05	6
Fielding Avg:	.977	.977	9
Runs Scored:	744		5 (tie)
Runs Allowed:	747		7

Starting Lineup

Ted Simmons, c
Dick Allen, 1b-3b
Julian Javier, 2b
Joe Torre, 3b-c
Dal Maxvill, ss
Lou Brock, lf
Jose Cardenal, cf
Joe Hague, rf-1b
Leron Lee, rf
Carl Taylor, rf
Vic Davalillo, cf
Mike Shannon, 3b

Pitchers

Bob Gibson, sp
Steve Carlton, sp
Mike Torrez, sp
Jerry Reuss, sp
Nelson Briles, sp-rp
Chuck Taylor, rp
Frank Linzy, rp

Attendance

1,629,736 (fifth in NL)

Club Leaders

Batting Avg:	Torre	.325
On-Base Pct:	Torre	.398
Slugging Pct:	Allen	.560
Home Runs:	Allen	34
RBIs:	Allen	101
Runs:	Brock	114
Stolen Bases:	Brock	51
Wins:	Gibson	23
Strikeouts:	Gibson	274
ERA:	Gibson	3.12
Saves:	Taylor	8

MARCH 18   Mike Shannon is diagnosed with kidney problems.

During a routine physical exam during spring training, it was discovered that Shannon suffered from glomerulonephritis, a rare disorder that is occasionally fatal. He spent a month in the hospital and was treated at home for another month before being cleared to play again. Shannon played in 52 games, batting only .213. Team physician Dr. Stan London announced in mid-August that Shannon's condition had deteriorated and he wouldn't be allowed to play for the rest of the season. As it turned out, he never played another game. In 1972, Shannon became one of the Cardinals' radio and television broadcasters, a job he holds to this day.

APRIL 8   In the season opener, the Cardinals defeat the Expos 7–2 in Montreal. The Cards tied the game 2–2 with a run in the eighth inning and broke it open with five in the ninth. Dick Allen, in his Cardinal debut, hit a home run and two doubles. Julian Javier collected three hits. Bob Gibson was the winning pitcher.

On the same day, the Cardinals sent Willie Montanez and Bob Browning to the Phillies to complete the Curt Flood trade. Montanez and Browning were substituted for Flood when he filed suit against organized baseball (see October 7, 1969). In the end, the trade sent Tim McCarver, Joe Hoerner, Byron Browne, Montanez, and Browning to Philadelphia for Dick Allen, Cookie Rojas, and Jerry Johnson. Allen was 28 when he came to the Cardinals with a .301 cumulative batting average and 177 home runs over the previous six seasons. He also came with a reputation for frequent drinking escapades, playing the horses, and divisiveness in the clubhouse. Allen gave the Cardinals one great season, batting .279 with 34 homers and 101 RBIs in 122 games before a leg injury shelved him for the final seven weeks of the season. The Cardinals dealt him to the Dodgers after the season in an ill-conceived trade (see October 5, 1970). Rojas and Johnson were of little help to the Cardinals and were traded again before the 1970 All-Star break. Montanez, who was a 22-year-old minor leaguer when he was sent to Philadelphia, proved to be the biggest loss. He hit 30 homers as a rookie outfielder for the Phillies in 1971 and fashioned a 14-year big-league career.

Transcendental Graphics/theruckerarchive.com

Curt Flood sacrificed prime years of his playing career to challenge baseball owners over the reserve clause. He played in just 13 games for the Washington Senators in 1971 after vetoing the Cardinals' deal to send him to Philadelphia after the 1969 season. Ultimately, however, he opened the door to free agency for generations of players.

APRIL 10   In the home opener, the Cardinals score seven runs in the seventh inning and defeat the Mets 7–3 before 45,960 at Busch Memorial Stadium.

Cardinals games on local television were broadcast in color for the first time in 1970.

APRIL 15   Mike Torrez pitches a one-hitter to defeat the Expos 10–0 at Busch Memorial Stadium. Torrez was six outs away from a no-hitter when Adolpho Phillips singled to lead off the eighth. Torrez was also 3 for 3 at the plate. It was his 11th win in a row over two seasons. Torrez won his last nine decisions in 1969 and his first two in 1970.

APRIL 26   Bob Gibson strikes out 15 batters during a 4–1 win over the Reds at Busch Memorial Stadium.

Gibson led the National League in wins in 1970, posting a 23–7 record and a 3.12 ERA to win the NL Cy Young Award. He fanned 274 batters in 294 innings. No other pitcher on the Cardinals won more than 10 games in 1970. Outside of Gibson, the staff combined for a 53–79 record.

MAY 5   The day after Ohio National Guardsmen shot and killed four students at Kent State University, the Cardinals play at Crosley Field for the last time and lose 5–1 to the Reds. The Reds moved into Riverfront Stadium on June 30, 1970.

The Cards started the season with 9 wins in their first 14 games but were 41–57 on July 26 after a stretch of 20 losses in the first 24 July games.

MAY 10   The Cardinals score four runs in the ninth inning to defeat the Braves 6–5 in Atlanta. Jose Cardenal drove in the final two runs with a bases-loaded single off Hoyt Wilhelm. Dick Allen started the rally with a homer.

MAY 11   Dick Allen's three-run, walk-off homer in the ninth inning off Jim Bunning is all the offense the Cardinals need in a 3–0 win over the Phillies at Busch Stadium. Steve Carlton pitched the shutout.

Carlton reported to spring training late because of a bitter holdout. August Busch had trouble adjusting to the cultural changes of the late 1960s and early 1970s, and with the newfound militancy of players who were demanding larger salaries, greater retirement benefits, better working conditions, and more freedom of personal expression. Carlton came to represent everything Busch hated about the changing times. During their salary dispute in the spring of 1970, Busch grumped, "I don't give a damn if Carlton ever pitches another baseball game for the Cardinals." They eventually agreed to a two-year deal, but the ill feelings remained, and Carlton didn't help matters with his 10–19 record and 3.72 ERA in 1970.

MAY 15   The Cardinals defeat the Cubs 1–0 at Busch Memorial Stadium. Mike Torrez (seven innings) and Billy McCool (two innings) combined on the shutout. Jose Cardenal drove in the lone run of the game with a single in the seventh inning.

MAY 19   The Cardinals trade Jerry Johnson to the Giants for Frank Linzy.

MAY 21   Steve Carlton strikes out 16 batters in eight innings but loses 4–3 at Philadelphia. The Cards trailed 3–0 heading into the ninth before scoring three times, two on a home run by Dick Allen, who was playing in Philadelphia for the first time since the Phillies had traded him. The Phils scored in the bottom of the ninth off three relievers, however, for the win.

Carlton struck out 16 or more batters three times in a Cardinal uniform, and the club lost all three. He fanned 16 on September 20, 1967, in a 3–1 loss to the Phillies in Philadelphia and fanned 19 Mets on September 15, 1969. The Mets won 4–3.

MAY 22   Many of the Cardinals are forced to evacuate from a hotel fire at the Sheraton in Philadelphia.

The fire broke out on the 15th floor, and smoke shot up to the 17th, 19th, and 20th floors, where most of the club was staying. Mike Shannon and pitching coach Billy Muffett awakened many on the ball club by kicking against their doors. The fire was brought under control quickly, and some players slept through the disturbance.

MAY 23   Bob Gibson strikes out 16 batters during a 3–1 win over the Phillies in Philadelphia. Dick Allen hit two homers to drive in all three St. Louis runs.

MAY 24   Dick Allen strikes out five times during a 10-inning, 6–5 loss to the Phillies in Philadelphia.

JUNE 2   The Cardinals defeat the Giants 12–1 before a crowd at Busch Memorial Stadium that totaled exactly 11,111. Dick Allen drove in seven runs with a single in the first inning, a homer with a man on base in the fifth, and a grand slam off Jerry Johnson in the eighth.

JUNE 4   In the first round of the amateur draft, the Cardinals select right-handed pitcher Jim Browning from Emma Sansom High School in Gadsden, Alabama.

Browning never made it past Class AA, marking the third consecutive season that the Cardinals drafted a player in the first round who failed to reach the majors. Future major leaguers drafted and signed by the Cardinals in 1970 were Mike Tyson (3rd round of the January draft), Rudy Arroyo (4th round of the secondary phase of the January draft), and June draftees Greg Terlecky (5th round), Don Durham (7th round), Marc Hill (10th round), John Denny (29th round), and Bake McBride (37th round). Four players (Tyson, Hill, Denny, and McBride) had big-league careers of 10 seasons or longer.

JUNE 7   Down 7–1, the Cardinals score two runs in the sixth inning and seven in the seventh to defeat the Padres 10–7 at Busch Memorial Stadium. Ted Simmons started the comeback with his first major league homer, a two-run shot in the sixth. Vic Davalillo pinch hit for Bob Gibson and opened the seventh inning with a single; he singled again later in the inning as the Cards batted around.

Davalillo collected 24 hits, including eight doubles, three triples, and a homer, in 73 at-bats as a pinch hitter in 1970.

JUNE 13   The Cardinals trade Cookie Rojas to the Royals for Fred Rico.

Acquired from the Phillies the previous October, Rojas was 31 years old when the 1970 season started. He hit only .106 in 23 games in St. Louis before being passed on to the Royals in a terrible trade. Finding new life in Kansas City, Rojas made the American League All-Star team for four consecutive seasons beginning in 1971. Rico never played a single game for the Cards.

JUNE 17	Bob Gibson comes within four outs of a no-hitter and strikes out 13 during an 8–0 win over the Padres in San Diego. The only hit off Gibson all night was a single by Ivan Murrell with two outs in the eighth inning.

JUNE 19   The Cardinals outlast the Cubs 5–3 in 17 innings in Chicago. The two seventeenth-inning runs scored on Ted Simmons's bases-loaded single.

JUNE 25   The Cardinals play at Forbes Field for the last time and lose 4–3 in 11 innings to the Pirates. The Pirates moved into Three Rivers Stadium on July 16, 1970.

JULY 1   The Cardinals trade Ted Abernathy to the Royals for Chris Zachary.

In another appallingly bad deal with their Missouri rivals, the Cardinals lost Abernathy, who gave Kansas City 12 saves over the remainder of the 1970 season and 23 more in 1971 while the Cardinal bullpen imploded. Zachary was 3–10 with a 5.32 ERA in St. Louis.

JULY 5   Bob Gibson wins his 10th in a row to run his season record to 12–3 by defeating the Expos 6–3 in Montreal.

JULY 19   Mike Torrez collects four hits, including a double, in four at-bats and pitches a complete game to defeat the Braves 3–1 at Busch Memorial Stadium.

JULY 20   Chuck Taylor faces the minimum 27 batters over nine innings, but the Cardinals lose 4–0 to the Reds in 10 innings in the second game of a doubleheader at Busch Memorial Stadium. Taylor allowed three hits but wiped out two runners on double plays and one on an attempted steal. The Reds won the game on Lee May's grand slam in the tenth off Bob Chlupsa. Cincinnati also won the first game, 4–3.

JULY 24   The Cardinals play at Riverfront Stadium for the first time and lose 4–0 to the Reds.

JULY 26   Johnny Bench hits three home runs off Steve Carlton during a 12–5 Reds win over the Cardinals in Cincinnati.

JULY 27   The Cardinals break an eight-game losing streak by beating the Reds 16–9 in Cincinnati.

AUGUST 1   Dick Allen hits a grand slam off Jack DiLauro in the seventh inning of a 14–7 win over the Astros in Houston.

AUGUST 8   The Cardinals score four runs in the ninth inning to defeat the Expos 11–10 at Busch Memorial Stadium. The game was tied 7–7 heading into the ninth when Montreal scored three times. The final two runs in the Cards' game-winning rally came on Joe Hague's two-run, walk-off homer.

AUGUST 9   Jerry Reuss pitches a two-hitter to defeat the Expos 4–0 in the second game of a doubleheader at Busch Memorial Stadium. The only hits off Reuss were singles by Rusty Staub in the fourth inning and John Bateman in the seventh. Montreal won the first game 7–6.

AUGUST 11 Pinch hitter Carl Taylor's walk-off grand slam climaxes a five-run rally in the ninth inning and beats the Padres 11–10 at Busch Memorial Stadium. Ron Herbel gave up the slam. San Diego led 8–1 before the Cards scored two in the seventh and three in the eighth. The Padres plated two runs in the ninth to take a 10–6 advantage before the incredible St. Louis comeback.

AUGUST 12

Bob Gibson strikes outs 13 batters in a 14-inning complete game to defeat the Padres 5–4 at Busch Memorial Stadium. The day after hitting a game-winning grand slam, Carl Taylor drove in the winning run again by drawing a bases-loaded walk in the fourteenth.

AUGUST 21

The Cardinals down the Padres 14–8 in San Diego.

AUGUST 22

Bob Gibson pitches a two-hitter to defeat the Padres 7–0 in San Diego. The only hits off Gibson were singles by Ed Spezio in the sixth and eighth innings.

AUGUST 23

The Cardinals score three runs in the ninth inning to beat the Padres 8–7 in San Diego. The last two runs scored on a single by Jose Cardenal, who had five RBIs on the day.

AUGUST 28

Jerry Reuss pitches a two-hitter to defeat the Dodgers 1–0 at Los Angeles. The only hits off Reuss were singles by Bill Sudakis in the fourth and seventh innings. Joe Torre provided the lone run of the game with a homer off Don Sutton in the ninth inning.

> Torre had a career-changing year in 1970. During the previous offseason, Torre put himself on the popular Stillman water diet with lots of protein, no carbohydrates, and eight glasses of water a day. He lost 25 pounds. Fans began asking for copies of the diet in such large numbers that the Cardinals sent out copies detailing the regimen. Torre also moved to third base, a position he hadn't played since high school, when Mike Shannon was unavailable because of his kidney ailment. Torre responded to the challenge by batting .325 with 203 hits, 21 homers, and 100 RBIs. He was the Cardinals' regular third baseman during his 1971 MVP season.

AUGUST 29

Lou Brock hits a two-out, two-run homer in the ninth inning to beat the Dodgers 3–2 in Los Angeles.

> Brock hit .304 with 202 hits, 114 runs, 13 homers, and 51 steals in 1970.

AUGUST 30

Leron Lee hits a two-run homer in the second to account for all of the Cardinals' runs needed to defeat the Dodgers 2–1 in Los Angeles.

> The win gave the Cardinals a 64–68 record, 23 wins in their last 34 games, and a shot at the pennant, 5½ games out of first place. The club ended the season on a 12–18 skid.

SEPTEMBER 6

Bob Gibson wins his 20th game of the season with a 7–2 decision over the Expos at Busch Memorial Stadium.

SEPTEMBER 8

The Cardinals play at Connie Mack Stadium for the last time and beat the Phillies 6–3. Dick Allen hadn't play in a game in a month because of an injured leg, but he insisted on starting in the Cards' last game in Philadelphia, where he played for seven years as a Phillie. Allen had two hits, including a homer, in three at-bats, and never played in another game as a Cardinal. The injury caused controversy in the Cardinals organization. He insisted on getting treated in Philadelphia. The Cards wanted Allen to recuperate in St. Louis. Shortly after the season was over, Allen was traded (see October 5, 1970).

The Phillies moved into Veterans Stadium in 1971.

SEPTEMBER 9   The Cardinals play at Three Rivers Stadium for the first time and defeat the Pirates 6–4.

SEPTEMBER 13   Joe Torre homers in the thirteenth inning to defeat the Mets 5–4 in New York.

SEPTEMBER 17   The Cardinals collect 22 hits and defeat the Cubs 9–2 in Chicago.

SEPTEMBER 23   Bob Gibson pitches a two-hitter for his 23rd win of the season, defeating the Cubs 2–1 in the second game of a doubleheader at Busch Memorial Stadium. The only Chicago hits were a triple by Glenn Beckert in the fourth inning and a single by Joe Pepitone in the seventh. The Cards completed the sweep with a victory by the same 2–1 score in the nightcap.

SEPTEMBER 26   Entering the game with 19 losses in the 1970 season, Steve Carlton dodges number 20 by beating the Expos 7–2 in Montreal.

The Cardinals' last 20-game loser was Jesse Haines, who was 13–20 in 1920.

SEPTEMBER 28   The Cardinals purchase Fred Norman from the Dodgers.

OCTOBER 5   The Cardinals trade Dick Allen to the Dodgers for Ted Sizemore and Bob Stinson.

Allen spent a year with the Dodgers before being traded to the White Sox, where he won the 1972 American League Most Valuable Player Award. At least the Dodgers had the good sense to trade Allen for Tommy John. All the Cardinals received for Allen was an average second baseman (Sizemore) and a third-string catcher (Stinson).

OCTOBER 20   The Cardinals trade Sam Campisi and Jim Kennedy to the Twins for Herman Hill and Charlie Wissler.

Hill died on December 14, 1970, while playing in the Venezuelan Winter League. He drowned in the Caribbean Sea near Valencia.

OCTOBER 21   The Cardinals trade Jim Campbell to the Red Sox for Dick Schofield.

NOVEMBER 30   The Cardinals trade Jerry DaVanon to the Orioles for Moe Drabowsky. On the same day, the Cardinals drafted Cecil Cooper from the Red Sox.

The Cards took Cooper to spring training in 1971 but were unimpressed and returned him to the Sox. Cooper went on to a career in which he put up 2,192 hits, 241 home runs, and a .298 batting average.

1971

Season in a Sentence

Behind Joe Torre's MVP season, 20 wins from Steve Carlton, and a no-hitter from Bob Gibson, the Cardinals hold first place as late as June 10 and win 90 games.

Finish • Won • Lost • Pct • GB

Second   90   72   .556   7.0

Manager

Red Schoendienst

Stats

Stats	Cards	NL	Rank
Batting Avg:	.275	.252	1
On-Base Pct:	.342	.319	1
Slugging Pct:	.385	.366	2
Home Runs:	95		9 (tie)
Stolen Bases:	124		1
ERA:	3.85	3.47	11
Fielding Avg:	.978	.979	8
Runs Scored:	739		2
Runs Allowed:	699		10 (tie)

Starting Lineup

Ted Simmons, c
Joe Hague, 1b
Ted Sizemore, 2b
Joe Torre, 3b
Dal Maxvill, ss
Lou Brock, lf
Matty Alou, cf-1b
Jose Cardenal, rf
Jose Cruz, cf
Julian Javier, 2b
Luis Melendez, rf-cf
Jim Beauchamp, 1b

Pitchers

Steve Carlton, sp
Bob Gibson, sp
Jerry Reuss, sp
Reggie Cleveland, sp
Chris Zachary, sp-rp
Moe Drabowsky, rp
Frank Linzy, rp
Don Shaw, rp
Chuck Taylor, rp

Attendance

1,604,671 (fourth in NL)

Club Leaders

Batting Avg:	Torre	.363
On-Base Pct:	Torre	.421
Slugging Pct:	Torre	.555
Home Runs:	Torre	24
RBIs:	Torre	137
Runs:	Brock	126
Stolen Bases:	Brock	62
Wins:	Carlton	20
Strikeouts:	Gibson	185
ERA:	Gibson	3.04
Saves:	Drabowsky	8

JANUARY 29   The Cardinals trade Nelson Briles and Vic Davalillo to the Pirates for Matty Alou and George Brunet.

Briles looked finished after he was 6–7 with a 6.22 ERA in 1970, but he rebounded to pitch in the World Series for the Pirates in 1971. Overall it was a good trade, however, as Alou hit .314 in 268 games for the Cardinals over three seasons.

APRIL 6   The Cardinals lose the season opener 2–1 in 10 innings to the Cubs in Chicago. The temperature was 39 degrees with a strong wind blowing in from center field. Billy Williams ended the contest with a walk-off homer off Bob Gibson. The Cards collected only three hits off Ferguson Jenkins, who pitched a complete game. Joe Torre hit a seventh-inning homer for the only Cardinal run.

Torre had one of the best offensive years ever by a Cardinal in 1971. He won the MVP Award by leading the NL in batting average (.363), hits (230), total bases (352), and RBIs (137) in addition to scoring 97 runs and smacking 24 homers. The hits and batting average figures are the best in a single season by any Cardinal from 1948 to the present. Torre's total-bases mark was the best from 1954 through 1998. The RBI total was tops in Cardinal annals from 1940 through 1998.

Joe Torre was a Cardinal for six seasons and hit 98 home runs in that time. He was traded after the 1974 season to the Mets. Torre has been a baseball player or manager for more than 40 years.

APRIL 7   The Cardinals take a 12–0 lead after four innings and breeze to a 14–3 win over the Cubs in Chicago.

APRIL 10   The Cardinals lose the home opener 6–4 to the Giants before 26,841 at Busch Memorial Stadium. Joe Torre hit a home run.

APRIL 25   The Cardinals score three runs in the ninth inning to beat the Phillies 5–4 at Busch Memorial Stadium. Joe Torre ended the contest with a bases-loaded single.

APRIL 28   Joe Torre extends his hitting streak to 22 games, although the Cardinals lose 9–1 to the Mets at Busch Memorial Stadium.

MAY 2   Steve Carlton pitches the Cardinals to a 1–0 win over the Expos at Busch Memorial Stadium.

               Carlton rebounded from his 10–19 season of 1970 to post a 20–9 mark and a 3.56 ERA in 1971.

MAY 3   The Cardinals play at Veterans Stadium for the first time and lose 3–2 to the Phillies.

MAY 21   Down 8–3, the Cardinals score in every inning from the third through the eighth and defeat the Padres 15–8 at Busch Memorial Stadium. Joe Torre scored four runs and drove in four.

MAY 27   Chris Zachary pitches a two-hitter to defeat the Cubs 10–0 at Busch Memorial Stadium. The only Chicago hits were a double by opposing pitcher Ferguson Jenkins in the third inning and a single by Chris Cannizzaro in the sixth. It was Zachary's first career complete game and his only one as a member of the Cardinals.

MAY 29   The Cardinals defeat the Braves 8–7 with a dramatic ninth-inning rally at Busch Memorial Stadium. Atlanta took a 7–5 lead with two runs in the top of the ninth before the Cards countered with two in their half. All three runs scored on Joe Torre's bases-loaded, walk-off triple.

MAY 30   Lou Brock extends his hitting streak to 26 games during an 8–3 victory over the Braves at Busch Memorial Stadium.

          At the end of May, the Cardinals had a record of 32–17 and a 2½-game lead over the Pirates. An 8–21 record in June, however, sent the Cards spiraling out of pennant contention before they had a brief run at Pittsburgh (see August 15, 1971).

JUNE 7   Down 6–2, the Cardinals score four runs in ninth inning and one in the tenth to stun the Braves 7–6 in Atlanta. In the ninth, Ted Sizemore drove in two runs with a double, and Jerry McNertney tied the game with a two-run pinch-double. Ted Simmons drove in the game-winner with a single.

JUNE 8   In the first round of the amateur draft, the Cardinals select first baseman Ed Kurpiel from Archbishop Molloy in Hollis, New York.

          Kurpiel was the fourth first-round pick in a row who failed to reach the majors. Future major leaguers the Cardinals drafted and signed in 1971 were Mike Vail (4th round) and Mike Potter (6th round) in the secondary phase of the January draft, and June draftees Larry Herndon (3rd round), Jerry Mumphrey (4th round), Jim Dwyer (11th round), and Keith Hernandez (42nd round) from Capuchino High School in Millsbrae, California. Despite being the 783rd player taken in the 1971 draft, Hernandez was one of the best selections the Cardinals ever made.

JUNE 10   The Cardinals drop out of first place with a 2–1 loss to the Pirates at Busch Memorial Stadium.

          The Cards never regained the top spot for the rest of the season.

JUNE 11   The Cardinals trade Leron Lee and Fred Norman to the Padres for Al Santorini.

          Norman went from the Padres to the Reds in June 1973 and pitched for Cincinnati in both the 1975 and 1976 World Series.

JUNE 15   The Cardinals trade Mike Torrez to the Expos for Bob Reynolds.

          This was a horribly one-sided deal. Torrez was only 24 when the Cardinals let him go. After the trade, he won 164 big-league games for six clubs before his career ended in 1984. Reynolds pitched only four games for the Cardinals and had a 10.29 ERA.

JUNE 17   Don Kessinger collects six hits in six at-bats to lead the Cubs to a 10-inning, 7–6 win over the Cardinals in Chicago.

JUNE 22   Steve Carlton strikes out 12 batters during a 6–5 win over the Dodgers in Los Angeles.

JUNE 25   The Cubs score 10 runs in the seventh inning off Don Shaw, Chuck Taylor, and Daryl Patterson and beat the Cardinals 12–0 at Busch Memorial Stadium.

JUNE 29   The Cardinals score seven runs in the third inning of an 8–3 win over the Pirates at Busch Memorial Stadium.

JULY 20   The Cardinals drop 14 games out of first place with a 5–1 loss to the Phillies at Busch Memorial Stadium.

JULY 24   The Cardinals outlast the Expos 8–7 in 14 innings in the first game of a doubleheader in Montreal. A single by Ted Simmons drove in the game-winner. Both teams scored twice in the twelfth. The Cards completed the sweep with a 9–3 victory in the nightcap. During the twin bill, Joe Torre collected five hits in seven at-bats, drew five walks, and drove in seven runs.

Simmons hit .303 with seven homers in 1971.

JULY 29   The Cardinals trade Jose Cardenal, Dick Schofield, and Bob Reynolds to the Brewers for Ted Kubiak and Chuck Loseth.

Cardenal had several more productive years ahead of him as a starting outfielder. Kubiak was never anything more than a utility infielder and played only 32 games as a Cardinal.

AUGUST 1   The Cardinals score three runs in the top of the twelfth inning to take a 6–3 lead over the Phillies before rain halts play in a bizarre game in Philadelphia.

Rain suspended play for an hour and 48 minutes in the top of the twelfth with the score 3–3 and two Cardinals on base. Play resumed, and the Cardinals scored three times. Rain then stopped play again for 31 minutes, and the umpires finally called the game off. According to the league rules then in force, the score reverted back to the last full inning played, which meant that the contest went into the books as an 11-inning, 3–3 tie. The Cardinals filed a protest and claimed the Phillies failed to put the playing field back into condition after the rain stopped. NL president Chub Feeney upheld the protest because of mechanical failure of the Zamboni that removed water from the artificial surface at Veterans Stadium. Debris blown onto the field during the storm clogged the machine. Feeney ruled the game suspended with the Cardinals leading 6–3. The contest was completed 37 days later (see September 7, 1971).

AUGUST 4   Bob Gibson collects his 200th career victory with a 7–2 decision over the Giants at Busch Memorial Stadium.

Gibson had a 16–13 record and a 3.04 ERA in 1971.

AUGUST 6   Down 6–1, the Cardinals explode for nine runs in the fifth inning and defeat the Giants 12–8 at Busch Memorial Stadium. The Cards collected eight consecutive singles in the big inning by Jose Cruz, Dal Maxvill, Ted Sizemore, Lou Brock, Julian Javier, Matty Alou, Joe Torre, and Ted Simmons.

Brock had the best overall season of his career in 1971. He led the NL in runs scored (126) and stolen bases (64) in addition to collecting 200 hits and batting .313.

AUGUST 7   Matty Alou beats out a bunt and scores in the tenth inning for the deciding run in a 3–2 win over the Dodgers at Busch Memorial Stadium. After Alou reached first, Dodger second baseman Jim Lefebvre huddled with pitcher Pete Mikkelsen halfway between the mound and second base, but they failed to call time. Alou suddenly took off for second, and Mikkelsen threw high to Lefebvre, who had backtracked to the bag. Alou continued on to third. Lefebvre charged after the ball but had difficulty picking it up in short-center, and Alou raced home to score ahead of Lefebvre's hurried throw.

AUGUST 14   Bob Gibson pitches the only no-hitter of his career, defeating the Pirates 11–0 at Three Rivers Stadium. In the ninth inning, Gibson retired Vic Davalillo on a grounder to Dal Maxvill at shortstop, Al Oliver on an easy roller to Ted Kubiak at second, and Willie Stargell on a called third strike. It was the first no-hitter thrown in Pittsburgh since 1907 and was Gibson's 201st career victory. He walked three and struck out ten.

Prior to his August 14, 1971, performance, Gibson had given up on the notion of pitching a no-hitter. "High-ball pitchers don't throw no-hitters," he often said, "and I'm a high-ball pitcher." Indeed, despite 251 career victories and 56 shutouts, Gibson had relatively few low-hit games during his career. He pitched only one one-hitter and seven two-hitters.

AUGUST 15   The Cardinals complete a four-game series sweep of the Pirates by scoring five runs in the eighth inning for a 6–4 win in Pittsburgh.

The win put the Cardinals only four games behind the first-place Pirates and gave them a 67–54 record. Trailing by 14 games on July 20, the Cards made up 10 games in 26 days. They lost their next five games, however, and never seriously challenged the Pirates again.

AUGUST 22   Lou Brock scores five times during a 13–4 romp over the Braves in Atlanta. Brock reached base on two singles and three walks.

AUGUST 23   Bob Gibson helps his own cause with a single in the ninth inning to break a 2–2 tie and left the Cardinals to a 3–2 win over the Astros in Houston.

AUGUST 28   Bob Gibson strikes out 13 batters during a 4–0 win over the Reds at Busch Memorial Stadium.

SEPTEMBER 1   The Cardinals trade Dan Ford and Fred Rico to the Twins for Stan Williams.

SEPTEMBER 5   The Cardinals collect 20 hits and defeat the Cubs 12–5 at Busch Memorial Stadium.

SEPTEMBER 6   Lou Brock and Tim McCarver fight during a 6–3 win over the Phillies in the first game of a doubleheader at Veterans Stadium. The Phillies were angry because Brock tried to steal with a 6–0 lead. In retaliation, Philadelphia pitcher Marty Muniz whistled a couple of close pitches at Brock. McCarver and Brock had words, and McCarver clipped him with a punch. McCarver was ejected. Brock finished the game with four stolen bases. The Phillies won the second tilt 2–1.

SEPTEMBER 7   The Cardinals play out their suspended August 1 game against the Phillies in Philadelphia before a regularly scheduled contest. The August 1 game was stopped with the Cardinals leading 6–3 in the top of the twelfth. The Phillies rallied for three runs in the bottom half, however, before the Cards scored three more in the thirteenth to win 9–6. In the regularly scheduled tilt, the Cardinals trailed 5–3 before scoring two runs in the ninth inning and two in the tenth to win 7–5. In the tenth, Ted Simmons tripled in the first run and scored on a ground-out.

SEPTEMBER 12   Bob Gibson records his 50th career shutout, beating the Cubs 4–0 in Chicago.

               Gibson finished his career with 56 shutouts, 13th all time and 7th since 1920.

SEPTEMBER 19   The Cardinals breeze to an 11–0 win over the Expos in Montreal.

SEPTEMBER 24   A walk-off grand slam by Joe Hague in the tenth inning beats the Expos 10–6 at Busch Memorial Stadium. The homer came off Mike Marshall. Montreal scored three times in the ninth to send the contest into extra innings.

SEPTEMBER 27   The Cardinals score five runs in the tenth inning to beat the Mets 6–1 in New York.

SEPTEMBER 28   Steve Carlton records his 20th win of the season with a 5–2 decision over the Mets in New York. It was Carlton's last game with the Cards (see February 25, 1972).

OCTOBER 18   The Cardinals trade Chuck Taylor, Harry Parker, Jim Beauchamp, and Tom Coulter to the Mets for Jim Bibby, Art Shamsky, Rich Folkers, and Charles Hudson.

1972

Season in a Sentence

In a fit of pique, August Busch orders the trades of Steve Carlton and Jerry Reuss, a strike cancels the first week of the season, and the Cardinals wind up with a losing record.

Finish • Won • Lost • Pct • GB

Fourth   75   81   .481 21.5

Manager

Red Schoendienst

Stats	Cards	NL	Rank
Batting Avg:	.260	.248	2
On-Base Pct:	.328	.325	5
Slugging Pct:	.355	.365	8
Home Runs:	70		12
Stolen Bases:	104		4
ERA:	3.42	3.45	6
Fielding Avg:	.977	.978	8
Runs Scored:	568		8
Runs Allowed:	600		6

Starting Lineup

Ted Simmons, c
Matty Alou, 1b
Ted Sizemore, 2b
Joe Torre, 3b
Dal Maxvill, ss
Lou Brock, lf
Jose Cruz, cf
Jose Melendez, rf-cf
Bernie Carbo, rf
Ed Crosby, ss-3b

Pitchers

Bob Gibson, sp
Rick Wise, sp
Reggie Cleveland, sp
Al Santorini, sp
Scipio Spinks, sp
Diego Segui, rp

Attendance

1,196,894 (eighth in NL)

Club Leaders

Batting Avg:	Alou	.314
On-Base Pct:	Brock	.359
Slugging Pct:	Simmons	.465
Home Runs:	Torre	11
RBIs:	Torre	81
Runs:	Brock	81
Stolen Bases:	Brock	63
Wins:	Gibson	19
Strikeouts:	Gibson	208
ERA:	Gibson	2.46
Saves:	Segui	9

JANUARY 7   The Cardinals sign Donn Clendenon following his release by the Mets.

FEBRUARY 25   The Cardinals trade Steve Carlton to the Phillies for Rick Wise.

Steve Carlton and August Busch were involved in a bitter contract dispute during the 1969–70 offseason, and Carlton signed for a two-year deal worth $45,000 a season. After compiling a 20–9 record in 1971, Carlton wanted a large raise. At the same time, as an inflation-checking device, President Richard Nixon ordered wage and price controls with annual salary increases fixed at no more than 5.5 percent. Busch was determined to follow Nixon's directives, even though professional athletes were exempt from the salary controls. Carlton believed his 20-win season should be enough to increase his salary to the $65,000 range. There was also Busch's personal dislike of the pitcher. It was a time when the generation gap was a chasm, and the 72-year-old Busch didn't understand the 27-year-old pitcher's fascination with martial arts and Eastern religions. The possibility of a strike (see April 7, 1972) also put Busch in a disagreeable mood. In the end, Busch ordered general manager Bing Devine to trade Carlton. Devine did so, swapping him to the Phillies for Rick Wise, who was also involved in a salary dispute. Ironically, Busch paid Wise the same salary that Carlton was asking. When the trade was completed, it looked to be about even. Over the *previous two seasons, Carlton had a 3.64 ERA. Wise's ERA over the same period was 3.45. Wise was also nine months younger than Carlton. As things turned out, it was an inequitable exchange, to say the least. In 1972, Carlton was 27–10 with a Philadelphia club that went 59–97. After leaving the Cardinals, he won 252 big-league games to finish his career 329–244. He seemed to save his best for his Cardinals matchups, compiling a 38–14 mark against his former club. In two seasons with the Redbirds, before a trade to the Red Sox, Wise had a 32–28 record but pitched without much support from hitters and relievers and had a 3.24 ERA.*

MARCH 24   The Cardinals trade Julian Javier to the Reds for Tony Cloninger.

MARCH 26   The Cardinals trade Frank Linzy to the Brewers for Rich Stonum.

APRIL 7   The Cardinals' scheduled home opener with the Phillies in St. Louis is canceled by baseball's first players strike. The strike ended on April 15, but the Cards missed out on six games in that span.

APRIL 15   In the strike-delayed season opener, the Cardinals lose 3–2 to the Expos before only 8,808 at Busch Memorial Stadium. Bob Gibson went six innings. Montreal broke a 2–2 tie with a run in the eighth inning off Al Santorini.

On the same day, the Cardinals traded Jerry Reuss to the Astros for Scipio Spinks and Lance Clemons. Like Carlton, Reuss was a young left-hander who angered August Busch by holding out for a higher salary than the Cardinals owner was willing to pay. Reuss also caused consternation among the club hierarchy by growing a beard. Busch ordered Reuss to shave it off. He refused. Busch ordered Bing Devine to trade the 22-year-old pitcher, a St. Louis native with a bright future. After the trade, Reuss won 198 more big-league games. In 10 months, from June 1971 through April 1972, the Cards dealt away Mike Torrez, Steve Carlton, and Jerry Reuss in terribly one-sided deals. After leaving St. Louis, the three pitchers combined to win 614 big-league games in exchange for four hurlers who won a grand total of 38 games in Cardinal uniforms. Spinks had three distinctions as a Redbird. First was his unusual first name. Spinks was named, as were generations of first-born Spinks men, for the Roman general who conquered Hannibal and burned Carthage. Spinks carried a stuffed gorilla he named "Mighty Joe Young" everywhere he went for good luck. Finally, after running through the third-base coach's stop sign, Spinks suffered a severe knee injury sliding into Johnny Bench in a game against the Reds on July 4, 1972. He was never again an effective pitcher.

APRIL 19   Facing his former teammates for the first time, Steve Carlton leads the Phillies to a 1–0 win over the Cardinals in Philadelphia in a duel with Bob Gibson.

Mike Walden and Mike Shannon replaced Jim Woods on the Cardinals radio and TV team in 1972, joining Jack Buck. Walden lasted only a year, but Shannon has remained with the Cardinals for more than three decades. August Busch gave Shannon a chance at broadcasting after a kidney ailment ended his playing career in 1970. Shannon had no broadcasting experience when he started, and the early years brought him more than his share of critics, but Cardinal fans today would have a difficult time imagining a game without his unique, passionate style and observations.

MAY 7   The Cardinals rip off five straight hits and score three runs in the ninth for a 5–4 defeat of the Braves at Busch Memorial Stadium. Pinch hitter Mike Fiore drove in the winning run with a single. It was Fiore's only hit in 10 at-bats with the Cards.

In 1972, the Cardinals jumped on the bandwagon along with all other major league clubs by discarding the traditional flannels in favor of the new double-knit uniform fabrics. The Pirates were the first team to use the double-knits in 1970. The material was lighter, more comfortable and more durable. Gone also were the jersey buttons and zippers; a built-in elastic sash replaced the standard belt. The traditional Cardinals emblem, the birds on the bat, remained unaltered on the new pullover style. Red, white, and blue trim was added around the collar, on the sleeve, on the belt sash, and down the sides of the trousers.

MAY 10   Ted Simmons hits a grand slam off Dave Roberts in the third inning that gives the Cardinals a 5–2 lead, but the Astros rally to defeat the Cardinals 10–7 at Busch Memorial Stadium.

After a strong 90-win season, the Cardinals had high hopes in 1972, but those were dashed by a 16–28 record by June 3. Optimism rebounded after they won 24 times in 30 games from June 4 through July 8, but the club finished the season 75–81 in the strike-shortened season.

MAY 19   The Cardinals trade Joe Hague to the Reds for Bernie Carbo.

When Scipio Spinks left the Cardinals, he gave his stuffed gorilla, "Mighty Joe Young," to Carbo. Carbo took the gorilla with him to Boston after a trade to the Red Sox, and it sat on the bench, still adorned in a miniature Cardinals uniform. "Mighty Joe Young" was considered a good-luck charm on the Sox' 1975 American League championship club.

MAY 31   Bob Gibson pitches the Cardinals to a 1–0 win over Ferguson Jenkins and the Cubs in Chicago. Lou Brock drove in the only run of the game on a single in the fifth inning.

Gibson started the season with losses in his first five decisions but finished with a 19–11 record, a 2.46 ERA, 23 complete games in 35 starts, and 208 strikeouts in 278 innings. Rick Wise had a 16–16 record and a 3.11 ERA in his first season with the club.

JUNE 4   Bob Gibson pitches his second consecutive shutout, defeating the Dodgers 4–0 in Los Angeles. Gibson capped the afternoon with a two-run homer in the ninth inning.

JUNE 6   In the first round of the amateur draft, the Cardinals select pitcher Dan Larson from Alhambra High School in Alhambra, California.

Larson was traded to the Astros before making his major league debut in 1976. During a seven-year career with three clubs, he had a 10–25 record and a 4.40 ERA. The only other future major leaguer the Cardinals drafted and signed in 1972 was Mike Proly, who was chosen in the ninth round.

JUNE 7   The Cardinals purchase Diego Segui from the Athletics.

JUNE 10   Ted Simmons homers off Mike Caldwell in the third inning of a 5–2 win over the
               Padres in San Diego.

JUNE 21   Four days after the break-in at Democratic Party National Committee offices at
               the Watergate complex in Washington, the Cardinals build an 11–0 lead after three
               innings and wallop the Padres 14–3 at Busch Memorial Stadium. It was Bob Gibson's
               211th career win, which broke the Cardinal club record of 210 that Jesse Haines set
               from 1920 through 1937.

JUNE 24   Luis Melendez hits a pinch-hit grand slam off Ray Sadecki in the fifth inning of an
               11–0 win over the Mets in New York.

JUNE 25   Scipio Spinks strikes out 13 batters in a 7–1 win over the Mets in the first game of a
               doubleheader in New York. The Cardinals completed the sweep with a 2–1 victory in
               the second contest.

JUNE 27   The Cardinals score a run in the eleventh inning against a five-man infield to beat the
               Expos 4–3 in the first game of a doubleheader at Busch Memorial Stadium. With the
               bases loaded and Lou Brock batting, Montreal manager Gene Mauch brought in an
               outfielder so that three players manned the right side of the infield. Brock foiled the
               strategy by hitting a ball just inside the first base line to drive in the winning run. The
               Expos won the second game 11–3.

               *Brock batted .311 and led the National League with 63 stolen bases in 1972.
               Ted Simmons batted .303 with 16 homers and 96 RBIs. Joe Torre had a fine
               season by hitting .289 with 11 home runs, but it was a huge drop from his MVP
               numbers of 1971.*

JULY 1   The Cardinals sweep the Phillies 6–4 and 1–0 in a doubleheader in Philadelphia. In
               the second game, Donn Clendenon accounted for the lone run of the game with a
               homer in the fourth inning off Ken Reynolds. Al Santorini (7$\frac{1}{3}$ innings) and Diego
               Segui (1$\frac{2}{3}$ innings) combined on the shutout.

JULY 11   Lou Brock collects five hits, including a double, in six at-bats, but the Cardinals lose
               5–4 in 15 innings to the Braves at Busch Memorial Stadium.

JULY 12   Bob Gibson pitches a shutout and clubs a home run to lead the Cardinals to a 7–0
               win over the Braves at Busch Memorial Stadium.

               *Gibson hit five homers in 1972 to tie his own club record for homers by a
               pitcher in a season. Gibson also hit five in 1965. His 24 career home runs are a
               Cardinal record for pitchers and rank seventh in major league history.*

JULY 13   Reggie Cleveland pitches a two-hitter to defeat the Braves 2–0 at Busch Memorial
               Stadium. The only Atlanta hits were singles by Rico Carty in the second inning and
               opposing pitcher Ron Reed in the third.

               The Canadian-born Cleveland hailed from Swift Current, Saskatchewan.

JULY 17   Bob Gibson strikes out 13 batters and beats the Astros 3–2 in Houston. It was
               Gibson's 10th win in a row.

JULY 21   Bob Gibson hits a sixth-inning homer and pitches the Cardinals to a 2–1 win over the Braves in Atlanta. It was Gibson's 11th win in a row.

JULY 25   Bob Gibson is the starter in the All-Star Game, played at Atlanta–Fulton County Stadium, and pitches two shutout innings. The National League won 4–3 in 10 innings.

AUGUST 2   Down 5–0, the Cardinals score five runs in the fourth inning and beat the Pirates 10–5 in a game stopped after 6½ innings by rain.

AUGUST 27 The Cardinals trade Matty Alou to the Athletics for Bill Voss and Steve Easton.

AUGUST 30 The Cardinals lose a 3–2 decision to the Giants at Busch Memorial Stadium in a game that turned on a freak play. With two outs and Luis Melendez the Redbird runner on third in the sixth inning, Cards infielder Dwain Anderson hit a roller that looked like a certain foul, but the ball hit a crease in the AstroTurf just short of third base, took a zany bounce off the back of the bag and stayed fair. Anderson hadn't broken from the batter's box and was an easy out at first. Melendez crossed the plate to no avail because Anderson was put out to end the inning. Bob Gibson struck out 14 batters in the defeat.

> *On the same day, the Cardinals trade Dal Maxvill to the Athletics for Joe Lindsey and Gene Dusen. The Alou and Maxvill trades during the last week of August for four prospects indicated that the Cardinals had thrown in the towel on the season. Alou and Maxvill were both on Oakland's 1972 World Series roster and earned World Championship rings. The four players acquired in the August 27 and August 30 trades played in a combined 11 games for the Cardinals, all of them by Bill Voss. Alou played for St. Louis again in 1973.*

SEPTEMBER 8 The Cardinals explode for five runs in the thirteenth inning, three on a Ted Simmons homer, to beat the Mets 9–4 in the second game of a doubleheader at Shea Stadium. New York won the opener 8–2.

> *Simmons is also believed to be the first player in major league history to play in a regular-season game without signing a contract. He had held out during spring training in 1972 while looking for a 100 percent raise to $35,000. As they had in the Steve Carlton negotiations, Cards management cited federal guidelines that raises had to be limited to 5.5 percent. Under the rules then in effect, players were bound to a club for life through the reserve clause. According to the language of the clause, if a player failed to sign a contract, a team had an option on his services for another year at a salary dictated by management. Simmons played under that option at the start of the 1972 season.*
>
> *According to the Players Association's Marvin Miller, the option was binding for only one year. The owners contended that the option was permanent and self-renewing. Simmons considered becoming the first player to challenge the option clause by failing to sign a contract, and then declaring himself a free agent at the end of the season, but on August 9, he signed a two-year pact with the Cardinals worth of total of $75,000. Two years later, Andy Messersmith and Dave McNally played all year without a contract and went to arbitration to seek free agency. On December 23, 1975, arbitrator Peter Seitz ruled that the option clause was valid for only one year and declared Messersmith and McNally free*

agents. In 1976, the players and owners negotiated an agreement in which any player with at least six years in the majors could become a free agent.

SEPTEMBER 13   Pinch-hitting in the thirteenth inning, Jorge Roque hit a home run to beat the Expos 5–4 in Montreal.

The homer was the first of only two that Roque struck in 139 at-bats during his big-league career. It was also Roque's only homer as a Cardinal.

SEPTEMBER 27   Al Santorini strikes out 13 batters in a 4–0 win over the Mets at Busch Memorial Stadium before a crowd of only 3,380.

As a result of the strike that delayed the beginning of the season, a slow start, and their eventual losing record, the Cardinals drew only 1,196,894 fans in 1972, a large drop from the 2,011,167 the club attracted in 1968. With the exception of 1981, another strike-shortened year, the 1972 total was the lowest at Busch in its 40-year history.

SEPTEMBER 28   In a decision by the Federal Trade Commission, Beatrice Foods Co. of Chicago is prohibited from using a commercial starring Lou Brock. The FTC charged Beatrice with using deceptive advertising because Brock told viewers that he got his speed from eating Milk Duds candies. The federal agency said the endorsements were based on a monetary relationship between Beatrice and Brock and not on nutritional superiority, creating the false impression that Milk Duds instilled, improved, and maintained athletic ability and performance.

SEPTEMBER 30   The Cardinals defeat the Cubs 2–1 in a 16-inning marathon in Chicago. In the sixteenth, Ted Simmons doubled and Ted Sizemore singled to score the deciding run. Lou Brock collected three hits to raise his career total to 2,000.

OCTOBER 26   The Cardinals trade Rudy Arroyo and Greg Milliken to the Dodgers for Larry Hisle.

This would have been a terrific trade if the Cardinals had hung on to Hisle (see November 29, 1972).

NOVEMBER 6   The Cardinals trade Jorge Roque to the Expos for Tim McCarver.

NOVEMBER 29   Three weeks after Richard Nixon defeats George McGovern in the presidential election, the Cardinals trade Larry Hisle and John Cumberland to the Twins for Wayne Granger.

Hisle was a regular in the Minnesota outfield for six years. In 1977 and 1978 combined, he batted .296 with 62 homers and 234 RBIs. Hisle hit more home runs in each of those two seasons than the Cardinals' entire starting outfield.

1973

Season in a Sentence

After losing 20 of their first 25 games, the Cardinals surge to a five-game lead in August, only to finish second in a weak NL East.

Finish • Won • Lost • Pct • GB

Second   81   81   .500   1.5

Manager

Red Schoendienst

Stats

Stats	Cards	NL	Rank
Batting Avg:	.259	.254	5
On-Base Pct:	.334	.329	5
Slugging Pct:	.357	.376	10
Home Runs:	75		12
Stolen Bases:	100		4
ERA:	3.25	3.66	2
Fielding Avg:	.975	.977	8
Runs Scored:	643		8
Runs Allowed:	603		3

Starting Lineup

Ted Simmons, c
Joe Torre, 1b-3b
Ted Sizemore, 2b
Ken Reitz, 3b
Mike Tyson, ss
Lou Brock, lf
Jose Cruz, cf
Jose Melendez, rf-cf
Tim McCarver, c
Bernie Carbo, rf

Pitchers

Rick Wise, sp
Reggie Cleveland, sp
Alan Foster, sp
Bob Gibson, sp
Tom Murphy, sp-rp
Diego Segui, rp
Al Hrabosky, rp
Orlando Pena, rp

Attendance

1,574,046 (fourth in NL)

Club Leaders

Batting Avg:	Simmons	.310
On-Base Pct:	Torre	.376
Slugging Pct:	Simmons	.438
Home Runs:	Simmons	13
	Torre	13
RBIs:	Simmons	91
Runs:	Brock	110
Stolen Bases:	Brock	70
Wins:	Wise	16
Strikeouts:	Wise	144
ERA:	Gibson	2.77
Saves:	Segui	17

APRIL 6   Three months after the United States ends its military involvement in Vietnam, the Cardinals lose 7–5 to the Pirates at Three Rivers Stadium. The Cards led 5–0 with Bob Gibson on the mound before Pittsburgh scored a run in the sixth inning, one in the seventh and five in the eighth.

Jerry Reuss was traded at the start of the 1972 season in large part because he had the audacity to grow a beard, but by 1973 facial hair was common in baseball. During the 1972 season, Oakland Athletics owner Charlie Finley paid his players to grow mustaches, becoming the first major leaguers since the first decade of the 20th century to sport facial hair. Among the Cardinals sporting mustaches in 1973 were Bernie Carbo, Luis Melendez, and Mike Tyson. They were the first Cardinal players with facial hair since Jake Beckley, who played for the club from 1904 through 1907.

APRIL 8   Lou Brock collects five hits in five at-bats in the second game of a doubleheader in Pittsburgh, but the Cardinals lose 5–3. The Cards also dropped the opener 4–3 in 10 innings.

APRIL 10   The scheduled home opener against the Mets is rained out.

APRIL 11   In the home opener, the Cardinals lose 5–4 to the Mets before 12,290 at Busch Memorial Stadium.

A new eight-foot-high inner fence at Busch reduced the power alleys from 386 feet to 376 and the center field distance from 414 feet to 404. The first home run to fall between the fences didn't come until July, when Willie Stargell hit one out in the Cards' 42nd home game of 1973. Only 49 homers landed in the opening before the team removed the inner fence after the 1976 season. Despite the smaller dimensions, Busch Memorial Stadium remained one of the toughest places to hit a home run in the National League. In 1973, players hit 57 homers there, 27 by the Cards and 30 by the opposition. In the club's road games that year, the Cardinals hit 48 home runs, and the home teams hit another 75.

APRIL 22   The Cardinals' record drops to 1–12 after a doubleheader loss to the Phillies by scores of 4–2 and 2–1 on Easter Sunday in Philadelphia.

MAY 8   The Cardinals' record falls to 5–20 with a 9–7 defeat at the hands of the Giants in San Francisco. On the same day, the Cardinals traded Al Santorini to the Braves for Tom Murphy.

The Cards recovered from the debacle of the opening 25 games by winning 56 of their next 86 to take a five-game lead in the NL East in early August.

MAY 11   The Cardinals wallop the Expos 12–0 at Busch Memorial Stadium.

Harry Walker and Jay Randolph joined Jack Buck and Mike Shannon in the radio and TV booth in 1973. A former player, coach, and manager with the Cardinals, Walker lasted only a year as a broadcaster. Randolph remained with the Cards until 1986.

MAY 30   The Cardinals win their eighth game in a row with a 5–2 decision over the Reds at Busch Memorial Stadium.

JUNE 2   Pinch hitting for Ken Reitz with the bases loaded in the eighth inning and the score 2–2, Tim McCarver hits a grand slam on Fred Gladding's first pitch to lift the Cardinals to a 6–2 win over the Astros at Busch Memorial Stadium. Gladding relieved Jim York and came into the game to face McCarver.

JUNE 3   Tim McCarver's walk-off single in the tenth inning beats the Astros 2–1 at Busch Memorial Stadium.

JUNE 5   In the first round of the amateur draft, the Cardinals select pitcher Joe Edelen from Gracemont High School in Gracemont, Oklahoma.

Edelen played just 27 big-league games and had a 6.75 ERA. The only future major leaguers drafted and signed by the Cardinals were Randy Wiles (5th round), John Tamargo (6th round), and Eric Rasmussen (32nd round).

JUNE 6   The Cardinals trade Jim Bibby to the Rangers for Mike Nagy and John Wockenfuss.

Bibby got a late start in professional baseball because he missed two seasons while in the military, including a tour in Vietnam, and didn't look like a prospect after posting a 1–5 record and a 5.11 ERA as a Cardinal. He was 28 when the Cardinals traded him but had a 110–96 record over the remainder of his career, which ended in 1984. With the Pirates in 1979 and 1980, Bibby had a combined won-lost mark of 31–10. His brother Henry played on three NCAA national basketball championship teams at UCLA and later played in the NBA. Henry's son Mike also had an NBA career after attending the University of Arizona. The Cards received nothing in exchange for Bibby. Wockenfuss never played a game in St. Louis. Nagy appeared in only nine contests and had an 0–2 record.

JUNE 13   A no-hitter eludes Rick Wise in an 8–0 win over the Reds at Riverfront Stadium. Wise was two outs from a no-hitter when Joe Morgan lined a single with one gone in the ninth for the only Cincinnati hit of the night. The Cards scored seven runs in the third inning, four of them on a grand slam by Luis Melendez off Jack Billingham.

Wise had previously pitched a no-hitter against the Reds in Cincinnati while a member of the Phillies in 1971.

JUNE 15   The Cardinals purchase Orlando Peña from the Orioles.

JUNE 18   Mike Tyson's homer in the third inning off Balor Moore beats the Expos 1–0 in a game at Busch Memorial Stadium called after five innings by rain. It was Tyson's first major league homer. Rick Wise pitched the shutout.

JUNE 21   Rick Wise is charged with driving under the influence after his car strikes a 16-year-old motorcyclist on a St. Louis County highway.

JUNE 27   Joe Torre hits for the cycle during a 15–4 win over the Pirates in Pittsburgh. Torre doubled off John Rooker in the first inning, homered against Luke Walker in the third, tripled in the fourth facing Bob Johnson, and singled off of Steve Blass in the ninth. The Cards collected 22 hits in the contest.

JULY 4   The Cardinals erupt for eight runs in the fourth inning and defeat the Pirates 11–3 at Busch Memorial Stadium.

JULY 15   The Cardinals defeat the Padres 5–4 in 15 innings in San Diego. Bernie Carbo doubled in the winning run. He entered the game as a pinch hitter in the thirteenth.

JULY 22   The Cardinals take first place by scoring three runs in the eighth inning to defeat the Dodgers 5–4 at Busch Memorial Stadium.

JULY 24   Rick Wise is the starting pitcher in the All-Star Game, won by the National League 7–1 at Royals Stadium in Kansas City. Wise allowed a run in two innings.

JULY 26   The Cardinals sweep the Mets 13–1 and 2–1 in a doubleheader at Busch Memorial Stadium. In the opener, Bob Gibson drove in five runs, including a grand slam off John Strohmayer.

AUGUST 5   The Cardinals increase their lead in the NL East to five games by taking a doubleheader from the Mets 3–2 and 4–1 in New York.

The wins gave the Cardinals a record of 61–50 after a 5–20 start to the 1973 season. After the August 5 sweep, however, the Redbirds lost their next 8 games and 11 of their next 12. One of the reasons for the collapse down the stretch was the loss of Bob Gibson to a leg injury, suffered on August 4. He didn't pitch again until September 29.

AUGUST 14   Down 5–0, the Cardinals score five runs in the sixth inning and four in the seventh to defeat the Astros 9–5 at Busch Memorial Stadium. The victory broke an eight-game losing streak.

AUGUST 18   The Cardinals send Dave Campbell and cash to the Astros for Tommie Agee.

AUGUST 19   Alan Foster pitches the Cardinals to a 1–0 win over the Padres at Busch Memorial Stadium.

AUGUST 21   Rick Wise helps his own cause by hitting a grand slam off Roric Harrison in the third inning, but his troubles on the mound lead to a loss to the Braves in Atlanta. The Cardinals scored seven times in the third to take a 7–0 lead, but the Braves came back with runs in their half, then added five more in the fifth and sixth to win.

AUGUST 24   Jose Cruz homers in the eleventh inning to beat the Reds 5–4 in Cincinnati.

AUGUST 27   Ken Reitz hits a three-run bases-loaded single in the fourteenth inning to defeat the Astros 6–3 in Houston. On the pitch before Reitz's hit, Tommie Agee was stealing home, but Reitz didn't see him. As Agee slid into home, Reitz hit a foul tip, sending Agee back to third.

                 Reitz was the Cardinals' starter at third base from 1973 through 1980, except for 1976 when he played for the Giants. Although an average hitter at best, Reitz was nicknamed "the Zamboni Machine" for his ability to suck grounders off the artificial turf at Busch Memorial Stadium.

AUGUST 29   The Cardinals purchase Eddie Fisher from the White Sox.

AUGUST 30   The Cardinals nip the Mets 1–0 in 10 innings at Busch Memorial Stadium. The winning run scored on a double by Lou Brock and a walk-off single by Jose Cruz facing Tom Seaver. Reggie Cleveland (nine innings) and Al Hrabosky (one inning) combined on the shutout.

                 Brock hit .297, scored 110 runs, collected 193 hits, and led the NL in stolen bases with 70 in 1973. Ted Simmons batted .310 with 13 homers and 91 RBIs.

SEPTEMBER 5   The Cardinals take a three-game lead in the NL East with a 5–3 win over the Pirates in Pittsburgh.

                 The win gave the Cards a 72–68 record. But the club fell out of first place by losing its next seven games, dropping three to the Cubs in Chicago, two to the Expos in St. Louis, and two more to the Pirates at home.

SEPTEMBER 6   The Cardinals purchase Matty Alou from the Yankees.

SEPTEMBER 17   Tommy Cruz makes his major league debut as a pinch runner during a 12-inning, 5–3 win over the Expos in Montreal.

                 There were three Cruz brothers on the Cardinals in 1973, natives of Arroyo, Puerto Rico. Jose (born in 1947), played for the Cards as an outfielder from 1970 through 1974. Hector (born in 1953) was with the club in 1973 and again from 1975 through 1977 as a third baseman and outfielder. Tommy (born in

1951) was also an outfielder. He played in only three games with the Cardinals before a trade to the Rangers. The three Cruz brothers never played together in the same game for the Cardinals.

SEPTEMBER 23   Joe Torre collects his 2,000th career hit with a single off George Stone during a 5–2 loss to the Mets in New York, Torre's hometown.

SEPTEMBER 25   The Cardinals lose 4–3 to the Cubs at Busch Memorial Stadium.

The loss was the Cardinals' 13th in their last 17 games and dropped the club four games behind the first-place Mets with five contests left on the schedule.

SEPTEMBER 26   Rick Wise pitches the Cardinals to a 1–0 win over the Cubs at Busch Memorial Stadium. Ted Simmons drove in the lone run of the game with a single in the first inning.

SEPTEMBER 27   Reggie Cleveland pitches a one-hitter and faces the minimum 27 batters to beat the Cubs 2–0 at Busch Memorial Stadium. The only Chicago base runner was Ken Rudolph, who singled with one out in the sixth inning. Rudolph was retired on a double play that started with Burt Hooton's sacrifice attempt. Lou Brock's two-run homer in the sixth inning accounted for both runs.

SEPTEMBER 28   The Cardinals defeat the Phillies 3–0 at Busch Memorial Stadium. It was the Cards' third consecutive shutout. Mike Thompson (four innings) and Diego Segui (five innings) combined on the shutout. Thompson was removed from the game without allowing a hit because he walked four batters. Diego Segui hurled the last five innings and surrendered just two base hits: a double by Bill Robinson in the eighth inning and a single by Willie Montanez in the eighth.

Thompson pitched 21 games for the Cards in 1973 and 1974, six of them starts, and had an 0–3 record. He was in the majors from 1971 through 1975 with Washington, St. Louis, and Atlanta and had a career 1–15 record. He walked 128 batters in 164²/₃ innings.

SEPTEMBER 30   On the final day of the regular season, the Cardinals win their fifth game in a row by defeating the Phillies 3–1 at Busch Memorial Stadium.

Despite an 81–81 record, the Cardinals still had a slim chance at the NL East pennant. At the close of play on September 30, the Mets were 81–79, and the Pirates were 80–81. The Mets had to make up two postponements by playing a doubleheader against the Cubs in Chicago on October 1. On the same day, the Pirates made up a rained-out contest versus the Padres in Pittsburgh. If the Mets lost twice, they would play the Cards in a one-game playoff to determine the NL East champion. A three-way tie would have been possible if the Mets had lost twice and the Pirates won.

OCTOBER 1   The Mets eliminate the Cardinals and Pirates and win the NL East by defeating the Cubs 6–4 in Chicago.

The Mets went on to upset the Reds in the National League Championship Series, then lost a seven-game World Series against the Athletics.

OCTOBER 25   The Cardinals sell Matty Alou to the Padres.

OCTOBER 26   The Cardinals trade Rick Wise and Bernie Carbo to the Red Sox for Reggie Smith and Ken Tatum. On the same day, the Cards sent Tommy Cruz and cash to the Rangers for Sonny Siebert.

> *This trade has to be rated about even, although Smith gave the Cardinals two fine seasons, making the All-Star team in both 1974 and 1975. The Cards would have come out ahead on the deal if they didn't made a mistake by trading Smith to the Dodgers in 1976 before he was named to two more All-Star squads and played in two World Series.*

DECEMBER 5   The Cardinals trade Tommie Agee to the Dodgers for Pete Richert.

DECEMBER 7   The Cardinals trade Reggie Cleveland, Diego Segui, and Terry Hughes to the Red Sox for Lynn McGlothlen, John Curtis, and Mike Garman.

> *In the second major deal with the Red Sox during the 1973–74 offseason, the Cardinals gained the advantage as McGlothlen, Curtis, and Garman each proved to be valuable additions for a couple of seasons.*

DECEMBER 8   The Cardinals trade Tom Murphy to the Brewers for Bob Heise.

1974

Season in a Sentence

In a year highlighted by Lou Brock's 118 stolen bases, the Cardinals finish a close second for the second year in a row.

Finish • Won • Lost • Pct • GB

Finish	Won	Lost	Pct	GB
Second	86	75	.534	1.5

Manager

Red Schoendienst

Stats

Stats	Cards	NL	Rank
Batting Avg:	.265	.255	3
On-Base Pct:			
Slugging Pct:	.365	.367	6
Home Runs:	83		12
Stolen Bases:	172		1
ERA:	3.48	3.62	6
Fielding Avg:	.977	.976	2
Runs Scored:	677		4
Runs Allowed:	643		5

Starting Lineup

Ted Simmons, c
Joe Torre, 1b
Ted Sizemore, 2b
Ken Reitz, 3b
Mike Tyson, ss
Lou Brock, lf
Bake McBride, cf
Reggie Smith, rf
Jose Cruz, rf-lf

Pitchers

Lynn McGlothlen, sp
Bob Gibson, sp
John Curtis, sp
Alan Foster, sp
Sonny Siebert, sp
Bob Forsch, sp
Al Hrabosky, rp
Mike Garman, rp
Rich Folkers, rp
Orlando Pena, rp

Attendance

1,838,413 (third in NL)

Club Leaders

Batting Avg:	McBride	.309
	Smith	.309
On-Base Pct:	Smith	.389
Slugging Pct:	Smith	.528
Home Runs:	Smith	23
RBIs:	Simmons	103
Runs:	Brock	105
Stolen Bases:	Brock	118
Wins:	McGlothlen	16
Strikeouts:	McGlothlen	142
ERA:	McGlothlen	2.69
Saves:	Hrabosky	9

MARCH 23   Six weeks after the kidnapping of Patty Hearst, the Cardinals trade Scipio Spinks to the Cubs for Jim Hickman.

> *Before the 1974 season began, Dick Meyer resigned his positions as executive vice president of the Cardinals and as president of Anheuser-Busch, Inc. Meyer resigned over a clash in policies at the brewery after the firing of executives during a period of downsizing. Meyer had been of one Busch's most trusted advisers and had been involved with the Cardinals since Busch bought the club in 1953. August Busch's title in the Cardinal hierarchy changed from president to chairman of the board and chief executive officer.*

APRIL 5   The Cardinals score two runs in the tenth inning and defeat the Pirates 6–5 on Opening Day before 24,210 at Busch Memorial Stadium. The game ended in bizarre fashion. The Cards went to bat in the bottom of the tenth trailing 5–4. With no outs, singles by Bake McBride, Ken Reitz, and Tim McCarver produced the tying run. Jose Cruz followed with a safe bunt, loading the bases. Lou Brock lined to right field, where Gene Clines trapped the ball. The runners held, fearing the ball would be caught, and Jim Dwyer, running for Reitz, was easily forced out on Clines's throw to catcher Mike Ryan. Ryan then threw to Richie Hebner at third, forcing McCarver, who had retreated to second. Hebner pegged the ball to second baseman Rennie Stennett, who tagged McCarver instead of stepping on second, which would have forced Cruz for a triple play. While the Pirates were arguing with the umpires that Stennett had tagged the bag, they failed to call time and Cruz alertly pushed on to second. Ted Sizemore then singled to drive in Cruz with the winning run. McBride collected three hits, including a double. Reitz also contributed three hits.

> *Bob Starr joined the Cardinals broadcast team in 1974, joining Jack Buck, Mike Shannon, and Jay Randolph. Starr remained with the Cards until 1979.*

APRIL 6   In his Cardinals debut, Sonny Siebert shuts out the Pirates 8–0 at Busch Memorial Stadium.

APRIL 13   In the Cardinals' seventh game of the season, Lou Brock steals his first two bases of 1974 during a 6–4 win over the Pirates in Pittsburgh.

> *When the 1973 season began, Brock had led the NL in steals seven times, runs twice, and doubles and triples once each, and had four seasons with 200 or more hits. He had also played in three World Series. Brock was bothered, however, by what he believed was a lack of respect for his accomplishments. He had been named to only three All-Star teams, and his highest finish in the MVP balloting was sixth, in 1968 and 1973. Although he was due to turn 35 in August and had never stolen more than 74 bases in a season, Brock set out on a quest in 1974 to break Maury Wills's single-season stolen-base record of 104, set in 1962 when Wills played for the Dodgers. With the record, Brock felt he would receive the recognition he deserved. Prior to 1974, Brock had never even attempted to steal more than 92 bases in a season. In 1974, he swiped 118 in 151 attempts. In addition, Brock batted .304, scored 105 runs, and collected 194 hits. After stealing his record 118 bases, Brock never again stole as many as half that number, dropping to 56 in both 1975 and 1976. Rickey Henderson stole 130 bases in 1982 to pass Brock as the single-season record holder. Brock still has the National League mark, however, and the second-highest figure in the modern era.*

MAY 7   Lynn McGlothlen pitches the Cardinals to a 1–0 win over the Reds in Cincinnati. Joe
               Torre drove in the lone run of the game with a sacrifice fly in the ninth inning.

               *In his first season with the Cardinals, McGlothlen had a 12–3 record on July 4
               and finished with a 16–12 mark and a 2.70 ERA.*

MAY 8   Reggie Smith drives in both runs and Lou Brock scores both in a 2–0 win over
               the Reds in Cincinnati. Smith drove in Brock with doubles in the sixth and eighth
               innings. John Curtis pitched the shutout.

               *In his first season with the Cardinals, Smith hit .309 with 23 homers and 100
               RBIs. He was one of three starting outfielders for the Cards who hit .300 or
               better in 1974. Lou Brock hit .306, and Bake McBride matched Smith's figure
               of .309. In the race for the highest batting average on the Cardinals in 1974,
               McBride nosed out Smith .309481 to .309478.*

MAY 24   The Cubs' failure to cover home plate during a rundown in the ninth inning gives
               the Cardinals a 1–0 victory at Wrigley Field. With Joe Torre on first base and Ted
               Simmons on third, Tim McCarver grounded to Billy Williams at first. Williams
               threw home, and catcher Tom Lunstedt closed in on Simmons before tossing the
               ball to third baseman Matt Alexander. Simmons turned toward the plate, raced past
               Lunstedt, and scored with Alexander chasing him in vain. Neither Rick Reuschel nor
               Williams covered the plate. Sonny Siebert pitched the shutout for the Redbirds.

JUNE 5   In the first round of the amateur draft, the Cardinals select shortstop Garry
               Templeton from Valley High School in Santa Ana, California.

               *Templeton was an immediate sensation, reaching the majors as the Cardinals'
               20-year-old starting shortstop in August 1976. Templeton looked like a sure Hall
               of Famer after his first five seasons in the majors, and while those projections
               failed to materialize, he was one of the Cardinals' best selections over the first
               40 years of the amateur draft. The Cards did draft a future Hall of Famer, Paul
               Molitor, out of St. Paul, Minnesota, in the 28th round. Molitor opted to attend
               the University of Minnesota, however, instead of signing with the St. Louis
               organization. He was drafted in the first round by the Brewers in 1977. Other
               players drafted and signed by the Cardinals in 1974 were John Urrea (first
               round of the regular phase in January) and Bill Caudill (eighth round in June).
               In addition, the Cardinals signed future second baseman Tommy Herr as an
               undrafted free agent.*

JUNE 10   Joe Torre hits a two-run homer in the eleventh inning to beat the Dodgers 4–2 in Los
               Angeles.

JUNE 11   Lynn McGlothlen (8²/₃ innings) and Al Hrabosky (¹/₃ of an inning) combine to beat the
               Dodgers 1–0 in Los Angeles. The run scored in the sixth inning. Lou Brock reached
               first base when Dodger catcher Steve Yeager interfered with Brock's swing. He moved
               to third on Ted Simmons's single and scored on another single by Bake McBride.

               *Nicknamed "The Mad Hungarian," Hrabosky was one of the most colorful
               players ever to don a St. Louis uniform. He became a cult hero to Cardinals
               fans. In 1974, he grew a Fu Manchu mustache and beard because he believed
               it intimidated hitters. "I start frowning and it comes down and I look meaner,"*

Hrabosky explained. "My wife doesn't like it, but baseball comes first." Before throwing his first pitch after arriving from the bullpen, Hrabosky would stand at the back of the mound and meditate for a few seconds, pound his glove, turn around, and ascend the mound with a scowl on his face. The routine started in the June 11, 1974, game against the Dodgers, and Hrabosky struck out Tom Paciorek on three pitches to end the game. During the 1974 season, Hrabosky had an 8–1 record and nine saves with a 2.95 ERA. Over his final 41 innings, Hrabosky allowed only one run.

JUNE 21   The Cardinals sell Pete Richert to the Phillies.

JUNE 30   Bake McBride hits a two-run homer in the eleventh inning to beat the Mets 5–3 in the second game of a doubleheader in New York. The Cards also won the opener, 5–2.

Arnold (Bake) McBride was the National League Rookie of the Year in 1974, batting .309 with 30 stolen bases. In 1,429 at-bats with the Cardinals prior to a 1977 trade to the Phillies, McBride hit .307 and could run 100 yards in 9.7 seconds, but he lacked power and suffered nagging knee injuries that prevented him from becoming a star. His father, also nicknamed Bake, pitched for the Kansas City Monarchs in the Negro Leagues.

JULY 12   The Cardinals score nine runs in the first inning and defeat the Braves 10–0 in the second game of a doubleheader at Busch Memorial Stadium. Bob Forsch pitched the shutout for his first major league win. Atlanta won the first tilt 7–3.

The decision was the first of 163 games that Forsch won in a Cardinals uniform, although he recorded more than 15 games in a season only once. The only two pitchers ahead of him in wins as a Cardinal are Hall of Famers Bob Gibson (251) and Jesse Haines (210). At the end of the 2005 season, Forsch also ranked fourth in games pitched (456), third in strikeouts (1,079), third in innings (2,658), and ninth in shutouts (19). He played for the club from 1974 through 1988. Forsch was drafted by the Cardinals in the 38th round in 1968 as a third baseman. He switched to pitching while with Cedar Rapids in the Midwest League in 1970. Bob's brother Ken, who is three years older, also had a long career as a major league pitcher, mainly with the Astros. The two are the only pair of brothers to pitch no-hitters in the major leagues. Bob pitched two of them, one in 1978 and another in 1983. He is the only Cardinal pitcher with a pair of no-hitters.

JULY 17   Bob Gibson records his 3,000th career strikeout by fanning Cesar Geronimo of the Reds during a 12-inning, 6–4 loss at Busch Memorial Stadium. Gibson was only the second pitcher in major league history to reach the 3,000-strikeout mark. The first was Walter Johnson, who fanned 3,508 from 1907 through 1927.

In an odd coincidence, Gibson struck out number 3,000 on the day that Dizzy Dean died, and on the 50th anniversary of Jesse Haines's no-hitter for the Cardinals on July 17, 1924. Geronimo was also the victim of Nolan Ryan's 3,000th career strikeout in 1980.

JULY 19   The Cardinals lose for the 13th time in a stretch of 14 games by dropping a 5–1 decision to the Astros at Busch Memorial Stadium.

The loss put the Cardinals' record at 44–49, three games behind the first-place Phillies.

JULY 20   The Cardinals break a six-game losing streak with three runs in the ninth inning to defeat the Astros 6–5 at Busch Memorial Stadium. Tim McCarver drove in the final two runs with a walk-off single. He entered the contest as a pinch hitter in the eighth inning.

JULY 21   The Forsch brothers face each other for the first time in a 9–1 win over the Astros at Busch Memorial Stadium. Bob pitched a complete game. Ken hurled the seventh and eighth innings in relief.

JULY 23   Reggie Smith homers in the National League's 7–2 victory in the All-Star game, played at Three Rivers Stadium in Pittsburgh. Smith homered in the seventh inning off Catfish Hunter.

JULY 29   Lou Brock steals his 700th career base during an 11–4 win over the Cubs in Chicago.

JULY 30   Reggie Smith drives in all four St. Louis runs for a 4–3 win over the Phillies in Philadelphia. Smith hit a triple in the first inning to put the Cards up 1–0, a homer in the sixth to break a 1–1 tie, and a two-run homer in the eighth with the club trailing 3–2.

AUGUST 4   After losing the opener in a doubleheader at Busch Memorial Stadium against the Phillies, the Cardinals rebound to take the nightcap 11–0. The split allowed the Cardinals to maintain a one-game lead over Philadelphia in the pennant race.

AUGUST 5   The Cardinals defeat the Phillies 3–2 in 13 innings at Busch Memorial Stadium. Ted Simmons tied the score 2–2 with a two-run homer in the ninth. Joe Torre's bases-loaded single off the left-field wall drove in the winner.

AUGUST 6   The Cardinals score seven runs in the third inning of a 9–4 win in the second game of a doubleheader against the Expos in Montreal. The Cards also won the opener, 5–4. Lou Brock stole his 75th base of the season to surpass his career best of 74, which he established in 1966.

AUGUST 9   On the day after Richard Nixon resigns, Ted Simmons hits a grand slam off Geoff Zahn in the sixth inning of a 5–3 win over the Dodgers at Busch Memorial Stadium. It was Simmons's 25th birthday.

AUGUST 12   Ted Sizemore draws five walks in seven plate appearances during a 13-inning, 6–5 win over the Padres at Busch Memorial Stadium. His fifth walk in the thirteenth loaded the bases and set the stage for Bake McBride's game-winning sacrifice fly.

AUGUST 15   The Cardinals trade Dan Larson and Ron Selak to the Astros for Claude Osteen.

AUGUST 16   Held to no runs and two hits through eight innings, the Cardinals erupt for two tallies in the ninth to defeat the Giants 2–1 at Busch Memorial Stadium. Joe Torre drove in the winning run with a single.

AUGUST 17   A two-run, walk-off homer by Reggie Smith in the ninth inning beats the Giants 5–3 at Busch Memorial Stadium.

The Cardinals made a sartorial change late in the 1974 season by switching from black shoes to red ones.

AUGUST 28	Lou Brock steals his 90th base of the season during a 5–1 win over the Padres in San Diego.

Between 1900 and 1974, the only players with 90 or more steals in a season were Ty Cobb with 96 in 1915 and Maury Wills with 104 in 1962 and 95 in 1965. Brock drew considerable criticism throughout his career because he often stole bases when his club had a large lead. That intensified in 1974 when he attempted to steal 151 times. But his stolen-base percentage that season was in line with his remarkably consistent career. Brock's success rate was 79 percent in 1969, 77 in 1970, 77 in 1971, 78 in 1972, 78 in 1973, 78 in 1974, 78 in 1975 and 75 in 1976.

AUGUST 29	After retiring the first 21 batters to face him, John Curtis settles for a one-hitter and a 3–1 win over the Padres in San Diego. The first base runner was Dave Winfield, who walked leading off the eighth. After Curtis surrendered another walk, Fred Kendall singled in a run to spoil both the no-hit and shutout bid. It also tied the score 1–1. The Cards won by scoring twice in the ninth.

AUGUST 30	Wearing number 18, Keith Hernandez makes his major league debut during an 8–2 loss to the Giants in San Francisco, which is Hernandez's hometown. Hitting seventh, he had a single and an RBI in two at-bats.

Hernandez switched to number 37 in 1976, his first year as the club's everyday first baseman. He held on to the position until a trade to the Mets in 1983. One of the best defensive first basemen in major league history with 11 Gold Gloves, Hernandez played on two different World Championship teams, including the Cards in 1982, and captured a batting title and MVP Award. His father, John, who became a San Francisco fireman, was a top prospect in the Cardinals' farm system during the 1940s until a beaning blurred his vision. Keith's brother Gary played four seasons in the Cardinal organization. Keith was a high school star as a junior at Capuchino High School in Millsbrae, California, a San Francisco suburb, but quit the baseball team during his senior year because of a dispute with the coach. As a result, he slipped to the 42nd round in the 1971 draft and became one of the best late-round bargains in big-league history. As a Cardinal, Hernandez batted .299 with 662 runs, 1,217 hits, 265 doubles, 81 homers, and 595 RBIs.

SEPTEMBER 1	Lou Brock steals four bases during an 8–1 win over the Giants in San Francisco. The four gave Brock 98 for the season.

On the same day, the Cardinals sold Tim McCarver to the Red Sox.

SEPTEMBER 5	The Cardinals purchase Ron Hunt from the Expos.

SEPTEMBER 6	Lou Brock steals his 100th and 101st bases of the season during a 5–0 win over the Mets at Busch Memorial Stadium.

SEPTEMBER 10	Two days after Gerald Ford pardons Richard Nixon, Lou Brock steals his 104th and 105th bases of 1974 to tie and break the modern single-season mark of 104 set by

Maury Wills in 1962. The steals, which Brock got during an 8–2 loss to the Phillies at Busch Memorial Stadium, were also the 739th and 740th of his career and gave him the modern National League lifetime record, previously 738 by Max Carey from 1910 through 1929.

His record-breaking 105th steal came in the seventh inning with Dick Ruthven as the pitcher and Bob Boone as the catcher. The game was halted to honor Brock. After teammates swarmed to congratulate him, a member of the grounds crew dug up second base. Negro Leagues star James "Cool Papa" Bell, a Hall of Famer and St. Louis native, then presented it to Brock. Also introduced was Emory Hines, Brock's coach at Southern University. Brock was handed a microphone and thanked the fans.

Photo File/Hulton Archive/Getty Images

Lou Brock came to the Cardinals in a deal with the Cubs for pitcher Ernie Broglio, the Cards' greatest trade of all time. He was a gifted base runner and managed to steal 938 bases in his 19-year career, though he never stole home. Brock was inducted into the Hall of Fame in 1985.

SEPTEMBER 11   At Shea Stadium, the Cardinals defeat the Mets 4–3 in 25 innings, the second-longest game in major league history. The contest lasted 7 hours and 4 minutes and ended at 3:13 AM. Among those in attendance were commissioner Bowie Kuhn and his wife. The couple stayed until the conclusion. The Cardinals trailed 3–1 with two outs in the ninth when Ken Reitz hit a two-run homer. The two clubs then combined for 15 consecutive scoreless innings. In the twenty-fifth, Bake McBride led off with an infield single. When New York pitcher Hank Webb threw wildly on a pickoff attempt, McBride raced to third. First baseman John Milner retrieved the ball in foul territory and threw to catcher Ron Hodges, who dropped the throw, allowing McBride to score.

St. Louis relievers Mike Garman, Al Hrabosky, Rich Folkers, Ray Bare, Claude Osteen, and Sonny Siebert combined for 19 scoreless innings. The two teams combined to use 50 players in the tilt, 26 of them by the Cardinals.

The only longer game in major league history was a 26-inning affair between the Boston Braves and the Brooklyn Dodgers on May 1, 1920. The contest was called by darkness with the score tied 1–1. Another 25-inning game took place on May 8 and 9, 1984, between the White Sox and Brewers. They had played 17 innings before umpires suspended the game because of a 1 AM curfew. The game continued the following evening with eight more innings. Chicago won 5–4.

SEPTEMBER 13   Two nights after a 25-inning marathon, the Cardinals play 17 innings and beat the Phillies 7–3 in Philadelphia. The Phillies used a National League–record 27 players. The Cardinals put 24 players into the box score. There were no runs scored from the fourth through the sixteenth. The Cards erupted for five runs in the seventeenth, and the Phils countered with one. St. Louis batters drew 16 walks.

SEPTEMBER 14   The Cardinals take the lead in the NL East from the Pirates with a 9–2 win over the Phillies in Philadelphia.

SEPTEMBER 17   The Cardinals take a 2½-game lead in the NL East with a 13-inning, 2–1 win over the Pirates at Pittsburgh. Ted Simmons drove in the winning run with a sacrifice fly. Al Hrabosky pitched four hitless innings of relief.

From September 11 through September 17, the Cardinals won six in a row while the Pirates lost six in succession. This allowed the Cardinals to leap from a 3½-game deficit to a 2½-game advantage in a week.

SEPTEMBER 20   Lou Brock and Bake McBride receive death threats from a man who claimed to bet $50,000 on the Pirates to win the NL East. The man's letter included numerous racial slurs and obscenities. He said he had an inoperable brain tumor and had one to two months to live, and that he planned to shoot Brock and McBride from the stands and commit suicide. The two Cardinals outfielders were assigned a special security detail for protection.

SEPTEMBER 21   The Cubs humiliate the Cardinals 19–4 at Busch Memorial Stadium.

SEPTEMBER 22   A fight breaks out during a 6–5 win over the Cubs at Busch Memorial Stadium. Bill Madlock took exception to Al Hrabosky's "psyche-out" routine on the mound (see June 11, 1974) and refused to get into the batter's box. Madlock wound up in an argument with Ted Simmons that quickly spread into a bench-clearing brawl.

SEPTEMBER 23   The Cardinals suffer a crucial loss in the pennant race, dropping a 1–0 decision in 10 innings to the Pirates at Busch Memorial Stadium. The Cards could have taken a 2½-game lead in the race with a win. Richie Hebner drove in the lone run of the game with a single off Lynn McGlothlen.

SEPTEMBER 24   The Cardinals drop out of first place with a 7–3 loss to the Pirates at Busch Memorial Stadium.

SEPTEMBER 25   The Cardinals retake first place with a dramatic 13–12 win in 11 innings over the Pirates at Busch Memorial Stadium. Down 5–0 in the first inning, the Cardinals took a 9–6 lead in the fifth, but Pittsburgh tied it 9–9 to send the contest into extra innings. The Pirates scored three times in the eleventh, but the Cardinals rallied for four in their half. Pinch hitter Jim Dwyer drove in the winning run with a sacrifice fly.

SEPTEMBER 29   The Cardinals beat the Cubs 7–3, and Lou Brock steals his 118th base of the season.

The Cards headed into the final three games of the season tied for first place with the Pirates.

OCTOBER 1   On the second-to-last day of the season, the Cardinals drop one game back of the Pirates with a 3–2 loss to the Expos in Montreal. The Cards led 2–1 before Mike Jorgensen hit a two-out, two-run homer off Bob Gibson in the eighth inning. The Pirates won 6–5 against the Cubs in Pittsburgh.

OCTOBER 2   On the final day of the season, the Cardinals are snowed out in Montreal while the Pirates clinch the NL East with a 10-inning, 5–4 win over the Cubs in Pittsburgh. The Cards had already checked out of their rooms at the Queen Elizabeth Hotel in Montreal, but they gathered in the lobby that night. If the Pirates had lost, the Cards and Bucs would have played a one-game playoff for the NL East championship. In St. Louis, KSD-TV sportscaster Ron Jacober listened to the Pirates-Cubs game and relayed what was happening at Three Rivers Stadium via telephone to Cards TV announcer Jay Randolph, who provided the club with the play-by-play. The Cubs scored four runs in the first inning to take a 4–0 lead and were still ahead 4–3 heading into the ninth, but catcher Steve Swisher let an apparent game-ending third strike from Rick Reuschel get past him for a passed ball and allowed the tying run to score. The Pirates plated the winning run an inning later.

The 1974 season was the second consecutive year that the Cardinals finished 1½ games out of first place. The Pirates lost the National League Championship Series to the Dodgers.

OCTOBER 13   The Cardinals trade Joe Torre to the Mets for Ray Sadecki and Tommy Moore.

With Keith Hernandez ready to take over at first base, the Cardinals no longer needed Torre. He returned to St. Louis as a manager from 1990 through 1995.

OCTOBER 14   The Cardinals trade Marc Hill to the Giants for Elias Sosa and Ken Rudolph.

OCTOBER 24   The Cardinals sell Jose Cruz to the Astros.

Cruz was 26 when he was sold to the Astros and had a .247 batting average and 26 homers in 1,208 career at-bats. He didn't appear to have a bright future, but Cruz became a star in Houston, where he topped the .300 mark in six seasons. In 1983, he led the league in hits. After leaving St. Louis, Cruz collected 1,953 hits, batted .291, and hit 139 homers despite playing home games in the Astrodome, a notoriously difficult park for hitters.

NOVEMBER 18   The Cardinals trade Sonny Siebert, Alan Foster, and Rich Folkers to the Padres for Ed Brinkman and Danny Breeden.

DECEMBER 6   The Cardinals trade Ed Kurpiel and Rudy Kinard to the Expos for Ron Fairly.

1975

Season in a Sentence

After narrowly missing the Eastern Division pennant in both 1973 and 1974, the Cardinals fall to a distant third.

Finish • Won • Lost • Pct • GB

Third (tie) 82   80   .506   10.5

Manager

Red Schoendienst

Stats

Stats	Cards	NL	Rank
Batting Avg:	.273	.257	1
On-Base Pct:	.326	.330	5
Slugging Pct:	.375	.369	4
Home Runs:	81		11
Stolen Bases:	116		5
ERA:	3.57	3.62	6
Fielding Avg:	.973	.975	8
Runs Scored:	662		6
Runs Allowed:	689		7

Starting Lineup

Ted Simmons, c
Reggie Smith, 1b-rf
Ted Sizemore, 2b
Ken Reitz, 3b
Mike Tyson, ss
Lou Brock, lf
Bake McBride, cf
Willie Davis, rf
Luis Melendez, cf-rf
Ron Fairly, 1b
Keith Hernandez, 1b
Mario Guerrero, ss

Pitchers

Lynn McGlothlen, sp
Bob Forsch, sp
Ron Reed, sp
John Denny, sp
Bob Gibson, sp-rp
Eric Rasmussen, sp
Al Hrabosky, rp
Mike Garman, rp
John Curtis, rp-sp

Attendance

1,695,270 (fifth in NL)

Club Leaders

Batting Avg:	Simmons	.332
On-Base Pct:	Simmons	.396
Slugging Pct:	Simmons	.491
Home Runs:	Smith	19
RBIs:	Simmons	100
Runs:	Simmons	80
Stolen Bases:	Brock	56
Wins:	Forsch	15
	McGlothlen	15
Strikeouts:	McGlothlen	146
ERA:	Forsch	2.68
Saves:	Hrabosky	22

MARCH 29   The Cardinals trade Danny Godby to the Red Sox for Danny Cater.

APRIL 7   The Cardinals lose the season opener 8–4 to the Expos before 31,769 at Busch Memorial Stadium. Bob Gibson struck out 12 batters but got tagged with the loss. Reggie Smith homered. Ted Sizemore collected three hits, including a double.

The 1975 Opening Day assignment was the 11th in a row for Gibson. In those 11 starts, he was 2–2 with seven no-decisions. The 1975 campaign was also Gibson's last in the majors. It was not a happy year. He was taken out of the starting rotation in early June and spent most of the last three months doing mop-up duty in the bullpen. Gibson had a 3–10 record and a 5.04 ERA.

APRIL 9   Bob Forsch faces the minimum 27 batters and allows only two hits in a 4–0 win over the Expos at Busch Memorial Stadium. The only Montreal hits were singles by Barry Foote in the second inning and Tony Scott in the seventh. Both were erased on double plays.

APRIL 17   Ted Simmons homers from both sides of the plate during a 14–7 loss to the Mets at Busch Memorial Stadium. Ted Sizemore made three errors in an inning to tie the major league record for second basemen.

Simmons batted .332 with 193 hits, 18 homers, and 100 RBIs in 1975.

MAY 4   Reggie Smith collects five hits in five at-bats with two homers, a double, and two singles, although the Cardinals lose 8–6 to the Cubs at Busch Memorial Stadium. Smith's two homers came from opposite sides of the plate. He hit a home run batting right-handed against Geoff Zahn and one left-handed off Oscar Zamora. Smith is also likely the only player in major league history to hit two homers off pitchers whose names begin with the letter Z in the same game.

Smith hit .302 with 19 homers in 1975.

MAY 9   The Cardinals trade Larry Herndon and Luis Gonzalez to the Giants for Ron Bryant.

Herndon was another valuable player that the Cardinals let get away during the 1970s. Although he was never a star, Herndon played in 1,537 big-league games and was better than many of the players patrolling the Cardinals' outfield during the late 1970s and early 1980s. Bryant played in only 10 games for the Cards and posted an 0–1 record.

MAY 10   The Cardinals break a scoreless tie by erupting for eight runs in the sixth inning and defeat the Giants 9–2 at Busch Memorial Stadium.

MAY 17   The Cardinals take a 14–0 lead after four innings and trounce the Giants 17–2 in San Francisco. The Cards collected 23 hits in the contest.

MAY 28   The Cardinals trade Ray Sadecki and Elias Sosa to the Braves for Ron Reed and Wayne Nordhagen.

Reed played basketball and baseball at Notre Dame and played two seasons in the NBA with the Detroit Pistons from 1965 through 1967. He was 9–8 in his lone season as a Cardinal.

MAY 27   Lou Brock hits for the cycle in a 7–1 win over the Padres at Busch Memorial
              Stadium. Facing Dave Freisleben, Brock singled in the first inning, homered in the
              third, and tripled in the fifth. Brock completed the cycle with a double off Alan
              Foster in the eighth.

JUNE 2   Lynn McGlothlen pitches the Cardinals to a 1–0 win over the Braves at Busch
              Memorial Stadium. Ted Simmons drove in the lone run of the game with a single in
              the fourth inning.

              *An outstanding all-around athlete, McGlothlen won the Louisiana High School
              Tennis Championship three years in a row.*

JUNE 4   The Cardinals trade Ed Brinkman and Tommy Moore to the Rangers for Willie
              Davis.

              *Although he was 35 when acquired by the Cardinals, Davis provided a spark
              by hitting .291 in 98 games as the starting right fielder. On the same day, the
              Cardinals selected pitcher David Johnson from Gaylord High School in Gaylord,
              Michigan, in the first round of the amateur draft. Johnson never advanced past
              Class AA. Future major leaguers drafted and signed by the Cardinals in 1975
              were Kelly Paris (2nd round), Mike Ramsey (3rd), Andy Replogle (9th), Jim
              Lentine (12th), and Alan Olmstead (13th). None of the five ever played well
              enough to hold down a regular job, however. The club did sign Ken Oberkfell as
              an undrafted free agent, however. Oberkfell started in the Cardinals' infield for
              five seasons beginning in 1979.*

JUNE 6   Bob Forsch pitches a two-hitter to defeat the Astros 6–0 in Houston. All six runs
              scored in the sixth inning. The only hits off Forsch were singles by Cesar Cedeño in
              the first inning and opposing pitcher Larry Dierker in the third.

JUNE 23   The Cardinals record two shutouts to beat the Mets 1–0 and 4–0 at Shea Stadium.
              In the opener, Ron Reed threw the shutout. The lone run scored in the first when
              Lou Brock led off with a walk, stole two bases, and scored on a sacrifice fly by Ron
              Fairly. In the second tilt, John Denny held New York scoreless. All four runs were
              scored on a pinch-hit grand slam by Ted Simmons in the eighth inning against Jon
              Matlack.

              *Denny had a 51–46 record with the Cardinals from 1974 through 1979. He
              was pleasant and philosophical under ordinary circumstances, but the least
              bit of adversity sent his competitive juices into a raging volcano. Plagued by
              inconsistencies in pitching performance that reflected his complex personality,
              Denny was traded to the Indians in 1979.*

JUNE 27   Bob Gibson records his 250th career win by defeating the Expos 6–4 in the first
              game of a doubleheader in Montreal. The Expos won the second game 5–4.

JULY 5   The Cardinals edge the Expos 1–0 in the second game of a doubleheader at Busch
              Memorial Stadium. John Curtis (eight innings) and Al Hrabosky (one inning)
              combined on the shutout. The lone run of the contest scored on a double by Reggie
              Smith in the fourth inning. Montreal won the opener 2–0.

              In 1975 Hrabosky became the first Cardinal pitcher to record at least 20 saves with an ERA under 2.00. He had a 13–3 record, 22 saves, and a 1.66 ERA in 97¹/₃ innings over 65 games.

JULY 7   The Cardinals tie a major league record when three outfielders throw out runners at home plate during an 8–6 win over the Giants at Busch Memorial Stadium. The runners were retired on throws from left fielder Lou Brock, center fielder Luis Melendez, and right fielder Willie Davis.

There have been only four instances in which a big-league club's outfield has thrown out three runners at home plate in a game. The July 7, 1975, game is the only time it has happened since 1905.

JULY 8   Ron Fairly hits a grand slam off Pete Falcone in the sixth inning, but the Cardinals lose 6–4 to the Giants at Busch Memorial Stadium.

JULY 12   To display their resentment over the failure of Dodgers manager Walter Alston to select Al Hrabosky for the National League All-Star team, the Cardinals hold "Hrabosky Hbanner Hday." The club encouraged fans to show their support for the colorful reliever by bringing banners to a Cardinals-Dodgers game televised nationally by NBC on a Saturday afternoon. The Cards won 2–1 by scoring a run in the ninth and another in the tenth. Hrabosky was the winning pitcher with two innings of scoreless relief.

JULY 13   Al Hrabosky is the winning pitcher for the second game in a row as the Cardinals defeat the Dodgers 2–1 at Busch Memorial Stadium.

JULY 17   The Cardinals down the Giants 1–0 in San Francisco. John Denny (seven innings) and Al Hrabosky (two innings) combined on the shutout. Ted Simmons drove in the only run of the game with a double in the ninth inning.

While growing up in Anaheim, California, Hrabosky worked as an attendant at Disneyland.

JULY 19   The Cardinals issue six intentional walks, a major league record for a nine-inning game, during a 5–2 loss to the Giants in San Francisco.

The loss gave the Cardinals a record of 43–46, 13 games off the pace set by the Pirates.

JULY 21   Eric Rasmussen pitches a shutout in his first major league start, defeating the Padres 4–0 in San Diego. Ted Simmons had a home run nullified during the contest for using an illegal bat. Umpire Art Williams said that Simmons's bat was grooved at the barrel end, which violated the rules.

Rasmussen never quite developed the way the Cardinals had hoped. He pitched for the club from 1975 through 1978 and had a 27–39 record before a trade sent him to the Padres. Rasmussen was 50–77 over the course of an eight-year career.

JULY 25   The Cardinals trade Jim Dwyer to the Expos for Larry Lintz.

AUGUST 6 The Cardinals open the first inning with six straight singles from Lou Brock, Willie Davis, Ron Fairly, Ted Simmons, Reggie Smith, and Ted Sizemore, and they go on to defeat the Padres 10–6 at Busch Memorial Stadium.

AUGUST 9   Lou Brock collects the 2,500th hit of his career during a 6–1 win over the Padres at Busch Memorial Stadium.

AUGUST 10   Trailing 2–1 heading into the bottom of the tenth inning, the Cardinals rally for two runs to defeat the Padres 3–2 at Busch Memorial Stadium. Ken Reitz tied the score with a home run. The consecutive singles, the last one by Lou Brock, produced the winning tally.

AUGUST 11   Willie Davis leaves the club to confer with his ex-wife, who was threatening to garnish his wages for the rest of the season due to non-payment of alimony and child support. Davis returned to the club eight days later after the two had reached an amicable solution.

             Davis credited his conversion to Buddhism for his ability to remain calm through the ordeal. In 1971, Davis became a member of the Soka Gakkai, a Nicheren Buddhist sect. He fingered prayer beads and chanted before every game.

AUGUST 17   The Cardinals defeat the Braves 8–1 in Atlanta.

             The win gave the Cardinals a 65–57 record and put them three games out of first place in a three-team race with the Pirates and Phillies. With a 22–11 record, the Cardinals cut 11 games off the Pittsburgh lead in just 29 days. The Cards could draw no closer, however, and finished in a tie for third place 10½ games out of first.

AUGUST 19   Lynn McGlothlen strikes out three batters on the minimum nine pitches in the second inning of a 2–1 win over the Reds at Busch Memorial Stadium. The victims were Cesar Geronimo, Darrell Chaney, and Gary Nolan.

AUGUST 23   Ted Simmons hits a grand slam off Phil Niekro in the fifth inning of a 7–2 win over the Braves at Busch Memorial Stadium.

AUGUST 24   Lou Brock steals the 800th and 801st bases of his career during a 6–2 win over the Braves at Busch Memorial Stadium.

AUGUST 25   The Cardinals are saved from possible defeat by rain at Busch Memorial Stadium. Cliff Johnson of the Astros homered in the top of the eleventh for a 4–3 lead, but rain stopped play before the inning could be completed. According to the rules at the time, the score reverted back to the end of the last inning and the contest went into the books as a 10-inning, 3–3 tie.

SEPTEMBER 1 Bob Gibson is honored at Busch Memorial Stadium prior to a 6–3 win over the Cubs before a crowd of 48,435. August Busch presented Gibson with a deluxe motor home. The 76-year-old club owner then personally chauffeured Gibson, his mother, and two daughters around the park as a climax to the hour-long program. Gibson was also given a CB radio and a case of champagne among many other gifts. Commissioner Bowie Kuhn made a speech, and proclamations were offered by Missouri governor Christopher Bond and the mayors of St. Louis, East St. Louis, and Gibson's hometown of Omaha. Emcee Jack Buck read a wire from President Gerald Ford.

SEPTEMBER 3   Pete LaCock hits a grand slam off Bob Gibson in the seventh inning of an 11–6 loss to the Cubs at Busch Memorial Stadium. It was the last pitch Gibson would throw as a major leaguer.

With the permission of team management, Gibson left the club on September 17 and went home to Omaha.

SEPTEMBER 22   A two-run homer by Ted Simmons in the twelfth inning beats the Expos 6–4 in the first game of a doubleheader in Montreal. The Expos won the second game 8–5.

SEPTEMBER 26   Bob Forsch pitches the Cardinals to a 1–0 win over the Pirates at Busch Memorial Stadium. The run scored in the first inning. Lou Brock opened with a single and on a hit-and-run play scored from first base on a single from Ted Simmons.

SEPTEMBER 30   The Cardinals trade Mike Barlow to the Astros for Mike Easler.

OCTOBER 20   The Cardinals trade Willie Davis to the Padres for Dick Sharon.

OCTOBER 28   The Cardinals trade Mike Garman and Bobby Hrapmann to the Cubs for Don Kessinger.

DECEMBER 8   The Cardinals trade Ken Reitz to the Giants for Pete Falcone.

Reitz returned to the Cardinals in another trade with the Giants on December 10, 1976.

DECEMBER 9   The Cardinals trade Ron Reed to the Phillies for Mike Anderson.

The Phillies changed Reed from a starter to a reliever, and he had eight solid seasons in which he pitched in the postseason six times in Philadelphia, including two World Series.

1976

Season in a Sentence

A youth movement produces a losing record and results in the end of Red Schoendienst's 12-year run as manager.

Finish • Won • Lost • Pct • GB

Fifth 72 90 .444 29.0

Manager

Red Schoendienst

Stats

Stats	Cards	• NL •	Rank
Batting Avg:	.260	.255	4
On-Base Pct:	.325	.323	5
Slugging Pct:	.359	.361	4
Home Runs:	63		12
Stolen Bases:	123		6
ERA:	3.60	3.50	8
Fielding Avg:	.973	.977	11
Runs Scored:	629		4
Runs Allowed:	671		8

Starting Lineup

Ted Simmons, c
Keith Hernandez, 1b
Mike Tyson, 2b
Hector Cruz, 3b
Don Kessinger, ss
Lou Brock, lf
Jerry Mumphrey, cf
Willie Crawford, rf
Bake McBride, cf
Vic Harris, 2b-cf
Garry Templeton, ss
Mike Anderson, rf
Joe Ferguson, c
Reggie Smith, 1b-of-3b

Pitchers

Lynn McGlothlen, sp
Pete Falcone, sp
John Denny, sp
Bob Forsch, sp
Al Hrabosky, rp
Mike Wallace, rp
Bill Grief, rp
Eric Rasmussen, rp-sp
John Curtis, rp-sp

Attendance

1,207,079 (sixth in NL)

Club Leaders

Batting Avg:	Brock	.301
On-Base Pct:	Simmons	.371
Slugging Pct:	Hernandez	.428
Home Runs:	Cruz	13
RBIs:	Simmons	75
Runs:	Brock	73
Stolen Bases:	Brock	56
Wins:	McGlothlen	13
Strikeouts:	Falcone	138
ERA:	Denny	2.52
Saves:	Hrabosky	13

MARCH 2   The Cardinals trade Ted Sizemore to the Dodgers for Willie Crawford.

APRIL 9   Lynn McGlothlen pitches a six-hit shutout on Opening Day, defeating the Cubs 5–0 before 30,671 at Busch Memorial Stadium.

> *The Cardinals were in the midst of a youth movement in 1976 with players such as Garry Templeton (age 20), Keith Hernandez (22), Pete Falcone (22), John Denny (23), Hector Cruz (23), Jerry Mumphrey (23), Eric Rasmussen (24), Mike Wallace (25), and Mike Anderson (25).*

APRIL 18   John Denny retires the first 18 batters he faces before giving up a run and six hits, but he emerges as the winning pitcher in a 2–1 decision over the Expos at Busch Memorial Stadium.

APRIL 19   The Cardinals lose a 17-inning marathon 4–3 to the Mets at Busch Memorial Stadium. Del Unser's homer off Mike Wallace drove in the winning run. Bake McBride collected five hits, including two doubles, in eight at-bats.

APRIL 20   The Cardinals lose 8–0 to the Mets at Busch Memorial Stadium in a game that featured a free-for-all over hit batsmen. After Del Unser homered in the first inning, Lynn McGlothlen hit him in the third. In the bottom of the inning, New York hurler Jon Matlack threw over McGlothlen's head. When Matlack led off the fourth, McGlothlen drilled him with a pitch that set off the brawl. The league suspended McGlothlen for five days.

APRIL 26   The Giants score seven runs in the first inning to take a 7–1 lead, but the Cardinals rally to win 15–7 in San Francisco.

Cardinals road uniforms changed from the traditional gray to light blue in 1976. The club went back to the gray uniforms in 1985.

APRIL 28   Infielder Doug Clarey hits a two-run homer in the sixteenth inning that beats the Giants 4–2 in San Francisco. Both teams scored in the fourteenth.

The homer was Clarey's only hit during his brief big-league career, which lasted nine games, mostly as a late-inning defensive replacement. He never started a game as a major leaguer. The dramatic sixteenth-inning homer against the Giants came in the second of Clarey's four at-bats in the majors and eight days after his 22nd birthday. He was on the Cardinals roster only because of an injury to Mike Tyson and was sent back to the minors as soon as Tyson was healthy enough to play.

MAY 22   Reggie Smith hits three consecutive homers and drives in five runs during a 7–6 win over the Phillies in Philadelphia. He hit the third batting right-handed against Tug McGraw in the ninth inning and broke a 6–6 tie. Smith connected in his previous two at-bats, hitting right-handed off Jim Kaat with two on in the fifth and from the left side against Ron Reed in the seventh, a blast that tied the game 6–6. Smith also made a sensational catch in the ninth to save at least one run from scoring.

The Cardinals had seven switch-hitters on the 1976 roster in Vic Harris, Don Kessinger, Jerry Mumphrey, Ted Simmons, Reggie Smith, John Tamargo, and Gerry Templeton.

MAY 28   Willie Crawford hits a grand slam off Craig Swan in the fifth inning of a 6–0 win over the Mets in New York. John Curtis didn't allow a hit until the seventh inning and settled for a three-hit shutout.

MAY 29   A homer by Reggie Smith in the tenth inning beats the Mets 3–2 in New York.

MAY 30   Down 5–2, the Cardinals score three runs in the ninth inning and one in the eleventh to beat the Mets 6–5 in New York. Ending an 0-for-20 slump, Don Kessinger drove in the tying run with a single in the ninth, then hit a sacrifice fly in the eleventh for the win.

JUNE 8   In the first round of the amateur draft, the Cardinals select first baseman Leon Durham from Woodward High School in Cincinnati.

Durham played in 1,067 major league games, but only 96 of them were with the Cardinals. They traded him to the Cubs following his 1980 rookie season because they had a better option at first base in Keith Hernandez. Future major leaguers drafted and signed by the Cardinals in 1976 were Dan O'Brien (3rd round of the January secondary phase) and June draftees Gene Roof (12th round), Ray Searage (22nd round), John Littlefield (30th round), and John Fulgham (1st round of the secondary phase).

JUNE 13   After being shut out in the opener 4–0, the Cards slug back to win the nightcap 12–9 in a doubleheader against the Reds in Cincinnati.

JUNE 15   The Cardinals trade Reggie Smith to the Dodgers for Joe Ferguson, Bob Detherage, and Ref Tisdale.

After 47 games in 1976, Smith was batting only .216, and the Cardinals gambled that Smith was finished as a productive player at the age of 31. The gamble backfired. Smith's decline in production was due to a persistent shoulder problem, which was corrected with surgery during the 1976–77 offseason. In 1977 and 1978 combined, Smith batted .302 with 61 homers on two Dodgers clubs that went to the World Series. In exchange, the Cardinals received a player they didn't need and two others who never appeared in a game in a St. Louis uniform. Ferguson was a primarily a catcher who could fill in as an outfielder. His playing time as a catcher was limited with Ted Simmons playing nearly every day, and Ferguson lacked the speed to cover Busch's vast AstroTurf outfield. In addition, Ferguson hit only .201 in 71 games with the Cards.

JULY 4   On the nation's bicentennial, the Cardinals lose 4–3 to the Expos at Busch Memorial Stadium.

JULY 6   The Cardinals score seven runs in the first inning and go on to defeat the Giants 13–7 at Busch Memorial Stadium.

JULY 21   Playing third base for the first time in his career, Ted Simmons makes an error in the tenth inning that leads to the winning run in a 7–6 loss to the Dodgers in Los Angeles.

JULY 22   Ted Simmons makes two errors at third base during an 8–4 loss to the Cubs at Busch Memorial Stadium.

The debacle ended the experiment of trying to turn Simmons into a third baseman at two games. He was booed lustily during the loss to the Cubs and blasted the fans in a tirade after the game. "Too many of them don't know what's going on," Simmons said. This led to more catcalls from the stands, as Simmons slumped from a .332 average and 18 homers in 1975 to a .291 average and five home runs in 1976. Despite the drop in production, Simmons was still the best player on the Cardinals in 1976.

AUGUST 1 John Denny holds the Cubs hitless for 7⅔ innings but allows a run in the eighth and one in the tenth to lose 2–1 at Wrigley Field. The first of five Chicago hits was a single by Jerry Morales with two outs in the eighth inning.

AUGUST 3 Don Kessinger drives in all five Cardinals runs in a doubleheader split against the Pirates in Pittsburgh. The Cards lost the first game 2–1 and won the second 4–2. Kessinger had two doubles and a single in seven at-bats.

AUGUST 6 | Lou Brock collects five hits in six at-bats, but the Cardinals lose 11–7 to the Padres at Busch Memorial Stadium. The Cards led 6–3 heading into the ninth before San Diego scored eight runs.

SEPTEMBER 1 | The Cardinals edge the Reds 1–0 in 11 innings at Busch Memorial Stadium. A walk to Don Kessinger with the bases loaded drove in the winning run. Eric Rasmussen (ten innings) and Al Hrabosky (one inning) combined on the shutout.

SEPTEMBER 3 | The Cardinals trade Mike Easler to the Angels for Ron Farkas.

Easler later acquired the nickname "The Hit Man" for his ability to stroke line drive after line drive, but at the time he was dealt by the Cardinals, Easler had only one big-league base hit in 27 at-bats, a .037 average. After leaving St. Louis, Easler collected 118 home runs and 1,077 hits for a .295 average for five clubs through 1987. Farkas never appeared in a major league game.

SEPTEMBER 5 | The Cardinals win 1–0 in 11 innings for the second time in less than a week, defeating the Cubs in Chicago. A pinch-single by Ron Fairly broke up the scoreless battle. John Denny (nine innings), Bill Grief (2/3 of an inning) and Al Hrabosky (1 2/3 innings) combined on the shutout.

SEPTEMBER 14 | The Cardinals sell Ron Fairly to the Athletics.

SEPTEMBER 19 | Down 5–4, the Cardinals explode for five runs in the ninth inning and win 9–7 against the Expos in the first game of a doubleheader in Montreal. Ted Simmons put the Cards into the lead with a bases-loaded triple. St. Louis added two insurance runs, which were needed when the Expos rallied for two in their half of the inning. The Redbirds lost the second tilt 1–0.

These were the last two games that the Cardinals played at Jarry Park. The Expos moved into Olympic Stadium in 1977.

OCTOBER 3 | On the final day of the season, the Cardinals lose two 1–0 decisions to the Pirates in a doubleheader in Pittsburgh, wasting fine pitching performances by John Denny and Pete Falcone.

Despite the loss, Denny pitched well enough to win the National League ERA title. He ended the season with 2.52 ERA in 207 innings, nosing out Doug Rau of the Dodgers, who finished at 2.57. Due to a lack of batting support similar to his October 3 loss, Denny had an 11–9 record to show for his efforts.

OCTOBER 5 | After 12 years as manager, Red Schoendienst loses his job.

Schoendienst was let go after a 72–90 season and a drop in attendance of nearly 500,000 between 1975 and 1976. He was accused by many in the Cardinal organization of being too easygoing and that the club needed a firmer hand to lead the youth movement. "These are times, regardless of one's capabilities, when a different perspective is in order," August Busch said. Schoendienst served as a coach for the Athletics in 1976 and 1977, then returned to St. Louis as a full-time coach with the Cardinals from 1979 through 1989 and on a part-time basis from 1990 through 1995. He also served two stints as interim manager for 37 games in 1980 and 24 games in 1990.

OCTOBER 7   The Cardinals hire 48-year-old Vern Rapp as manager.

Rapp was one of the most controversial managers in club history. His 179-game reign was almost constantly in turmoil. A graduate of Cleveland High School in St. Louis, Rapp never reached the majors as a player and was a manager in the minors as early as 1955. He worked in the Yankees, Cardinals, Reds, and Expos chains and had a long series of successes. August Busch believed that the club needed a hard-nosed disciplinarian in contrast to the laid-back attitude of Red Schoendienst. Rapp ran the Reds' top farm club in Indianapolis from 1969 through 1975 and helped groom players who would contribute to four pennant winners and two World Championships. The Reds were the most conservative organization in baseball with a policy of no mustaches or beards and strict rules about hair and sideburn length. There was also a rigid dress code both on and off the field. Rapp believed that a well-groomed player was a disciplined player and that these rules were part of the fabric of a winning team. He wanted to enforce the same regulations in St. Louis, a notion August Busch fervently supported. Players were less than enthusiastic about the idea, particularly Bake McBride, who had to shave off his mutton chop sideburns, and Al Hrabosky, who believed that his Fu Manchu was part of his pitching arsenal. In Rapp's first year, the Cardinals were 83–79, an 11-game improvement over 1976, but he managed to alienate almost every athlete on the team in the process (see July 21, 1977).

OCTOBER 20   The Cardinals trade Willie Crawford, John Curtis, and Vic Harris to the Giants for Mike Caldwell, John D'Acquisto, and Dave Rader.

NOVEMBER 6   Four days after Jimmy Carter defeats Gerald Ford in the presidential election, the Cardinals trade Bill Grief, Sam Mejias, and Angel Torres to the Expos for Tony Scott, Steve Dunning, and Pat Scanlan.

NOVEMBER 23   The Cardinals trade Joe Ferguson and Bob Detherage to the Astros for Larry Dierker and Jerry DaVanon.

Dierker came to the Cardinals at the age of 30 with 137 career wins. He looked like a fine addition to the rotation, but Dierker broke his leg during spring training and posted only a 2–6 record as a Cardinal.

DECEMBER 10   The Cardinals trade Lynn McGlothlen to the Giants for Ken Reitz.

McGlothlen was only 26 when traded, but his days as a consistently effective pitcher were over. He died in 1984 at the age of 34 in a fire in Louisiana.

1977

Season in a Sentence

Although the club wins 11 more games than in 1976 in Vern Rapp's first season as manager, battles over grooming policies receive as much press as battles on the diamond.

Finish • Won • Lost • Pct • GB

Third   83   79   .512   18.0

Manager

Vern Rapp

Stats

Stats	Cards	NL	Rank
Batting Avg:	.270	.262	4
On-Base Pct:	.332	.331	6
Slugging Pct:	.388	.396	6
Home Runs:	96		11
Stolen Bases:	134		5
ERA:	3.81	3.91	7
Fielding Avg:	.978	.977	5
Runs Scored:	737		4
Runs Allowed:	688		6

Starting Lineup

Ted Simmons, c
Keith Hernandez, 1b
Mike Tyson, 2b
Ken Reitz, 3b
Garry Templeton, ss
Lou Brock, lf
Jerry Mumphrey, cf-lf-rf
Hector Cruz, rf
Tony Scott, cf

Pitchers

Bob Forsch, sp
Eric Rasmussen, sp
John Denny, sp
Pete Falcone, sp
Tom Underwood, sp
Al Hrabosky, rp
Roger Metzger, rp
Clay Carroll, rp
John Urrea, rp
Rawly Eastwick, rp

Attendance

1,659,287 (fourth in NL)

Club Leaders

Batting Avg:	Templeton	.322
On-Base Pct:	Simmons	.408
Slugging Pct:	Simmons	.500
Home Runs:	Simmons	21
RBIs:	Simmons	95
Runs:	Templeton	94
Stolen Bases:	Brock	35
Wins:	Forsch	20
Strikeouts:	Rasmussen	120
ERA:	Forsch	3.48
	Rasmussen	3.48
Saves:	Hrabosky	10

MARCH 23   Two months after Americans were transfixed by the television miniseries *Roots*, the Cardinals trade Lerrin LaGrow to the White Sox for Clay Carroll.

MARCH 28   The Cardinals trade Bill Caudill to the Reds for Joel Youngblood.

The Reds and Cubs also passed on Caudill before he became one of the top relievers in the American League. Caudill recorded 78 saves for the Mariners and Athletics from 1982 through 1984. Youngblood played only 25 games for the Cards and batted .185.

MARCH 29   The Cardinals complete a trade with the Reds for the second day in a row, dealing Mike Caldwell to Cincinnati for Pat Darcy.

The Reds sent Caldwell to the Brewers in June, and he became one of the top starters in the American League. He had a record of 22–9 for Milwaukee in 1978 and was 82–48 from 1978 through 1982. Darcy never pitched another game after the trade.

APRIL 7   The Cardinals score four runs in the first inning and win the season opener 12–6 against the Pirates in Pittsburgh. Keith Hernandez hit a homer and a double and drove in four runs. John Denny was the winning pitcher.

The Cardinals closed the 1976 season with shutout losses in the last three games against the Pirates at Three Rivers Stadium. The Cards opened 1977 by scoring 28 runs in a three-game sweep of the Pirates in the same ballpark.

APRIL 15   The Cardinals lose the home opener 7–0 before 41,226 at Busch Memorial Stadium. John Rooker pitched the shutout.

Between the 1976 and 1977 seasons, the team replaced the original AstroTurf covering installed in 1970. The new one covered the entire playing surface except for the sliding pits around the bases.

APRIL 20   Ted Simmons drives in all four runs on a three-run homer in the sixth inning and a run-scoring single in the eighth to lead the Cardinals to a 4–2 win over the Mets at Busch Memorial Stadium.

Simmons hit .318 with 21 homers in 1977.

APRIL 27   The Cardinals rout the Cubs 21–3 in Chicago. The big inning was the fifth when the Cards scored eight runs to take a 14–1 lead. Garry Templeton scored five runs.

Only 21, Templeton looked like a sure Hall of Famer in 1977 with a .322 average, 200 hits, 18 triples, and 8 homers. His 18 triples were the most of any major leaguer between Willie Mays in 1957 and George Brett in 1979. Templeton continued his top-level production for many more years. On his 25th birthday, he had already collected 815 hits, carried a .307 batting average, and led the NL in triples three times. Because of injuries, immaturity, and emotional instability, however, Templeton's career began a slow and steady decline when he should have been reaching his peak.

MAY 6   Al Hrabosky sets off a brawl by hitting Cesar Cedeño with a pitch in the ninth inning of a 4–1 win over the Astros at Busch Memorial Stadium. Joaquin Andujar of Houston and Roger Freed of the Cards were ejected for overzealous participation in the melee. The contest was delayed for nearly 10 minutes.

MAY 9   A walk-off homer by Ted Simmons in the tenth inning beats the Reds 6–5 at Busch Memorial Stadium.

MAY 10   Three Cardinals pitchers combine on a one-hitter for a 10–1 win over the Reds at Busch Memorial Stadium. Starter John D'Acquisto pitched four hitless innings but walked five and allowed a run. Vern Rapp took D'Acquisto out for a pinch hitter in the bottom of the fourth as the Cards scored twice to take a 2–1 lead. Buddy Schultz pitched four innings and allowed the only Cincinnati hit, a double by Ken Griffey with two outs in the eighth. Al Hrabosky hurled the ninth.

MAY 13   A three-run homer by Ken Reitz in the ninth inning beats the Braves 3–0 in Atlanta. Bob Forsch (eight innings) and Al Hrabosky (one inning) combined on the shutout.

Forsch had a record of 20–7 and an ERA of 3.48 for the Cards in 1977.

MAY 15   Dave Rader collects five hits, including three doubles, but the Cardinals lose 15–12 to the Braves in Atlanta.

Rader had a total of only 30 hits in 66 games as a Cardinal.

MAY 21   Vern Rapp suspends Al Hrabosky indefinitely for "sheer insubordination." The suspension occurred after Hrabosky, who had been feuding with the manager over hair codes and other assorted issues, refused a request to meet with Rapp. Rapp lifted the suspension on May 23.

MAY 27   Ken Reitz hits a grand slam off Santo Alcala in the fourth inning of a 7–3 win over the Expos at Busch Memorial Stadium.

MAY 29   Larry Parrish hits three homers at Busch Memorial Stadium to lead the Expos to a 14–4 win over the Cardinals.

MAY 30   The Cardinals score nine runs in the sixth inning of a 14–0 pasting of the Cubs at Busch Memorial Stadium.

The Cards closed out May with a 28–18 record.

JUNE 3   The Cardinals play at Olympic Stadium in Montreal for the first time and lose 2–0 to the Expos.

JUNE 7   In the first round of the amateur draft, the Cardinals select catcher Terry Kennedy from Florida State University.

Kennedy was the son of Bob Kennedy, a major league outfielder during the 1940s and 1950s. At the time Terry was drafted with the sixth overall pick, Bob was the Cubs' general manager. Terry rose quickly through the Cardinals' minor league system, but Ted Simmons blocked his path to the majors. Kennedy was traded to the Padres at the end of the 1980 season and remained in the big leagues until 1991. Other future major leaguers the Cardinals drafted and signed in 1977 were Joe DeSa (3rd round), Jim Gott (4th round), Andy Rincon (5th round), Jeff Doyle (6th round), Neil Fiala (32nd round), and Tye Waller (4th round of the January draft).

JUNE 15   The Cardinals trade Bake McBride and Steve Waterbury to the Phillies for Tom Underwood, Dane Iorg, and Rick Bosetti. On the same day, the Cards dealt Joel Youngblood to the Mets for Mike Phillips.

McBride couldn't get along with Vern Rapp, which led to the outfielder's departure. McBride was in Philadelphia's starting outfield for five seasons, hit better than .300 twice, and played on a World Championship club in 1980.

JUNE 28   Ken Reitz drives in eight runs during a 13–3 thrashing of the Pirates in the second game of a doubleheader at Busch Memorial Stadium. Reitz hit two homers and a single. One of the homers was a grand slam off Grant Jackson in the fourth inning. The Cards also won the opener, 6–1.

JULY 5   Mike Tyson hits a grand slam off John Candelaria in the fourth inning of a 7–3 win over the Pirates in Pittsburgh.

JULY 6 | The Cardinals score seven runs in the seventh inning, but it's too late to prevent an 11–8 loss to the Pirates in Pittsburgh.

JULY 12 | Cardinal right fielder Roger Freed drops Ted Sizemore's fly ball with two outs in the ninth inning to hand the Phillies a 5–4 win over the Cardinals in Philadelphia.

JULY 14 | The Cardinals score three runs in the ninth inning and two in the eleventh and defeat the Phillies 7–6 in Philadelphia.

JULY 19 | Garry Templeton hits a double and scores a run during the National League's 7–5 win in the All-Star Game, played at Yankee Stadium.

JULY 21 | August Busch lifts the ban on facial hair for the rest of the 1977 season while extending Vern Rapp's contract as manager one more year, through the end of 1978.

Rapp and his players had been in almost constant disagreement over the manager's grooming edicts since the first day of spring training. Hrabosky was at the forefront of the controversy because he believed that his Fu Manchu mustache intimidated hitters and was necessary for him to pitch well. At the time Busch allowed him to grow his mustache again, Hrabosky had been cuffed around by National League hitters all season. Busch read a long statement to the press, and indirectly to Hrabosky, at the time of the announcement: "You said in the newspaper that you can only get batters out by being psyched up with your mustache and beard. Then go ahead and grow it. But, boy, are you going to look like a fool if you don't get the batters out. . . . You painted me into a corner and no one does that to me." The St. Louis Post-Dispatch ran a daily "Hair Meter" for weeks afterward showing Al's Stats after he grew back his beard. For the record, Hrabosky, sans beard, pitched 37 games and 53 innings and allowed 49 hits and 24 walks and had a 4.58 ERA. After growing back his facial hair, there was little noticeable difference as Hrabosky appeared in 28 games and 33 innings and surrendered 33 hits and 17 walks with a 4.09 ERA.

JULY 23 | The Cardinals score two runs in the eleventh inning to beat the Astros 4–3 at Busch Memorial Stadium. Hector Cruz doubled in the tying run and scored on a single by Jerry Mumphrey.

JULY 29 | The Cardinals score nine runs in the second inning and defeat the Reds 10–3 in the second game of a doubleheader at Riverfront Stadium. Keith Hernandez hit a grand slam off Jack Billingham. Cincinnati won the first game 6–5.

AUGUST 8 | The Cardinals beat the Mets 4–2 in New York.

The win gave the Cards a 62–50 record and a position in fourth place, four games behind the first place Phillies. The Cards could get no closer to first, however, and although they rose to third in the NL East, they finished the season 18 games back.

AUGUST 13 | The Cardinals beat the Mets 1–0 in 10 innings in Montreal. Mike Anderson drove in the winning run with a bases-loaded single. John Urrea (seven innings) and Butch Metzger (three innings) combined on the shutout.

AUGUST 17   On the day after Elvis Presley dies in Memphis, Bob Forsch pitches a two-hitter to beat the Mets 2–0 at Busch Memorial Stadium. The only New York hits were singles by Bruce Bosclair in the first inning and Lenny Randle in the sixth.

AUGUST 19   Mike Tyson drives in six runs on a homer, a double, and a single during a 12–4 rout of the Padres at Busch Memorial Stadium.

AUGUST 20   The Cardinals trade Don Kessinger to the White Sox for Steve Staniland.

AUGUST 22   The Cardinals stun the Dodgers with seven runs in the ninth inning to win 8–6 at Busch Memorial Stadium. Roger Freed's two-run, pinch-hit, walk-off homer capped the rally.

AUGUST 25   During a 4–2 loss to the Giants at Busch Memorial Stadium, Lou Brock steals the 890th and 891st bases of his career, leaving him one shy of Ty Cobb's modern career record of 892.

Brock stole 35 bases in 59 attempts in 1977.

AUGUST 29   Lou Brock steals the 892nd and 893rd bases of his career to pass Ty Cobb and break the modern record during a 4–3 loss to the Padres in San Diego. Cobb played in the majors from 1905 through 1928. Brock tied the mark with a steal in the first inning. As the first batter of the game, he walked against Dave Freisleben, broke for second base on the next pitch, and made it easily as catcher Dave Roberts's throw went into center field. Brock advanced to third, where he was mobbed by teammates. The game was halted momentarily, and Brock has second base presented to him. He broke the record in the seventh by swiping second with the Cards leading 3–2. Brock reached on a fielder's choice and went to second on Freisleben's next offering to the plate. Once again, Cardinals surged on to the field to congratulate Brock, who yanked up second base with a big smile and held it aloft. The Padres produced a field mic to allow Brock to address the crowd, which gave him a round of applause. The ceremonies held up the game for five minutes. When Brock took his place in left field in the bottom of the seventh, members of the San Diego bullpen surrounded him to get his autograph. At the point, Vern Rapp took Brock out of the game and replaced him with Rick Bosetti.

Cobb took 3,033 games to steal 892 bases. Brock needed just 2,376 games to eclipse his mark. He broke only the modern record—post-1900. Until 1977, the man with the most steals in history was Billy Hamilton, who swiped 937 from 1888 through 1901. Prior to 1898, however, scoring rules were different. A runner who went from first to third on a single, for example, could be credited with a stolen base. Brock passed Hamilton with the final steal of his career (see September 23, 1979).

AUGUST 31   The Cardinals trade Clay Carroll to the White Sox for Silvio Martinez, Nels Nyman, and Dave Hamilton.

Martinez looked like a budding star after a 9–8 record in 1978 and 15–8 in 1979 before elbow problems surfaced.

SEPTEMBER 3   Keith Hernandez hits a grand slam off Gary Lavelle in the eighth inning that gives the Cardinals a 5–4 lead, but the Giants rally to win 6–5 in 14 innings in San Francisco.

SEPTEMBER 12   After a parade in downtown St. Louis, Lou Brock Night at Busch Memorial Stadium honors his career stolen-base record set on August 29. August Busch gave Brock a ring with "893" in diamonds. Brock didn't steal a base in that night's game but collected three singles in an 11–9 win over the Cubs. Ken Reitz ended the game with a two-run homer off Bruce Sutter with two outs in the ninth.

SEPTEMBER 15   Trailing 6–1, the Cardinals explode for seven runs in the sixth inning and beat the Pirates 10–7 in the second game of a doubleheader at Busch Memorial Stadium. Pittsburgh won the opener 4–3.

SEPTEMBER 18   A grand slam by Keith Hernandez off Warren Brusstar is the big blow in a nine-run second inning as the Cardinals rout the Phillies 12–5 at Busch Memorial Stadium. Lou Brock collected five hits, including a double, in five at-bats.

                The Cardinals were 52–31 at home and 31–48 on the road in 1978.

SEPTEMBER 26   A clubhouse confrontation between Wayne Twitchell of the Expos and Al Hrabosky follows Montreal's 9–5 victory over the Cardinals at Busch Memorial Stadium. Enraged because Hrabosky had hit teammate Warren Cromartie with a pitch after the Expos scored four runs in the ninth inning, Twitchell was waiting outside the clubhouse when Hrabosky and the Redbirds left the field and confronted him about Cromartie's pelting. "I was drastically outnumbered," Twitchell said, explaining how the argument stopped short of blows.

SEPTEMBER 27   Bob Forsch earns his 20th win of the season with a 5–3 decision over the Expos at Busch Memorial Stadium. Forsch helped his own cause with a two-run double.

                John Denny was ejected before they played the National Anthem. Umpire Paul Runge noticed Denny "leaning across the rail" to talk to fans near the St. Louis dugout in violation of a National League rule. When Runge ordered Denny to return to the dugout, the pitcher got testy and was given the thumb.

SEPTEMBER 30   Lou Brock steals the 900th base of his career during a 7–2 win over the Mets in the first game of a doubleheader at Busch Memorial Stadium. New York won the second contest 6–3.

DECEMBER 6   The Cardinals trade Tom Underwood and Victor Cruz to the Blue Jays for Pete Vuckovich and John Scott.

                The Cardinals came out ahead in the deal as Vuckovich was 39–31 and had a 3.20 ERA for the club over three seasons before a trade to the Brewers. With his Fu Manchu, long hair, crazed expression on the mound, and Eastern European ancestry, Vuckovich was a worth successor to Al Hrabosky. "He borders a little on Frankenstein," Ted Simmons said of Vuckovich. "When he pitches he puts himself in another world." Vuckovich's free-spirited nature might have stemmed from several near-death experiences. He was born with the umbilical cord around his neck. When he was 1½, undiagnosed appendicitis led to peritonitis. He had a benign tumor removed from his head a year later during a delicate eight-hour operation. When he was 21, he was speeding on a rain-slickened road and rolled his Camaro down an 80-foot embankment. Shortly thereafter, Vuckovich almost died when he was electrocuted while installing a 15,000-volt reactor in his work for an electrical contractor. After his playing career ended, Vuckovich played a Yankee slugging first baseman in the movie Major League.

DECEMBER 8   The Cardinals send Dave Rader and Hector Cruz to the Cubs for Jerry Morales, Steve Swisher, and cash.

DECEMBER 9   The Cardinals trade Al Hrabosky to the Royals for Mark Littell and Buck Martinez, then send Martinez to the Brewers for George Frazier.

Hrabosky was dealt after a season of battling management over his Fu Manchu. The trade was about even as Hrabosky and Littell each gave their new clubs a couple of solid seasons before developing arm trouble. Hrabosky came back to the Cardinals as a telecaster in 1985, a job he still holds.

1978

Season in a Sentence

The Cardinals compile their worst winning percentage since 1924 and change managers from hyper-intensive Vern Rapp to laid-back Ken Boyer.

Finish • Won • Lost • Pct • GB

Fifth   69   93   .426   21.0

Managers

Vern Rapp (6–11), Jack Krol (1–1), and Ken Boyer (62–81).

Stats

Stats	Cards	• NL •	Rank
Batting Avg:	.249	.254	9
On-Base Pct:	.306	.323	12
Slugging Pct:	.358	.372	9
Home Runs:	79		9
Stolen Bases:	97		9
ERA:	3.58	3.58	6
Fielding Avg:	.979	.978	4
Runs Scored:	600		11
Runs Allowed:	657		8

Starting Lineup

Ted Simmons, c
Keith Hernandez, 1b
Mike Tyson, 2b
Ken Reitz, 3b
Garry Templeton, ss
Jerry Mumphrey, lf-rf-cf
George Hendrick, cf
Jerry Morales, rf
Lou Brock, lf
Tony Scott, lf
Mike Phillips, 2b

Pitchers

Johnny Denny, sp
Bob Forsch, sp
Pete Vuckovich, sp-rp
Silvio Martinez, sp
Mark Littell, rp
Buddy Schultz, rp
John Urrea, rp-sp

Attendance

1,278,212 (eighth in NL)

Club Leaders

Batting Avg:	Simmons	.287
On-Base Pct:	Simmons	.377
Slugging Pct:	Simmons	.512
Home Runs:	Simmons	22
RBIs:	Simmons	80
Runs:	Hernandez	90
Stolen Bases:	Templeton	34
Wins:	Denny	14
Strikeouts:	Vuckovich	149
ERA:	Vuckovich	2.54
Saves:	Littell	11

APRIL 7   The Cardinals win the season opener 5–1 over the Phillies in Philadelphia. Bob Forsch went 7¹/₃ innings for the win. Ken Reitz hit a home run. In his Cards debut, Jerry Morales collected three hits.

APRIL 10   In the home opener, the Cardinals thrash the Pirates 11–2 before 19,241 at Busch Memorial Stadium.

APRIL 16   Bob Forsch pitches a no-hitter to defeat the Phillies 5–0 on a day in which the temperature at Busch Memorial Stadium is in the low 40s. Forsch walked two and struck out three. A controversial scoring decision marred the no-hit job, however. In the eighth inning, a grounder off Garry Maddox's bat slid under third baseman Ken Reitz's glove. It took 10 seconds for official scorer Neil Russo of the *St. Louis Post-Dispatch* to rule that it was an error. The Phillies claimed that Reitz never touched the ball and that it should have been a hit. Reitz said that the ball skimmed off his glove and that it was an error all the way. In the ninth, Jay Johnstone was retired on a grounder to shortstop Garry Templeton, Bake McBride on a ground ball to Mike Phillips at second, and Larry Bowa on an easy roller to Reitz.

Forsch's no-hitter was the first in a National League game in St. Louis since 1924 when Jesse Haines threw one for the Cardinals, and the first in a major league contest in the city since 1953. Bobo Holloman of the Browns, making his first big-league start, pitched a no-hitter in an American League tilt against the Philadelphia Athletics that year at old Busch Stadium. Later in the 1978 season, Forsch tied a modern club record by losing nine games in a row and finished with an 11–17 record.

APRIL 19   Both teams collect only two hits in a game the Mets win 2–0 at Busch Memorial Stadium. Mark Littell started for the Cards and allowed two runs and two hits in five innings. Littell allowed singles to Lenny Randle in the first inning and Bruce Bosclair in the third, and both led to runs. Pete Vuckovich followed with four hitless innings of relief. Pat Zachry pitched a complete game for New York.

APRIL 25   The Cardinals fire Vern Rapp as manager. Coach Jack Krol was named interim manager until a replacement could be hired.

The ax fell on Rapp when the club had a 6–11 record. He was 89–90 overall with the club. During spring training, Rapp had well-publicized shouting matches with Garry Templeton and Buddy Schultz. The tipping point came nine days before Rapp was fired. Ted Simmons tried to loosen up the clubhouse after a tough loss by cranking up the stereo. Rapp believed in quiet contemplation after a defeat and lit into Simmons, calling the All-Star catcher a "loser." When Rapp refused to appear on his daily pregame radio show with Jack Buck, the announcer had time to fill and broke the story about the Rapp-Simmons confrontation. While Rapp was knowledgeable about baseball and had an impressive record managing in the minors, he didn't seem to have the knack for handling major leaguers. Rapp managed again with the Reds in 1984 but was fired before the end of the season.

APRIL 26   In the first game following the dismissal of Vern Rapp, the Cardinals jump on the Expos for a 12–2 win at Montreal.

Transcendental Graphics/theruckerarchive.com

Ted Simmons caught for the Cardinals for 13 seasons during which he gave the team consistent production as well as a sure glove behind the plate.

APRIL 28   The Cardinals hire Ken Boyer as manager.

Boyer played for the Cardinals as an All-Star and MVP third baseman from 1955 through 1965. He finished out his years as a player with the Mets, White Sox, and Dodgers and returned to the Cardinals organization as a minor league manager in 1970. Boyer was a coach with the club in 1971 and 1972, then went back to the minors as a manager from 1973 through 1976 before going to work for the Orioles. At the time he was hired to manage the Cardinals, Boyer was 46 years old and the manager of Baltimore's Triple AAA club in Rochester. A drastic contrast to the micromanaging of Vern Rapp, Boyer had a laid-back approach. He was unable to salvage the 1978 season, but the Cardinals improved to 86–76 under Boyer in 1979. The club slid again in 1980, however, and he was fired 51 games into the season. Boyer died of lung cancer at the age of 51 in September 1982.

APRIL 29   Eric Rasmussen pitches the Cardinals to a 1–0 win over the Dodgers at Busch Memorial Stadium. Ken Reitz drove in the game's only run with a sacrifice fly in the seventh inning.

MAY 6   John Denny pitches a two-hitter to beat the Padres 1–0 in San Diego. Garry Templeton drove in the lone run of the game with a single off Gaylord Perry in the seventh inning. The only hits off Denny were a double by Dave Winfield in the second inning and a single by Derrel Thomas in the sixth.

MAY 23   The Cardinals lose their 11th game in a row, dropping a 4–1 decision to the Expos at Busch Memorial Stadium.

The Cardinals lost 16 of 17 from May 12 through May 29.

MAY 24   The Cardinals break their 11-game losing streak behind a two-hitter from John Denny to win 2–0 against the Expos at Busch Memorial Stadium. A single by Ted Simmons in the third inning drove in both runs. The only two Montreal hits were singles by Andre Dawson in the sixth inning and Gary Carter in the seventh.

Simmons hit .287 with 40 doubles and 22 homers in 1978.

MAY 26   Silvio Martinez pitches a no-hitter for the Cardinals' American Association farm club in Springfield, Missouri, beating Omaha 4–0. The performance earned Martinez a call-up to the majors (see May 30, 1978).

On the same day, the Cardinals traded Eric Rasmussen to the Padres for George Hendrick. The Cards pulled off a great deal to acquire the enigmatic Hendrick, who was in the starting lineup through the end of the 1984 season. Hendrick led the Cardinals in home runs four times, RBIs five times, and slugging percentage three times and batted over .300 in 1979, 1980, and 1983. He was 28 years old and in his eighth big-league season when he came to St. Louis with a reputation as underachieving, unaggressive, and undisciplined. The Cardinals learned he was merely misunderstood, in part because Hendrick rarely talked to reporters. Although he put up All-Star numbers with the Redbirds, some raised questions about Hendrick's effort. His quiet, casual demeanor led many to accuse him of not hustling. Others said that despite his relaxed style, Hendrick was highly competitive and was a vocal leader in the clubhouse. That Whitey Herzog kept Hendrick on the club for four and a half seasons after Herzog took over as manager in June 1980 speaks volumes. Herzog demanded that his players be hard-nosed and hustle on every play, and he didn't hesitate to get rid of anyone who failed to meet those expectations, including stars such as Ted Simmons, Garry Templeton, and Keith Hernandez.

MAY 27   Ted Simmons is ejected after hitting a home run during a game against the Cubs at Busch Memorial Stadium. The homer tied the score 2–2 in the ninth, but Simmons argued with umpire Paul Runge over a previous strike call as he crossed the plate. The Cubs went on to win 3–2 in 10 innings.

MAY 30   In his first major league start and first appearance with the Cardinals, Silvio Martinez pitches a one-hitter for an 8–2 victory over the Mets at Shea Stadium. Martinez had a no-hitter until Steve Henderson tagged the first pitch of the seventh inning for a homer. The Mets added another run in the ninth without benefit of a hit.

Prior to the May 30 gem, Martinez had pitched in 10 big games, all in relief with the White Sox in 1977.

JUNE 8 — In the first round of the amateur draft, the Cardinals select first baseman Robert Hicks from Tate High School in Pensacola, Florida.

> *Hicks failed to advance past Class AA. None of the players drafted in 1978 ever played a game for the Cardinals. The only future major leaguer drafted and signed was George Bjorkman, who appeared in 29 contests for the Astros in 1983.*

JUNE 9 — The Cardinals celebrate the 25th anniversary of the ownership of Anheuser-Busch with a pregame gala program before an 11–7 loss to the Astros at Busch Memorial Stadium.

JUNE 15 — The Cardinals sell Jim Dwyer to the Giants.

JUNE 16 — Tom Seaver pitches a no-hitter against the Cardinals for a 4–0 Reds win in Cincinnati. George Hendrick made the last out of the game with a grounder to Dan Driessen at first base.

JUNE 30 — The Cardinals are held to three hits over 10 innings by Ross Grimsley but win 2–1 over the Expos in Montreal. Mike Tyson drove in the winning run with a double.

JULY 7 — Leading off the first inning, Garry Templeton homers on John Candelaria's first pitch, but it proves to be the only Cardinal run in a 2–1 loss to the Pirates at Busch Memorial Stadium.

JULY 8 — Silvio Martinez pitches a one-hitter for a 4–0 win over the Pirates at Busch Memorial Stadium. The only Pittsburgh hit was a single by Omar Moreno with one out in the first inning.

JULY 26 — Silvio Martinez pitches a two-hitter to defeat the Giants 2–1 at Candlestick Park. The only San Francisco hits were doubles by Terry Whitfield and Darrell Evans in the fifth inning.

AUGUST 12 — John Denny (seven innings) and Roy Thomas (two innings) combine on a one-hitter to defeat the Mets 5–1 in New York. The hit came on a disputed call by first-base umpire Paul Pryor. In the seventh inning, John Stearns hit a slow bouncer to second baseman Mike Tyson, who threw to first. Pryor ruled that Roger Freed had pulled his foot off the bag before taking the throw. The Cardinals believed that Stearns was out, and even if the runner had been safe, the play should have been ruled an error on Freed. Denny was lifted for a pinch hitter in the top of the eighth.

> *The Cardinals bottomed out with a record of 40–68 before going on a spurt with 17 wins in 22 games from August 5 through August 27. The Cards ended the season with a 69–93 mark. The .424 winning percentage was the lowest of any team since the 1924 club posted a .422 mark and 65–89 record.*

AUGUST 21 — The Cardinals collect 23 hits and lambaste the Reds 14–9 in Cincinnati.

AUGUST 25 — George Hendrick drives in seven runs on two doubles and a grand slam in the third inning off Larry McWilliams as the Cardinals outlast the Braves 11–10 in Atlanta.

AUGUST 27   The Cardinals romp to a 14–3 win over the Braves in Atlanta.

AUGUST 31   Wayne Garrett hits a pinch-hit grand slam off Doug Bair in the ninth inning, but it's too late to prevent an 11–6 loss to the Reds at Busch Memorial Stadium.

SEPTEMBER 15   After losing 12 games in a row to the Cubs since the start of the season, the Cardinals erupt for five runs in the twelfth inning to win 6–2 at Wrigley Field after a Chicago rally in the bottom half falls short. Mike Phillips highlighted the five-run inning with a three-run homer. It was the only home run that Phillips hit all year.

SEPTEMBER 21   The Cardinals announce that Lou Brock will play in 1979.

There was some question whether Brock would come back for another year because he suffered through an awful season in 1978, in which he turned 39 in June. Brock desperately wanted to end his career with at least 3,000 hits and entered 1978 needing 166 to reach that goal. He collected only 66 hits, however, while batting just .221.

SEPTEMBER 25   Silvio Martinez pitches a two-hitter to beat the Mets 3–0 at Shea Stadium. The only New York hits were singles by John Stearns in the second inning and Steve Henderson in the eighth.

OCTOBER 18   John Claiborne replaces Bing Devine as general manager.

Devine originally served as general manager from 1957 through 1964 and was fired shortly before building a club that won three NL pennants and two World Championships in a span of five seasons (see August 13, 1964). He was brought back in December 1967. His second term as general manager lasted far too long, as a significant majority of Devine's trades had a detrimental effect on the club's future. Claiborne, who was 39 when hired as the general manager, wasn't the answer, however. A native of St. Louis who attended Cleveland High School and Washington University in the city, the Cardinals originally hired him in 1968 as an administrative assistant under Devine. Later Claiborne was an assistant general manager in Oakland and Boston. He was ousted in a reorganization of the Red Sox. At the time Claiborne became the Cardinals' general manager, he was working in private business. His record on trades was even worse than Devine's. Claiborne lasted only 22 months on the job.

DECEMBER 4   The Cardinals trade Jerry Morales and Aurelio Lopez to the Tigers for Bob Sykes and Jack Murphy.

Lopez was an overweight 30-year-old reliever when traded, but the Cardinals should have kept him. He was Detroit's closer for several seasons and had a 10–1 record on the Tigers' 1984 World Championship team.

DECEMBER 5   The Cardinals trade Pete Falcone to the Mets for Tom Grieve and Kim Seaman.

1979

Season in a Sentence

In Lou Brock's last season, the Cardinals hold first place as late as June 12 and win 17 more games than in the 1978 debacle.

Finish • Won • Lost • Pct • GB

Third   86   76   .531   12.0

Manager

Ken Boyer

Stats

	Cards	• NL •	Rank
Batting Avg:	.278	.261	1
On-Base Pct:	.335	.328	3
Slugging Pct:	.401	.385	5
Home Runs:	100		9
Stolen Bases:	116		7
ERA:	3.72	3.73	6
Fielding Avg:	.980	.978	4
Runs Scored:	731		3 (tie)
Runs Allowed:	693		6

Starting Lineup

Ted Simmons, c
Keith Hernandez, 1b
Ken Oberkfell, 2b
Ken Reitz, 3b
Garry Templeton, ss
Lou Brock, lf
Tony Scott, cf
George Hendrick, rf
Jerry Mumphrey, lf
Mike Tyson, 2b
Dane Iorg, lf-rf

Pitchers

Pete Vuckovich, sp
Silvio Martinez, sp
Bob Forsch, sp
John Denny, sp
John Fulgham, sp
Mark Littell, rp
Darold Knowles, rp
Will McEnaney, rp

Attendance

1,627,256 (seventh in NL)

Club Leaders

Batting Avg:	Hernandez	.344
On-Base Pct:	Hernandez	.417
Slugging Pct:	Hernandez	.513
Home Runs:	Simmons	26
RBIs:	Hernandez	105
Runs:	Hernandez	116
Stolen Bases:	Scott	37
Wins:	Vuckovich	15
	Denny	15
Strikeouts:	Vuckovich	145
ERA:	Martinez	3.27
Saves:	Littell	13

JANUARY 16   The Cardinals sign Darold Knowles, most recently with the Expos, as a free agent.

MARCH 10   The Cardinals sign Bernie Carbo, most recently with the Red Sox, as a free agent.

MARCH 27   Garry Templeton creates controversy during a radio interview with Mike Shannon. Upset over a pay cut he received during the previous offseason, the Cardinal shortstop said that he was going to play "conservatively" during the upcoming season and demanded to be traded. "I'm not going to play hard," Templeton said. "I'm not going to do my best." One newspaper reporter quoted Templeton saying, "For an extra $30,000 I'll play like they never saw before." In addition to his contract, Templeton was upset that the Cardinals were trying to change his style of play on defense after leading major league shortstops in errors with 40 in 1978. Templeton apologized for his remarks and went out to have a season in which he hit .314 with 211 hits, 105 runs, 26 stolen bases, 9 homers, and a league-leading 19 triples. The triples total was the highest by a Cardinal since Stan Musial hit 20 in 1946. Templeton is the only National Leaguer in history to lead the league in triples three years in a row. He also gave back to the community by purchasing 50 box seats for every summer game for underprivileged and handicapped children.

APRIL 6   Six days after the nuclear disaster at Three Mile Island, the Cardinals open the season with an 8–1 win over the Phillies before 40,526 at Busch Memorial Stadium. John Denny pitched a complete game and battery-mate Ted Simmons homered. Ken Reitz collected two doubles and a single and drove in three runs. Tony Scott also drove in three with a triple, double, and single.

The Cardinals introduced a new mascot in 1979 named "Fredbird." Feathered mascots became all the rage during the 1970s beginning with the San Diego Chicken and the Phillie Phanatic.

APRIL 7   Ken Forsch pitches a no-hitter for the Astros, defeating the Braves 6–0 in Houston.

Bob Forsch had pitched a no-hitter for the Cardinals on April 16, 1977, making the Forsch brothers the only pair of siblings to pitch no-hitters in the majors. Bob hurled another in 1983.

APRIL 9   Set to turn 40 in June, Lou Brock announces that the 1979 season will be his last in the majors.

Brock entered the 1979 season needing 100 hits to reach the 3,000 mark for his career. In 1978, he collected only 66 hits and batted .221, so his chances of making it to 3,000 looked grim. Brock wanted to go out in a blaze of glory and rededicated himself during the 1978–79 offseason with a new training regimen. It paid off; he had a torrid start in 1979. At the end of May, he had 45 hits in 118 at-bats for a .381 average. Brock picked up hit number 3,000 on August 13. He finished the season with 123 hits and a .304 batting average.

APRIL 11   During a flight delay, Cardinals players cause damage at the St. Louis airport.

The Cardinals had to wait 10 hours for a flight to Pittsburgh when their plane was denied clearance to take off because of a vicious storm. TWA supplied a special VIP lounge for the club, but some players damaged folding chairs, tore lettering off the walls, ripped out telephones, and broke a wooden door. The team fined Ken Reitz, Keith Hernandez, and Silvio Martinez for their roles in the fracas and ordered them to make restitution for the $1,000 in damage done to the waiting area.

APRIL 15   The Cardinals explode for five runs in the tenth inning and beat the Pirates 9–4 in Pittsburgh.

The Cardinals took the numbers off the fronts of their uniforms in 1979 and placed them on the sleeves. The numbers returned to the jersey fronts in 1981.

APRIL 18   The Cardinals outlast the Cubs 3–2 in 14 innings in Chicago. The winning run scored on a double by Keith Hernandez and a single by Tony Scott.

Hernandez emerged as a full-fledged star in 1979 by leading the NL in batting average (.344), runs (116), and doubles (48) in addition to hitting 11 triples and 11 homers and driving in 105 runs. He won the MVP in a vote that ended in a tie with Willie Stargell.

APRIL 23   The Cardinals score two runs in the ninth inning and one in the tenth off Phil Niekro to beat the Braves 3–2 in Atlanta. A single by Jerry Mumphrey drove in the winning run.

APRIL 24   Ted Simmons homers with two outs in the tenth inning to defeat the Braves 6–5 in Atlanta.

Simmons hit .285 with 26 homers in 1979.

APRIL 28   The Cardinals wallop the Reds 12–1 in Cincinnati.

MAY 1   A dramatic walk-off, pinch-hit grand slam by Roger Freed in the eleventh inning beats the Astros 7–6 at Busch Memorial Stadium. Houston scored three times in the top of the eleventh before the Cards struck back. After loading the bases on two singles and a walk, Freed blasted a 3–2 pitch into the left field bleachers.

MAY 9   Tony Scott collects five hits, including a triple and a double, in seven at-bats, but the Cardinals lose 5–4 in 16 innings to the Astros in Houston.

MAY 11   Jeff Burroughs breaks up Bob Forsch's no-hit bid with a home run in the seventh inning. Forsch allowed three hits in $7^2/_3$ innings but wound up losing 3–0 to the Braves at Busch Memorial Stadium.

MAY 15   John Denny pitches a two-hitter to beat the Expos 1–0 at Busch Memorial Stadium. Mike Phillips drove in the winning run with a walk-off single in the ninth inning off Steve Rogers. The only Montreal hits were singles by Warren Cromartie in the first inning and Larry Parrish in the second.

MAY 19   The Cardinals score six runs in the twelfth inning and beat the Mets 9–4 in New York.

JUNE 1   After the Dodgers score a run in the top of the eleventh, the Cardinals come back with two in their half to win 8–7 at Busch Memorial Stadium. The rally was accomplished despite a base-running blunder by Tony Scott. Scott smashed a drive off the wall to drive in the tying run but thought the ball had gone over for a home run and was tagged out trotting into second base. Pinch hitter Dane Iorg drove in the winning run with a single.

JUNE 3   Pete Vuckovich strikes out 12 batters during a 6–4 win over the Dodgers in Los Angeles.

JUNE 5   In the first round of the amateur draft, the Cardinals select outfielder Andy Van Slyke from New Hartford High School in New Hartford, New York.

Van Slyke reached the majors in 1983 and played four seasons with the Cardinals before a poorly conceived trade sent him to the Pirates. Others future major leaguers the Cardinals drafted and signed in 1979 were Tom Dozier (11th round), Mark Salas (18th round), Terry Clark (23rd round), and Ralph Citarella (1st round of the secondary phase).

JUNE 10   The Cardinals take sole possession of first place with a 3–2 win over the Padres at Busch Memorial Stadium.

The win gave the Cards a record of 31–21.

JUNE 11   Ted Simmons hits homers both sides of the plate and drives in six runs to lead the

Cardinals to a 9–7 win over the Dodgers in Los Angeles. His grand slam in the third inning off Jerry Reuss while batting right-handed gave the Cards a 4–3 lead. From the left side of the plate, Simmons homered in the ninth inning off Lerrin LaGrow with a man on base to break a 7–7 tie.

JUNE 13   Trailing 9–1, the Cardinals score seven runs in the ninth inning, but the uprising falls short resulting in a 9–8 loss to the Dodgers in Los Angeles. Tony Scott hit a grand slam off Rick Sutcliffe.

The loss also knocked the Cards out of first place. The club never regained the top spot in the NL East.

JUNE 27   Silvio Martinez pitches a one-hitter to defeat the Expos 5–0 at Busch Memorial Stadium. Martinez was four outs from a no-hitter when Duffy Dyer delivered a single with two outs in the eighth inning. The only other base runner was Andre Dawson, who reached on an error in the second inning.

JULY 1   Terry Kennedy is a hero in both ends of a doubleheader at Busch Memorial Stadium as the Cardinals sweep the Phillies 13–7 and 2–1. In the eighth inning of the first game, he hit a grand slam off Tug McGraw. It was Kennedy's first career homer. The Cards scored six times in the eighth to break a 7–7 tie. In the second tilt, Kennedy's walk-off, pinch-hit single drove in the winning run. Mark Littell was the winning pitcher in both games.

JULY 6   In a rare display of power, the Cardinals hit eight home runs during a doubleheader and sweep the Braves 9–5 and 5–4 in 10 innings in Atlanta. The Cards hit four homers in each game. Lou Brock set the tone by hitting Eddie Solomon's first pitch for a homer leading off the first inning of the opener. Garry Templeton hit two homers in the second game, the second one a game-winner in the tenth. The other St. Louis homers came from Bernie Carbo, Mike Phillips, Jerry Mumphrey, Ken Reitz, and Mike Tyson. It was Phillips's only homer all year.

Garry Templeton was selected as a reserve on the National League All-Star team, but he refused to play in the game because he was angry over not being elected as the starter. "If I ain't startin', I ain't departin'," Templeton said.

JULY 13   Silvio Martinez pitches the Cardinals to a 1–0 win over the Astros in Houston.

JULY 21   The Cardinals score nine runs in the third inning on two doubles, seven singles, and a walk and rout the Reds 12–3 at Busch Memorial Stadium.

AUGUST 9   John Denny pitches a two-hitter to defeat the Mets 4–0 at Shea Stadium. The only New York hits were a single by Lee Mazzilli in the first inning and a double by Joel Youngblood in the fifth.

AUGUST 10 The Cardinals sweep the Cubs 13–8 and 5–3 at Busch Memorial Stadium.

AUGUST 13 Lou Brock collects his 3,000th career hit during a 3–2 win over the Cubs at Busch Memorial Stadium. Brock came into the contest with 2,998 hits. A single off Dennis Lamp in the first inning put gave him 2,999. He went into the record book in the fourth on a 2–2 pitch when he slashed a drive off Lamp's hand. The drive glanced to

Lamp's left, and Brock skittered across first base as third baseman Steve Ontiveros had no play.

AUGUST 17   John Fulgham pitches a two-hitter for a 3–0 win over the Giants at Busch Memorial Stadium. Fulgham retired the first 16 batters to face him before Mike Sadek singled with one out in the sixth. Willie McCovey collected the other San Francisco hit with a single in the seventh.

A native of St. Louis, Fulgham was 10–6 with a 2.53 ERA as a 23-year-old rookie in 1979. He was 4–6 in 1980 before tearing a rotator cuff. The injury ended his career.

AUGUST 18   With the Cardinals trailing the Giants 4–3 at Busch, manager Ken Boyer ignores the percentages and sends left-handed Dane Iorg to the plate against lefty Vida Blue with two on and one out in the ninth. Iorg responded by driving in both runners with a single for a 5–4 Cardinal win.

AUGUST 31   The Cardinals outlast the Padres 8–7 in 15 innings in San Diego. Keith Hernandez drove in the winning run with a double. Dan O'Brien was the winning pitcher in his only win in a 13-game big-league career.

SEPTEMBER 9   The Cardinals stage Lou Brock Day with pregame ceremonies before a 4–1 loss to the Expos. A crowd of 47,244 turned out at Busch Memorial Stadium. The Cardinals presented Brock with a 33-foot cabin cruiser worth an estimated $125,000. He also received a Chevrolet Monte Carlo from radio station KMOX and a silver tray from teammates.

SEPTEMBER 22   Lou Brock ties Billy Hamilton for the all-time stolen lead with the 937th steal of his career during a 6–3 win in the first game of a doubleheader in New York.

Each of Brock's major league stolen bases was at second or third base. He never stole home.

SEPTEMBER 23   Lou Brock passes Billy Hamilton as the all-time stolen base career leader by swiping number 938 during a 10-inning, 7–4 win over the Mets in New York.

Brock never stole another base. Since 1979, a recheck of Hamilton's stolen base records has reduced his total to 914. Rickey Henderson shattered Brock's mark by stealing 1,406 bases, but Brock still ranks second all time.

SEPTEMBER 25   George Hendrick collects five hits, including a homer and a double, in five at-bats, leading the Cardinals to a 9–5 win over the Pirates in Pittsburgh.

Hendrick batted .300 with 16 homers in 1979.

SEPTEMBER 28   Garry Templeton becomes the only player in major league history to collect 100 hits from both sides of the plate with three hits from the right side during a doubleheader against the Mets at Busch Memorial Stadium. The Cards lost both games, 6–2 and 7–6 in 11 innings.

Templeton collected his 94th hit of the season from the right side on September 22. Upon learning that no one had ever gotten 100 hits from both sides in the same season, he began batting right-handed against right-handed pitching to get the record.

SEPTEMBER 30   Lou Brock plays his last major league and is hitless in four at-bats during a 4–2 loss to the Mets at Busch Memorial Stadium.

OCTOBER 17   The Cardinals trade Mike Tyson to the Cubs for Donnie Moore.

DECEMBER 7   A month after Iranian militants seize the US Embassy in Tehran, the Cardinals trade John Denny and Jerry Mumphrey to the Indians for Bobby Bonds.

The trade proved to be an abject disaster. Bonds was 33 but was coming off a season in which he hit 25 homers, scored 93 runs, drove in 85, and stole 34 bases. From 1969 through 1979, Bonds averaged 104 runs scored, 28 homers, 86 RBIs, and 39 stolen bases per season. As a Cardinal, Bonds played in 86 games and batted .203 and hit five homers before drawing his release. Denny continued to be inconsistent throughout the remainder of his career, which lasted seven more years, but he was an above-average pitcher and his peak included a 1983 season in which he won the Cy Young Award with the Phillies. Mumphrey would have fit in nicely with the Cardinals teams of the 1980s, which featured speedy outfielders who hit for average. After leaving St. Louis, he played nine more seasons in the majors and batted .295 over 1,063 games.

THE STATE OF THE CARDINALS

The Cardinals' fortunes took a dramatic turn for the better on June 9, 1980, when Whitey Herzog was named manager. Before the year ended, he had the dual duties of general manager and field manager. With a flurry of trades, Herzog built a club that won National League pennants in 1982, 1985, and 1987 and the World Series in 1982. The club was inconsistent, however. Season win totals from 1982 through 1989 were 92, 79, 84, 101, 79, 95, 76, and 86. Overall, the Cardinals were 825–734 during the 1980s, for a winning percentage of .529—best in the National League. NL pennant winners outside of St. Louis were the Phillies (1980 and 1983), Dodgers (1981 and 1988), Padres (1984), Mets (1986), and Giants (1989). NL East champions were the Phillies (1980 and 1983), Expos (1981), Cubs (1984 and 1989), and Mets (1986 and 1988).

THE BEST TEAM

The 1982 outfit had a 92–70 regular-season record and has been the only Cardinals team to claim a world title since 1968. The 1985 Cards were 101–61 but lost the World Series in seven games to the Royals, who went 91–71 that year.

THE WORST TEAM

A year after going to the World Series, the team was 76–86 and finished in fifth place in 1988.

THE BEST MOMENT

On October 14, 1985, Ozzie Smith hit a walk-off home run in Game Five of the NLCS against the Dodgers' Tom Niedenfuer—"Go crazy, folks! Go crazy!"

THE WORST MOMENT

The low point of the 1980s was umpire Don Denkinger's blown call in the ninth inning of Game Six of the 1985 World Series and the Cardinals' subsequent meltdown against the Royals to blow a shot at the World Championship.

THE ALL-DECADE TEAM • YEARS W/CARDS

Darrell Porter, c	1981–85
Keith Hernandez, 1b	1974–83
Tom Herr, 2b	1979–88
Terry Pendleton, 3b	1984–90
Ozzie Smith, ss	1982–96
Vince Coleman, lf	1985–90
Willie McGee, cf	1982–90, 1996–1999
George Hendrick, rf	1978–84
Bob Forsch, p	1974–88
John Tudor, p	1985–88, 1990
Joaquin Andujar, p	1981–85
Todd Worrell, p	1985–89, 1992

Other outstanding Cardinals of the 1980s included first baseman Jack Clark (1985–87), third baseman–second baseman Ken Oberkfell (1977–84), left fielder Lonnie Smith (1982–85), right fielder Andy Van Slyke (1983–86), and pitchers Bruce Sutter (1981–84) and Danny Cox (1983–88). Ozzie Smith is in the Hall of Fame. Hernandez and Sutter put up Cooperstown-caliber numbers, and Clark and Darrell Porter should receive some consideration for Cooperstown.

THE DECADE LEADERS

Batting Avg:	Hernandez	.306
On-Base Pct:	Hernandez	.396
Slugging Pct:	Hendrick	.468
Home Runs:	Hendrick	89
RBIs:	Hendrick	440
Runs:	Smith	583
Stolen Bases:	Coleman	472
Wins:	Forsch	84
Strikeouts:	Forsch	555
ERA:	Tudor	2.55
Saves:	Sutter	127

THE HOME FIELD

Anheuser-Busch made the Civic Center Corporation, which had operated Busch Memorial Stadium since 1966, a subsidiary in 1981, resulting in better maintenance and upkeep of the ballpark. The facility quickly gained the reputation of being one of baseball's cleanest facilities. In addition to being repainted nearly every year and scrubbed down before every game, the stadium got new AstroTurf and a new scoreboard, complete with video-replay capabilities, before the 1983 season. Also in 1983, the official name of the stadium changed from Busch Memorial Stadium to Busch Stadium. The baseball Cardinals became the lone tenants of the park in March 1988 when the football Cardinals bolted for Phoenix.

THE GAME YOU WISH YOU HAD SEEN

The Cardinals defeated the Brewers 6–3 in Game Seven of the 1982 World Series, played on October 20.

THE WAY THE GAME WAS PLAYED

The 1980s had a little something for everybody. Trends surfacing in the 1970s continued, with teams emphasizing speed over power. The Cardinals were at the forefront of this shift. The 1982 World Champions finished last in the majors in home runs and first in the National League in steals. Earned run averages hovered around 3.60. But 1987 combined the speed numbers of the dead-ball era with the power numbers of the 1950s. NL teams averaged more than 150 steals and 150 homers, the only time that has ever occurred. But the offensive bubble burst shortly afterward, and in 1988 and 1989, the NL experienced its lowest batting averages in nearly 20 years.

THE MANAGEMENT

August Busch was the owner of the Cardinals from February 1953 until his death in September 1989. August Busch III succeeded his father as chairman of the board. Whitey Herzog was named general manager in August 1980 following John Claiborne's dismissal. After serving as both general manager and field manager for part of 1980 and all of 1981, Herzog exited his general manager role in April 1982. The new general manager was Joe McDonald. After McDonald's resignation in January 1985, Dal Maxvill became GM. The Cards had four changes in field managers in 1980: Ken Boyer, Jack Krol, Herzog,

Red Schoendienst, and then Herzog again. Krol and Schoendienst ran the club on interim bases. Herzog held the position until 1990.

THE BEST PLAYER MOVE

The Cardinals pulled off a number of brilliant trades during the 1980s. The best player acquired in a trade was Ozzie Smith from the Padres during the 1981–82 offseason. The Willie McGee–for–Bob Sykes deal that same offseason was the most one-sided in favor of the Cardinals.

THE WORST PLAYER MOVE

The Cardinals sent former MVP Keith Hernandez packing to the Mets in June 1983 for Neil Allen and Rick Ownbey.

1980

Season in a Sentence

The Cardinals finish first in runs scored but last in ERA and change managers four times between June and October.

Finish • Won • Lost • Pct • GB

Fourth   74   88   .457   17.0

Managers

Ken Boyer (18–33), Jack Krol (0–1), Whitey Herzog (38–35), and Red Schoendienst (18–19)

Stats

Stats	Cards	NL	Rank
Batting Avg:	.275	.259	1
On-Base Pct:	.331	.323	1
Slugging Pct:	.400	.374	1
Home Runs:	101		8
Stolen Bases:	117		9
ERA:	3.93	3.60	12
Fielding Avg:	.981	.978	2
Runs Scored:	738		1
Runs Allowed:	710		11

Starting Lineup

Ted Simmons, c
Keith Hernandez, 1b
Ken Oberkfell, 2b
Ken Reitz, 3b
Garry Templeton, ss
Leon Durham, lf-rf
Tony Scott, cf
George Hendrick, rf-cf
Dane Iorg, lf
Terry Kennedy, c-lf
Bobby Bonds, lf
Tom Herr, 2b

Pitchers

Pete Vuckovich, sp
Bob Forsch, sp
Bob Sykes, sp
Silvio Martinez, sp
John Fulgham, sp
John Littlefield, rp
Jim Kaat, rp
Don Hood, rp

Attendance

1,385,147 (seventh in NL)

Club Leaders

Batting Avg:	Hernandez	.321
On-Base Pct:	Hernandez	.408
Slugging Pct:	Simmons	.505
Home Runs:	Hendrick	25
RBIs:	Hendrick	109
Runs:	Hernandez	111
Stolen Bases:	Templeton	31
Wins:	Vuckovich	12
Strikeouts:	Vuckovich	132
ERA:	Vuckovich	3.40
Saves:	Littlefield	9

APRIL 10   Pete Vuckovich wins a 1–0 duel over the Pirates with a three-hitter before an Opening Day crowd of 43,867 at Busch Memorial Stadium. After putting the first two batters in the ninth on base, Vuckovich struck out Tim Foli, Dave Parker, and Willie Stargell to end the game. After walking, Bobby Bonds scored the lone run of the game in the third inning on a double by George Hendrick.

Bonds wore number 25 throughout most of his major league career with six different clubs, but when he came to St. Louis, George Hendrick already had number 25. Instead, Bonds wore 00 in his only year with the Cardinals, which seemed appropriate to many fans in light of his on-field contributions.

APRIL 17   George Hendrick drives in six runs to spark an attack that beats the Pirates 12–9 in Pittsburgh. Hendrick had a homer and three singles.

Hendrick hit .302 with 25 homers and 109 RBIs in 1980.

APRIL 28   Keith Hernandez collects five hits, including a double, in five at-bats to lead the Cardinals to a 10–1 rout of the Phillies in Philadelphia.

Hernandez hit .321 with 16 homers, 99 RBIs, and 111 runs scored in 1980.

APRIL 30   The Cardinals purchase Jim Kaat from the Yankees.

Kaat was 41 years old and in his 22nd major league season when he arrived in St. Louis. Kaat pitched out of the Cardinal bullpen for three seasons.

MAY 2   On the day that Mt. St. Helens erupts in Washington State, the Cardinals explode for seven runs in the seventh inning and defeat the Astros 9–1 at Busch Memorial Stadium.

Dan Kelly replaced Bob Starr in the Cardinals' radio and television booth in 1980. Kelly joined Jack Buck, Mike Shannon, and Jay Randolph.

MAY 6   The Cardinals break a 3–3 tie with six runs in the fifth inning and defeat the Giants 10–7 at Busch Memorial Stadium.

MAY 7   The Cardinals maul the Giants 12–2 at Busch Memorial Stadium.

MAY 9   The Cardinals reach double figures for the third game in a row with a 15–7 win over the Dodgers at Busch Memorial Stadium.

MAY 31   August Busch visits the clubhouse and warns of impending changes if the club doesn't start winning. The Cardinals had lost 16 of their last 18 games. They responded with an 8–6 win over the Expos.

JUNE 3   In the first round of the amateur draft, the Cardinals select pitcher Don Collins from Ferguson High School in Newport News, Virginia.

Collins never made it past Class A ball. The Cardinals didn't select anyone in the 1980 draft that became a big-league regular. The only players they drafted and signed who reached the majors were Kevin Hagen (fourth round of the January draft), Ricky Horton (fourth round in June), and Jim Adduci (seventh round). The Cards did draft two relievers who went on to have long careers—Dan Plesac and Rick Aguilera—but both opted to attend college rather than sign with St. Louis. In 1983, the Brewers drafted and signed Plesac, and Aguilera went to the Mets.

JUNE 4   Ken Reitz leads off the tenth inning with a homer off Neil Allen to beat the Mets 1–0 in New York. At the age of 41, Kaat pitched all 10 innings for a complete-game shutout. It was his first complete game and first shutout in two years. It was also the last of his 31 career shutouts.

JUNE 8   Bobby Bonds ties a National League record by drawing six walks during a doubleheader at Olympic Stadium. He walked four times in the first game and two in the second. Montreal won both games, 6–4 and 9–4.

Manager Ken Boyer was fired between the two games. Coach Jack Krol served as interim manager for the second contest. The Cards started the year 13–13 but went into a nose dive and were 18–33 when Boyer was canned. General manager John Claiborne flew to Montreal to deliver the bad news to Boyer. He had a 166–191 record as manager from 1978 through 1980.

Meanwhile, back in St. Louis 48-year-old Dorrel (Whitey) Herzog was named as manager in a press conference at Grant's Farm, August Busch's home. Herzog's hiring was one of the most important in club history. He won three National

League pennants, more than any other manager in Cardinal history, and a World Championship. Herzog had been a journeyman outfielder for four American League clubs from 1956 through 1963. He managed the Rangers in 1973, the Angels in 1974, and the Royals from 1975 through 1979. In Kansas City, Herzog guided the Royals to three straight division championships in 1976, 1977, and 1978, but he was fired because he didn't get along with owner Ewing Kauffman. Herzog was never afraid to speak his mind, and August Busch had a long history of hiring outspoken individuals. Herzog managed the Cardinals until 1990.

Getty Images Sport/Getty Images

Whitey Herzog aligned the stars for the Cardinals where previous managers had failed. With carte blanche from the ownership to rebuild the team, both through the front office and on the field, Herzog became a St. Louis icon and ranks second among Cardinals managers behind Tony La Russa.

 ## Whitey Ball

The Cardinals of the 1980s were one of the most unusual teams in baseball history. The club won three pennants with the lowest home run totals in baseball and stolen-base figures since the dead-ball era. With Whitey Herzog directing the club from the bench, the style of play became known as "Whitey ball." Hired to run the Cardinals in June 1980, Herzog tailored his club around the dimensions and the surface of Busch Stadium, with distant fences and AstroTurf, by acquiring players with blazing speed. During a 10-year span from 1982 through 1991, the Cardinals ranked last in the majors in home runs. Over the same period, the club was first in the NL in stolen bases seven times and first in the majors five times.

This list shows home run and stolen-base totals during the period in which Herzog was manager and the Cardinals' rank among the 12 National League teams. The last year on the list was 1991, the year after Herzog resigned as manager. In 1992, the Cardinals moved in the fences and began building a team based on power, culminating with the arrival of Mark McGwire in a trade with the Athletics in July 1997. McGwire hit 70 home runs in 1998, more than some of the Herzog-era clubs.

Year	Home Runs	NL Rank	Stolen Bases	NL Rank	Notes
1980	101	8	117	9	a
1981	50	10	88	7	b
1982	67	12*	200	1	c
1983	83	12*	207	1	
1984	75	12*	220	1+	
1985	87	11	314	1+	c, d
1986	58	12*	262	1+	
1987	94	12*	248	1+	c
1988	71	12*	234	1+	
1989	73	12*	155	2	
1990	73	12*	221	2	
1991	68	12*	202	2	

*   The Cardinals ranked last in the majors.
+   The Cardinals ranked first in the majors.
a   Herzog became manager of the Cardinals on June 9, 1980.
b   The season was shortened to 103 games by a player's strike.
c   The Cardinals won the NL pennant.
d   The 314 stolen bases were the most of any major league club since the New York Giants swiped 319 in 1912.

JUNE 9   In Whitey Herzog's first game as manager, George Hendrick hits a three-run homer in the tenth inning to beat the Braves 8–5 in Atlanta. The Cardinals led 5–0 in the sixth inning before allowing the Braves back in the game.

JUNE 15   The Cardinals win a 13-inning, 10–9 thriller against the Reds at Busch Memorial Stadium. Cincinnati scored six times in the ninth inning to take an 8–5 lead, but the Cards tallied three in their half on a three-run single by George Hendrick. The Reds took a 9–8 lead in the top of the thirteenth before the Redbirds countered with two in the bottom of the inning to win. Terry Kennedy drove in both of the extra-inning runs with a walk-off double.

JUNE 20   Terry Kennedy drives in six runs on a pair of three-run homers in the first and seventh innings to lead the Cardinals to a 7–5 win over the Reds in Cincinnati. He hit the second homer with the Cards trailing 5–4.

JUNE 22   The Cardinals rout the Reds 12–2 in Cincinnati.

JUNE 28   The Cardinals score four runs in the ninth inning to defeat the Cubs 8–6 in the first game of a doubleheader at Wrigley Field. Leon Durham drove in the tying and go-ahead runs with a double. Chicago won the second contest 2–1.

JULY 4   George Hendrick hammers a walk-off homer in the tenth inning to beat the Phillies 1–0 at Busch Memorial Stadium. Bob Sykes pitched all 10 innings for the complete-game shutout.

JULY 8   George Hendrick smacks an RBI single that ties the score 2–2 in the sixth inning of the All-Star Game, played at Dodger Stadium in Los Angeles. The National League went on to win 4–2.

JULY 11   The Cardinals score four runs in the ninth inning to beat the Expos 5–3 in Montreal. A pinch-double by Keith Smith drove in the tying and go-ahead runs.

              Smith collected only 7 hits in 44 at-bats as an outfielder for the Cardinals over two seasons for a .159 batting average.

JULY 12   Down 6–1, the Cardinals score one run in the sixth inning, one in the seventh, two in the ninth, and two in the twelfth to win 8–6 over the Mets in New York. In the ninth inning, Garry Templeton tripled in one run and scored on Leon Durham's sacrifice fly. Ken Oberkfell broke the 6–6 tie with a triple in the twelfth.

              Oberkfell hit .303 for the Cardinals in 1980. He grew up in Maryville, Missouri, near St. Louis and was signed out of high school in 1975 as an undrafted free agent. As a second baseman and third baseman for the Cards, Oberkfell hit .292 in 724 games over eight seasons.

JULY 17   The Cardinals explode for 10 runs in the third inning and beat the Padres 15–3 at Busch Memorial Stadium.

AUGUST 6   The Cardinals score seven runs in the third inning to take a 12–0 lead and dispatch the Phillies 14–0 in Philadelphia.

AUGUST 11   Blasting eight runs in the first inning, the Cardinals massacre the Expos 16–0 at Busch Memorial Stadium. Dane Iorg collected three doubles and a triple to tie a Cardinal club record for most extra-base hits in a game.

AUGUST 18   The Cardinals score eight runs in the second inning and defeat the Reds 10–1 in Cincinnati in a contest stopped by rain after 6½ innings.

              On the same day, John Claiborne was fired as general manager after only 22 months on the job. In a statement, August Busch said that the dismissal was the result of his "basic disagreement" with Claiborne regarding the progress of the team. No replacement was immediately named (see August 29, 1980).

AUGUST 21   The Cardinals' flight from Cincinnati to Atlanta nearly turns into disaster at the Atlanta airport. Just as the plane was about to touch down, the pilot pushed the throttle full and pulled up because another plane had not cleared the runway.

AUGUST 28   Dane Iorg drives in seven runs with two doubles and a single during an 11–2 win over the Braves at Busch Stadium.

AUGUST 29   Whitey Herzog gives up his reins as manager to become the Cardinals' general manager. Red Schoendienst was named interim manager for the remainder of the 1980 season. "I sure as heck didn't come here to be a general manager," Herzog said, "but I can do more for the Cardinals as general manager than as field manager." (See October 24, 1980.)

SEPTEMBER 2   The Cardinals tie a National League record with four sacrifice flies during a 12–4 win over the Reds at Busch Memorial Stadium. Dane Iorg recorded two of the sacrifice flies, and Mike Phillips and Keith Hernandez collected the other two.

SEPTEMBER 12   Leon Durham hits a grand slam off Warren Brusstar in the fifth inning of a 7–4 win over the Phillies in the first game of a doubleheader in Philadelphia. In the second game, the Cardinals broke a scoreless tie to score five runs in the eleventh inning for a 5–0 win. With the score 1–0, Keith Hernandez hit a bases-loaded triple and scored on a single by George Hendrick. Making his major league debut, Alan Olmstead was the starting pitcher and hurled 9$^1/_3$ shutout innings. John Littlefield completed the shutout.

A native of St. Louis who attended Hazelwood East High School, Olmstead's big-league career lasted only five games. He had a 1–1 record and a 2.86 ERA in 34$^2/_3$ innings.

SEPTEMBER 19   The Cardinals earn an exciting 9–8 victory over the Expos at Busch Memorial Stadium. Down 7–2, St. Louis tied the contest with five runs in the seventh. After Montreal scored in the top of the ninth, the Cards came back with two in their half on two singles and George Hendrick's two-run, walk-off double.

Jim Kaat missed the last week of the season when he punctured his ear drum while using a Q-tip.

SEPTEMBER 25   Ted Simmons drives in six runs on a single, a solo homer, and a grand slam to lead the Cardinals to a 10–2 win over the Pirates in Pittsburgh. He hit the grand slam in the seventh off Don Robinson.

OCTOBER 5   On the last day of the season, Keith Hernandez falls just short of winning his second straight batting title by going 1 for 4 in a 3–2 win over the Mets at Busch Memorial Stadium. Hernandez finished the season at .321. Bill Buckner of the Cubs led the league with a .324 mark. Despite missing 44 games with a broken bone in his hand, Garry Templeton was third in the NL in batting average. He hit .319 and stole 31 bases in 1980.

OCTOBER 24   Whitey Herzog returns to his job as the Cardinals' field manager.

After being elevated to general manager on August 29, Herzog set about finding a field manager for the 1981 season. After casting about for candidates, he decided he was the most qualified person for the job and took on the dual roles of general manager and field manager. The Cardinals hired former Mets general manager Joe McDonald as an executive assistant to ease some of Herzog's front-office burdens.

DECEMBER 7   The Cardinals sign Darrell Porter, most recently with the Royals, as a free agent.

Porter played for Herzog in Kansas City and hit 20 homers to go with his 112 RBIs and .291 average in 1979. Porter made the All-Star team in 1980 for the fourth time in his career, although his numbers slipped drastically. Much of the problem stemmed from a severe addition to drugs and alcohol. Porter publicly admitted the problem and went into rehabilitation. A top-level defensive catcher, Porter's signing allowed the Cardinals to trade Ted Simmons and Terry Kennedy, two good-hitting catchers with average gloves (see December 8,

1980, and December 12, 1980). Porter hit only .237 in 1,652 at-bats over five seasons for the Cardinals, but he hit 54 homers. While his offensive numbers paled in comparison to Simmons's, Porter had on-base percentages and slugging percentages well above the league average for catchers. In 2001, Bill James ranked Porter as the 18th best catcher in baseball history. Despite his positive contributions in 12 seasons as a starting catcher in the majors, fans never fully appreciated Porter's skills, particularly in St. Louis, where they were angry over the trade of the popular Simmons and heaped almost constant abuse on Porter from the stands.

DECEMBER 8   A month after Ronald Reagan defeats Jimmy Carter in the presidential election, the Cardinals trade Terry Kennedy, Steve Swisher, John Littlefield, John Urrea, Mike Phillips, Kim Seaman, and Alan Olmstead to the Padres for Rollie Fingers, Gene Tenace, Bob Shirley, and Bob Geren.

When asked by August Busch for an assessment of the ball club at the end of the 1980 season, Whitey Herzog was blunt: "I've never seen such a bunch of misfits. Nobody would run out a ball. Nobody in the bullpen wanted the ball." Herzog was appalled not only with the lack of hustle and self-discipline, but also the blatant drug and alcohol abuse and rampant egos. "You've got a bunch of mean people, some very sorry human beings," Herzog told Busch. "It's the first time I've ever been afraid to walk through my own clubhouse." With Busch Stadium's deep fences and AstroTurf field, Herzog wanted to emphasize speed and defense over power. He also desired a corps of relievers that could close the door in the eighth and ninth innings. Most important, he wanted guys who were tough and unselfish. Herzog wasted little time in disassembling the disappointing ball club, and the December 8 trade was Herzog's first step in cleaning house. In a span of less than a week, he would totally remake the Cardinals.

DECEMBER 9   The Cardinals trade Leon Durham, Ken Reitz, and Tye Waller to the Cubs for Bruce Sutter.

The slow-moving Durham and Reitz didn't fit into Herzog's plan the club. Durham would be a regular for the Cubs for seven seasons, but the only position he could field adequately was first base, and the Cards already had Keith Hernandez. With a devastating split-finger fastball and a lumberjack beard, Sutter was one of the best closers in baseball. He led the NL in saves three times in four seasons as a Cardinal.

DECEMBER 12   The Cardinals trade Rollie Fingers, Ted Simmons, and Pete Vuckovich to the Brewers for Sixto Lezcano, David Green, Lary Sorensen, and Dave LaPoint.

The Cardinals traded two future Cy Young Award winners in one deal. Fingers, a future Hall of Famer the Cardinals had acquired from the Padres four days earlier, won the award in 1981. Vuckovich took the Cy Young trophy in 1982. Simmons was a regular with the Brewers for five seasons as a catcher and designated hitter. None of the four players the Cards acquired won any awards. Green was the biggest disappointment. A native of Nicaragua, Green had been compared to Willie Mays and Roberto Clemente. Green was listed as a 20-year-old when the Cardinals picked him up, but he might have been as old as 24. In five seasons with the Cardinals, he batted just .273 with 26 homers in 1,104 at-bats.

1981

Season in a Sentence

The Cardinals compile the best record in the NL East but fail to reach the playoffs in a year convoluted by a midseason strike and a split season.

Finish • Won • Lost • Pct • GB

*	59	43	.578	*

* In the first half of the season, the Cardinals finished 30–20 in second place, 1½ games behind. In the second half, the Cardinals were 29–23 and finished in second place, half a game behind.

Manager

Whitey Herzog

Stats

Stats	Cards • NL • Rank		
Batting Avg:	.265	.255	3
On-Base Pct:	.339	.319	3
Slugging Pct:	.377	.364	3
Home Runs:	50		10
Stolen Bases:	88		7
ERA:	3.63	3.49	8
Fielding Avg:	.981	.978	1
Runs Scored:	464		2 (tie)
Runs Allowed:	380		8

Starting Lineup

Darrell Porter, c
Keith Hernandez, 1b
Tom Herr, 2b
Ken Oberkfell, 3b
Garry Templeton, ss
Dane Iorg, lf
George Hendrick, cf-rf
Sixto Lezcano, rf-lf
Tony Scott, cf
Gene Tenace, c
Mike Ramsey, ss
Tito Landrum, lf-rf

Pitchers

Bob Forsch, sp
Lary Sorensen, sp
John Martin, sp
Joaquin Andujar, sp
Silvio Martinez, sp
Bruce Sutter, rp
Jim Kaat, rp
Bob Shirley, rp-sp

Attendance

1,010,247 (sixth in NL)

Club Leaders

Batting Avg:	Hernandez	.306
On-Base Pct:	Hernandez	.401
Slugging Pct:	Hendrick	.485
Home Runs:	Hendrick	18
RBIs:	Hendrick	61
Runs:	Hendrick	67
Stolen Bases:	Herr	23
Wins:	Forsch	10
Strikeouts:	Sutter	57
ERA:	Forsch	3.18
Saves:	Sutter	25

JANUARY 15   Five days before American hostages in Iran are released from captivity, Bob Gibson is elected to the Hall of Fame on the first ballot.

APRIL 11   Two weeks after Ronald Reagan is shot in John Hinckley Jr.'s assassination attempt, the Cardinals lose the season opener 5–2 to the Phillies before 38,473 at Busch Memorial Stadium.

The Cards pulled off a triple play in the eighth. With the bases loaded, Gary Matthews hit a low line drive to shortstop Garry Templeton. Although the umpire ruled a clean catch, Templeton thought the ball had been trapped and threw to catcher Darrell Porter, who relayed to Keith Hernandez at first. The umpire there ruled that Mike Schmidt had retouched first, and Hernandez threw to second baseman Tommy Herr to nail Schmidt for the second out. Herr then fired to third baseman Ken Oberkfell, who tagged Bake McBride to complete the triple play.

APRIL 18   Six days after the launch of Columbia, the first space shuttle, Keith Hernandez is the victim of Tom Seaver's 3,000th career shutout, but the Cardinals win 10–4 over the Reds in Cincinnati.

APRIL 26   The Cardinals win their eighth game in a row with a 3–2 decision over the Pirates in Pittsburgh.

The Cardinals had a record of 12–3 on May 3.

MAY 9   The Cardinals drub the Pirates 13–0 at Busch Memorial Stadium.

MAY 12   Tom Herr's tenth-inning suicide squeeze bunt scores Gene Tenace from third base with the winning run in a 2–1 decision over the Astros in Houston.

Herr took over as the starting second baseman for the Cardinals in 1981 as Ken Oberkfell moved to third. Herr was the starter at second for seven years, including three World Series teams.

MAY 14   Down 6–1, the Cardinals score two runs in the seventh inning and four in the ninth to stun the Astros 7–6 in Houston. George Hendrick delivered two-run doubles in both the eighth and ninth.

Hendrick hit .284 with 18 homers in 1981.

MAY 19   The Cardinals outlast the Astros 15–12 at Busch Memorial Stadium. Down 7–2 in the fourth inning, the Cards battled back to take a 10–9 lead with three runs in the sixth and put the game on ice with five more in the seventh.

MAY 31   The Cardinals drop from first place to third in one day with a 6–1 loss to the Phillies in Philadelphia.

JUNE 3   The Cardinals get a thrilling 3–2 win in 11 innings over the Expos at Busch Memorial Stadium. With the Redbirds trailing 2–1 in the tenth, George Hendrick tied it with a homer. Orlando Sanchez tripled and scored the winning run in the eleventh on Tommy Herr's single.

JUNE 6   Keith Hernandez's grand slam off John Littlefield in the eighth inning caps an 11–1 win over the Padres at Busch Memorial Stadium. The victory put the Cards back into first place by half a game.

Hernandez hit .306 with eight homers in 1981.

JUNE 7   The Cardinals again drop out of first place with a 5–1 loss to the Padres at Busch Memorial Stadium.

On the same day, the Cardinals traded Tony Scott to the Astros for Joaquin Andujar. Tempestuous, eccentric, capricious, unique, quotable, often brilliant, and always entertaining, Andujar was one of the most exciting and excitable characters ever to don a Cardinal uniform. "I go to the field like a Japanese kamikaze," he once said in explaining his pitching philosophy using one of his many humorous non sequiturs. "I am one tough Dominican." The Astros were happy to find a club that would take Andujar off their hands and accepted the journeyman outfielder Scott in return. Andujar was 28 and had a 42–48 lifetime record, and Houston didn't believe he could be a consistent winner. He found new life in St. Louis with a 68–53 record over five seasons. Andujar was 15–10 in 1982, 20–14 in 1984, and 21–12 in 1985. Control was the key to his improvement after arriving in St. Louis. As an Astro, he averaged 3.90 walks per nine innings. As a Cardinal, he reduced that figure to 2.41.

JUNE 8 — In the first round of the amateur draft, the Cardinals select shortstop Bobby Meacham from San Diego State University.

The Cardinals traded Meacham to the Yankees a year later, and he had a six-year big-league career as a utility infielder. Other future major leaguers the Cardinals drafted and signed in 1981 were Tom Nieto (third round), Curt Ford (fourth round), Jeff Keener (seventh round), Danny Cox (thirteenth round), and Randy Hunt (first round of the secondary phase).

JUNE 11 — With a midnight strike deadline looming, the Cardinals defeat the Dodgers 2–1 at Busch Memorial Stadium. The only two St. Louis runs scored on a two-run inside-the-park homer by George Hendrick off Fernando Valenzuela in the first inning. Pedro Guerrero attempted a shoestring catch on Hendrick's drive, and the ball rolled all the way to the wall. The Phillies beat the Astros 6–4 to maintain a one-game lead over the Redbirds. No one knew it at the time, but the Phillies clinched a berth in the postseason with the win (see August 6, 1981).

JUNE 12 — The major league players begin a strike that lasts 50 days and wipes out nearly two months of the 1981 baseball season. The strike reduced the Cardinals' schedule to 103 games.

JULY 28 — Anheuser-Busch, Inc., gains controlling interest in the Civic Center Redevelopment Corporation, which owns Busch Memorial Stadium. The move was made to give the Cardinals authority over the maintenance and upkeep of the stadium as well as the profits from concessions and parking. Following the acquisition, the ball club made certain that the park was repainted almost every year and scrubbed down after every game, making it one of the cleanest facilities in baseball.

JULY 31 — Two days after Prince Charles marries Lady Diana Spencer in London, the players and owners hammer out an agreement that ends the strike.

AUGUST 6 — The owners vote to split the 1981 pennant race, with the winners of the two halves of the season competing in an extra round of playoffs for the division title. This had major implications for the Cardinals because the club finished the first half only one game behind the Phillies.

AUGUST 9 — Bruce Sutter earns a save in the All-Star Game by retiring three American Leaguers in order in the ninth inning for a 5–4 National League win at Municipal Stadium in Cleveland.

In his first season with the Cardinals, Sutter had a 3–5 record, a 2.62 ERA, and a league-leading 25 saves.

AUGUST 10 — In the first regular-season game following the strike, the Cardinals down the Phillies

7–3 in Philadelphia. During the game, Pete Rose collected his 3,631st career hit to break Stan Musial's record for most hits in the National League.

AUGUST 23   The Cardinals collect 20 hits and thump the Dodgers 11–7 at Busch Memorial Stadium.

AUGUST 26   The Cardinals score eight runs in the fifth inning and defeat the Giants 9–4 at Busch Memorial Stadium.

Whitey Herzog fined Garry Templeton $5,000 and suspended him indefinitely for making obscene gestures at fans during the game. Before the game, Templeton said that he was too tired to play, but Herzog put him in the lineup at shortstop anyway. Templeton responded with a halfhearted effort. In the first inning Templeton struck out, but Giant catcher Milt May dropped the ball. Templeton jogged slowly toward first before veering toward the Cardinal dugout. The crowd began booing, and Templeton responded with his middle fingers raised. After two similar gestures later in the game, Templeton was ejected by umpire Bruce Froemming prior to the fourth inning. As Templeton got to the Cardinal dugout, Herzog grabbed him by the shirt and backed him against a wall before players swooped in to break up the scuffle. A day later, Templeton agreed to seek psychiatric help and was hospitalized and treated for what was diagnosed as depression. He returned to the lineup on September 15, but his absence probably cost the Cardinals a berth in the postseason.

AUGUST 27   A homer by George Hendrick in the thirteenth inning beats the Padres 3–2 in San Diego. Hendrick drove in all three St. Louis runs.

SEPTEMBER 3   Sixto Lezcano's two-run homer highlights a three-run ninth inning that produces a 5–3 win over the Dodgers in Los Angeles.

SEPTEMBER 12   A two-run, walk-off homer by Julio Gonzalez in the thirteenth inning beats the Mets 4–2 at Busch Memorial Stadium.

The homer was the first by Gonzalez in the majors since 1978 and his only one in 1981.

SEPTEMBER 15   In his first game back following his August 26 suspension, Garry Templeton collects four hits in five at-bats during a 3–2 win over the Expos in the first game of a doubleheader at Olympic Stadium. Montreal won the second game 4–3.

SEPTEMBER 17   Darrell Porter hits a grand slam off Steve Rogers in the third inning during a 7–4 win over the Expos on Montreal.

The win gave the Cardinals a 21–14 record and a 3½-game in the NL East second-half pennant race. There were 17 games to go.

SEPTEMBER 19   The Cardinals trade Joe Edelen and Neil Fiala to the Reds for Doug Bair.

SEPTEMBER 23   The Cardinals drop out of first place with a 9–4 loss to the Phillies at Busch Memorial Stadium.

SEPTEMBER 24   The Phillies score 11 runs in the third inning off Lary Sorensen, Bob Shirley, and

Mark Littell to thrash the Cardinals 14–6 at Busch Memorial Stadium. After the game, Pete Rose was issued a summons for disturbing the peace after pounding his bat on top of the dugout to frighten two fans who had been shouting obscenities at him and throwing beer at Phillies players. The altercation occurred in the eighth inning.

Sorensen's parents named him Lary with one r because they liked four-letter names. They named his siblings Gary, Lynn, and Gail. Shirley's high school catcher was Seattle Seahawks wide receiver Steve Largent.

SEPTEMBER 29   The Cardinals beat the Expos 8–4 at Busch Memorial Stadium to retake first place by half a game.

SEPTEMBER 30   The Cardinals' stay in first place lasts only one day after the club loses 8–5 to the Phillies at Philadelphia. Seven St. Louis pitchers combined to walk 13 batters. There were three games left in the season.

OCTOBER 1   The Cardinals are all but eliminated from the postseason with a crushing 8–7 loss to the Pirates in near-freezing temperatures in Pittsburgh. The Cards rallied from a 7–2 deficit to tie the contest in the ninth inning. The Pirates won the game with a run in the bottom of the ninth off Bruce Sutter.

The Cardinals finished the 1981 season with the best record in the NL East with 59 wins, 43 losses, and one tie. The Expos had the next-best mark at 60–48. But the Cards were shut out of the postseason because they failed to win either of the two halves of the strike-torn campaign. The Phillies won the first half, and the Expos won the second.

St. Louis finished one game back of the Phillies in the first half, and one-half game behind the Expos in the second.

OCTOBER 21   The Cardinals trade Bob Sykes to the Yankees for Willie McGee.

The Cards picked up McGee in one of the most one-sided trades in club history. He was an obscure 23-year-old outfielder when the Cardinals acquired him and had yet to play above the Class AA level. The quiet, unassuming McGee started the 1982 season in the minors but was called up during the second week of May after an injury to David Green. McGee made his presence felt by batting .296 in 123 games as a rookie and fit right in with the need for speed and line drive hitting at Busch Memorial Stadium. In 12 seasons with the club from 1982 through 1990 and again from 1996 through 1999, he played 1,549 games and collected 735 runs, 1,615 hits, 248 doubles, 83 triples, and 294 stolen bases and had a .296 batting average. McGee also won three Gold Gloves and the 1985 NL MVP. Sykes never appeared in another game in the majors following the trade.

NOVEMBER 20   In a three-team deal, the Cardinals trade Lary Sorensen and Silvio Martinez to the Indians and receive Lonnie Smith from the Phillies.

The Cardinals gave up almost nothing to acquire Smith, who hit .307 for the 1982 World Champion Cardinals while stealing 68 bases and leading the National League in runs with 120. Smith followed with a .321 average in 1983 before drug problems curtailed his effectiveness.

DECEMBER 10   The Cardinals trade Garry Templeton, Sixto Lezcano, and Luis DeLeon to the Padres for Ozzie Smith, Steve Mura, and Alan Olmstead.

> *The trade wasn't officially completed until February 11, 1982, until Smith's and Templeton's contract problems could be worked out. The deal was a huge gamble for the Cardinals, but it paid off. Templeton looked like a future Hall of Famer in December 1981, but his questionable defense, work ethic, immaturity, and behavioral problems earned him a ticket out of town. Templeton was a starter in San Diego for nine years but never put up the batting numbers there that he had in St. Louis. Arguably the greatest defensive shortstop in baseball history, it was Smith who earned a plaque in Cooperstown. Although weak with the bat early in his career, Smith built himself into a contributor on offense. From 1985 through 1993, Smith hit .281 with a .359 on-base percentage and an average of 36 steals per season. He started in 12 All-Star Games and won 13 Gold Gloves. As a Cardinal, Smith ranks third in games played with 1,990, trailing only Stan Musial and Lou Brock. He is also sixth in hits (1,944), eighth in doubles (338), and third in steals (433).*

1982

Season in a Sentence

Despite hitting the fewest home runs in the major leagues, the club's "Whitey ball" strategy produces a World Championship.

Finish • Won • Lost • Pct • GB

First   92   70   .568   +5.0

National League Championship Series—The Cardinals defeated the Atlanta Braves three games to none

World Series—The Cardinals defeated the Milwaukee Brewers four games to three

Manager

Whitey Herzog

Stats	Cards	NL	Rank
Batting Avg:	.264	.258	2
On-Base Pct:	.337	.322	1
Slugging Pct:	.364	.373	8
Home Runs:	67		12
Stolen Bases:	200		1
ERA:	3.37	3.60	3
Fielding Avg:	.981	.978	1
Runs Scored:	685		5
Runs Allowed:	609		1

Starting Lineup

Darrell Porter, c
Keith Hernandez, 1b
Tom Herr, 2b
Ken Oberkfell, 3b
Ozzie Smith, ss
Lonnie Smith, lf
Willie McGee, cf
George Hendrick, rf
Mike Ramsey, 2b-3b-ss
Dane Iorg, lf
David Green, cf
Gene Tenace, c

Pitchers

Joaquin Andujar, sp
Bob Forsch, sp
Steve Mura, sp
Dave LaPoint, sp-rp
John Stuper, rp
Bruce Sutter, rp
Doug Bair, rp
Jim Kaat, rp

Attendance

2,111,906 (fourth in NL)

Club Leaders

Batting Avg:	L. Smith	.307
On-Base Pct:	Hernandez	.397
Slugging Pct:	Hendrick	.450
Home Runs:	Hendrick	19
RBIs:	Hendrick	104
Runs:	L. Smith	120
Stolen Bases:	L. Smith	68
Wins:	Andujar	15
	Forsch	15
Strikeouts:	Andujar	137
ERA:	Andujar	2.47
Saves:	Sutter	36

APRIL 6   In the season opener, the Cardinals score five runs in the first inning off Nolan Ryan and wallop the Astros 14–3 in Houston. Bob Forsch was the winning pitcher. Darrell Porter hit a three-run homer, and Keith Hernandez clubbed two doubles and a single, scored three runs, and drove in three. A pair of Smiths made their debuts with the Cardinals. Lonnie scored three runs, and Ozzie collected two hits in five at-bats and drove in a pair of runs.

Hernandez hit .299 with seven homers and 94 RBIs in 1982.

APRIL 10   In the home opener, the Cardinals lose 11–7 to the Pirates before 40,878 at Busch Memorial Stadium. In his first game as a Cardinal in St. Louis, Lonnie Smith hit a home run.

On the same day, Joe McDonald replaced Whitey Herzog as general manager.

Herzog had grown weary of the dual role of general manager–field manager and wanted to limit his role to that of guiding the club from the dugout. Herzog liked making trades but hated talking to agents and negotiating contracts. At the time, McDonald was Herzog's top assistant.

APRIL 11 After the first two hitters in the ninth are retired, the Cardinals rally for two runs to beat the Pirates 7–6 at Busch Memorial Stadium. After a walk to Orlando Sanchez, Julio Gonzalez drove in the first run with a triple and scored on a Dane Iorg single.

APRIL 18 Down 5–3, the Cardinals score two runs in the ninth inning and one in the eleventh to beat the Phillies 6–5 at Busch Memorial Stadium. David Green was the hero, driving in the tying run in the ninth inning with a single before delivering another RBI single in the eleventh to end the game. It was the Cardinals' eighth win in a row.

APRIL 24 The Cardinals win their twelfth game in a row with a 7–4 decision over the Phillies in Philadelphia.

APRIL 25 Behind the pitching of Steve Carlton, the Phillies end the Cardinals' 12-game winning streak with an 8–4 win in Philadelphia.

MAY 15 The Cardinals score four runs in the top of the tenth, three on a Lonnie Smith homer, but have to survive a three-run Braves rally in the bottom half to win 7–6 in Atlanta.

MAY 19 Catcher Gene Tenace fails to force the runner at home plate with the bases loaded, enabling the Padres to shade the Cardinals 5–4 in 10 innings in San Diego. With one out, Sixto Lezcano hit a grounder to Cards third baseman Dane Iorg. The throw home beat Alan Wiggins racing in from third, but Tenace, charged with an error, pulled his foot off the bag as the winning run scored.

MAY 29 A bizarre play in which Ozzie Smith singles into a double play highlights a 4–2 loss to the Padres at Busch Memorial Stadium. Joaquin Andujar set the stage by lining a single to center. Smith followed with a single to right. Andujar rounded second but stopped in his tracks when San Diego right fielder Sixto Lezcano's throw came in behind him. After a brief rundown, third baseman Luis Salazar tagged out Andujar, who then jarred the ball from Salazar's glove. Padres shortstop Garry Templeton, uncertain whether Andujar had been retired, swiped at the loose ball and scooped it toward third base. However, no one was covering the bag and Smith charged toward third. Left fielder Alan Wiggins retrieved the ball and threw to Templeton, who tagged out Smith after he rounded the base too far.

MAY 30 The Cardinals win a thrilling 10-inning, 6–5 decision over the Padres at Busch Memorial Stadium. Trailing 3–0, the Cardinals scored three in the ninth to send the game into extra innings. Lonnie Smith doubled in two runs, moved to third on a fielder's choice, and scored on a Tommy Herr sacrifice fly. San Diego scored two in the tenth, but the Cards put together another three-run rally in the bottom half to win 6–5. Smith again played a starring role by driving in the first run with a double and scoring on Mike Ramsey's single. Dane Iorg drove in the winning run with a pinch-single.

MAY 31 The Cardinals score 10 runs in the fourth inning and beat the Giants 11–6 at Busch Memorial Stadium.

JUNE 2

Joaquin Andujar pitches the Cardinals to a 1–0 win over the Giants at Busch Memorial Stadium. The lone run of the game scored in the third on a single by Keith Hernandez.

Andujar was 15–10 with a 2.47 ERA in 1982. The June 2 contest was one of his five shutouts.

JUNE 7

In the first round of the amateur draft, the Cardinals select pitcher Todd Worrell from Biola College.

Only three players drafted and signed by the Cardinals in 1982 reached the majors, but all three were future All-Stars. Worrell reached the majors in 1985 and proved his worth with a starring role in both the pennant race and postseason. Still technically a rookie in 1986, Worrell was the NL Rookie of the Year. The Cardinals also selected Vince Coleman, the 1985 Rookie of the Year, in the 10th round of the 1982 draft. Terry Pendleton was chosen in the 7th round. The team took a fourth All-Star, Rob Dibble, in the 11th round, but Dibble opted for college instead. The Reds drafted and signed Dibble in 1983.

JUNE 29

George Hendrick drives in seven runs, four of them on a grand slam in the eighth inning off Ed Farmer, to lead the Cardinals to a 15–3 drubbing of the Phillies in Philadelphia.

Hendrick hit .282 with 19 homers and 104 RBIs in 1982.

JULY 20

In a strange game at Busch Memorial Stadium, the Cardinals lose 8–6 to the Braves. Atlanta scored five runs in the top of the first inning before the Cards countered with six in their half, then failed to score for the remainder of the game.

AUGUST 2

The Cardinals leave 24 men on base during a 17-inning, 4–2 loss to the Pirates at Busch Memorial Stadium. Tommy Herr collected five hits, including a double, in nine at-bats.

Prior to clinching the pennant, the Cardinals never lost more than three games in a row all season.

AUGUST 22

Third-string catcher Glenn Brummer pulls off a daring, surprise steal of home in the twelfth inning with two outs and two strikes on the hitter to give the Cardinals a 5–4 win over the Giants at Busch Memorial Stadium. Brummer was in the game only because Gene Tenace had been removed for a pinch runner and Darrell Porter had been taken out for a pinch hitter. Brummer singled with one out, moved to second on a single by Willie McGee and to third on a two-out infield hit by Ozzie Smith. With David Green batting and Gary Lavelle pitching, Brummer broke for the plate and slid under the tag by Milt May. Brummer ran on his own on a play that clearly violated all the tenets of conventional baseball, but it worked and became one of the catalysts in the Cardinals' drive to the pennant.

Brummer stole only four bases in 178 career games. His 1982 teammates gave him a home plate with the autographs of all of the members of the team.

SEPTEMBER 1

In his first major league at-bat, Kelly Paris starts the game-winning rally that beats the Dodgers 6–5 in Los Angeles. Paris led off the thirteenth inning with a pinch single, moved to second on a sacrifice, and scored on Ozzie Smith's two-out single.

Paris had only three hits in 29 at-bats as a Cardinal for a .103 average.

SEPTEMBER 4   Lonnie Smith sets a club record by stealing five bases, but the Cardinals lose 5–4 to the Giants in San Francisco when Jack Clark hits a three-run, walk-off homer in the ninth inning off Bruce Sutter.

Despite the loss on September 4, Sutter had a great year in 1982. He was 9–8 with 36 saves and a 2.90 ERA in 70 games and 102$^{1}/_{3}$ innings.

SEPTEMBER 6   A two-out, walk-off, pinch single by George Hendrick in the ninth inning gives the Cardinals a 1–0 victory over the Expos at Busch Memorial Stadium. Joaquin Andujar pitched the shutout.

The Cardinals drew 2,111,906 in 1982, breaking the previous club record of 2,090,145 set in 1967.

SEPTEMBER 8   Bob Forsch pitches the Cardinals to a 1–0 win over the Expos at Busch Memorial Stadium. A triple by Keith Hernandez in the third inning drove in the lone run.

SEPTEMBER 12   The Cardinals lose 4–1 to the Mets on Butch Yatkeman Day at Busch Memorial Stadium.

Yatkeman began working for the Cardinals in 1923 when he was a batboy and had been the equipment manager since 1931 when he was honored in pregame ceremonies. Yatkeman received a car and a diamond-studded watch among an avalanche of gifts in recognition of his six decades of service to the club. He retired at the end of the 1982 season.

SEPTEMBER 13   The Cardinals are pushed out of first place with a 2–0 loss to the Phillies in Philadelphia. Steve Carlton pitched the complete-game shutout.

SEPTEMBER 14   The Cardinals retake first place with a 2–0 triumph over the Phillies at Busch Memorial Stadium. Darrell Porter accounted for both runs by smacking a homer with a man on in the fourth inning. John Stuper (7$^{1}/_{3}$ innings) and Bruce Sutter (1$^{2}/_{3}$ innings) combined on the shutout.

The Cards remained in first place for the rest of the season.

SEPTEMBER 19   The Cardinals take a 4½-game lead in the NL East race with 13 contests left in the schedule by taking a 3–1 decision over the Mets in New York. The win completed a five-game sweep at Shea Stadium that included two twinight doubleheaders. The five wins came in a 46-hour span.

SEPTEMBER 20   The Cardinals extend their winning streak to 8 games and their lead in the NL East to 5½ games with a 4–1 victory over the Phillies at Busch Memorial Stadium.

In a nine-game span from September 12 through September 20, the Cardinals allowed only nine runs in nine games.

SEPTEMBER 27   Willie McGee's three-run, inside-the-park homer in the first inning highlights a 4–2 win over the Expos in Montreal that clinches the Cardinals' first NL East pennant.

OCTOBER 3   On the last day of the season, Julio Gonzalez homers in the fourteenth inning to beat the Cubs 5–4 in Chicago. The homer was the only one Gonzalez hit in 1982 and the last of four that he hit during his major league career.

The Cardinals met the Braves in the National League Championship Series. Managed by Joe Torre, Atlanta won the first 13 games of 1982 and finished the regular season with a record of 89–73. The series was a best-of-five affair.

OCTOBER 6   The NLCS opens with the Braves playing the Cardinals at Busch Memorial Stadium, but rain stops play before the game becomes official. The Braves led 1–0 after 4½ innings. It was the first postponement at Busch Memorial Stadium since August 1976. The teams would not complete the game.

OCTOBER 7   The Cardinals win the first official game of the 1982 NLCS with a 7–0 win over the Braves at Busch Memorial Stadium before a crowd of 53,008. Forsch not only pitched a complete-game, three-hit shutout but also collected two singles and a sacrifice fly. Willie McGee tripled and scored a run in the third inning on a sacrifice fly by Ozzie Smith. McGee should have had an inside-the-park homer but missed third-base coach Chuck Hiller's signal waving him home. The Cards broke the game open with five runs in the sixth.

OCTOBER 8   Game Two, scheduled for Busch Memorial Stadium, is postponed by rain.

OCTOBER 9   The Cardinals rally from a 3–1 deficit with runs in the sixth, eighth, and ninth innings to beat the Braves 4–3 before 53,408 in Game Two at Busch Memorial Stadium. David Green, who entered the game as a left fielder in a double switch in the eighth, opened the ninth with a single. Green moved to second on Tommy Herr's sacrifice fly and scored on a single by Ken Oberkfell. Bruce Sutter contributed two innings of hitless relief and was the winning pitcher.

OCTOBER 10   The Cardinals win the National League pennant with a 6–2 win over the Braves in Atlanta, completing the three-game sweep. Willie McGee homered, tripled, and drove in three runs.

Darrell Porter was the MVP of the NLCS with five hits, three of them doubles, in nine at-bats after batting .231 during the regular season. He would also be the MVP in the World Series. Bruce Sutter retired all 13 batters he faced, topping a pitching staff that allowed only five runs. The win put the Cards in the World Series for the first time since 1968. The opponent was the Milwaukee Brewers, a franchise appearing in the World Series for the first—and to date only—time. In a battle between the country's foremost beer capitals, the 1982 Fall Classic matched a team called the Brewers and owned by a man named Bud (Selig), against a club owned by a brewer who made Bud (August Busch). It was also a clash of styles. Managed by Harvey Kuenn, the Brewers were dubbed "Harvey's Wallbangers," leading the majors in home runs with 218 while stealing 84 bases. The Cardinals, emphasizing speed, defense, and pitching in a game plan known as "Whitey ball," were last in the majors in homers with 67 while swiping 200 bases. The Brewers were 95–67 during the regular season in 1982, then won the ALCS over the Angels. Milwaukee lost the first two games of the series but then won three in a row.

OCTOBER 12   The Brewers rout the Cardinals 10–0 in Game One of the World Series before 53,723 at Busch Memorial Stadium. Mike Caldwell threw a three-hitter, Paul Molitor collected five hits, and Robin Yount picked up four.

The designated hitter was used in all seven games in 1982, marking the first time that the Cardinals participated in a championship game using the rule passed by the American League in 1973. (From 1976 through 1986, the DH was used for every game in even-numbered years. From 1987 to the present, the rule has been employed in games played in American League ballparks.) Whitey Herzog played Gene Tenace, Dane Iorg, Steve Braun, David Green, and Lonnie Smith in the DH role. Iorg collected 9 hits in 17 at-bats for an average of .529.

OCTOBER 13   The Cardinals rally from a three-run deficit to win Game Two 5–4 before 53,723 at Busch Memorial Stadium. The Brewers took a 3–0 lead in the top of the third before the Cardinals woke up and scored twice in the bottom half. Tom Herr doubled in the first run and scored on a single by Ken Oberkfell. After Milwaukee scored in the fifth, Darrell Porter tied the score 4–4 with a two-run double in the sixth. In the eighth, the Cardinals loaded the bases on Lonnie Smith's walk. Most observers believed that Pete Ladd's 3–2 pitch to Smith was an incorrect call by umpire Bill Haller. Another Ladd walk, to pinch hitter Steve Braun, pushed across the winning run.

Of the 25 players on the Cardinals' 1982 World Series roster, only 8 played for the club before Whitey Herzog became manager in June 1980. The eight were Bob Forsch, George Hendrick, Keith Hernandez, Tom Herr, Dane Iorg, Jim Kaat, Ken Oberkfell, and Mike Ramsey. By the time the Cardinals reached the Fall Classic again in 1985, only Forsch and Herr remained.

OCTOBER 15   The Cardinals take a two-games-to-one lead with a 6–2 victory over the Brewers at County Stadium in Milwaukee. Willie McGee was the star. He robbed Paul Molitor of an extra-base hit in the first inning with a catch in deep center field. In the fifth, he broke a scoreless tie by swatting a three-run homer off Pete Vuckovich. McGee hit another homer in the seventh, then took a homer away from Gorman Thomas with a leaping catch in the ninth.

There have been only four World Series matchups between two teams from the Midwest since 1945, and the Cardinals have participated in all four. The others were between the Cardinals and Tigers in 1968, the Cardinals and Royals in 1985, and the Cardinals and Twins in 1987.

OCTOBER 16   The Brewers even the series with a 7–5 win over the Cardinals in Milwaukee. The Cardinals seemed to have the game in hand with a 5–1 lead, but the Brewers scored six runs in the seventh off four pitchers.

OCTOBER 17   In Game Five, the Brewers move within one game of a World Championship with a 6–4 win over the Cardinals in Milwaukee. The Cardinals had 15 hits but stranded 12 runners. Keith Hernandez and George Hendrick each collected three hits and drove in two runs.

The 1982 World Series wasn't a defensive masterpiece, as there were 18 errors by the two clubs, 11 of them committed by the Brewers.

OCTOBER 19   The Cardinals force a seventh game by walloping the Brewers 13–1 before 53,723 at

Busch Memorial Stadium. Rookie John Stuper pitched a complete game in which he threw his final pitch more than five hours after his first one. The contest was delayed by rain for 26 minutes in the fifth inning and 2 hours and 13 minutes in the sixth. Stuper pitched the game only five days after the death of his father. Keith Hernandez drove in four runs on a homer and a single. Darrell Porter also homered. Lonnie Smith was called out attempting to steal home in the third, but television replays seemed to indicate that he was safe.

Prior to every home World Series in 1982, 1985, and 1987, August Busch rode onto the field atop the Budweiser beer wagon, pulled around the stadium by eight Clydesdales. During each game, the wagon emerged from the Cards bullpen with Busch waving a red cowboy hat as organist Ernie Hays played the Budweiser anthem, "Here Comes the King."

OCTOBER 20 The Cardinals claim their first World Championship since 1967 with a 6–3 win over the Brewers in Game Seven, played before 53,723 at Busch Memorial Stadium. The Brewers led 3–1 heading into the bottom of the sixth inning and were 12 outs from winning the series when the Cardinals scored three runs. The Cards loaded the bases, and Keith Hernandez stepped to the plate on his 29th birthday facing Milwaukee reliever Bob McClure. Hernandez and McClure grew up in homes 100 feet from each other in San Francisco and played ball together as kids. Hernandez won the battle over his boyhood chum by driving in two runs on a single to

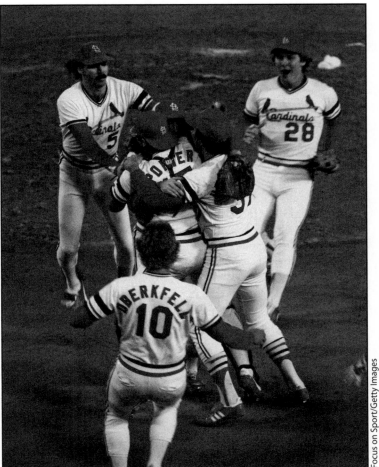

Catcher Darrell Porter embraces reliever Bruce Sutter after Sutter struck out Gorman Thomas to take the World Series over the Brewers in seven games. Keith Hernandez (behind Porter), Tom Herr (#28), Ken Oberkfell (#10), and Mike Ramsey (#5) rush in to celebrate.

Focus on Sport/Getty Images

tie the score, and he crossed the plate with the go-ahead run on a single by George Hendrick. The Cardinals added two insurance runs in the eighth. Pitching in pain,

Joaquin Andujar went seven innings and was the winning pitcher. Five days earlier, Andujar had been removed from Game Three in the seventh inning when he took a line drive off his kneecap. Bruce Sutter nailed down the save by retiring all six batters he faced. He got his last out on a swinging strikeout by Gorman Thomas.

DECEMBER 1   Gene Tenace signs with the Pirates as a free agent.

DECEMBER 14   The Cardinals trade Stan Javier and Bobby Meacham to the Yankees for Marty Mason, Steve Fincher, and Bob Helsom.

1983

Season in a Sentence

A year after winning the World Championship, the pitching staff implodes, and the Cardinals sink to fourth place in the NL East with a losing record.

Finish • Won • Lost • Pct • GB

Fourth   79   83   .488 11.0

Manager

Whitey Herzog

Stats

Stats	Cards	NL	Rank
Batting Avg:	.270	.255	2
On-Base Pct:	.337	.325	2
Slugging Pct:	.384	.376	4
Home Runs:	83		12
Stolen Bases:	207		1
ERA:	3.79	3.83	10
Fielding Avg:	.976	.978	8
Runs Scored:	679		5
Runs Allowed:	710		10 (tie)

Starting Lineup

Darrell Porter, c
George Hendrick, 1b-rf
Tom Herr, 2b
Ken Oberkfell, 3b
Ozzie Smith, ss
Lonnie Smith, lf
Willie McGee, cf
David Green, rf
Andy Van Slyke, lf-3b
Keith Hernandez, 1b
Mike Ramsey, 2b

Pitchers

John Stuper, sp
Dave LaPoint, sp
Bob Forsch, sp
Joaquin Andujar, sp
Neil Allen, sp
Danny Cox, sp
Bruce Sutter, rp
Jeff Lahti, rp
Dave Von Ohlen, rp

Attendance

2,317,914 (third in NL)

Club Leaders

Batting Avg:	L. Smith	.321
On-Base Pct:	L. Smith	.381
Slugging Pct:	Hendrick	.493
Home Runs:	Hendrick	18
RBIs:	Hendrick	97
Runs:	L. Smith	83
Stolen Bases:	L. Smith	43
Wins:	Stuper	12
	LaPoint	12
Strikeouts:	Andujar	125
ERA:	Stuper	3.68
Saves:	Sutter	21

APRIL 5   The Cardinals receive their World Series rings in pregame ceremonies before losing 7–1 to the Pirates in front of an Opening Day crowd of 43,509 at Busch Stadium.

There were many changes at the St. Louis ballpark in 1983, beginning with the name. Busch Memorial Stadium became simply Busch Stadium. New AstroTurf was installed, as well as a new scoreboard complete with video-replay capabilities.

APRIL 13   George Hendrick collects five hits, including two homers, in five at-bats to lead the Cardinals to a 9–1 win over the Pirates in Pittsburgh.

Hendrick hit .318 with 18 homers and 97 RBIs in 1983.

APRIL 14   The Cardinals score seven runs in the first inning that account for all their runs in a 7–1 victory over the Mets at Busch Stadium.

APRIL 29   The game between the Cardinals and Giants at Busch Stadium is suspended at the end of the fourteenth inning because the automatic tarp fails to function after a rain delay. The game was completed the following evening.

APRIL 30   The suspended game of April 29 is finished, with the Cardinals winning 6–5 in 16 innings. San Francisco won the regularly scheduled contest 5–0.

The Cardinals finished April with a 10–6 record and were 26–18 on June 1. The club was in first place as late as July 19 with 46 wins and 44 losses. Despite a record around the .500 mark, the Cards still had a shot at the pennant in mid-September.

MAY 10   Tom Herr hits his first major league home run in the 1,161st at-bat of his career during an 8–4 win over the Giants in San Francisco.

MAY 18   The Cardinals explode for eight runs in the seventh inning and beat the Astros 9–5 at Busch Stadium.

MAY 27   The Cardinals win an 18-inning marathon by a 3–1 score over the Astros in Houston. There were no runs scored by either team from the sixth through the seventeenth. In the eighteenth, Lonnie Smith and Keith Hernandez both doubled to break the tie. A single by Willie McGee provided an insurance run.

JUNE 6   In the first round of the amateur draft, the Cardinals select third baseman Jim Lindeman from Bradley University.

Lindeman played 351 games as a reserve outfielder–first baseman over nine years, four of them with the Cardinals. The only other players the Cards drafted and signed in 1983 were Tom Pagnozzi in the 8th round and John Costello in the 24th.

JUNE 7   Bob Forsch pitches a two-hitter to beat the Phillies 2–1 at Veterans Stadium. George Hendrick accounted for both St. Louis runs with a first-inning homer. The only Philadelphia hits were a homer by Mike Schmidt in the second inning and a single by Bo Diaz in the eighth.

JUNE 11   Lonnie Smith enters a St. Louis treatment center for a drug problem. After rehabilitation at Hyland Center at St. Anthony's Hospital, he returned to the club on July 10.

JUNE 15   The Cardinals trade Keith Hernandez to the Mets for Neil Allen and Rick Ownbey.

There seemed to be little explanation for a trade that sent a former MVP near the top of his game to the Mets for two mediocre pitchers, but it came out later that Herzog and Hernandez had a strained relationship over Hernandez's involvement in drugs, the primary reason for his exit from St. Louis. Also, Herzog loved guys who scrapped and rolled around in the dirt, and Hernadez was never that kind of player. While with the Mets, Hernandez kicked his drug habit and was a regular for five more years, played in three more All-Star Games, and won another World Series. The Cards received next to nothing in the deal. Allen was an average pitcher at best, while Ownbey compiled a 1–6 record as a Cardinal.

JUNE 21   In his debut with the Cardinals, Neil Allen throws eight shutout innings and is the winning pitcher in a 6–0 decision over his former Mets teammates in New York.

JUNE 22   The Cardinals trade Doug Bair to the Phillies for Dave Rucker.

JULY 1   The Cardinals unleash a 22-hit barrage and defeat the Pirates 13–6 in Pittsburgh.

JULY 4   Darrell Porter hits a grand slam off Jim Bibby in the third inning of an 11–4 win over the Pirates in the second game of a doubleheader at Three Rivers Stadium. Pittsburgh won the first game 7–2.

Porter hit .262 with 15 homers in 1983.

JULY 6   Whitey Herzog manages the National League to a 13–3 loss in the All-Star Game, played at Comiskey Park in Chicago.

JULY 14   Trailing 4–3, the Cardinals score three runs in the ninth inning, then survive a Giants rally in the bottom half to win 6–5 in San Francisco. Floyd Rayford broke the 4–4 tie with a two-run pinch-homer.

In 1983, Anheuser-Busch was the primary or partial sponsor of radio or television play-by-play for 23 of the 26 major league clubs. The only ones not associated with Anheuser-Busch were the Brewers, Blue Jays, and Expos.

JULY 27   The Cardinals steal nine bases during a 7–6 win over the Giants in San Francisco. Lonnie Smith led the way with three steals. Ken Oberkfell and Willie McGee each swiped two, and Bill Lyons and David Green had one each.

JULY 28   The Cardinals sweep the Expos 3–2 (10 innings) and 10–1 in Montreal.

AUGUST 6   In his major league debut, Danny Cox starts against the Phillies and pitches 10 shutout innings at Veterans Stadium, allowing seven hits. Cox ended up with a no decision, however, because he was lifted for a pinch hitter in the top of the eleventh with the score 0–0. The Cards lost 1–0 when Bruce Sutter allowed a run in the bottom of the eleventh. Steve Carlton pitched the shutout for Philadelphia.

Cox was born in Northampton, England, where his father was stationed with the US Army.

AUGUST 10   A homer by David Green caps a four-run thirteenth inning, enabling the Cardinals to beat the Cubs 9–5 in Chicago.

AUGUST 18   Andy Van Slyke's walk-off homer beats the Astros 5–4 at Busch Stadium.

AUGUST 25   George Hendrick homers on Steve Bedrosian's first pitch after the Braves reliever enters the game in the ninth inning. The shot gave the Cardinals a 2–1 win at Busch Stadium.

SEPTEMBER 11   Ten days after the Soviets shoot down a Korean passenger plane, resulting in the deaths of 269 people, Willie McGee's RBI single provides the winning run in a 2–1 victory over the Cubs in Chicago.

The win kept the Cardinals in a tight four-team race in the NL East. The Expos were in first, the Phillies in second half a game back, the Cardinals third, 1½ games behind, and the Pirates two games out in fourth place. The Cards lost 9 of their next 10 games, however, and dropped out of the race.

SEPTEMBER 23   Steve Carlton wins the 300th game of his career, leading the Phillies to a 6–2 win over the Cardinals at Busch Stadium.

SEPTEMBER 25   Joaquin Andujar's 16-year-old live-in baby sitter is found dead in Andujar's St. Louis apartment. Her death was attributed to natural causes.

SEPTEMBER 26   Bob Forsch pitches his second career no-hitter, defeating the Expos 3–0 at Busch Stadium. Forsch threw 96 pitches, retired the last 22 batters to face him, walked none, and struck out six. The only two Montreal base runners were Gary Carter, who was hit by a pitch, and Chris Speier, who reached on an error by third baseman Ken Oberkfell. Both occurred in the second inning. Terry Crowley led off the ninth and struck out looking at a 2–2 pitch. Umpires ejected Crowley for arguing the call. Terry Francona followed with a routine fly ball to right fielder David Green. Manny Trillo made the final out on a grounder to Oberkfell. The victory was Forsch's first as a starter in two months. He had been relegated to the bullpen for much of August and September because of his ineffectiveness in a starting role.

Forsch is the only individual to pitch two no-hitters as a Cardinal, and he pitched the only two no-hitters of nine innings or more in the 40-year history of the second Busch Stadium. His threw his first no-hitter on April 16, 1978. Oddly, Forsch pitched the no-hitters in two of the worst seasons of his career: He was 11–17 in 1978 and 10–12 in 1983. He posted a lifetime record of 168–136.

SEPTEMBER 27   The Cardinals pull off an unusual triple play during a 10–4 loss to the Expos at Busch Stadium. With the bases loaded in the fourth inning, Andre Dawson hit a hard shot to second baseman Jeff Doyle, who threw to Ozzie Smith at shortstop for the forceout at second. Smith threw to first baseman Jim Adduci to get Dawson for the second out. Terry Francona, the runner at second, thought Doyle had caught the ball on the fly and that the throw to second for the forceout had doubled him off second. Francona wandered away from the base and was called out by the umpires after he had gone into the dugout.

Doyle played only 13 big-league games, all with the Cardinals. Adduci appeared in only 10 games as a Redbird.

OCTOBER 3   In the final game of the season, Lonnie Smith collects two hits in four at-bats during a 9–6 win over the Cubs at Busch Stadium, but he finishes second to Bill Madlock of the Pirates in the batting race. Madlock sat out the final game to preserve his .323 average.

Despite the losing season, the Cardinals drew 2,317,914 into Busch Stadium in 1983 to set a club attendance record.

1984

Season in a Sentence

The Cardinals are first among the 26 big-league teams in stolen bases and last in the majors in home runs.

Finish · Won · Lost · Pct · GB

Finish	Won	Lost	Pct	GB
Third	84	78	.519	12.5

Manager

Whitey Herzog

Stats

Stats	Cards ·	NL ·	Rank
Batting Avg:	.252	.255	8
On-Base Pct:	.319	.322	6
Slugging Pct:	.351	.369	11
Home Runs:	75		12
Stolen Bases:	220		1
ERA:	3.58	3.59	7
Fielding Avg:	.982	.978	1
Runs Scored:	652		7
Runs Allowed:	645		6

Starting Lineup

Darrell Porter, c
David Green, 1b
Tommy Herr, 2b
Terry Pendleton, 3b
Ozzie Smith, ss
Lonnie Smith, lf
Willie McGee, cf
George Hendrick, rf
Andy Van Slyke, rf-lf-cf
Tito Landrum, lf-rf
Ken Oberkfell, 3b

Pitchers

Joaquin Andujar, sp
Dave LaPoint, sp
Danny Cox, sp
Kurt Kepshire, sp
Bruce Sutter, rp
Jeff Lahti, rp
Neil Allen, rp
Dave Rucker, rp
Ricky Horton, sp-rp

Attendance

2,037,448 (fourth in NL)

Club Leaders

Batting Avg:	McGee	.291
On-Base Pct:	L. Smith	.349
Slugging Pct:	Green	.416
Home Runs:	Green	15
RBIs:	Hendrick	69
Runs:	McGee	82
Stolen Bases:	L. Smith	50
Wins:	Andujar	20
Strikeouts:	Andujar	147
ERA:	Andujar	3.30
Saves:	Sutter	45

FEBRUARY 22   Four months after a bomb rips through a Marine compound in Beirut, killing 241, and four months after the US invasion of Grenada, the Cardinals sign Art Howe, most recently with the Astros, as a free agent.

APRIL 3   The Cardinals open the season with an 11–7 win over the Dodgers in Los Angeles. The Dodgers scored three runs in the first inning, but the Cards came back, scoring six of their runs off Fernando Valenzuela. Darrell Porter collected three hits, including a triple and a homer. Willie McGee had a home run, two singles, and three RBIs. Danny Cox was the winning pitcher with three scoreless innings of relief.

The Cardinals were on pay cable for the first time in 1984. There were 52 games on Sports Time cable in addition to 37 contests on KSDK-TV, formerly KSD-TV. Bob Carpenter was added to the broadcast team. Carpenter has had three stints as a Cardinals broadcaster: 1984, 1995 through 2001, and 2004 to the present.

APRIL 7 — Making his major league debut as a relief pitcher in the sixth inning, Ricky Horton gives up a homer and a double on his first two pitches. Jeffrey Leonard hit the home run, and Chili Davis connected for the double. The Cards lost 11–0 to the Giants in San Francisco.

APRIL 13 — The Cardinals play their home opener on Friday the 13th and win 4–1 over the Pirates before 45,453 at Busch Stadium. Ozzie Smith's three-run homer in the seventh broke a 1–1 tie.

The Cardinals retired uniform number 85 in conjunction with August Busch's 85th birthday in 1984.

APRIL 15 — The Cardinals edge the Pirates 1–0 at Busch Stadium. Bob Forsch (4¹/₃ innings), Dave Rucker (two innings), Jeff Lahti (one inning), and Bruce Sutter (1²/₃ innings) combined on the shutout.

Sutter had a sensational year in 1984, with 45 saves, a 1.54 ERA, and a 5–7 record.

APRIL 22 — David Palmer of the Expos pitches a rain-shortened, five-inning perfect game at Busch Stadium, beating the Cardinals 4–0. The game was stopped by a downpour in the top of the sixth inning after Palmer had retired all 15 batters he had faced.

APRIL 27 — Joaquin Andujar hits a dramatic home run during an 8–2 win over the Expos at Olympic Stadium. In the fifth inning with the score 2–2, Montreal pitcher Steve Rogers brushed Andujar back in retaliation for his throwing a pitch over Bryan Little's head earlier in the game. On the first pitch following the brushback, Andujar hit the ball over the fence.

Andujar was the National League's only 20-game winner in 1984, posting a record of 20–14 and a 3.34 ERA. He also led the NL innings pitched (261¹/₃) and shutouts (4).

MAY 12 — George Hendrick breaks up a no-hit bid by the Reds' Mario Soto by hitting a two-out, two-strike homer in the ninth for the Cardinals' only hit in a contest at Riverfront Stadium. Hendrick's blast also tied the score 1–1, but Cincinnati scored in the bottom of the ninth to win 2–1.

MAY 15 — Joaquin Andujar hits a grand slam off Jeff Dedmon in the eighth inning of a 9–1 win over the Braves at Busch Stadium. Andujar called his shot. After an intentional walk loaded the bases, he pointed to the right-field wall before delivering the homer.

As a hitter, Andujar collected five homers in 607 at-bats during his major league career, but his batting average was just .127, and he struck out 315 times.

MAY 20

A two-run, walk-off homer by Darrell Porter in the ninth inning beats the Reds 3–2 at Busch Stadium. Porter also drove in the first St. Louis run with a double in the seventh that tied the game 1–1.

MAY 27

The Cardinals score seven runs in the first inning, lead 11–6 after three innings, and defeat the Braves 12–9 in Atlanta.

JUNE 3

Dave LaPoint pitches the Cardinals to a 1–0 win over the Mets in New York. It was LaPoint's first career shutout. Ken Oberkfell drove in the lone run of the game with a single in the fourth inning.

JUNE 4

In the first round of the amateur draft, the Cardinals select pitcher Mike Dunne from Bradley University. It was the second year in a row that the Cardinals chose a Bradley alum in the first round. They picked Jim Lindeman in 1983.

> *Dunne was traded to the Pirates before appearing in a game for the Cardinals. He was 13–6 as a rookie in 1987 but ended his career 25–30. Other future major leaguers drafted and signed by the Cardinals in 1984 were Matt Kinzer (2nd round), Scott Arnold (5th round), Lance Johnson (6th round), Greg Mathews (10th round), Craig Wilson (20th round), Jeff Fassero (22nd round), and Mike Fitzgerald (1st round of the secondary phase).*

JUNE 15

The Cardinals trade Ken Oberkfell to the Braves for Mike Jorgensen and Ken Dayley. On the same day, the Cardinals sold Dane Iorg to the Royals.

> *Oberkfell was no longer necessary once Terry Pendleton took over the starting job at third base. Dayley was a valuable reliever for seven seasons in St. Louis and pitched in two World Series.*

JUNE 20

David Green's two-run homer in the ninth inning off Jeff Reardon scores the only runs in a 2–0 win over the Expos in Montreal.

> *Green was considered by many to be the most talented athlete on the Cardinal clubs of the early 1980s, but he never developed into a dependable everyday player. Personal problems were a contributing factor. Green hailed from Nicaragua, which at the time was torn asunder by civil war. With the help of August Busch's contacts in the State Department, Green brought his mother to St. Louis during the summer of 1983, but she didn't like the climate and moved to Florida. Homesick, she returned to Nicaragua and died shortly after returning to her homeland. One of Green's brothers was imprisoned in Nicaragua. In addition, Green was associated with a convicted drug dealer and spent a month in a rehab center for alcoholics during the 1984 season.*

JUNE 23

Willie McGee has a career day by hitting for the cycle and driving in six runs during a game televised nationally by NBC-TV, but he's upstaged by Ryne Sandberg as the Cardinals lose 12–11 to the Cubs in 11 innings at Wrigley Field. The Cards led 9–3 in the sixth but allowed Chicago back in the game. With the score 9–8 and two outs in the ninth, Sandberg homered off Bruce Sutter to send the contest into extra innings. McGee completed the cycle in the tenth with an RBI single, and he scored on David Green's single to give the Redbirds an 11–9 advantage. Sandberg stepped to the plate again and hit a two-run homer off Sutter to tie the tilt again, 11–11. The Cubs won it in the eleventh on a walk-off pinch-single by Dave Owen.

JUNE 29 — Ricky Horton is four outs from a no-hitter before allowing two hits in a 5–0 win over the Padres in San Diego. The first hit off Horton was a double by Kevin McReynolds with two outs in the eighth. The other hit was a single in the ninth by Alan Wiggins.

JULY 1 — The Cardinals trade Mike Ramsey to the Expos for Chris Speier and cash.

JULY 8 — Down 6–2, the Cardinals stun the Dodgers with four runs in the ninth inning and two in the twelfth to win 8–6 in Los Angeles. Andy Van Slyke was the hero of the comeback with a three-run homer in the ninth and an RBI single in the twelfth.

JULY 13 — Chris Speier's three-run homer in the tenth inning lifts the Cardinals to a 7–4 win over the Padres at Busch Stadium. Speier was in the game at shortstop because Ozzie Smith sustained a broken wrist when he was hit by a pitch in the sixth inning.

JULY 17 — The Cardinals lose a 7–2 decision to the Giants at Busch Stadium in a contest highlighted by a confrontation between Joaquin Andujar and San Francisco pitcher Mike Krukow. In the third inning, Krukow threw two inside pitches to Andujar. Plate umpire Art Williams warned Krukow, who argued briefly with the umpire and then yelled at Andujar. The two pitchers charged each other but were quickly separated.

JULY 18 — Darrell Porter hits a two-out, walk-off grand slam off Bob Lacey in the eleventh inning to beat the Giants 8–4 at Busch Stadium.

JULY 30 — Tito Landrum's two-run, walk-off homer in the tenth inning beats the Mets 3–1 at Busch Stadium.

AUGUST 10 — The Cardinals score three runs in the tenth inning, the last two on Willie McGee's homer, to beat the Phillies 3–0 in Philadelphia. Kurt Kepshire (eight innings) and Bruce Sutter (two innings) combined on the shutout.

AUGUST 19 — The Cardinals trade Chris Speier to the Twins for Jay Petitbone.

AUGUST 28 — Darrell Porter breaks a 2–2 tie in the tenth inning with a bases-loaded triple, sparking the Cardinals to a 5–3 win over the Braves in Atlanta.

AUGUST 31 — Lonnie Smith hits a grand slam off Nolan Ryan in the first inning of a 7–5 win over the Astros at Busch Stadium.

SEPTEMBER 4 — The Cardinals bury the Mets 12–2 at Busch Stadium.

SEPTEMBER 5 — The Cardinals shock the Phillies by scoring four runs in the ninth inning to win 6–5 at Busch Stadium. All four runs scored with two outs. Andy Van Slyke tied the game with a two-run pinch-single. Willie McGee drove in the winning run with a one-base hit. It was McGee's fifth hit of the game in five at-bats. He collected four singles and a triple.

SEPTEMBER 16 — After the Pirates take a 7–6 lead in the top of the tenth inning, David Green's two-run single in the bottom half beats the Pirates 8–7 at Busch Stadium.

SEPTEMBER 19 — Danny Cox pitches the Cardinals to a 1–0 win over the Expos at Busch Stadium. The lone run scored in the sixth inning on a sacrifice fly by Terry Pendleton after Ozzie Smith tripled. Joaquin Andujar pitched the shutout.

Pendleton was forced out of the lineup during the last week of the season when his knee swelled up after being bitten by an insect.

SEPTEMBER 28   Joaquin Andujar records his 20th win of the season with a 10-inning, 4–1 decision over the Cubs in Chicago. Andujar allowed only one run and two hits over nine innings. He was lifted for a pinch hitter when the Cards scored three times. Bruce Sutter pitched the tenth for his 45th save of the season. That tied the major league record at the time, set by Dan Quisenberry of the Royals in 1983.

SEPTEMBER 30   On the last day of the season, Bruce Sutter fails in his bid for a then–major league record 46th save. He entered the game in the eighth inning with the Cardinals ahead 1–0 against the Cubs in Chicago, but Sutter allowed two runs in the ninth to lose 2–1.

Sutter's record lasted only until 1986, when Dave Righetti saved 46 games for the Yankees. The 45-save mark has since been surpassed many times, including Lee Smith (47 in 1991) and Jason Isringhausen (47 in 2004) of the Cardinals.

NOVEMBER 4   Fred Kuhlmann is named president and chief executive officer of the Cardinals.

With the appointment, Kuhlmann became the number two man in the Cardinals organization behind August Busch. Kuhlmann took some of the day-to-day responsibilities of running the club away from Busch, who was 85. Kuhlmann had recently retired from an executive position at Anheuser-Busch.

DECEMBER 7   Five weeks after Ronald Reagan wins a second term as president by defeating Walter Mondale, the Braves sign Bruce Sutter to a contract as a free agent.

Sutter saved 45 games in 1984 and wanted a long-term deal that would make him one of the highest-paid players in baseball. The Cardinals made Sutter a lucrative offer, but Braves owner Ted Turner made a better one—six years and $10 million. It was considered to be the richest deal in professional sports up to that time. He was due to turn 32 before Opening Day, however, and was overworked in accumulating those 45 saves, making 71 appearances and pitching 122$\frac{1}{3}$ innings, both career highs. Sutter wasn't able to maintain his brilliance. After signing with the Braves, he pitched only three more seasons and posted a 4.54 ERA.

DECEMBER 12   The Cardinals trade George Hendrick and Steve Barnard to the Pirates for John Tudor and Brian Harper.

Hendrick was 35 when the Cardinals traded him, and he declined rapidly after leaving St. Louis. He was never again an everyday player and hit just .243 over the remaining four seasons of his career. Tudor, on the other hand, was brilliant, posting a record of 62–26 in five seasons as a Cardinal, including 35–9 at Busch Stadium. His .705 winning percentage is the best of any pitcher in club history with at least 60 decisions.

1985

Season in a Sentence

The Cardinals are given little chance of competing for a pennant in preseason forecasts, but they reach the World Series and advance to the brink of a World Championship before losing to the Royals.

Finish • Won • Lost • Pct • GB

First   101   61   .623   +3.0

National League Championship Series—The Cardinals defeat the Los Angeles Dodgers four games to two

World Series—The Cardinals lose to the Kansas City Royals four games to three

Manager

Whitey Herzog

Stats

Stats	Cards	NL	Rank
Batting Avg:	.264	.252	1
On-Base Pct:	.338	.321	1
Slugging Pct:	.379	.374	6
Home Runs:	87		11
Stolen Bases:	314		1
ERA:	3.10	3.59	2
Fielding Avg:	.983	.979	1
Runs Scored:	747		1
Runs Allowed:	572		2

Starting Lineup

Tom Nieto, c
Jack Clark, 1b
Tommy Herr, 2b
Terry Pendleton, 3b
Ozzie Smith, ss
Vince Coleman, lf
Willie McGee, cf
Andy Van Slyke, rf
Darrell Porter, c
Tito Landrum, of

Pitchers

John Tudor, sp
Joaquin Andujar, sp
Danny Cox, sp
Kurt Kepshire, sp
Bob Forsch, sp
Jeff Lahti, rp
Ken Dayley, rp
Bill Campbell, rp
Ricky Horton, rp

Attendance

2,637,563 (third in NL)

Club Leaders

Batting Avg:	McGee	.353
On-Base Pct:	Clark	.393
Slugging Pct:	Clark	.502
Home Runs:	Clark	22
RBIs:	Herr	110
Runs:	McGee	114
Stolen Bases:	Coleman	110
Wins:	Andujar	21
	Tudor	21
Strikeouts:	Tudor	169
ERA:	Tudor	1.93
Saves:	Lahti	19

JANUARY 3   The Cardinals fire general manager Joe McDonald.

The move was unexpected and came as a shock to both McDonald and Whitey Herzog, who brought McDonald from the Mets organization to St. Louis. A replacement was named seven weeks later (see February 25, 1985).

JANUARY 7   Lou Brock is elected to the Hall of Fame on the first ballot.

JANUARY 23   The Cardinals sign Mike LaValliere, most recently with the Phillies, as a free agent.

FEBRUARY 1   The Cardinals trade David Green, Dave LaPoint, Gary Rajsich, and Jose Uribe to the Giants for Jack Clark.

Although the Cardinals had to surrender four players to acquire Clark, who played only three years in St. Louis, the deal had a positive impact on the club. Clark played first base on two World Series teams. In his first season with the Cards, Clark hit .281 with 22 homers.

FEBRUARY 25   The Cardinals hire Dal Maxvill as general manager.

Maxvill was a good-field, no-hit shortstop for the Cardinals from 1962 through 1972. He played on three World Series teams for the Cards and another one with the Athletics. A native of Granite City, Illinois, just across the Mississippi River from St. Louis, Maxvill had served as a coach with the Athletics (1975), Mets (1978), Cardinals (1979–80), and Braves (1982–84) when he was selected to run the Cards front office. Maxvill was the general manager of the Cardinals until 1994.

APRIL 2   The Cardinals trade Argenis Salazar and John Young to the Mets for Jose Oquendo and Mark Davis.

Oquendo became a cult figure in St. Louis and played all nine positions as a Cardinal over nine seasons. He has been a coach for the Cardinals since 1999.

APRIL 6   The Cardinals trade Dave Rucker to the Phillies for Bill Campbell and Ivan DeJesus.

APRIL 9   Gary Carter's homer off Neil Allen in the tenth inning gives the Mets a 6–5 win over the Cardinals in New York in the opening game of the 1985 season. It was Carter's first game as a Met. Jack Clark hit a home run in his first at-bat as a Cardinal. Tom Herr collected two singles and a double. Vice President George Bush threw out the first pitch.

The preseason forecasts gave the Cardinals almost no chance of winning a pennant. Those predictions seemed accurate when the Cards lost their first four games of 1985.

APRIL 15   The Cardinals win the home opener 6–1 against the Expos before a crowd of 42,986 at Busch Stadium. Bob Forsch pitched a complete game, and Ozzie Smith hit a homer.

Smith batted .276 with six homers in 1985.

APRIL 21   Terry Pendleton hits a grand slam off Rod Scurry in the seventh inning of a 6–0 win over the Pirates at Busch Stadium.

MAY 15   The Cardinals score six runs in the first inning and thrash the Padres 14–4 in San Diego.

The Cardinals returned to the traditional gray uniforms on the road in 1985 after wearing light blue in away games from 1976 through 1984.

MAY 17   Trailing 6–5 with two outs and no one on base in the ninth inning, the Cardinals collect five consecutive singles and beat the Astros 8–6 in Houston. The singles were struck by Willie McGee, Tom Herr, Jack Clark, Andy Van Slyke, and Terry Pendleton.

On the same day, the Cardinals traded Lonnie Smith to the Royals for John Morris. Smith appeared to be in an irreversible decline when traded, but he had several more productive years ahead of him. He is the only individual to appear in the World Series for four different franchises, playing for the Phillies in 1980, the Cardinals in 1982, the Royals in 1985, and the Braves in 1991 and 1992. Morris was never anything more than a reserve outfielder.

MAY 20   The Cardinals wallop the Braves 14–0 at Busch Stadium.

MAY 28   The Cardinals score seven runs in the fourth inning and defeat the Braves 9–3 in Atlanta.

MAY 31   Danny Cox retires the first 23 batters he faces in a 5–0 win over the Reds at Busch Stadium. Cox flirted with a perfect game until Dave Concepcion singled with two outs in the eighth. Ron Oester followed with another single in the same inning, and Cox had to settle for a two-hit shutout.

Cox had the best season of his career with an 18–9 record and a 2.88 earned run average.

JUNE 3   In the first round of the amateur draft, the Cardinals select pitcher Joe Magrane from the University of Arizona.

Magrane led the NL in ERA in 1988 and was 18–9 in 1989, but an injured elbow prevented a bright future. He went 25–42 for his career after the 1989 season. Other future major leaguers drafted and signed by the Cardinals in June 1985 were Tim Jones (2nd round), Steve Peters (5th round), Ray Stevens (6th round), and Howard Hilton (22nd round). Alex Cole was picked in the second round of the January draft.

JUNE 7   The Cardinals break a 1–1 tie with six runs in the thirteenth inning and beat the Mets 7–2 at Busch Stadium.

JUNE 8   Tom Herr hits a homer off Tom Gorman in the ninth inning for the lone run in a 1–0 triumph over the Mets in New York. John Tudor pitched the shutout.

Herr hit only eight homers in 1985, but he drove in 110 runs, scored 97, and batted .302.

JUNE 9   Terry Pendleton hits an inside-the-park grand slam off Joe Sambito in the fifth inning of an 8–2 win in the second game of a doubleheader against the Mets at Shea Stadium. The homer was the result of a collision between New York center fielder Terry Blocker and right fielder Danny Heep. The two crashed as Pendleton's drive hit Blocker's glove. Before the Mets outfielders could recover, Pendleton had rounded the bases. The Cards lost the first game 6–1.

JUNE 14   The Cardinals outlast the Cubs 11–10 in Chicago.

JUNE 22   The Cardinals take sole possession of first place with a 10-inning, 2–1 win over the

Cubs at Busch Stadium. Curt Ford drove in the winning run with a pinch-single in his first major league at-bat.

JUNE 23   John Tudor pitches a two-hitter to defeat the Cubs 7–0 at Busch Stadium. The only Chicago hits were singles by Steve Lake in the third inning and Ryne Sandberg in the fourth.

Tudor had an extraordinary season in 1985, his first as a Cardinal. He had a 1–7 record on May 30. A high school friend who had been following Tudor on cable television noticed the Cardinal hurler wasn't freezing his front leg long enough before delivering the ball to the plate, thus causing the leg to arrive well before his arm released the ball. Tudor corrected the problem, and over the remainder of the regular season, he won 20 of 21 decisions to finish the year with a 21–8 record and a 1.93 ERA in 275 innings. Tudor also led the league in shutouts with 10. The only Cardinal pitcher in the modern era with more shutouts was Bob Gibson, who had 13 in 1968. While posting the 20–1 record after May 30, Tudor's ERA was a remarkable 1.37.

JULY 8   Joaquin Andujar runs his record to 15–3 in the Cardinals' 79th game of 1985, a 6–1 victory over the Giants at Busch Stadium.

Andujar refused his invitation to play in the All-Star Game because National League manager Dick Williams of the defending champion Padres selected San Diego's LaMarr Hoyt as the starting pitcher. Andujar finished the season with a 21–12 record and a 3.40 ERA in 269²/₃ innings, but he was horrible down the stretch. After winning his 20th game on August 23, Andujar went 1–5 with a 6.35 ERA.

JULY 21   Steve Braun hits a two-run pinch-homer in the tenth inning to beat the Dodgers 4–2 in Los Angeles.

JULY 25   Trailing 6–0, the Cardinals score one run in the sixth inning, three in the seventh, and five in the ninth to defeat the Padres 9–6 in San Diego.

JULY 30   Willie McGee collects five hits, including a double and a homer, in six at-bats during an 11–3 win over the Cubs in Chicago.

McGee had a career year in 1985, winning the National League MVP Award. He led the NL in batting average (.353), hits (216), and triples (18), in addition to scoring 114 runs, stealing 56 bases, and hitting 10 home runs.

AUGUST 1   The Cardinals steal four bases on one pitch during a 14-inning, 9–8 loss to the Cubs at Wrigley Field. In the third inning, Vince Coleman dived head-first into third base while Willie McGee swiped second. Coleman overslid the bag, however, and after regaining his feet, realized that he couldn't get back to third and headed for home. Third baseman Ron Cey threw to catcher Jody Davis, who ran Coleman back toward third and threw to Cey. Coleman reversed his field, ran past Davis, and, because pitcher Scott Sanderson was covering third instead of home, scored easily. Meanwhile, McGee went to third. Both Coleman and McGee were credited with two stolen bases on the play.

Prior to Coleman's arrival, the major league record for stolen bases by a rookie was 73. Coleman, who ran a 9.4 100-yard dash while at Florida A&M, shattered that mark with 110 steals in 1985 while winning the Rookie of the Year Award. In addition to leading the league in stolen bases, Coleman hit .267 and scored 107 runs. He started the season at the Cardinals' Class AAA affiliate in Louisville but was called up after an injury sidelined Tito Landrum. Coleman was expected to stay on the roster only until Landrum recovered, but he never went back to the minors. In his first game, on April 18, Coleman was 1 for 3 with two stolen bases. In his second game, the following day, he had four hits, including a double and a triple, and drove in the winning run as the Cardinals defeated the Pirates 5–4 at Busch Stadium. His 110 steals in 1985 have been topped in modern times only by Rickey Henderson (130 in 1982) and Lou Brock (118 in 1974). Coleman didn't stop there. He swiped 107 bases in 1986 and 109 in 1987 to record three of the six highest single-season stolen-bases marks since 1900. Coleman is also the only individual in modern times to steal at least 100 bases three years in a row. He led the NL in steals six seasons in a row. Coleman played on the Florida A&M football team as a punter. His cousin Greg Coleman, who also matriculated at the school, was a punter in the NFL for 12 seasons.

AUGUST 6   The Cardinals' game against the Cubs in St. Louis is postponed by a players strike. The August 7 contest between the same two clubs was also called off. The strike ended on August 8, and both games were made up with doubleheaders.

AUGUST 8   John Tudor pitches a one-hitter to defeat the Cubs 8–0 at Busch Stadium. The only Chicago hit was a single by Leon Durham in the fifth inning.

AUGUST 10   Willie McGee collects 7 hits in 10 at-bats in a doubleheader sweep of the Phillies in Philadelphia. In the opener, McGee was 3 for 5 in a 5–4 Cardinal victory. In the second tilt, he went 4 for 5 in a 13–4 win. One of his hits was a three-run homer.

AUGUST 15   Kurt Kepshire retires the first 18 batters he faces before giving up five hits, but he is the winning pitcher in a 3–1 decision over the Pirates in the front end of a doubleheader at Busch Stadium. The Cards also won the nightcap, 4–3 in 12 innings.

AUGUST 20   The Astros clobber the Cardinals 17–2 in Houston.

AUGUST 21   A three-run pinch-homer by Darrell Porter in the ninth inning beats the Astros 7–4 in Houston.

AUGUST 23   Joaquin Andujar wins his 20th game of the season with a 6–2 decision over the Braves in Atlanta.

AUGUST 29   The Cardinals trade Mark Jackson to the Reds for César Cedeño.

Cedeño was a 34-year-old outfielder in his 15th season when the Cardinals acquired him. Once considered baseball's next great superstar, he played in his fourth career All-Star Game when he was 25, but he never appeared in another one. Cedeño played only 28 games as a Cardinal but etched his name in club lore because of his contributions in the 1985 pennant drive. In 76 at-bats, he hit an astonishing .434 with six home runs in one of the best late-season pickups by any club in baseball history. After 1985, Cedeño played in only 37 more big-league games, all of them with the Dodgers, and batted .231 without a single home run.

SEPTEMBER 1   John Tudor pitches a shutout to defeat the Astros 5–0 at Busch Stadium.

SEPTEMBER 5   Danny Cox pitches a two-hitter to defeat the Cubs 6–1 at Wrigley Field. The only Chicago hits were a double by Shawon Dunston in the first inning and a triple by Bob Dernier in the sixth.

SEPTEMBER 6   John Tudor pitches his second consecutive shutout, defeating the Braves 8–0 in Atlanta. César Cedeño hit a pinch-hit grand slam off Gene Garber in the sixth inning.

SEPTEMBER 11   John Tudor needs 10 innings to pitch his third consecutive shutout, beating the Mets 1–0 in New York. César Cedeño provided the lone run of the game with a home run off Jesse Orosco on an 0–2 pitch leading off the tenth.

Tudor pitched 31 consecutive scoreless innings in four starts from September 1 through September 16.

SEPTEMBER 15   César Cedeño collects five hits, including a homer and two doubles, in five at-bats to lead the Cardinals to a 5–1 win over the Cubs in Chicago.

SEPTEMBER 16   The Cardinals take first place with an 8–4 and 3–1 sweep of the Pirates in Pittsburgh.

The Cards remained in first place for the rest of the season but didn't clinch the pennant until the final weekend.

SEPTEMBER 19   Vince Coleman steals his 100th base of the season during a 6–3 loss to the Phillies in Philadelphia.

SEPTEMBER 21   Trailing 5–0, the Cardinals rally to beat the Expos 7–6 at Busch Stadium. A two-run homer by Jack Clark in the seventh inning put the Cards in the lead. On the previous pitch, he re-injured his rib cage trying to check his swing, but Clark fought through the pain to deliver the homer.

SEPTEMBER 22   Down 5–4 with two outs and no one on base in the ninth inning, Willie McGee singles and Tom Herr homers for a 6–5 win over the Expos at Busch Stadium.

SEPTEMBER 26   John Tudor records his 20th win and 10th shutout of 1985 with a 5–0 decision over the Phillies at Busch Stadium. It was also Tudor's 10th consecutive victory.

John Tudor and Joaquin Andujar were the first Cardinal teammates to win at least 20 games in the same season since Mort Cooper and Johnny Beazley accomplished the feat in 1942. No two pitchers have won 20 in the same season in St. Louis since 1985.

SEPTEMBER 27   The Mets lose while the Cardinals are rained out in Montreal. At the end of the day, the Cards led the Mets by 4½ games to nine contests left on the schedule.

SEPTEMBER 28   Vince Coleman steals four bases during a 10-inning, 4–2 win over the Expos in Montreal.

As a team, the Cardinals stole 314 bases in 1985. It was not only a club record, but also the most of any major league team since the New York Giants swiped 319 in 1912. The 1985 Cards clubbed only 87 homers, the second fewest in the majors that year. The blazing speed trumped the lack of power as the Cardinals led the NL in runs scored with 747. The leading base stealers for the Cards in 1985 were Vince Coleman (110), Willie McGee (56), Andy Van Slyke (34), Tom Herr (31), Ozzie Smith (31), Terry Pendleton (17), and Lonnie Smith (12).

OCTOBER 1   In the showdown for the NL East pennant, the Mets cut the Cardinals' lead to two games with an 11-inning, 1–0 win at Busch Stadium. Darryl Strawberry rocketed a homer off Ken Dayley in the eleventh for the lone run of the game. The ball struck the digital clock in the right-field stands. John Tudor pitched 10 shutout innings. Ron Darling (nine innings) and Jesse Orosco (two innings) threw for the Mets.

OCTOBER 2   The Cardinals' lead in the NL East drops to one game with a 5–2 loss to the Mets at Busch Stadium.

OCTOBER 3   The Cardinals salvage the third contest of the series against the Mets with a 4–3 win at Busch Stadium. The victory put the Cards two games ahead of New York with three games left to play.

OCTOBER 5   The Cardinals clinch the pennant with a 7–1 win over the Cubs at Busch Stadium. John Tudor was the winning pitcher, earning his eleventh consecutive victory.

The Cardinals' opponent in the National League Championship Series in 1985 was the Los Angeles Dodgers. Managed by Tommy Lasorda, the Dodgers were 95–67 in 1985 and won the NL West by 5½ games. In 1985 both League Championship Series were settled in a best-of-seven format for the first time. From 1969 through 1984, the LCS was a best-of-five affair.

OCTOBER 9   The Cardinals open the NLCS with a 4–1 loss to the Dodgers in Los Angeles. John Tudor, who won 20 of his last 21 regular-season decisions, was the losing pitcher, surrendering four runs in 5²/₃ innings. Fernando Valenzuela was the winner with relief help from Tom Niedenfuer.

OCTOBER 10   The Dodgers take Game Two of the NLCS by defeating the Cardinals 8–2 in Los Angeles. Joaquin Andujar pitched 4¹/₃ innings and allowed six hits.

Things looked bleak for the Cards following the loss. Not only was the club down two games to none after being outscored 12–3, but the Dodgers had scored 10 runs in 10 innings off the Redbirds' two best starting pitchers.

OCTOBER 12   The Cardinals begin their comeback with a 4–2 win over the Dodgers in Game Three before 53,708 at Busch Stadium. The Cardinals scored two runs in each of the first two innings, two by Vince Coleman. He unnerved the Dodgers by leading off the first with a single and immediately stealing second. Dodger pitcher Bob Welch tried to pick Coleman off second but threw the ball into center field, and Coleman sped all the way home. In the second, Coleman walked and moved to third on an errant pickoff attempt by catcher Mike Scioscia. Tom Herr provided the second run of the second inning with a homer. Danny Cox was the winning pitcher, and Terry Pendleton made two dazzling defensive plays.

Game Three of the NLCS proved to be Coleman's last appearance in the 1985 postseason. In a freak accident, the fastest man in baseball was disabled by Busch Stadium's slow-moving automatic tarpaulin. While performing stretching exercises just prior to Game Four, the tarp, which weighed nearly a ton, rolled over Coleman's left leg up to his thigh. He was trapped for 30 seconds before the grounds crew could roll the tarp back over the leg. Coleman was removed from the field on a stretcher and was diagnosed with a bone chip near his left knee.

OCTOBER 13   The Cardinals even the series by scoring nine runs in the second inning and routing the Dodgers 12–2 before 53,708 at Busch Stadium. Tito Landrum, who replaced Vince Coleman in left field, collected four hits in five at-bats and drove in three runs. Jack Clark collected three hits, and John Tudor was the winning pitcher.

OCTOBER 14   The Cardinals move within one victory of the NL pennant when Ozzie Smith hits a walk-off homer in the ninth inning to defeat the Dodgers 3–2 before 53,708 at Busch Stadium. The Cardinals scored twice in the first inning on a pair of walks and a two-run double by Tom Herr off Fernando Valenzuela. The Dodgers tied the game with two runs in the fourth against Bob Forsch. The game remained knotted until the ninth. Tom Niedenfuer relieved Valenzuela. Niedenfuer retired Willie McGee and faced Smith. The slick-fielding shortstop shocked the nationwide television audience and those at the ballpark by lashing a line drive on a 1–2 pitch down the right-field line for a home run. Smith leaped for joy when he saw the ball hit the cement pillar above the right-field wall and literally danced around the bases. On the radio, Jack Buck immortalized the moment with his most famous call: "Smith corks one into right down the line. It may go! Go crazy, folks! Go crazy! It's a home run, and the Cardinals have won the game by the score of 3–2 on a home run by the Wizard!"

Entering the game, Smith had 13 career homers in 4,225 regular-season at-bats and 50 postseason at-bats. The switch-hitter had never hit a homer from the left side of the plate as a major leaguer in more than 3,000 at-bats. During the 1986 and 1987 seasons, Smith batted 1,114 times without a single homer. His next home run didn't occur until 1988 after a stretch of 1,327 homerless regular-season at-bats. Smith's first regular-season home run batting left-handed was on June 12, 1987, in his 4,612th at-bat from that side of the plate. Over his career, Smith hit five regular-season homers from the left side in 6,287 at-bats. Oddly, Coleman's injury contributed to the epic home run. With Coleman out of the lineup, Smith moved from eighth in the batting order to second, which put him in position to hit the game-winner in Game Five.

OCTOBER 16   Jack Clark provides the heroics with a ninth-inning homer to lift the Cardinals to the NL pennant with a 7–5 over the Dodgers in Los Angeles. The Cards trailed 4–1 heading into the seventh. Willie McGee put St. Louis within a run with a two-run single off Orel Hershiser. Tom Niedenfuer replaced Hershiser, and the first batter he faced was Ozzie Smith, who had touched the Dodger reliever for a homer on the last pitch of Game Five. Smith responded with a triple to score McGee and tie the contest at 4–4. The Dodgers took the lead again in the eighth, however, when Mike Marshall homered off Todd Worrell. Niedenfuer was still on the mound in the ninth. Willie McGee singled and stole second. Ozzie Smith walked, and both he and McGee moved up a base on Tom Herr's ground-out. With first base open, Tommy Lasorda elected to pitch to Clark. On the first pitch from Niedenfuer, Clark hit a 450-foot home run into the left-field bleachers to give the Cards a 7–5 lead. Ken Dayley retired all three batters he faced in the ninth, two on strikeouts, to give the Cards the win.

The Cardinals faced the Kansas City Royals in the World Series in a matchup known as the "I-70 Series" for the interstate highway connecting the two Missouri cities. To add to the intrigue, Whitey Herzog faced the club he had managed from 1975 through 1979. The 1985 Royals were managed by Dick Howser, posted a 91–71 record, and won the AL West by one game over the California Angels. In the ALCS, the Royals trailed the Blue Jays three games to one before winning three in a row to move on to the Fall Classic. The Royals would rally from a 3–1 deficit again in the World Series.

OCTOBER 19   The Cardinals win Game One of the 1985 World Series 3–1 over the Royals in Kansas City. After the Royals took a 1–0 lead in the second inning, the Cardinals scored single runs in the third, sixth, and ninth innings. John Tudor pitched 6$\frac{2}{3}$ innings for the victory. Todd Worrell earned the save with 2$\frac{1}{3}$ innings of relief.

Worrell was thrust into the key role less than two months after making his major league debut on August 27. A native of Arcadia, California, Worrell attended tiny Biola College—the Biblical Institute of Los Angeles—with designs on one day working with young people in the church and had no thoughts on playing professional baseball. After finishing his education, he was drafted by the Cardinals in 1982. He was a struggling starter in the minors until a conversion to relief early in the 1985 season. Worrell was elevated to the big leagues just four days before the August 31 deadline to set the postseason roster, and by the end of the regular season, he had earned a spot as the Cardinals' closer.

Willie McGee was the 1985 MVP and continually came through in the clutch. From 1982 to 1990 with the Cardinals he batted .297 and stole 274 bases. The Cards, opting to go with younger players, traded him to the Athletics in August 1990 for Felix Jose, Stan Boyer, and Daryl Green. He returned for an encore from 1996 to 1999.

Focus on Sport/Focus on Sport/Getty Images

OCTOBER 20   Trailing 2–0, the Cardinals erupt for four runs in the ninth inning and take Game Two 4–2 at Kansas City. Royals pitcher Charlie Leibrandt headed into the ninth working on a two-hit shutout and had retired 13 batters in a row. Willie McGee led off with a double, but Leibrandt quickly retired two batters. Jack Clark singled in a run, and Landrum punched a double down the right-field line with Clark going to third. César Cedeño was walked intentionally to load the bases. Terry Pendleton dropped a soft liner down the left-field line for a three-run double, and the Cards had a two-run lead. Jeff Lahti pitched the ninth for the save.

With two wins at Royals Stadium, the Cardinals' World Championship seemed to be in the bag. Prior to 1985, no team had ever won the first two games on the road, then lost a seven-game postseason series.

OCTOBER 22   The Royals win their first game of the 1985 World Series with a 6–1 decision over the Cardinals before 53,634 at Busch Stadium. Bret Saberhagen pitched a complete game for Kansas City.

Players on both the 1982 and 1985 World Series rosters of the Cardinals were Joaquin Andujar, Steve Braun, Bob Forsch, Tom Herr, Jeff Lahti, Willie McGee, Darrell Porter, and Ozzie Smith. Forsch, Herr, McGee, and Smith also played for the Cardinals in the 1987 Fall Classic.

OCTOBER 23   The Cardinals pull within one game of the World Championship with a 3–0 win over the Royals before 53,634 at Busch Stadium. John Tudor pitched the five-hit shutout. Tito Landrum hit a solo homer in the second inning, and Willie McGee added another one in the third.

OCTOBER 24   With the champagne on ice, the Royals delay the Cardinals' celebration by winning Game Five by a 6–1 score before 53,634 at Busch Stadium. Todd Worrell provided the lone bright spot for St. Louis by striking out all six batters he faced while pitching the sixth and seventh innings. The six consecutive strikeouts tied a World Series record.

OCTOBER 26   Three outs from the World Championship, the Cardinals lose a controversial 2–1 decision to the Royals in Kansas City. The score was 0–0 after seven innings. Danny Cox and Charlie Leibrandt were pitching superbly. The Cards broke through for a run in the eighth. After Terry Pendleton singled and César Cedeño walked, pinch hitter Terry Harper delivered a run-scoring single. The 1–0 margin remained until the ninth. During the 1985 regular season and postseason, the Cards had a 91–0 record when leading after eight innings. With Todd Worrell on the mound, pinch hitter Jorge Orta led off with a bouncer to first baseman Jack Clark. Clark tossed to Worrell, who was covering first. In an inexplicable call, umpire Don Denkinger ruled Orta safe. Television replays showed that not only did Worrell beat Orta to the base, but Orta also stepped on the pitcher's foot.

Frazzled by Denkinger's decision, the Cardinals made one galling mistake after another to blow the game. The next hitter, Steve Balboni, lifted a pop foul that Clark and catcher Darrell Porter let drop untouched in front of the dugout. Balboni singled to left. Jim Sundberg, trying to sacrifice, hit into a force at third. A passed ball with Hal McRae at the plate moved the runners up. Worrell then walked McRae to load the bases. Pinch hitter Dane Iorg, who had played for the Cardinals from 1977 through 1984, arched a blooper into short right, scoring the tying and winning runs.

Sundberg slid around Porter's tag, although Andy Van Slyke's throw to the plate appeared to be there in plenty of time for Porter to make the play.

OCTOBER 27 — Still seething over the Game Six loss, the Cardinals lose Game Seven 11–0 to the Royals in Kansas City. It was over in a hurry, as the Royals scored two runs in the second inning, three in the third, and six in the fifth. John Tudor, making his third start of the series, was relieved in the third. He angrily smashed an electric fan in the dugout and opened a nasty gash in his left hand that required stitches. In the fateful fifth, the Cardinals used five pitchers. Joaquin Andujar and Whitey Herzog were both ejected arguing the ball and strike calls of home plate umpire Don Denkinger, who had blown the call at first the previous evening. Bret Saberhagen pitched the shutout.

The name Don Denkinger is not one to utter in polite company near St. Louis, and many in Cardinal Nation still blame the umpire for the loss in the 1985 World Series. But the Cardinals' anemic offense should shoulder much of the blame. The club scored only 13 runs in the seven games.

OCTOBER 29 — Joaquin Andujar is suspended for the first 10 games of the 1986 season as a result of his Game Seven tantrum, in which he twice bumped Don Denkinger.

DECEMBER 10 — The Cardinals trade Joaquin Andujar to the Athletics for Mike Heath and Tim Conroy.

Andujar had posted a record of 41–26 over the previous two seasons, but his meltdown during the 1985 World Series and links to a convicted Pittsburgh drug dealer led to the trade. Dealing Andujar was a huge gamble, but he won only 17 more big-league games after leaving St. Louis. The two players acquired in the deal contributed next to nothing as Cardinals, however. The club expected Heath to compete for the starting catcher position, but he was an extreme disappointment. He batted .205 in 65 games and flipped off Cardinal fans with an obscene gesture during a game in April 1986. The team dealt Heath to the Tigers the following August.

1986

Season in a Sentence

After scoring the most runs in the National League and winning the pennant in 1985, the Cardinals score the fewest runs in the league in 1986 and finish the season with a losing record.

Finish • Won • Lost • Pct • GB

Third   79   82   .491   28.5

Manager

Whitey Herzog

Stats

Stats	Cards	NL	Rank
Batting Avg:	.236	.253	12
On-Base Pct:	.311	.324	12
Slugging Pct:	.327	.380	12
Home Runs:	58		12
Stolen Bases:	262		1
ERA:	3.37	3.72	4
Fielding Avg:	.981	.978	1
Runs Scored:	601		12
Runs Allowed:	611		3

Starting Lineup

Mike LaValliere, c
Jack Clark, 1b
Tom Herr, 2b
Terry Pendleton, 3b
Ozzie Smith, ss
Vince Coleman, lf
Willie McGee, cf
Andy Van Slyke, rf
Curt Ford, rf-lf
Tito Landrum, rf
Mike Heath, c
Clint Hurdle, 1b

Pitchers

Bob Forsch, sp
John Tudor, sp
Danny Cox, sp
Greg Mathews, sp
Tim Conroy, sp
Tim Worrell, rp
Pat Perry, rp
Ricky Horton, rp

Attendance

2,471,974 (third in NL)

Club Leaders

Batting Avg:	Smith	.280
On-Base Pct:	Smith	.376
Slugging Pct:	Van Slyke	.452
Home Runs:	Van Slyke	13
RBIs:	Van Slyke	61
	Herr	61
Runs:	Coleman	94
Stolen Bases:	Coleman	107
Wins:	Forsch	14
Strikeouts:	Cox	108
ERA:	Cox	2.90
Saves:	Worrell	36

MARCH 30   On Easter Sunday, Danny Cox breaks his ankle jumping down from a three-foot-high seawall on St. Petersburg Beach while on a fishing expedition and suffers a broken ankle. He was on the disabled list until April 29.

APRIL 8   The Cardinals win the season opener 2–1 against the Cubs before 48,672 at Busch Stadium. Andy Van Slyke drove in both runs with a single in the fourth inning. John Tudor pitched a complete game.

> *Ozzie Smith liked to celebrate the beginning of big games such as Opening Day by doing back flips on his way to shortstop, but in 1986 Cardinal management forbade it. Before the opener, Smith ran onto the field alongside his son O. J., who provided the acrobatics by executing a somersault.*

APRIL 9   The Civic Center Corporation, the owner of Busch Stadium and a subsidiary of Anheuser-Busch, announces plans to expand the capacity of the stadium by adding 3,000 seats and 14 luxury boxes. The expansion was an attempt to persuade the football Cardinals to continue using the facility. New seats were installed throughout Busch, increasing the capacity from 50,138 to 53,138 for baseball, and from 51,392 to 54,392 for football. More women's restrooms were also added in response to complaints from fans. Midway through the opening game in 1986, a group of women, tired of waiting in long lines to use the facilities, invaded one of the men's restrooms and booted out the men for the duration of the contest. The football Cardinals moved to Phoenix before the 1988 campaign despite the improvements.

APRIL 11   The Cardinals sign Ray Burris as a free agent following his release by the Brewers.

APRIL 12   John Tudor wins his 18th consecutive regular-season game at Busch Stadium over two seasons with a 6–3 decision over the Expos.

Ken Wilson joined the Cardinals' television team in 1986. He remained with the club until 1990.

APRIL 18   Two days after the United States bombs Libya in response to terrorist attacks, John Tudor wins his 15th consecutive regular-season game with a 4–2 decision over the Expos in Montreal.

Tudor had a regular-season record of 23–1 from June 1, 1985, through April 18, 1986.

APRIL 19   The Cardinals defeat the Expos 9–6 in a 17-inning marathon in Montreal. The Cards scored in the ninth inning to tie the game 4–4 and send it into extra innings. Each team scored in both the thirteenth and fourteenth innings. Reliever Tim Conroy, in his first major league at-bat and in his first game with the Cardinals, walked on a 3–2 pitch from Floyd Youmans to break the 6–6 tie in the seventeenth. Willie McGee added a two-run single.

The Cardinals started the 1986 season with a 7–1 record, then lost seven in a row. By July 10, the defending NL champion Cardinals had a record of 34–49.

MAY 1   Vince Coleman ties a major league record with three sacrifice flies, in the fifth, seventh, and ninth innings of a game against the Padres in San Diego. Oddly, those were the only three St. Louis runs in a 4–3 loss.

Jeff Lahti pitched the final four games of his career in 1986. He went on the disabled list on April 24 with a damaged shoulder. He seemed to be on the road to recovery when he re-injured the shoulder in January 1987 falling down a flight of stairs while carrying boxes.

MAY 8   The Cardinals erupt for 20 hits and pound the Padres 13–3 at Busch Stadium.

The 13 runs output was a rare outburst in 1986. The Cardinals were first in runs scored in the NL in 1985, scoring 747 times. In 1986, the Cards were last in the NL in runs with 601. The club also dropped from first in both batting average and on-base percentage in 1985 to last in 1986. Almost every hitter suffered a decline from the previous season, but none more so than Willie McGee. After winning the MVP Award in 1985 with a .353 average, he batted only .256 in 1986. The Redbirds hit only 58 homers in 1986, the fewest by the franchise in a non-strike year since 1933. The figure of 0.36 homers per game was the lowest of any Cardinal club since 1920. The opposition hit 135 homers off Cardinal pitching in 1986.

MAY 10   In his Cardinals debut, Ray Burris pitches the Cardinals to a 6–3 win over the Giants at Busch Stadium and delivers a three-run double in his first at-bat since 1983.

JUNE 3   In his major league debut, Greg Mathews is one out from a shutout when he gives up a run with two outs in the ninth, but he comes away with a 3–1 win over the Astros in Houston.

              On the same day, the Cardinals selected second baseman Luis Alicea from Florida State University in the first round of the amateur draft. Alicea played the first 5 years of his 13-year major league career with the Cardinals. Other future major leaguers the Cards drafted and signed in 1986 were Todd Zeile (2nd round), Bien Figueroa (3rd round), Larry Carter (10th round), Mike Perez (12th round), and Mark Grater (23nd round).

JUNE 4   Tom Herr provides the lone run of a 1–0 victory over the Cubs with a second-inning homer off Scott Sanderson. Ray Burris (eight innings) and Todd Worrell (one inning) combined on the shutout.

JUNE 7   John Tudor pitches a two-hitter to defeat the Cubs 3–2 at Busch Stadium. The only Chicago hits were a homer by Ryne Sandberg in the fourth inning and Bob Dernier in the fifth.

JUNE 13   The Cardinals need 10 innings to beat the Cubs 1–0 in the first game of a doubleheader at Wrigley Field. The lone run of the game was the result of a triple by Mike LaValliere and an infield out by Terry Pendleton. Greg Mathews (nine innings) and Todd Worrell (one inning) combined on the shutout. Chicago won the second tilt 3–2 in 11 innings.

              Although he pitched in the 1985 World Series, Todd Worrell was still considered a rookie in 1986. According to the rules, a pitcher with fewer than 50 regular-season innings pitched in the majors at the start of a season retained his rookie status. Worrell had pitched 21²/₃ innings in 1985. He won the 1986 Rookie of the Year Award by saving 36 games with a 9–10 record and a 2.08 ERA in 103²/₃ innings over 74 appearances.

JUNE 20   Both leadoff hitters start the first inning with homers in a 9–2 Cardinal win over the Phillies in Philadelphia. Curt Ford homered off Charles Hudson, and Jeff Stone added a home run against Bob Forsch.

JUNE 23   Tom Herr collects five hits, including a double, in five at-bats and drives in both Cardinal runs in an 11-inning, 2–1 victory over the Pirates at Busch Stadium. Herr tied the score with an RBI single in the fifth inning and won the contest with another run-scoring single in the eleventh. The heroics came a few hours after his wife gave birth to the couple's second son, named Jordan Thomas.

JUNE 24   Jack Clark tears a ligament in his right thumb with an ill-advised head first dive into third base during a 5–2 win over the Pirates at Busch Stadium. The injury put Clark out of action for the rest of the season.

JUNE 30   Vince Coleman steals four bases, but the Cardinals lose 7–0 to the Mets at Busch Stadium.

Once it became apparent that the Cardinals had no chance of winning a pennant, Whitey Herzog gave Coleman the green light to run whenever the speedster desired in order to beat Rickey Henderson's single-season stolen-base record of 130, set with the Athletics in 1982. Coleman fell short with 107 steals. If he had been a better hitter, Coleman might have surpassed the Henderson mark. He batted only .232 and had a .304 on-base percentage in 1986.

JULY 8 — The Cardinals edge the Dodgers 1–0 in Los Angeles. Mike LaValliere's single in the seventh inning drove in the lone run. Tim Conroy (six innings) and Ricky Horton (three innings) teamed up on the shutout.

JULY 15 — Whitey Herzog manages the National League to a 3–2 loss in the All-Star Game, played at the Astrodome in Houston.

JULY 17 — The Cardinals trim the Dodgers 12–2 at Busch Stadium.

JULY 19 — On a Saturday afternoon in which the official temperature in St. Louis reaches 102 degrees, the Cardinals beat the Dodgers 2–1 at Busch Stadium.

JULY 22 — The Cardinals break a 2–2 tie with eight runs in the fourth inning and defeat the Giants 10–7 at Busch Stadium.

A brawl occurred with two outs in the top of the seventh when Giants pitcher Frank Williams brushed back Vince Coleman. On the next pitch, Williams hit Coleman in the foot and was ejected. After both benches cleared and came out to home plate, Whitey Herzog and San Francisco skipper Roger Craig argued. The two began bumping, then pushing, each other and set off numerous wrestling matches among players. Tom Herr suffered a cut that required eight stitches to close.

AUGUST 4 — Vince Coleman steals four bases during a 3–2 win over the Phillies at Busch Stadium. The winning run scored in the ninth inning on Terry Pendleton's squeeze bunt, which scored Ozzie Smith from third base.

Smith batted .280 in 1986.

AUGUST 10 — Bob Forsch hits a grand slam off Mike Bielecki in the fifth inning of a 5–4 win over the Pirates at Busch Stadium. Forsch's slam gave the Cards a 5–0 lead, but he allowed four runs before being lifted for a reliever in the eighth inning.

On the same day, the Cardinals traded Mike Heath to the Tigers for Ken Hill and Mike Laga.

AUGUST 15 — A two-run single by John Morris in the tenth inning breaks a 1–1 tie against the Mets in New York. Each team added another run to make the final 4–2.

AUGUST 16 — John Morris is the hero in extra innings again with a run-scoring triple in the eleventh that breaks a 1–1 tie and leads to a 3–1 win over the Mets in New York.

AUGUST 30 — Tim Conroy carries a no-hitter into the eighth inning before allowing two runs and three hits in a 5–2 win over the Reds at Busch Stadium. The first Cincinnati hit was a double by Bo Diaz leading off the eighth.

SEPTEMBER 5   Appearing as a pinch hitter, Fred Manrique hits a home run in his first at-bat as a Cardinal to help St. Louis to an 8–5 win over the Braves in Atlanta.

The homer was the only extra-base hit Manrique collected in 13 games and 17 at-bats as a member of the Cardinals.

SEPTEMBER 15   The Cardinals edge the Mets 1–0 in 13 innings at Busch Stadium. The only run of the game scored on Curt Ford's bases-loaded walk on a 3–2 pitch from Roger McDowell. John Tudor (3 innings), Ken Dayley (7 innings), Pat Perry (1 2/3 innings), and Todd Worrell (1 1/3 innings) combined on the shutout. Tudor left the game with an injury.

During the game, Mike Laga of the Cardinals became the only batter ever to hit a ball out of Busch Stadium during its 40-year history. The ball left the park in foul territory about two-thirds of the way down the first-base line and 130 feet above field level. It landed in a flower bed outside the employee parking lot. The crowd gave Laga a standing ovation before he struck out on the next pitch. It was his only claim to fame as a Cardinal. Laga played three seasons with the club and hit just .154 in 76 games.

1987

Season in a Sentence

The Cardinals rebound from a losing campaign in 1986 to reach the World Series for the third time in six years.

Finish • Won • Lost • Pct • GB

First   95   67   .586   +3.0

National League Championship Series—The Cardinals defeated the San Francisco Giants four games to three

World Series—The Cardinals lost to the Minnesota Twins four games to three

Manager

Whitey Herzog

Stats

Stats	Cards	NL	Rank
Batting Avg:	.263	.261	6
On-Base Pct:	.343	.331	1
Slugging Pct:	.378	.404	9
Home Runs:	94		12
Stolen Bases:	248		1
ERA:	3.91	4.05	5
Fielding Avg:	.982	.979	1
Runs Scored:	798		2
Runs Allowed:	693		4

Starting Lineup

Tony Peña, c
Jack Clark, 1b
Tom Herr, 2b
Terry Pendleton, 3b
Ozzie Smith, ss
Vince Coleman, lf
Willie McGee, cf
Curt Ford, rf
Jose Oquendo, rf-2b-ss
Jim Lindeman, rf
Steve Lake, c

Pitchers

Danny Cox, sp
Greg Mathews, sp
Bob Forsch, sp
Joe Magrane, sp
John Tudor, sp
Todd Worrell, rp
Ricky Horton, rp
Bill Dawley, rp
Ken Dayley, rp
Pat Perry, sp

Attendance

3,072,122 (first in NL)

Club Leaders

Batting Avg:	Smith	.303
On-Base Pct:	Clark	.459
Slugging Pct:	Clark	.597
Home Runs:	Clark	35
RBIs:	Clark	106
Runs:	Coleman	121
Stolen Bases:	Coleman	109
Wins:	Three tied w/	11
Strikeouts:	Mathews	108
ERA:	Magrane	3.54
Saves:	Horton	33

APRIL 1   The Cardinals trade Andy Van Slyke, Mike LaValliere, and Mike Dunne to the Pirates for Tony Peña.

The Cardinals believed that Van Slyke had all of the tools to become an All-Star-caliber player, but by the end of spring training, the club had run out of patience. At the time of the trade, he was 26 years old, had played in 521 big-league games, and had a .259 batting average with 41 homers. Van Slyke fulfilled his promise in Pittsburgh and played in two All-Star games. It was a bad deal all around. Dunne won 13 games for a mediocre Pittsburgh club in 1987, although arm trouble prevented any further success. Peña was a three-year starter in St. Louis and played in a World Series and an All-Star Game in a Cardinals uniform, but LaValliere actually put up better offensive numbers over the remainder of his career than Peña.

In 1987 Ozzie Smith had an outstanding year, posting career bests in batting average (.303), slugging percentage (.383), hits (182), runs (104), RBIs (75), doubles (40), and walks (89), as well as a .987 fielding percentage (tied for his career high). He turned 111 double plays and earned the 8th of his 13 Gold Gloves.

APRIL 7   In the opening game of the season, the Cardinals defeat the Cubs 9–3 in Chicago. Tito Landrum collected three hits in three at-bats. John Tudor was the winning pitcher, with help from Bill Dawley, who pitched four innings of scoreless relief.

The Cardinals went from first in the National League in runs scored in 1985 (747) to last in 1986 (601) to second in 1987 (798). The up-and-down trend continued in 1988 when the Cards scored only 578 runs, good for eleventh in a 12-team league.

APRIL 9   Vince Coleman steals four bases during a 4–2 win over the Cubs in Chicago.

Vince Coleman stole 109 bases, scored 121 runs, and batted .289 in 1987.

APRIL 14   In the home opener, the Cardinals lose 9–4 to the Expos before 48,458 at Busch Stadium.

Tony Peña broke his thumb in his third game as a Cardinal. He was out of action for six weeks.

APRIL 18   Tom Herr hits a walk-off grand slam off Jesse Orosco, climaxing a five-run tenth inning that results in a 12–8 win over the Mets on "Seat Cushion Night" at Busch Stadium. As Herr rounded the bases, thousands of cushions sailed onto the field. The

Mets took an 8–7 lead in the top of the tenth before Tom Pagnozzi drove in the tying run with a single, setting the stage for Herr's game-winning blast. Herr finished the contest with six RBIs.

APRIL 19   On Easter Sunday, John Tudor is injured in a freak accident during a 4–2 win over the Mets at Busch Stadium. Mets catcher Barry Lyons ran into the Cardinal dugout in pursuit of a foul pop and landed on Tudor, breaking a bone below the pitcher's right kneecap. Ironically, Tudor was hurt attempting to protect Lyons. He could have gotten out of the way in time to avoid the collision but saw that Lyons was going headfirst into the bench and tried to block his path. Tudor was out for three and a half months.

MAY 7   The Cardinals break a scoreless tie with eight runs in the fourth inning and go on to win a 17–10 slugfest against the Padres in San Diego. The Cards led 14–0 after 6½ innings before allowing the Padres to score five runs in the seventh and five more in the ninth. Skeeter Barnes hit a homer in his first at-bat in a St. Louis uniform.

The home run was the only hit that Barnes collected as a Cardinal. He had just four at-bats in four games with the club. The home run on May 7 was his only one as a major leaguer between 1984 and 1991.

MAY 17   Tom Pagnozzi hits a grand slam off Guy Hoffman in the fifth inning of a 10–2 win over the Reds at Busch Stadium.

Pagnozzi played his entire 12-year major league career with the Cardinals.

MAY 20   The Cardinals take first place with a 5–4 win over the Braves in Atlanta. Trailing 4–1, the Cards scored a run in the sixth inning, two in the seventh, and one in the ninth.

The Redbirds remained in first place for the rest of the year but didn't clinch the pennant until the last week of the season.

MAY 24   Jack Clark hits a grand slam off Mike Scott in the second inning of an 8–2 win over the Astros in Houston.

Clark led the NL in on-base percentage (.461), slugging percentage (.597), and walks (136) in 1987 in addition to batting .285 with 35 homers and 106 RBIs. He was the only Cardinal to hit 35 or more homers in a season between Stan Musial (35 in 1954) and Mark McGwire (70 in 1998). Clark finished third in the NL MVP voting in 1987. Ozzie Smith was second in the balloting behind Andre Dawson of the Cubs. Smith batted .303 with 104 runs, 40 doubles, 75 RBIs, and 36 stolen bases in addition to his usual sterling defensive play.

JUNE 2   In the first round of the amateur draft, the Cardinals select pitcher Cris Carpenter from the University of Georgia.

Not to be confused with ace Chris Carpenter, who joined the Cardinals in 2004, Cris Carpenter had a 21–15 record with the Cardinals, mostly as a reliever, from 1988 through 1992. Other future major leaguers the Cardinals drafted and signed in 1987 were Jeremy Hernandez (2nd round), Ray Lankford (3rd round), Rod Brewer (5th round), and Tim Sherrill (18th round).

JUNE 5   Greg Mathews ($7^{1}/_{3}$ innings) and Todd Worrell ($1^{2}/_{3}$ innings) combine on a two-hitter to defeat the Cubs 5–1 at Wrigley Field. Jody Davis collected both Chicago hits with a double in the first inning and a single in the fourth.

JUNE 7   The Cardinals outlast the Cubs 13–9 in Chicago.

JUNE 8   Vince Coleman steals four bases during a 12–8 victory over the Phillies in Philadelphia.

JUNE 16   The Cardinals score nine runs in the sixth inning and overpower the Pirates 11–1 at Busch Stadium.

              The Cardinals won the pennant in 1987 using 12 different players in right field, 10 of them as starters. Curt Ford started the most games, 50, at the position.

JUNE 18   Jack Clark cracks a two-run, walk-off homer in the tenth inning, his second home run of the game, to lift the Cardinals to an 8–6 win over the Pirates at Busch Stadium.

JUNE 27   The Cardinals splatter the Expos 15–5 in Montreal.

JULY 7   Jack Clark ties a National League record with six walks during a doubleheader against the Dodgers at Busch Stadium. The Cardinals won both games 5–4, with the second one going 10 innings. In the nightcap, the Cards trailed 4–2 when Steve Lake hit a two-run homer to tie the score 4–4. In the tenth, Clark delivered a walk-off single.

JULY 10   Jack Clark's walk-off homer in the thirteenth inning gives the Cardinals a 7–5 win over the Giants at Busch Stadium. Both teams scored in the twelfth inning. The victory was the ninth in a row for the Cards.

JULY 19   Jack Clark hits a homer in the tenth inning to beat the Padres 5–4 in San Diego. Earlier, Clark had hit a three-run blast to give St. Louis a 3–1 lead.

JULY 23   A 9–6 win over the Dodgers in Los Angeles gives the Cardinals a 9½-game lead in the NL East with a record of 61–32.

              The Cards nearly frittered away the lead by going 34–35 the rest of the way. By September, the club was involved in the three-way tussle for first place with the Mets and the Expos.

JULY 30   The Cardinals trade Dave LaPoint to the White Sox for Bryce Hulstrom.

AUGUST 1   Down 6–4, the Cardinals score two runs in the ninth inning and one in the tenth to beat the Pirates 8–7 at Busch Stadium. Vince Coleman's walk-off single gave the Cards their final run.

AUGUST 7   Jose Oquendo pitches in the eighth inning of a 15–5 loss to the Phillies in Philadelphia and allows three runs. Also during the eighth, Whitey Herzog deployed Ricky Horton in right field, Willie McGee at shortstop, and Tito Landrum at first base. It was the only time that those three individuals played those positions over the course of their big-league careers.

Oquendo played eight different positions in 1987, missing only catcher, and started at every position but pitcher and catcher. In addition to his one contest as a pitcher, he played in 37 games in right field, 32 at second base, 23 at shortstop, 8 at third base, 8 in left field, 3 in center, and 3 at first.

AUGUST 13   The Cardinals tie a major league record for the longest game without a putout by any of the outfielders, losing 4–2 in 13 innings to the Phillies at Busch Stadium.

AUGUST 26   Vince Coleman ends his streak of 1,721 at-bats without a home run during a 5–4 win over the Astros at Busch Stadium. It was Coleman's second career homer. The first was an inside-the-parker in 1985.

AUGUST 30   The Cardinals score three runs in the ninth inning to beat the Braves 4–3 at Busch Stadium. RBI doubles by Terry Pendleton and Willie McGee led to Jose Oquendo's squeeze bunt, which brought across the winning run.

AUGUST 31   The Cardinals trade Pat Perry to the Reds for Scott Terry.

SEPTEMBER 9   The Cardinals' lead in the NL East shrinks to 1½ games after an 8–3 loss to the Expos in Montreal.

Jack Clark tears a tendon in his ankle, an injury with considerable consequences for the Cardinals' playoff hopes (see October 6, 1987).

SEPTEMBER 11   Down 4–1, the Cardinals score three runs in the ninth and two in the tenth to stun the Mets 6–4 in New York. In the ninth, Willie McGee hit a two-strike, two-out, run-scoring single to keep the Cardinals alive, and Terry Pendleton followed with a two-run homer to tie the score 4–4. The win put the Cardinals 2½ games in front of the Mets in the NL East race.

McGee hit .285 with 11 homers and 105 RBIs in 1987.

SEPTEMBER 22   Whitey Herzog uses unusual strategy during a 3–2 win over the Phillies at Busch Stadium. After Todd Worrell gave up a homer in the ninth to Mike Schmidt to reduce the Cardinals' lead to one, Herzog brought Bill Dawley in to pitch and moved Worrell to left field. After Dawley fanned Von Hayes, Worrell moved back to the mound to earn the save.

The Cardinals set a club record by drawing 3,072,122 fans in Busch Stadium in 1987. The only franchise to draw 3 million or more prior to 1987 was the Los Angeles Dodgers. The Mets also drew more than 3 million in 1987 (3,034,129).

SEPTEMBER 29   The Cardinals all but wrap up the NL East title with a doubleheader sweep of the Expos at Busch Stadium. Both wins were shutouts. In the first game, Joe Magrane beat Montreal 1–0. The only run scored on Tom Herr's sacrifice fly in the sixth inning. Greg Mathews (six innings) and Todd Worrell (three innings) combined on the 3–0 victory in the second tilt.

The Cardinals won 95 games in 1987, but no individual pitcher won more than 11. The leading winners on the Cardinals were Bob Forsch (11–7), Danny Cox (11–9), and Greg Mathews (11–11). John Tudor went 10–2.

October 1 — The Cardinals clinch the NL East pennant with an 8–2 win over the Expos at Busch Stadium.

The Cardinals met the San Francisco Giants in the National League Championship Series. Managed by Roger Craig, the Giants reached the postseason for the first time since 1971 with a 90–72 record.

October 6 — The Cardinals open the NLCS with a 5–3 win over the Giants before 55,331 at Busch Stadium. The score was 2–2 when the Cards scored three times in the sixth inning. Terry Pendleton broke the tie with an RBI single. Greg Mathews drove in the other two tallies with another single. He also pitched 7^1/$_3$ innings and allowed three runs, two of them earned. Mathews didn't know he was starting until about three hours before game time, when scheduled starter Danny Cox was sidelined with a stiff neck. Not expecting to pitch, Mathews had played 18 holes of golf earlier in the day.

Jack Clark was another casualty. He was limited to two at-bats in the 1987 postseason because of a tendon tear in his ankle suffered on September 9.

October 7 — The Giants tie the series with a 5–0 win in Game Two, played before 55,331 at Busch Stadium. Dave Dravecky was the winning pitcher with a two-hit complete-game shutout. The only Cardinal hits were singles by Jim Lindeman in the second inning and Tom Herr in the fourth.

October 9 — The Cardinals rally from a four-run deficit to beat the Giants 6–5 at Candlestick Park in San Francisco. After five innings, the Cards were down 4–0 and hadn't scored in 16 consecutive innings. Jim Lindeman, who was playing first base in place of Jack Clark, hit a two-run homer in the sixth. The Cards added four runs in the seventh, one on Lindeman's sacrifice fly, and held off a Giants rally in the ninth. Ozzie Smith collected three hits.

During the 1987 regular season, Lindeman hit .208 with eight homers in 207 at-bats. During the postseason, he was 9 for 28, an average of .321.

October 10 — The Giants even the series again with a 4–2 win in San Francisco. Jeffrey Leonard homered for the Giants. He hit a home run in each of the first four games of the series.

October 11 — The Giants move within one game of reaching the World Series for the first time since 1962 by taking the fifth game of the NLCS with a 6–3 win over the Cardinals in San Francisco. The Cards led 3–2 before the Giants scored four runs in the fourth inning off Bob Forsch.

October 13 — The Cardinals stave off elimination by beating the Giants 1–0 in Game Six before 55,331 at Busch Stadium. John Tudor (7^1/$_3$ innings), Todd Worrell (1 inning), and Ken Dayley (^{2}/$_3$ of an inning) combined on the shutout. Dave Dravecky, who two-hit the Cards in Game Two, was the hard-luck losing pitcher. The lone run of the game scored in the second inning. Tony Peña led off with a triple that Giants right fielder Candy Maldonado lost in the lights. One out later, Jose Oquendo hit a sacrifice fly. Worrell started the ninth with a strikeout against Will Clark, but Whitey Herzog brought in left Ken Dayley to face left-handed batter Harry Spilman and switch-hitter Jose Uribe. Worrell moved to right field in case he was needed for one more batter. He wasn't. Dayley retired Chris Speier, who was batting for Spilman, and Uribe to seal the victory.

OCTOBER 14   The Cardinals move on to the World Series by defeating the Giants 6–0 in Game Seven before 55,331 at Busch Stadium. Danny Cox pitched the complete-game shutout. Jose Oquendo, who entered the game with two career homers in 903 regular-season at-bats, hit a 3–2 pitch from Atlee Hammaker over the wall in the second inning with two runners on base. The Cardinals' pitching staff closed out the NLCS with 22 consecutive scoreless innings.

> *The Cardinals played the Minnesota Twins in the World Series. Managed by Tom Kelly, the Twins won a weak AL West field with an 85–77 record, two games ahead of the Royals. Minnesota was outscored 806–786 during the regular season. Four AL East clubs had better records than the Twins, topped by the Tigers' 98–64 mark. The club reached the World Series by upsetting Detroit in five games in the American League Championship Series. Despite their mediocre record, the Twins were tough at home, posting a 56–25 regular-season record. In the World Series, games one, two, six, and seven were scheduled for the Metrodome. The Twins had yet to win a World Series since their move from Washington, DC, where the club was known as the Senators, at the end of the 1960 season. The only previous World Series in Minnesota was in 1965, which the Twins lost to the Dodgers in seven games. The only prior World Championship for the franchise was in 1924, when the Senators defeated the New York Giants.*

OCTOBER 17   The Twins thrash the Cardinals 10–1 in the opening game of the 1987 World Series, played at the Metrodome in Minneapolis. The Cards scored their lone run in the second inning before the Twins exploded for seven runs in the fourth inning off Joe Magrane and Bob Forsch. Dan Gladden hit a grand slam off Forsch. The big inning ended a streak of 25 consecutive scoreless innings in the postseason by St. Louis pitchers. Frank Viola was the winning pitcher.

> *The game was the first in World Series history to be played indoors.*

OCTOBER 18   The Cardinals fall behind two games to none with an 8–4 loss to the Twins in Minneapolis. The Twins again struck a huge blow in the fourth inning, scoring six runs to take a 7–0 lead.

OCTOBER 20   The Cardinals finally win a game in the 1987 World Series by defeating the Twins 3–1 before 55,347 at Busch Stadium in Game Three. All three runs scored in the seventh inning to erase a 1–0 deficit. Vince Coleman drove in the first two runs with a single, stole second, and scored on an Ozzie Smith single. John Tudor pitcher seven innings for the win, and Todd Worrell went the final two frames for the save.

OCTOBER 21   The Cardinals even the series with a 7–2 win over the Twins before 55,347 at Busch Stadium in Game Four. This time it was the Cardinals' turn for fourth-inning fireworks. They scored six runs. Tom Lawless stunned the crowd by hitting a three-run homer on an 0–1 pitch from Frank Viola to break a 1–1 tie. Doing his best Reggie Jackson impersonation, Lawless stood at the plate to watch his drive sail toward the outfield and flipped his bat into the air when the ball cleared the fence.

> *Lawless was traded even up for Pete Rose in a 1984 deal between the Reds and the Expos. Any comparison to Rose ends there. Lawless had a .207 career average with only two homers and 24 RBIs in 531 at-bats between 1982 and 1990. He played for the Cards between 1985 and 1988. Lawless batted just 25*

times during the 1987 regular season and had only two hits for an .080 batting average and no RBIs. Due to an injury to Terry Pendleton, however, Lawless played three games at third base during the World Series against the Twins in a platoon with Jose Oquendo. Lawless's homer was his only hit in the 1987 Fall Classic. Before that, his last home run had come on April 25, 1984, when he played for the Reds.

OCTOBER 22   The Cardinals move within one game of a World Championship by defeating the Twins 4–2 before 55,347 at Busch Stadium in Game Five. The Cards broke open a scoreless game with three runs in the sixth off Bert Blyleven. Tony Peña collected three hits in the contest.

OCTOBER 24   The Twins force a Game Seven by beating the Cardinals 11–5 in Game Six in Minneapolis. Tom Herr homered in the first inning off Les Straker to give the Cardinals a 1–0 lead. The Cards were still ahead 5–2 heading into the bottom of the fourth and were 18 outs away from sipping champagne. The Twins foiled those plans by scoring four runs in the fifth and four more in the sixth. The sixth-inning runs crossed the plate on Kent Hrbek's grand slam off Ken Dayley.

OCTOBER 25   The Cardinals lose Game Seven 4–2 to the Twins in Minneapolis. Jim Lindeman and Steve Lake stroked RBI singles in the second inning to give the Cards a 2–0 lead. The Twins came back, however, with single runs in the second and fifth innings off Joe Magrane, in the sixth against Danny Cox, and in the eighth off Todd Worrell. Over the last seven innings, only two St. Louis batters reached base. Frank Viola, making his third start in the Series, went eight innings for the win. Jeff Reardon supplied the save by retiring all three batters in the ninth. Willie McGee made the last out on a bouncer to Gary Gaetti at third base.

Despite the 4–3 split in the seven-game series, the games themselves weren't particularly close. None was settled by less than a two-run margin, and the latest tie score in any of the contests was a 1–1 deadlock in the seventh inning of the third game. The home team won all seven games. The Twins were 4–0 in the Metrodome, scoring 33 runs, and 0–3 at Busch Stadium, with just 5 tallies. Counting the postseason, the Twins were 62–25 in Minneapolis and 31–57 elsewhere. The din inside the Metrodome rattled the opposition, including the Cardinals in the World Series, and the off-white ceiling often confused visiting outfielders. Enthusiastic Twins fans' "Homer Hankies" didn't help.

1988

Season in a Sentence

For the second time in three years, the Cardinals follow a World Series appearance with a losing season.

Finish • Won • Lost • Pct • GB

Fifth   76   86   .469 25.0

Manager

Whitey Herzog

Stats

Stats	Cards	NL	Rank
Batting Avg:	.249	.248	4
On-Base Pct:	.312	.313	6
Slugging Pct:	.337	.363	12
Home Runs:	71		12
Stolen Bases:	234		1
ERA:	3.47	3.45	9
Fielding Avg:	.981	.979	1
Runs Scored:	578		11
Runs Allowed:	633		9

Starting Lineup

Tony Peña, c
Bob Horner, 1b
Jose Oquendo, 2b-3b
Terry Pendleton, 3b
Ozzie Smith, ss
Vince Coleman, lf
Willie McGee, cf
Tom Brunansky, rf
Luis Alicea, 2b
Tom Pagnozzi, c
Pedro Guerrero, 1b

Pitchers

Jose DeLeon, sp
Joe Magrane, sp
John Tudor, sp
Danny Cox, sp
Todd Worrell, rp
Ken Dayley, rp
Scott Terry, rp
Steve Peters, rp
Larry McWilliams, rp-sp

Attendance

2,892,799 (third in NL)

Club Leaders

Batting Avg:	McGee	.292
On-Base Pct:	Smith	.350
Slugging Pct:	Brunansky	.428
Home Runs:	Brunansky	22
RBIs:	Brunansky	79
Runs:	Smith	80
Stolen Bases:	Coleman	81
Wins:	DeLeon	13
Strikeouts:	DeLeon	208
ERA:	Magrane	2.18
Saves:	Worrell	32

JANUARY 6   Two months after the end of the six-month Congressional hearings investigating the Iran-Contra scandal, Jack Clark signs with the Yankees as a free agent.

The club's failure to sign Clark was a mistake. He was injured often during his three seasons with the Cardinals, but he was also the club's only home run threat. Clark had four productive years ahead of him, clubbing 106 homers for the Yankees, Padres, and Red Sox from 1988 through 1991.

JANUARY 14   The Cardinals sign Bob Horner as a free agent.

The Cardinals compounded the mistake of letting Jack Clark escape by signing Horner to replace him as the club's first baseman and cleanup hitter. In 1987, Horner played for the Yakult Swallows in Japan. With St. Louis, Horner hit .257 with 3 homers in 206 at-bats.

FEBRUARY 9   The Cardinals send Ricky Horton, Lance Johnson, and cash to the White Sox for Jose DeLeon.

In yet another terrible transaction by the Cardinal front office, the club dealt 24-year-old Lance Johnson, who went on to start in center field for eight seasons with the White Sox and Mets. He was a league leader in hits twice and in triples five seasons. DeLeon had an impressive start with the Cardinals but was wildly inconsistent, posting an overall 43–57 record. He posted a 13–10 record in 1988 and a 16–12 mark in 1989, when he led the NL in strikeouts, but followed with seasons of 7–19, 5–9, and 2–7. From June 25, 1990, until his release from the Cardinals on August 31, 1992, DeLeon had an 8–30 record.

MARCH 14   The National Football League approves the St. Louis franchise's move to Phoenix. The transfer left the baseball Cardinals as the only occupants of Busch Stadium.

APRIL 4   The Cardinals lose the season opener 5–4 to the Reds in 12 innings in Cincinnati. Joe Magrane was the starting pitcher and hit a three-run homer off Mario Soto in the fourth inning to break a 1–1 deadlock. He was the first Cardinal pitcher to homer on Opening Day since Jack Powell in 1901. But Magrane allowed the Reds to tie the score 4–4, in part because he unwisely threw home on a comebacker to nail the runner from third with two outs. Magrane had an easy out at first. Larry McWilliams allowed the game-winning run in the twelfth.

APRIL 8   The Cardinals lose 4–3 to the Pirates in the home opener before 51,647 at Busch Stadium.

The Cards stumbled out of the gate in 1988 with a 3–10 record, rose to 32–26 on June 8, and then slipped again to finish the year with 76 wins and 86 losses.

APRIL 22   The Cardinals trade Tom Herr to the Twins for Tom Brunansky.

Brunansky was another player acquired to fill the Cardinals' power needs after Jack Clark's departure. Brunansky hit 43 homers in 320 games as a Cardinal, but he hit only 11 of those at Busch Stadium.

MAY 1   John Tudor (six innings) and Scott Terry (three innings) combine on a one-hitter to defeat the Dodgers 9–0 at Los Angeles. Tudor was taken out of the game with a no-hitter in progress. He was still recovering from a shoulder injury and was on a 75-pitch limit. At the end of the sixth, Tudor had thrown 68 pitches. The only Dodger hit was Kirk Gibson's single off Terry in the seventh inning.

From June 1, 1985, through June 23, 1988, Tudor had a 47–12 won-lost record and a 2.28 ERA in 608$\frac{1}{3}$ innings.

MAY 7   John Tudor extends his streak of consecutive no-hit innings to 13 in beating the Dodgers 2–1 at Busch Stadium. After throwing six no-hit innings on May 1, Tudor didn't allow any hits over the first seven innings of the May 7 start. Mike Marshall collected the first Los Angeles hit with a single to lead off the eighth inning. Two more hits led to a run, which tied the score 1–1. The Cardinals won the contest in the ninth inning on Tom Brunansky's walk-off single.

MAY 12   The Cardinals take a come-from-behind 13–12 decision from the Giants at Busch Stadium. Trailing 8–3, the Cards scored six runs in the sixth inning. San Francisco added three tallies in the seventh to pull ahead 11–9, but the Redbirds roared back with four runs in their half to take the lead for good.

MAY 14   Jose Oquendo is the losing pitcher as the Cardinals fall 7–5 in a 19-inning marathon to the Braves. Oquendo entered the game in the ninth as a first baseman. After pitching the fifteenth, Cardinal reliever Randy O'Neal had to come out because of a sore shoulder. He was the seventh Cardinal pitcher in the game. The only three hurlers left on the roster were starters and weren't available. Herzog had also used all of his position players. With no appealing options available, he sent Oquendo to the mound. Jose DeLeon, who had pitched 8²/₃ innings the night before, went to the outfield. He played right field against right-handed batters and left field against left-handed batters, switching back and forth with Tom Brunansky. Amazingly, Oquendo shut out the Braves in the sixteenth, seventeenth, and eighteenth innings. In the nineteenth, Ken Griffey Sr. hit a two-out, two-run double to give Atlanta the victory.

The May 12, 1988, contest was the longest National League game ever played in St. Louis, including at Sportsman's Park and Robison Field. The Browns also played a 19-inning game at Sportsman's Park, losing to the Indians 4–3 on July 1, 1952.

MAY 17   The Cardinals score three runs in the eleventh to beat the Cubs 3–0 in Chicago. Luis Alicea's two-out, two-run single took a bad hop and broke the 0–0 tie. John Tudor (nine innings), Scott Terry (one inning), and Todd Worrell (one inning) combined on a three-hit shutout.

Terry began his professional career in 1980 as a 20-year-old outfielder in the Reds organization. He switched to pitching in 1983 and reached the majors in 1986. Terry played six seasons in the big leagues, five of them with the Cardinals, and had a 24–28 record.

MAY 21   A three-run, walk-off homer by Tony Peña in the eleventh inning beats the Astros 7–4 at Busch Stadium.

From his catching position, Peña squatted at the plate with his right leg stretched out in front of him in a stance unlike any catcher's before or since. He could give the pitcher a low target that way and block pitches in the dirt, as his glove was just a foot off the ground at times, but his left leg was so powerful and agile that he could explode out that stance and throw or chase down a bunt. Peña won four Gold Gloves during his career.

MAY 24   Vince Coleman collects five hits, including a double, in five at-bats to lead the Cardinals to an 11-inning, 3–2 win over the Reds at Busch Stadium. The winning run scored on a bases-loaded walk to Jose Oquendo.

MAY 25   Larry McWilliams pitches a two-hitter to beat the Reds 6–0 at Busch Stadium. The only Cincinnati hits were singles by Buddy Bell in the fourth inning and Dave Collins in the sixth.

JUNE 2   The Cardinals squeak past the Phillies 3–2 in 14 innings in Philadelphia. Tom Brunansky, running on the pitch, scored from second base with the winning run when Tony Peña hit an infield chopper. Peña slid safely into first base as Brunansky hustled home.

On the same day, the Cardinals selected pitcher John Ericks from the University of Illinois, pitcher Brad DuVall from Virginia Tech University, and outfielder Brian Jordan from the University of Richmond in the first round of the amateur draft. The Cards had two extra picks due to free agent compensation. DuVall never advanced beyond Class A, Ericks had a brief three-year career in the big leagues, and Jordan played in the majors for well over a decade. The Buffalo Bills also drafted Jordan in the seventh round of the NFL draft in 1989. He never played for the Bills, but he was a defensive back with the Atlanta Falcons from 1989 through 1991. After giving up football to concentrate on a baseball career, he played outfield with the Cardinals for seven seasons beginning in 1992. Other future major leaguers St. Louis signed and drafted in 1988 were Rheal Cormier (sixth round), Mark Clark (ninth round), and Joe Hall (tenth round).

JUNE 3   Tom Brunansky homers in the tenth inning to lift the Cardinals to a 5–4 win over the Phillies in Philadelphia.

JUNE 23   John Tudor pitches a two-hitter to beat the Phillies 2–0 at Busch Stadium. The only Philadelphia hits were singles by Steve Jeltz in the third inning and Bob Dernier in the ninth.

JUNE 27   The Cardinals and the Expos tie a major league record with three extra-inning homers during a 6–3 Montreal win at Busch Stadium. With the score tied 2–2, Tim Wallach of the Expos and Tom Brunansky of the Cards both homered in the thirteenth. Hubie Brooks won the contest with a three-run blast in the fourteenth.

JULY 3   A two-out, two-run homer by Tom Brunansky in the ninth inning rallies the Cardinals to a 5–4 win over the Padres in San Diego.

JULY 4   John Tudor shoves his glove into an ABC-TV cameraman's lens in the Cardinals dugout after being taken out for a reliever during a 5–3 loss to the Dodgers in Los Angeles. Tudor apologized the following day.

JULY 9   The Giants humiliate the Cardinals 21–2 in San Francisco.

JULY 12   Whitey Herzog manages the National League to a 2–1 loss in the All-Star Game, played at Riverfront Stadium in Cincinnati.

             From 1960 through 1988, the National League had a 26–5–1 record in the All-Star Game. (In 1960, 1961, and 1962 baseball held two All-Star Games each season. The second game in 1961 ended in a 1–1 tie.) During the stretch, Whitey Herzog was 0–3 managing the NL squad, losing in 1983, 1986, and 1988.

JULY 14   The Cardinals sign Dan Quisenberry as a free agent following his release by the Royals.

             Quisenberry led the AL in saves five times between 1980 and 1985, but he seemed washed up when he arrived in St. Louis. He gave the Cardinals one good season with a 2.64 ERA in 63 games in 1989.

JULY 19   Chicago Bears coach Mike Ditka takes batting practice with the Cardinals before a 3–2 win over the Dodgers at Busch Stadium.

JULY 22   A two-run, walk-off homer by Jose Oquendo in the eleventh beats the Giants 4–2 in Busch Stadium.

JULY 24   Two bench-clearing brawls break out during the eighth inning of a 5–0 loss to the Giants at Busch Stadium.

The first episode involved the Giants' Will Clark and the Cardinals' Ozzie Smith and Jose Oquendo, who was playing second base. With Clark on first base and one out, Candy Maldonado grounded to Smith, whose throw to Oquendo forced Clark at second. As Clark slid, he hit Oquendo's legs some six to eight feet behind the base. Oquendo in turn kicked Clark and slapped his batting helmet. Clark jumped to his feet and grabbed Oquendo. Smith punched Clark from behind. Third baseman Terry Pendleton, pitcher Scott Terry, and Maldonado joined in the fray, both teams poured out of the dugouts, and fights broke out all over the field. After order was restored, Terry buzzed a pitch near Mark Aldrete's head, and both benches emptied again. No punches were thrown in the second incident, but Smith and Giants catcher Bob Brenly got into a heated argument.

AUGUST 10   John Tudor pitches the Cardinals to a 1–0 win over the Phillies in Philadelphia. Terry Pendleton drove in only run with a single in the first inning.

AUGUST 12   Joe Magrane pitches a one-hitter to beat the Cubs 4–0 at Wrigley Field. The only Chicago hit was Vern Law's second-inning single.

Magrane won the National League ERA title with a figure of 2.18 in 165$\frac{1}{3}$ innings. Despite the low earned run average, his offensive support was pathetic, and Magrane had a 5–9 won-lost record. Three of his five wins were shutouts. The five wins were the fewest ever for an ERA leader in either league. The son of a professor in cancer research at Morehead State University, Magrane pitched for the Cards from 1987 through 1993 and was a favorite of sportswriters because he was always ready with an intelligent, quick-witted quip to help fill space in the papers. He was 18–9 with a 2.91 ERA in 1989, but arm trouble short-circuited a promising career. Magrane missed the entire 1991 season and most of 1992. He pitched his last game before his 30th birthday and finished his stay in the majors with a 57–67 record. After his playing career ended, Magrane took his oddball sense of humor into the broadcasting booth, working for the Angels, Devil Rays, and ESPN.

AUGUST 16   The Cardinals trade John Tudor to the Dodgers for Pedro Guerrero.

After Bob Horner failed to work out following Jack Clark's trip to the Yankees as a free agent, the Cards were in desperate need of a slugging first baseman. Guerrero was 32 years old and had declined from his peak with the Dodgers, but he started for the Cardinals at first base until 1991 and gave the club one great year, 1989, when he batted .311 with 17 homers, 117 RBIs, and a league-leading 42 doubles. Injuries prevented Tudor from being effective in Los Angeles. He returned to the Cardinals as a free agent in 1990.

AUGUST 28   Ken Dayley, one strike from a save, is taken out of the game after the Reds' Chris Sabo hits a long foul ball. The drive prompted Whitey Herzog to bring Todd Worrell in the bullpen. Worrell recorded the third strike on one pitch to close out a 5–3 win in Cincinnati.

The 1988 season was the seventh in a row that the Cardinals stole at least 200 bases. The last team to accomplish the feat prior to the Cards was the Tigers, from 1909 through 1915. St. Louis swiped 200 bases in 1982, 207 in 1983, 220 in 1984, 314 in 1985, 262 in 1986, 248 in 1987, and 234 in 1988. The Redbirds led the NL in the category all seven seasons. In 1989, the club dropped to 155 but recorded 221 in 1990, 202 in 1991, and 206 in 1992.

August 31   The Cardinals trade Bob Forsch to the Astros for Denny Walling.

September 6   Jose DeLeon strikes out 12 batters during a 1–0 win over the Expos at Busch Stadium. Vince Coleman drove in the lone run of the game with a single in the third inning.

DeLeon struck out 208 batters in 225⅓ innings while posting a 13–10 record and a 3.67 ERA. Thanks to his strikeout total, the Cardinals' pitching staff was eighth in strikeouts in 1988. Whitey Herzog tailored not only his offense and defense to fit the ballpark but his pitching staff as well. With a field covered by artificial turf and speedy defenders, Herzog liked pitchers who kept the ball down. Strikeouts were not a priority. From 1980 through 1987, Cardinals pitchers finished last in a 12-team league 6 times and were 11th once and 10th the other year.

September 8   The Cardinals edge the Phillies 1–0 at Busch Stadium. The lone run scored on a bases-loaded walk to Ozzie Smith in the fifth inning. Larry McWilliams (6⅔ innings), Ken Dayley (⅓ of an inning) and Todd Worrell (2 innings) teamed on the shutout.

September 24   Jose Oquendo catches for one inning during a 14–1 loss to the Mets at Busch Stadium. Steve Peters was the pitcher and retired New York in a 1–2–3 inning.

Oquendo became the first National Leaguer to play all nine positions in a season since Gene Paulette of the Cardinals in 1918. He played 69 games at second base, 47 at third base, 17 at shortstop, 16 at first base, 9 in right field, 4 in center field, 2 in left, 1 as a pitcher (see May 14, 1988), and 1 as a catcher. He started at every position except pitcher and catcher.

December 16   Six weeks after George Bush defeats Michael Dukakis in the presidential election, the Cardinals trade Steve Lake and Curt Ford to the Phillies for Mike Thompson.

December 19   The Cardinals sign Bob Tewksbury, most recently with the Cubs, as a free agent.

Tewksbury proved to be an excellent pickup. He posted a 67–46 record in six seasons with the Cardinals.

1989

Season in a Sentence

The Cardinals draw more than three million fans to Busch Stadium and stay in the race until mid-September before sinking to third place.

Finish • Won • Lost • Pct • GB

Third   86   76   .531   7.0

Manager

Whitey Herzog

Stats

Stats	Cards	• NL •	Rank
Batting Avg:	.258	.246	2
On-Base Pct:	.323	.315	1
Slugging Pct:	.363	.365	7
Home Runs:	73		12
Stolen Bases:	155		3
ERA:	3.36	3.50	4
Fielding Avg:	.982	.979	1
Runs Scored:	632		9
Runs Allowed:	608		4

Starting Lineup

Tony Peña, c
Pedro Guerrero, 1b
Jose Oquendo, 2b
Terry Pendleton, 3b
Ozzie Smith, ss
Vince Coleman, lf
Milt Thompson, cf
Tom Brunansky, rf
Willie McGee, cf

Pitchers

Joe Magrane, sp
Jose DeLeon, sp
Ken Hill, sp
Scott Terry, sp
Ted Power, sp-rp
Todd Worrell, rp
Ken Dayley, rp
Frank DiPino, rp
Dan Quisenberry, rp
John Costello, rp

Attendance

3,080,980 (first in NL)

Club Leaders

Batting Avg:	Guerrero	.311
On-Base Pct:	Guerrero	.391
Slugging Pct:	Guerrero	.477
Home Runs:	Brunansky	20
RBIs:	Guerrero	117
Runs:	Pendleton	83
Stolen Bases:	Coleman	65
Wins:	Magrane	18
Strikeouts:	DeLeon	201
ERA:	Magrane	2.91
Saves:	Worrell	20

FEBRUARY 28   Red Schoendienst is elected to the Hall of Fame by the Veterans Committee.

APRIL 3   Ten days after the Exxon Valdez spills oil into Alaska's Price William Sound, the Cardinals lose the season opener 8–4 to the Mets in New York. Pedro Guerrero drove in all four St. Louis runs, three on a third-inning homer off Dwight Gooden to give the Cards a 3–2 lead. Joe Magrane couldn't hold the advantage, however, and allowed seven runs in $3^2/_3$ innings.

APRIL 9   The Cardinals rout the Phillies 15–3 in Philadelphia.

APRIL 14   In the home opener, the Cardinals lose 9–4 to the Mets before 51,257 at Busch Stadium. New York scored seven runs in the fifth inning off Joe Magrane to break a 1–1 tie. John Morris homered for the Cards.

The next day, Magrane went on the 15-day disabled list with colitis. He returned on May 1 and finished the season with an 18–9 record and a 2.91 ERA.

APRIL 21   Jose DeLeon pitches a two-hitter to defeat the Expos 1–0 at Busch Stadium. The only Montreal hits were singles by Otis Nixon in the first inning and Mark Aldrete in the ninth. The lone run of the game scored on John Morris's walk-off pinch-single in the ninth.

APRIL 29   Jose Oquendo's walk-off single with two outs in the eleventh beats the Dodgers 1–0 at Busch Stadium. Ken Hill (8 innings), Ken Dayley ($^1/_3$ of an inning), Todd Worrell ($1^2/_3$ innings), and Cris Carpenter (1 inning) teamed on the shutout.

Given a chance to play every day at one position instead of as a roving utility man, Oquendo appeared in 158 games as a second baseman and batted .291. He also led all NL second basemen in fielding percentage, putouts, assists, and double plays. Double play partner Ozzie Smith batted .273.

MAY 4   The Cardinals collect 21 hits and rout the Dodgers 12–0 in Los Angeles.

MAY 10   Joe Magrane ($8^2/_3$ innings) and Todd Worrell ($^1/_3$ of an inning) combine on a two-hitter to defeat the Padres 3–1 at Busch Stadium. The only San Diego hits were a double by Carmelo Martinez in the seventh inning and a single by Jack Clark in the ninth, both off Magrane.

MAY 11   The Cardinals take sole possession of first place with a 6–5 win over the Padres at Busch Stadium.

The win gave the Cards a 19–13 record, but the club lost its next 5 games and 15 of its next 20. The Cardinals failed to regain first place but contended for the NL East pennant until mid-September.

MAY 20   The Cardinals outlast the Braves 1–0 in 13 innings in Atlanta. Ozzie Smith tripled and scored the only run of the game on Terry Pendleton's two-out single. Scott Terry (six innings), Matt Kinzer (one inning), Cris Carpenter (three innings), Ken Dayley (two innings), and Dan Quisenberry (one inning) combined on the shutout.

The 1989 Cardinals had three players who punted on college football teams. The three were Vince Coleman (Florida A&M), Matt Kinzer (Purdue), and Cris Carpenter (Georgia).

MAY 21   The Cardinals explode for five runs in the tenth inning to defeat the Braves 6–1 in Atlanta.

MAY 29   After holding the Astros hitless until Terry Puhl singles with one out in the seventh inning, Ken Hill gives up three more hits and three runs and loses 3–2 at Busch Stadium.

JUNE 4   The Cubs beat the Cardinals 11–3 at Busch Stadium in a contest marred by a bench-clearing brawl. Mark Grace of the Cubs charged the mound when Frank DiPino brushed him back in the fifth inning. Grace missed the next two weeks with a shoulder injury from the brawl.

JUNE 5   In the first round of the amateur draft, the Cardinals select outfielder Paul Coleman from Frankston High School in Frankston, Texas.

Coleman was the sixth overall pick in the draft but was a bust and never advanced past Class AA. With the seventh choice in the draft, the White Sox picked Frank Thomas. Those the Cardinals drafted and signed in 1989 who reached the majors were Mike Milchin (2nd round), Tripp Cromer (3rd round), Bill Hurst (20th round), Steve Dixon (31st round), and Frank Cimorelli (37th round), but none of them became big-league regulars.

JUNE 8	The Cardinals break a 2–2 tie with five runs in the ninth inning to defeat the Expos 7–2 in Montreal.
JUNE 9	The Cardinals defeat the Cubs 1–0 in Chicago. Pedro Guerrero drove in the lone run of the game with a double in the first inning. Jose DeLeon (8 innings) Ken Dayley ($1/3$ of an inning), and Todd Worrell ($2/3$ of an inning) teamed on the shutout.
JUNE 11	The Cardinals score eight runs in the seventh inning and defeat the Cubs 10–7 in Chicago. Ozzie Smith collected five hits, including two doubles, in five at-bats.
JUNE 14	The Cardinals win 10–0 over the Expos at Busch Stadium.
JUNE 24	Vince Coleman steals his 39th and 40th consecutive bases during a 5–2 loss to the Pirates in Pittsburgh to break Dave Lopes's major league record of 38, which he set with the Dodgers in 1975. Coleman's streak began on September 18, 1988 (see July 26, 1989).
JULY 6	The Cardinals drub the Dodgers 14–2 at Busch Stadium.
JULY 15	A two-run double by Pedro Guerrero in the eighth inning off Fernando Valenzuela accounts for the only runs in a 2–0 win over the Dodgers in Los Angeles. Joe Magrane pitched the shutout.
JULY 25	Jose Oquendo runs his hitting streak to 23 games during a 4–2 loss to the Cubs at Busch Stadium. Vince Coleman was called out for a base-running blunder in the fourth inning: He cut across the diamond to return to second base after he had gone too far around third on a fly ball.
JULY 26	Vince Coleman drives in both runs, and Terry Pendleton scores twice in a 2–0 victory over the Cubs at Busch Stadium. Coleman also stole three bases to extend his major league record of consecutive stolen bases to 50, dating back to September 18, 1988. He swiped bases on his last 6 attempts in 1988 and the first 44 of 1989. Jose DeLeon (8 innings), Ken Dayley ($1/3$ of an inning), and Todd Worrell ($2/3$ of an inning) combined on the shutout (see July 28, 1989).
JULY 28	Vince Coleman's record of 50 consecutive successful attempted steals ends during a 2–0 win over the Expos in Montreal. Montreal catcher Nelson Santovenia threw out Coleman in the fourth inning.
JULY 29	Vince Coleman is called out for interference twice while running the bases during a 2–0 loss to the Expos at Olympic Stadium. In the third inning, while at first base, Coleman was tagged on a pick-off attempt by Andrea Galarraga, but the Montreal first baseman dropped the ball. Coleman swatted at the ball and took off for second. It didn't work. Umpire Eric Gregg called Coleman out for interference. In the eighth, he tried to break up a double play by grabbing the Expos' Damaso Garcia's shirt to prevent a relay throw to first. Umpire John Kibler caught it and called Coleman out.
AUGUST 6	The Cardinals rally for four runs in the tenth inning to stun the Phillies 5–4 at Busch Stadium. The Cards scored in the ninth on Terry Pendleton's homer to tie the score 1–1 and send the game into extra innings. Philadelphia scored three runs in the top of the tenth. With one out in the bottom half, Vince Coleman singled, Ozzie Smith

walked, and Pedro Guerrero, Tom Brunansky, and Jose Oquendo followed with RBI singles to tie the score. With the bases loaded and two outs, Whitey Herzog had Joe Magrane pinch hit for Todd Worrell because there was no one left on the bench. Magrane drew a walk from Jeff Parrett to drive in the winning run. Worrell was the winning pitcher despite giving up three runs in one inning of work.

AUGUST 16   A run-scoring single by Cardinal shortstop Tim Jones caps a three-run, eighth-inning rally that defeats the Braves 3–2 at Busch Stadium. Later in the inning, Jones was thrown out at the plate on a hard tag by Atlanta catcher John Russell. Jones and Russell engaged in a brief shoving match, and both benches emptied.

AUGUST 22   Ted Power holds the Braves hitless for the first 7⅓ innings, and the Cardinals close out a 10–5 win at Atlanta. The first hit off Power was a single by John Russell with one out in the eighth. Before getting the third out of the inning, Power gave up two more hits, both of them homers, and five runs. Power was lifted for a reliever but was the winning pitcher.

The Cardinals led the National League in fielding percentage six consecutive seasons from 1984 through 1989 to tie a major league record. The only other club to lead a league in fielding six years in a row was the Red Sox from 1916 through 1921.

AUGUST 30   The Cardinals suffer a crushing 2–0 loss to the Reds in 13 innings at Busch Stadium. Jose DeLeon was the starting pitcher for the Cards and went 11 innings. He allowed just one base runner and faced the minimum 33 batters. Luis Quinones got the only Cincinnati hit off DeLeon, a single in the fourth inning, but was erased on a double play. DeLeon retired the last 22 batters he faced. Todd Worrell relieved DeLeon and allowed the two thirteenth-inning runs. The Cardinals set a major league record (since tied) for the most men left on base in a shutout—16.

DeLeon was 16–12 with a 3.05 ERA in 1989. He led the NL in strikeouts with 201.

SEPTEMBER 2   The Cardinals thrash the Astros 13–5 at Busch Stadium.

SEPTEMBER 8   Down 7–1, the Cardinals score one run in the fifth inning, four in the seventh, and five in the eighth and beat the Cubs 11–8 in Chicago. Pedro Guerrero hit a three-run homer to break the 8–8 tie.

The win put the Cardinals half a game behind the Cubs in the NL East pennant race.

SEPTEMBER 9   With a chance to take first place, the Cardinals lose 3–2 in 10 innings to the Cubs in Chicago.

SEPTEMBER 10   Four Cubs pitchers combine to strike out 18 Cardinals during a 4–1 Chicago win at Wrigley Field.

The loss left the Cardinals 2½ games back of the first-place Cubs. The September 10 defeat was the second in a seven-game losing streak that dropped the club out of the race.

SEPTEMBER 14 · A "crowd" of 1,519, the smallest in the 40-year history of Busch Stadium, watches the Cardinals lose 4–3 to the Pirates. The game was making up a contest halted the previous evening with the score 0–0 after five innings. The rescheduling wasn't announced until after midnight for a game played in the early afternoon on an open date. During the contest, smoke curled into the ballpark from a fire at the nearby Cupples Station warehouse. "It was like a graveyard with lights," Whitey Herzog quipped. The previous low was 3,380 against the Mets on September 27, 1972.

Despite the low attendance figure on September 14, the Cardinals set a club record in 1989 by drawing 3,080,980, breaking the old mark of 3,072,122 set in 1987. The 1989 record stood until the Cards attracted 3,194,092 in 1998, the year of the McGwire-Sosa home run race.

SEPTEMBER 29 · Cardinals owner August Busch dies at the age of 90 at his home at Grant's Farm in suburban St. Louis.

August Busch left a legacy in St. Louis, not only in baseball, but in industry and the city's cultural institutions. Busch was a philanthropist, civic leader, and breeder of the world-famous Clydesdale horses. His Cardinals won six NL pennants and three World Championships during his 37 seasons as owner of the club. Busch also took over a small, ailing brewery in 1946 following the death of his father and turned it into the world's largest. Under his direction, the brewery grew from producing 3 million barrels of beer annually to 78.5 million, nearly twice that of the nearest competitor, at the time of his death.

The loss left a void at the top of the Cardinals organization. Busch's son, August Busch III, took over as the Cards' chairman of the board, but he had little interest in running a baseball team and devoted the vast majority of his time to the brewery. Those assigned to oversee the Cardinals operation from 1989 through 1995, when the brewery sold the club, were corporate suits like Fred Kuhlmann, Stuart Meyer, and Mark Lamping. The early 1990s were marked by the departure of free agents and a lack of bold and creative moves necessary to build a contending team.

NOVEMBER 27 · Six weeks after an earthquake strikes San Francisco during the World Series, Tony Peña signs with the Red Sox as a free agent.

Peña had four more seasons ahead of him as a starter, but the Cardinals were in a youth movement and had Todd Zeile and Tom Pagnozzi in the pipeline ready to take over as catchers.

NOVEMBER 28 · The Cardinals sign Bryn Smith, most recently with the Expos, as a free agent.

DECEMBER 14 · The Cardinals sign John Tudor as a free agent after his stint with the Dodgers.

Tudor pitched only 14$\frac{1}{3}$ innings in 1989 because of elbow, shoulder, and knee injuries, each of which required surgery. He was 12–4 with a 2.40 ERA for the Cardinals in 1990 but retired at the end of the season, at age 36, because the accumulating injuries had robbed him of his fastball and he wanted to leave the game as a success.

THE STATE OF THE CARDINALS

The Cardinals never developed much consistency during the 1990s and generally ran in the middle of the pack in the National League. No club lost more than 92 games nor won more than 88. The Cardinals won the NL Central in 1996 and advanced to the NLCS against the Braves. Overall, the Cards were 758–794, the first time that the club had more losses than wins over the course of a decade since the 1910s. The winning percentage of .488 ranked eighth in the National League. NL champions were the Reds (1990), Braves (1991, 1992, 1995, 1996, and 1999), Phillies (1993), Marlins (1997), and Padres (1998). During the Cards' last four seasons in the NL East, the champions were the Pirates (1990, 1991, and 1992) and Phillies (1993). After moving to the Central Division, the leaders aside from St. Louis were the Reds (1995) and Astros (1997, 1998, and 1999). There were no champions in 1994 because of the players' strike.

THE BEST TEAM

In their first season under Tony La Russa, the Cardinals won the NL Central in 1996 and posted an 88–74 record. After sweeping the Padres in the Division Series, the Cards lost the NLCS in seven games to the Braves.

THE WORST TEAM

The 1990 Cardinals were 70–92 and finished in last place. The awful year led to Whitey Herzog's departure.

THE BEST MOMENT

The best moment of the 1990s was Mark McGwire's embracing the Maris family after he hit his 62nd home run of the 1998 season on September 8.

THE WORST MOMENT

The Cardinals appeared to be headed for the World Series after taking a three-games-to-one lead in the 1996 NLCS against the Braves, but they lost games five, six, and seven by a combined score of 32–1.

THE ALL-DECADE TEAM • YEARS W/CARDS

Tom Pagnozzi, c	1987–98
Mark McGwire, 1b	1997–2001
Jose Oquendo, 2b	1986–95
Todd Zeile, 3b	1989–95
Ozzie Smith, ss	1982–96
Bernard Gilkey, lf	1990–95
Ray Lankford, cf	1990–2001, 2004
Brian Jordan, rf	1992–98
Bob Tewksbury, p	1989–94
Lee Smith, p	1990–93
Donovan Osborne, p	1992–93, 1995–99
Andy Benes, p	1996–97, 2000–02

Ozzie Smith is the only player to make the Cardinals' All-Decade Team in both the 1980s and 1990s and also is the only Hall of Famer. McGwire is likely to be elected to the Hall of Fame in 2007, his first year of eligibility. Lee Smith also has a shot at the Hall of Fame before his eligibility expires in 2017. The pitchers listed on the 1990s All-Decade Team reflects the Cardinals inability to establish a consistent starting pitching rotation.

THE DECADE LEADERS

Batting Avg:	McGwire	.292
On-Base Pct:	McGwire	.448
Slugging Pct:	McGwire	.726
Home Runs:	Lankford	181
RBIs:	Lankford	703
Runs:	Lankford	781
Stolen Bases:	Lankford	239
Wins:	Tewksbury	66
Strikeouts:	Osborne	535
ERA:	Tewksbury	3.49
Saves:	Smith	160

THE HOME FIELD

A state-of-the-art sound system and a new large video screen were installed at Busch Stadium in 1993. Grass replaced the artificial turf in 1996. The Family Pavilion, featuring a variety of games and attractions, and Homer's Landing, a picnic area in left field, also opened. The predominate color scheme changed from blue to green. In 1997, the Cardinals installed a hand-operated scoreboard 17 feet high and 270 feet wide and flag decks in the outfield's upper deck commemorating the franchise's World Series Championships and retired uniform numbers. Those additions reduced capacity from 57,769 to 49,676 but made the ballpark more fan-friendly and conducive to watching baseball.

THE GAME YOU WISH YOU HAD SEEN

Mark McGwire broke Roger Maris's single-season home run record on September 8, 1998, with number 62.

THE WAY THE GAME WAS PLAYED

Baseball experienced one of its pivotal transitions in the 1990s, as offensive numbers soared higher than ever before. Fueled by the home run, pitching weakened by rapid league expansion, a smaller strike zone, and smaller ballparks, the average number of runs scored per game in the National League jumped from 7.9 in 1989 to 10.0 in 1999. Teams averaged 114 home runs in 1989 and 181 in 1999. Mark McGwire was at the center of this offensive explosion. Though he set the record for home runs hit as a rookie with 49 in 1987, he wouldn't surpass that mark until 1996, thanks in part to a few years battling injuries. Home run fever reached a crescendo in 1998, when McGwire and Sammy Sosa battled amiably to be the first to pass Roger Maris's 37-year-old single-season home run record. After years of bigger, more impersonal stadiums designed for multiple uses, capped by the Toronto Blue Jays' mammoth SkyDome (complete with hotel), which opened in 1989, the Baltimore Orioles sparked a return to the neighborhood parks of old with Camden Yards. Other franchises soon followed with their own retro ballparks, grass fields, and cozy-sounding names. Uniform designs reflected this, as teams moved from the polyester pullover jerseys of the '70s and '80s to button-front styles with belts and more traditional tailoring.

THE MANAGEMENT

August Busch died in September 1989, leaving a vacuum at the top of the Cardinals organization. His son, August Busch III, had the title of chairman of the board but possessed little interest in running the club and devoted most of his time to the brewery. At the start of the 1990s, Fred Kuhlmann was the president and chief executive officer and headed the Cardinals' day-to-day operations. Anheuser-Busch, which had owned the club since 1953, sold the team to a group of investors headed by William O. DeWitt Jr. on March 21, 1996. DeWitt assumed the title of chairman of the board/general partner. General managers were Dal Maxvill (1985–1994) and Walt Jocketty (1994–present). Field managers were Whitey Herzog (1980–90), Red Schoendienst (1990), Joe Torre (1990–95), Mike Jorgensen (1995), and Tony La Russa (1996–present).

THE BEST PLAYER MOVE

The Cardinals acquired Mark McGwire from the Athletics on July 31, 1997, for T. J. Mathews, Eric Ludwick, and Blake Stein.

THE WORST PLAYER MOVE

After he put up awful numbers in 1992, his only season with the Cardinals, the club seemed to have little reason to hang on to Andres Galarraga. He signed with Colorado as a free agent and went on to play in four more All-Star games with the Rockies and Braves.

1990

Season in a Sentence

Whitey Herzog resigns in July in frustration over his inability to motivate an underachieving team, and the Cardinals finish in last place for the first time since 1918.

Finish • Won • Lost • Pct • GB

Sixth   70   92   .432   25.0

Managers

Whitey Herzog (33–47), Red Schoendienst (13–11), and Joe Torre (24–34)

Stats

Stats	Cards	NL	Rank
Batting Avg:	.256	.256	8
On-Base Pct:	.323	.324	8
Slugging Pct:	.358	.383	11
Home Runs:	73		12
Stolen Bases:	221		1
ERA:	3.87	3.79	8
Fielding Avg:	.979	.980	6
Runs Scored:	599		11
Runs Allowed:	698		8

Starting Lineup

Todd Zeile, c
Pedro Guerrero, 1b
Jose Oquendo, 2b
Terry Pendleton, 3b
Ozzie Smith, ss
Vince Coleman, lf
Willie McGee, cf
Milt Thompson, rf
Tom Pagnozzi, c
Rex Hudler, rf-lf

Pitchers

Joe Magrane, sp
John Tudor, sp
Bob Tewksbury, sp
Bryn Smith, sp
Jose DeLeon, sp
Lee Smith, rp
Frank DiPino, rp
Ken Dayley, rp
Tom Niedenfuer, rp
Scott Terry, rp

Attendance

2,573,225 (third in NL)

Club Leaders

Batting Avg:	McGee	.335
On-Base Pct:	McGee	.382
Slugging Pct:	McGee	.437
Home Runs:	Zeile	15
RBIs:	Guerrero	80
Runs:	McGee	76
Stolen Bases:	Coleman	77
Wins:	Tudor	12
Strikeouts:	DeLeon	164
ERA:	Tudor	2.40
Saves:	L. Smith	27

FEBRUARY 15   The owners lock the players out of spring training because of a lack of progress during negotiations for a new basic agreement.

FEBRUARY 27   The Cardinals trade Alex Cole and Steve Peters to the Padres for Omar Oliveras.

MARCH 18   The labor dispute between the players and owners is resolved.

Spring training camps opened on March 20. The season, scheduled to open on April 1, was delayed a week, with missed games made up on open dates with doubleheaders and by extending the close of the campaign by three days.

APRIL 9   The Cardinals defeat the Expos 6–5 in 11 innings in the season opener before 48,752 at Busch Stadium. Willie McGee's two-run double in the ninth sent the game into extra innings, and his walk-off single in the eleventh drove in the winning run. Terry Pendleton collected three hits during the contest.

The letters "AAB" were stitched onto the left sleeves on the Cardinals' uniforms in 1990 in honor of August Busch, who died in September 1989.

APRIL 13   The Cardinals wallop the Phillies 11–0 in Philadelphia.

APRIL 21   Pedro Guerrero hits a grand slam off Terry Mulholland in the third inning of a 10-inning, 7–6 loss to the Phillies at Busch Stadium.

MAY 4   The Cardinals trade Tom Brunansky to the Red Sox for Lee Smith.

The Cards were willing to trade one of their few home run threats because closer Todd Worrell was out for the season with an elbow injury. (Worrell missed the entire 1991 season as well.) Smith was in his 10th big-league season when the Cardinals acquired him, and he had already accumulated 238 of his career 478 saves, a major league record. He immediately stepped into the closer role with the Redbirds and gave the club four terrific seasons. In 1990, he saved 27 games for St. Louis with an ERA of 2.10.

MAY 10   Down 5–0, the Cardinals score seven runs in the fifth inning and four in the sixth to defeat the Padres 11–5 in San Diego.

MAY 24   Vince Coleman's walk-off homer in the twelfth inning defeats the Giants 3–2 in San Francisco.

JUNE 3   Vince Coleman steals four bases during a 7–4 win over the Cubs at Busch Stadium. The Cards were 8 for 8 in stolen bases during the game. In addition to Coleman's four steals, Ozzie Smith swiped three, and Willie McGee stole one.

JUNE 4   In the first round of the amateur draft, the Cardinals select pitcher Donovan Osborne from the University of Nevada-Las Vegas and shortstop Aaron Holbert of Jordan High School in Long Beach, California.

Osborne was a rookie sensation in 1992 with an 11–9 record but like many young pitchers was affected by arm trouble. He was 47–45 in seven seasons with the Cardinals. Holbert has had an odd professional career. He played one game for the Cardinals in 1996. After nine seasons in the minors, he didn't play in his second big-league game until 2005, when the Reds called him up. In 1990 the Cardinals also signed and drafted Marc Ronan (3rd round), Scott Baker (7th round), Terry Bradshaw (9th round), Tom Urbani (13th round), and Duff Brumley (24th round).

JUNE 6   After the Phillies score two runs in the tenth inning, but the Cardinals come back with three in their half to win 12–11 at Busch Stadium. Willie McGee drove in the tying and winning runs with a walk-off double. The Cards had a 7–2 lead after six innings and fell behind 9–7 before scoring twice in the ninth to send the game into extra innings.

Frank DiPino was the winning pitcher. It was his 14th consecutive win dating to June 9, 1988. DiPino won his first 2 decisions of the winning streak with the Cubs and the last 12 with the Cardinals. He had a 9–0 record in 1989. When the 14-game streak began, DiPino had an 18–35 lifetime record.

JUNE 8   The Expos demolish the Cardinals 18–2 in Montreal.

JUNE 13   Willie McGee, a three-time Gold Glove winner, makes three errors in center field during a 6–5 loss to the Pirates at Busch Stadium.

JUNE 17   Jose DeLeon (7$\frac{1}{3}$) innings and Frank DiPino (1$\frac{2}{3}$ innings) combine on a two-hitter to defeat the Expos 7–1 on a 96-degree day at Busch Stadium. The only Montreal hits were a homer by Spike Owen in the first inning and a single by Nelson Santovenia in the fifth.

JUNE 26   Terry Pendleton collects five hits, including a double, in six at-bats, but the Cardinals lose 8–6 to the Mets in 11 innings at Busch Stadium.

JUNE 29   Fernando Valenzuela no-hits the Cardinals for a 6–0 Los Angeles win at Dodger Stadium. After Willie McGee walked, Pedro Guerrero ended the game by grounding into a double play. On the same day, Dave Stewart pitched a no-hitter for the Athletics against the Blue Jays.

JULY 1   Trailing 5–0, the Cardinals score two runs in the fourth inning and four in the sixth to beat the Dodgers 6–5 at Los Angeles.

JULY 4   Vince Coleman draws a seven-game suspension after striking umpire Ed Montague in the nose with the bill of his batting helmet during an argument in the course of a 9–2 loss to the Giants in San Francisco.

JULY 6   Whitey Herzog resigns as manager of the Cardinals. Coach Red Schoendienst was named interim manager.

   Herzog decided to resign even though there were 2½ years remaining on his contract. The resignation followed a three-game sweep at the hands of the Giants in San Francisco that dropped the club's record to 33–47. "I was totally embarrassed by the way our team played. I just feel badly for the ball club, the organization and the fans," Herzog said. "I'm the manager. I take full responsibility. I can't get the guys to play. That's the first time I've felt like that in 17 years of managing." Herzog left with an 822–728 record as a manger of the Cardinals (see August 1, 1990).

JULY 15   The Cardinals play a Sunday-night game at Busch Stadium for the first time and lose 5–3 to the Giants. ESPN televised the game nationally.

JULY 24   Vince Coleman steals four bases during a 9–4 win over the Cubs at Busch Stadium. He stole home with Willie McGee batting and two outs in the eighth, beating pitcher Mike Bielecki's throw to the plate.

   Coleman stole four bases in a game eight times as a Cardinal.

JULY 25   The Cardinals score eight runs in the first inning and cruise to a 9–0 win over the Cubs at Busch Stadium.

JULY 29   Willie McGee homers in the seventh inning off David Cone to provide the lone run in a 1–0 win over the Mets in New York. Joe Magrane (7$\frac{2}{3}$ innings) and Lee Smith (1$\frac{1}{3}$ innings) combined on the shutout.

AUGUST 1   Joe Torre is named manager of the Cardinals.

Torre was a longtime friend of general manager Dal Maxvill. Torre was 50 when the Cardinals hired him. He had played in the majors from 1960 through 1977 as a catcher, first baseman, and third baseman, including a stint with the Cards from 1969 through 1975 when he won the 1971 NL MVP. He had previously managed the Mets (1977–81) and Braves (1982–84), but only two of those eight teams finished their seasons with winning records. The best of the lot was the 1982 Braves, which were 89–73 and won the NL West before the Cards swept them in the NLCS. From 1985 through 1990, Torre was a broadcaster for the Angels. He was unable to move the Cardinals into pennant contention as manager and was fired in May 1995 after posting a 351–354 record.

AUGUST 2   In Joe Torre's debut as manager of the Cardinals, the club wins 4–2 over the Phillies in Philadelphia. Willie McGee's 22-game hitting streak came to an end when he went 0 for 3.

AUGUST 8   Six days after Iraq invades Kuwait and the day after Operation Desert Shield troops leave for Saudi Arabia, the Cardinals lose 4–3 to the Cubs in 15 innings in Chicago. The contest was scoreless after nine innings. Both teams scored twice in the tenth inning and once in the thirteenth.

AUGUST 16   Pedro Guerrero tangles with Astros pitcher Danny Darwin in the seventh inning of a 4–2 win at Busch Stadium. Guerrero and Darwin had words after Darwin threw inside to Guerrero in the sixth inning. In the seventh, Guerrero punched Darin in the face after the Houston hurler reached base on an infield hit. Both benches cleared, but there were no other incidents, although Guerrero and Darwin exchanged angry words after the game outside the clubhouse area. Several police officers were called as a precautionary measure.

AUGUST 17   Bob Tewksbury allows only one base runner during a 5–0 win over the Astros at Busch Stadium. Tewksbury retired the first 21 batters to face him before Franklin Stubbs doubled leading off the eighth. Tewksbury shook off the loss of his perfect-game bid by retiring the remaining six Houston batters in order. He threw only 80 pitches.

AUGUST 21   Ray Lankford makes his major league debut. He collected two hits, including a double, in four at-bats during a 7–3 loss to the Braves at Busch Stadium.

Lankford played in the Cardinals' outfield from 1990 through 2001 and again in 2004. He was the nephew of Carl Nichols, who was five years older and played in the majors with the Orioles and Astros from 1986 through 1991. Because of a troubled home environment, Lankford moved in with the Nichols family in Modesto, California, when he was 11. When he reached the majors, many were comparing Lankford to Barry Bonds. While that prediction failed to come true, Lankford was nonetheless a productive player for a decade. As a Cardinal, he hit 228 homers and stole 250 bases to become the only player in club history to pass the 200 mark in both categories. At the end of the 2005 season, Lankford was third all time in home runs behind only Stan Musial (475) and Ken Boyer (255). Lankford also collected hits, 1,479 hits, 339 doubles, 52 triples, 928 runs, and 829 RBIs.

AUGUST 27   A jury in Covington, Kentucky, just across the Ohio River from Cincinnati, clears
             Cardinal players Frank DiPino and Tom Pagnozzi of disorderly conduct charges
             stemming from a May 19 brawl at a service station. The players said they went to
             the aid of a woman who had been attacked by an off-duty Dayton, Kentucky, police
             officer. The incident occurred after the Cardinals lost to the Reds 1–0 at Riverfront
             Stadium.

AUGUST 29   The Cardinals trade Willie McGee to the Athletics for Felix Jose, Stan Royer, and
             Daryl Green.

             *Despite playing the final five weeks of the season in the American League,
             McGee won his second National League batting title in 1990 with a .335
             average. He played in the majors until 1999, batting .291 following the trade to
             Oakland, and spent the last four seasons of his career in a second engagement
             with the Cardinals. The Cards traded McGee because they were out of the
             pennant race, and with his contract set to expire at the end of the season, they
             obtained three prospects to bolster the youth movement. Also, Ray Lankford
             appeared ready to take over McGee's position in center field. Jose made the
             All-Star team in 1991 at the age of 25 and gave the Cardinals two solid seasons
             before a trade to the Royals following the 1992 season.*

SEPTEMBER 4 The Cardinals edge the Mets 1–0 at Busch Stadium. Terry Pendleton drove in the
             lone run of the game with a double in the fourth inning. Joe Magrane (five innings),
             Omar Oliveras (three innings), and Lee Smith (one inning) combined on the shutout.

SEPTEMBER 20 The Cardinals score three runs in the ninth inning to beat the Phillies 5–4 at Busch
             Stadium. Ray Lankford's walk-off single drove in the winning run.

SEPTEMBER 25 Bernard Gilkey is the only Cardinal base runner, but St. Louis wins 1–0 over the
             Phillies at Philadelphia. Facing Terry Mulholland, Gilkey led off the first inning
             with a triple and scored on a sacrifice fly by Geronimo Peña. Mulholland retired
             26 batters in a row before Gilkey doubled with two outs in the ninth. Joe Magrane
             (seven innings), Mike Perez (one inning), and Ken Dayley (one inning) teamed on the
             shutout.

DECEMBER 3   Terry Pendleton signs with the Braves as a free agent.

             *Pendleton was 30 years old and hit just .230 in 121 games in 1990. His career
             batting average was .259. The Cards had little interest in re-signing him, but
             over the next two seasons, Pendleton had seasons in Atlanta that far surpassed
             any he put together in St. Louis. In 1991, Pendleton led the league in batting
             average (.319) and hits (187) and won the NL MVP Award. In 1992, he hit .311
             with 199 hits and 105 RBIs. The Braves went to the World Series both seasons.*

DECEMBER 5   Vince Coleman signs with the Mets as a free agent.

             *Coleman wasn't a big loss. He played seven more seasons, but never as a regular
             because of injuries and diminished effectiveness. In 1993, while playing for the
             Mets in a series in Los Angeles, Coleman threw a lit M-80 firecracker out of a
             car window at fans, injuring two children and a woman.*

1991

Season in a Sentence

With an exciting group of young players, the Cardinals rebound from a 92-loss season to post 84 wins.

Finish • Won • Lost • Pct • GB

Second   84   78   .519 14.0

Manager

Joe Torre

Stats

	Cards	• NL •	Rank
Batting Avg:	.255	.250	4
On-Base Pct:	.324	.320	4
Slugging Pct:	.357	.373	11
Home Runs:	68		12
Stolen Bases:	202		2
ERA:	3.69	3.69	7
Fielding Avg:	.982	.980	1
Runs Scored:	651		6
Runs Allowed:	648		6

Starting Lineup

Tom Pagnozzi, c
Pedro Guerrero, 1b
Jose Oquendo, 2b
Todd Zeile, 3b
Ozzie Smith, ss
Milt Thompson, lf
Ray Lankford, cf
Felix Jose, rf
Bernard Gilkey, lf
Gerald Perry, 1b
Rex Hudler, lf-cf
Geronimo Peña, 2b

Pitchers

Bryn Smith, sp
Bob Tewksbury, sp
Ken Hill, sp
Omar Olivares, sp
Jose DeLeon, sp
Lee Smith, rp
Juan Agosto, rp
Scott Terry, rp
Cris Carpenter, rp

Attendance

2,448,699 (second in NL)

Club Leaders

Batting Avg:	Jose	.305
On-Base Pct:	O. Smith	.380
Slugging Pct:	Zeile	.412
Home Runs:	Zeile	11
RBIs:	Zeile	81
Runs:	O. Smith	96
Stolen Bases:	Lankford	44
Wins:	B. Smith	12
Strikeouts:	Hill	121
ERA:	DeLeon	2.71
Saves:	L. Smith	47

JANUARY 9   The Cardinals sign Jamie Moyer following his release by the Rangers.

Moyer pitched only eight games with the Cardinals, posting a 5.74 ERA and an 0–5 record, which dropped his career won-lost mark to 34–54. He was a free agent at the end of the 1991 season, and the Cards made no attempt to sign him. Despite his poor performance with the club, the Cardinals should have brought him back. After spending the entire 1992 season in the minors, Moyer was 171–98 for the Orioles, Red Sox, and Mariners from 1993 through 2005.

FEBRUARY 12   A month after the United States and its allies attack Iraq to start the Persian Gulf War, the Cardinals sign Rich Gedman, most recently with the Astros, as a free agent.

Gedman proved to be one of the worst free-agent signings in club history. In two seasons with the Cardinals, he batted .166 with four homers in 199 at-bats.

APRIL 9   Six weeks after President Bush orders a cease fire to end the Persian Gulf War against Iraq, the Cardinals win the season opener 4–1 over the Cubs on a cloudy, 42-degree day in Chicago. Three runs in the eighth inning broke a 1–1 tie. Bryn Smith pitched seven innings for the win.

Jack Buck's son Joe, then 21 years old, joined the Cardinals' radio team in 1991 after spending two seasons as the play-by-play voice of the Louisville Redbirds. Jack Buck continued as the Cardinals' voice until 2001. In 2002, Joe became the play-by-play announcer on Fox's NFL broadcasting team, the first play-by-play announcer to handle Major League Baseball and NFL coverage since Al Michaels in the 1980s. Through 2005, Buck had called eight World Series, six All-Star games, and a Super Bowl on national television.

APRIL 15   The Cardinals score three runs in the ninth inning to defeat the Mets 5–4 in New York. Pedro Guerrero led off the ninth with his second home run of the game. Todd Zeile tripled in the second run, then scored on Tom Pagnozzi's sacrifice fly. Lee Smith struck out all three batters he faced for the save.

Zeile was a catcher throughout his minor league career and earned a starting job at the position as a rookie in 1990. Joe Torre thought that Tom Pagnozzi was a better defensive catcher, however, and Zeile moved to third base late in the 1990 season. Zeile resisted the move, but Torre himself had made the transition from catching to third base and believed that Zeile could do the same. He hit .280 with 11 homers in 1991, but his inexperience at third showed, and he led the NL in errors at third with 25. Zeile seemed poised to become a star, but he never developed into the player the Cardinals had envisioned. Although he never played in an All-Star Game, he did appear in 2,158 big-league games over 16 seasons. Zeile played seven seasons with the Cardinals before a trade to the Cubs in May 1995. By the time his career ended in 2004, he had played for 11 different teams. In addition to playing for the Cardinals and Cubs, Zeile appeared in games for the Phillies, Orioles, Dodgers, Marlins, Rangers, Mets, Rockies, Yankees, and Expos. He married US Olympic gymnast Julianne McNamara in 1984.

APRIL 18   The scheduled home opener against the Phillies at Busch Stadium is rained out.

APRIL 19   The Cardinals start the home season with a 3–1 win over the Phillies before 21,468 at Busch Stadium.

APRIL 20   The Cardinals roll over the Phillies 12–1 at Busch Stadium.

APRIL 21   Ray Lankford scores from second base on a ground-out to beat the Phillies 7–6 in 10 innings at Busch Stadium. Running on a pitch that Gerald Perry grounded into a forceout at second, Lankford rounded third and knocked the ball loose from Phillies catcher Darren Daulton on the play at the plate. The Cards trailed 6–1 before scoring four runs in the seventh inning, one in the ninth, and one in the tenth.

APRIL 22   Felix Jose's two-run, walk-off homer with one out in the ninth inning beats the Cubs 3–2 at Busch Stadium.

Jose hit .305 with 40 doubles and eight homers for the Cardinals in 1991.

MAY 1   Playing for the Oakland Athletics against the Texas Rangers, Rickey Henderson steals the 939th base of his career, breaking Lou Brock's record.

MAY 8   The Braves batter the Cardinals 17–1 in Atlanta.

MAY 13	Ken Hill (eight innings) and Lee Smith (one inning) combine on a two-hitter to defeat the Reds 1–0 at Busch Stadium. Jeff Reed collected the only Cincinnati hits with singles in the third and eighth innings.

Lee Smith set a National League record for most saves in a season with 47 in 1991. He had a 6–3 record and a 2.34 ERA in 74 innings over 63 games. His NL saves record was broken by Randy Myers of the Cubs, who had 53 in 1993. Smith's club record was tied by Jason Isringhausen, who had 47 in 2004.

MAY 18	The Cardinals pummel the Astros 12–2 at Busch Stadium.
MAY 26	The Cardinals collect 23 hits and wallop the Mets 14–4 in New York. Tom Pagnozzi drove in six runs on a triple, a double, and two singles.
MAY 27	One game after picking up 23 hits, the Cards are held to just one hit by Doug Drabek for a 5–0 loss to the Pirates at Busch Stadium.
MAY 29	The Cardinals are the victims of a one-hitter for the second game in three days as Zane Smith of the Pirates pitches Pittsburgh to a 6–0 win at Busch Stadium.
JUNE 1	Milt Thompson's bizarre broken-bat single in the tenth inning ends a 6–5 win over the Mets at Busch Stadium. With Gerald Perry on third base, Thompson's bat splintered when he made contact with a John Franco pitch. The ball and half of Thompson's bat whizzed toward first baseman Dave Magadan at the same time. Magadan had to make a split-second decision. If he fielded the ball, he risked serious injury from being struck by the flying bat. If he ducked out of the way, Thompson's hit would win the game for the Cardinals. Magadan chose to duck, and Perry crossed the plate with the winning run.

Perry played for the Cardinals from 1991 through 1995. He is the club's all-time record holder in career pinch hits with 70.

JUNE 3	The Cardinals select third baseman Dmitri Young from Rio Mesa High School in Oxnard, California, pitcher Allen Watson from New York Tech, and pitcher Brian Barber from Dr. Phillips High School in Orlando, Florida. The Cards had three first-round picks due to free-agent compensation.

Young played for the Cardinals for two seasons before he was dealt to the Reds. Watson played three seasons in St. Louis and had a 51–55 lifetime record with five clubs over eight seasons. Barber's career in the majors lasted only 26 games. Other future major leaguers the Cardinals drafted and signed in 1991 were DaRond Stovall (5th round), John Mabry (6th round), Doug Creek (7th round), Allen Battle (10th round), Mike DiFelice (11th round), Mike Busby (14th round), John Frascatore (24th round), and Rigo Beltran (36th round).

JUNE 4	Milt Thompson is the hero for driving in all three runs of a 3–2, 11-inning win against the Dodgers at Busch Stadium. Thompson hit a sacrifice fly in the ninth off Orel Hershiser to tie the score 4–1. After Los Angeles went ahead with a run in the top of the eleventh, Thompson hit a two-out, two-run triple to win the game.
JUNE 13	The Cardinals wallop the Padres 12–1 at Busch Stadium.

JUNE 14	President Bush watches the Cardinals lose 2–1 to the Dodgers in Los Angeles.
JUNE 25	The Cardinals rally from a 5–0 deficit to beat the Phillies 10–9 at Busch Stadium. Ozzie Smith drove in the tying and winning runs with a single in the eighth inning.

Smith batted .285 and scored 96 runs in 1991.

JUNE 26	The Cardinals wallop the Phillies 14–1 at Busch Stadium.
JUNE 27	Ken Hill goes 7⅓ innings without allowing a hit before the Cardinals close out a 4–2 win over the Phillies at Busch Stadium. The first Philadelphia hit was a triple by Dickie Thon with one out in the eighth. Hill allowed just that one hit and one run. Lee Smith surrendered a run and two hits in the ninth but came away with the save.
JUNE 28	The Cardinals collect 21 hits and rout the Cubs 14–6 in Chicago.
JULY 1	The Cardinals edge the Phillies 1–0 in Philadelphia. Todd Zeile drove in the lone run of the game with a single in the fifth inning. Bryn Smith (seven innings), Cris Carpenter (one inning), and Lee Smith (one inning) combined on the shutout.
JULY 16	Ozzie Smith's two-run single in the ninth inning beats the Reds 8–7 in Cincinnati.
JULY 22	The Cardinals score seven runs in the sixth inning and defeat the Astros 9–1 at Busch Stadium.
AUGUST 3	Todd Zeile leads off the tenth inning with a walk-off home run that beats the Pirates 6–5 at Busch Stadium.

Zeile led the Cardinals in home runs in 1991 with 11. It was the lowest total to lead the club since 1920, when Austin McHenry hit a team-high 10.

AUGUST 6	Trailing 6–1, the Cardinals score one run in the third inning, three in the fifth, one in the sixth, and one in the tenth to defeat the Expos 7–6 at Busch Stadium. Ray Lankford keyed the comeback with two triples and a double and drove in the winning run.
AUGUST 22	A fight breaks out during an 8–0 loss to the Mets in the second game of a double-header at Shea Stadium. After giving up back-to-back homers to Kevin Elster and Kevin McReynolds, Cardinal pitcher Willie Fraser fired his next pitch at Howard Johnson's back. Johnson marched to the mound, and both benches emptied. Johnson halted, but Mets catcher Rick Cerone tore through Pedro Guerrero and swung at Fraser. Guerrero then wrestled Cerone to the ground before peace was restored. The Cardinals won the opener 7–3.
AUGUST 25	Lee Smith earns the 300th save of his career by pitching the ninth inning of a 5–2 win over the Dodgers at Busch Stadium.
AUGUST 27	After defeating the Giants 5–4 at Busch Stadium, the Cardinals pull to within four games of the first-place Pirates and have a 69–55 record.

The Cards lost 9 of their next 11 games to quickly drop out of the pennant race.

SEPTEMBER 1   The Cardinals pummel the Giants 14–1 in San Francisco.

SEPTEMBER 12   The Cardinals slip past the Pirates 1–0 at Busch Stadium. A bases-loaded walk to Felix Jose in the sixth inning accounted for the lone run of the game. Ken Hill ($6^2/_3$ innings), Bob McClure ($1/_3$ of an inning), Scott Terry ($2/_3$ of an inning), and Lee Smith ($1^1/_3$ innings) teamed on the shutout.

SEPTEMBER 15   Ray Lankford hits for the cycle during a 7–2 win over the Mets at Busch Stadium. Lankford doubled in the first inning, singled in the third, and tripled in the fifth off Pete Schourek, then completed the cycle with a home run in the seventh facing Wally Whitehurst. Lankford also scored four runs and stole a base.

Lankford led the NL in triples in 1991 with 15.

SEPTEMBER 22   Ken Hill ($8^1/_3$ innings) and Lee Smith ($2/_3$ of an inning) combine on a two-hitter to beat the Mets 2–1 at Shea Stadium. Daryl Boston collected both New York hits with a double in the sixth inning and a home run in the ninth, both off Hill.

SEPTEMBER 30   The Cardinals wallop the Expos 11–1 at Busch Stadium.

OCTOBER 1   Lee Smith breaks Bruce Sutter's club record with his 46th save of the season, closing out a 3–1 win over the Expos at Busch Stadium.

NOVEMBER 25   The Cardinals trade Ken Hill to the Expos for Andres Galarraga.

Hill had a 22–32 record as a Cardinal but found his groove in Montreal, going 41–21 over three seasons. The Cards brought him back in another trade with the Expos in April 1995, but Hill was only 6–7 with a 5.06 ERA before the club dealt him to the Indians in July. Galarraga was a bust with the Cardinals. He broke his wrist in the second game of the season and batted .243 with 10 homers in 95 games in 1992. He was a free agent at the end of the season, and the Redbirds made little attempt to sign him. Galarraga inked a contract with the Rockies and hit .370 in Colorado to win the 1993 batting title. In eight seasons with the Rockies and Braves from 1993 through 2000, Galarraga batted .312 with 244 homers and 800 RBIs despite missing one full season (1999) because of cancer.

1992

Season in a Sentence

The youth movement remains stuck in neutral, as key injuries and a lack of power prevent the club from building on the improvement shown the previous season.

Finish • Won • Lost • Pct • GB

Third   83   79   .512   13.0

Manager

Joe Torre

Stats

Stats	Cards	NL	Rank
Batting Avg:	.262	.252	1
On-Base Pct:	.325	.318	3
Slugging Pct:	.375	.368	6
Home Runs:	94		10
Stolen Bases:	208		1
ERA:	3.38	3.51	4
Fielding Avg:	.985	.981	1
Runs Scored:	631		6
Runs Allowed:	604		4

Starting Lineup

Tom Pagnozzi, c
Andres Galarraga, 1b
Luis Alicea, 2b
Todd Zeile, 3b
Ozzie Smith, ss
Bernard Gilkey, lf
Ray Lankford, cf
Felix Jose, rf
Milt Thompson, lf
Geronimo Peña, 2b
Brian Jordan, lf-rf

Pitchers

Bob Tewksbury, sp
Donovan Osborne, sp
Rheal Cormier, sp
Omar Olivares, sp
Mark Clark, sp
Jose DeLeon, sp-rp
Lee Smith, rp
Mike Perez, rp
Cris Carpenter, rp
Bob McClure, rp
Todd Worrell, rp

Attendance

2,418,483 (third in NL)

Club Leaders

Batting Avg:	O. Smith	.295
	Jose	.295
On-Base Pct:	Lankford	.371
Slugging Pct:	Lankford	.480
Home Runs:	Lankford	20
RBIs:	Lankford	86
Runs:	Lankford	87
Stolen Bases:	O. Smith	43
Wins:	Tewksbury	16
Strikeouts:	Olivares	124
ERA:	Tewksbury	2.16
Saves:	L. Smith	43

APRIL 6   In the season opener, the Cardinals lose 4–2 to the Mets in 10 innings before 45,174 at Busch Stadium. Bobby Bonilla hit a two-run homer in the tenth off Lee Smith to win the game. It was Bonilla's second homer of the game.

The Cardinals lost two second basemen early in the season. In spring training, Geronimo Peña tripped over a glove that was left on the grass and broke his clavicle. On Opening Day, Jose Oquendo suffered a dislocated shoulder. Peña returned in late May, but Oquendo played only 14 games all season.

APRIL 8   Brian Jordan collects two hits and drives in four runs in his major league debut leading the Cardinals to a 15–7 win over the Mets at Busch Stadium.

The Cardinals moved in the fences at Busch Stadium in 1992. The foul lines remained at 330 feet, but the power alleys went from 386 feet to 375, and center field from 414 feet to 402. In addition, the height of the wall dropped from 10½ feet to 8. With a more convenient target, the Cardinals hit 55 homers at Busch Stadium in 1992, the most at home since the ballpark opened in 1966.

APRIL 23   The Cardinals lose a tough 1–0 decision to the Mets in thirteen innings in New York.

The winning run scored when Juan Agosto hit Daryl Boston with a pitch with the bases loaded.

The Cardinals changed their uniforms slightly in 1992. From 1972 through 1991, the uniform shirt was of a pullover style with a red and navy blue stripe around the sleeve. In 1992, a button-front jersey replaced the pullover, with no stripes on the sleeves.

APRIL 24   Ray Lankford keys a two-run rally in the ninth inning that beats the Expos 4–3 at Busch Stadium. Lankford doubled in the tying run and scored on a single by Ozzie Smith.

Smith hit .295 for the Cardinals in 1992.

Bob Tewksbury was the staff ace for the Cardinals teams of the early 1990s. Though he was often on the DL, Tewksbury managed a 67–46 record during his time in St. Louis.

Gary Newkirk/Getty Images Sport/Getty Images

APRIL 25   The Cardinals outlast the Expos 2–1 in 17 innings at Busch Stadium. Bob Tewksbury pitched the last two innings and knocked in the winning run with a single in the seventeenth. Tewksbury, who finished his career with a .132 batting average, hit because the Cardinals had run out of position players to pinch hit and there were no pitchers left in the bullpen.

Tewksbury entered the season at the age of 31 with a lifetime record of 32–34 and a 3.67 ERA. As recently as 1990, he had spent much of his time in the minors. Using pinpoint control, Tewksbury was a revelation in 1992 with a 16–5 record and a 2.16 ERA. He walked only 20 batters in 233 innings. Tewksbury's rate of 0.77 walks per nine innings was the lowest of any major league pitcher in a season since 1933.

APRIL 26   Ozzie Smith steals the 500th base of his career during a 6–0 loss to the Expos at Busch Stadium.

Smith finished his career with 580 stolen bases. There are only 13 players with more steals since 1900.

MAY 6   Seven days after riots begin in the South Central section of Los Angeles, resulting in the deaths of 52 people, Felix Jose hits a walk-off homer with two outs in the eleventh to beat the Giants 5–4 at Busch Stadium.

The riots, which began April 29, swept South Central Los Angeles after a jury acquitted officers on all but one count in the beating of black motorist Rodney King. The Cardinals got out of Los Angeles just in time, concluding a series with the Dodgers on April 28. The Dodgers had four home games against the Phillies and Expos postponed by the week-long riots.

MAY 9   Down 9–0 after 3½ innings and 11–3 after 4½ with John Smoltz pitching for Atlanta, the Cardinals rally with two runs in the fifth, four in the seventh, and three in the eighth to beat the Braves 12–11 at Busch Stadium. Gerald Perry contributed a three-run pinch-double in the seventh. Felix Jose tied the score with a two-run homer. Luis Alicea drove in the winning run with a single.

Alicea put together an odd set of stats in 1992: 11 triples in just 265 at-bats but only 9 doubles.

MAY 10   Trailing 5–2, the Cardinals score one run in the seventh inning, one in the eighth, and two in the ninth to defeat the Braves 6–5 at Busch Stadium. Tom Pagnozzi drove in the tying and winning runs with a two-out, two-run, walk-off single.

MAY 15   A two-run homer by Felix Jose sparks a four-run in the ninth inning that gives the Cardinals a 7–5 win over the Astros in Houston.

MAY 17   Felix Jose drives in five runs, including a third-inning grand slam off Pete Harnisch, to lead the Cardinals to a 7–5 win over the Astros in Houston.

MAY 24   Tom Pagnozzi's walk-off homer in the ninth inning defeats the Astros 4–3 at Busch Stadium. The victory put the Cardinals into first place.

MAY 25   Felix Jose's walk-off single in the ninth inning beats the Dodgers 6–5 at Busch Stadium.

The win gave the Cardinals a 26–18 record and a 1½-game lead in the NL East race.

MAY 26   Ozzie Smith collects his 2,000th career hit during a 5–2 loss to the Dodgers at Busch Stadium.

MAY 29   The Padres score two times in the ninth inning to beat the Cardinals 2–1 at Busch Stadium. Rookie Cardinal pitcher Donovan Osborne had retired 24 batters in a row and was one out from a shutout when Tony Gwynn doubled. Osborne was replaced by Lee Smith, who surrendered a two-base hit to Fred McGriff and a single to Garry Sheffield to lose the game.

JUNE 1   In the first round of the amateur draft, the Cardinals select pitcher Sean Lowe from Arizona State University.

Lowe reached the majors in 1997 and was 0–5 with a 10.72 ERA in two seasons with the Cardinals. Other future major leaguers the Cardinals drafted and signed in 1992 were Mike Gulan (2nd round), Steve Montgomery (3rd round), Keith Johns (6th round), Scarborough Green (10th round), Frank Lankford (18th round), Brady Raggio (20th round), Joe McEwing (28th round), Kirk Bullinger (32nd round), and T. J. Mathews (36th round).

JUNE 3   The Cardinals drop out of first place with an 8–3 loss to the Reds in Cincinnati.

The Cards failed to regain the top spot for the remainder of the season. The club was as close as 3½ games out on July 11 but faded to third place, 13 games behind the Pirates. Their inability to beat Pittsburgh derailed their pennant hopes. From June 30 through September 21, St. Louis lost 13 games in a row to the Pirates, 6 of them by a one-run margin. The Cards gave up only 45 runs in those 13 defeats, an average of 3.5 per game, but scored just 18 times.

JUNE 16   Ozzie Smith is placed on the 15-day disabled list because of the chicken pox. Smith became infected after contracting the virus from his son and daughter.

JULY 2   The Cardinals edge the Giants 1–0 in San Francisco. Ray Lankford drove in the lone run of the game with a double in the sixth inning. Donovan Osborne (7⅓ innings), Todd Worrell (⅔ of an inning), and Lee Smith (1 inning) combined on the shutout.

Lankford hit .293 with 40 doubles and 20 homers in 1992.

JULY 4   For the second time in three days, the Cardinals slip past the Giants 1–0 in San Francisco. The Independence Day victory took 13 innings to complete. Todd Zeile drove in the lone run of the game with a single. Bob Tewksbury (eight innings), Cris Carpenter (two innings), Todd Worrell (one inning), Mike Perez (one inning), and Lee Smith (one inning) teamed on the shutout.

JULY 6   Commissioner Fay Vincent orders the Cardinals and Cubs to move to the National League's Western Division beginning with the 1993 season. The two clubs were to move west while the Reds and Braves were slated to shift to the Eastern Division. Vincent said that he ruled in the best interests of baseball at the urging of the National League owners.

In March, the NL owners voted 10–2 in favor of moving the four clubs, thus giving the league geographic logic. The Cardinals were in favor of the move to the East. One of the two negative votes came from the Cubs organization, which, as one of the directly affected parties, had to give its assent before the move became official. The Cubs sued the commissioner on July 7 in US District Court and asked for a preliminary injunction barring Vincent from enforcing his decision. The injunction was granted on July 23. Vincent resigned as commissioner on September 7 under pressure from major league owners, and the National League scrapped the realignment plan on September 24. Beginning in 1994, the American and National Leagues split into three divisions, with the Cubs and Cardinals joining the NL Central.

JULY 8   The Cardinals win 1–0 on the West Coast for the third time in seven days, beating the Padres in San Diego. Tom Pagnozzi provided all of the offense by clubbing a homer with two outs in the ninth off Randy Myers. Omar Oliveras (8 innings), Bob McClure (1/3 of an inning) and Lee Smith (2/3 of an inning) combined on the shutout.

Smith led the NL in saves for the second year in a row with 43. He also had a 4–9 record a 3.12 ERA.

JULY 14   Ozzie Smith hits a double in the All-Star Game, but the National League loses 13–8 in San Diego.

JULY 29   Bernard Gilkey's three-run, walk-off homer in the ninth inning beats the Expos 4–1 at Busch Stadium. It was his first homer of the season. In the eighth, Gilkey leaped over the fence to rob Larry Walker of a home run.

AUGUST 15   Andres Galarraga drives in five runs, including a grand slam in the eighth inning off John Wetteland to lead the Cardinals to a 6–4 win over the Expos at Olympic Stadium. The slam came with the Cards trailing 4–2. Montreal pitcher Wes Gardner tied a major league record in the first inning by hitting three batters. Ray Lankford, Galarraga, and Luis Alicea all were plunked in a span of five batters.

AUGUST 16   The Cardinals play their 16th consecutive errorless game to set a major league record during a 5–2 win over the Expos. The streak started on July 30. Tracy Woodson collected four hits, including his first home run since 1988, in five at-bats.

AUGUST 19   The Cardinals rout the Astros 12–1 at Busch Stadium.

AUGUST 28   The Cardinals defeat the Dodgers 1–0 at Busch Stadium. Andres Galarraga drove in the game's only run with a sacrifice fly in the first inning. Mark Clark (seven innings), Todd Worrell (one inning), and Lee Smith (one inning) teamed on the shutout.

SEPTEMBER 1   Solo homers by Geronimo Peña in the first inning and Tom Pagnozzi in the fifth beat the Padres 2–0 in San Diego. Donovan Osborne (seven innings), Todd Worrell (one inning), and Lee Smith (one inning) teamed on the shutout.

SEPTEMBER 7   Bernard Gilkey's homer leading off the tenth inning defeats the Expos 8–7 in Montreal.

SEPTEMBER 13   Ray Lankford hits a grand slam off Jim Bullinger in the fifth inning, and Felix Jose adds a bases-loaded triple in the sixth to spark a 10–3 win over the Cubs at Busch Stadium.

SEPTEMBER 17   Bernard Gilkey smacks a two-run homer in the ninth inning that beats the Mets 3–2 in New York.

SEPTEMBER 19   The Cardinals outlast the Cubs 11–10 in 10 innings in the second game of a doubleheader at Wrigley Field. Stan Royer drove in the winning run with a single. Chicago won the first game 6–5.

SEPTEMBER 20   Two reserve players given a rare chance to start lead the Cardinals to a 16–4 victory over the Cubs in Chicago. Rod Brewer collected five hits in five at-bats and scored four runs. Stan Royer was 4 for 4, scored four runs, drove in four, and hit his first major league homer. The Cards collected 22 hits in the contest.

SEPTEMBER 24   All seven runs of a 4–3 win over the Mets at Busch Stadium score in the fourteenth inning. The contest was scoreless before Jeff Kent broke the deadlock with a three-run homer in the fourteenth off Bryn Smith. The Cardinals rallied for four in their half of the inning for a stunning victory. Felix Jose drove in the first two with a pinch-single, Ozzie Smith tied the contest with a two-run single, and Todd Zeile drove in the winning run with another base hit.

NOVEMBER 17   Two weeks after Bill Clinton defeats George Bush in the presidential election, the Cardinals lose Chuck Carr, Cris Carpenter, and Scott Baker to the Marlins in the expansion draft.

DECEMBER 9   The Cardinals lose two free agents as Todd Worrell signs with the Dodgers and Milt Thompson inks a deal with the Phillies.

                Worrell pitched out of the Dodger bullpen for five seasons. He led the National League in saves with 44 in 1996.

1993

Season in a Sentence

The Cardinals stay on the heels of the first-place Phillies until a late-July slump.

Finish • Won • Lost • Pct • GB

Third   87   75   .537   10.0

Manager

Joe Torre

Stats	Cards	NL	Rank
Batting Avg:	.272	.264	4
On-Base Pct:	.344	.330	2
Slugging Pct:	.395	.399	8
Home Runs:	118		12
Stolen Bases:	153		2
ERA:	4.09	4.04	8
Fielding Avg:	.975	.978	10
Runs Scored:	758		5
Runs Allowed:	744		9 (tie)

Starting Lineup

Tom Pagnozzi, c
Gregg Jefferies, 1b
Luis Alicea, 2b
Todd Zeile, 3b
Ozzie Smith, ss
Bernard Gilkey, lf
Ray Lankford, cf
Mark Whiten, rf
Geronimo Peña, 2b
Erik Pappas, c
Brian Jordan, lf-rf

Pitchers

Bob Tewksbury, sp
Rene Arocha, sp
Donovan Osborne, sp
Rheal Cormier, sp
Joe Magrane, sp
Allen Watson, sp
Lee Smith, rp
Mike Perez, rp
Omar Olivares, rp
Les Lancaster, rp

Attendance

2,844,328 (sixth in NL)

Club Leaders

Batting Avg:	Jefferies	.342
On-Base Pct:	Jefferies	.408
Slugging Pct:	Jefferies	.485
Home Runs:	Whiten	25
RBIs:	Zeile	103
Runs:	Gilkey	99
Stolen Bases:	Jefferies	46
Wins:	Tewksbury	17
Strikeouts:	Tewksbury	97
ERA:	Arocha	3.78
Saves:	L. Smith	43

FEBRUARY 22   The Cardinals trade Felix Jose and Craig Wilson to the Royals for Gregg Jefferies and Ed Gerald.

The Cards pulled off a great short-term deal in acquiring Jefferies. He reached the majors at the age of 20 and seemed destined for greatness, but he never reached his superstar potential as a Met or a Royal. Jefferies was 25 when he reached St. Louis and gave the Cards two terrific seasons, making the All-Star team as a first baseman in each of them. He hit .342 with 16 homers in 1993 and .321 with 12 home runs in 1994. Jefferies moved on to the Phillies as a free agent after the '94 season. Jose was another player many tabbed as a future MVP candidate, but he declined rapidly after moving to the American League and by 1995 was a bench player.

MARCH 31   Five weeks after a terrorist bomb explodes in the parking garage of the World Trade Center, killing six people, the Cardinals trade Mark Clark to the Indians for Mark Whiten and Juan Andujar.

Whiten became available after a horrific boating accident killed two Indians pitchers and put another one out indefinitely with injuries. Cleveland acquired Clark to replenish the staff. Whiten etched his name into Cardinal lore with his batting explosion on September 7, 1993, in which he clubbed 4 homers and drove in 12 runs. Overall, he hit .253 with 25 home runs and 99 RBIs in 1993, his first of two seasons in St. Louis. After the 1994 season, the Cards traded Whiten to the Red Sox.

APRIL 6   The Cardinals lose 2–1 to the Giants in the season opener before 50,892 at Busch Stadium. In his San Francisco debut, Barry Bonds broke a 1–1 tie with a sacrifice fly off Bob Tewksbury.

Tewksbury was 17–10 with a 3.83 ERA in 1993. He walked only 20 batters in 213²/₃ innings.

APRIL 10   Ozzie Smith drives in both runs during a 2–1 victory over the Reds at Busch Stadium. Smith gave the Cardinals a 1–0 lead with an RBI single in the eighth inning and drove in the winning tally with another single in the tenth.

APRIL 13   Lee Smith breaks the all-time save record with the 358th of his career, passing Jeff Reardon, by closing out a 9–7 win over the Dodgers in Los Angeles with a scoreless ninth.

Smith finished his career with 478 saves, still a major league record at the conclusion of the 2005 season. He played with the Cardinals from 1990 through 1993 and accumulated 160 saves in St. Louis. Smith also held the club record at the end of the 2005 campaign. Jason Isringhausen was second with 140.

APRIL 14   The Cardinals outlast the Dodgers 2–1 in 15 innings in Los Angeles. Gregg Jefferies drove in the winning run with an infield single that scored Brian Jordan from third base. Donovan Osborne (7¹/₃ innings), Omar Olivares (1²/₃ innings), Ron Murphy (2 innings), Mike Perez (2 innings), Les Lancaster (1 inning), and Lee Smith (1 inning) combined to allow the Dodgers' only four hits.

Omar Olivares's father, Ed, played for the Cardinals in 1960 and 1961 and hit .143 in 24 games as an outfielder.

APRIL 20   The day after the raid on the Branch Davidian compound in Waco, Texas, the Cardinals play the Rockies for the first time and win 5–0 at Busch Stadium.

APRIL 28   The Cardinals play a regular-season game in Colorado for the first time and beat the Rockies 7–6 with two runs in the ninth inning. Rod Brewer drove in the winning run with a pinch-single.

The game was played at Mile High Stadium in Denver. The Rockies moved to Coors Field in 1995.

MAY 14   The Cardinals play the Marlins for the first time and win 7–2 at Busch Stadium.

The Cardinals started the 1993 with seven wins in their first nine games, dropped to 25–25 on June 1 to fall 10 games behind the Phillies, then won 30 of their next 42 to vault back into the pennant race. The Cards were 55–37 on July 19 and only three games back of Philadelphia but would draw no closer, going 32–38 over the final 70 games to finish 10 games out of first.

MAY 16   Todd Zeile's bases-loaded, walk-off single in the ninth inning beats the Marlins 1–0 at Busch Stadium. Donovan Osborne (eight innings) and Lee Smith (one inning) combined on the shutout.

              Zeile batted .277 with 17 homers and 105 RBIs in 1993.

MAY 22   By starting in a 4–2 loss to the Pirates in Pittsburgh, Ozzie Smith breaks Larry Bowa's National League record for most games played at shortstop in a career with 2,223.

              Smith finished his career with 2,511 games at shortstop, which ranks second in major league history. The only player with more contests at short is Luis Aparicio, who played in 2,581 with the White Sox, Orioles, and Red Sox from 1956 through 1973.

JUNE 3   In the first round of the amateur draft, the Cardinals select pitcher Alan Benes of Creighton University.

              Alan's older brother by four years, Andy, was playing for the Padres in his fifth season in the majors when Alan was drafted. Alan was 13–10 with the Cardinals in 1996, but any hopes he had for success as a big leaguer were ruined by arm troubles. Overall, he played six seasons in St. Louis. Andy played for the Cardinals in 1996 and 1997 and again from 2000 through 2002. With Andy's 18–10 record, the Benes brothers combined to win 31 games in 1996. The two were teammates with the Redbirds in 1996, 1997, 2000, and 2001.

JUNE 11   Bernard Gilkey's home run in the fifth inning off Kent Bottenfield is the lone run of a 1–0 win over the Expos at Busch Stadium. Joe Magrane (7²/₃ innings), Pete Kilgus (¹/₃ of an inning), and Lee Smith (1 inning) teamed on the shutout.

              Gilkey hit .305 with 16 homers and 99 runs scored in 1993.

JUNE 12   The Cardinals rout the Expos 13–3 at Busch Stadium.

JUNE 17   Ozzie Smith collects five hits, including three doubles, in five at-bats and drives in six runs during an 11–10 win over the Cubs in Chicago.

JUNE 21   The Cardinals play the Marlins in Miami for the first time and win 4–3 at Joe Robbie Stadium.

JUNE 23   Rookie Cardinal pitcher Rene Arocha, a hero in Miami's Cuban-American community, pitches 5¹/₃ innings and drives in two runs with his first major league hit and is the winning pitcher in a 4–3 decision over the Marlins at Joe Robbie Stadium. The game was Arocha's first in Miami, where he lived after defecting two years earlier. A crowd of 37,936 cheered each time Arocha's name was mentioned, and he was given a standing ovation when he left the contest.

              Arocha spent his entire four-year major league career with the Cardinals and posted an 18–17 record.

JULY 1   Brian Jordan drives in five runs, including a grand slam in the third inning off Mark Davis, leading the Cardinals to a 14–5 trouncing of the Phillies at Busch Stadium.

The Cards scored five runs in the first inning, two in the second, and seven in the third to take a 14–0 lead.

JULY 6   The Cardinals score two runs in the ninth inning to beat the Braves 5–4 at Busch Stadium. Gregg Jefferies drove in Luis Alicea with the tying run and scored on Todd Zeile's walk-off single.

JULY 19   On the field where he played three years as a safety with the Atlanta Falcons, Brian Jordan hits two homers to lead the Cardinals to a 4–0 win over the Atlanta Braves at Atlanta–Fulton County Stadium.

JULY 20   The start of the Cardinals-Braves game in Atlanta is delayed for two hours by a fire. The blaze started at 6 PM, an hour and 40 minutes before game time, in a chafing dish in one of the suites at Atlanta–Fulton County Stadium. The fire quickly spread through several of the suites, the press box, and the box seats one level below. Many of the St. Louis players were taking batting practice and ran into the outfield as black smoke poured onto the diamond. Once play got under way, the Braves won 8–5.

JULY 23   Down 6–3, the Cardinals take the lead with eight runs in the sixth inning and move on to defeat the Rockies 13–11 at Denver. Nine consecutive batters reach base in the inning.

JULY 28   Todd Zeile hits a grand slam off Terry Mulholland in the first inning to give the Cardinals a 4–0 lead, but the Phillies bounce back to win 14–6 in Philadelphia.

AUGUST 4   The Cardinals break a 1–1 tie with six runs in the third inning and beat the Marlins 10–2 in Miami. Florida walked six batters in the inning, and Luis Alicea hit a grand slam off Richie Lewis.

AUGUST 6   The Cardinals score in each of the first six innings and rout the Marlins 16–6 at Busch Stadium.

AUGUST 10   Immediately after a 31-minute rain delay, Brian Jordan and Mark Whiten homer on consecutive pitches from Joel Johnston to defeat the Pirates 4–2 in Pittsburgh. The Cardinals won despite hitting into a triple play in the eighth inning.

AUGUST 11   Mark Whiten becomes the first visiting player to homer into the upper deck at Three Rivers Stadium, which opened in 1970, during an 8–6 loss to the Pirates. Whiten didn't hit another home run until he tagged four in a game on September 7.

AUGUST 24   The Padres score 13 runs in the first inning and cruise to a 17–4 win over the Cardinals in San Diego. Allen Watson started and allowed eight runs in one-third of an inning by surrendering four walks and four extra-base hits. Todd Burns gave up the other five first-inning runs.

In his first major league season, Watson started 1993 with a 6–0 record, then lost seven in a row to finish with a 6–7 record.

AUGUST 28   A Gregg Jefferies home run off Pedro Martinez in the tenth inning beats the Dodgers 3–2 in Los Angeles.

AUGUST 31   Bernard Gilkey's two-run, walk-off triple in the ninth inning beats the Reds 7–6 at Busch Stadium.

On the same day, the Cardinals traded Lee Smith to the Yankees for Richard Batchelor. Smith saved 43 games in 1993, but his ERA was 4.50, and he was near the end of his career.

SEPTEMBER 7   In the best single-game performance in Cardinals history, Mark Whiten hits 4 home runs and drives in 12 runs, both of which tied major league records, during a 15–2 victory over the Reds in the second game of a twinight doubleheader at Riverfront Stadium. Whiten tied another record for most RBIs in a doubleheader with 13. The twin bill was scheduled because of a June 4 rainout between the Cards and Reds. In the opener, the Cardinals scored seven runs in the eighth inning to take a 13–9 lead. Whiten contributed a sacrifice fly. But Cincinnati rallied with three runs in the eighth and two in the ninth to win 14–13. The two ninth-inning runs scored on a fly ball that Whiten, playing right field, misplayed into a triple. In the first inning of the season game, Whiten hit a 408-foot opposite-field grand slam off Larry Luebbers to left center field on a 2–0 pitch. It was Whiten's first homer since August 11. In the sixth, he hit a 397-foot, three-run blast to right-center field on the first pitch from Mike Anderson. Whiten connected off Anderson again in the seventh with two runners on base on a 2–1 pitch that traveled 388 feet and cleared the right-field wall. In the ninth, Whiten hit a 441-foot shot to right-center against Rob Dibble. When Whiten hit the final home run, at about 1 AM, there were only about 2,000 fans left in the ballpark. A switch-hitter, Whiten hit all four homers from the left side of the plate.

Through the end of the 2005 season, there have been 15 players who have hit four home runs in a game. Whiten is the only Cardinal to accomplish the feat. He was the first Cardinal batter to hit more than two homers in a game since Reggie Smith hit three in 1976. It didn't happen again until Mark McGwire clubbed three in a game in 1998. Whiten finished his career, which he spent with 8 different clubs over 11 years, with 105 homers. Of the 15 who hit four homers in a game, the only ones with fewer career homers than Whiten were Bobby Lowe (71), Pat Seerey (86), and Ed Delahanty (101). Whiten's 12 RBIs in a game tied the major league record set by Jim Bottomley of the Cardinals in 1924. His 13 RBIs during the doubleheader tied the mark set by Nate Colbert of the Padres in 1972.

SEPTEMBER 9   Todd Zeile's grand slam off Terry Bross in the sixth inning of a 9–4 win over the Giants in San Francisco.

SEPTEMBER 14   Mark Whiten hits homers from both sides of the plate during a 12–9 loss to the Expos at Busch Stadium in an odd game in which each team scored nine runs in the last three innings. Whiten homered off lefty Kirk Rueter in the seventh inning and right-hander Mel Rojas in the eighth.

On the same day, Major League Baseball announced its three-division alignment, plus an extra round of playoff games, to be put into effect during the 1994 season. The Cardinals were placed in the Central Division with Chicago, Cincinnati, Houston, and Pittsburgh. The Brewers joined the Central Division in 1998 when they moved to the National League, making it the only six-team division in either league.

SEPTEMBER 19   Mark Whiten's two-out, two-run, walk-off double in the ninth beats the Pirates 7–6 at Busch Stadium.

SEPTEMBER 29   The Cardinals go 17 innings only to lose a 1–0 crusher to the Mets in New York. Jeff Kent's two-out double off Les Lancaster scored the winning run. Over the first 16 innings, Rheal Cormier (seven innings), Pete Kilgus (two innings), Mike Perez (two innings), Les Guetterman (two innings), Rob Murphy (two innings), and Lancaster (one inning) pitched shutout ball allowing only four hits.

> *Cormier hailed from the Canadian town of Moncton, New Brunswick. During the offseason, he worked as a lumberjack.*

DECEMBER 6   Andres Galarraga signs with the Rockies as a free agent.

1994

Season in a Sentence

During a miserable summer, the Cardinals lose 19 of their last 27 games before a strike ends the season on August 12.

Finish • Won • Lost • Pct • GB

Third (tie)   53   61   .465   13.0

Manager

Joe Torre

Stats

Stats	Cards	NL	Rank
Batting Avg:	.263	.267	9
On-Base Pct:	.342	.336	4
Slugging Pct:	.414	.415	7
Home Runs:	108		8 (tie)
Stolen Bases:	76		7
ERA:	5.14	4.21	13
Fielding Avg:	.982	.980	4
Runs Scored:	535		6
Runs Allowed:	581		13

Starting Lineup

Tom Pagnozzi, c
Gregg Jefferies, 1b
Geronimo Peña, 2b
Todd Zeile, 3b
Ozzie Smith, ss
Bernard Gilkey, lf
Ray Lankford, cf
Mark Whiten, rf
Luis Alicea, 2b
Brian Jordan, cf-lf
Jose Oquendo, ss
Terry McGriff, c

Pitchers

Bob Tewksbury, sp
Allen Watson, sp
Vicente Palacios, sp-rp
Kevin Foster, sp
Mike Morgan, sp
Mike Perez, rp
Rene Arocha, rp
Rich Rodriguez, rp
John Habyan, rp
Rob Murphy, rp
Bryan Eversgerd, rp

Attendance

1,866,544 (seventh in NL)

Club Leaders

Batting Avg:	Jefferies	.325
On-Base Pct:	Jefferies	.391
Slugging Pct:	Jefferies	.489
Home Runs:	Zeile	19
	Lankford	19
RBIs:	Zeile	75
Runs:	Lankford	89
Stolen Bases:	Gilkey	15
Wins:	Tewksbury	12
Strikeouts:	Tewksbury	79
ERA:	Palacios	4.44
Saves:	Perez	12

JANUARY 31   Three weeks after Nancy Kerrigan is attacked by assailants connected to rival skater Tonya Harding, the Cardinals sign Rick Sutcliffe, most recently with the Orioles, as a free agent.

Sutcliffe came to the Cardinals with a lifetime record of 165–135, but he was 37 years old and near the end of his career. He was 6–4 in one season in St. Louis with a 6.52 ERA.

APRIL 3   The Cardinals open the season against the Reds at Riverfront Stadium on Easter in a game nationally televised on ESPN. With the temperature at 39 degrees for the evening game, Ray Lankford led off the first inning with a home run off Jose Rijo on a 3–2 pitch. Lankford later added a double and a single in the 6–4 St. Louis victory. Bob Tewksbury was the winning pitcher.

Tewksbury started the 1994 season with seven consecutive victories. From September 25, 1991, through May 11, 1994, Tewksbury had a 41–15 record.

APRIL 11   The Cardinals' scheduled home opener against the Dodgers in postponed by rain.

APRIL 12   The Cardinals get the home season under way but lose 7–3 to the Dodgers before 46,947 at Busch Stadium.

APRIL 17   Geronimo Peña homers from both sides of the plate during a 5–0 win over the Padres at Busch Stadium. Peña homered off right-hander Alan Ashby in the third inning and left-hander Mark Davis in the seventh.

APRIL 22   The Cardinals score two runs in the ninth inning to defeat the Astros 6–5 at Busch Stadium. With one out, Mitch Williams loaded the bases with walks, then hit Bernard Gilkey with a pitch to force in the tying run. Todd Zeile drove in the winning tally with a walk-off single.

Zeile hit .267 with 19 homers in the strike-shortened 1994 season. Ray Lankford also hit .267 with 19 home runs that year.

MAY 1   Ray Lankford homers on the first pitch of the game from Brian Williams of the Astros, setting the stage for a 6–5 Cardinal win at Houston.

MAY 4   Trailing 5–1, the Cardinals score three runs in the eighth inning and two in the ninth to defeat the Rockies in Denver. The two ninth-inning tallies came on Bernard Gilkey's home run.

MAY 6   Down 2–1 in the ninth, the Cardinals load the bases and score on two walks to beat the Mets 3–2 in New York. John Franco issued passes to pinch hitter Gerald Perry on a 3–2 pitch, and to Terry McGriff, another pinch hitter, on a 3–1 offering.

MAY 10   Ray Lankford's walk-off homer in the eleventh inning beats the Cubs 7–6 at Busch Stadium. The Cardinals led 6–0 after four innings before allowing Chicago to tie the score.

MAY 17   Six Cardinal pitchers combine on a two-hit shutout to defeat the Pirates 2–0 at Three Rivers Stadium. The carousel on the mound tied a National League record for most pitchers used in a shutout. Tom Urbani ($7^2/_3$ innings) started the game and allowed one hit. He was followed by John Habyan, who walked the only batter he faced, Rob Murphy ($1/3$ of an inning), Mike Perez ($1/3$ of an inning), Rich Rodriguez ($1/3$ of an inning), and Rene Arocha ($11/3$ inning). It was Urbani's second career win. He entered the contest with a 1–5 record. Carlos Garcia collected both Pittsburgh hits with a single in the fourth off Urbani and a single in the ninth against Arocha.

MAY 18   Ray Lankford homers in the tenth inning to beat the Pirates 4–3 in Pittsburgh.

MAY 22   Trailing 9–6, the Cardinals score four runs to beat the Marlins 10–9 in Miami. Gregg Jefferies drove in the tying and winning runs with a two-run double. Luis Alicea collected five hits, including a triple and a double, in six at-bats. The Cards trailed 7–2 in the second inning when a brawl erupted. After Jeff Conine hit the third Florida homer off Allen Watson in the third inning, the Cardinal pitcher hit Orestes Destrade with a pitch. As Destrade charged the mound, Watson threw a glove at him, opening a cut on Destrade's nose. Destrade punched Watson in the face, and both benches emptied. After the game, Destrade dismissed Watson as a "wimpy, gutless college boy."

MAY 24   The Cardinals set a major league record for most runners left on base without scoring a run by stranding 16 in a 4–0 loss to the Phillies at Busch Stadium. The Cards collected nine hits, including two doubles, and drew eight walks.

JUNE 2   In the first round of the amateur draft, the Cardinals select pitcher Bret Wagner from Wake Forest University.

Wagner never reached the majors. The Cardinals chose and signed future major leaguers Carl Dale (2nd round), Curtis King (5th round), Blake Stein (6th round), Placido Polanco (19th round), Jose Leon (22nd round), Keith McDonald (24th round), and Keith Glauber (42nd round), but only Polanco became a big-league regular.

JUNE 4   Ray Lankford's walk-off homer on the first pitch of the ninth inning beats the Giants 2–1 at Busch Stadium.

On June 13 the Cardinals were 32–28, good for third place, two games out of first. The season went downhill rapidly, however. The club was 21–33 the rest of the way before the strike ended the season.

JUNE 16   The Cardinals tie a major league record by turning seven double plays, but lose 7–5 to the Pirates in 10 innings at Busch Stadium. First baseman Gregg Jefferies figured in six of the double plays.

JUNE 18   A day after 95 million Americans tune in to the eight-hour police chase of O. J. Simpson and his Ford Bronco, Tom Pagnozzi hits a grand slam off Blas Minor in the sixth inning of a 9–0 win over the Pirates at Busch Stadium.

JUNE 30   The Cardinals overcome a 6–0 deficit to win 9–7 over the Rockies in a brawl-filled game at Busch Stadium. After hitting a three-run homer off Curtis Leskanic in the third inning, Geronimo Peña was hit by a Darren Holmes pitch in the sixth. Peña charged the mound and punched Holmes as both benches emptied. Peña was ejected, and Jose Oquendo took over at second base. Oquendo broke the 7–7 tie by driving in the go-ahead runs with a single in the seventh inning.

July 1   In his first game back after missing six games with a heel injury, Gregg Jefferies collects four hits, including two homers, in four at-bats, to lead the Cardinals to an 11–4 win over the Rockies in St. Louis. Ray Lankford, Mark Whiten, and Geronimo Peña also homered by the Cards. It was the first time that the Cardinals hit five homers in a game at Busch Stadium.

July 8   Mark Whiten drives in both runs of a 2–0 win over the Braves in Atlanta with a single in the fourth inning. Bob Tewksbury pitched the shutout.

July 12   Gregg Jefferies leads off the bottom of the first inning of the All-Star Game with a double, sparking the National league to a 10-inning, 8–7 win at Three Rivers Stadium in Pittsburgh.

July 18   The Cardinals blow an 11-run lead and lose 15–12 to the Astros at the Astrodome. St. Louis took an 11–0 lead with three runs in the first inning, four in the second, and four in the third. Houston rallied, however, by scoring two runs in the fourth inning, two in the fifth, and 11 in the sixth before the Cards scored a meaningless run in the ninth. The Astros orchestrated their comeback against pitchers Allen Watson, Cris Carpenter, Brian Eversgerd, and Steve Dixon. The 11-run rally tied a National League record for the largest deficit overcome to win a game. The Cardinals came from 11 back to beat the Giants 14–12 on June 15, 1952, and the Phillies trailed 12–1 before defeating the Cubs 18–16 in 10 innings on April 17, 1976.

          Dixon pitched only six major league games over two seasons. In five innings, he walked 13 batters and allowed 16 runs for an ERA of 28.80.

July 19   One day after the Cardinals blew an 11-run lead, Cardinal hurler Vicente Palacios throws a one-hitter to topple the Astros 10–0 at Houston. He pitched the gem on his 31st birthday. Palacios retired the last 21 batters to face him after Andujar Cedeño led off the third inning with a single.

July 30   Before 53,514, the largest regular-season crowd in the history of Busch Stadium, the Cardinals defeat the Cubs 10–7.

August 4 Todd Zeile hits a grand slam off Mel Rojas in the ninth inning of a 7–3 win over the Expos in Montreal.

August 8 Todd Zeile drives in six runs during an 11–1 trouncing of the Marlins in Miami.

August 11 With the strike deadline looming, the Cardinals defeat the Marlins 8–6 in Miami.

August 12 With about 70 percent of the season completed, the major league players go on strike.

          The strike, baseball's eighth interruption since 1972, had been anticipated all season. The owners wanted to put a lid on escalating payrolls by capping salaries and revising, if not eliminating, salary arbitration procedures. The players, who were obviously not interested in these reforms, had only one weapon once talks broke down: a strike.

September 1 The Cardinals name 36-year-old Mark Lamping as president of the organization.

A St. Louis native and a graduate of St. Louis University, Lamping was put in charge of the club's business and facility operations. Prior to assuming his position with the Cardinals, he had served as Anheuser-Busch's group director of sports marketing and as the commissioner of the Continental Basketball Association. Lamping brought much-needed youth, vitality, and vision to an organization that had grown stagnant. Among his accomplishments was helping to transform Busch Stadium into a more fan-friendly venue. At Lamping's insistence, the Cardinals also caught up with the changing times by actively pursuing free agents. The club hired Walt Jocketty at the end of the 1994 season and Tony La Russa a year later, and the Cardinals once again became one of baseball's most successful franchises. Although Anheuser-Busch sold the club in December 1995, Lamping stayed on under the new ownership and was still president of the Cardinals in 2005.

SEPTEMBER 14   The owners of the 28 major league clubs vote 26–2 to cancel the remainder of the season, including the playoffs and the World Series.

SEPTEMBER 21   The Cardinals fire Dal Maxvill as general manager.

The dismissal of Maxvill, who had been general manager since 1985, was the first major act under Mark Lamping's leadership. "What I've learned," Lamping said, "is that no one is happy with where the team is at this point. I just did not believe that maintaining the status quo got us any closer to winning a world championship." (See October 15, 1994.)

SEPTEMBER 25   A crowd of nearly 50,000 turns out at Busch Stadium for "Fan Appreciation Day." Hall of Famers Stan Musial and Red Schoendienst attended, and fans were allowed to run the bases and tour the clubhouse.

OCTOBER 15   The Cardinals hire 43-year-old Walt Jocketty as general manager.

Jocketty was not the Cardinals' first choice. The club actively pursued Phillies general manager Lee Thomas, but Thomas took himself out of consideration. Jocketty proved to be an excellent choice. In more than a decade as general manager, he seldom hesitated to make bold moves and has shown an ability to improve the club at all levels. Prior to coming to St. Louis, Jocketty worked in the Oakland Athletics organization for 14 years as club director in minor league development and scouting during a period in which the franchise won three AL pennants and a World Championship. Jocketty's career in St. Louis has been marked by his ability to acquire big names in trades. Among those he brought to St. Louis in deals with other clubs have been, in chronological order, Todd Stottlemyre, Mark McGwire, Edgar Renteria, Pat Hentgen, Darryl Kile, Fernando Viña, Jim Edmonds, Will Clark, Woody Williams, Chuck Finley, Scott Rolen, Larry Walker, and Mike Mulder.

DECEMBER 7   The Cardinals trade Luis Alicea to the Red Sox for Nate Minchey and Jeff McNeely.

DECEMBER 10   The Cardinals announce that the artificial turf at Busch Stadium will be removed and replaced by grass before the start of the 1996 season. The club played home games on AstroTurf from 1970 through 1995.

DECEMBER 12   The Cardinals sign Tom Henke, most recently with the Rangers, and Danny Jackson, most recently with the Phillies, as free agents.

Henke was 37 on Opening Day in 1995 but gave the Cardinals one top-notch season as a closer. He made the All-Star team and posted a 1.82 ERA, a 1–1 record, and 36 saves. Despite the success, Henke retired at the end of the season. Jackson signed for three years at $10.8 million after posting a 14–6 record for the Phillies in 1994, but he was treated for thyroid cancer before the 1995 season and was still weak when the campaign started. Later he injured an ankle. In three seasons in St. Louis, Jackson was 5–15 with a 5.78 ERA.

DECEMBER 14   Gregg Jefferies signs with the Phillies as a free agent.

Jefferies made the All-Star team in both of his seasons with the Cardinals and turned them into a lucrative four-year deal with Philadelphia. As a Phillie, Jefferies never came close to matching his St. Louis numbers.

1995

Season in a Sentence

The Cardinals undergo a massive roster overhaul, field an anemic offense, fire two managers, and hire Tony La Russa after the season.

Finish • Won • Lost • Pct • GB

Fourth   62   81   .434 22.5

In the wild-card race, the Cardinals were in 10th place, 14.5 games behind

Managers

Joe Torre (20–27) and Mike Jorgensen (42–54)

Stats	Cards	NL	Rank
Batting Avg:	.247	.263	14
On-Base Pct:	.316	.334	14
Slugging Pct:	.374	.408	14
Home Runs:	107		13
Stolen Bases:	79		10
ERA:	4.09	4.18	6
Fielding Avg:	.980	.980	8
Runs Scored:	563		14
Runs Allowed:	658		6

Starting Lineup

Danny Sheaffer, c
John Mabry, 1b-rf
Jose Oquendo, 2b
Scott Cooper, 3b
Tripp Cromer, ss
Bernard Gilkey, lf
Ray Lankford, cf
Brian Jordan, rf
Tom Pagnozzi, c
Ozzie Smith, ss
David Bell, 2b
Darnell Coles, 3b-1b
Todd Zeile, 1b

Pitchers

Mark Petkovsek, sp
Allen Watson, sp
Ken Hill, sp
Mike Morgan, sp
Donovan Osborne, sp
Tom Urbani, sp-rp
Danny Jackson, sp
Tom Henke, rp
Jeff Parrett, rp
Tony Fossas, rp
Rich DeLucia, rp
Rene Arocha, rp

Attendance

1,756,727 (seventh in NL)

Club Leaders

Batting Avg:	Gilkey	.298
On-Base Pct:	Gilkey	.358
Slugging Pct:	Lankford	.513
Home Runs:	Lankford	25
RBIs:	Lankford	82
Runs:	Jordan	83
Stolen Bases:	Jordan	24
	Lankford	24
Wins:	DeLucia	8
Strikeouts:	Osborne	82
ERA:	Petkovsek	4.00
Saves:	Henke	36

Doug Pensinger/Getty Images Sport/Getty Images

Ray Lankford posted big numbers for the Cardinals from 1990 to 2001. In his 12 consecutive seasons with the Cards, Lankford hit 222 home runs and had nearly a .300 batting average.

JANUARY 13   Major league owners vote to use replacement players during the 1995 season if the players' strike, begun on August 12, 1995, is not settled.

The Cardinals opened spring training in February at St. Petersburg, Florida, with replacement players and used them until the strike came to an end on April 2.

APRIL 2   The 234-day strike of Major League Baseball players comes to an end.

The opening of the season, originally scheduled to begin on April 3, was pushed back to April 26 with each team playing 144 games. The replacement players were either released or sent to the minors.

APRIL 5   The Cardinals trade Bryan Eversgerd, Kirk Bullinger, and DaRond Stovall to the Expos for Ken Hill.

APRIL 8   The Cardinals trade Mark Whiten and Rheal Cormier to the Red Sox for Scott Cooper and Cory Bailey. On the same day, Bob Tewksbury signed with the Rangers as a free agent.

Cooper had a great night in his first game as a Cardinal (see April 26, 1995) but was an extreme disappointment. He hit only .230 with three homers in 374 at-bats in 1995.

APRIL 12   The National Football League approves the transfer of the Los Angeles Rams to St. Louis.

The Rams played four regular-season games at Busch Stadium in 1995 before the opening of the Trans World Dome (now known as the Edward Jones Dome) on November 12.

APRIL 26   Nine days after the bombing of a federal office building in Oklahoma City, resulting in the deaths of 168 people, the Cardinals open the season with a 7–6 win over the Phillies before 33,539 at Busch Stadium. The Cards trailed 5–0 in the third inning and 6–5 heading into the ninth. Third baseman Scott Cooper, a St. Louis native in his Cardinals debut, drove in the tying and winning runs with a walk-off single. Cooper collected four RBIs on the night. Brian Jordan hit a homer and drove in the other three runs.

The 1–0 record following the opener was the only time the Cardinals were above .500 all year. A complete lack of offensive punch was the major culprit. The Cards finished last in a 14-team league in runs, batting average, on-base percentage, and slugging percentage. The starting pitching wasn't much better. The leader in wins on the 1995 Cardinals was reliever Rich DeLucia with eight.

APRIL 30   A three-run homer by Danny Sheaffer in the sixth inning accounts for all of the runs in a 3–0 win over the Mets in New York. Tom Urbani (six innings), Rich DeLucia (two innings), and Tom Henke (one inning) combined on the shutout.

MAY 10   The Cardinals wallop the Cubs 11–1 at Busch Stadium.

JUNE 1   In the first round of the amateur draft, the Cardinals select pitcher Matt Morris from Seton Hall University and third baseman Chris Haas from St. Mary's High School in Paducah, Kentucky. The Cardinals had one extra pick in the first round due to free-agent compensation.

Haas never reached the majors, but the Cardinals more than made up for the miscalculation by choosing Morris. In 2005, Morris won his 100th career game. Others the Cardinals drafted and signed in 1995 were Matt DeWitt (10th round), Britt Reames (17th round), Chris Richard (19th round), Kerry Robinson (34th round), and Cliff Politte (54th round).

JUNE 5   The Cardinals play at Coors Field for the first time and win 9–5 over the Rockies.

JUNE 16   On a busy day, the Cardinals fire Joe Torre as manager, hire Mike Jorgensen to replace him, and trade Todd Zeile to the Cubs for Mike Morgan, Paul Torres, and Francisco Morales.

Torre was dismissed with the Cardinals holding a record of 20–27. He was 351–354 as manager in St. Louis from 1990 through 1995. It was the third time that Torre had been fired as manager. His previous stints were with the Mets and Braves. At the time the Cards canned him, Torre's career record in 14 seasons as a manager was 894–1,003. At that point, he never had managed a team in the

World Series, nor had he appeared in one in 18 seasons as a player. The Yankees saw something in Torre, however, and hired him as manager on November 2, 1995. In his first season in pinstripes, Torre managed the Yanks to a World Championship. It was the start of one of the most successful runs in big-league history. Torre also managed the Yankees to World Championships in 1998, 1999, and 2000 and to the World Series appearances in 2001 and 2003 before losing.

Jorgensen was a big-league first baseman from 1969 through 1985. His last two seasons were as a Cardinal. At the time he was hired as manager, Jorgensen was 46 years old and the club's director of player development. He managed the Cards to a 42–54 record for the remainder of the 1995 season before Tony La Russa replaced him. Jorgensen went back to his old job in player development.

JULY 2   Danny Jackson's record on the season drops to 0–9 after losing a 7–6 decision to the Cubs in Chicago. Jackson was the first Cardinal pitcher to start a season with nine consecutive losses since Art Fromme in 1907.

JULY 3   Mike Morgan pitches a no-hitter for the first $8^{1}/_{3}$ innings before settling for a 6–0 win over the Expos at Busch Stadium. Morgan started the ninth by inducing Curtis Pride to fly out. After Tony Tarasco walked, Wil Cordero collected the only Montreal hit with an infield single. Third baseman Scott Cooper barehanded Cordero's chopper but threw past first base. Cordero reached second on a play that was ruled a hit and an error. Morgan was then taken out of the game, and Jeff Parrett recorded the final two outs.

Morgan set a major league record by playing for 12 teams during his major league career. In addition to the Cardinals, Morgan appeared in games for the Athletics, Yankees, Blue Jays, Mariners, Orioles, Dodgers, Cubs, Reds, Twins, Rangers, and Diamondbacks between 1978 and 2002.

JULY 25   Brian Jordan has a big day against the Mets with two homers and a walk-off single to lead the Cardinals to an 8–7 win at Busch Stadium.

JULY 27   The Cardinals trade Ken Hill to the Indians for David Bell, Rick Heiserman, and Pepe McNeal.

David Bell was part of a three-generation baseball family. His grandfather Gus Bell played in the majors from 1950 through 1964. David's father, Buddy was a big-leaguer from 1972 through 1989. David brother Mike was also in the majors for 19 games in 2000. David played for the Cardinals from 1995 through 1998 and was still active in the majors in 2005.

JULY 31   Hurricane Erin cancels the Cardinals-Marlins game in Miami.

AUGUST 6   John Mabry fakes a bunt, then singles through a drawn-in infield to score the winning run in the thirteenth inning of a 4–3 win over the Cubs at Busch Stadium. Both teams scored in the twelfth inning, with a St. Louis run coming on a home run by Darnell Coles.

AUGUST 10   The Cardinals win a forfeit against the Dodgers in Los Angeles.

With one out in the bottom of the ninth and the Cardinals leading 2–1, the umpire stopped the game after some in the raucous sellout crowd of 53,361 on Ball Night littered the field with balls for the third time. The game was delayed six minutes in the top of the seventh, and again in the ninth after Dodger outfielder Raul Mondesi and manager Tom Lasorda were ejected after Mondesi struck out. The umpires ordered the Cardinals to leave the field while the balls were picked up. After another delay of five minutes, the Cards went back on the field, and a few more balls were thrown. One just missed hitting center fielder Brian Jordan in the head. At that point, the umpires called the game. It was the first forfeit in the major leagues since 1979, and the first in the National League since the Cardinals forfeited to the Phillies on July 18, 1954.

AUGUST 21   Brian Jordan's three-run, walk-off homer with two out in the ninth inning beats the Reds 8–6 at Busch Stadium. The Cards trailed 6–2 before mounting the comeback with two runs in the seventh inning and one in the eighth to set the stage for Jordan's heroics.

AUGUST 25   Bernard Gilkey leads off the first inning with a homer on the first pitch from Brian Rekar, sparking the Cardinals to an 8–3 win over the Rockies in Denver.

AUGUST 26   Trailing 4–0, the Cardinals stun the Rockies with five runs in the ninth inning, the last four on Danny Sheaffer's grand slam off Bruce Ruffin to win 5–4 in Denver.

SEPTEMBER 11   The Cardinals rout the Giants 13–4 at Busch Stadium.

SEPTEMBER 12   Ray Lankford homers for the fourth consecutive game, leading the Cardinals to a 10–4 win over the Giants at Busch Stadium.

SEPTEMBER 15   Ozzie Smith sets a record for most career double plays by a shortstop with his 1,554th during a 7–6 loss to the Dodgers in Los Angeles.

                 By the end of his career in 1996, Smith had completed 1,590 double plays. He also set the major league mark for most assists (8,375) and most total chances (12,624) by a shortstop in a career.

SEPTEMBER 25   Bernard Gilkey breaks up the no-hit bid of Frank Castillo of the Cubs with two outs in the ninth inning of a 7–0 loss to Chicago at Wrigley Field. Castillo had an 0–2 count on Gilkey and was one strike from a no-hitter. After the count went to 2–2, Gilkey hit an opposite-field triple into right field. Castillo retired the next hitter for a one-hitter.

OCTOBER 23   Three weeks after O. J. Simpson is found not guilty of the double murder of his ex-wife and her companion, the Cardinals hire 51-year-old Tony La Russa as manager.

                 La Russa hit only .199 without a single homer in 132 games as a player over six big-league seasons. Throughout his playing career, La Russa continued his education. He attended the University of Tampa and the University of South Florida during the offseason and obtained a degree in industrial engineering. He attended law school at Florida State University, graduated in 1978, and passed the bar in 1979. Baseball took priority, however, and La Russa received his first major league managing job with the White Sox in 1979. In 1983, the Sox won the Western Division title with a record of 99–63. The .611 winning percentage was the best of any White Sox team since 1920. It wasn't matched again until 2005. By 1986, however, La Russa was fired after a series of disagreements with general manager Ken Harrelson. A month later, he accepted a job as manager of the Athletics. He led the Oakland club to the World Series in 1988, 1989, and 1990, winning a World Championship in 1989. By 1995 the A's had fallen into last place. Cardinals general manager Walt Jocketty, who had worked with La Russa in Oakland, was able to lure him to St. Louis because of long-term rebuilding in Oakland, the uncertainty over the Athletics' new ownership, and the manager's high regard for the Cardinals' rich tradition. In La Russa's first season, the Cards won the division championship. After a few bumpy years in the late 1990s, La Russa brought the Redbirds back to prominence with almost yearly postseason appearances in the 21st century.

OCTOBER 25   Anheuser-Busch announces its intention to sell the Cardinals.

The statement came as a complete surprise. The company had owned the Cardinals since 1953. "We concluded it was in the best interest of everyone, including the Cardinals and the fans, to seek a new owner," brewery chairman August Busch III said. Anheuser-Busch offered the team as a package that also included Busch Stadium and two downtown parking garages near the stadium (see December 22, 1995).

DECEMBER 14   The Cardinals trade Allen Watson, Rich DeLucia, and Doug Creek to the Giants for Royce Clayton and Chris Wimmer.

DECEMBER 15   The Cardinals sign Willie McGee, most recently with the Giants, as a free agent.

McGee had previously played for the Cardinals from 1982 through 1990. His second tour of duty with the club lasted four years, until his retirement in 1999. The signing reunited the last remnants of the Cardinals' perennial playoff teams of the '80s, McGee and Ozzie Smith. Even in his later years, McGee had a knack for coming through in the clutch, and fans hadn't forgotten his shoestring catches, humble personality, and quiet leadership from his last stint in St. Louis. Many remained indignant, even angry, that McGee had been shipped off to Oakland in 1990 like livestock, after all he had done for the Redbirds. When he returned, he received a standing ovation every time he came to bat.

DECEMBER 18   The Cardinals sign Gary Gaetti, most recently with the Royals, as a free agent.

DECEMBER 21   The Cardinals purchase Rick Honeycutt from the Athletics.

DECEMBER 22   A group headed by William O. DeWitt Jr. purchases the Cardinals from Anheuser-Busch, pending the approval of National League owners. The sale became official on March 21, 1996.

DeWitt's father, William O. DeWitt Sr., was a baseball fixture for 50 years. The senior DeWitt began his career in baseball as an office boy for the Cardinals at the age of 15 in 1916. By 1936, he was vice president and general manger of the St. Louis Browns and led the club to its only World Series appearance, in 1944. He also owned the Browns, along with his brother Charles, from 1949 through 1951 before selling the club to Bill Veeck. DeWitt was general manager of the Tigers and Reds during the 1950s and 1960s and owned the Reds from 1962 through 1966. William DeWitt Jr. naturally grew up around baseball. He was nine years old when the midget Eddie Gaedel used William Jr.'s uniform in Bill Veeck's famous publicity stunt (see August 18, 1951). After earning degrees from both Yale and Harvard, William Jr. was a part owner of the Cincinnati Stingers in the World Hockey Association during the 1970s and had vast business interests. Others involved in the purchase of the Cardinals from Anheuser-Busch included St. Louis attorney Frederick O. Hanser and banking executive Andrew N. Baur. Hanser was a great-grandson of Adolph Diaz, who owned stock in the Cardinals from 1917 through 1947. DeWitt, Hanser, and Baur all attended St. Louis Country Day School and were lifelong friends, attending many Cardinals games together before purchasing the club. The group has been largely anonymous in St. Louis, however, preferring to stay behind the scenes and allow Tony La Russa and Walt Jocketty to run the club.

DECEMBER 23   The Cardinals sign Andy Benes, most recently with the Padres, and Ron Gant, most recently with the Reds, as free agents.

One of Tony La Russa's first priorities was to rebuild the starting rotation. Benes was a major step in that process. Andy joined his brother Alan on the Cardinals' pitching staff. In 1996, Andy had a record of 18–10 with a 3.83 ERA. The same season, Alan contributed a 13–10 mark and a 4.90 ERA. Gant gave the Cardinals one good year but unfortunately had been signed to a hefty five-year deal that strained the club's budget. In 1996, Gant hit 30 homers and became the first Cardinal outfielder to hit at least 30 in a season since Stan Musial hit 35 in 1954. Gant's power outburst masked a .249 batting average and defensive deficiencies, however. His signing led the Cardinals to trade Bernard Gilkey to the Mets in another bad deal (see January 22, 1996). They dealt Gant to the Phillies after the 1998 season following a drop in production. The Cards sweetened the deal by paying Philadelphia $5 million to take on the two remaining years of Gant's contract.

1996

Season in a Sentence

In Tony La Russa's first year as manager, the Cardinals overcome a sluggish start to win the NL Central before blowing a three-games-to-one edge over the Braves in the National League Championship Series.

Finish • Won • Lost • Pct • GB

First   88   74   .543   +6.0

National League Division Series—The Cardinals defeated the San Diego Padres three games to none

National League Championship Series—The Cardinals lost to the Atlanta Braves four games to three

Manager

Tony La Russa

Stats

Stats	Cards	• NL •	Rank
Batting Avg:	.267	.262	4
On-Base Pct:	.332	.333	6
Slugging Pct:	.407	.408	6
Home Runs:	142		12
Stolen Bases:	149		4
ERA:	3.97	4.21	6
Fielding Avg:	.980	.979	8
Runs Scored:	759		7
Runs Allowed:	706		6

Starting Lineup

Tom Pagnozzi, c
John Mabry, 1b
Luis Alicea, 2b
Gary Gaetti, 3b
Royce Clayton, ss
Ron Gant, lf
Ray Lankford, cf
Brian Jordan, rf
Willie McGee, rf
Ozzie Smith, ss
Danny Sheaffer, c
Mark Sweeney, lf

Pitchers

Andy Benes, sp
Todd Stottlemyre, sp
Donovan Osborne, sp
Alan Benes, sp
Mike Morgan, sp
Dennis Eckersley, rp
T. J. Mathews, rp
Tony Fossas, rp
Rick Honeycutt, rp
Cory Bailey, rp
Mark Petkovsek, rp

Attendance

2,654,718 (fourth in NL)

Club Leaders

Batting Avg:	Jordan	.310
On-Base Pct:	Lankford	.366
Slugging Pct:	Gant	.504
Home Runs:	Gant	30
RBIs:	Jordan	104
Runs:	Lankford	100
Stolen Bases:	Lankford	35
Wins:	Benes	18
Strikeouts:	Stottlemyre	194
ERA:	Osborne	3.53
Saves:	Eckersley	30

JANUARY 9   The Cardinals trade Allen Battle, Bret Wagner, Jay Witasick, and Carl Dale to the Athletics for Todd Stottlemyre.

JANUARY 11   The Cardinals sign Mike Gallego, most recently with the Athletics, as a free agent.

JANUARY 22   The Cardinals trade Bernard Gilkey to the Mets for Eric Ludwick, Erik Hiljus, and Yudith Ozario.

Gilkey had a career year with the Mets, batting .317 with 30 homers, 117 RBIs, and 108 runs scored in 1996 before going into a dramatic slide. None of the three players acquired in the deal was of any help to the Cardinals.

FEBRUARY 13   The Cardinals trade Steve Montgomery to the Athletics for Dennis Eckersley.

Eckersley was 41 years old when the Cardinals acquired him. Playing for La Russa with the Athletics from 1987 through 1995, Eckersley established his Hall of Fame credentials by becoming one of the most dominant relief pitchers in history. In two inconsistent seasons as the Cards' closer, Eckersley had a 3.58 ERA in 120 games and 66 saves, but his won-lost record was an abysmal 1–11.

FEBRUARY 26   Donovan Osborne suffers a broken rib in an auto accident in St. Petersburg. Osborne turned his car into the path of a pickup truck. He missed the first two weeks of the regular season.

MARCH 17   The Cardinals sign Luis Alicea, most recently with the Red Sox, as a free agent.

APRIL 1   In Tony La Russa's debut as Cardinal manager, the club loses 7–6 to the Mets on Opening Day at Shea Stadium. New York led 6–3 until scoring four times in the seventh inning, three of them on a home run by Bernard Gilkey, who was playing in his first game for the Mets following his trade from the Cardinals. Willie McGee homered and drove in three runs, and Ray Lankford collected three hits. Ozzie Smith didn't play because of a tender right hamstring. Smith started at shortstop in every Cardinals opener from 1982 through 1995. Royce Clayton took over Smith's spot.

Tony La Russa was the fourth lawyer to manage the Cardinals. The others were Miller Huggins (1913–17), Jack Hendricks (1918), and Branch Rickey (1919–25).

APRIL 5   The day after "Unabomber" Theodore Kaczynski is arrested in Montana, the Cardinals defeat the Braves 5–4 in Atlanta. Ron Gant drove in the winning run with a bases-loaded walk.

APRIL 8   In the home opener, the Cardinals lose 4–3 in 10 innings to the Expos before 52,841 at Busch Stadium. Facing Pedro Martinez, Gary Gaetti homered in his first at-bat as a Cardinal at Busch Stadium.

APRIL 14   Down 5–0, the Cardinals score three runs in the third inning and three in the fifth to defeat the Phillies 6–5 at Busch Stadium.

APRIL 16   Orlando Merced and Derek Bell of the Pirates both hit grand slams against the Cardinals during a 13–3 Pittsburgh win in St. Louis. It was the only time in the 40-year history of Busch Stadium that a team hit two grand slams in a game. Merced hit his slam in the first inning off Andy Benes. Bell connected with the bases loaded against Tom Urbani in the sixth.

APRIL 19   The Cardinals tie a National League record by using six pitchers in a shutout, defeating the Phillies 1–0 in Philadelphia. The pitchers were Mark Petkovsek (4 innings), Tony Fossas (1 inning), T. J. Mathews (1²/₃ innings), Rick Honeycutt (¹/₃ of an inning), Cory Bailey (1 inning), and Dennis Eckersley (1 inning). Royce Clayton drove in the game's only run with a two-out single in the ninth.

APRIL 20   For the second game in a row, the Cardinals defeat the Phillies 1–0 at Veterans Stadium with a two-out single in the ninth inning. Brian Jordan drove in the winner.

Alan Benes (eight innings) and Dennis Eckersley (one inning) combined on a two-hitter. The only Philadelphia hits were singles by Mark Whiten in the fifth inning and Mickey Morandini in the eighth.

MAY 3   The Cardinals break a 15-game losing streak in San Diego, dating back to July 1992, with a 3–1 win over the Padres.

MAY 8   Ron Gant hits a pinch-hit grand slam off Mark Gardner during a seven-run sixth inning, but the Cardinals lose 10–7 to the Giants at Busch Stadium.

MAY 9   Trailing 8–5, the Cardinals erupt for 11 runs in the eighth inning and defeat the Giants 16–8 at Busch Stadium. Willie McGee hit a grand slam off Doug Creek during the big inning.

MAY 13   Andy Benes is ejected after igniting a bench-clearing brawl. He hit Gary Sheffield with a pitch during a 5–2 loss to the Marlins in Miami. The Cards led 1–0 in the sixth when Benes hit Sheffield on the left arm. Sheffield crumpled to the ground in pain, then stood, picked up his bat, slammed it to the ground, and started toward Benes. Catcher Tom Pagnozzi restrained Sheffield, who clenched his fists and yelled at Benes. T. J. Mathews relieved Benes. Mathews walked the next batter to load the bases, then gave up a grand slam to Terry Pendleton.

MAY 15   Todd Stottlemyre strikes out 13 batters during a 6–0 win over the Marlins in Miami.

MAY 18   John Mabry hits for the cycle, but the Rockies score five runs in the ninth inning off Dennis Eckersley to beat the Cardinals 9–8 in Denver. Eckersley allowed a two-run homer to Ellis Burks and a three-run, walk-off blast to John Vander Wal. Mabry's cycle came in sequential order. Facing Marvin Freeman, Mabry singled in the second inning, doubled in the third, and tripled in the fifth before hitting a home run off Mike Muñoz in the seventh.

MAY 19   The Cardinals lose 10–3 to the Rockies in Denver to drop their record to 17–26 on the season. The Cards were in last place in the NL Central but just four games out of first.

After losing seasons in 1994 and 1995, another one appeared to be in the offing after the May 19 defeat. The Redbirds went 71–48 the rest of the season, however.

JUNE 1   Trailing 4–2 against the Astros at Busch Stadium, the Cardinals tie the game 4–4 on Luis Alicea's two-run homer in the ninth and win 5–4 on Tom Pagnozzi's walk-off home run in the tenth.

JUNE 2   Astros pitcher Darryl Kile ties a major league record by hitting four Cardinal batters during a 2–0 St. Louis win at Busch Stadium. Those Kile plunked were Ray Lankford, Ron Gant, Danny Sheaffer, and Luis Alicea.

JUNE 4   In the first round of the amateur draft, the Cardinals select pitcher Braden Looper from Wichita State University.

Looper pitched only one season for the Cardinals before a trade to Florida, where he established himself as one of the better closers in baseball with the

Marlins. Thus far, the 1996 draft has been one of the worst in club history. The only other players the Cardinals drafted and signed that have reached the majors are Brent Butler (3rd round) and Stubby Clapp (36th round).

JUNE 14   Gary Gaetti hits two home runs and a double to lead the Cardinals to a 13–4 rout of the Mets at Busch Stadium. One of Gaetti's homers was a grand slam off Paul Byrd in the eighth inning. In his first game back after spending five weeks on the disabled list with a hamstring strain, Ron Gant hit a home run off Jason Isringhausen to lead off the first inning.

JUNE 15   The Cardinals trade Pat Borders to the Angels for Ben VanRyn.

JUNE 19   Ozzie Smith announces his retirement effective at the end of the season.

JUNE 24   Ron Gant homers on the first pitch of the game from John Smoltz, and Brian Jordan drives in six runs during a 9–2 win over the Braves in Atlanta. Jordan homered, singled, and hit a sacrifice fly.

JULY 6   John Mabry collects five hits in five at-bats during a 9–5 win over the Pirates in Pittsburgh.

JULY 12   At windy Wrigley Field, the Cardinals tie the club record for most homers in a game with seven, leading to a 13–3 rout of the Cubs. Ron Gant and Gary Gaetti each hit two homers, while Ray Lankford, John Mabry, and Brian Jordan added the rest. The only other time the Cards hit seven home runs in a game was on May 7, 1940.

JULY 13   Brian Jordan drives in six runs with a grand slam and a two-run homer to spark the Cardinals to an 11–5 win over the Cubs in Chicago. Jordan hit it in the six inning off Tanyon Sturtze.

           From June 23 through July 24, Jordan drove in 44 runs over 28 games. He finished the season batting .310 with 17 homers and 104 RBIs.

JULY 21   Tom Pagnozzi's walk-off homer in the tenth inning beats the Cubs 6–5 at Busch Stadium.

AUGUST 2   Ron Gant's grand slam off Bobby Jones in the fifth inning provides all four Cardinals runs in a 4–3 win over the Mets in New York.

AUGUST 7   Gary Gaetti's walk-off homer with one out in the ninth inning is the lone run in a 1–0 win over the Padres at Busch Stadium. Mel Stottlemyre (eight innings) and Mark Petkovsek (one inning) combined on the shutout.

AUGUST 16 Andy Benes wins his tenth consecutive game with a 6–2 decision over the Marlins at Busch Stadium.

           After a 1–7 start to the 1996 season, Benes was 17–3 the rest of the way.

AUGUST 23 Ray Lankford's home run in the third inning off Darryl Kile is the only run in a 1–0 win over the Astros in Houston. Donovan Osborne (seven innings) T. J. Mathews (one inning), and Dennis Eckersley (one inning) teamed on the shutout.

AUGUST 29   The Cardinals lose 10–9 to the Marlins in Miami to fall to 69–65, 2½ games behind the Astros.

AUGUST 26   Donovan Osborne is arrested on charges of public intoxication and criminal trespass after refusing to leave a Houston nightclub.

SEPTEMBER 1   Trailing 6–2, the Cardinals score two runs in the fifth inning, six in the seventh, and four in the eighth to beat the Rockies 15–6 at Busch Stadium.

SEPTEMBER 2   The Cardinals pull within half a game of first place behind Houston with an 8–7 win over the Astros in 10 innings at Busch Stadium. The Cards trailed 7–3 in the fourth inning before mounting a comeback. Veterans Willie McGee, age 37, and Ozzie Smith, 41, both relegated to bench roles in 1996, were the stars of the game. McGee played in place of the injured Ron Gant and singled in Smith for the winning run. It was McGee's fourth hit of the game. Spelling Royce Clayton, Smith hit a home run and two singles and scored four runs.

Among those in attendance were Republican Party presidential candidate Bob Dole and his vice presidential running mate, Jack Kemp. Both left in the fourth inning due to campaign commitments.

SEPTEMBER 3   The Cardinals take over first place with a 12–3 win over the Astros at Busch Stadium.

SEPTEMBER 4   The Cardinals complete a three-game sweep of the Astros at Busch Stadium and take a 1½-game lead in the NL Central with a 6–4 victory over Houston.

The Cardinals were 11–2 against the Astros in 1996.

SEPTEMBER 7   Donovan Osborne helps his own cause with a grand slam off Alan Ashby in the fifth inning to lead the Cardinals to an 8–3 win over the Padres at Busch Stadium. Osborne's slam broke a 1–1 tie. It was the Cardinals' eighth win in a row.

SEPTEMBER 10   The Cardinals edge the Giants 1–0 in San Francisco. Ray Lankford's double in the sixth inning scored the game's only run. Mark Petkovsek (5 innings), Tony Fossas (1 inning), Cory Bailey (⅓ of an inning), Rick Honeycutt (1⅓ innings), and Dennis Eckersley (1⅓ innings) teamed on the shutout.

SEPTEMBER 19   The Cardinals complete a three-game sweep of the Cubs at Busch Stadium with a 13-inning, 5–4 win. Tom Pagnozzi's single over a five-man infield drove in the winning run. Benches cleared in the fifth inning following an exchange of hit batsmen.

The win gave the Cardinals a five-game lead in the NL Central.

SEPTEMBER 24   The Cardinals clinch the NL Central with a 7–1 win over the Pirates in Pittsburgh. It was their first division title since 1987.

The Cardinals met the San Diego Padres in the National League Division Series, which began on October 1. Managed by Bruce Bochy, the Padres were 91–71 in 1996 and won the NL West by one game over the Dodgers.

SEPTEMBER 25   Reserve outfielder Terry Bradshaw collects four hits, including a double, in five at-bats during an 11-inning, 8–7 over the Pirates in Pittsburgh.

The four hits proved to be the last four of Bradshaw's career. He finished his two-year stay in the majors with 17 hits in 62 at-bats for a .262 average.

SEPTEMBER 28   The Cardinals celebrate Ozzie Smith Day at Busch Stadium. The event attracted 52,876, the largest crowd for a day game in the 40-year history of the facility. In pregame ceremonies, Smith received a dozen testimonials, a half-dozen standing ovations, and two red sports cars. When he took his position at shortstop in the first inning, Smith executed one of his trademark back flips. He went 1 for 4 during a 5–2 win over the Reds.

Smith finished his career with 1,257 runs, 2,460 hits, and 580 stolen bases. The only players since 1900 to top him in all three categories are Lou Brock, Max Carey, Ty Cobb, Eddie Collins, Rickey Henderson, Joe Morgan, Tim Raines, and Honus Wagner.

OCTOBER 1   The Cardinals open the Division Series with a 3–1 win over the Padres before 54,193 at Busch Stadium. All three St. Louis runs scored on a homer by Gary Gaetti in the first inning off Joey Hamilton. Todd Stottlemyre pitched $6^2/_3$ innings for the win.

OCTOBER 3   The Cardinals win Game Two with a 5–4 decision over the Padres before 56,752 at Busch Stadium. Ron Gant broke a 1–1 tie with a three-run double in the fifth inning, but San Diego tied the game 4–4 with two runs in the sixth and one in the eighth. In the bottom of the eighth, Brian Jordan and John Mabry walked. Both moved up on a wild pitch before Tom Pagnozzi hit a soft dribbler back to Padres pitcher Trevor Hoffman, whose throw to the plate was too late to catch the hard-charging Jordan. Dennis Eckersley, celebrating his 42nd birthday, earned the save by pitching the ninth. Fellow reliever Rick Honeycutt, also 42, was the winning pitcher.

Andy and Alan Benes were only the second pair of brothers to pitch in the same postseason for the same team. The first was Dizzy and Paul Dean for the Cardinals in 1934.

OCTOBER 5   After trailing 4–1 at the end of the fifth inning, the Cardinals storm back to complete the three-game Division Series sweep of the Padres in with 7–5 win in San Diego. Brian Jordan was the star. With the score tied in the bottom of the eighth, two outs and a man on second, Jordan made a diving catch of a Jody Reed liner. Then in the ninth, with one out, Jordan hit a two-run homer to seal the victory. It was his third hit of the game. Ron Gant also homered during the contest.

The Cardinals met the Atlanta Braves in the National League Championship Series. Managed by Bobby Cox, the Braves were the defending World Champions, having defeated the Indians in the 1995 World Series. In 1996, Atlanta was 96–66 during the regular season and beat the Dodgers three straight in the Division Series. During the regular season, the Cardinals were 4–9 against the Braves and lost all six meetings at Busch Stadium.

OCTOBER 9   The Cardinals open the NLCS with a 4–2 loss to the Braves in Atlanta. The Braves broke a 2–2 tie with two runs in the eighth inning off Mark Petkovsek.

OCTOBER 10   The Cardinals even the series with an 8–3 win over the Braves in Atlanta. The Cards broke open a 3–3 game with five runs in the seventh inning. After Greg Maddux intentionally walked Brain Jordan, Gary Gaetti promptly made him pay by hitting a grand slam. Ron Gant also homered for St. Louis.

OCTOBER 12   The Cardinals take a two-games-to-one lead in the NLCS with a 3–2 win over the Braves before 56,769 at Busch Stadium. Ron Gant drove in all three St. Louis runs with a pair of home runs off Tom Glavine. Gant hit a two-run blast in the first inning and a solo shot in the sixth.

In 1994, the Braves had released Gant after he broke his leg in a dirt-bike accident.

OCTOBER 13   The Cardinals move within one game of advancing to the World Series with a 4–3 victory over the Braves before 56,764 at Busch Stadium. The Cards trailed 3–0 before scoring three times in the seventh inning and one in the eighth. The Redbirds collected only one hit off Denny Neagle over the first six innings. The Cards tied the score in the seventh with two outs. With the bases empty John Mabry singled, Tom Pagnozzi walked, and Dmitri Young hit a pinch-hit triple and scored on an infield single by Royce Clayton. In the eighth Brian Jordan broke the tie with a home run off Steve McMichael.

On the same day, the Yankees won the American League Championship Series over the Orioles four games to one. All the Cardinals had to do to meet former manager Joe Torre in the World Series was beat the Braves once in three tries.

OCTOBER 14   The Cardinals suffer a 14–0 thrashing at the hands of the Braves in Game Five before 56,782 at Busch Stadium. Atlanta jumped on the Cards early with five runs in the first inning and two in the second off Todd Stottlemyre. The Braves collected 22 hits in the contest.

OCTOBER 16   The Braves force a seventh game by defeating the Cardinals 3–1 in Atlanta.

The 1996 NLCS marked the final time that the Cardinals played at Atlanta–Fulton County Stadium. The Braves moved into Turner Field in 1997.

OCTOBER 17   The Braves win the seventh game 15–0 over the Cardinals in Atlanta. It was over early, as the Braves scored six runs in the first inning off Donovan Osborne. Ozzie Smith made his last major league appearance by fouling out as a pinch hitter in the sixth inning.

The Braves outscored the Cardinals 32–1 in the last three games of the NLCS. Atlanta won the first two games of the World Series against the Yankees 12–1 and 4–0 in New York, then dropped four games in a row.

OCTOBER 23   Cardinals players, coaches, and staff begin a round of antibiotic shots after possible exposure to hepatitis A virus from eating a postgame meal at Bartolino's South, a restaurant in St. Louis County, on October 13. The Cards went to the establishment to celebrate their Game Four win in the National League Championship Series. The team said that no one had been reported ill, but four employees of the restaurant were diagnosed with hepatitis A, leading to a recommendation from health officials that the Cardinals take precautionary measures against contracting the virus.

NOVEMBER 20   Two weeks after Bill Clinton wins a second term as president over Bob Dole, the Cardinals sign Delino DeShields, most recently with the Dodgers, as a free agent.

DECEMBER 12   The Cardinals announce changes at Busch Stadium for the upcoming 1997 season.

Unlike the other multipurpose "cookie-cutter" stadium built for both baseball and football during the 1960s and 1970s, the Cardinals had the advantage of owning the facility and not having a football team to accommodate. This afforded them the opportunity to give Busch Stadium more of a baseball feel without consulting government authorities or another club. The most significant change at Busch Stadium was the addition of a 17-foot-high, 270-foot-wide, hand-operated scoreboard in the upper deck in center field that featured inning-by-inning line scores from each major league game. On both sides of the scoreboard were flag decks commemorating the franchise's World Series Championships and retired uniform numbers. Other modifications included the move of the bullpens from a position outside the foul lines to a spot behind the outfield fence, the change of the blue Anheuser-Busch color scheme to a more traditional "ballpark" green, and new picnic and family areas. Hundreds of new seats were placed at field level closer to the action, and others were reconfigured so that they faced the infield. The capacity of Busch Stadium was reduced from 57,769, including standing room, to 49,676.

Retired Numbers

Through the 2005 season, the Cardinals have retired nine uniform numbers.

1—Ozzie Smith

Smith's number 1 was retired subsequent with his retirement at the end of the 1996 season. Smith wore the number 1 from 1978 through 1981 with the San Diego Padres and in each of his 15 seasons in St. Louis. The last player prior to Smith to wear number 1 was Garry Templeton, from 1977 through 1981. Templeton was traded to the Padres for Smith.

2—Red Schoendienst

When Schoendienst was a rookie with the Cardinals in 1945, he was given number 6, which Stan Musial had worn from 1941 through 1944. The number was available in 1945 because Musial was in the Navy. When Musial returned from the service in 1946, Schoendienst was assigned number 2, which he wore until his trade to the Giants in June 1956. Schoendienst came back to St. Louis as a player in 1961 and was again given number 2. Hal Smith wore number 2 in 1960 but was reassigned number 9 when Schoendienst came back to the Cards. As a player, manager, and coach, he wore number 2 from 1961 through the 1990s and saw it retired in 1996.

6—Stan Musial

Musial arrived in St. Louis during a September call-up in 1941. He was given number 6 by equipment manager Butch Yatkeman simply because it was the available jersey that fit Musial the best. Earlier in the 1941 season, it had been worn by Harry Walker and Pep Young. With the exception of 1945, when Red Schoendienst used number 6 while Musial was in the service, no one with the Cardinals has used the number since. It was the first number the Cardinals retired, in 1963, when Musial's playing career ended.

9—Enos Slaughter

Slaughter wore number 9 from his rookie year in 1938 until he was traded to the Yankees just prior to the 1954 season. The Cardinals retired the number in his honor in 1996. Others who wore number 9 include Debs Garms (1943–1945, while Slaughter was in military service), Bill Virdon, Bobby Del Greco, Jim King, Ray Katt, Tim McCarver, Hal Smith, Minnie Minoso, Bob Uecker, Roger Maris, Joe Torre, Ken Rudolph, Vern Rapp, Steve Swisher, coach Hub Kittle, Terry Pendleton, and Torre again when he returned as manager in the 1990s.

14—Ken Boyer

Boyer wore number 14 as a player from 1955 through 1965, as a coach in 1971 and 1972, and as manager from 1978 through 1980. Before 1955, the last player to wear 14 was Gerry Staley, from 1947 through 1954. Boyer didn't live to see the number retired, which the Cardinals did in 1984. He died in 1982. Others who wore number 14 include George Kernek, Ron Davis, Steve Huntz, Ed Crosby, Terry Hughes, Dave Ricketts, Luis Alvarado, Dave Rader, Julio Gonzalez, and Rafael Santana.

17—Dizzy Dean
The Cardinals first assigned permanent uniform numbers in June 1932, and Dean was given number 17, which he wore until a trade to the Cubs just prior to the 1938 season. The Cards retired number 17 just after Dean's death in 1974. Others who wore number 17 before it was retired included Hal Epps, Joe Stripp, Lynn King, Erv Dusak, Frank Demaree, Augie Bergamo, Joe Garagiola, Harry Walker, Wally Westlake, Les Fusselman, Sal Yvars, Vic Raschi, Mel Wright, Vinegar Bend Mizell, Ed Olivares, Jerry Buchek, Fred Whitfield, Jim Beauchamp, Carl Warwick, Bobby Tolan, Vic Davalillo, Matty Alou, and Bill Voss.

20—Lou Brock
When Brock was brought to St. Louis in a trade with the Cubs in June 1964, he got number 20. Before that, the last player to wear number 20 was Gary Kolb. The team retired Brock's number when he retired, in 1979.

45—Bob Gibson
Number 45 was Gibson's third number as a Cardinal. He wore number 58 in 1959 and number 31 at the start of the 1960 season. After he was sent to the minors in May 1960, the Cards gave number 31 to Curt Simmons, whom they had acquired from the Phillies. When Gibson came back in July, he received number 45, last worn during a regular-season game by Dean Stone in 1959. Gibson retired in 1975, and number 45 went with him.

85—August Busch
Number 85 was retired in 1985 in honor of longtime owner August Busch's 85 birthday.

In addition to the nine individuals listed above, three others have also been honored by the Cardinals and are listed among the retired numbers in the outfield seats at Busch Stadium. Number 42 was retired in 1997 throughout major league baseball in honor of Jackie Robinson. Rogers Hornsby, who played with the Cardinals from 1916 through 1926 and again in 1933, is listed by name only because the bulk of his career was spent before permanent numbers were sewn on the backs of major league uniforms. Hornsby's name was added in 1997. The most recent to be honored is legendary broadcaster Jack Buck, who served as radio and television announcer from 1954 through 2001. Buck's signature call, "That's a winner!" was placed among the retired uniform numbers following his death in June 2002.

In 2005, Mark McGwire's number 25 was in "suspended animation." It had not been assigned to a player since McGwire's retirement in 2001. In addition, Darryl Kile's number 57 was not been given to another player since Kile's death in 2002.

1997

Season in a Sentence

After guaranteeing that the Cardinals would repeat as NL Central champs, Tony La Russa watches his club lose 89 games.

Finish • Won • Lost • Pct • GB

Fourth   73   89   .451   11.0

In the wild-card race, the Cardinals were in ninth place, 19 games back

Manager

Tony La Russa

Stats	Cards	• NL •	Rank
Batting Avg:	.255	.263	13
On-Base Pct:	.326	.333	13
Slugging Pct:	.396	.410	10
Home Runs:	144		8
Stolen Bases:	164		3
ERA:	3.88	4.21	5
Fielding Avg:	.980	.981	9
Runs Scored:	689		11
Runs Allowed:	708		5

Starting Lineup

Mike DiFelice, c
Dmitri Young, 1b
Delino DeShields, 2b
Gary Gaetti, 3b
Royce Clayton, ss
Ron Gant, lf
Ray Lankford, cf
Willie McGee, rf
John Mabry, rf-1b
Tom Lampkin, c
Mark McGwire, 1b

Pitchers

Matt Morris, sp
Todd Stottlemyre, sp
Andy Benes, sp
Alan Benes, sp
Donovan Osborne, sp
Dennis Eckersley, rp
Tony Fossas, rp
Dennis Frascatore, rp
Mark Petkovsek, rp

Attendance

2,634,014 (fourth in NL)

Club Leaders

Batting Avg:	DeShields	.295
	Lankford	.295
On-Base Pct:	Lankford	.411
Slugging Pct:	Lankford	.585
Home Runs:	Lankford	31
RBIs:	Lankford	98
Runs:	Lankford	94
Stolen Bases:	DeShields	55
Wins:	Morris	12
	Stottlemyre	12
Strikeouts:	Benes	175
ERA:	Benes	2.89
Saves:	Eckersley	36

JANUARY 20   Luis Alicea signs with the Angels as a free agent.

APRIL 1   The Cardinals open the season with a 2–1 loss to the Expos at Olympic Stadium. Montreal pinch hitter Sherman Obando drew a bases-loaded walk in the ninth inning off Tony Fossas to bring the winning run across the plate.

Uniform numbers disappeared from the fronts of the Cardinals' jerseys in 1997 and 1998 before making a return in 1999.

APRIL 6   The Cardinals fall to 0–6 on the 1997 season, the worst start in club history, with a 3–2 loss to the Astros in Houston.

The Cardinals scored only 12 runs in the six season-opening losses. The Cardinals were 18–27 on May 23, then evened their record at 41–41 on July 2. In a weak NL Central field, the .500 record was good enough to lead the division by one game. It was also the only day all year that St. Louis had a record of .500 or better. The Cards were 32–48 the rest of the way.

APRIL 8   The Cardinals win for the first time in 1997 with a 2–1 decision over the Expos in the home opener before 47,542 at Busch Stadium. The temperature was 45 degrees at game time and had fallen to 37 when Willie McGee ended the contest with a pinch-hit home run in the ninth inning.

APRIL 10   The game between the Cardinals and Expos at Busch Stadium is postponed by snow.

APRIL 11   Dennis Eckersley strikes out all three batters he faces in the ninth inning to preserve a 4–2 win over the Astros at Busch Stadium.

APRIL 13   The Cardinals tie a National League record with four consecutive doubles in the fourth inning of a 6–2 win over the Astros at Busch Stadium. Dmitri Young, Ron Gant, Gary Gaetti, and John Mabry each hit one off of Mike Hampton.

APRIL 19   The Cardinals participate in the first-ever regular-season game in Hawaii by sweeping a doubleheader against the Padres in Honolulu by scores of 1–0 and 2–1. In the opener, Matt Morris (one inning), Mark Petkovsek (six innings), T. J. Mathews (one inning), and Dennis Eckersley (one inning) teamed on the shutout. Matt Morris left the game early with an injury. In the nightcap, Andy Benes hurled a three-hit complete game.

The Cardinals had to fly from Miami, where they were finishing a series against the Marlins on April 17, to Honolulu for the games.

APRIL 20   The Cardinals conclude the series in Honolulu with an 8–2 loss to the Padres.

Every team in Major League Baseball retired number 42 in 1997 in honor of Jackie Robinson. The last Cardinal to wear number 42 was Jose Oliva in 1995.

APRIL 22   Down 4–3 with two outs and no one on base in the ninth inning, the Cardinals rally for three runs off Todd Worrell to win 6–4 against the Dodgers in Los Angeles. In his first game back from the disabled list, Ray Lankford singled and stole second and third to set up the game-winning rally. After Brian Jordan walked, Gary Gaetti delivered a two-run double and scored on John Mabry's double.

MAY 7   The Cardinals score nine runs in the seventh inning of a 14–7 win over the Phillies at Busch Stadium. Ray Lankford hit a grand slam off Erik Plantenburg.

Lankford hit .295 with 31 homers and 98 RBIs in 1997.

MAY 16   The Cardinals play at Turner Field for the first time and lose a heartbreaking 13-inning, 1–0 decision to the Braves. Alan Benes lost his no-hitter on Michael Tucker's two-out double in the ninth inning, and the Braves scored in the thirteenth on Andruw Jones's infield dribbler. In the ninth, Benes got Keith Lockhart on a soft liner to Royce Clayton at shortstop before retiring Kenny Lofton on a grounder. One out from a no-hitter, Benes surrendered the double to Tucker on an 0–1 pitch. Benes closed out the ninth by fanning Fred McGriff and was lifted for a pinch hitter in the top of the tenth. John Frascatore, the fourth Cardinal reliever, allowed the winning run in the thirteenth.

MAY 17   Ray Lankford hits a grand slam off Brad Clontz in the eighth inning, but the Cardinals lose 11–6 to the Braves in Atlanta.

MAY 21   Both benches clear during a 3–2 loss to the Pirates at Three Rivers Stadium after a fight between Cardinals catcher Mike DiFelice and Pittsburgh outfielder Mark Johnson. DiFelice swung at Johnson after a collision at home plate.

MAY 24   Andy Benes strikes out 12 batters in seven innings during a 9–3 win over the Giants in San Francisco.

JUNE 2   In the first round of the amateur draft, the Cardinals select shortstop Adam Kennedy from Cal State Northridge.

> *Kennedy was traded to the Angels just prior to the 2000 season in a deal that brought Jim Edmonds to St. Louis. Other future major leaguers the Cardinals drafted and signed in 1997 were Rick Ankiel (2nd round), Jason Karnuth (6th round), Justin Brunette (20th round), and Jose Rodriguez (24th round). Projected as a possible number one overall selection in the 1997 draft, Ankiel lasted until the end of the second round because he reportedly wanted as much as $6 million to sign. The Cardinals got him for $2.5 million, which, at the time was still a record for a drafted player who didn't become a free agent.*

JUNE 3   John Mabry drives in six runs during a 15–4 win over the Rockies at Busch Stadium. Mabry hit a home run and two singles. Royce Clayton collected five of the Cardinals' 21 hits with four singles and a double in six at-bats.

JUNE 7   Ray Lankford hits two homers to lead the Cardinals to a 3–1 win over the Dodgers in Los Angeles. It was the fourth straight game in which Lankford hit a home run.

JUNE 9   John Mabry runs his hitting streak to 20 games during a 9–1 win over the Padres in San Diego.

JUNE 13   The Cardinals are scheduled to play an American League team during the regular season for the first time, but the contest against the Indians at Busch Stadium is rained out.

> *On the same day, the Cardinals traded Danny Jackson, Rich Batchelor, and Mark Sweeney to the Padres for Fernando Valenzuela, Phil Plantier, and Scott Livingstone. Valenzuela was released on July 15 after compiling an 0–4 record and a 5.56 ERA as a Cardinal.*

JUNE 14   The Cardinals play a regular-season interleague game for the first time and split a doubleheader with the Indians at Busch Stadium. Cleveland won the opener 8–3, while the Cards took the second tilt 5–2.

JUNE 16   The Cardinals play the Brewers during the regular season for the first time and lose 1–0 at County Stadium in Milwaukee. The Cardinals previously played at County Stadium from 1953 through 1965, when it was the home of the Braves.

> *The Brewers moved to the National League in 1998.*

JUNE 25   Gary Gaetti's two-run, walk-off homer with one out in the ninth inning beats the Cubs 3–1 at Busch Stadium.

JUNE 30   The Cardinals play the Twins during the regular season for the first time and win 2–1 at Busch Stadium.

JULY 1   Tom Lampkin's two-run homer in the fourth inning off LaTroy Hawkins accounts all of the runs in a 2–0 victory over the Twins at Busch Stadium. Todd Stottlemyre (seven innings), T. J. Mathews (one inning), and Dennis Eckersley (one inning) teamed on the shutout.

JULY 2   Willie McGee hits a walk-off home run in the tenth inning to defeat the Twins 2–1 at Busch Stadium.

McGee hit only three homers in 1997, and two of them ended games. The other walk-off blast occurred on April 8.

JULY 4   The Cardinals drop into a tie for first place with the Pirates with a tough 10-inning, 7–5 loss to Pittsburgh at Busch Stadium. Left fielder Ron Gant lost a fly ball in the sun with two outs in the ninth that allowed the Pirates to tie the score. Mark Smith's two-run homer off Dennis Eckersley in the tenth scored the winning runs. The two clubs wore replicas of Negro Leagues uniforms during the contest. The Cardinals donned the jerseys of the St. Louis Stars, and the Pirates appeared in uniforms modeled after those of the Homestead Grays.

The Cardinals dropped out of first the following day and failed to regain the top spot in the NL Central in 1997.

JULY 15   Ray Lankford becomes the only batter to hit two homers into the upper deck at Cinergy Field in Cincinnati during a 7–4 Cardinals victory over the Reds. He hit both of them off Brett Tomko in consecutive at-bats in the first and third innings. The facility, which opened in 1970 as Riverfront Stadium, was torn down after the 2002 season.

The feat was so rare that the only other players to hit two upper-deck homers over the course of a full season were Reds sluggers George Foster in 1977 and Greg Vaughn in 1999.

JULY 26   On a Saturday afternoon in which the temperature in St. Louis reaches 100 degrees, the Cardinals beat the Marlins 2–1 at Busch Stadium.

JULY 31   The Cardinals trade T. J. Mathews, Eric Ludwick, and Blake Stein to the Athletics for Mark McGwire.

The impact of the acquisition of McGwire for three undistinguished players cannot be understated. When he came to St. Louis, McGwire was 33 years old and had 363 career homers. He first gained national attention in 1987 when he set the all-time major league record for most home runs by a rookie with 49 for the A's. It would be nine years before McGwire reached that home run figure again as he battled injuries and prolonged slumps. His nadir was 1991, when he hit .201 with 22 home runs in 154 games. He seemed to be back on track in 1996 with a .312 average and 52 home runs. He had hit 34 homers for the Athletics in 1997 when they dealt him to the Cardinals. McGwire came cheaply because his contract was due to expire at the end of the season and the A's had almost no hope of signing him. Oakland had a record of 42–68 and was hopelessly out of postseason contention.

The trade reunited McGwire with Tony La Russa, who managed him from the start of his playing career through 1995, and it was a gamble for the Cardinals, because they too, had no guarantee that McGwire would help them reach the playoffs (they were seven games out of first) or return to St. Louis in 1998. McGwire was a native Californian and was known to favor going to a West Coast team. To many people's surprise, he inked a three-year deal, with an option for $11 million in a fourth season, that would keep him in St. Louis. The recipient of fan adulation as soon as he arrived in the city, McGwire loved the family atmosphere, enthusiasm, and baseball tradition in St. Louis, and he had a strong relationship with La Russa. The Cardinals reaped the benefits of the deal in 1998, when McGwire mania swept the nation as he chased Roger Maris's single-season home run record. McGwire's remarkable 70–home run season brought a huge amount of national attention to St. Louis and packed the stadium night after night. His affection for the city and his high-profile charity work made McGwire a bona fide civic hero. In addition, his stirring public-service announcement on TV about the sexual abuse of children aired during the 1998 postseason. He followed his record-breaking season with 65 more homers in 1999. In 1,739 at-bats with the Cardinals before his retirement in 2001, McGwire hit 220 home runs.

AUGUST 1   Mark McGwire makes his debut with the Cardinals and is hitless in three at-bats during a 4–1 loss to the Phillies in Philadelphia.

AUGUST 8   In his first home game with the Cardinals, Mark McGwire hits a 441-foot home run, helping St. Louis to a 6–1 win over the Phillies at Busch Stadium. McGwire received a standing ovation when he batted in the first inning, although at the time he was hitting .080 as a Cardinal with 2 singles in 25 at-bats.

                McGwire had only 3 hits in his first 35 at-bats with the Cardinals before his bat ignited. In 1997, McGwire batted .253 with 24 homers in 173 at-bats with the Cardinals. Combined with his 34 homers with Oakland, he had 58 home runs on the season.

AUGUST 15   Mark McGwire hits a game-tying, two-run homer in the ninth, and Delino DeShields smacks a homer leading off the twelfth to defeat the Braves 3–2 at Busch Stadium.

                DeShields hit .295 with 11 homers and a league-leading 14 triples in 1997.

AUGUST 19   The Cardinals score eight runs in the second inning and smash the Expos 12–5 in Montreal.

AUGUST 22   Mark McGwire hits two tape-measure homers during a 7–3 victory over the Marlins in Miami. One of his blasts traveled an estimated 500 feet, and the other 462 feet.

AUGUST 28   After spotting the Expos five runs in the top of the first inning, the Cardinals rally to win 11–5 at Busch Stadium.

AUGUST 29   The Cardinals and Royals meet for the first time during the regular season, and the Cardinals win 9–7 in Kansas City. The crowd included a large contingent of vocal Cardinals fans. Willie McGee, the only player in the game who appeared in the 1985 World Series between the two Missouri rivals, hit a bases-loaded triple during a four-run eighth inning that gave the Cardinals a 9–6 lead.

AUGUST 30   A bench-clearing brawl erupts in the fourth inning of a 16–5 loss to the Royals in Kansas City. After Jermaine Dye hit a grand slam to give the Royals a 14–1 lead, Mark Petkovsek hit Johnny Damon in the leg with the next pitch, and Damon charged the mound. In the ensuing fight, Andy Benes ripped open the front of Kansas City starter Tim Belcher's jersey while manager Tony Muser and coach Jamie Quirk wrestled with Cardinal players on the ground.

SEPTEMBER 1   The day after Princess Diana dies after a car accident in Paris, the Cardinals play the White Sox during the regular season for the first time and lose 5–4 at Busch Stadium.

SEPTEMBER 2   Mark McGwire hits a home run estimated at 502 feet off the scoreboard in left center during the first inning of a 6–3 win over the White Sox at Busch Stadium.

SEPTEMBER 6   The Cardinals score a single run in seven different innings before erupting for three tallies in the thirteenth to defeat the Rockies 10–7 in Denver. The Cards scored in the first, third, fourth, sixth, seventh, eighth, and twelfth.

SEPTEMBER 10   Mark McGwire hits his 50th home run of 1997, but the Cardinals lose 7–6 to the Giants in San Francisco.

With the homer, McGwire became the first player since Babe Ruth in 1927 and 1928 to hit at least 50 home runs in back-to-back seasons. McGwire needed 11 homers in his last 17 games to tie Roger Maris's single-season home run record of 61, set with the Yankees in 1961.

SEPTEMBER 14   The Cardinals score seven runs in the third inning and defeat the Padres 10–4 at Busch Stadium.

SEPTEMBER 15   Ray Lankford hits a two-run homer in the bottom of the fifteenth inning, but it's not enough to overcome a three-run Dodger rally in the top of the inning and prevent a 7–6 loss at Busch Stadium.

SEPTEMBER 16   Mark McGwire hits a home run estimated at 517 feet during a 7–6 loss to the Dodgers at Busch Stadium.

On the same day, the Cardinals signed McGwire to a three-year contract worth $28 million that would allow him to remain with the Cardinals through the 2000 season.

SEPTEMBER 17   Mark McGwire hits his 53rd home run of 1997, the most of any major leaguer since Roger Maris hit 61 in 1961, during a 12–9 win over the Cubs in Chicago.

SEPTEMBER 25   Tony La Russa ties a major league record by using nine pinch hitters during a 14-inning, 4–3 loss to the Reds at Busch Stadium. The pinch hitters were Ron Gant, Willie McGee, Tom Lampkin, Tom Pagnozzi, John Mabry, Todd Stottlemyre, Jeff Berbinger, Scott Livingstone, and Eli Marrero. The Cardinals used 26 players in all.

SEPTEMBER 27   On the second-to-last day of the season, Mark McGwire hits his 56th and 57th home runs of the year during a 12–4 victory over the Cubs at Busch Stadium.

SEPTEMBER 28   In the season finale, Mark McGwire ties the major league record for most home runs by a right-handed batter in a season with his 58th during a 2–1 win over the Cubs at Busch Stadium. Previous right-handed hitters with 58 home runs in a season were Jimmie Foxx of the Philadelphia Athletics in 1932 and Hank Greenberg of the Detroit Tigers in 1938.

NOVEMBER 10   The Cardinals trade Dmitri Young to the Reds for Jeff Brantley.

The Cardinals had hopes that Brantley could handle the role of closer, but his career was essentially over when he came to St. Louis. A former first-round draft choice, Young failed to develop to the satisfaction of the Cardinals, but he was only 23 when he was traded. Since leaving St. Louis, Young has been a starter as a first baseman, outfielder, and designated hitter with the Reds and the Tigers.

NOVEMBER 18   In the expansion draft, the Cardinals lose Mike DiFelice and Kerry Robinson to the Devil Rays.

DECEMBER 9   Dennis Eckersley signs with the Red Sox as a free agent.

Eckersley pitched one more ineffective season before retiring.

DECEMBER 16   The Cardinals sign Kent Mercker, most recently with the Reds, as a free agent.

1998

Season in a Sentence

Mark McGwire brings national attention to St. Louis with his successful pursuit of Roger Maris's single-season home run record.

Finish • Won • Lost • Pct • GB

Third   83   79   .512   19.0

In the wild-card race, the Cardinals were tied for fourth place, 6½ games back

Manager

Tony La Russa

Stats

Stats	Cards	NL	Rank
Batting Avg:	.258	.262	10
On-Base Pct:	.341	.331	5
Slugging Pct:	.441	.410	3
Home Runs:	223		1
Stolen Bases:	133		4
ERA:	4.31	4.23	11
Fielding Avg:	.979	.980	12
Runs Scored:	810		5
Runs Allowed:	782		9

Starting Lineup

Eli Marrero, c
Mark McGwire, 1b
Delino DeShields, 2b
Gary Gaetti, 3b
Royce Clayton, ss
Ron Gant, lf
Ray Lankford, cf
Brian Jordan, rf
John Mabry, lf-rf-3b
Willie McGee, lf-rf
Tom Lampkin, c
Fernando Tatis, 3b

Pitchers

Kent Mercker, sp
Todd Stottlemyre, sp
Matt Morris, sp
Donovan Osborne, sp
Juan Acevedo, rp
John Painter, sp
John Frascatore, rp
Kent Bottenfield, sp-rp

Attendance

3,194,092 (fourth in NL)

Club Leaders

Batting Avg:	Jordan	.316
On-Base Pct:	McGwire	.470
Slugging Pct:	McGwire	.752
Home Runs:	McGwire	70
RBIs:	McGwire	147
Runs:	McGwire	130
Stolen Bases:	DeShields	26
	Lankford	26
Wins:	Mercker	11
Strikeouts:	Stottlemyre	147
ERA:	Stottlemyre	3.51
Saves:	Acevedo	15

JANUARY 6   The Cardinals sign Kent Bottenfield, most recently with the Cubs, as a free agent.

JANUARY 19   The Cardinals unveil plans for bronze sculptures outside the main gates at Busch Stadium. Sculptures of Stan Musial and Bob Gibson were added in 1998, Lou Brock and Red Schoendienst in 1999, and Enos Slaughter and Ozzie Smith in 2000. Later came Dizzy Dean, George Sisler, Jack Buck, and Rogers Hornsby.

FEBRUARY 3   The Diamondbacks sign Andy Benes as a free agent.

Benes had agreed to a $30 million, five-year contract with the Cardinals, but management's Player Relations Committee voided it, concluding the deal was signed after the December 7 deadline. Benes joined the expansion Diamondbacks for three years and $16 million. He rejoined the Cardinals in 2000.

MARCH 29   The Cardinals trade Juan Acevedo to the Mets for Rigo Beltran.

The Cardinals held spring training in Jupiter, Florida, for the first time in 1998. The Cards' training headquarters was in St. Petersburg, Florida, from 1938 through 1997, with the exception of three years during World War II.

MARCH 31   The Cardinals play a regular-season game in March for the first time and win 6–0 over the Dodgers before 47,972 at Busch Stadium. Mark McGwire began his assault on Roger Maris's home run record by breaking a scoreless tie with a grand slam off Ramon Martinez in the fifth inning. Gary Gaetti contributed two singles and a double. Todd Stottlemyre pitched seven shutout innings for the win.

APRIL 2   In the second game of the season, Mark McGwire hits his second dramatic homer of 1998 with a three-run, walk-off blast in the twelfth inning to defeat the Dodgers 8–5 at Busch Stadium.

APRIL 3   Mark McGwire homers for the third straight game, but the Cardinals lose 13–5 to the Dodgers at Busch Stadium.

APRIL 4   Mark McGwire becomes just the second player in major league history to homer in the first four games of the season with a towering three-run shot during an 8–6 win over the Padres at Busch Stadium. The only other player to homer in his first four games was Willie Mays in 1971. McGwire hit homers in six straight games counting the last two of the 1997 season.

APRIL 7   Leading 9–1 after 5½ innings, the Cardinals hang on to defeat the Rockies 12–11 in Denver.

            The Cardinals introduced an alternative cap design in 1998. The cap was navy blue with a red bill and featured the traditional redbird perched on a bat.

APRIL 8   The Cardinals beat the Rockies 13–9 in another Coors Field slugfest.

            Catcher Eli Marrero missed the early part of the season when a low-grade malignant tumor was found in his thyroid gland. He battled back from radiation treatments sooner than expected and became the starter after the All-Star break. Marrero had a complete recovery and was still active in the majors in 2005.

APRIL 14   Mark McGwire hits three homers during a 15–5 rout of the Diamondbacks in St. Louis. It was the only time that a Cardinal player hit three homers in a game in the 40-year history of Busch Stadium. It was also the first ever meeting between the Cardinals and Diamondbacks. McGwire hit a two-run homer in the third inning and a solo homer in the fifth, both off Jeff Suppan, and another two-run shot in the eighth against Barry Manuel. The Cardinals broke a 5–5 tie with six runs in the seventh.

APRIL 29   After falling behind 5–0 in the second inning, the Cardinals rally to beat the Expos 13–7 at Busch Stadium. The Cards took the lead with five runs in the sixth.

MAY 8   Mark McGwire hits his 400th career homer during a 9–2 Cardinals loss to the Mets in New York.

MAY 11   Todd Stottlemyre strikes out 13 batters and allows no runs and two hits over eight innings during a 7–0 win over the Brewers at Busch Stadium. Stottlemyre retired the last 18 batters to face him, 11 of them on strikeouts. Jeff Brantley closed out the game with a perfect ninth inning. The only Milwaukee hits were a double by Jeromy Burnitz in the first inning and a single by Bob Hamelin in the third. The contest was also the first regular-season meeting between the Cardinals and Brewers in St. Louis.

MAY 12   Mark McGwire hits a home run estimated at 527 feet during a 10-inning, 6-5 win over the Brewers at Busch Stadium. Delino DeShields drove in the winning run with a walk-off single.

DeShields hit .290 with seven homers in 1998.

MAY 15   Brady Raggio gives up eight consecutive singles and puts 11 men on base in succession with nine hits and two walks in the first inning of an 8–7 loss to the Marlins at Busch Stadium. Raggio was shelled even though the Marlins benched Garry Sheffield, Bobby Bonilla, and Charles Johnson awaiting the finalization of a trade with the Dodgers.

Raggio was 2–3 with an 8.10 ERA in 46²/₃ innings in the majors over two seasons. Although he failed to establish a successful big-league career, Raggio has to be given credit for making it that far considering a disastrous accident that nearly killed him. On Halloween night in 1992 while a minor leaguer in the Cardinals' system, Raggio stepped off a cliff and fell 70 feet. Partying in Santa Barbara, California, he went to walk down a flight of stairs to the beach but missed and plunged into the darkness. Raggio broke his right kneecap, lower right leg, and left elbow. He missed the entire 1993 season recuperating from his injuries.

MAY 16   Mark McGwire tops his blast of May 12 with a 545-foot homer during a 5–4 win over the Marlins at Busch Stadium.

MAY 17   Brian Jordan collects five hits, including a homer, in five a-bats, in a 13–4 win over the Marlins at Busch Stadium.

Jordan hit .316 with 25 home runs in 1998.

MAY 19   Mark McGwire hits three homers and drives in six runs to lead the Cardinals to a 14–8 victory over the Phillies in Philadelphia. McGwire struck a three-run homer in the third inning and a solo shot in the fifth off Tyler Green, then added a two-run blast in the eighth facing Wayne Gomes. McGwire's third homer broke an 8–8 tie.

McGwire hit nine homers in eight games from May 18 through May 25.

MAY 22   Mark McGwire hits a home run into "Big Mac Land," a section of seats in the upper deck next to the left-field foul pole at Busch Stadium, during a 12-inning, 4–3 win over the Braves.

As a result of a tie-in between the Cardinals and McDonald's, each time a player homered into "Big Mac Land," all of those in attendance received a free Big Mac sandwich. McGwire, who made nothing from the promotion, admitted that he wasn't a fan of Big Macs. "I've never had one in my whole life," McGwire said. "I've never touched one. I don't like that special sauce and all the other stuff."

MAY 30   Mark McGwire hits his 27th home run in the Cardinals' 53rd game of the season, an 8–3 win over the Padres in San Diego.

McGwire tied a club record for most home runs in a month with 16 in May 1998. He tied his own record in July 1999.

JUNE 2   In the first round of the amateur draft, the Cardinals select outfielder J. D. Drew from Florida State University and pitcher Ben Diggins from Bradshaw Mountain High School in Dewey, Arizona. The Cardinals had one extra pick in the first round due to free-agent compensation.

The Phillies drafted Drew in the first round in 1997 as the second overall pick, but the two sides couldn't agree on a contract. He went back into the draft in 1998 and was chosen ninth overall by St. Louis. Drew played for the Cardinals through the 2003 season before a trade to the Braves. Diggins didn't sign with the Cardinals, and the Brewers drafted him in 1999. It was just as well that he didn't sign with the Cards because he proved to be a wasted pick. Other future major leaguers the Cardinals drafted and signed in 1998 included Chad Hutchinson (2nd round), Bud Smith (4rth round), Jack Wilson (9th round), Les Walrond (13th round), and Esix Snead (18th round).

JUNE 8   The Cardinals play the White Sox in Chicago for the first time and lose 8–6 at Comiskey Park.

JUNE 9   Leading 7–0 in the fifth inning and 8–4 with two outs and no one on in the bottom of the ninth, the Cardinals wind up losing 10–8 in 11 innings to the White Sox in Chicago. Robin Ventura homered in both the ninth and eleventh innings.

JUNE 12   The Cardinals play a regular-season game in Phoenix for the first time and defeat the Diamondbacks 9–4 at Bank One Ballpark. The Cards scored eight runs in the third inning, four of them on a grand slam by Mark McGwire off Andy Benes.

JUNE 22   The Cardinals play the Tigers for the first time during the regular season and win 4–1 at Busch Stadium.

On the same day, the Cardinals purchased Bobby Witt from the Rangers.

JUNE 24   The Cardinals play in Cleveland during the regular season for the first time and lose 14–3 to the Indians at Jacobs Field.

JUNE 26   The Cardinals play in Minneapolis during the regular season for the first time and lose 5–1 to the Twins at the Metrodome.

JUNE 28   Bob Tewksbury uses 44-mile-per-hour lob pitches against Mark McGwire, who fails to hit the ball past first base during a 3–2 loss to the Twins in Minneapolis.

JUNE 30   The Royals play a regular-season game in St. Louis for the first time and beat the Cardinals 6–1 at Busch Stadium.

Mark McGwire's homer was the lone Cardinal run of the game. It was his 37th of the season at the halfway point in the 162-game schedule. In order to tie Roger Maris for the single-season home run record, McGwire needed 24 homers in the second half. Sammy Sosa's hot June gave McGwire some competition in the pursuit of Maris's mark. Sosa set an all-time major league record for most homers in month by swatting 20 in June 1998. On June 30, Sosa had 33 home runs.

JULY 9   Todd Stottlemyre bats eighth in the order during a 5–4 loss to the Astros at Busch Stadium.

Tony La Russa batted his pitchers in the eighth slot in the batting order for the rest of the season. The Cardinal manager said the ploy "gives us a better shot to score runs. It's an extra guy on base in front of Ray (Lankford), Mark (McGwire) and Brian (Jordan). The more guys on base, the less they will be able to pitch around Mark." For the record, the Cardinals scored 4.98 runs per game with the pitcher batting ninth and 4.96 with the pitcher hitting eighth.

JULY 11   After the Astros take a 3–2 lead in the top of the eleventh, Mark McGwire hits a two-run, walk-off homer in the bottom half for a 4–3 win at Busch Stadium.

JULY 17   Mark McGwire hits his 41st and 42nd homers of 1998, including a 511-foot shot into the upper deck, to pace the Cardinals to a 4–1 win over the Dodgers at Busch Stadium.

JULY 20   Mark McGwire ties the club record for homers in a season with his 43rd during a 13–1 pounding of the Padres in San Diego. Johnny Mize set the record in 1940. Ray Lankford hit a grand slam in the ninth inning off Roberto Ramirez.

JULY 26   Mark McGwire breaks Johnny Mize's club record for homers in a season with his 44th during a 3–1 win over the Rockies in Denver.

JULY 28   Ray Lankford's grand slam off Mike Myers in the eighth inning puts the Cardinals ahead of the Brewers 10–8, but Milwaukee counters with five runs in the ninth inning to win 13–10 at Busch Stadium.

Lankford hit .293 with 31 homers and 105 RBIs in 1998.

JULY 31   The Cardinals trade Royce Clayton and Todd Stottlemyre to the Rangers for Fernando Tatis and Darren Oliver.

AUGUST 7   After the Cubs score three runs in the top of the first inning, the Cardinals erupt for 11 runs in their half and win 16–3 at Busch Stadium.

AUGUST 8   Ray Lankford stages an incredible turnaround during a 13-inning, 9–8 win over the Cubs at Busch Stadium. Lankford struck out five times in his first five trips to the plate. With the Cards trailing 7–5 in the eleventh, Lankford hit a two-out, two-run homer. After both teams scored in the twelfth, Lankford drove in the winning run with a single in the thirteenth.

Lankford's homer was the Cardinals' 145th of the season, breaking the record of 144 set in 1997. The Cards finished the 1998 season with 223 homers to lead the National League in the category for the first time since 1944. It fact, it was the first time that the Cardinals finished in the top half of the NL in home runs since 1967, when the club was fourth in homers in a 10-team league. And the record 223 homers in 1998 weren't all because of Mark McGwire. Even after taking away McGwire's 70 home runs, the club had 153 homers during the season, which still would have exceeded the previous mark of 144. Others who contributed to the club record included Lankford (31), Ron Gant (26), and Brian Jordan (25). The Cardinals finished sixth in the National League in runs scored, however, as the offense relied too heavily on the home run. Mark McGwire's pursuit of Roger Maris's home run record took the minds of the fans away from the fact the Cardinals as a team were disappointing, falling out of contention for a postseason berth by early June. The injury-riddled starting pitching rotation was a major culprit. Kent Mercker was the leading winner with 11 despite a 5.07 ERA.

AUGUST 12   After the Mets score three runs in the ninth inning to tie the score 4–4 and send the game into extra innings, the Cardinals win 5–4 with a run in the fourteenth. Ray Lankford drove in the game winner with a single.

AUGUST 14   Five different Cardinals homer during a 10–5 win over the Cardinals at Busch Stadium. Ray Lankford, Tom Lampkin, Delino DeShields, Brian Jordan, and Fernando Tatis all hit dingers.

AUGUST 19   The Cubs and Cardinals meet at Wrigley Field with Mark McGwire and Sammy Sosa tied for the home run lead with 47 apiece. Sosa hit his 48th home run of the year in the fifth inning, but McGwire delivered the counterpunch with his 48th of the season in the eighth inning to tie the game and his 49th in the tenth to beat the Cubs 8–6.

AUGUST 20   Mark McGwire hits his 50th and 51st home runs of the season during a doubleheader against the Mets in New York. The Cards won the first game 2–0, then lost 5–4.

AUGUST 23   Fernando Tatis collects five hits, including a home run, in five at-bats, but the Cardinals lose 4–3 to the Pirates in Pittsburgh.

AUGUST 26   Mark McGwire hits a 509-foot home run during a 10-inning, 7–6 loss to the Marlins at Busch Stadium.

AUGUST 30   Mark McGwire hits a 501-foot home run during an 8–7 victory over the Braves at Busch Stadium. It was McGwire's 55th homer of the season, leaving him one short of the National League record set by Hack Wilson of the Cubs in 1930.

SEPTEMBER 1 Mark McGwire ties and breaks Hack Wilson's National League single-season home run with his 56th and 57th of 1998 during a 7–1 win over the Marlins in Miami. McGwire began the night tied with Sammy Sosa for the major league home run lead.

SEPTEMBER 2 Mark McGwire hits his 58th and 59th home run of 1998 during a 14–4 walloping of the Marlins in Miami. McGwire's blasts overshadowed the efforts of Cardinals pitcher Kent Mercker, who hit a grand slam off Jesus Sanchez in the fourth inning.

SEPTEMBER 5 Mark McGwire hits his 60th homer of the season during a 7–0 win over the Reds at Busch Stadium. The homer, struck off Dennys Reyes, put McGwire one away from Roger Maris's single-season record.

SEPTEMBER 6 In his bid to tie Roger Maris, Mark McGwire goes 0 for 3 with a walk during a 5–2 win over the Reds at Busch Stadium.

             Next up was a two-game series against the Cubs at Busch Stadium on September 7 and 8.

SEPTEMBER 7 In the pregame press conference prior to the Cardinals-Cubs matchup at Busch Stadium, Mark McGwire and Sammy Sosa sip bottled water and swap one-liners, seeming to enjoy every minute of the media attention surrounding their race for the home run record. Entering the contest, McGwire had 60 homers, and Sosa had 58. During the game, McGwire hit his 61st home run of 1998 to tie the all-time record for most home runs in a season during the 3–2 Cardinals win. He hit the home run in the first inning off Mike Morgan. The drive carried 430 feet to left field. The ball had some hook but curled inside the foul pole, ricocheted off one of the windows on the Stadium Club, and fell into section 281. As he crossed the plate, McGwire hugged his 10-year-old son, Matthew, who arrived 30 minutes before game time. Also in attendance were McGwire's parents. His father, John, was celebrating his 61st birthday on the day Mark hit his 61st homer. Five of the six children of the late Roger Maris were also in the stands. Their mother was hospitalized with a "heart flutter." After hitting the homer, McGwire saluted in the direction of the Maris family.

SEPTEMBER 8   On national television, Mark McGwire passes Roger Maris with his 62nd home run of 1998 with a blast in the fourth inning off Steve Trachsel of the Cubs during a 6–1 Cardinals win at Busch Stadium. The homer was a line drive to left field that began to sink as it neared the eight-foot-high fence. The ball made it by less than two feet. At 341 feet, it was McGwire's shortest home run of the season and touched off an emotional celebration, not just in St. Louis, but around the country. In a daze, McGwire missed first base and was headed toward second before coach Dave McKay reminded him that he had neglected to touch the bag. Rounding the bases slowly while savoring every second, McGwire shook hands with the Cubs infielders and catcher Scott Servais. Once again, McGwire paused to lift his son in the air and was hugged by his friendly rival, Sammy Sosa, who had sprinted in from right field to home plate. McGwire also went to the front row of the stands to embrace the Maris family, which included all six children and Roger's widowed wife, as red-and-white streamers floated gently into the outfield grass and fireworks boomed overhead. The game was delayed for 11 minutes. The ball was picked up by groundskeeper Tim Forneris, who later gave it to McGwire. Sosa went homerless in the contest to remain at 58 on the season.

> In a postgame party on the field, McGwire was given a 1962 red Corvette. He and his son took a slow victory drive around the field as the crowd cheered. The drama was far from over, however, with 18 games left in the season. Even though McGwire broke Maris's 1961 mark, there was a possibility that Sammy Sosa could wind up as the all-time single-season record holder when the 1998 campaign ended.

SEPTEMBER 13   Sammy Sosa hits his 61st and 62nd home runs of the 1998 season during a 10-inning, 11–10 win over the Brewers in Chicago. The two homers tied McGwire for the league lead.

SEPTEMBER 15   Mark McGwire hits home run number 63 during an 8–6 loss to the Pirates at Busch Stadium. He hit the home run off Jason Christensen in a rare pinch-hitting role.

SEPTEMBER 16   Sammy Sosa's grand slam off Brian Boehringer in the eighth inning breaks a 2–2 tie in a 6–3 Cubs win over the Padres in San Diego. Sosa drove in all six Cubs runs. The homer was Sosa's 63rd of the season, tying him once again with Mark McGwire for the league lead.

SEPTEMBER 18   Mark McGwire hits home run number 64 during a 5–2 win over the Brewers in Milwaukee. This one came off of Rafael Roque in the fourth inning.

SEPTEMBER 20   Mark McGwire's home run total reaches 65 during an 11–6 win over the Brewers in Milwaukee with a first-inning blast off Scott Karl. Facing Rod Henderson, who was making his major league debut, McGwire lost another potential home run when a fan appeared to interfere with a drive into the center field bleachers. In a controversial decision, second base umpire Bob Davidson ruled that the fan had reached over the wall, and McGwire was credited with a ground-rule double. The fan thought to have touched the ball was Michael Chopes, a 31-year-old high school gym teacher from Waterford, Wisconsin, who was ejected from the stadium and fined $518 for trespassing. Replays showed that two fans, standing along the railing in front of the seats, had indeed reached out but never made contact with the ball until it passed the fence and fell into a gap between the padded outfield wall and the seats.

SEPTEMBER 23   Sammy Sosa breaks out of an 0-for-23 slump by hitting his 64th and 65th homers of 1998, tying Mark McGwire for the lead during an 8–7 Cubs loss to the Brewers in Milwaukee.

SEPTEMBER 25   Sammy Sosa hits his 66th home run of the season, and 45 minutes later, Mark McGwire answers with his 66th off Shane Bennett in the fifth inning of a 6–5 win over the Expos at Busch Stadium. Both McGwire and Sosa had two regular-season games remaining on the schedule. Sosa failed to hit another home run, while McGwire added four more.

McGwire's home run chase helped set an attendance record at Busch Stadium. The Cardinals drew 3,194,092 fans at home, breaking the old mark of 3,080,980 set in 1989.

SEPTEMBER 26   Mark McGwire homers twice during a 7–6 loss to the Expos at Busch Stadium to lift his season total to 68. McGwire homered off Dustin Hermanson in the fourth inning and Kirk Bullinger in the seventh.

McGwire hit 38 homers at Busch Stadium and 32 on the road in 1998.

SEPTEMBER 27   In the final game of the season, Mark McGwire hits two home runs during a 6–3 win over the Expos at Busch Stadium to give him 70 on the season. He homered off Mike Thurman in the second inning and Carl Pavano in the seventh.

In addition to hitting 70 home runs, McGwire set club records for walks (162) and intentional walks (28). His 1998 on-base percentage of .470 was the highest of any Cardinal since Rogers Hornsby in 1925. McGwire's slugging percentage of .752 was the second best in club history behind Hornsby's .756 in 1925. He drove in 147 runs, the best in St. Louis since Joe Medwick collected 154 in 1937. And his runs scored (130) and total bases (383) were both the best of any Cardinal since Stan Musial in 1948. McGwire had more home runs (70) than singles (61) in 1998. Babe Ruth held the all-time record for home runs in a season for 42 years. Ruth first gained the mark in 1919 when he hit 29 as a member of the Red Sox but broke his own record three times as a New York Yankee with 54 in 1920, 59 in 1921, and 60 in 1927. Ruth's 60 homers were the standard until Roger Maris hit 61 in 1961. Maris was the record holder for 37 seasons. McGwire's record lasted just three years: Barry Bonds clubbed 73 home runs for the Giants in 2001.

NOVEMBER 19   The Cardinals send Ron Gant, Jeff Brantley, Cliff Politte, and cash for Ricky

Bottalico and Garret Stephenson. On the same day, the Cardinals signed Eric Davis, most recently with the Orioles, as a free agent.

NOVEMBER 23   Brian Jordan signs with the Braves as a free agent.

DECEMBER 4   Delino DeShields signs with the Orioles as a free agent.

DECEMBER 14   The Cardinals trade Braden Looper, Armando Almanza, and Pablo Ozuna to the Marlins for Edgar Renteria.

> *Only the fourth native of Colombia to reach the majors, Renteria was the hero of Florida's 1997 World Championship team by driving in the winning run in the ninth inning of Game Seven against Cleveland. The Marlins quickly dismantled the championship club by trading almost all of their star players for prospects on the orders of owner Wayne Huizenga, who was trying to shed salary. The Cardinals were one of the beneficiaries as Renteria was the starting shortstop in St. Louis for six seasons and played in three All-Star Games and the 2004 World Series.*

Doug Pensinger/Getty Images Sport/Getty Images

In the Cardinals' final game of the season, Mark McGwire's hits his 70th home run against the Expos. While McGwire smashed a 37-year record for most home runs in a season, his record stood for only three years before Barry Bonds homered 73 times in 2001. It's unclear how much help either player received from illegal performance-enhancing drugs, but both, particularly Bonds, have undergone intense scrutiny.

The Road to 70

Through 1997, only two hitters had topped 60 home runs in the major leagues. Babe Ruth hit 60 homers in 1927, and Roger Maris surpassed him with 61 in 1961. Maris stood virtually unopposed as the single-season home run king for more than 30 years. Until 1996, his closest challengers were Willie Mays, with 52 in 1965, George Foster, with 52 in 1977, and Cecil Fielder, who clubbed 51 in 1990.

Beginning in the mid-1990s, an offensive explosion gripped baseball that included an increase in home runs. Ken Griffey Jr. struck 49 for the Mariners in 1996 and hit another 56 in 1997. Mark McGwire, who hit 56 homers in 1996 for the Athletics, put up 58 in 1997 in a season split between the A's and Cardinals.

Both were besieged by questions during spring training in 1998 about the possibility of breaking Maris's home run record. No one was mentioning Maris and Sammy Sosa in the same sentence. After all, Sosa's career high at that point was 40, in 1996. He had 36 in 1997.

McGwire disappointed no one. On May 24, he had 24 homers in 48 games, a pace that would give him 81 homers on the season. On the same day, Sosa had 9 homers in 49 games, a 30-home run pace. Sosa then embarked on a home run streak unmatched in baseball history. From May 25 through June 25, he hit 25 homers in 29 games. In the month of June alone he hit 20, breaking the old mark for home runs in a month set by the Tigers' Rudy York, who hit 18 in August 1937. Suddenly Sammy became SAMMY!

Tremendous adulation was heaped upon both players. Fans in every ballpark greeted every McGwire plate appearance with a sustained standing ovation, and Sosa won people's hearts with his infectious enthusiasm and public insistence that McGwire was the man of the moment. McGwire, for his part, contended that

Sosa deserved to win the league's MVP. As both players approached, and eventually passed, Maris's mark, baseball enjoyed much greater attention than it had in the past, and it extended all across the country, not just in St. Louis and Chicago. The home run chase helped win back many fans still jaded by the strike that wiped out part of the 1994 and 1995 seasons. In addition, the McGwire-Sosa competition attracted casual fans and those who previously had little interest in the game.

McGwire and Sosa finished August with 55 homers apiece, one short of Hack Wilson's NL record, set with the Cubs in 1930. McGwire hit two homers on September 1 to break Wilson's record and his 60th on September 5, tying Babe Ruth's 1927 standard in the Cardinals' 142nd game.

The Cardinals and the Cubs met in a two-game series in St. Louis on September 7 and 8. Heading into the series, McGwire had 60 homers and Sosa 58. McGwire rose to the occasion by tying Maris with his 61st homer on September 7 off Mike Morgan and his 62nd a day later facing Steve Trachsel.

Sosa tied McGwire by hitting his 62nd on September 13. McGwire struck number 62 on the 15th, and Sammy tied him again a day later. McGwire hit number 64 on the 18th and 65 on the 20th. Sosa matched him again, hitting two homers on the 23rd to reach 65, then passed McGwire with his 66th in the Astrodome off Jose Lima on September 252. Just 45 minutes later in Montreal, the lead evaporated when McGwire hit his 66th. It was the 21st time that the two had homered on the same day. In the final two games of the season, played on September 26 and 27, McGwire hit four homers to finish the season with 70. Sosa remained stuck on 66. Ken Griffey Jr. had a 56–home run season that would have created headlines in any year except 1998.

1999

Season in a Sentence

"Home Run Race II" between Mark McGwire and Sammy Sosa helps distract fans from a Cardinals club that loses 86 games.

Finish • Won • Lost • Pct • GB

Fourth   75   86   .466   21.5

In the wild-card race, the Cardinals finished in eighth place, 21 games back

Manager

Tony La Russa

Stats	Cards	NL	Rank
Batting Avg:	.262	.268	13
On-Base Pct:	.338	.342	11
Slugging Pct:	.426	.429	9
Home Runs:	194		5
Stolen Bases:	134		8
ERA:	4.74	4.56	11
Fielding Avg:	.979	.980	12
Runs Scored:	809		10
Runs Allowed:	838		12

Starting Lineup

Eli Marrero, c
Mark McGwire, 1b
Joe McEwing, 2b-lf
Fernando Tatis, 3b
Edgar Renteria, ss
Ray Lankford, lf
J. D. Drew, cf
Willie McGee, rf-lf
Darren Bragg, cf-rf
Alberto Castillo, c
Placido Polanco, 2b
Eric Davis, rf
Thomas Howard, rf

Pitchers

Kent Bottenfield, sp
Darren Oliver, sp
Jose Jiminez, sp
Kent Mercker, sp
Garrett Stephenson, sp
Ricky Bottalico, rp
Manny Aybar, rp
Lance Painter, rp
Rick Croushore, rp
Juan Acevedo, rp
Mike Mohler, rp

Attendance

3,225,334 (third in NL)

Club Leaders

Batting Avg:	Lankford	.306
On-Base Pct:	McGwire	.424
Slugging Pct:	McGwire	.697
Home Runs:	McGwire	66
RBIs:	McGwire	147
Runs:	McGwire	118
Stolen Bases:	DeShields	37
Wins:	Bottenfield	18
Strikeouts:	Bottenfield	124
ERA:	Bottenfield	3.97
Saves:	Bottalico	20

JANUARY 12   Guernsey's, an auction house in Manhattan, auctions the baseball that Mark McGwire hit for his 70th home run of 1998 for $3,005,000. An anonymous buyer purchased the ball by telephone. The 70th home run ball had been caught by Phil Ozersky, a medical researcher who earned $30,000 a year. Ozersky turned down $1 million immediately after catching the ball. The same individual who purchased McGwire's 70th home run ball also bought the ball Sammy Sosa hit for number 66 for $150,000.

On the same day, the Cardinals sign Darren Bragg, most recently with the Red Sox, as a free agent.

JANUARY 20   Bobby Witt signs with the Devil Rays as a free agent.

FEBRUARY 17   Five days after Bill Clinton is acquitted following his impeachment trial in the House of Representatives, the Cardinals sign Shawon Dunston, most recently with the Giants, as a free agent.

APRIL 5   The Cardinals open the season with a 10–8 loss to the Brewers before 47,806 at Busch Stadium. There were two lengthy rain delays during the evening. Mark McGwire and Fernando Tatis hit home runs. Shawon Dunston, in his first game as a Cardinal, collected two singles and a double. Eli Marrero had three hits, including two doubles.

Dan McLaughlin joined the Cardinals' broadcast team in 1999 as a television play-by-play announcer.

APRIL 8   Fernando Tatis hits his third homer in the third game of the season as the Cardinals win 3–2 against the Brewers at Busch Stadium.

APRIL 16   Mark McGwire doubles against a four-man outfield to spark a five-run fourth inning that beats Houston 5–3 at the Astrodome. Second baseman Craig Biggio moved to a position between left field and center field.

APRIL 17   The Cardinals score seven runs in the eighth inning and beat the Astros 8–5 in Houston.

APRIL 23   Fernando Tatis becomes the only player in major league history to hit two grand slams in a single inning during a 12–5 win over the Dodgers in Los Angeles. Tatis also set a major league record for most RBIs during an inning with eight. He hit both slams in an 11-run third inning, both off Chan Ho Park. Tatis's first came with the Cardinals trailing 2–0 on a 2–0 pitch with no outs. Tatis faced Park again with the bases filled and two outs later in the third, and he homered into the left-field pavilion on a 3–2 pitch.

The home run outburst came in Tatis's 226th big-league game. He had only 24 previous home runs. None of them was a grand slam, and Tatis had only one previous multi-homer game, in 1997 as a Texas Ranger. Through 2005, only 14 players have hit two grand slams in one game. Just two of them have occurred in a National League game. The other two–grand slam game in the NL was by Atlanta Braves pitcher Tony Cloninger in 1966.

APRIL 27   The Cardinals defeat the Rockies 7–5 at Busch Stadium.

The victory gave the Cardinals a 12–6 record and a 1½-game lead in the NL Central. The Cards were 42–42 on July 7 and 5½ games out of first, but within weeks they were hopelessly out of contention for a postseason berth. By the end of the season, many fans in Cardinal Nation were calling loudly for a new manager. After four seasons with in St. Louis, La Russa's record with the Cards was 319–328.

APRIL 28   Eight days after 15 die in a shooting at Columbine High School in Littleton, Colorado, Larry Walker hits three homers and drives in eight runs for the Colorado Rockies during a 9–7 defeat of the Cardinals at Busch Stadium.

The Cardinals drew 3,225,334 fans at home in 1999, breaking the old mark of 3,194,092 set the previous season.

MAY 2   J. D. Drew ties a Cardinals record by scoring five runs during a 16–5 win over the Expos in Montreal. Drew reached base on a single, double, triple, and two walks.

MAY 4	Mark McGwire hits a grand slam off Greg Maddux in the second inning of a 9–1 win over the Braves in Atlanta.
MAY 7	Shawon Dunston hits a two-run, walk-off homer in the ninth inning that beats the Pirates 4–2 at Busch Stadium. Pittsburgh scored two runs in the top of the ninth to tie the contest.
MAY 9	Shawon Dunston hits a grand slam off Jose Silva in the first inning, but the Cardinals lose 12–9 to the Pirates at Busch Stadium.
MAY 16	Ray Lankford hits a two-run, walk-off homer in the ninth inning that beats the Dodgers 5–4 at Busch Stadium. It was Lankford's second homer of the game.
MAY 22	Mark McGwire becomes only the third player to hit a ball out of Dodger Stadium during a 5–4 win over the Dodgers. The ballpark opened in 1962. The drive bounced off the roof of the left-field pavilion and was estimated to have traveled 484 feet. The only other two to hit a home run out of Dodger Stadium were Willie Stargell in 1969 and 1973, and Mike Piazza in 1997.
MAY 23	An 8–3 win over the Dodgers in Los Angeles is marred by a fight. In the ninth inning, Dodger pitcher Terry Arnold hit Shawon Dunston in the back with a fastball. Dunston, the third Cardinal to be hit in the game and the second in the inning, rushed the mound and tackled Arnold before they were engulfed by players from both dugouts and bullpens.
MAY 25	The Giants wallop the Cardinals 17–1 at Busch Stadium.
JUNE 2	In the first round of the amateur draft, the Cardinals select pitcher Chance Caple from Texas A&M University, pitcher Nick Stocks from Florida State University, and first baseman Chris Duncan from Canton del Oro High School in Tucson, Arizona. The Cards had two extra picks because of free-agent compensation.

> *To date, the Cardinals have failed to get one good player out of the three picks. Duncan made his major league debut in 2005 as a September call-up. The other two have yet to reach the majors. Although the first-rounders have failed to produce, the Cards made one of the best draft selections in club history in the 13th round by picking Albert Pujols. A native of the Dominican Republic, Pujols later attended Fort Osage High School in Independence, Missouri, and Maple Woods (Mo.) Community College. Other future big-leaguers the Cardinals drafted and signed in 1999 were Josh Pearce (2nd round), Jimmy Journell (4th round), Coco Crisp (7th round), Mike Crudale (24th round), and Bo Hart (33rd round).*

JUNE 4	The Cardinals play the Tigers in Detroit for the first time during the regular season and lose 4–1 at Tiger Stadium.
JUNE 8	The Cardinals lose 11–10 to the Royals in Kansas City.
JUNE 9	The Cardinals lose after reaching double digits in runs for the second game in a row, dropping a 17–13 decision to the Royals in Kansas City.

JUNE 12   The Cardinals win 8–7 in 14 innings against the Tigers at Busch Stadium. Edgar Renteria's two-out, bases-loaded single drove in the winning run. The Cards trailed 7–2 before scoring three runs in the seventh inning and two in the eighth to send the contest into extra innings.

JUNE 22   Mark McGwire drives in the game-winner, a single in the fourteenth inning, to beat the Astros 4–3 at Busch Stadium.

JUNE 26   Rookie Cardinal pitcher Jose Jiminez pitches a no-hitter to beat Randy Johnson and the Diamondbacks 1–0 in Phoenix. Jiminez entered the game with a 1999 season record of 3–7 and a 6.69 ERA. He was the first Cardinal to pitch a no-hitter since Bob Forsch in 1983. The lone run of the game scored in the top of the ninth on an RBI double by Thomas Howard off Johnson, who struck out 14 during the evening. Right fielder Eric Davis saved the no-hitter with two diving catches, including a one-out grab in the ninth inning of a sinking liner off the bat of David Delucci. Jiminez then got Tony Womack for the final out on a slow roller to Joe McEwing at second base. Jiminez walked two, struck out eight, and faced only 28 batters.

               Jiminez finished the 1999 season with a 5–14 record with a 5.85 ERA. Through the end of the 2005 season, Jiminez had a lifetime record of 24–44 and a 4.92 ERA (see June 30, 1999).

JUNE 30   In his first start since his no-hitter, Jose Jiminez is tagged for seven runs and seven hits in an 11–3 loss to the Astros in Houston (see July 5, 1999).

JULY 1   The Cardinals play in the Astrodome for the last time and win 10–4 over the Astros.

JULY 4   Rookie Joe McEwing extends his hitting streak to 25 games during a 17–5 loss to the Diamondbacks at Busch Stadium.

               McEwing became a fan favorite in St. Louis because of his hustle. His 25-game hitting streak is the best in Cardinals history by a rookie and the ninth best overall. In 1999, McEwing played seven different positions: 66 games at second base, 32 in left field, 23 in center, 19 in right, 6 at third, 2 at second, and 1 at shortstop.

JULY 5   In his second start since his no-hitter, Jose Jiminez pitches a two-hitter to defeat the Diamondbacks 1–0 at Busch Stadium. It was also his second 1–0 win in three starts, and both were against Randy Johnson. Jiminez retired the first 13 batters to face him before Steve Finley doubled. The only other Arizona hit was a single by Andy Fox off Jiminez's glove in the sixth inning.

               The shutouts on June 26 and July 5, 1999, were the only two shutout of Jiminez's career.

JULY 7   Darren Bragg hits a two-run, walk-off homer in the bottom of the ninth inning to beat the Reds 2–1 at Busch Stadium.

               Kent Bottenfield entered the 1999 season with a lifetime record of 18–27, but he was 14–3 at the All-Star break. He finished the season at 18–7 with a 3.97 ERA.

JULY 16   Mark McGwire hits a pair of three-run homers for a total of six RBIs, but the Cardinals lose 9–8 to the White Sox at Busch Stadium.

JULY 22   The Cardinals score three runs in the ninth inning to beat the Reds 6–5 in Cincinnati. Fernando Tatis tied the game with a two-run homer. Mark McGwire broke the deadlock with another home run.

JULY 27   The Cardinals score seven runs in the second inning to take a 7–2 lead but lose 10–8 to the Giants in San Francisco.

JULY 28   The Cardinals play at 3Com Park, formerly Candlestick Park, for the last time and defeat the Giants 6–3.

JULY 31   The Cardinals trade Shawon Dunston to the Mets for Craig Paquette.

Dunston returned to the Cardinals as a free agent in 2000.

AUGUST 2   Mark McGwire hits his 498th career home run and his first triple since June 2, 1988, during a 6–5 win over the Padres at Busch Stadium. McGwire reached third after right fielder Tony Gwynn had robbed McGwire of a homer by leaping above the fence.

McGwire went 4,618 at-bats between triples. He hit six during his 16-year career.

AUGUST 4   Two players close in on milestones as the Cardinals defeat the Padres 7–6 at Busch Stadium. Mark McGwire hit his 499th career home run, and Tony Gwynn collected three hits to bring his career total to 2,998. St. Louis fans gave Gwynn a standing ovation after each hit.

AUGUST 5   Mark McGwire hits his 500th and 501st lifetime homers, and Tony Gwynn collects his 2,999th career hit as the Padres roll past the Cardinals 10–3 at Busch Stadium. Both of McGwire's homers came off Andy Ashby.

Gwynn picked up his 3,000th career hit in Montreal on August 6.

AUGUST 9   Fernando Tatis hits a grand slam off Billy Brewer in the third inning of a 12–6 win over the Phillies in Philadelphia. The slam tied the club record for most grand slams in a season with three. Jim Bottomley set the mark in 1925, and Keith Hernandez tied it in 1977.

The series against the Phillies at Veterans Stadium marked J. D. Drew's first appearance in Philadelphia. Drew was drafted by the Phils with the second overall pick in 1997 but spurned their offer and declined to sign a contract. The Cardinals chose him in the 1998 draft. Amid a massive police and security presence, Drew had to dodge debris, including batteries, and non-stop abuse from Phillies fans during the three-game series in the City of Brotherly Love.

AUGUST 15 Craig Paquette's two-run, two-out double beats the Cubs 6–5 at Busch Stadium. The game concluded a three-game series between the Cardinals and Cubs in which Mark McGwire and Sammy Sosa each hit three homers. When the Cubs left St. Louis, McGwire led Sosa 47–46 in the major league home run race.

AUGUST 22 Mark McGwire hits an opposite-field homer estimated at 502 feet during an 8–5 win in the first game of a doubleheader against the Mets at Shea Stadium. The drive left a dent in the right-center-field scoreboard 60 feet above ground level. It was McGwire's 50th home run of the season. New York won the second tilt 7–5.

AUGUST 24	The Cardinals trade Kent Mercker to the Red Sox for Mike Matthews and David Benham.
SEPTEMBER 5	After allowing the Brewers to tie the game 9–9 with three runs in the bottom of the ninth inning, the Cardinals score four times in the tenth to win 13–9 in Milwaukee.
SEPTEMBER 17	Mark McGwire hits a grand slam in the fourth inning of an 11–8 win over the Astros at Busch Stadium. The slam was the first of three St. Louis consecutive home runs off Jose Lima. Thomas Howard homered on the next pitch, and Fernando Tatis followed with another homer. It was the first time that the Cardinals hit three straight homers since 1964. The Cards entered the fourth trailing 4–0 and scored nine runs.

Tatis had a career year in 1999 that far exceeded his output before or since. He hit 34 homers, drove in 107 runs, scored 104, and batted .298. Tatis's listed age was only 24 in 1999, and he seemed to have several All-Star-caliber seasons in front of him, but he was out of the majors by 2004.

SEPTEMBER 18	The Cardinals beat up on the Astros for the second day in a row, winning 13–6 at Busch Stadium.
SEPTEMBER 26	Mark McGwire hits his 60th home run of 1999 during a 7–5 loss in 12 innings to the Reds in Cincinnati.

With a week left in the season, Sammy Sosa had 61 homers, and Mark McGwire 60.

SEPTEMBER 27	Mark McGwire hits his 61st home run during a 9–7 loss to the Reds in Cincinnati.
SEPTEMBER 29	Mark McGwire homers in both games of a doubleheader against the Padres at Busch Stadium to give him 63 on the season. The Cards won the first game 4–3 and lost the second 6–5.
OCTOBER 2	In the second-to-last game of the season, Mark McGwire hits his 64th home run of the season during a 6–3 loss to the Cubs at Busch Stadium.
OCTOBER 3	In the season finale, Mark McGwire hits his 65th home run of 1999, and Sammy Sosa clubs his 63rd during a 9–5 Cardinals win over the Cubs in a contest at Busch Stadium called after 4½ innings by rain. McGwire hit his 65th homer off Steve Trachsel, who also allowed his record-breaking 62nd home run on September 8, 1998.

McGwire hit six homers in his final seven games in 1999 to win the McGwire-Sosa home run derby for the second year in a row. McGwire's 135 homers in consecutive seasons is the major league record. In addition to his 65 home runs in 1999, he led the NL in RBIs with 147. McGwire also scored 118 runs and batted .278.

NOVEMBER 11	The Cardinals trade Lance Painter, Alberto Castillo, and Mike DeWitt to the Blue Jays for Pat Hentgen and Paul Spoljaric.

Hentgen, who won the Cy Young Award with the Blue Jays in 1996, was 15–12 in his only season as a Cardinal.

NOVEMBER 16   The Cardinals trade Manny Aybar, Jose Jiminez, Rick Croushore, and Brent Butler to the Rockies for Darryl Kile and Dave Veres.

> *The Cardinals pulled off a terrific deal that helped the club in the short term. Kile was 19–7 for the Astros in 1997 before signing with the Rockies as a free agent. He spent two unhappy seasons in the thin air in Colorado with a record of 21–30. Closer to sea level in St. Louis, Kile was 20–9 for the Cardinals in 2000 and followed with a 16–11 mark in 2001. He was 5–4 in 2002 before his sudden death at the age of 33, from a heart condition. Kile was found dead in his bed at the Westin Hotel in Chicago where the Cardinals were staying during a series with the Cubs (see June 22, 2002). Veres gave the Cardinals three good seasons out of the bullpen.*

DECEMBER 20   The Cardinals trade Juan Acevedo, Matt Parker, and Eliezer Alfonzo to the Brewers for Fernando Viña.

> *The Cardinals pulled off another excellent deal, as Viña was the club's starting second baseman for four years.*

DECEMBER 21   Darren Bragg signs with the Rockies as a free agent.

THE STATE OF THE CARDINALS

Through the 2005 season, the Cardinals had a 575–397 record during the 21st century, a .592 winning percentage good for best in the National League, edging the Atlanta Braves (573–399, .590). The only major league club with a better record from 2000 through 2005 was the Yankees (582–386, .601). Six different franchises have won the World Series in the first six years of the new millennium, but St. Louis isn't among them, although the Cardinals reached the postseason in five of those six seasons (four times as the NL Central title holders and once as the wild card). The Redbirds appeared in the National League Championship Series four times but won only in 2004 and were swept by the Red Sox in the Fall Classic. Overall, Tony La Russa's Cardinals were 17–18 in the postseason from 2000 through 2005. NL champions outside of St. Louis have been the Mets (2000), Diamondbacks (2001), Giants (2002), Marlins (2003), and Astros (2005). NL Central champs, other than the Cards, were the Astros (2001) and the Cubs (2003).

THE BEST TEAM

The 2004 Cardinals were 105–57, a winning percentage of .648 that was the best of any St. Louis club since 1944. The 2004 edition was the first to win an NLCS since 1987 but lost four straight to Boston in the World Series.

THE WORST TEAM

The only Cardinals team from 2000 through 2005 that failed to make a postseason appearance was the 2003 outfit, which was 85–77, but finished only three games out of first place.

THE BEST MOMENT

The best moment came in Game Five of the 2005 NLCS when Albert Pujols capped an incredible two-out, three-run ninth-inning rally with a home run to beat the Astros 5–4 in Houston. The euphoria lasted only 48 hours, however, as the Cards were eliminated in Game Six.

THE WORST MOMENT

On June 22, 2002, just four days after the death of broadcasting legend Jack Buck, pitcher Darryl Kile was found dead in his Chicago hotel room.

THE ALL-DECADE TEAM • YEARS W/CARDS

Mike Matheny, c	2000–04
Albert Pujols, 1b	2001–05
Fernando Viña, 2b	2000–03
Scott Rolen, 3b	2002–05
Edgar Renteria, ss	1999–2004
Reggie Sanders, lf	2004–05
Jim Edmonds, cf	2000–05
J. D. Drew, rf	1999–2003
Matt Morris, p	1997–98, 2000–05
Darryl Kile, p	2000–02
Chris Carpenter, p	2004–05
Jason Isringhausen, p	2002–05

Pujols has not only been the Cardinals' best first baseman over the first six seasons of the 2000s, but the best left fielder as well. He is listed here at first base. The only players on the All-Decade Team who began their professional career with the Cards were Pujols, Morris, and Drew. The rest arrived in trades or as free agents.

THE DECADE LEADERS

Batting Ave:	Albert Pujols	.332
On-Base Pct:	Albert Pujols	.416
Slugging Pct:	Albert Pujols	.621
Home Runs:	Jim Edmonds	210
RBIs:	Albert Pujols	621
Runs:	Albert Pujols	629
Stolen Bases:	Edgar Renteria	111
Wins:	Matt Morris	82
Strikeouts:	Matt Morris	758
ERA:	Darryl Kile	3.54
Saves:	Jason Isringhausen	140

THE HOME FIELD

The final game at Busch Stadium was played on October 19, 2005, ending 40 years of Cardinals history at the ballpark. As fans left the stadium, they could peer into the construction site of the new Busch Stadium, opened in 2006 just south of the old stadium.

THE GAME YOU WISH YOU HAD SEEN

On the brink of elimination in the 2004 NLCS, Jim Edmonds hit a twelfth-inning home run in Game Six to defeat the Astros 6–4.

THE WAY THE GAME WAS PLAYED

The offensive explosion baseball experienced during the late 1990s continued into this century, as did the trend toward baseball-only ballparks with grass fields. In the NL new ballparks opened in San Francisco, Houston, Pittsburgh, Milwaukee, Cincinnati, Philadelphia, San Diego, and St. Louis between 2000 and 2006. Another was on the drawing board in Washington.

THE MANAGEMENT

As of 2006, the Cardinals had had the same management team in place at the top of the organization for more than 10 years in a remarkable display of stability. William O. DeWitt Jr. was serving as chairman of the board, Frederick O. Hanser as vice chairman, Mark Lamping as president, Walt Jocketty as general manager, and Tony La Russa as field manager.

THE BEST PLAYER MOVE

The acquisition of Jim Edmonds in a trade with the Angels for Kent Bottenfield and Adam Kennedy in March 2000 ranks among the best in club history.

THE WORST PLAYER MOVE

None of the deals completed by the Cardinals from 2000 through 2005 has been disastrous. The worst two thus far sent Jack Wilson to the Pirates for Jason Christiansen in 2000 and Coco Crisp to the Indians for Chuck Finley in 2002. Both deals have the potential to backfire as Wilson and Crisp have become regulars for their new clubs, although the Cardinals had better players at shortstop than Wilson and better outfielders on the roster than Crisp through the 2005 season.

2000

Season in a Sentence

Despite losing Mark McGwire to injuries for half of the season, the Cardinals hit 235 homers and win the NL Central before losing to the Mets in the NLCS.

Finish • Won • Lost • Pct • GB

First   95   67   .586 +10.0

National League Division Series—The Cardinals defeated the Atlanta Braves three games to none

National League Championship Series—The Cardinals lost to the New York Mets four games to one

Managers

Tony La Russa

Stats

Stats	Cards	NL	Rank
Batting Avg:	.270	.266	6
On-Base Pct:	.356	.345	4
Slugging Pct:	.455	.432	3
Home Runs:	235		2
Stolen Bases:	87		11
ERA:	4.38	4.63	7
Fielding Avg:	.981	.981	7
Runs Scored:	887		4
Runs Allowed:	771		7

Starting Lineup

Mike Matheny, c
Mark McGwire, 1b
Fernando Viña, 2b
Craig Paquette, 3b
Edgar Renteria, ss
Ray Lankford, lf
Jim Edmonds, cf
J. D. Drew, rf
Fernando Tatis, 3b
Placido Polanco, 2b
Eric Davis, rf
Shawon Dunston, cf-lf
Will Clark, 1b
Thomas Howard, rf

Pitchers

Darryl Kile, sp
Garrett Stephenson, sp
Pat Hentgen, sp
Andy Benes, sp
Rick Ankiel, sp
Dave Veres, rp
Mike James, rp
Heathcliff Slocumb, rp

Attendance

3,336,493 (first in NL)

Club Leaders

Batting Avg:	Viña	.300
On-Base Pct:	Edmonds	.411
Slugging Pct:	Edmonds	.583
Home Runs:	Edmonds	42
RBIs:	Edmonds	108
Runs:	Edmonds	129
Stolen Bases:	Viña	121
Wins:	Kile	20
Strikeouts:	Ankiel	194
ERA:	Ankiel	3.50
Saves:	Veres	29

JANUARY 7   Six days after the dawn of the new millennium and the end of worries about the Y2K problem, the Cardinals sign Andy Benes, most recently with the Diamondbacks, as a free agent.

Benes played three seasons in his second tour of duty with the Cardinals and posted a record of 24–20.

FEBRUARY 3   Four days after the St. Louis Rams win the Super Bowl with a 23–16 decision over the Tennessee Titans, the Cardinals sign Shawon Dunston, most recently with the Mets, as a free agent.

MARCH 18   The Cardinals trade Joe McEwing to the Mets for Jesse Orosco.

Orosco pitched in a major league record 1,252 games, but only 6 of them were with the Cardinals. He completed just 2¹/₃ innings. In the big leagues from 1979 through 2003, Orosco also played for the Mets, Dodgers, Indians, Brewers, Orioles, Dodgers, Padres, Yankees, and Twins.

MARCH 23   The Cardinals trade Kent Bottenfield and Adam Kennedy to the Angels for Jim Edmonds.

Edmonds was 29 years old when he joined the team and was coming off of an injury-marred season in which he batted .250 with five homers. The Angels considered him a divisive influence in the clubhouse. The trade for Edmonds has proved to be one of the best in Cardinals history. In his first six seasons in St. Louis, through 2005, he batted .292 with 210 homers and 590 RBIs.

APRIL 3   In the season opener, the Cardinals defeat the Cubs 7–1 before 48,156 at Busch Stadium. Mark McGwire didn't play because of a sore back. Craig Paquette, McGwire's replacement at first base, lined a three-run homer in the first inning. Eric Davis also homered, and Fernando Viña contributed two singles and a triple. Darryl Kile, in his Cardinal debut, pitched six innings for the win.

Major League Baseball wanted the Cardinals to open the season in Tokyo in a two-game series against the Mets. A majority of Cards players, led by Mark McGwire, vetoed the trip to Japan, however. The Mets played the Cubs at the Tokyo Dome on March 29 and 30.

APRIL 6   J. D. Drew hits two homers, including a grand slam off Brian Williams in the fourth inning, during a 13–3 win over the Cubs at Busch Stadium. During the seven-run third inning, Fernando Tatis, Drew, and Mike Matheny hit back-to-back homers off Kyle Farnsworth.

APRIL 9   Six different Cardinals hit six home runs during an 11–2 win over the Brewers at Busch Stadium. J. D. Drew, Shawon Dunston, Edgar Renteria, Craig Paquette, Mark McGwire, and Jim Edmonds all went deep.

In his first 201 games at Busch Stadium, McGwire hit 100 home runs.

APRIL 10   The Cardinals play at Enron Field (now known as Minute Maid Park) in Houston for the first time and defeat the Astros 8–7.

Jim Edmonds set a club record by reaching base in 12 consecutive plate appearances from April 10 through 12 on nine hits and three walks. Of the nine hits, two were homers, three were doubles, and four were singles. Few players ever have made a bigger impact in their first season with a club than Edmonds. He became the first Cardinal outfielder to hit at least 40 homers in a season (42) and added 108 RBIs, 129 runs, a .295 batting average, and a Gold Glove.

APRIL 11   Trailing 6–4, the Cardinals score seven runs in the seventh inning on Thomas Howard's grand slam off Chris Holt and a three-run blast from Edgar Renteria to defeat the Astros 10–6 in Houston.

The Cardinals started the 2000 season with a 7–1 record and scored 70 runs in the eight games.

APRIL 13   The Rockies score 10 runs in the second inning, all off Darryl Kile, during a 12–6 win over the Cardinals in Denver. Overall, Kile surrendered 11 runs, 8 earned, in 1²/₃ innings.

Kile recovered from the debacle to post a 20–9 record and a 3.91 earned run average in 2000.

APRIL 15   The Cardinals-Rockies game in Denver is postponed by snow.

APRIL 16   Fernando Viña collects five hits, including a double, in five at-bats, but the Cardinals lose 14–13 to the Rockies in the second game of a doubleheader in Denver. The Cards won the opener 9–3.

APRIL 20   Eli Marrero hits a grand slam off Brian Boehringer in the first inning of a 14–1 win over the Padres at Busch Stadium. Marrero added another homer later in the game.

APRIL 23   Placido Polanco hits a grand slam off Scott Karl in the second inning of a 6–3 win over the Rockies in a game at Busch Stadium shortened to seven innings by rain.

The Cardinals hit 55 home runs in 25 April games in 2000. The Cards smacked a club-record 235 homers during the season, led by Jim Edmonds (42), Mark McGwire (32), Ray Lankford (26), Fernando Tatis (18), J. D. Drew (18), Edgar Renteria (16), Craig Paquette (15), Shawon Dunston (12), and Will Clark (12).

MAY 7   Eric Davis hits a grand slam off Denny Neagle in the fifth inning of a 9–7 loss to the Reds in Cincinnati.

The Cardinals hit a club-record 12 grand slams in 2000.

MAY 8   The Cardinals play at Pac Bell Park (known SBC Park by 2005) in San Francisco for the first time and lose 6–4 to the Giants.

MAY 9   The Cardinals score eight runs in the second inning and defeat the Giants 13–6 in San Francisco.

MAY 14   Craig Paquette collects five hits, one of them a home run, in five at-bats during a 12–10 win over the Dodgers at Busch Stadium.

MAY 18   Mark McGwire hits three homers, which drive in all seven of the Cardinals' runs, in a 7–2 win over the Phillies in Philadelphia. McGwire clubbed a three-run homer in the first and a two-run bomb in the second, both off Curt Schilling, and a two-run homer in the eighth facing Wayne Gomes.

MAY 20   The Cardinals score seven runs in the eighth inning and five in the ninth to close out a 19–4 trouncing of the Pirates in Pittsburgh.

MAY 24   Mark McGwire hits his sixth homer in a span of six games during a 5–1 win over the Marlins at Busch Stadium.

McGwire hit 20 homers in the Cardinals' first 45 games in 2000. After slugging 70 home runs in 1998 and 65 in 1999, McGwire seemed to be well on the way to challenging those figures.

MAY 29   Garrett Stephenson runs his record on the 2000 season to 8–0 with a 3–0 decision over the Diamondbacks in Phoenix.

Stephenson entered the season as a 28-year-old with a 14–12 lifetime record. His 8–0 start was the best in Cardinals history by a starting pitcher and the third best overall. Howie Krist was 10–0 in 1941 with four wins as a starter and six as a relief pitcher. Frank DiPino was 9–0 as a reliever in 1989. Stephenson finished the 2000 season with a 16–9 record but missed the entire 2001 season with reconstructive elbow surgery and never fully recovered. He was 9–18 with the Cardinals in 2002 and 2003.

MAY 30   Shawon Dunston hits a grand slam off Omar Daal in the sixth inning of a 6–1 victory over the Diamondbacks in Phoenix.

JUNE 5   In the first round of the amateur draft, the Cardinals select outfielder Shaun Boyd of Vista High School in Oceanside, California, and pitcher Blake Williams of Southwest Texas State University. The Cards had one extra pick in the first round due to free-agent compensation. Thus far, the only three players the Cardinals drafted and signed in 2000 that have reached the majors have been Yadier Molina (4th round), Carmen Cali (10th round), and John Gall (11th round).

JUNE 11   Pat Hentgen takes a no-hitter into the seventh inning and defeats the Tigers 7–3 in Detroit.

JUNE 22   Trailing 8–1 to the Giants after 4½ innings at Busch Stadium, the Cardinals rally to win 11–10. Shawon Dunston keyed the comeback with six RBIs on two homers and a double. Craig Paquette drove in the winner with a walk-off single in the ninth.

JUNE 23   Mark McGwire hits his 550th career home run and 28th of 2000 during a 6–1 win over the Dodgers at Busch Stadium. The contest finished 8 hours and 47 minutes after the scheduled 1:15 PM start because of rain delays totaling 5 hours and 55 minutes.

JUNE 24   Larry Sutton, recalled from the minors earlier in the day to replace an injured J. D. Drew, hits a walk-off pinch-single to beat the Dodgers 2–1 at Busch Stadium.

JULY 4   Six days after six-year-old Elian Gonzalez returns to Cuba following a bitter legal battle, Keith McDonald hits a home run in his first major league at-bat during a 14–3 win over the Reds at Busch Stadium. McDonald batted in the eighth inning as a pinch hitter.

JULY 6   Keith McDonald becomes only the second batter to homer in his first two major league at-bats. Placed in the lineup as a catcher in his first big-league start, he homered in the second inning of a 12–6 loss to the Reds at Busch Stadium. McDonald previously homered in his first at-bat two nights earlier as a pinch hitter.

The only other player to homer in his first two at-bats in the majors was Bob Nieman of the St. Louis Browns on September 14, 1951. McDonald had one of the more peculiar careers in big-league history. He was 27 when he reached the majors and was born in Yokosuka, Japan. Despite his fast start, McDonald played in only eight major league games and accumulated just nine at-bats over two seasons (2000–01). After hitting homers in his first two at-bats, McDonald collected only one more hit in the majors—also a home run. His final big-league batting record was three hits, three homers, a .333 batting average, a .455 on-base percentage, and a 1.333 slugging percentage.

JULY 7   Mark McGwire goes on the disabled list with tendinitis in his knee.

              At the halfway point in the season, McGwire had 30 homers, 69 RBIs, and a .309 batting average. He returned from the disabled list on September 7 but had only 15 more at-bats.

JULY 13   Starting the game batting ninth as the designated hitter, Shawon Dunston hits a grand slam off Jesus Peña in the seventh inning during a 13–5 victory over the White Sox in Chicago.

JULY 14   Eduardo Perez hits a grand slam off Bob Howry in the eighth inning of a 9–4 win over the White Sox in Chicago.

JULY 15   Eric Davis collects five hits in five at-bats, but the Cardinals lose 15–7 to the White Sox in Chicago.

JULY 17   Outfielder Chris Richard homers on the first pitch he sees as a major leaguer during an 8–3 win over the Twins in Minneapolis. Richard was called up from the minors to replace J. D. Drew, who went on the disabled list.

              Richard was traded to the Orioles 12 days later after playing six games with the Cards. His only other hit with the club was a single.

JULY 21   The Cardinals rout the Astros 12–1 in Houston.

JULY 23   Andy Benes ties a major league record for most home runs allowed in an inning with four during a 15–7 loss to the Astros in Houston. Benes allowed homers in the second inning to Bill Spiers, Jeff Bagwell, Lance Berkman, and Richard Hidalgo in a span of six batters. Berkman also homered off Andy's brother Alan in the eighth.

JULY 25   Fernando Tatis homers off Russ Springer in the sixth inning of a 7–3 win over the Diamondbacks at Busch Stadium.

JULY 29   The Cardinals trade Chris Richard and Mark Nussbeck to the Orioles for Mike Timlin and cash. On the same day, the Cards dealt Jack Wilson to the Pirates for Jason Christiansen.

              Wilson became the Pirates' starting shortstop in 2001, a job he still held in 2005.

JULY 31   The Cardinals trade Jose Leon to the Orioles for Will Clark and cash.

AUGUST 2   In his first start with the Cardinals, Will Clark collects a homer and two singles to lead the Cardinals to a 10–7 win over the Expos in Montreal.

              The Cardinals acquired Clark in the July 31 trade with Baltimore to take over at first base after Mark McGwire was sidelined with a knee injury. Clark was once one of the most hated players in Cardinal Nation. While with the Giants, he got into a fight with Ozzie Smith and Jose Oquendo (see July 24, 1988). Subsequently, Clark was booed every time he appeared at Busch Stadium until he left for the American League in 1994. Clark became an immediate favorite in St. Louis once he joined the Cardinals, however. In his first four starts with the Cards, he hit four homers, one in each contest, along with nine hits and seven RBIs in 14 at-bats. Overall, he hit .345 with 12 home runs, 15 doubles, and 42 RBIs in 171 at-bats with the club. Despite the success, he retired at the end of the season at the age of 36.

AUGUST 12   Will Clark draws a bases-loaded walk in the twelfth inning for Curtis Leskanic to force across the winning run in a 2–1 victory over the Brewers in Milwaukee.

The Cardinals had a 50–33 record and a 10-game advantage in the NL Central on July 5 when the club hit a rough patch by losing 20 of the next 32 to cut the lead to 4½. Beginning with the August 12 triumph, the Cards were 28–9 before clinching the division title on September 20.

AUGUST 18   Trailing 6–0, the Cardinals score a run in the sixth inning, three in the seventh, two in the eighth, and one in the ninth to win 7–6 over the Phillies at Busch Stadium. Carlos Hernandez drove in the winning run with a walk-off single.

SEPTEMBER 1   Jim Edmonds hits a walk-off homer to beat the Mets 6–5 at Busch Stadium.

SEPTEMBER 3   Jim Edmonds hits his second walk-off homer against the Mets in three days with an eleventh-inning blast that concludes a 4–3 victory at Busch Stadium.

SEPTEMBER 10   The Cardinals play at County Stadium in Milwaukee for the last time and lose 4–3 to the Brewers.

SEPTEMBER 12   The Cardinals wallop the Pirates 11–1 in Pittsburgh.

SEPTEMBER 13   The Cardinals play at Three Rivers Stadium for the last time and defeat the Pirates 9–5.

During the six-game road trip through Milwaukee and Pittsburgh, Mark McGwire started each game but was replaced after the top of the first inning. Still recovering from his injured knee, McGwire wasn't yet ready to play on defense and was limited to one at-bat per game. To ensure that McGwire would get an at-bat and have proper time to warm up his injured knee, Tony La Russa batted him in either the first or second slot in the order. McGwire was listed as the second baseman in four games, the left fielder in one, and as the shortstop in the sixth, but he never took the field at those positions.

SEPTEMBER 16   Fernando Tatis hits a grand slam off Daniel Garibay in the third inning of a 7–6 win over the Cubs at Busch Stadium.

SEPTEMBER 20   The Cardinals clinch the NL Central with an 11–6 win over the Astros at Busch Stadium. Jim Edmonds hit a grand slam off Jim Holt in the third inning.

The Cardinals' 95–67 record in 2000 was tied with the Braves for the second best in the NL in 2000. The Giants were 97–65.

SEPTEMBER 24   Will Clark drives in all five St. Louis runs, four on a fifth-inning grand slam off Todd Van Poppel, but the Cardinals lose 10–5 in Chicago.

SEPTEMBER 26 Padres pitchers tie a major league record by hitting three batters in the eighth inning of a 7–1 Cardinals win in San Diego. Heathcliff Slocumb beaned Mark McGwire, and Dave Maurer hit Ray Lankford and Will Clark.

SEPTEMBER 28 Darryl Kile records his 20th win of the season with a 7–6 decision over the Padres in San Diego.

SEPTEMBER 29 Mike Matheny suffers a household injury that prevents him from playing in the postseason. Matheny cut his right ring finger with a hunting knife, a birthday gift he had just opened, and had surgery to repair two severed flexor tendons and a nerve.

OCTOBER 1 With the help of the Braves' 10–5 loss to the Rockies in Atlanta, the Cardinals clinch home-field advantage in the first round of the playoffs by beating the Reds 6–2 at Busch Stadium. Both the Cards and the Braves had 95–67 records, but St. Louis had a better record in head-to-head competition. The Redbirds won four of the seven regular-season meetings between the two clubs. Managed by Bobby Cox, the Braves were the defending NL champions, had reached every NLCS from 1991 through 1999, and had won five of them.

OCTOBER 3 In the first game of the Division Series, the Cardinals defeat the Braves 7–5 before 52,378 at Busch Stadium. The Cards scored six runs in the first inning off Greg Maddux on five singles, two errors, and a misplayed fly ball. Rick Ankiel almost gave the lead away in the fourth inning by walking four batters, throwing five wild pitches (a modern major league record), and allowing four runs in a bizarre breakdown. Not only did Ankiel miss the strike zone, but he also bounced several pitches past Carlos Hernandez and fired others well over the catcher's head and off the backstop. The last time a pitcher threw five wild pitches in an inning in any regular-season or postseason game was 1890. Four relievers allowed only one run over the last 6⅔ innings. Jim Edmonds collected a homer and two singles.

Less than three months past his 21st birthday, Ankiel was a surprise pick by Tony La Russa as the Game One starter. Darryl Kile was expected to have the honor. Ankiel was 3–0 with a 1.65 ERA in his last five starts and 11–7 with a 3.50 ERA overall in 2000. He also struck out 194 batters to break the Cardinals' rookie record of 191, set by Dizzy Dean in 1932. Kile was 20–9, but his 3.91 ERA was higher than Ankiel's.

OCTOBER 5 The Cardinals rout the Braves 10–5 in Game Two before 52,389 at Busch Stadium. After the Braves scored twice in the top of the first off Darryl Kile, the Cards rallied for three in their half on Will Clark's home run and never trailed again. Tom Glavine gave up seven St. Louis runs, and by the end of the fourth inning, the score was 8–2. Jim Edmonds contributed three doubles and a spectacular over-the-shoulder catch on the warning track. Mark McGwire hit a pinch-homer in the eighth.

OCTOBER 7 The Cardinals sweep the Braves in three games with a 7–1 win at Turner Field in Atlanta. Facing Kevin Millwood, Fernando Viña hit the game's second pitch for a home run. In the sixth, Viña hit a two-run single. Jim Edmonds homered in the third. Edmonds had 8 hits during the series, including 2 homers and 4 doubles, in 14 at-bats.

The Cardinals played the New York Mets in the National League Championship Series. Managed by Bobby Valentine, the Mets were the wild-card entry. They recorded a 94–68 regular-season record and advanced by defeating the Giants in four games in the Division Series.

OCTOBER 11   The Cardinals open the NLCS with a 6–2 loss to the Mets before 52,255 at Busch Stadium. The Mets scored two runs in the first inning off Darryl Kile and never trailed again. The only two St. Louis runs scored in the ninth.

OCTOBER 12   The Cardinals lose Game Two 6–5 to the Mets before 52,250 at Busch Stadium. Rick Ankiel was the starter, but his location problems, which had begun in Game One of the Division Series, continued. Ankiel walked three, threw two wild pitches, and heaved several more pitches to the backstop, leading to two New York runs, before La Russa yanked him with two outs in the first. The Cards twice rallied from a two-run deficit to tie the game 3–3 with two tallies in the sixth and knotted the contest again with two more in the eighth. Will Clark, normally a sure-handed first baseman, booted a Robin Ventura ground ball at the beginning of the ninth. Joe McEwing pinch ran for Ventura and later scored on Jay Payton's single.

OCTOBER 14   The Cardinals defeat the Mets 8–2 at Shea Stadium in Game Three. The Cards never trailed after scoring twice in the first. Andy Benes went eight innings for the win.

OCTOBER 15   The Cardinals fall behind three games to one with a 10–6 loss to the Mets in New York. Jim Edmonds gave the Cards a 2–0 lead with a two-run homer in the first, but the Mets scored four times in their half and three in the second off Darryl Kile. Will Clark's fifth-inning home run put them within two, 8–6, but the Cards couldn't score again.

OCTOBER 16   The Mets move on to the World Series with a 7–0 rout in New York in Game Five of the 2000 NLCS. Rick Ankiel's nightmare continued. He entered the game in the seventh but walked two and threw two wild pitches in two-thirds of an inning. Both benches emptied in the eighth when Dave Veres hit Mets center fielder Jay Payton in the helmet with a pitch, but order was quickly restored. In an all–New York World Series, the Mets lost to the Yankees in five games.

DECEMBER 8   With the result of the November 7 presidential election between George Bush and Al Gore still in doubt, Shawon Dunston signs with the Giants as a free agent.

DECEMBER 14   Two days after the US Supreme Court declares George Bush the winner in the presidential election, the Cardinals trade Fernando Tatis and Britt Reames to the Expos for Dustin Hermanson and Steve Kline.

Kline pitched for four seasons with the Cardinals and was known as much for his resin- and sweat-stained cap as he was for his pitching.

DECEMBER 19   Pat Hentgen signs with the Orioles as a free agent.

DECEMBER 23   Eric Davis signs with the Giants as a free agent.

2001

Season in a Sentence

Sparked by an incredible rookie season from Albert Pujols, the Cardinals win 50 of their last 74 games and reach the playoffs before losing in the first round.

Finish · Won · Lost · Pct · GB

First (tie)   93   69   .574   0

The Cardinals finished the season in a tie for first place with the Astros, but Houston was declared the NL Central champion because Houston had the better record in head-to-head competition (9–7). The Cardinals won the wild card by three games over the Giants.

National League Division Series—The Cardinals lost to the Arizona Diamondbacks three games to two

Manager

Tony La Russa

Stats

Stats	Cards	NL	Rank
Batting Avg:	.270	.261	3
On-Base Pct:	.339	.331	4
Slugging Pct:	.441	.425	5
Home Runs:	199		7
Stolen Bases:	91		7
ERA:	3.93	4.36	3
Fielding Avg:	.982	.982	10
Runs Scored:	814		4
Runs Allowed:	684		3

Starting Lineup

Mike Matheny, c
Albert Pujols, 1b-3b-lf-rf
Fernando Viña, 2b
Placido Polanco, 3b
Edgar Renteria, ss
Craig Paquette, lf-rf
Jim Edmonds, cf
J. D. Drew, rf
Mark McGwire, 1b
Ray Lankford, lf
Eli Marrero, c
Kerry Robinson, lf-cf
Bobby Bonilla, 1b

Pitchers

Matt Morris, sp
Darryl Kile, sp
Dustin Hermanson, sp
Andy Benes, sp
Bud Smith, sp
Dave Veres, rp
Steve Kline, rp
Mike Timlin, rp
Gene Stechschulte, rp
Mike Matthews, rp

Attendance

3,113,091 (third in NL)

Club Leaders

Batting Avg:	Pujols	.329
On-Base Pct:	Pujols	.403
Slugging Pct:	Pujols	.610
Home Runs:	Pujols	37
RBIs:	Pujols	130
Runs:	Pujols	112
Stolen Bases:	Viña	17
	Renteria	17
Wins:	Morris	22
Strikeouts:	Morris	185
ERA:	Kile	3.09
Saves:	Veres	15

JANUARY 5   The Cardinals announce the signing of free agents Bobby Bonilla (most recently with the Braves), Bernard Gilkey (from the Red Sox), and John Mabry (from the Padres). Gilkey and Mabry played previously with the Cardinals.

APRIL 2   The Cardinals open the season in Denver and lose 8–0 to the Rockies. Albert Pujols made his major league debut. Batting seventh and playing left field, Pujols had a single in three at-bats.

The Cards lost all three games of the opening series in Colorado by a combined score of 32–11, then won five in a row.

APRIL 6   Fernando Viña collects five hits, including a triple, in five at-bats, during a 12–9 win over the Diamondbacks in Phoenix. The Cardinals broke a 2–2 tie with eight runs in the fifth inning. Albert Pujols hit his first major league home run during the contest.

When spring training began, Pujols was 21 years old and virtually unknown, even in St. Louis. Not only had he never appeared in a big-league game, but he also had played just one season as a professional and only 24 games above the Class A level. Despite the lack of experience, Pujols responded with one of the greatest rookie seasons in baseball history. Playing in 161 games, he hit .329 with 194 hits, 37 homers, 47 doubles, 130 RBIs, and 112 runs scored. Pujols established rookie records for RBIs, total bases (360), and extra-base hits (88). He also played all over the field in 2001, appearing in 55 games at third base, 42 at first, 39 in left field, and 39 in right. Pujols was the NL Rookie of the Year and also finished fourth in the MVP voting. Other Cardinal batting stars in 2001 included Jim Edmonds and Fernando Viña. Edmonds batted .304 and had 30 homers and 110 RBIs. Viña hit .303 and clubbed nine homers. Both Edmonds and Viña won Gold Gloves.

APRIL 8   In his first start of the 2001 season, Rick Ankiel strikes out eight batters and walks three over five innings during a 9–4 win over the Diamondbacks in Phoenix.

Ankiel was under the microscope all during spring training in 2001 because of his erratic tosses during the 2000 postseason. Camera operators followed him even as he warmed up.

APRIL 9   In the home opener, the Cardinals defeat the Rockies 3–2 before 48,702 at Busch Stadium. The winning run scored in the ninth on a wild pitch by ex-Cardinal hurler Jose Jiminez. Albert Pujols, playing in his first game in St. Louis, hit a home run.

Before the contest, 80-year-old Stan Musial played the National Anthem on his harmonica along with Richard Hayman, conductor of the St. Louis Symphony Pops.

APRIL 12   Dustin Hermanson holds the Cardinals hitless for 6²/₃ innings, but the Cardinals lose 6–4 at Busch Stadium. The first Colorado hit was a two-out, two-run homer by Larry Walker in the seventh inning. Two pitches later, Todd Helton homered to give the Rockies a 3–2 lead.

APRIL 17   Pitcher Gene Stechschulte, acting as a pinch hitter, homers in his first major league at-bat, and first baseman Bobby Bonilla, acting as a pitcher, gives up a home run to the first batter he faces as a pitcher in a bizarre 17–4 loss to the Diamondbacks in Phoenix. Stechschulte, who had played in 25 previous big-league games as a reliever but had never batted, was sent to the plate as a pinch hitter in the sixth inning and hit a home run off Armando Reynoso. Not only did Stechschulte homer in his first at-bat, but on the first pitch as well. Bobby Bonilla, appearing in the last season of his 16-year career, took the mound in the ninth for the first time ever. Erubiel Durazo, the first batter he faced, hit a home run. Bonilla allowed two runs in the inning.

APRIL 29   The Cardinals win a 12–1 blowout against the Mets at Busch Stadium. The Cards scored seven runs in the third inning to take an 11–0 lead.

MAY 2   Ray Lankford hits a two-run homer in the eleventh inning to lead the Cardinals to a 4–2 win over the Marlins in Miami.

MAY 10   Rick Ankiel throws five pitches to the backstop in three innings during an 11–5 win over the Pirates at Busch Stadium.

The following day, the Cardinals sent Ankiel to their Class AAA farm club in Memphis because of his inexplicable wildness. Ankiel made six starts for the Cardinals in 2001, walked 25 batters in 24 innings, and had a 7.13 ERA. He pitched three games in Memphis, issuing an astonishing 17 bases on balls and 12 wild pitches in just 4^1/$_3$ innings. Sent all the way to Johnson City in the low Class A Appalachian League, Ankiel appeared to have his problems worked out with 158 strikeouts and 18 walks in 87^2/$_3$ innings and a 1.33 ERA. He also hit 10 homers, the fourth highest figure in the league, in 105 at-bats as a part-time designated hitter. Ankiel missed the entire 2002 season with an elbow strain, however, and had Tommy John surgery in July 2003. He made it back to the majors in 2004, but only for five games. The final chapter of Rick Ankiel's days as a baseball player has yet to be written. Still only 25 years old in the spring of 2005, he gave up pitching and went back to the minors as an outfielder in the hopes of one day continuing his major league career.

MAY 13   The Cardinals win a 13–4 laugher over the Cubs at Busch Stadium.

MAY 15   The Cardinals play at PNC Park in Pittsburgh for the first time and win 8–3 over the Pirates. It was the Cards' eighth win in a row.

MAY 17   The Cardinals extend their winning streak to 10 games with a 12–2 decision over the Pirates in Pittsburgh.

The Cards outscored the opposition 80–22 during the winning streak. The win vaulted the Redbirds into first place by one game, at 24–15.

MAY 22   The Cardinals play at Miller Park in Milwaukee for the first time and lose 5–0 to the Brewers.

MAY 25   With the Cardinals one strike from defeat, Craig Paquette hits a three-run homer on a 1–2 pitch with two outs in the ninth inning to beat the Reds 5–4 in Cincinnati.

JUNE 5   In the first round of the amateur draft, the Cardinals select pitcher Justin Pope of the University of South Florida. The first two players the Cardinals drafted and signed in 2001 to reach the majors were second rounder Dan Haren and fifth-round pick Skip Schumaker.

JUNE 7   Matt Morris has a no-hitter going after six innings with a 3–0 lead but runs into trouble by allowing one run in the seventh and two in the eighth. The Cardinals wind up losing 4–3 to the Cubs in Chicago.

JUNE 15   Bobby Bonilla hits a pinch-hit grand slam off Kelly Wunsch in the seventh inning of a 10–3 win over the White Sox at Busch Stadium.

JULY 7   Mark McGwire hits a grand slam off Steve Woodard in the fourth inning that gives the Cardinals a 6–2 lead, but the Indians rally to win 7–6 in 10 innings in Cleveland.

JULY 13   The Cardinals lose 4–1 to the Tigers at Busch Stadium. The loss dropped the Cards to 43–45 on the 2001 season, nine games behind the first-place Astros.

The Cardinals went 50–24 the rest of the way to reach the postseason.

JULY 18   Bobby Bonilla collects his 2,000th career hit during a 17–11 loss to the Astros in Houston.

AUGUST 2   The Cardinals trade Ray Lankford to the Padres for Woody Williams.

Williams pitched four seasons for the Cardinals and had a 45–22 record. Lankford was in his 12th season as a Cardinal and was near the end as a player. He sulked after being platooned and became a clubhouse distraction. Lankford returned to the Cardinals for a farewell season in 2004.

AUGUST 3   Matt Morris gives up five runs in the first inning but follows it up with six innings of shutout ball as the Cardinals rally to beat the Marlins 7–5 in the first game of a doubleheader at Busch Stadium. Florida won the second tilt 6–4.

On the same day, a jury in Gainesville, Florida, ordered Anheuser-Busch to pay $50 million, plus $22.6 million in interest, to Roger Maris's family for improperly taking away a beer distributorship in 1997. The lawsuit charged the brewery with breach of contract and breach of implied covenant of good faith and fair dealings. August Busch gave Maris the distributorship after Maris retired from baseball in 1968. He died in 1985, and his family continued operating the business in Gainesville and Ocala. Later in the month, the Maris family sued Anheuser-Busch again, this time for $5 billion. The second lawsuit charged that the company had smeared Maris's reputation by saying that the family's beer distributorship had poor business practices, sold outdated beer, falsified documents, and engaged in fraud. The two parties settled out of court in August 2005.

AUGUST 10   Trailing 5–0 after three innings, the Cardinals rally to beat the Mets 7–6 in 10 innings in New York. Craig Paquette drove in the winning run with a sacrifice fly.

AUGUST 11   Mark McGwire hits his 574th career home run during a 6–3 win over the Mets in New York. The homer put McGwire past Harmon Killebrew into fifth place all time in home runs. Home run number 574 also ended an odd streak for McGwire. Each of his 10 hits from July 18 through August 11 was a home run.

McGwire retired at the end of the 2001 season with 583 homers. At the time, he trailed only Hank Aaron (755), Babe Ruth (714), Willie Mays (660), and Frank Robinson (586). Over the next the four years, McGwire was passed by Barry Bonds (708 at the end of the 2005 season) and Sammy Sosa (590 at the end of 2005).

AUGUST 19   The Cardinals win their eleventh game in a row with a 9–0 decision over the Phillies at Busch Stadium.

The winning streak put the Cardinals back in contention for a berth in the postseason. At the end of the day, the Cards were 68–55 and 2½ games behind the Astros in the NL Central.

AUGUST 29   The Cardinals outlast the Padres 16–14 at Busch Stadium. The Cards scored nine runs in the second inning to take a 9–4 lead and never relinquished the advantage, although there were some tense moments in the ninth when San Diego scored three times.

AUGUST 30
The Cardinals lead 11–0 after three innings and wallop the Padres 13–3 at Busch Stadium.

SEPTEMBER 2
The Cardinals fall seven games behind the Astros in the NL Central with 26 contests left on the schedule after losing 7–3 to the Dodgers in Los Angeles. The Cards were three games behind the Cubs in the wild-card race.

SEPTEMBER 3
Cardinal rookie Bud Smith pitches a no-hitter to defeat the Padres 4–0 in San Diego. Smith was 21 years old and making only his 11th big-league start. It was also his first complete game. Smith had failed to make it past the seventh inning in his previous starts. A native of Southern California, Smith's mother, stepfather, 14 other immediate family members, and 10 high school buddies were among those in attendance. He started the ninth inning by retiring Rickey Henderson on a groundout. After D'Angelo Jiminez walked, Edgar Renteria backhanded Ryan Klesko's grounder for the second out. Smith sealed the no-hitter by fielding Phil Nevin's hard comebacker. He pumped his fist in the air and ran halfway to first base before flipping the ball to Albert Pujols. Smith threw 134 pitches, walked four, and struck out seven.

Smith finished the 2001 season with a 6–3 record and a 3.63 ERA. He looked to be a star for many years to come but was 1–5 with a 6.94 ERA in 2002, went to the Phillies in the Scott Rolen trade, and underwent two shoulder surgeries. Ironically, the 134 pitches he threw in the no-hitter might have contributed to his injury problems. Barring an unlikely return to the majors after 2005, Smith's seven big-league victories will be tied for the second fewest for a pitcher with a no-hitter. Bobo Holloman, who threw a no-hitter in his first start in the majors for the St. Louis Browns in 1953, had three wins. George Davis of the 1914 Boston Braves also had seven career victories.

SEPTEMBER 5
Woody Williams pitches a two-hitter against his former Padres teammates and wins 2–0 in San Diego. Williams retired the first 18 batters he faced and the minimum 27 over nine innings. The only hits off Williams were singles by D'Angelo Jiminez in the seventh inning and Ben Davis in the ninth. The Cards retired both on the base paths.

SEPTEMBER 8
Tony La Russa ties a National League record for most pitchers used in a nine-inning game with nine during a 6–5 win over the Dodgers at Busch Stadium. Starter Alan Benes went six innings. The eight relievers were Luther Hackman, Steve Kline, Dave Veres, Mike James, Mike Matthews, Mike Timlin, Jeff Tabaka, and Gene Stechschulte.

Kline appeared in 89 games in 2001, a Cardinal record for a pitcher. His ERA over 75 innings was 1.80.

SEPTEMBER 9
Jim Edmonds hits a grand slam off Chan Ho Park in the fourth inning of an 8–1 win over the Dodgers at Busch Stadium.

SEPTEMBER 11
Two hijacked commercial airliners strike and destroy the twin towers of the World Trade Center in New York in the worst terrorist attack ever on American soil. A third hijacked plane destroyed a portion of the Pentagon, and a fourth crashed in rural Pennsylvania. Some 3,000 were killed, including about 2,800 at the World Trade Center.

Almost immediately, commissioner Bud Selig canceled the slate of games scheduled for that day, including the Cardinals-Brewers matchup in Milwaukee. Later in the week, Selig announced that all games through Sunday, September 16 would be postponed. The contests were made up by extending the regular season a week. When play resumed, an air of heightened security and patriotism imbued every game. Fans endured close scrutiny by stadium personnel. "God Bless America" replaced "Take Me Out to the Ball Game" as the song of choice during the seventh-inning stretch.

SEPTEMBER 17   In the first game following the September 11 terrorist attacks, the Cardinals defeat the Brewers 2–1 at Busch Stadium. In his first start since his no-hitter on September 3, Bud Smith allowed only three hits in seven innings. He skipped a start after throwing 134 pitches in that outing, then waited for baseball to resume play following 9/11.

The game drew a crowd of 30,528 and had a patriotic flavor. It took almost 10 minutes for a large contingent of police and firefighters to take their positions before the National Anthem, and fans stood and cheered the entire game. They cheered again after a 21-fireworks salute before the contest.

SEPTEMBER 19   Matt Morris earns his 20th win of the 2001 season with an 8–2 decision over the Brewers at Busch Stadium. Morris struck out a career-high 13 in seven innings.

Morris was 22–8 with a 3.18 ERA in 2001. His 22 wins were the most by a Cardinal pitcher since Bob Gibson won 23 in 1970. Darryl Kile also had a great year in 2001, with a 16–11 record and a 3.09 earned run average.

SEPTEMBER 21   Albert Pujols hits a grand slam off Omar Olivares that breaks a 5–5 tie, giving the Cardinals a 9–5 victory over the Pirates in Pittsburgh. It was the Cardinals' eighth win in a row.

SEPTEMBER 22   The Cardinals extend their winning streak to nine games with a 4–1 decision over the Pirates in Pittsburgh.

SEPTEMBER 28   The Cardinals trounce the Pirates 14–3 at Busch Stadium.

With eight contests left on the schedule, the Cardinals trailed the Astros by three games in the NL Central race and led the Giants by three games in the wild-card chase.

OCTOBER 1   The Cardinals move into a tie for first place with a 5–1 win over the Brewers in Milwaukee. Both the Cardinals and the Astros had records of 91–66. The Cards led the Giants by four games in the wild-card race.

OCTOBER 4   The Cardinals take a one-game lead in the NL Central with a 10–3 win over the Brewers in Milwaukee. Matt Morris won his 22nd game of the year. Mark McGwire hit his 583rd career home run, connecting against Rocky Coppinger. It was the last home run of McGwire's career (see November 11, 2001). The Astros lost 10–2 to the Giants in Houston. In that game, Barry Bonds tied Mark McGwire's single-season home run record of 70 set in 1998.

The Cardinals headed into the final weekend with three games against the Astros in St. Louis to decide the NL Central title. The Cards needed to win two of three to win the division.

OCTOBER 5   The Cardinals drop back into a tie for first place with a 2–1 loss to the Astros at Busch Stadium. The Cards clinched a postseason berth, however, when the Giants lost 11–10 to the Dodgers in San Francisco, ensuring that St. Louis would be the wild-card entry should the club lose the division title. During the loss to the Dodgers, Barry Bonds broke Mark McGwire's single-season home run record by clubbing his 71st and 72nd homers of 2001.

Bonds added number 73 on October 7, the last day of the season.

OCTOBER 6   The Cardinals win 10–6 over the Astros at Busch Stadium to take a one-game lead in the NL Central race.

OCTOBER 7   On the day that the United States launches a sustained air campaign in Afghanistan against al-Qaeda, the Cardinals lose a chance at winning the NL Central by dropping a 9–2 decision to the Astros at Busch Stadium. The Cardinals and the Astros both finished the season with records of 93–69, but Houston was declared the division winner based on head-to-head competition (9–7).

The Cardinals met the Arizona Diamondbacks in the National League Division Series. A 1998 expansion team managed by Bob Brenly, the Diamondbacks were in their fourth season and won the NL West with a 92–70 record.

OCTOBER 9   The Cardinals lose Game One of the National League Championship Series 1–0 to the Diamondbacks in Phoenix. The starting pitchers were Matt Morris and Curt Schilling. The two tied for the National League lead in regular-season victories with 22. Schilling pitched a three-hit, complete-game shutout. Morris allowed a run and six hits in seven innings. The Diamondbacks' run scored in the fifth inning. Morris grazed Damian Miller with a pitch, Schilling laid down a sacrifice, and Steve Finley singled.

OCTOBER 10   The Cardinals even the series with a 4–1 triumph over Randy Johnson and the Diamondbacks in Phoenix. Woody Williams (seven innings) and Steve Kline (two innings) combined to allow one run and five hits. Albert Pujols put the Cardinals ahead 2–0 with a two-run homer off Johnson in the first inning.

OCTOBER 12   The Diamondbacks take a two-games-to-one lead in the Division Series with a 5–3 victory over the Cardinals before 52,273 at Busch Stadium. Jim Edmonds put the Cards ahead with a two-run homer in the fourth inning. Arizona scored one in the sixth and four in the seventh to take a 5–2 lead, however. Craig Counsell broke the 2–2 tie with a three-run homer off Mike Matthews.

OCTOBER 13   The Cardinals force a deciding fifth game by beating the Diamondbacks 4–1 before 52,194 at Busch Stadium. After rain delayed the start of the game for 3½ hours, both teams scored in the first inning. The Cards put the game away with a run in the second inning and two in the third. Fernando Viña hit a homer and two singles. Bud Smith went five innings for the win with relief help from Dustin Hermanson (three perfect innings) and Steve Kline (one inning).

OCTOBER 14   The Diamondbacks win the Division Series with a 2–1 decision over the Cardinals in Phoenix. Reggie Sanders put Arizona in the lead with a homer in the fourth inning off Matt Morris, and J. D. Drew tied the contest 1–1 with a home run in the eighth against Curt Schilling. Morris was lifted after eight innings because of a blister on his right thumb. Dave Veres started the ninth and gave up a double to Matt Williams, who was lifted for pinch runner Midre Cummings. Damian Miller sacrificed Cummings to third. Tony La Russa brought in Steve Kline to replace Veres. Kline intentionally walked Greg Colbrunn. Tony Womack tried to lay down a suicide squeeze but failed to make contact, and Cummings was tagged out. Colbrunn moved up to second base on the play. Womack made up for missing the bunt by delivering a series-winning single.

The Diamondbacks moved on to defeat the Braves in five games in the National League Championship Series and the Yankees in seven games in the World Series.

NOVEMBER 11   Mark McGwire announces his retirement. Slowed by a bad knee, McGwire hit 29 homers in 299 at-bats in 2001, but batted only .187. McGwire had agreed to a $30 million, two-year contract extension in spring training that would cover the 2002 and 2003 seasons, but he never signed the deal. "After a considerable discussion with those close to me, I have decided not to sign the extension, as I am unable to perform at a level equal to the salary the organization would be paying me. I believe I owe it to the Cardinals and the fans of St. Louis to step aside so a talented free agent can be brought in as the final piece of what I expect can be a World Championship–caliber team," McGwire said.

DECEMBER 10   The Cardinals sign Jason Isringhausen, most recently with the Athletics, as a free agent.

In four seasons through 2005, Isringhausen has established himself as one of the best closers in club history with 140 saves. At the start of 2006, Isringhausen ranked second among Cardinal pitchers in career saves, trailing only Lee Smith, who recorded 160.

DECEMBER 18   The Cardinals sign Tino Martinez, most recently with the Yankees, as a free agent.

The Cards acquired Martinez to play first base following Mark McGwire's retirement. The club didn't expect Martinez to match McGwire's numbers, but he was a disappointment with a .267 batting average and 37 homers in two seasons in St. Louis.

2002

Season in a Sentence

The Cardinals stumble out of the gate with a 14–19 record in early May but overcome the deaths of Jack Buck and Darryl Kile in June and a starting pitching rotation in disarray to make it as far as the NLCS.

Finish • Won • Lost • Pct • GB

First   97   65   .597   +13.0

National League Division Series—The Cardinals defeated the Arizona Diamondbacks three games to none

National League Championship Series—The Cardinals lost to the San Francisco Giants four games to one

Manager

Tony La Russa

Stats

Stats	Cards	NL	Rank
Batting Avg:	.268	.259	2
On-Base Pct:	.338	.331	4
Slugging Pct:	.425	.410	2
Home Runs:	175		3
Stolen Bases:	86		10 (tie)
ERA:	3.70	4.11	4
Fielding Avg:	.983	.982	6
Runs Scored:	787		2
Runs Allowed:	648		3

Starting Lineup

Mike Matheny, c
Tino Martinez, 1b
Fernando Viña, 2b
Placido Polanco, 3b
Edgar Renteria, ss
Albert Pujols, lf
Jim Edmonds, cf
J. D. Drew, rf
Eli Marrero, rf-lf-cf
Scott Rolen, 3b
Miguel Cairo, lf-2b
Kerry Robinson, lf
Mike DiFelice, c
Eduardo Perez, rf

Pitchers

Matt Morris, sp
Jason Simontacchi, sp
Woody Williams, sp
Chuck Finley, sp
Andy Benes, sp
Darryl Kile, sp
Jason Isringhausen, rp
Dave Veres, rp
Steve Kline, rp
Mike Crudale, rp
Mike Timlin, rp

Attendance

3,011,756 (fourth in NL)

Club Leaders

Batting Avg:	Pujols	.314
On-Base Pct:	Edmonds	.420
Slugging Pct:	Pujols	.561
	Edmonds	.561
Home Runs:	Pujols	34
RBIs:	Pujols	127
Runs:	Pujols	118
Stolen Bases:	Renteria	22
Wins:	Morris	17
Strikeouts:	Morris	171
ERA:	Morris	3.42
Saves:	Isringhausen	32

April 1   The Cardinals open the season with a 10–2 win over the Rockies before 48,397 at Busch Stadium. Matt Morris went seven innings for the win. Albert Pujols hit a three-run double in the fourth, and Mike DiFelice added a home run.

Pujols followed his rookie season by becoming the first player ever to bat at least .300 with 30 homers, 100 RBIs, and 100 runs scored in each of his first two major league season. In 2002, he batted .314 and had 34 home runs, 127 RBIs, and 118 runs scored. Pujols was the runner-up to Barry Bonds in the MVP voting.

April 9   The Cardinals defeat the Brewers 6–5 at Busch Stadium.

April 10   Eduardo Perez hits a walk-off homer in the eleventh inning to beat the Brewers 6–5 at Busch Stadium. The Cardinals trailed 5–0 before scoring three runs in the third inning, one in the fourth, and one in the ninth to set the stage for the dramatic victory.

APRIL 11   The Cardinals defeat the Brewers 6–5 at Busch Stadium for the third game in a row.

APRIL 13   Darryl Kile (six innings), Luther Hackman (two innings), and Jason Isringhausen (one inning) combine on a two-hitter to defeat the Astros 2–1 at Busch Stadium. Isringhausen closed out the game by striking out the only three batters he faced on the minimum nine pitches. The victims were Daryle Ward, Jose Vizcaino, and Julio Lugo. The only other Cardinal pitchers to strike out three batters in an inning were Bob Gibson in 1969 and Lynn McGlothlen in 1975. The only two Houston hits in the contest were singles by Brad Ausmus in the third and Daryle Ward in the seventh. Eli Marrero singled home the winning run with two outs in the ninth.

Marrero made the unusual transformation from catcher to outfielder in 2002. He started the season with 11 hits in his first 15 at-bats and finished with a .262 average and 18 homers.

APRIL 17   Jim Edmonds hits a grand slam off Curt Schilling with the Cardinals trailing 3–2 in the fifth inning, sparking the club to an 8–4 win over the Diamondbacks in Phoenix.

Edmonds hit .311 with 28 homers, made his usual series of highlight-reel catches in center field, and won a Gold Glove in 2002.

MAY 7   The Cardinals lose 8–0 to the Cubs in Chicago.

The loss dropped the Cardinals' 2002 record to 14–19. The club was in fourth place, 5½ games out of first. The worst problem was the starting pitching. The Cards used 11 different starters in the first 30 games of the season. By the end of the season, the Cardinals had employed 26 pitchers, 14 of them as starters. The most intriguing hurler was Jason Simontacchi, who made his major league debut in May at age 28. He pitched for the Italian Olympic team in 2000 and had stints in both Venezuela and an independent league. Simontacchi won his first five big-league decisions and finished 2002 with an 11–5 record.

MAY 11   Trailing 8–0, the Cardinals score three runs in the fifth inning, two in the sixth, and five in the eighth to beat the Reds 10–8 in Cincinnati. All five eighth-inning runs scored with two outs. Placido Polanco hit a two-run double, Fernando Viña drove in a run with another double to tie the score, and J. D. Drew added a two-run homer.

MAY 17   Darryl Kile (seven innings), Gene Stechschulte (one inning), and Jason Isringhausen (one inning) combine on a two-hitter to defeat the Reds 3–1 at Busch Stadium. The only two Cincinnati hits were a single by Jason LaRue in the sixth inning and a double by Austin Kearns in the seventh.

MAY 22   J. D. Drew hits a walk-off homer in the ninth inning to defeat the Astros 3–2 at Busch Stadium.

MAY 26   Fernando Viña hits a grand slam off Josh Fogg in the second inning of a 7–3 win over the Pirates in Pittsburgh. Jim Edmonds hit a 438-foot homer that bounced off a walkway and into the Allegheny River.

JUNE 4   In their first selection in the amateur draft, the Cardinals select shortstop Calvin Hayes from East Rowan High School in Salisbury, North Carolina, in the third round. The Cards forfeited their choices in the first and second rounds due to free-agent compensation.

The first 2002 draftee to reach the majors was Brad Thompson, taken in the 16th round.

JUNE 10   The Cardinals play the Mariners during the regular season for the first time and lose 10–0 at Safeco Field in Seattle.

JUNE 11   Albert Pujols hits a grand slam off James Baldwin in the sixth inning of a 7–4 win over the Mariners in Seattle.

JUNE 16   The Cardinals move into a tie for first place with a 5–1 win over the Royals at Busch Stadium.

The Cards remained on top of the NL Central for the rest of the season. The club had an 83–46 record over the last 129 games of the campaign.

JUNE 18   The Cardinals play the Angels during the regular season for the first time and win 7–2 at Busch Stadium.

Legendary broadcaster and St. Louis institution Jack Buck died on the same day, at the age of 77, following a long illness during which he was hospitalized for nearly six months. Buck was the club's radio and television announcer from 1954 through 2000. His son Joe joined his father in the booth in 1991 to continue the family business. For four and a half hours on June 20, the Cardinals held a public viewing of Buck's closed casket at home plate at Busch Stadium. The team also cut the initials "JFB" in the grass just beyond the center field wall and again behind second base.

Elsa/Getty Images Sport/Getty Images

Darryl Kile pitched for the Cardinals from 2000 to 2002. His won-lost record was 41–24 before he passed away from atherosclerosis, a narrowing of the coronary arteries, in mid-season.

JUNE 22   Only four days after the death of Jack Buck, Darryl Kile is found dead at the team hotel in Chicago. He was 33. Kile was survived by his wife, Flynn; five-year-old twins, a son, Kannon, and a daughter, Sierra; and a 10-month-old son, Ryker.

At 12:25 PM, a little more than two hours before game time, several Cardinals realized that Kile wasn't at the ballpark and called the Westin Hotel and asked to check on him. The hotel security director and maintenance man went to Kile's suite. The pitcher was found in his bed. Police estimated that Kile had been dead for 8 to 10 hours. The game against the Cubs at Wrigley Field was postponed. Kile showed no health problems during a routine physical in spring training, although he complained of shoulder pain and weakness the night before he died. He had no history of heart problems and was not on medication, but his father died of a heart attack in his mid-40s in 1993. An autopsy showed he likely died from blocked coronary arteries.

JUNE 23   A day after the death of Darryl Kile, the grieving Cardinals lose 8–3 to the Cubs in Chicago in a game played on national television on Sunday night on ESPN. Kile was the scheduled starter.

At a memorial service held at the team hotel in the morning, the club voted unanimously to play with the blessing of Flynn Kile, Darryl's wife. The game had an eerie feel from the outset. Organ music that usually filled Wrigley Field during batting practice and between innings was silent. The flags were at half-staff. Kile's name and number 57 were on the marquee outside Wrigley for the entire day, and the only thing on the park's electronic message board was a bright yellow "57." A moment of silence was held for him before the game. The entire Cardinal team received a standing ovation as it left the field after batting practice.

JUNE 25   In the first home game following Darryl Kile's death, the Cardinals lose 2–0 to the Brewers.

Several Cardinals wept openly during a memorial service and a video tribute before the game. Between innings, Kile's career highlights and accomplishments were listed on the video board. Kile's jersey hung in the tunnel leading to the clubhouse. Team personnel wore small black circular patches with Kile initials and number on the left sleeve. In addition was a patch to commemorate the death of longtime broadcaster Jack Buck.

JULY 2   Placido Polanco, Jim Edmonds, and Albert Pujols hit back-to-back-to-back homers against Kevin Jarvis in the second inning of an 11–5 win over the Padres at Busch Stadium.

JULY 7   Placido Polanco collects five hits in five at-bats during a 12–6 win over the Dodgers at Busch Stadium.

JULY 19   The Cardinals trade Luis Garcia and Coco Crisp to the Indians for Chuck Finley.

In his 17th and final big-league season, 39-year-old Finley came to the Cardinals with 193 lifetime wins and went 7–4 down the stretch. Crisp became a regular in the Cleveland outfield.

JULY 28   The Cardinals score six runs in the ninth inning to stun the Cubs 10–9 in a game televised nationally on ESPN on Sunday night. Down 6–0, the Cards scored four runs in the sixth inning but allowed Chicago to increase its lead to 9–4. In the ninth, the Cards made the score 9–7 on Miguel Cairo's RBI double and run-scoring singles from Jim Edmonds and Tino Martinez. The thrilling climax came when Edgar Renteria hit a towering, three-run, walk-off homer.

Renteria hit .305 with 11 homers and won a Gold Glove in 2002.

JULY 29
The Cardinals trade Placido Polanco, Bud Smith, and Mike Timlin to the Phillies for Scott Rolen and Doug Nickle.

Rolen was in the last year of his contract and wanted no part of re-signing with the Phillies after being booed often by Philadelphia's fickle fans, who constantly compared his play with the impossibly high standard set by Mike Schmidt. Like many before him, including players such as Mark McGwire, Rolen was willing to forego free agency to sign a long-term deal with the Cardinals for the club's family atmosphere and adoring fan base.

AUGUST 10
Albert Pujols hits a grand slam off Shawn Estes in the first inning of a 5–4 win over the Mets at Busch Stadium.

AUGUST 15
Cardinal pitchers walk 11 batters, but the club wins 11–5 over the Pirates in Pittsburgh. The Cards broke a 5–5 tie with six runs in the ninth.

AUGUST 18
Edgar Renteria hits a grand slam off Vicente Padilla in the sixth inning of a 5–1 win over the Phillies in Philadelphia.

AUGUST 22
The Cardinals score three runs in the ninth inning, the last two on a walk-off double by Fernando Viña, to beat the Pirates 5–4 at Busch Stadium.

AUGUST 25
The Cardinals send Jason Jarmuth, Jared Blasdell, and cash to the Cubs for Jeff Fassero.

AUGUST 27
Chuck Finley pitches a two-hitter to defeat the Reds 5–0 in the second game of a doubleheader in Cincinnati. The Cards scored all five of their runs in the first inning. Juan Castro got both of the hits off Finley, singles in the sixth and ninth innings. The Reds won the opener 5–4.

AUGUST 29
The Cardinals play at Cinergy Field (formerly Riverfront Stadium) in Cincinnati for the last time and lose 7–0.

AUGUST 30
Just three hours before a 6–3 Cardinal win over the Cubs in Chicago, the players and owners come to a new labor agreement that prevents a strike.

AUGUST 31
Eli Marrero homers in both ends of a day-night doubleheader in Chicago to help the Cardinals sweep the Cubs 8–1 and 10–4. Marrero's second homer was a grand slam off Jason Bere in the third inning.

SEPTEMBER 4
Down 5–0, the Cardinals score four runs in the third inning on Edgar Renteria's grand slam, single tallies in the fifth, sixth, and seventh, and three in the eighth to beat the Reds 10–5 at Busch Stadium. Renteria's homer was off Ryan Dempster.

SEPTEMBER 6   In a matchup of the Benes brothers, the Cardinals score all 11 of their runs in the third inning and defeat the Cubs 11–2 in Chicago. Alan Benes started for the Cubs and gave up eight runs in 2$^1/_3$ innings. Andy Benes contributed to his brother's demise with two hits. Andy was one out from a complete-game shutout when he gave up two runs.

SEPTEMBER 11   The Cardinals extend their winning streak to eight games with a 4–3 decision over the Brewers in Milwaukee. The victory gave the Cards a 6½-game lead in the NL Central pennant race.

SEPTEMBER 17   The Cardinals break a 4–4 tie with seven runs in the eighth inning, four on a grand slam by Tino Martinez off Sean Lowe, to win 11–4 over the Rockies in Denver.

SEPTEMBER 20   The Cardinals clinch the NL Central with a 9–3 win over the Astros at Busch Stadium. The Cards celebrated near the mound with Albert Pujols carrying the jersey of the late Darryl Kile onto the field.

SEPTEMBER 23   The Cardinals score 10 runs in the seventh inning and defeat the Diamondbacks 13–1 at Busch Stadium.

SEPTEMBER 28   Chuck Finley records his 200th, and last, career win with a 3–1 decision over the Brewers at Busch Stadium.

The Cardinals met the Arizona Diamondbacks in the National League Division Series for the second year in a row. In 2001, the Cards lost to Arizona three games to two. Managed by Bob Brenly, the 2002 Diamondbacks were the defending World Champions and had a 98–64 record during the regular season.

OCTOBER 1   The Cardinals open the playoffs with a 12–2 triumph over the Diamondbacks in Phoenix. Jim Edmonds got the scoring under way with a two-run homer in the first inning off Randy Johnson. The Cards broke a 2–2 tie in the fourth inning with three runs, two of them on a homer by Scott Rolen. Fernando Viña collected three hits and scored twice. Matt Morris went seven innings for the win.

Morris was the Cardinals' top pitcher in 2002 with a 17–9 record and a 3.42 ERA.

OCTOBER 3   The Cardinals win Game Two 2–1 over the Diamondbacks in Phoenix. J. D. Drew homered in the third off Curt Schilling to give the Cards a 1–0 lead. After Arizona tied the score with an unearned run in the eighth, St. Louis won the contest in the ninth. Edgar Renteria singled, moved to second on a sacrifice by Mike Matheny, and scored on a Miguel Cairo single. Cairo was in the game at third base because Scott Rolen was injured when base runner Alex Cintron blindsided him. Rolen suffered a sprained shoulder and missed the remainder of the postseason.

In the first two games of the series, the Cards defeated Arizona's two aces. Randy Johnson (24–5) and Curt Schilling (23–7) had a combined 47–12 record in 2002.

OCTOBER 5   The Cardinals complete a three-game sweep of the Diamondbacks with a 6–3 victory before 52,189 at Busch Stadium. Miguel Cairo, subbing for the injured Scott Rolen, collected three hits, including a double, in three at-bats in addition to two RBIs and two runs scored. Arizona scored first with two runs in the second, but the Redbirds surged ahead with a run in the second inning, another in the third, and two in the fourth. Albert Pujols threw out two runners at the plate from left field. After the final out, St. Louis players celebrated near second base with Matt Morris carrying the jersey of the late Darryl Kile onto the field.

The Cardinals met the San Francisco Giants in the National League Championship Series. Managed by Dusty Baker, the Giants went 95–66 in 2002 to earn a wild-card berth. In the first round, the Giants upset the Braves in five games.

OCTOBER 9   The Cardinals lose the NLCS opener 9–6 to the Giants before 52,175 at Busch Stadium. Starter Matt Morris allowed seven runs in 4$\frac{1}{3}$ innings to put St. Louis in a 7–1 hole. Albert Pujols, Miguel Cairo, and J. D. Drew homered during the futile comeback.

In the fifth inning, Tony La Russa and Dusty Baker were arguing with their faces only inches apart as umpire Randy Marsh tried to intervene. The incident began when Giants center fielder Kenny Lofton took offense at a close pitch from Cardinal hurler Mike Crudale. Lofton had homered in the third, and many Cardinals believed he was showboating by stopping to admire the shot. After ducking away from the pitch, Lofton yelled at Crudale and catcher Mike Matheny. Marsh stepped between Lofton and Crudale as both benches emptied. No punches were thrown, but several on each team scuffled: Baker and La Russa, Barry Bonds and Eduardo Perez; and Lofton and Scott Rolen. Both La Russa and Baker were fined an undisclosed amount by Major League Baseball.

OCTOBER 10   The Giants win Game Two 4–1 before 52,195 at Busch Stadium. The big right-hander Jason Schmidt dominated the Cardinals' offense with eight strikeouts and just one walk in 7$\frac{2}{3}$ innings. The game marked starter Woody Williams's first appearance since September 20 due to an injury to his left side.

OCTOBER 12   The Cardinals take the third game of the NLCS 5–4 at Pac Bell Park in San Francisco. The Cards took a 2–1 lead with a pair of runs in the third inning and added to the advantage with a solo homer from Mike Matheny in the fourth and another from Jim Edmonds in the fifth. Barry Bonds tied the score, however, with a three-run homer off Chuck Finley that sailed into McCovey Cove in the bottom of the fifth. The Cards broke the deadlock with an Eli Marrero homer in the sixth.

The Game Three and Game Four starting pitchers for the Cardinals made their final big-league appearances in the 2002 NLCS. Both Finley and Andy Benes retired before the 2003 season started.

OCTOBER 13   The Giants take a three-games-to-one lead with a 4–3 victory in San Francisco. Fernando Viña started a two-run rally in the first inning with a double. The Giants tied the contest with two tallies in the sixth off Andy Benes. It was still 2–2 with two outs and no one base in the eighth when Tony La Russa made the controversial decision to intentionally walk Barry Bonds. Benito Santiago foiled the strategy with a two-run homer. The Cardinals scored a run in the ninth to close the gap to 4–3 and had a runner on third with one out, but Albert Pujols and J. D. Drew struck out against Rob Nen to end the game.

After the contest, Garrett Stephenson got in a shoving match with an abusive fan before walking onto the team bus.

OCTOBER 14   The Giants move on to the World Series by defeating the Cardinals 2–1 in San Francisco. Neither Matt Morris nor Kirk Rueter allowed any runs in the first six innings. The Cards scored first in the seventh on a Mike Matheny double, Matt Morris's sacrifice, and a sacrifice fly from Fernando Viña. The Giants tied the game in the eighth on two singles, a hit batsman, and a sacrifice fly by Barry Bonds. Kenny Lofton drove in the winning run in the ninth with the third single of the inning.

The Giants lost the World Series to the Anaheim Angels in seven games.

DECEMBER 13   The Cardinals sign Chris Carpenter, most recently with the Blue Jays, as a free agent.

When the Cardinals signed him, Carpenter was 27 years old and had a lifetime 49–50 record and a history of arm trouble. The Cards signed him with the full knowledge that Carpenter would miss the entire 2003 season with shoulder surgery, but the gamble paid huge dividends. In the first two seasons following his return, Carpenter was one of the best pitchers in the NL. He was 15–5 with a 3.46 ERA in 2004 and 21–5 with a 2.83 ERA in 2005.

DECEMBER 17   The Cardinals sign Joe Girardi, most recently with the Rockies, as a free agent.

DECEMBER 18   The Cardinals sign Cal Eldred, most recently with the White Sox, as a free agent.

2003

Season in a Sentence

The Cardinals possess a championship-quality offense and defense, but a lack of pitching prevents a return to the postseason.

Finish • Won • Lost • Pct • GB

Third   85   77   .525   3.0

In the wild-card race, the Cardinals tied for fourth place, six games back

Manager

Tony La Russa

Stats

Stats	Cards	NL	Rank
Batting Avg:	.279	.262	2
On-Base Pct:	.350	.332	1
Slugging Pct:	.454	.417	2
Home Runs:	196		2 (tie)
Stolen Bases:	82		5
ERA:	4.60	4.28	11
Fielding Avg:	.987	.983	1
Runs Scored:	876		2
Runs Allowed:	796		11

Starting Lineup

Mike Matheny, c
Tino Martinez, 1b
Bo Hart, 2b
Scott Rolen, 3b
Edgar Renteria, ss
Albert Pujols, lf-1b
Jim Edmonds, cf
J. D. Drew, rf
Orlando Palmeiro, lf-rf
Miguel Cairo, 2b-lf
Fernando Viña, 2b
Eduardo Perez, rf
Kerry Robinson, lf-rf-cf

Pitchers

Woody Williams, sp
Brett Tomko, sp
Matt Morris, sp
Garrett Stephenson, sp
Jason Isringhausen, rp
Steve Kline, rp
Cal Eldred, rp
Jeff Fassero, rp
Jason Simontacchi, rp-sp

Attendance

2,910,371 (fourth in NL)

Club Leaders

Batting Avg:	Pujols	.359
On-Base Pct:	Pujols	.439
Slugging Pct:	Pujols	.667
Home Runs:	Pujols	43
RBIs:	Pujols	124
Runs:	Pujols	137
Stolen Bases:	Renteria	37
Wins:	Williams	18
Strikeouts:	Williams	153
ERA:	Williams	3.67
Saves:	Isringhausen	22

JANUARY 3   Dave Veres signs with the Cubs as a free agent.

MARCH 31   Twelve days after US forces invade Iraq, the Cardinals open the 2003 season with an 11–9 win over the Brewers before 49,561 at Busch Stadium. Trailing 7–5 heading into the bottom of the eighth, the Cards scored six runs, three of them on a Scott Rolen home run, before St. Louis survived a two-run Milwaukee rally in the ninth. Eduardo Perez and Tino Martinez also homered. Edgar Renteria drove in three runs.

Renteria had a career year in 2003, batting .330 with 13 homers, 47 doubles, and 100 RBIs. He also earned a Gold Glove.

APRIL 4   Jim Edmonds ties a club record for most extra-base hits in a game with two homers and two doubles, but the Cardinals lose 6–5 in 13 innings to the Astros at Busch Stadium.

APRIL 8   Mike Matheny's three-run homer in the thirteenth inning beats the Rockies 15–12 in Denver. Colorado scored six runs in the sixth inning to lead 11–7. The Cards then pulled ahead 12–11 with five runs in the seventh, only to have the Rockies tie the contest in the bottom half. Jim Edmonds contributed a homer and two doubles during the contest.

> *Combined with his two homers and two doubles on April 4, Edmonds became one of only five players in major league history to collect seven extra-base hits in consecutive games, and the only one to accomplish the feat since 1954. The four-day gap between games was due to Edmonds's being held out of the starting lineup on April 5, a rainout on April 6 and an off day on April 7. One of the other four players with seven extra-base hits in consecutive games was Red Schoendienst with the Cardinals in 1948.*

APRIL 16 — The Cardinals post a 12–2 win over the Brewers in Milwaukee.

APRIL 21 — Tino Martinez and Diamondback pitcher Miguel Batista are ejected for precipitating a bench-clearing brawl during a 1–0 Cardinals loss in Phoenix.

> *Batista hit Martinez in the shoulder blade with a pitch in the fifth inning. The two jawed at each other while Martinez slowly made his way to first. Martinez was forced at second base, and while trotting off the field, made a right turn to attack Batista. As Martinez threw a punch, Batista fired the ball at him but missed. Both benches quickly cleared. Batista, backpedaling throughout the brawl, was herded into left field by Arizona manager Bob Brenly.*

APRIL 27 — The Cardinals win a 20-inning marathon 7–6 against the Marlins in Miami in a contest that lasted six hours and seven minutes. Fernando Viña drove in the winning run in the twentieth with a single. He was 0 for 9 before the hit. It was the longest Cardinals game played since 1974. The Cards scored three runs in the ninth inning for a seemingly insurmountable 6–1 lead, but the Marlins countered with five tallies in the bottom half to tie the score 6–6. Cardinal relievers were solid the rest of the way, however, with eleven consecutive shutout innings. Steve Kline earned the win with three perfect innings. Tino Martinez collected five hits in eight at-bats.

APRIL 29 — The Cardinals score seven runs in the eighth inning to win 13–3 over the Mets at Busch Stadium.

APRIL 30 — The Cardinals strafe Mets pitching for the second day in a row, winning 13–4 at Busch Stadium.

MAY 1 — Jim Edmonds hits a walk-off homer in the tenth inning to defeat the Mets 6–5 at Busch Stadium.

> *Edmonds hit 39 homers, batted .275, and won his sixth Gold Glove in 2003. He had 28 homers at the All-Star break, but a shoulder injury, apparently suffered in the All-Star Game Home Run Derby, slowed Edmonds in the second half.*

MAY 5 — The Cardinals play at Great American Ball Park in Cincinnati for the first time and lose 5–4 to the Reds.

MAY 8 — Aaron Boone hits three homers off Cardinal pitchers during an 8–6 loss to the Reds in Cincinnati.

MAY 9

Fernando Viña hits a grand slam off Carlos Zambrano in the second inning of a 6–3 win over the Cubs in Chicago.

MAY 11

The clash between the Cardinals and Cubs in Chicago is postponed with the Cardinals leading 11–9 in the top of the fifth inning. The game was called after a 64-minute rain delay. None of the statistics in the contest counted.

MAY 16

J. D. Drew smashes a home run estimated at 514 feet during a 7–4 win over the Cubs at Busch Stadium. The mammoth shot hit the top of the right-field video board.

MAY 22

Albert Pujols homers for the fourth game in a row, although the Cardinals lose 5–2 to the Astros in Houston.

MAY 23

The Cardinals take a thrilling 10–8 victory from the Pirates in 10 innings in Pittsburgh. The Cards were down 7–2 before scoring three in the eighth inning. Still trailing 7–5 with two out in the ninth, Scott Rolen hit a two-strike pitch for a three-run homer to put St. Louis ahead 8–7. The Pirates scored in the bottom half to send the game into extra innings, however. J. D. Drew broke the 8–8 tie with a run-scoring triple. Albert Pujols collected five hits, including two doubles, in five at-bats.

JUNE 3

The Cardinals play the Blue Jays for the first time during the regular season and win 11–5 at Busch Stadium.

> *On the same day, the Cardinals selected catcher Daric Barton from Marina High School in Huntington Beach, California, in the first round of the amateur draft. Barton was traded to the Athletics with two other players in December 2004 for Mark Mulder. The first player from the 2003 draft to appear in a game for the Cardinals was 15th rounder Anthony Reyes.*

JUNE 5

Woody Williams holds the Blue Jays hitless for 7^1/$_3$ innings during a 13–5 Cardinals win at Busch Stadium. The only hit off Williams over eight innings was a single by Orlando Hudson with one out in the eighth inning. Dustin Hermanson relieved Williams and allowed five runs in the ninth without retiring a batter. Williams also hit a triple during the contest.

> *Williams won 10 games in a row over two seasons counting his last three decisions in 2002 and a 7–0 start in 2003. He finished 2003 with an 18–9 record and a 3.87 ERA.*

JUNE 6

The Cardinals play a regular-season game against the Orioles for the first time and win 8–6 at Busch Stadium. The two franchises were once St. Louis rivals. The Orioles were known as the St. Louis Browns from 1902 through 1953 before moving to Baltimore.

JUNE 7

The Cardinals come out on the wrong end of an 8–1 game at Busch Stadium. To commemorate the only all–St. Louis World Series, in 1944, the two former city rivals wore replica uniforms from that season, with the Orioles donning those of the Browns.

> *During an eight-game span that ended June 7, Albert Pujols collected 19 hits in 29 at-bats, an average of .655.*

JUNE 8	Scott Rolen has a grand slam among his four hits during an 11–10 win over the Orioles at Busch Stadium. He hit the shot off Rick Bauer in the sixth inning.
	Rolen hit .286 with 28 homers and drove in 104 runs in 2003.
JUNE 10	The Cardinals play the Red Sox for the first time during the regular season and win 9–7 at Fenway Park with two runs in the ninth inning. The two franchises met previously in the 1946 and 1967 World Series.
JUNE 12	Jim Edmonds hits a three-run homer in the thirteenth inning for a roller coaster victory against the Red Sox in Boston. Edmonds's blast gave the Cards an 8–5 lead before the club withstood a two-run rally in the bottom half for an 8–7 win. The Cards led 3–0 but allowed three runs in the ninth. J. D. Drew put St. Louis ahead again with a two-run homer in the tenth, but the club squandered the advantage by surrendering two in the bottom half.
JUNE 13	In the first ever regular-season meeting between the Cardinals and the Yankees, Roger Clemens picks up his 300th career victory with a 5–2 decision in New York. The two franchises met previously in the World Series in 1926, 1928, 1942, 1943, and 1964.
JUNE 14	Tino Martinez hits a pair of two-run homers versus his former Yankee teammates, but the Cardinals lose 13–4 in New York.
	Second baseman Bo Hart made his major league debut on June 19 following an injury to Fernando Viña and became an immediate sensation. Hart had 7 hits in his first 10 at-bats and 18 in his first 35 at-bats, but he soon cooled off. He finished the season with a .277 average in 2003, batted just 13 times in 2004, and didn't appear in a big-league game in 2005.
JUNE 26	The Cardinals score seven runs in the third inning and defeat the Reds 11–7 at Busch Stadium.
JUNE 28	The Cardinals maintain their hold on first place with a 13–9 win over the Royals in Kansas City. Jim Edmonds tied the club record for most extra-base hits in a game with two homers and two doubles. It was the second time in 2003 that Edmonds had four extra-base hits in a game (see April 4, 2003). Edmonds hit five homers in four games from June 25 through June 28.
	The Cardinals were in first place from June 25 through July 8; on August 23 and 24; and again from August 28 through September 2.
JUNE 29	The Cardinals rout the Royals 13–6 in Kansas City. Albert Pujols collected four hits, including two homers. On a day in which Negro Leagues players were honored, among them 100-year-old Ted Radcliffe, the Cardinals wore replica uniforms of the 1928 St. Louis Stars, and the Royals donned those of the 1924 Kansas City Monarchs.
JULY 3	The Cardinals score eight runs in the second inning and defeat the Giants 9–5 at Busch Stadium.
JULY 4	The Cardinals survive three homers from Moises Alou to defeat the Cubs 11–8 in Chicago.

JULY 12 — Albert Pujols hits a two-run, walk-off homer in the eleventh inning to beat the Padres 9–7 at Busch Stadium.

JULY 13 — Both benches clear in the first inning of a 3–1 win over the Padres at Busch Stadium. The Padres' Adam Eaton hits Albert Pujols in the shoulder blade on the slugger's first pitch of the day, one day after Pujols lingered at home plate in the wake of his game-winning homer (see July 12, 2003).

JULY 15 — Albert Pujols drives in a run with a fifth-inning single to give the National League a 5–1 lead in the All-Star Game, but the American League rallies to win 8–7 at U.S. Cellular Field in Chicago.

JULY 20 — Nine homers, five of them by the Dodgers, fly out of Dodger Stadium during a 10–7 Cardinals victory. Woody Williams gave up four homers and hit one himself. Williams hit his homer in the fourth inning and broke a 5–5 tie.

JULY 21 — Matt Morris breaks his hand on a Mark Kotsay line drive in the first inning of a 10-inning, 5–4 loss to the Padres in San Diego.

> *Morris didn't pitch again until August 23, his return delayed a week by an ankle injury foolishly suffered during hotel horseplay with teammates.*

JULY 23 — The Cardinals play at Qualcomm Stadium in San Diego for the last time and defeat the Padres 8–4.

JULY 26 — Jason Isringhausen induces a bases-loaded triple in a 13–8 win over the Pirates at Busch Stadium.

JULY 27 — The Cardinals score three runs in the ninth inning to defeat the Pirates 4–3 at Busch Stadium. Albert Pujols drove in the winning run with a walk-off single.

JULY 30 — The Cardinals wallop the Expos 11–1 in Montreal.

AUGUST 2 — Bo Hart hits a grand slam in the fourth inning off Jae Weong Seo that lifts the Cardinals to a 7–1 lead over the Mets at Shea Stadium. New York gave them a scare by scoring five runs in the ninth inning before the Cards emerged with a 10–9 win.

AUGUST 10 — Braves shortstop Rafael Furcal pulls off only the 12th unassisted triple play in baseball history during a 3–2 Cardinals win at Busch Stadium. With St. Louis runners on first and second in the fifth, the score 1–1, and Woody Williams batting, Furcal leaped high in the air to snare Williams's liner. Furcal then stepped on second to double Mike Matheny and tagged out Orlando Palmeiro as he made a futile attempt to get back to first base.

AUGUST 16 — Albert Pujols extends his hitting streak to 30 games during a 5–4 loss to the Phillies in Philadelphia.

> *Pujols missed the next four games with flu-like symptoms (see August 22, 2003).*

AUGUST 17 — The Cardinals play at Veterans Stadium for the last time and lose 6–4 to the Phillies.

AUGUST 19   Trailing 5–3, the Cardinals score 10 runs in the eighth inning and win 13–5 over the Pirates at Busch Stadium. Scott Rolen drove in six runs in the game. Five of them were in the big inning, in which he had a three-run double and a two-run single.

AUGUST 20   The Pirates smack seven homers during a 14–0 thrashing of the Cardinals at Busch Stadium. Reggie Sanders hit two homers, one of them a grand slam, during a 10-run Pittsburgh fifth inning. Rob Mackowiak hit two homers for the Bucs, and Brian Giles, Jason Kendall, and Jeff D'Amico added one each.

AUGUST 21   Jim Edmonds hits a three-run, walk-off homer to beat the Pirates 6–3 at Busch Stadium. The homer came two pitches after Pittsburgh third baseman Jose Hernandez muffed Edmonds's foul pop near the stands.

AUGUST 22   Albert Pujols returns to the lineup but goes hitless in five at-bats during a 9–4 loss to the Phillies at Busch Stadium. His hitting streak ended at 30 games.

   Pujols's 30-game hitting streak is tied for the second longest in Cardinals history. Rogers Hornsby hit in 33 straight games in 1922, and Stan Musial had a 30-game streak in 1950.

AUGUST 28   Kerry Robinson hits a walk-off homer in the ninth inning for a 3–2 win over the Cubs at Busch Stadium.

   Writer Buzz Bissinger chronicled this series against the Cubs, and Robinson's shot, in 3 Nights in August (Houghton Mifflin), a tribute to La Russa's managerial prowess. The homer was the only one that Robinson struck in 2003 and the last of three that he collected in 575 at-bats with the Cardinals. A native of St. Louis, Robinson liked unusual uniform numbers. He wore number 13 and number 0 with the Cardinals from 2001 through 2003, after wearing number 00 with the Reds in 1999.

AUGUST 30   Jim Edmonds robs Cincinnati's Russell Branyan of a homer during a 6–3 win over the Reds by leaping high above, and reaching over, the center-field wall at Great American Ball Park. Edmonds caught the ball as it descended past the top of the fence and hung on to it as he pulled his glove back into play. It was the second night in a row that Edmonds had robbed the Reds of a home run. The previous evening he made another leaping catch of a Kelly Stinnett drive, although the Cards lost 6–5.

AUGUST 31   Albert Pujols drives in all five runs on a pair of home runs in a 5–0 victory over the Reds in Cincinnati. Pujols hit a two-run homer off Dan Serafini in the sixth inning and a three-run shot against Danny Graves in the eighth.

SEPTEMBER 3 J. D. Drew hits a grand slam off Felix Sanchez in the sixth inning to give the Cards a 6–3 lead, but the Cubs rally to win 8–7 at Wrigley Field. The tension-filled contest featured a shouting match between Tony La Russa and Cubs manager Dusty Baker, and starting pitchers Danny Haren and Matt Clement hitting each other with pitches. The bad blood between La Russa and Baker extended back to the previous season's NLCS, when Baker was the manager of the Giants (see October 9, 2002).

   The loss knocked the Cards out of first place. The club failed to regain the top spot in the division in 2003.

SEPTEMBER 6   The Cardinals drub the Reds 13–6 at Busch Stadium.

SEPTEMBER 14   The Astros complete a three-game sweep of the Cardinals with a 4–1 win at Houston. The defeats left the Cards 5½ games out of first place with 12 contests left on the schedule, virtually eliminating any chance that St. Louis would host a postseason series.

> *As the Cardinals faded from contention, there were reports of dissension in the Cardinals clubhouse as several veterans had verbal confrontations with the demanding Tony La Russa. Many of those who had disagreements with him, including Tino Martinez and Fernando Viña, were gone by 2004.*

SEPTEMBER 18   The Cardinals wallop the Brewers 13–0 at Busch Stadium.

SEPTEMBER 20   Albert Pujols hits a walk-off homer against the Astros at Busch Stadium for a 3–2 win.

SEPTEMBER 28   On the last day of the season, Albert Pujols wins the NL batting title with two hits in five at-bats during a 9–5 win over the Diamondbacks in Phoenix. Pujols nosed out Todd Helton .35871 to .35849 in the closest race in NL history and the third closest in the major league record books. Helton went 2 for 4 on the same day during the Rockies' 10-inning, 10–8 victory over the Padres in San Diego.

> *In addition to batting .359, Pujols hit 43 homers, drove in 124 runs, and scored 137 to become the first player in major league history with at least 30 homers, 100 RBIs, 100 runs, and a .300 batting average in each of his first three seasons. He also had 212 hits and 51 doubles. The only other Cardinal with 200 hits and 40 homers in the same season was Rogers Hornsby in 1922. Pujols was also the first St. Louis hitter to top the 50 mark for doubles since Stan Musial had 53 in 1953. For the second year in a row, Pujols was the runner-up to Barry Bonds in the MVP balloting.*

NOVEMBER 20   The Cardinals trade Tino Martinez and cash to the Devil Rays for Evan Rust and J. P. Davis.

DECEMBER 10   Fernando Viña signs with the Tigers as a free agent.

DECEMBER 13   The Cardinals trade J. D. Drew and Eli Marrero to the Braves for Jason Marquis, Ray King, and Adam Wainwright.

DECEMBER 16   The Cardinals announce the signing of free agents Reggie Sanders, most recently with the Pirates, and Jeff Suppan, from the Red Sox.

2004

Season in a Sentence

The Cardinals win 105 regular-season games, the most of any St. Louis team since 1944, and reach the World Series for the first time since 1987 before being swept by the Red Sox.

Finish • Won • Lost • Pct • GB

First   105   57   .649 +13.0

National League Division Series—The Cardinals defeated the Los Angeles Dodgers three games to one

National League Championship Series—The Cardinals defeated the Houston Astros four games to three

World Series—The Cardinals lost to the Boston Red Sox four games to none

Manager

Tony La Russa

Stats

Stats	Cards	NL	Rank
Batting Avg:	.278	.263	1
On-Base Pct:	.344	.333	4
Slugging Pct:	.460	.423	1
Home Runs:	214		3
Stolen Bases:	111		2
ERA:	3.75	4.30	2
Fielding Avg:	.985	.983	6
Runs Scored:	855		1
Runs Allowed:	659		1

Starting Lineup

Mike Matheny, c
Albert Pujols, 1b
Tony Womack, 2b
Scott Rolen, 3b
Edgar Renteria, ss
John Mabry, lf-rf
Jim Edmonds, cf
Reggie Sanders, rf-lf
Ray Lankford, lf
Marlon Anderson, 2b-lf
Roger Cedeño, lf-rf
So Taguchi, lf-rf
Hector Luna, ss-2b-3b
Larry Walker, rf

Pitchers

Jeff Suppan, sp
Matt Morris, sp
Jason Marquis, sp
Chris Carpenter, sp
Woody Williams, sp
Jason Isringhausen, rp
Ray King, rp
Steve Kline, rp
Cal Eldred, rp
Kiko Calero, rp

Attendance

3,048,427 (sixth in NL)

Club Leaders

Batting Avg:	Pujols	.331
On-Base Pct:	Edmonds	.418
Slugging Pct:	Pujols	.657
Home Runs:	Pujols	46
RBIs:	Rolen	124
Runs:	Pujols	133
Stolen Bases:	Womack	26
Wins:	Suppan	16
Strikeouts:	Carpenter	152
ERA:	Carpenter	3.46
Saves:	Isringhausen	47

JANUARY 9   Ray Lankford returns to the Cardinals as a free agent.

JANUARY 12   Jeff Fassero signs with the Rockies as a free agent.

JANUARY 17   Formal groundbreaking takes place for the Cardinals' new ballpark, which opened in April 2006. With Anheuser-Busch purchasing the naming rights, the new facility was the third Cardinals home field to be named Busch Stadium.

> *Occupying space just south of Busch Stadium on land that was formerly a parking lot, the new ballpark was the culmination of more than six years of planning. The cost was $345 million, $300 million of which the Cardinals financed. It was designed by HOK Sport with Jim Chibnall serving as the lead architect. The third Busch Stadium was part of a trend of baseball-only stadiums that began with the opening of Camden Yards in Baltimore in 1992. From 1992 through 2006, there were 15 ballparks constructed exclusively for baseball, 11 of them in the National League, and they combined many of the elements of the*

classic ballparks of the early 20th century with the amenities 21st-century fans have come to expect. Unlike the closed circle of the previous Busch Stadium, the new one is open, giving fans numerous views of the city, particularly beyond the outfield to the Gateway Arch. Inspired partly by the architecture of landmark local buildings, the new Busch Stadium's many arched entrances reference the neighboring Cupples Station warehouse district. The warm brick tones mirror the colors of the Wainwright Building. The exposed steel trusses bear the influence of the historic Eads Bridge. The angle of the roof is similar to that of the first Busch Stadium, also known as Sportsman's Park, which was located at Grand and Dodier and closed in 1966. The site of the second Busch Stadium is slated to become the Ballpark Village neighborhood beyond Clark Street. The only thing separating the back of the left-field bleachers from Clark Street is a patio and about 100 feet of wrought-iron fence, allowing unobstructed views of the game for fans and motorists passing by. The Ballpark Village neighborhood is also targeted for development, with residential property, restaurants, and other businesses that will contain outfield views from balconies and rooftops.

MARCH 21   The Cardinals trade Matt Duff to the Red Sox for Tony Womack.

APRIL 3   The Cardinals send Chris Widger and Wilson Delgado to the Mets for Roger Cedeño and cash.

APRIL 5   With President George Bush looking on, the Cardinals lose the season opener 8–6 to the Brewers before 49,149 at Busch Stadium. Scott Podsednik broke a 4–4 tie with a three-run homer off Matt Morris, and the Cardinals were unable to close the gap.

After visiting both clubhouses before the game, Bush threw out the ceremonial first pitch to Mike Matheny. Bush watched the first five innings from a private box.

APRIL 8   Hector Luna homers in his first major league at-bat during an 11–5 loss to the Brewers at Busch Stadium. Starting at second base, Luna homered in the second inning.

Luna was the sixth Cardinal to homer in his first major league at-bat. The others were Eddie Morgan (1934), Wally Moon (1954), Keith McDonald (2000), Chris Richard (2000), and Gene Stechschulte (2001).

APRIL 9   The Cardinals hit five homers and defeat the Diamondbacks 13–6 in Phoenix. Reggie Sanders hit two of the home runs, with Scott Rolen, Ray Lankford, and Albert Pujols adding the rest. All five homers were struck in the first three innings off Casey Daigle, who was making his major league debut. Chris Carpenter was the winning pitcher. It was his first win as a Cardinal and his first in the majors since July 29, 2002. Carpenter missed the entire 2003 season following shoulder surgery.

APRIL 16   The Cardinals build an 11–3 lead after three innings and trounce the Rockies 13–5 at Busch Stadium.

APRIL 21   The Cardinals hit five home runs to power past the Astros 12–6 in Houston. Jim Edmonds hit a grand slam off Ricky Stone in the sixth inning. Reggie Sanders, Marlon Anderson, Scott Rolen, and Ray Lankford hit the others.

APRIL 22   Hector Luna's suicide squeeze in the twelfth inning scores Reggie Sanders from third base and beats the Astros 2–1 in Houston.

APRIL 29   Jim Edmonds hits a walk-off homer on an 0–2 pitch leading off the thirteenth inning to defeat the Phillies 5–4 at Busch Stadium.

Tony La Russa is one of two managers to win at least 700 games with two different franchises. La Russa had 798 wins with the Athletics and 894 with the Cardinals at the start of the 2006 season. Sparky Anderson had 863 wins with the Reds and 1,311 at the helm of the Tigers.

MAY 2   Scott Rolen lines a walk-off, bases-loaded single in the tenth inning to provide the lone run in a 1–0 win over the Cubs at Busch Stadium. Matt Morris (nine innings) and Jason Isringhausen (one inning) combined on the shutout.

Rolen batted .314 with 34 homers, 124 RBIs, and 109 runs scored and earned his sixth career Gold Glove in 2004. Albert Pujols hit 46 homers, and Jim Edmonds added 42. It was the first time that the Cardinals had two players with 40 or homers in a season and three with at least 30. Pujols also batted .331, drove in 123 runs, and led the NL in runs scored (133) and total bases (389). He had 196 hits and 51 doubles to become the first Cardinal with 50 or more doubles in a season since Joe Medwick in 1936 and 1937. In addition to his 42 homers, Edmonds batted .301, drove in 111 runs, and scored 102. In the NL MVP voting, Pujols was third, Rolen fourth, and Edmonds fifth.

MAY 4   Mike Matheny saves a 6–5 win over the Phillies in Philadelphia with a sterling defensive play. With the bases loaded and two outs in the ninth and a Phillie runner on third, Jason Isringhausen struck out Pat Burrell swinging on a high fastball. The ball deflected off Matheny's glove all the way to the backstop. The Cardinal catcher chased it down and, with no play at the plate, fired a long throw to first to get Burrell by a half-step. It was the first time that the Cardinals played at game at Citizens Bank Park. Chris Carpenter gave up consecutive homers to Burrell, Jim Thome, and Bobby Abreu in the fifth.

MAY 8   The Cardinals lose 2–0 to the Expos in Montreal to fall to 15–16 on the 2004 season.

The May 8 loss represented the low point of the season. From May 27 through September 5, the Cardinals had a record of 69–22.

MAY 9   The Cardinals play in Montreal for the last time and win 5–2 over the Expos at Olympic Stadium.

The Expos moved after the 2004 season to Washington, where they were renamed the Nationals.

MAY 19   The Cardinals slip past the Mets 1–0 in New York. Scott Rolen drove in the lone run of the game on a double with two outs in the eighth inning. Jeff Suppan (six innings), Cal Eldred (two innings), and Steve Kline (one inning) combined on the shutout.

MAY 27   Albert Pujols has no official at-bats in five plate appearances. He drew four walks and hit a sacrifice fly during a 6–3 win over the Pirates at Busch Stadium.

MAY 28 — The Cardinals score the winning run in the tenth inning on a balk by Octavio Dotel to defeat the Astros 2–1 in Houston.

MAY 30 — Albert Pujols collects four hits, including two homers, in five at-bats to lead the Cardinals to a 10–3 win over the Astros in Houston.

JUNE 1 — Albert Pujols collects five hits, including two homers and a double, during an 8–1 victory over the Pirates in Pittsburgh.

JUNE 2 — In the first round of the amateur draft, the Cardinals select pitcher Chris Lambert from Boston College.

JUNE 3 — Both managers are ejected with two outs in top of the ninth inning of a 4–2 Cardinals win over the Pirates at PNC Park. The incident stemmed from a high inside pitch from Pittsburgh reliever Mike Gonzalez that sent Tony Womack into the dirt. After Tony La Russa directed comments toward Pirates manager Lloyd McClendon, McClendon stormed out of the dugout to confront La Russa. Plate umpire Brian Gorman and first-base umpire Dale Scott tried to restrain McClendon, who forged ahead. La Russa came onto the field, and the umpires stood between the managers as they exchanged heated words along the first-base line near the Cardinals dugout. The benches and bullpens emptied, and there was physical contact, but no players were ejected.

JUNE 9 — A bench-clearing fracas highlights the Cardinals' 12–4 win over the Cubs at Wrigley Field. In the fifth inning, Matt Morris buzzed Derek Lee with a pitch. Lee pointed at Morris and the St. Louis dugout when he got back up, and Morris screamed right back. Plate umpire Ed Rapuano pulled Lee back as the Cubs and Cardinals slowly started coming out of their dugouts, and Lee walked away from the plate. He started back toward the mound after someone said something to him, and both teams rushed forward, although no punches were thrown. Edgar Renteria hit a grand slam off Mark Prior in the fourth.

JUNE 10 — The Cubs score 10 runs in the fourth inning off Dan Haren and Cal Eldred during a 12–3 win over the Cardinals in Chicago.

JUNE 11 — In the first ever meeting between the Cardinals and the Texas Rangers, the Cardinals move into first place in the NL Central with a 12–7 victory at the Ballpark in Arlington.

JUNE 13 — The Cardinals build a 12–0 lead after three innings and drub the Rangers 13–2 in Arlington.

JUNE 16 — The Cardinals play the Athletics for the first time and win 8–4 at Busch Stadium.

JUNE 17 — The Cardinals score three runs in the ninth inning and defeat the Athletics 5–4 at Busch Stadium.

JUNE 18 — Albert Pujols hits a walk-off homer in the tenth inning to defeat the Reds 4–3 at Busch Stadium. The Cards tied the score in the ninth inning on a walk and three hits.

JUNE 20 — Ken Griffey Jr. hits his 500th career homer during a 6–0 Reds win over the Cardinals at Busch Stadium. Matt Morris surrendered the milestone.

Mike Crummley, a 19-year-old college student from Mount Carmel, Illinois, caught the ball. Crummley gave the ball back to Griffey, who rewarded him with an all-expenses-paid trip to the All-Star Game in Houston. At Griffey's behest, Crummley also shagged fly balls during the All-Star Game Home Run Derby.

JULY 2   The Cardinals play the Mariners for the first time at Busch Stadium and win 11–2.

JULY 10   The Cardinals extend their winning streak to eight games with a 5–2 decision over the Cubs at Busch Stadium. Jim Edmonds homered in his fourth consecutive game.

JULY 11   Jim Edmonds ties a club record by homering in his fifth straight game, but the Cardinals lose 5–2 to the Cubs at Busch Stadium.

JULY 13   Albert Pujols hits two doubles in three at-bats and drives in a run during the All-Star Game, but the National League loses 9–4 at Minute Maid Park in Houston.

JULY 20   Albert Pujols collects three homers, a double, and a single in five at-bats to rally the Cardinals from a six-run deficit to defeat the Cubs 11–8 at Wrigley Field. He hit the homer off Glendon Rusch with no one on base in the third inning and the Cardinals trailing 7–1. Pujols hit another home run in the seventh facing Kyle Farnsworth to narrow the Chicago lead to 8–7. Pujols broke the 8–8 tie with a two-run shot off LaTroy Hawkins on a hit-and-run play. After Reggie Sanders added another St. Louis homer, Hawkins was ejected for arguing umpire Tim Tschida's balls and strikes.

JULY 21   The Cardinals edge the Brewers 1–0 at Busch Stadium. Edgar Renteria drove in the run with a sacrifice fly in the sixth inning. Woody Williams (seven innings), Ray King (one inning), and Jason Isringhausen (one inning) teamed on the shutout.

            Isringhausen tied Lee Smith's club record for most saves in a season with 47 in 2004. Izzy had a 4–2 record and a 2.87 ERA.

JULY 29   The Cardinals outlast the Reds 11–10 in Cincinnati.

AUGUST 1   Matt Morris allows eight runs against the Giants in San Francisco to put the Cardinals in an 8–0 hole. The Cards battled back but lost 8–7, the final two runs coming in the ninth inning.

AUGUST 4   Albert Pujols hits a walk-off homer to defeat the Expos 5–4 at Busch Stadium.

AUGUST 6   The Cardinals trade Luis Martinez to the Rockies for Larry Walker.

            Walker received a standing ovation before his first at-bat as a Cardinal at Busch Stadium, then received another one after striking out on three pitches. Buoyed by the unqualified adoration of red-clad St. Louis fans, Walker hit .280 with 11 homers in 150 at-bats over the remainder of the 2004 season.

AUGUST 9   Edgar Renteria collects five hits, including a double, in five at-bats during a 6–2 win over the Mets at Busch Stadium.

AUGUST 10   The Cardinals collect only two hits, but both are homers that lead to a 2–1 defeat of the Marlins in 10 innings in Miami. Albert Pujols hit a home run off Josh Beckett in the sixth inning, and Jim Edmonds won the contest with a blast off Guillermo Mota in the tenth.

AUGUST 11   Jeff Suppan (8 innings), Steve Kline ($^1/_3$ of an inning), and Jason Isringhausen ($^2/_3$ of an inning) combine on a two-hitter to defeat the Marlins 1–0 in Miami. Suppan gave up both hits, a single to Alex Gonzalez in the sixth inning and an infield dribbler by Juan Pierre in the ninth. Edgar Renteria drove in the Cardinals' run with a single in the sixth.

AUGUST 17   Larry Walker hits a grand slam off Danny Graves during a six-run Cardinal eighth that leads to a 7–2 victory over the Reds at Busch Stadium.

AUGUST 20   Julian Tavarez is ejected from the first game of a doubleheader against the Pirates at Busch Stadium after the umpires accuse him of having a "foreign substance" on his hat. The Cards swept the twin bill 5–4 and 5–3.

Major League Baseball suspended Tavarez for 10 days. After an appeal, MLB reduced the suspension to 8 days.

AUGUST 22   Larry Walker hits his second grand slam in less than a week with a bases-loaded smash off Brian Meadows in the eighth inning of an 11–4 win over the Pirates at Busch Stadium.

SEPTEMBER 2   Matt Morris pitches a two-hitter to defeat the Dodgers 3–0 at Busch Stadium. The only Los Angeles hits were singles by opposing pitcher Jose Lima in the third inning and Robin Ventura in the fifth.

SEPTEMBER 4   Jim Edmonds hits his 300th career homer during a 5–1 win over the Dodgers at Busch Stadium. Kazuhisa Ishii surrendered the milestone. Jason Marquis was the winning pitcher. It was his 11th victory in a row.

Edmonds hit 9 homers in a 10-game span from August 25 through September 4.

SEPTEMBER 5   The Cardinals extend their winning streak to nine games with an 11-inning, 6–5 decision over the Dodgers at Busch Stadium. Reggie Sanders drove in the winning run with a walk-off single.

SEPTEMBER 6   The Cardinals play at Petco Park in San Diego for the first time and lose 7–3 to the Padres.

SEPTEMBER 12   Larry Walker collects four hits, including two doubles, in five at-bats during a 7–6 win over the Dodgers in Los Angeles.

SEPTEMBER 18   The Cardinals clinch the division title with a 7–0 win over the Diamondbacks at Busch Stadium.

SEPTEMBER 19   Rick Ankiel makes his first major league appearance since May 10, 2001, by pitching two hitless innings with one walk and four strikeouts during a 3–2 loss to the Diamondbacks at Busch Stadium.

SEPTEMBER 23   The Cardinals win their 100th game of 2004 with a 4–2 decision over the Brewers in Milwaukee.

The Cardinals played the Los Angeles Dodgers in the National League Championship Series. Managed by Jim Tracy, the Dodgers were 93–69 in 2004. It was the club's first postseason appearance since 1996.

OCTOBER 5   The Cardinals open the playoffs with an 8–3 win over the Dodgers before 52,227 at Busch Stadium. Albert Pujols got the scoring under way with a solo homer in the first inning. The Cards put the game away with five runs in the third to take a 6–0 lead with the help of home runs from Larry Walker and Jim Edmonds. Mike Matheny went deep in the fourth. Larry Walker hit his second home run, and the fifth for the Redbirds, in the seventh.

OCTOBER 7   The Cardinals win 8–3 for the second game in a row to take a two-games-to-none lead over the Dodgers in front of 52,228 fans at Busch Stadium. Los Angeles scored all of its runs on solo homers off Jason Marquis. The score was 3–3 when the Cardinals scored three times in the fifth with two outs. Edgar Renteria drove in the tie-breaking run with a single. Mike Matheny drove in four insurance runs with a pair of two-run singles in the fifth and seventh.

OCTOBER 9   The Dodgers stay alive in the Division Series by defeating the Cardinals 4–0 in Los Angeles. Jose Lima pitched the five-hit shutout.

OCTOBER 10   The Cardinals take the Division Series three games to one with a 6–2 victory over the Dodgers in Los Angeles. Reggie Sanders tied the score 1–1 in the second inning with a home run on a 1–2 pitch. After both teams scored in the third, the Cards went ahead 5–2 in the fourth on Albert Pujols's three-run homer. Pujols added a solo homer in the seventh. Jeff Suppan earned the victory by pitching seven innings.

At the end of the series, the teams congratulated each other on the field. It was an idea that Larry Walker pitched to Tony La Russa, who worked out the details with Dodger counterpart Jim Tracy.

The Cardinals played the Houston Astros in the National League Championship Series. Managed by Phil Garner, the Astros finished the season with a 92–70 record and won 36 of their last 46 games to earn a wild-card berth. Houston defeated the Braves in five games in the Division Series.

OCTOBER 13   The Cardinals open the NLCS with a 10–7 win over the Astros before 52,323 at Busch Stadium. Houston scored twice in the first inning, but the Cardinals matched that figure in the bottom half on a two-run homer by Albert Pujols. Woody Williams gave up two runs in the fourth inning but started a two-run rally in the fifth with a double. Larry Walker doubled in Williams, then scored on a single by Scott Rolen. The Redbirds broke the 4–4 tie with six runs in the sixth, the last three on a bases-loaded double by Jim Edmonds.

OCTOBER 14   The Cardinals win Game Two of the NLCS 6–4 over the Astros before 52,347 at Busch Stadium. The two teams played in a constant drizzle with temperatures in the 40s. The Astros led 3–0 until the Cardinals broke through with four runs in the fifth inning on a pair of two-run homers by Larry Walker and Scott Rolen. Houston tied the game 4–4 in the seventh, but the Cards broke the deadlock with two in the eighth when Albert Pujols and Rolen hit solo home runs.

The Cardinals welcomed Rolen's LCS outburst. The third baseman had been quiet in the Division Series, going 0 for 12 with six walks and three strikeouts. Rolen has a .190 average for his career in the postseason (2002 and 2004).

OCTOBER 16   The Astros take Game Three with a 5–2 decision over the Cardinals in Houston. Larry Walker hit a solo homer in the first off Roger Clemens before Houston countered with three runs in its half. Jim Edmonds homered in the second, but Clemens and Brad Lidge shut down the Cardinals the rest of the way.

OCTOBER 17   The Astros even the series with a 6–5 win over the Cardinals at Houston in Game Four. The Cards struck quickly with three runs in the first inning, two of them on a home run by Albert Pujols off Roy Oswalt. St. Louis still led 5–3 after 5½ innings but couldn't hold the advantage. The Astros scored two runs in the sixth inning and one in the seventh. Carlos Beltran broke the 5–5 tie with a homer off Julian Tavarez.

Tavarez punched the dugout wall after returning to the bench and broke his left ring finger and fifth metacarpal. He played the rest of the postseason with a protective wrap on his glove hand. Tavarez was also fined $10,000 by Major League Baseball for throwing a pitch at Jeff Bagwell's head during the game.

OCTOBER 18   The Cardinals stand one loss from elimination after losing Game Five 3–0 to the Astros in Houston. Through 8½ innings, the pitching was brilliant as the two teams scored no runs and collected only two hits. Houston's Brandon Backe pitched eight

Jonathan Daniel/Getty Images Sport/Getty Images

Jim Edmonds's twelfth-inning, walk-off home run wins Game Six and forces a Game Seven in the 2004 NLCS. Edmonds has been a solid home run hitter since coming to the Cards in 2000 and through 2005 ranked fifth on the team's all-time home run list.

innings, allowing just one hit, and Brad Lidge retired the Cards 1-2-3 in the ninth. The only St. Louis base hit during the game was Tony Womack's single with two outs in the sixth. Woody Williams surrendered only one hit, a first-inning single by Jeff Bagwell, during seven shutout innings. Jason Isringhausen added a perfect eighth. Isringhausen fell apart in the ninth, however. Carlos Beltran led off the inning with a single, then stole second. Isringhausen intentionally walked Lance Berkman, and Jeff Kent hit a long three-run, walk-off homer on the first pitch.

OCTOBER 21   The Cardinals force a seventh game with a 12-inning, 6–4 victory over the Astros before 52,144 at Busch Stadium. Houston scored in the top of the first, but Albert Pujols put the Cards back in it with a two-run homer in the bottom half. After the Astros tied the score in the top of the third, the Redbirds scored two more in their half to lead 4–2. The Astros weren't finished, however, and added runs in the fourth and another in the ninth as Jason Isringhausen blew a save opportunity for the second game in a row. It remained 4–4 until the twelfth, when Jim Edmonds hit a two-out, two-run, walk-off homer. Edgar Renteria and Reggie Sanders each contributed three hits to the victory.

OCTOBER 21   The Cardinals earn their first trip to the World Series since 1987 with a 5–2 win over the Astros in Game Seven before 52,140 at Busch Stadium. Craig Biggio led off the first inning with a homer off Jeff Suppan, and Houston was still ahead 2–1 after 5½ innings. The game stayed close in large part because of Jim Edmonds's defense, a sensational diving catch in center field with his back to the plate. The Cards took the lead with three runs in the sixth off Roger Clemens. All three runs scored with two outs. Albert Pujols drove in the tying run and scored on a homer by Scott Rolen. The Cards added an insurance run in the ninth.

The home team won all seven games in the series.

The Cardinals met the Boston Red Sox in the World Series. Most of the pre-Series hype focused on the "Curse of the Bambino" and Boston's inability to win a World Championship since 1918. The Cardinals were contributors, winning the 1946 and 1967 Fall Classics over Boston in seven games. Managed by Terry Francona, the Sox were 98–64 in 2004 and entered the playoffs as a wild card. In the American League Championship Series, the Red Sox pulled off the impossible by losing the first three games to the Yankees then winning four in a row. Boston was the first team in major league history to overcome an 0–3 deficit in a postseason series.

OCTOBER 23   The Cardinals lose the first game of the World Series 11–9 to the Red Sox at Fenway Park. The Red Sox scored four runs in the first inning and three in the third off Woody Williams to take a 7–2 lead. The Cards battled back to tie the game 7–7 in the sixth. Boston scored two in the seventh, and again the Cards tied the contest with two in the eighth. The Sox put the game away, however, with two tallies in the bottom of the eighth off Julian Tavarez. Larry Walker was the big hitter for St. Louis with a homer, two doubles, and a single in five at-bats.

The Cardinals' starting pitchers in the 2004 World Series were Williams, Matt Morris, Jeff Suppan, and Jason Marquis. (Chris Carpenter missed the postseason with a biceps injury.) The four combined to allow 18 runs, all earned, in 17⅓ innings.

OCTOBER 24   The Red Sox take Game Two from the Cardinals 6–2 in Boston. Albert Pujols collected three of the Cards' five hits with two doubles and a single.

OCTOBER 26   The Red Sox take a three-games-to-none lead in the World Series with a 4–1 win over the Cardinals before 52,016 at Busch Stadium. Larry Walker scored St. Louis's only run on a homer in the ninth inning. The Cards blew a big chance in the third when Jeff Suppan led off with an infield single and Edgar Renteria sent the pitcher to third with a double. Larry Walker grounded to second, but Suppan inexplicably headed back to third after breaking for the plate and was thrown out when first baseman David Ortiz rifled the ball to third baseman Bill Mueller.

Stan Musial threw out the ceremonial first pitch to Bob Gibson.

OCTOBER 27   The Red Sox complete a four-game sweep of the Cardinals with a 3–0 decision before 52,037 at Busch Stadium. The Sox scored a run in the first inning and two in the third. The Cards collected only four hits and scored just four runs in the last three games of the series.

Jim Edmonds (1 for 15) and Scott Rolen (0 for 15) combined to bat .033 during the World Series.

DECEMBER 8   Five weeks after George Bush defeats John Kerry in the presidential election, Woody Williams signs with the Padres as a free agent.

DECEMBER 14   Mike Matheny signs as a free agent with the Giants.

DECEMBER 17   Edgar Renteria signs with the Red Sox as a free agent.

DECEMBER 18   The Cardinals trade Dan Haren, Kiko Calero, and Daric Barton to the Athletics for Mark Mulder.

DECEMBER 20   Steve Kline signs with the Orioles as a free agent.

DECEMBER 21   Tony Womack signs with the Yankees as a free agent.

DECEMBER 23   The Cardinals sign David Eckstein, most recently with the Angels, as a free agent.

Eckstein became a fan favorite in his first season with the Cardinals, batting .294 as the Cardinals' leadoff hitter and providing sure-handed defense up the middle.

2005

Season in a Sentence

The Cardinals reach the 100-win mark and post the best record in the National League for the second year in a row, but they lose to the Astros in the Championship Series.

Finish • Won • Lost • Pct • GB

First   100   62   .617 +11.0

National League Division Series—The Cardinals defeated the San Diego Padres three games to none

National League Championship Series—The Cardinals lost to the Houston Astros four games to two

Manager

Tony La Russa

Stats

Stats	Cards	NL	Rank
Batting Avg:	.270	.262	2
On-Base Pct:	.339	.330	3
Slugging Pct:	.423	.414	4
Home Runs:	170		7
Stolen Bases:	83		7
ERA:	3.49	4.22	1
Fielding Avg:	.984	.983	7
Runs Scored:	805		3
Runs Allowed:	634		1

Starting Lineup

Yadier Molina, c
Albert Pujols, 1b
Mark Grudzielanek, 2b
Abraham Nuñez, 3b
David Eckstein, ss
Reggie Sanders, lf
Jim Edmonds, cf
Larry Walker, rf
So Taguchi, lf-rf-cf
John Mabry, rf-lf
Scott Rolen, 3b
John Rodriguez, lf

Pitchers

Chris Carpenter, sp
Mark Mulder, sp
Jeff Suppan, sp
Matt Morris, sp
Jason Marquis, sp
Jason Isringhausen, rp
Ray King, rp
Julian Tavarez, rp
Al Reyes, rp
Randy Flores, rp

Attendance

3,542,271 (second in NL)

Club Leaders

Batting Avg:	Pujols	.330
On-Base Pct:	Pujols	.430
Slugging Pct:	Pujols	.609
Home Runs:	Pujols	41
RBIs:	Pujols	117
Runs:	Pujols	129
Stolen Bases:	Pujols	16
Wins:	Carpenter	21
Strikeouts:	Carpenter	213
ERA:	Carpenter	2.83
Saves:	Isringhausen	39

JANUARY 6   The Cardinals sign Mark Grudzielanek, most recently with the Cubs, as a free agent.

MARCH 9   Unable to harness his control problems on the mound, Rick Ankiel announces that he will to attempt to make it back to the majors as an outfielder.

APRIL 5   Playing the Astros, their 2004 NLCS opponent, the Cardinals win the season opener 7–3 in Houston. All three outfielders homered. Jim Edmonds started the scoring with a three-run homer in the first inning. Later, Larry Walker and Reggie Sanders added home runs. The St. Louis victory ended a long winning streak by Houston at Minute Maid Park. The Astros had won their last 18 regular-season home games in 2004 and were 5–1 in the postseason.

Edmonds batted .263 with 29 homers in 2005.

APRIL 8   In the home opener, the Cardinals defeat the Phillies 6–5 before 50,074 at Busch Stadium. The Cards trailed 5–1 after five innings before mounting the comeback.

Larry Walker tied the game 5–5 with a bases-loaded walk from Aaron Fultz, and Albert Pujols followed with another walk to force in the go-ahead run. David Eckstein reached base five times in five plate appearances with two singles, two walks, and a hit by pitch.

Pujols had another incredible season in 2005, batting .330 with 41 homers, 117 RBIs, and 129 runs scored. Pujols is one of only four players to drive in at least 100 runs in each of his first five seasons in the majors. The other three are Joe DiMaggio, Al Simmons, and Ted Williams.

APRIL 12   Jason Marquis hits a bases-loaded triple in the second inning to key a 5–1 win over the Reds at Busch Stadium.

APRIL 18   The Cardinals explode for nine runs in the ninth inning to cap an 11–1 win over the Pirates at PNC Park. Mark Mulder (eight innings) and Jimmy Journell (one inning) combined on a two-hitter. The only two Pittsburgh hits were a single by Freddy Sanchez in the fifth inning and a double by Craig Wilson in the sixth.

APRIL 23   Mark Mulder pitches a 10-inning complete game to defeat the Astros 1–0 in 43-degree weather at Busch Stadium. Roger Clemens pitched seven shutout innings for Houston. Larry Walker drove in the Cardinals' run with a walk-off single.

Mulder was the first Cardinal pitcher to go at least 10 innings in a game since Jose DeLeon in 1989.

APRIL 27   Mark Grudzielanek hits for the cycle in a 6–3 win over the Brewers at Busch Stadium. Facing Victor Santos, Grudzielanek led off the first inning with a homer, then singled and scored in the second and hit an RBI double in the fourth. He completed the cycle with a triple off Jorge de la Rosa in the sixth. Chris Carpenter contributed 12 strikeouts in $7^2/_3$ innings.

MAY 2   The Cardinals stage the most incredible ninth-inning rally in their long history by scoring seven runs to beat the Reds 10–9 in Cincinnati. With the Cards down 9–3 at the top of the inning, Reds reliever David Weathers walked Yadier Molina and Abraham Nuñez. After Roger Cedeño struck out, David Eckstein singled to load the bases. Albert Pujols hit into a force-out, scoring Molina. Reggie Sanders kept the rally alive by singling in Nuñez, and Jim Edmonds got Reds fans murmuring when he hit a three-run homer off Danny Graves to make it 9–8. John Mabry drove in the tying and winning runs with a two-run homer, also off Graves. It was the first time that the Cardinals had entered the ninth inning of a game trailing by six runs or more and come away with a victory.

The Cardinals' comeback marked the tipping point for Reds closer Danny Graves, who spoke out in the press about fans' booing after the game. His comments brought on more boos and calls from fans and culminated in his flipping off a fan after a particularly rough 9–2 loss to the Cleveland Indians on May 22 in which he gave up five ninth-inning runs. The Reds designated Graves for assignment the next day.

MAY 8   On Mother's Day, the Cardinals explode for 11 runs in the first inning and rout the Padres 15–5 at Busch Stadium.

MAY 9   Mark Mulder strikes out 12 batters in seven innings to lead the Cardinals to a 4–2 victory over the Dodgers at Busch Stadium.

MAY 20   John Mabry hits a grand slam off Zack Greinke in the first inning of a 7–6 win over the Royals in Kansas City.

JUNE 4   The Cardinals score eight runs in the third inning to break a 1–1 tie and hang on to defeat the Astros 11–9 in Houston. Reggie Sanders keyed the attack with a grand slam off Wandy Rodriguez in addition to collecting three doubles to tie a Cardinal record for most extra-base hits in a game.

JUNE 7   In a rematch of the 2004 World Series opponents, the Cardinals defeat the Red Sox 7–1 at Busch Stadium. It was the first time that the Cardinals and Red Sox played each other in St. Louis during the regular season.

               On the same day, the Cardinals selected outfielder Colby Rasmus from Russell County High School in Alabama in the first round of the amateur draft.

JUNE 10   The Cardinals play the Yankees in St. Louis for the first time during the regular season and win 8–1 at Busch Stadium.

JUNE 13   The Cardinals play the Blue Jays in Toronto for the first time and lose 4–1.

JUNE 14   Chris Carpenter pitches a one-hitter to defeat the Blue Jays 7–0 in Toronto. The only hit off Carpenter was a double by Russ Adams with two outs in the sixth inning. Carpenter played for the Blue Jays from 1997 through 2002.

JUNE 17   The Cardinals play the Devil Rays for the first time during the regular season and win 6–4 in St. Petersburg.

JUNE 26   The Cardinals hit into six double plays in a 10-inning, 5–4 loss to the Pirates at Busch Stadium. One of the double plays started when Yadier Molina passed Abraham Nuñez between first and second. With runners at first and second and one out, Molina hit a drive off the fence in right-center. Nuñez, who was on first, apparently thought right fielder Matt Lawton had caught the ball and was retreating to first as Molina rounded the bag and passed him. Molina was called out for passing him, and the stunned Nuñez was tagged out while standing near second base.

JULY 6   David Eckstein's suicide squeeze scores So Taguchi in the ninth inning to give the Cardinals a 2–1 win over the Giants in San Francisco.

JULY 12   Tony La Russa manages the National League to a 7–5 loss in the All-Star Game, played at Comerica Park in Detroit.

               La Russa is 3–1 as a manager in All-Star Games, 3-0 in the American League and 0–1 in the National League.

JULY 31   Jim Edmonds enters the game in the seventh inning and delivers an RBI double and a two-run homer in the eleventh inning for a 7–5 win over the Dodgers in Los Angeles.

AUGUST 7   David Eckstein hits a walk-off grand slam off Chris Reitsma with one out in the ninth inning to defeat the Braves 5–3 at Busch Stadium. Albert Pujols put St. Louis on the board in the eighth inning with a solo shot, his 31st of the year.

Eckstein's game-winning blast came on Organ Transplant Awareness Day. His father, Whitey, received a kidney transplant later in the month from a family friend. Three of Eckstein's siblings also have required kidney transplants.

AUGUST 19   Trailing 4–0, the Cardinals score five times in the ninth inning to shock the Giants 5–4 at Busch Stadium. Yadier Molina pulled the Cards within a run by blasting a three-run homer. Jim Edmonds ended the contest with a two-out, two-run double.

AUGUST 25   Tony La Russa moves past Sparky Anderson into third place on the list of career wins by a manager with a 6–3 win over the Pirates in Pittsburgh. The victory was La Russa's 2,195th in a career that began in 1979 with Bill Veeck's Chicago White Sox. The only managers with more wins are Connie Mack (3,731) and John McGraw (2,763).

AUGUST 26   The Cardinals play the Nationals in Washington for the first time and lose 4–1 at RFK Stadium. It was the Cardinals' first regular-season game in Washington since 1899.

AUGUST 27   Jason Marquis pitches a two-hitter and his first career shutout, defeating the Nationals 6–0 at RFK Stadium. The only Washington hits were singles by Marlon Byrd and Christian Guzman.

SEPTEMBER 3   Five days after Hurricane Katrina devastates New Orleans and the Gulf Coast, Chris Carpenter records his 20th win with a 4–2 decision over the Astros in Houston.

SEPTEMBER 8   Chris Carpenter pitches the first seven innings of a 5–0 win over the Mets at Busch Stadium to record his 13th win in a row. His record was 21–4.

The 13-game winning streak was the second longest in Cardinals history during a single season. The only longer one was Bob Gibson's 15-game streak in 1968. Carpenter finished the season with a 21–5 record, a 2.83 ERA, and 213 strikeouts in $241^2/_3$ innings.

SEPTEMBER 15 The Cardinals clinch the NL Central title with a 6–1 win over the Cubs in Chicago. The contest was called by rain with two outs in the bottom of the ninth after a 58-minute delay.

OCTOBER 2   The Cardinals play their last regular-season game at Busch Stadium, a 7–5 victory against the Reds. Matt Morris gave up consecutive homers to Felipe Lopez, Adam Dunn, and Austin Kearns in the third inning. It was the Cards' 100th win of the 2005 season. It was the first time the Redbirds had won 100 or more games in consecutive seasons since 1942 through 1944.

Mike Shannon, who had seen all 40 years of Busch Stadium history as a player and broadcaster, threw out the ceremonial first pitch. Among those introduced before the game were Stan Musial, Bob Gibson, Lou Brock, Red Schoendienst, Ozzie Smith, Willie McGee, Vince Coleman, Tom Herr, Jack Clark, Mark McGwire, Whitey Herzog, Ted Simmons, Steve Carlton, Keith Hernandez, Bruce Sutter, Lonnie Smith, Todd Worrell, and John Tudor.

The Cardinals met the Padres in the National League Division Series. Managed by Bruce Bochy, the Padres were 82–80 in 2005, the worst record ever by a playoff team.

OCTOBER 4   The Cardinals open the Division Series with an 8–5 win over the Padres before 52,349 at Busch Stadium. Reggie Sanders starred with six RBIs. His two-run single in the third inning put the Cards up 4–0, and his grand slam in the fifth against Jake Peavy on a 3–0 pitch provided St. Louis with an 8–0 cushion. Jim Edmonds also helped with a homer, double, and single. The Cards survived a scare in the ninth when San Diego scored three runs and loaded the bases with two outs.

Sanders drove in 10 runs in the three-game series against the Padres.

OCTOBER 6   The Cardinals take a two-games-to-none lead in the Division Series with a 6–2 victory over the Padres before 52,599 at Busch Stadium. Mark Mulder took a line drive from Joe Randa off of his left arm in the second inning, but he shook it off and went 6$\frac{1}{3}$ innings, allowing only one run for the win.

OCTOBER 8   The Cardinals close out the Division Series with a 7–4 win over the Padres at Petco Park in San Diego to complete the three-game sweep. The Cards led 7–0 after 4½ innings before withstanding a Padres rally. David Eckstein homered in the winning cause.

The Cardinals played the Astros in the National League Championship Series in a rematch of 2004. Managed by Phil Garner, Houston reached the playoffs as a wild card with an 89–73 record.

OCTOBER 12   The Cardinals open the NLCS with a 5–3 win over the Astros before 52,332 at Busch Stadium. Reggie Sanders started the scoring with a 445-foot, two-run homer in the first inning off Andy Pettitte. The Cards led 5–0 after five, and Chris Carpenter looked every bit the ace as he gave up two runs on five hits over eight innings. Houston put up another run in the ninth against closer Jason Isringhausen.

OCTOBER 13   The Astros even the NLCS with a 4–1 win over the Cardinals before 52,358 in Game Two at Busch Stadium. Matching up against Roy Oswalt, Mark Mulder turned in a strong performance—one earned run over seven innings—but he got little help from the Cardinal offense. Albert Pujols accounted for the lone St. Louis run with a homer in the sixth inning. The team went 0 for 8 with runners in scoring position.

OCTOBER 15   The Cardinals lose to Roger Clemens and the Astros 4–3 in Houston and fall behind two games to one in the NLCS. Mike Lamb broke a 2–2 tie with a two-run homer off starter Matt Morris in the sixth inning. Clemens gave up two runs on six hits in six innings. The Cards scored in the ninth off Brad "Lights Out" Lidge and had a runner on second with two outs when David Eckstein flied out to end the game. It was the first run that the Cardinals had scored off Lidge in 31 innings over 24 appearances, dating back to September 2003.

OCTOBER 16   The Astros anticipate reaching the World Series with a 2–1 win over the Cardinals in Houston. The Astros broke a 1–1 tie with a run in the seventh inning on an unearned run. Umpire Phil Cuzzi tossed Tony La Russa in the bottom of the seventh and then Jim Edmonds in the top of the eighth for questioning balls and strikes. John Rodriguez stepped in for Edmonds and hit a 3–2 pitch well over 400 feet to dead center, where Willy Tavarez tracked it down while running up Tal's Hill. The Cards again had a chance in the ninth when Albert Pujols and Larry Walker both singled off Brad Lidge, but Morgan Ensberg threw out Pujols at home on a Reggie Sanders dribbler, and John Mabry grounded into a flawlessly executed double play that nobody could have expected Eric Bruntlett and Adam Everett to turn. Chad Qualls notched the victory for the Astros.

OCTOBER 17   The Cardinals are one strike away from a season-ending loss before a thrilling three-run, ninth-inning rally beats the Astros 5–4 in Houston. The Cards took a 2–1 lead in the fourth inning when Mark Grudzielanek flared a single into the outfield with the bases loaded and two outs. Houston took the lead back when Lance Berkman sliced a three-run home run into the Crawford Boxes off Chris Carpenter in the seventh. The Cards still trailed 4–2 entering the ninth when Brad Lidge took the mound for the third night in a row. On the previous two evenings, Lidge had earned saves despite some shaky moments. Lidge retired the first two batters before David Eckstein took his place in the batter's box with the crowd at Minute Maid Park anticipating a pennant celebration. The count was 1–2 when Eckstein singled through the hole between short and third. Jim Edmonds walked on five pitches. Then Pujols put the Cardinals ahead 5–4 with a 412-foot, three-run homer that cleared the train tracks above the left-field wall, one of the most dramatic blasts in postseason history. Jason Isringhausen pitched a scoreless ninth to preserve the victory.

Ronald Martinez/Getty Images Sport/Getty Images

The combination of Albert Pujols's three-run home run in the top of the ninth and Jason Isringhausen's scoreless bottom half clinches Game Six of the 2005 NLCS for the Cards.

OCTOBER 19   The euphoria over Albert Pujols's home run lasts only 48 hours as the Astros end the Cardinals' season with a 5–1 win before 52,438 in the final game played at Busch Stadium. The Astros score two runs in the third inning, and the Cardinals' offense never got going. The Cards collected only four hits off Roy Oswalt and two relievers. Albert Pujols went 0 for 4, and starter Mark Mulder gave up three runs in the first four innings.

NOVEMBER 7   The demolition of Busch Stadium begins.

Hundreds of observers lined adjacent streets, occupied rooftops, and looked on from nearby hotels to view the first swings of a five-ton wrecking ball. The southern half of the stadium was scheduled to be demolished first to allow the completion of the new Busch Stadium in time for the Cardinals home opener on April 10, 2006. The rest of the old stadium was scheduled for demolition by June 30. All of the concrete was slated to be crushed, then used to fill the playing field of the old park up to street level.

NOVEMBER 10   Chris Carpenter is named the 2005 National League Cy Young Award winner. He was the first Cardinal to win the award since Bob Gibson in 1970.

NOVEMBER 16   Albert Pujols is named the 2005 National League Most Valuable Player Award winner. Pujols finished fourth in the MVP balloting following his rookie season in 2001, second to Barry Bonds in both 2002 and 2003, and third in 2004.

DECEMBER 8   The Cardinals trade Ray King to the Rockies for Larry Bigbie and Aaron Miles.

DECEMBER 12   Matt Morris signs with the Giants as a free agent.

DECEMBER 13   The Cardinals announce the signing of Ricardo Rincon to a two-year, $2.9 million deal after his stint with the Oakland A's.

DECEMBER 15   The Cardinals announce the signing of Braden Looper, a reliever for the Mets in 2005, to a three-year, $13.5 million deal.

The Cardinals drafted Looper in the first round in 1996.

DECEMBER 23   The Cardinals sign outfielder Juan Encarnacion to a three-year contract for a reported $15 million. Encarnacion stepped into Larry Walker's spot in right field. The team also picked up Junior Spivey, most recently with the Nationals, in a one-year deal to replace second baseman Mark Grudzielanek, who signed with Kansas City.

By the Numbers

CARDINALS ALL-TIME OFFENSIVE LEADERS 1882–2005

	Games			Runs			Doubles	
1	Stan Musial	3,026	1	Stan Musial	1,949	1	Stan Musial	725
2	Lou Brock	2,289	2	Lou Brock	1,427	2	Lou Brock	434
3	Ozzie Smith	1,990	3	Rogers Hornsby	1,089	3	Joe Medwick	377
4	Enos Slaughter	1,820	4	Enos Slaughter	1,071	4	Rogers Hornsby	367
5	Red Schoendienst	1,795	5	Red Schoendienst	1,025	5	Enos Slaughter	366
6	Curt Flood	1,738	6	Ozzie Smith	991	6	Red Schoendienst	352
7	Ken Boyer	1,667	7	Ken Boyer	988	7	Jim Bottomley	344
8	Willie McGee	1,661	8	Ray Lankford	928	8	Ray Lankford	339
9	Rogers Hornsby	1,580	9	Jim Bottomley	921	9	Ozzie Smith	338
	Ray Lankford	1,580	10	Curt Flood	845	10	Ted Simmons	332
11	Julian Javier	1,578	11	Arlie Latham	832	11	Frankie Frisch	286
12	Ted Simmons	1,564	12	Frankie Frisch	831	12	Curt Flood	271
13	Marty Marion	1,502	13	Charlie Comiskey	816	13	Pepper Martin	270
14	Jim Bottomley	1,392	14	Joe Medwick	811	14	Ken Boyer	269
15	Frankie Frisch	1,311	15	Willie McGee	760	15	Keith Hernandez	265
16	Terry Moore	1,298	16	Pepper Martin	756	16	Terry Moore	263
17	Joe Medwick	1,216	17	Ted Simmons	736	17	Marty Marion	261
18	Dal Maxvill	1,205	18	Terry Moore	719	18	Willie McGee	255
19	Pepper Martin	1,189		Julian Javier	719	19	Chick Hafey	242
20	Tim McCarver	1,181	20	Tip O'Neill	697	20	Albert Pujols	227

	At-Bats			Hits			Triples	
1	Stan Musial	10,972	1	Stan Musial	3,630	1	Stan Musial	177
2	Lou Brock	9,125	2	Lou Brock	2,713	2	Rogers Hornsby	143
3	Ozzie Smith	7,160	3	Rogers Hornsby	2,110	3	Enos Slaughter	135
4	Red Schoendienst	6,841	4	Enos Slaughter	2,064	4	Lou Brock	121
5	Enos Slaughter	6,775	5	Red Schoendienst	1,980	5	Jim Bottomley	119
6	Ken Boyer	6,334	6	Ozzie Smith	1,944	6	Ed Konetchy	93
7	Curt Flood	6,318	7	Ken Boyer	1,855	7	Willie McGee	83
8	Rogers Hornsby	5,881	8	Curt Flood	1,853	8	Joe Medwick	81
9	Willie McGee	5,734	9	Jim Bottomley	1,727	9	Pepper Martin	75
10	Ted Simmons	5,725	10	Ted Simmons	1,704	10	Tip O'Neill	70
11	Julian Javier	5,631	11	Willie McGee	1,683	11	Garry Templeton	69
12	Ray Lankford	5,417	12	Joe Medwick	1,590	12	Johnny Mize	66
13	Jim Bottomley	5,314	13	Frankie Frisch	1,577	13	Red Schoendienst	65
14	Marty Marion	5,313	14	Ray Lankford	1,479	14	Jack Smith	63
15	Frankie Frisch	5,059	15	Julian Javier	1,450	15	Frankie Frisch	61
16	Joe Medwick	4,747	16	Marty Marion	1,402		Ken Boyer	61
17	Terry Moore	4,700	17	Terry Moore	1,318	17	Charlie Comiskey	58
18	Charlie Comiskey	4,389	18	Bill White	1,241	18	Vince Coleman	56
19	Bill White	4,165	19	Pepper Martin	1,227	19	Julian Javier	55
20	Pepper Martin	4,117	20	Keith Hernandez	1,217	20	Ray Lankford	52

Home Runs

1	Stan Musial	475
2	Ken Boyer	255
3	Ray Lankford	228
4	Mark McGwire	220
5	Jim Edmonds	210
6	Albert Pujols	201
7	Rogers Hornsby	193
8	Jim Bottomley	181
9	Ted Simmons	172
10	Johnny Mize	158
11	Joe Medwick	152
12	Enos Slaughter	145
13	Bill White	140
14	Lou Brock	129
15	Chick Hafey	127
16	George Hendrick	122
17	Ripper Collins	106
	Whitey Kurowski	106
19	Joe Torre	98
	Curt Flood	84

Walks

1	Stan Musial	1,599
2	Ozzie Smith	876
3	Enos Slaughter	838
4	Ray Lankford	780
5	Lou Brock	681
6	Rogers Hornsby	660
7	Ken Boyer	631
8	Ted Simmons	624
9	Keith Hernandez	585
10	Miller Huggins	572
11	Jim Edmonds	551
12	Jim Bottomley	509
13	Red Schoendienst	497
14	Mark McGwire	470
15	Marty Marion	451
16	Frankie Frisch	448
17	Curt Flood	439
18	Tom Herr	438
19	Johnny Mize	424
20	Yank Robinson	419

Stolen Bases

1	Lou Brock	888
2	Vince Coleman	549
3	Ozzie Smith	433
4	Arlie Latham	369
5	Charlie Comiskey	336
6	Willie McGee	318
7	Tommy McCarthy	270
8	Yank Robinson	221
9	Jack Smith	203
10	Ray Lankford	199
11	Frankie Frisch	195
12	Tommy Dowd	187
13	Miller Huggins	174
14	Lonnie Smith	173
15	Tom Herr	152
16	Ed Konetchy	151
17	Curt Welch	148
	Edgar Renteria	148
19	Pepper Martin	146
20	Shorty Fuller	140

RBIs

1	Stan Musial	1,951
2	Enos Slaughter	1,148
3	Jim Bottomley	1,105
4	Rogers Hornsby	1,072
5	Ken Boyer	1,001
6	Ted Simmons	929
7	Ray Lankford	829
8	Joe Medwick	823
9	Lou Brock	814
10	Frankie Frisch	720
11	Willie McGee	678
12	Ozzie Smith	664
13	Johnny Mize	653
14	Red Schoendienst	651
15	Curt Flood	633
16	Bill White	631
17	Albert Pujols	621
18	Chick Hafey	618
19	Marty Marion	605
20	Keith Hernandez	595

Strikeouts

1	Lou Brock	1,469
2	Ray Lankford	1,449
3	Willie McGee	926
4	Ken Boyer	859
5	Jim Edmonds	853
6	Julian Javier	801
7	Stan Musial	698
8	Vince Coleman	628
9	Curt Flood	606
10	Bill White	601
11	Mark McGwire	553
12	Keith Hernandez	536
13	Mike Shannon	525
14	Marty Marion	520
15	Rogers Hornsby	480
16	Joe Torre	476
17	Dal Maxvill	470
18	Ted Simmons	453
19	George Hendrick	448
20	Pepper Martin	438

Batting Average

(minimum 2,000 plate appearances)

1	Rogers Hornsby	.359
2	Tip O'Neill	.343
3	Johnny Mize	.336
4	Joe Medwick	.335
5	Albert Pujols	.332
6	Stan Musial	.331
7	Chick Hafey	.326
8	Jim Bottomley	.325
9	Patsy Donovan	.314
10	Frankie Frisch	.312
11	George Watkins	.309
12	Joe Torre	.308
13	Ripper Collins	.307
14	Tommy McCarthy	.306
15	Ernie Orsatti	.306
16	Milt Stock	.305
17	Garry Templeton	.305
18	Enos Slaughter	.305
19	Joe Cunningham	.304
20	Austin McHenry	.302

On-Base Percentage

(minimum 2,000 plate appearances)

1	Mark McGwire	.427
2	Rogers Hornsby	.427
3	Johnny Mize	.419
4	Stan Musial	.417
5	Albert Pujols	.417
6	Joe Cunningham	.413
7	Tip O'Neill	.406
8	Jim Edmonds	.406
9	Miller Huggins	.402
10	Ray Blades	.395
11	Solly Hemus	.392
12	Yank Robinson	.392
13	Jim Bottomley	.387
14	Keith Hernandez	.385
15	Enos Slaughter	.384
16	Joe Torre	.382
17	Chick Hafey	.379
18	J. D. Drew	.377
19	Taylor Douthit	.373
20	Joe Medwick	.372

Slugging Percentage

(minimum 2,000 plate appearances)

1	Mark McGwire	.683
2	Albert Pujols	.621
3	Johnny Mize	.600
4	Jim Edmonds	.584
5	Rogers Hornsby	.568
6	Chick Hafey	.568
7	Stan Musial	.559
8	Joe Medwick	.545
9	Jim Bottomley	.537
10	Ripper Collins	.517
11	J. D. Drew	.498
12	Tip O'Neill	.489
13	Ray Lankford	.481
14	Ken Boyer	.475
15	Brian Jordan	.474
16	George Watkins	.474
17	Bill White	.472
18	George Hendrick	.470
19	Enos Slaughter	.463
20	Ray Blades	.460

Joe Medwick

Transcendental Graphics/theruckerarchive.com

CARDINALS ALL-TIME PITCHING LEADERS 1882–2005

	Wins			Winning Percentage			Games Started	
1	Bob Gibson	251		(minimum 100 decisions)		1	Bob Gibson	482
2	Jesse Haines	210	1	Dave Foutz	.704	2	Bob Forsch	401
3	Bob Forsch	163	2	Silver King	.694	3	Jesse Haines	388
4	Bill Sherdel	153	3	Bob Caruthers	.692	4	Bill Doak	319
5	Bill Doak	144	4	Mort Cooper	.677	5	Bill Sherdel	244
6	Dizzy Dean	134	5	Dizzy Dean	.641	6	Harry Brecheen	224
7	Harry Brecheen	128	6	Lon Warneke	.629	7	Ted Breitenstein	221
8	Dave Foutz	114	7	Matt Morris	.620	8	Slim Sallee	214
9	Silver King	111	8	Harry Brecheen	.618	9	Larry Jackson	209
10	Bob Caruthers	108	9	Al Brazle	.602	10	Matt Morris	206
11	Slim Sallee	106	10	George Munger	.602	11	Dizzy Dean	196
12	Mort Cooper	105	11	Howie Pollet	.599	12	Max Lanier	187
13	Max Lanier	101	12	Max Lanier	.594	13	Wild Bill Hallahan	186
	Larry Jackson	101	13	Jack Stivetts	.593		Mort Cooper	186
	Matt Morris	101	14	Bob Tewksbury	.593	15	Vinegar Bend Mizell	185
16	Howie Pollet	97	15	Jumbo McGinnis	.591	16	Howie Pollet	177
	Al Brazle	97	16	Bob Gibson	.591	17	Steve Carlton	172
18	Ted Breitenstein	94	17	Wild Bill Hallahan	.578	18	Curt Simmons	171
19	Wild Bill Hallahan	93	18	Murry Dickson	.571	19	Dave Foutz	166
20	Gerry Staley	89	19	Jesse Haines	.571	20	Ray Sadecki	165
			20	Flint Rhem	.563			

	Losses			Games			Complete Games	
1	Bob Gibson	174	1	Jesse Haines	554	1	Bob Gibson	255
2	Jesse Haines	158	2	Bob Gibson	528	2	Jesse Haines	209
3	Bill Doak	136	3	Bill Sherdel	465	3	Ted Breitenstein	197
4	Bill Sherdel	131	4	Bob Forsch	455	4	Dave Foutz	156
5	Bob Forsch	127	5	Al Brazle	441	5	Silver King	154
6	Ted Breitenstein	125	6	Bill Doak	376	6	Bob Caruthers	151
7	Slim Sallee	107	7	Todd Worrell	348	7	Jumbo McGinnis	145
8	Larry Jackson	86	8	Lindy McDaniel	336	8	Bill Doak	144
9	Bob Harmon	81	9	Larry Jackson	330		Bill Sherdel	144
10	Harry Brecheen	79	10	Al Hrabosky	329	10	Dizzy Dean	141
11	Gerry Staley	76	11	Ken Dayley	327	11	Slim Sallee	123
12	Dizzy Dean	75	12	Slim Sallee	317	12	Harry Brecheen	122
13	Vinegar Bend Mizell	70	13	Gerry Staley	301	13	Mort Cooper	105
14	Max Lanier	69	14	Steve Kline	300	14	Jack Powell	101
15	Wild Bill Hallahan	68	15	Harry Brecheen	292	15	Willie Sudhoff	100
16	Lee Meadows	67	16	Ted Wilks	282	16	Jack Stivetts	99
17	Howie Pollet	65	17	Max Lanier	277	17	Howie Pollet	96
18	Al Brazle	64	18	Dizzy Dean	273	18	Jack Taylor	90
	Ray Sadecki	64	19	Wild Bill Hallahan	259	19	Kid Gleason	86
20	Flint Rhem	63	20	Ted Breitenstein	250	20	Max Lanier	85

Shutouts

1	Bob Gibson	56
2	Bill Doak	32
3	Mort Cooper	28
4	Harry Brecheen	25
5	Jesse Haines	24
6	Dizzy Dean	23
7	Max Lanier	20
	Howie Pollet	20
9	Bob Forsch	19
10	Jumbo McGinnis	18
	Ernie Broglio	18
12	Slim Sallee	17
13	Dave Foutz	16
	Curt Simmons	16
	Steve Carlton	16
16	Larry Jackson	15
17	Lon Warneke	14
18	Wild Bill Hallahan	13
	George Munger	13
	Joaquin Andujar	13

Walks

1	Bob Gibson	1,336
2	Jesse Haines	870
3	Ted Breitenstein	839
4	Bob Forsch	790
5	Bill Doak	740
6	Wild Bill Hallahan	648
7	Bill Sherdel	595
8	Bob Harmon	594
9	Vinegar Bend Mizell	568
10	Max Lanier	524
11	Harry Brecheen	505
12	Al Brazle	492
13	Jack Stivetts	479
	Larry Jackson	479
15	Mort Cooper	478
16	Howie Pollet	473
	Ernie Broglio	473
18	Slim Sallee	467
19	Six tied at	449

Strikeouts/9 Innings

(minimum 1,000 innings pitched)

1	Bob Gibson	7.22
2	Steve Carlton	6.77
3	Matt Morris	6.44
4	Ernie Broglio	5.98
5	Jack Stivetts	5.92
6	Vinegar Bend Mizell	5.83
7	Dizzy Dean	5.67
8	Ray Sadecki	5.42
9	Ray Washburn	5.22
10	Wild Bill Hallahan	4.86
11	Larry Jackson	4.84
12	Max Lanier	4.73
13	Mort Cooper	4.61
14	Joaquin Andujar	4.51
15	Harry Brecheen	4.31
16	Curt Simmons	4.28
17	Murry Dickson	4.24
18	George Munger	4.20
19	Howie Pollet	4.08
20	Dave Foutz	3.82

Innings Pitched

1	Bob Gibson	3,884.1
2	Jesse Haines	3,203.2
3	Bob Forsch	2,658.2
4	Bill Sherdel	2,450.2
5	Bill Doak	2,387.0
6	Ted Breitenstein	1,925.1
7	Slim Sallee	1,905.1
8	Harry Brecheen	1,790.1
9	Dizzy Dean	1,737.1
10	Larry Jackson	1,672.1
11	Mort Cooper	1,480.1
12	Dave Foutz	1,457.2
13	Max Lanier	1,454.2
14	Wild Bill Hallahan	1,453.1
15	Silver King	1,433.2
16	Howie Pollet	1,401.2
17	Bob Caruthers	1,395.0
18	Matt Morris	1,377.1
19	Al Brazle	1,376.2
20	Jumbo McGinnis	1,325.0

Strikeouts

1	Bob Gibson	3,117
2	Dizzy Dean	1,095
3	Ted Breitenstein	1,079
4	Matt Morris	986
5	Jesse Haines	979
6	Steve Carlton	951
7	Bill Doak	938
8	Larry Jackson	899
9	Harry Brecheen	857
10	Vinegar Bend Mizell	789
11	Wild Bill Hallahan	784
12	Bill Sherdel	779
13	Max Lanier	764
14	Jose DeLeon	763
15	Mort Cooper	758
16	Ernie Broglio	747
17	Jack Stivetts	691
18	Ray Sadecki	665
19	Ray Washburn	663
20	Slim Sallee	652

ERA

(minimum 1,000 innings pitched)

1	Slim Sallee	2.67
2	Dave Foutz	2.67
3	Silver King	2.71
4	Jumbo McGinnis	2.73
5	Bob Caruthers	2.75
6	Mort Cooper	2.77
7	Max Lanier	2.84
8	Harry Brecheen	2.91
9	Bob Gibson	2.91
10	Bill Doak	2.93
11	Dizzy Dean	2.99
12	Lee Meadows	3.00
13	Jack Stivetts	3.01
14	Howie Pollet	3.06
15	Steve Carlton	3.10
16	Curt Simmons	3.25
17	Al Brazle	3.31
18	Joaquin Andujar	3.33
19	Ray Washburn	3.34
20	Murry Dickson	3.38

Saves

1	Lee Smith	160
2	Jason Isringhausen	140
3	Todd Worrell	129
4	Bruce Sutter	127
5	Dennis Eckersley	66
6	Lindy McDaniel	64
7	Al Brazle	60
	Joe Hoerner	60
9	Al Hrabosky	59
10	Dave Veres	48
11	Ken Dayley	39
12	Tom Henke	36
13	Dizzy Dean	30
14	Ted Wilks	29
15	Mark Littell	28
16	Slim Sallee	26
	Diego Segui	26
18	Bill Sherdel	25
19	Barney Schultz	21
	Hal Woodeshick	21

Bob Gibson

Transcendental Graphics/theruckerarchive.com

CARDINALS ALL-TIME ROSTER

A

Abbott, Ody	1910
Abernathy, Ted	1970
Acevedo, Juan	1998–99
Adams, Babe	1906
Adams, Buster	1939, 1943, 1945–46
Adams, Jim	1890
Adams, Joe	1902
Adams, Sparky	1930–33
Adduci, Jim	1983
Adkinson, Henry	1895
Agee, Tommie	1973
Agosto, Juan	1991–92
Ainsmith, Eddie	1921–23
Alba, Gibson	1988
Alberts, Cy	1910
Alexander, Grover	1926–29
Alexander, Nin	1884
Alicea, Luis	1988, 1991–94, 1996
Allen, Dick	1970
Allen, Ethan	1933
Allen, Neil	1983–85
Alou, Matty	1971–73
Alston, Walter	1936
Altman, George	1963
Alvarado, Luis	1974, 1976
Alyea, Brant	1972
Amaro, Ruben	1958
Ames, Red	1915–19
Anderson, Craig	1961
Anderson, Dwain	1972–73
Anderson, Ferrell	1953
Anderson, George	1918
Anderson, John	1962
Anderson, Marlon	2004
Anderson, Mike	1976–77
Andrews, John	1973
Andrews, Nate	1937, 1939
Andujar, Joaquin	1981–85
Ankenman, Pat	1936
Ankiel, Rick	1999–2001, 2004
Antonelli, John	1944–45
Arndt, Harry	1905–07
Arnold, Scott	1988

Arocha, Rene	1993–95
Arroyo, Luis	1955
Arroyo, Rudy	1971
Aust, Dennis	1965–66
Ayala, Benny	1977
Aybar, Manny	1997–99

B

Backman, Les	1909–10
Bailey, Bill	1921–1922
Bailey, Cory	1995–96
Bair, Doug	1981–83, 1985
Baird, Doug	1917–19
Bakenhaster, Dave	1964
Baker, Bill	1948–49
Baker, Steve	1983
Baldwin, O. F.	1908
Ball, Art	1894
Bannon, Jimmy	1893
Barbeau, Jap	1909–10
Barber, Brian	1995–96
Barclay, George	1902–04
Bare, Ray	1972, 1974
Barfoot, Clyde	1922–23
Bargar, Greg	1986
Barkley, Sam	1885
Barlow, Mike	1975
Barnes, Frank	1957–58, 1960
Barnes, Skeeter	1987
Barrett, Frank	1939
Barrett, Red	1945–46
Barry, Shad	1906–08
Bartosch, Dave	1945
Batchelor, Rich	1993, 1996–97
Bates, Frank	1899
Battle, Allen	1995
Bauta, Ed	1960–63
Bautista, Jose	1997
Baxter, John	1907
Beall, Johnny	1918
Beard, Ralph	1954
Beauchamp, Jim	1963, 1970–71
Beazley, Johnny	1941–42, 1946
Beck, Zinn	1913–16
Beckley, Jake	1904–07

Beckmann, Bill	1942	Bollweg, Don	1950–51
Beebe, Fred	1906–09	Bonds, Bobby	1980
Beecher, Ed	1897	Bonilla, Bobby	2001
Beers, Clarence	1948	Bonner, Frank	1895
Bell, David	1995–98	Booker, Rod	1987–89
Bell, Hi	1924, 1926–27,	Borbon, Pedro	1980
	1929–30	Borbon, Pedro, Jr.	2003
Les Bell	1923–1927	Bordagaray, Frenchy	1937–38
Bellman, John	1889	Borders, Pat	1996
Beltran, Rigo	1997	Bosetti, Rick	1977
Benes, Alan	1995–97, 1999–2001	Bottalico, Ricky	1999
Benes, Andy	1996–97, 2000–02	Bottenfield, Kent	1998–99
Benes, Joe	1931	Bottomley, Jim	1922–32
Bennett, Pug	1906–07	Bowman, Bob	1939–40
Benson, Vern	1951–53	Boyer, Cloyd	1949–52
Benton, Sid	1922	Boyer, Ken	1955–65
Berblinger, Jeff	1997	Boyle, Jack	1887–89, 1891
Bergamo, Augie	1944–45	Bradford, Buddy	1975
Berly, Jack	1924	Bradshaw, Terry	1995–96
Bernard, Joe	1909	Bragg, Darren	1999
Bertaina, Frank	1970	Brain, Dave	1903–05
Berte, Harry	1903	Branch, Harvey	1962
Bescher, Bob	1915–17	Brandt, Jackie	1956
Betcher, Frank	1910	Brantley, Jeff	1998
Betts, Harry	1903	Brashear, Roy	1902
Betzel, Bruno	1914–18	Bratcher, Joe	1924
Bibby, Jim	1972–73	Braun, Steve	1981–85
Bierbauer, Lou	1897–98	Brazle, Al	1943, 1946–54
Bilko, Steve	1949–54	Brecheen, Harry	1940, 1943–52
Billings, Dick	1974–75	Breitenstein, Ted	1891–96, 1901
Bird, Frank	1892	Bremer, Herb	1937–39
Blades, Ray	1922–28, 1930–32	Bresnahan, Roger	1909–12
Blake, Harry	1899	Bressler, Rube	1932
Blake, Sheriff	1937	Bressoud, Ed	1967
Blank, Connie	1909	Brewer, Rod	1990–93
Blasingame, Don	1955–59	Bridges, Marshall	1959–60
Blatnik, Johnny	1950	Bridges, Rocky	1960
Blattner, Buddy	1942	Briggs, Grant	1892
Blaylock, Bob	1956, 1959	Briles, Nelson	1965–70
Blaylock, Gary	1959	Brinkman, Ed	1975
Bliss, John	1908–12	Brock, John	1917–18
Bloomfield, Clyde	1963	Brock, Lou	1964–79
Boardman, Charlie	1915	Brodie, Steve	1892–93
Boever, Joe	1985–86	Broglio, Ernie	1959–64
Bohne, Sammy	1916	Bronkie, Herman	1918
Bokelman, Dick	1951–53	Brosnan, Jim	1958–59
Bolden, Bill	1919	Brottern, Tony	1916, 1918

Broughton, Cal	1885	Byerly, Bud	1943–45
Brown, Buster	1905–07	Byers, Bill	1904
Brown, Ed	1882	Byrne, Bobby	1907–09
Brown, Jim	1915		
Brown, Jimmy	1937–43	**C**	
Brown, Three Finger	1903	Cabrera, Al	1913
Brown, Tom	1895	Cairo, Miguel	2001–03
Browne, Byron	1969	Calero, Kiko	2003–04
Browning, Cal	1960	Calhoun, John	1902
Browning, Pete	1894	Cali, Carmen	2004–05
Brummer, Glenn	1981–84	Callahan, Jim	1898
Brunansky, Tom	1988–90	Camacho, Ernie	1990
Brunet, George	1971	Camnitz, Harry	1911
Brunette, Justin	2000	Camp, Llewellyn	1892
Bruno, Tom	1978–79	Campau, Count	1890
Bryant, Ron	1975	Campbell, Bill	1985
Bucha, Johnny	1948, 1950	Campbell, Billy	1905
Buchek, Jerry	1961, 1963–66	Campbell, Dave	1973
Bucher, Jim	1938	Campbell, Jim	1970
Buckels, Gary	1994	Campisi, Sal	1969–70
Buckley, Dick	1892–94	Cannizzaro, Chris	1960–61
Buelow, Fritz	1899–1900	Canseco, Ozzie	1992–93
Burbrink, Nelson	1955	Capilla, Doug	1976–77
Burch, Al	1906–07	Carabello, Ramon	1995
Burda, Bob	1962, 1971	Carbo, Bernie	1972–73, 1979–80
Burdette, Lew	1963–64	Cardenal, Jose	1970–71
Burgess, Tom	1954	Carleton, Tex	1932–34
Burk, Sandy	1912–13	Carlton, Steve	1965–71
Burke, Jimmy	1899, 1903–05	Carmel, Duke	1959–60, 1963
Burke, Joe	1890	Carpenter, Chris	2004–05
Burke, Leo	1963	Carpenter, Cris	1988–92
Burkett, Jesse	1899–1901	Carpenter, Hick	1892
Burkhart, Ken	1945–48	Carr, Chuck	1992
Burnett, John	1907	Carroll, Clay	1977
Burns, Ed	1912	Carroll, Cliff	1892
Burns, Farmer	1912	Carsey, Kid	1897–98
Burns, Todd	1993	Cartwright, Ed	1890
Burrell, Harry	1891	Caruthers, Bob	1884–87, 1892
Burris, Ray	1986	Castiglione, Pete	1953–54
Burton, Ellis	1958, 1960	Castillo, Alberto	1999
Busby, Mike	1996–99	Cater, Danny	1975
Bush, Guy	1938	Cather, Ted	1912–14
Bushong, Doc	1885–87	Cedeño, Cesar	1985
Busse, Ray	1973	Cedeño, Roger	2004–05
Butler, Art	1914–16	Cepeda, Orlando	1966–68
Butler, John	1904	Chamberlain, Elton	1888–90
Butler, Johnny	1929	Chambers, Bob	1910

Chambers, Cliff	1951–53	Connor, Joe	1895
Chambers, John	1937	Connor, Roger	1894–97
Chant, Charlie	1976	Conroy, Tim	1986–87
Charles, Chappy	1908–09	Conwell, Ed	1911
Cheney, Tom	1957, 1959	Cook, Paul	1891
Childs, Cupid	1899	Coolbaugh, Mike	2002
Childs, Pete	1901	Coolbaugh, Scott	1994
Chittum, Nelson	1958	Cooley, Duff	1893–96
Chlupsa, Bob	1970–71	Cooney, Jimmy	1924–25
Christiansen, Jason	2000–01	Cooper, Mort	1938–45
Ciaffone, Larry	1951	Cooper, Scott	1995
Cicotte, Al	1961	Cooper, Walker	1940–45, 1956–57
Cimoli, Gene	1959	Copeland, Mays	1935
Cimorelli, Frank	1994	Corbett, Joe	1904
Citarelli, Ralph	1983–84	Corhan, Roy	1916
Clapp, Stubby	2001	Cormier, Rheal	1991–94
Clarey, Doug	1976	Corrales, Pat	1966
Clark, Danny	1927	Corridon, Frank	1910
Clark, Jack	1985–87	Cosman, Jim	1966–67
Clark, Jim	1911–12	Costello, John	1988–90
Clark, Mark	1991–92	Coulter, Tom	1969
Clark, Mike	1952–53	Coveney, John	1903
Clark, Phil	1958–59	Cox, Bill	1936
Clark, Will	2000	Cox, Danny	1983–88
Clarke, Josh	1905	Crabtree, Estel	1933, 1941–42
Clarke, Stan	1990	Craig, Roger	1964
Clarkson, Dad	1893–95	Crandall, Doc	1913
Clayton, Royce	1996–98	Crawford, Forrest	1906–07
Clemens, Doug	1960–64	Crawford, Glenn	1945
Clements, Jack	1898	Crawford, Pat	1933–34
Clemons, Lance	1972	Crawford, Willie	1976
Clemons, Verne	1919–24	Creek, Doug	1995
Clendenon, Donn	1972	Creel, Jack	1945
Cleveland, Reggie	1969–73	Creely, Gus	1890
Cloninger, Tony	1972	Creger, Bernie	1947
Clough, Ed	1924–26	Crespi, Creepy	1938–42
Cole, Dick	1951	Criger, Lou	1899–1900
Coleman, John	1895	Crimian, Jack	1951–52
Coleman, Percy	1897	Critchley, Morrie	1882
Coleman, Vince	1985–90	Cromer, Tripp	1993–95
Coleman, Walter	1895	Crooks, John	1892–93, 1898
Coles, Darnell	1995	Crosby, Ed	1970, 1972–73
Collins, Phil	1935	Cross, Jeff	1942, 1946–48
Collins, Ripper	1931–36	Cross, Lave	1898–1900
Collum, Jackie	1951–53, 1956	Cross, Monte	1896–97
Coluccio, Bob	1978	Crotty, Joe	1882
Comiskey, Charlie	1882–89, 1891	Crouch, Bill	1941, 1945

Croushore, Rick	1998–99	DeCinces, Doug	1987
Crowe, George	1959–61	Decker, Frank	1882
Crudale, Mike	2002–03	Decker, George	1898
Cruise, Walton	1914, 1916–19	DeFate, Tony	1917
Crumling, Gene	1945	DeGroff, Rube	1905–06
Cruz, Hector	1973, 1975–77	DeJean, Mike	2003
Cruz, Ivan	2002	DeJesus, Ivan	1985
Cruz, Jose	1970–74	Delahanty, Joe	1907–09
Cruz, Tommy	1973	DeLancey, Bill	1932, 1934–35, 1940
Cuellar, Mike	1964	Delaney, Art	1924
Culver, George	1970	DeLeon, Jose	1988–92
Cumberland, John	1972	DeLeon, Luis	1981
Cunningham, Joe	1954, 1956–61	Delgado, Wilson	2002–03
Cunningham, Ray	1931–32	Del Greco, Bobby	1956
Cuppy, Nig	1899	Delker, Eddie	1929, 1931–32
Currie, Clarence	1902–03	Dell, Wheezer	1912
Currie, Murphy	1916	DeLucia, Rich	1995
Curtis, John	1974–76	Demaree, Frank	1943
Cuthbert, Ned	1882–83	DeMontreville, Lee	1903
		Dennis, Don	1965–66
D		Denny, John	1974–79
D'Acquisto, John	1977	Derringer, Paul	1931–33
Dale, Gene	1911–12	Derry, Russ	1949
Damaska, Jack	1963	DeSa, Joe	1980
Daniels, Pete	1898	DeShields, Delino	1997–98
Daringer, Rolla	1914–15	Devlin, Jim	1888–89
Dark, Al	1956–58	Diaz, Einar	2005
Darling, Dell	1891	Dickerman, Leo	1924–25
Davalillo, Vic	1969–70	Dickson, Murry	1939–40, 1942–43,
Davanon, Jerry	1969–70, 1974, 1977		1946–48, 1956–57
Davis, Curt	1938–40	Diering, Chuck	1947–51
Davis, Eric	1999–2000	Dierker, Larry	1977
Davis, Jumbo	1889–90	DiFelice, Mike	1996–97, 2002
Davis, Jim	1957	Dillard, Pat	1900
Davis, Daisy	1884	Dillhoefer, Pickles	1919–21
Davis, Kiddo	1934	Dimmel, Mike	1979
Davis, Ron	1968	DiPino, Frank	1989–90, 1992
Davis, Spud	1928, 1934–36	Distel, Dutch	1918
Davis, Willie	1975	Dixon, Steve	1993–94
Dawley, Bill	1987	Doak, Bill	1913–24, 1929
Day, Boots	1969	Dockins, George	1945
Day, Pea Ridge	924–25	Dolan, Cozy	1914–15
Dayley, Ken	1984–90	Dolan, John	1893
Deal, Cot	1950, 1954	Dolan, Tom	1883–84, 1888
Dean, Dizzy	1930, 1932–37	Donahue, Red	1895–97
Dean, Paul	1934–39	Donahue, She	1904
Deasley, Pat	1883–84	Donlin, Mike	1899–1900

Donnelly, Blix	1944–46	Eckstein, David	2005
Donnelly, Jim	1890, 1898	Edelen, Joe	1891
Donovan, Patsy	1900–03	Edmonds, Jim	2000–05
Dorr, Bert	1882	Edwards, Johnny	1968
Douglass, Klondike	1896–97	Egan, Wish	1905–06
Douthit, Taylor	1923–31	Ehret, Red	1895
Dowd, Tommy	1893–98	Eldred, Cal	2003–05
Dowling, Dave	1964	Elliott, Harry	1953, 1955
Doyle, Carl	1940	Ellis, Jim	1969
Doyle, Jeff	1983	Ellis, Rube	1909–12
Doyle, John	1882	Ely, Bones	1893–95
Drabowsky, Moe	1971–72	Endicott, Bill	1946
Dressen, Lee	1914	Ennis, Del	1957–58
Dressler, Rob	1978	Enwright, Charlie	1909
Drew, J. D.	1998–2003	Epps, Hal	1938, 1940
Driessen, Dan	1987	Erautt, Eddie	1953
Drissel, Mike	1885	Esper, Duke	1897–98
Druhot, Carl	1906–07	Essegian, Chuck	1959
Duff, Mike	2002	Evans, LeRoy	1897
Duffee, Charlie	1889–90	Evans, Steve	1909–13
Duliba, Bob	1959–60, 1962	Eversgerd, Bryan	1994, 1998
Duncan, Chris	2005	Ewing, Bob	1912
Duncan, Taylor	1977	Ewing, John	1883
Dunham, Wiley	1902	Ewing, Reuben	1921
Dunlap, Grant	1953		
Dunleavy, John	1903–05	**F**	
Dunston, Shawon	1999–2000	Fagin, Fred	1895
Durham, Don	1972	Fairly, Ron	1975–76
Durham, Joe	1959	Falcone, Pete	1976–78
Durham, Leon	1980, 1989	Fallon, George	1943–45
Durocher, Leo	1933–37	Fanok, Harry	1963–64
Duryea, Jesse	1891	Farrell, Doc	1930
Dusak, Erv	1941–42, 1946–51	Farrell, John	1902–05
Dwyer, Frank	1892	Fassero, Jeff	2002–03
Dwyer, Jim	1973–75, 1977–78	Faszholz, Jack	1953
Dyer, Eddie	1922–27	Fenwick, Bobby	1973
		Ferguson, Joe	1976
E		Ferrarese, Don	1962
Eagan, Bill	1891	Fiala, Neil	1981
Earle, Billy	1890	Figueroa, Bien	1992
Earley, Bill	1986	Finley, Chuck	2002
Earnshaw, George	1936	Fiore, Mike	1972
Easton, Jack	1891–92	Fisburn, Sam	1919
Eastwick, Rawly	1977	Fisher, Bob	1918–19
Echols, Johnny	1939	Fisher, Chauncey	1901
Eckersley, Dennis	1996–97	Fisher, Eddie	1973
Eckert, Al	1935	Fisher, Showboat	1930

Fitzgerald, Mike	1988	Gaiser, Fred	1908
Flack, Max	1922–25	Galarraga, Andres	1992
Flanigan, Tom	1958	Gall, John	2005
Flood, Curt	1958–69	Gallego, Mike	1996–97
Flood, Tim	1899	Galloway, Bad News	1912
Flores, Randy	2004–05	Galvin, Pud	1892
Flowers, Ben	1955–56	Gannon, Bill	1898
Flowers, Jake	1923, 1926, 1931–32	Gant, Ron	1996–98
Folkers, Rich	1972–74	Garagiola, Joe	1946–51
Ford, Curt	1985–88	Gardella, Dan	1950
Ford, Hod	1932	Gardner, Glenn	1945
Forsch, Bob	1974–88	Garibaldi, Art	1936
Fossas, Tony	1995–97	Garman, Mike	1974–75
Foster, Alan	1973–74	Garms, Debs	1943–45
Fournier, Jake	1920–22	Garrett, Wayne	1978
Foutz, Dave	1884–87	Gedman, Rich	1991–92
Fowler, Jesse	1924	Gelbert, Charley	1929–32, 1935–36
Francis, Earl	1965	Genins, Frank	1892
Francona, Tito	1965–66	Gerhardt, Joe	1890
Frank, Charlie	1893–94	Gettel, Al	1955
Frankhouse, Fred	1927–30	Gettinger, Tom	1889–90
Franklin, Micah	1997	Getzein, Charlie	1892
Franks, Herman	1939	Geyer, Rube	1910–13
Frascatore, John	1994–95, 1997–98	Giannelli, Ray	1995
Fraser, Willie	1991	Gibson, Bob	1959–75
Frazier, George	1978–80	Gilbert, Billy	1908–09
Frazier, Joe	1954–56	Gilbert, Shawn	1998
Freed, Roger	1977–79	Gilham, George	1920–21
Freeman, Julie	1888	Gilhooley, Frank	1911–12
Freese, Gene	1958	Gilkey, Bernard	1990–95
Freigau, Howard	1922–25	Gill, Jim	1889
Frey, Benny	1932	Gillenwater, Carmen	1940
Frisch, Frankie	1927–37	Gilpatrick, George	1898
Frisella, Dan	1976	Gilson, Hal	1968
Fromme, Art	1906–08	Girardi, Joe	2003
Fulgham, John	1979–80	Giusti, Dave	1969
Fuller, Harry	1891	Glasscock, Jack	1892–93
Fuller, Shorty	1889–91	Glaviano, Tommy	1949–52
Fullis, Chick	1934, 1936	Gleason, Bill	1882–87
Fulmer, Charles	1884	Gleason, Jack	1882–83
Fusselback, Ed	1882	Gleason, Kid	1892–94
Fusselman, Les	1952–53	Glenn, Bob	1920
		Glenn, Harry	1915
		Glenn, John	1960

G

Gaetti, Gary	1996–98	Godby, Danny	1974
Gagliano, Phil	1963–70	Golden, Roy	1910–11
Gainer, Del	1922	Goldsby, Walt	1884

Goldsmith, Hal	1929
Gonzalez, Jose	1984
Gonzalez, Julio	1981–82
Gonzalez, Mike	1915–18, 1924–25, 1931–32
Goodenough, Bill	1893
Goodfellow, Mike	1887
Goodwin, Marv	1917, 1919–22
Gore, George	1892
Gorman, Herb	1952
Gorman, Jack	1883
Gornicki, Hank	1941
Gotay, Julio	1960–62
Grabowski, Al	1929–30
Grady, Mike	1897, 1904–06
Grammas, Alex	1954–56, 1959–62
Granger, Wayne	1968, 1973
Grant, Mudcat	1969
Grater, Mark	1991
Gray, Dick	1959–60
Greason, Bill	1954
Green, David	1981–84, 1987
Green, Gene	1957–59
Green, Scarborough	1997
Grief, Bill	1976
Griessenbeck, Tim	1920
Grieve, Tom	1979
Griffin, Sandy	1893
Griffith, Clark	1891
Grim, Bob	1960
Grimes, Burleigh	1930–31, 1933–34
Grimes, John	1897
Grimm, Charlie	1918
Griner, Dan	1912–16
Grissom, Marv	1959
Groat, Dick	1963–65
Grodzicki, Johnny	1941, 1946–47
Grudzielanek, Mark	2005
Grzenda, Joe	1972
Guerrero, Mario	1975
Guerrero, Pedro	1988–92
Guetterman, Lee	1993
Gulan, Mike	1997
Gumbert, Harry	1941–44
Gunson, Joe	1893
Gutteridge, Don	1936–40
Guzman, Santiago	1969–72

H

Habenicht, Bob	1951
Habyan, John	1994–95
Hackett, Jim	1902–03
Hackman, Luther	2000–02
Haddix, Harvey	1952–56
Hafey, Chick	1924–31
Hageman, Casey	1914
Hagen, Kevin	1983–84
Hague, Joe	1968–72
Hahn, Don	1975
Hahn, Fred	1952
Haid, Hal	1928–30
Haigh, Ed	1892
Haines, Jesse	1920–37
Hall, Charley	1916
Hallahan, Wild Bill	1925–26, 1929–36
Hallman, Bill	1897
Hamilton, Dave	1978
Haney, Fred	1929
Haney, Larry	1973
Harding, Lou	1886
Haren, Dan	2003–04
Harley, Dick	1897–98
Harmon, Bob	1909–13
Harmon, Chuck	1956–57
Harper, Brian	1985
Harper, George	1928
Harper, Jack	1900–01
Harrell, Ray	1935, 1937–38
Harris, Vic	1976
Hart, Bill	1896–97
Hart, Bo	2003–05
Hart, Bob	1890
Hartenstein, Chuck	1970
Hartman, Fred	1897, 1902
Hassler, Andy	1984–85
Hatton, Grady	1956
Hauser, Arnold	1910–13
Hawke, Bill	1892–93
Hawley, Pink	1892–94
Hazleton, Doc	1902
Healy, Francis	1934
Hearn, Bunny	1910–11
Hearn, Jim	1947–50
Heath, Mike	1986
Heathcote, Cliff	1918–22

Heidemann, Jack	1974	Holbert, Aaron	1996
Heidrick, Emmett	1899–1901	Holland, Mul	1929
Heinkel, Don	1969	Holly, Ed	1906–07
Heintzelman, Tom	1973–74	Holm, Wattie	1924–29, 1932
Heise, Bob	1974	Holmes, Darren	2000
Heise, Clarence	1934	Holmes, Ducky	1898
Hemond, Scott	1995	Holmes, Ducky	1906
Hemphill, Charlie	1899	Hood, Don	1906
Hemus, Solly	1949–56, 1959	Hopkins, Slim	1907
Hendrick, George	1978–84	Hopp, Johnny	1939–45
Hendrick, Harvey	1932	Hopper, Bill	1913–14
Henke, Tom	1995	Horner, Bob	1988
Henshaw, Roy	1938	Hornsby, Rogers	1915–26, 1933
Hentgen, Pat	2000	Horstman, Oscar	1917–19
Hermanson, Dustin	2001, 2003	Horton, Rick	1984–87, 1989–90
Hernandez, Carlos	2000	Householder, Paul	1984
Hernandez, Keith	1974–83	Houseman, John	1897
Herndon, Larry	1974	Howard, David	1998–99
Herr, Ed	1888, 1890	Howard, Doug	1975
Herr, Tom	1979–88	Howard, Earl	1918
Hertweck, Neal	1952	Howard, Thomas	1999–2000
Heusser, Ed	1935–36	Howe, Art	1984–85
Heydon, Mike	1901	Howell, Richard	1912
Hickman, Jim	1974	Howerton, Bill	1949–51
Hicks, Jim	1969	Hoy, Dummy	1891
Higginbotham, Irv	1906, 1908–09	Hrabosky, Al	1970–77
Higgins, Bill	1890	Hudgens, Jimmy	1923
Higgins, Dennis	1971–72	Hudler, Rex	1990–92
Higgins, Festus	1909–10	Hudson, Charles	1972
High, Andy	1928–31	Hudson, Nat	1886–89
Hildebrand, Palmer	1913	Huelsman, Frank	1897
Hilgendorf, Tom	1969–70	Huggins, Miller	1910–16
Hill, Carmen	1929–30	Hughes, Dick	1966–68
Hill, Hugh	1904	Hughes, Terry	1973
Hill, Ken	1988–91, 1995	Hughes, Tom	1959
Hill, Marc	1973–74	Hughey, Jim	1898, 1900
Hilton, Howard	1990	Hulett, Tim	1995
Himes, John	1905–06	Hulswitt, Rudy	1909–10
Hitchcock, Sterling	2003	Humphreys, Bob	1963–64
Hitt, Bruce	1917	Hunt, Ben	1913
Hobbie, Glenn	1964	Hunt, Joel	1931–32
Hock, Ed	1920	Hunt, Randy	1985
Hodnett, Charlie	1883	Hunt, Ron	1974
Hoelskoetter, Art	1905–08	Hunter, Brian	1998
Hoerner, Joe	1966–69	Hunter, Herb	1921
Hogan, Eddie	1882	Huntz, Steve	1967, 1969
Hogan, Marty	1894–95	Huntzinger, Walter	1926

Hurdle, Clint	1986
Hutchinson, Bill	1897
Hutchinson, Chad	2001
Hutchinson, Ira	1940–41
Hyatt, Ham	1915
Hynes, Pat	1903

I

Iorg, Dane	1977–84
Irwin, Walt	1921
Isringhausen, Jason	2002–05

J

Jablonski, Ray	1953–54, 1959
Jackson, Al	1966–67
Jackson, Danny	1995–97
Jackson, Larry	1955–62
Jackson, Mike	1971
Jacobs, Mike	1919–20
Jacobs, Tony	1955
James, Bob	1909
James, Charlie	1960–64
James, Mike	2000–01
Janvrin, Hal	1919–21
Jarvis, Kevin	2005
Jasper, Hi	1916
Jaster, Larry	1965–68
Javier, Julian	1960–71
Jeffcoat, Hal	1959
Jefferies, Gregg	1993–94
Jensen, Marcus	1999
Jiminez, Jose	1998–99
Johnson, Adam	1918
Johnson, Billy	1951–53
Johnson, Bob	1969
Johnson, Darrell	1980
Johnson, Jerry	1970
Johnson, Ken	1947–50
Johnson, Lance	1987
Johnson, Si	1936–38
Johnson, Syl	1926–33
Johnson, Tyler	2005
Jones, Cowboy	1899–1901
Jones, Gordon	1954–56
Jones, Howie	1921
Jones, Nippy	1946–51
Jones, Red	1940

Jones, Sam	1957–58, 1963
Jones, Tim	1988–93
Jonnard, Buster	1929
Jordan, Brian	1992–98
Jorgensen, Mike	1984–85
Jose, Felix	1990–92
Joseph, Kevin	2002
Journell, Jimmy	2003, 2005
Judy, Lyle	1935
Jurisch, Al	1944–45
Jutze, Skip	1972

K

Kaat, Jim	1980–83
Kane, Jere	1890
Karger, Ed	1906–08
Kamuth, Jason	2001
Kasko, Eddie	1957–58
Katt, Ray	1956, 1958–59
Kaufmann, Tony	1927–28, 1930–31, 1935
Kavanagh, Marty	1918
Kazak, Eddie	1948–52
Keely, Bob	1944–45
Keen, Vic	1926–27
Keener, Joe	1982–83
Keister, Bill	1900
Kelleher, John	1912
Kelleher, Mick	1972–73, 1975
Kellner, Alex	1959
Kellum, Win	1905
Kelly, Bill	1910
Kelly, John	1907
Kelly, Pat	1998
Kemmler, Rudy	1886
Kennedy, Adam	1999
Kennedy, Jim	1970
Kennedy, Terry	1978–80
Keough, Marty	1985
Kepshire, Kurt	1984–86
Kerins, John	1890
Kernek, George	1965–66
Kessinger, Don	1976–77
Kile, Darryl	2000–02
Kilgus, Pete	1983
Kimball, Newt	1940
Kime, Hal	1920

Kimmick, Walt	1919	Lahti, Jeff	1982–86
Kinder, Ellis	1956	Lake, Eddie	1939–41
King, Charlie	1959	Lake, Steve	1986–88
King, Curtis	1997–99	Lally, Bud	1897
King, Jim	1957	Lamabe, Jack	1967
King, Lynn	1935–36, 1939	Lamline, Fred	1915
King, Ray	2005	Lampkin, Tom	1997–98
King, Silver	1887–89	Lancaster, Les	1993
Kinlock, Walt	1895	Landrith, Hobie	1957–58
Kinslow, Tom	1899	Landrum, Don	1960–62
Kinzer, Matt	1989	Landrum, Tito	1980–87
Kinzey, Walt	1895	Lang, Don	1948
Kircher, Mike	1920–21	Lanier, Max	1938–46, 1949–51
Kissinger, Bill	1895–97	Lankford, Ray	1990–2001, 2004
Klein, Lou	1943, 1945–46, 1949	LaPalme, Paul	1955–56
Kleinke, Nub	1945, 1947	LaPoint, Dave	1981–84, 1987
Kline, Ron	1960	LaPointe, Ralph	1948
Kline, Steve	2001–04	Lamore, Bob	1918
Kling, Rudy	1902	Lary, Lyn	1939
Klusman, Billy	1890	Lasseter, Don	1957
Kluttz, Clyde	1946	Latham, Arlie	1883–89, 1896
Knicely, Alan	1986	LaValliere, Mike	1985–86
Knight, Jack	1922	Lavan, Doc	1919–24
Knode, Mike	1920	Lavin, Johnny	1884
Knouff, Ed	1887–88	Lawless, Tom	1985–88
Knowles, Darold	1979–80	Lawrence, Brooks	1954–55
Koeningsmark, Willis	1919	Leahy, Tom	1905
Kolb, Gary	1960, 1962–63	Lee, Leron	1969–71
Konetchy, Ed	1907–13	Lee, Manuel	1995
Konstanty, Jim	1956	Lentine, Jim	1978–80
Kopshaw, George	1923	Leonard (first name unknown)	1892
Koy, Ernie	1940–41	Lersch, Barry	1974
Krausse, Lew	1973	Leslie, Roy	1919
Krehmeyer, Charlie	1884–85	Lewandowski, Dan	1951
Krieger, Kurt	1949, 1951	Lewis, Bill	1933
Krist, Howie	1937–38, 1941–43, 1946	Lewis, Fred	1883–84
		Lewis, Johnny	1964
Krueger, Otto	1900–02	Lezcano, Sixto	1981
Kubiak, Ted	1971	Liddle, Don	1956
Kuehne, Willie	1892	Lillard, Gene	1940
Kurosaki, Ryan	1975	Lillis, Bob	1961
Kurowski, Whitey	1941–49	Lincoln, Mike	2004
Kuzava, Bob	1957	Lindell, Johnny	1950
		Lindeman, Jim	1986–89
L		Lindsey, Jim	1929–34
Laga, Mike	1986–88	Lint, Royce	1954
LaGrow, Lerrin	1976	Lintz, Larry	1975

Linzy, Frank	1970–71
Little, Jeff	1980
Little, Mark	1998
Littlefield, Dick	1956
Littlefield, John	1980
Littlejohn, Carlisle	1927–28
Litwhiler, Danny	1943–44, 1946
Livingston, Paddy	1917
Livingstone, Scott	1997
Locke, Larry	1962
Lockman, Whitey	1956
Loftus, Tom	1883
Lohrman, Bill	1942
Long, Jeoff	1963–64
Long, Tommy	1915–17
Looper, Braden	1998
Lopatka, Art	1945
Lopez, Aurelio	1978
Lotz, Joe	1918
Lovenguth, Lynn	1957
Lovett, John	1903
Lowdermilk, Grover	1909, 1911
Lowdermilk, Lou	1911–12
Lowe, Sean	1997–98
Lowrey, Peanuts	1950–54
Lucid, Con	1897
Ludwick, Eric	1996–97
Ludwig, Bill	1908
Luebbers, Larry	1999
Luna, Hector	2004–05
Luna, Memo	1954
Lush, Ernie	1910
Lush, Johnny	1907–10
Lyons, Bill	1983–84
Lyons, Denny	1891, 1895
Lyons, George	1920
Lyons, Harry	1887–88
Lyons, Hersh	1941

M

Mabe, Bob	1958
Mabry, John	1994–98, 2001, 2004–05
MacKenzie, Ken	1963
Mackinson, Johnny	1955
Maclin, Lonnie	1993
Macon, Max	1938

Magee, Bill	1901
Magee, Lee	1911–14
Maglie, Sal	1958
Magrane, Joe	1987–90, 1992–93
Mahaffey, Art	1966
Mahoney, Mike	1898
Mahoney, Mike	2005
Mails, Duster	1925–26
Mallory, Jim	1945
Mancuso, Gus	1928, 1930–32, 1941–42
Mann, Les	1921–23
Mansell, Tom	1883
Manrique, Fred	1986
Maranville, Rabbit	1926–27
Marbet, Walt	1913
Marion, Marty	1940–50
Maris, Roger	1967–68
Marolewski, Fred	1953
Marquis, Jason	2004–05
Marrero, Eli	1997–2003
Marshall, Charlie	1941
Marshall, Doc	1906–08
Marshall, Joe	1906
Martin, Freddie	1946, 1949–50
Martin, John	1980–83
Martin, Morrie	1957–58
Martin, Pepper	1928, 1930–40, 1944
Martin, Stu	1936–40
Martinez, Marty	1972
Martinez, Silvio	1978–81
Martinez, Teddy	1975
Martinez, Tino	2002–03
Mason, Ernie	1894
Matheny, Mike	2000–04
Mathews, Greg	1986–88, 1990
Mathews, T. J.	1995–97, 2001
Matthews, Mike	2000–02
Mattick, Wally	1918
Mauch, Gene	1952
Maupin, Harry	1898
Maxvill, Dal	1962–72
May, Jakie	1917–21
McAdams, Jack	1911
McAuley, Ike	1917
McBride, Bake	1973–77
McBride, George	1905–06

McBride, Pete	1899	McSorley, Trick	1886
McCaffrey, Harry	1882–83	McSweeney, Paul	1891
McCarthy, Joe	1906	McWilliams, Larry	1988
McCarthy, Tommy	1888–91	Meadows, Lee	1915–19
McCarty, Lew	1920–21	Medwick, Joe	1932–40, 1947–48
McCarver, Tim	1959–61, 1963–69, 1973–74	Meek, Dad	1889–90
McCauley, Pat	1893	Mejia, Miguel	1996
McClure, Bob	1991–92	Mejia, Roberto	1997
McCool, Billy	1970	Mejias, Sam	1976
McCormick, Jim	1892	Melendez, Luis	1970–76
McCurdy, Harry	1922–23	Melter, Steve	1909
McDaniel, Lindy	1955–62	Menze, Ted	1918
McDaniel, Von	1957–58	Mercer, John	1912
McDermott, Mickey	1961	Mercker, Kent	1998–99
McDermott, Mike	1897	Merritt, Lloyd	1957
McDonald, Keith	2000–01	Mertes, Sam	1906
McDougal, John	1895–96	Mesner, Steve	1941
McDougal, Sandy	1905	Metzger, Butch	1977
McEnaney, Will	1979	Mickelson, Ed	1950
McEwing, Joe	1998–99	Mierkowicz, Ed	1950
McFadden, Guy	1895	Miggins, Larry	1948, 1952
McFarland, Ed	1896–97	Mikkelsen, Pete	1968
McGann, Dan	1900–01	Miksis, Eddie	1957
McGarr, Chippy	1888	Millard, Frank	1890
McGee, Bill	1935–41	Miller, Bob	1957, 1959–61
McGee, Willie	1982–90, 1996–99	Miller, Charlie	1913–14
McGeehan, Dan	1911	Miller, Doggie	1894–95
McGill, Willie	1891	Miller, Dots	1914–17, 1919
McGinley, Jim	1904–05	Miller, Dusty	1890, 1899
McGinnis, Jumbo	1882–86	Miller, Eddie	1950
McGlothlen, Lynn	1974–76	Miller, Elmer	1912
McGlynn, Stoney	1906–08	Miller, Kohly	1892
McGraw, Bob	1927	Miller, Stu	1952–54, 1956
McGraw, John	1900	Milligan, Jocko	1888–89
McGraw, Tom	1997	Mills, Buster	1934
McGriff, Terry	1994	Milton, Larry	1903
McGrillis, Mark	1892	Minoso, Minnie	1962
McGwire, Mark	1997–2001	Mitchell, Bobby	1882
McHenry, Austin	1918–22	Mitchell, Charlie	1928–30
McIvor, Otto	1911	Mize, Johnny	1936–41
McKay, Cody	2004–05	Mizell, Vinegar Bend	1952–53, 1956–60
McKean, Ed	1899	Moford, Herb	1955
McLaurin, Ralph	1908	Mohler, Mike	1999–2000
McLean, Larry	1904, 1913	Molina, Gabe	2002–03
McNertney, Jerry	1971–72	Molina, Yadier	2004–05
McQuaid, Marty	1891	Mollwitz, Fritz	1919
		Moon, Wally	1954–58

Mooney, Jim	1933–34
Moore, Donnie	1980
Moore, Gene	1933–35
Moore, Randy	1937
Moore, Terry	1935–42, 1946–48
Moore, Tommy	1975
Moore, Whitey	1942
Morales, Jerry	1978
Moran, Charley	1903, 1908
More, Forrest	1909
Morgan, Bobby	1956
Morgan, Eddie	1936
Morgan, Joe	1964
Morgan, Mike	1995–96
Moriarty, Gene	1892
Morris, John	1986–90
Morris, Matt	1997–98, 2000–05
Morris, Walter	1908
Morse, Hap	1911
Morton, Charlie	1882
Moryn, Walt	1960–61
Mowrey, Mike	1909–13
Moyer, Jamie	1991
Mueller, Heinie	1920–26
Muffett, Billy	1957–58
Mulder, Mark	2005
Mullane, Tony	1883
Mumphrey, Jerry	1974–79
Munger, George	1943–44, 1946–52
Munyan, John	1890–91
Murris, Les	1936
Mura, Steve	1982
Murch, Simmy	1904–05
Murchison, Tim	1917
Murdoch, Wilbur	1908
Murphy, Ed	1901–03
Murphy, Howard	1909
Murphy, Joe	1886–87
Murphy, John	1902
Murphy, Mike	1912
Murphy, Morgan	1896–97
Murphy, Rob	1993–94
Murphy, Tom	1973
Murray, Red	1906–08
Musial, Stan	1941–44, 1946–63
Myers, Bert	1896
Myers, Hy	1923–25
Myers, Lynn	1938–39

N

Nagy, Mike	1973
Nahem, Sam	1941
Narron, Sam	1935, 1942–43
Nash, Ken	1914
Naymick, Mike	1944
Neale, Joe	1890–91
Nelson, Mel	1960, 1968–69
Nelson, Rocky	1949–51, 1956
Nicol, George	1890
Nicol, Hugh	1883–86
Nichols, Art	1901–03
Nichols, Kid	1904–05
Niebergall, Charlie	1921, 1923–24
Niedenfuer, Tom	1990
Niehaus, Dick	1913–15
Niehoff, Bert	1918
Nieman, Bob	1960–61
Nieto, Tom	1984–85
Niland, Tom	1896
Noonan, Pete	1906–07
Noren, Irv	1957–59
Norman, Fred	1970–71
North, Lou	1917, 1920–24
Northey, Ron	1947–49
Nossek, Joe	1969–70
Nuñez, Abraham	2005
Nunn, Howie	1959
Nye, Rich	1970

O

Oakes, Rebel	1910–13
Oberbeck, Henry	1883
Oberkfell, Ken	1977–84
O'Brien, Dan	1978–79
O'Brien, Johnny	1958
O'Connor, Jack	1899–1900
O'Connor, Paddy	1914
O'Dea, Ken	1942–46
O'Farrell, Bob	1925–28, 1933, 1935
Ogrodowski, Bruce	1936–37
O'Hara, Bill	1910
O'Hara, Tom	1906–07
Ohme, Kevin	2003
O'Leary, Charley	1913

Oliva, Jose	1995	Parker, Roy	1919
Olivares, Ed	1960–61	Parmelee, Roy	1938
Olivares, Omar	1990–94	Parrett, Jeff	1995–96
Oliver, Darren	1998–99	Parrott, Tom	1896
Oliver, Gene	1959, 1961–63	Partenheimer, Stan	1945
Olivo, Diomedes	1963	Pasquella, Mike	1919
Olmstead, Al	1980	Patterson, Daryl	1971
O'Neal, Randy	1987–88	Patton, Harry	1910
O'Neill, Dannie	1893	Paulette, Gene	1917–19
O'Neill, Jack	1902–03	Paulsen, Gil	1925
O'Neill, Mike	1901–04	Paynter, George	1894
O'Neill, Tip	1884–89, 1891	Pearce, George	1917
Oquendo, Jose	1986–95	Pearce, Josh	2002–04
Ordaz, Luis	1997–99	Pears, Frank	1893
Orengo, Joe	1939–40	Pearson, Alex	1902
Orosco, Jesse	2000	Pearson, Jason	2003
O'Rourke, Charlie	1959	Peel, Homer	1927, 1930
O'Rourke, Patsy	1908	Peete, Charlie	1956
O'Rourke, Tim	1894	Peitz, Heinie	1892–95, 1913
Orsatti, Ernie	1927–35	Peitz, Joe	1894
Ortega, William	2001	Pena, Geronimo	1990–95
Osborne, Donovan	1992–93, 1995–99	Peña, Tony	1987–89
Osteen, Champ	1908–09	Pendleton, Terry	1984–90
Osteen, Claude	1974	Pepper, Ray	1932–33
Otten, Jim	1980–81	Perdue, Hub	1914–15
Otten, Joe	1895	Perez, Eduardo	1999–2000, 2002–03
Owen, Mickey	1937–40	Perez, Mike	1990–94
Ownbey, Rick	1984, 1988	Perritt, Pol	1912–14
		Perry, Gerald	1991–95
P		Perry, Pat	1985–87
Pabst, Ed	1890	Perlica, Bill	1921–23
Packard, Gene	1917–18	Peters, Steve	1987–89
Padden, Dick	1901	Petkovsek, Mark	1995–98
Padgett, Don	1937–41	Pfeffer, Jeff	1921–24
Pagnozzi, Tom	1987–98	Phelps, Ed	1909–10
Paine, Phil	1958	Phillips, Ed	1953
Painter, Lance	1997–99, 2003	Phillips, Mike	1977–80
Palacios, Vicente	1994–95	Phyle, Bill	1906
Palmer, Lowell	1972	Piche, Ron	1966
Palmeiro, Orlando	2003	Pickett, Charlie	1910
Papai, Al	1948, 1950	Pinckney, George	1892
Papi, Stan	1974	Pinson, Vada	1969
Pappas, Erik	1993–94	Pippen, Cotton	1936
Paquette, Craig	1999–2001	Plantier, Phil	1997
Parent, Freddy	1899	Plodinec, Tim	1972
Paris, Kelly	1892	Poholsky, Tom	1950–51, 1954–56
Parker, Harry	1970–71, 1975	Polanco, Placido	1998–2002

Politte, Cliff	1998
Pollet, Howie	1941–43, 1946–51
Popp, Bill	1902
Porter, Colin	2004
Porter, Darrell	1981–85
Porter, J. W.	1959
Potter, Mike	1976–77
Potter, Nels	1936
Powell, Jack	1899–1901
Power, Ted	1989
Presko, Joe	1951–54
Proly, Mike	1976
Puccinelli, George	1930, 1932
Pujols, Albert	2001–05
Pulsipher, Bill	2005
Purkey, Bob	1965
Puttman, Ambrose	1906

Q

Quest, Joe	1883–84
Quinlan, Finners	1913
Quinn, Jack	1893–96, 1898, 1900
Quirk, Jamie	1983
Quisenberry, Dan	1988–89

R

Radebaugh, Roy	1911
Rader, Dave	1977
Radinsky, Scott	1999–2000
Raffensberger, Ken	1939
Raggio, Brady	1997–98
Rajsich, Gary	1984
Raleigh, John	1909–10
Ramirez, Milt	1970–71
Ramsey, Mike	1978, 1980–84
Ramsey, Toad	1889–90
Rand, Dick	1953, 1955
Raschi, Vic	1954–55
Rasmussen, Eric	1975–76, 1982–83
Raub, Tommy	1906
Rayford, Floyd	1983
Raymond, Bugs	1907–08
Reames, Britt	2000
Rebel, Art	1945
Redding, Phil	1912–13
Reed, Milt	1911
Reed, Ron	1975

Reeder, Bill	1949
Reese, Jimmy	1932
Reilly, Tom	1908–09
Reinhart, Art	1919, 1925–28
Reis, Jack	1911
Reitz, Ken	1972–75, 1977–80
Renteria, Edgar	1999–2004
Repass, Bob	1939
Repulski, Rip	1953–56
Rettger, George	1891
Reuss, Jerry	1969–71
Reyes, Al	2004–05
Reyes, Anthony	2005
Reynolds, Bob	1971
Reynolds, Ken	1975
Rhem, Flint	1924–28, 1930–32, 1934, 1936
Rhoads, Bob	1903
Rhodes, Charlie	1906, 1908–09
Ribant, Dennis	1969
Rice, Del	1945–55, 1960
Rice, Hal	1948–53
Richard, Clyde	2000
Richard, Lee	1976
Richardson, Bill	1901
Richardson, Gordie	1964
Richert, Pete	1974
Richmond, Don	1951
Ricketts, Dave	1963, 1965, 1967–69
Ricketts, Dick	1959
Ricks, John	1891, 1894
Rieger, Elmer	1910
Riggert, Joe	1914
Riggs, Lew	1934
Rincon, Andy	1980–82
Ring, Jimmy	1927
Riviere, Tink	1921
Roberts, Skipper	1913
Robinson, Hank	1914–15
Robinson, Kerry	2001–03
Robinson, Wilbert	1900
Robinson, Yank	1885–89, 1891
Roche, Jack	1914–15, 1917
Rodriguez, John	2005
Rodriguez, Jose	2000, 2002
Rodriguez, Nerio	2002
Rodriguez, Rich	1994–95

Roe, Preacher	1938	Scheinblum, Richie	1974
Roettger, Wally	1927–29, 1931	Schindler, Bill	1920
Rojas, Cookie	1970	Schmidt, Freddy	1944, 1946–47
Rojek, Stan	1951	Schmidt, Walter	1925
Rolen, Scott	2002–05	Schmidt, Willard	1952–53, 1965–67
Rolling, Ray	1912	Schoendienst, Red	1945–56, 1961–63
Romano, Johnny	1967	Schofield, Dick	1953–58, 1968, 1971
Romonosky, John	1953	Schreckengost, Ossee	1899
Ronan, Marc	1993	Schriver, Pop	1901
Roof, Gene	1981–83	Schulte, Heinie	1927, 1936
Roque, Jorge	1970–72	Schulte, Johnny	1927
Roseman, Chief	1890	Schultz, John	1891
Rothrock, Jack	1934–35	Schulz, Walt	1920
Royer, Stan	1991–94	Schumaker, Skip	2005
Rucker, Dave	1983–84	Schupp, Ferdie	1919–21
Rudolph, Ken	1975–78	Scoffic, Lou	1936
Russell, Jack	1940	Scott, George	1920
Russell, Paul	1894	Scott, Tony	1977–81
Ryan, J.	1895	Seabol, Scott	2005
Ryan, John	1901–03	Seaman, Kim	1979–80
Ryba, Mike	1935–38	Segui, Diego	1972–73
		Sell, Epp	1922–23
S		Selph, Carey	1929
Sabo, Chris	1995	Sessi, Walter	1941, 1946
Sadecki, Ray	1960–66, 1975	Seward, George	1882
Sadowski, Bob	1960	Sexton, Jimmy	1893
Salas, Mark	1984	Shannon, Mike	1962–70
Sallee, Slim	1908–16	Shannon, Spike	1904–06
Samuls, Ike	1895	Shannon, Wally	1959–60
Sanchez, Orlando	1981–83	Shantz, Bobby	1962–64
Sanders, Ray	1942–45	Shaw, Al	1907–09
Sanders, Reggie	2004–05	Shaw, Don	1971–72
Sanders, Wes	1903–04	Shay, Danny	1904–05
Santana, Rafael	1983	Shea, Gerry	1905
Santorini, Al	1971–73	Sheaffer, Danny	1995–97
Sarni, Bill	1951–52, 1954–56	Sheckard, Jimmy	1913
Saturria, Luis	2000–01	Sheehan, Bill	1895–96
Sauer, Ed	1949	Shepardson, Ray	1924
Sauer, Hank	1956	Sherdel, Bill	1918–30, 1932
Savage, Ted	1965–67	Sherrill, Tim	1990–91
Sawatski, Carl	1960–63	Shields, Charlie	1907
Scarsone, Steve	1997	Shields, Vince	1924
Schaffer, Jimmie	1961–62	Shinners, Ralph	1925
Schang, Bobby	1927	Shirley, Bob	1981
Schappert, John	1882	Shotton, Burt	1919–23
Scheffing, Bob	1951	Shoun, Clyde	1938–42
Schieb, Carl	1954	Shoupe, John	1882

Shugart, Frank	1893–94	Speier, Chris	1984
Siebert, Dick	1937–38	Spencer, Daryl	1960–61
Siebert, Sonny	1974	Spezio, Ed	1964–68
Simmons, Curt	1960–66	Spinks, Scipio	1972–73
Simmons, Ted	1968–80	Sprague, Ed	1973
Simontacchi, Jason	2002–04	Spring, Jack	1964
Simpson, Dick	1968	Springer, Russ	2003
Sisler, Dick	1946–47, 1952–53	Sprinz, Joe	1933
Sizemore, Ted	1971–75	Stainback, Tuck	1938
Skinner, Bob	1964–66	Staley, Gerry	1947–54
Slade, Gordon	1933	Staley, Harry	1895
Slattery, Jack	1906	Stallard, Tracy	1965–66
Slaughter, Enos	1938–42, 1946–53	Stallcup, Virgil	1952–53
Slocumb, Heathcliff	1999–2000	Standridge, Pete	1911
Smiley, Bill	1882	Stanky, Eddie	1952–53
Smith, Bill	1958–59	Stanton, Harry	1900
Smith, Bob	1957	Starr, Ray	1932
Smith, Bobby Gene	1957–59, 1962	Stechschulte, Gene	2000–02
Smith, Bryn	1990–92	Steele, Bill	1910–14
Smith, Bud	2002–02	Steele, Bob	1916–17
Smith, Charley	1966	Stein, Bob	1972–73
Smith, Earl	1928–30	Stenzel, Jake	1898–99
Smith, Frank	1956	Stephens, Ray	1990–91
Smith, Fred	1917	Stephenson, Bobby	1955
Smith, Germany	1898	Stephenson, Garrett	1999–2000, 2002–03
Smith, Hal	1956–61	Stewart, Stuffy	1916–17
Smith, Jack	1915–26	Stinson, Bob	1971
Smith, Jud	1893	Stivetts, Jack	1889–91
Smith, Keith	1979–80	Stobbs, Chuck	1958
Smith, Lee	1990–93	Stock, Milt	1919–23
Smith, Lonnie	1982–85	Stone, Dean	1959
Smith, Ozzie	1982–96	Stone, Tige	1923
Smith, Reggie	1974–76	Storke, Alan	1909
Smith, Tom	1898	Stottlemyre, Todd	1996–98
Smith, Travis	2002	Stout, Allyn	1931–33
Smith, Wally	1911–12	Street, Gabby	1931
Smith, Willie	1994	Strief, George	1883–84
Smoot, Homer	1902–06	Stricker, Cub	1892
Smyth, Red	1917–18	Stripp, Joe	1938
Snyder, Frank	1912–19, 1927	Struve, Al	1884
Sodowsky, Clint	1999	Stuart, Johnny	1922–25
Soff, Ray	1986–87	Stuper, John	1982–84
Solomon, Eddie	1976	Sudhoff, Willie	1897–1901
Sorensen, Lary	1981	Sudgen, Joe	1898
Sosa, Elias	1975	Sullivan, Dan	1885
Sothoron, Allen	1924–26	Sullivan, Harry	1909
Southworth, Billy	1926–27, 1929	Sullivan, Joe	1896

Sullivan, Sleeper	1882–83	Thompson, Gus	1906
Sullivan, Suter	1898	Thompson, Mark	1999–2000
Summers, Kid	1893	Thompson, Mike	1973–74
Sunkel, Tom	1937, 1939	Thompson, Milt	1989–1992
Suppan, Jeff	2004–05	Thornton, John	1892
Surkont, Max	1956	Tiefanauer, Bobby	1952, 1955, 1961
Sutcliffe, Rick	1994	Timlin, Mike	2000–02
Sutherland, Gary	1978	Tinning, Bud	1935
Sutter, Bruce	1981–84	Tolan, Bobby	1965–68
Sutthoff, Jack	1899	Tomko, Brett	2003
Sutton, Johnny	1977	Toney, Fred	1923
Sutton, Larry	2000–01	Toporcer, Specs	1921–28
Sweeney, Mark	1995–97	Torre, Joe	1969–74
Sweeney, Pete	1889–90	Torrez, Mike	1067–71
Swindells, Charlie	1904	Toth, Paul	1962
Swisher, Steve	1978–80	Trekell, Harry	1913
Sykes, Bob	1979–81	Triplett, Coaker	1941–43
Sylvester, Lou	1887	Trost, Mike	1890
		Trotter, Bill	1944
		Tucker, Tommy	1898

T

Tabaka, Jeff	2001	Tudor, John	1985–88, 1990
Taguchi, So	2002–05	Tuero, Oscar	1918–20
Tamargo, John	1976–78	Tunnell, Lee	1987
Tate, Lee	1958–59	Turner, Tuck	1896–98
Tatis, Fernando	1998–2000	Twineham, Old Hoss	1893–94
Taussig, Don	1961	Tyson, Mike	1972–79
Tavarez, Julian	2004–05		

U

Taylor, Carl	1970	Uecker, Bob	1964–65
Taylor, Ed	1903	Underwood, Tom	1977
Taylor, Jack	1898	Urban, Jack	1959
Taylor, Jack	1904–06	Urbani, Tom	1993–96
Taylor, Joe	1958	Urrea, John	1977–80
Taylor, Ron	1963–65	Ury, Lou	1903
Teachout, Bud	1932		

V

Tebeau, Patsy	1899–1900		
Templeton, Garry	1976–81	Valenzuela, Benny	1958
Tenace, Gene	1981–82	Valenzuela, Fernando	1997
Terlecky, Greg	1975	Vance, Dazzy	1933–34
Terry, Scott	1987–91	Van Dyke, Bill	1892
Terwillinger, Wayne	1932	Vann, John	1913
Tewksbury, Bob	1989–94	Van Noy, Jay	1951
Thacker, Moe	1963	Van Slyke, Andy	1983–86
Thevenow, Tommy	1924–28	Verban, Emil	1944–46
Thielman, Jake	1905–06	Veres, Dave	2000–02
Thomas, Roy	1978–80	Vergez, Johnny	1936
Thomas, Tom	1899–1900	Vick, Ernie	1922, 1924–26
Thompson, Brad	2005		

Villanueva, Hector	1993
Viña, Fernando	2000–03
Vines, Bob	1924
Virdon, Bill	1955–56
Visner, Joe	1891
Von Ohlen, Dave	1983–84
Voss, Bill	1972
Vuckovich, Pete	1978–80

W

Wade, Ben	1954
Wagner, Leon	1960
Wainhouse, Dave	2000
Wainwright, Adam	2005
Walker, Bill	1933–36
Walker, Duane	1988
Walker, Harry	1940–43, 1946–47, 1950–51, 1955
Walker, Joe	1923
Walker, Larry	2004–05
Walker, Oscar	1882
Walker, Roy	1921–22
Walker, Tom	1976
Wallace, Bobby	1899–1901, 1917–18
Wallace, Mike	1975–76
Waller, Elliott	1980
Walling, Denny	1988–90
Ward, Dick	1935
Warneke, Lon	1937–42
Warner, John	1905
Warwick, Bill	1925–26
Warwick, Carl	1961–62, 1964–65
Washburn, Ray	1961–69
Waslewski, Gary	1969
Waterbury, Steve	1976
Watkins, George	1930–33
Watson, Allen	1993–95
Watson, Mitt	1916–17
Weaver, Art	1902–03
Webb, Skeeter	1932
Wehmeier, Herm	1956–58
Weiland, Bob	1937–40
Welch, Curt	1885–87
Wells, Jake	1890
Werden, Perry	1892–93
Werle, Bill	1952
Westlake, Wally	1951–52

Weyhing, Gus	1900
Wheeler, Dick	1918
Wheeler, Harry	1884
Whelan, Jim	1913
Whisenant, Pete	1955
Whistler, Lew	1893
White, Ade	1937
White, Bill	1888
White, Bill	1959–65, 1969
White, Ernie	1940–43
White, Gabe	2005
White, Hal	1953–54
White, Jerry	1986
White, Rick	2002
Whitehead, Burgess	1933–35
Whiten, Mark	1993–94
Whitfield, Fred	1962
Whitney, Art	1891
Whitrock, Bill	1890
Whitted, Possum	1912–14
Wicker, Bob	1901–03
Widger, Chris	2003
Wight, Bill	1958
Wigington, Fred	1923
Wilber, Del	1946–49
Wilhelm, Hoyt	1957
Wilie, Denney	1911–12
Wilkins, Rick	2000
Wilks, Ted	1944–51
Williams, Jimy	1966–67
Williams, Otto	1902–03
Williams, Stan	1971
Williams, Steamboat	1914, 1916
Williams, Woody	2001–04
Williamson, Howie	1928
Willis, Joe	1911–13
Willis, Ron	1966–69
Willis, Vic	1910
Wilson, Charlie	1932–33, 1935
Wilson, Jimmie	1928–33
Wilson, Owen	1914–16
Wilson, Zeke	1899
Winford, Jim	1932, 1934–37
Wingo, Ivy	1911–14
Winsett, Tom	1935
Wise, Rick	1972–73
Withrow, Corky	1963

Witt, Bobby	1998
Wolf, Chicken	1892
Wolter, Harry	1907
Womack, Tony	2004
Wood, John	1896
Woodburn, Gene	1911–12
Woodeshick, Hal	1965–67
Woodson, Tracy	1992–93
Woodward, Frank	1919
Woodridge, Floyd	1955
Worrell, Todd	1985–89, 1992
Worthington, Red	1934
Wright, Jamey	2002
Wright, Mel	1954–55

Y

Yan, Esteban	2003
Yerkes, Steve	1901–03
Yochim, Ray	1948–49
Young, Babe	1948
Young, Bobby	1948
Young, Cy	1899–1900
Young, Dmitri	1996–97
Young, Gerald	1994
Young, Joe	1892
Young, Pep	1941, 1945
Youngblood, Joel	1977
Yuhas, Eddie	1952–53
Yvars, Sal	1953–54

Z

Zachary, Chris	1971
Zacher, Elmer	1910
Zackert, George	1911–12
Zearloss, Dave	1904–05
Zeile, Todd	1989–95
Zeller, Bart	1970
Zies, Bill	1891
Zimmerman, Eddie	1906
Zmich, Ed	1910–11

Managers

Blades, Ray	1939–40
Boyer, Ken	1978–80
Bresnahan, Roger	1909–12
Buckenberger, Al	1895
Burke, Jimmy	1905
Campau, Count	1890
Caruthers, Bob	1892
Comiskey, Charlie	1883–89, 1891
Connor, Roger	1896
Crooks, Jack	1892
Cuthbert, Ned	1882
Diddlebock, Harry	1896
Donovan, Patsy	1901–03
Dowd, Tommy	1896–97
Dyer, Eddie	1946–50
Frisch, Frankie	1933–38
Gerhardt, Joe	1890
Glasscock, Jack	1892
Gonzalez, Mike	1938, 1940
Gore, George	1892
Hack, Stan	1958
Hallman, Bill	1897
Heilbroner, Louis	1900
Hemus, Solly	1959–61
Hendricks, Jack	1918
Herzog, Whitey	1980–90
Hornsby, Rogers	1925–26
Huggins, Miller	1913–17
Hutchinson, Fred	1956–58
Hurst, Tim	1898
Jorgensen, Mike	1995
Keane, Johnny	1961–64
Kerins, John	1890
Krol, Jack	1978, 1980
La Russa, Tony	1996–2005
Latham, Arlie	1896
Marion, Marty	1951
McCarthy, Tommy	1890
McCloskey, John	1906–08
McKechnie, Bill	1928–29
Miller, Doggie	1894
Nichols, Kid	1904–05
Nicol, Hugh	1897
O'Farrell, Bob	1927
Phelan, Lew	1895
Quinn, Jack	1895
Rapp, Vern	1977–78
Rickey, Branch	1919–25
Robison, Stanley	1905
Roseman, Chief	1890
Schoendienst, Red	1965–76, 1980, 1990
Southworth, Billy	1929, 1940–45
Stanky, Eddie	1952–55
Street, Gabby	1929–33
Stricker, Cub	1892
Sullivan, Ted	1883
Tebeau, Patsy	1899–1900
Torre, Joe	1990–95
Von der Ahe, Chris	1892, 1895–97
Walker, Harry	1955
Watkins, Bill	1893
Williams, Jimmy	1884

Coaches

Aufenio, Tony	1973
Baylor, Don	1992
Becker, Joe	1965–66
Benson, Vern	1961–64, 1970–75
Blades, Ray	1930–32, 1951
Boyer, Ken	1971–72
Braun, Steve	1990
Cardenal, Jose	1994–95
Chambliss, Chris	1993–95
Coleman, Joe	1991–94
Collins, Dave	1991–92
Cooper, Walker	1957
Cunningham, Joe	1982
DeJohn, Mark	1996–2001
Dent, Bucky	1991–94
Duncan, Dave	1996–2005
Easler, Mike	1999–2001
Gibson, Bob	1995
Gomez, Preston	1976
Gonzalez, Mike	1934–46
Hack, Stan	1957–58
Hacker, Rich	1986–90
Hassey, Ron	1996
Hendrick, George	1996–97
Hiller, Chuck	1981–83
Hollingsworth, Al	1957–58
Hopp, Johnny	1956
Hubbard, Jack	1993

Johnson, Darrell	1960–61	Schoendienst, Red	1962–64, 1979–95
Kahn, Lou	1954–55	Schultz, Barney	1971–75
Katt, Ray	1959–61	Schultz, Joe	1963–68
Kaufman, Tony	1947–50	Shotton, Burt	1923–25
Keane, Johnny	1959–61	Sisler, Dick	1966–70
Killefer, Bill	1926	Smith, Hal	1962
Kissell, George	1969–75	Sothoron, Al	1927–28
Kittle, Hub	1981–83	Sugden, Joe	1921–25
Knowles, Darold	1983	Thomas, Lee	1972, 1983
Koenig, Fred	1976	Thomas, Ray	1922
Krol, Jack	1977–80	Thompson, Tim	1981
Lachemann, Rene	1997–99	Turner, Tink	1924
Lanier, Hal	1981–85	Vernon, Mickey	1965
Lansford, Carney	1997–98	Walker, Dixie	1953, 1955
Lewis, Johnny	1973–76, 1984–89	Walker, Harry	1959–62
Leyva, Nick	1984–88	Wares, Buzzy	1930–52
Marion, Marty	1950	Williams, Otto	1926
Mason, Marty	2000–05	Zeller, Bart	1970
Maxvill, Dal	1979–80	Zimmer, Tom	1976
McKay, Dave	1996–2005		
McKechnie, Bill	1927		
McRae, Hal	2005		
Milliken, Bob	1965–70, 1976		
Moore, Terry	1949–52, 1956–58		
Mozzali, Mo	1977–78		
Muffett, Billy	1967–70		
Neale, Greasy	1929		
O'Leary, Charley	1913–17		
Onslow, Jack	1928		
Oquendo, Jose	1999–2005		
Osteen, Claude	1977–80		
Page, Mitchell	2001–04		
Parker, Dave	1998		
Peitz, Heinie	1913		
Pettini, Joe	2002–05		
Pitts, Gaylen	1991–95		
Pollet, Howie	1959–64		
Posedel, Bill	1954–57		
Quirk, Jamie	1984		
Reynolds, Tommy	1996		
Ricketts, Dave	1974–75, 1978–81		
Riddle, John	1952–55		
Riggins, Mark	1995		
Riggleman, Jim	1989–90		
Roarke, Mike	1984–90		
Ruberto, Sonny	1977–78		
Ryba, Mike	1951–54		

Books of Interest

Each book in the **Baseball Behind the Seams** series focuses on a single position, exploring it with the kind of depth serious fans crave. Through extensive research, including interviews with hundreds of players past and present, the authors have brought together the most original and informative series ever published on the game.

Each book in the series covers

- The physical and mental qualities of the position
- The position's history
- The plays, and how to make them
- Profiles of the position's top all-time players
- The best defenders of the position
- A day in the life of one player, from arriving at the ball park to the final out
- Lists of Gold Gloves, MVPs, and Rookies of the Year
- Fun and quirky facts about the position

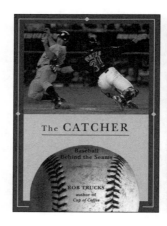

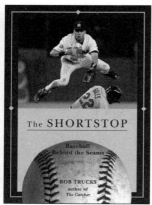

The Catcher
By Rob Trucks
$14.99 Paperback
ISBN: 1-57860-164-9

The Starting Pitcher
By Rob Trucks
$14.99 Paperback
ISBN: 1-57860-163-0

The First Baseman
By Tom Keegan
$14.95 Paperback
ISBN: 1-57860-261-0

The Shortstop
By Rob Trucks
$14.95 Paperback
ISBN: 1-57860-262-9

Available at local and online booksellers or at www.emmisbooks.com.
Emmis Books, 1700 Madison Road, Cincinnati, Ohio 45206

Books of Interest

The Baseball Uncyclopedia:
A Highly Opinionated, Myth-Busting Guide to the Great American Game
By Michael Kun and Howard Bloom

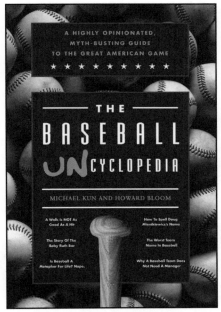

ISBN: 1-57860-233-5
$14.95 Paperback

"Incredibly funny and so easy to relate to. A baseball book that reminds us it's just a game in the much bigger game of life."
—Karl Ravech, Host, ESPN's *Baseball Tonight*

The Baseball Uncyclopedia reveals the truth about the tall tales, ill-formed opinions, and widely held misunderstandings that baseball fans have clung to for generations.

Michael Kun and Howard Bloom explain that, contrary to popular belief, an American League team is *not* required to use a designated hitter. They argue that it's *not* always wrong to root against the home team. They heap scorn upon those who believe Joe DiMaggio was *ever* "The Greatest Living Baseball Player." They also offer tips on appropriate ballpark heckling and issue a condemnation of the writer responsible for Reggie Jackson's *Love Boat* appearance. And they reveal shocking information about Moises Alou's personal habits that will dismay even the most jaded baseball devotee.

Packed with surprising baseball facts as well as the musings of two baseball fanatics, crammed almost to bursting with argument starters, bet settlers, and absurd pop-culture references, *The Baseball Uncyclopedia* offers a sound rebuke to anyone who thinks a baseball book can't be smart, funny and informative all at the same time.